Simpson's
Contemporary Quotations

Compiled by

James B Simpson

Foreword by

Daniel J Boorstin

Houghton Mifflin Company

Boston   1988

Other books and compilations by James B Simpson

Best Quotes of '54, '55, '56 · 1957
The Hundredth Archbishop of Canterbury · 1962
Contemporary Quotations · 1964

With Edward M Story
The Long Shadows of Lambeth X · 1969
Stars in His Crown · 1976
Discerning God's Will · 1979

With Robert A K Runcie
Seasons of the Spirit · 1983

Library of Congress Cataloging-in-Publication Data

Simpson, James Beasley.
Simpson's contemporary quotations.

Includes indexes.
1. Quotations, English.   I. Title.
PN6083.S53   1988   818'.02   87–37867
ISBN 0–395–43085–2

Index by Edward M Story with James P Marciano

*In loving memory of my sister Bobbye
and for Michael, Steven and Andrew, whose generation
will voice the contemporary quotations of the future.*

Contents

COMMUNICATIONS & THE ARTS

Foreword

This uniquely twentieth-century kind of reference book could be called "Quotations from Familiar People." Only our times have made a volume like this possible, and necessary. These quotations tell us what our contemporaries have said since 1950. The multiplying news magazines, television and radio programs, best-selling authors, and public relations and advertising campaigns have multiplied the familiar people. We recognize their faces, their voices, even their gestures, but we seldom remember exactly what they have said. As celebrities, they are best known for their well-knownness. These floods of familiar people overwhelm us with their images without leaving a memorable or usable residue of their words. What they said is gone with the wind, or with the flip of a television dial. In this book James B Simpson clothes the familiar people in their own words. And so he reminds us of what they might have preferred to leave forgotten, and what we, to our loss, are likely to have forgotten.

In this way Simpson offers us a delightfully "contemporary" pleasure that we seldom find in quotations from the more remote past. Classical authors—Plato, Shakespeare, Milton or Tennyson—impress us by their cogency, their profundity or their eloquence. But quotations from the people whom we have come to know in our own time can have an added, subtly human dimension—the irony and conceit, pride and mock humility, and megalomania of those who said it. Among our contemporaries we can be amused and surprised and instructed not only by what was said but by who said it and when. The boasts of Alexander the Great or Cromwell may be raw material for historians, but when Idi Amin says "I am the hero of Africa," or the Soviet premier Leonid I Brezhnev says "God will not forgive us if we fail," they enlighten us as they never intended.

From an earlier age, the most widely circulating dictionary of quotations is that by John Bartlett (1820–1905). Son of a Plymouth, Massachusetts, sea captain, Bartlett never went beyond grade school and educated himself as a bookseller in the University Bookstore in Cambridge. When learned professors could not locate even in the great Harvard College Library the passage they were looking for or vaguely remembered, they would go to him for help. "Ask John Bartlett" became familiar around Harvard Square, and Bartlett began keeping a commonplace book of the most frequently sought quotations. He also invented a new system of chess notation. An ardent fisherman, Bartlett produced a definitive bibliography of "Books on Angling, including Ichthyology, Pisciculture, Etc." He found a place in classical American literature in the poem "To John Bartlett, Who Had Sent Me a Seven Pound Trout," by his friend, the eminently quotable James Russell Lowell. Then Bartlett earned his own immortality as an angler for aphorisms. His *Familiar Quotations* (1855) went through nine editions in his lifetime and lives on today in its fifteenth edition (1980). That admirable book has become a prototype for American books of quotations, and Bartlett, like Webster, seems to have become a common noun. Perhaps one day Simpson will attain the same distinction.

Bartlett's book was aptly titled. He did not try to focus attention on quotations of which his readers had never heard, but rather aimed to help readers locate the author and the precise form of vaguely or imperfectly remembered lines. His book was for people who had shared an education in the ancient and modern classics—to help them give precision to their memory. Bartlett's was a bookish book for bookish people, or at least for all who wanted to seem more bookish than they really were.

Simpson's book has a quite different origin and a different range, for a new age. Nowadays few Americans have had a classical education and too few share the common discourse of Western literature. The very idea of literary familiarity is at the risk of becoming obsolete. Bartlett, we hope, will continue to help save us from that peril. But Simpson is by contemporaries for contemporaries, in an era when people are less familiar with the classics than with the media. And for people overwhelmed by images, with few words to match. This is not a bookish book, but it *is* a book for literate people. In fact it aims to restore a literate dimension to an age of images. Simpson can also increase our respect for the word, our interest in the word and our reverence for the immortal word. For the words in this book will likely outlive the images of many of the people from whom they come.

Versatile personal experience in the contemporary media—print and electronic—alerted and qualified James B Simpson to record the wittier, more eloquent, more revealing spokesmen of these last decades. This collection was not hatched in a cozy bookshop, nor are these quotations the answers to queries of bookish American Cantabrigians. Precisely a century after the first edition of Bartlett, James B Simpson compiled his *Best Quotes of '54, '55, '56*, which in the next 30 years grew into the present volume. No New Englander but a native of Arkansas, he attended Northwestern University just outside Chicago. Not a bookseller but a journalist, he wrote for the Associated Press and United Press International, was a television network consultant, had a full ration of the advertising world as an account executive, then a stint in corporate public relations. These experiences finally inspired him to still another view of the immortal word, and he became an Episcopal priest.

This book provides a lively, if atomized, running commentary on the public life of the last decades, and a generous sample of the pretentiousness, conceit, hypocrisy, eloquence—and nobility—of our best-known contemporaries. Here we can remind ourselves of the wit and wisdom produced in our own time, while we enjoy the self-contradictions of politicians and the whimsies of cultural gurus. Many a juicy boast leaves a sour taste which we can savor. Since Simpson gives dates and sources for his quotations, he helps us put words in their time and place and so adds the vivid immediacy lacking from the classical past. Incidentally he helps us sense the elusiveness of history, and he makes us wonder how many historic reputations have been saved by the lucky loss of off-the-cuff pontifications.

Happily, too, this book is a documented retort to the doomsayers who find wit and eloquence only in the deeper past. These pages solace us with proof that quotable wisdom did not go out with the coming of the horseless carriage. Our age proves to be neither so crass nor so uneloquent as some would have us believe.

Simpson gives us the opportunity to do for ourselves what Bartlett left to the sifting generations. While Bartlett deferred to "the test of time," which meant the verdict of teachers, authors, scholars and librarians, Simpson spreads a wider net and gives each of us jurisdiction over the speakers' immortality. This book challenges the reader to separate wit, eloquence, acuteness and profundity from mere familiarity, shallow paradox or cuteness. And so it can help us sharpen our judgment and deepen our understanding of the people who have shaped our contemporary life.

Just as every generation has its style of utterance, so each has its own style of quotation. Leafing through the *Congressional Record*, we discover a stark contrast between the rhetoric of the Age of Bartlett and the rhetoric of the Age of Simpson. The floors of Congress in the nineteenth century echoed with quotations from classical authors and standard poets, the materials of "familiar" quotations. More recent politicians are wary of the look of pedantry or of sounding "literary." They are more likely to quote their contemporaries—sports figures, television stars or best-selling authors.

"Well-stolen is half-written," said Arnold Schönberg in what might have been the motto for today's public speaker. In Washington, a city of ghosted speakers and ghostwriters, it is assumed that people in power have not written what they utter. Of course the speechwriter is the most often quoted and least often acknowledged wit of our time. The acknowledged quotation becomes a rare and valued public confession. With a quotation we make it plain that we are letting someone else who says it better, say it for us. Most of us, unlike the president of the United States, the secretary of state or the CEO of a large corporation, cannot afford a "spokesman." But we can all afford a quotation, which gives us many of the same advantages. Then we too can deny that *we* said it, or if we prefer we can claim credit for choosing so graceful a way of saying it. And for us too the opportunities for convenient ambiguities are endless. Are we praising or blaming, complaining or rejoicing, being outspoken, oblique, direct or ironic? Or is this our own way of refusing to make a statement? Our quotation can help us be newsworthy by piquing the listener's curiosity about our intentions or our motives. While many of the quotations in this book have the iridescence of wit, they also have the transparency of the colloquial, and so they are especially well qualified to speak for us.

"Brush up your Shakespeare!" is shockingly undemocratic advice to the speechgiver or speechwriter today. And this book, besides being contemporary and up-to-date, is emphatically democratic. In fact, only in a society without an intellectual or any other kind of aristocracy could such quotations have been produced or such a collection be compiled. This is not a harvest of profundities by the most respected authors. And this book helps us glimpse the democratic future. If, as Andy Warhol suggested, our democracy will not really be fulfilled until that time in the future when "everyone will be famous for 15 minutes," Simpson gives us a foretaste of the wit and wisdom of that age, and shows how some of our contemporaries have already seized their 15 minutes.

What our democratic America, our world of flooding images and fleeting utterances, characteristically produces is not literary wit but the *occasional* wit, the utterance sparked by anybody at all from almost anybody else. This wit is conspicuously contemporary. It is the by-product of a particular, usually ephemeral occasion—an interview, a press release, a television conversation, a newspaper column, oft-repeated rumor or gossip. It comes from every public person's opportunity and desire to get his image across. It springs out of the marketplace, the ballot box, the political debate, the radio speaker or the television screen, the airport kiosk or the current best seller. It does not aim at longevity, much less immortality. But it has its own peculiar charm, its own spontaneity, its own self-depreciation and self-adulation. It is not solemn, but it sometimes turns out to be serious. Simpson's book is a current anthology of this *occasional* wit which nobody else seems to be collecting, much less arranging so we can find it. Using this book will not make you seem learned. But it can help you reap continuing amusement and instruction—with quotable words—from the fleeting moments and ephemeral images of our times.

Daniel J Boorstin

Preface

Telephotos from throughout the world were streaming to the picture desk of United Press International in New York, by day and far into the night, in the early 1950s when I was an editor there and where, as an extra job, I began putting aside quotations for one of the earliest panel shows, *Who Said That?* I met the faces in the news; next I sought their words. In captions and in scripts, I included both sources and dates so that the fuller stories could be searched out later; in this book of nearly 10,000 quotations by some 4,000 people, spanning the years 1950 through 1987, I have followed the same procedure in the attributions.

Looking back on those busy days of juggling two sets of deadlines, during which time I experienced a double impact from world events, I can still readily behold the faces that peered at us daily as the news broke. I see a montage of mid-twentieth-century personalities against a vast canvas of action—a pale Alger Hiss in a federal courtroom, the Soviet Union's Jacob Malik striding out of the United Nations, Belgium's King Leopold III abdicating, Althea Gibson playing championship tennis, Nijinsky dead at age 60 and George Orwell at 46. Although I had quickly become mesmerized by newspictures, I had also come to realize that the words of these key players were often more telling than their faces. Faces change, but remarks remain, often taking on more profound meaning as time passes. In this sense, quotations take up where pictures leave off. Whether you turn to quotations for information or pleasure, you will, in the words of a fellow chronicler, historian Arthur M Schlesinger Jr, "discover your own lives."

Moving from wire photos to NBC and later to the radio news desk of the Associated Press, I deepened my concentration on the acquisition of quotations by people prominent and unknown. Besides writing hourly newscasts for the AP national wire, I constantly studied the teletype dispatches from abroad, read nine daily newspapers and listened to scores of broadcasts. I well remember Truman's Missouri accent, Elizabeth II's girlish speech, Eisenhower's convoluted syntax, Joseph McCarthy's bluster, Helen Keller's courage, Frank Lloyd Wright's tart criticisms, Tallulah Bankhead's *dahling*s.

Early on it became clear that the scope of my quotations research was greedily consuming large chunks of the days, months, even years of my life. In a marathon of reading to acquire 50 to 70 good quotes a week, I found that my days had disintegrated into a blur; my weekends were nonexistent. Yet I reveled in and loved the work. In that extraordinary post-World War II period when the world seemed to be trying to make up for lost time, I had a virtual galaxy of notable quotables from which to choose. Churchill, for one, sent me running to the typewriter every time he opened his mouth. Also on stage were de Gaulle, Khrushchev, MacArthur, Clare Boothe Luce, Robert Frost and Adlai Stevenson, to name but a few.

By 1957, drawing on files that had become voluminous, I completed my first book, *Best Quotes of '54, '55, '56.* Published by Thomas Y Crowell, it contained 1,866 utterances by 784 people ranging from Marcel Achard to Fred Zusy. "We need not depend on Bartlett and those who compile the best quotations of the past," said the Preface provided by my mentor and friend, news commentator H V Kaltenborn, who went on to say, "There is wit and wisdom abroad in the land today. It is reported in all we read and hear. Each day brings a new harvest." *Newsweek* described it as "a book whose editor and origins are as distinctive to our age as Bartlett and his Harvard patrons were to the 1850s." Indeed, John Bartlett and I are distinctive representatives of our times, but there are contrasts, too. Toiling by the light of an oil lamp, bookseller Bartlett reached back to the Bible and Shakespeare. Almost a century later, working in Rockefeller Center, I obtained many of my quotes via satellite. In the early years of our respective projects Bartlett and I advanced to other positions. He became a Boston publisher, a logical extension of his original pursuit. I, on the other hand, was ordained to the Episcopal priesthood after a career in advertising and public relations. But both of us discovered wider vistas that added immeasurably to our larders of quotations.

In 1964 Crowell published my second compilation, *Contemporary Quotations*, a book of over 2,900 remarks made by more than 1,300 people in public life. The outbreaks of assassinations were beginning, and entirely new subjects commanded attention: astronautics, the Berlin Wall, civil rights, desegregation, drugs, ecology, the Pill. In the Preface to the 1964 book I wrote with considerable conviction that "our era boasts eloquent spokesmen from every level of society, and . . . their words should not be buried in the formidable and sometimes inaccessible files of newspapers and magazines." The existence of computerized databases notwithstanding, I feel this statement is still valid.

During the late 1970s columnist William Safire noted in the New York *Times Book Review* that "the useful 'Contemporary Quotations' by James Simpson has been out of print . . . (despite some quotable lines in the last 15 years)." His interest spurred me to continue the acquisition of quotes. The result of my never-ending quest lies in your hands today: a compilation of notable, memorable utterances from thousands of people worldwide, covering the years 1950 to 1987, but with special emphasis on the period from 1964 to the present. During 37 years I have read over 65,000 newspapers, more than 10,000 magazines and numerous books in my spare time. In short, the world is still my beat.

Because an increasing number of good quotes derive from television programs, most evenings I keep a tape recorder at hand or I request transcripts afterward. I videotape shows that are broadcast at odd hours. While it is important to read widely in order to glean quotable gems, it is equally important to read with discipline. Overreading results in overquotation, and overquotation can mean a collection of the near memorable, not the most memorable. Some days are more quoteworthy than others. The newspapers of Sunday, September 13, 1987, yielded an unusually large catch of 17 quotes. (When I added them to the manuscript three months later, 15 of

them had retained their validity.) Conversely, there are rare days, such as Sunday, November 30, 1987—a holiday weekend—when nothing of lasting value turns up. This very unpredictability, together with the inescapable subjectivity of the compiler, serves as a check and balance against insertion of the mediocre instead of the brilliant, the insignificant instead of the significant, the ephemeral instead of the timeless. A single day's reading also may unearth the vulgar as well as the lofty. To fail to record the off-color is to deny the realities of contemporary life. Therefore you will find some of it here. I might add that for each of the few lines in this volume that may be deemed racy by some readers, I have legions more in a file marked "naughty quotations," the contents of which will have to wait for a later time. My Houghton Mifflin editors certainly weren't stuffy; at one point, however, old-fashioned gallantry did cause me to question whether or not a particularly earthy line should be broached by an Anglican cleric to a Boston lady.

In any case, while I have sought to include remarks relating to events of record—remarks found in formal addresses, declarations and official statements—balanced by the counterpoint of the off-the-cuff quip or the brilliant epigram, I have *celebrated* in this collection spontaneity, color and originality of expression, no matter what the source. I have found that even the United States Supreme Court can be as winning in its language as a Macy's copywriter. Apropos to this, attorney Murray Gartner laughed aloud one day while reading Justice William J Brennan Jr's solemn observation that "sex, a great and mysterious motive force in human life, has indisputably been a subject of absorbing interest to mankind through the ages."

You may not think that you collect quotes, but we all do, and we play them back in our own minds whenever we need them. We select the memorable from family, friends, teachers, employers and the people next door. Proud parents quote their children; years later children quote their parents. Favorite quotes are likely to come to mind unexpectedly. For instance, I am waiting at a traffic light when out of nowhere surfaces Phyllis Battelle's quip that Barbara Hutton "for her fifth wedding . . . wore black and carried a scotch and soda." A far more serious quote comes up as I saunter to the post office: Barbara W Tuchman's assertion that "history is the unfolding of miscalculations." In my ministry I have frequently turned to Carl Jung's observation that he had never treated a patient over 35 "whose problem in the last resort was not that of finding a religious outlook on life." Many have been the nights that I have fallen asleep pondering a quotation from Albert Camus that a friend had discovered with a shout of glee, "In the depth of winter, I finally learned that within me lay an invincible summer." All of us undoubtedly have had the experience of coming across a yellowed clipping in a desk drawer or wallet, finding it still to be reassuring. Harry Truman carried a crumpled copy of Tennyson's lines from "The Parliament of Man." I have long had in the corner of my shaving mirror a quote from that elusive fellow Anonymous, who said, "The greatest possible contribution which any of us can make to the world is just to be ourselves at our best." Scores of favorites—in this book and elsewhere—I commend to you as lively, enduring company.

The quotations found in this, a totally new book, represent the articulate, often rambunctious voices of our time. Their murmuring, shouting, pleading, exhorting words reflect the issues and answers expressed by those concerned with a war in Southeast Asia; with a flourishing drug culture; with increasing acts of global terrorism; with a series of wars in the Middle East, Afghanistan and Central America; with human rights and equality; with the South African situation; with famine in Ethiopia; with Watergate; with détente and glasnost; with sexual permissiveness; with the specter of AIDS. The voices of the past 24 years speak of Agent Orange; of corporate takeovers; of pot and of poppers; of jets; of Contras, condos and condoms; of women bishops; of traveling popes. *Simpson's Contemporary Quotations*, from Hank Aaron to Vladimir Zworykin, includes the words of Henry Kissinger and Edward Koch, Corazon Aquino and Zhou Enlai, Truman Capote and Gore Vidal, Lillian Hellman and Nadine Gordimer, Shana Alexander and Joan Didion, Coretta Scott King and Joseph Brodsky, Desmond Tutu and Elie Wiesel, John Lennon and Bruce Springsteen, Ralph Nader and Ronald Reagan, Pope John Paul II and Robert Runcie, Gloria Steinem and Frank Sinatra, Sandra Day O'Connor and William ("Refrigerator") Perry and thousands more.

Simpson's Contemporary Quotations is published at a time when quotes have been increasingly used by major newspapers and magazines as devices to seize and hold readers' interest. As an example, on Sunday, November 10, 1985, the New York *Times* used three quotes as headlines, quotes that conveyed the gist of a trio of stories on the front page of the drama section. In a 32-month period *Time* used six covers linking quotations with pictures of the speakers. On the cover of the November 12, 1984, issue, a portrait of the assassinated Indira Gandhi was underlined with her prophetic words, "If I die today, every drop of my blood will invigorate the nation." And on July 20, 1987, *Time* ran a cover photo of Lt Col Oliver North along with his statement, "I was authorized to do everything that I did." *Newsweek* recently instituted the delightful new feature "Overheard," in which the reader encounters the best quotes of the preceding days along with a collection of the best political cartoons. It is my hope that media editors and reporters, speechwriters, attorneys, judges, executives, students, instructors and general readers will find this book—organized by categories and indexed by sources and by subjects and key lines—useful. In any case, it represents a self-imposed torture, "a splendid misery," as Thomas Jefferson called the presidency. Part of that misery has been my concern that all quotes and their attributions are scrupulously accurate. Over time, quotes are often erroneously attributed to people we believe might have said such and such, even if they didn't. Henry Ford, Mother Teresa and Samuel Goldwyn come to mind. In this sense, I once asked a brother priest, Christopher Morley Jr, about a line attributed to his father on a greeting card: "There is only one success—to be able to spend your life in your own way." His reply: "It doesn't *sound* like him." Yet, our printed evidence attests to the belief that he did say it; hence, Morley is listed here as the speaker of the line.

Father Morley is one of many whose opinions and help I have enlisted during the course of this project. The staff of Monmouth County Library's Eastern Branch at Shrewsbury, New Jersey, has been unfailingly responsive. A good friend and parishioner, Charlotte Rader, helped with original organization, while Georgia Maas and John J Bridson ably furthered correspondence and verification of data. Toward the end, Sally Seibert, a star researcher, also worked with Father Edward M Story, who indexed both the 1964 and the 1988 books.

At Houghton Mifflin executive editor Anne H Soukhanov supplied the counsel, encouragement and belief so vital to long-term undertakings. Coordinating editor Kaethe Ellis directed the book from manuscript to print, providing at the same time the painstaking attention to fact and stylistic detail essential to excellent editing and requisite to all lucky authors. Assistant editor James P Marciano and associate editor Susan M Innes worked long hours in editing and checking this collection, as did other Houghton Mifflin Reference Department editors Pamela B DeVinne, David R Pritchard and Rosemary E Previte, assisted by Paul G Evenson, Laurie McCrohon,

Cara E Murray and Heidi R Stahl. My Publisher honors me by including my name in the title for this great babble of words and torrent of talk cascading down the years.

In the final letting go of this edition I recall a New Year's Eve that was thick with the melancholy ruminations for which that "between-the-years" holiday is notorious. It was 1949 and my undergraduate days were close behind me. I heard the stroke of midnight, the turn of the decade, and hoped it might somehow mark the start of a great adventure, of consuming commitment. Like the answer to a prayer, immediately ahead was the beginning of a joyful march through more than four and a half decades in a wild, abandoned romance with the words of others. As I have bent to my task, I have often thought of those who might use this book, and of dashing off postcards to them, saying "Having a wonderful time, wish you were here." Well, now you are.

As for the persistent question "Who said that?" it lives still. It floated on the mists of time ages before it inspired the long-running television show of the same name, the program that gave me my breakthrough. And to the unrelenting inquiry "Who said that?" this book replies.

James B Simpson †
Washington DC
Lent 1988

Explanatory Notes

The quotations in this book are divided into three major categories and sixty subcategories, including Heads of State, Science, Love, Poets, Coaches, Officials & Owners. This is an ideal arrangement for discovering quotations about a specific topic or for browsing in pleasurable search of an apt phrase. The Contents (pages iv–v) and the guidewords at the top of each page will direct you to the section you are seeking.

Author & Source Names

In each section and subsection author and source names appear in alphabetical order before the quoted selections. Authors and sources frequently appear in more than one section. The Index by Sources (see below) lists each author and source in this book.

Brief identifications of authors are included where required. The identification usually reflects the status of the author at the time his or her words were written or spoken.

Order of Entries

Multiple quotations from an individual author or source within a particular section are in chronological order, with the earliest quote appearing first. If more than one quotation comes from a particular year, quotations from books precede those from monthly magazines and both precede quotations from weekly magazines.

Attributions

Attributions give the fullest possible information to help you pinpoint the quotation in its appropriate context or discover more in the original source. Judicial opinions, major speeches and quotations recalled in obituaries include, where possible, the actual date of the opinion or speech or the actual date of death.

In attributions all months and years appear in shortened form. Day, month and year are given in inverted order; for example, 8 Jun 87.

The abbreviation *ib*, short for *ibidem*, "in the same place," is used when a quotation has the same author and the same attribution as the preceding quote. It may also be used when the author and publication are the same as in the preceding quotation, even though the date of publication is different.

Abbreviations

Standard abbreviations are used in identifications and attributions for military ranks (such as Adm for Admiral), for professional titles (such as Dr for Doctor) and for state names where needed (such as CA for California). Months of the year and radio and television networks have also been abbreviated.

Indexes

Since this book is organized by categories, many quotations will be found by simply looking up the section you want in the list of Contents. To aid you further in searching out just the right quotation, there are two completely separate Indexes at the end of the book.

In the Index by Sources (starting on page 409) you will find an alphabetical list of the authors and sources of quotations, from Henry ("Hank") Aaron to Vladimir Zworykin. Page references will guide you to just the right places to find all the quotes from, for example, Ronald Reagan or "that elusive fellow," Anonymous.

In addition, a listing of particularly interesting topics will be found in the Index by Subjects and Key Lines (starting on page 441). In this Index references include both a page number and a quotation number, for example:

> Academy Awards, 274:22, 275:22 . . .

Quotation numbers—beginning with 1 for the first complete quotation on each page—appear to the left of individual quotations.

A particularly helpful feature of the Index by Subjects and Key Lines is the inclusion of hundreds of well-known and not-so-well-known phrases and lines from public officials, noted commentators and humble folk. Many of these Key Lines will be instantly recognizable:

> "Eagle has landed," 136:19
> "I'm not a crook," 11:1

Others may be less familiar, but will whet your appetite for discovering "Who said that?":

> "dust is a protective coating," 206:9
> "my tongue is smiling," 301:5
> "nag it, gnaw it . . . flatter it," 355:11

In both Indexes *see* and *see also* cross-references have been included where needed.

All in all, these Indexes, used in conjunction with the list of categories given in the Contents, will yield a fascinating look at the quotations of our present time.

He that giveth his mind . . . will keep the sayings of the renowned, and where subtle parables are, he will be there also. He will seek out the secrets of grave sentences, and be conversant in dark parables. He shall serve among great men, and appear before princes; he will travel through strange countries . . . When the great Lord will, he shall be filled with the spirit of understanding; he shall pour out wise sentences, and give thanks unto the Lord in his prayer.

Ecclesiasticus 39:1–4, 6

The World

POLITICS & GOVERNMENT

Heads of State

KONRAD ADENAUER, Chancellor of West Germany

1 The rare case where the conquered is very satisfied with the conqueror.
> On Allied occupation of West Berlin, NY *Times* 21 Mar 60

2 Only the stupidest calves choose their own butcher.
> On Western wheat shipments to the USSR, NY *Herald Tribune* 6 Oct 63

IDI AMIN, President of Uganda

3 I am the hero of Africa.
> *Newsweek* 12 Mar 73

CORAZON C AQUINO, President of the Philippines

4 They came out in the millions to show their dogged support for the woman the dictatorship claimed it had defeated in the election.
> As victor in election ending Ferdinand E Marcos's 20-year regime, NY *Times* 27 Feb 86

5 All the world wondered as they witnessed . . . a people lift themselves from humiliation to the greatest pride.
> *ib*

6 The nation was awakened by that deafening shot.
> Dedicating a marker at Manila Airport where her husband Benigno was assassinated on August 21, 1983, *US News & World Report* 1 Sep 86

7 You have spent many lives and much treasure to bring freedom to many lands that were reluctant to receive it. And here you have a people who won it by themselves and need only the help to preserve it.
> To US Congress, *Time* 29 Sep 86

8 It is not I who have been consigned to the bedroom of history.
> Alluding to remark by Ferdinand E Marcos that a woman's place was in the bedroom, NY *Times* 1 Dec 86

CLEMENT ATTLEE, Prime Minister of Great Britain

9 Few thought he was even a starter.
There were many who thought themselves smarter.
But he ended PM, CH and OM,
An earl and a Knight of the Garter.
> On his political career, news summaries 8 Apr 56

VINCENT AURIOL, President of France

10 The work was killing me; they called me out of bed at all hours of the night to receive resignations of prime ministers.
> On leaving office, news summaries 1 Feb 54

BENJAMIN NNAMDI AZIKIWE, President of Nigeria

11 It is better we disintegrate in peace and not in pieces.
> *Newsweek* 8 Aug 66

BEATRIX, Queen of the Netherlands

12 I realize that much will be asked of me, yet I am resolved to accept it as a great and splendid task.
> On succeeding to the throne, NY *Times* 1 May 80

13 Nature is under control but not disturbed.
> On opening a new Dutch sea barrier, *ib* 5 Oct 86

MENACHEM BEGIN, Prime Minister of Israel

14 Israel is still the only country in the world against which there is a written document to the effect that it must disappear.
> On PLO charter, statement to the press, Washington DC, 22 Mar 78

DAVID BEN GURION, Prime Minister of Israel

15 In Israel, in order to be a realist you must believe in miracles.
> CBS TV 5 Oct 56

16 The trebling of the population in this small and impoverished country, flowing with milk and honey but not with sufficient water, rich in rocks and sand dunes but poor in natural resources and vital raw materials, has been no easy task: Indeed, practical men, with their eyes fixed upon things as they are, regarded it as an empty and insubstantial utopian dream.
> NY *Herald Tribune* 28 Apr 63

17 Israel has created a new image of the Jew in the world—the image of a working and an intellectual people, of a people that can fight with heroism.
> *Time* 9 Jun 67

18 Ours is a country built more on people than on territory. The Jews will come from everywhere: from France, from Russia, from America, from Yemen. . . . Their faith is their passport.
> Recalled by Shimon Peres on 100th anniversary of Ben Gurion's birth, NY *Times* 5 Oct 86

ZULFIKAR ALI BHUTTO, President of Pakistan

19 Pakistan was once called the most allied ally of the United States. We are now the most nonallied.
> NY *Times* 6 Jul 73

P W BOTHA, President of South Africa

20 Not only will we survive [sanctions], we will emerge stronger on the other side.
> NY *Times* 28 Sep 86

LEONID I BREZHNEV, Soviet Premier

21 God will not forgive us if we fail.
> To President Jimmy Carter at June 1979 summit meeting, recalled when Mikhail S Gorbachev also invoked the deity, NY *Times* 2 Sep 85

KOFI BUSIA, Prime Minister of Ghana

22 I don't like hypocrisy—even in international relations.
> Interview 2 Feb 70

1

1 Diplomacy . . . means the art of nearly deceiving all your friends, but not quite deceiving all your enemies.
ib

JIMMY CARTER, 39th US President

2 You have given me a great responsibility: to stay close to you, to be worthy of you and to exemplify what you are.
Inaugural address 20 Jan 77

3 I personally think that he did violate the law, that he committed impeachable offenses. But I don't think that he thinks he did.
On former President Richard M Nixon, to reporters after press conference 12 May 77

4 The experience of democracy is like the experience of life itself—always changing, infinite in its variety, sometimes turbulent and all the more valuable for having been tested by adversity.
To Indian Parliament 2 Jan 78

5 If you fear making anyone mad, then you ultimately probe for the lowest common denominator of human achievement.
To Future Farmers of America, Kansas City, 9 Nov 78

6 Human rights is the soul of our foreign policy, because human rights is the very soul of our sense of nationhood.
At White House ceremony commemorating 30th anniversary of UN Declaration of Human Rights 6 Dec 78

7 For the first time in the history of our country the majority of our people believe that the next five years will be worse than the past five years.
Address to the nation 15 Jul 79

8 An act of terrorism totally outside the bounds of international law and diplomatic tradition. . . . a crisis [that] calls for firmness and restraint.
On embassy personnel taken hostage in Iran, 15 Nov 79

9 Aggression unopposed becomes a contagious disease.
On Soviet intervention in Afghanistan, address to the nation 4 Jan 80

10 America did not invent human rights. In a very real sense . . . human rights invented America.
Farewell address 14 Jan 81

11 For this generation, ours, life is nuclear survival, liberty is human rights, the pursuit of happiness is a planet whose resources are devoted to the physical and spiritual nourishment of its inhabitants.
ib

FIDEL CASTRO, President of Cuba

12 I began revolution with 82 men. If I had [to] do it again, I do it with 10 or 15 and absolute faith. It does not matter how small you are if you have faith and plan of action.
NY *Times* 22 Apr 59

13 If there ever was in the history of humanity an enemy who was truly universal, an enemy whose acts and moves trouble the entire world, threaten the entire world, attack the entire world in any way or another, that real and really universal enemy is precisely Yankee imperialism.
To International Cultural Congress, Havana, 12 Jan 68

KONSTANTIN U CHERNENKO, Soviet Premier

14 Those who try to give us advice on matters of human rights do nothing but provoke an ironic smile among us. We will not permit anyone to interfere in our affairs.
Time 2 Jul 84

WINSTON CHURCHILL, Prime Minister of Great Britain

15 One does not leave a convivial party before closing time.
Responding to queries on when he would retire as prime minister, news summaries 22 Mar 54

16 To jaw-jaw is better than to war-war.
On visit to Washington DC 26 Jun 54

17 I have never accepted what many people have kindly said—namely that I inspired the nation. Their will was resolute and remorseless, and as it proved, unconquerable. It fell to me to express it.
On World War II, 80th birthday address to Parliament 30 Nov 54

18 It was the nation and the race dwelling all round the globe that had the lion's heart. I had the luck to be called upon to give the roar.
ib

19 I also hope that I sometimes suggested to the lion the right place to use his claws.
ib

20 It may be that we shall by a process of sublime irony have reached a stage in this story where safety will be the sturdy child of terror, and survival the twin brother of annihilation.
On the hydrogen bomb, news summaries 3 Mar 55

21 It is a remarkable comment on our affairs that the former prime minister of a great sovereign state should thus be received as an honorary citizen of another.
On receiving honorary US citizenship, NY *Times* 10 Apr 63

22 Meeting Franklin Roosevelt was like opening your first bottle of champagne; knowing him was like drinking it.
Recalled on Churchill's death 24 Jan 65

23 If the Almighty were to rebuild the world and asked me for advice, I would have English Channels round every country. And the atmosphere would be such that anything which attempted to fly would be set on fire.
1952 comment quoted by Lord Moran *Churchill: Taken from the Diaries of Lord Moran* Houghton Mifflin 66

24 I always seem to get inspiration and renewed vitality by contact with this great novel land of yours which sticks up out of the Atlantic.
To Vice President Richard M Nixon during 1954 dinner in Washington DC, quoted in *RN: Memoirs of Richard Nixon* Grosset & Dunlap 78

25 In wartime, truth is so precious that she should always be attended by a bodyguard of lies.
Quoted by Thomas Griffith "Ducking the Truth" *Time* 24 Dec 84

26 "No comment" is a splendid expression. I am using it again and again.
ib

1 [Their] insatiable lust for power is only equaled by their incurable impotence in exercising it.

> On opposition government after World War II, quoted by John Colville *The Fringes of Power* Norton 85

2 No lover ever studied every whim of his mistress as I did those of President Roosevelt.

> Recalling 1942 Anglo-American disputes over a second front, *ib*

3 The Russians will try all the rooms in a house, enter those that are not locked, and when they come to one that cannot be broken into, they will withdraw and invite you to dine genially that same evening.

> On postwar negotiations with the Soviets, quoted by Walter Isaacson and Evan Thomas *The Wise Men* Simon & Schuster 86

CHARLES DE GAULLE, President of France

4 I was France.

> On leadership of Free France resistance during World War II, *The Complete War Memoirs of Charles de Gaulle*, translated by Jonathan Griffin, Simon & Schuster 55

5 France cannot be France without greatness.

> *ib*

6 Now I shall return to my village and there will remain at the disposition of the nation.

> Press conference 19 May 58

7 The national task that had been incumbent upon me for 18 years is hereby confirmed.

> On election as president of the Fifth Republic 28 Dec 58

8 The great leaders have always stage-managed their effects.

> *The Edge of the Sword* Criterion Books 60

9 My dear and old country, here we are once again together faced with a heavy trial.

> On uprising in Algeria, NY *Times* 30 Jan 60

10 Once upon a time there was an old country, wrapped up in habit and caution. . . . We have to transform our old France into a new country and marry it to its time.

> *ib* 15 Jun 60

11 You start out giving your hat, then you give your coat, then your shirt, then your skin and finally your soul.

> On dealing with the Soviets, NY *Herald Tribune* 22 Sep 61

12 Diplomats are useful only in fair weather. As soon as it rains they drown in every drop.

> Quoted by former aide Constantin Melnick, *Newsweek* 1 Oct 62

13 Treaties are like roses and young girls. They last while they last.

> On Franco-German treaty talks, *Time* 12 Jul 63

14 A great country worthy of the name does not have any friends.

> *ib* 28 May 65

15 To govern is always to choose among disadvantages.

> NY *Times* 14 Nov 65

16 When I want to know what France thinks, I ask myself.

> *Time* 17 Dec 65

17 I have heard your views. They do not harmonize with mine. The decision is taken unanimously.

> Quoted by Jean Raymond Tournoux *De Gaulle and Pétain: Sons of France* Viking 66

18 The better I get to know men, the more I find myself loving dogs.

> Quoted in *Time* 8 Dec 67

19 I have tried to lift France out of the mud. But she will return to her errors and vomitings. I cannot prevent the French from being French.

> *ib*

20 You may be sure that the Americans will commit all the stupidities they can think of, plus some that are beyond imagination.

> *ib*

21 I respect only those who resist me, but I cannot tolerate them.

> NY *Times* 12 May 68

22 I have against me the bourgeois, the military and the diplomats, and for me, only the people who take the Métro.

> *ib*

23 Patriotism is when love of your own people comes first; nationalism, when hate for people other than your own comes first.

> Recalled on leaving the presidency, *Life* 9 May 69

24 As an adolescent . . . I was convinced that France would have to go through gigantic trials, that the interest of life consisted in one day rendering her some signal service and that I would have the occasion to do so.

> Recalled on his death, *Newsweek* 23 Nov 70

25 I predict you will sink step by step into a bottomless quagmire, however much you spend in men and money.

> On Vietnam War, 1961 statement to President John F Kennedy, quoted in *Memories of Hope* Press Ltd 76

26 [He is] a lion with a lion's countenance.

> After 1960 meeting with Israeli Prime Minister David Ben Gurion, quoted by Shimon Peres NY *Times* 5 Oct 86

DENG XIAOPING, Chinese Premier

27 By following the concept of "one country, two systems," you don't swallow me up nor I you.

> On policy adopted for Hong Kong, quoted in NY *Times* 2 Jan 85

28 It doesn't matter if a cat is black or white, so long as it catches mice.

> On liberalization of Communist Party rules, quoted in *Time* 6 Jan 86

29 Young leading cadres have risen up by helicopter. They should really rise step by step.

> On influential proponents of the Cultural Revolution in the 1960s, *ib*

JOHN G DIEFENBAKER, Prime Minister of Canada

30 I am not anti-American. But I am strongly pro-Canadian.

> NY *Times* 13 Jul 58

ALEC DOUGLAS-HOME, Prime Minister of Great Britain

1 There are two problems in my life. The political ones are insoluble and the economic ones are incomprehensible.

NY *Times* 9 Jan 64

FRANÇOIS ("PAPA DOC") DUVALIER, President of Haiti

2 I know the Haitian people because I *am* the Haitian people.

Recalled on his death 21 Apr 71

JEAN CLAUDE ("BABY DOC") DUVALIER, President of Haiti

3 People of Haiti, I am the heir to the political philosophy, the doctrine and the revolution which my late father incarnated as president-for-life [and] I have decided to continue his work with the same fierce energy and the same intransigence.

On assuming presidency after his father's death, radio address 21 Apr 71

4 It is the destiny of the people of Haiti to suffer.

Quoted by V S Naipaul *The Return of Eva Perón* Knopf 80

5 The president is here, strong and firm as a monkey's tail.

Assuring Haitians that he would not flee the country, although he did so a week later, NY *Times* 1 Feb 86

ANTHONY EDEN, Prime Minister of Great Britain

6 If you've broken the eggs, you should make the omelette.

Letter to his brother during Suez Crisis, quoted by Elizabeth Longford *The Queen: The Life of Elizabeth II* Knopf 83

DWIGHT D EISENHOWER, 34th US President

7 Whatever America hopes to bring to pass in the world must first come to pass in the heart of America.

Inaugural address 20 Jan 53

8 Every gun that is made, every warship launched, every rocket fired, signifies in the final sense a theft from those who hunger and are not fed, those who are cold and are not clothed.

To Amer Society of Newspaper Editors 16 Apr 53

9 From behind the Iron Curtain, there are signs that tyranny is in trouble and reminders that its structure is as brittle as its surface is hard.

State of the Union address 7 Jan 54

10 From this day forward, the millions of our school-children will daily proclaim in every city and town, every village and rural schoolhouse, the dedication of our nation and our people to the Almighty.

On signing law for inclusion of the words "under God" in the Pledge of Allegiance, 14 Jun 54

11 I have one yardstick by which I test every major problem—and that yardstick is: Is it good for America?

On farm bill veto, address to the nation 16 Apr 56

12 Farming looks mighty easy when your plow is a pencil and you're a thousand miles from the corn field.

Address at Peoria IL 25 Sep 56

13 I could have spoken from Rhode Island where I have been staying . . . But I felt that, in speaking from the house of Lincoln, of Jackson, and of Wilson, my words would better convey both the sadness I feel in the action I was compelled today to make and the firmness with which I intend to pursue this course until the orders of the federal court at Little Rock can be executed without unlawful interference.

On sending troops to enforce integration in Little Rock AR High School, address to the nation broadcast from White House 24 Sep 57

14 This desk of mine is one at which a man may die, but from which he cannot resign.

Quoted by a friend, *Parade* 2 Feb 58

15 Oh, that lovely title, ex-president.

NY *Post* 26 Oct 59

16 I feel like the fellow in jail who is watching his scaffold being built.

On construction of reviewing stands for inauguration of his successor John F Kennedy, NY *Times* 6 Dec 60

17 Unlike presidential administrations, problems rarely have terminal dates.

State of the Union address 12 Jan 61

18 No one should ever sit in this office over 70 years old, and that I know.

On leaving office in 1961 at age 70, quoted in *Newsweek* 2 Mar 87

ELIZABETH II, Queen of England

19 I declare before you all that my whole life, whether it be long or short, shall be devoted to your service and the service of our great imperial family to which we all belong.

Twenty-first birthday address, recalled five years later on her succession to the throne 6 Feb 52

20 The upward course of a nation's history is due in the long run to the soundness of heart of its average men and women.

Christmas address 25 Dec 54

21 I cannot lead you into battle. I do not give you laws or administer justice but I can do something else—I can give my heart and my devotion to these old islands and to all the peoples of our brotherhood of nations.

First televised Christmas address 25 Dec 57

22 It is as queen of Canada that I am here. Queen of Canada and all Canadians, not just one or two ancestral strains.

Recognizing dissent of French-Canadians, address 9 Jul 73

23 We lost the American colonies because we lacked the statesmanship to know the right time and the manner of yielding what is impossible to keep.

In Philadelphia on six-day Bicentennial visit, *Newsweek* 19 Jul 76

24 It is easy enough to define what the Commonwealth is not. Indeed this is quite a popular pastime.

Silver Jubilee address 7 Jun 77

25 I myself prefer my New Zealand eggs for breakfast.

After she was pelted with eggs during a walkabout on New Zealand visit, new summaries 26 Feb 86

GERALD R FORD, 38th US President

1 My fellow Americans, our long national nightmare is over.
> On succeeding Richard M Nixon as president 9 Aug 74

2 Our constitution works. Our great republic is a government of laws, not of men.
> *ib*

3 I am acutely aware that you have not elected me as your president by your ballots, so I ask you to confirm me with your prayers.
> *ib*

4 A government big enough to give you everything you want is a government big enough to take from you everything you have.
> Address to Congress 12 Aug 74

5 As I rejected amnesty, so I reject revenge. I ask all Americans who ever asked for goodness and mercy in their lives, who ever sought forgiveness for their trespasses, to join in rehabilitating all the casualties of the tragic conflict of the past.
> On Americans who avoided conscription during the Vietnam War, to Veterans of Foreign Wars, Chicago, 19 Aug 74

6 An American tragedy in which we all have played a part.
> On Watergate, announcing pardon of former President Richard M Nixon 8 Sep 74

7 It can go on and on, or someone must write "The End" to it. I have concluded that only I can do that. And if I can, I must.
> *ib*

INDIRA GANDHI, Prime Minister of India

8 All my games were political games; I was, like Joan of Arc, perpetually being burned at the stake.
> On her childhood, NY *Times* 5 Nov 71

9 You cannot shake hands with a clenched fist.
> Quoted in *Christian Science Monitor* 17 May 82

10 If I die a violent death, as some fear and a few are plotting, I know that the violence will be in the thought and the action of the assassins, not in my dying.
> Handwritten statement found in her residence and later used on plaque in the garden where she was assassinated on October 31, 1984, opened to the public 27 May 85

RAJIV GANDHI, Prime Minister of India

11 She was mother not only to me but to the whole nation. She served the Indian people to the last drop of her blood.
> On succeeding his mother as prime minister 31 Oct 84

12 For some days, people thought that India was shaking. But there are always tremors when a great tree falls.
> Address three weeks after his mother's assassination, NY *Times* 20 Nov 84

MIKHAIL S GORBACHEV, Soviet Premier

13 Surely, God on high has not refused to give us enough wisdom to find ways to bring us an improvement . . . in relations between the two great nations on earth.
> *Time* 9 Sep 85

14 Certain people in the United States are driving nails into this structure of our relationship, then cutting off the heads. So the Soviets must use their teeth to pull them out.
> *ib*

15 Sometimes . . . when you stand face to face with someone, you cannot see his face.
> Following summit meeting with Ronald Reagan in Iceland, press conference 12 Oct 86

16 Without glasnost there is not, and there cannot be, democratism, the political creativity of the masses and their participation in management.
> February 1986 address to Party Congress on new policy of openness, NY *Times* 9 Nov 86

17 What we need is Star Peace and not Star Wars.
> To Indian Parliament, New Delhi, *ib* 28 Nov 86

18 Our enemy sees us clearly. . . . They will not start a war. They're worried about one thing: If democracy develops here, if we succeed, we will win.
> On relations with the US, *Time* 5 Jan 87

19 It is better to discuss things, to argue and engage in polemics than make perfidious plans of mutual destruction.
> Comment after Moscow talks with US Secretary of State George P Shultz, NY *Times* 19 Apr 87

YAKUBU GOWON, President of Nigeria

20 The trouble with military rule is that every colonel or general is soon full of ambition. The navy takes over today and the army tomorrow.
> Chicago *Daily News* 29 Aug 70

EDWARD HEATH, Prime Minister of Great Britain

21 Abhorrence of apartheid is a moral attitude, not a policy.
> At Lord Mayor's banquet, London, 16 Nov 70

CHAIM HERZOG, President of Israel

22 I do not bring forgiveness with me, nor forgetfulness. The only ones who can forgive are dead; the living have no right to forget.
> On first visit of an Israeli head of state to Bergen-Belsen, West Germany, where 50,000 persons died in Nazi concentration camp, NY *Times* 12 Apr 87

HIROHITO, Emperor of Japan

23 That most unfortunate war, which I deeply deplore.
> 1975 comment on World War II, quoted in NY *Times* 12 Jul 84

24 I made efforts to swallow tears and to protect the species of the Japanese nation.
> September 9, 1945, letter to Crown Prince Akihito after surrender to Allied forces, quoted in *ib* 28 Apr 86

HERBERT HOOVER, 31st US President

25 When there is a lack of honor in government, the morals of the whole people are poisoned.
> Recalled on eve of his 90th birthday, NY *Times* 9 Aug 64

26 Many years ago, I concluded that a few hair shirts were part of the mental wardrobe of every man. The president differs from other men in that he has a more extensive wardrobe.
> Quoted by Brooks Atkinson *ib* 17 Oct 64

1 I outlived the bastards.
> When asked about those who blamed him for the Depression, quoted by William O Douglas *The Court Years 1939–75* Random House 80

2 I'm the only person of distinction who's ever had a depression named for him.
> Quoted by Richard Norton Smith *An Uncommon Man* Simon & Schuster 84

HUSSEIN, King of Jordan

3 It is my firm belief that I have a link with the past and a responsibility to the future. I cannot give up. I cannot despair. There's a whole future, generations to come. I have to keep trying.
> Quoted by Curtis Wilkie "The Durable Monarch" Boston *Globe* 28 Jun 87

LYNDON B JOHNSON, 36th US President

4 I will do my best. That is all I can do. I ask for your help—and God's.
> On arriving in Washington DC on the evening of John F Kennedy's assassination, 22 Nov 63

5 I'd rather give my life than be afraid to give it.
> On decision to walk in Kennedy's funeral procession 25 Nov 63

6 We have talked long enough in this country about equal rights. . . . It is time now to write the next chapter—and to write it in the books of law.
> To Congress 27 Nov 63

7 This administration here and now declares unconditional war on poverty.
> State of the Union address 8 Jan 64

8 I want to make a policy statement. I am unabashedly in favor of women.
> On appointing 10 women to top government positions as part of his pledge to end a "stag government," 4 Mar 64

9 To conclude that women are unfitted to the task of our historic society seems to me the equivalent of closing male eyes to female facts.
> At White House swearing-in ceremony of women appointees 13 Apr 64

10 We have the opportunity to move not only toward the rich society and the powerful society, but upward to the Great Society.
> Address at University of Michigan 22 May 64

11 We Americans know—although others appear to forget—the risk of spreading conflict. We still seek no wider war.
> On ordering retaliatory action against North Vietnam Communist forces after renewed attacks on US destroyers in Gulf of Tonkin, address to the nation 4 Aug 64

12 They call upon us to supply American boys to do the job that Asian boys should do.
> Urging a policy of restraint in Vietnam, 12 Aug 64

13 When I was a boy . . . we didn't wake up with Vietnam and have Cyprus for lunch and the Congo for dinner.
> To Conference on Educational Legislation 1 Mar 65

14 A rioter with a Molotov cocktail in his hands is not fighting for civil rights any more than a Klansman with a sheet on his back and mask on his face. They are both more or less what the law declares them: lawbreakers, destroyers of constitutional rights and liberties and ultimately destroyers of a free America.
> To White House Conference on Equal Employment Opportunity held during rioting in Watts section of Los Angeles, 20 Aug 65

15 Our purpose in Vietnam is to prevent the success of aggression. It is not conquest, it is not empire, it is not foreign bases, it is not domination. It is, simply put, just to prevent the forceful conquest of South Vietnam by North Vietnam.
> Accepting Freedom House Award, *Time* 4 Mar 66

16 Our numbers have increased in Vietnam because the aggression of others has increased in Vietnam. There is not, and there will not be, a mindless escalation.
> *ib*

17 It is the common failing of totalitarian regimes that they cannot really understand the nature of our democracy. They mistake dissent for disloyalty. They mistake restlessness for a rejection of policy. They mistake a few committees for a country. They misjudge individual speeches for public policy.
> Answering North Vietnamese charge that US could not endure a long, inconclusive war, address at San Antonio 29 Sep 67

18 I report to you that our country is challenged at home and abroad: that it is our will that is being tried and not our strength; our sense of purpose and not our ability to achieve a better America.
> State of the Union address 17 Jan 68

19 I believe, with abiding conviction, that this people—nurtured by their deep faith, tutored by their hard lessons, moved by their high aspirations—have the will to meet the trials that these times impose.
> *ib*

20 What we won when all of our people united . . . must not be lost in suspicion and distrust and selfishness and politics. . . . Accordingly, I shall not seek, and I will not accept, the nomination of my party for another term as president.
> Address to the nation 31 Mar 68

21 I'm tired. I'm tired of feeling rejected by the American people. I'm tired of waking up in the middle of the night worrying about the war.
> To a friend following his withdrawal speech, quoted in *Newsweek* 15 Apr 68

22 The presidency has made every man who occupied it, no matter how small, bigger than he was; and no matter how big, not big enough for its demands.
> NY *Times* 26 Mar 72

23 Being president is like being a jackass in a hailstorm. There's nothing to do but stand there and take it.
> Recalled on his death 22 Jan 73

24 I won't have you electioneering on my doorstep. Every time you get in trouble in Parliament you run over here with your shirttail hanging out.
> To Prime Minister Harold Wilson, quoted by William Safire *Safire's Political Dictionary* Random House 78

25 The Russians feared Ike. They didn't fear me.
> On Korean War in contrast to Vietnam War, quoted by Richard M Nixon *Time* 29 Jul 85

1 If you let a bully come in your front yard, he'll be on your porch the next day and the day after that he'll rape your wife in your own bed.

On appeasement, quoted by Walter Isaacson and Evan Thomas *The Wise Men* Simon & Schuster 86

2 I don't believe I'll ever get credit for anything I do in foreign affairs, no matter how successful it is, because I didn't go to Harvard.

To Hugh Sidey, quoted by *ib*

CONSTANTINE KARAMANLIS, Premier of Greece

3 We are given to the cult of personality; when things go badly we look to some messiah to save us. . . . If by chance we think we have found one, it will not be long before we destroy him.

NY *Times* 17 Nov 74

KENNETH KAUNDA, President of Zambia

4 The power which establishes a state is violence; the power which maintains it is violence; the power which eventually overthrows it is violence.

Quoted in Colin M Morris ed *Kaunda on Violence* Collins 80

JOHN F KENNEDY, 35th US President

5 When at some future date the high court of history sits in judgment on each one of us—recording whether in our brief span of service we fulfilled our responsibilities to the state—our success or failure, in whatever office we may hold, will be measured by the answers to four questions—were we truly men of courage . . . were we truly men of judgment . . . were we truly men of integrity . . . were we truly men of dedication?

As president-elect, to Massachusetts legislature, NY *Times* 10 Jan 61

6 Let the word go forth from this time and place, to friend and foe alike, that the torch has been passed to a new generation of Americans—born in this century, tempered by war, disciplined by a hard and bitter peace, proud of our ancient heritage and unwilling to witness or permit the slow undoing of those human rights to which this nation has always been committed and to which we are committed today at home and around the world.

Inaugural address 20 Jan 61

7 Let every nation know, whether it wishes us well or ill, that we shall pay any price, bear any burden, meet any hardship, support any friend, oppose any foe to assure the survival and the success of liberty.

ib

8 Let us never negotiate out of fear. But let us never fear to negotiate.

ib

9 In the long history of the world, only a few generations have been granted the role of defending freedom in its hour of maximum danger. I do not shrink from this responsibility—I welcome it.

ib

10 And so, my fellow Americans: Ask not what your country can do for you—ask what you can do for your country.

ib

11 All this will not be finished in the first hundred days. Nor will it be finished in the first thousand days, nor in the life of this administration, nor even perhaps in our lifetime on this planet. But let us begin.

ib

12 To state the facts frankly is not to despair the future nor indict the past. The prudent heir takes careful inventory of his legacies and gives a faithful accounting to those whom he owes an obligation of trust.

On outgoing administration, State of the Union address 30 Jan 61

13 Geography has made us neighbors. History has made us friends. Economics has made us partners, and necessity has made us allies. Those whom God has so joined together, let no man put asunder.

To Canadian Parliament 17 May 61

14 Tell him, if he doesn't mind, we'll shake hands.

On meeting Soviet Premier Nikita S Khrushchev in Vienna 4 Jun 61

15 I hear it said that West Berlin is militarily untenable—and so was Bastogne, and so, in fact, was Stalingrad. Any danger spot is tenable if men—brave men—will make it so.

Address to the nation 25 Jul 61

16 The freedom of the city is not negotiable. We cannot negotiate with those who say, "What's mine is mine and what's yours is negotiable."

ib

17 Khrushchev reminds me of the tiger hunter who has picked a place on the wall to hang the tiger's skin long before he has caught the tiger. This tiger has other ideas.

NY *Times* 24 Dec 61

18 My father always told me that all businessmen were sons of bitches, but I never believed it till now.

On steel industry executives who increased prices, to staff members 11 Apr 62

19 The path we have chosen for the present is full of hazards, as all paths are. . . . The cost of freedom is always high, but Americans have always paid it. And one path we shall never choose, and that is the path of surrender, or submission.

Announcing blockade of Cuba to stop delivery of Soviet missiles, address to the nation 22 Oct 62

20 There are many people in the world who really don't understand—or say they don't—what is the great issue between the free world and the Communist world. . . . Let them come to Berlin!

At West Berlin City Hall 26 Jun 63

21 All free men, wherever they may live, are citizens of Berlin. And therefore, as a free man, I take pride in the words *"Ich bin ein Berliner!"*

ib

22 I don't think the intelligence reports are all that hot. Some days I get more out of the New York *Times*.

Recalled on his death 22 Nov 63

23 If anyone is crazy enough to want to kill a president of the United States, he can do it. All he must be prepared to do is give his life for the president's.

Quoted by Pierre Salinger *With Kennedy* Doubleday 66

1 [Like] dealing with Dad—all give and no take.

On negotiating with Soviet Premier Nikita S Khrushchev, quoted by Peter Collier and David Horowitz *The Kennedys* Summit 84

2 You never know what's hit you. A gunshot is the perfect way.

When asked how he would choose to die, *ib*

MOHAMMED DAUD KHAN, President of Afghanistan

3 I feel the happiest when I can light my American cigarettes with Soviet matches.

Newsweek 30 Jul 73

AYATOLLAH RUHOLLA KHOMEINI, spiritual leader of Iran

4 One thing I congratulate everyone on is the great explosion which has occurred in Washington's Black House and the very important scandal which has gripped leaders of America.

On disclosure of US arms sales to Iran, NY *Times* 21 Nov 86

5 [Americans] are the great Satan, the wounded snake.

On Americans, NBC TV 8 Dec 86

NIKITA S KHRUSHCHEV, Soviet Premier

6 Whether you like it or not, history is on our side. We will bury you!

To Western ambassadors at reception in Moscow 17 Nov 56

7 Revolutions are the locomotives of history.

To Supreme Soviet, *Pravda* 8 May 57

8 If you live among dogs, keep a stick. After all, this is what a hound has teeth for—to bite when he feels like it!

On military preparedness, interview in Japanese newspaper 9 Jul 57

9 Support by United States rulers is rather in the nature of the support that the rope gives to a hanged man.

Interview in Egyptian newspaper 25 Nov 57

10 We say the name of God, but that is only habit.

Time 6 Jan 58

11 The more bombers, the less room for doves of peace.

Moscow Radio 14 Mar 58

12 Don't you have a machine that puts food into the mouth and pushes it down?

To Vice President Richard M Nixon during "kitchen debate" in model home at Amer National Exhibition, Moscow, news summaries 25 Jul 59

13 Bombs do not choose. They will hit everything.

At Moscow rally, NY *Herald Tribune* 12 Aug 61

14 [It] would be like inviting them to eat milk with an owl.

Explaining that people must not be asked to join a commune if they think of it "as a table set with empty plates around which sit high-minded and fully equal people," NY *Times* 7 Mar 62

15 I once said, "We will bury you," and I got into trouble with it. Of course we will not bury you with a shovel. Your own working class will bury you.

To Westerners, address at Split, Yugoslavia, 24 Aug 63

16 If you start throwing hedgehogs under me, I shall throw a couple of porcupines under you.

On US criticism of Berlin Wall, NY *Times* 7 Nov 63

17 I want to talk to these people because they stay in power and you change all the time.

Asking to meet with Italian businessmen instead of government officials, *Life* 24 Nov 67

18 There are still some people who think that we have Stalin to thank for all our progress, who quake before Stalin's dirty underdrawers, who stand at attention and salute them.

Khrushchev Remembers, translated and edited by Strobe Talbott, Little, Brown 70

19 I'll step on your corns any time I want.

On East Berlin and failed US invasion of Cuba, to President John F Kennedy at 1961 Vienna summit meeting, quoted by Ralph G Martin *A Hero for Our Time* Macmillan 83

HELMUT KOHL, Chancellor of West Germany

20 I have been underestimated for decades. I've done very well that way.

On eve of victory for his coalition, NY *Times* 25 Jan 87

ADOLFO LÓPEZ MATEOS, President of Mexico

21 A woman is a citizen who works for Mexico. We must not treat her differently from a man, except to honor her more.

On emancipation of women, *Time* 12 Oct 59

DIOSDADO MACAPAGAL, President of the Philippines

22 I have sat at the sumptuous tables of power, but I have not run away with the silverware.

On his political career, *Time* 24 Nov 61

HAROLD MACMILLAN, Prime Minister of Great Britain

23 There might be 1 finger on the trigger, but there will be 15 fingers on the safety catch.

On breakdown of summit conference on nuclear disarmament, to House of Commons 31 May 60

24 A strange, a perverted creed that has a queer attraction both for the most primitive and for the most sophisticated societies.

On Communism, NY *Herald Tribune* 15 Oct 61

25 Once the bear's hug has got you, it is apt to be for keeps.

On Soviet domination, *ib*

26 It is the duty of Her Majesty's government . . . neither to flap nor to falter.

London *Observer* 19 Nov 61

27 I was determined that no British government should be brought down by the action of two tarts.

On Profumo Affair, news summaries 13 Jun 63

28 Britain's most useful role is somewhere between bee and dinosaur.

On mixing strength with efficiency, recalled on his death 29 Dec 86

29 [It was] not at all like an experience in the modern world. More like meeting George III at Brighton.

On 1953 meeting with President Dwight D Eisenhower in Bermuda to discuss the Middle East, *ib*

30 It's no use crying over spilt summits.

On Soviet cancellation of summit conference after 1960 downing of US spy plane, *ib*

1 Sixty-three years ago . . . the unemployment figure was 29 percent. Last November [it] was 28 percent. A rather sad end to one's life.
> On his home borough Stockton-on-Tees, quoted in *Newsweek* 12 Jan 87

2 I was a sort of son to Ike, and it was the other way round with Kennedy.
> On relationship with Presidents Dwight D Eisenhower and John F Kennedy, quoted in *Time* 12 Jan 87

MAO ZEDONG, Chinese premier

3 Passivity is fatal to us. Our goal is to make the enemy passive.
> *Time* 18 Dec 50

4 Communism is not love. Communism is a hammer which we use to crush the enemy.
> *ib*

5 Revolution is not a dinner party, not an essay, nor a painting, nor a piece of embroidery; it cannot be advanced softly, gradually, carefully, considerately, respectfully, politely, plainly and modestly.
> *ib*

6 Let a hundred flowers bloom.
> Address acknowledging contradictions within Communist society 27 Feb 57

7 All reactionaries are paper tigers.
> News summaries 31 Aug 60

8 Swollen in head, weak in legs, sharp in tongue but empty in belly.
> On intellectuals, quoted by Fu-sheng Mu *The Wilting of the Hundred Flowers* Praeger 63

9 Despise the enemy strategically, but take him seriously tactically.
> In handbook for revolutionaries, quoted in *Time* 22 Mar 63

10 I voted for you during your last election.
> To President Richard M Nixon, quoted in *RN: Memoirs of Richard Nixon* Grosset & Dunlap 78

11 People like me sound like a lot of big cannons.
> *ib*

12 [Khrushchev] should get a one-ton medal.
> On forcing China to work alone in developing nuclear power, quoted in NY *Times* 5 May 85

FERDINAND E MARCOS, former President of the Philippines

13 It is not a choice of life, it is a choice of death. If this is life, I'd rather die.
> On exile in Hawaii, NBC TV 9 Dec 86

GOLDA MEIR, Prime Minister of Israel

14 We have always said that in our war with the Arabs we had a secret weapon—no alternative.
> *Life* 3 Oct 69

15 The Egyptians could run to Egypt, the Syrians into Syria. The only place we could run was into the sea, and before we did that we might as well fight.
> *ib*

16 It is true we have won all our wars, but we have paid for them. We don't want victories anymore.
> *ib*

17 [The Soviet government] is the most realistic regime in the world—no ideals.
> Interview 7 Oct 69

18 Arab sovereignty in Jerusalem just cannot be. This city will not be divided—not half and half, not 60–40, not 75–25, nothing.
> *Time* 19 Feb 73

19 It's no accident many accuse me of conducting public affairs with my heart instead of my head. Well, what if I do? . . . Those who don't know how to weep with their whole heart don't know how to laugh either.
> *Ms* Apr 73

20 Let me tell you something that we Israelis have against Moses. He took us 40 years through the desert in order to bring us to the one spot in the Middle East that has no oil!
> At dinner honoring West German Chancellor Willy Brandt, NY *Times* 10 Jun 73

21 To be or not to be is not a question of compromise. Either you be or you don't be.
> When asked during a White House visit about the question of Israel's future, *ib* 12 Dec 74

22 I don't know why you use a fancy French word like *détente* when there's a good English phrase for it—cold war.
> *Newsweek* 19 Jan 76

23 What do you gain, Soviet Union, from this miserable policy? Where is your decency? Would it be a disgrace for you to give up this battle?
> On suppression of freedom for Jews in the USSR, to World Conference on Soviet Jewry, Brussels, NY *Times* 20 Feb 76

24 I never did anything alone. Whatever was accomplished in this country was accomplished collectively.
> To Egyptian President Anwar el-Sadat during his unprecedented visit to Israel, news summaries 21 Nov 77

25 Above all, this country is our own. Nobody has to get up in the morning and worry what his neighbors think of him. Being a Jew is no problem here.
> On 30th anniversary of founding of Israel, *International Herald Tribune* 11 May 78

26 We do not rejoice in victories. We rejoice when a new kind of cotton is grown and when strawberries bloom in Israel.
> Recalled on her death 8 Dec 78

ISKANDER MIRZA, President of Pakistan

27 Democracy is hypocrisy without limitation.
> *Time* 20 Oct 58

FRANÇOIS MITTERRAND, President of France

28 A man loses contact with reality if he is not surrounded by his books.
> On why he continued to live in Rue de Bièvre, using the Elysée Palace only for official functions, London *Times* 10 May 82

29 France is delighted at this new opportunity to show the world . . . that when one has the will one can succeed in joining peoples who have been brought close by history.
> Announcing plans for joint British-French railroad tunnel under English Channel, NY *Times* 21 Jan 86

JOSEPH MOBUTO, President of Zaire

1 I no longer have a borrowed soul. I no longer have borrowed thoughts or ideas. I no longer speak in a borrowed language.

> On changing his country's name from Democratic Republic of the Congo to Zaire, quoted in San Francisco *Examiner & Chronicle* 25 Jun 72

MIR HUSSEIN MOUSSAVI, Prime Minister of Iran

2 The Americans still think that feudalism rules the world and therefore demand that Iran explain its handling of the hijacking affair. Iran explains nothing to anyone but God.

> On refusal to extradite hijackers, NY *Times* 13 Dec 84

BRIAN MULRONEY, Prime Minister of Canada

3 The biggest trading partner of the United States is not West Germany or Japan, it's right here.

> Demand that Reagan administration make greater efforts to honor commitments on trade and acid rain, NY *Times* 22 Jan 87

GAMAL ABDEL NASSER, President of Egypt

4 We're a sentimental people. We like a few kind words better than millions of dollars given in a humiliating way.

> Refusing economic aid from the West, *Réalités* Jan 58

5 People do not want words—they want the sound of battle . . . the battle of destiny.

> To National Assembly 20 Jan 69

6 There is no longer a way out of our present situation except by forging a road toward our objective, violently and by force, over a sea of blood and under a horizon blazing with fire.

> To Parliament 6 Nov 69

JAWAHARLAL NEHRU, Prime Minister of India

7 The only alternative to coexistence is codestruction.

> London *Observer* 29 Aug 54

8 Democracy is good. I say this because other systems are worse.

> NY *Times* 25 Jan 61

9 I have become a queer mixture of the East and the West, out of place everywhere, at home nowhere.

> On influence of his British education, recalled on his death 27 May 64

RICHARD M NIXON, 37th US President

10 Certainly in the next 50 years we shall see a woman president, perhaps sooner than you think. A woman can and should be able to do any political job that a man can do.

> To League of Women Voters, Washington DC, 16 Apr 69

11 My concern today is not with the length of a person's hair but with his conduct.

> On campus radicals, at General Beadle State College, Madison SD, 3 Jun 69

12 The student who invades an administration building, roughs up a dean, rifles the files and issues "nonnegotiable demands" may have some of his demands met by a permissive university administration. But the greater his "victory" the more he will have undermined the security of his own rights.

> *ib*

13 This is the greatest week in the history of the world since the Creation.

> Saluting crew of the Apollo 11 four days after the first manned landing on the moon, aboard USS *Hornet* 24 Jul 69

14 If we take the route of the permanent handout, the American character will itself be impoverished.

> Proposal to reform welfare programs, address to the nation 8 Aug 69

15 Tonight—to you, the great silent majority of my fellow Americans—I ask for your support.

> On his Vietnam War policy, address to the nation 3 Nov 69

16 You see these bums, you know, blowing up campuses . . . storming around about this issue.

> On student protesters against Vietnam War, remark on leaving Pentagon meeting 1 May 70

17 There are some people, you know, they think the way to be a big man is to shout and stomp and raise hell—and then nothing ever really happens. I'm not like that . . . I never shoot blanks.

> *Look* 19 Oct 71

18 My strong point is not rhetoric, it isn't showmanship, it isn't big promises—those things that create the glamour and the excitement that people call charisma and warmth.

> CBS TV 2 Jan 72

19 My strong point, if I have a strong point, is performance. I always do more than I say. I always produce more than I promise.

> *ib*

20 The presidency has many problems, but boredom is the least of them.

> 60th birthday interview 9 Jan 73

21 I believe in the battle—whether it's the battle of a campaign or the battle of this office, which is a continuing battle.

> Interview two days after his second inauguration, 22 Jan 73

22 As this long and difficult war ends, I would like to address a few special words to . . . the American people: Your steadfastness in supporting our insistence on peace with honor has made peace with honor possible.

> On the Vietnam War, address to the nation 23 Jan 73

23 Under the doctrine of separation of powers, the manner in which the president personally exercises his assigned executive powers is not subject to questioning by another branch of government.

> Statement issued from the White House 12 Mar 73

24 I want you to stonewall it.

> To staff on news of break-in at Watergate headquarters of Democratic Party, taped conversation 22 Mar 73

25 There will be no whitewash in the White House.

> On Watergate investigation, press conference 17 Apr 73

26 I doubt if any of them would even intentionally double-park.

> On suspects in Watergate break-in, LA *Times* 1 May 73

27 If I were to make public these tapes, containing blunt and candid remarks on many different subjects, the confidentiality of the office of the president would always be suspect.

> Address to the nation 15 Aug 73

1 People have got to know whether or not their president is a crook. Well, I'm not a crook. I earned everything I've got.
> To Associated Press Managing Editors Assn, Disneyland, 17 Nov 73

2 There is a time to be timid. There is a time to be conciliatory. There is a time, even, to fly and there is a time to fight. And I'm going to fight like hell.
> On Congressional moves toward impeachment, press conference 27 Jan 74

3 Unless a president can protect the privacy of the advice he gets, he cannot get the advice he needs.
> *ib*

4 The 1976 Bicentennial is not going to be invented in Washington, printed in triplicate by the Government Printing Office [and] mailed to you by the United States Postal Service.
> Calling for citizens to supersede government in preparing observance of nation's 200th birthday, address to the nation 10 Mar 74

5 My own view is that taping of conversations for historical purposes was a bad decision on the part of all the presidents. I don't think Kennedy should have done it. I don't think Johnson should have done it, and I don't think we should have done it.
> To Executives Club, Chicago, NY *Times* 16 Mar 74

6 I have never been a quitter. To leave office before my term is completed is opposed to every instinct in my body. But as president I must put the interests of America first . . . Therefore, I shall resign the presidency effective at noon tomorrow.
> Address to the nation 8 Aug 74

7 This [is] a burden I shall bear for every day of the life that is left to me.
> On Watergate, statement to the press 8 Sep 74

8 I brought myself down. I impeached myself by resigning.
> Television interview with David Frost 4 May 77

9 I let the American people down.
> *ib*

10 When the president does it, that means that it is not illegal.
> Arguing for extenuating circumstances, *ib*

11 I had never expected that the China initiative would come to fruition in the form of a Ping-Pong team.
> On first friendly overture by People's Republic of China in March 1972, *RN: Memoirs of Richard Nixon* Grosset & Dunlap 78

12 My telephone calls and meetings and decisions were now parts of a prescribed ritual aimed at making peace with the past; his calls, his meetings and his decisions were already the ones that would shape America's future.
> On transfer of power to his successor Gerald R Ford after Nixon's decision to resign, *ib*

13 I took a look around the office. . . . I walked out and closed the door behind me. I knew that I would not be back there again.
> On leaving the Executive Office Building on August 8, 1974, *ib*

14 "Good luck, Mr President," I said to him. "As I told you when I named you, I know the country is going to be in good hands with you in the Oval Office."
> Farewell to Gerald R Ford on August 9, 1974, *ib*

15 The memory of that scene for me is like a frame of film forever frozen at that moment: the red carpet, the green lawn, the white house, the leaden sky. . . . The new president and his first lady.
> *ib*

16 I turned into the helicopter . . . the red carpet was rolled up. . . . The White House was behind us now.
> *ib*

17 What starts the process, really, are laughs and slights and snubs when you are a kid. . . . If your anger is deep enough and strong enough, you learn that you can change those attitudes by excellence, personal gut performance.
> Quoted by Ken W Clawson Washington *Post* 9 Aug 79

18 It's a piece of cake until you get to the top. You find you can't stop playing the game the way you've always played it.
> *ib*

19 So you are lean and mean and resourceful and you continue to walk on the edge of the precipice because over the years you have become fascinated by how close you can walk without losing your balance.
> *ib*

20 Get a good night's sleep and don't bug anybody without asking me.
> To re-election campaign manager Clark MacGregor, recorded on tape later made public, *Christian Science Monitor* 14 Aug 80

21 No event in American history is more misunderstood than the Vietnam War. It was misreported then, and it is misremembered now.
> *No More Vietnams* Arbor House 85, quoted in NY *Times* 28 Mar 85

22 Rarely have so many people been so wrong about so much.
> *ib*

23 People see me and they think, "He's risen from the dead."
> *Newsweek* 19 May 86

24 They say, "Gee, you look great." That means they thought you looked like hell before.
> *ib*

25 When I retire I'm going to spend my evenings by the fireplace going through those boxes. There are things in there that ought to be burned.
> 1971 statement recalled by John Ehrlichman, *Parade* 30 Nov 86

JULIUS K NYERERE, Prime Minister of Tanganyika/ Tanzania

26 Freedom to many means immediate betterment, as if by magic. . . . Unless I can meet at least some of these aspirations, my support will wane and my head will roll just as surely as the tickbird follows the rhino.
> *Time* 15 Dec 61

27 Small nations are like indecently dressed women. They tempt the evil-minded.
> *Reporter* 9 Apr 64

MOHAMMED REZA PAHLAVI, Shah of Iran

28 *Shah* is a kind of magic word with the Persian people.
> NY *Times* 25 Sep 67

1 Let me tell you quite bluntly that this king business has given me personally nothing but headaches.
ib 27 Oct 67

2 My advisers built a wall between myself and my people. I didn't realize what was happening. When I woke up, I had lost my people.
To Egyptian President Anwar el-Sadat, after the shah's overthrow, *Time* 10 Dec 79

3 My main mistake was to have made an ancient people advance by forced marches toward independence, health, culture, affluence, comfort.
Recalled on his death 27 Jul 80

LESTER B PEARSON, Prime Minister of Canada

4 I accept now with equanimity the question so constantly addressed to me, "Are you an American?" and merely return the accurate answer, "Yes, I am a Canadian."
1941 statement recalled on his election as prime minister, news summaries 31 Dec 63

5 This is the flag of the future, but it does not dishonor the past.
On his country's new Maple Leaf flag, to House of Commons 15 Dec 64

6 We have achieved the most amazing things, a few million people opening up half a continent. But we have not yet found a Canadian soul except in time of war.
On lack of national identity, *Time* 5 May 67

SHIMON PERES, Prime Minister of Israel

7 Nothing had excited me—the huge cars, the entourages, the bodyguards, the policeman jumping to attention, all meant nothing to me . . . till I came to the old man's office.
On becoming prime minister two decades after his mentor David Ben Gurion, *People* 15 Oct 84

8 Why cross an ocean when you can cross a river? Why should we sail to Washington when we can meet right away 10 miles from here?
On Middle East peace initiative by Jordan's King Hussein, *Time* 17 Jun 85

9 Leading the Jewish people is not easy—we are a divided, obstinate, highly individualistic people who have cultivated faith, sharp-wittedness and polemics to a very high level.
"In Homage to Ben Gurion" NY *Times* 5 Oct 86

10 It is not only the psychology of the people that makes them so exacting—their geographical situation has been equally problematic.
ib

11 He altered the image of the Jew from that of rabbi, merchant, wanderer, to that of scientist, farmer and soldier.
On David Ben Gurion, *ib*

12 He restored the Bible to its people, he restored the people to the Bible.
ib

JUAN D PERÓN, President of Argentina

13 It is not that we were so good, but those who followed us were so bad that they made us seem better than we were.
1972 interview in Spain, recalled on his return to power, NY *Times* 14 Jul 73

14 We are no longer interested in elections except as a means to reach our objectives.
ib

15 The order of the day for every Peronist . . . is to answer a violent action with another action still more violent.
Recalled on his death 1 Jul 74

SOUVANNA PHOUMA, Premier of Laos

16 I am a good friend to Communists abroad but I do not like them at home.
On the art of remaining neutral, *Life* 3 Nov 61

GEORGES POMPIDOU, President of France

17 France is a widow.
On death of Charles de Gaulle, *Newsweek* 23 Nov 70

18 The rest of the world cannot be expected to regulate its life by a clock which is always slow.
On US dollar as a "basic monetary yardstick . . . that constantly loses value as a result of purely internal politics," Washington *Post* 26 May 71

MUAMMAR QADDAFI, Libyan head of state

19 If Abu Nidal is a terrorist, then so is George Washington.
Reply to President Ronald Reagan in defense of Palestinian terrorist, *Newsweek* 20 Jan 86

20 I am sailing out along parallel 32.5 to stress that this is the Libyan border. This is the line of death where we shall stand and fight with our backs to the wall.
On planning confrontation with US Sixth Fleet in Mediterranean, NY *Times* 26 Jan 86

21 American soldiers must be turned into lambs and eating them is tolerated.
Address two months after US bombing raid on Tripoli, *ib* 15 Jun 86

22 We are capable of destroying America and breaking its nose.
ib

23 The man who carried out the attack is still in power and still insane, so we shall expect another attack any minute.
On President Ronald Reagan, quoted in *US News & World Report* 27 Oct 86

RONALD REAGAN, 40th US President

24 This administration is totally colorblind.
On appropriating funds to investigate killing of black children in Atlanta, 13 Mar 81

25 We have the means to change the laws we find unjust or onerous. We cannot, as citizens, pick and choose the laws we will or will not obey.
On dismissing 12,000 striking air traffic controllers, to United Brotherhood of Carpenters and Joiners, Chicago, 3 Sep 81

26 The Soviet Union would remain a one-party nation even if an opposition party were permitted—because everyone would join that party.
To British Parliament 8 Jun 82

27 Democracy is not a fragile flower; still it needs cultivating.
Introducing Project Democracy to foster democratic ideals in authoritarian regimes, *ib*

1 The ultimate determinant in the struggle now going on for the world will not be bombs and rockets but a test of wills and ideas—a trial of spiritual resolve: the values we hold, the beliefs we cherish and the ideals to which we are dedicated.
ib

2 [We seek] a constitutional amendment to permit voluntary school prayer. God should never have been expelled from America's classrooms in the first place.
State of the Union address 25 Jan 83

3 I call upon the scientific community in our country, those who gave us nuclear weapons, to turn their great talents now to the cause of mankind and world peace: to give us the means of rendering these nuclear weapons impotent and obsolete.
Introducing the Strategic Defense Initiative, address to the nation 23 Mar 83

4 Tonight we are launching an effort which holds the promise of changing the course of human history.
ib

5 My belief has always been . . . that wherever in this land any individual's constitutional rights are being unjustly denied, it is the obligation of the federal government—at point of bayonet if necessary—to restore that individual's constitutional rights.
Press conference 17 May 83

6 They don't worship at the altar of forced busing and mandatory quotas. They don't believe you can remedy past discrimination by mandating new discrimination.
Defending his nominees for Civil Rights Commission, quoted by Jean Nathan Miller "Ronald Reagan and the Techniques of Discrimination" *Atlantic* Feb 84

7 If I thought there was some reason to be concerned about them, I wouldn't be sleeping in this house tonight.
When asked about continued presence of Soviet nuclear submarines along US coastlines, press conference 22 May 84

8 Damn it, Pierre, what do you want me to do? We'll go sit with empty chairs to get those guys back to the table.
To Pierre Trudeau, prime minister of Canada, who pressed for détente with the USSR when Soviet leadership changed, Washington *Post* 15 Jun 84

9 My fellow Americans: I'm pleased to tell you today that I've signed legislation that will outlaw Russia forever. We begin bombing in five minutes.
Comment while testing a microphone before a broadcast 11 Aug 84

10 Anyone that's ever had their kitchen done over knows that it never gets done as soon as you wish it would.
Attempting to explain delay in installing security devices in US embassy in Beirut after bombing that claimed many lives, NY *Times* 26 Sep 84

11 The war in Vietnam threatened to tear our society apart, and the political and philosophical disagreements that separated each side continue, to some extent. It's been said that these memorials reflect a hunger for healing.
On privately financed Vietnam Veterans Memorial and statue in Washington DC, Veterans Day address 11 Nov 84

12 Some of your countrymen were unable to distinguish between their native dislike for war and the stainless patriotism of those who suffered its scars. But there has been a rethinking [and] now we can say to you, and say as a nation, thank you for your courage.
ib

13 Some say it will bring war to the heavens, but its purpose is to deter war, in the heavens and on earth.
On Strategic Defense Initiative, State of the Union address 6 Feb 85

14 The freedom fighters of Nicaragua . . . are the moral equal of our Founding Fathers and the brave men and women of the French Resistance.
To National Conservative Political Action Conference 1 Mar 85

15 The vote on the Peacekeeper is also a vote on Geneva. Rejecting the Peacekeeper will knock the legs out from under the negotiating table.
On importance of the MX missile, which he had dubbed "the Peacekeeper," in arms negotiations, *Newsweek* 18 Mar 85

16 Someone must stand up to those who say, "Here's the key, there's the Treasury, just take as many of those hard-earned tax dollars as you want."
On vetoing a bill that would have extended $2 billion in federal loan guarantees to farmers, *Time* 18 Mar 85

17 I will veto again and again until spending is brought under control.
ib

18 People don't start wars, governments do.
On eve of Geneva arms negotiations meeting, *ib*

19 I have only one thing to say to the tax increasers. Go ahead—make my day.
Picking up dialogue from Clint Eastwood's 1983 movie *Sudden Impact, ib* 25 Mar 85

20 Most [tax revisions] didn't improve the system, they made it more like Washington itself: complicated, unfair, cluttered with gobbledygook and loopholes designed for those with the power and influence to hire high-priced legal and tax advisers.
Address to the nation 28 May 85

21 Even Albert Einstein reportedly needed help on his 1040 form.
ib

22 The distance between the present system and our proposal is like comparing the distance between a Model T and the space shuttle. And I should know; I've seen both.
ib

23 The little dictator who went to Moscow in his green fatigues to receive a bear hug did not forsake the doctrine of Lenin when he returned to the West and appeared in a two-piece suit.
On Daniel Ortega Saavedra, president of Nicaragua, *Time* 17 Jun 85

24 The current tax code is a daily mugging.
Labor Day address, Independence MO, 2 Sep 85

25 America's view of apartheid is simple and straightforward: We believe it is wrong. We condemn it. And we are united in hoping for the day when apartheid will be no more.
On ordering sanctions against South Africa, announcement from the Oval Office 9 Sep 85

1 These young Americans sent a message to terrorists everywhere . . . "You can run but you can't hide."
> On US pilots who captured four terrorists who had hijacked a ship in the Mediterranean, paraphrasing Joe Louis's 1946 comment, press conference 11 Oct 85

2 If we don't want to see the map of Central America covered in a sea of red, eventually lapping at our own borders, we must act now.
> Appeal to Congress for $100 million in aid for Nicaraguan rebels, White House statement 5 Mar 86

3 My fellow Americans, I must speak to you tonight about a mounting danger in Central America that threatens the security of the United States. This danger will not go away; it will grow worse, much worse, if we fail to take action now.
> On aid for Nicaraguan rebels, address to the nation 16 Mar 86

4 As long as there are guns, the individual that wants a gun for a crime is going to have one and going to get it. The only person who's going to be penalized and have difficulty is the law-abiding citizen, who then cannot have [it] if he wants protection—the protection of a weapon in his home, for home protection.
> On his support for removal of gun controls, White House interview 22 Mar 86

5 I've often wondered how some people in positions of this kind . . . manage without having had any acting experience.
> Interview with Barbara Walters ABC TV 24 Mar 86

6 I have come to the conclusion that the 22nd Amendment [limiting the presidency to two terms] was a mistake. Shouldn't the people have the right to vote for someone as many times as they want to vote for him?
> ib

7 I think the presidency is an institution over which you have temporary custody.
> When asked what he would tell students about the presidency, interview with Hugh Sidey "In Search of History" Time 7 Apr 86

8 The White House is the leakiest place I've ever been in.
> On special measures to ensure secrecy of plans to bomb Libya, press conference 9 Apr 86

9 We know that this mad dog of the Middle East has a goal of a world revolution.
> On Muammar Qaddafi of Libya, ib

10 Today we have done what we had to do. If necessary, we shall do it again.
> Address to the nation an hour after US air attack on Muammar Qaddafi's Tripoli headquarters in reprisal for terrorist bombing of Berlin nightclub and other incidents in which American lives were lost, 14 Apr 86

11 [Qaddafi] counted on America to be passive. He counted wrong.
> ib

12 I don't have too much time for fiction.
> On memoirs of former budget director David A Stockman, NY Times 18 Apr 86

13 The nine most terrifying words in the English language are, "I'm from the government and I'm here to help."
> Opening Chicago press conference with acknowledgment of farmers' need for federal assistance, 12 Aug 86

14 Isn't it strange that . . . people build walls to keep an enemy out, and there's only one part of the world and one philosophy where they have to build walls to keep their people in?
> On the Berlin Wall, ib

15 There is bitter bile in my throat.
> Blaming a newspaper, "that rag in Beirut," for leaking reports of US arms sales to Iran, Time 8 Dec 86

16 I've never seen the sharks circling like they now are with blood in the water.
> Acknowledging criticism engendered by revelations that money from arms sales to Iran had gone to Contra forces in Nicaragua, ib

17 I do not feel betrayed. . . . He has a fine record. He is a national hero.
> On Oliver L North's work on the National Security Council, ib

18 My only criticism is that I wasn't told everything.
> ib

19 I just don't think it's good for us to be run out of town.
> Refusing to cancel Secretary of State George P Shultz's visit to Moscow after discovery of bugs in new US embassy building, ib 20 Apr 87

ANWAR EL-SADAT, President of Egypt

20 Russians can give you arms but only the United States can give you a solution.
> Newsweek 13 Jan 75

JOSEPH STALIN, Soviet Premier

21 If any foreign minister begins to defend to the death a "peace conference," you can be sure his government has already placed its orders for new battleships and airplanes.
> Recalled on his death 5 Mar 53

MARGARET THATCHER, Prime Minister of Great Britain

22 One hopes to achieve the zero option, but in the absence of that we must achieve balanced numbers.
> On Soviet and Allied missiles in Europe, NY Times 20 Jan 83

23 I'm not a good butcher but I've had to learn to carve the joint. People expect a new look.
> On changes in her cabinet after landslide victory, ib 11 Jun 83

24 I have a habit of comparing the phraseology of communiqués, one with another across the years, and noting a certain similarity of words, a certain similarity of optimism in the reports which followed the summit meetings and a certain similarity in the lack of practical results during the ensuing years.
> London Times 1 Jun 84

25 Platitudes? Yes, there are platitudes. Platitudes are there because they are true.
> ib

26 If you go into what I call a bubble boom, every bubble bursts.
> On national economy, ib

27 I like Mr Gorbachev, we can do business together.
> On meeting Mikhail S Gorbachev in London before he became Soviet premier, news summaries 17 Dec 84

1 We didn't have to do the minuets of diplomacy. We got down to business.
> On Mikhail S Gorbachev, CBS TV 11 Mar 85

2 I have made it quite clear that a unified Ireland was one solution that is out. A second solution was a confederation of two states. That is out. A third solution was joint authority. That is out—that is a derogation of sovereignty.
> After meeting with Irish Prime Minister Garret Fitz-Gerald to discuss ways of ending conflict in Northern Ireland, NY *Times* 20 Nov 85

3 I always cheer up immensely if an attack is particularly wounding because I think, well, if they attack one personally, it means they have not a single political argument left.
> On criticism, London *Daily Telegraph* 21 Mar 86

4 If you lead a country like Britain, a strong country, a country which has taken a lead in world affairs in good times and in bad, a country that is always reliable, then you have to have a touch of iron about you.
> On references to her as the Iron Lady, *ib*

5 I do not know anyone who has got to the top without hard work. That is the recipe. It will not always get you to the top, but should get you pretty near.
> *ib*

6 If you want to cut your own throat, don't come to me for a bandage.
> To Robert Mugabe, prime minister of Zimbabwe, who called for sanctions against South Africa, quoted in *Time* 7 Jul 86

7 What is success? I think it is a mixture of having a flair for the thing that you are doing; knowing that it is not enough, that you have got to have hard work and a certain sense of purpose.
> *Parade* 13 Jul 86

8 To wear your heart on your sleeve isn't a very good plan; you should wear it inside, where it functions best.
> On governing, interview with Barbara Walters *20/20* ABC TV 18 Mar 87

9 A world without nuclear weapons would be less stable and more dangerous for all of us.
> To Soviet Premier Mikhail S Gorbachev, *Time* 27 Apr 87

OMAR TORRIJOS HERRERA, President of Panama

10 I don't like Communism because it hands out wealth through rationing books.
> NY *Times* 7 Sep 77

PIERRE ELLIOTT TRUDEAU, Prime Minister of Canada

11 Canada will be a strong country when Canadians of all provinces feel at home in all parts of the country, and when they feel that all Canada belongs to them.
> To Liberal Convention, Ottawa, 5 Apr 68

12 We wish nothing more, but we will accept nothing less. Masters in our own house we must be, but our house is the whole of Canada.
> *ib*

13 The state has no business in the bedrooms of the nation.
> Appeal for revised divorce laws, NY *Times* 16 Jun 68

14 Living next to you is in some ways like sleeping with an elephant. No matter how friendly and even-tempered is the beast, if I can call it that, one is affected by every twitch and grunt.
> On relations with the US, *ib* 26 Mar 69

15 My life is one long curve, full of turning points.
> *New Yorker* 5 Jul 69

16 I bear solemn witness to the fact that NATO heads of state and of government meet only to go through the tedious motions of reading speeches, drafted by others, with the principal objective of not rocking the boat.
> First major address after leaving office, accepting Albert Einstein International Peace Prize, quoted in NY *Times* 14 Nov 84

HARRY S TRUMAN, 33rd US President

17 If I'd known how much packing I'd have to do, I'd have run again.
> On leaving the White House, *Time* 26 Jan 53

18 Any man who has had the job I've had and didn't have a sense of humor wouldn't still be here.
> News summaries 19 Apr 55

RICHARD VON WEIZSÄCKER, President of West Germany

19 There were many ways of not burdening one's conscience, of shunning responsibility, looking away, keeping mum. When the unspeakable truth of the Holocaust then became known at the end of the war, all too many of us claimed that they had not known anything about it or even suspected anything.
> On 40th anniversary of end of World War II, quoted in NY *Times* 12 May 85

20 All of us, whether guilty or not, whether old or young, must accept the past. . . . It is not a case of coming to terms with the past. That is not possible. It cannot be subsequently modified or undone.
> *ib*

21 Whoever refuses to remember the inhumanity is prone to new risks of infection.
> *ib*

22 Seeking to forget makes exile all the longer; the secret of redemption lies in remembrance.
> *ib*

HAROLD WILSON, Prime Minister of Great Britain

23 Given a fair wind, we will negotiate our way into the Common Market, head held high, not crawling in. Negotiations? Yes. Unconditional acceptance of whatever terms are offered us? No.
> Address in Bristol 20 Mar 67

24 The main essentials of a successful prime minister [are] sleep and a sense of history.
> *The Governance of Britain* Harper & Row 77

ZHOU ENLAI, Chinese Premier

25 All diplomacy is a continuation of war by other means.
> *Saturday Evening Post* 27 Mar 54

26 China and North Vietnam are closely united to each other, like the lips and the teeth.
> In Hanoi 5 Mar 71

1 For us, it is all right if the talks succeed, and it is all right if they fail.
> On President Richard M Nixon's visit to China 5 Oct 71

2 China is an attractive piece of meat coveted by all . . . but very tough, and for years no one has been able to bite into it.
> To Chinese Communist Party Congress, NY *Times* 1 Sep 73

Officials & Other Personages

ELLIOTT ABRAMS, US Assistant Secretary of State for Inter-American Affairs

3 There isn't any way for the people of Nicaragua to find out what's going on in Nicaragua.
> Announcing US technical aid to Nicaraguan rebels for powerful new radio station to promote anti-Sandinista ideas, NY *Times* 9 Nov 86

4 I never said I had no idea about most of the things you said I said I had no idea about.
> At Iran-Contra hearings 3 Jun 87

DEAN ACHESON, US Secretary of State

5 I will undoubtedly have to seek what is happily known as gainful employment, which I am glad to say does not describe holding public office.
> On retiring to private life, *Time* 22 Dec 52

6 The greatest mistake I made was not to die in office.
> After listening to funeral eulogies for his successor John Foster Dulles, news summaries 27 Mar 59

7 Great Britain has lost an empire and has not yet found a role.
> Address at West Point 5 Dec 62

8 The most important aspect of the relationship between the president and the secretary of state is that they both understand who is president.
> Quoted by Dean Rusk NBC TV 26 Mar 69

9 I have a curious and apprehensive feeling as I watch JFK that he is sort of an Indian snake charmer.
> Letter to former President Harry S Truman about President John F Kennedy, quoted in David S McLellan and David C Acheson eds *Among Friends* Dodd, Mead 80

10 Washington is like a self-sealing tank on a military aircraft. When a bullet passes through, it closes up.
> Quoted by Walter Isaacson and Evan Thomas *The Wise Men* Simon & Schuster 86

SPIRO T AGNEW, US Vice President

11 The lessons of the past are ignored and obliterated in a contemporary antagonism known as the generation gap.
> Denouncing Moratorium Day protest against Vietnam War, NY *Times* 20 Oct 69

12 A spirit of national masochism prevails, encouraged by an effete corps of impudent snobs who characterize themselves as intellectuals.
> *ib*

EZRA TAFT BENSON, US Secretary of Agriculture

13 We're not advocating the plowing under of every fourth farmer.
> On presidential recommendation that so-called marginal farmers should turn to other work, news summaries 2 Feb 54

CHARLES E BOHLEN, US diplomat

14 A noncommunist premier with communist ministers would be like a woman trying to stay half pregnant.
> On Winston Churchill's suggestion that the West share spheres of influence with Joseph Stalin in postwar government of the Balkans, quoted by Walter Isaacson and Evan Thomas *The Wise Men* Simon & Schuster 86

ROBERT H BORK, Acting US Attorney General

15 I was thinking of resigning [since] I did not want to be perceived as a man who did the president's bidding to save my job. I [have] had some time to think about it since. I think I did the right thing.
> 1973 statement on his firing of Watergate special prosecutor Archibald Cox on October 20, 1973, recalled on his appointment to the Supreme Court, NY *Times* 2 Jul 87

KINGMAN BREWSTER, US Ambassador to Great Britain

16 It is satisfying for the descendant of a dissident refugee from Elizabeth I to present his credentials to Elizabeth II.
> London *Observer* 3 Jul 77

17 The function of a briefing paper is to prevent the ambassador from saying something dreadfully indiscreet. I sometimes think its true object is to prevent the ambassador from saying anything at all.
> To English-Speaking Union, Edinburgh, 8 Sep 77

18 We all live in a televised goldfish bowl.
> Lecture, St George's Chapel, Windsor, 5 May 78

19 I'm very curious to know what the hell they're saying on the phone, but I'd be more worried if they weren't talking.
> On direct contact between heads of state, London *Observer* 10 Jun 79

MORTIMER CAPLIN, Commissioner, Internal Revenue Service

20 There is one difference between a tax collector and a taxidermist—the taxidermist leaves the hide.
> *Time* 1 Feb 63

CHARLES, Prince of Wales

21 Something as curious as the monarchy won't survive unless you take account of people's attitudes. . . . After all, if people don't want it, they won't have it.
> Quoted by Anthony Sampson *The Changing Anatomy of Britain* Random House 83

CLARK M CLIFFORD, US Secretary of Defense

22 I am not conscious of falling under any of those ornithological divisions.
> When asked if he considered himself a hawk or a dove, NY *Times* 2 Jan 68

BARBER B CONABLE JR, US Congressman

23 Exhaustion and exasperation are frequently the handmaidens of legislative decision.
> *Time* 22 Oct 84

24 [Congress is] functioning the way the Founding Fathers intended—not very well. They understood that if you move too quickly, our democracy will be less responsible to the majority.
> *ib*

1 I don't think it's the function of Congress to function well. It should drag its heels on the way to decision.
ib

J Edward Day, US Postmaster General

2 We cannot put the face of a person on a stamp unless said person is deceased. My suggestion, therefore, is that you drop dead.
Letter, never mailed, to a petitioner who wanted himself portrayed on a postage stamp, NY *Times* 7 Mar 62

John Dean, White House special counsel

3 I began by telling the president that there was a cancer growing on the presidency and that if the cancer was not removed . . . the president himself would be killed by it.
To Senate Watergate hearings 25 Jun 73

4 You really have to experience the feeling of being with the president in the Oval Office. . . . It's a disease I came to call Ovalitis.
After conviction for participation in Watergate cover-up, news summaries 1 Jan 75

Bernadette Devlin, Member of British Parliament

5 It wasn't long before people discovered the final horrors of letting an urchin into Parliament.
On being elected at age 21, *The Price of My Soul* Knopf 69

Michael V DiSalle, former Director, US Office of Price Stabilization

6 The only way to keep food prices down is to "keep them down on the farm" after they've seen parity.
Quoted in San Francisco *Examiner* 22 Apr 73

Robert J Dole, US Senator

7 If you're hanging around with nothing to do and the zoo is closed, come over to the Senate. You'll get the same kind of feeling and you won't have to pay.
Address on budget deficit to conference of NY local officials, NY *Times* 9 May 85

8 As long as there are only 3 to 4 people on the floor, the country is in good hands. It's only when you have 50 to 60 in the Senate that you want to be concerned.
ib

Raymond J Donovan, US Secretary of Labor

9 If you're in the contracting business in this country, you're suspect. If you're in the contracting business in New Jersey, you're indictable. If you're in the contracting business in New Jersey and are Italian, you're convicted.
In confirmation hearings before Senate Labor Committee 27 Jan 81

10 Give me back my reputation!
As former secretary, on acquittal after nine-month trial on charges of larceny and fraud, to the prosecutor, *Time* 8 Jun 87

Alec Douglas-Home, Foreign Secretary of Great Britain

11 Why employ intelligent and highly paid ambassadors and then go and do their work for them? You don't buy a canary and sing yourself.
NY *Times* 21 Apr 61

Yuri V Dubinin

12 I only understand positive statements in English.
On becoming Soviet ambassador to the US, quoted in NY *Times* 21 May 86

John Foster Dulles, US Secretary of State

13 The ability to get to the verge without getting into the war is the necessary art. . . . if you are scared to go to the brink, you are lost.
Quoted by James Shepley "How Dulles Averted War" *Life* 16 Jan 56

14 We walked to the brink and we looked it in the face.
On US involvement in Korea, Indochina and Formosa, *ib*

Abba Eban, Foreign Minister of Israel

15 Israel is not an aviary.
When asked if his country's policy was hawkish or dovish, NY *Post* 8 Jul 67

16 I think that this is the first war in history that on the morrow the victors sued for peace and the vanquished called for unconditional surrender.
·NY *Times* 9 Jul 67

17 Men and nations do behave wisely, once all other alternatives have been exhausted.
Vogue 1 Aug 67

Edward, Duke of Windsor

18 It didn't work out.
On brief reign in 1936 as King Edward VIII, quoted on *60 Minutes* CBS TV 8 Jun 80

M Kathryn Eickhoff, Chief Economist, US Office of Management and Budget

19 You just don't see people running through the streets to have the deficit cut.
On public's indifference toward the $2-trillion national debt, NY *Times* 15 Sep 85

Allen J Ellender, US Senator

20 First we just gave them these surpluses. Next we agreed to pay freight on transportation to ports. Then we agreed to mill the grain and package it. The next thing [you know] we'll be asked to cook it and serve it.
On complaints by charitable organizations about food donated to them by the US, 1 Apr 56

Gerald R Ford, US Vice President

21 A coalition of groups . . . is waging a massive propaganda campaign against the president of the United States. . . . an all-out attack. Their aim is total victory for themselves and total defeat [for him].
On Watergate crisis, to Amer Farm Bureau Federation, Washington *Post* 17 Jan 74

22 It's the quality of the ordinary, the straight, the square, that accounts for the great stability and success of our nation. It's a quality to be proud of. But it's a quality that many people seem to have neglected.
Time 28 Jan 74

23 The political lesson of Watergate is this: Never again must America allow an arrogant, elite guard of political adolescents to by-pass the regular party

organization and dictate the terms of a national election.

> On the Committee for the Re-election of the President, NY *Times* 31 Mar 74

1 I cannot imagine any other country in the world where the opposition would seek, and the chief executive would allow, the dissemination of his most private and personal conversations with his staff, which, to be honest, do not exactly confer sainthood on anyone concerned.

> On taping of conversations in White House office of President Richard M Nixon, address at University of Michigan, Ann Arbor, *ib* 4 May 74

BARNEY FRANK, US Congressman

2 This bill is the legislative equivalent of crack. It yields a short-term high but does long-term damage to the system and it's expensive to boot.

> On antidrug bill passed by House of Representatives, NY *Times* 12 Sep 86

HANS FRANK, Governor General of Poland

3 A thousand years will pass and the guilt of Germany will not be erased.

> Statement before being hanged for World War II crimes, quoted by William L Shirer *The Rise and Fall of the Third Reich* Simon & Schuster 60

J WILLIAM FULBRIGHT, US Senator

4 We have the power to do any damn fool thing we want to do, and we seem to do it about every 10 minutes.

> On Senate's right to change its mind, *Time* 4 Feb 52

EVAN G GALBRAITH, US Ambassador to France

5 The State Department desperately needs to be vigorously harnessed. It has too big a role to play in the formulation of foreign policy, and foreign policy is too important to be left up to foreign service officers.

> On resigning after four years as ambassador, NY *Times* 13 Feb 85

6 There's something about the Foreign Service that takes the guts out of people.

> *ib*

STEVEN GARFINKEL, Director, US Information Security Oversight Office

7 There are more secrets, but there is not more secrecy.

> On increase of espionage within government, NY *Times* 15 Apr 86

PETER C GOLDMARK JR, NY State Budget Director

8 Welfare is hated by those who administer it, mistrusted by those who pay for it and held in contempt by those who receive it.

> NY *Times* 24 May 77

ANDREI A GROMYKO, Soviet Foreign Minister

9 Every night, whisper "peace" in your husband's ear.

> To Nancy Reagan, at White House reception 28 Sep 84

10 My personality doesn't interest me.

> Refusing to answer personal questions, *Newsweek* 1 Oct 84

11 [The world may end up] under a Sword of Damocles . . . on a tightrope over the abyss.

> Criticizing US Strategic Defense Initiative, *Time* 11 Mar 85

12 Comrades, this man has a nice smile, but he's got iron teeth.

> On Mikhail S Gorbachev, quoted in NY *Times* 17 Jun 85

ALEXANDER M HAIG JR, US Secretary of State

13 As of now, I am in control here in the White House.

> After President Ronald Reagan was wounded in an assassination attempt while Vice President George Bush was away from Washington DC, statement to the press 30 Mar 81

DORCAS HARDY, Director, Social Security System

14 The one with the primary responsibility to the individual's future is that individual.

> *Christian Science Monitor* 5 Mar 87

15 The business of government should be businesslike.

> *ib*

W AVERELL HARRIMAN, US diplomat

16 Conferences at the top level are always courteous. Name-calling is left to the foreign ministers.

> News summaries 1 Aug 55

17 [Americans wanted to] settle all our difficulties with Russia and then go to the movies and drink Coke.

> On wariness of sharing global responsibilities with the Soviets, quoted by Walter Isaacson and Evan Thomas *The Wise Men* Simon & Schuster 86

18 [He's] a margarine Communist.

> Prediction that Chairman Mao of China would break with Soviets, *ib*

19 I always read everything on the desks of people I went to see in Moscow, London, Paris . . . I found it quite useful.

> On his ability to read upside down, recalled on his death 26 Jul 86

PATRICIA ROBERTS HARRIS, US Secretary of Housing and Urban Development

20 Senator, I am one of them. You do not seem to understand who I am. I am a black woman, the daughter of a dining-car worker . . . If my life has any meaning at all, it is that those who start out as outcasts can wind up as being part of the system.

> Reply to Senator William Proxmire when asked if she would be able to defend the interests of the poor, *Newsweek* 24 Jan 77

ARTHUR A HARTMAN, US Ambassador to USSR

21 It is unacceptable to subject Americans in Moscow to any substance that is not present in the general environment.

> On "spy dust," powdery chemical used to track movements of US diplomats, NY *Times* 15 Feb 86

ORRIN G HATCH, US Senator

22 The marble columns will stand tall like silent sentinels and the busts of the great Americans which line the upper wall will study our every move—

sometimes approvingly, more often than not with raised eyebrows. As always.

On waning days of 98th Congress, NY *Times* 17 Oct 84

DENIS HEALEY, Chancellor of the Exchequer

1 [It will] squeeze the rich until the pips squeak.

On presenting budget to Parliament, *Illustrated London News* May 78

RICHARD M HELMS, Director, CIA

2 I have one president at a time. I only work for you.

To President Richard M Nixon, who had promised not to use top-secret information to incriminate Helms, his predecessor or the CIA, quoted in *RN: Memoirs of Richard Nixon* Grosset & Dunlap 78

DONALD A HICKS, Research Director, US Defense Dept

3 Freedom works both ways. They're free to keep their mouths shut. . . . I'm also free not to give the money.

Suggesting that federal research grants be denied scientists who oppose the Strategic Defense Initiative, Washington *Post* 13 May 86

JIM HIGHTOWER, Texas Agricultural Commissioner

4 Little ol' boy in the Panhandle told me the other day you can still make a small fortune in agriculture. Problem is, you got to start with a large one.

On the financial crisis of the American farmer, to Chamber of Commerce, Dallas, NY *Times* 9 Mar 86

5 The only difference between a pigeon and the American farmer today is that a pigeon can still make a deposit on a John Deere.

ib

6 Do something. If it doesn't work, do something else. No idea is too crazy.

Instructions to staff of activists dedicated to restoring farm profits, *ib*

LUTHER H HODGES, US Secretary of Commerce

7 If ignorance paid dividends, most Americans could make a fortune out of what they don't know about economics.

Wall Street Journal 14 Mar 62

ANNA ROSENBERG HOFFMAN, US Assistant Secretary of Defense

8 No form letters are sent out from this office. No husband was ever Section Three, Paragraph II-a, to his wife.

Newsweek 27 Feb 51

GEORGE M HUMPHREY, US Secretary of the Treasury

9 You can't set a hen in one morning and have chicken salad for lunch.

On the impossibility of quick economic change, *Time* 26 Jan 53

10 It's a terribly hard job to spend a billion dollars and get your money's worth.

Look 23 Feb 54

WILLIAM G HYLAND, former national security adviser

11 Protectionism is the ally of isolationism, and isolationism is the Dracula of American foreign policy.

Commencement address at Washington University, St Louis, NY *Times* 17 May 87

PETER JAY, former British Ambassador to US

12 He is just as entitled to be underwhelmed by the prospect of reigning over a fourth-class nation as the rest of us are by the prospect of living in it.

On Charles, Prince of Wales, "Great is Little Britain" *London Illustrated News* Apr 86

CLAUDIA ("LADY BIRD") JOHNSON

13 The first lady is, and always has been, an unpaid public servant elected by one person, her husband.

Quoted in *US News & World Report* 9 Mar 87

LYNDON B JOHNSON, US Vice President

14 The Negro says, "Now." Others say, "Never." The voice of responsible Americans . . . says, "Together." There is no other way.

Memorial Day address, Gettysburg PA, 30 May 63

15 Until justice is blind to color, until education is unaware of race, until opportunity is unconcerned with the color of men's skins, emancipation will be a proclamation but not a fact.

ib

MAX M KAMPELMAN, chief US arms negotiator

16 We must be prepared to stay at the negotiating table one day longer than the Soviets.

Time 11 Mar 85

17 A dialogue is more than two monologues.

ib 6 May 85

PAUL KEATING, Federal Treasurer of Australia

18 I try to use the Australian idiom to its maximum advantage.

On his use of colorful language in Parliament, *Wall Street Journal* 14 Nov 86

GEORGE F KENNAN, US diplomat

19 [One sometimes feels] a guest of one's time and not a member of its household.

On view of himself as a pragmatist, quoted by Walter Isaacson and Evan Thomas *The Wise Men* Simon & Schuster 86

20 The best [an American] can look forward to is the lonely pleasure of one who stands at long last on a chilly and inhospitable mountaintop where few have been before, where few can follow and where few will consent to believe he has been.

On trying to understand the Soviets, *ib*

21 [The accords were] fig leaves of democratic procedure to hide the nakedness of Stalinist dictatorship.

On postwar agreements to govern Eastern Europe, *ib*

ROBERT F KENNEDY, US Attorney General

22 I thought they'd get one of us, but Jack, after all he's been through, never worried about it . . . I thought it would be me.

On learning of his brother's assassination, quoted by Peter Collier and David Horowitz *The Kennedys* Summit 84

23 Did the CIA kill my brother?

To CIA Director John A McCone as speculation grew over US involvement in Bay of Pigs invasion, *ib*

HENRY A KISSINGER

1 No foreign policy—no matter how ingenious—has any chance of success if it is born in the minds of a few and carried in the hearts of none.
  As national security adviser, to International Platform Assn 2 Aug 73

2 High office teaches decision making, not substance. [It] consumes intellectual capital; it does not create it. Most high officials leave office with the perceptions and insights with which they entered; they learn how to make decisions but not what decisions to make.
  White House Years Little, Brown 79

3 The statesman's duty is to bridge the gap between his nation's experience and his vision.
  Years of Upheaval Little, Brown 82

4 In crises the most daring course is often safest.
  ib

5 [The] American temptation [is] to believe that foreign policy is a subdivision of psychiatry.
  Commencement address at University of South Carolina, *Time* 17 Jun 85

6 If I should ever be captured, I want no negotiation—and if I should request a negotiation from captivity they should consider that a sign of duress.
  Expressing strong opposition to bargaining with terrorists, *US News & World Report* 7 Oct 85

7 You can't make war in the Middle East without Egypt and you can't make peace without Syria.
  Quoted by Ted Koppel *Nightline* ABC TV 21 May 86

8 Whatever must happen ultimately should happen immediately.
  On handling of Iran-Contra scandal, *Time* 8 Dec 86

9 Any fact that needs to be disclosed should be put out now or as quickly as possible, because otherwise . . . the bleeding will not end.
  ib

EDWARD KOCH, Mayor of NYC

10 In a neighborhood, as in life, a clean bandage is much, much better than a raw or festering wound.
  On plan to improve the image of the Bronx by covering the windows of abandoned city-owned buildings with decals depicting pleasant interiors, NY *Times* 12 Nov 83

DELBERT L LATTA, US Congressman

11 I hold in my hand 1,379 pages of tax simplification.
  On tax reform, quoted in *US News & World Report* 23 Dec 85

DREW LEWIS, presidential envoy

12 Saying sulfates do not cause acid rain is the same as saying that smoking does not cause lung cancer.
  On meeting with New England governors to discuss industrial pollution, NY *Times* 14 Sep 85

HENRY CABOT LODGE JR

13 I guess it wouldn't discourage a real mob for very long, but it packs all the authority you can put in a desk drawer.
  On keeping a small revolver in his desk while ambassador to South Vietnam, *Time* 15 May 64

NIALL MACDERMOT, Financial Secretary of British Treasury

14 "State intelligence," like "military intelligence" and "woman friend," is a contradiction in terms.
  Quote 23 Jan 66

WILLIAM B MACOMBER, former US Ambassador to Jordan and Turkey

15 When it comes to an important portion of American ambassadorial appointments, we are still in the era of the Charge of the Light Brigade.
  On campaign donations in exchange for ambassadorial appointments, NY *Times* 20 Nov 84

JEB STUART MAGRUDER, former Chairman, Committee to Re-elect the President

16 I know what I have done, and Your Honor knows what I have done. . . . Somewhere between my ambition and my ideals, I lost my ethical compass.
  Confessing perjury in Watergate investigation, *Time* 3 Jun 74

GRAHAM A MARTIN, former US Ambassador to South Vietnam

17 In the end, we simply cut and ran. The American national will had collapsed.
  On 10th anniversary of fall of Saigon, NY *Times* 30 Apr 85

VINCENT MASSEY, Governor-General of Canada

18 What we do should have a Canadian character. Nobody looks his best in somebody else's clothes.
  Recalled on his death, *Time* 12 Jan 68

CHARLES McC MATHIAS JR, US Congressman

19 Most of us are honest all the time, and all of us are honest most of the time.
  On Congressional ethics, *Time* 31 Mar 67

JAMES A McCLURE, US Senator

20 In that hearing, we didn't hear anything.
  On why there were no leaks from a closed hearing, NY *Times* 24 Jan 87

ROBERT S McNAMARA, US Secretary of Defense

21 Neither conscience nor sanity itself suggests that the United States is, should or could be the global gendarme.
  To Amer Society of Newspaper Editors, NY *Times* 19 May 66

22 Coercion, after all, merely captures man. Freedom captivates him.
  ib

EDWIN MEESE 3RD, White House counsel

23 [An expert is] somebody who is more than 50 miles from home, has no responsibility for implementing the advice he gives, and shows slides.
  NY *Times* 24 Jan 84

24 Nicaragua is fast becoming a terrorist country club.
  On evidence that Nicaragua gave shelter to German, Italian, Irish, Spanish and Arab terrorists, news summaries 14 Sep 85

PAT NIXON

1 Being first lady is the hardest unpaid job in the world.
> Interview in Monrovia, Liberia, 15 Mar 72

OLIVER L NORTH, former staff member of National Security Council

2 I don't think there is another person in America that wants to tell this story as much as I do.
> Invoking Fifth Amendment right against self-incrimination in testimony to House committee investigating arms sales to Iran, NY *Times* 10 Dec 86

3 I came here to tell you the truth, the good, the bad and the ugly.
> Testifying at Iran-Contra hearings after being granted limited immunity, 7 Jul 87

4 I am here to accept responsibility for that which I did. I will not accept responsibility for that which I did not do.
> *ib*

5 I haven't, in the 23 years that I have been in the uniformed services of the United States of America ever violated an order—not one.
> *ib*

6 I thought using the Ayatollah's money to support the Nicaraguan resistance . . . was a neat idea.
> On diversion of funds from arms sales to Iran 8 Jul 87

CLARENCE M PENDLETON JR, Chairman, US Commission on Civil Rights

7 The looniest idea since Looney Tunes came on the screen.
> On comparable pay for comparable work, NY *Times* 17 Nov 84

MILDRED PERLMAN, NY Civil Service Commission

8 You start by saying no to requests. Then if you have to go to yes, OK. But if you start with yes, you can't go to no.
> NY *Times* 1 Dec 75

PETER G PETERSON, former US Secretary of Commerce

9 The experience may have been costly, but it was also priceless.
> On his term in the Cabinet, *Quote* 18 Jan 73

PRINCE PHILIP, Duke of Edinburgh

10 If we are to recover prosperity we shall have to find ways of emancipating energy and enterprise from the frustrating control of timid ignoramuses.
> Quoted by Anthony Sampson *The Anatomy of Britain* Harper & Row 62

IGNACIO PICHARDO PAGAZA, Comptroller General of Mexico

11 The phenomenon of corruption is like the garbage. It has to be removed daily.
> NY *Times* 17 Apr 87

AQUILINO Q PIMENTEL, Minister of Local Government, the Philippines

12 There appears to have been a call for blood. . . . It might as well be mine, not hers. Hers is more important.
> Accepting dismissal by President Corazon C Aquino, NY *Times* 4 Dec 86

JOHN M POINDEXTER, former national security adviser

13 I made a very deliberate decision not to ask the president so that I could insulate him from the decision and provide some future deniability for the president if it ever leaked out.
> On diverting funds from arms sales, at Iran-Contra hearings 15 Jul 87

NANCY REAGAN

14 Today, there is a drug and alcohol abuse epidemic in this country. And no one is safe from it—not you, not me and certainly not our children, because this epidemic has their names written on it.
> Address to the nation with President Reagan 14 Sep 86

15 There is no moral middle ground. Indifference is not an option. . . . For the sake of our children, I implore each of you to be unyielding and inflexible in your opposition to drugs.
> *ib*

16 I don't think most people associate me with leeches or how to get them off. But I know how to get them off. I'm an expert at it.
> To Amer Camping Assn, Washington DC 2 Mar 87

DONALD T REGAN, White House chief of staff

17 I read all these stories that I don't know anything about politics. But I must know something. I've had some good victories in Congress, and I've survived this town for four years.
> NY *Times* 25 Jan 85

18 At dinner parties I sit below the salt now. There are a lot of interesting people there.
> *Time* 18 Mar 85

19 It's an ear job, not an eye job.
> *ib*

20 We do many things at the federal level that would be considered dishonest and illegal if done in the private sector.
> On efforts to alter federal budget, NY *Times* 25 Aug 86

21 Some of us are like a shovel brigade that follow a parade down Main Street cleaning up.
> On Iceland summit meeting between Ronald Reagan and Mikhail S Gorbachev, *ib* 16 Nov 86

22 By no means was it really teed up for him.
> On President Ronald Reagan's advance knowledge of arms sales to Iran, statement to Senate-appointed commission, quoted by William Safire "Teed Off over Teed Up" *ib* 19 Apr 87

23 I was trying to tell the commission that the issue had not been really defined well enough to be ready for the president.
> *ib*

24 When one goes through combat-patrol work, one quickly learns that the best target is the person who "stands on the skyline. . . ." Indians knew it, Indian scouts knew it, soldiers, sailors and all marines know it. . . . A chief of staff is supposed to know it, but sometimes there is no way a chief of staff can stay off the skyline.
> *ib*

ELLIOT L RICHARDSON

1 Conscience is the voice of values long and deeply infused into one's sinew and blood.

On resigning as US attorney general rather than approve presidential firing of a Richardson appointee, *Life* Special Report 73

ELEANOR ROOSEVELT

2 Always be on time. Do as little talking as humanly possible. Remember to lean back in the parade car so everybody can see the president. Be sure not to get too fat, because you'll have to sit three in the back seat.

On campaign behavior for first ladies, NY *Times* 11 Nov 62

DEAN RUSK, US Secretary of State

3 Let me say with a Georgia accent that we cannot solve this problem if it requires a diplomatic passport to claim the rights of an American citizen.

On restaurants that admitted dark-skinned diplomats but not US blacks, *Life* 1 Jan 62

4 We were eyeball-to-eyeball and the other fellow just blinked.

On the Cuban missile crisis, *Saturday Evening Post* 8 Dec 62

5 When you solve a problem, you ought to thank God and go on to the next one.

On the Cuban missile crisis, *Look* 6 Sep 66

6 The United States is not just an old cow that gives more milk the more it's kicked in the flanks.

Telling Senate Foreign Relations Committee that the US would not deliver a nuclear ultimatum to Vietnam, NY *Times* 5 May 67

7 The fidelity of the United States to security treaties is not just an empty matter. It is a pillar of peace in the world.

On 10th anniversary of fall of Saigon, *ib* 30 Apr 85

8 Give a member of Congress a junket and a mimeograph machine and he thinks he is secretary of state.

Quoted in *Time* 6 May 85

JEANNE SAUVÉ

9 I was asked to prepare a little program and I never stopped.

On how she became first woman governor-general of Canada, London *Times* 29 Nov 85

JOHN F SEIBERLING, US Congressman

10 The American people want to preserve their American heritage, and they have the quaint belief that public lands belong to them as much as to the people of the state where the lands are located.

On legislation to preserve large tracts of Idaho and other states as wilderness areas, NY *Times* 15 Jul 84

GEORGE P SHULTZ, US Secretary of State

11 I learned in business that you had to be very careful when you told somebody that's working for you to do something, because the chances were very high he'd do it. In government, you don't have to worry about that.

NY *Times* 14 Oct 84

12 Oh, you know. I am secretary of state. My trips aren't successful. I just talk to people.

On global diplomacy, *ib* 17 May 85

13 [It was an attempt] to stick the Congress's finger in King Hussein's eye.

On US Senate's nonbinding resolution to ban further arms sales to Jordan, press conference 4 Jun 85

14 Nothing ever gets settled in this town. . . . a seething debating society in which the debate never stops, in which people never give up, including me. And so that's the atmosphere in which you administer.

On not being told about arms sales to Iran, to House investigating committee, NY *Times* 9 Dec 86

GERRY E STUDDS, US Congressman

15 It is the Edsel of the 1980s. It is overpriced, it has been oversold, it will not perform as advertised.

On Strategic Defense Initiative, NY *Times* 21 Jun 85

GEORGE C WALLACE, Governor of Alabama

16 I draw the line in the dust and toss the gauntlet before the feet of tyranny, and I say segregation now, segregation tomorrow, segregation forever.

1963 inaugural address, quoted in *Life* 26 Dec 69

VERNON A WALTERS, US Ambassador to UN

17 The fact that I was a bachelor provided two opportunities or two handles that they might get on me, namely, girls or boys.

On eluding traps for blackmail while a military attaché in France during the 1960s, *Silent Missions* Doubleday 78

18 Americans have always had an ambivalent attitude toward intelligence. When they feel threatened, they want a lot of it, and when they don't, they regard the whole thing as somewhat immoral.

ib

EARL WARREN, Chief Justice, US Supreme Court

19 We may not know the whole story in our lifetime.

On assassination of President John F Kennedy, quoted by Don Hewitt *Minute by Minute* Random House 85

JAMES G WATT, US Secretary of the Interior

20 I have a black, a woman, two Jews and a cripple. And we have talent.

Comment on his staff that led to his resignation, to US Chamber of Commerce 21 Sep 83

JAIME WHEELOCK, Minister of Agriculture, Nicaragua

21 We prefer the loss of the coffee to the loss of the country.

On diverting 20,000 student volunteers from harvest work to bolster defense against a possible US invasion, *Newsweek* 19 Nov 84

Politicians & Critics

HAROLD A ACKERMAN, Judge, US District Court, New Jersey

22 You reached for that honey pot and you got stung.

On conviction of former Atlantic City Mayor Michael J Matthews for extortion, NY *Times* 1 Jan 85

1 You served the people shamefully. The people . . . thought they were electing a mayor.
ib

KONRAD ADENAUER, Chancellor of West Germany

2 Kennedy cooked the soup that Johnson had to eat.
On the Vietnam War, NY *Times* 24 Jan 73

SHANA ALEXANDER

3 What troubles me is not that movie stars run for office, but that they find it easy to get elected. It should be difficult. It should be difficult for millionaires, too.
Life 8 Jul 66

SVETLANA ALLILUYEVA

4 It is human nature that rules the world, not governments and regimes.
On seeking asylum in the US in 1967, recalled when she returned to Russia, NY *Times* 3 Nov 84

AMERICAN BAR ASSOCIATION

5 The United States may become the first great power to falter because it lost its ability to collect taxes.
Quoted in *Wall Street Journal* 10 Apr 84

ANONYMOUS

6 The prime minister wishes to be obscene and not heard.
Opposition member's charge that Prime Minister Pierre Trudeau had mouthed an obscenity in Canadian House of Commons during debate on February 16, 1971, quoted in John Robert Colombo ed *Colombo's Canadian Quotations* Hurtig 74

7 Some leaders are born women.
Saying on a T-shirt worn at UN observance of International Women's Day, quoted in news summaries 18 Mar 83

8 She's a handbag economist who believes you pay as you go.
On Margaret Thatcher, quoted in *New Yorker* 10 Feb 86

9 What if Adams should die and Eisenhower becomes president of the United States?
On President Dwight D Eisenhower's chief of staff Sherman Adams, recalled on Adams's death, NY *Times* 28 Oct 86

10 If we don't fight now, nothing will change. But if enough of us get killed, something may happen.
Hungarian youth, quoted by Timothy Foote on 30th anniversary of 1956 citizens' uprising against Soviet troops, *Smithsonian* Nov 86

11 Hey, hey, LBJ, how many boys did you kill today?
Chant of protesters picketing White House during Vietnam War, quoted on *Lyndon Johnson* PBS TV 8 Apr 87

HANNAH ARENDT

12 The most radical revolutionary will become a conservative the day after the revolution.
New Yorker 12 Sep 70

13 The trouble with lying and deceiving is that their efficiency depends entirely upon a clear notion of the truth that the liar and deceiver wishes to hide.
Crises of the Republic Harcourt Brace Jovanovich 72

RICHARD ARMEY, US Congressman

14 It's nothing but an eight-story microphone plugged into the Politburo.
On new US embassy building in Moscow found riddled with Soviet spying devices, *Time* 20 Apr 87

CLEMENT ATTLEE

15 The House of Lords is like a glass of champagne that has stood for five days.
Quoted by Leon A Harris *The Fine Art of Political Wit* Dutton 64

16 One layer was certainly 17th century. The 18th century in him is obvious. There was the 19th century, and a large slice, of course, of the 20th century; and another, curious layer which may possibly have been the 21st.
Comparing Winston Churchill to a cake, quoted by William Manchester *The Last Lion* Little, Brown 83

J EVANS ATTWELL

17 We are not going to have a racehorse pulling a milk wagon.
On appointing former Senate majority leader Howard H Baker Jr as head of the Washington office of his Texas law firm, NY *Times* 11 Dec 84

MARGARET ATWOOD

18 If the national mental illness of the United States is megalomania, that of Canada is paranoid schizophrenia.
The Journals of Susanna Moodie Oxford 70, quoted in John Robert Colombo ed *Colombo's Canadian Quotations* Hurtig 74

BEN BAGDIKIAN

19 He has been called "the Wizard of Ooze" and a man possessed of tonsils marinated in honey.
On Senator Everett M Dirksen, NY *Times* 14 Mar 65

HOWARD H BAKER JR, US Senator

20 The central question is simply put: What did the president know and when did he know it?
To John Dean, White House special counsel, at Watergate hearings 28 Jun 73

RUSSELL BAKER

21 A new star with a tremendous national appeal, the skill of a consummate showman.
On President John F Kennedy at his first televised press conference, NY *Times* 26 Jan 61

ALBEN W BARKLEY, former US Vice President

22 The best audience is intelligent, well-educated and a little drunk.
Recalled on his death 30 Apr 56

BERNARD BARUCH

23 Vote for the man who promises least; he'll be the least disappointing.
Quoted by Meyer Berger *Meyer Berger's New York* Random House 60

CAROL BELLAMY, President, NY City Council

24 I think he is an entertainer. I would prefer if he were a performer.
On Mayor Edward Koch, NY *Times* 31 Jan 85

GEORGES BIDAULT

1 I have plumbed the depth of human cowardice and I realized that there is only one way to be right, and that is to be in power.

> Statement in 1962 shortly before he was exiled for attempting to overthrow Charles de Gaulle as president, recalled on Bidault's death 27 Jan 83

2 If we had not been dealing with the devil in person, we could have saved Algeria.

> On de Gaulle, *ib*

3 Africa is destined to anarchy. It is turning into 36 Haitis, with 36 Duvaliers, full of Cadillacs, beggars and snarling dogs.

> *ib*

JIMMY BRESLIN

4 The first funeral for Andrew Goodman was at night and it was a lot of work. To begin with they had to kill him.

> On last rites for a 21-year-old civil-rights worker slain and secretly buried in Mississippi with two of his associates, NY *Herald Tribune* 10 Aug 64

5 Politics, where fat, bald, disagreeable men, unable to be candidates themselves, teach a president how to act on a public stage.

> *Table Money* Ticknor & Fields 86

DAVID BRINKLEY

6 This is the first convention of the space age—where a candidate can promise the moon and mean it.

> On 1960 Democratic National Convention, quoted in *Newsweek* 13 Mar 61

JOSEPH BRODSKY

7 No matter under what circumstances you leave it, home does not cease to be home. No matter how you lived there—well or poorly.

> On leaving the USSR, NY *Times* 1 Oct 72

JAMES BROOKE

8 The blunt-spoken New Englander ran the White House as "the abominable 'no' man."

> On President Dwight D Eisenhower's chief of staff Sherman Adams, recalled on Adams's death, NY *Times* 28 Oct 86

GEORGE BROWN, Foreign Secretary of Great Britain

9 I've got nothing against men wearing striped pants and black jackets if they want to, and they can wear Anthony Eden hats to their hearts' content. It's the wearing of striped pants in the soul that I object to, and having a Homburg hat where your heart ought to be.

> Quoted in *Christian Science Monitor* 19 Aug 66

JOHN MASON BROWN

10 The more I observed Washington, the more frequently I visited it, and the more people I interviewed there, the more I understood how prophetic L'Enfant was when he laid it out as a city that goes around in circles.

> *Through These Men* Harper 56

ART BUCHWALD

11 Just when you think there's nothing to write about, Nixon says, "I am not a crook." Jimmy Carter says, "I have lusted after women in my heart." President Reagan says, "I have just taken a urinalysis test, and I am not on dope."

> At Humor and the Presidency Symposium, Ford Museum, Grand Rapids MI, *Time* 29 Sep 86

GEORGE BURNS

12 Too bad that all the people who know how to run the country are busy driving taxicabs and cutting hair.

> *Life* Dec 79

BARBARA BUSH

13 I can't say it, but it rhymes with *rich*.

> On her husband's opponent, Democratic vice-presidential candidate Geraldine Ferraro; she later telephoned Ferraro to apologize for referring to her as a *witch*, NY *Times* 15 Oct 84

GEORGE BUSH, US Vice President

14 I haven't chosen her yet.

> When asked what criteria he would use in selecting a 1988 vice-presidential candidate, to Republican meeting in NYC 27 Mar 87

CAPITOL STEPS, political satirists

15 Hark, when Gerald Ford was king,
We were bored with everything.
Unemployment 6 percent.
What a boring president.
Nothing major needed fixin'
So he pardoned Richard Nixon.

> Lyrics for performance at Humor and the Presidency Symposium, Ford Museum, Grand Rapids MI, *Time* 22 Sep 86

JIMMY CARTER, 39th US President

16 I now understand more clearly than I ever had before why you won in November 1980 and I lost.

> Thanking his successor Ronald Reagan for address during dedication of Carter Presidential Center in Atlanta, NY *Times* 2 Oct 86

HERVÉ DE CHARETTE, French cabinet minister

17 The French at heart are monarchists. They like to prostrate themselves in front of the monarch, whom they now call president, and every seven years or so they guillotine him.

> NY *Times* 26 Nov 87

LAWTON CHILES, US Senator

18 We have entered the era of the "imperial" former presidency with lavish libraries, special staffs and benefits, around-the-clock Secret Service protection for life and other badges of privilege.

> On his legislation to cut cost of presidential perquisites, *Wall Street Journal* 27 Jul 84

GEORGE J CHURCH

19 He is running not for election but for the history books.

> On President Ronald Reagan halfway through his second term, *Time* 29 Sep 86

WINSTON CHURCHILL

1 In war, you can only be killed once, but in politics, many times.
> Recalled on his death 24 Jan 65

2 Baldwin thought Europe was a bore, and Chamberlain thought it was only a greater Birmingham.
> 1953 comment quoted by Lord Moran *Churchill: Taken from the Diaries of Lord Moran* Houghton Mifflin 66

RAMSEY CLARK, former US Attorney General

3 If Rosa Parks had not refused to move to the back of the bus, you and I might never have heard of Dr Martin Luther King.
> On effectiveness of individual protests, NY *Times* 14 Apr 87

CLARK M CLIFFORD

4 We're going through a kind of ancient, barbaric war dance now—it's almost an ultimate in absurdity.
> On investigation of arms sales to Iran, *Christian Science Monitor* 9 Dec 86

FRANCIS X CLINES

5 If castaway cigar butts once were the floor symbol of the male-dominated convention, the equivalent symbol this year is a litter of women's pumps.
> On Democratic National Convention in San Francisco, NY *Times* 18 Jul 84

RICHARD CORRIGAN

6 On Capitol Hill Congress runs by an internal clock: Legislative days are not counted the way calendar days are, and the seasons are marked not by the earth's orbit but by whether Congress is in session or out.
> "Technology Focus" *National Journal* 25 Oct 86, quoted in NY *Times* 31 Oct 86

7 However time may be measured at the Naval Observatory, the clock seems to tick slowly here when Congress is out of town.
> *ib*

MARIO CUOMO, Governor of NY

8 We must get the American public to look past the glitter, beyond the showmanship, to the reality, the hard substance of things. And we'll do it . . . not so much with speeches that will bring people to their feet as with speeches that bring people to their senses.
> Keynote address to Democratic National Convention in San Francisco 16 Jul 84

9 I said I didn't want to run for president. I didn't ask you to believe me.
> NY *Times* 12 Feb 85

10 You campaign in poetry. You govern in prose.
> *New Republic* 8 Apr 85

11 I have no plans, and no plans to plan.
> On presidential ambitions, NY *Times* 14 Sep 86

JOHN C DANFORTH, US Senator

12 I was to Japanese visitors to Washington what the Mona Lisa is to Americans visiting Paris.
> On his criticism of trade deficit with Japan, NY *Times* 14 Sep 86

ROBERTSON DAVIES

13 The average politician goes through a sentence like a man exploring a disused mine shaft—blind, groping, timorous and in imminent danger of cracking his shins on a subordinate clause or a nasty bit of subjunctive.
> *The Papers of Samuel Marchbanks* Viking 86, quoted in Boston *Globe* 5 Aug 86

BETTE DAVIS

14 I sent my flowers across the hall to Mrs Nixon but her husband remembered what a Democrat I am and sent them back.
> On occupying one of the VIP suites at New York Hospital–Cornell Medical Center, Joan Rivers show 8 Apr 87

JOHN DAWKINS, Member of Australian Parliament

15 I heard his library burned down and that both books were destroyed—and one of them hadn't even been colored in yet.
> On fellow member Wilson Tuckey, quoted in *Wall Street Journal* 14 Nov 86

CHARLES DE GAULLE, President of France

16 I have come to the conclusion that politics are too serious a matter to be left to the politicians.
> Quoted by Clement Attlee *Twilight of Empire* Barnes 62

17 Roosevelt, a false witness; Truman, a merchant; Eisenhower, I am told that on the golf links he is better [with a putter] than he is with the long shots and that doesn't surprise me; Kennedy, the style of a hairdresser's assistant—he combed his way through problems; Johnson, a truck driver or a stevedore—or a legionnaire.
> *Time* 28 Feb 69

LEN DEIGHTON

18 In Mexico an air conditioner is called a politician because it makes a lot of noise but doesn't work very well.
> *Mexico Set* Knopf 85

DENG XIAOPING, Chinese Premier

19 The United States brags about its political system, but the president says one thing during the election, something else when he takes office, something else at midterm and something else when he leaves.
> Quoted by John F Burns "Deng Asserts Ties to West Are Vital to Fight Poverty" NY *Times* 2 Jan 85

THOMAS E DEWEY

20 My decision on this matter is as certain and final as death and the staggering New Deal taxes.
> Letter to his 1948 campaign manager announcing that he would never again seek the presidency, quoted in *Time* 2 Jan 50

GUSTAVO DÍAZ ORDOZ

21 I like to operate like a submarine on sonar. When I am picking up noise from both the left and right, I know my course is correct.
> While campaigning for presidency of Mexico, *US News & World Report* 13 Jul 64

JOHN G DIEFENBAKER, Prime Minister of Canada

1 The Liberals are the flying saucers of politics. No one can make head nor tail of them and they never are seen twice in the same place.
> Address at London, Ontario, 5 May 62

LLOYD DOGGETT

2 Sometimes when you get in a fight with a skunk, you can't tell who started it.
> On his opponent for a seat in the Texas legislature, *Time* 5 Nov 84

ROBERT J DOLE, US Senator

3 History buffs probably noted the reunion at a Washington party a few weeks ago of three ex-presidents: Carter, Ford and Nixon—See No Evil, Hear No Evil and Evil.
> To Washington Gridiron Club dinner 26 Mar 83

4 We'll all be riding that streetcar of desire.
> On 1988 Republican National Convention in New Orleans, NY *Times* 24 Jan 87

SEAN DONLON, Irish Ambassador to US

5 Democrats give away their old clothes; Republicans wear theirs. Republicans employ exterminators; Democrats step on the bugs. Democrats eat the fish they catch; Republicans stuff 'em and hang 'em on the wall.
> Quoted in Washington *Post* 23 Oct 81

T C DOUGLAS, leader of Canadian New Democratic Party

6 The Liberals talk about a stable government but we don't know how bad the stable is going to smell.
> News summaries 30 Oct 65

MAUREEN DOWD

7 His House colleagues still call him "Jackie One Note"—joking that if you ask him how to solve the problem of teenage pregnancy, he'll tell you to cut taxes.
> "Is Jack Kemp Mr Right?" NY *Times* 28 Jun 87

MARK DUFFY

8 In Louisiana we don't bet on football games . . . We bet on whether a politician is going to be indicted or not.
> On winning wager that Governor Edwin W Edwards would be charged with racketeering and fraud, NY *Times* 3 Mar 85

JOHN P EAST, US Senator

9 The average American doesn't know the difference between a Contra and a caterpillar or between a Sandinista and a sardine.
> Opposing House-Senate conference agreement to continue ban on covert aid to Nicaraguan Contras, NY *Times* 12 Oct 84

EDMONTON JOURNAL

10 The eyes are Paul Newman blue. His hair has the swoop of the Robert Redford style and the voice the resonance of a Lorne Greene school of broadcasting. The jaw is by Gibraltar.
> On Brian Mulroney, newly elected prime minister of Canada, quoted in NY *Times* 6 Sep 84

EDWIN W EDWARDS, Governor of Louisiana

11 [He's] so slow that he takes an hour and a half to watch *60 Minutes.*
> On 1983 Republican opponent David C Treen, NY *Times* 22 Oct 83

12 People say I've had brushes with the law. That's not true. I've had brushes with overzealous prosecutors.
> On 12th grand jury probe in a decade, *ib* 24 Oct 83

13 [I could not lose unless I was] caught in bed with a dead girl or a live boy.
> On 1983 race against David C Treen, recalled on his grand jury indictment for racketeering and fraud, *Time* 11 Mar 85

JOHN EHRLICHMAN, White House special assistant

14 I think we ought to let him hang there, let him twist slowly, slowly in the wind.
> To presidential counsel John Dean on acting FBI Director L Patrick Gray, taped conversation 7 Mar 73

15 I was under the assumption that it would be conducted as a normal investigation, not as some kind of a second-story job.
> On break-in of office of Daniel Ellsberg's psychiatrist after Ellsberg's leak of the Pentagon Papers, Washington *Post* 26 Jul 73

DWIGHT D EISENHOWER, 34th US President

16 Neither a wise man nor a brave man lies down on the tracks of history to wait for the train of the future to run over him.
> Presidential campaign speech, quoted in *Time* 6 Oct 52

17 We are tired of aristocratic explanations in Harvard words.
> 1952 campaign remark that was recalled after more than a dozen Harvard men were named to high positions in the Eisenhower administration, *ib* 26 Jan 53

18 I thought it completely absurd to mention my name in the same breath as the presidency.
> Recalling his initial reaction to suggestions that he run for office, *Mandate for Change* Doubleday 63

19 [I despise people who] go to the gutter on either the right or the left and hurl rocks at those in the center.
> *Time* 25 Oct 63

20 I shall make that trip. I shall go to Korea.
> 1952 campaign promise that was credited with winning the election, quoted in *Life* 5 Jul 68

SAM ERVIN, US Senator

21 Divine right went out with the American Revolution and doesn't belong to the White House aides. What meat do they eat that makes them grow so great?
> News conference during Watergate investigation, *Time* 16 Apr 73

22 I'm not going to let anybody come down at night like Nicodemus and whisper something in my ear that no one else can hear. That is not executive privilege; it is poppycock.
> At Senate Watergate hearings, *US News & World Report* 28 May 73

23 If the many allegations made to this date are true, then the burglars who broke into the headquarters of the Democratic National Committee at the Watergate were, in effect, breaking into the home of every citizen.
> *ib*

1 There is nothing in the Constitution that authorizes or makes it the official duty of a president to have anything to do with criminal activities.
>At Senate Watergate hearings, Washington *Post* 12 Jul 73

2 I used to think that the Civil War was our country's greatest tragedy, but I do remember that there were some redeeming features in the Civil War in that there was some spirit of sacrifice and heroism displayed on both sides. I see no redeeming features in Watergate.
>*ib* 24 Jul 73

LORD ESHER (Oliver S B Brett)

3 We are fortunate to have inherited an institution which we certainly should never have had the intelligence to create. We might have been landed with something like the American Senate.
>On the House of Lords, *Wall Street Journal* 2 May 63

ROWLAND EVANS JR

4 The Kennedy organization doesn't run, it purrs.
>On John F Kennedy's presidential campaign, quoted by Ralph G Martin *A Hero for Our Time* Macmillan 83

JAMES A FARLEY

5 A rigged convention is one with the other man's delegates in control. An open convention is when your delegates are in control.
>Quoted in *Convention and Election Almanac* issued by NBC 64

JULES FEIFFER

6 I used to think I was poor. Then they told me I wasn't poor, I was needy. They told me it was self-defeating to think of myself as needy, I was deprived. Then they told me underprivileged was overused. I was disadvantaged. I still don't have a dime. But I have a great vocabulary.
>1965 cartoon, quoted by William Safire *Safire's Political Dictionary* Random House 78

DIANNE FEINSTEIN, Mayor of San Francisco

7 Toughness doesn't have to come in a pinstripe suit.
>On women's role in government, *Time* 4 Jun 84

GERALDINE A FERRARO

8 Vice president—it has such a nice ring to it!
>Accepting Walter F Mondale's invitation to be his Democratic Party running mate, NY *Times* 13 Jul 84

9 Modern life is confusing—no "Ms take" about it.
>Explaining her preference for her maiden name as an attorney and her husband's name Zaccaro in private life, *ib*

10 You people married to Italian men, you know what it's like.
>On her husband's refusal to disclose his tax returns, *ib* 13 Aug 84

11 I'd call it a new version of voodoo economics, but I'm afraid that would give witch doctors a bad name.
>On Republican Party platform, *ib* 25 Aug 84

12 I should have had a circuitous answer that was a non-answer.
>On initial replies about her family's finances, *Life* Oct 84

TREVOR FISHLOCK

13 She ate a television journalist for breakfast and, feeling peckish, bit off some reporters' heads at a press conference.
>On Prime Minister Margaret Thatcher during a visit to Canada, London *Times* 28 Sep 83

DAVID FROST

14 Vote Labor and you build castles in the air. Vote Conservative and you can live in them.
>*That Was the Year That Was* BBC TV 31 Dec 62

CARLOS FUENTES

15 What the United States does best is to understand itself. What it does worst is understand others.
>*Time* 16 Jun 86

J WILLIAM FULBRIGHT, US Senator

16 The junior senator from Wisconsin, by his reckless charges, has so preyed upon the fears and hatreds and prejudices of the American people that he has started a prairie fire which neither he nor anyone else may be able to control.
>On Senator Joseph R McCarthy's charges of Communism in high places, news summaries 30 Nov 54

17 The biggest lesson I learned from Vietnam is not to trust [our own] government statements. I had no idea until then that you could not rely on [them].
>Recalling his years as chairman of US Senate Foreign Relations Committee during Vietnam War, NY *Times* 30 Apr 85

18 I'm sure that President Johnson would never have pursued the war in Vietnam if he'd ever had a Fulbright to Japan, or say Bangkok, or had any feeling for what these people are like and why they acted the way they did. He was completely ignorant.
>*ib* 26 Jun 86

JOHN KENNETH GALBRAITH

19 Politics is not the art of the possible. It consists in choosing between the disastrous and the unpalatable.
>*Ambassador's Journal* Houghton Mifflin 69

20 Nothing is so admirable in politics as a short memory.
>Quoted in *A Guide to the 99th Congress* LTV Corp 85

GEORGE H GALLUP

21 Polling is merely an instrument for gauging public opinion. When a president or any other leader pays attention to poll results, he is, in effect, paying attention to the views of the people. Any other interpretation is nonsense.
>News summaries 1 Dec 79

JOHN NANCE GARNER, former US Vice President

22 You have to do a little bragging on yourself even to your relatives—man doesn't get anywhere without advertising.
>News summaries 15 Feb 54

BOB GELDOF

1 It's really very simple, Governor. When people are hungry they die. So spare me your politics and tell me what you need and how you're going to get it to these people.
> Discussing African famine relief with deputy governor of Eastern Region of the Sudan, NY *Times* 26 Jan 85

DAVID R GERGEN

2 When he hung up on Nancy Reagan, that's when he crossed his final threshold.
> On resignation of White House chief of staff Donald T Regan during Iran arms sales investigation, *Nightline* ABC TV 27 Feb 87

JACK GESCHEIDT

3 The *News* says, Khadafy
The *Times* says, Qaddafi
Time says, Gaddafi
Newsweek, Kaddafi;
MOO-a-mar
Mo-AH-mar;
LIB-ya
LIB-ee-a;
Let's blow the whole thing off.
> On variations in spelling of name of Libyan leader Muammar Qaddafi, NY *Times* 18 May 86

IAN GILMOUR, British Conservative Party leader

4 Politicians trim and tack in their quest for power, but they do so in order to get the wind of votes in their sails.
> *The Body Politic* Hutchinson 69

BARRY M GOLDWATER, US Senator

5 Extremism in the defense of liberty is no vice. . . . Moderation in the pursuit of justice is no virtue.
> Accepting Republican presidential nomination 16 Jul 64

6 To insist on strength . . . is not war-mongering. It is peace-mongering.
> NY *Times* 11 Aug 64

7 It's political Daddyism and it's as old as demagogues and despotism.
> On President Lyndon B Johnson's promise of federal aid without additional cost, *ib* 27 Nov 64

8 I wouldn't trust Nixon from here to that phone.
> *Newsweek* 29 Sep 86

DORIS KEARNS GOODWIN

9 Once a president gets to the White House, the only audience that is left that really matters is history.
> On presidential libraries, NY *Times* 13 Oct 85

10 They all start competing against Lincoln as the greatest president. And the [library] building becomes the symbol, the memorial to that dream.
> *ib*

NADINE GORDIMER

11 Mumbling obeisance to abhorrence of apartheid [is] like those lapsed believers who cross themselves when entering a church.
> On US policy of "constructive engagement" in South Africa, NY *Times* 8 Sep 85

HENRY GRAFF, Professor of History, Columbia University

12 He has a chance to make somebody move over on Mount Rushmore. He's working for his place on the coins and the postage stamps.
> On President Ronald Reagan at start of his second term, *Newsweek* 28 Jan 85

ROGER L GREEN, Brooklyn Assemblyman and Chairman, Black and Puerto Rican Legislative Caucus

13 Everyone appears to be noticing only the statue's torch and not the manacles on her ankles.
> On centennial of Statue of Liberty, NY *Times* 30 May 86

MEG GREENFIELD

14 In Washington it is an honor to be disgraced. . . . you have to have *been* somebody to fall.
> *Newsweek* 2 Jun 86

ALEXANDER M HAIG JR

15 I probably carry more scar tissue on my derrière than any other candidate—that's political scar tissue.
> On his qualifications for entering the 1988 presidential campaign, *MacNeil/Lehrer Newshour* 24 Mar 87

16 I'm the only American alive or dead who presided unhappily over the removal of a vice president and a president.
> On his service at the White House during Richard M Nixon's presidency, *ib*

H R HALDEMAN, White House special assistant

17 Once the toothpaste is out of the tube, it's hard to get it back in.
> On Watergate disclosures, news summaries 30 Aug 73

18 Every president needs an SOB—and I'm Nixon's.
> *ib*

PETE HAMILL

19 Say what you will about him . . . Ed Koch is still the best show in town.
> On NYC Mayor Edward Koch, "Act III" NY *Daily News* 1 Sep 85

20 He steps on stage and draws the sword of rhetoric, and when he is through, someone is lying wounded and thousands of others are either angry or consoled.
> *ib*

GRACE HANSEN

21 I feel I'm as qualified for office as any of the other comedians who are running.
> On her 1970 gubernatorial race against incumbent Tom McCall, recalled on her death, Eugene OR *Register-Guard* 14 Jan 85

22 For some time I've had my eye on Tom McCall's seat—which is a great deal more than he's had on it.
> *ib*

GARY HART, US Senator

23 This is one Hart that you will not leave in San Francisco.
> After his unsuccessful bid for the presidency at the 1984 Democratic National Convention in San Francisco, London *Financial Times* 21 Jul 84

1 There is always some fig leaf being used.

> On excuses for armed intervention abroad, *Time* 7 Apr 86

2 Follow me around. I don't care. . . . If anybody wants to put a tail on me, go ahead. They'd be very bored.

> As presidential candidate, from interview that appeared the same day the Miami *Herald* reported that a woman had spent the night at his Washington town house, NY *Times* 3 May 87

3 I think there is one higher office than president and I would call that patriot.

> On first television interview following his withdrawal from the presidential race, *Nightline* ABC TV 8 Sep 87

DENIS HEALEY, former Chancellor of the Exchequer

4 La Pasionaria of middle-class privilege.

> On Prime Minister Margaret Thatcher, *New Yorker* 10 Feb 86

WILLIAM RANDOLPH HEARST

5 A politician will do anything to keep his job—even become a patriot.

> Recalled on his death 14 Aug 51

LILLIAN HELLMAN

6 I cannot and will not cut my conscience to fit this year's fashions.

> Letter to House Committee on Un-American Activities, *Nation* 31 May 52

7 Truth made you a traitor as it often does in a time of scoundrels.

> On McCarthy era, *Scoundrel Time* Little, Brown 76

A P HERBERT, Member of British Parliament

8 I am sure that the party system is right and necessary. . . . there must be some scum.

> *Independent Member* Doubleday 51

THEODORE M HESBURGH, President, Notre Dame

9 Voting is a civic sacrament.

> *Reader's Digest* Oct 84

STEPHEN HESS

10 The presidency is a huge echo chamber magnifying every little thing he does.

> On President Ronald Reagan, *Time* 6 Feb 84

CHARLTON HESTON

11 To the world, you are America.

> To Ronald Reagan at a Hollywood charity ball given in the president's honor, NY *Times* 2 Dec 85

GILBERT HIGHET

12 What is politics but persuading the public to vote for this and support that and endure these for the promise of those?

> "The Art of Persuasion" *Vogue* Jan 51

GEORGE HILL

13 She is said to be inclined to cough noisily when he goes on too long at the rostrum; but this is a traditional prerogative of the political wife, and rather more necessary in this instance than in most.

> On Glenys Kinnock, wife of Neil Kinnock, Labor Party candidate for prime minister, London *Times* 19 Feb 87

STANLEY HOFFMANN, Director, Harvard Center for European Studies

14 Arms control has to have a future, or none of us does. But it doesn't necessarily have to come in big packages of 600-page treaties.

> *Newsweek* 1 Oct 84

SIMON HOGGART

15 The nanny seemed to be extinct until 1975, when, like the coelacanth, she suddenly and unexpectedly reappeared in the shape of Margaret Thatcher.

> "At the Top: Margaret Thatcher" *Vanity Fair* Aug 83

16 She is the first head of government in history to give a whole country its second childhood.

> *ib*

CHUCK HOLLANDER, National Student Assn

17 Hippiedom is more than a choice of lifestyle. It's an apolitical systemicide.

> *Time* 7 Jul 67

HERBERT HOOVER, 31st US President

18 Honor is not the exclusive property of any political party.

> Quoted in *Christian Science Monitor* 21 May 64

LUCY HOWARD

19 In the heat of a political lifetime, Ronald Reagan innocently squirrels away tidbits of misinformation and then, sometimes years later, casually drops them into his public discourse, like gum balls in a quiche.

> *Newsweek* 11 Nov 85

JAMES C HUMES

20 Churchill wrote his own speeches. When a leader does that, he becomes emotionally invested with his utterances. . . . If Churchill had had a speech writer in 1940, Britain would be speaking German today.

> NY *Times* 15 Jun 86

HUBERT H HUMPHREY, US Senator

21 Underneath the beautiful exterior there was an element of ruthlessness and toughness that I had trouble either accepting or forgetting.

> On presidential campaign of John F Kennedy, *The Education of a Public Man* Doubleday 76

ALDOUS HUXLEY

22 Idealism is the noble toga that political gentlemen drape over their will to power.

> Recalled on his death, NY *Herald Tribune* 24 Nov 63

HAROLD L ICKES

23 I am against government by crony.

> On resigning in 1946 as secretary of the interior, recalled on his death 3 Feb 52

WALTER ISAACSON and EVAN THOMAS

24 Big, pink and lumbering, waving a trunklike arm, he indulged his love of phrase making with such clinkers as "our merific inheritances," "marcesant monarchyu," "nautical nimbus."

> On Senator Arthur H Vandenberg as chairman of Foreign Relations Committee, *The Wise Men* Simon & Schuster 86

1 [John Foster Dulles] stirred whiskey with a thick forefinger, his socks drooped, his suits were green-hued, his ties were indifferent and his breath was chronically bad. Hunched forward as he talked, he droned on in a flat voice, pronouncing Anthony Eden "Ant–ny."
ib

HENRY M JACKSON, US Senator

2 The best politics is no politics.
On need for bipartisan approach to foreign affairs, to Amer Bar Assn, Chicago, 3 Feb 80

JESSE JACKSON

3 I cast my bread on the waters long ago. Now it's time for you to send it back to me—toasted and buttered on both sides.
Addressing black voters, *New York* 30 Jan 84

4 My constituency is the desperate, the damned, the disinherited, the disrespected and the despised.
Address to Democratic National Convention in San Francisco, 17 Jul 84

5 If there are occasions when my grape turned into a raisin and my joy bell lost its resonance, please forgive me. Charge it to my head and not to my heart.
ib

6 I am not a perfect servant. I am a public servant doing my best against the odds. As I develop and serve, be patient. God is not finished with me yet.
ib

7 Our flag is red, white and blue, but our nation is a rainbow—red, yellow, brown, black and white—and we're all precious in God's sight.
ib

8 America is not like a blanket—one piece of unbroken cloth, the same color, the same texture, the same size. America is more like a quilt—many patches, many pieces, many colors, many sizes, all woven and held together by a common thread.
ib

9 The white, the Hispanic, the black, the Arab, the Jew, the woman, the Native American, the small farmer, the businessperson, the environmentalist, the peace activist, the young, the old, the lesbian, the gay and the disabled make up the American quilt.
ib

10 We must not measure greatness from the mansion down, but from the manger up.
ib

11 From seeds of his body blossomed the flower that liberated a people and touched the soul of a nation.
Funeral oration for Martin Luther King Sr 15 Nov 84

JIANG QING, Gang of Four member

12 Man's contribution to human history is nothing more than a drop of sperm.
Newsweek 20 Feb 84

CLAUDIA ("LADY BIRD") JOHNSON

13 A politician ought to be born a foundling and remain a bachelor.
Time 1 Dec 75

LYNDON B JOHNSON, 36th US President

14 Every man has a right to a Saturday night bath.
London *Observer* 13 Mar 60

15 There are plenty of recommendations on how to get out of trouble cheaply and fast. Most of them come down to this: Deny your responsibility.
At Democratic fund-raising affair, news summaries 30 Sep 67

16 All that Hubert needs over there is a gal to answer the phone and a pencil with an eraser on it.
On Vice President Hubert H Humphrey, recalled on Johnson's death 22 Jan 73

17 Jack was out kissing babies while I was out passing bills. Someone had to tend the store.
On John F Kennedy's selection as Democratic presidential nominee, quoted by Ralph G Martin *A Hero for Our Time* Macmillan 83

18 I seldom think of politics more than 18 hours a day.
Quoted in *A Guide to the 99th Congress* LTV Corp 85

19 A man can take a little bourbon without getting drunk, but if you hold his mouth open and pour in a quart, he's going to get sick on it.
On political persuasion, "Love It or Loathe It, Here's the Wit and Wisdom of LBJ" *People* 2 Feb 87

20 The CIA is made up of boys whose families sent them to Princeton but wouldn't let them into the family brokerage business.
ib

21 When things haven't gone well for you, call in a secretary or a staff man and chew him out. You will sleep better and they will appreciate the attention.
ib

RYSZARD KAPUSCINSKI

22 Money changes all the iron rules into rubber bands.
On fall of the shah of Iran, *Shah of Shahs* Harcourt Brace Jovanovich 85

GEORGE F KENNAN

23 The best thing we can do if we want the Russians to let us be Americans is to let the Russians be Russian.
US–Soviet Relations: The First 50 Years WNET TV 17 Apr 84

EDWARD M KENNEDY, US Senator

24 Come out of the rose garden.
Challenging President Jimmy Carter to a public debate, news summaries 10 Feb 80

25 Well, here I don't go again.
On decision not to run in 1988 presidential campaign, press conference 20 Dec 85

26 Frankly, I don't mind not being president. I just mind that someone else is.
To Washington Gridiron Club dinner 22 Mar 86

JACQUELINE KENNEDY

27 He didn't even have the satisfaction of being killed for civil rights. . . . it had to be some silly little Communist.
To her mother Janet Auchincloss on the evening of November 22, 1963, quoted by William Manchester *The Death of a President* Harper & Row 67

JOHN F KENNEDY, 35th US President

1 To exclude from positions of trust and command all those below the age of 44 would have kept Jefferson from writing the Declaration of Independence, Washington from commanding the Continental Army, Madison from fathering the Constitution, Hamilton from serving as secretary of the treasury, Clay from being elected speaker of the House and Christopher Columbus from discovering America.
> NY *Times* 5 Jul 60

2 We stand today on the edge of a new frontier—the frontier of the 1960s—a frontier of unknown opportunities and perils—a frontier of unfulfilled hopes and threats.
> Accepting the Democratic presidential nomination 15 Jul 60

3 The new frontier of which I speak is not a set of promises—it is a set of challenges. It sums up not what I intend to offer the American people, but what I intend to ask of them. It appeals to their pride, not their pocketbook—it holds out the promise of more sacrifice instead of more security.
> *ib*

4 I hope that no American . . . will waste his franchise and throw away his vote by voting either for me or against me solely on account of my religious affiliation. It is not relevant.
> On being a Roman Catholic, *Time* 25 Jul 60

JOSEPH P KENNEDY

5 I have no political ambitions for myself or my children.
> Recalled on his death 18 Nov 69

JOSEPH P KENNEDY II, US Congressman

6 If you have 30 cousins, it's pretty easy.
> On fund-raising for his campaign, *Time* 8 Sep 86

7 I've had a tough time learning how to act like a congressman. Today I accidentally spent some of my own money.
> Quoted in *Newsweek* 9 Feb 87

ROBERT F KENNEDY

8 It will help erase the idea that politics is a second-rate profession and a dirty business.
> On John F Kennedy Library, *Newsweek* 9 Mar 64

9 Now I can go back to being ruthless again.
> On winning race for US Senate, *Esquire* Apr 65

ROSE KENNEDY

10 It's *our* money, and we're free to spend it any way we please.
> On her son John F Kennedy's presidential campaign, quoted by Ralph G Martin *A Hero for Our Time* Macmillan 83

MARTIN LUTHER KING JR

11 If you will protest courageously, and yet with dignity and Christian love, when the history books are written in future generations, the historians will have to pause and say, "There lived a great people—a black people—who injected new meaning and dignity into the veins of civilization."
> Address at Montgomery AL, news summaries 31 Dec 55

12 Discrimination is a hellhound that gnaws at Negroes in every waking moment of their lives to remind them that the lie of their inferiority is accepted as truth in the society dominating them.
> To Southern Christian Leadership Conference, Atlanta, 16 Aug 67

JEANE J KIRKPATRICK, US Ambassador to UN

13 Look, I don't even agree with *myself* at times.
> On leaving Democratic Party to register as a Republican, NBC TV 3 Apr 85

14 [Democrats] can't get elected unless things get worse—and things won't get worse unless they get elected.
> *Time* 17 Jun 85

15 A government is not legitimate merely because it exists.
> On Sandinista government in Nicaragua, *ib*

HENRY A KISSINGER

16 Nixon had three goals: to win by the biggest electoral landslide in history; to be remembered as a peacemaker; and to be accepted by the "Establishment" as an equal. He achieved all these objectives at the end of 1972 and the beginning of 1973. And he lost them all two months later—partly because he turned a dream into an obsession.
> On president Richard M Nixon and the Watergate break-in, *Years of Upheaval* Little, Brown 82

17 It was a Greek tragedy. Nixon was fulfilling his own nature. Once it started it could not end otherwise.
> To James St Clair on August 8, 1974, after President Nixon's televised announcement of his resignation, *ib*

18 The Vietnam War required us to emphasize the national interest rather than abstract principles. . . . What President Nixon and I tried to do was unnatural. And that is why we didn't make it.
> On 10th anniversary of end of the Vietnam War, *Wall Street Journal* 11 Mar 85

19 When you meet the president, you ask yourself, "How did it ever occur to anybody that he should be governor much less president?"
> On President Ronald Reagan, *US* 2 Jun 86

STANLEY KLEIN, FBI terrorism expert

20 Talk in a normal voice. Terrorists are suspicious of whispering.
> On how to behave if taken hostage, to conference of business travelers, NY *Times* 10 Oct 86

EDWARD KOCH, Mayor of NYC

21 I'm not the type to get ulcers. I give them.
> NY *Times* 20 Jan 84

22 If you don't like the president, it costs you 90 bucks to fly to Washington to picket. If you don't like the governor, it costs you 60 bucks to fly to Albany to picket. If you don't like me, 90 cents.
> *ib* 28 Feb 85

23 We're in the hands of the state legislature and God, but at the moment, the state legislature has more to say than God.
> On requesting additional funds for NYC, *ib* 27 Jun 86

1 The knife of corruption endangered the life of New York City. The scalpel of the law is making us well again.

> On recent scandals, State of the City Address, *ib* 25 Jan 87

2 If you turn your back on these people, you yourself are an animal. You may be a well-dressed animal, but you are nevertheless an animal.

> Calling for civic compassion in AIDS epidemic, *ib* 16 Mar 87

TED KOPPEL

3 Here is a guy who's had a stake driven through his heart. I mean, really nailed to the bottom of the coffin with a wooden stake, and a silver bullet through the forehead for good measure—and yet he keeps coming back.

> On former President Richard M Nixon, *New York* 13 Aug 84

WILLIAM KOVACH

4 We cannot encourage a process that has a political saliva test administered by candidates.

> On allowing campaign managers to veto proposed panelists for presidential debates, *Time* 22 Oct 84

CHARLES KRAUTHAMMER

5 A three-year diet of rubber chicken and occasional crow.

> On campaigning for the presidency, "The Appeal of Ordeal" *Time* 14 May 82

6 Post-Watergate morality, by which anything left private is taken as presumptive evidence of wrongdoing.

> "Pietygate: School for Scandal" *ib* 10 Sep 84

7 If we insist that public life be reserved for those whose personal history is pristine, we are not going to get paragons of virtue running our affairs. We will get the very rich, who contract out the messy things in life; the very dull, who have nothing to hide and nothing to show; and the very devious, expert at covering their tracks and ambitious enough to risk their discovery.

> *ib*

8 Take all your dukes and marquesses and earls and viscounts, pack them into one chamber, call it the House of Lords to satisfy their pride and then strip it of all political power. It's a solution so perfectly elegant and preposterous that only the British could have managed it.

> "Celebrities in Politics: A Cure" *ib* 21 Apr 86

RICHARD LAMM, Governor of Colorado

9 Christmas is a time when kids tell Santa what they want and adults pay for it. Deficits are when adults tell the government what they want—and their kids pay for it.

> To National League of Cities, Seattle, 10 Dec 85

10 Politics, like theater, is one of those things where you've got to be wise enough to know when to leave.

> On stepping down after 12 years in office, *US News & World Report* 26 Jan 87

LYNDON LAROUCHE JR

11 [The Leesburg Garden Club is a] nest of Soviet fellow travelers . . . clacking busybodies in a Soviet jellyfish front, sitting here in Leesburg oozing out their funny little propaganda and making nuisances of themselves.

> NY *Times* 11 Apr 86

HAROLD D LASSWELL, Professor of Law and Political Science, Yale

12 Political science without biography is a form of taxidermy.

> Quoted by Arnold A Rogow *James Forrestal* Macmillan 64

PAUL LAXALT, US Senator

13 A politician taking campaign money from gamblers in Nevada is like one taking campaign money from the auto people in Michigan. Gambling is our legal business.

> On campaigning in Nevada, NY *Times* 21 Oct 84

IRVING LAYTON

14 In Pierre Elliott Trudeau, Canada has at last produced a political leader worthy of assassination.

> *The Whole Bloody Bird* McClelland 69

MAX LERNER

15 The politics of surprise leads through the Gates of Astonishment into the Kingdom of Hope.

> On announcement of presidential visit to China, quoted by Richard M Nixon *RN: Memoirs of Richard Nixon* Grosset & Dunlap 78

DON LESSEM

16 The former "first brat" [has] become a Yippie among yuppies.

> On Amy Carter's radical activities, Boston *Globe* 28 Jun 87

DAVID LEVINE

17 [My philosophy] is that politicians should be jumped on as often as possible.

> On his cartoons, *Time* 24 Sep 84

ANN F LEWIS, National Director, Americans for Democratic Action

18 Politicians have the same occupational hazard as generals—focusing on the last battle and overreacting to that.

> NY *Times* 24 Sep 86

LIBYA RADIO

19 Oh, heroes of our Arab nation, let your missiles and suicide cells pursue American terrorist embassies and interests wherever they may be!

> Exhorting Arab suicide squads to attack US targets in the Middle East, quoted in *Time* 7 Apr 86

G GORDON LIDDY, White House special assistant

20 Why is it there are so many more horses' asses than there are horses?

> On Watergate hearings, news summaries 30 Aug 73

WALTER LIPPMANN

1 Successful . . . politicians are insecure and intimidated men. They advance politically only as they placate, appease, bribe, seduce, bamboozle or otherwise manage to manipulate the demanding and threatening elements in their constituencies.
The Public Philosophy Little, Brown 55

2 Brains, you know, are suspect in the Republican Party.
Recalled on his death 14 Dec 74

3 Once you touch the biographies of human beings, the notion that political beliefs are logically determined collapses like a pricked balloon.
From his 1913 book *A Preface to Morals*, quoted by Ronald Steel *Walter Lippmann and the American Century* Atlantic–Little, Brown 80

4 Certainly he is not of the generation that regards honesty as the best policy. However, he does regard it as a policy.
On President Richard M Nixon, quoted in *Newsweek* 12 May 80

LONDON DAILY TELEGRAPH

5 [She seems] a cross between Isadora Duncan and Lawrence of Arabia.
On Prime Minister Margaret Thatcher during NATO maneuvers, quoted in *Time* 29 Dec 86

EARL LONG, Governor of Louisiana

6 I consider myself 40 percent Catholic and 60 percent Baptist. . . . but I'm in favor of *every* religion, with the possible exception of snake-chunking. Anybody that so presumes on how he stands with Providence that he will let a snake bite him, I say he deserves what he's got coming to him.
Quoted in *New Yorker* 4 Jun 60

7 The kind of thing I'm good at is knowing every politician in the state and remembering where he itches. And I know where to scratch him.
ib

RUSSELL B LONG, US Senator

8 Tax reform means "Don't tax you, don't tax me, tax that fellow behind the tree."
News summaries 31 Dec 76

9 I really think that it's better to retire, in Uncle Earl's terms, when you still have some snap left in your garters.
Referring to Earl Long, former governor of Louisiana, NY *Times* 18 Mar 85

10 [A tax loophole is] something that benefits the other guy. If it benefits you, it is tax reform.
Recalled on his retirement, *Time* 10 Nov 86

CLARE BOOTHE LUCE

11 Communism is the opiate of the intellectuals [with] no cure except as a guillotine might be called a cure for dandruff.
Newsweek 24 Jan 55

GEORGE LUNDBERG, Editor, Amer Medical Assn *Journal*

12 An era of chemical McCarthyism is at hand, and "guilty until proven innocent" is the new slogan.
On drug testing, *US News & World Report* 15 Dec 86

HAROLD MACMILLAN

13 He is forever poised between a cliché and an indiscretion.
On position of British foreign secretary, *Newsweek* 30 Apr 56

14 At home, you always have to be a politician; when you're abroad, you almost feel yourself a statesman.
Look 15 Apr 58

15 I have never found, in a long experience of politics, that criticism is ever inhibited by ignorance.
Wall Street Journal 13 Aug 63

16 You can hardly say boo to a goose in the House of Commons now without cries of "Ungentlemanly," "Not fair" and all the rest.
Quoted by Leon A Harris *The Fine Art of Political Wit* Dutton 64

17 If people want a sense of purpose they should get it from their archbishop. They should certainly not get it from their politicians.
Quoted by Henry Fairlie *The Life of Politics* Methuen 69

18 [She is] a brilliant tyrant surrounded by mediocrities.
On Prime Minister Margaret Thatcher, *Newsweek* 12 Jan 87

EDWARD MAHE

19 Senate races are about ideology. Governors are about jobs and contracts and schools and bridges and more contracts.
On study showing that a majority of voters care more about gubernatorial races than about Senate races, NY *Times* 12 Oct 86

WYNAND MALAN, South African politician

20 I did not clash with the National Party, I clashed with my conscience. And in the end, conscience wins.
On resigning from the party because of its continued support of apartheid, *Time* 4 May 87

ANDREW H MALCOLM

21 A Chicago alderman once confessed he needed physical exercise but didn't like jogging, because in that sport you couldn't hit anyone.
NY *Times* 5 May 85

WILLIAM MANCHESTER

22 It would be inaccurate to say that Churchill and I conversed. . . . Like Gladstone speaking to Victoria, he addressed me as though I were a one-man House of Commons. It was superb.
On his initial meeting with Winston Churchill, recounted in *The Last Lion* Little, Brown 83

NELSON MANDELA

23 Only free men can negotiate; prisoners cannot enter into contracts. Your freedom and mine cannot be separated.
Refusing to bargain for freedom after 21 years in prison, *Time* 25 Feb 85

DONALD R MANES, former Queens Borough President

24 I apologize for what was said even though I didn't say it.
On report that he called NYC Mayor Edward Koch a crook, WQXR Radio 3 Feb 86

IMELDA MARCOS

1 I think that's a very kinky issue with the panties and bras. That's the thing that they will display: shoes, panties and bras.

On exhibition of thousands of pairs of shoes and other articles of clothing left behind when she and her husband fled the Philippines, NY *Times* 10 Apr 86

STANLEY MARCUS

2 Running those poor steers back and forth in the heat is ridiculous. . . . What they ought to do is put the steers in the convention hall and run the delegates.

On efforts in Dallas to project a Western image during the Republican National Convention, NY *Times* 28 Aug 84

RALPH G MARTIN

3 Handshaking is friendly until your hands bleed. Confetti looks festive until you're forced to spit out mouthfuls hurled directly into your face. Applause is wonderful until you can hardly hear yourself speak. A crush of screaming women is flattering until they tear your clothes.

On campaigning, *A Hero for Our Time* Macmillan 83

GROUCHO MARX

4 Politics is the art of looking for trouble, finding it everywhere, diagnosing it incorrectly and applying the wrong remedies.

Recalled on his death 19 Aug 77

JANE MAYER

5 The campaign kickoff was so dismal that it needed a plastic surgeon instead of a press agent to put a face on it.

On Mondale-Ferraro presidential campaign, *Wall Street Journal* 11 Sep 84

EUGENE J MCCARTHY, US Senator

6 Have you ever tried to split sawdust?

Reply to charge that he had divided the Democratic Party, NBC TV 23 Oct 69

JOSEPH R MCCARTHY, US Senator

7 While I cannot take the time to name all of the men in the State Department who have been named as members of the Communist Party and members of a spy ring, I have here in my hand a list of 205 that were known to the secretary of state as being members of the Communist Party and who nevertheless are still working and shaping the policy of the State Department.

February 9, 1950, address at Wheeling WV that began a period of unfounded accusations, quoted by Richard H Rovere *Senator Joe McCarthy* Harcourt, Brace 59

8 McCarthyism is Americanism with its sleeves rolled.

Theme in successful campaign for re-election to US Senate in 1952, *ib*

MARY MCCARTHY

9 Congress—these, for the most part, illiterate hacks whose fancy vests are spotted with gravy and whose speeches, hypocritical, unctuous and slovenly, are spotted also with the gravy of political patronage.

On the Contrary Farrar, Straus & Cudahy 61

JOHN T MCCUTCHEON

10 The political cartoon is a sort of pictorial breakfast food. It has the cardinal asset of making the beginning of the day sunnier.

NY *Times* 3 Dec 75

RALPH MCGILL

11 One of the shameful chapters of this country was how so many of the comfortable—especially those who profited from the misery of others—abused her . . . But she got even in a way that was almost cruel. She forgave them.

Quoted by Helen Gahagan Douglas *The Eleanor Roosevelt We Remember* Hill & Wang 63

JOE MCGINNISS

12 We forgave, followed and accepted because we liked the way he looked. And he had a pretty wife. Camelot was fun, even for the peasants, as long as it was televised to their huts.

On President John F Kennedy, *The Selling of the President 1968* Trident 69

GEORGE MCGOVERN, US Senator

13 [I am] 1,000 percent for Tom Eagleton and I have no intention of dropping him from the ticket.

On his 1972 presidential running mate Thomas F Eagleton after disclosure of Eagleton's health problems, statement issued less than a week before McGovern asked him to resign, quoted by Theodore H White *The Making of the President 1972* Atheneum 73

14 To those who charge that liberalism has been tried and found wanting, I answer that the failure is not in the idea, but in the course of recent history. The New Deal was ended by World War II. The New Frontier was closed by Berlin and Cuba almost before it was opened. And the Great Society lost its greatness in the jungles of Indochina.

Lecture at Oxford University, NY *Times* 22 Jan 73

15 The whole campaign was a tragic case of mistaken identity.

On his unsuccessful 1972 presidential campaign, *ib* 6 May 73

16 The trouble was, all people saw on television were a few of my outspoken supporters out front; and they came away thinking that was me.

ib

17 When people ask if the United States can afford to place on trial the president, if the system can stand impeachment, my answer is, "Can we stand anything else?"

Advocating impeachment of Richard M Nixon, San Francisco *Examiner* 29 Nov 73

SHEILA MCKECHNIE, Director, Shelter National Campaign for the Homeless Ltd, London

18 People who are homeless are not social inadequates. They are people without homes.

Christian Science Monitor 7 May 85

GEORGE MEANY

19 We heard from the abortionists and we heard from the people who looked like Jacks, acted like Jills and had the odors of Johns.

On 1972 Democratic National Convention, quoted in *Wall Street Journal* 11 Jul 84

ROBERT G MENZIES, former Prime Minister of Australia

1 Never forget posterity when devising a policy. Never think of posterity when making a speech.
The Measure of the Years Cassell 70

2 The long-established and noble rule of Law, one of the greatest products of the character and tradition of British history, has suffered a deadly blow. Blackmail has become respectable.
On British government's cancellation of English tour by South African cricket players after public protests, recalled on his death 15 May 78

HENRY MILLER

3 One has to be a lowbrow, a bit of a murderer, to be a politician, ready and willing to see people sacrificed, slaughtered, for the sake of an idea, whether a good one or a bad one.
Quoted in George Plimpton ed *Writers at Work* Viking 63

JEAN NATHAN MILLER

4 Through his mastery of storytelling techniques, he has managed to separate his character, in the public mind, from his actions as president. . . . He has, in short, mesmerized us with that steady gaze.
"Ronald Reagan and the Techniques of Deception" *Atlantic* Feb 84

5 The best advice one can offer to both press and public is the suggestion Ronald Reagan himself gave to students in Chicago . . . "Don't let me get away with it. Check me out. Don't be the sucker generation."
ib

WILLIAM ("FISHBAIT") MILLER, Congressional doorkeeper

6 Eighty percent were hypocrites, 80 percent liars, 80 percent serious sinners . . . except on Sundays. There is always boozing and floozying. . . . I don't have enough time to tell you everybody's name.
60 Minutes CBS TV 24 Apr 77

GEORGE J MITCHELL, US Senator

7 Although he's regularly asked to do so, God does not take sides in American politics.
At Iran-Contra hearings 13 Jul 87

JOHN N MITCHELL, Director, Committee for the Re-election of the President

8 In my mind, the re-election of Richard Nixon, compared with what was available on the other side, was so much more important that I put it in just that context.
On why he did not advise the president of the Watergate break-in, LA *Times* 11 Jul 73

MARTHA MITCHELL

9 [Nixon] bleeds people. He draws every drop of blood and then drops them from a cliff. He'll blame any person he can put his foot on.
Late night telephone call to UPI White House reporter Helen Thomas, quoted in LA *Times* 28 Aug 73

HERBERT MITGANG

10 Johnson himself turned out to be so many different characters he could have populated all of *War and Peace* and still had a few people left over.
On President Lyndon B Johnson, in review of Merle Miller's *Lyndon: An Oral Biography* Putnam 80, NY *Times* 15 Aug 80

IRVIN MOLOTSKY

11 In a few days they are on the walls of the recipients, mementos of a once-in-a-lifetime visit to the president of the United States, pretty good cementers of future support.
On what White House photographer Michael Evans called "grip-and-grin" photographs of Ronald Reagan and visiting dignitaries, "Of Presidential Image and Presidential Focus" NY *Times* 15 Mar 85

WALTER F MONDALE

12 I don't want to spend the next two years in Holiday Inns.
Withdrawing from 1976 presidential campaign 21 Nov 74

13 I said I didn't want to spend most of my life in Holidays Inns, but I've checked and they've all been redecorated. They're marvelous places to stay and I've thought it over and that's where I'd like to be.
On accepting nomination as candidate for vice president, news summaries 16 Jul 76

14 In our system, at about 11:30 on election night, they just push you off the edge of the cliff—and that's it. You might scream on the way down, but you're going to hit the bottom, and you're not going to be in elective office.
On loss to Ronald Reagan in 1984 presidential election, NY *Times* 4 Mar 87

15 Do you want to tear your life apart and get rid of everything you've known as a lifestyle? Like seeing your family? Being with your friends? A fishing trip? A hunting trip? A night's sleep?
Comments to prospective presidential candidates, quoted in *Newsweek* 30 Mar 87

LANCE MORROW

16 The real 1960s began on the afternoon of November 22, 1963 . . . It came to seem that Kennedy's murder opened some malign trap door in American culture, and the wild bats flapped out.
Time 14 Nov 83

17 In the pageant of unity [at the Democratic National Convention], one speaker after another recited a Whitmanesque litany of races and classes and minorities and interests and occupations—or unemployments. Some speakers, in fact, made the nation sound like an immense ingathering of victims—terrorized senior citizens, forsaken minorities, Dickensian children—warmed by the party's Frank Capra version of America: Say, it's a wonderful life!
"All Right, What Kind of People Are We?" *ib* 30 Jul 84

18 His campaign sounded a note of the bogusly grand. Hart is Kennedy typed on the eighth carbon.
After Gary Hart's withdrawal from the 1988 presidential campaign, *ib,* 18 May 87

ROBERT MOSES

19 If you elect a matinee idol mayor, you're going to have a musical comedy administration.
On John V Lindsay as mayor of NYC, NY *Times* 8 Jan 78

BILL MOYERS

20 Ideas are great arrows, but there has to be a bow. And politics is the bow of idealism.
Time 29 Oct 65

1 I work for him despite his faults and he lets me work for him despite my deficiencies.

> As press secretary to President Lyndon B Johnson, NY *Times* 3 Apr 66

2 Hyperbole was to Lyndon Johnson what oxygen is to life.

> *ib* 11 Sep 75

DANIEL P MOYNIHAN, US Senator

3 Citizen participation [is] a device whereby public officials induce nonpublic individuals to act in a way the officials desire.

> *The Public Interest* Fall 69

4 Somehow liberals have been unable to acquire from life what conservatives seem to be endowed with at birth: namely, a healthy skepticism of the powers of government agencies to do good.

> NY *Post* 14 May 69

5 The single most exciting thing you encounter in government is competence, because it's so rare.

> NY *Times* 2 Mar 76

EDWARD R MURROW

6 No one can terrorize a whole nation, unless we are all his accomplices.

> On Senator Joseph R McCarthy's accusations about Communists in government, *See It Now* CBS TV 7 Mar 54

7 If none of us ever read a book that was "dangerous," had a friend who was "different" or joined an organization that advocated "change," we would all be just the kind of people Joe McCarthy wants. Whose fault is that? Not really [McCarthy's]. He didn't create this situation of fear. He merely exploited it, and rather successfully.

> *ib*

8 The politician in my country seeks votes, affection and respect, in that order. . . . With few notable exceptions, they are simply men who want to be loved.

> October 19, 1959, address at London Guildhall, quoted by A M Sperber *Murrow* Freundlich 86

9 The politician is . . . trained in the art of inexactitude. His words tend to be blunt or rounded, because if they have a cutting edge they may later return to wound him.

> *ib*

10 After last night's debate, the reputation of Messieurs Lincoln' and Douglas is secure.

> On September 26, 1960, televised debate between presidential candidates John F Kennedy and Richard M Nixon, *ib*

11 Difficulty is the excuse history never accepts.

> On President John F Kennedy's inaugural address, *ib*

RALPH NADER

12 Our founders did not oust George III in order for us to crown Richard I.

> On President Richard M Nixon during Watergate investigation, news summaries 23 Oct 73

13 President Reagan was elected on the promise of getting government off the backs of the people and now he demands that government wrap itself around the waists of the people.

> On proposed legislation requiring air bags or automatic seat belts in all automobiles, NY *Times* 12 Jul 84

14 The networks are not some chicken-coop manufacturing lobby whose calls nobody returns.

> On NBC President Robert C Wright's proposal that company employees support a political action committee, quoted by Edwin Diamond *New York* 19 Jan 87

V S NAIPAUL

15 Argentine political life is like the life of an ant community or an African forest tribe: full of events, full of crisis and deaths, but life is always cyclical, and the year ends as it begins.

> Quoted by Lydia Chavez NY *Times* 15 Dec 85

EARL NEWSOM

16 Today's public opinion, though it may appear as light as air, may be tomorrow's legislation—for better or for worse.

> Quoted in Amer Petroleum Institute newsletter Winter 63

NEW YORK HERALD TRIBUNE

17 Truman lost his temper, MacArthur lost his job, Acheson lost his war, a million and a half people lost their lives and Stalin didn't even lose a night's sleep.

> On Korean War and early 1950s, 6 Apr 64

REINHOLD NIEBUHR

18 The sad duty of politics is to establish justice in a sinful world.

> Quoted by Jimmy Carter *Why Not the Best?* Broadman 75

RICHARD M NIXON, 37th US President

19 Any lady who is first lady likes being first lady. I don't care what they say, they like it.

> *Newsweek* 22 Mar 71

20 My view is that one should not break up a winning combination.

> On choice of Spiro T Agnew as vice-presidential running mate, CBS TV 2 Jan 72

21 If an individual wants to be a leader and isn't controversial, that means he never stood for anything.

> Dallas *Times-Herald* 10 Dec 78

22 I wish I could give you a lot of advice, based on my experience of winning political debates. But I don't have that experience. My only experience is at losing them.

> Letter to Robert Gray, Ronald Reagan's deputy campaign manager, quoted by Robert Sam Anson *Exile: The Unquiet Oblivion of Richard M Nixon* Simon & Schuster 84

23 I wouldn't bet the farm on it, but I'd bet the main house. I wouldn't even bet the outhouse on Mondale.

> On Ronald Reagan's chances of defeating Walter Mondale in the 1984 presidential election, *Time* 21 May 84

24 What does that candyass think I sent him over there for?

> On Secretary of the Treasury George P Shultz's refusal to authorize tax audits of Nixon's critics, quoted by Ronald Steel "Shultz's Way" NY *Times* 11 Jan 87

JON NORDHEIMER

25 Louisiana has [no] monopoly on rogues, rapscallions, shakedowns and kickbacks. . . . Nor is it the

only place where a few officials have endeared themselves to the electorate by means of the utter disorder of their private lives.

NY *Times* 3 Mar 85

MICHAEL OAKESHOTT

1 In political activity . . . men sail a boundless and bottomless sea; there is neither harbor for shelter nor floor for anchorage, neither starting point nor appointed destination.

"Rabble without a Cause" London *Times* 21 May 85

KIRK O'DONNELL

2 [Political theory] provides a common language with which people in this town communicate with each other.

On Washington DC, NY *Times* 18 Jan 83

3 Instant analysis is the occupational disease. . . . There are no smokestacks, there's no black lung. Politics is the only industry.

ib

THOMAS P ("TIP") O'NEILL, Speaker of the House

4 Am I wrong in listening to women who live in Nicaragua and follow the Sermon on the Mount? Or am I supposed to just sit here and believe generals?

On crediting testimony of Maryknoll nuns against US aid to Nicaraguan Contras, quoted by Jimmy Breslin NY *Daily News* 29 Jun 86

ALAN PATON

5 I envision someday a great, peaceful South Africa in which the world will take pride, a nation in which each of many different groups will be making its own creative contribution.

Quoted in *New Yorker* 17 Dec 60

6 The Afrikaner has nowhere to go, and that's why he would rather destroy himself than capitulate.

On resistance to social change by descendants of the Dutch settlers in South Africa, *Christian Science Monitor* 17 Jan 78

LESTER B PEARSON, Prime Minister of Canada

7 We'll jump off that bridge when we come to it.

Quoted in John Robert Colombo ed *Colombo's Canadian Quotations* Hurtig 74

8 Politics is the skilled use of blunt objects.

From 1972 CBC TV presentation *The Tenth Decade, ib*

CLAIBORNE PELL, US Senator

9 My opponent called me a cream puff. . . . Well, I rushed out and got the baker's union to endorse me.

On his first political campaign, NY *Times* 3 Feb 87

10 The secret is to always let the other man have your way.

ib

CHARLES PETERS

11 Bureaucrats write memoranda both because they appear to be busy when they are writing and because the memos, once written, immediately become proof that they were busy.

How Washington Really Works Addison-Wesley 80

12 The more bureaucrats do wrong to the public, the more favors congressmen can do for their constitu-

ents as they right the wrongs—or as they appear to try to right them.

ib

PRINCE PHILIP, Duke of Edinburgh

13 Most of the monarchies of Europe were really destroyed by their greatest and most ardent supporters. It was the most reactionary people who tried to hold onto something without letting it develop and change.

Quoted by John Pearson *The Selling of the Royal Family* Simon & Schuster 86

CABELL PHILLIPS

14 One gathers from talking with him, indeed, that he looks back upon the whole episode regretfully, as a virtuous husband might upon an extramarital fling with the office widow.

On Henry A Wallace's attitude toward his term as vice president, NY *Times* 6 Oct 63

HOWARD PHILLIPS, Chairman, Conservative Caucus

15 [The Reagan] administration's foreign policy has been to kiss the Russian bear's bottom, and he keeps turning the other cheek.

On swap of journalist Nicholas Daniloff for accused Soviet agent Gennadi Zakharov, *Time* 13 Oct 86

16 If [George P] Shultz continues as secretary of state, then Reagan has basically accepted the role not even of Queen Elizabeth but of the Queen Mother.

On investigation of arms sales to Iran, *Newsweek* 8 Dec 86

WILLIAM PROXMIRE, US Senator

17 The biggest danger for a politician is to shake hands with a man who is physically stronger, has been drinking and is voting for the other guy.

NY *Herald Tribune* 16 Feb 64

18 He knows the tax code as thoroughly as the pope knows the Lord's Prayer.

On Senator Russell B Long, recalled on Long's retirement, *Time* 10 Nov 86

JEANETTE RANKIN, 1st US Congresswoman

19 We're half the people; we should be half the Congress.

Calling for more women in public office, *Newsweek* 14 Feb 66

SAM RAYBURN, Speaker of the House

20 They may be just as intelligent as you say. But I'd feel a helluva lot better if just one of them had ever run for sheriff.

To Vice President Lyndon B Johnson on associates of President John F Kennedy, quoted by Lance Morrow "After 20 Years, the Question: How Good a President?" *Time* 14 Nov 83

21 Wait a minute.

Advice recalled by Jack Valenti as "the three most important words in the English language," quoted by Peter W Kaplan "Are Movies a Fabulous Invalid, Too?" NY *Times* 5 May 85

RONALD REAGAN, 40th US President

22 The thought of being president frightens me. I do not think I want the job.

As governor of California, news summaries 31 Dec 73

1 To sit back hoping that someday, someway, someone will make things right is to go on feeding the
crocodile, hoping he will eat you last—but eat you
he will.
> News summaries 7 Nov 74

2 Politics I supposed to be the second-oldest profession. I have come to realize that it bears a very close
resemblance to the first.
> LA *Herald-Examiner* 3 Mar 78

3 With our eyes fixed on the future, but recognizing
the realities of today. . . . we will achieve our destiny to be as a shining city on a hill for all mankind
to see.
> To Conservative Political Action Conference 17 Mar 78

4 I was alarmed at my doctor's report: He said I was
sound as a dollar.
> As Republican presidential nominee 17 Jul 80

5 I believe Moses was 80 when God first commis-
sioned him for public service.
> On running for president at age 73, address at Dixon IL
> 6 Feb 84

6 Thomas Jefferson once said, "We should never
judge a president by his age, only by his works."
And ever since he told me that I stopped worrying.
> *ib*

7 There were so many candidates on the platform that
there were not enough promises to go around.
> On Democratic presidential primary debate in New
> Hampshire, *Newsweek* 6 Feb 84

8 Republicans believe every day is the Fourth of July,
but Democrats believe every day is April 15.
> NY *Times* 10 Oct 84

9 If I had as much make-up on as he did, I'd have
looked younger, too.
> On "age issue" during television debates with Walter F
> Mondale, *Wall Street Journal* 11 Oct 84

10 Shouldn't someone tag Mr Kennedy's bold new
imaginative program with its proper age? Under the
tousled boyish haircut is still old Karl Marx—first
launched a century ago. There is nothing new in the
idea of a government being Big Brother.
> 1960 letter to Richard M Nixon disclosed in final weeks
> of 1984 presidential campaign, NY *Times* 27 Oct 84

11 I'll be like Scarlett O'Hara—I'll think about it tomorrow.
> Refraining from endorsement of Vice President George
> Bush for 1988 Republican presidential nomination, *ib* 12
> Feb 85

12 Die-hard conservatives thought that if I couldn't get
everything I asked for, I should jump off the cliff
with the flag flying—go down in flames. No, if I can
get 70 or 80 percent of what it is I'm trying to
get . . . I'll take that and then continue to try to get
the rest in the future.
> On criticism of early political compromises, *ib* 6 Oct 85

13 You know, it was only a generation ago that actors
couldn't be buried in the churchyard.
> Expressing belief that people underestimated him be-
> cause of his acting background, *ib*

14 Recession in when your neighbor loses his job. Depression is when you lose yours. And recovery is
when Jimmy Carter loses his.
> 1980 campaign remark recalled when Reagan participat-

ed in dedication of Carter Presidential Center in Atlanta, *ib*
2 Oct 86

JAMES RESTON

15 Half circus and half Supreme Court.
> On national political conventions, NY *Times* 12 Jul 60

16 How Kennedy knew the precise drop in milk consumption in 1960, the percentage rise in textile im-
ports from 1957 to 1960 and the number of speeches
cleared by the Defense Department is not quite
clear, but anyway, he did. He either overwhelmed
you with decimal points or disarmed you with a
smile and a wisecrack.
> On President John F Kennedy's press conferences,
> quoted by Ralph G Martin *A Hero for Our Time* Mac-
> millan 83

17 An election is a bet on the future, not a popularity
test of the past.
> NY *Times* 10 Oct 84

ELLIOT L RICHARDSON

18 Washington is . . . a city of cocker spaniels. It's a
city of people who are more interested in being pet-
ted and admired, loved, than rendering the exercise
of power.
> NY *Times* 13 Jul 82

ALAN RICHMAN

19 She enjoys driving her restless mind in the express
lane.
> On Senator Paula Hawkins of Florida, *People* 20 Oct 86

HYMAN G RICKOVER

20 If you're going to sin, sin against God, not the bureaucracy. God will forgive you but the bureaucracy
won't.
> Quoted by William A Clinkscales Jr after Senate com-
> mittee delayed confirming him as director of the Selec-
> tive Service System, NY *Times* 3 Nov 86

PAT ROBERTSON

21 The first words I spoke as a baby were *Mommy*,
Daddy and *constituency*.
> On growing up in a prominent Virginia political family,
> NY *Times* 12 Feb 87

ANDY ROONEY

22 The only people who say worse things about politicians than reporters do are other politicians.
> *60 Minutes* CBS TV 7 Oct 84

23 I just wish we knew a little less about his urethra
and a little more about his arms sales to Iran.
> On press coverage of President Ronald Reagan's pros-
> tate operation, *ib* 11 Jan 87

ELEANOR ROOSEVELT

24 Where, after all, do universal human rights begin?
In small places, close to home—so close and so
small that they cannot be seen on any map of the
world.
> Quoted in NY *Times* 26 Dec 65

ETHEL AND JULIUS ROSENBERG

25 We are the first victims of American fascism.
> Letter released by their attorney on the day they were
> electrocuted for espionage, news summaries 19 Jun 53

RICHARD H ROVERE

1 He stamped with his name a tendency, a whole cluster of tendencies in American life. The name survives. To many Americans, whatever is illiberal, anti-intellectual, repressive, reactionary, totalitarian or merely swinish will hereafter be *McCarthyism*. The word is imprecise, but it conveys a meaning and a powerful image.

> On Senator Joseph R McCarthy, "The Frivolous Demagogue" *Esquire* Jun 58

2 He was a master of the scabrous and the scatological.

> *ib*

3 McCarthy invented the Multiple Lie—the lie with so many tiny gears and fragile connecting rods that reason exhausted itself in the effort to combat it.

> *ib*

ROBERT RUNCIE, Archbishop of Canterbury

4 Apartheid is an insult to God and man whom God dignifies.

> Address during April 1982 tour of Nigeria, *Seasons of the Spirit* Eerdmans 83

MARK RUSSELL

5 He'll tell you he's a Texan
Though he's got those Eastern ways,
Eatin' lots of barbecue
With a sauce that's called béarnaise.

> On George Bush's 1980 campaign, "Two-Gun Georgie Bush," set to tune of "Yellow Rose of Texas," quoted in NY *Times* 7 Oct 84

WILLIAM SAFIRE

6 I want my questions answered by an alert and experienced politician, prepared to be grilled and quoted—not my hand held by an old smoothie.

> On artful dodging of difficult questions by President Ronald Reagan, NY *Times* 16 Aug 84

7 No one flower can ever symbolize this nation. America is a bouquet.

> On Congressional designation of the rose as the official US flower, *ib* 25 Sep 86

8 One difference between French appeasement and American appeasement is that France pays ransom in cash and gets its hostages back while the United States pays ransom in arms and gets additional hostages taken.

> *ib* 13 Nov 86

9 The first ladyship is the only federal office in which the holder can neither be fired nor impeached.

> *ib* 2 Mar 87

10 Decide on some imperfect Somebody and you will win, because the truest truism in politics is: You can't beat Somebody with Nobody.

> "The Perfect Candidate" *ib* 16 Apr 87

ANTHONY SAMPSON

11 The real rulers of England are not so much in the center of a solar system as in a cluster of interlocking circles, each one largely preoccupied with its own professionalism and expertise and touching others only at one edge. . . . They are not a single Establishment but a ring of Establishments, with slender connections.

> *The Anatomy of Britain* Harper & Row 62

12 In the person of the prime minister several different strands come together. Dukes, Eton, Balliol, the Guards, clubs, the Church and Whitehall all jostle together behind that mustache.

> On Harold Macmillan, *ib*

LORD SAMUEL (Edwin Herbert Samuel)

13 Where there are two PhDs in a developing country, one is head of state and the other is in exile.

> NY *Times* 5 Jul 64

LORD SANDWICH (Alexander V E P Montague)

14 Lord Hailsham said the other day that the machinery of government was creaking. My Lords, it is not even moving sufficiently to emit a noise of any kind.

> NY *Times* 21 Apr 63

ARTHUR SCARGILL, Marxist leader of British miners

15 [That] most dangerous duo, President Ray-Gun and the plutonium blonde, Margaret Thatcher.

> Quoted in *Time* 3 Dec 84

JAMES R SCHLESINGER, former US Secretary of Defense

16 The notion of a defense that will protect American cities is one that will not be achieved, but it is that goal that supplies the political magic, as it were, in the president's vision.

> To Senate Foreign Relations Committee, NY *Times* 7 Feb 87

17 Americans historically have embraced crusades—such as World War II—as well as glorious little wars. The difficulty is that the most likely conflicts of the future fall between crusades and such brief encounters as Grenada or Mayagüez.

> *ib*

SERGE SCHMEMANN

18 In some circles Stalin has in fact been making a comeback. . . . His portrait hangs above the dashboard of trucks, a symbol of blue-collar nostalgia for a tough leader.

> NY *Times* 31 Oct 86

DAVID SCHOENBRUN

19 There never was a France like the Madonna that Charles de Gaulle worships in the fresco of his imagination.

> *The Three Lives of Charles de Gaulle* Atheneum 66

PATRICIA SCHROEDER, US Congresswoman

20 I have a brain and a uterus, and I use both.

> On being an elected official and a mother, NY *Times* 6 May 77

21 I was cooking breakfast this morning for my kids, and I thought, "He's just like a Teflon frying pan: Nothing sticks to him."

> August 1983 description of President Ronald Reagan, quoted by Michael Kenney Boston *Globe* 24 Oct 84

22 Spine transplants are what we really need to take Reagan on.

> On the military budget, NY *Times* 14 Jan 85

WALTER SHAPIRO

1 Geraldine Ferraro was undergoing one of the worst ordeals of a media age—trial by disclosure.

> On investigation of her family's finances, *Newsweek* 27 Aug 84

DAVID K SHIPLER

2 The Holocaust never quite leaves Israeli Jews alone. Arabs use it against them and they use it against Arabs. Jews use it against other Jews. Even the president of the United States, it seems, can use it against the prime minister of Israel.

> *Arab and Jew: Wounded Spirits in a Promised Land* Times Books 86

3 Watching foreign affairs is sometimes like watching a magician; the eye is drawn to the hand performing the dramatic flourishes, leaving the other hand—the one doing the important job—unnoticed.

> "For Israel and US, A Growing Military Partnership" NY *Times* 15 Mar 87

HUGH SIDEY

4 A White House dinner is the American family assembled, from labor leaders to billionaires, actors, architects, academicians and athletes.

> "Talking Peace and Pork Chops" *Time* 23 Jan 84

5 When people travel here from across the country, they shed jealousies and politics and prejudices. . . . The mighty climb down. The humble are elevated.

> *ib*

6 [China's Premier] Zhao Ziyang, for all of his billion constituents, seemed in the evening's lovely flow like a favorite uncle, smiling a little too much, wanting to be a bit American, talking about peace and pork chops.

> *ib*

7 In this era of world leadership, the metal detector is the altar and the minicam may be god.

> "The New Style of Exposure" *ib* 18 Jun 84

8 In just 20 years terrorism, communications, the jet plane and the increase of wealth and knowledge have forced, to varying degrees, world leaders into a haunted and secret peerage whose links with the people they guide are meticulously cleansed and staged.

> *ib*

9 The problems seem so easy out there on the stump. Deficits shrink with a rhetorical flourish.

> On closing days of the 1984 presidential campaign, "Now Comes the Hard Part" *ib* 5 Nov 84

10 We love the blather and boast, the charge and countercharge of campaigning. Governing is a tougher deal.

> *ib*

11 The prime minister found something hopeful in the man's eyes and manner. The 30 or so people who run this world analyze one another that way and then make decisions of life and death for us. Scary, but true.

> On Margaret Thatcher's first meeting with Mikhail S Gorbachev, "Measure of the Man" *ib* 25 Mar 85

WILLIAM E SIMON, former US Secretary of the Treasury

12 Bad politicians are sent to Washington by good people who don't vote.

> Quoted in *A Guide to the 99th Congress* LTV Corp 85

ALAN K SIMPSON, US Senator

13 There is no "slippery slope" toward loss of liberties, only a long staircase where each step downward must first be tolerated by the American people and their leaders.

> NY *Times* 26 Sep 82

14 Welcome to the pit [and] the great hunters who have been out to tack the pelt of Bill Rehnquist on the wall of the den.

> To Supreme Court nominee Antonin Scalia on his appearance before the Senate Judiciary Committee after the committee's prolonged hearings to confirm William H Rehnquist as chief justice, *ib* 8 Aug 86

15 Here we can brag and bluster and blather and almost like a comic book character you could invent, Captain Bombast, pull the cape around the shoulders and shout the magic words, "Get him." And rise above it all in a blast of hot air.

> Characterizing his committee, *ib*

16 Stonewalling, wiretapping, cover-up, Lord's sake, if there isn't one of us here at this table that hasn't dabbled in that mystery.

> *ib*

17 He has to do the heavy lifting and the windows and the wash, and also protect the president.

> On role of Ronald Reagan's White House chief of staff Donald T Regan, *ib* 19 Feb 87

18 [You were doing a] sadistic little disservice to your country.

> To reporters who shouted questions about the Iran arms deal to President Reagan as he boarded a helicopter, *Time* 30 Mar 87

19 You'd like to stick it in his gazoo.

> *ib*

JOHN J SIRICA, Judge, US District Court, District of Columbia

20 An attempt is already underway to revise history— to leave the impression that the former president had nothing to do with Watergate. But there is no doubt about his obstruction of justice after the Watergate break-in.

> NY *Times* 12 Aug 79

MICHAEL SMALL

21 To their credit, neither candidate said anything that would damage his campaign, and neither bit his opponent.

> On mock debate between a German shepherd and a rottweiler, staged by Walter F Mondale's family the night before the actual debate in Louisville KY, *People* 5 Nov 84

DAVID SMITH

22 It's the season to scam, gate, bash and amokize every noun around Washington.

> On the Iran-Contra scandal, NY *Times* 28 Mar 87

23 Contrascam, Olliegate, president-bashing, Iranamok—place any person or group in Column A, and the drearisome foursome in Column B. Then generate headlines to your heart's content.

> *ib*

1 One might label this sorry affair Iranscambashamok.
ib

MARGARET CHASE SMITH, US Senator

2 When people keep telling you that you can't do a thing, you kind of like to try it.
Announcing her presidential candidacy, *Time* 7 Feb 64

STEVEN SMITH

3 You've got to understand their reasoning. They think of this historian as one of their pocket-people, whom they feel they can count on.
On Kennedy family's approval of biographers, quoted by Peter Collier and David Horowitz *The Kennedys* Summit 84

ALEXANDER SOLZHENITSYN

4 I was in a state of witless shock, as though flames had suddenly enwrapped and paralyzed me so that for a moment I had no mind, no memory.
On arrest by Russian secret police, *The Oak and the Calf* Harper & Row 80

THEODORE C SORENSEN

5 The ambassador was never present, but his presence was never absent.
On Joseph P Kennedy's influence on his son John's presidential campaign, quoted by Ralph G Martin *A Hero for Our Time* Macmillan 83

6 Presidential candidates don't chew gum.
Aside to John F Kennedy overheard at a Nebraska airport, *ib*

7 I think he's informing himself, reaching out and getting ideas and information and advice. I haven't the slightest doubt that internally taking shape in that marvelous brain of his is a philosophy of foreign affairs. But it would be premature to say that one is fully formed.
On NY Governor Mario Cuomo, NY *Times* 1 May 86

ROGER STARR

8 Reality is the best possible cure for dreams.
On the near financial collapse of NYC in the mid 1970s, *The Rise and Fall of New York City* Basic Books 85

DAVID STEEL, leader of British Liberal Party

9 The cabinet has been shaken about a bit, but it's the same old jar of jellybeans.
On Prime Minister Margaret Thatcher's restructuring of her Conservative cabinet, *Newsweek* 16 Sep 85

10 [She has turned] the British bulldog into a Reagan poodle.
On Thatcher's decision to permit US bombers to take off from British bases for attack on Libya, *Time* 28 Apr 86

RONALD STEEL

11 Politics as battle has given way to politics as spectacle.
"The Vanishing Campaign Biography" NY *Times* 5 Aug 84

12 We are not a cynical people. The will to believe lingers on. We like to think that heroes can emerge from obscurity, as they sometimes do; that elections do matter, even though the process is at least part

hokum; that through politics we can change our society and maybe even find a cause to believe in.
ib

13 He has not yet become an elder statesman, though his foreign policy credentials are considerable, but he is certainly our ancient mariner, forever tugging at our sleeve to let him tell his tale of what really happened.
On Richard M Nixon, *New York Review of Books* 30 May 85

14 He forever perplexes and annoys. Every time you think he is about to show the statesmanship for which his intelligence and experience have equipped him, he throws a spitball.
ib

GLORIA STEINEM

15 What has the women's movement learned from [Geraldine Ferraro's] candidacy for vice president? Never get married.
On personal and financial problems of Ferraro's family during 1984 presidential campaign, quoted in Boston *Globe* 14 May 87

ADLAI E STEVENSON

16 [They are] the dinosaur wing of the party.
On the Republican's extreme conservatives, address at Salt Lake City, news summaries 14 Oct 52

17 The general has dedicated himself so many times, he must feel like the cornerstone of a public building.
On his opponent Dwight D Eisenhower, *ib* 1 Nov 52

18 It is an ancient political vehicle, held together by soft soap and hunger and with front-seat drivers and back-seat drivers contradicting each other in a bedlam of voices, shouting "go right" and "go left" at the same time.
On the Republican Party, *ib* 15 Nov 52

19 I don't envy the driver and I don't think the American people will care to ride in his bus very far.
ib

20 To act coolly, intelligently and prudently in perilous circumstances is the test of a man—and also a nation.
Opposing US defense of islands off Chinese mainland, *ib* 11 Apr 55

21 Nixon is finding out there are no tails on an Eisenhower jacket.
On the 1960 presidential campaign, *ib* 30 Aug 60

22 The elephant has a thick skin, a head full of ivory, and as everyone who has seen a circus parade knows, proceeds best by grasping the tail of its predecessor.
ib

23 It will be helpful in our mutual objective to allow every man in America to look his neighbor in the face and see a man—not a color.
Foreword to booklet on interracial relations prepared by Anti-Defamation League of B'nai B'rith, quoted in NY *Times* 22 Jun 64

24 You know, you really can't beat a household commodity—the ketchup bottle on the kitchen table.
On running for president against Dwight D Eisenhower, recalled on Stevenson's death 14 Jul 65

1 He is the kind of politician who would cut down a redwood tree, then mount the stump and make a speech for conservation.
On Richard M Nixon, *ib*

DAVID A STOCKMAN

2 A veritable incubator of short cuts, schemes and devices to overcome the truth.
On his job as director of US Office of Management and Budget, *The Triumph of Politics* Harper & Row 86

3 He operated on the echo principle: He told the president what he wanted to hear.
On White House chief of staff Donald T Regan, *ib*

THEODORE STRAUSS

4 The vanquished themselves prove that history has not lied; like tourists in hell, they took snapshots.
On photographs of Nazi concentration camps, ABC TV 6 Mar 68

ROBERT A TAFT, US Senator

5 You really have to get to know Dewey to dislike him.
On Republican presidential candidate Thomas E Dewey, recalled on Taft's death 31 Jul 53

MARGARET THATCHER, Prime Minister of Great Britain

6 No woman in my time will be prime minister or chancellor or foreign secretary—not the top jobs. Anyway, I wouldn't want to be prime minister; you have to give yourself 100 percent.
On appointment as government spokesperson for education, London *Sunday Telegraph* 26 Oct 69

7 In politics if you want anything said, ask a man. If you want anything done, ask a woman.
People 15 Sep 75

8 What Britain needs is an iron lady.
Campaign slogan, quoted in *Newsweek* 14 May 79

9 Unless we change our ways and our direction, our greatness as a nation will soon be a footnote in the history books, a distant memory of an offshore island, lost in the mists of time like Camelot, remembered kindly for its noble past.
Campaign speech in Bolton, *ib*

10 Of course it's the same old story. Truth usually is the same old story.
On her stand for sound money and competitive industry to cut inflation and unemployment, *Time* 16 Feb 81

11 We were told our campaign wasn't sufficiently slick. We regard that as a compliment.
On winning an unprecedented third term as prime minister, NY *Times* 12 Jun 87

PAUL THEROUX

12 The Peace Corps is a sort of Howard Johnson's on the main drag into maturity.
Sunrise with Seamonsters Houghton Mifflin 84

NORMAN THOMAS

13 [President John F] Kennedy said that if we had nuclear war we'd kill 300 million people in the first hour. [Secretary of Defense Robert S] McNamara, who is a good businessman and likes to save, says it would be only 200 million.
Recalled on his death 19 Dec 68

14 The struggle against demagoguery scarcely fits the St George-against-the-dragon myth . . . Our democratic St George goes out rather reluctantly with armor awry.
Quoted on 30th anniversary of US Senate's censure of Joseph R McCarthy, NY *Times* 2 Dec 84

15 The struggle is confused; our knight wins by no clean thrust of lance or sword, but the dragon somehow poops out, and decent democracy is victor.
ib

LORD THOMSON OF FLEET (Roy Herbert Thomson)

16 I've got money so I'm a Conservative.
Recalled on his death 4 Aug 76

LORD THORNEYCROFT (Peter Thorneycroft), British Conservative Party leader

17 The choice in politics isn't usually between black and white. It's between two horrible shades of gray.
London *Sunday Telegraph* 11 Feb 79

FRANK TRIPPETT

18 Democratic government's capacity for Byzantine deviousness is probably best told by that epochal best-teller, the Pentagon Papers—that "hemorrhage" of classified matter, as Henry Kissinger ruefully called it—which dramatized, in 47 volumes, just how far a government could go in clandestine and illicit duplicity.
"The Public Life of Secrecy" *Time* 17 Jan 83

HARRY S TRUMAN, 33rd US President

19 In my opinion eight years as president is enough and sometimes too much for any man to serve in that capacity.
Announcement that he would not seek election to a second full term, 29 Mar 52

20 That precedent should continue—not by a Constitutional amendment but by custom based on the honor of the man in the office.
ib

21 Therefore to re-establish that custom, although by a quibble I could say I've only had one term, I am not a candidate and will not accept the nomination for another term.
ib

22 You and I are stuck with the necessity of taking the worst of two evils or none at all. So—I'm taking the *immature* Democrat as the best of the two. Nixon is impossible.
Letter to Dean Acheson on 1960 presidential campaign 26 Aug 60

23 I remember when I first came to Washington. For the first six months you wonder how the hell you ever got here. For the next six months you wonder how the hell the rest of them ever got here.
Recalled on his death 26 Dec 72

24 He's one of the few in the history of this country to run for high office talking out of both sides of his mouth at the same time and lying out of both sides.
On Richard M Nixon, quoted by Merle Miller *Plain Speaking: An Oral Biography of Harry S Truman* Berkley 74

1 He wasn't used to being criticized, and he never did get it through his head that's what politics is all *about*. He was used to getting his ass kissed.

On President Dwight D Eisenhower, *ib*

2 Why, this fellow don't know any more about politics than a pig knows about Sunday.

On 1952 presidential candidate Dwight D Eisenhower, quoted by Richard M Nixon *RN: Memoirs of Richard Nixon* Grosset & Dunlap 78

MARGARET TRUMAN

3 He took pride in belonging to the world's most exclusive club: the United States Senate.

To joint session of Congress on centenary of the birth of her father President Harry S Truman 8 May 84

4 He was prouder still to be a member of that even more restricted group, Uncle Sam Rayburn's Board of Education—the Bourbon and Branch Water College of Congressional Knowledge.

ib

5 He loved politicians—even Republicans.

ib

T L TSIM

6 The destiny of Hong Kong is now the same as the destiny of China. There is no escaping.

On 1984 agreement between Britain and China that life in the crown colony would continue virtually unchanged when it reverted to Chinese rule in 1997, NY *Times* 27 Sep 84

ED TURNER

7 A 6-Kleenex, 40-goose-bumper shot in the warm, golden tones of a cereal commercial.

On Ronald Reagan's 1984 campaign film, *Wall Street Journal* 21 Aug 84

DESMOND TUTU, Bishop of Johannesburg

8 Be nice to whites, they need you to rediscover their humanity.

NY *Times* 19 Oct 84

9 I am a leader by default, only because nature does not allow a vacuum.

Christian Science Monitor 20 Dec 84

10 When a pile of cups is tottering on the edge of the table and you warn that they will crash to the ground, in South Africa you are blamed when that happens.

NY *Times* 3 Jan 85

11 For goodness sake, will they hear, will white people hear what we are trying to say? Please, all we are asking you to do is to recognize that we are humans, too.

ib

12 I am not interested in picking up crumbs of compassion thrown from the table of someone who considers himself my master. I want the full menu of rights.

Today NBC TV 9 Jan 85

13 Those who invest in South Africa should not think they are doing us a favor; they are here for what they get out of our cheap and abundant labor, and they should know that they are buttressing one of the most vicious systems.

Quoted by LA Mayor Tom Bradley in letter to the editor LA *Times* 13 May 85

JACK VALENTI, White House special assistant

14 I sleep each night a little better, a little more confidently, because Lyndon Johnson is my president.

In frontispiece to Jack Shepherd and Christopher S Wren comps *Quotations from Chairman LBJ* Simon & Schuster 68

GORE VIDAL

15 In writing and politicking, it's best not to think about it, just do it.

Quoted in *A Guide to the 99th Congress* LTV Corp 85

JOHN VINOCUR

16 On a strawberry sundae of a day, all daisies and June sun and pastoral posing by world leaders on the Lancaster House lawn.

On summit conference in London, NY *Times* 9 Jun 84

17 Like boilerplate, the final statements bear hundreds of hammer marks and rivets. And in their leaden way, they are perhaps as good a reflection of the mood that dominates the meetings at Lancaster House as the photogenic scenes behind the building this afternoon when President Reagan seemed to want to mow the old building's lawn.

ib

LOUDON WAINWRIGHT

18 Displaying a bland, even an eerie, disregard for what appeared to be the facts of the situation, he fell back on an old habit of looking ahead to the next defeat.

On perennial presidential candidate Harold E Stassen, *Life* 20 Mar 64

TERRY WAITE

19 Freeing hostages is like putting up a stage set, which you do with the captors, agreeing on each piece as you slowly put it together; then you leave an exit through which both the captor and the captive can walk with sincerity and dignity.

On trips to Middle East as emissary of the Archbishop of Canterbury to negotiate the release of hostages held by terrorists, ABC TV 3 Nov 86

GEORGE C WALLACE, Governor of Alabama

20 Being governor don't mean a thing anymore in this country. We're nothing. Just high-paid ornaments is all. I'm thinking of running for president myself.

Life 22 Jul 66

21 After much prayerful consideration, I feel that I must say I have climbed my last political mountain.

On retiring from Alabama politics, NY *Times* 3 Apr 86

22 I'm the lamest lame duck there could be.

At farewell to political supporters after his retirement as governor, news summaries 22 Nov 86

HAROLD WASHINGTON, Mayor of Chicago

23 We have destroyed the dinosaur.

On defeating the Democratic machine in his 1983 election as mayor, quoted in *Time* 31 Mar 86

RUSSELL WATSON

24 After starting her career as a beauty queen on the fleshy fringes of show business, Imelda grew into bigger roles, playing Jackie to her husband's Jack, Bonnie to his Clyde, Evita to his strongman.

On Imelda Marcos, former first lady of the Philippines, "How to Spend a Billion" *Newsweek* 24 Mar 86

1 Enriched beyond the dreams of any normal person's avarice, she accumulated possessions with a single-minded lust that calls to mind those ancient Romans who gorged themselves, then vomited so they could gorge again.
> *ib*

JOSEPH N WELCH

2 Until this moment, Senator, I think I had never gauged your cruelty or your recklessness. . . . Have you no sense of decency, sir, at long last? Have you left no sense of decency?
> To Senator Joseph J McCarthy at the Army-McCarthy hearings after McCarthy had gratuitously smeared a young associate of Welch's, news summaries 9 Jun 54

THEODORE H WHITE

3 I happen to think that American politics is one of the noblest arts of mankind; and I cannot do anything else but write about it.
> NY *Times* 22 Jun 65

4 The gusto of one, the indignation of the other; the challenge of the one party, the response of the other; the eloquence and the comedy, the passion and the issues were ours—no other country can provide them.
> *ib*

5 He is like a good prewar house—solidly built. They don't build them that way anymore. He's also been repainted several times.
> On Richard M Nixon's return to presidential politics, *Time* 16 Feb 68

6 His passion has aroused the best and the beast in man. And the beast waited for him in the kitchen.
> On assassination of presidential candidate Robert F Kennedy in the kitchen of the Ambassador Hotel in Los Angeles, *The Making of the President 1968* Atheneum 69

7 The best time to listen to a politician is when he's on a stump on a street corner in the rain late at night when he's exhausted. Then he doesn't lie.
> NY *Times* 5 Jan 69

8 The flood of money that gushes into politics today is a pollution of democracy.
> *Time* 19 Nov 84

9 There is no excitement anywhere in the world, short of war, to match the excitement of an American presidential campaign.
> On his role as "a storyteller of elections" in series of books on presidential campaigns, recalled on his death 15 May 86

10 A liberal is a person who believes that water can be made to run uphill. A conservative is someone who believes everybody should pay for his water. I'm somewhere in between: I believe water should be free, but that water flows downhill.
> *ib*

11 With the end of the nominating process, American politics leaves logic behind.
> *Newsweek* 26 May 86

12 Politics in America is the binding secular religion.
> *Time* 29 Dec 86

RALPH WHITEHEAD JR

13 If Mike Dukakis were an automobile, he'd be a Honda Civic. Compact, efficient, reliable—short on style but long on utility.
> On 1988 presidential candidate Michael S Dukakis, governor of Massachusetts, Boston *Globe* 17 Mar 87

TOM WICKER

14 [It is] a product of the media and by the media, if not just for the media.
> On Senator Gary Hart's campaign for the 1984 Democratic presidential nomination, NY *Times* 13 Mar 84

AMY WILENTZ

15 The upcoming primaries will be a test of their old family football cheer: "Clap your hands! Stamp your feet! 'Cause Daddy's team can't be beat."
> On concurrent Congressional campaigns of two of Robert F Kennedy's children, *Time* 8 Sep 86

GEORGE F WILL

16 They define themselves in terms of what they oppose.
> On conservatives, *Newsweek* 30 Sep 74

17 Voters don't decide issues, they decide *who* will decide issues.
> *ib* 8 Mar 76

18 The unpleasant sound Bush is emitting as he traipses from one conservative gathering to another is a thin, tinny "arf"—the sound of a lap dog.
> On Vice President George Bush, Washington *Post* 30 Jan 86

19 All God's chillun got shoes or can get them in Mrs Marcos's closet, which is large enough to house Mr and Mrs Duvalier, itinerant nonlaborers.
> On the 1986 flight into exile of Imelda Marcos of the Philippines, leaving behind a horde of shoes, and Haiti's ouster of President Jean Claude "Baby Doc" Duvalier, *Newsweek* 5 Jan 87

20 Stalin's henchman [V M] Molotov, 96, died old and in bed, a privilege he helped to deny to millions.
> *ib*

JEANETTE WILLIAMS

21 It's like raping Alice in Wonderland.
> On eve of her husband Harrison A William Jr's expulsion from the Senate, NBC TV 3 Mar 82

HAROLD WILSON, Prime Minister of Great Britain

22 There is something utterly nauseating about a system of society which pays a harlot 25 times as much as it pays its prime minister, 250 times as much as it pays its members of Parliament and 500 times as much as it pays some of its ministers of religion.
> To the House of Commons during Profumo Affair, news summaries 31 Mar 63

JAMES Q WILSON, Professor of Government, Harvard

23 There are no more liberals . . . They've all been mugged.
> *Time* 21 Jan 85

TOM WOLFE

24 Radical chic invariably favors radicals who seem primitive, exotic and romantic, such as the grape

workers who are not merely radical and "of the soil" but also Latin; the Panthers, with their leather pieces, Afros, shades and shoot-outs; and the Red Indians, who, of course, had always seemed primitive, exotic and romantic.

On the fashionable rich who celebrated and supported radical views, *Radical Chic* Farrar, Straus & Giroux 70

1 At the outset, at least, all three groups had something else to recommend them, as well: They were headquartered 3,000 miles away from the East Side of Manhattan.

ib

STEVIE WONDER

● 2 [South Africa is] the land with tears in her eyes.

At UN ceremony honoring his work against apartheid in South Africa, NY *Times* 14 May 85

HARRIETT WOODS

3 The price of running for the Senate today is spending more time than you'd like to spend asking people for more money than they'd like to give.

On campaigning for US Senate seat in Missouri, quoted by Steven V Roberts "Politicking Goes High-Tech" NY *Times* 2 Nov 86

JAMES C WRIGHT JR, US Congressman

4 Here is an animal with a hide two feet thick, and no apparent interest in politics. What a waste.

On the rhinoceros, NY *Times* 9 Dec 86

5 I have gone out already breaking the ice and floating ideas, saying the unsayable, and lightning has not struck me down.

On becoming speaker of the House, quoted by Tom Wicker "The Wright Stuff" *ib* 11 Mar 87

ROBERT C WRIGHT

6 Employees who earn their livings and support their families from the profits of our business must recognize the need to invest some portion of their earnings to ensure that the company is well represented in Washington.

Memo to NBC employees on his desire for a company political action committee, quoted by Edwin Diamond *New York* 19 Jan 87

7 Employees who elect not to participate . . . should question their own dedication to the company and their expectations.

ib

STEFAN CARDINAL WYSZYNSKI

8 You covered my windows with blotting paper so that people would not see the primate of Poland; but no one will be able to shield those windows from the world.

A Freedom Within: The Prison Notes of Cardinal Wyszynski Hodder & Stoughton 85, quoted by Timothy Garton Ash London *Times* 17 Jan 85

YEVGENY YEVTUSHENKO

9 But what if it doesn't work . . . ?
and they jammed sticks
In the wheels of the first locomotive
To make sure it wouldn't work.

On "timid bureaucrats" in a move regarded as "jumping off the bandwagon" of Soviet Premier Mikhail S Gorbachev, NY *Times* 10 Sep 85

DAVID R YOUNG, aide to US Secretary of State Henry A Kissinger

10 I'm a plumber. I fix leaks.

On his assignment to prevent security leaks, quoted by Theodore H White *Breach of Faith: The Fall of Richard Nixon* Atheneum 75

WHITNEY MOORE YOUNG JR

11 There is no such thing as a moderate in the civil-rights movement; everyone is a radical. The difference is whether or not one is all rhetoric or relevant.

Recalled on his death 11 Mar 71

12 Personally, I am not nonviolent, but I'm not a fool either. I can count.

ib

13 Should I . . . stand on 125th Street cussing out Whitey to show I am tough? Or should I go downtown and talk to an executive of General Motors about 2,000 jobs for unemployed Negroes?

ib

UNITED NATIONS

Officials & Delegates

AFRO-ASIAN DECLARATION ON COLONIALISM

14 All peoples have the right of self-determination.

NY *Times* 15 Dec 60

MIGUEL A ALBORNOZ, Ecuador

15 In the developing countries the United Nations doesn't mean frustration, confrontation or condemnation. It means environmental sanitation, agricultural production, telecommunications, the fight against illiteracy, the great struggle against poverty, ignorance and disease. That's what the United Nations is about.

On the UN as it neared its 40th anniversary, NY *Times* 22 Sep 85

NORA ASTORGA, Nicaragua

16 We said nonsense but it was important nonsense.

On conversing cordially with US Ambassador Vernon A Walters even though their countries were at odds, NY *Times* 28 Sep 86

WARREN R AUSTIN, United States

17 As we take our places in the General Assembly and at the Council meetings, let us begin all our work in the name of God, for the solution of all our problems is a spiritual one.

To General Assembly, gathered for the first time in new headquarters, news summaries 14 Oct 52

18 To craftsmanship we shall add statesmanship in the capitol of peace.

ib

ANGIE BROOKS-RANDOLPH, Liberia, President of General Assembly

19 The United Nations believes we cannot continue to ignore 800 million people. . . . to solve the problem we must have two Chinas.

LA *Herald-Examiner* 27 Feb 70

LORD CARADON (Hugh Mackintosh Foot), Great Britain

1 Now that he has changed the weather
Lion and lamb can vote together.
God bless the Russian delegation,
I waive consecutive translation.

> Poem read to Security Council in tribute to Soviet representative Vasily V Kuznetsov, NY *Times* 20 Jun 68

2 Better to make prime ministers out of prisoners than prisoners out of prime ministers.

> Reply to criticism by Soviet representative, *International Herald Tribune* 5 Jun 79

3 I wanted to say in the Security Council, "There is no cause for alarm. The rumbling sound that you hear is the normal noise of the Soviet ambassador being lowered and locked into a fixed position." But I never got to say it, the time was never quite right.

> Mimicking British pilots' explanation to passengers on lowering of landing gear, *ib*

HUMAYUN RASHEED CHOUDHURY, Bangladesh, President of General Assembly

4 If everyone did this, it would save us hundreds of thousands of dollars.

> On Angolan Foreign Minister Afonso Van Dunem's decision to stop speaking 10 minutes into his 40-minute speech that was also available in print, NY *Times* 27 Sep 86

ANDREW COHEN, Great Britain

5 To campaign against colonialism is like barking up a tree that has already been cut down.

> *Quote* 23 Feb 58

JOSÉ CORREA, Nicaragua

6 We do not believe in having happiness imposed upon us.

> Reply to Soviet representative, NY *Times* 20 Jul 60

DECLARATION OF THE RIGHTS OF THE CHILD

7 Whereas mankind owes to the child the best it has to give . . .

> Opening words of resolution approved by General Assembly's Social, Humanitarian and Cultural Committee, NY *Times* 20 Oct 59

8 The child shall be entitled from his birth to a name and a nationality.

> *ib*

9 He shall be entitled to grow up and develop in health; to this end special care and protection shall be provided both to him and to his mother, including adequate prenatal and postnatal care.

> *ib*

10 The child who is physically, mentally or socially handicapped shall be given the special treatment, education and care required by his particular condition.

> *ib*

11 The child is entitled to receive education, which shall be free and compulsory at least in the elementary stages.

> *ib*

12 The child shall in all circumstances be among the first to receive protection and relief.

> *ib*

FRANÇOIS GIULIANI, spokesman for Secretary-General

13 Protocol is everything.

> NY *Times* 24 Jul 83

ARTHUR J GOLDBERG, United States

14 Law not served by power is an illusion; but power not ruled by law is a menace which our nuclear age cannot afford.

> Commencement address at Catholic University of America, *Time* 17 Jun 66

ANDREI A GROMYKO, USSR

15 Greece is a sort of American vassal; the Netherlands is the country of American bases that grow like tulip bulbs; Cuba is the main sugar plantation of the American monopolies; Turkey is prepared to kowtow before any United States proconsul and Canada is the boring second fiddle in the American symphony.

> NY *Herald Tribune* 30 Jun 53

16 Thank you, Comrade President.

> Closing remark to Corneliu Manescu of Rumania, first president of General Assembly from a Communist-bloc country, 23 Sep 67

DAG HAMMARSKJÖLD, Sweden, Secretary-General

17 Everything will be all right—you know when? When people, just people, stop thinking of the United Nations as a weird Picasso abstraction and see it as a drawing they made themselves.

> *Time* 27 Jun 55

18 Constant attention by a good nurse may be just as important as a major operation by a surgeon.

> On UN's role in keeping peace in the Middle East, news summaries 18 Mar 56

19 "Freedom from fear" could be said to sum up the whole philosophy of human rights.

> On 180th anniversary of Virginia Declaration of Human Rights, *Quote* 20 May 56

20 I never discuss discussions.

> After talks with Soviet leaders, *Look* 19 Sep 56

21 The Assembly has witnessed over the last weeks how historical truth is established; once an allegation has been repeated a few times, it is no longer an allegation, it is an established fact, even if no evidence has been brought out in order to support it.

> Responding to Soviet Premier Nikita S Khrushchev's attack in General Assembly, NY *Times* 4 Oct 60

22 Those who invoke history will certainly be heard by history. And they will have to accept its verdict.

> *ib*

23 It is a little bit humiliating when I have to say that Chou En-lai to me appears as the most superior brain I have so far met in the field of foreign politics. . . . so much more dangerous than you imagine because he is so much better a man than you have ever admitted.

> Letter to a friend, quoted by Brian Urquhart *Hammarskjöld* Knopf 72

24 The big, shoe-thumping fellow continues as a dark thunderhead to threaten all unrepentant non-Communists with hail and thunder.

> Letter to a friend about Khrushchev, *ib*

LOUIS LANCE JOSEPH, Australia

1 [It was] quite simply a massacre in the sky.

On death of 269 persons aboard Korean airliner shot down when it entered Soviet airspace, to Security Council, NY *Times* 3 Sep 83

TOSHIKAZU KASE, Japan

2 I'll put it this way—now the prodigal has returned home after squandering a fortune. The prodigal has reformed.

Comment after Japan was elected a member of the UN, NY *World-Telegram & Sun* 21 Dec 56

JEANE J KIRKPATRICK, United States

3 I was a woman in a man's world. I was a Democrat in a Republican administration. I was an intellectual in a world of bureaucrats. I talked differently. This may have made me a bit like an ink blot. People projected around me.

On her resignation after four years as US ambassador, NY *Times* 1 Feb 85

4 When the Syrian ambassador acted up, what I really felt like saying to him was, "Go to your room!"

Quoted in *US* 2 Jun 86

CHARLES M LICHENSTEIN, United States

5 If in the judicious determination of the members of the United Nations they feel they [are] not welcome and treated with the hostly consideration that is their due, the United States strongly encourages member states to seriously consider removing themselves and this organization from the soil of the United States.

Responding to Soviet charges after the downing of a Korean passenger plane by Soviet jets prompted the US to deny Andrei Gromyko permission to land at Kennedy and Newark airports, NY *Times* 20 Sep 83

6 We will put no impediment in your way and we will be at dockside bidding you a farewell as you set off into the sunset.

ib

TRYGVE LIE, Norway, Secretary-General

7 I shall take all the troubles of the past, all the disappointments, all the headaches, and I shall pack them in a bag and throw them in the East River.

On retiring as Secretary-General, news summaries 31 Dec 53

HENRY CABOT LODGE JR, United States

8 This organization is created to prevent you from going to hell. It isn't created to take you to heaven.

On purpose of UN, news summaries 28 Jan 54

9 It has been well said that a hungry man is more interested in four sandwiches than four freedoms.

Appealing to Senate Appropriations Committee for renewed support of UN technical assistance programs, news summaries 29 Mar 55

10 The primary, the fundamental, the essential purpose of the United Nations is to keep peace. Everything it does which helps prevent World War III is good. Everything which does not further that goal, either directly or indirectly, is at best superfluous.

NY *Journal-American* 1 May 58

11 As you begin your tour of the United States, you may as well know that one American national trait which irritates many Americans and must be convenient for our critics is that we relentlessly advertise our imperfections.

To Soviet Premier Nikita S Khrushchev, news summaries 18 Sep 59

12 May the United Nations ever be vigilant and potent to defeat the swallowing up of any nation, at any time, by any means—by armies with banners, by force or by fraud, by tricks or by midnight treachery.

At dedication of plaque honoring 37,000 servicemen who died while fighting under UN's unified command in Korean War, NY *Times* 28 Jun 60

13 The fact that the talk may be boring or turgid or uninspiring should not cause us to forget the fact that it is preferable to war.

On the UN, recalled on his death 27 Feb 85

14 Membership of the United Nations gives every member the right to make a fool of himself, and that is a right of which the Soviet Union in this case has taken full advantage.

After Soviets denounced the US for aggressive actions, *ib*

PAUL J F LUSAKA, Zambia, President of General Assembly

15 There was no south, there was no north, no east and no west—just the 11 apostles.

After conference with 10 former General Assembly presidents, NY *Times* 13 Jun 85

RODERIC M J LYNE, Great Britain

16 You can accidentally but deliberately bump into someone at a party whose office you cannot enter.

On diplomatic entertaining, NY *Times* 4 Oct 85

ANTONIO MONTEIRO, Portugal

17 It's group therapy for the world.

On series of debates that mark the start of each General Assembly session, NY *Times* 27 Sep 86

CONOR CRUISE O'BRIEN, former UN representative to Katanga

18 The United Nations cannot do anything, and never could; it is not an animate entity or agent. It is a place, a stage, a forum and a shrine. . . . a place to which powerful people can repair when they are fearful about the course on which their own rhetoric seems to be propelling them.

New Republic 4 Nov 85

19 The main thing that endears the United Nations to member governments, and so enables it to survive, is its proven capacity to fail, and to be seen to fail.

ib

20 You can safely appeal to the United Nations in the comfortable certainty that it will let you down.

ib

ANTHONY PARSONS, Great Britain

21 On the third Tuesday of every September, floodgates are opened in a tall building on the East River in New York and a Niagara of rhetoric gushes forth for three months.

"Waffles But Still Worthwhile" London *Times* 6 Oct 79

1 Our view would be that the patient died yesterday at midday.

On British-Argentine negotiations over the Falkland Islands after Secretary-General Javier Pérez de Cuéllar remarked, "The patient is in intensive care but still alive," news summaries 21 May 82

ABDUL RAHMAN PAZWAK, Afghanistan, President of General Assembly

2 Few, if any, calamities in our time have befallen the world without some advance notice . . . from this rostrum. Thus, if fools and folly rule the world, the end of man in our time may come as a rude shock, but it will no longer come as a complete surprise.

On retiring 19 Sep 67

JAVIER PÉREZ DE CUÉLLAR, Peru, Secretary-General

3 The patient is in intensive care but still alive.

Personifying the British-Argentine peace negotiations over the Falkland Islands, news summaries 21 May 82

ALEX QUAISON-SACKEY, Ghana, President of General Assembly

4 There is now a balance of terror.

On worldwide representation of nations at the UN, *Quote* 27 Jun 65

IVOR RICHARD, Great Britain

5 The United Nations is messy because the world is messy.

On retiring after five years as British ambassador, NY *Times* 18 May 79

6 The United Nations will not abolish sin, but it can make it more difficult for the sinners.

ib

7 You cannot spend five years here and not appreciate that the gap between a skilled car worker and the Duke of Westminster is as nothing when compared with the differential between the car worker in Coventry and the Tanzanian peasant.

ib

ELEANOR ROOSEVELT, United States

8 Without the United Nations our country would walk alone, ruled by fear instead of confidence and hope.

Recalled on her death 7 Nov 62

ROSEMARY SPENCER, US Protocol Officer

9 Of course, everybody wants the permanent representative at their functions. You can only split the permanent representative 10 ways. Scheduling is a problem.

NY *Times* 2 Oct 81

ADLAI E STEVENSON, United States

10 The first principle of a free society is an untrammeled flow of words in an open forum.

NY *Times* 19 Jan 62

11 This the first time I ever heard it said that the crime is not the burglary, but the discovery of the burglar.

Comment to Soviet Ambassador Valerian A Zorin, who charged that the US threatened peace by exposing Soviet missile shipments to Cuba, 25 Oct 62

12 Do you, Ambassador Zorin, deny that the USSR has placed and is placing medium- and intermediate-range missiles and sites in Cuba? Yes or no? Don't wait for the translation. Yes or no?

ib

13 You are in the courtroom of world opinion. . . . You have denied they exist, and I want to know if I understood you correctly. . . . I am prepared to wait for my answer until hell freezes over. And I am also prepared to present the evidence in this room!

ib

14 I believe in the forgiveness of sin and the redemption of ignorance.

Reply to a heckler who asked him to state his beliefs in a UN Day address at Dallas, *Time* 1 Nov 63

15 I don't want to send them to jail. I want to send them to school.

On pickets who attacked him in Dallas, *ib*

16 After four years at the United Nations I sometimes yearn for the peace and tranquillity of a political convention.

NY *Times* 14 Aug 64

U THANT, Burma, Secretary-General

17 The war we have to wage today has only one goal and that is to make the world safe for diversity.

On international tolerance, Dag Hammarskjöld Memorial Lecture, Columbia University, quoted in NY *Times* 8 Jan 64

18 I don't like to be disturbed at home; I tell the cable office not to call me before 6:30 AM, unless there's a war.

On beginning his ninth year as Secretary-General, *ib* 3 Nov 69

SEMYON K TSARAPKIN, USSR

19 I am not a gentleman. I am a representative of the Soviet Union here.

Answer to US Ambassador Henry Cabot Lodge Jr's inquiry on why "the gentleman" was asking for the floor; Lodge replied, "The two are not necessarily exclusive," news summaries 26 Jun 54

VERNON A WALTERS, United States

20 The United Nations has become a place where many countries seek to achieve a lynching of the United States by resolution.

On becoming US ambassador, NY *Times* 31 May 85

21 I'd describe myself as a pragmatist tinged with idealism.

ib

22 It is an endless procession of surprises. The expected rarely occurs and never in the expected manner.

On UN social circuit, *ib* 4 Oct 85

23 I'm a participant in the doctrine of constructive ambiguity.

On preference for keeping a low profile, *Christian Science Monitor* 18 Apr 86

24 I don't think we should tell them what we're going to do in advance. Let them think. Worry. Wonder. Uncertainty is the most chilling thing of all.

On how US should deal with terrorists and terrorism, *ib*

RUDIGER VON WECHMAR, West Germany, former President of General Assembly

1 Cut the fat, cut the fat.
   Recommendation for UN, NY *Times* 13 Jun 85

RICHARD A WOOLCOTT, Australia

2 Apart from a good mind, the two most important assets for a United Nations diplomat are a good tailor and a strong liver.
   NY *Times* 4 Oct 85

ANDREW YOUNG, United States

3 That was not a lie, it was just not the whole truth.
   On disclosing an unauthorized meeting with the Palestine Liberation Organization that resulted in Young's resignation 14 Aug 79

VALERIAN A ZORIN, USSR

4 I am not in an American courtroom, sir, and therefore do not wish to answer a question that is put to me in the fashion in which a prosecutor puts questions. In due course, sir, you will have your reply.
   Comments to US Ambassador Adlai E Stevenson when challenged to deny that the USSR had offensive missiles in Cuba, 25 Oct 62

Observers & Critics

CORAZON C AQUINO, President of the Philippines

5 As our country bled . . . its leader's wife came to this podium piously to call for a new human order, this when thousands of Filipinos were political prisoners.
   To General Assembly, speaking from the same lectern used a year earlier by Imelda Marcos, 22 Sep 86

6 One must be frank to be relevant.
   Chiding UN for lack of support in opposing the Ferdinand Marcos regime, *ib*

ZULFIKAR ALI BHUTTO, Foreign Minister of Pakistan

7 Let's build a monument for the veto. Let's build a monument for impotence and incapacity.
   Denouncing Security Council after invasion of Pakistan by India, NY *Times* 16 Dec 71

JACQUES CHIRAC, Premier of France

8 Terrorism has become the systematic weapon of a war that knows no borders or seldom has a face.
   To General Assembly 24 Sep 86

9 Terrorism [takes] us back to ages we thought were long gone if we allow it a free hand to corrupt democratic societies and destroy the basic rules of international life.
   ib

ALISTAIR COOKE

10 Who is this rare bird, perched at the eerie dead center of the world's hurricane, whom all men delight to praise? A Machiavelli with a Boy Scout's exterior? A gross flatterer? A Talleyrand subtler than Khrishna Menon? A monstrous appeaser? Clean is the word for Hammarskjöld.
   On Dag Hammarskjöld, NY *Herald Tribune* 5 Oct 57

NORMAN COUSINS

11 We will not have peace by afterthought.
   1956 editorial on importance of preservation rather than breaches of world peace, recalled in summary of his comments, *Saturday Review* 15 Apr 80

12 If the United Nations is to survive, those who represent it must bolster it; those who advocate it must submit to it; and those who believe in it must fight for it.
   ib

JOHN FOSTER DULLES, US Secretary of State

13 The United Nations was not set up to be a reformatory. It was assumed that you would be good before you got in and not that being in would make you good.
   On UN Charter, news summaries 9 Jul 54

ABBA EBAN, Foreign Minister of Israel

14 When I was first here, we had the advantages of the underdog. Now we have the disadvantages of the overdog.
   On representing his country after its repulse of Egyptian invaders in the Six-Day War, *New Yorker* 1 Jul 67

15 Lest Arab governments be tempted out of sheer routine to rush into impulsive rejection, let me suggest that tragedy is not what men suffer but what they miss.
   Calling for peace in Middle East, to General Assembly, NY *Times* 9 Oct 68

16 Time and again these governments have rejected proposals today—and longed for them tomorrow.
   ib

DWIGHT D EISENHOWER, 34th US President

17 I feel impelled to speak today in a language that in a sense is new—one which I, who have spent so much of my life in the military profession, would have preferred never to use. That new language is the language of atomic warfare.
   Address to UN seeking establishment of international atomic energy agency, 8 Dec 53

18 The United States pledges . . . its determination to help solve the fearful atomic dilemma—to devote its entire heart and mind to finding the way by which the miraculous inventiveness of man shall not be dedicated to his death but consecrated to his life.
   ib

19 If the United Nations once admits that international disputes can be settled by using force, then we will have destroyed the foundation of the organization and our best hope of establishing a world order.
   On Israel's invasion of Egypt, address to the nation 20 Feb 57

20 In most communities it is illegal to cry "fire" in a crowded assembly. Should it not be considered serious international misconduct to manufacture a general war scare in an effort to achieve local political aims?
   On Middle East crisis, address to General Assembly 13 Aug 58

WILLIAM FAULKNER

21 The last sound on the worthless earth will be two human beings trying to launch a homemade spaceship and already quarreling about where they are going next.
   To UNESCO Commission, NY *Times* 3 Oct 59

ESTHER B FEIN

1 If the United Nations is a country unto itself, then the commodity it exports most is words.
NY *Times* 14 Oct 85

THOMAS M FRANCK, Director of Center for International Studies, NY University

2 We could probably win more often . . . if we were willing to . . . deploy seasoned personnel and equip them with sufficient carrots and sticks.
Nation against Nation: What Happened to the UN Dream and What the US Can Do about It Oxford 85

HAILE SELASSIE, Emperor of Ethiopia

3 Today I stand before the world organization which has succeeded to the mantle discarded by its discredited predecessor.
Opening a special session of the General Assembly in Addis Ababa, thus becoming the first ruler to address both the League of Nations and the UN, 4 Oct 63

4 Throughout history it has been the inaction of those who could have acted, the indifference of those who should have known better, the silence of the voice of justice when it mattered most, that has made it possible for evil to triumph.
ib

DAVID HARE

5 When they speak, dead frogs fall out of their mouths.
On some UN representatives, *A Map of the World* Faber & Faber 83

POPE JOHN PAUL II

6 You will forgive me, ladies and gentlemen, for evoking this memory, but I would be untrue to the history of this century, I would be dishonest with regard to the great cause of man which we all wish to service, if I should keep silence—I who come from the country on whose living body Auschwitz was at one time constructed.
Appeal for lasting freedom from concentration camps, address to General Assembly 2 Oct 79

7 The United Nations organization has proclaimed 1979 as the Year of the Child. . . . Are the children to receive the arms race from us as a necessary inheritance?
ib

LYNDON B JOHNSON, 36th US President

8 Peace is a journey of a thousand miles and it must be taken one step at a time.
To General Assembly 17 Dec 63

JUAN CARLOS, King of Spain

9 Europe cannot confine itself to the cultivation of its own garden.
To General Assembly 22 Sep 86

JOHN F KENNEDY, 35th US President

10 My God, in this job he's got the nerve of a burglar.
On Ambassador Adlai E Stevenson, *Time* 24 Feb 61

11 We prefer world law in the age of self-determination to world war in the age of mass extermination.
To General Assembly 25 Sep 61

12 We cannot expect that all nations will adopt like systems, for conformity is the jailer of freedom and the enemy of growth.
ib

NIKITA S KHRUSHCHEV, Soviet Premier

13 All the sparrows on the rooftops are crying about the fact that the most imperialist nation that is supporting the colonial regime in the colonies is the United States of America.
To General Assembly 1 Oct 60

14 What innocence, may I ask, is being played here when it is known that this virtuous damsel has already got a dozen illegitimate children?
ib

HAROLD MACMILLAN, former Prime Minister of Britain

15 A colonial governor who ran out of countries.
On Lord Caradon, British ambassador, *International Herald Tribune* 5 Jun 79

GOLDA MEIR, Foreign Minister of Israel

16 My delegation cannot refrain from speaking on this question—we who have such an intimate knowledge of boxcars and of deportations to unknown destinations that we cannot be silent.
On Soviet actions in Hungary, to General Assembly, news summaries 21 Nov 56

ROBERT G MENZIES, Prime Minister of Australia

17 It is . . . a simple but sometimes forgotten truth that the greatest enemy to present joy and high hopes is the cultivation of retrospective bitterness.
To General Assembly, NY *Times* 6 Oct 60

JAMES MORRIS

18 There it stands ablaze, like a slab of fire, with its parade of white flagstaffs gleaming in the street light, and the humped black limousines patient at the door.
On the UN building, NY *Times* 2 Oct 60

19 When at last you . . . cross the road to the United Nations, it is like traversing some unmarked but crucial frontier.
ib

DAVID ORMSBY-GORE, 5th Baron Harlech, Minister of State, Great Britain

20 It would indeed be the ultimate tragedy if the history of the human race proved to be nothing more noble than the story of an ape playing with a box of matches on a petrol dump.
Christian Science Monitor 25 Oct 60

POPE PAUL VI

21 You have before you a humble man; your brother; and among you all, representatives of sovereign states, the least invested, if you wish to think of him thus, with a minuscule, as it were symbolic, temporal sovereignty, only as much as is necessary to be free to exercise his spiritual mission and to assure all those who deal with him that he is independent of every other sovereignty of this world.
To General Assembly 4 Oct 65

1 You must strive to multiply bread so that it suffices for the tables of mankind, and not rather favor an artificial control of birth, which would be irrational, in order to diminish the number of guests at the banquet of life.
ib

2 No more war! Never again war! . . . If you wish to be brothers, drop your weapons.
ib

SHIMON PERES, Prime Minister of Israel

3 The sons of Abraham have become quarrelsome, but remain family nonetheless.
Address to General Assembly in which he invited Jordan to peace talks. 21 Oct 85

ENOCH POWELL, Member of British Parliament

4 It is the very capital and new Jerusalem of humbug.
Listener 28 May 81

RONALD REAGAN, 40th US President

5 Maybe all those delegates should have six months . . . in Moscow and then six months in New York, and it would give them an opportunity to see two ways of life. . . . I think the gentleman [Charles Lichenstein] who spoke the other day had the hearty approval of most people in America in his suggestion that we weren't asking anyone to leave, but if they chose to leave, good-bye.
Press conference 21 Sep 83

6 The founders [of the United Nations] sought to replace a world at war with a world of civilized order. They hoped that a world of relentless conflict would give way to a new era, one where freedom from violence prevailed. . . . But the awful truth is that the use of violence for political gain has become more, not less, widespread in the last decade.
To General Assembly following Soviet downing of a Korean passenger plane. 26 Sep 83

7 What has happened to the dreams of the United Nations's founders? What has happened to the spirit which created the United Nations? The answer is clear: Governments got in the way of the dreams of the people.
ib

8 Dreams became issues of East versus West. Hopes became political rhetoric. Progress became a search for power and domination. Somewhere the truth was lost that people don't make war, governments do.
ib

9 The founders of the United Nations expected that member nations would behave and vote as individuals after they had weighed the merits of an issue— rather like a great, global town meeting. The emergence of blocks and the polarization of the United Nations undermine all that this organization initially valued.
ib

10 As caring, peaceful peoples, think what a powerful force for good we could be. Distinguished delegates, let us regain the dream the United Nations once dreamed.
ib

CARLOS P ROMULO, Ambassador to US and former representative from Philippines

11 I had hoped it would be the conscience of the world and it is.
On the UN, 16 years after he had addressed its founding session with the words, "Let us make this floor the last battlefield." *I Walked with Heroes* Holt, Rinehart & Winston 61

12 Can you imagine a policeman being required to secure the assent of parties to a street fight before breaking up the conflict?
On situation of the UN in 1984, recalled on his death 15 Dec 85

A M ROSENTHAL

13 Within a pitifully short time, the China that sat on the Council and was supposed to represent a billion people represented nothing but a steamy Pacific island.
Recalling effect of Chinese Revolution on Security Council representation, NY *Times* 25 Sep 85

14 There is a secret agreement between the United States and the Soviet Union . . . a simple but lucid treaty holding that when one side does something particularly fatheaded and self-destructive the other will respond by shooting itself in the foot within a period of from 17 to 30 days.
ib 14 Dec 86

HARRY S TRUMAN, 33rd US President

15 Our conference in 1945 did much more than draft an international agreement among 50 nations. [We] set down on paper the only principles which will enable civilized human life to continue to survive on this globe.
On UN's 10th anniversary, NY *Herald Tribune* 25 Jun 55

AFONSO VAN DUNEM, Foreign Minister of Angola

16 Mr President, I have decided not to speak the entire speech which I have.
To General Assembly when he was 10 minutes into a 40-minute speech that was also available in print, NY *Times* 27 Sep 86

STEVIE WONDER

17 The bell for freedom still rings,
The hammer for justice still pounds,
As long as there's light,
There's still a day,
And I know that we can find our way.
"The Bell for Freedom," song composed for UN ceremony honoring his work against apartheid in South Africa, NY *Times* 14 May 85

MOHAMMED YAZID, spokesman for Algerian rebels

18 Some of us throw bombs, I throw ideas. We have men to do the shooting but I do the shouting.
NY *Times* 18 Mar 61

ARMED FORCES

Officers & Enlistees

GEN CREIGHTON W ABRAMS JR, US Army

19 They've got us surrounded again, the poor bastards.
On World War II Battle of the Bulge, recalled on his appointment to command post in Vietnam. *Time* 16 Feb 68

ANONYMOUS

1 Sir, a doolie is that insignificant whose rank is measured in negative units, one whose potential for learning is unlimited.

> Self-description of Air Force Academy freshmen, referred to as "doolies," quoted in *Time* 19 Jan 62

2 [For reading chests], disregard all Legions of Merit, Air Medals, Distinguished Service Medals. Discount Silver Stars if the officer was high-ranking when it was awarded and if unaccompanied by a Purple Heart.

> US Marine Corps colonel's formula for interpretation of campaign ribbons on uniforms, quoted in *Newsweek* 9 Jul 84

3 They couldn't shoot down a high-flying banana.

> Pentagon spokesman commenting on Libyan shells that fell short of US forces in the Mediterranean, quoted in news summaries 16 Apr 86

SGT PHILLIP ARTEBURY, US Army

4 I'm no hero. Heroes are for the Late Show.

> "Dear Mom" letter inscribed on NY Vietnam War Memorial 85

COL CHARLES A BECKWITH, US Army

5 My men and I have decided that our boss, the president of the United States, is as tough as woodpecker lips.

> Message to President Carter after aborted attempt to free US hostages in Iran, quoted by Jimmy Carter *Keeping Faith* Bantam 83

GEN OMAR N BRADLEY, US Army

6 I am convinced that the best service a retired general can perform is to turn in his tongue along with his suit and to mothball his opinions.

> News summaries 17 May 59

MAJ JOSIAH BUNTING, US Army retired

7 Ennoblement is earned by merit in the American Army.

> *The Lionheads* Popular Library 72

8 The depleted ranks of peers are annually replenished by fresh appointments from the ranks of its higher squirearchy, the appointments being made from a list annually prepared in the pentagonal Camelot.

> *ib*

9 Among these senior warriors, a major general commanding a division in Vietnam is an earl, a Marcher Lord, and he maintains a briefing court, a formal masculine assembly which meets regularly and according to a fixed protocol to enable him to take counsel of his greater feudatories and his household knights. All here is order, degree, heraldry, pomp, deference.

> *ib*

10 These men are worthy heirs to the tradition of Washington and Lee and Marshall, men who know their business, and who because they hate war, have soldiered well.

> On soldiers in Vietnam, *ib*

ADM ARLEIGH BURKE, US Navy

11 The major deterrent [to war] is in a man's mind.

> *US News & World Report* 3 Oct 60

LT WILLIAM L CALLEY JR, US Army

12 That was the order of the day.

> On killing Vietnamese civilians at My Lai in 1968, news summaries 23 Feb 71

13 They were all enemy. They were all to be destroyed.

> *ib*

JIMMY CARTER, 39th US President

14 My decision to register women . . . confirms what is already obvious throughout our society—that women are now providing all types of skills in every profession. The military should be no exception.

> Proposing that both men and women be required to register for conscription, 8 Feb 80

GEN BEN CHIDLAW, Commander, US Continental Air Defense Command

15 More than 3 million square miles of territory to protect, 10 thousand miles of border to guard and a fence to build 10, 11 or 12 miles high. . . . It is better to have less thunder in the mouth and more lightning in the hand.

> *Time* 20 Dec 54

WINSTON CHURCHILL

16 If Hitler invaded hell I would make at least a favorable reference to the devil in the House of Commons.

> *The Grand Alliance* Houghton Mifflin 50

17 Before Alamein we never had a victory. After Alamein we never had a defeat.

> *The Hinge of Fate* Houghton Mifflin 50

18 There was unanimous, automatic, unquestioned agreement around our table.

> On decision at Potsdam Conference about US use of atom bomb on Japan, *Triumph and Tragedy* Houghton Mifflin 53

19 When the war of the giants is over the wars of the pygmies will begin.

> On the end of World War II, *ib*

20 Really I feel less keen about the Army every day. I think the Church would suit me better.

> Postscript on a letter home during early training at Sandhurst, quoted by William Manchester *The Last Lion* Little, Brown 83

21 War is a game that is played with a smile. If you can't smile, grin. If you can't grin, keep out of the way till you can.

> *ib*

GEN MARK W CLARK, US Army

22 I return with feelings of misgiving from my third war—I was the first American commander to put his signature to a paper ending a war when we did not win it.

> On retiring as commander of UN forces in Korea, NY *Herald Tribune* 21 Oct 53

MAX CLELAND, former head of US Veterans Administration

23 Within the soul of each Vietnam veteran there is probably something that says "Bad war, good soldier." [Only now are Americans beginning to] separate the war from the warrior.

> On dedication of Vietnam Veterans Memorial, Washington DC, *Time* 22 Nov 82

MOHAMMED DAOUD, Afghani rebel commander

1 History tells me that when the Russians come to a country they don't go back.

> Comments of 21-year-old leader of 50 men who had fought the Soviet-backed Afghan army since 1980, NY *Times* 28 Mar 85

COL GEORGE DAY, US Army

2 After about 25 medals, you run out of shoulder to put them on.

> Comment of the most-decorated living veteran, *Life* Jul 86

GEN CHARLES DE GAULLE

3 And don't forget to get killed.

> To Romain Gary, permitting his return to combat in World War II, quoted by Romain Gary "To Mon Général" *Life* 9 May 69

4 You'll live. Only the best get killed.

> *ib*

CHARLES EARLY, World War II veteran

5 There were wrecks everywhere—wrecks of vehicles everywhere, wrecks of men everywhere.

> On 40th anniversary of Battle of Iwo Jima, quoted by Clyde Haberman NY *Times* 20 Feb 85

DWIGHT D EISENHOWER, 34th US President

6 When you put on a uniform, there are certain inhibitions that you accept.

> As US Army general, on learning that President Harry S Truman had relieved Gen Douglas MacArthur of command, 11 Apr 51

7 The most terrible job in warfare is to be a second lieutenant leading a platoon when you are on the battlefield.

> 17 Mar 54

8 That was not the biggest battle that ever was, but for me it always typified one thing—the dash, the ingenuity, the readiness at the first opportunity that characterizes the American soldier.

> On 10th anniversary of the Battle of the Remagen Bridge, 8 Mar 55

9 The purpose is clear. It is safety with solvency. The country is entitled to both.

> Urging unification of ground, sea and air commands, 17 Apr 58

10 It is far more important to be able to hit the target than it is to haggle over who makes a weapon or who pulls a trigger.

> *ib*

11 The sergeant *is* the Army.

> NY *Times* 24 Dec 72

COL RALPH GAUER, US Army Intelligence

12 It's going to be a "come-as-you-are" war.

> On future warfare, *Newsweek* 9 Jul 84

GEN JAMES M GAVIN, US Army

13 If you want a decision, go to the point of danger.

> Quoted by Ralph G Martin *A Hero for Our Time* Macmillan 83

LT GEN ALFRED M GRAY, US Marine Corps

14 There's no such thing as a crowded battlefield. Battlefields are lonely places.

> Address to officers, *Newsweek* 9 Jul 84

15 [I go] where the sound of thunder is.

> On 34-year career that had given him more time in the field than most generals, including 2 years in Korea and 5 in Vietnam, *ib*

16 I don't run democracy. I train troops to defend democracy and I happen to be their surrogate father and mother as well as their commanding general.

> To new officers, *ib*

17 All of you are assistant mothers and fathers. That is an awesome responsibility.

> *ib*

LT GEN HUBERT R HARMON, Superintendent, Air Force Academy

18 The academy's long-range mission will be to train generals, not second lieutenants.

> *Newsweek* 6 Jun 55

GEN LEWIS B HERSHEY, Director, Selective Service System

19 When we know as much about people as hog specialists know about hogs, we'll be better off.

> News summaries 18 Jun 56

20 Between a fellow who is stupid and honest and one who is smart and crooked, I will take the first. I won't get much out of him, but with that other guy I can't keep what I've got.

> On retirement after 30 years as director of conscription, NY *Times* 30 Jan 70

HO CHI MINH

21 You will kill 10 of our men, and we will kill 1 of yours, and in the end it will be you who tire of it.

> Recalled on his death 3 Sep 69

BRIG GEN ELIZABETH P HOISINGTON, US Army

22 If I had learned to type, I never would have made brigadier general.

> Comment of highest-ranking officer in Women's Army Corps, NY *Times* 20 Jun 70

REAR ADM GRACE MURRAY HOPPER, US Navy

23 I handed my passport to the immigration officer, and he looked at it and looked at me and said, "What are you?"

> On being the oldest officer on active duty in the US armed forces, *60 Minutes* CBS TV 24 Aug 86

REX HUNT, British Governor of Falkland Islands

24 I think it very uncivilized to invade British territory. You are here illegally.

> To Argentine general, *Life* Jan 83

LYNDON B JOHNSON, 36th US President

25 We did not choose to be the guardians of the gate, but there is no one else.

> On continued intervention in Vietnam, address to the nation 28 Jul 64

26 The Air Force comes in every morning and says, "Bomb, bomb, bomb" . . . And then the State Department comes in and says, "Not now, or not there, or too much, or not at all."

> To Adlai Stevenson, quoted by Philip L Geyelin *Lyndon B Johnson and the World* Praeger 66

1 I feel like I just grabbed a big juicy worm with a right sharp hook in the middle of it.

> To press secretary Bill Moyers after November 24, 1963, Vietnam briefing, quoted in *Newsweek* 10 Feb 75

2 Curtis Le May wants to bomb Hanoi and Haiphong. You know how he likes to go around bombing.

> To Walter Lippmann, quoted by Ronald Steel *Walter Lippmann and the American Century* Atlantic–Little, Brown 80

3 You wake up . . . at 3:30 to see if they're back.

> On following news of attacks during Vietnam War, quoted by Hugh Sidey "Lyndon Johnson's Personal Alamo" *Time* 15 Apr 85

4 Hell, it's just like the Alamo, and you damn well needed somebody. Well, by God, I'm going to go and thank the Lord that I've got men who want to go with me, from [Secretary of Defense] McNamara right on down to the littlest private who's carrying a gun.

> *ib*

5 If one little old general in shirt sleeves can take Saigon, think about 200 million Chinese comin' down those trails. No sir, I don't want to fight them.

> On consequences of invading northward where a huge army was massed, *ib*

6 I'm willin' for any solution—religious, political. I'm not going to keep offerin' to negotiate so much because they turn us down each time. It indicates a weakness on our part.

> *ib*

7 I don't know what it will take out there—500 casualties maybe, maybe 500,000. It's the aughts that scare me.

> *ib*

8 It is always a strain when people are being killed. I don't think anybody has held this job who hasn't felt personally responsible for those being killed.

> *ib*

ADM C TURNER JOY, US Navy

9 The field of combat was a long, narrow, green-baize covered table. The weapons were words.

> On a year of truce talks in Korea, news summaries 31 Dec 52

CAPT DOUGLAS J KATZ, Director of Professional Development, US Naval Academy

10 This is the last chance where he or she has sole control over his destiny. After this, it's the needs of the service.

> On senior cadets' option to choose type of duty, NY *Times* 30 Jan 86

JOHN F KENNEDY, 35th US President

11 There is always inequity in life. Some men are killed in war and some men are wounded, and some men are stationed in the Antarctic and some are stationed in San Francisco. It's very hard in military or personal life to assure complete equality. Life is unfair.

> To reservists anxious to be released from active duty, 21 Mar 62

12 I look forward to . . . a future in which our country will match its military strength with our moral restraint, its wealth with our wisdom, its power with our purpose.

> Last major public address, at Amherst College 26 Oct 63

WILL KETTERSON, spokesman for US Air Force Academy

13 Quibbling is the creation of a false impression in the mind of the listener by cleverly wording what is said, omitting relevant facts or telling a partial truth when one does so with the intent to deceive or mislead.

> On suspension of highest-ranking junior-class cadet for an offense considered to be the same as lying, NY *Times* 25 Sep 85

GEN BELA KIRALY, Commander, Hungarian National Guard

14 Even pirates, before they attack another ship, hoist a black flag.

> On Ambassador Yuri V Andropov's pretense of peace while Soviet forces were preparing to crush 1956 uprising in Hungary, recalled on Andropov's death 9 Feb 84

JOHN F LEHMAN JR, Secretary of the Navy

15 Contrary to the parlor-room Pershings around [Washington], we have a fully integrated multiservice unified command structure.

> NY *Times* 12 Oct 85

CAPT ROBERT LEWIS, US Army Air Corps

16 As the bomb fell over Hiroshima and exploded, we saw an entire city disappear. I wrote in my log the words: "My God, what have we done?"

> Comments of copilot of the *Enola Gay*, recalled on approach of 10th anniversary of bombing, NBC TV 19 May 55

GEN DOUGLAS MACARTHUR, US Army

17 The world has turned over many times since I took the oath on the plain at West Point, and the hopes and dreams have long since vanished; but I still remember the refrain of one of the most popular barracks ballads of that day which proclaimed most proudly that old soldiers never die; they just fade away.

> After being relieved of duties by President Harry S Truman, address to Congress 19 Apr 51

18 And like the old soldier in that ballad, I now close my military career and just fade away, an old soldier who tried to do his duty as God gave him the sight to see that duty.

> *ib*

19 I can recall no parallel in history where a great nation recently at war has so distinguished its former enemy commander.

> On receiving one of Japan's highest decorations, NY *Times* 22 Jun 60

20 Duty, honor, country: Those three hallowed words reverently dictate what you ought to be, what you can be, what you will be. They are your rallying point to build courage when courage seems to fail, to regain faith when there seems to be little cause for faith, to create hope when hope becomes forlorn.

> On receiving West Point's Sylvanus Thayer Award for service to the nation, 12 May 62

21 In my dreams I hear again the crash of guns, the rattle of musketry, the strange, mournful mutter of

the battlefield. But in the evening of my memory always I come back to West Point. Always there echoes and re-echoes: duty, honor, country.
ib

1 The outfit soon took on color, dash and a unique flavor which is the essence of that elusive and deathless thing called soldiering.
On Rainbow Division in World War I, *Life* 24 Jan 64

2 Could I have but a line a century hence crediting a contribution to the advance of peace, I would yield every honor which has been accorded by war.
Recalled on his death 5 Apr 64

3 Where-oh-where was that welcome they told us of? Where was that howling mob to proclaim us monarchs of all we surveyed? . . . Those bright eyes and slim ankles that had been kidding us in our dreams? Nothing—nothing like that. One little urchin asked us who we were and when we said—we are the famous 42nd—he asked if we had been to France.
On Rainbow Division's return to NYC on April 25, 1919, *ib*

4 We are bound no longer by the straitjacket of the past [and] nowhere is the change greater than in our profession of arms. . . . What, you may well ask, will be the end of all of this? I would not know! But I would hope that our beloved country will drink deep from the chalice of courage.
To army comrades assembled for his 82nd birthday, recalled on his death, NY *Journal-American* 7 Apr 64

5 I suppose, in a way, this has become part of my soul. It is a symbol of my life. Whatever I have done that really matters, I've done wearing it. When the time comes, it will be in [this] that I journey forth. What greater honor could come to an American, and a soldier?
On the uniform of the US Army, recalled on his death, *Life* 17 Apr 64

6 I've looked that old scoundrel death in the eye many times but this time I think he has me on the ropes.
On entering Walter Reed Army Medical Center for surgery that ended in his death, *ib*

7 In war, you win or lose, live or die—and the difference is just an eyelash.
In posthumous memoirs, "Reminiscences" *ib* 10 Jul 64

8 They died hard, those savage men—like wounded wolves at bay. They were filthy, and they were lousy, and they stunk. And I loved them.
On troops who died in defense of Bataan and Corregidor in early days of World War II, *ib*

9 These proceedings are closed.
Concluding Japan's surrender in Tokyo Bay on September 2, 1945, thereby ending World War II, quoted by Alistair Cooke *America* Knopf 73

10 My first recollection is that of a bugle call.
Quoted by William Manchester *American Caesar* Little, Brown 78

MAO ZEDONG, Chinese premier

11 The enemy advances, we retreat.
The enemy camps, we harass.
The enemy tires, we attack.
The enemy retreats, we pursue.
Slogan for his troops, recalled on his death 9 Sep 76

GEN GEORGE C MARSHALL, US Army

12 Morale is the state of mind. It is steadfastness and courage and hope. It is confidence and zeal and loyalty. It is élan, esprit de corps and determination.
Recalled on his death 16 Oct 59

13 Don't fight the problem, decide it.
Favorite advice, quoted by Walter Isaacson and Evan Thomas *The Wise Men* Simon & Schuster 86

ROBERT S MCNAMARA, Secretary of Defense

14 I don't object to its being called "McNamara's war." I think it is a very important war and I am pleased to be identified with it and do whatever I can to win it.
On the Vietnam War, NY *Times* 25 Apr 64

15 One cannot fashion a credible deterrent out of an incredible action.
On nuclear weapons, *The Essence of Security* Hodder & Stoughton 68

CDR JAMES MEACHAM, US Navy

16 I'm not talking about confusion and inefficiency, which to a certain extent are products of all wars, but about muddle-headed thinking, cover-your-ass orders, lies and outright foolishness on the very highest levels.
1968 letter from Vietnam to his wife used by CBS TV in preparing 1982 documentary *The Uncounted Enemy: A Vietnam Deception*, which prompted Gen William C Westmoreland to sue CBS for $120 million, NY *Times* 4 Jan 85

GOLDA MEIR, Prime Minister of Israel

17 We don't thrive on military acts. We do them because we have to, and thank God we are efficient.
Vogue Jul 69

GEN JOHN H ("IRON MIKE") MICHAELIS, US Army

18 You're not here to die for your country. You're here to make those so-and-sos die for theirs.
To troops fighting in Korea, recalled on his death, *Time* 11 Nov 85

FIELD MARSHAL BERNARD LAW MONTGOMERY, 1st Viscount Montgomery of Alamein, British Army

19 Decisions! And a general, a commander in chief who has not got the quality of decision, then he is no good.
CBS TV 28 Apr 59

MAJ GEN JOHN JEREMY MOORE, British Army

20 The Falkland Islands are once more under the government desired by their inhabitants. God save the Queen.
Radioing news to London on successful mission against invading Argentine forces, *Life* Jan 83

ADM THOMAS MOORER, US Navy retired

21 The Xerox machine is one of the biggest threats to national security ever devised.
Time 17 Jun 85

GAMAL ABDEL NASSER, President of Egypt

22 They defended the grains of sand in the desert to the last drop of their blood.
Praising Egyptian forces after the Six-Day War against Israel, NY *Times* 10 Jun 67

RICHARD M NIXON, 37th US President

1 Tell them to send everything that can fly.

> On support for Israel in 1973 action against Egypt and Syria, *RN: Memoirs of Richard Nixon* Grosset & Dunlap 78

MAJ MICHAEL DAVIS O'DONNELL, First Aviation Brigade, US Army

2 And in that time
When men decide and feel safe
To call the war insane,
Take one moment to embrace
Those gentle heroes
You left behind.

> From a 1970 poem written three months before his death in Vietnam, chosen for inscription across top of NY Vietnam War Memorial, *Newsweek* 20 May 85

TATSUYA OHTAWA, Japanese pilot

3 We were about to change an island of dreams into a living hell.

> On 40th anniversary of Pearl Harbor attack, *Washington Post* 7 Dec 81

GEN BRUCE PALMER JR, US Army

4 [It was] the first clear failure in our history.

> On 10th anniversary of fall of South Vietnam, NY *Times* 15 Apr 85

LESTER B PEARSON, Prime Minister of Canada

5 I was in the Victoria Library in Toronto in 1915, studying a Latin poet, and all of a sudden I thought, "War can't be this bad." So I walked out and enlisted.

> Quoted by Robinson Beal *The Pearson Phenomenon* Longman 64

ADM ARTHUR W RADFORD, US Navy, Chairman, Joint Chiefs of Staff

6 A decision is the action an executive must take when he has information so incomplete that the answer does not suggest itself.

> *Time* 25 Feb 57

RONALD REAGAN, 40th US President

7 We pray for the wisdom that this hero be America's last unknown.

> On the Unknown Soldier of the Vietnam War, 25 May 84

8 The Soviet troops that came to the center of this continent did not leave when peace came. They are still there, uninvited, unwanted, unyielding, almost 40 years after the war.

> To veterans gathered at Pointe du Hoc, France, for 40th anniversary of invasion of Normandy, 6 Jun 84

9 The only weapon we have is MAD—Mutual Assured Destruction. Why don't we have MAS instead—Mutual Assured Security?

> Declaring intention to proceed with research for Strategic Defense Initiative, independent of whatever arms-reduction agreement might be reached with the Soviets, NY *Times* 12 Feb 85

10 We're talking about a weapon that won't kill people. It'll kill weapons.

> On testing and development of Strategic Defense Initiative, *Newsweek* 30 Sep 85

ADM HYMAN G RICKOVER, US Navy

11 One of the most wonderful things that happened in our *Nautilus* program was that everybody knew it was going to fail—so they let us completely alone so we were able to do the job.

> On development of first nuclear submarine, *Reader's Digest* Jul 58

12 The more you sweat in peace, the less you bleed in war.

> 1983 retirement speech, recalled on his death 8 Jul 86

GEN MATTHEW B RIDGWAY, US Army

13 Sometimes, at night, it was almost as if I could hear the assurance that God the Father gave to another soldier, named Joshua: "I will not fail thee nor forsake thee."

> Recalling his World War II command of 82nd Airborne Division on D-day, *Time* 28 May 84

COL JOHN W RIPLEY, US Marine Corps

14 They're the ones I want. They're the strugglers; they've had to cope with adversity.

> On desirability of some Naval Academy cadets who rank near the bottom of their class, NY *Times* 30 Jan 86

GEN BERNARD ROGERS, NATO Supreme Allied Commander Europe

15 The last thing we want to do is make Europe safe for a conventional war.

> Opposing removal of medium-range missiles because it could encourage nonnuclear conflict, *Time* 16 Mar 87

LT COL JAMES N ROWE, US Army Special Forces

16　Hide, screaming incomprehension
of the inevitable;
for it is inevitable
　　　　and it is coming.

> Poem written in 1961 after 3-night dream sequence depicting his capture by the North Vietnamese almost exactly as it occurred on October 29, 1963, *Five Years to Freedom* Ballantine 71

REAR ADM JAMES E SERVICE, US Naval War College

17 We get officers here who have spent their careers looking through gunsights or periscopes or binoculars. We want to expand the size of their horizons and to show them that they alone are not going to win the war.

> NY *Times* 25 Nov 84

CAPT JOHN E SHEPHARD JR, Assistant Professor of Political Science, US Military Academy

18 The problem, evidently, was that God and President Truman did not see eye to eye.

> On President Truman's recall of Gen Douglas MacArthur from Korea and MacArthur's subsequent statement that he had "tried to do his duty as God gave him the sight to see that duty," *Wall Street Journal* 26 Mar 87

MAJ GEN C T SHORTIS, British Director of Infantry

19 The infantry doesn't change. We're the only arm [of the military] where the weapon is the man himself.

> NY *Times* 4 Feb 85

GEN DAVID M SHOUP, Commandant, US Marine Corps

1 Remember, God provides the best camouflage several hours out of every 24.

> On night fighting, NY *Herald Tribune* 5 Jan 61

FIELD MARSHAL WILLIAM JOSEPH SLIM, British Army

2 I tell you . . . as officers, that you will neither eat, nor drink, nor smoke, nor sit down, nor lean against a tree until you have personally seen that your men have first had a chance to do these things. If you will do this for them, they will follow you to the ends of the earth. And if you do not, I will bust you in front of your regiments.

> Recalled on his death, NY *Times* 15 Dec 70

GEN WALTER BEDELL SMITH, Chief of Staff, US Army

3 To tell you the truth, I thought of all the damned paperwork this was going to mean in the morning.

> Recalling his presence at signing of armistice ending World War II in Europe, NY *Times* 8 May 65

ADM JAMES STOCKDALE, US Navy retired

4 [They can] shout down the head of the physics department at Cal Tech.

> Expressing confidence in civilian control of weapons procurement, *Newsweek* 9 Jul 84

COL HARRY SUMMERS, US Army

5 If your job is to fix trucks, the bottom line is how many trucks you fix. The combat Army has a totally different ethic: Accomplish your mission and take care of your men.

> *Newsweek* 9 Jul 84

GEN MAXWELL D TAYLOR, US Army

6 Unless you are prepared to use our planes to knock out Cuban planes, then you shouldn't have started the thing in the first place.

> On Bay of Pigs invasion, quoted by Ralph G Martin *A Hero for Our Time* Macmillan 83

7 Here was this vast machinery of government and they didn't know how it ran, where you put in the gas, where you put in the oil, where you turn the throttle.

> On inexperience of President John F Kennedy and his staff during Bay of Pigs crisis, *ib*

8 When I began to use my cricket, the first man I met in the darkness I thought was a German until he cricketed. . . . We threw our arms around each other, and from that moment I knew we had won the war.

> On 1944 invasion of Normandy, quoted in *Time* 28 May 84

MARGARET THATCHER, Prime Minister of Great Britain

9 It is only when you look now and see success that you say that it was good fortune. It was not. We lost 250 of our best young men. I felt every one.

> On Falkland Islands War with Argentina, *New Yorker* 10 Feb 86

10 It was sheer professionalism and inspiration and the fact that you really cannot have people marching into other people's territory and staying there.

> *ib*

VICE ADM NILS THUNMAN, US Deputy Chief of Naval Operations

11 The oceans are becoming more opaque, not less. . . . Nobody can find us.

> Contending that submarine fleet is invulnerable despite spying, *Time* 17 Jun 85

HARRY S TRUMAN, 33rd US President

12 The Marine Corps is the Navy's police force and as long as I am president that is what it will remain. They have a propaganda machine that is almost equal to Stalin's.

> Quoted in *Time* 18 Sep 56

ADM STANSFIELD TURNER, US Navy

13 We talked for a few more minutes and then the president turned to the vice president and said he'd just narrowed the candidates to one. And my 31-year naval career flew out the window.

> On being asked in 1977 by President Jimmy Carter to head the CIA, NY *Times* 16 Jun 85

GEN NATHAN F TWINING, Chief of Staff, US Air Force

14 If our air forces are never used, they have achieved their finest goal.

> News summaries 31 Mar 56

LT GEN WALTER F ULMER, US Army

15 The essence of a general's job is to assist in developing a clear sense of purpose . . . to keep the junk from getting in the way of important things.

> *Newsweek* 9 Jul 84

16 We've got some very good things to do without screwing around with sleeves.

> Telling officers to disregard regulation that fatigue uniform sleeves should be rolled up outside in so that solid-colored linings wouldn't spoil camouflage effect, *ib*

UNITED STATES ARMY

17 Babies satisfactorily born.

> Coded message to Potsdam Conference on successful test of atomic bomb at Alamogordo NM, an event that set in motion Allied plans for attack on Hiroshima, quoted by Winston Churchill *Triumph and Tragedy* Houghton Mifflin 53

18 Wordlessly, the Corps clenches and unclenches its fists, trying to devise a way of sending him appropriate greetings. Alas, there are no words magnificent enough.

> Framed message from West Point cadets marking Gen Douglas MacArthur's 84th birthday, recalled on his death 5 Apr 64

LT RICHARD VAN DE GEER, US Air Force

19 I can envision a small cottage somewhere, with a lot of writing paper, and a dog, and a fireplace and maybe enough money to give myself some Irish coffee now and then and entertain my two friends.

> Letter to a friend before he was killed on May 15, 1975, officially the last American to die in Vietnam War, *Time* 15 Apr 85

20 It isn't very easy for me to even tell myself what the motivation was to come here. I went into this searching for something. I have it now. If I could, I would probably go home. Adios, my friend.

> Tape-recorded message to his closest friend, received the day of Van de Geer's death, *Newsweek* 20 May 85

GEN JOHN W VESSEY JR, US Army, Chairman, Joint Chiefs of Staff

1 [My job is] to give the president and secretary of defense military advice before they know they need it.
> NY *Times* 15 Jul 84

2 "Resource-constrained environment" [are] fancy Pentagon words that mean there isn't enough money to go around.
> *ib*

3 More has been screwed up on the battlefield and misunderstood in the Pentagon because of a lack of understanding of the English language than any other single factor.
> *ib*

4 Our strategy is one of preventing war by making it self-evident to our enemies that they're going to get their clocks cleaned if they start one.
> To soldiers at Schofield Barracks in Hawaii, *ib*

5 You have to set your "shove-it" tolerance someplace. But you also have to recognize that you, too, may be wrong, and that in two weeks' time you'll be "old what's-his-name" and won't be able to influence the situation at all.
> On retiring after 46 years of service, *ib* 3 Sep 85

6 Don't get small units caught in between the forces of history.
> Lesson learned from death of 237 US servicemen in terrorist bombing in Beirut, *ib*

ADM JAMES D WATKINS, former US Chief of Naval Operations

7 [This is] an era of violent peace.
> Quoted by Richard Halloran "A Silent Battle Surfaces" NY *Times* 7 Dec 86

CASPAR W WEINBERGER, US Secretary of Defense

8 I think women are too valuable to be in combat.
> To Defense Advisory Committee on Women in the Services, *US News & World Report* 19 May 86

9 [Here] rests the soul of our nation—here also should be our conscience.
> Veterans Day address at Arlington National Cemetery, NY *Times* 11 Nov 86

GEN WILLIAM C WESTMORELAND, US Army

10 War is fear cloaked in courage.
> *McCall's* Dec 66

11 Vietnam was the first war ever fought without any censorship. Without censorship, things can get terribly confused in the public mind.
> *Time* 5 Apr 82

JOHN WHEELER, Chairman, Vietnam Veterans Memorial Committee

12 I had a picture of a seven-year-old throwing a Frisbee around on the grass . . . but it's treated as a spiritual place.
> On Vietnam Veterans Memorial, Washington DC, *Time* 15 Apr 85

GEN YIGAEL YADIN, Israeli Chief of Staff

13 The civilian is a soldier on 11 months' annual leave.
> On readiness of reserve forces who have one month of intensive training a year, NY *Times* 25 May 86

ADM ELMO ZUMWALT JR, former US Chief of Naval Operations

14 We checked with the Army and Air Force about the possible injurious effects on humans of Agent Orange . . . We were told there were none. You trust those things.
> On defoliant he ordered used during Vietnam War, from *My Father, My Son*, with Lt Elmo Zumwalt 3rd, Macmillan 86, excerpted in NY *Times* 24 Aug 86

15 I ordered the spraying of Agent Orange.
> *ib*

16 Knowing what I now know, I still would have ordered the defoliation to achieve the objectives it did, of reducing casualties.
> *ib*

17 That does not ease the sorrow I feel for Elmo, or the anguish his illness, and Russell's disability, give me. It is the first thing I think of when I awake in the morning, and the last thing I remember when I go to sleep at night.
> On his son, suffering from cancer, and his grandson, born with a severe learning disability, conditions thought to have been caused by his son's exposure to Agent Orange, *ib*

LT ELMO ZUMWALT 3RD

18 I am a lawyer and I don't think I could prove in court . . . that Agent Orange is the cause of all the medical problems . . . reported by Vietnam veterans, or of their children's serious birth defects. But I am convinced that it is.
> On his cancer and his son's learning disability, from *My Father, My Son*, with Adm Elmo Zumwalt Jr, Macmillan 86, excerpted in NY *Times* 24 Aug 86

19 I realize that what I am saying may imply that my father is responsible for my illness and Russell's disability. . . . I do not doubt for a minute that the saving of American lives was always his first priority. Certainly thousands, perhaps even myself, are alive today because of his decision to use Agent Orange.
> *ib*

Observers & Critics

ANONYMOUS

20 This embattled shore, portal of freedom, is forever hallowed by the ideas, valor and sacrifice of our fellow countrymen.
> Monument inscription on Normandy coast, quoted by John Vinocur "D-day Plus 40 Years" NY *Times* 13 May 84

LES ASPIN, US Congressman

21 Before we give you billions more, we want to know what you've done with the trillion you've got.
> Letter to Secretary of Defense Caspar W Weinberger after Aspin became chairman of House of Representatives Armed Services Committee, NY *Times* 5 Feb 85

DANIEL BERRIGAN SJ

22 Don't just do something, stand there.
> On importance of thought as well as action in 1960s war protests, recalled in Springfield MA *Valley Advocate* 17 Nov 86

WILLIAM BROYLES JR

1 "Why me?" That is the soldier's first question, asked each morning as the patrols go out and each evening as the night settles around the foxholes.
Memorial Day tribute, NY *Times* 26 May 86

2 What has brought unique, irreplaceable me—out of all the possibilities of life—here, now, to this? Was all my youth—the paper route after school, the stolen moments in the back seats of borrowed cars, the football workouts, the cramming for finals—meant to end this way, dying in a muddy paddy?
ib

ROBERT W BUCHHEIM, National Research Council

3 This is dangerous material. It was designed to be dangerous. It is very dangerous.
On chemical weapons, NY *Times* 22 Nov 84

ALISTAIR COOKE

4 These doomsday warriors look no more like soldiers than the soldiers of the Second World War looked like conquistadors. The more expert they become the more they look like lab assistants in small colleges.
On personnel of antiballistic missile complex, *America* Knopf 73

NELSON DeMILLE

5 It was no more than a black slash in the ground, a poignant contrast to the lofty white marble and limestone of this monumental city. It was cut into a gently rising slope of grass . . . An al fresco mortuary.
On Vietnam Veterans Memorial, Washington DC, *Word of Honor* Warner 85

6 It's a gravestone.
ib

DAVID DIAZ

7 They say you can read faces. Well, if that is true, you can read the entire Vietnamese War in the crowds here.
On dedication of NY Vietnam War Memorial, NBC TV 5 May 85

BERNARD EDELMAN

8 They were called grunts, and many of them, however grudgingly, were proud of the name. They were the infantrymen, the foot soldiers of the war.
Dear America: Letters Home from Vietnam Norton 85

OWEN EDWARDS

9 A chest full of medals is nothing more than a résumé in 3-D and Technicolor.
On interviewing a US Marine general, NY *Times* 14 Jul 85

JANET FLANNER ("Genet")

10 When you look at the startling ruins of Nuremberg, you are looking at a result of the war. When you look at the prisoners on view in the courtroom, you are looking at 22 of the causes.
On Nuremberg trials of war criminals, *Janet Flanner's World: Uncollected Writings 1932–75* Harcourt Brace Jovanovich 79

OTTO FRIEDRICH

11 The lessons that it teaches . . . are fundamentally the lessons that all great battles teach . . . That even the most carefully prepared plans often go wrong. That lucky breaks are very important.
On 40th anniversary of D-day Allied invasion of France, *Time* 28 May 84

12 [It teaches] that war is cruel and wasteful but sometimes necessary. That a blundering victory is more to be valued than a heroic defeat. That might and right sometimes come to the same end. All these things happened on June 6, 1944.
ib

MICHAEL GLENDON JR

13 Hi, Daddy. I love you. This is Michael. I'm seven now.
Telephone conversation welcoming home Maj Michael Glendon, who had been shot down over North Vietnam in 1966, quoted by George Esper and the Associated Press *The Eyewitness History of the Vietnam War 1961–75* Ballantine 83

PETER GOLDMAN

14 Playing poker in their Quonset hut on Tinian, killing the last hours of the preatomic age.
On US bomber crew scheduled to carry first atomic bomb, *Newsweek* 29 Jul 85

15 The bodies lay on the ground like damaged goods from a warehouse.
On Hiroshima after bombing, *ib*

16 It was as if Japan had fallen victim to a case of collective amnesia.
On Japanese cordiality to Americans after bombings of Hiroshima and Nagasaki, *ib*

PETER GRIER

17 He smiles with the faraway, sea-remembering smile of all desk admirals.
On Adm James D Watkins, first nuclear submariner to become Chief of Naval Operations, *Christian Science Monitor* 4 Jun 86

18 It looks like a condominium with a cannon and tracks.
On introduction of US Army's 25-ton Bradley Fighting Vehicle, *ib* 19 Aug 86

ARLO GUTHRIE

19 Proceeded on down the hall,
Gettin' more injections,
Inspections, detections, neglections,
And all kinds of stuff
That they was doin' to me.
Vietnam-era ballad on Army physical examination, "Alice's Restaurant," quoted in *Newsweek* 5 May 86

THEODORE M HESBURGH, President, Notre Dame

20 It's like having a cobra in the nursery with your grandchildren. . . . You get rid of the cobra or you won't have any grandchildren.
On nuclear weapons, *60 Minutes* CBS TV 14 Mar 82

ERNEST F HOLLINGS, US Senator

21 If they've been put there to fight, there are far too few. If they've been put there to be killed, there are far too many.
On US Marines in Lebanon, *Time* 26 Dec 83

ALLAN KELLER

1 The only war is the war you fought in. Every veteran knows that.

NY *World-Telegram & Sun* 24 Aug 65

NGUYEN CAO KY

2 Americans are big boys. You can talk them into almost anything. [Just] sit with them for half an hour over a bottle of whiskey and be a nice guy.

1965 statement quoted by Robert C Mason, *Chickenhawk* Viking 83

MRS MAHONEY

3 Dear Pete, Just a short note. Please don't do anything foolish. Seriously, Pete, please take care of yourself and don't be a hero. I don't need a Medal of Honor winner. I need a son. Love, Mom

Letter to her son Lt Peter P Mahoney, US Army, engraved on NY Vietnam War Memorial, *Newsweek* 20 May 85

WILLIAM MANCHESTER

4 He was a great thundering paradox of a man.

On Gen Douglas MacArthur, *American Caesar* Little, Brown 78

5 Japanese naval officers in dress whites are frequent guests at [Pearl Harbor's] officers' mess [and] are very polite. . . . They always were. Except, of course, for that little interval there between 1941 and 1945.

Good-bye, Darkness: A Memoir of the Pacific War Little, Brown 80

6 I wondered vaguely if this was when it would end, whether I would pull up tonight's darkness like a quilt and be dead and at peace evermore.

On an enemy attack, *ib*

7 Men . . . do not fight for flag or country, for the Marine Corps or glory or any other abstraction. They fight for one another. [And] if you came through this ordeal, you would age with dignity.

ib

8 The French had collapsed. The Dutch had been overwhelmed. The Belgians had surrendered. The British army, trapped, fought free and fell back toward the Channel ports, converging on a fishing town whose name was then spelled Dunkerque. Behind them lay the sea. It was England's greatest crisis since the Norman Conquest, vaster than those precipitated by Philip II's Spanish Armada, Louis XIV's triumphant armies or Napoleon's invasion barges massed at Boulogne. This time Britain stood alone.

Preamble to *The Last Lion* Little, Brown 83

EDWARD MARSH

9 In war, resolution; in defeat, defiance; in victory, magnanimity; in peace, good will.

Epigram on World War I, used by Winston Churchill in his volumes on World War II, recalled on Marsh's death 13 Jan 53

10 In defeat, unbeatable; in victory, unbearable.

On Viscount Montgomery, *ib*

JOHN C METZLER, Superintendent, Arlington National Cemetery

11 I will tell each person what I have told others in the past—that exactly who the men on the hill are is not as important as the fact that they are there. Being there, they are not only representative of other men who died unknown, but of all men who have fought for America. For that reason, they belong to all of us.

Comment prior to burial of Unknown Soldiers of World War II and Korean War, *Cosmopolitan* May 58

JAMES A MICHENER

12 [They were] a group of two dozen nurses completely surrounded by 100,000 unattached American men.

On the heroines he chose for his 1947 book *Tales of the South Pacific*, Memphis *Commercial Appeal* 31 Dec 51

13 I was a Navy officer writing about Navy problems and I simply stole this lovely Army nurse and popped her into a Navy uniform, where she has done very well for herself.

ib

LANCE MORROW

14 Like robots suffering an obscure sorrow, they carried the casket of the new Unknown Soldier, the one from Vietnam. [It] was a different kind of war for the United States [in] a shattering time, a bomb that originated a world away and went off in the middle of the American mind. [Now] the prevailing note was one of acceptance and reconciliation, as if in burying the Unknown Soldier, the nation were also interring another measure of its residual bitterness.

"War and Remembrance: A Bit of the Bitterness Is Buried Along with an Unknown Soldier" *Time* 11 Jun 84

15 As they marched, the crowds lining the route broke into applause, a sweet and deeply felt spontaneous pattering that was a sort of communal embrace. Welcome home.

ib

MALCOLM MUGGERIDGE

16 In Europe the ubiquitous GI, with his camera like a third eye, created wherever he went a little America, air-conditioned, steam-heated and neon-lighted. In American eyes he was a liberator and defender of freedom. In other eyes he often seemed part of an American army of occupation. To all he symbolized Europe's enfeeblement and the shift of world power and wealth across the Atlantic.

The Titans: United States of America BBC TV 16 Jan 62

NEW YORK TIMES

17 Transfixed by the mysterious marble panels, glassy black windows reflecting the present and overlooking the past.

On visitors to Washington DC's Vietnam Veterans Memorial "The Black Gash of Shame" 14 Apr 85

18 A memorial at once national and personal. In each sharply etched name one reads the price paid by yet another family. In the sweeping pattern of names, chronological by day of death, 1959 to 1975, one reads the price paid by the nation.

ib

1 Ten years after the war, America may not yet comprehend the loss of those 58,000 lives; but it has at least found a noble way to remember them.
ib

RALPH DELAHAYE PAINE JR

2 The burden the Navy has carried so brilliantly in the Pacific will inevitably be shared more and more with the Army and its air forces. But the Navy has performed its historic duty; the Navy got them there.
"The War: The Pacific Sweep" *Fortune* Jul 45, reprinted in 50th anniversary issue 11 Feb 80

DREW PEARSON

3 His smile and manner are the moss on a character of granite.
On Gen Earle G Wheeler, Chairman, Joint Chiefs of Staff, NY *Times* 29 Feb 68

ROGER PINEAU and JOHN COSTELLO

4 [He was] speared like a frog and hung out to dry for the rest of the war.
On Capt Joseph J Rochefort, whose deciphering of Japanese codes was a crucial factor in US victory at the Battle of Midway but who was not given credit by Washington intelligence officers, quoted in NY *Times* 17 Nov 85

MAURICE PINGUET, Professor of French Literature, University of Tokyo

5 Good son, good student, good soldier: The young pilot of the kamikaze special unit was less the martyr of a fanatic faith than of his own good heart and good will.
On World War II suicide pilots as part of ancient Japanese philosophy and culture, from *Voluntary Death in Japan*, published in Paris and quoted by *International Herald Tribune* 3 Dec 85

WILLIAM PROXMIRE, US Senator

6 Move over, $7,000 coffeepots! Stand aside, $400 hammers! We now have the $792 doormat!
On inordinantly high cost of materiel, NY *Times* 4 Oct 85

7 The poor taxpayer may wipe his shoes on a $3 doormat when he goes home, but not the Navy. It is, damn the cost, full feet ahead on a doormat you would be ashamed to get muddy.
ib

ROBERT ROEMER, project director, Grumman Corp

8 It's roughly like throwing an arrow backward.
On Grumman X-29A planes run by 3 computers making 40 adjustments per second, *Time* 10 Sep 84

GREG RUSHFORD, investigator for US House Select Committee on Intelligence

9 [They] acted like used-car salesmen rolling the mileage back.
On military personnel who calculated enemy strength in Vietnam, NY *Times* 1 Feb 85

WILLIAM SAFIRE

10 Modern war needs modern lingo.
Observing that "today's attackerese" refers to more than old terms such as *conduct a raid, mount an attack* or *deliver a blow*, NY *Times* 4 May 86

JAMES SHEEHAN

11 [It] would be like turning the Liberty Bell upside-down and making it a planter.
On US Navy's opposition to sale of the *Olympia*, Cdr George Dewey's flagship in the 1898 Battle of Manila Bay, NY *Times* 2 Feb 86

ALAN K SIMPSON, US Senator

12 He's a million rubber bands in his resilience.
Expressing respect for Secretary of Defense Caspar W Weinberger, whose budget was being reviewed, NY *Times* 3 Feb 85

KIRKE L SIMPSON

13 Under the wide and starry skies of his own homeland, America's unknown dead from France sleeps tonight, a soldier home from the wars.
On the burial of the Unknown Soldier of World War I at Arlington VA, recalled on Simpson's death, NY *Times* 17 Jun 72

14 Alone, he lies in the narrow cell of stone that guards his body; but his soul has entered into the spirit that is America. Wherever liberty is held close in men's hearts, the honor and the glory and the pledge of high endeavor poured out over this nameless one of fame will be told and sung by Americans for all time.
ib

FRANK SNEPP, former agent, CIA

15 Disinformation is most effective in a very narrow context.
Christian Science Monitor 26 Feb 85

16 You take a fraction of reality and expand on it. It's very seldom totally at odds with the facts. . . . It's shaving a piece of reality off.
On disinformation, *ib*

BENJAMIN SPOCK

17 I'm not a pacifist. I was very much for the war against Hitler and I also supported the intervention in Korea, but in this war we went in there to steal Vietnam.
After indictment on charges of aiding and abetting resistance to Selective Service laws, news summaries 5 Jan 68

RICHARD STUBBING, US Office of Management and Budget

18 It's a middle-class welfare program for engineers.
On lack of competitive bidding that helps contractors keep large payrolls, NY *Times* 15 May 85

EVAN THOMAS

19 American boys should not be seen dying on the nightly news. Wars should be over in three days or less, or before Congress invokes the War Powers Resolution. Victory must be assured in advance. And the American public must be all for it from the outset.
On "unreal extremes" of modern warfare, "Week of the Big Stick" *Time* 7 Apr 86

TIME MAGAZINE

20 The rescuers had to rescue themselves.
On ill-fated attempt to free hostages in Iran, 5 May 80

BARBARA W TUCHMAN

1 A relentless talent for tactlessness.
> On Germany's entrance into World War I, *The Guns of August* Macmillan 62

2 The fleet sailed to its war base . . . in the North Sea, headed not so much for some rendezvous with glory as for rendezvous with discretion.
> On defense of coastline prior to outbreak of war, *ib*

3 Nothing so comforts the military mind as the maxim of a great but dead general.
> *ib*

JOHN VINOCUR

4 The sense of war, the extraordinary bravery of the Allied armies, the numbers, the losses, the real suffering that disappears in time and commemorative oratory, are not marked out in any red guidebook of the emotions, but they are present if you look.
> "D-day Plus 40 Years" NY *Times* 13 May 84

5 At the edge of the cliffs, the wind is a smack, and D-day becomes wildly clear: climbing that cutting edge into the bullets.
> *ib*

6 The American cemetery at Saint-Laurent-sur-Mer is a great lawn at the edge of the sea, white marble crosses and Stars of David against an open horizon. . . . very American in the best sense: no phony piety, simple, easy.
> *ib*

PATRICIA L WALSH

7 We don't need to fabricate anything because the truth will make you weep.
> On experiences as a civilian nurse in Vietnam, NY *Times* 12 Feb 85

JOHN WHEELER

8 It was the defining event . . . and remains a thousand degrees hot.
> On the Vietnam War, *Touched with Fire* Avon 85

JAMES WILDE

9 The stench of death massaged my skin; it took years to wash away.
> On reporting the Vietnam War, *Time* 15 Apr 85

PETER WYDEN

10 Cataclysms from the Old Testament came to Truman's mind: "It may be the fire destruction prophesied in the Euphrates Valley era after Noah and his ark."
> *Day One: Before Hiroshima & After* Simon & Schuster 84

11 Churchill also resorted to biblical terms. . . . He brimmed over with exuberance: "What was gunpowder? Trivial. What was electricity? Meaningless. The atomic bomb is the Second Coming in wrath."
> *ib*

LAW

Attorneys & the Practice of Law

RENATA ADLER

12 In the strange heat all litigation brings to bear on things, the very process of litigation fosters the most profound misunderstandings in the world.
> *Reckless Disregard* Knopf 86

SHANA ALEXANDER

13 The law changes and flows like water, and . . . the stream of women's rights law has become a sudden rushing torrent.
> *Shana Alexander's State-by-State Guide to Women's Legal Rights* Wollstonecraft 75

14 The players are from central casting: a small-town lawyer with the biggest case of his lifetime, an uptight young prosecutor in steel-rimmed glasses, a folksy and politically correct judge, a long parade of faltering witnesses, a defendant who looks like Constance Bennett and, for a jury, a double row of Archie and Edith Bunkers, a third of them black.
> On murder trial of Jean Harris, *Very Much a Lady* Little, Brown 83

AMERICAN CIVIL LIBERTIES UNION

15 Liberty is always unfinished business.
> Annual Report 55/56

ANONYMOUS

16 Quote Learned but follow Gus.
> On Learned Hand, who sat in US Court of Appeals at the same time as his more practical cousin Augustus Hand, quoted in NY *Times* 8 Mar 87

HARRY S ASHMORE

17 We are going to have to decide what kind of people we are—whether we obey the law only when we approve of it or whether we obey it no matter how distasteful we may find it.
> On integration of Little Rock High School, Arkansas *Gazette* 4 Sep 57

ROBERT BADINTER, French Minister of Justice

18 One does not plead for a dead man, because the lawyer of a dead man is nothing but a man who remembers.
> On capital punishment, London *Times* 19 Sep 81

F LEE BAILEY

19 Can any of you seriously say the Bill of Rights could get through Congress today? It wouldn't even get out of committee.
> *Newsweek* 17 Apr 67

20 I use the rules to frustrate the law. But I didn't set up the ground rules.
> NY *Times* 20 Sep 70

HOWARD H BAKER JR, US Senator

21 You've got to guard against speaking more clearly than you think.
> Quoting his father's reaction to Baker's first court appearance, Washington *Post* 24 Jun 73

ROGER N BALDWIN

22 [Our goal is] a society with a minimum of compulsion, a maximum of individual freedom and of voluntary association and the abolition of exploitation and poverty.
> Recalled on his death 26 Aug 81

RICHARD J BARTLETT, former Dean, Albany Law School, Union University

1 Once someone uses the term "reasonable person," it's awfully hard to define it.

> On defense of Bernhard H Goetz, accused of shooting four youths he believed were attempting to rob him, NY *Times* 9 Jul 86

WILLIAM F BAXTER, Assistant US Attorney General

2 I've never met a litigator who didn't think he was winning—right up until the moment the guillotine dropped.

> News summaries 8 Jan 82

MELVIN BELLI

3 There is never a deed so foul that something couldn't be said for the guy; that's why there are lawyers.

> LA *Times* 18 Dec 81

4 [A lawyer's] performance in the courtroom is responsible for about 25 percent of the outcome; the remaining 75 percent depends on the facts.

> US *News & World Report* 20 Sep 82

SIDNEY BERNARD

5 Jury duty [is] a bog of quicksand on the path to justice.

> "The Waiting Game" NY *Journal-American* 30 Dec 65

ALEXANDER M BICKEL, Professor of Legal History, Yale

6 [The judiciary is] the least dangerous branch of our government.

> Quoted in *Christian Science Monitor* 11 Feb 86

ROSE ELIZABETH BIRD, Chief Justice, California Supreme Court

7 You salivate on signal; they want a Pavlovian justice.

> On state law for periodic election and re-election of judges, a statute that a year later resulted in her removal from the bench, NY *Times* 22 Dec 85

HUGO L BLACK, Associate Justice, US Supreme Court

8 The layman's constitutional view is that what he likes is constitutional and that which he doesn't like is unconstitutional.

> NY *Times* 26 Feb 71

HARRY A BLACKMUN, Associate Justice, US Supreme Court

9 Who is to say that 5 men 10 years ago were right whereas 5 men looking the other direction today are wrong.

> On prior court decisions, especially 5–4 votes, LA *Herald-Examiner* 20 Apr 70

10 We're all eccentrics. We're nine prima donnas.

> *Time* 6 Feb 84

11 If one's in the doghouse with the Chief, he gets the crud. He gets the tax cases and some of the Indian cases, which I like, but I've had a lot of them.

> Alluding to strained relations with Chief Justice Warren E Burger, NY *Times* 22 Dec 86

DEREK BOK, President, Harvard

12 There is far too much law for those who can afford it and far too little for those who cannot.

> Report to Board of Overseers 21 Apr 83

ROBERT H BORK, Judge, US Court of Appeals, District of Columbia Circuit

13 [It is] a ship with a great deal of sail but a very shallow keel.

> On constitutional law, NY *Times* 4 Jan 85

14 [Law is] vulnerable to the winds of intellectual or moral fashion, which it then validates as the commands of our most basic concept.

> *ib*

WILLIAM J BRENNAN JR, Associate Justice, US Supreme Court

15 We current justices read the Constitution in the only way that we can: as 20th-century Americans.

> Address at Georgetown University, NY *Times* 13 Oct 85

16 We look to the history of the time of framing and to the intervening history of interpretation. But the ultimate question must be, what do the words of the text mean in our time.

> *ib*

CLAUS VON BÜLOW

17 This was a tragedy and it satisfied all of Aristotle's definitions of tragedy. Everyone is wounded, some fatally.

> To Harvard Law School forum after his acquittal at trials for attempted murder of his wife, NY *Times* 16 Mar 86

WARREN E BURGER, Chief Justice, US Supreme Court

18 Concepts of justice must have hands and feet . . . to carry out justice in every case in the shortest possible time and the lowest possible cost. This is the challenge to every lawyer and judge in America.

> To Amer Bar Assn 1 Oct 72

19 We are more casual about qualifying the people we allow to act as advocates in the courtroom than we are about licensing electricians.

> Address at Fordham University Law School, news summaries 28 Dec 73

20 The courtrooms of America all too often have Piper Cub advocates trying to handle the controls of Boeing 747 litigation.

> *ib*

21 The trial of a case [is] a three-legged stool—a judge and two advocates.

> To Amer Bar Assn 12 Feb 78

22 Doctors . . . still retain a high degree of public confidence because they are perceived as healers. Should lawyers not be healers? Healers, not warriors? Healers, not procurers? Healers, not hired guns?

> *ib* 12 Feb 84

23 It is not unprofessional to give free legal advice, but advertising that the first visit will be free is a bit like a fox telling chickens he will not bite them until they cross the threshold of the hen house.

> *ib* 11 Aug 86

24 Judges . . . rule on the basis of law, not public opinion, and they should be totally indifferent to pressures of the times.

> Quoted by Charlotte Saikowski "The Power of Judicial Review" *Christian Science Monitor* 11 Feb 87

DAN M BURT

1 No individual should find the foot of a behemoth on his neck for no reason at all, without the ability to lift that foot off.
> On Gen William C Westmoreland's libel suit against CBS TV, NY *Times* 31 May 84

GUIDO CALABRESI, Professor of Law, Yale

2 There is something particularly appealing about teaching a subject that seems to deal with the lowest kind of relationships—accidents, ambulance chasing—because you can show students that these raise the most fundamental questions about the structure of society.
> *Time* 14 Mar 77

WILLIAM J CAMPBELL, Judge, US District Court, Northern Illinois

3 Today, the grand jury is the total captive of the prosecutor who, if he is candid, will concede that he can indict anybody, at any time, for almost anything, before any grand jury.
> *Newsweek* 22 Aug 77

RAMSEY CLARK, US Attorney General

4 A right is not what someone gives you; it's what no one can take from you.
> NY *Times* 2 Oct 77

ROY M COHN

5 My scare value is high. My arena is controversy. My tough front is my biggest asset.
> On his career as an attorney, recalled on his death 2 Aug 86

6 I don't write polite letters. I don't like to plea-bargain. I like to fight.
> *ib*

7 I bring out the worst in my enemies and that's how I get them to defeat themselves.
> Quoted by William Safire NY *Times* 4 Aug 86

LYNN COMPTON, Chief Deputy District Attorney, Los Angeles

8 I think the law became an ass the day it let the psychiatrists get their hands on [it].
> Summation at Sirhan Sirhan's trial for assassination of Robert F Kennedy, LA *Times* 14 Apr 69

ARCHIBALD COX, Professor of Law, Harvard

9 Through the centuries, men of law have been persistently concerned with the resolution of disputes . . . in ways that enable society to achieve its goals with a minimum of force and maximum of reason.
> News summaries 30 Dec 73

DONALD R CRESSEY, Professor of Criminology, University of California, Santa Barbara

10 Things in law tend to be black and white. But we all know that some people are a little bit guilty, while other people are guilty as hell.
> *Center Magazine* May/Jun 78

11 You cannot bring in a verdict that the defendant is a little bit guilty.
> *ib*

MARIO CUOMO, Governor of NY

12 If you can manipulate news, a judge can manipulate the law. A smart lawyer can keep a killer out of jail, a smart accountant can keep a thief from paying taxes, a smart reporter could ruin your reputation—unfairly.
> NBC TV 21 Aug 86

CHARLES CURTIS

13 Fraud is the homage that force pays to reason.
> *A Commonplace Book* Simon & Schuster 57

14 Bias and prejudice are attitudes to be kept in hand, not attitudes to be avoided.
> *ib*

ALAN M DERSHOWITZ, Professor of Law, Harvard

15 Judges are the weakest link in our system of justice, and they are also the most protected.
> *Newsweek* 20 Feb 78

16 All sides in a trial want to hide at least some of the truth.
> *US News & World Report* 9 Aug 82

17 The defendant wants to hide the truth because he's generally guilty. The defense attorney's job is to make sure the jury does not arrive at that truth.
> *ib*

18 The prosecution . . . wants to make sure the process by which the evidence was obtained is not truthfully presented, because, as often as not, that process will raise questions.
> *ib*

19 The judge also has a truth he wants to hide: He often hasn't been completely candid in describing the facts or the law.
> *ib*

LORD PATRICK DEVLIN, Judge of the High Court

20 The judges of England have rarely been original thinkers or great jurists. Many have been craftsmen rather than creators.
> Quoted by Anthony Sampson *Anatomy of Britain Today* Harper & Row 65

21 The most important thing for a judge is—curiously enough—judgment.
> *ib*

WILLIAM O DOUGLAS, Associate Justice, US Supreme Court

22 The 5th Amendment is an old friend and a good friend. . . . one of the great landmarks in men's struggle to be free of tyranny, to be decent and civilized.
> *An Almanac of Liberty* Doubleday 54

23 Common sense often makes good law.
> In court ruling 25 Mar 57

24 Since when have we Americans been expected to bow submissively to authority and speak with awe and reverence to those who represent us?
> Statement on unfair arrests for disorderly conduct, recalled on his retirement 12 Nov 75

25 We who have the final word can speak softly or angrily. We can seek to challenge and annoy, as we need not stay docile and quiet.
> *ib*

1 One who comes to the Court must come to adore, not to protest. That's the new gloss on the 1st Amendment.

> To Justice Potter Stewart on why Vietnam War veterans were arrested for peaceful protest on steps of the Supreme Court building, *The Court Years 1939–75* Random House 80

2 At the constitutional level where we work, 90 percent of any decision is emotional. The rational part of us supplies the reasons for supporting our predilections.

> *ib*

3 The Constitution is not neutral. It was designed to take the government off the backs of people.

> *ib*

4 It seemed to me that I had barely reached the Court when people were trying to get me off.

> On attempts to impeach him, *ib*

ADRIAN G DUPLANTIER, Louisiana State Senator

5 We are about to make motherhood a crime. No civilized government in the history of mankind has ever done this.

> Comment before legislators voted to make the bearing of more than one illegitimate child a criminal act, NY *Herald Tribune* 15 Jun 60

RONALD D DWORKIN, Professor of Law, NY University

6 Moral principle is the foundation of law.

> *Law's Empire* Belknap Press/Harvard 86, quoted in *Christian Science Monitor* 20 May 86

7 Integrity is the key to understanding legal practice. . . . Law's empire is defined by attitude, not territory or power or process.

> *ib*

MARIAN WRIGHT EDELMAN

8 We are willing to spend the least amount of money to keep a kid at home, more to put him in a foster home and the most to institutionalize him.

> Quoted by Margie Casady "Society's Pushed-Out Children" *Psychology Today* Jun 75

THOMAS EHRLICH, Dean, Stanford Law School

9 [There] is an increasing sense of what can be called "legal pollution."

> On courts and legislatures "too prone to take on problems that they have no business getting into," *US News & World Report* 21 Jul 75

DWIGHT D EISENHOWER, 34th US President

10 The clearest way to show what the rule of law means to us in everyday life is to recall what has happened when there is no rule of law.

> Address on first observance of Law Day 5 May 58

11 I deplore the need or the use of troops anywhere to get American citizens to obey the orders of constituted courts.

> On Arkansas's defiance of Supreme Court school desegregation ruling, 14 May 58

12 There is no person in this room whose basic rights are not involved in any successful defiance to the carrying out of court orders.

> *ib*

AUSTIN ELLIOT

13 Whoever said "Marriage is a 50–50 proposition" laid the foundation for more divorce fees than any other short sentence in our language.

> "Some Observations on the Attorney-Secretary Function" *Law Office Economics and Management* Nov 64

MARTIN ERDMANN, NYC Legal Aid Society

14 Appellate Division judges [are] the whores who became madams.

> *Life* 12 Mar 71

SAM ERVIN, US Senator

15 I'll have you understand I am running this court, and the law hasn't got a damn thing to do with it!

> Recalling an old magistrate's words to a young attorney, quoted by Thad Stem Jr and Alan Butler comps *Senator Sam Ervin's Best Stories* Moore 73

16 The rain it raineth on the just
And also on the unjust fella;
But chiefly on the just, because
The unjust steals the just's umbrella.

> *ib*

17 [Polygraph tests] are 20th-century witchcraft.

> Quoted by Susan Dentzer "Can You Pass the Job Test?" *Newsweek* 5 May 86

BENJAMIN F FAIRLESS, President, US Steel

18 What five members of the Supreme Court say the law is may be something vastly different from what Congress intended the law to be.

> Address at Boston 18 May 50

19 If we persist in that kind of a system of law . . . virtually every business in America, big and small, is going to have to be run from Sing Sing, Leavenworth or Alcatraz.

> *ib*

GEOFFREY FISHER, Archbishop of Canterbury

20 In a civilized society, all crimes are likely to be sins, but most sins are not and ought not to be treated as crimes. . . . Man's ultimate responsibility is to God alone.

> *Look* 17 Mar 59

21 There is a sacred realm of privacy for every man and woman where he makes his choices and decisions—a realm of his own essential rights and liberties—into which the law, generally speaking, must not intrude.

> *ib*

MACKLIN FLEMING

22 Procrastination is a sin of lawyers, trial judges, reporters, appellate judges, in brief, everyone connected with the machinery of criminal law.

> *LA Times* 24 Jul 74

ABE FORTAS, Associate Justice, US Supreme Court

23 For a justice of this ultimate tribunal, the opportunity for self-discovery and the occasion for self-revelation is usually great.

> Quoted on his appointment to US Supreme Court, *Newsweek* 9 Aug 65

1 Judging is a lonely job in which a man is, as near as may be, an island entire.
ib

FELIX FRANKFURTER, Associate Justice, US Supreme Court

2 All our work, our whole life is a matter of semantics, because words are the tools with which we work, the material out of which laws are made, out of which the Constitution was written. Everything depends on our understanding of them.
Reply to counsel who said a challenge from the bench was "just a matter of semantics," *Reader's Digest* Jun 64

3 Litigation is the pursuit of practical ends, not a game of chess.
News summaries 9 Aug 64

4 As a member of this court I am not justified in writing my private notions of policy into the Constitution, no matter how deeply I may cherish them or how mischievous I may deem their disregard.
ib

5 Judicial judgment must take deep account . . . of the day before yesterday in order that yesterday may not paralyze today.
Quoted in *National Observer* 1 Mar 65

6 It must take account of what it decrees for today in order that today may not paralyze tomorrow.
ib

DAVID FROST and ANTONY JAY

7 The whole paraphernalia of the criminal law and the criminal courts is based on the need of the upper class to keep the lower class in its place.
The English Avon 68

8 This is what has to be remembered about the law: Beneath that cold, harsh, impersonal exterior there beats a cold, harsh, impersonal heart.
ib

9 Nobody wants literate people to go to prison—they have a distressing way of revealing what it's actually like and destroying our illusions about training and rehabilitation with nasty stories about sadism and futility and buckets of stale urine.
ib

JACOB D FUCHSBERG, former President, Amer Trial Lawyers Assn

10 The average juror . . . wraps himself in civic virtue. He's a judge now. He tries to act the part and do the right thing.
News summaries 6 Jun 69

JOHN W GARDNER

11 All laws are an attempt to domesticate the natural ferocity of the species.
San Francisco *Examiner & Chronicle* 3 Jul 74

LAWRENCE GIBBS, Commissioner, Internal Revenue Service

12 A taxpaying public that doesn't understand the law is a taxpaying public that can't comply with the law.
Wall Street Journal 3 Mar 87

OSCAR B GOODMAN

13 The Constitution is a fragile document. Today it has been bruised if not broken.
On US Senate's conviction in impeachment of his client US District Court Judge Harry E Claiborne of Nevada, NY *Times* 10 Oct 86

ALBERT GORE JR, US Senator

14 When you have the facts on your side, argue the facts. When you have the law on your side, argue the law. When you have neither, holler.
Washington *Post* 23 Jul 82

WILLIAM T GOSSETT, President, Amer Bar Assn

15 The rule of law can be wiped out in one misguided, however well-intentioned, generation.
Address 11 Aug 69

MILTON S GOULD

16 When you soar like an eagle, you attract the hunters.
On his clients, corporate executives under government investigation, *Time* 8 Dec 67

GENE GUERRERO, Georgia State Director, Amer Civil Liberties Union

17 Can you imagine the Founding Fathers saying that the major source of authority in [your] life can make you drop your pants and urinate as a condition of getting or keeping a job?
On examination for drug use as an invasion of privacy, quoted by Susan Dentzer "Can You Pass the Job Test?" *Newsweek* 5 May 86

LORD HAILSHAM OF MARYLEBON (Quintin Hogg)

18 A reasonable doubt is nothing more than a doubt for which reasons can be given. The fact that 1 or 2 men out of 12 differ from the others does not establish that their doubts are reasonable.
In support of changing jury vote necessary for conviction from unanimous to 10–2, *Time* 19 May 67

MARY HAMILTON

19 I will not answer until I am addressed correctly.
To an Alabama prosecutor who addressed her by her first name, an action that the US Supreme Court later ruled against as a familiarity contrary to the law barring segregation in courtrooms, *Newsweek* 13 Apr 64

LEARNED HAND

20 If we are to keep our democracy, there must be one commandment: Thou shalt not ration justice.
To NY Legal Aid Society 16 Feb 51

21 There is no surer way to misread any document than to read it literally.
Recalled on his death 18 Aug 61

22 Proceed. You have my biased attention.
To attorney who asked to review a motion already heard, *ib*

23 The spirit of liberty is the spirit which is not too sure that it is right.
ib

24 [The judge's authority] depends upon the assumption that he speaks with the mouth of others.
Quoted by William J Brennan Jr, Associate Justice, US Supreme Court, NY *Times* 6 Oct 63

1 The momentum of his utterances must be greater than any which his personal reputation and character can command.
ib

2 The public needs the equivalent of Chevrolets as well as Cadillacs.
On trend toward popular marketing of legal services, quoted in *USA Today* 2 Feb 84

GIDEON HAUSNER

3 No one can demand that you be neutral toward the crime of genocide. If . . . there is a judge in the whole world who can be neutral toward this crime, that judge is not fit to sit in judgment.
Defending legality of trial of war criminal Adolf Eichmann, NY *Times* 27 Jun 61

MORTON J HORWITZ, Professor of Law, Harvard

4 [Law is] an odd profession that presents its greatest scholarship in student-run publications.
On law-school reviews, *Newsweek* 15 Sep 75

PAUL E JOHNSON

5 A ruling like this will cause prejudice in people who have never been prejudiced before.
On losing Supreme Court appeal against affirmative action employer who awarded a job to a woman with 4 years of experience and a test score of 73 as compared with his 13 years of experience and a score of 75, *Time* 6 Apr 87

NEAL JOHNSTON, Chief of Staff, NY City Council

6 The screening process through which law firms choose new partners is perhaps as well considered as anything this side of a papal election.
NY *Times* 6 Mar 83

LUCILLE KALLEN

7 A lawyer's relationship to justice and wisdom . . . is on a par with a piano tuner's relationship to a concert. He neither composes the music, nor interprets it—he merely keeps the machinery running.
Introducing C B Greenfield Crown 79

IRVING R KAUFMAN, Judge, US Court of Appeals, 2nd Circuit

8 To the extent that the judicial profession becomes the daily routine of deciding cases on the most secure precedents and the narrowest grounds available, the judicial mind atrophies and its perspective shrinks.
To Institute of Judicial Administration 26 Aug 69

9 What most impresses us about great jurists is not their tenacious grasps of fine points, honed almost to invisibility; it is the moment when we are suddenly aware of the sweep and direction of the law, and its place in the lives of men.
ib

10 No other profession is subject to the public contempt and derision that sometimes befalls lawyers. . . . the bitter fruit of public incomprehension of the law itself and its dynamics.
Quoted in San Francisco *Examiner & Chronicle* 17 Apr 77

11 The judge is forced for the most part to reach his audience through the medium of the press whose reporting of judicial decisions is all too often inaccurate and superficial.
ib

12 Courtrooms contain every symbol of authority that a set designer could imagine. Everyone stands up when you come in. You wear a costume identifying you as, if not quite divine, someone special.
Time 5 May 80

13 The judicial system is the most expensive machine ever invented for finding out what happened and what to do about it.
ib

14 The ideal is to have the losing party feel that he is not the victim of the judge, but simply the object of a profession that is the same for all.
ib

15 The [Supreme] Court's only armor is the cloak of public trust; its sole ammunition, the collective hopes of our society.
"Keeping Politics out of the Court" NY *Times* 9 Dec 84

ROBERT F KENNEDY, US Attorney General

16 I'm tired of chasing people.
On plans to pursue other interests after more than a decade as a criminal investigator, counsel and public official, NY *Times* 6 May 64

MARTIN LUTHER KING JR

17 It may be true that the law cannot make a man love me, but it can keep him from lynching me, and I think that's pretty important.
Wall Street Journal 13 Nov 62

18 An individual who breaks a law that conscience tells him is unjust, and who willingly accepts the penalty of imprisonment in order to arouse the conscience of the community over its injustice, is in reality expressing the highest respect for the law.
Why We Can't Wait Harper & Row 64

PAUL H KING, Judge, District Court, Dorchester MA

19 The police are not going to run this court. The defendants are not going to run this court. The defense attorneys are not going to run this court. The district attorney is not going to run this court. I'm going to run this court.
Reaction to 50 off-duty police officers who protested his bail procedures in 1980, Boston *Globe* 14 Nov 86

EDWARD KOCH, Mayor of NYC

20 If you seek violence, we will seek to put you in jail.
To labor and management in hotel dispute, NY *Times* 2 Jun 85

21 You don't have to love them. You just have to respect their rights.
On signing law barring discrimination on basis of sexual orientation, *US News & World Report* 14 Apr 86

STEVEN KUMBLE

22 The key thing that makes national law firms work is synergy; with the right combination, one and one can make three.
NY *Times* 4 Oct 84

JEROME KURTZ, former Commissioner, Internal Revenue Service

1 If a person is an economic being and figures out the odds, then there is a very high incentive to cheat. That is, of course, putting aside honor, duty and patriotism.

Wall Street Journal 10 Apr 84

RUSSELL R LEGGETT, Judge, Westchester County Court

2 You will be judges of the fact. You are the sole and exclusive judges of what the truth is. You will bring with you here your common sense.

To prospective jurors in murder trial of Jean Harris for the death of Dr Herman Tarnower, quoted in her book *Stranger in Two Worlds* Macmillan 86

3 Your verdict will be "Guilty" or "Not Guilty." Your job is not to find innocence.

ib

LEE LOEVINGER

4 Too much may be the equivalent of none at all.

Lecture at NY University warning that legal apparatus may collapse from its own weight, news summaries 16 Dec 78

PAUL LOMBARD

5 A deceased man has the right to breathe life into the womb of his wife and prove that love is stronger than death.

Argument on behalf of a woman who sought to obtain sperm deposited at a sperm bank by her husband prior to his death, NY *Times* 2 Aug 84

JONATHAN LUBELL

6 Given the state of libel law, whenever a public figure gets to face a jury, it is a victory.

On representing Lt Col Anthony Herbert in unsuccessful libel suit against CBS TV, similar to action brought by Gen William C Westmoreland, *Time* 22 Oct 84

MICHAEL MAGGIO

7 All you can do is to say three Hail Marys and three Our Fathers and throw the letters in. God will play a larger role in this than a lawyer.

Filing visa applications made under special provision for citizens of countries showing decrease in immigration to the US, NY *Times* 22 Jan 87

DAVID MARGOLICK

8 He takes hundreds of recent law graduates at their most vulnerable, dependent state and guides them, soothes them, suffers with them, flatters them, advises them, exhorts them, humors them and holds their hands over the last hurdle before they enter the practice of law.

On eight-week course offered by John M Pieper to students preparing for NY State bar exams, NY *Times* 16 Jul 84

MICHELLE TRIOLA MARVIN

9 If a man wants to leave a toothbrush at my house, he can damn well marry me.

On winning $104,000 California Superior Court case against common-law husband Lee Marvin, a decision regarded as a precedent for reciprocal property rights of unwed couples, NY *Times* 19 Apr 79

PHYLLIS MCGINLEY

10 When blithe to argument I come,
   Though armed with facts, and merry,
May Providence protect me from
   The fool as adversary,
Whose mind to him a kingdom is
   Where reason lacks dominion,
Who calls conviction prejudice
   And prejudice opinion.

"Moody Reflections" in *Times Three: Selected Verse from Three Decades* Viking 60

EDWIN MEESE 3RD, US Attorney General

11 [A Supreme Court] decision does not establish a "supreme law of the land" that is binding on all persons and parts of government, henceforth and forevermore.

Address at Tulane University, quoted in NY *Times* 23 Oct 86

12 The implication that everyone would have to accept its judgments uncritically, that it was a decision from which there could be no appeal, was astonishing.

On Supreme Court's assertion in 1958 that its earlier ruling requiring desegregation established "the supreme law of the land," *ib*

DAVID MELINKOFF, Professor of Law, UCLA

13 Lawyers as a group are no more dedicated to justice or public service than a private public utility is dedicated to giving light.

San Francisco *Examiner & Chronicle* 22 Jun 73

MURRAY MEYERSON

14 Just think of the pleasure it would give a wealthy man to cut off his free-spending brother, then to explain it all in living color.

On videotaped wills, *International Herald Tribune* 16 May 79

HENRY G MILLER, President, NY State Bar Assn

15 The legal system is often a mystery, and we, its priests, preside over rituals baffling to everyday citizens.

"The Lawyer is Number 2, Not Number 1" NY *Times* 26 Jan 85

NEWTON MINOW

16 In Germany, under the law everything is prohibited except that which is permitted. In France, under the law everything is permitted except that which is prohibited. In the Soviet Union, everything is prohibited, including that which is permitted. And in Italy, under the law everything is permitted, especially that which is prohibited.

On his comparative study of legal systems, *Time* 18 Mar 85

HOYT A MOORE

17 No one is under pressure. There wasn't a light on when I left at 2 o'clock this morning.

Quoted by a partner in his Manhattan law firm, Cravath, Swaine & Moore, *Time* 24 Jun 64

ROBERT MORGENTHAU, District Attorney, NYC

18 I would rather have my fate in the hands of 23 representative citizens of the county than in the hands of a politically appointed judge.

Defending secrecy of grand jury proceedings, *Time* 8 Apr 85

PETER MORRISON

1 I don't know of any other industry, except the movie business, that has so many stars. Every lawyer thinks he's special.
> NY *Times* 26 Nov 84

FRANCIS T MURPHY, President, Federation of NY State Judges

2 Society is pressed to its ancient defense against the violent criminal: the fear of swift and severe punishment. Either we take that road now, or we will live in the sickly twilight of a soulless people too weak to drive predators out of their own house.
> Calling on fellow judges to sentence anyone convicted of a serious crime, regardless of insufficient space in jails, NY *Times* 23 Apr 84

3 No more essential duty of government exists than the protection of the lives of its people. Fail in this, and we fail in everything.
> *Harper's* Jul 84

JON NEWMAN, Judge, US Court of Appeals, 2nd Circuit

4 [American liberty] is premised on the accountability of free men and women for what they have done, not for what they may do.
> On unconstitutionality of preventive detention, quoted in editorial "Fat Tony and the Bail Principle" NY *Times* 29 Nov 86

NEWSWEEK

5 Getting excused from jury duty without sufficient reason amounts to thumbing your nose at a distressed neighbor and at the most effective friend a free man ever had, the American courts.
> Public-service advertisement 24 Aug 64

6 It's called jury *duty*, not jury inconvenience. It is an obligation, not an interruption.
> *ib*

NEW YORK TIMES

7 They like to be seen wearing the robes of judicial restraint.
> Editorial on conservatism of Supreme Court Justices Warren E Burger, William H Rehnquist and Lewis F Powell Jr, "Good Old Federalism" 21 Feb 85

8 The Supreme Court does not deny them power; it says only that they should swing the bat in the legislative arena instead of the courts.
> On states' rights, *ib*

ROBERT N C NIX

9 Be prepared, be sharp, be careful, and use the King's English well. And you can forget all the [other rules] unless you remember one more: Get paid.
> Advice to young lawyers, recalled on inauguration of his son Robert N C Nix Jr as Chief Justice of Pennsylvania, NY *Times* 7 Jan 84

RICHARD M NIXON, 37th US President

10 Our chief justices have probably had more profound and lasting influence on their times and on the direction of the nation than most presidents.
> On appointment of Warren E Burger as Chief Justice of US Supreme Court, 21 May 69

LOUIS NIZER

11 When a man points a finger at someone else, he should remember that four of his fingers are pointing at himself.
> *My Life in Court* Doubleday 62

12 I know of no higher fortitude than stubborness in the face of overwhelming odds.
> *ib*

13 [Preparation] is the be-all of good trial work. Everything else—felicity of expression, improvisational brilliance—is a satellite around the sun. Thorough preparation is that sun.
> *Newsweek* 11 Dec 78

14 Yes, there's such a thing as luck in trial law but it only comes at 3 o'clock in the morning. . . . You'll still find me in the library looking for luck at 3 o'clock in the morning.
> *Reader's Digest* Oct 84

SANDRA DAY O'CONNOR, Associate Justice, US Supreme Court

15 My hope is that 10 years from now, after I've been across the street at work for a while, they'll all be glad they gave me that wonderful vote.
> On being confirmed unanimously by US Senate 21 Sep 81

STEWART ONEGLIA, US Department of Justice

16 [They are] social pariahs, irrationally ostracized by their communities because of medically baseless fears of contagion.
> On civil rights of AIDS patients, NY *Times* 26 Jun 86

PAUL O'NEIL

17 A criminal lawyer, like a trapeze performer, is seldom more than one slip from an awful fall.
> On attorney Edward Bennett Williams, *Life* 22 Jun 59

18 No splints yet invented will heal a lawyer's broken reputation.
> *ib*

JOSÉ ORTEGA Y GASSET

19 Law is born from despair of human nature.
> Recalled on his death 18 Oct 55

MARGUERITE OSWALD

20 This young man—whether he's my son or a stranger—repeatedly declares, "I didn't do it, I didn't do it." And he's shot down. That's not the American way of life. A man is innocent until he's proved guilty.
> On death of her son Lee Harvey Oswald less than 48 hours after the assassination of President John F Kennedy, NY *Post* 19 Feb 64

EDWARD PACKARD JR

21 Law students are trained in the case method, and to the lawyer everything in life looks like a case.
> *Columbia Forum* Spring 67

22 The lawyer's first thought in the morning is how to handle the case of the ringing alarm clock.
> *ib*

ROSA PARKS

1 All I was doing was trying to get home from work.

> On her refusal to move to the back of a bus, an action leading to a boycott in Birmingham AL that sparked the civil-rights movement, recalled on 30th anniversary of her arrest, NBC TV 1 Dec 85

REGINALD WITHERS PAYNE, Judge of the High Court

2 The difficulty about a gentlemen's agreement is that it depends on the continued existence of the gentlemen.

> NY *Times* 9 Feb 64

ROSCOE POUND, Dean Emeritus, Harvard Law School

3 Law is experience developed by reason and applied continually to further experience.

> *Christian Science Monitor* 24 Apr 63

4 Law must be stable, and yet it cannot stand still.

> Quoted by Kenneth R Redden and Enid L Veron *Modern Legal Glossary* Michie 80

LEWIS F POWELL JR, Associate Justice, US Supreme Court

5 I go onto the Court with deep personal misgivings whether I'll like it. In fact, I rather suppose I won't. . . . but it has a very special place in the life and attitude of any lawyer of my age, and for those of my generation it is a revered institution, the pinnacle of our profession.

> Washington *Post* 24 Oct 71

6 For the most part . . . we function as nine small independent law firms.

> NY *Times* 9 Dec 84

THOMAS REED POWELL

7 If you think that you can think about a thing, inextricably attached to something else, without thinking of the thing it is attached to, then you have a legal mind.

> Recalled on his death 16 Aug 55

PETER S PRESCOTT

8 Political crimes. . . . leap forth [from the courtroom], teeth bared, threatening the tranquillity of the republic, and the people fall on them with great gnashings and groanings.

> On continuing interest in 1950 perjury conviction of Alger Hiss, *Newsweek* 3 Apr 78

ANNA QUINDLEN

9 Night court is to the usual courtroom administration of justice what madras is to white oxford cloth.

> NY *Times* 24 Apr 82

JANE BRYANT QUINN

10 Lawyers [are] operators of the toll bridge across which anyone in search of justice has to pass.

> *Newsweek* 9 Oct 78

RONALD REAGAN, 40th US President

11 State problems should involve state solutions.

> Restating a well-known viewpoint while at the same time supporting a federal law that would establish a national minimum age for drinking, address at Oradell NJ 20 Jun 84

WILLIAM H REHNQUIST, Associate Justice, US Supreme Court

12 The Supreme Court is an institution far more dominated by centrifugal forces, pushing toward individuality and independence, than it is by centripetal forces pulling for hierarchical ordering and institutional unity.

> Address at University of Minnesota Law School, NY *Times* 20 Oct 84

13 Somewhere "out there," beyond the walls of the courthouse, run currents and tides of public opinion which lap at the courtroom door.

> Address at Suffolk University Law School, Boston, *ib* 17 Apr 86

GEORGE RHYNE, World Conference on World Peace through Law

14 What we lawyers want to do is to substitute courts for carnage, dockets for rockets, briefs for bombs, warrants for warheads, mandates for missiles.

> *Wall Street Journal* 27 Jun 63

JOHN ROBERTSON, Professor of Law, University of Texas

15 Hiring a surrogate mother can be viewed as part of a constitutional right of married couples to reproduce.

> NY *Times* 6 Oct 86

SOLLY ROBINS

16 We pioneered the field of catastrophe law.

> On representing the government of India in negligence suit against Union Carbide Corp for industrial disaster at Bhopal, NY *Times* 12 Mar 85

FRED RODELL, Professor of Law, Yale

17 [The law is like the killy-loo bird, a creature that] insisted on flying backward because it didn't care where it was going but was mightily interested in where it had been.

> NY *Times* 27 Jun 84

RICHARD ROME, Kansas magistrate

18 From her ancient profession she's been busted,
And to society's rules she must be adjusted,
If from all this a moral doth unfurl,
It's that pimps do not protect the working girl.

> On prostitution conviction that drew disapproval from feminist groups, *National Observer* 4 Oct 75

BERTRAND RUSSELL

19 Obscenity is whatever happens to shock some elderly and ignorant magistrate.

> *Look* 23 Feb 54

20 What is new in our time is the increased power of the authorities to enforce their prejudices.

> Quoted on *Who Said That?* BBC TV 8 Aug 58

CARL SANDBURG

21 Why is there always a secret singing when a lawyer cashes in? Why does a hearse horse snicker hauling a lawyer away?

> Quoted in NY *Times* 13 Jan 85

ANTONIN SCALIA, Associate Justice, US Supreme Court

22 [The Freedom of Information Act is] the Taj Mahal of the Doctrine of Unanticipated Consequences, the

Sistine Chapel of Cost-Benefit Analysis Ignored.
> Recalled on his appointment to Supreme Court, *Time* 30 Jun 86

LESLIE SCARMAN

1 Law reform is far too serious a matter to be left to the legal profession.
> To NYC Bar Assn, *Record* Jan 55

ROBERT SCHMITT

2 The average lawyer is essentially a mechanic who works with a pen instead of a ball peen hammer.
> *Americans for Legal Reform Newsletter* Spring 84

IRVING S SHAPIRO, Chairman, E I du Pont de Nemours

3 Litigation should be a last resort, not a knee-jerk reflex.
> *Christian Science Monitor* 5 Dec 78

ARIEL SHARON, former Defense Minister of Israel

4 A lie . . . should be tried in a place where it will attract the attention of the world.
> On bringing libel suit against *Time* magazine in NYC, NY *Times* 20 Nov 84

JOHN J SIRICA, Judge, US District Court, District of Columbia

5 In all candor, the Court fails to perceive any reason for suspending the power of courts to get evidence and rule on questions of privilege in criminal matters simply because it is the president of the United States who holds the evidence.
> Statement on obtaining Watergate tapes from President Richard M Nixon, *Christian Science Monitor* 15 Sep 74

JAMES SISSERSON

6 [It's] like suing God in the Vatican.
> On chances of a Florida court ruling against Walt Disney Productions, *Time* 11 May 85

ELIOT DUNLAP SMITH

7 The law is the only profession which records its mistakes carefully, exactly as they occurred, and yet does not identify them as mistakes.
> Quoted by Louis Brown "Legal Autopsy" Amer Judicial Society *Journal* Nov 54

SMITHTOWN NY TOWN BOARD

8 Unhealthy noise shall include, but not be limited to, that noise created by a dog barking for fifteen (15) continuous minutes.
> Amendment to noise ordinance, NY *Times* 23 Aug 84

ALEXANDER SOLZHENITSYN

9 I have spent all my life under a Communist regime, and I will tell you that a society without any objective legal scale is a terrible one indeed. But a society with no other scale but the legal one is not quite worthy of man either.
> Commencement address at Harvard 8 Jun 78

JOHN STERLING

10 [The] ideal client is the very wealthy man in very great trouble.
> "Lawyers and the Laws of Economics" *ABA Journal* Apr 60

ADLAI E STEVENSON

11 I think that one of the most fundamental responsibilities . . . is to give testimony in a court of law, to give it honestly and willingly.
> When asked why he had signed an affidavit supporting Alger Hiss after his conviction for perjury, recalled on Stevenson's death 14 Jul 65

12 Law is not a profession at all, but rather a business service station and repair shop.
> *The Papers of Adlai Stevenson* Little, Brown 72

POTTER STEWART, Associate Justice, US Supreme Court

13 Swift justice demands more than just swiftness.
> *Time* 20 Oct 58

14 Fairness is what justice really is.
> *ib*

LLOYD PAUL STRYKER

15 A trial is still an ordeal by battle. For the broadsword there is the weight of evidence; for the battle-ax the force of logic; for the sharp spear, the blazing gleam of truth; for the rapier, the quick and flashing knife of wit.
> Recalled on his death 21 Jun 55

16 Trying a case the second time is like eating yesterday morning's oatmeal.
> *ib*

17 A tendency toward enthusiasm and a chivalrous instinct have more than once been weighed as evidence of a lack of judgment.
> *ib*

BRENDAN J SULLIVAN JR

18 I'm not a potted plant. I'm here as the lawyer. That's my job.
> On being told to allow his client Lt Col Oliver L North to object for himself if he wished to do so, at Iran-Contra hearings 9 Jul 87

GLEN TATHAM, Zimbabwe park warden

19 To kill a man for shooting an animal is a very delicate matter.
> On executions of poachers of rare Zimbabwe valley rhinoceros, NY *Times* 6 May 86

TIME MAGAZINE

20 Late every night in Connecticut, lights go out in the cities and towns, and citizens by tens of thousands proceed zestfully to break the law.
> On Connecticut law against contraceptives, 10 Mar 61

21 Of course, there is always a witness to the crime—but as though to make the law completely unenforceable, Connecticut forbids spouses from testifying against one another.
> *ib*

HARRY S TRUMAN, 33rd US President

22 Whenever you put a man on the Supreme Court he ceases to be your friend.
> Recalled on his 75th birthday, NY *Times* 8 May 59

JOHN TURNER, Attorney General of Canada

23 Substantive and procedural law benefits and protects landlords over tenants, creditors over debtors,

lenders over borrowers, and the poor are seldom among the favored parties.
> To Canadian Bar Assn 7 Dec 69

MORRIS K UDALL, US Congressman

1 One puts on black robes to scare the hell out of white people, while the other puts on white robes to scare the hell out of blacks.
> Contrasting US Supreme Court justices and Ku Klux Klan members, Washington Gridiron Club dinner 27 Mar 82

GORE VIDAL

2 Litigation takes the place of sex at middle age.
> Quoted by Kenneth R Redden and Enid L Veron *Modern Legal Glossary* Michie 80

SOL WACHTLER, Judge, NY State Court of Appeals

3 You can, if you wish, think of it like the universe: Each case is a sun, and all the judges, lawyers and administrative personnel represent planets revolving around the case in fixed orbit, never getting closer.
> NY *Times* 22 Apr 85

JOYCE WADLER

4 [He was] a lawyer who usually operated with the delicacy of a Lexington Avenue express train.
> On Thomas Puccio, defense counsel in trial of Claus von Bülow, accused of attempting to murder his wife, *New York* 3 Jun 85

EARL WARREN, Chief Justice, US Supreme Court

5 In civilized life, law floats in a sea of ethics.
> NY *Times* 12 Nov 62

6 The man of character, sensitive to the meaning of what he is doing, will know how to discover the ethical paths in the maze of possible behavior.
> Quoted in editorial on moral codes, *Christian Science Monitor* 21 May 64

7 The police must obey the law while enforcing the law.
> Condemning use of involuntary confessions, quoted in Milwaukee *Journal* 20 Sep 64

8 You sit up there, and you see the whole gamut of human nature. Even if the case being argued involves only a little fellow and $50, it involves justice. That's what is important.
> Recalled on his death, *Time* 22 Jul 74

9 If Nixon is not forced to turn over tapes of his conversations with the ring of men who were conversing on their violations of the law, then liberty will soon be dead in this nation.
> Quoted by William O Douglas *The Court Years 1939–75* Random House 80

10 The old Court you and I served so long will not be worthy of its traditions if Nixon can twist, turn and fashion . . . If Nixon gets away with that, then Nixon makes the law as he goes along—not the Congress nor the courts.
> *ib*

HERMAN WEINKRANTZ, Judge, NYC Criminal Court

11 This court will not deny the equal protection of the law to the unwashed, unshod, unkempt and uninhibited.
> Ruling that disapproval of hippies would not interfere with their civil rights, NY *Times* 1 Jul 68

BYRON R WHITE, Associate Justice, US Supreme Court

12 We're the only branch of government that explains itself in writing every time it makes a decision.
> *Time* 8 Oct 84

MARY BETH WHITEHEAD

13 [He considers me] just a uterus with legs.
> On NJ Superior Court Judge Harvey R Sorkow, who denied her the right to rear the child she had conceived as a surrogate mother, NY *Times* 8 Apr 87

HARRISON A WILLIAMS JR, former US Senator

14 A "dishonest crime" is when somebody else creates the situation for which you are convicted.
> On his prison sentence for accepting illegal funds, WNET TV 15 Jan 86

DOROTHY WRIGHT WILSON, Dean, University of Southern California Law Center

15 If criminals wanted to grind justice to a halt, they could do it by banding together and all pleading not guilty.
> On plea-bargaining and the criminal justice system, LA *Times* 11 Aug 74

JAMES Q WILSON, Professor of Government, Harvard

16 Arresting a single drunk or a single vagrant who has harmed no identifiable person seems unjust, and in a sense it is. But failing to do anything about a score of drunks or a hundred vagrants may destroy an entire community.
> *Thinking about Crime* Random House 77, quoted in *Time* 11 Mar 85

LORD WOLFENDEN (John Frederick Wolfenden), Chair, Committee on Homosexual Offenses and Prostitution

17 Homosexual behavior between consenting adults in private should no longer be a criminal offense.
> *Wolfenden Report*, issued by Her Majesty's Stationers 5 Sep 57

EVELLE J YOUNGER, Attorney General of California

18 An incompetent attorney can delay a trial for years or months. A competent attorney can delay one even longer.
> LA *Times* 3 Mar 71

FRANKLIN E ZIMRING, Professor of Law, University of Chicago

19 Because of plea-bargaining, I guess we can say, "Gee, the trains run on time." But do we like where they are going?
> *Time* 28 Aug 78

Judicial Opinions

SIDNEY H ASCH, Judge, NY State Supreme Court, Appellate Division

20 Where sexual proclivity does not relate to job function, it seems clearly unconstitutional to penalize an individual in one of the most imperative of life's endeavors, the right to earn one's daily bread.
> Majority opinion in 3–1 ruling that upheld municipal authority to bar private agencies from discrimination on the basis of sexual orientation, 7 May 85

MARIANNE O BATTANI, Judge, Wayne County Circuit Court, Detroit

1 We really have no definition of *mother* in our lawbooks. *Mother* was believed to have been so basic that no definition was deemed necessary.

> Ruling that the biological mother of an infant conceived outside the womb is the "true" mother as opposed to the woman who carries the child to term, 14 Mar 86

DAVID L BAZELON, Judge, US Court of Appeals, District of Columbia Circuit

2 The majority decision constitutionalizes a distinction between a red leather pouch and a paper bag that is necessarily based at least in some part on economic and class differences and perceptions.

> Dissenting opinion in 2–1 ruling that recognized luggage but not paper bags as a personal sanctuary, 17 Apr 80

3 In some of our subcultures, paper bags are often used to carry intimate personal belongings. And the sight of some of our less fortunate citizens carrying their belongings in brown paper bags is too familiar to permit such crass biases to diminish protection of privacy.

> *ib*

HUGO L BLACK, Associate Justice, US Supreme Court

4 Criticism of government finds sanctuary in several portions of the 1st Amendment. It is part of the right of free speech. It embraces freedom of the press.

> Dissenting opinion in 6–3 ruling that forbade a person summoned before a Congressional committee to refuse to answer the question, "Are you a member of the Communist Party?" 27 Feb 61

5 I was brought up to believe that Scotch whisky would need a tax preference to survive in competition with Kentucky bourbon.

> Dissenting opinion in 6–2 ruling that limited power of states to tax and restrict the liquor business, 1 Jun 64

6 Recalling that it is a Constitution intended to endure for ages to come, we also remember that the Founders wisely provided the means for that endurance: Changes in the Constitution, when thought necessary, are to be proposed by Congress or conventions and ratified by the states. The Founders gave no such amending power to this Court.

> Dissenting opinion in 6–3 ruling that prohibited racial discrimination in restaurants, 22 Jun 64

7 Our Constitution was not written in the sands to be washed away by each wave of new judges blown in by each successive political wind.

> Dissenting opinion in 6–2 ruling that upheld federal law making possession of heroin sufficient evidence of illegal importation of drugs, 20 Jan 70

8 The flagrant disregard in the courtroom of elementary standards of proper conduct should not and cannot be tolerated.

> Unanimous opinion that a disorderly defendant may forfeit his constitutional right to be present in court, NY *Times* 1 Apr 70

9 We believe trial judges confronted with disruptive, contumacious, stubbornly defiant defendants must be given sufficient discretion to meet the circumstances in each case.

> *ib*

10 It would degrade our country and our judicial system to permit our courts to be bullied, insulted and humiliated and the orderly progress thwarted and obstructed by defendants brought before them charged with crimes.

> *ib*

11 Paramount among the responsibilities of a free press is the duty to prevent any part of the government from deceiving the people and sending them off to distant lands to die of foreign fevers and foreign shot and shell.

> Concurring opinion in 6–3 ruling that upheld the press's right to publish the Pentagon Papers, 30 Jun 71

12 In my view, far from deserving condemnation for their courageous reporting, the New York *Times*, the Washington *Post* and other newspapers should be commended for serving the purpose that the Founding Fathers saw so clearly.

> *ib*

13 In revealing the workings of government that led to the Vietnam War, the newspapers nobly did precisely that which the Founders hoped and trusted they would do.

> *ib*

HARRY A BLACKMUN, Associate Justice, US Supreme Court

14 The states are not free, under the guise of protecting maternal health or potential life, to intimidate women into continuing pregnancies.

> Majority opinion in 7–2 ruling that established the constitutional legality of abortion, 22 Jan 73

15 The mandated description of fetal characteristics at two-week intervals, no matter how objective, is plainly overinclusive. [It is] not medical information that is always relevant to the woman's decision, and it may serve to confuse and punish her and to heighten her anxiety.

> *ib*

16 Controversy over the meaning of our nation's most majestic guarantees frequently has been turbulent. . . . Abortion raises moral and spiritual questions over which honorable persons can disagree sincerely and profoundly. But those disagreements did not then and do not now relieve us of our duty to apply the Constitution faithfully.

> *ib*

17 If there is any truth to the old proverb that "one who is his own lawyer has a fool for a client," the Court . . . now bestows a *constitutional* right on one to make a fool of himself.

> Dissenting opinion in 6–3 ruling that allowed a defendant to refuse counsel, 30 Jun 75

18 The flaw in the statute [is] that in all its applications, it operates on a fundamentally mistaken premise that high solicitation costs are an accurate measure of fraud.

> Majority opinion in 5–4 ruling that struck down a Maryland statute regulating how much charities may spend on fund raising, 26 Jun 84

19 By placing discretion in the hands of an official to grant or deny a license, such a statute creates a threat of censorship that by its very existence chills free speech.

> *ib*

1 What the Court really has refused to recognize is the fundamental interest all individuals have in controlling the nature of their intimate associations.

> Dissenting opinion in 5–4 ruling that upheld the right to prohibit deviant sexual behavior, 30 Jun 86

2 The right of an individual to conduct intimate relationships in the intimacy of his or her own home seems to me to be the heart of the Constitution's protection of privacy.

> ib

3 It is precisely because the issue raised by this case touches the heart of what makes individuals what they are that we should be especially sensitive to the rights of those whose choices upset the majority.

> ib

4 [Disapproval of homosexuality cannot justify] invading the houses, hearts and minds of citizens who choose to live their lives differently.

> ib

ROBERT H BORK, Judge, US Court of Appeals, District of Columbia Circuit

5 By depriving the charged person of any defenses [the rulings] mean that sexual dalliance, however voluntarily engaged in, becomes harassment whenever an employee sees fit, after the fact, so to characterize it.

> Dissenting opinion in 7–3 ruling that held employers responsible for sexual harassment of one employee by another, 14 May 85

WILLIAM J BRENNAN, Associate Justice, US Supreme Court

6 Sex and obscenity are not synonymous. Obscene material is material which deals with sex in a manner appealing to prurient interest.

> Dissenting opinion in 5–4 ruling that established a new legal standard for obscenity, 24 Jun 57

7 Sex, a great and mysterious motive force in human life, has indisputably been a subject of absorbing interest to mankind through the ages.

> ib

8 We hold that the Constitution does not forbid the states minor intrusions into an individual's body under stringently limited conditions.

> Majority opinion in 5–4 ruling that blood tests of drunken drivers do not constitute self-incriminating evidence, 20 Jun 66

9 This Court inescapably has the duty, as the ultimate arbiter of the meaning of our Constitution, to say whether, when individuals condemned to death stand before our bar, "moral concepts" require us to hold that the law has progressed to the point where we should declare that the punishment of death, like punishments on the rack, the screw and the wheel, is no longer morally tolerable in our society.

> Dissenting opinion in 7–2 ruling that upheld the death penalty, 2 Jul 76

10 Death is not only an unusually severe punishment, unusual in its pain, in its finality and in its enormity, but it serves no penal purpose more effectively than a less severe punishment; therefore the principle inherent in the clause that prohibits pointless infliction of excessive punishment when less severe punishment can adequately achieve the same purposes invalidates the punishment.

> ib

11 Appellant constituted a legitimate class of one, and this provides a basis for Congress's decision to proceed with dispatch with respect to his materials.

> Majority opinion in 7–2 ruling that upheld Congressional seizure of Richard M Nixon's presidential papers, 28 Jun 77

12 We cannot . . . let colorblindness become myopia which masks the reality that many "created equal" have been treated within our lifetimes as inferior both by the law and by their fellow citizens.

> Dissenting opinion in 5–4 ruling in the Bakke case that prohibited racial quotas in university admissions policies, 28 Jun 78

13 No longer is the female destined solely for the home and the rearing of the family and only the male for the marketplace and the world of ideas.

> Majority opinion in 6–3 ruling that laws barring alimony for men are unconstitutional, 5 Mar 79

14 It would be ironic indeed if a law triggered by a nation's concern over centuries of racial injustice and intended to improve the lot of those who had "been excluded from the American dream for so long" constituted the first legislative prohibition of all voluntary, private, race-conscious efforts to abolish traditional patterns of racial segregation and hierarchy.

> Majority opinion in 5–2 ruling that a training program reserving places for blacks did not constitute illegal reverse discrimination, 27 Jun 79

15 It is difficult to understand precisely what the state hopes to achieve by promoting the creation and perpetuation of a subclass of illiterates within our boundaries, surely adding to the problems and costs of unemployment, welfare and crime. It is thus clear that whatever savings might be achieved by denying these children an education, they are wholly insubstantial in light of the costs involved to these children, the state and the nation.

> Majority opinion in 5–4 ruling that young illegal aliens have a constitutional right to public schooling, 15 Jun 82

16 Use of a mentally ill person's involuntary confession is antithetical to the notion of fundamental fairness embodied in the due process clause.

> Dissenting opinion in 7–2 ruling that confessions from the mentally ill may be used against them even if those confessions are not the product of free will, 10 Dec 86

17 Congress acknowledged that society's accumulated myths and fears about disability and disease are as handicapping as are the physical limitations that flow from actual impairment.

> Majority opinion in 7–2 ruling that people with contagious diseases are covered by law that prohibits discrimination against the handicapped in federally aided programs, 3 Mar 87

WARREN E BURGER, Chief Justice, US Supreme Court

18 It is indeed an odd business that it has taken this Court nearly two centuries to "discover" a constitutional mandate to have counsel at a preliminary hearing.

> Dissenting opinion in 6–2 ruling that declared right of the accused to court-appointed counsel at pretrial hearings, 22 Jun 70

1 There can be no assumption that today's majority is "right" and the Amish and others like them are "wrong." A way of life that is odd or even erratic but interferes with no rights or interests of others is not to be condemned because it is different.

> Majority opinion in 6–1 ruling that freed members of religious sects from compulsory school attendance, 15 May 72

2 For better or worse, editing is what editors are for; and editing is selection and choice of material. That editors—newspaper or broadcast—can and do abuse this power is beyond doubt, but that is no reason to deny the discretion Congress provided.

> Majority opinion in 7–2 ruling that allowed radio and television stations to refuse to sell time for political or controversial advertisements, 29 May 73

3 Calculated risks of abuse are taken in order to preserve higher values.

> ib

4 The president's need for complete candor and objectivity from advisers calls for great deference from the courts.

> Unanimous opinion on the Nixon tapes that ruled the needs of the judicial process may outweigh presidential privilege, 24 Jul 74

5 However, when the privilege depends solely on the broad, undifferentiated claim of public interest in the confidentiality of such conversations, a confrontation with other values arises.

> ib

6 Free speech carries with it some freedom to listen.

> Majority opinion in 7–1 ruling that prohibited the closing of courtrooms to the press, 2 Jul 80

7 We reject the contention that in the remedial context the Congress must act in a wholly "colorblind" fashion. . . . It is fundamental that in no organ of government, state or federal, does there repose a more comprehensive remedial power than in the Congress, expressly charged by the Constitution with competence and authority to enforce equal protection guarantees.

> Majority opinion in 6–3 ruling that upheld a federal law allotting 10 percent of public works contracts to minority businesses, ib

8 There can be no doubt that the practice of opening legislative sessions with prayer has become part of the fabric of our society.

> Majority opinion in 6–3 ruling that both Congress and state legislatures may pay a chaplain to open sessions with prayer, 5 Jul 83

9 Respondent's expectation that his garden was protected from observation is unreasonable and is not an expectation that society is prepared to honor.

> Majority opinion in 5–4 ruling that upheld aerial surveillance without a warrant of a fenced backyard where police suspected marijuana was being grown, 19 May 86

10 We may have lured judges into roaming at large in the constitutional field.

> Dissenting opinion in 5–4 ruling that reaffirmed opinion establishing constitutional right to abortion, 11 Jun 86

11 To hold that the act of homosexual sodomy is somehow protected as a fundamental right would be to cast aside millennia of moral teaching.

> Concurring opinion in 5–4 ruling that upheld the right to prohibit deviant sexual behavior, 30 Jun 86

CANADIAN SUPREME COURT

12 Kneeling to receive Communion is not a criminal offense.

> Ruling against arrest of Roman Catholics in Nova Scotia for "disturbing the solemnity of a church service" by refusing to follow new directive to stand while receiving the Eucharist, news summaries 30 Sep 85

TOM C CLARK, Associate Justice, US Supreme Court

13 In the relationship between man and religion, the state is firmly committed to a position of neutrality.

> Majority opinion in 8–1 ruling that religious exercises in public schools are unconstitutional, 17 Jun 63

14 To so interpret the language of the act is to extract more sunbeams from cucumbers than did Gulliver's mad scientist.

> Dissenting opinion in 7–2 ruling that upheld the constitutionality of loyalty oaths, 1 Jun 64

15 To conjure up such ridiculous questions, the answers to which we all know or should know are in the negative, is to build up a whimsical and farcical straw man which is not only grim but Grimm.

> ib

16 A defendant on trial for a specific crime is entitled to his day in court, not in a stadium or a city or nationwide arena.

> Majority opinion in 5–4 ruling that the principles of a fair trial are violated when telecasting is allowed, 7 Jun 65

17 The heightened public clamor resulting from radio and television coverage will inevitably result in prejudice. Trial by television is, therefore, foreign to our system.

> ib

LYNN COMPTON, Judge, California Court of Appeals, 2nd District

18 Whatever choice Elizabeth Bouvia may ultimately make, I can only hope that her courage, persistence and example will cause our society to deal realistically with the plight of those unfortunate individuals to whom death beckons as a welcome respite from suffering.

> Unanimous opinion that the right to refuse medical treatment is basic and fundamental in the case of a quadriplegic cerebral palsy victim who requested she not be force-fed, 16 Apr 86

LAWRENCE H COOKE, Judge, NY State Court of Appeals

19 Ordinarily, death will be determined according to the traditional criteria of irreversible cardiorespiratory repose. When, however, the respiratory and circulatory functions are maintained by mechanical means, their significance, as signs of life, is at best ambiguous.

> Unanimous opinion that a person may be deemed legally dead when the brain has ceased to function, even if heartbeat and breathing are being maintained artificially, 30 Oct 84

RICHARD L CURRY, Judge, Cook County Circuit Court, Chicago

20 The scheme which has major-league baseball trashing a residential community and tinkering with the quality-of-life aspirations of countless households so

that television royalties might more easily flow into the coffers of 25 distant sports moguls is not consonant with present-day concepts of right and justice.

> Supporting citizens' protest against night baseball at Chicago's Wrigley Field, 25 Mar 85

WILLIAM O DOUGLAS, Associate Justice, US Supreme Court

1 We do not sit as a superlegislature to weigh the wisdom of legislation.

> Majority opinion in 8–1 ruling that upheld right of states to legislate internal affairs, 3 Mar 52

2 We are a religious people whose institutions presuppose a Supreme Being.

> Majority opinion in 6–3 ruling that allowed release of public school students for religious instruction, 28 Apr 52

3 The right to be let alone is indeed the beginning of all freedoms.

> Dissenting opinion in 7–1 ruling that allowed radios to be played on streetcars, 26 May 52

4 The critical point is that the Constitution places the right of silence beyond the reach of government.

> Dissenting opinion in 7–2 ruling that upheld Immunity Act of 1954, 26 Mar 56

5 Free speech is not to be regulated like diseased cattle and impure butter. The audience . . . that hissed yesterday may applaud today, even for the same performance.

> Dissenting opinion in 5–4 ruling that banned sale of obscene books, 24 Jun 57

6 We deal with a right of privacy older than the Bill of Rights—older than our political parties, older than our school system.

> Majority opinion in 6–2 ruling that overturned state birth control laws, 7 Jun 65

7 Marriage is a coming together for better or for worse, hopefully enduring, and intimate to the degree of being sacred.

> *ib*

8 The association promotes a way of life, not causes; a harmony in living, not political faiths; a bilateral loyalty, not commercial or social projects. Yet it is an association for as noble a purpose as any involved in any prior decisions.

> *ib*

9 If discrimination based on race is constitutionally permissible when those who hold the reins can come up with "compelling" reasons to justify it, then constitutional guarantees acquire an accordionlike quality.

> Dissenting opinion in 7–2 ruling that upheld discriminatory university admissions policies, 23 Apr 74

ABE FORTAS, Associate Justice, US Supreme Court

10 Needless, heedless, wanton and deliberate injury of the sort inflicted by *Life*'s picture story is not an essential instrument of responsible journalism.

> Draft of 1966 opinion upholding suit for invasion of privacy brought against *Life* magazine for picturing home of family held hostage by escaped convicts, quoted by Bernard Schwartz *Unpublished Opinions of the Warren Court* Oxford 85

FELIX FRANKFURTER, Associate Justice, US Supreme Court

11 [It is anomalous] to hold that in order to convict a man the police cannot extract by force what is in his mind, but can extract what is in his stomach.

> Unanimous opinion that reversed conviction of an alleged drug addict because evidence was obtained by forced stomach pumping, 2 Jan 52

12 Lincoln's appeal to "the better angels of our nature" failed to avert a fratricidal war. But the compassionate wisdom of Lincoln's first and second inaugurals bequeathed to the Union, cemented with blood, a moral heritage which, when drawn upon in times of stress and strife, is sure to find specific ways and means to surmount difficulties that may appear to be insurmountable.

> Concurring opinion in unanimous ruling that ordered racial desegregation of schools in Little Rock AR, 29 Sep 58

13 Time and experience have forcefully taught that the power to inspect dwelling places, either as a matter of systematic area-by-area search or, as here, to treat a specific problem, is of indispensable importance in the maintenance of community health; a power that would be greatly hobbled by the blanket requirement of the safeguards necessary for a search of evidence of criminal acts.

> Majority opinion in 5–4 ruling that allowed health inspectors to enter a private home without a search warrant, 4 May 59

ARTHUR J GOLDBERG, Associate Justice, US Supreme Court

14 The basic guarantees of our Constitution are warrants for the here and now, and unless there is an overwhelmingly compelling reason, they are to be promptly fulfilled.

> Unanimous opinion that ordered Memphis TN to desegregate immediately its recreational facilities, NY *Times* 27 May 63

15 The concept of neutrality can lead to . . . a brooding and pervasive devotion to the secular and a passive, or even active, hostility to the religious. Such results are not only not compelled by the Constitution, but, it seems to me, are prohibited by it.

> Concurring but mitigating opinion in 8–1 ruling that declared religious exercises in public schools unconstitutional, 17 Jun 63

STEWART F HANCOCK JR, Judge, NY State Court of Appeals

16 Coercion results from the fact that the state establishes the rate that the customer must pay, and the rate includes an allowance for the objected-to contributions.

> Majority opinion in 5–2 ruling that it is unconstitutional for state-regulated utilities to contribute customers' money to causes they may oppose, 19 Dec 86

JOHN MARSHALL HARLAN, Associate Justice, US Supreme Court

17 The Constitution is not a panacea for every blot upon the public welfare. Nor should this Court, ordained as a judicial body, be thought of as a general haven for reform movements.

> Dissenting opinion in 6–3 ruling that required both houses of state legislatures to be apportioned on a population basis, 15 Jun 64

ROBERT H JACKSON, Associate Justice, US Supreme Court

1 In our country are evangelists and zealots of many different political, economic and religious persuasions whose fanatical conviction is that all thought is divinely classified into two kinds—that which is their own and that which is false and dangerous.

> Concurring opinion in 5–2 ruling that upheld Labor Management Relations Act of 1947 barring labor leaders from membership in the Communist Party, 8 May 50

2 The petitioner's problem is to avoid Scylla without being drawn into Charybdis.

> Majority opinion in 5–4 ruling that prohibited federal jurisdiction over utility rates, 7 May 51

3 Men are more often bribed by their loyalties and ambitions than by money.

> Dissenting opinion in 6–3 ruling that upheld authority of department heads in awarding government contracts, 26 Nov 51

4 We can afford no liberties with liberty itself.

> Dissenting opinion in 5–3 ruling that upheld the constitutionality of forced deportation, 7 Apr 52

5 The day that this country ceases to be free for irreligion, it will cease to be free for religion.

> Dissenting opinion in 6–3 ruling that allowed release of public school children for religious instruction, 28 Apr 52

6 We are not unaware that we are not final because we are infallible; we know that we are infallible only because we are final.

> Concurring opinion in 6–3 ruling that upheld Supreme Court as the court of last appeal, 9 Feb 53

7 In this court the parties changed positions as nimbly as if dancing a quadrille.

> Majority opinion in 6–3 ruling that armed forces personnel have no constitutional right to a particular assignment based on education or preparation, 9 Mar 53

8 The validity of a doctrine does not depend on whose ox it gores.

> Dissenting opinion in 5–3 ruling that upheld state laws setting statute of limitations on cases of wrongful death, 18 May 53

THURGOOD MARSHALL, Associate Justice, US Supreme Court

9 If the 1st Amendment means anything, it means that a state has no business telling a man, sitting alone in his own house, what books he may read or what films he may watch.

> Unanimous opinion that the 1st Amendment guarantees the right to possess in one's home material that might be regarded as obscene in public, 7 Apr 69

10 Our whole constitutional heritage rebels at the thought of giving government the power to control men's minds.

> ib

11 Surely the fact that a uniformed police officer is wearing his hair below his collar will make him no less identifiable as a policeman.

> Dissenting opinion in 7–2 ruling that upheld the right of police departments to order officers to have short haircuts and no beards, NY Times 6 Apr 76

12 Mere access to the courthouse doors does not by itself assure a proper functioning of the adversary process.

> Majority opinion in 8–1 ruling that allowed defendants who plead not guilty by reason of insanity to seek a psychiatrist's help in preparing and presenting their cases, 26 Feb 85

13 [It is] a historic step toward eliminating the shameful practice of racial discrimination in the selection of juries.

> Majority opinion in 7–2 ruling that made it more difficult for blacks to be excluded from juries trying black defendants, 30 Apr 86

14 [Ending racial discrimination in jury selection] can be accomplished only by eliminating peremptory challenges entirely.

> ib

15 [Jurors who are opposed to capital punishment are] more likely to believe that a defendant's failure to testify is indicative of his guilt, more hostile to the insanity defense, more mistrustful of defense attorneys and less concerned about the danger of erroneous convictions.

> Dissenting opinion in 6–3 ruling that opponents of the death penalty may be barred from juries in capital cases, 5 May 86

MASSACHUSETTS SUPREME JUDICIAL COURT

16 [It is time to end] antediluvian assumptions concerning the role and status of women in marriage.

> Ruling that wives have a right to sue their husbands, 30 Jul 80

JAMES B M McNALLY, Judge, NY State Supreme Court, Appellate Division

17 Slovenliness is no part of my religion, nor is it conducive to rest. Scripture commands cleanliness.

> Unanimous opinion declaring it legal to use a coin-operated laundry on Sunday, NY Times 19 Jun 59

SANDRA DAY O'CONNOR, Associate Justice, US Supreme Court

18 A moment of silence is not inherently religious.

> Concurring opinion in 6–3 ruling that an Alabama law authorizing voluntary prayer or meditation in public schools violated the 1st Amendment by encouraging religious practice, 4 Jun 85

19 It is difficult to discern a serious threat to religious liberty from a room of silent, thoughtful schoolchildren.

> ib

20 Statutes authorizing unreasonable searches were the core concern of the framers of the 4th Amendment.

> Minority opinion in 5–4 ruling that broadened an exception to the 4th Amendment rule barring use of unconstitutionally seized evidence in criminal trials, 9 Mar 87

21 It is a measure of the framers' fear that a passing majority might find it expedient to compromise 4th Amendment values that these values were embodied in the Constitution itself.

> ib

22 We hold that the reckless disregard for human life implicit in knowingly engaging in criminal activity known to carry a grave risk of death represents a highly culpable mental state . . . that may be taken into account in making a capital sentencing judgment

when that conduct causes its natural, though also not inevitable, lethal result.

> Majority opinion in 5–4 ruling that some accomplices in crimes leading to death may be executed even if they did not personally kill or intend to kill, 21 Apr 87

LAWRENCE PIERCE, Judge, US Court of Appeals, 2nd Circuit

1 Although the employer may perhaps lawfully destroy its own reputation, its employees should be and are barred from destroying their employer's reputation by misappropriating their employer's informational property.

> Majority opinion in 2–1 ruling that upheld conviction of former *Wall Street Journal* reporter for insider trading, 27 May 86

LEWIS F POWELL JR, Associate Justice, US Supreme Court

2 The guarantee of equal protection cannot mean one thing when applied to one individual and something else when applied to a person of another color. If both are not accorded the same protection, then it is not equal.

> Majority opinion in 5–4 ruling that affirmed the constitutionality of college admission programs favoring minorities, 28 Jun 78

3 The states' role in our system of government is a matter of constitutional law, not of legislative grace.

> Dissenting opinion in 5–4 ruling that upheld imposition of federal standards for mass transit workers, 19 Feb 85

WILLIAM H REHNQUIST, Associate Justice, US Supreme Court

4 A father's interest in having a child—perhaps his only child—may be unmatched by any other interest in his life. It is truly surprising that the state must assign a greater value to a mother's decision to cut off a potential human life by abortion than to a father's decision to let it mature into a live child.

> Minority opinion in 6–3 ruling that prohibited states from requiring women to obtain their husbands' consent for abortions, 1 Jul 76

5 Pregnancy is of course confined to women, but it is in other ways significantly different from the typical covered disease or disability.

> Majority opinion in 6–3 ruling that allowed private employers to refuse to compensate women for absences due to pregnancy, 7 Dec 76

6 This result . . . will daily stand as a veritable sword of Damocles over every succeeding president and his advisers.

> Dissenting opinion in 7–2 ruling that upheld Congressional seizure of Richard M Nixon's presidential papers, 28 Jun 77

7 The Constitution requires that Congress treat similarly situated persons similarly, not that it engage in gestures of superficial equality.

> Majority opinion in 6–3 ruling that upheld military draft for males only, 25 Jun 81

8 [The majority has created] a scenario in which the government appears as the Big Bad Wolf and Pacifica as Little Red Riding Hood. A more appropriate analogy [would be] Faust and Mephistopheles.

> Dissenting opinion in 5–4 ruling that lifted ban on editorializing by public broadcasting's Pacifica Foundation, 3 Jul 84

9 The considered professional judgment of the Air Force is that the traditional outfitting of personnel in standardized uniforms encourages the subordination of personal preferences and identities in favor of the overall group mission.

> Majority opinion in 5–4 ruling that allowed the military to prohibit an Orthodox Jewish officer from wearing a yarmulke indoors while in uniform, 25 Mar 86

10 [Jury selection] is best based upon seat-of-the-pants instincts, which are undoubtedly crudely stereotypical and may in many cases be hopelessly mistaken.

> Dissenting opinion in 7–2 ruling that made it more difficult for blacks to be excluded from juries trying black defendants, 30 Apr 86

11 [To restrict political spending] is much like allowing a speaker in a public hall to express his views while denying him the use of an amplifying system.

> Majority opinion in 7–2 ruling that struck down $1,000 legal limit on spending by political action committees on behalf of presidential candidates, 18 Jun 86

CHARLES RICHEY, Judge, US District Court, District of Columbia

12 The court must admit that it is not comfortable with racially based distinctions. [But] no decision of [the Supreme] Court has ever adopted the proposition that the Constitution must be colorblind.

> Rejecting Justice Department's argument that a 1984 Supreme Court decision "precludes the use of any race-conscious affirmative action plan," 1 Apr 85

H LEE SAROKIN, Judge, US District Court, New Jersey

13 Why should a claim for a damaged leg survive one's death where a claim for a damaged name does not? After death, the leg cannot be healed, but the reputation can. To say that a man's defamed reputation dies with him is to ignore the realities of life and the bleak legacy he leaves behind.

> Ruling that the family of a deceased man may sue for libel to clear his name, 13 Jan 83

14 The invidious effects of such mass, roundup urinalysis is that it casually sweeps up the innocent with the guilty.

> Ruling that mandatory testing of government employees to determine presence of illegal drugs is unconstitutional, 18 Sep 86

ANTONIN SCALIA, Associate Justice, US Supreme Court

15 There is nothing new in the realization that the Constitution sometimes insulates the criminality of a few in order to protect the privacy of us all.

> Majority opinion in 6–3 ruling that refused to expand police powers to search or seize evidence that they suspect may be stolen, 3 Mar 87

16 A search is a search, even if it happens to disclose nothing but the bottom of a turntable.

> *ib*

17 We are unwilling to send police and judges into a new thicket of 4th Amendment law, to seek a creature of uncertain description that is neither a plain-view inspection nor yet a "full-blown search."

> *ib*

18 The Court today completes the process of converting [Title VII of the Civil Rights Act of 1964] from a guarantee that race or sex will not be the basis for

employment determinations, to a guarantee that it often will.

> Dissenting opinion in 6–3 ruling that employers may sometimes favor women and members of minorities over better-qualified men and whites in hiring and promoting in order to achieve better balance in their work forces, 25 Mar 87

1 Ever so subtly, without even alluding to the last obstacles preserved by earlier opinions that we now push out of our path, we effectively replace the goal of a discrimination-free society with the quite incompatible goal of proportionate representation by race and by sex in the workplace.

> *ib*

2 A law can be both economic folly and constitutional.

> Concurring opinion in 6–3 ruling that upheld state law restricting hostile takeover offers for companies incorporated within that state, 21 Apr 87

HARVEY R SORKOW, Judge, New Jersey Superior Court

3 To make a new concept fit into an old statute makes tortured law with tortured results.

> Ruling in the Baby M case that a surrogacy agreement was a valid contract and did not violate prior laws governing adoption, custody and the cessation of parental rights, 31 Mar 87

JOHN PAUL STEVENS, Associate Justice, US Supreme Court

4 When the commission finds that a pig has entered the parlor, the exercise of its regulatory power does not depend on proof that the pig is obscene.

> Majority opinion in 5–4 ruling that allowed the Federal Communications Commission to prohibit the broadcasting of words that are offensive but fall short of the Court's definition of obscenity, 3 Jul 78

5 The 4th Amendment protects the individual's privacy in a variety of settings. In none is the zone of privacy more clearly defined than when bounded by the unambiguous physical dimensions of an individual's home—a zone that finds its roots in clear and specific constitutional terms: "the right of the people to be secure in their . . . houses . . . shall not be violated."

> Majority opinion in 6–3 ruling that required police to have a warrant before entering a suspect's home to make an arrest, 15 Apr 80

6 It is not our job to apply laws that have not yet been written.

> Majority opinion in 5–4 ruling that allowed consumers to use videotape recorders to tape television programs for their own use, 17 Jan 84

7 Although it may not be a castle, [it is the] functional equivalent of a hotel room, a vacation and retirement home or a hunting and fishing cabin.

> Dissenting opinion in 6–3 ruling that upheld the search of a motor home by police without a warrant, 13 May 85

8 Just as the right to speak and the right to refrain from speaking are complementary components of a broader concept of individual freedom of mind, so also the individual's freedom to choose his own creed is the counterpart of his right to refrain from accepting the creed established by the majority.

> Majority opinion in 6–3 ruling that an Alabama law authorizing voluntary prayer or meditation in public schools violated the 1st Amendment by encouraging religious practice, 4 Jun 85

9 The government must pursue a course of complete neutrality toward religion.

> *ib*

10 They may not be conscripted against their will as the foot soldiers in a federal crusade.

> Majority opinion in 5–3 ruling that struck down Reagan administration regulations requiring life-prolonging medical treatment for infants with severe handicaps, 9 Jun 86

11 To show a "well-founded fear of persecution," an alien need not prove that it is more likely than not that he or she will be persecuted in his or her home country.

> Majority opinion in 6–3 ruling that the government must ease its rule for deciding whether aliens are eligible for political asylum, 9 Mar 87

POTTER STEWART, Associate Justice, US Supreme Court

12 It must always be remembered that what the Constitution forbids is not all searches and seizures, but unreasonable searches and seizures.

> Majority opinion in 5–4 ruling that prohibited the federal government from using evidence improperly seized by state officials, 27 Jun 60

13 The 4th Amendment and the personal rights it secures have a long history. At the very core stands the right of a man to retreat into his own home and there be free from unreasonable governmental intrusion.

> Unanimous opinion that Constitution bars police from electronic eavesdropping, 5 Mar 61

14 For me this is not something that can be swept under the rug and forgotten in the interest of forced Sunday togetherness.

> Dissenting opinion in 6–3 ruling that upheld blue laws, 29 May 61

15 I shall not today attempt further to define the kinds of material . . . but I know it when I see it.

> Concurring opinion in 6–3 ruling that overturned ban on pornographic films, 22 Jun 64

16 At the very least, the freedom that Congress is empowered to secure . . . includes the freedom to buy whatever a white man can buy, the right to live wherever a white man can live. If Congress cannot say that being a freeman means at least this much, then the 13th Amendment made a promise it cannot keep.

> Majority opinion in 7–2 ruling that upheld a 102-year-old law prohibiting racial discrimination in the sale and rental of real estate, 17 Jun 68

17 The dichotomy between personal liberties and property rights is a false one. Property does not have rights. People have rights.

> Majority opinion in 4–3 ruling that upheld a district court's refusal to hear a case involving property rights, 23 Mar 72

18 In fact, a fundamental interdependence exists between the personal right to liberty and the personal right in property.

> *ib*

19 These death sentences are cruel and unusual in the same way that being struck by lightning is cruel and unusual.

> Concurring opinion in 5–4 ruling that struck down state death penalty laws, 29 Jun 72

1 The Court today holds the Congress may say that some of the poor are too poor even to go bankrupt. I cannot agree.

> Dissenting opinion in 5–4 ruling that a person must pay a $50 legal fee when filing for bankruptcy, 10 Jan 73

2 May the state fence in the harmless mentally ill solely to save its citizens from exposure to those whose ways are different? One might as well ask if the state, to avoid public unease, could incarcerate all who are physically unattractive or socially eccentric.

> Unanimous opinion that mental patients cannot be confined in institutions against their will and without treatment if they are not dangerous and if they are capable of surviving on their own, 26 Jun 75

3 To force a lawyer on a defendant can only lead him to believe that the law contrives against him.

> Majority opinion in 6–3 ruling that a defendant may not be forced to accept state-appointed counsel, 30 Jun 75

4 It may be assumed that parents have a 1st Amendment right to send their children to educational institutions that promote the belief that racial segregation is desirable, and that the children have an equal right to attend such institutions. But it does not follow that the practice of excluding racial minorities from such institutions is also protected by the same principle.

> Majority opinion in 7–2 ruling that prohibited private schools from excluding children because of their race, 25 Jun 76

5 We are concerned here only with the imposition of capital punishment for the crime of murder, and when a life has been taken deliberately by the offender, we cannot say that the punishment is invariably disproportionate to the crime. It is an extreme sanction suitable to the most extreme of crimes.

> Majority opinion in 7–2 ruling that the death penalty is a constitutionally acceptable form of punishment for premeditated murder, 2 Jul 76

6 A person's mere propinquity to others independently suspected of criminal activity does not . . . give rise to probable cause to search that person.

> Majority opinion in 6–3 ruling that a warrant to search a particular place does not automatically authorize police to search anyone who happens to be there, 29 Nov 79

7 Regardless of whether the freedom of a woman to choose to terminate her pregnancy for health reasons lies at the core or the periphery of the due process [of] liberty . . . it simply does not follow that a woman's freedom of choice carries with it a constitutional entitlement to the financial resources to avail herself of the full range of protected choices.

> Majority opinion in 5–4 ruling that upheld the Congressional ban on federal payments for abortion, 30 Jun 80

8 Abortion is inherently different from other medical procedures because no other procedure involves the purposeful termination of a potential life.

> ib

9 [It took many decades after adoption of the 14th Amendment] before the states and the federal government were finally directed to eliminate detrimental classifications based on race. Today, the Court derails this achievement and places its imprimatur on the creation once again by government of privileges based on birth.

> Dissenting opinion in 6–3 ruling that upheld a federal law setting aside 10 percent of public works contracts for minority businesses, 2 Jul 80

VITO J TITONE, Judge, NY State Court of Appeals

10 It cannot be said that nude sunbathing on a beach is a form of expression likely to be understood by the viewer as an attempt to convey a particular point of view.

> Unanimous opinion that nude sunbathing is not a constitutionally protected form of expression, 21 Oct 86

MATTHEW TOBRINER, Judge, California Supreme Court

11 Man's drive for self-expression, which over the centuries has built his monuments, does not stay within set bounds; the creations which yesterday were the detested and the obscene become the classics of today.

> Ruling that Henry Miller's *Tropic of Cancer* was not pornographic, *Wall Street Journal* 3 Feb 64

12 The quicksilver of creativity will not be solidified by legal pronouncement; it will necessarily flow into new and sometimes frightening fields.

> ib

UNITED STATES COURT OF APPEALS, DISTRICT OF COLUMBIA CIRCUIT

13 Man has discovered no technique for long preserving free government except that the executive be under the law.

> 5–2 ruling that President Richard M Nixon must turn over to investigators the tape recordings he was withholding, NY *Times* 14 Oct 73

14 Sovereignty remains at all times with the people and they do not forfeit through elections the rights to have the law construed against and applied to every citizen.

> ib

FREDERICK M VINSON, Chief Justice, US Supreme Court

15 There is a vast difference—a constitutional difference—between restrictions imposed by the state which prohibit the intellectual commingling of students, and the refusal of individuals to commingle where the state presents no such bar.

> Unanimous opinion that black students admitted to state universities may not be restricted in their access to university facilities and functions, 5 Jun 50

SOL WACHTLER, Judge, NY State Court of Appeals

16 A marriage license should not be viewed as a license for a husband to forcibly rape his wife with impunity.

> Unanimous opinion that a man may be prosecuted for raping his wife, 20 Dec 84

17 A married woman has the same right to control her own body as does an unmarried woman.

> ib

18 In the past, those who had ideas they wished to communicate to the public had the unquestioned right to disseminate those ideas in an open marketplace.

Now that the marketplace has a roof over it and is called a mall, we should not abridge that right.

> Dissenting opinion in 5–2 ruling that permitted owners of shopping malls to restrict the distribution of leaflets, 19 Dec 85

1 We cannot lightly . . . allow the perpetrator of a serious crime to go free simply because that person believed his actions were reasonable and necessary to prevent some perceived harm.

> Ruling that Bernhard H Goetz should be prosecuted for shooting four youths whom he feared were about to rob him, 8 Jul 86

2 [It] would allow citizens to set their own standards for the permissible use of force.

> *ib*

EARL WARREN, Chief Justice, US Supreme Court

3 In these days, it is doubtful that any child may reasonably be expected to succeed in life if he is denied the opportunity of an education.

> Unanimous opinion in Brown *v* Board of Education of Topeka that declared segregated schools unconstitutional, 17 May 54

4 Such an opportunity, where the state has undertaken to provide it, is a right which must be made available to all on equal terms.

> *ib*

5 Separate educational facilities are inherently unequal.

> *ib*

6 We come then to the question presented: Does segregation of children in public schools solely on the basis of race, even though the physical facilities and other "tangible" factors may be equal, deprive the children of the minority group of equal education opportunities? We believe that it does.

> *ib*

7 To separate [children] from others of similar age and qualifications solely because of their race generates a feeling of inferiority as to their status in the community that may affect their hearts and minds in a way unlikely ever to be undone.

> *ib*

8 We conclude that in the field of public education the doctrine of "separate but equal" has no place.

> *ib*

9 All provisions of federal, state or local law requiring or permitting discrimination in public education must yield.

> Unanimous opinion that ordered the desegregation of public schools, 31 May 55

10 The police must obey the law while enforcing the law.

> Unanimous opinion that confessions obtained under duress must be excluded from criminal proceedings, 22 Jun 59

11 Life and liberty can be as much endangered from illegal methods used to convict those thought to be criminals as from the actual criminals themselves.

> *ib*

12 The censor's sword pierces deeply into the heart of free expression.

> Dissenting opinion in 5–4 ruling that allowed municipalities to ban the showing of motion pictures that do not meet certain moral standards, 23 Jan 61

13 Legislatures represent people, not acres or trees.

> Majority opinion in 6–3 ruling that required both houses of state legislatures to be apportioned on a population basis, 15 Jun 64

14 Prior to any questioning, the person must be warned that he has a right to remain silent, that any statement he does make may be used as evidence against him and that he has a right to the presence of an attorney, either retained or appointed.

> Majority opinion in 6–3 ruling in the Miranda case that prohibited prosecution from using information obtained in violation of a suspect's 5th Amendment rights, 13 Jun 66

15 There is no requirement that police stop a person who enters a police station and states that he wishes to confess a crime or a person who calls the police to offer a confession [because] volunteered statements of any kind are not barred by the 5th Amendment.

> *ib*

CLINTON R WEIDNER, Judge, Court of Common Pleas, Cumberland County PA

16 By analogy, Miss Frick might as well try to enjoin publication and distribution of the Holy Bible because, being a descendant of Eve, she does not believe that Eve gave Adam the forbidden fruit in the Garden of Eden and . . . her senses are offended by such a statement about an ancestor of hers.

> Dismissing Helen Frick's lawsuit charging that her father Henry Clay Frick had been libeled by a historian's biography, NY *Times* 26 May 67

BYRON R WHITE, Associate Justice, US Supreme Court

17 [Rape] is highly reprehensible, both in a moral sense and in its almost total contempt for the personal integrity and autonomy of the female victim and for the latter's privilege of choosing those with whom intimate relations are to be established.

> Majority opinion in 6–2 ruling that forbade death penalty for rape, 29 Jun 77

18 Short of homicide, [rape] is the "ultimate violation of self."

> *ib*

19 To exclude all jurors who would be in the slightest way affected by the prospect of the death penalty would be to deprive the defendant of the impartial jury to which he or she is entitled under the law.

> Majority opinion in 8–1 ruling that overturned a Texas law barring opponents of the death penalty from jury duty in capital cases, 25 Jun 80

20 The Court, casually, but candidly, abandons the functional approach to immunity that has run through all of our decisions. Indeed, the majority turns this rule on its head by declaring that because the functions of the president's office are so varied and diverse and some of them so profoundly important, the office is unique and must be clothed with office-wide, absolute immunity. This is a policy, not law, and in my view, very poor policy.

> Dissenting opinion in 5–4 ruling that granted former President Richard M Nixon immunity from civil suits concerning damages he might have caused while in office, 24 Jun 82

21 Maintaining order in the classrooms has never been easy [and] it is evident that the school setting requires some easing of the restrictions to which

searches by public authorities are ordinarily subject.
> Majority opinion in 6–3 ruling that allowed the search of students for drugs or weapons, 15 Jan 85

1 The 1st Amendment protects the right to speak, not the right to spend.
> Dissenting opinion in 7–2 ruling that struck down $1,000 legal limit on spending by political action committees on behalf of presidential candidates, 18 Mar 85

2 Where the suspect poses no immediate threat to the officer and no threat to others, the harm resulting from the failing to apprehend him does not justify the use of deadly force to do so.
> Majority opinion in 6–3 ruling that forbade police to shoot to kill fleeing suspects who are not armed, 27 Mar 85

3 The risk of racial prejudice infecting a capital sentencing proceeding is especially serious in light of the complete finality of the death sentence.
> Majority opinion in 7–2 ruling that allowed a defendant facing capital punishment to have prospective jurors questioned on prejudice, 30 Apr 86

4 However one answers the metaphysical or theological question whether the fetus is a "human being" or the legal question whether it is a "person" as that term is used in the Constitution, one must at least recognize, first, that the fetus is an entity that bears in its cells all the genetic information that characterizes a member of the species *Homo sapiens* and distinguishes an individual member of that species from all others and, second, that there is no nonarbitrary line separating a fetus from a child or, indeed, an adult human being.
> Dissenting opinion in 5–4 ruling that reaffirmed the constitutional right to abortion, 11 Jun 86

5 Respondent would have us announce . . . a fundamental right to engage in homosexual sodomy. This we are quite unwilling to do.
> Majority opinion in 5–4 ruling that upheld the right to prohibit deviant sexual behavior, 30 Jun 86

6 The Court is most vulnerable and comes nearest to illegitimacy when it deals with judge-made constitutional law having little or no cognizable roots in the language or design of the Constitution.
> *ib*

7 The law . . . is constantly based on notions of morality, and if all laws representing essentially moral choices are to be invalidated under the due process clause, the courts will be very busy indeed.
> *ib*

ROBERT N WILENTZ, Chief Justice, New Jersey Supreme Court

8 It is the upheaval of prior norms by a society that has finally recognized that it must change its habits and do whatever is required, whether it means a small change or a significant one, in order to stop the senseless loss inflicted by drunken drivers.
> Majority opinion in 6–1 ruling that a host may be held liable for serving alcohol to persons later involved in drunk-driving incidents, 27 Jun 84

9 The common characteristics of a battered wife [include] her inability to leave despite such constant beatings; her "learned helplessness"; her lack of anywhere to go; her feeling that if she tried to leave, she would be subjected to even more merciless treatment; her belief in the omnipotence of her battering husband; and sometimes her hope that her husband will change his ways.
> Majority opinion in 6–1 ruling that called for a new trial for a woman convicted of killing her abusive husband, 24 Jul 84

Criminology

GAIL ABARBANELA, Rape Treatment Center, Santa Monica

10 If a girl says no and the boy perceives it as yes, he acts on his belief and you have trouble.
> On date rape, news summaries 25 May 85

DAVID ABRAHANSEN, psychoanalyst

11 The American dream is, in part, responsible for a great deal of crime and violence because people feel that the country owes them not only a living but a good living.
> Quoted in San Francisco *Examiner & Chronicle* 18 Nov 75

12 Frustration is the wet nurse of violence.
> *ib*

PETER ACKROYD

13 Murderers will try to recall the sequence of events, they will remember exactly what they did just before and just after. . . . But they can never remember the actual moment of killing. . . . This is why [they] will always leave a clue.
> *Hawksmoor* Harper & Row 86

FREDA ADLER

14 [Rape] is the only crime in which the victim becomes the accused.
> *Sisters in Crime* McGraw-Hill 75

15 Woman throughout the ages has been mistress to the law, as man has been its master.
> *ib*

POLLY ADLER

16 What it comes down to is this: The grocer, the butcher, the baker, the merchant, the landlord, the druggist, the liquor dealer, the policeman, the doctor, the city father and the politician—these are the people who make money out of prostitution, these are the real reapers of the wages of sin.
> *A House Is Not a Home* Rinehart 53

ELI ADORNO

17 Do you think someone who is about to rape you is going to stop and think about a condom?
> On uselessness of issuing condoms to fellow prisoners in Riker's Island penitentiary, quoted in NY *Times* 5 Mar 87

MEHMET ALI AGCA

18 To me [the pope] was the incarnation of all that is capitalism.
> On attempted assassination of Pope John Paul II, *Time* 18 Feb 85

19 Bulgaria is guilty.
> On plot to kill the pope, news summaries 7 Jun 85

MARGERY ALLINGHAM

1 Chemists employed by the police can do remarkable things with blood. They can . . . weave it into a rope to hang a man.
The Tiger in the Smoke Doubleday 52

ELIZABETH ANDREWS, Buckingham Palace maid

2 Bloody hell, Ma'am, what's he doing in here?
On discovering an early-morning intruder in bedroom of Queen Elizabeth II, quoted in London *Observer* 18 Jul 82

GENNARO ANGUILO, Boston organized crime boss

3 When a guy knocks ya down, never get up unless he's gonna kill ya.
From compilation of FBI tapes in "Anguilo's Republic" *New England Monthly* Jul 86, quoted in *Harper's* Oct 86

4 When a man assumes leadership, he forfeits the right to mercy.
ib

5 I wouldn't be in a legitimate business for all the . . . money in the world.
ib

ANONYMOUS

6 There was a blue wall of silence.
On lack of official response to reports of police brutality, NY *Daily News* 6 May 85

7 Crack down on crack.
Police motto for campaign against potent new drug. NY *Times* 21 May 86

8 It's like fishing from a bucket filled with fish.
On US Border Patrol's task of stopping illegal immigration from Mexico, *ib* 3 Aug 86

9 Even the bugs have bugs.
On police and organized crime spying, *NBC Evening News* NBC TV 8 Sep 86

BILL ARMONTROUT, Warden, Missouri State Penitentiary

10 I look at the criminal justice system as a sewer pipe and I'm just at the end of it. The police did their job, the courts did their job, now I have to do my job.
On his role as executioner, *Wall Street Journal* 6 Nov 84

WILLIAM ATTWOOD

11 *Payola* is the year's new word. It doesn't sound as ugly as *bribe*, but it means the same thing.
Look 29 Mar 60

BRUCE BABBITT, former Governor of Arizona

12 [It] is like living in a wilderness of mirrors. No fact goes unchallenged.
On 10-year controversy surrounding murder of investigative reporter Don Bolles, *Wall Street Journal* 23 Feb 87

BRUCE A BAIRD, AARON R MARCU and FRANK H SHERMAN, US Prosecuting Attorneys, NYC

13 Carmine Persico was born in August 1933 and killed his first human being in 1951, before his 18th birthday.
Sentencing memorandum on organized crime boss Carmine Persico, quoted in NY *Times* 18 Nov 86

JOSEPH BALL, President, Amer College of Trial Lawyers

14 Most of the clients that I represent in a criminal case I detest.
LA *Herald-Examiner* 23 Aug 70

15 The more I become involved emotionally in my client's cause, the less I am able to do for him.
ib

J HOPPS BARKER, Florida State Probation and Parole Commission

16 When you punish someone, you pay for it later. There was a time when pickpockets were publicly hanged, but other pickpockets took advantage of the large crowds attracted to the executions to ply their trade.
McCall's May 65

PEGGY BARLOW

17 Television nearly always showed the bandits in masks and using violence, but I wanted to go about it in a kind and gentle way.
Comment of 70-year-old widow who tried to rob London's National Westminster Bank, London *Times* 6 Oct 84

18 Agatha Christie would have been in her element with the plot.
ib

SYDNEY BIDDLE BARROWS

19 Never say anything on the phone that you wouldn't want your mother to hear at your trial.
Advice to women she employed in escort service, *Mayflower Madam*, with William Novak, Arbor House 86

20 I was naughty. I wasn't bad. Bad is hurting people, doing evil. Naughty is not hurting anyone. Naughty is being amusing.
Quoted by Marian Christy "'Mayflower Madam' Tells All" Boston *Globe* 10 Sep 86

21 I ran the wrong kind of business, but I did it with integrity.
ib

ED BATES, Sheriff, Madera County CA

22 I long for the days of good honest crooks.
On the kidnapping of 26 children and their bus driver, news summaries 19 Jul 76

REX BEABER, clinical psychologist, UCLA

23 The little child in each of us would kill any person who infringed our slightest right.
Time 8 Apr 85

DAVID BERKOWITZ, known as "Son of Sam"

24 It was a command. I had a sign and I followed it. Sam told me what to do and I did it.
Confession to police of killing six persons and wounding seven others on orders from his dog Sam. *Time* 22 Aug 77

25 And huge drops of lead
Poured down upon her head
Until she was dead.
Yet the cats still come out at night to mate;
And the sparrows still sing in the morning.
Poem found in suspect's car, *ib*

1 I am a spirit roaming the night. Thirsty, hungry, seldom stopping to rest, anxious to please Sam. I love my work.

> Letter to Jimmy Breslin, quoted in *ib*

WALTER AUGUSTUS BOWE, gang member

2 We could knock the head and the arms off that damned old bitch.

> On plot to destroy the Statue of Liberty, NY *Times* 17 Feb 65

JIMMY BRESLIN

3 Out in the ocean, a rope is put around the man's neck. The other end of the rope is attached to an old jukebox and it is thrown overboard. The man invariably follows.

> On organized crime murders, *The Gang That Couldn't Shoot Straight* Viking 69

4 The number 1 rule of thieves is that nothing is too small to steal.

> NBC TV 15 May 74

5 Precious was one of a large number of people on the street, many of whom appeared to be women; some, like Precious, actually were.

> On prostitutes and transvestites of Manhattan's West Side, NY *Daily News* 22 Mar 87

SUSAN BROWNMILLER

6 We are unalterably opposed to the presentation of the female body being stripped, bound, raped, tortured, mutilated and murdered in the name of commercial entertainment and free speech.

> On pornography, *Against Our Will: Men, Women and Rape* Simon & Schuster 75

WARREN E BURGER, Chief Justice, US Supreme Court

7 Guilt or innocence becomes irrelevant in the criminal trials as we flounder in a morass of artificial rules poorly conceived and often impossible [to apply].

> As judge, US Court of Appeals, District of Columbia Circuit, news summaries 26 May 69

8 Crime and the fear of crime have permeated the fabric of American life.

> To Amer Bar Assn, Houston, 8 Feb 81

9 A far greater factor [than abolishing poverty] is the deterrent effect of swift and certain consequences: swift arrest, prompt trial, certain penalty and—at some point—finality of judgment.

> On lowering the crime rate, *ib*

10 There may be some incorrigible human beings who cannot be changed except by God's own mercy to that one person.

> *ib*

TRUMAN CAPOTE

11 The quietness of his tone italicized the malice of his reply.

> On convicted murderer Perry Smith, *In Cold Blood* Random House 66

JOHN CASEY, NYC police officer

12 It's 90 percent boredom and 10 percent sheer terror.

> On Emergency Service Unit, quoted in NY *Times* 11 Feb 85

MARK DAVID CHAPMAN

13 I've pent up all my aggression, kept swallowing it and swallowing it.

> Statement to his attorney in first week after fatally shooting John Lennon, *People* 23 Feb 87

14 I found out Lennon was more accessible.

> On choosing to shoot Lennon instead of other public figures, *ib*

15 I remember thinking, "The bullets are working" . . . I think I felt a little regret that they were working.

> *ib* 2 Mar 87

CARYL CHESSMAN, convicted murderer

16 The California executioner keeps banker's hours. He never kills before 10 o'clock in the morning, never after 4 in the afternoon.

> Letter written in San Quentin Prison on eve of his execution, quoted in NY *Post* 3 May 60

JAMES CHILES

17 The rise of computer crime and armed robbery has not eliminated the lure of caged cash.

> "Age-Old Battle to Keep Safes Safe from Creepers, Soup Men and Yeggs" *Smithsonian* Jul 84

18 Safe-breaking and vault-breaking are at least as old as the pyramids and burial chambers of Egypt. . . . Poking holes in vaults and safes for profit appears to be as durable as greed.

> *ib*

19 Burglars know there's more than one way to skin a vault.

> *ib*

20 Organized crime is the dirty side of the sharp dollar.

> *ib*

AGATHA CHRISTIE

21 Oh dear, I never realized what a terrible lot of explaining one has to do in a murder!

> From her 1956 play *Spider's Web*, recalled on her death 12 Jan 76

BILL CLARK, Brooklyn detective

22 You want to make a guy comfortable enough to confess to murder.

> *New York* 24 Dec 84

RAMSEY CLARK, US Attorney General

23 A humane and generous concern for every individual, his health and his fulfillment, will do more to soothe the savage heart than the fear of state-inflicted death, which chiefly serves to remind us how close we remain to the jungle.

> Urging abolishment of the death penalty for federal crimes, to Senate Judiciary Committee, NY *Times* 3 Jul 68

24 Our history shows that the death penalty has been unjustly imposed, innocents have been killed by the state, effective rehabilitation has been impaired, judicial administration has suffered. It is the poor, the weak, the ignorant, the hated who are executed [and] racial discrimination occurs in the administration of capital punishment.

> *ib*

FRANCIS X CLINES

1 A show of police force worthy of a banana republic is the latest attraction on the cobbled streets of Georgetown.

> On police patrols in Washington DC neighborhood, NY *Times* 15 Apr 85

EARLE COHEN, hotel owner

2 Newport is not happy about it. Newport will never be happy about it.

> On trial of Claus von Bülow for attempted murder of his wife, NY *Times* 4 Apr 85

ARMAND COURVILLE

3 If the Mafia exists in Montreal, it's probably like the Knights of Columbus.

> Testifying at Quebec Police Commission inquiry on organized crime, Toronto *Globe & Mail* 27 May 75

ROBERT J CREIGHTON, FBI Agent

4 A fire scene is very fragile, especially in a tropical environment. You've got to get to the evidence before the heat, wind and rain do.

> On investigating arson in Puerto Rico hotel fire that killed 96 people, NY *Times* 7 Jan 87

MARIO CUOMO, Governor of NY

5 The mugger who is arrested is back on the street before the police officer, but the person mugged may not be back on the street for a long time, if ever.

> Calling for hiring of more police, *New Republic* 8 Apr 85

6 I'd say, "That's it, Charlie, you're going to be by yourself for a hundred years."

> Favoring life sentences without parole instead of capital punishment, *Time* 2 Jun 86

GERALD CVETKO, police officer

7 We don't have professional burglars here. We have opportunists.

> On burglary in South Plainfield NJ, NY *Times* 15 Mar 79

8 Burglars, judging by our statistics, define opportunity as an unoccupied, unlocked house stocked with portable television sets.

> *ib*

RICHARD J DALEY, Mayor of Chicago

9 The policeman isn't there to create disorder; the policeman is there to preserve disorder.

> Quoted by Laurence J Peter *Why Things Go Wrong: The Peter Principle Revisited* Morrow 84

EDMUND DAVIES

10 Let us clear any romantic notion of daredeviltry from our minds. It is nothing less than a sordid crime of violence inspired by vast greed.

> On sentencing 12 men convicted in Britain's Great Train Robbery, the theft of more than £20 million from the Royal Mail, *Time* 24 Apr 64

WILLIAM J DEAN

11 In New York City we need police officers to protect even the dead.

> On desecration of graves in Potter's Field, *Time* 29 Aug 83

WILFRED DENNO, Warden, Sing Sing Prison, NY

12 It may sound incredible, but they seemed more interested in the ball game.

> On reaction of death row inmates to abolishment of capital punishment in the state, NY *Times* 2 Jun 65

PETE ("THE GREEK") DIOPOULIS

13 A good hit man has no conscience at all.

> *60 Minutes* CBS TV 25 Apr 76

F W DUPREE

14 From Jesse James to Loeb and Leopold, from the perpetrators of the St Valentine's Day's massacre to the Lindbergh kidnapper and beyond, our celebrated delinquents have become a part of the national heritage.

> *New York Review of Books* 3 Feb 66

15 They figure in a sort of *musée imaginaire*, half Madame Tussaud's, half Smithsonian, of American crime.

> *ib*

ADOLF EICHMANN

16 To sum it all up, I must say that I regret nothing.

> While awaiting trial in Israel for death of 6 million Jews during World War II, *Life* 5 Dec 60

DORIS ANN FOSTER, convicted murderer

17 Death row is a state of mind.

> London *Times* 31 Aug 84

JAMES ALAN FOX, Professor of Criminal Justice, Northeastern University

18 The typical mass murderer is extraordinarily ordinary.

> Quoted in NY *Times* 27 Aug 84

ALADENA T ("JIMMY THE WEASEL") FRATIANNO, convicted murderer

19 Some people are a little better [at it] than others.

> When asked if he was a good killer, *60 Minutes* CBS TV 6 Jan 80

LYNETTE ("SQUEAKY") FROMME

20 Anybody can kill anybody.

> On her attempted assassination of President Gerald R Ford, news summaries 30 Sep 75

JOHN WAYNE GACY, convicted serial killer

21 [All the police] are going to get me for is running a funeral parlor without a license.

> Quoted by James Alan Fox and Jack Levin *Mass Murder* Plenum 85

THOMAS E GADDIS

22 Alcatraz, the federal prison with a name like the blare of a trombone, [is] a black molar in the jawbone of the nation's prison system.

> *Birdman of Alcatraz* Random House 55

DAVID GATES

23 The pseudonymous perpetrator of America's only unsolved airline hijacking [is] a folk hero as shadowy as Deep Throat and as morally troublesome as Jesse James.

> On celebration of D B Cooper Day in Ariel WA, *Newsweek* 26 Dec 83

WILLARD GAYLIN, psychiatrist

1 A street thug and a paid killer are professionals—beasts of prey, if you will, who have dissociated themselves from the rest of humanity and can now see human beings in the same way that trout fishermen see trout.

The Killing of Bonnie Garland Simon & Schuster 82

JEAN GENET

2 I give the name *violence* to a boldness lying idle and enamored of danger.

The Thief's Journal Grove 64

3 Violence is a calm that disturbs you.

ib

4 I recognize in thieves, traitors and murderers, in the ruthless and the cunning, a deep beauty—a sunken beauty.

ib

STEPHEN GILLERS, law professor, NYU

5 [Some] trials . . . look as much like the trial of an ordinary criminal case as a Hitchcock film looks like a home movie.

"Von Bülow, and Other Soap Operas" NY *Times* 5 May 85

RUDOLPH W GIULIANI, US Attorney, Southern District, NY

6 It's about time law enforcement got as organized as organized crime.

Quoted by Peter Stoler "The Sicilian Connection" *Time* 15 Oct 84

7 If we take back the labor unions, the legitimate businesses, eventually they become just another street gang. Spiritually, psychologically, they've always been just a street gang.

Quoted by Robert D McFadden "The Mafia of the 1980s: Divided and Under Siege" NY *Times* 11 Mar 87

MILLS E GODWIN, Governor of Virginia

8 Men of faith know that throughout history the crimes committed in liberty's name have been exceeded only by those committed in God's name.

On burning of crosses by Ku Klux Klan members, *Quote* 1 Jan 67

BERNARD H GOETZ

9 When you are surrounded by four people, one of them smiling, taunting, demanding, terrorizing, you don't have a complete grasp or perfect vision.

On shooting four youths who allegedly accosted him on a NYC subway, *Newsweek* 11 Mar 85

RONALD GOLDSTOCK, Director, NY State Organized Crime Task Force

10 The people who join the mob now are second- and third-generation and don't have the values their predecessors had.

NY *Times* 21 Mar 87

11 They prey on their own with extortion and protection rackets, in a culture where people don't go to the police and where most police don't speak the language.

On Chinese organized crime members, *ib*

JOHN GOTTI, organized crime leader

12 Don't carry a gun. It's nice to have them close by, but don't carry them. You might get arrested.

Quoted in NY *Times* 3 Dec 86

CHESTER GOULD

13 I decided that if the police couldn't catch the gangsters, I'd create a fellow who could.

On his comic strip *Dick Tracy*, recalled on his death 11 May 85

WILLIAM R GREER

14 Officers from the 44th Precinct in the High Bridge section of the Bronx arrested two men in a blue van who were trying to make off with the corner of 161st Street and Jerome Avenue.

On growing theft of paving stones, NY *Times* 12 Jan 85

PETE HAMILL

15 There is a growing feeling that perhaps Texas *is* really another country, a place where the skies, the disasters, the diamonds, the politicians, the women, the fortunes, the football players and the murders are all bigger than anywhere else.

After sniper at University of Texas killed 14 people and injured 30, Boston *Globe* 2 Aug 66

JEAN HARRIS, convicted murderer

16 [We were] two persons who never argued over anything except the use of a subjunctive.

Testimony in trial for her fatal shooting of Dr Herman Tarnower, NY *Times* 30 Jan 81

17 I had led a private life and wanted to die a private death.

On intention to kill herself after a final visit to Dr Tarnower, *ib* 31 Jan 81

18 Overnight I became a cottage industry.

On intense journalistic interest in her arrest and trial, *Stranger in Two Worlds* Macmillan 86

19 It would be ugly to watch people poking sticks at a caged rat. It is uglier still to watch rats poking sticks at a caged person.

On life in prison, *ib*

20 [The prison guards are] capable of committing daily atrocities and obscenities, smiling the smile of the angels all the while.

ib

21 Slippery bunch, angels, hiding their nasty little sins behind curtsies and compliments, Bibles and badges.

ib

22 What do you do in hell? Every day within this grim, ridiculous cinder block pile I play Horatio at small bridges, having easily convinced myself that what stands at risk on the other side is Human Decency, always in capital letters, or even that ephemeral little Tinker Bell called justice.

ib

LAWRENCE S HARRIS, North Carolina State Medical Examiner

23 Are we taking the drunken drivers off the road only to turn them into drunken pedestrians?

On traffic deaths of persons whose driver's licenses had been revoked for drunk driving, NY *Times* 30 Jun 86

G H HATHERILL, Commander, Scotland Yard

1 There are only about 20 murders a year in London and not all are serious—some are just husbands killing their wives.

News summaries 1 Jul 54

GIDEON HAUSNER

2 He is responsible because of the conspiracy and the plots for all that happened to the Jewish people—from the shores of the Arctic Ocean to the Aegean Sea, from the Pyrenees to the Urals.

Summation in trial of war criminal Adolf Eichmann, NY *Times* 27 Jun 61

3 In Maidanek, Poland, there was only one place where the children were treated kindly; at the entrance to the gas chamber each one was handed a sweet.

ib

WALTER HEADLEY, Chief of Police, Miami

4 I'm so used to pressure I'm afraid if it stopped I'd get the bends.

NY *Times* 17 Nov 68

LINDA HEATH, psychologist

5 Readers like the grass to be browner on the other side of the fence, and the browner the better.

On study showing that newspaper reports of violent crimes committed in other states appear to reassure readers of their own safety, quoted in NY *Times* 9 Sep 84

HENRY HILL, accused mob member

6 I'm an average nobody. I get to live the rest of my life like a schnook.

After providing information on other mobsters in exchange for a new identity, quoted by Nicholas Pileggi *Wiseguy* Simon & Schuster 86

MORTON A HILL SJ, member of President's Commission on Pornography

7 It is a Magna Carta for pornography.

1970 comment about Attorney General's Report on Pornography that concluded pornography is harmless and should be legalized, recalled after 1986 report declared that pornography could lead to violence. NY *Times* 23 Oct 86

JOHN W HINCKLEY JR

8 Guns are neat little things, aren't they? They can kill extraordinary people with very little effort.

Statement introduced by Hinckley's attorney in insanity defense for March 30, 1981, attempted assassination of President Ronald Reagan, quoted in *Time* 17 May 82

9 Your prodigal son has left again to exorcise some demons.

Farewell note to parents in February 1981. *ib*

10 Jodie Foster may continue to outwardly ignore me for the rest of my life, but I have . . . made her one of the most famous actresses in the world.

On actress who rebuffed his calls and letters, quoted in NY *Times* 9 Jul 82

ALGER HISS

11 In the future the way that Whittaker Chambers was able to carry out forgery by typewriter will be disclosed.

On how stolen documents were allegedly forged, news summaries 25 Jan 50

XAVIERA HOLLANDER

12 If my business could be made legal. . . . I and women like me could make a big contribution to what Mayor Lindsay calls "Fun City," and the city and state could derive the money in taxes and licensing fees that I pay off to crooked cops and political figures.

The Happy Hooker Dell 72

MARK HOLTHAUS, social worker

13 Guys die down here on a regular basis—that's the reality. They die here for a nickel. They are killed for a piece of change or because somebody looks at somebody wrong.

On frequent murders of homeless people on Los Angeles's Skid Row, NY *Times* 3 Nov 86

J EDGAR HOOVER, Director, FBI

14 Banks are an almost irresistible attraction for that element of our society which seeks unearned money.

News summaries 7 Apr 55

15 We are a fact-gathering organization only. We don't clear anybody. We don't condemn anybody.

Look 14 Jun 56

16 Just the minute the FBI begins making recommendations on what should be done with its information, it becomes a Gestapo.

ib

ROBERT HUGHES

17 [The prisons are] the monuments of Australia—the Paestums [of] an extraordinary time—an effort to exile en masse a whole class.

On 18th-century British practice of transporting criminals to Australia, quoted in NY *Times* 25 Jan 87

18 Transportation made sublimation literal. It conveyed evil to another world.

The Fatal Shore Knopf 86, quoted in *Time* 2 Feb 87

DEREK HUMPHRY, Director, Hemlock Society

19 Ninety-nine percent of requested deaths go unrecorded. It's a secret crime.

On mercy killings, *Newsweek* 9 Sep 85

BRUCE JACKSON, Professor of Law and Jurisprudence, State University of NY, Buffalo

20 America has the longest prison sentences in the West, yet the only condition long sentences demonstrably cure is heterosexuality.

NY *Times* 12 Sep 68

RICHARD LEOFRIC JACKSON, President, Interpol

21 I am devoted to detective novels. They make such a nice change from my work.

Saturday Evening Post 28 Oct 61

1 I particularly like your American ones, where the hero is invariably amorous, alcoholic and practically indestructible.
ib

ROGER A JASKE, convicted murderer

2 Mercenary looking for male Caucasian partner 18–25. Willing to accept the risk. Must have guts, be able to travel and start work immediately. No special skills required. High pay guaranteed. Ask for Sundance.
Ad placed to arrange his rescue from a courtroom; he was foiled by undercover police who answered the ad, NY *Times* 10 Mar 86

ANN JONES

3 The story of women who kill is the story of women.
Women Who Kill Holt, Rinehart & Winston 80

4 Unlike men, who are apt to stab a total stranger in a drunken brawl or run amuck with a high-powered rifle, we women usually kill our intimates: We kill our children, our husbands, our lovers.
ib

JOSEPH KALLINGER, convicted murderer

5 Picking our first victim seemed as right as going to church on Sunday.
On acting with his son in the murder of his older son and another boy, quoted by Flora Rheta Schreiber *The Shoemaker* Simon & Schuster 83

KITTY KELLEY

6 [He] ordered killings as easily as he ordered linguine.
On Chicago organized crime boss Sam Giancana, *His Way* Bantam 86

RICHARD KELLY, US Congressman

7 Does it show?
On stuffing his pockets with $25,000 in cash, to FBI agents posing as Arab businessmen during Abscam probe, videotape recording 8 Jan 80

STEPHEN P KENNEDY, Police Commissioner, NYC

8 A policeman's gun is his cross and he carries it always.
Saturday Evening Post 8 Sep 56

9 In the dark all men were the same color. In the dark our fellow man was seen more clearly than in the normal light of a New York night.
On "zero" crime rate during a blackout in Manhattan, *Time* 31 Aug 59

JAMES C KIMBROUGH, Judge, Superior Court, Lake County IN

10 We would not want our children to be beaten with extension cords, but we would not expect them to go out and kill little old ladies because of it.
On abused girl who fatally stabbed an aged woman, NY *Times* 2 Nov 86

MARTIN LUTHER KING JR

11 It is incontestable and deplorable that Negroes have committed crimes; but they are derivative crimes. They are born of the greater crimes of the white society.
To Southern Christian Leadership Conference 16 Aug 67

PAUL H KING, Judge, District Court, Dorchester MA

12 When they drag me down the aisle the final time I'll be singing "I Did It My Way."
On being barred from the bench for allegedly flouting the Massachusetts domestic abuse law, Boston *Globe* 14 Nov 86

PETER KIRK, Professor of Criminalistics, University of California

13 I hate this "crime doesn't pay" stuff. Crime in the United States is perhaps one of the biggest businesses in the world today.
Wall Street Journal 16 Feb 60

EDWARD KOCH, Mayor of NYC

14 The person who is bent on killing you will follow you wherever you are.
On murder of John Lennon, quoted in NY *Times* 10 Dec 80

ANNA M KROSS, Corrections Commissioner, NYC

15 Let time serve you, don't serve time!
Address at Riker's Island penitentiary, NY *Herald Tribune* 29 Dec 65

J WALLACE LaPRADE, FBI agent

16 We will not close that case until we know that he is not findable or found. And not findable means we find his bones.
On search for man accused of murdering his own wife, mother and three children in Westfield NJ, NY *Times* 2 Jun 74

JONATHAN LARSEN

17 His achievements read like the graffiti on the walls of a hangman's changing room.
On Rudolph W Giuliani, US attorney for Southern District, NY, "The Avenger" *Manhattan Inc* Feb 85

18 The criminal justice system [is] accurately symbolized by a large sculpture that sits at the foot of the United States attorney's building: four metal circles that interlock. The wheels of justice, as it were, frozen in legal and social gridlock.
ib

JOHN LE CARRÉ

19 You should have died when I killed you.
Lines for a bureaucrat speaking to a reassigned agent. *A Perfect Spy* Knopf 86

NATHAN LEOPOLD, convicted murderer

20 What a rotten writer of detective stories life is!
Life Plus 99 Years Doubleday 58

G GORDON LIDDY

21 They were afraid, never having learned what I taught myself: Defeat the fear of death and welcome the death of fear.
On fending off attacks by fellow prisoners after conviction for Watergate activities, *Will* St Martin's 79

LAWRENCE LIEF, industrial security analyst

22 Those you trust the most can steal the most.
Quoted by David Pauly "Stealing from the Boss" *Newsweek* 26 Dec 83

DAVID LIVINGSTONE

1 It's been busier than ever . . . I guess they were having a going-out-of-business sale.

> On increase in drug traffic from neighborhood home following court order to evict dealers. NY *Times* 11 Dec 86

LONDON POLICE

2 We have reason to believe you have committed an offense.

> Printed form for overtime parking, quoted by John Crosby NY *Herald Tribune* 4 Nov 63

HENRY LEE LUCAS, convicted serial murderer

3 Once I've done a crime, I just forget it. I go from crime to crime.

> On belief that he may have committed as many as 360 murders, 142 of which had been verified. *Life* Aug 84

CHARLES MANSON, convicted murderer

4 From the world of darkness I did loose demons and devils in the power of scorpions to torment.

> From his unsuccessful plea for parole from life sentence for ritualistic murders, NY *Times* 9 Feb 86

5 I'd probably try to stop the rain forests from being cut down. I'd probably join the revolution down south somewhere and try to save my life on the planet Earth. I might go to Libya. I might go see the Ayatollah. I might go to France, catch somebody in France I'm upset with.

> What he would do if paroled. *ib*

ROBERT MARK, Commissioner, London Metropolitan Police

6 The criminal trial today is . . . a kind of show-jumping contest in which the rider for the prosecution must clear every obstacle to succeed.

> Washington *Post* 23 Nov 71

JIM MATTOX, Attorney General of Texas

7 He was not afraid. He jumped up on the table with a smile and said he was ready for the rocket to take off so he could finally go home—and he did.

> On execution of Eliseo Moreno, convicted of killing 6 people during 50-hour rampage, NY *Times* 5 Mar 87

ED McBAIN

8 A detective sees death in all the various forms at least five times a week.

> *Ten Plus One* Simon & Schuster 63

9 He sees death in convicted thieves, the burglars, the muggers, the con men, the pimps, a death imposed by law, the gradual death of confinement behind bars.

> *ib*

10 He sees death in the prostitutes who have witnessed the death of honor, and daily multiply the death of love, who bleed away their own lives 50 times a day beneath the relentless stabbings of countless conjugations.

> *ib*

11 He sees it in the juvenile street gangs, who live in fear of death and who propagate fear by inflicting death to banish fear. And he sees it at its worst, as the result of violent emotions bursting into the mind and erupting from the hands.

> *ib*

OWEN J McCLAIN, Yonkers NY police officer

12 We don't believe the nation is smothered with tainted Tylenol.

> On death of a young woman from cyanide-laced over-the-counter medication. NY *Times* 12 Feb 86

ROBERT D McFADDEN

13 The old images seem like a caricature now: the shadowy world of secret rituals, the aging dons behind high-walled estates, the passion for vengeance and power over other men. For years, the Mafia was the stuff of novels and movies and whispers on Mulberry Street.

> "The Mafia of the 1980s: Divided and Under Siege" NY *Times* 11 Mar 87

14 Behind the façades of respectability, family life and surprisingly modest homes [are] fathers who hate drugs but sell tons of heroin, gambling czars who lose heavily on the horses, murderers who take offense at off-color language around women and Runyonesque characters with funny nicknames who beat people to death with hammers.

> On evidence presented in trials of organized crime figures. *ib*

15 The myths die hard, especially within the Mafia.

> *ib*

JOHN McGEORGE, Australian psychiatrist

16 A woman has a much better chance than a man of acquittal on a murder charge. . . . If she happens to be a blonde her chances rise about 45 percent.

> *Quote* 12 Mar 60

17 With attractive women . . . juries sometimes have to be restrained from handing them a medal for their crimes.

> *ib*

ANN McMILLAN, psychologist

18 Sometimes it's not going to matter who raises them. If the parents were Mary and Joseph, it would still turn out the same.

> On background of serial killers, quoted in *Newsweek* 26 Nov 84

EDWIN MEESE 3RD, US Attorney General

19 The idea that the police cannot ask questions of the person that knows most about the crime is an infamous decision.

> On Supreme Court's 1966 Miranda decision requiring police to advise criminal suspects of their right to remain silent. NY *Times* 1 Sep 85

J REID MELOY, forensic psychologist

20 Once they start to murder, the act becomes habitual. As it becomes habitual, it becomes easier.

> On serial killers. *Time* 9 Sep 85

KARL A MENNINGER

21 Is it hard for the reader to believe that suicides are sometimes committed to forestall the committing of murder? There is no doubt of it. Nor is there any doubt that murder is sometimes committed to avert suicide.

> *The Crime of Punishment* Viking 68

1 We need criminals to identify ourselves with, to secretly envy and to stoutly punish. They do for us the forbidden, illegal things we wish to do.
> *ib*

2 Police are not all bad guys. Nobody is all bad guys.
> *ib*

W WALTER MENNINGER

3 [Members of the commission] simply state that smoking marijuana in the privacy of your home should be perfectly legal—as long as no one gave it to you [or] sold it to you and you didn't grow it yourself.
> On report by President's Commission on Marijuana and Drug Abuse, San Francisco *Examiner & Chronicle* 23 Apr 72

MARIO MEROLA, District Attorney, Bronx NY

4 These guys commit their crimes with a pencil instead of a gun.
> On corporate crime, NY *Times* 9 Jun 85

5 Pretty soon, there will not be any debate in this city about overcrowded prisons. AIDS will take care of that.
> On reluctance to prosecute AIDS victims, *ib* 5 Mar 87

RICHARD MESSENER, NYC police officer

6 This is your wine and cheese crowd, and nothing ever goes wrong at such events.
> On picnickers attending summer philharmonic concerts in Central Park, NY *Times* 25 Jul 84

GEORGE METESKY

7 One thing I can't understand is why the newspapers labeled me the Mad Bomber. That was unkind.
> On his arrest for placing 20 bombs in public places over a 17-year period, NY *Journal-American* 22 Jan 57

GREGORY MILLER, Assistant US Attorney

8 When artwork is involved, it's almost assumed that it's going to travel. It's too hot to stay here.
> On calling in FBI after the theft of a painting from Philadelphia Museum of Art, NY *Times* 1 Jan 85

ELISEO MORENO, convicted murderer

9 I'm here because I'm guilty. . . . I'm willing to pay according to the laws of Texas because I know I'm guilty.
> On scheduled execution for killing 6 people during 50-hour rampage, NY *Times* 5 Mar 87

JACK MORGAN, City Prosecutor, Tulsa OK

10 Being kissed is an occupational hazard of police work.
> On policewoman who said she was kissed by a man "trying to get out of a ticket," quoted in NY *Times* 12 Dec 77

JAMES D C MURRAY, defense attorney

11 Juvenile delinquency starts in the highchair and ends in the death chair.
> NY *World-Telegram & Sun* 8 Sep 56

BESS MYERSON

12 The accomplice to the crime of corruption is frequently our own indifference.
> Quoted by Claire Safran "Impeachment?" *Redbook* Apr 74

VLADIMIR NABOKOV

13 You can always count on a murderer for a fancy prose style.
> *Lolita* Putnam 58

NEVADA DEPARTMENT OF PRISONS

14 After each execution, sinks, plugs, pot and entire inside of cabinet should be washed down with warm water and a detergent; add two ounces of aqua ammonia to each gallon of water.
> On cleaning of gas chamber after an execution, quoted by John Gregory Dunne *Esquire* Oct 86

NEW YORK TIMES

15 The eternal man in the street says the street's no place for anyone anymore.
> Editorial on series of unprovoked assaults, 29 Dec 80

EUGENE H NICKERSON, Judge, US District Court, Eastern NY

16 She can refresh his recollection with a piece of green cheese, if that will help.
> Permitting prosecutor's use of another person's testimony to refresh a witness's memory, NY *Times* 4 Dec 86

JOHN NORTON, Public Safety Commissioner, Pittsburgh

17 There is absolutely no doubt in my mind that rap music spurs violence.
> *Time* 1 Sep 86

JOAN O'SULLIVAN

18 Today, the Harvard-educated proprietor of a boutique brothel on the East Side would be photographed attending first nights and would discuss her next book on television chat shows with respectful psychoanalysts who would treat her, not without justification, as a professional colleague.
> Possible result of the legalization of prostitution, London *Times* 11 Feb 85

19 [The madam] would contribute her favorite recipes to *Cosmopolitan* magazine. And she would eventually achieve complete respectability by either posing for a *Playboy* centerfold or being elected to Congress.
> *ib*

MARINA OSWALD

20 Sometimes in the dark of night I begin to think. And I wonder if Lee started all this violence.
> On 10th anniversary of the death of her husband Lee Harvey Oswald, alleged assassin of President John F Kennedy, *People* 4 Mar 74

21 The memory is like a cat scratching my heart.
> *ib*

ROBERT PERRY, prosecuting attorney

22 For a plot hatched in hell, don't expect angels for witnesses.
> In summation to jury at conspiracy trial of John De Lorean, 6 Aug 84

NICHOLAS PILEGGI

1 Ever since Damon Runyon wrote the first preppy handbook for the city's Guys and Dolls, back in the 1930s, New York's tough-talking, double-breasted, blue-serge hoods have been the prototype for gangsters all over the world.
"The Boss of Bosses" *New York* 24 Dec 84

2 He had never lit a fire that wasn't a felony.
On a smalltime hoodlum, *Wiseguy* Simon & Schuster 86

PRESIDENTIAL COMMISSION ON ORGANIZED CRIME

3 The need to launder money has led organized crime to avail itself of the full range of banking services normally associated with legitimate, multinational business.
Calling for new federal laws to curb use of financial institutions to launder illegally gained money, NY *Times* 31 Oct 84

RICHARD RAMÍREZ, confessed murderer

4 I killed about 20 people. I was a super criminal. No one could catch me. [Then] they caught me.
Confession to a Los Angeles jail guard, NY *Times* 9 May 86

5 I love to kill people.
ib

RONALD REAGAN, 40th US President

6 The criminal element now calculates that crime really does pay.
To crime victims invited to the White House 18 Apr 84

ROBERT RICE

7 Crime is a logical extension of the sort of behavior that is often considered perfectly respectable in legitimate business.
The Business of Crime Farrar, Straus & Cudahy 56

ANGELO RIZZO

8 He's just a kid, and he's dying fast. . . . trapped inside a cell sick as a dog and made to lay in his own filth. All he did was drugs. Mass killers get treated better.
On fellow inmate in AIDS cell block at Riker's Island penitentiary, NY *Times* 5 Mar 87

SUSAN LISA ROSENBERG, radical protester

9 We're caught, but we're not defeated. Long live the armed struggle!
On arrest as a Weatherman Underground figure suspected in $1.6-million Brink's robbery, NY *Times* 1 Dec 84

BENJAMIN RUGGIERO

10 Keep a neat appearance at all times . . . a wise guy doesn't have a bushy mustache and long hair.
Advice to man about to be initiated into an organized crime family, NY *Times* 11 Mar 87

BERTRAND RUSSELL

11 Americans need rest, but do not know it. I believe this to be a large part of the explanation of the crime wave in the United States.
Quoted by Alan Wood *Bertrand Russell* Simon & Schuster 58

DIANA E RUSSELL

12 A large percentage of the male population has a propensity to rape.
The Politics of Rape Stein & Day 84

WILLIAM SAFIRE

13 One out of 10 guests turns out to be a lexi-klept.
On people who steal dictionaries from hotels, NY *Times* 12 Apr 87

14 Departing guests leave The Word and grab the words.
On preference for dictionaries over Bibles, *ib*

ANTHONY SALERNO

15 If it wasn't for me, there wouldn't be no mob left. I made all the guys. And everybody's a good guy. This guy don't realize that.
Wiretapped conversation about a disrespectful young mobster, NY *Times* 11 Mar 87

JACK SCAFF

16 The idea is to make the woman so repulsive that the attacker runs away. It sounds funny until you smell it.
On perfume for protection against assaults, *Wall Street Journal* 11 Sep 85

MARC SCHREUDER

17 My mother asked me to.
Testimony on motive for murder of his grandfather, quoted by Shana Alexander *Nutcracker* Doubleday 85

SCOTLAND YARD

18 This appeal is urgently directed to all those women whose means of livelihood places them in danger.
Warning possible future victims of a prostitute murderer, NY *Times* 28 Apr 64

ALFRED SETT, LA County Sheriff's Dept

19 Los Angeles is the serial mass murder capital of the world.
After a killer had shot to death 10 Skid Row people in 2 months, NY *Times* 3 Nov 86

GAIL SHEEHY

20 It is a silly question to ask a prostitute why she does it. . . . These are the highest-paid "professional" women in America.
Hustling Delacourt 73

THOMAS L SHEER, FBI bureau chief, NYC

21 They move into a legitimate business and they take it over and compete with other businesses, but if they feel they are losing out, they will revert to breaking legs. True American corporate competition does not include breaking legs.
On organized crime members, NY *Times* 11 Mar 87

R Z SHEPPARD

22 Some of the characters in the story had a fortune in fantasy lives.
On case known as the Main Line murders, "Pennsylvania Death Trip" *Time* 23 Feb 87

GEORGE SIMPSON, English judge

1 These long-haired, mentally unstable, petty little sawdust Caesars only find courage like rats, by hunting in packs.

> On weekend of gangs battling with fists, knives and clubs, NY *Herald Tribune* 19 May 64

SIRHAN SIRHAN

2 They can gas me, but I am famous. I have achieved in one day what it took Robert Kennedy all his life to do.

> On fatal shooting of Senator Robert F Kennedy, *Time* 13 Apr 81

BARRY SLOTNICK

3 If the district attorney wanted, a grand jury would indict a ham sandwich.

> Quoted by Sydney Biddle Barrows *Mayflower Madam*, with William Novak, Arbor House 86

JOHN JUSTIN SMITH

4 Nathan Leopold walked out of Stateville Prison Thursday into the wonderful world of free men. He promptly got sick.

> On release of a convicted murderer after 33 years in prison, Chicago *Daily News* 13 Mar 58

PERRY SMITH, convicted murderer

5 I thought he was a very nice gentleman. . . . I thought so right up to the moment I cut his throat.

> Quoted by Truman Capote *In Cold Blood* Random House 66

ALEXANDER SOLZHENITSYN

6 I can say without affectation that I belong to the Russian convict world no less . . . than I do to Russian literature. I got my education there, and it will last forever.

> *The Oak and the Calf* Harper & Row 80

CLYDE STOW, forensic pathologist

7 Having a policeman dig up a skeleton is like having a chimpanzee do a heart transplant.

> On careful exhumation of skeleton believed to be that of Nazi "angel of death" Joseph Mengele, ABC TV 7 Jun 85

WILLIE SUTTON

8 There was the South Ozone National Bank looking as though it had been waiting for me.

> Quoted by Quentin Reynolds *I, Willie Sutton: The Personal Story of the Most Daring Bank Robber and Jail Breaker of Our Time* Farrar, Straus 53

9 It is a rather pleasant experience to be alone in a bank at night.

> *ib*

MICHAEL TELLING

10 If I had my own private chapel, I could have laid her down to rest and perhaps given her a cross.

> On decapitation, concealment and disposal of the body of his wife, London *Times* 27 Jun 84

EMMANUEL TENEY, Professor of Psychiatry, Wayne State University, Detroit

11 Murder is not the crime of criminals, but that of law-abiding citizens.

> *Time* 12 Aug 66

STUDS TERKEL

12 Chicago is not the most corrupt American city, it's the most theatrically corrupt.

> Dick Cavett show PBS TV 9 Jun 78

OTTIS ELWOOD TOOLE

13 I killed people I didn't think was worth living anyhow.

> On his confessed series of 50 murders that began when he was age 14, *Life* Aug 84

JOE VALACHI, convicted racketeer

14 In the circle in which I travel, a dumb man is more dangerous than a hundred rats.

> Expressing confidence in his ability to testify to US Senate subcommittee, NY *Herald Tribune* 27 Sep 63

15 You live by the gun and knife, and die by the gun and knife.

> Secret code of crime syndicate, NY *Times* 21 Oct 63

16 You can imagine my embarrassment when I killed the wrong guy.

> Quoted in Robert Singer comp *The Bad Guys' Quote Book* Avon 84

DUDLEY VARNEY, LA homicide detective

17 There could be a guy signing his name on the ass of some dead body back on the East Coast, and we wouldn't know about it.

> On lack of time to read nationwide teletype messages, *Newsweek* 26 Nov 84

ANTHONY VIDLER, architect

18 Any precinct captain in New York could have told the grandmother that latches of that nature could not guard against the wolf.

> On design of lock on Little Red Riding Hood's grandmother's cottage, NY *Times* 5 Mar 84

JOHN P VUKASIN JR, Judge, US District Court, Northern California

19 [He was] not a Soviet apologist. [He] did not believe in anything at all. He is the type of modern man whose highest expression lies in his amorality.

> Prior to sentencing former US Navy officer Jerry A Whitworth for espionage, NY *Times* 29 Aug 86

JOSEPH WAMBAUGH

20 Perhaps it had nothing to do with sin and everything to do with sociopathy, that most incurable of human disorders because all so afflicted consider themselves *blessed* rather than cursed.

> On partnership of Main Line murderers, *Echoes in the Darkness* Morrow 87, quoted in *Time* 23 Feb 87

BENJAMIN WARD, NYC Police Commissioner

21 If you come to New York to buy crack, bring carfare and be prepared to take the bus back.

> On stopping 43 motorists and impounding 30 automobiles cruising in areas where drugs were sold, NY *Times* 5 Aug 86

HERBERT WARD, Episcopal priest

22 Child abuse casts a shadow the length of a lifetime.

> Annual report, St Jude's Ranch, Boulder City NV, 85

EDWIN WARNER

1 People have always accused kids of getting away with murder. Now that is all too literally true.
"The Youth Crime Plague" *Time* 11 Jul 77

KEITH WHEELER

2 They are pure, unduplicatable Chicago. . . . they help explain why—in Chicago—it is unwise to take your eyes off any asset smaller than a locomotive.
On the Panczko brothers, arrested 214 times in 25 years, *Life* 6 Aug 65

HERBERT EMERSON WILSON

3 The safe that night looked like a soft one [and] the explosion made no more noise than a pig's grunt.
On his first break-in of a Detroit department store, quoted by James Chiles "Age-Old Battle to Keep Safes Safe from Creepers, Soup Men and Yeggs" *Smithsonian* Jul 84

4 In all my years on the prowl, I never got over the thrill of hearing the first boom and seeing what it did to a massive block of steel.
ib

BUSINESS

Executives

AGHA HASAN ABEDI, President, Bank of Credit and Commerce International, Luxembourg

5 The conventional definition of management is getting work done through people, but real management is developing people through work.
Leaders Jul 84

TADASHI ADACHI, President, Chamber of Commerce of Japan

6 If the lion and dragon fight, they will both die.
On the belief that the shame of failure is exceeded only by the shame of causing someone else's failure, *Newsweek* 17 May 65

DONALD G ADAMS, Vice President, Addressograph-Multigraph Corp

7 Copying has become a national disease.
On the heavy use of photocopying machines, *Newsweek* 7 Sep 64

ANONYMOUS

8 The most important marketer in our company is the man or woman on the loading dock who decides not to drop the damned box into the back of the truck.
Executive of a high-tech company, quoted by Thomas J Peters and Nancy K Austin *A Passion for Excellence* Random House 85, excerpted in *Fortune* 13 May 85

9 If my boss calls, be sure to get his name.
Comment of ABC executive, quoted by William S Rukeyser in report on the swift shifts of personnel in television management, *Fortune* 14 Apr 86

ELIZABETH ARDEN, cosmetics executive

10 Dear, never forget one little point. It's my business. You just work here.
To her husband, quoted by Alfred Lewis and Constance Woodworth *Miss Elizabeth Arden* Coward, McCann & Geoghegan 72

MARY KAY ASH, Chairman, Mary Kay Cosmetics Inc

11 If you think you can, you can. And if you think you can't, you're right.
NY *Times* 20 Oct 85

MORTON BAHR, President, Communications Workers of America

12 We are beginning to recognize that it is more important to organize the unorganized than to argue about who will get the workers when they are organized.
On cooperation in labor negotiations, NY *Times* 4 May 86

SYDNEY BIDDLE BARROWS

13 The more you act like a lady, the more he'll act like a gentleman.
Instructions to employees of her escort service, *Mayflower Madam*, with William Novak, Arbor House 86

BRUCE BARTON, Chairman, Batten, Barton, Durstine & Osborn

14 In good times, people want to advertise; in bad times, they have to.
Town & Country Feb 55

BERNARD BARUCH

15 Always do one thing less than you think you can do.
On maintaining good health, *Newsweek* 28 May 56

WILLIAM BERNBACH, advertising executive

16 An idea can turn to dust or magic, depending on the talent that rubs against it.
NY *Times* 6 Oct 82

BARRY BINGHAM JR

17 There were board meetings when my wife was doing needlepoint, one sister was addressing Christmas cards and another didn't bother to attend.
On breakdown of the family media business, *Fortune* 17 Feb 86

ROGER BLOUGH, President, US Steel Corp

18 Steel prices cause inflation like wet sidewalks cause rain.
Forbes 1 Aug 67

FRANK BORMAN, Chief Executive Officer, Eastern Airlines

19 Capitalism without bankruptcy is like Christianity without hell.
Quoted in *US* 21 Apr 86

WILLIAM BOURKE, Executive Vice President, Ford Motor Co

20 Other people set off firecrackers. We drop atomic bombs.
On forced resignation of company president Lee Iacocca, NY *Times* 18 Jul 78

RICHARD BRANSON, Chairman, Virgin Atlantic Airlines

21 Like getting into a bleeding competition with a blood bank.
On competing with British Airways, London *Times* 20 Sep 84

EDGAR BRONFMAN, Chairman, Seagram Co

22 To turn $100 into $110 is work. To turn $100 million into $110 million is inevitable.
Newsweek 2 Dec 85

L E J BROUWER, Senior Managing Director, Royal Dutch/ Shell Oil Co

1 Oil is seldom found where it is most needed, and seldom most needed where it is found.
Time 4 May 70

CHARLES BROWER, President, Batten, Barton, Durstine & Osborn

2 There is no such thing as "soft sell" and "hard sell." There is only "smart sell" and "stupid sell."
Comments to national convention of sales executives, news summaries 20 May 58

ARTHUR BRYAN, Chairman, Josiah Wedgwood & Sons Ltd

3 Hiccups in the international business scene are not new to us. Wedgwood china has survived upheavals before—the Napoleonic Wars, the Franco-Prussian War, the world wars. We do have a sense of continuity.
Quoted in NY *Times* 30 Mar 80

LEO BURNETT, Chairman, Leo Burnett Co Inc

4 When you reach for the stars, you may not quite get one, but you won't come up with a handful of mud either.
Reader's Digest Jan 85

H S M BURNS, President, Shell Oil Co

5 A good manager is a man who isn't worried about his own career but rather the careers of those who work for him.
Quoted by Osborn Elliott *Men at the Top* Harper 59

6 Take care of those who work for you and you'll float to greatness on their achievements.
ib

DONALD C BURR, Chairman, People Express Airlines Inc

7 Coffee stains on the flip-down trays mean [to the passengers] that we do our engine maintenance wrong.
Quoted by Thomas J Peters and Nancy K Austin *A Passion for Excellence* Random House 85, excerpted in *Fortune* 13 May 85

CLIVE CHAJET, President, Lippincott & Margulies

8 There is an idea, broadly held on Wall Street, that names with X's are more memorable and tend to capture the attention of analysts. It is not held by us.
On advising clients about corporate name changes, quoted by Lisa Belkin "How American Can Became Primerica" NY *Times* 8 Mar 87

LORD CHANDOS (Oliver Lyttelton), international banking and metals executive

9 In business a reputation for keeping absolutely to the letter and spirit of an agreement, even when it is unfavorable, is the most precious of assets, although it is not entered in the balance sheet.
Memoirs of Lord Chandos: An Unexpected View From the Summit New American Library 63

10 Power in a corporation becomes residual and dwells in the background. It is the ability to exercise nice matters of judgment.
ib

ALVIN CHERESKIN, President, AC & R advertising agency

11 Sex! What is that but *life*, after all? We're all of us selling sex, because we're all selling life.
Quoted by Kennedy Fraser "As Gorgeous As It Gets" *New Yorker* 15 Sep 86

JOHN CHERRY, Florida undertaker

12 Celestis is a postcremation service. . . . We further reduce and encapsulate them, identify each by name, Social Security number and a religious symbol and place them into the payloader.
Comments of one of a group of morticians arranging to send human ashes into a permanent orbit 1,900 miles above the earth, NY *Times* 25 Jan 85

L L COLBERT, President, Chrysler Corp

13 When I've had a rough day, before I go to sleep I ask myself if there's anything more I can do right now. If there isn't, I sleep sound.
Newsweek 22 Aug 55

BARBER B CONABLE JR, President, World Bank

14 Women do two thirds of the world's work. . . . Yet they earn only one tenth of the world's income and own less than one percent of the world's property. They are among the poorest of the world's poor.
To annual meeting of World Bank and International Monetary Fund, NY *Times* 1 Oct 86

FAIRFAX CONE, advertising executive

15 Advertising is what you do when you can't go see somebody. That's all it is.
Christian Science Monitor 20 Mar 63

E GERALD CORRIGAN

16 I am very careful about bringing people into my confidence. I want to see the color of their eyes.
On becoming president of Federal Reserve Bank in Minneapolis, NY *Times* 30 Dec 84

HARLOW H CURTICE, President, General Motors Corp

17 General Motors has no bad years, only good years and better years.
Quoted by Alfred P Sloan Jr *My Years with General Motors* Doubleday 64

KITTY D'ALESSIO, President, Chanel Inc

18 As times change, you want to really revere your heredity, but you don't want to be a shrine. . . . to light candles and kneel.
On conflict between tradition and modernity after she succeeded company founder Coco Chanel, NY *Times* 28 Jul 85

19 Open the windows, let in the year we're living in.
ib

LEON A DANCO, President, Center for Family Business

20 They look upon retirement as something between euthanasia and castration.
On company founders who view "giving up" as tantamount to planning their own funerals, NY *Times* 11 Jun 86

JERRY DELLA FEMINA, advertising executive

21 Thank you for making me *nouveau riche*.
Engraving on silver box presented to attorney Mort Janklow after successful sale of Della Femina's advertising agency, *New York* 2 Feb 87

1 It goes back to all of us wanting to be in Hollywood. We're all dying to win an Oscar.

> On plethora of awards in advertising industry, *Wall Street Journal* 26 Mar 87

RICHARD DONAT, store manager, Marshall Field & Co, Chicago

2 Another day, another million dollars.

> On the Christmas shopping season, *Wall Street Journal* 29 Nov 84

FREDERICK HUDSON ECKER, Chairman, Metropolitan Life

3 I don't think anybody yet has invented a pastime that's as much fun, or keeps you as young, as a good job.

> Recalled on his death at age 96, 20 Mar 64

BILL EVANS, President, Clio Awards

4 We use the people who are in the bullpen producing.

> On importance of having young judges in advertising competition, *Wall Street Journal* 26 Mar 87

5 It's like having a designer dress compared with one from Woolworth's. Which one is more impressive when you go to the debutante ball?

> On the Clio's prestige as one of the oldest and best-known advertising awards, *ib*

JONI EVANS, President, Trade Division, Simon & Schuster

6 People assume you slept your way to the top. Frankly, I couldn't sleep my way to the middle.

> Comments to conference of women executives on her beginnings as a reader of manuscripts, NY *Times* 22 Jul 86

HAL FAIR, National Product Coordinator, Brother International Corp

7 Don't expect the typewriter to ever completely disappear.

> On the widespread use of word processors, NY *Times* 23 Nov 84

JIM FISHEL, direct-mail specialist

8 She doesn't want to touch it. She doesn't want to smell it. She doesn't want to hear it. Lord love her. She's a Mail Order Freak.

> Advertisement for direct marketing, quoted by Philip H Dougherty "Advertising: The Fishels of Fairfax at Compton" NY *Times* 30 Dec 80

BERNICE FITZ-GIBBON, Director of Advertising, Macy's

9 Teenagers travel in droves, packs, swarms. . . . To the librarian, they're a gaggle of geese. To the cook, they're a scourge of locusts. To department stores they're a big beautiful exaltation of larks. . . . all lovely and loose and jingly.

> NY *Times* 6 Jun 60

B C FORBES

10 If you don't drive your business, you will be driven out of business.

> *Forbes* 1 Apr 74

MALCOLM S FORBES

11 Executives who get there and stay suggest solutions when they present the problems.

> *Forbes* 12 May 80

GEORGE KEITH FUNSTON, President, New York Stock Exchange

12 Automation does not make optimism obsolete.

> Address at George Peabody College for Teachers, Vanderbilt University, Nashville TN, 11 Mar 64

CORNELIUS GALLAGHER, Realtor

13 After all, the three major sources of apartments are death, divorce and transfer.

> On reading obituaries for leads in the tight Manhattan housing market, NY *Times* 2 May 85

HAROLD S GENEEN, former Chairman, International Telephone and Telegraph

14 In the business world, everyone is paid in two coins: cash and experience. Take the experience first; the cash will come later.

> *Managing*, with Alvin Moscow, Doubleday 84

15 Every company has two organizational structures: The formal one is written on the charts; the other is the everyday relationship of the men and women in the organization.

> *ib*

16 Management must manage!

> *ib*

17 Managers in all too many American companies do not achieve the desired results because nobody makes them do it.

> *ib*

18 It is much more difficult to measure nonperformance than performance.

> On why management sometimes accepts underachievement, *ib*

19 Performance stands out like a ton of diamonds. Nonperformance can always be explained away.

> *ib*

20 You can know a person by the kind of desk he keeps. . . . If the president of a company has a clean desk . . . then it must be the executive vice president who is doing all the work.

> *ib*

21 The worst disease which can afflict business executives in their work is not, as popularly supposed, alcoholism; it's egotism.

> *ib*

22 It is an immutable law in business that words are words, explanations are explanations, promises are promises—but only performance is reality.

> *ib*

23 If you keep working you'll last longer and I just want to keep vertical. . . . I'd hate to spend the rest of my life trying to outwit an 18-inch fish.

> On establishing a new business after retiring from ITT, NY *Times* 18 Nov 84

J PAUL GETTY

24 No one can possibly achieve any real and lasting success or "get rich" in business by being a conformist.

> *International Herald Tribune* 10 Jan 61

25 Oil is like a wild animal. Whoever captures it has it.

> Quoted by Robert Lenzner *The Great Getty* Crown 85

1 There are one hundred men seeking security to one able man who is willing to risk his fortune.
ib

2 I buy when other people are selling.
ib

3 The meek shall inherit the earth, but not the mineral rights.
ib

4 If you can count your money, you don't have a billion dollars.
ib

STEVEN GILLIATT, Director of Design, Lippincott & Margulies

5 A one-syllable word sounds better with Inc. A longer word has better rhythm with Corporation.
On making corporate name changes, quoted by Lisa Belkin "How American Can Became Primerica" NY *Times* 8 Mar 87

6 [A logo] should look just as good in 15-foot letters on top of company headquarters as it does one sixteenth of an inch tall on company stationery.
ib

ROBERT GREENLEAF, Director of Management Research, AT&T

7 Many attempts to communicate are nullified by saying too much.
Servant Leadership: A Journey into the Nature of Legitimate Power and Greatness Paulist Press 77

8 Even the frankest and bravest of subordinates do not talk with their boss the same way they talk with colleagues.
ib

DEIL O GUSTAFSON, real estate executive

9 Inequality of knowledge is the key to a sale.
Newsweek 20 May 74

ROBERT W HAACK, President, New York Stock Exchange

10 The public may be willing to forgive us for mistakes in judgment but it will not forgive us for mistakes in motive.
Wall Street Journal 17 Oct 67

MARION HARPER JR, President, McCann-Erickson

11 I have been captured by what I chased.
On marketing organization that grew out of his advertising agency, *Newsweek* 30 Mar 64

JOHN B HARTNETT, Chairman, Xerox Corp

12 A word beginning with X . . . the more we thought about it, the more we were ready to try it. And we got it into the dictionary.
On the trademark *Xerox*, recalled on his death 3 Jun 82

KEN HAYASHIBARA, Japanese manufacturer

13 If the person is over 40 years old, I tell him he should do something because it is first good for Japan, good for the company, good for his family and finally good for him. If the person is under 40, I tell him he should do it because first it is good for him, good for his family, good for the company and finally good for Japan.
On social changes introduced during US military occupation of Japan, NY *Times* 9 May 84

H L HUNT, Texas oil billionaire

14 I didn't go to high school, and I didn't go to grade school either. Education, I think, is for refinement and is probably a liability.
60 Minutes CBS TV 1 Apr 69

NELSON BUNKER HUNT, Texas billionaire

15 People who know how much they're worth aren't usually worth that much.
Testimony to Congressional subcommittee, *Time* 12 May 80

ROBERT HUNTER, Director, National Insurance Consumer Organization

16 At the top of the cycle you write [policies for] everybody, no matter how bad, and at the bottom you cancel everybody, no matter how good. It's a manic-depressive cycle.
On the insurance business, quoted by George J Church "Sorry, Your Policy Is Cancelled" *Time* 24 Mar 86

LEE IACOCCA

17 One of the things the government can't do is run anything. The only things our government runs are the post office and the railroads, and both of them are bankrupt.
As president of Ford Motor Co, *Quote* 17 Jun 73

18 People want economy and they will pay any price to get it.
NY *Times* 13 Oct 74

19 When future historians look back on our way of curing inflation . . . they'll probably compare it to bloodletting in the Middle Ages.
Fortune 27 Jun 83

20 We at Chrysler borrow money the old-fashioned way. We pay it back.
As chairman of Chrysler Corp, which borrowed $1.2 billion under US Loan Guarantee Act of 1979 and repaid the loan seven years before it was due, news summaries 13 Jul 83

21 I gotta tell ya, with our $2.4 billion in profits last year, they gave me a great big bonus. Really, it's almost obscene.
Addressing market analysts in Detroit, quoted in *Time* 1 Apr 85

22 If a guy is over 25 percent jerk, he's in trouble. And Henry was 95 percent.
On Henry Ford II, *ib*

23 Are we going to be a services power? The double-cheeseburger-hold-the-mayo kings of the whole world?
To Japan Society of NY, *Fortune* 7 Jul 86

ERIC JOHNSTON, President, US Chamber of Commerce

24 The dinosaur's eloquent lesson is that if some bigness is good, an overabundance of bigness is not necessarily better.
Warning businesses against excessive growth, *Quote* 23 Feb 58

J BRUCE JOHNSTON, Executive Vice President, US Steel Corp

25 There are not enough seats in the steel lifeboat for everybody.
From a letter warning striking employees that the company was facing "an economic showdown with non-union competitors, bankrupt competitors and foreign competitors," NY *Times* 10 Aug 86

ERNEST A JONES, advertising executive

1 Only for the phony is commercialism—the bending of creativity to common utility—a naughty word. To the truly creative, it is a bridge to the great audience, a means of sharing rather than debasing.
> Address at Cranbrook Academy of Art, NY *Herald Tribune* 2 Jun 64

2 Creativity not committed to public purpose is merely therapy or ego satisfaction.
> *ib*

HENRY J KAISER, industrialist

3 Problems are only opportunities in work clothes.
> Recalled on his death 24 Aug 67

FREDERICK R KAPPEL, Chairman, AT&T

4 The Bell System is like a damn big dragon. You kick it in the tail, and two years later it feels it in its head.
> Quoted by J Robert Moskin "The Surprising Story of Ma Bell" *Look* 28 Aug 62

JOSEPH P KENNEDY, former US Ambassador to Britain

5 Whenever you're sitting across from some important person, always picture him sitting there in a suit of long red underwear. That's the way I always operated in business.
> Quoted by Lawrence O'Brien *No Final Victories* Doubleday 74

MARILYN MOATS KENNEDY, Managing Partner, Career Strategies, Chicago

6 Politics is the process of getting along with the querulous, the garrulous and the congenitally unlovable.
> Quoted in "Playing Office Politics" *Newsweek* 16 Sep 85

LANE KIRKLAND, President, AFL–CIO

7 To hear the Japanese plead for free trade is like hearing the word *love* on the lips of a harlot.
> NY *Times* 28 Jul 85

8 We must be part of the general staff at the inception, rather than the ambulance drivers at the bitter end.
> On bargaining disputes that impede contract negotiations, *ib* 4 May 86

CARL A KROCH, Chairman, Kroch's & Brentano's Inc, Chicago

9 The independent bookstore—you know we're almost dinosaurs.
> On turning over the 80-year-old family firm to its employees, NY *Times* 22 Jun 86

EDWIN HERBERT LAND, founder, Polaroid Corp

10 The bottom line is in heaven!
> When asked what a new product called Polavision might contribute to "the bottom line," *Boston Business* Fall 86

ESTÉE LAUDER, cosmetics executive

11 When you stop talking, you've lost your customer. When you turn your back, you've lost her.
> To conference of sales personnel, quoted by Kennedy Fraser "As Gorgeous As It Gets" *New Yorker* 15 Sep 86

12 Touch a face. Touch a hand. Say, "This is for you, this is what I want *you* to wear."
> *ib*

13 If you don't sell, it's not the product that's wrong, it's *you.*
> *ib*

MARY WELLS LAWRENCE, advertising executive

14 In this business, you can never wash the dinner dishes and say they are done. You have to keep doing them constantly.
> On need for fresh approaches, *Time* 3 Oct 66

JOHN L LEWIS, President, United Mine Workers

15 I don't think the federation has a head; its neck has just grown up and haired over.
> On World Federation of Trade Unions, recalled in news summaries 11 Jan 80

RAYMOND LOEWY

16 Good design keeps the user happy, the manufacturer in the black and the aesthete unoffended.
> Comment of "the father of streamlining," recalled on his death 14 Jul 86

BERNARD LOOMIS, toy manufacturing executive

17 The trouble with research is that it tells you what people were thinking about yesterday, not tomorrow. It's like driving a car using a rearview mirror.
> *International Herald Tribune* 9 Oct 85

FRANK P LOUCHHEIM, Chairman, Right Associates, management placement firm

18 "You're fired!" No other words can so easily and succinctly reduce a confident, self-assured executive to an insecure, groveling shred of his former self.
> "The Art of Getting Fired" *Wall Street Journal* 16 Jul 84

19 Handled creatively, getting fired allows an executive . . . to actually experience a sense of relief that he never wanted the job he has lost.
> *ib*

F R MANN, retired Chairman, National Container Corp

20 There's a little bit of the dictator in all of us. Fortunately, I was blessed with a disproportionately generous share.
> NY *Times* 16 Jun 76

HERBERT MARCUS, cofounder, Neiman-Marcus

21 There is never a good *sale* for Neiman-Marcus unless it's a good *buy* for the customer.
> 1926 comment to his son, quoted by Stanley Marcus *Minding the Store* Little, Brown 74

TOM McELLIGOTT, advertising executive

22 You're never too bad to win.
> On plethora of awards in advertising industry, *Wall Street Journal* 26 Mar 87

ROBERT MILLER, Chairman, Chrysler Financial Corp

23 Are these guys really Robin Hood and his Merry Men as they claim, or Genghis Khan and the Mongol hordes?
> On corporate raiders, address at Harvard Business School, *US News & World Report* 26 Jan 87

ROGER MILLER, Codirector, Mergers and Acquisitions, Salomon Brothers Inc

1 Junk bonds are the Holy Grail for hostile takeovers.
NY *Times* 14 Apr 85

GEORGE MORROW, President, Morrow Inc

2 Being in the microcomputer business is like going 55 miles an hour 3 feet from a cliff.
On his company's bankruptcy. *Fortune* 14 Apr 86

CHARLES G MORTIMER, President, General Foods Corp

3 Today convenience is the success factor of just about every type of product and service that is showing steady growth.
To Amer Marketing Assn, quoted by NY *Herald Tribune* 14 May 59

4 The creeping notion that additives are badditives.
Calling for campaign against the ban on food coloring, *Wall Street Journal* 29 Dec 60

CLINT W MURCHISON, Texas financier

5 Money is like manure. If you spread it around, it does a lot of good, but if you pile it up in one place, it stinks like hell.
Quoted by his son Clint Murchison Jr. *Time* 16 Jun 61

PAUL NEILD, Managing Director, Phillips & Drew, London

6 The aristocracy is in decline in the City, and the cloth-cap professionals are in the ascent. And we will take over.
On aggressive new breed in London's financial district. NY *Times* 25 Sep 86

DONALD NEUENSCHWANDER, Chairman, Medical Center Bank, Houston

7 You can't be all things to all people. But I can be all things to the people I select.
Commenting on his bank, whose clients are physicians and wealthy customers, *Time* 3 Dec 84

ALBERT NEWGARDEN, Arthur Young & Co

8 Accountants are perpetually fighting their shiny pants, green eyeshades, number-cruncher image.
Wall Street Journal 26 Apr 84

DAVID OGILVY, advertising executive

9 The most important word in the vocabulary of advertising is TEST. If you pretest your product with consumers, and pretest your advertising, you will do well in the marketplace.
Confessions of an Advertising Man Atheneum 63

10 Never stop testing, and your advertising will never stop improving.
ib

11 Leaders . . . grasp nettles.
To Amer Marketing Assn 10 May 72

WILLIAM S PALEY, founder, CBS

12 There's a certain amount of disorder that has to be reorganized.
On return as CBS chairman after his retirement. Boston *Globe* 16 Sep 86

COLA PARKER, President, National Assn of Manufacturers

13 We have gone completely overboard on security. Everything has to be secured, jobs, wages, hours—

although the ultimate in security is jail, the slave labor camp and the salt mine.
News summaries 9 Dec 55

PAUL J PAULSON, President, Doyle Dane Bernbach

14 You can learn a lot from the client. . . . Some 70 percent doesn't matter, but that 30 percent will kill you.
NY *Times* 4 May 79

JAMES CASH PENNEY, founder, JC Penney Corp

15 I wouldn't be human if I didn't feel pride and something that transcends pride—humility.
At dedication of his company's Manhattan headquarters, NY *Herald Tribune* 30 May 65

TOMMY PERSE, co-owner, Maxfield boutique, Los Angeles

16 The store forces people to cleanse their mind and allows them to do the major damage to their credit cards that we appreciate so much.
On effect of minimalist décor, *Newsweek* 10 Nov 86

T BOONE PICKENS, Chairman, Mesa Petroleum Co

17 Chief executives, who themselves own few shares of their companies, have no more feeling for the average stockholder than they do for baboons in Africa.
Harvard Business Review May/Jun 86

GIFFORD PINCHOT III, management consultant

18 Corporate risk takers are very much like entrepreneurs. They take personal risks to make new ideas happen.
Intrapreneuring Harper & Row 85

ROBERT PLISKIN, Vice President, Benton & Bowles

19 Market research can establish beyond the shadow of a doubt that the egg is a sad and sorry product and that it obviously will not continue to sell. Because after all, eggs won't stand up by themselves, they roll too easily, are too easily broken, require special packaging, look alike, are difficult to open, won't stack on the shelf.
To National Packaging Forum 16 Oct 63

B EARL PUCKETT, President, Allied Stores Corp

20 It is our job to make women unhappy with what they have.
Recalled on his death, *Newsweek* 23 Feb 76

CLARENCE B RANDALL

21 The leader must know, must know that he knows and must be able to make it abundantly clear to those about him that he knows.
Making Good in Management McGraw-Hill 64

ROSSER REEVES, Chairman, Ted Bates & Co Inc

22 If he isn't a salesman, he can't write selling copy. If he isn't a writer, he can't be a salesman in print.
On the making of a copywriter, *Advertising Age* 19 Apr 65

23 Some of the people that float around in this business and are allegedly great copywriters at great salaries, we wouldn't pay $50 a week to at this agency. I think a great many copywriters in this business earn their living because they haven't been caught.
ib

CHARLES REVSON, founder of Revlon Inc

1 I don't meet competition. I crush it.
    Time 16 Jun 58

AL RIES, Chairman, Trout & Ries Advertising Inc

2 Today, communication itself is the problem. We
have become the world's first overcommunicated
society. Each year we send more and receive less.
    Positioning: The Battle for Your Mind, with Jack Trout,
    McGraw-Hill 80

3 Changing the direction of a large company is like
trying to turn an aircraft carrier. It takes a mile before anything happens. And if it was a wrong turn,
getting back on course takes even longer.
    ib

4 Don't overlook the importance of worldwide thinking. A company that keeps its eye on Tom, Dick and
Harry is going to miss Pierre, Hans and Yoshio.
    ib

ROBERTO RISSO

5 If I can get every rich girl with a rose garden to use
guano, that's it.
    On his attempt to market $80,000 worth of Peruvian bat
    dung as the "Rolls Royce of fertilizers," *Wall Street
    Journal* 24 Jul 84

FELIX G ROHATYN, Chairman, Municipal Assistance Corp,
NYC

6 Two-tier tender offers, Pac-Man and poison-pill defenses, crown-jewel options, greenmail, golden par-
achutes, self-tenders—all have become part of our
everyday business.
    Quoted by William Safire NY *Times* 27 Jan 85

7 [Bankruptcy would be] like stepping into a tepid
bath and slashing your wrists: You might not feel
yourself dying, but that's what would happen.
    ib 2 Jul 85

WILLIAM ROOTES, industrialist

8 No other manmade device since the shields and
lances of the knights quite fulfills a man's ego like
an automobile.
    Quoted on *Who Said That?* BBC TV 14 Jan 58

RAYMOND RUBICAM, cofounder, Young & Rubicam Inc

9 The best identification of a great advertisement is
that its public is not only strongly sold by it, but that
both the public and the advertising world remember
it for a long time as an admirable piece of work.
    Quoted by David Ogilvy *Confessions of an Advertising
    Man* Atheneum 63

DAVID SARNOFF, Chairman, RCA

10 I hitched my wagon to an electron rather than the
proverbial star.
    NY *Times* 4 Apr 58

JIM SCHWARTZ, stockholder in Manhattan's East Side
Sauna

11 From a business point of view, we make as much
money from one person having sex with one person
as one person having sex with 40.
    On remaining open for business despite the AIDS epi-
    demic, NY *Times* 14 Oct 85

ROBERT F SIX, President, Continental Airlines

12 "My door is always open—bring me your problems." This is guaranteed to turn on every whiner,
lackey and neurotic on the property.
    Quoted in Robert W Kent ed *Money Talks* Pocket
    Books 86

RANDY SMITH, marketing official, People Express Airlines
Inc

13 We built the Model T; it was black and a lot of people bought it. But we found out not everybody wanted it.
    On no-frills flying, NY *Times* 25 Jun 86

ROGER B SMITH, Chairman, General Motors Corp

14 We hope this car will be less labor intensive, less
material intensive, less everything intensive than
anything we have done before.
    On the Saturn model, *Time* 21 Jan 85

BENJAMIN SONNENBERG, public relations pioneer

15 I supply the Listerine to the commercial dandruff on
the shoulders of corporations.
    Time 12 Feb 79

A ALFRED TAUBMAN, owner of 650 A&W Root Beer
Stands and Chairman, Sotheby Galleries

16 There is more similarity in a precious painting by
Degas and a frosted mug of root beer than you ever
thought possible.
    NY *Times* 3 Feb 85

17 God help us if we ever take the theater out of the
auction business or anything else. It would be an
awfully boring world.
    Wall Street Journal 18 Sep 85

BERNARD TRESNOWSKI, Director, Blue Cross and Blue
Shield Assn

18 In the past, employers were like an absentee host
who paid the bill but never showed up at the table.
Now they are intimately involved in planning the
menu.
    On new role of employers in determining health care,
    Newsweek 2 Jul 84

DONALD J TRUMP, real estate developer

19 When I build something for somebody, I always add
$50 million or $60 million onto the price. My guys
come in, they say it's going to cost $75 million. I say
it's going to cost $125 million, and I build it for $100
million. Basically, I did a lousy job. But they think
I did a great job.
    To 1984 meeting of US Football League owners, NY
    Times 1 Jul 86

TED TURNER

20 If I only had a little humility, I'd be perfect.
    Quoted in news summaries 8 Jun 80

JAMES R UFFELMAN, President, Technimetrics Inc

21 The work is often deadly and boring, but it requires
a keen intelligence, and the only way I can compete
with large corporations is to treat my employees better, move them up faster, give them more money
and put mirrors in the bathrooms.
    Wall Street Journal 21 Aug 84

1 If you can make an employee happy by spending $800 on a comfortable office chair, what's $800?

ib

KAREN VALENSTEIN, Vice President, E F Hutton Group Inc

2 I never go out of my way to screw someone, but I'm always looking over my shoulder.

Quoted by Jane Gross "Against the Odds" NY *Times* 6 Jan 85

3 There's a place for corporate wives, but there's no place for corporate husbands.

ib

KENNETH J VAUGHAN, former Director, Winnebago Industries Inc

4 John K probably won't stop working for Winnebago until six weeks after he dies.

On the company's founder John K Hanson, NY *Times* 18 May 86

AN WANG

5 Success is more a function of consistent common sense than it is of genius.

Boston Magazine Dec 86

6 I founded Wang Laboratories . . . to show that Chinese could excel at things other than running laundries and restaurants.

ib

GORDON WEBBER, Vice President, Benton & Bowles

7 To dare every day to be irreverent and bold. To dare to preserve the randomness of mind which in children produces strange and wonderful new thoughts and forms. To continually scramble the familiar and bring the old into new juxtaposition.

Advertising Age 31 Oct 60

WILLIAM K WHITEFORD, Chairman, Gulf Corp

8 Smell that! That's gasoline you smell in there. You can't buy any perfume in the world that smells as sweet.

Forbes 1 May 64

KING WHITNEY JR, President, Personnel Laboratory Inc

9 Change has considerable psychological impact on the human mind. To the fearful it is threatening because it means that things may get worse. To the hopeful it is encouraging because things may get better. To the confident it is inspiring because the challenge exists to make things better. Obviously, then, one's character and frame of mind determine how readily he brings about change and how he reacts to change that is imposed on him.

To a sales meeting, quoted by *Wall Street Journal* 7 Jun 67

WALTER B WRISTON

10 When you retire . . . you go from who's who to who's that, [like] stepping off the pier [or] achieving statutory senility.

On retiring as chairman of Citibank Corp, NY *Times* 21 Apr 85

PETE ZAMARELLO, real estate developer

11 I'd rather be a pimp with a purple hat . . . than be associated with banks.

In bankruptcy court in Anchorage, *Wall Street Journal* 24 Feb 87

12 I will not build nothing in Alaska, even my tomb.

ib

Observers & Critics

DEAN ACHESON

13 Time spent in the advertising business seems to create a permanent deformity like the Chinese habit of foot-binding.

Quoted in David S McLellan and David C Acheson eds *Among Friends* Dodd, Mead 80

WOODY ALLEN

14 Eighty percent of success is showing up.

Quoted by Thomas J Peters & Robert H Waterman *In Search of Excellence* Harper & Row 82

ANONYMOUS

15 He carves you up but leaves the skin around the body.

Comments of a Ford Motor Co executive on Philip Caldwell, president of international operations, quoted in NY *Times* 13 Mar 77

16 The problem when solved will be simple.

Sign on the wall of General Motors research laboratory, Dayton, quoted by Al Ries and Jack Trout *Positioning: The Battle for Your Mind* McGraw-Hill 81

17 You know what the difference is between a dead skunk and a dead banker on the road? There's skid marks by the skunk.

Quoted by Andrew H Malcolm *Final Harvest: An American Tragedy* Times Books 86

18 Oilfield prayer: Lord, let there be one more Boom. And don't let us screw it up.

Sign in Texas diner, quoted in "A Dream Dies in Texas" *People* 10 Nov 86

19 Either lead, follow or get out of the way.

Sign on desk of broadcasting executive Ted Turner, pictured in *Fortune* 5 Jan 87

PETER BAIDA

20 I have received memos so swollen with managerial babble that they struck me as the literary equivalent of assault with a deadly weapon.

"Management Babble" *American Heritage* Apr 85

LISA BELKIN

21 Dozens of meetings, hundreds of man-hours, millions of dollars and months of angst . . . went into the name change. . . . the most sweeping of changes brought about by the most persnickity attention to detail.

"How American Can Became Primerica" NY *Times* 8 Mar 87

22 Corporate identity specialists . . . spend their time rechristening other companies, [conducting] a legal search [and] a linguistic search to insure that the name is not an insult in another language.

ib

PAULA BERNSTEIN

1 Today's corporate family is headed by a "father" who finds the child he never had, the child he always wanted, at the office and guides him (sometimes her) up the ladder.

> Employing metaphors of family life to explain office scenarios, *Family Ties, Corporate Bonds* Doubleday 85

DEREK BOK, President, Harvard

2 The oldest of the arts and the youngest of the professions.

> Conferring the degree Master of Business Administration, quoted by Kingman Brewster, US Ambassador, in address to British Institute of Management 13 Dec 77

FRANCIS J BRACELAND, Chief Psychiatrist, Institute for Living, Hartford CT

3 Whereas the well-functioning executive encourages the best in brains and skills, the one who is paranoid or even less morbidly insecure must have inadequates about him, men who will take punishment.

> "Living with Executive Tensions" *National Observer* 28 Dec 64

JIMMY BRESLIN

4 Men in the uniform of Wall Street retirement: black Chesterfield coat, rimless glasses and the *Times* folded to the obituary page.

> *The Gang Who Couldn't Shoot Straight* Viking 69

5 People born in Queens, raised to say that each morning they get on the subway and "go to the city," have a resentment of Manhattan, of the swiftness of its life and success of the people who live there.

> *Table Money* Ticknor & Fields 86

6 Those of Manhattan are the brokers on Wall Street and they talk of people who went to the same colleges; those from Queens are margin clerks in the back offices and they speak of friends who live in the same neighborhood.

> *ib*

KINGMAN BREWSTER, US Ambassador to Britain

7 Incomprehensible jargon is the hallmark of a profession.

> To British Institute of Management 13 Dec 77

D W BROGAN

8 Man does not live by bread alone, even presliced bread.

> On decline of US baking industry, quoted in *Forbes* 1 Mar 64

HELEN GURLEY BROWN

9 No office anywhere on earth is so puritanical, impeccable, elegant, sterile or incorruptible as not to contain the yeast for at least one affair, probably more. You can say it couldn't happen *here*, but just let a yeast raiser into the place and first thing you know—bread!

> *Sex and the Office* Geis 64

ROBERT FARRAR CAPON

10 The shock of unemployment becomes a pathology in its own right.

> "Being Let Go" NY *Times* 5 Aug 84

DALE CARNEGIE

11 The ideas I stand for are not mine. I borrowed them from Socrates. I swiped them from Chesterfield. I stole them from Jesus. And I put them in a book. If you don't like their rules, whose would you use?

> On his 1936 book *How to Win Friends and Influence People, Newsweek* 8 Aug 55

DICK CAVETT

12 Show people tend to treat their finances like their dentistry. They assume the man handling it knows what he is doing.

> On investigation of his investment broker, *Time* 6 May 85

CENTURY CLUB OF NEW YORK

13 If this were the best of all possible worlds and the spirit of the Century were perfectly honored here, no business would ever be discussed in the clubhouse. In any case, business papers should never be displayed in the common rooms of the first, second and third floors.

> Announcement from the House Committee, *Century Customs: The Spirit and The Letter* 85

JOHN CLEESE

14 I find it rather easy to portray a businessman. Being bland, rather cruel and incompetent comes naturally to me.

> On appearing in industrial-training films, quoted in *Newsweek* 15 Jun 87

WILLIAM G CONNOLLY

15 The mortgage market changes virtually from day to day, so you can wait a few weeks and, if you haven't committed suicide in the meantime, try again, even with the same lenders.

> *The New York Times Guide to Buying or Building a Home* Quadrangle 79

JOHN C DANFORTH, Chairman, US Senate Subcommittee on Trade

16 Japan is a great nation. It should begin to act like one.

> Address in Tokyo 13 Jan 86

RICHARD G DARMAN, US Deputy Secretary of the Treasury

17 "Corpocracy" [is] large-scale corporate America's tendency to be like the government bureaucracy.

> NY *Times* 9 Nov 86

GIANNI DE MICHELIS, Minister of Labor, Italy

18 Culture is Italy's oil, and it must be exploited.

> Quoted by Roberto Suro "Saving the Treasures of Italy" NY *Times* 21 Dec 86

ALMA DENNY

19 The feminist surge will crest when a lady named Arabella, flounces and ruffles and all, can rise to the top of a Fortune 500 corporation.

> NY *Times* 30 Aug 85

NED DEWEY, Harvard Business School, Class of '49

20 These kids are smart. But I'd as soon take a python to bed as hire one.

> On recent graduates, *Business Week* 24 Mar 86

1 He'd suck my brains, memorize my Rolodex and use my telephone to find some other guy who'd pay him twice the money.

ib

PHILIP H DOUGHERTY

2 It is embellished with a print of Cabbage Patch Kids in muted hues of pink, blue and green, done not quite in Empire style and without either a court train or redingote, but flared about the bottom in an alençon lace effect [and] sprinkled throughout with tiny pink dots not unlike stephanotis adorning the Plaza Hotel's Grand Ballroom.

On introduction of world's first designer diaper with the claim that "babies go gaga over it," NY *Times* 1 Oct 84

PETER F DRUCKER

3 Innovation is the specific instrument of entrepreneurship. . . . the act that endows resources with a new capacity to create wealth.

Innovation and Entrepreneurship Harper & Row 85, quoted in *Harvard Business Review* May/Jun 86

PETER EVANS

4 He needed to make deals. . . . a deal meant an opponent, an opponent meant confrontation and confrontation was the source of his strength.

On Aristotle Onassis, *Ari* Summit 86

5 He could not live without adversaries, no more than a tree can live without soil; like mangrove trees, which make their own soil, he could create enemies from within himself.

ib

D W EWING

6 A zealous sense of mission is only possible where there is opposition to it.

"Tension Can Be an Asset" *Harvard Business Review* Sep/Oct 64

CLIFTON FADIMAN

7 He has made a profession out of a business and an art out of a profession.

On Alfred A Knopf, recalled on Knopf's death 11 Aug 84

ED FINKELSTEIN

8 A consultant is someone who takes your watch away to tell you what time it is.

NY *Times* 29 Apr 79

CHARLES FOUNTAIN

9 In the acquire-or-be-acquired corporate mayhem of the 1980s, the mantle of management has passed to investment bankers and number-crunchers whose vision extends no further than the next quarterly earnings statement.

Christian Science Monitor 10 Dec 86

10 Were David Sarnoff alive today, there would almost surely be no place for him in the company [RCA] he had shepherded to greatness.

ib

KENNEDY FRASER

11 For the camera and for posterity, Stanley Marcus and Estée Lauder greeted each other with an embrace . . . a pair of elderly merchant monarchs who had tested each other's titanic shrewdness for decades formally exchanging a kiss of peace.

On launching a new perfume at Neiman-Marcus in Dallas, "As Gorgeous As It Gets" *New Yorker* 15 Sept 86

ROBERT FROST

12 Take care to sell your horse before he dies. The art of life is passing losses on.

From "The Ingenuities of Debt" in *The Poetry of Robert Frost* Holt, Rinehart & Winston 79

MERYL GARDNER, Assistant Professor of Marketing, NY University

13 Just as there is a trend toward high tech today, there is another trend toward high touch—homemade and wholesome.

On Ben & Jerry's Homemade Inc, a Vermont ice-cream company, NY *Times* 29 Mar 85

ERIC GELMAN

14 Sharks have been swimming the oceans unchallenged for thousands of years; chances are, the species that roams corporate waters will prove just as hardy.

"Macho Men of Capitalism" *Newsweek* 1 Oct 84

JOHN GIBBONS, Chairman, Congressional Office of Technology Assessment

15 They recruit their managers from the factory floor; we get ours out of law schools.

On Japanese success in world trade, NY *Times* 28 Jul 85

LOUIS J GLICKMAN, real estate owner

16 The best investment on earth is earth.

NY *Post* 3 Sep 57

JACK GOULD

17 One does not allow the plumbers to decide the temperature, depth and timing of a bath.

Declaring that "old line carriers" such as AT&T should not be allowed to dominate national communications, NY *Times* 7 Aug 66

PAUL GRAY

18 Paperbacks blink in and out of print like fireflies. They also, as older collectors have ruefully discovered, fade and fall apart even more rapidly than their owners.

Time 3 May 82

EDGAR A GUEST

19 I take the family shopping round
The markets of the world.

Poem on cover of 1934 Fall/Winter Sears, Roebuck Catalogue, quoted in profile of Sears Chairman Edward Riggs Telling, *Time* 20 Aug 84

ANDREW HACKER, Professor of Political Science, Queens College

20 Advertising has always been the Peck's Bad Boy of American business . . . urging us to buy things we probably don't need and often can't afford.

NY *Times* 24 Jun 84

1 Every time a message seems to grab us, and we think, "I just might try it," we are at the nexus of choice and persuasion that is advertising.
ib

ALAN HARRINGTON

2 A corporation prefers to offer a job to a man who already has one . . . To obtain entry into paradise, in terms of employment, you should be in a full state of grace.
Life In the Crystal Palace Knopf 59

JOSEPH HELLER

3 I think in every country that there is at least one executive who is scared of going crazy.
Something Happened Knopf 74

MICHAEL DeCOURCY HINDS

4 Single-family homes in New York generally come in two price ranges: expensive and unbelievably expensive.
"Living with Tenants: An Owner's Guide" NY *Times* 5 May 85

JEAN HOLLANDS, psychotherapist

5 The person who says "I'm not political" is in great danger. . . . Only the fittest will survive, and the fittest will be the ones who understand their office's politics.
Quoted in "Playing Office Politics" *Newsweek* 16 Sep 85

ROBERT HUGHES

6 It was the basilica of gossip, the Vatican of inside dope.
On Gramercy Park residence of NY public relations pioneer Benjamin Sonnenberg, *Time* 12 Feb 79

IOWA CITY PRESS-CITIZEN

7 If there's one thing that is clear from Monday's tragic series of murder and suicide, it is that the farm crisis is not numbers and deficits and bushels of corn. It is people and pride and tears and blood.
On financially troubled farmer who killed a bank president and two others before taking his own life, quoted in NY *Times* 12 Dec 85

HAYES B JACOBS

8 Contentment, in Telephone Ad-land, is a conversation, and happiness is a warm receiver.
On AT&T advertisements, NY *Times* 1 Mar 64

JOSEPH D JAMAIL JR

9 There are more pompous, arrogant, self-centered mediocre . . . people running corporate America . . . Their judgments and misjudgments have made me rich.
On $10.5-billion settlement he won for Pennzoil Co against Texaco Inc, NY *Times* 21 Nov 85

GEORGE KATONA, Director, University of Michigan Business Survey Research Bureau

10 Business is like sex. When it's good, it's very, very good; when it's not so good, it's still good.
Wall Street Journal 9 Apr 69

MERVYN A KING, professor, London School of Economics

11 When I was a graduate student at Harvard, I learned about showers and central heating. Ten years later, I learned about breakfast meetings. These are America's three great contributions to civilization.
On value of "power breakfasts," quoted in NY *Times* 4 Mar 87

ROBERT KRULWICH

12 As soon as the boss decides he wants his workers to do something, he has two problems: making them do it and monitoring what they do.
"Motivating the Help" NY *Times* 4 Jul 82

H LANCE LESSMAN, arbitrage assistant to Ivan Boesky

13 If you perceive the pregnancy early, then you don't get beat up too badly if you're wrong, and you make a fortune if you're right.
Quoted by Connie Bruck in profile of Boesky, "My Master Is My Purse" *Atlantic* Dec 84

PETER H LEWIS

14 The new version has page previewing known as WYSIWYG (pronounced wizzy-wig, for What You See Is What You Get).
On new program from Microsoft, "A Way With Words" NY *Times* 4 Nov 86

SINCLAIR LEWIS

15 Damn the great executives, the men of measured merriment, damn the men with careful smiles . . . oh, damn their measured merriment.
From his 1925 novel *Arrowsmith*, recalled on his death 10 Jan 51

ASSAR LINDBECK, Nobel Prize Committee for economics

16 The true test of a brilliant theory [is] what first is thought to be wrong is later shown to be obvious.
On Franco Modigliani's award-winning theory of corporate finance, NY *Times* 16 Oct 85

JOANNE LIPMAN

17 Hollywood has its Oscars. Television has its Emmys. Broadway has its Tonys. And advertising has its Clios. And its Andys, Addys, Effies and Obies. And 117 other assorted awards. And those are just the big ones.
"Ad Creators Collect Prizes Ad Nauseam, Almost Ad Infinitum" *Wall Street Journal* 26 Mar 87

STEVE LOHR

18 A new breed of broker making $300,000 a year in London . . . hot traders [who] are likely to be thirtyish, a bit cheeky and more interested in piling up commissions than meeting club cronies for a late afternoon brandy at Boodle's or White's.
On changing financial community in Great Britain, "London's Brokers Start Taking Off the Gloves" NY *Times* 25 Sep 86

JAY W LORSCH, professor, Harvard Business School

19 I think a lot more decisions are made on serendipity than people think. Things come across their radar screens and they jump at them.
Quoted in "For a Company Chief, When There's a Whim There's Often a Way" *Wall Street Journal* 1 Oct 84

RUSSELL LYNES

20 Cynicism is the intellectual cripple's substitute for

intelligence. It is the dishonest businessman's substitute for conscience. It is the communicator's substitute, whether he is advertising man or editor or writer, for self-respect.
> To Amer Assn of Advertising Agencies 25 Apr 63

ANDREW H MALCOLM

1 Farmers now are members of a capital-intensive industry that values good bookwork more than backwork. So several times a year almost every farmer must seek operating credit from the college fellow in the white shirt and tie—in effect, asking financial permission to work hard on his own land.
> "Murder on the Family Farm" NY *Times* 23 Mar 86

LEON MANDEL, Editor, *Autoweek*

2 Lights shine more brightly at Ford, but they go out overnight.
> On short careers of Ford Motor Co executives, NY *Times* 3 Oct 84

DEXTER MASTERS

3 In the jungle of the marketplace, the intelligent buyer must be alert to every commercial sound, to every snapping of a selling twig, to every rustle that may signal the uprising arm holding the knife pointed toward the jugular vein.
> *The Intelligent Buyer and the Telltale Seller* Knopf 66

MARTIN MAYER

4 Except for the con men borrowing money they shouldn't get and the widows who have to visit with the handsome young men in the trust department, no sane person ever enjoyed visiting a bank.
> *The Money Bazaars* Dutton 84

5 This is the twilight of the banks. It would be a more cheerful spectacle if we could envision the dawn of the institutions that will replace them.
> *ib*

MARSHALL MCLUHAN

6 Advertising is the greatest art form of the 20th century.
> *Advertising Age* 3 Sep 76

EDWARD SHEPHERD MEAD

7 Not even computers will replace committees, because committees buy computers.
> *Wall Street Journal* 18 Jun 64

JESSE MEYERS, Publisher, *Beverage Digest*

8 [The battle is for the] shelf space in our stomachs.
> On competition between soft-drink bottlers, *Fortune* 7 Jan 85

MORTON MINTZ

9 The human being who would not harm you on an individual, face-to-face basis, who is charitable, civic-minded, loving and devout, will wound or kill you from behind the corporate veil.
> On the marketing of a damaging birth-control device, *At Any Cost: Corporate Greed, Women and the Dalkon Shield* Pantheon 85

JESSICA MITFORD

10 Gracious dying is a huge, macabre and expensive joke on the American public.
> On funeral directors, *The American Way of Death* Simon & Schuster 63

WALTER F MONDALE

11 What do we want our kids to do? Sweep up around Japanese computers?
> To electrical workers union, Washington *Post* 7 Oct 82

TED MORGAN

12 In America, the land of the permanent revolution, ulcers and cancer often become, for the men at the top, the contemporary equivalent of the guillotine.
> On Robert Lacey's *Ford: The Men and the Machine* Little, Brown 86, NY *Times* 13 Jul 86

13 [It is a story] to satisfy the expectations of the average man, who wants awful things to happen to overprominent people.
> *ib*

JAN MORRIS

14 The language of economics is seldom limpid, but in H Street they usually manage to remove from it the very last flickering colophon of charm.
> On the World Bank in Washington DC, *The Road to Huddersfield* Pantheon 63

FRANK MUMNY

15 To write a book is a task needing only pen, ink and paper; to print a book is rather more difficult, because genius often expresses itself illegibly; to read a book is more difficult still, for one has to struggle with sleep; but to sell a book is the most difficult task of all.
> "The Romance of Bookselling" *The Reader's Adviser* Bowker 60

RALPH NADER

16 For almost 70 years the life insurance industry has been a smug sacred cow feeding the public a steady line of sacred bull.
> Testimony to US Senate subcommittee, NY *Times* 19 May 74

17 I don't think meals have any business being deductible. I'm for separation of calories and corporations.
> *Wall Street Journal* 15 Jul 85

BRUCE NUSSBAUM

18 The organization man is dead. He thrived when smokestack America thrived. When airlines, banks and telephones were highly regulated. When Japan built shoddy cars. When computers were huge and an apple was something you ate.
> "The New Corporate Elite" *Business Week* 21 Jan 85

JACK O'LEARY

19 Simon and Schuster runs a sales contest every year. The winners get to keep their jobs.
> On high turnover of salespeople, *Newsweek* 2 Jul 84

C NORTHCOTE PARKINSON

20 Work expands to fill the time available for its completion.
> *Economist* 19 Nov 55

KEN PATTON, NYC Economic Development Administrator

21 We have yet to find a significant case where the company did not move in the direction of the chief executive's home.
> On corporate relocations, NY *Times* 5 Feb 71

LAURENCE J PETER

1 In a hierarchy, every employee tends to rise to his level of incompetence; the cream rises until it sours.
The Peter Principle Morrow 69

2 Work is accomplished by those employees who have not yet reached their level of incompetence.
ib

3 Competence, like truth, beauty and contact lenses, is in the eye of the beholder.
ib

4 Incompetence knows no barriers of time or place.
Why Things Go Wrong: The Peter Principle Revisited Morrow 84

5 Equal opportunity means everyone will have a fair chance at becoming incompetent.
ib

THOMAS J PETERS and NANCY K AUSTIN

6 The brand of leadership we propose has a simple base of MBWA (Managing By Wandering Around). To "wander," with customers and vendors and our own people, is to be in touch with the first vibrations of the new.
A Passion for Excellence Random House 85, excerpted in *Fortune* 13 May 85

DIANE RAVITCH, professor, Columbia University Teachers College

7 The person who knows "how" will always have a job. The person who knows "why" will always be his boss.
Commencement address at Reed College, Portland OR, *Time* 17 Jun 85

RONALD REAGAN, 40th US President

8 Inflation is as violent as a mugger, as frightening as an armed robber and as deadly as a hit man.
At Republican Party fund-raising dinner, LA *Times* 20 Oct 78

ROBERT REINHOLD

9 As welcome as a rattlesnake at a square dance.
On Thomas R Procopio, FDIC "liquidator-in-charge" during Texas bank failure, "US Helps Texans Survive Death of Bank" NY *Times* 14 Oct 84

RANDALL ROBINSON, TransAfrica lobby

10 They are supplying the legs on which this monster walks.
On US firms doing business with South Africa, *Time* 25 Nov 85

WILLIAM SAFIRE

11 The CEO era gave rise to the CFO (not certified flying object, as you might imagine, but chief financial officer) and, most recently, the CIO, chief investment officer, a nice boost for the bookkeeper you can't afford to give a raise, unless he is a member of the Congress of Industrial Organizations, in which case you can stick your title in your ear.
"Hail to the CEO" NY *Times* 28 Sep 86

ANTHONY SAMPSON

12 The great body of managers . . . spend their whole careers climbing up inside one great Leviathan, with little contact with anyone outside.
The Anatomy of Britain Harper & Row 62

PAUL SAMUELSON

13 Profits are the lifeblood of the economic system, the magic elixir upon which progress and all good things depend ultimately. But one man's lifeblood is another man's cancer.
To Forum of European and Amer Economists, Harvard, *Time* 16 Aug 76

ARTHUR M SCHLESINGER JR

14 Anti-intellectualism has long been the anti-Semitism of the businessman.
Partisan Review 4 Mar 53

E R SHIPP

15 The rest is hamburger history.
On the aftermath of Ray Kroc's 1961 buy-out of the original McDonald's holdings, NY *Times* 27 Feb 85

GERALD M SLATON, personnel consultant

16 There are the daddies, who want to be in charge, the mommies, who do the nurturing, and the various children vying for their attention.
Quoted in "Playing Office Politics" *Newsweek* 16 Sep 85

JOSEPH SMITH, consumer research specialist

17 The laundry has its hands on *my* dirty shirts, sheets, towels and tablecloths, and who knows what tales they tell.
On business relationships with people in service industries, quoted by Margot Slade "Butchers, Bakers and Intimacy" NY *Times* 11 Aug 86

LEE SMITH

18 The subordinate is likely to feel that the examiner has taken a sample of his bone marrow.
On the reason Keizo Saji, chairman of Suntory Ltd, asks "Why?" five times in rapid succession during meetings, *Fortune* 7 Jan 84

GERRY SPENCE, trial lawyer

19 What the insurance companies have done is to reverse the business so that the public at large insures the insurance companies.
Time 24 Mar 86

GEORGE STEINER, Professor of Comparative Literature, University of Geneva

20 More and more lower-middle-income families either live their lives in debt or leave the city altogether. The boom is strictly at the penthouse level.
To Royal Society of Arts, London, NY *Times* 26 May 85

TIME MAGAZINE

21 The world's biggest company is a bundle of paradoxes wrapped in a string of superlatives. It makes a product that cannot be bought and lives on a commodity that cannot be seen.
On AT&T, 29 May 64

1 Kodak is one of a growing number of recession-plagued companies that are trying to make their payrolls lean without being mean.

On early-retirement policies, 21 Feb 83

ANDREW TOBIAS

2 In a world where the time it takes to travel (supersonic) or to bake a potato (microwave) or to process a million calculations (microchip) shrinks inexorably, only three things have remained constant and unrushed: the nine months it takes to have a baby, the nine months it takes to untangle a credit card dispute and the nine months it takes to publish a hardcover book.

"Hot Leads and Lead Time" Savvy May 80

ROBERT TOWNSEND

3 If you don't do it excellently, don't do it at all. Because if it's not excellent, it won't be profitable or fun, and if you're not in business for fun or profit, what the hell are you doing there?

Farther Up the Organization Knopf 84

4 One of the most important tasks of a manager is to eliminate his people's excuses for failure.

ib

5 Most people in big companies are administered, not led. They are treated as personnel, not people.

ib

6 "Top" management is supposed to be a tree full of owls—hooting when management heads into the wrong part of the forest. I'm still unpersuaded they even know where the forest is.

ib

7 If you have to have a policy manual, publish the Ten Commandments.

ib

JAY L TUROFF, Chairman, NYC Taxi and Limousine Commission

8 When a man owns the tin, he has a vested interest in it.

On independent taxi drivers who purchase the required tin medallions from the city for as much as $100,000, NY Times 16 Dec 85

GORE VIDAL

9 Until the rise of American advertising, it never occurred to anyone anywhere in the world that the teenager was a captive in a hostile world of adults.

Rocking the Boat Little, Brown 62

PAUL A VOLCKER, Chairman, Federal Reserve System

10 What's the subject of life—to get rich? All of those fellows out there getting rich could be dancing around the real subject of life.

Newsweek 24 Feb 86

JOAN WALKER

11 It took at least 200 people, in 5 states, 4 months to turn out a Ford Thunderbird commercial that lasted 90 seconds.

NY Herald Tribune 5 Jul 64

MIKE WALLACE

12 There are more queens crowned in one night in Dallas than in 400 years in Westminster Abbey.

On sales incentive awards from Mary Kay Cosmetics, 60 Minutes CBS TV 25 Jul 82

THOMAS L WHISLER, Professor of Business, University of Chicago

13 Men are going to have to learn to be managers in a world where the organization will come close to consisting of all chiefs and one Indian. The Indian, of course, is the computer.

Christian Science Monitor 21 Apr 64

WILLIAM H WHYTE JR

14 The onlooker had better wipe the sympathy off his face. What he has seen is a revolution, not the home of little cogs and drones. What he has seen is the dormitory of the next managerial class.

On Levittown, Long Island, and similar suburbs, Fortune May 53

LEON WIESELTIER

15 Her book about the money in sex gives you the feeling of the sex in money.

On Sydney Biddle Barrows's Mayflower Madam, with Michael Novak, Arbor House 86, Vanity Fair Dec 86

16 The effort was to summon to the bosoms of her personnel the sort of man that Barrows likes to call "nice." Nice meant rich.

ib

DAVID WILD

17 Greenmail is, quite logically, blackmail of a different color.

On how takeover buyers increase stock prices for resale to management, "The Tax Adviser" Esquire Apr 85

MICHAEL WINERIP

18 If Jack Kerouac had set out to find a real bookstore in the suburbs, he would still be on the road, Phileas Fogg would still be in the air, the Ancient Mariner wouldn't have had time to tell anyone his story.

On bookstore chains, NY Times 28 Oct 86

WALTER WRISTON

19 Our banking system grew by accident; and whenever something happens by accident, it becomes a religion.

Business Week 20 Jan 75

BERNARD WYSOCKI

20 Confusing for AT&T shareholders, frustrating for many AT&T customers, a mixed blessing for AT&T competitors and a boon, if sometimes a boondoggle, for a small army of lawyers, consultants and stockbrokers.

On breakup of AT&T, in review of W Brooke Tunstall's Disconnecting Parties McGraw-Hill 85, Wall Street Journal 8 Apr 85

PHILIP YOUNG, economist, Pace University, NYC

21 For Hispanics, the store is the end, the goal. For Koreans, it's entry level.

On motivation of ethnic merchants, NY Times 19 Mar 85

Memorable Advertising

ALKA-SELTZER

1 Plop plop, fizz fizz, oh what a relief it is!®

2 I can't believe I ate the whole thing.

ALLSTATE INSURANCE

3 You're in good hands with Allstate.®

AMERICAN BROADCASTING COMPANY (ABC)

4 Out is no place to be tonight.
   Advertising 1975 TV movie *Love Among the Ruins*

AMERICAN EXPRESS CREDIT CARD

5 Don't leave home without it.®

AMERICAN SAFETY COUNCIL

6 There are a million and one excuses for not wearing a safety belt. Some are real killers.

AMERICAN TELEPHONE & TELEGRAPH (AT&T)

7 Reach out and touch someone.®

8 Let your fingers do the walking.
   Advertising Yellow Pages

AMTRAK

9 See America at see level.

ARPEGE PERFUMES

10 Promise her anything, but give her Arpege.

AVIS CAR RENTAL

11 We try harder.®

BANK LEUMI TRUST COMPANY OF NY

12 If it took six days to create the world, why should it take four weeks to get a loan?

BLACKGLAMA MINK

13 What becomes a legend most?®

BOLLA WINES

14 Wine is a little like love; when the right one comes along, you know it.

BOOK-OF-THE-MONTH CLUB

15 America's Bookstore®

BRIM DECAFFINATED COFFEE

16 Fill it to the rim with Brim.

BURGER KING

17 Have it your way.®

CALVIN KLEIN JEANS

18 Nothing comes between me and my Calvins.

CANTERBURY CATHEDRAL

19 St Augustine founded it. Becket died for it. Chaucer wrote about it. Cromwell shot at it. Hitler bombed it. Time is destroying it. Will you save it?
   Advertising restoration fund

CARTIER JEWELRY

20 Les must de Cartier.®

CHARMIN TOILET TISSUE

21 Please don't squeeze the Charmin.®

CHEMICAL BANK–NEW YORK TRUST COMPANY

22 When a woman's need is financial, her reaction is Chemical.

CHEVROLET

23 See the USA in your Chevrolet.

CLAIROL HAIR COLOR

24 Does she . . . or doesn't she?®

25 Hair color so natural only her hairdresser knows for sure.®

26 If I've only one life, let me live it as a blonde!

COCA-COLA

27 The pause that refreshes.

28 It's the real thing.

29 Have a Coke and a smile.

COTY PERFUMES

30 Want him to be more of a man? Try being more of a woman!

CUNARD CRUISES

31 Getting there is half the fun.

DE BEERS CONSOLIDATED MINES

32 A diamond is forever.

DOUBLEMINT GUM

33 Double your pleasure.® Double your fun.

DU PONT

34 Better things for better living through chemistry.

FEDERAL EXPRESS

35 When it absolutely, positively has to be there overnight.

36 When there's no tomorrow.
   On same-day delivery of document facsimiles

FLORIDA CITRUS COMMISSION

37 A day without orange juice is like a day without sunshine.

FORD

38 There's a Ford in your Future.

39 Ford has a better idea.

40 Quality is Job 1.

FOUR ROSES

41 America's most gifted whiskey.

FRIENDS OF ANIMALS

42 Extinct is forever.

GENERAL ELECTRIC

43 Progress is our most important product.

1 GE . . . We bring good things to life.®

INTERNATIONAL LADIES' GARMENT WORKERS' UNION

2 Look for the union label.

JELL-O

3 It sits as lightly on a heavy meal as it does on your conscience.

JOCKEY UNDERWEAR

4 The best seat in the house.

KENTUCKY FRIED CHICKEN

5 Buy a bucket of chicken and have a barrel of fun.

6 We do chicken right.

KOOL-AID

7 Moms depend on Kool-Aid like kids depend on Moms.

LIPTON TEA

8 Lipton's gets into more hot water than anything.

LORD & TAYLOR

9 Taking the "if" out of "gift."
Advertising personalized shopping service

LORD WEST FORMAL WEAR

10 A woman's most important accessory—her escort.

MAIDENFORM

11 I dreamed I stopped traffic in my Maidenform bra.

M&MS

12 The milk chocolate melts in your mouth—not in your hand.®

MAYTAG APPLIANCES

13 Our repairmen are the loneliest guys in town.

McDONALD'S

14 You deserve a break today.®

METROPOLITAN LIFE INSURANCE

15 A child is someone who passes through your life and then disappears into an adult.

NATIONAL COUNCIL ON THE HANDICAPPED

16 A curb is a wall to a handicapped person.

NEW SCHOOL FOR SOCIAL RESEARCH, NYC

17 The New School—it will change your mind!

NEW YORK CITY OPERA

18 Come to the opera for a song.
Advertising subscription tickets

NEW YORK CITY TRANSIT AUTHORITY

19 After all, to make a beautiful omelet, you have to break an egg.
Advertising subway reorganization

NEW YORK TIMES

20 "All the news that's fit to print."®

9-LIVES CAT FOOD

21 Hmph! Din-din. I'll eat when I'm ready.
Voice-over for Morris the cat

22 The cat who doesn't act finicky soon loses control of his owner.

PAN-AMERICAN COFFEE BUREAU

23 Good coffee is like friendship: rich and warm and strong.

PARAMOUNT PICTURES

24 The Eyes and Ears of the World.®
Slogan recalled after the last showing of motion-picture newsreels. *Time* 29 Dec 67

PATEK PHILIPPE WATCHES

25 Patek Philippe doesn't just tell you the time. It tells you something about yourself.

PEPPERIDGE FARM

26 It's like ice cream that's gone to heaven.
Advertising parfait cake

27 Pepperidge Farm remembers.

PILLSBURY

28 Nothin' says lovin' like somethin' from the oven.

RALSTON PURINA

29 All you add is love.
Advertising Dog Chow

30 Don't treat your puppy like a dog.
Advertising Puppy Chow

RED CROSS

31 The greatest tragedy is indifference.

REEBOK ATHLETIC SHOES

32 Because life is not a spectator sport.®

ROLAIDS

33 How do you spell relief? R-O-L-A-I-D-S.

ROLLS-ROYCE

34 At 60 miles an hour the loudest noise in the new Rolls-Royce comes from the electric clock.

SCANDINAVIAN LINES CRUISES

35 HMS *Scandinavia*: she's oceans of fun.

SCHAEFER BEER

36 Schaefer is the one beer to have when you're having more than one.

SEAGRAM'S

37 Dryest gin in town. Ask any Martini.

SQUIBB PHARMACEUTICALS

38 Adam and Eve ate the first vitamins, including the package.
Advocating balanced diet rather than reliance on vitamin pills

STEINWAY PIANOS

39 You'll rarely attend a concert that's not attended by Steinway.

40 The instrument of the immortals.

TAREYTON CIGARETTES

1 I'd rather fight than switch.

TEACHERS

2 No Scotch improves the flavor of water like Teachers.

TEXACO

3 You can trust your car to the man who wears the star.

TITANIC BEER

4 Goes down better than the real thing.

TRIVIAL PURSUIT BOARD GAMES

5 Every American is entitled to Life, Liberty and the Pursuit of Trivia.

UNITED AIR LINES

6 Fly the friendly skies of United.®

UNITED NEGRO COLLEGE FUND

7 "A mind is a terrible thing to waste."®

UNITED STATES ARMY

8 Be all that you can be.™

VIRGINIA SLIMS CIGARETTES

9 You've come a long way, baby.®

WALL STREET JOURNAL

10 The daily diary of the American dream.

WATERFORD GLASS

11 Born in fire, blown by mouth and cut by hand with heart.

12 Even when a piece of Waterford is dated, it's timeless.

WENDY'S

13 Where's the beef?®

WINSTON CIGARETTES

14 Winston tastes good like a cigarette should.®

WISK LAUNDRY DETERGENT

15 Ring around the collar.

YARDLEY LAVENDER SOAP

16 The soap that's kept women in hot water for 200 years—and they've loved every minute.

EDUCATION

Educators & Participants

ANONYMOUS

17 If you promise not to believe everything your child says happens at this school, I'll promise not to believe everything he says happens at home.
> Note to students' parents from an English schoolmaster, quoted in *Wall Street Journal* 4 Jan 85

SYLVIA ASHTON-WARNER

18 The truth is that I am enslaved. . . . in one vast love affair with 70 children.
> On life of a teacher, *Spinster* Simon & Schuster 59

19 I see the mind of the 5-year-old as a volcano with two vents: destructiveness and creativeness.
> *Teacher* Simon & Schuster 63

ASSOCIATION OF AMERICAN COLLEGES

20 It is a supermarket where students are shoppers and professors are merchants of learning. Fads and fashions, the demands of popularity and success, enter where wisdom and experience should prevail.
> *Integrity in the College Curriculum*, report on weakness of undergraduate programs, quoted in NY *Times* 11 Feb 85

THOMAS BAILEY, Florida State Superintendent of Schools

21 There must be such a thing as a child with average ability, but you can't find a parent who will admit that it is his child.
> *Wall Street Journal* 17 Dec 61

22 Start a program for gifted children, and every parent demands that his child be enrolled.
> *ib*

EDWARD C BANFIELD, Professor of Government, Harvard

23 A good professor is a bastard perverse enough to think what *he* thinks is important, not what government thinks is important.
> *Life* 9 Jun 67

JACQUES BARZUN, Dean of Graduate School, Columbia University

24 Teaching is not a lost art, but the regard for it is a lost tradition.
> *Newsweek* 5 Dec 55

25 The test and the use of man's education is that he finds pleasure in the exercise of his mind.
> "Science vs the Humanities" *Saturday Evening Post* 3 May 58

WILLIAM J BENNETT, US Secretary of Education

26 [The shortage of student loans] may require . . . divestiture of certain sorts—stereo divestiture, automobile divestiture, three-weeks-at-the-beach divestiture.
> NY *Times* 12 Feb 85

27 If my own son, who is now 10 months, came to me and said, "You promised to pay for my tuition at Harvard; how about giving me $50,000 instead to start a little business?" I might think that was a good idea.
> *ib*

28 The secretary of education does not work for the education establishment. The secretary works for the American people.
> *Christian Science Monitor* 12 Mar 85

29 Our common language is . . . English. And our common task is to ensure that our non-English-speaking children learn this common language.
> NY *Times* 26 Sep 85

1 The elementary school must assume as its sublime and most solemn responsibility the task of teaching every child in it to read. Any school that does not accomplish this has failed.
> Report on condition of elementary schools, quoted in *ib* 3 Sep 86

2 Most certification today is pure "credentialism." [It] must begin to reflect our demand for excellence, not our appreciation of parchment.
> *ib*

MARY MCLEOD BETHUNE, President Emeritus, Bethune-Cookman College, Daytona Beach FL

3 The drums of Africa still beat in my heart. They will not let me rest while there is a single Negro boy or girl without a chance to prove his worth.
> News summaries 19 May 55

BARBARA ARONSTEIN BLACK, Dean, Columbia Law School

4 Where I am today has *everything* to do with the years I spent hanging on to a career by my fingernails.
> On appointment as dean after raising a family and then returning to studies, NY *Times* 2 Jan 86

DEREK BOK, President, Harvard

5 I won't say there aren't any Harvard graduates who have never asserted a superior attitude. But they have done so to our great embarrassment and in no way represent the Harvard I know.
> *M* Jun 84

LEON BOTSTEIN, President, Bard College

6 At best, most college presidents are running something that is somewhere between a faltering corporation and a hotel.
> *Center* Mar 77

FRANK L BOYDEN, Headmaster, Deerfield Academy, MA

7 Work 'em hard, play 'em hard, feed 'em up to the nines and send 'em to bed so tired that they are asleep before their heads are on the pillow.
> News summaries 2 Jan 54

8 I never reprimand a boy in the evening—darkness and a troubled mind are a poor combination.
> *Life* 30 Nov 62

ERNEST BOYER, President, Carnegie Foundation for Advancement of Teaching

9 A poor surgeon hurts 1 person at a time. A poor teacher hurts 130.
> *People* 17 Mar 86

KINGMAN BREWSTER, President, Yale

10 If I take refuge in ambiguity, I assure you that it's quite conscious.
> On appointment as president, quoted in NY *Herald Tribune* 14 Oct 63

11 Universities should be safe havens where ruthless examination of realities will not be distorted by the aim to please or inhibited by the risk of displeasure.
> Inaugural address 11 Apr 64

12 Maybe you are the "cool" generation . . . If coolness means a capacity to stay calm and use your head in the service of ends passionately believed in, then it has my admiration.
> Baccalaureate address 12 Jun 66

PETER BRODIE, classics teacher, Foxcroft School, Middleburg VA

13 What is important—what lasts—in another language is not what is said but what is written. For the essence of an age, we look to its poetry and its prose, not its talk shows.
> NY *Times* 18 Jul 84

14 One attraction of Latin is that you can immerse yourself in the poems of Horace and Catullus without fretting over how to say, "Have a nice day."
> *ib*

15 There is a negative proof of the value of Latin: No one seems to boast of not knowing it.
> *ib*

MARY INGRAHAM BUNTING, President, Radcliffe College

16 When her last child is off to school, we don't want the talented woman wasting her time in work far below her capacity. We want her to come out running.
> On establishing institute for women's independent study, *Life* 13 Jan 61

LES BURTON, Assistant Superintendent of Security, Houston Public School System

17 Mostly we see .22 pistols, little .25 automatics or .38 revolvers, but we did have one kid bring a fully loaded .357 Magnum to school.
> On establishing metal-detector searches at classroom doors, NY *Times* 25 May 86

HERBERT BUTTERFIELD, Vice Chancellor, Cambridge

18 The academic mind can eat away the very basis of its own assurance . . . produce contortions when it tries to bend over backward . . . allow itself to be dismayed by the picture it has created of relentless historical process.
> Address on his retirement 2 Oct 61

19 The very fact of its finding itself in agreement with other minds perturbs it, so that it hunts for points of divergence, feeling the urgent need to make it clear that at least it reached the same conclusions by a different route.
> *ib*

GUIDO CALABRESI, Dean, Yale Law School

20 You never replace a great scholar who retires. If you try to do that, you end up with burnt-out volcanoes.
> On A Bartlett Giamatti's retirement as president of Yale, NY *Times* 12 Dec 85

BRAD CARTER, Chairman, Religious Studies Department, Southern Methodist University

21 They wanted a great university without building a great university. They knew a lot about football, but not a lot about academia.
> On National Collegiate Athletic Assn's suspension of SMU's football program for recruiting violations, NY *Times* 5 Mar 87

DORA CHAPLIN, Professor of Christian Education, General Theological Seminary, NYC

1 Everyone knows a good deal about one child—himself.
> *The Privilege of Teaching* Morehouse-Barlow 62

SIDNEY M B COULLING, Professor of English, Washington and Lee University

2 Of all the threats to Phi Beta Kappa . . . probably none is more pervasive than that of the so-called counterculture, with its elevation of instinct over intellect, mysticism over reason, consciousness over scholarship, sensitivity over discipline.
> *Wall Street Journal* 7 Mar 71

ARCHIBALD COX, Professor of Law, Harvard

3 A great many college graduates come here thinking of lawyers as social engineers arguing the great Constitutional issues.
> San Francisco *Examiner & Chronicle* 6 Jun 82

PAUL CUBETA, Director, Bread Loaf School of English, Middlebury College, VT

4 Perhaps our greatest responsiblity is to repledge our continuing devotion to perpetuating a legacy of language in an age when the spoken word is suspected as "a glib and oily art," manipulative doublespeak; when the written word—badly written, of course—is unread; and when "vibrations" are alleged to be, not inarticulate throbbing, but true communication where every sentence begins with "I feel" and ends with "you know."
> *Christian Science Monitor* 2 Aug 76

JOHN SLOAN DICKEY, President, Dartmouth

5 The American male at the peak of his physical powers and appetites, driving 160 big white horses across the scenes of an increasingly open society, with weekend money in his pocket and with little prior exposure to trouble and tragedy, personifies "an accident going to happen."
> "Conscience and the Undergraduate" *Atlantic* Apr 55

6 There is no more vulnerable human combination than an undergraduate.
> *ib*

OTIS C EDWARDS, Episcopal priest

7 To be loose with grammar is to be loose with the worst woman in the world.
> Lecture at Nashotah House Episcopal Seminary, Nashotah WI, 10 Jan 66

DWIGHT D EISENHOWER, 34th US President

8 Some years ago I became president of Columbia University and learned within 24 hours to be ready to speak at the drop of a hat, and I learned something more, the *trustees* were expected to be ready to speak at the *passing* of the hat.
> To joint meeting of Philippine and US Chambers of Commerce 17 Jun 60

ELLIOT EISNER, professor, Stanford School of Education

9 We have inadvertently designed a system in which being good at what you do as a teacher is not formally rewarded, while being poor at what you do is seldom corrected nor penalized.
> *NY Times* 3 Sep 85

SISTER EVANGELIST RSM

10 I have one rule—attention. They give me theirs and I give them mine.
> On teaching high-school students, Billings MT *Gazette* 4 May 80

JOHN FISCHER, Dean, Teachers College, Columbia University

11 The essence of our effort to see that every child has a chance must be to assure each an equal opportunity, not to become equal, but to become different—to realize whatever unique potential of body, mind and spirit he or she possesses.
> San Francisco *Examiner* 19 Mar 73

CLAUDE M FUESS

12 I was still learning when I taught my last class.
> After 40 years at Phillips Academy, Andover MA, *Independent Schoolmaster* Atlantic Monthly Press 52

JOHN KENNETH GALBRAITH

13 The commencement speech is not, I think, a wholly satisfactory manifestation of our culture.
> Commencement address at American University, Washington DC, *Time* 18 Jun 84

14 Commencement oratory . . . must eschew anything that smacks of partisan politics, political preference, sex, religion or unduly firm opinion. Nonetheless, there must be a speech: Speeches in our culture are the vacuum that fills a vacuum.
> *ib*

DAVID P GARDNER, President, University of Utah, Salt Lake City

15 Much that passes for education . . . is not education at all but ritual. The fact is that we are being educated when we know it least.
> *Vital Speeches* 15 Apr 75

16 We learn simply by the exposure of living, and what we learn most natively is the tradition in which we live.
> *ib*

JOHN GARGIN, Professor of Political Science, Kent State University, OH

17 Most of our students are here to get the credentials they believe are central to admission to the Dream. Everyone does the rhetoric bit—Fascist pig this and that—but push them and they ask you to write recommendations for jobs with banks and insurance companies.
> *NY Times* 17 Oct 76

A BARTLETT GIAMATTI, President, Yale

18 A liberal education is at the heart of a civil society, and at the heart of a liberal education is the act of teaching.
> "The American Teacher" *Harper's* Jul 80

19 Teaching is an instinctual art, mindful of potential, craving of realizations, a pausing, seamless process.
> *ib*

20 Teachers believe they have a gift for giving; it drives them with the same irrepressible drive that drives others to create a work of art or a market or a building.
> *ib*

1 On a good day, I view the job [of president] as directing an orchestra. On the dark days, it is more like that of a clutch—engaging the engine to effect forward motion, while taking greater friction.
> NY *Times* 6 Mar 83

2 It is not enough to offer a smorgasbord of courses. We must insure that students are not just eating at one end of the table.
> *ib*

3 There are many who lust for the simple answers of doctrine or decree. They are on the left and right. They are not confined to a single part of the society. They are terrorists of the mind.
> Final baccalaureate address, *ib* 26 May 86

VIRGINIA GILDERSLEEVE, Dean Emeritus, Barnard College

4 I was resolved to sustain and preserve in my college the bite of the mind, the chance to stand face to face with truth, the good life lived in a small, various, highly articulate and democratic society.
> *Many a Good Crusade* Macmillan 54

X 5 The ability to think straight, some knowledge of the past, some vision of the future, some skill to do useful service, some urge to fit that service into the well-being of the community—these are the most vital things education must try to produce.
> *ib*

ROBERT F GOHEEN, President, Princeton

6 If you feel that you have both feet planted on level ground, then the university has failed you.
> Baccalaureate address, *Time* 23 Jun 61

7 In the realm of ideas it is better to let the mind sally forth, even if some precious preconceptions suffer a mauling.
> Commencement address, NY *Times* 19 Jun 66

SAMUEL GOULD, Chancellor, University of California, Santa Barbara

8 If the state of oratory that inundates our educational institutions during the month of June could be transformed into rain for southern California, we should all be happily awash or waterlogged.
> *Time* 27 Jun 60

HANNA HOLBORN GRAY, President, University of Chicago

9 There was a perception that life here was—I won't say gray, that's hard for me—but beige.
> On a guidebook's observation that "studying is the U of C student's favorite pastime," *Time* 28 May 84

10 The university's characteristic state may be summarized by the words of the lady who said, "I have enough money to last me the rest of my life, unless I buy something."
> *Christian Science Monitor* 25 Nov 86

A WHITNEY GRISWOLD, President, Yale

11 A Socrates in every classroom.
> On his ambitious standard for faculty, *Time* 11 Jun 51

12 Could *Hamlet* have been written by a committee, or the *Mona Lisa* painted by a club? Could the New Testament have been composed as a conference report? Creative ideas do not spring from groups. They spring from individuals. The divine spark leaps from the finger of God to the finger of Adam.
> Baccalaureate address 8 Jun 57

S I HAYAKAWA, President, San Francisco State College

13 How anybody dresses is indicative of his self-concept. If students are dirty and ragged, it indicates they are not interested in tidying up their intellects either.
> LA *Herald-Examiner* 8 Apr 73

THEODORE M HESBURGH, President, Notre Dame

14 Anyone who refuses to speak out off campus does not deserve to be listened to on campus.
> Quoted by Clark Kerr NY *Times* 18 Sep 84

JOEL H HILDEBRAND, Emeritus Professor of Chemistry, University of California, Berkeley

15 The invention of IQ did a great disservice to creativity in education. . . . Individuality, personality, originality, are too precious to be meddled with by amateur psychiatrists whose patterns for a "wholesome personality" are inevitably their own.
> NY *Times* 16 Jun 64

RICHARD HOFSTADTER, Professor of American History, Columbia University

16 The delicate thing about the university is that it has a mixed character, that it is suspended between its position in the eternal world, with all its corruption and evils and cruelties, and the splendid world of our imagination.
> 1968 commencement address, quoted in "Parting Shots: A Century of Commencement Speeches" *Saturday Review* 12 May 79

17 A university's essential character is that of being a center of free inquiry and criticism—a thing not to be sacrificed for anything else.
> *ib*

18 A university is not a service station. Neither is it a political society, nor a meeting place for political societies. With all its limitations and failures, and they are invariably many, it is the best and most benign side of our society insofar as that society aims to cherish the human mind.
> *ib*

MICHAEL K HOOKER, Chancellor, University of Maryland

19 What I'm concerned about is the people who *don't* dwell on the meaninglessness of their lives, or the meaningfulness of it—who just pursue mindless entertainment.
> Quoted by Rushworth M Kidder *Christian Science Monitor* 1 Oct 86

HAROLD HOWE II, former US Commissioner of Education

20 Teenagers go to college to be with their boyfriends and girlfriends; they go because they can't think of anything else to do; they go because their parents want them to and sometimes because their parents don't want them to; they go to find themselves, or to find a husband, or to get away from home, and sometimes even to find out about the world in which they live.
> *Newsweek* 26 Apr 76

SHIRLEY M HUFSTEDLER, US Secretary of Education

21 I'm bilingual. I speak English and I speak educationese.
> *Newsweek* 12 May 80

ROBERT M HUTCHINS, Chancellor, University of Chicago

1 Education is a kind of continuing dialogue, and a dialogue assumes . . . different points of view.
> On academic freedom, *Time* 8 Dec 52

2 It is not so important to be serious as it is to be serious about the important things. The monkey wears an expression of seriousness which would do credit to any college student, but the monkey is serious because he itches.
> *Quote* 3 Aug 58

3 It has been said that we have not had the three R's in America, we had the six R's: remedial readin', remedial 'ritin' and remedial 'rithmetic.
> NY *Herald Tribune* 22 Apr 63

4 There is only one justification for universities, as distinguished from trade schools. They must be centers of criticism.
> Recalled on his death 14 May 77

LOUIS JOHANNOT, Headmaster, Institut Le Rosey, Switzerland

5 The only reason I always try to meet and know the parents better is because it helps me to forgive their children.
> *Life* 7 May 65

STANLEY KATZ, Master, Rockefeller College, Yale

6 You couldn't just slap it into place. You had to do it right, make the ivy fit.
> On establishment of the college, NY *Times* 30 Apr 84

BARNABY C KEENEY, President, Brown University

7 The scramble to get into college is going to be so terrible in the next few years that students are going to put up with almost anything, even an education.
> *Time* 29 Aug 55

8 At college age, you can tell who is best at taking tests and going to school, but you can't tell who the best people are. That worries the hell out of me.
> Recalled on his death 18 Jun 80

GEORGE F KENNAN, Professor Emeritus, Institute for Advanced Study, Princeton NJ

9 The very concept of history implies the scholar and the reader. Without a generation of civilized people to study history, to preserve its records, to absorb its lessons and relate them to its own problems, history, too, would lose its meaning.
> On receiving Gold Medal for History from the Amer Academy and Institute of Arts and Letters, NY *Times* 27 May 84

10 Not only the studying and writing of history but also the honoring of it both represent affirmations of a certain defiant faith—a desperate, unreasoning faith, if you will—but faith nevertheless in the endurance of this threatened world—faith in the total essentiality of historical continuity.
> *ib*

CLARK KERR, President, University of California, Berkeley

11 A university anywhere can aim no higher than to be as British as possible for the sake of the undergraduates, as German as possible for the sake of the public at large—and as confused as possible for the preservation of the whole uneasy balance.
> Lecture at Harvard, "The Uses of the University," quoted in NY *Times* 26 Apr 63

ROBERT J KIBBEE, Chancellor, City University of NY

12 The quality of a university is measured more by the kind of student it turns out than the kind it takes in.
> NY *Times* 27 Jul 71

13 Over the years, we have come to identify quality in a college not by whom it serves but by how many students it excludes. Let us not be a sacred priesthood protecting the temple, but rather the fulfillers of dreams.
> In defense of open admissions, recalled on his death 16 Jun 82

GRAYSON KIRK, President, Columbia University

14 The most important function of education at any level is to develop the personality of the individual and the significance of his life to himself and to others. This is the basic architecture of a life; the rest is ornamentation and decoration of the structure.
> *Quote* 27 Jan 63

SUSANNA KLEIN, senior, Wellesley College

15 I have lived in three dormitories over four years and I have never seen a naked man, other than in the privacy of my own room.
> Defending classmates against charges of "sexual immorality" brought by a student's father, NY *Times* 1 May 76

16 As for "unnatural sex habits," it only occurs to me that with the removal of all men from campus, you might witness more so-called unnatural acts than previously.
> *ib*

JONATHAN KOZOL

17 Pick battles big enough to matter, small enough to win.
> *On Being a Teacher* Continuum 81

LEON LESSINGER, Dean, College of Education, USC

18 Human beings are full of emotion, and the teacher who knows how to use it will have dedicated learners. It means sending dominant signals instead of submissive ones with your eyes, body and voice.
> *Newsweek* 8 Mar 76

WILMARTH S LEWIS, Selections Committee, Yale

19 The Yale president must be a Yale man. Not too far to the right, too far to the left or a middle-of-the-roader. Ready to give the ultimate word on every subject under the sun from how to handle the Russians to why undergraduates riot in the spring. Profound with a wit that bubbles up and brims over in a cascade of brilliance. You may have guessed who the leading candidate is, but there is a question about him: Is God a Yale man?
> 1950 statement recalled in 1970s when Yale considered a woman president, NY *Times* 24 Apr 77

FRANK J MACCHIAROLA, Schools Chancellor, NYC

20 If Chrysler had an assembly line in which the same number of cars got through as kids do in our school system, people would be scandalized.
> NY *Times* 9 Jan 83

CHARLES C MARSHALL III, former member, Students for a Democratic Society

1 I think a lot of it was puberty.
> On student rioting of 1960s, *Time* 14 Apr 80

SYBIL MARSHALL

2 I had learned to respect the intelligence, integrity, creativity and capacity for deep thought and hard work latent somewhere in every child; they had learned that I differed from them only in years and experience, and that as I, an ordinary human being, loved and respected them, I expected payment in kind.
> On 18 years as teacher in a one-room school in rural England, *An Experiment in Education* Cambridge 63

BENJAMIN E MAYS, former President, Morehouse College, Atlanta GA

3 The tragedy of life doesn't lie in not reaching your goal. The tragedy lies in having no goal to reach.
> Quoted by Marian Wright Edelman in commencement address at Barnard College, NY *Times* 16 May 85

CHRISTA MCAULIFFE, teacher, Concord NH

4 I cannot join the space program and restart my life as an astronaut, but this opportunity to connect my abilities as an educator with my interests in history and space is a unique opportunity to fulfill my early fantasies.
> From her winning essay in NASA's nationwide search for the first teacher to travel in space, released after her death with six others aboard the space shuttle Challenger 28 Jan 86

R M MCCALLUM, Master, Pembroke College, Oxford

5 Fulbright is responsible for the greatest movement of scholars across the face of the earth since the fall of Constantinople in 1453.
> On US Senator J William Fulbright's sponsorship of Fulbright scholarships, *Saturday Evening Post* 23 Mar 63

CHARLES MCCURDY JR, Executive Secretary, State Universities Assn

6 Would that this institution—or some institution—could become the University of Utopia. What will it be like? It will be the most enlightened institution of higher learning in the world today. . . . Its only purpose is to educate. What a radically novel idea for an institution of higher learning!
> Address at Gustavus Adolphus College, St Peter MN, 1 Jun 57

WILLIAM H MCNEILL, Professor of History, University of Chicago

7 My job is to bore you and let the hardness of your seat and the warmth of your robe prepare you for what is to come.
> Commencement address at Bard College 26 May 84

JOHN MERRIMAN, Professor of History and Master, Branford College, Yale

8 Yale is more than going to classes. Yale is staggering on in the best fashion possible.
> On 10-week strike of workers, NY *Times* 1 Dec 84

EDMUND S MORGAN, Professor of History, Yale

9 Children whose curiosity survives parental discipline and who manage to grow up before they blow up are invited to join the Yale faculty. Within the university they go on asking their questions and trying to find the answers . . . it is a place where the world's hostility to curiosity can be defied.
> "What Every Yale Freshman Should Know" *Saturday Review* 23 Jan 60

V S NAIPAUL

10 Ignorant people in preppy clothes are more dangerous to America than oil embargoes.
> After a year of teaching at Wesleyan University, *Time* 21 May 79

MAURICE NATANSON, Professor of Philosophy, Yale

11 What a teacher doesn't say . . . is a telling part of what a student hears.
> NY *Times* 6 Jan 85

NATIONAL CONFERENCE ON HIGHER EDUCATION

12 Awareness need never remain superficial in an educated man, whereas unawareness is certain to be ignorance probably compounded by arrogance.
> Report prepared for annual meeting, Chicago, 20 Apr 64

NEW YORK CITY BOARD OF EDUCATION

13 It's like being grounded for 18 years.
> Poster warning against teen pregnancy, pictured in NY *Times* 12 Oct 86

14 Don't make a baby if you can't be a father.
> *ib*

EWALD B NYQUIST, NY State Education Commissioner

15 Equality is not when a female Einstein gets promoted to assistant professor: Equality is when a female schlemiel moves ahead as fast as a male schlemiel.
> NY *Times* 9 Oct 75

JACK W PELTASON, President, Amer Council on Education

16 The Greeks had their laurel wreaths. The English have their honors list. The French are always wearing ribbons in their lapels. In this country honorary degrees from universities serve that function.
> NY *Times* 27 May 84

JAMES A PERKINS, President, Cornell

17 The acquisition of knowledge is the mission of research, the transmission of knowledge is the mission of teaching and the application of knowledge is the mission of public service.
> From Stafford Little Lectures at Princeton, quoted in NY *Times* 3 Nov 66

JOHN PHILLIPS, President, National Assn of Independent Colleges and Universities

18 The real test is whether we are going to have an efficient, program-oriented department or just another federal bureaucracy run by a group of people with their feet caught in their underwear.
> On new US Department of Education, *Newsweek* 12 May 80

NATHAN M PUSEY, President, Harvard

1 The teacher's task is not to implant facts but to place the subject to be learned in front of the learner and, through sympathy, emotion, imagination and patience, to awaken in the learner the restless drive for answers and insights which enlarge the personal life and give it meaning.
NY *Times* 22 Mar 59

2 We live in a time of such rapid change and growth of knowledge that only he who is in a fundamental sense a scholar—that is, a person who continues to learn and inquire—can hope to keep pace, let alone play the role of guide.
The Age of the Scholar Belknap Press/Harvard 63

JOHN A RASSIAS, Professor of Romance Languages, Dartmouth

3 Language study is a route to maturity. Indeed, in language study as in life, if a person is the same today as he was yesterday, it would be an act of mercy to pronounce him dead and to place him in a coffin, rather than in a classroom.
Quote 26 May 74

4 Language is a living, kicking, growing, flitting, evolving reality, and the teacher should spontaneously reflect its vibrant and protean qualities.
ib

PHILIP RIEFF, Professor of Sociology, University of Pennsylvania

5 Scholarship is polite argument.
NY *Herald Tribune* 1 Jan 61

MANLEY E ROGERS, Director of Admissions, West Point

✗6 Robert E Lee didn't make it the first time and Jefferson Davis took the vacancy. Pershing didn't make it for two years, MacArthur couldn't get in the first year and Eisenhower took an extra year of high school to get in. [Patton] took three years to get in and five to get out.
On prominent alumni who were not initially accepted by West Point, NY *Times* 7 May 85

7 Harvard doesn't consider anyone a loss until he dies without a diploma, because they say he can always come back and finish.
On West Point's 33 percent attrition rate compared with that of private institutions, *ib*

RUTHERFORD D ROGERS, librarian, Yale

8 We're drowning in information and starving for knowledge.
On the enormous number of books, periodicals and other documents published each year, quoted in NY *Times* 25 Feb 85

HENRY ROSOVSKY, former Dean, Faculty of Arts and Sciences, Harvard

9 Harvard admissions is an exercise in social engineering.
Quoted by Colin Campbell "The Harvard Factor" NY *Times* 20 Jul 86

GEORGE C ST JOHN, Headmaster, Choate School, Wallingford CT

10 We save a boy's soul at the same time we are saving his algebra.
Recalled on his death 21 Jan 66

ST JOHN'S COLLEGE, Annapolis MD

11 The great books can only repeat what they have to say, without furnishing the clarification that we desire.
Philosophy of education as stated in college catalogue, quoted by Robert Kanigel "Where Great Books Are the Teachers" NY *Times* 21 Sep 86

BENNO C SCHMIDT JR, President, Yale

12 Yale is a crucible in American life for the accommodation of intellectual achievement, of wisdom, of refinement, with the democratic ideals of openness, of social justice and of equal opportunity.
On election as president, quoted in NY *Times* 11 Dec 85

13 Yale's greatness carries an urgent need to guard against the fall of excellence into exclusivity, of refinement into preciousness, of elegance into class and convention.
ib

14 To take the measure of oneself by reference to one's colleagues leads to envy or complacency rather than constructive self-examination.
On competition in academia, *Christian Science Monitor* 12 Dec 85

CHARLES SEYMOUR, President, Yale

15 We seek the truth and will endure the consequences.
Recalled on his death 11 Aug 63

GEORGE N SHUSTER, President Emeritus, Hunter College

16 You ought not to educate a woman as if she were a man, or to educate her as if she were not.
The Ground I Walked On Farrar, Straus 61

ALAN SIMPSON, President, Vassar College

17 An educated man . . . is thoroughly inoculated against humbug, thinks for himself and tries to give his thoughts, in speech or on paper, some style.
On becoming president, *Newsweek* 1 Jul 63

✗18 Any education that matters is liberal. All the saving truths, all the healing graces that distinguish a good education from a bad one or a full education from a half empty one are contained in that word.
Address at 100th commencement 31 May 64

19 [The word *liberal*] distinguishes whatever nourishes the mind and spirit from the training which is merely practical or professional or from the trivialities which are no training at all.
ib

HAROLD TAYLOR, President, Sarah Lawrence College

20 A student is not a professional athlete. . . . He is not a little politician or junior senator looking for angles . . . an amateur promoter, a glad-hander, embryo Rotarian, café-society leader, quiz kid or man about town. A student is a person who is learning to fulfill his powers and to find ways of using them in the service of mankind.
News summaries 3 Sep 56

21 Most of the most important experiences that truly educate cannot be arranged ahead of time with any precision.
"The Private World of the Man with a Book" *Saturday Review* 7 Jan 61

JOHN THORN, Headmaster, Winchester College

1 Whatever else I do before finally I go to my grave, I hope it will not be looking after young people.
> Quoted by Martin O'Brien "Inside Britain's Brainiest School" *M* Feb 85

HUGH TREVOR-ROPER, Professor of Modern History, Oxford

2 The function of a genius is not to give new answers, but to pose new questions which time and mediocrity can resolve.
> *Man and Events* Harper 57

BARBARA M WHITE, President, Mills College

3 The basic purpose of a liberal arts education is to liberate the human being to exercise his or her potential to the fullest.
> *Christian Science Monitor* 8 Sep 76

EUGENE S WILSON, Dean of Admissions, Amherst

4 Only the curious will learn and only the resolute overcome the obstacles to learning. The quest quotient has always excited me more than the intelligence quotient.
> *Reader's Digest* Apr 68

MARY J WILSON, elementary school teacher

5 I'm never going to be a movie star. But then, in all probability, Liz Taylor is never going to teach first and second grade.
> *Newsweek* 4 Jul 76

HENRY M WRISTON, President Emeritus, Brown University

6 Those who misrepresent the normal experiences of life, who decry being controversial, who shun risk, are the enemies of the American way of life, whatever the piety of their vocal professions and the patriotic flavor of their platitudes.
> *Wall Street Journal* 1 Jun 60

7 A guidance counselor who has made a fetish of security, or who has unwittingly surrendered his thinking to economic determinism, may steer a youth away from his dream of becoming a poet, an artist, a musician or any other of thousands of things, because it offers no security, it does not pay well, there are no vacancies, it has no "future."
> *ib*

8 Among all the tragic consequences of depression and war, this suppression of personal self-expression through one's life work is among the most poignant.
> *ib*

NANCY ZERBY

9 The girls aren't going to know what they're doing because they're freshmen, and the school's not going to know what it's doing because we're girls.
> On being among the first women admitted to Yale, NY *Times* 30 Apr 69

Observers & Critics

J DONALD ADAMS

10 There are times when I think that the ideal library is composed solely of reference books. They are like understanding friends—always ready to meet your mood, always ready to change the subject when you have had enough of this or that.
> NY *Times* 1 Apr 56

EDWARD ALBEE

11 American critics are like American universities. They both have dull and half-dead faculties.
> To NY Cultural League, news summaries 6 May 69

CHRISTOPHER ANDREAE

12 Ignorance is a *right*! Education is eroding one of the few democratic freedoms remaining to us.
> *Christian Science Monitor* 21 Feb 80

ANONYMOUS

13 A major cause of deterioration in the use of the English language is very simply the enormous increase in the number of people who are using it.
> Quoted by Robert McCrum, William Cran and Robert MacNeil *The Story of English* Viking 86

BERNARD BARUCH

14 I am quite sure that in the hereafter she will take me by the hand and lead me to my proper seat.
> On one of his early teachers, news summaries 29 Aug 55

SIMONE DE BEAUVOIR

15 These worthy schoolteachers were not overburdened with diplomas, but as far as devotion and morality were concerned, they were second to none; they wore plum-colored silk blouses that caressed my cheeks when they pressed me to their bosoms.
> On her early teachers, *When Things of the Spirit Come First* Pantheon 82

JIM BENCIVENGA

16 The single-room worlds remain strong icons at the heart of our national memory, permanent as any church spire piercing the New England sky.
> On country schools, *Christian Science Monitor* 13 Feb 85

17 From facing down rattlesnakes in broom closets with the spring thaw to fending off ranch-hand bullies (or lovelorn cowboys), teachers had to be wise in the ways of the world.
> *ib*

BERNARD BERENSON

18 German is of stone, limestone, pudding stone, marble, granite even, and so to a considerable degree is English, whereas French is bronze and gives out a metallic resonance with tones that neither German nor English tolerate.
> Quoted by Meryle Secrest *Being Bernard Berenson* Holt, Rinehart & Winston 79

LEONARD BERNSTEIN

19 [It was] an initiation into the love of learning, of learning how to learn, that was revealed to me by my BLS masters as a matter of interdisciplinary cognition—that is, learning to know something by its relation to something else.
> On Boston Latin School, NY *Times* 22 Nov 84

LISA BIRNBACH

1 The University of Miami is not a campus with visible school spirit, just visible tan lines.
Lisa Birnbach's College Book Ballentine 84

DANIEL J BOORSTIN, Librarian of Congress

2 Knowledge is not simply another commodity. On the contrary, Knowledge is never used up. It increases by diffusion and grows by dispersion.
To House Appropriations Subcommittee, quoted in NY *Times* 23 Feb 86

HAL BOYLE

3 Professors simply can't discuss a thing. Habit compels them to deliver a lecture.
News summaries 31 Dec 86

WILLIAM E BROCK, US Secretary of Labor

4 It's an insane tragedy that 700,000 people get a diploma each year and can't read the damned diploma.
To Senate Committee on Labor and Human Resources, NY *Times* 14 Jan 87

JOHN MASON BROWN

5 She knows what is the best purpose of education: not to be frightened by the best but to treat it as part of daily life.
Tribute to classical scholar Edith Hamilton, *Publishers Weekly* 17 Mar 58

JEROME BRUNER

6 The shrewd guess, the fertile hypothesis, the courageous leap to a tentative conclusion—these are the most valuable coins of the thinker at work. But in most schools guessing is heavily penalized and is associated somehow with laziness.
The Process of Education Harvard 60

WILLIAM F BUCKLEY JR

7 The majority of the senior class of Vassar does not desire my company and I must confess, having read specimens of their thought and sentiments, that I do not desire the company of the majority of the senior class of Vassar.
Withdrawing as commencement speaker after students protested his conservative record, NY *Times* 20 May 80

ROBERT W BURCHFIELD

8 American English is the greatest influence of English everywhere.
On completing lexicographical work on *A Supplement to the Oxford English Dictionary*, quoted in *Newsweek* 2 Jun 86

WARREN E BURGER, Chief Justice, US Supreme Court

9 [We must have] a program to "learn the way out of prison."
Calling for programs that teach convicts to read and write, to Amer Bar Assn, Houston, 8 Feb 81

CARNEGIE CORPORATION OF NEW YORK

10 Teachers will not come to the school knowing all they have to know, but knowing how to figure out what they need to know, where to get it and how to help others make meaning out of it.
On establishment of a committee to set teaching standards, *A Nation Prepared*, report quoted in NY *Times* 16 May 86

11 Teachers must think for themselves if they are to help others think for themselves.
ib

WINSTON CHURCHILL

12 Study history, study history. In history lies all the secrets of statecraft.
Quoted by James Humes *Churchill* Stein & Day 80

13 I got into my bones the essential structure of the ordinary British sentence—which is a noble thing.
On studying remedial English for three terms, quoted by William Manchester *The Last Lion* Little, Brown 83

CYRIL CONNOLLY

14 [The headmistress] was an able instructress in French and history and we learned with her as fast as fear could teach us.
From his essay "Such, Such Were the Joys," quoted in *Newsweek* 19 Mar 84

NORMAN COUSINS

15 A library, to modify the famous metaphor of Socrates, should be the delivery room for the birth of ideas—a place where history comes to life.
Amer Library Assn *Bulletin* Oct 54

16 The main failure of education is that it has not prepared people to comprehend matters concerning human destiny.
Saturday Review 15 Apr 78

JEAN SPARKS DUCEY, librarian

17 People ought to listen more slowly!
On confused requests such as "Do you have the wrath of grapes?" and "I want a book about the Abdominal Snowman," *Christian Science Monitor* 9 Dec 86

JOHN FOSTER DULLES, US Secretary of State

18 I wouldn't attach too much importance to these student riots. I remember when I was a student at the Sorbonne in Paris, I used to go out and riot occasionally.
On Indonesian demonstrations, news summaries 15 Apr 58

BEVERLY FRANKEL FIELDS

19 He made us feel we were present at a feast of wit, fed by his good sense, and thrilled to be, for that brief time, in on the jest.
On Bergen Evans, *Northwestern University Alumni News* Jan 85

RUDOLF FLESCH

20 Johnny couldn't read . . . for the simple reason that nobody ever showed him how.
Why Johnny Can't Read Harper 55

E M FORSTER

21 They go forth with well-developed bodies, fairly developed minds and undeveloped hearts. An undeveloped heart—not a cold one. The difference is important.
On British public school students, *Life* 2 Apr 51

ROBERT FROST

22 Education is the ability to listen to almost anything without losing your temper or your self-confidence.
Reader's Digest Apr 60

1 Education doesn't change life much. It just lifts trouble to a higher plane of regard.
Quote 9 July 61

2 College is a refuge from hasty judgment.
ib

J WILLIAM FULBRIGHT, US Senator

3 The exchange program is the thing that reconciles me to all the difficulties of political life.
On Fulbright scholarships established after World War II. *New Yorker* 10 May 58

4 It's the one activity that gives me some hope that the human race won't commit suicide, though I still wouldn't count on it.
ib

5 To avoid a nuclear war. . . . you may think that's pretentious but that's its main purpose.
On rationale for establishing Fulbright scholarships, NY *Times* 26 Jun 86

6 In the long course of history, having people who understand your thought is much greater security than another submarine.
ib

VARTAN GREGORIAN, President, NY Public Library

7 It meant that New York philanthropists, New York society, would now rediscover the library. . . . that learning, books, education have glamour, that self-improvement has glamour, that hope has glamour.
On Brooke Astor's decision to devote herself to raising money for the library, NY *Times* 20 May 84

8 The book is here to stay. What we're doing is symbolic of the peaceful coexistence of the book and the computer.
On computerization of card catalog, *Time* 25 Feb 85

9 Libraries keep the records on behalf of all humanity. . . . the unique and the absurd, the wise and [the] fragments of stupidity.
New Yorker 14 Apr 86

HENRY ANATOLE GRUNWALD

10 Everything can be learned, including, to a very large extent, to be what you are not. You can learn to be pretty if you are plain, charming if you are dull, thin if you are fat, youthful if you are aging, how to write though you are inarticulate, how to make money though you are not good with figures.
Time 5 Jul 76

11 Nagging questions remain: Where is the line between making the most of one's potential and reaching for the unattainable? Where is the line between education as a tool and education as a kind of magic? The line is blurred and that is why when education fails, disillusionment is so bitter.
ib

EDITH HAMILTON

12 To be able to be caught up into the world of thought—that is educated.
Saturday Evening Post 27 Sep 58

SYDNEY J HARRIS

13 Nothing is as easy to make as a promise this winter to do something next summer; this is how commencement speakers are caught.
Chicago *Daily News* 20 Feb 58

GENE R HAWES

14 Intellect won, though not easily or decisively. Gradually, painfully, the upper-class colleges severed as amicably as possible their links with the least-qualified members of the prominent families.
Analysis of Social Register and Ivy League college enrollments, NY *Times* 14 Mar 64

LARRY HAWKINS, founder, Institute for Athletics and Education

15 We need programs that will teach athletes how to *spell* "jump shot" rather than how to shoot it.
Quoted by Preston Greene "A Mind *Is* a Terrible Thing to Waste" *Christian Science Monitor* 13 Aug 86

GILBERT HIGHET

16 A teacher must believe in the value and interest of his subject as a doctor believes in health.
The Art of Teaching Knopf 50

E D HIRSCH JR

17 We have ignored cultural literacy in thinking about education . . . We ignore the air we breathe until it is thin or foul. Cultural literacy is the oxygen of social intercourse.
Cultural Literacy: What Every American Needs to Know Houghton Mifflin 87

ERIC HOFFER

18 The education explosion is producing a vast number of people who want to live significant, important lives but lack the ability to satisfy this craving for importance by individual achievement. The country is being swamped with nobodies who want to be somebodies.
Wall Street Journal 23 Mar 78

HERBERT HOOVER, 31st US President

19 No greater nor more affectionate honor can be conferred on an American than to have a public school named after him.
At dedication of Herbert Hoover Junior High School, San Francisco, 5 Jun 56

JOHN K HUTCHENS

20 I do not mean to suggest that our handsome, newly enlarged library is to be a headquarters of busy bookworms, old and young, routinely absorbing knowledge by the hour while birds sing outside and the Mets fight it out for last place in the National League. On the contrary, a good library is a joyful place where the imagination roams free, and life is actively enriched.
In program for benefit to aid Free Reading Room of Rye NY 28 Oct 67

JESSE JACKSON

21 [Today's students] can put dope in their veins or hope in their brains. . . . If they can conceive it and believe it, they can achieve it. They must know it is not their aptitude but their attitude that will determine their altitude.
Washington *Post* 21 May 78

LYNDON B JOHNSON, 36th US President

1 We have entered an age in which education is not just a luxury permitting some men an advantage over others. It has become a necessity without which a person is defenseless in this complex, industrialized society. . . . We have truly entered the century of the educated man.
> As vice president, commencement address at Tufts University, 9 Jun 63

2 Poverty must not be a bar to learning and learning must offer an escape from poverty.
> Calling for an educational system that "grows in excellence as it grows in size," commencement address at University of Michigan 22 May 64

3 I believe the destiny of your generation—and your nation—is a rendezvous with excellence.
> Commencement address at College of the Holy Cross, Worcester MA, 10 Jun 64

4 I greet you as the shapers of American society.
> To National Educational Assn 3 Jul 65

ALFRED KAZIN

5 If we practiced medicine like we practice education, we'd look for the liver on the right side and left side in alternate years.
> Quoted by US Secretary of Education William J Bennett in address to National Press Club 27 Mar 85

HELEN KELLER

6 A child . . . must feel the flush of victory and the heart-sinking of disappointment before he takes with a will to the tasks distasteful to him and resolves to dance his way through a dull routine of textbooks.
> NY Times 12 Sep 65

JOHN F KENNEDY, 35th US President

7 The human mind is our fundamental resource.
> Message to Congress on state of education 20 Feb 61

8 A child miseducated is a child lost.
> State of the Union address 11 Jan 62

9 It might be said now that I have the best of both worlds. A Harvard education and a Yale degree.
> On receiving honorary degree from Yale, NY Times 12 Jun 62

10 I want to emphasize in the great concentration which we now place upon scientists and engineers how much we still need the men and women educated in the liberal tradition, willing to take the long look, undisturbed by prejudices and slogans of the moment, who attempt to make an honest judgment on difficult events.
> Address at University of North Carolina 12 Oct 62

11 Modern cynics and skeptics . . . see no harm in paying those to whom they entrust the minds of their children a smaller wage than is paid to those to whom they entrust the care of their plumbing.
> Address on 90th anniversary of Vanderbilt University 19 May 63

ROGER G KENNEDY, Director, National Museum of Amer History

12 Our business here is revelation. . . . to reveal those objects Americans have kept on purpose in ways that permit them to be freshly perceived.
> On exhibition of items such as Judy Garland's ruby slippers, NY Times 19 Oct 84

CHARLES F KETTERING

13 My definition of an educated man is the fellow who knows the right thing to do at the time it has to be done. . . . You can be sincere and still be stupid.
> Quoted by T A Boyd Professional Amateur Dutton 57

LINCOLN KIRSTEIN

14 Harvard was a kind of luxurious afternoon.
> Looking back on Harvard's Class of '30, New Yorker 15 Dec 86

EDWARD KOCH, Mayor of NYC

15 The fireworks begin today. Each diploma is a lighted match. Each one of you is a fuse.
> Commencement address to graduates of Polytechnic Institute of NY, during which fire broke out briefly, NY Times 10 Jun 83

C S LEWIS

16 The real Oxford is a close corporation of jolly, untidy, lazy, good-for-nothing humorous old men, who have been electing their own successors ever since the world began and who intend to go on with it. They'll squeeze under the Revolution or leap over it when the time comes, don't you worry.
> Quoted in Jan Morris ed The Oxford Book of Oxford Oxford 78

ARTHUR LUBOW

17 Behind closed doors each winter the college admissions committee riffles through the folders of concerto-writing East Coast preppies, football stars from the Corn Belt and ghetto valedictorians.
> On Harvard's selection of students, Newsweek 10 Jul 78

18 Diversity wasn't always cultivated along the banks of the Charles.
> On effort since the 1950s to make Harvard a less homogeneous institution, ib

ARCHIBALD MACLEISH

19 Once you permit those who are convinced of their own superior rightness to censor and silence and suppress those who hold contrary opinions, just at that moment the citadel has been surrendered. For the American citadel is a man. Not man in general. Not man in the abstract. Not the majority of men. But man. That man. His worth. His uniqueness.
> 1951 commencement address at Wellesley College, quoted in "Parting Shots: A Century of Commencement Speeches" Saturday Review 12 May 79

JOHN MASEFIELD

20 There are few earthly things more beautiful than a university . . . a place where those who hate ignorance may strive to know, where those who perceive truth may strive to make others see.
> News summaries 10 Jun 63

CHARLES McC MATHIAS JR, US Senator

21 I cannot help but wonder whether, by continuing and expanding the school lunch program, we aren't witnessing, if not encouraging, the slow demise of yet another American tradition: the brown bag. . . . Perhaps we are beholding yet another break in the chain that links child to home.
> Time 16 Aug 76

1 The brown bag, of course, had its imperfections. While some kids carried roast beef sandwiches, others had peanut butter. I have no way of knowing if all of those brown bags contained "nutritionally adequate diets." But I do know that those brown bags and those lunch pails symbolized parental love and responsibility.
ib

H L MENCKEN

2 A professor must have a theory as a dog must have fleas.
Quoted by Geoffrey H Hartman *Easy Pieces* Columbia University 85

WILLIAM MENNINGER

3 It is just as important, perhaps more important, for the teacher to have the benefit of personal counseling when he needs it as it is for the student.
To National Assn of Secondary School Principals, news summaries 24 Feb 54

THOMAS MERTON

4 October is a fine and dangerous season in America. . . . a wonderful time to begin anything at all. You go to college, and every course in the catalogue looks wonderful.
Recalled on his death 10 Dec 68

SUE MITTENTHAL

5 As the youngsters grow attached to their teachers and classmates . . . they can finally say good-bye to their mothers without re-enacting the death scene from *Camille*.
NY *Times* 6 Sep 84

BERNARD LAW MONTGOMERY, 1st Viscount Montgomery of Alamein

6 I was well beaten myself, and I am better for it.
On corporal punishment in schools, news summaries 8 Nov 55

TED MORGAN

7 The elective system . . . offered a bewildering freedom of choice, leaving some graduates with the impression that they had nibbled at dozens of canapés of knowledge and never had their fill.
On Harvard's experimentation with elective courses, *FDR* Simon & Schuster 85

DANIEL P MOYNIHAN, US Senator

8 The United States in the 1980s may be the first society in history in which children are distinctly worse off than adults.
On problems in US education system, NY *Times* 6 May 86

STEPHEN NEILL

9 The bad teacher imposes his ideas and his methods on his pupils, and such originality as they may have is lost in the second-rate art of imitation.
A Genuinely Human Existence Doubleday 59

10 The good teacher . . . discovers the natural gifts of his pupils and liberates them by the stimulating influence of the inspiration that he can impart. The true leader makes his followers twice the men they were before.
ib

NEW YORK TIMES

11 Lunch is eaten on its front steps. The proper and the improper disport themselves in its backyard. All civilization enters its reading room at the beck of a card.
Editorial on 75th anniversary of NY Public Library, "The Lions' House" 20 May 86

RICHARD M NIXON, 37th US President

12 It is not too strong a statement to declare that this is the way civilizations begin to die . . . None of us has the right to suppose it cannot happen here.
On tumult on college campuses, address 22 Mar 69

13 Violence or the threat of violence [must] never be permitted to influence the actions or judgments of the university community. Once it does, the community, almost by definition, ceases to be a university. It is for this reason that from time immemorial expulsion has been the primary instrument of university discipline.
ib

SEÁN O'FAOLÁIN

14 It is really the undergraduate who makes a university, gives it its lasting character, smell, feel, quality, tradition . . . whose presence creates it and whose memories preserve it.
Harvard Alumni Bulletin 24 Oct 64

VANCE PACKARD

15 You can't tell a millionaire's son from a billionaire's.
On democracy at prep schools, *The Status Seekers* McKay 59

GEORGES POMPIDOU, President of France

16 The most dangerous thing about student riots is that adults take them seriously.
Life 20 Feb 70

NELSON A ROCKEFELLER, Governor of NY

17 There are many other possibilities more enlightening than the struggle to become the local doctor's most affluent ulcer case.
Urging Syracuse University graduates to enter public service, *Quote* 3 Jul 66

ROCKEFELLER BROTHERS FUND

18 A degree is not an education, and the confusion on this point is perhaps the gravest weakness in American thinking about education.
Prospect for America Doubleday 61

STEVEN RUNCIMAN

19 Faced by the mountainous heap of the minutiae of knowledge and awed by the watchful severity of his colleagues, the modern historian too often takes refuge in learned articles or narrowly specialized dissertations, small fortresses that are easy to defend from attack.
London *Times* 7 Jul 83

20 I believe that the supreme duty of the historian is to write history, that is to say, to attempt to record in one sweeping sequence the greater events and movements that have swayed the destiny of man.
ib

MICHAEL SADLER

1 Education is the established church of the United States. It is one of the religions that Americans believe in. It has its own orthodoxy, its pontiffs and its noble buildings.
    Quoted in NY *Times* 1 Sep 56

WILLIAM SAFIRE

2 I think we have a need to know what we do not need to know.
    "Class Cleavage" NY *Times* 1 Jun 86

3 What we don't need to know for achievement, we need to know for our pleasure. Knowing how things work is the basis for appreciation, and is thus a source of civilized delight.
    ib

NORMAN ST JOHN-STEVAS, Member of British Parliament

4 How amazing that the language of a few thousand savages living on a fog-encrusted island in the North Sea should become the language of the world.
    Quoted by Jack Valenti NY *Times* 10 Jul 84

ELOISE SALHOLZ

5 Living up to basic ethical standards in the classroom—discipline, tolerance, honesty—is one of the most important ways children learn how to function in society at large.
    "Morals Mine Field" *Newsweek* 13 Oct 86

ANTHONY SAMPSON

6 In Britain, the segregated world of public schools crops up in all kinds of institutions: A boy can pass from Eton to the Guards to the Middle Temple to Parliament and still retain the same male world of leather armchairs, teak tables and nicknames. They need never deal closely with other kinds of people, and some never do.
    The Anatomy of Britain Harper & Row 62

CHARLES SCRIBNER JR

7 Language is the soul of intellect, and reading is the essential process by which that intellect is cultivated beyond the commonplace experiences of everyday life.
    Publishers Weekly 30 Mar 84

8 Beyond the formative effects of reading on the individuals composing society, the fact that they have read the same books gives them experiences and ideas in common. These constitute a kind of shorthand of ideas which helps make communication quicker and more efficient. That is what we mean when we say figuratively of another person, "We speak the same language."
    ib

C A SIMPSON, Dean, Christ Church College, Oxford

9 It is a rare thing for a student to be taught by only one tutor. If he should by rare chance have been indoctrinated by Mr A, he will certainly be liberated by Mr B.
    Answering charge that US students at Oxford might acquire a preference for the British system, *Saturday Evening Post* 23 Mar 63

B F SKINNER

10 Education is what survives when what has been learned has been forgotten.
    "Education in 1984" *New Scientist* 21 May 64

MURIEL SPARK

11 All my pupils are the crème de la crème. Give me a girl of an impressionable age, and she is mine for life.
    The Prime of Miss Jean Brodie Dell 64

JOSEPH STALIN

12 Education is a weapon whose effects depend on who holds it in his hands and at whom it is aimed.
    Recalled on his death 5 Mar 53

ADLAI E STEVENSON

13 We must recover the element of quality in our traditional pursuit of equality. We must not, in opening our schools to everyone, confuse the idea that all should have equal chance with the notion that all have equal endowments.
    To United Parents Assn, NY *Times* 6 Apr 58

14 Respect for intellectual excellence, the restoration of vigor and discipline to our ideas of study, curricula which aim at strengthening intellectual fiber and stretching the power of young minds, personal commitment and responsibility—these are the preconditions of educational recovery in America today; and, I believe, they have always been the preconditions of happiness and sanity for the human race.
    ib

TIME MAGAZINE

15 Balliol College is a Victorian Gothic pile of no great distinction. . . . Yet it sits at the head of Oxford's intellectual table—a proud hatchery of prime ministers, archbishops, cardinals and viceroys.
    On the college's 700th anniversary, 12 Jul 63

16 Whether or not Balliol really was 700—an agreed age more than a historic fact—they cheerily drank the ancient toast, *Floreat domus de Balliol*, meaning roughly, boola, boola Balliol.
    ib

17 Shocked to the tips of its sweat socks.
    Recalling Dartmouth's switch to coeducation in 1972, 12 Mar 79

GARDNER TUCKER

18 A towered city, set within a wood,
    Far from the world, upon a mountain crest,
    There storms of life burst not, nor cares intrude,
    There Learning dwells, and Peace is Wisdom's guest.
    Quoted in William Strode and William Butt eds *Sewanee: The University of the South* Harmony House 84

JOHN UPDIKE

19 Four years was enough of Harvard. I still had a lot to learn, but had been given the liberating notion that now I could teach myself.
    Quoted in *Life* Sep 86

EVELYN WAUGH

20 We class schools . . . into four grades: leading school, first-rate school, good school and school.
    Recalled on his death 10 Apr 66

1 The truth is that Oxford is simply a very beautiful city in which it is convenient to segregate a certain number of the young of the nation while they are growing up.

> Quoted in Donat Gallagher ed *A Little Order: Selections from His Journalism* Little, Brown 81

ORSON WELLES

2 He is as unaffected as Albert Einstein.

> On Joel Kufferman at age 6, recalled in reunion of child prodigies who appeared on the radio show *The Quiz Kids*, CBS TV 16 Nov 86

MARK WHITE, Governor of Texas

3 The rest of the world is sweeping past us. The oil and gas of the Texas future is the well-educated mind. But we are still worried about whether Midland can beat Odessa at football.

> Supporting law that bans failing students from participating in extracurricular activities, NY *Times* 25 Nov 85

THEODORE H WHITE

4 Generally students are the best vehicles for passing on ideas, for their thoughts are plastic and can be molded and they can adjust the ideas of old men to the shape of reality as they find it in villages and hills of China or in ghettos and suburbs of America.

> *In Search of History: A Personal Adventure* Harper & Row 78

GEORGE F WILL

5 A society that thinks the choice between ways of living is just a choice between equally eligible "lifestyles" turns universities into academic cafeterias offering junk food for the mind.

> *Newsweek* 29 May 78

6 In the 1940s a survey listed the top seven discipline problems in public schools: talking, chewing gum, making noise, running in the halls, getting out of turn in line, wearing improper clothes, not putting paper in wastebaskets. A 1980s survey lists these top seven: drug abuse, alcohol abuse, pregnancy, suicide, rape, robbery, assault. (Arson, gang warfare and venereal disease are also-rans.)

> *ib* 5 Jan 87

W WILLARD WIRTZ, US Secretary of Labor

7 Commencement speakers have a good deal in common with grandfather clocks: Standing usually some six feet tall, typically ponderous in construction, more traditional than functional, their distinction is largely their noisy communication of essentially commonplace information.

> Commencement address at University of Iowa, *Time* 19 Jun 65

JOHN WOLFENDEN

8 Schoolmasters and parents exist to be grown out of.

> London *Sunday Times* 13 Jun 58

JOHN A WOLTER, Director, Geography and Map Division, Library of Congress

9 Remember civics? It wasn't this bouillabaisse they call social studies today.

> *Time* 16 Sep 85

LOUIS BOOKER WRIGHT, Director, Folger Shakespearean Library, Washington DC

10 We're trying to show that we're not a little bit of England in America, but a place for Americans to gain a better perspective on their own history.

> News summaries 9 May 55

11 All the fundamental concepts which make up the kind of people we are today had their modern conception in the Tudor and Stuart periods. For us, that's the milk in the coconut.

> *ib*

MEDICINE

Physicians & the Medical World

DR PIETER V ADMIRAAL

12 The very word *euthanasia* is never used because of the madman Hitler.

> On stigma attached to euthanasia in Germany, France and Sweden, quoted by Francis X Clines "Dutch Are Quietly Taking the Lead in Euthanasia" NY *Times* 31 Oct 86

13 We in Holland know the word means "a mild death, a dignified death." And therefore we use it.

> *ib*

14 I say to my patient, "I wish you a very good journey to an unknown you've never seen."

> To his patients who choose euthanasia, *ib*

DR DAVID ALLMAN, President, Amer Medical Assn

15 The dedicated physician is constantly striving for a balance between personal, human values, scientific realities and the inevitabilities of God's will.

> "The Brotherhood of Healing," address to National Conference of Christians and Jews 12 Feb 58

16 Life is precious to the old person. He is not interested merely in thoughts of yesterday's good life and tomorrow's path to the grave. He does not want his later years to be a sentence of solitary confinement in society. Nor does he want them to be a death watch.

> *ib*

AMERICAN DENTAL ASSOCIATION

17 Brush them and floss them and take them to the dentist, and they will stay with you. Ignore them, and they'll go away.

> Advertisement in *Time* 11 Feb 85

DR GEORGE J ANNAS, Professor of Health Law, Boston University School of Medicine

18 The more things doctors are able to do, the more likely that at least a few doctors won't do them. And the result will be more people suing for negligence.

> *Wall Street Journal* 7 Jun 85

ANONYMOUS

19 Drill, fill and bill.

> Standard of old-fashioned dentistry, quoted in *Newsweek* 5 May 86

20 Please come to my being alive party.

> Patient's invitation to physician after treatment for drug addiction, quoted in advertisement for St Vincent's Hospital and Medical Center, NY *Times* 7 May 86

Dr Vincent Askey, President, Amer Medical Assn

1 When it comes to your health, I recommend frequent doses of that rare commodity among Americans—common sense.
> Address at Bakersfield CA 20 Oct 60

2 We are rapidly becoming a land of hypochondriacs, from the ulcer-and-martini executives in the big city to the patent medicine patrons in the sulfur-and-molasses belt.
> ib

Dr Michael M Baden, Chief Medical Examiner, NYC

3 A cancer is not only a physical disease, it is a state of mind.
> NY *Times* 17 Jun 79

Dr Leonard Bailey

4 More than 100 people are involved in a transplant operation . . . and we can't waste time and resources if there is a chance the caretakers aren't up for an awesome responsibility.
> On initial refusal to perform a heart transplant on an infant whose unwed parents appeared unable to provide long and intensive care, NY *Times* 15 Jun 86

5 You can't serve up hearts like cherries jubilee.
> *Time* 23 Jun 86

Dr Tazewell Banks, Director of Heart Program, DC General Hospital

6 It would be better if they told their children, "Go out and play in traffic."
> On parents who allow their children to eat foods rich in unsaturated fats at fast-food restaurants, NY *Times* 15 Nov 85

Dr Alvan Barach, developer of the first practical oxygen tent

7 Remember to cure the patient as well as the disease.
> Recalled on his death 15 Dec 77

Dr Christiaan N Barnard, South African surgeon

8 It is infinitely better to transplant a heart than to bury it to be devoured by worms.
> *Time* 31 Oct 69

Bernard Baruch

9 I am interested in physical medicine because my father was. I am interested in medical research because I believe in it. I am interested in arthritis because I have it.
> NY *Post* 1 May 59

Dr Thomas J Bassler, pathologist

10 Two out of every three deaths are premature; they are related to loafer's heart, smoker's lung and drinker's liver.
> Quoted by James Fixx *The Complete Book of Running* Random House 77

Dr Anne C Bayley

11 It was like coming home from work and finding that your spaniel had turned into a wolf . . . so against one's expectations.
> On Kaposi's sarcoma as it changed to an AIDS-related virus in Zambia, NY *Times* 9 Dec 85

Cal Beacock

12 A bunch of germs were whooping it up
In the Bronchial Saloon.
The bacillus handling the larynx
Was jazzing a gag-time tune,
While back of the tongue in a solo game
Sat Dangerous Ah Kerchoo.
And watching his luck was his light of love
The malady known as Flu.
> From *The Pundit*, published by International Save the Pun Foundation, quoted in *Reader's Digest* Jan 86

Dr Arthur Benjamin

13 We all basically go back to being a child when we're in a dentist's chair.
> *Newsweek* 5 May 86

Dr Harry Benjamin

14 I ask myself, in mercy, or in common sense, if we cannot alter the conviction to fit the body, should we not, in certain circumstances, alter the body to fit the conviction?
> To Jan Morris, who as a man approached Dr Benjamin for sex-change surgery, quoted in NY *Times* 27 Aug 86

Dr Norman Bethune

15 How beautiful the body is . . . How terrible when torn. The little flame of life sinks lower and lower and, with a flicker, goes out. It goes out like a candle goes out. Quietly and gently. It makes its protest at extinction, then submits. It has its say, then is silent.
> From 1940 article on his experiences in China, quoted in *New Frontiers* Fall 52

Jeff Bleckner

16 It attacks the most precious thing we have as human beings, our mental faculties.
> On Alzheimer's disease, quoted by Stephen Farber NY *Times* 11 Mar 85

Shannon Boff

17 I think I'm going into retirement. Any more babies coming from me are going to be keepers.
> Comments of a 23-year-old woman who had twice been a surrogate mother, quoted in *Time* 28 Apr 86

Dr Joseph F Boyle, President-elect, Amer Medical Assn

18 We believe that doctors have the same concerns as their patients and will share in all the sacrifices that are necessary to keep the economy strong.
> Appeal to physicians to help the economy by voluntarily freezing their fees for a year, NY *Times* 24 Feb 84

Dr Sandy Burstein

19 What is most interesting in family practice is not what the problem is but what motivates people to seek help for it. Something in the family, a hidden factor, will make the mundane interesting.
> *New Yorker* 23 Jul 84

Dr John Button Jr

20 We sit at breakfast, we sit on the train on the way to work, we sit at work, we sit at lunch, we sit all afternoon . . . a hodgepodge of sagging livers, sinking gallbladders, drooping stomachs, compressed intestines and squashed pelvic organs.
> To Amer Osteopathic Assn, quoted in *Newsweek* 6 Aug 56

DR ARTHUR CAPLAN, Associate Director, Hastings Center, Hastings-on-Hudson, NY

1 Bodies aren't the same as Coca-Cola cans.
> Quoted by Lindsey Gruson "Signs of Traffic in Cadavers Seen, Raising Ethical Issues" NY *Times* 25 Sep 86

2 The use of fetuses as organ and tissue donors is a ticking time bomb of bioethics.
> On fetal-cell surgery, quoted by Joe Levine "Help from the Unborn" *Time* 12 Jan 87

CHARLES, Prince of Wales

3 The whole imposing edifice of modern medicine, for all its breathtaking successes, is, like the celebrated Tower of Pisa, slightly off balance. It is frightening how dependent on drugs we are all becoming and how easy it is for doctors to prescribe them as the universal panacea for our ills.
> Address at 150th anniversary dinner of the British Medical Assn, quoted in NY *Times* 9 Jan 85

DR DONALD J CIAGLIA, Assistant Professor of Community Medicine, University of Rochester, NY

4 They learn that once they enter the court, they are in someone else's operating room.
> On teaching legal procedures to medical students, NY *Times* 5 Mar 86

DR JAMES CIMINO, Medical Director, Calvary Hospital, NY Institute for the Terminally Ill

5 You die as you've lived. If you were paranoid in life, you'll probably be paranoid when you're dying.
> NY *Times* 6 Mar 79

MATT CLARK

6 In Alzheimer's [disease] the mind dies first: Names, dates, places—the interior scrapbook of an entire life—fade into mists of nonrecognition.
> "A Slow Death of the Mind" *Newsweek* 3 Dec 84

DR CYRIL CLARKE, Director of Research, Royal College of Physicians

7 You could say people are living longer because of the decline in religion. Not many people believe in the hereafter, so they keep going.
> On increasing number of people reaching the age of 100, London *Times* 27 Dec 86

DR STANLEY N COHEN, geneticist, Stanford

8 Nature [is] that lovely lady to whom we owe polio, leprosy, smallpox, syphilis, tuberculosis, cancer.
> Quoted by David N Leff in letter to the editor NY *Times* 15 Mar 87

DR JOHN P CONOMY, Chairman of Neurology, Cleveland Clinic Foundation

9 It's very hard to live a productive life when a piece of your brain is missing. And that's what stroke is, a hole in the brain.
> *Wall Street Journal* 16 Jul 84

NORMAN COUSINS

10 The more serious the illness, the more important it is for you to fight back, mobilizing all your resources—spiritual, emotional, intellectual, physical.
> *Anatomy of an Illness* Norton 79

11 Your heaviest artillery will be your will to live. Keep that big gun going.
> *ib*

12 Laughter is a form of internal jogging. It moves your internal organs around. It enhances respiration. It is an igniter of great expectations.
> *ib*

DR THERESA CRENSHAW, President, Amer Assn of Sex Educators, Counselors and Therapists

13 You're not just sleeping with one person, you're sleeping with everyone *they* ever slept with.
> Interviewed on *Men, Women, Sex and AIDS* NBC TV 13 Jan 87

DR BRUCE B DAN

14 Sedentary people have shriveled hearts and most of us who do not exercise have an atrophied body.
> On evidence that even moderate exercise helps prolong life, quoted in NY *Times* 27 Jul 84

15 We can now prove that large numbers of Americans are dying from sitting on their behinds.
> *ib*

DR MICHAEL E DE BAKEY

16 If you can think of how much love there would be in hundreds of hearts, then that is how much love there is in a plastic heart and when you grow up you will understand how very much love that is.
> In reply to a child who asked, "Does a plastic heart have love in it?" *Newsweek* 6 Jun 66

DR WILLIAM C DEVRIES

17 I would have picked up the artificial heart and thrown it on the floor and walked out and said he's dead if the press had not been there.
> On his frustration in implanting the first artificial heart. NY *Times* 12 Apr 83

18 We all felt the majesty of the body. . . . As we saw the artificial heart beat . . . the feeling was not aren't we great, but aren't we small.
> *ib*

DR SEYMOUR DIAMOND

19 Patients with migraines know precisely when and how often and how long their headaches strike. They often come in with long lists. When you have a patient with lists, you have a patient with migraine.
> Quoted in Washington *Post* 28 Dec 79

DR FRANCIS DUDLEY-HART

20 Some consulting rooms are full of complainers . . . professionals for whom pain is a career.
> To British Medical Assn. quoted in London *Daily Telegraph* 17 Jul 74

DAVID W DUNLAP

21 The subject no longer has to be mentioned by name. Someone is sick. Someone else is feeling better now. A friend has just gone back into the hospital. Another has died. The unspoken name, of course, is AIDS.
> NY *Times* 23 Apr 85

DR ROBERT S ELIOT, Professor of Cardiology, University of Nebraska

1 Rule Number 1 is, don't sweat the small stuff. Rule Number 2 is, it's all small stuff. And if you can't fight and you can't flee, flow.

On coping with stress, *Time* 6 Jun 83

DR ALEXANDER FLEMING

2 A good gulp of hot whiskey at bedtime—it's not very scientific, but it helps.

On treatment of the common cold, news summaries 22 Mar 54

DR HENRY W FLOURNOY

3 Every baby has turned into a ticking time bomb that can go off in your hand.

On refusing to treat a pregnant lawyer who had been the prosecuting attorney in two malpractice suits against another obstetrician, NY *Times* 18 May 86

THEODOR GEISEL ("Dr Seuss")

4 When at last we are sure
You've been properly pilled,
Then a few paper forms
Must be properly filled
So that you and your heirs
May be properly billed.

You're Only Old Once! Random House 86

PETER GOLDMAN and LUCILLE BEACHY

5 He is one in a sad new specialty in our medicine, a thin white line of plague doctors doing battle with the most fearsome epidemic of our time.

On physicians who treat patients with AIDS, "One Against the Plague" *Newsweek* 21 Jul 86

DR BURTON GREBIN, Executive Director, St Mary's Hospital for Children, Bayside, Queens

6 The death of a child is the single most traumatic event in medicine. To lose a child is to lose a piece of yourself.

On opening of NYC's first facility for terminally ill children, NY *Times* 30 Oct 84

JANE GROSS

7 Rarely does anyone speak of fear for his own life, as if an unspoken etiquette prevails.

On regular meetings of persons who have lost their lovers to AIDS, "AIDS: The Next Phase" NY *Times* 16 Mar 87

8 Over and over, these men cry out against the weight of so many losses—not just a lover dead, but friends and friends of friends, dozens of them, until it seems that AIDS is all there is and all there ever will be.

ib

DR GUNNAR GUNDERSEN, former President, Amer Medical Assn

9 When I began practice . . . I was relatively safe in assuming [that abdominal pain] was appendicitis or green apples. Today it is also highly probable that the patient is suffering from the fact that his wife of 40 years wants to leave him for the Peace Corps or Richard Burton.

Commencement address at Strich School of Medicine, Loyola University, Chicago, 7 Jun 62

10 While the patient wants the best and most modern treatment available, he is also badly in need of the old-fashioned friend that a doctor has always personified and which you must continue to be.

ib

DR MICHAEL J HALBERSTAM

11 [The joy of medicine is] the challenge of making a solid diagnosis, the delight in besting (if only momentarily) an intern or resident, the satisfaction (if rare) of actually helping someone, the sheer cantankerousness of being able to tell the bureaucracy to "stuff it."

Recalled on his death 5 Dec 80

MURRAY HAYDON, artificial heart recipient

12 Would you please turn on the television. I'd like to see if I'm still alive and how I'm doing.

News summaries 19 Feb 85

DR ROBERT P HEANEY, endocrinologist, Creighton University, Omaha NE

13 It's just like remodeling an office. The body tears out partitions, puts up dry walls and paints.

On how the body takes calcium from its bones when there is a shortage of calcium in the blood stream, *Newsweek* 27 Jan 86

DR HERMAN HELLERSTEIN, School of Medicine, Case Western Reserve University, Cleveland OH

14 Coronary heart disease is a silent disease and the first manifestation frequently is sudden death.

Newsweek 6 Aug 84

DR ELMER HESS, President, Amer Medical Assn

15 If a man is good in his heart, then he is an ethical member of any group in society. If he is bad in his heart, he is an unethical member. To me, the ethics of medical practice is as simple as that.

American Weekly 24 Apr 55

16 There is no greater reward in our profession than the knowledge that God has entrusted us with the physical care of his people.

ib

DR ARTHUR HOLLEB, Vice President for Medical Affairs, Amer Cancer Society

17 We do not know what we mean by cure because there is a great difference between cure and long-term survival.

On the society's slogan "We want to cure cancer in your lifetime," NY *Times* 17 Apr 79

DR CHARLES BRENTON HUGGINS, Professor of Surgery, University of Chicago

18 One pits his wits against apparently inscrutable nature, wooing her with ardor [but] nature is blind justice who cannot recognize personal identity.

On scientific research, *National Observer* 21 Nov 66

19 [Nature] can refuse to speak but she cannot give a wrong answer.

ib

1 We wanted to see if hormone therapy would do for elderly gentlemen what it would do for their best friends, elderly male dogs.

On cancer research, Chicago *Sun Times* 27 Nov 66

DR ERNEST JOHNSON, Ohio State University

2 Back fusions are like killing a fly on the windowpane with a sledgehammer. The fly is dead, but you've also broken the glass.

Quoted in "That Aching Back" *Time* 14 Jul 80

LYNDON B JOHNSON, 36th US President

3 Every citizen will be able, in his productive years when he is earning, to insure himself against the ravages of illness in his old age.

On signing Medicare Act, NY *Times* 21 Jul 65

DR DAVID JONES

4 Doctors coin money when they do procedures [but] family medicine doesn't have any procedures.

New Yorker 23 Jul 84

5 Cystoscopies . . . gastroscopies . . . biopsies. They can do three or four of those and make five or six hundred dollars in a single day [but] we get nothing when we use our time to understand the lives of our patients.

ib

DR SARA MURRAY JORDAN, gastroenterologist

6 Every businessman over 50 should have a daily nap and nip—a short nap after lunch and a relaxing high-ball before dinner.

Reader's Digest Oct 58

7 Nobody should smoke cigarettes—and smoking with an ulcer is like pouring gasoline on a burning house.

ib

8 A much more effective and lasting method of face-lifting than surgical technique is happy thinking, new interests and outdoor exercise.

ib

9 In medicine, as in statecraft and propaganda, words are sometimes the most powerful drugs we can use.

NY *Times* 23 Nov 59

DR HUGO A KEIM, orthopedist

10 If you believe in evolution . . . you can trace all of our lower back problems to the time when the first hominid stood erect.

Quoted in "That Aching Back" *Time* 14 Jul 80

11 If you're a creationist, you can look at it this way: When Eve offered Adam the apple, he stood up to accept it.

ib

GERALDINE KIDSTON, mother of a drug victim

12 I guess he got into what we now call designer drugs.

Testimony to Senate committee on the need for protection against unregulated drugs, NY *Times* 19 Jul 85

DR JOHN KIRKLIN, heart surgeon, Mayo Clinic, Rochester MN

13 Surgery is always second best. If you can do something else, it's better.

Time 3 May 63

14 Surgery is limited. It is operating on someone who has no place to go.

ib

DR C EVERETT KOOP, US Surgeon General

15 You can't talk of the dangers of snake poisoning and not mention snakes.

On need to discuss sexual conduct as part of AIDS education in schools, quoted by John Leo "Sex and Schools" *Time* 24 Nov 86

MARTHA WEINMAN LEAR

16 No other surgery affects people in quite this way. For it is unthinkable, finally, that one's heart should be cut open. It is the one unthinkable cut.

On her husband's double by-pass coronary operation, *Heartsounds* Simon & Schuster 80

17 Women agonize . . . over cancer; we take as a personal threat the lump in every friend's breast.

ib

DR FREDERICK LEBOYER, French obstetrician

18 Yes, hell exists. It is not a fairy tale. One indeed burns there. This hell is not at the end of life. It is here. At the beginning. Hell is what the infant must experience before he gets to us.

Comments from proponent of "birth without violence," NY *Times* 8 Dec 74

19 This tragic brow, these closed eyes, eyebrows raised and knotted.

ib

20 This howling mouth, this head which rolls back and tries to escape.

ib

21 These hands which stretch out, implore, beg, then rise to the head in a gesture of calamity.

ib

22 These feet which kick furiously, legs which bend in to protect a tender stomach. This flesh which is but a mass of spasms, starts and shakes.

ib

23 He doesn't speak, the newborn? Why his entire being shouts out, "Don't touch me! Don't touch me!" And yet at the same time, imploringly, begging, "Don't leave me! Don't leave me!" . . . This is birth. This is the torture, the Calvary.

ib

DR THOMAS C LEE, Professor of Surgery, Georgetown University Medical School

24 Eagles: When they walk, they stumble. They are not what one would call graceful. They were not designed to walk. They fly. And when they fly, oh, how they fly, so free, so graceful. They see from the sky what we never see. Steve, you are an eagle.

Inscription given with painting of an eagle to a paraplegic medical student, quoted in Washington *Post* 29 May 80

DAVID N LEFF, Editor in Chief, *Biotechnology Newswatch*

25 The gene-spliced product is safer by far than the natural one.

On superiority of genetically engineered hormones to those taken from cadavers, letter to the editor NY *Times* 15 Mar 87

1 This genie can't be pushed back into the bottle.
> On impossibility of halting genetic research, *ib*

DR C WALTON LILLEHEI, heart surgeon

2 The Wright brothers' first flight was shorter than a Boeing 747's wing span. We've just begun with heart transplants.
> NY *Post* 16 Dec 69

DR IAN LUSTBADER

3 When you get that close to the abyss, you can always jump tomorrow.
> On critically ill patients who may decide whether or not artificial means will be used to prolong their lives, NY *Times* 16 Jan 85

DR WALTER MARTIN, President, Amer Medical Assn

4 The very success of medicine in a material way may now threaten the soul of medicine.
> "Medicine and the Public Welfare," inaugural address 23 Jun 54

THOMAS MATTHEWS

5 [Condoms] are like raincoats in the Sahara.
> On futility of issuing condoms at NYC's Riker's Island Prison to prevent spread of AIDS, NY *Times* 5 Mar 87

WILLIAM F MAY, Professor of Medical Ethics, Southern Methodist University

6 You convert the whole medical system into a giant jaws and the individual's only possible response is a yelp of protest.
> On acquisition of bodily parts for transplants and research, quoted by Lindsey Gruson "Signs of Traffic in Cadavers Seen, Raising Ethical Issues" NY *Times* 25 Sep 86

JOHN McPHEE

7 If the social status of a urologist, a nephrologist, a gastroenterologist, can send a wistful moment through the thoughts of a family practitioner, that is nothing compared with this hovering ghost, this image afloat above the family practitioner's head: Superdoc, the Great American GP, *omniscie ubiquitous*.
> "A Reporter at Large: Heirs of General Practice" *New Yorker* 23 Jul 84

8 The doctor listens in with a stethoscope and hears sounds of a warpath Indian drum.
> On prenatal examinations, *ib* 6 Aug 84

DR WILLIAM MONTAGNA, dermatological researcher, Brown University

9 Interest in hair today has grown to the proportions of a fetish. Think of the many loving ways in which advertisements refer to scalp hair—satiny, glowing, shimmering, breathing, living. Living indeed! It is as dead as rope.
> NY *Herald Tribune* 11 Apr 63

ASHLEY MONTAGU

10 One goes through school, college, medical school and one's internship learning little or nothing about goodness but a good deal about success.
> *Northwestern University Alumni News* Summer 75

11 There have been some medical schools . . . in which somewhere along the assembly line, a faculty member has informed the students, not so much by what he said but by what he did, that there is an intimate relation between curing and caring.
> *ib*

12 Human beings are the only creatures who are able to behave irrationally in the name of reason.
> NY *Times* 30 Sep 75

13 The [doctor] has been taught to be interested not in health but in disease. What the public is taught is that health is the cure for disease.
> *ib*

JAN MORRIS (James Morris)

14 I told him everything and it was from him that I learned what my future would be.
> On consultation with Dr Harry Benjamin, who coined the term *transsexualism* and performed Morris's sex-change operation, recalled on Benjamin's death, NY *Times* 27 Aug 86

DR BERNARD NATHANSON

15 We can see the child moving rather serenely in the uterus. . . . The child senses aggression in its sanctuary. . . . We see the child's mouth wide open in a silent scream.
> From narration of *The Silent Scream*, 1984 film on the abortion of a 12-week-old fetus, quoted in NY *Times* 11 Mar 85

EDWARD R NIDA, US Food and Drug Administration

16 How you lose or keep your hair depends on how wisely you choose your parents.
> On barring sale of nonprescription cures for baldness, NY *Times* 15 Jan 85

DR JOEL J NOBEL, cofounder, Emergency Care Research Institute

17 The purpose of medicine is to prevent significant disease, to decrease pain and to postpone death when it is meaningful to do so. Technology has to support these goals—if not, it may even be counterproductive.
> On the development and maintenance of high-technology medical systems, NY *Times* 1 Jan 85

DR WILLIS POTTS, heart surgeon

18 The heart is a tough organ: a marvelous mechanism that, mostly without repairs, will give valiant service up to a hundred years.
> *The Surgeon and the Child* Saunders 59

DR JOSEPH PURSCH, Medical Director, Comprehensive Care Corp

19 Coroners (they always have the final word) know why cocaine's nickname is *killer*.
> "Cocaine in the Board Room" *Leaders* Jul 84

20 Cocaine is quickly supplanting alcohol as the most dangerous occupational hazard in executive suites.
> *ib*

21 The irony is that as the user gets sicker, he is less able to see it. The magic of the powder is that every noseful tells you that you don't really have a problem.
> *ib*

STEVEN RADLAUER

1 When you are exhausted from trying to beat the odds against recovery, when you want only to cash in your chips and let them fall where they may, you do not ask your doctor to gamble with your life but to *stop* gambling.

> Letter to the editor NY *Times* 5 Nov 86

2 The physician who overrules the request, insisting instead on rolling the medical dice again and again in an effort to see how long the inevitable can be postponed, is the one who is gambling.

> *ib*

RONALD REAGAN, 40th US President

3 I've noticed that everybody that is for abortion has already been born.

> As presidential candidate, quoted in NY *Times* 22 Sep 80

4 Surgeons now speak of "the patient" in the womb [and] for the first time . . . we're able to see with our own eyes, on film, the abortion of a 12-week-old unborn child. [It] provides chilling documentation of the horror of abortion.

> On 1984 film *The Silent Scream*, to antiabortion demonstrators, Washington DC, 22 Jan 85

DONNA REGAN, surrogate mother

5 They're borrowing one tiny little egg and some space.

> On surrogate motherhood, *Newsweek* 4 Nov 85

DR ARNOLD RELMAN, Editor, New England Journal of Medicine

6 Health care is being converted from a social service to an economic commodity, sold in the marketplace and distributed on the basis of who can afford to pay for it.

> Criticizing the takeover of public hospitals by commercial businesses, NY *Times* 25 Jan 85

PATRICK REYNOLDS, grandson of tobacco manufacturer R J Reynolds

7 Am I biting the hand that feeds me? If the hand that once fed me is the tobacco industry, then that hand has killed 10 million people and may kill millions more.

> On the eve of testifying before Congressional hearing on the banning of cigarette advertising, NY *Times* 17 Jul 86

MARION ROACH

8 She was losing her mind in handfuls.

> On her mother, a victim of Alzheimer's disease, *Another Name for Madness* Houghton Mifflin 85

DR OLIVER SACKS, British neurologist

9 There is only one cardinal rule: One must always *listen* to the patient.

> Quoted by Walter Clemons "Listening to the Lost" *Newsweek* 20 Aug 84

10 If migraine patients have a common and legitimate second complaint besides their migraines, it is that they have not been listened to by physicians. Looked at, investigated, drugged, charged, but not listened to.

> *ib*

DR JONAS SALK

11 It is courage based on confidence, not daring, and it is confidence based on experience.

> On administering the experimental vaccine for polio to himself and his wife and three sons, news summaries 9 May 55

12 I feel that the greatest reward for doing is the opportunity to do more.

> On receiving Congressional Medal for Distinguished Civilian Achievement 23 Apr 58

DR CECILY SAUNDERS

13 I think very soon the right to die will become the duty to die.

> On euthanasia, *60 Minutes* CBS TV 24 Jul 83

MARGARET SCHROEDER

14 I wish Bill had written down on the consent form at what point he would want to say, "Stop this, I've had enough."

> On her husband William Schroeder, artificial-heart recipient, after he suffered a series of strokes, *People* 16 Dec 85

DR ALBERT SCHWEITZER

15 I wanted to be a doctor that I might be able to work without having to talk because for years I had been giving myself out in words.

> Recalled on his death 4 Sep 65

16 This new form of activity [medicine] I could not represent to myself as talking about the religion of love, but only as an actual putting it into practice.

> *ib*

17 Whosoever is spared personal pain must feel himself called to help in diminishing the pain of others.

> *ib*

18 Serious illness doesn't bother me for long because I am too inhospitable a host.

> Quoted by Norman Cousins *Anatomy of an Illness* Norton 79

NORBERT SEGARD

19 I am not going to fight against death but for life.

> On suffering from cancer, London *Times* 2 Feb 81

DR HANS SELYE, Director, Institute of Experimental Medicine and Surgery, University of Montreal

20 Man should not try to avoid stress any more than he would shun food, love or exercise.

> *The Stress of Life* McGraw-Hill 56, quoted in *Newsweek* 31 Mar 58

21 Every stress leaves an indelible scar, and the organism pays for its survival after a stressful situation by becoming a little older.

> *Emphasis*, paper from Smith, Kline & French, Winter 69

DR RICHARD SELZER

22 I contemplate the body, dead and diseased as well as alive and healthy.

> *Mortal Lessons* Simon & Schuster 77

1 The heart is pure theater . . . throbbing in its cage palpably as any nightingale.
ib

2 The liver, that great maroon snail: No wave of emotion sweeps it. Neither music nor mathematics gives it pause in its appointed tasks.
ib

3 You do not die all at once. Some tissues live on for minutes, even hours, giving still their little cellular shrieks, molecular echoes of the agony of the whole corpus.
ib

4 Surgery is the red flower that blooms among the leaves and thorns that are the rest of medicine.
Letters to a Young Doctor Simon & Schuster 82, quoted in NY *Times* 29 Aug 82

DR MARK SIEGLER, Director, Center for Clinical Medical Ethics, University of Chicago

5 The coming together of two laudable movements—death with dignity and cost containment—concerns me. You start with those in a permanent vegetative state. Then you move to the mentally retarded, the permanently senile, seriously ill defective newborns and the physically handicapped. Patients have a right to die. But do they have a duty to die?
Quoted in NY *Times* 18 Aug 86

DR GEORGE D SNELL

6 I was on a hunt for 30 years. I wore a laboratory gown, not a Maine guide's red wool jacket.
On winning the 1980 Nobel Prize for his explanation of how cell structure relates to organ transplants, *Life* Feb 81

DR BENJAMIN SPOCK

7 You know more than you think you do.
First sentence of *Baby and Child Care*, quoted in *Ladies' Home Journal* Mar 60

8 In automobile terms, the child supplies the power but the parents have to do the steering.
ib

9 I really learned it all from mothers.
On the 40th-anniversary edition of his book that had already sold more than 28 million copies, *Time* 8 Apr 85

DR MARTIN R STEINBERG, Director, Mt Sinai Hospital, NYC

10 The most important thing we have learned about the aged is the necessity to give them the shortest possible period "down," the longest period "up." When a patient is "up," he is a citizen, an individual. When he is "down," he and his doctor are in trouble. . . . "Down" is bad, "up" is life.
Saturday Evening Post 20 May 67

PINCHAS STOLPER, Executive Vice President, Union of Orthodox Jewish Congregations of America

11 A person is entitled to be buried whole.
On acquisition of bodily parts for transplants and research, quoted by Lindsey Gruson "Signs of Traffic in Cadavers Seen, Raising Ethical Issues" NY *Times* 25 Sep 86

JEROME H STONE, President, National Alzheimer's Disease and Related Disorders Assn

12 It is the disease that robs the mind of the victim and breaks the hearts of the family.
NY *Times* 23 Nov 83

DR LEWIS THOMAS, President, Memorial Sloan-Kettering Institute for Cancer Research

13 The great secret of doctors, known only to their wives, but still hidden from the public, is that most things get better by themselves; most things, in fact, are better in the morning.
NY *Times* 4 Jul 76

CALVIN TRILLIN

14 Keeping off a large weight loss is a phenomenon about as common in American medicine as an impoverished dermatologist.
Alice, Let's Eat Random House 78

UNITED STATES SURGEON GENERAL

15 Warning: Quitting smoking now greatly reduces serious risk to your health.
One of four warnings printed on cigarette packages, quoted by NY *Times* 12 Feb 86

DR CECIL VAUGHN, St Luke's Hospital, Phoenix

16 There's a greater law than the FDA, and that is an obligation of a doctor to try to do anything he can to save a life when he thinks that there's a chance.
Defending a decision to implant an experimental mechanical heart without the approval of the US Food and Drug Administration, NY *Times* 8 Mar 85

CLAUDIA WALLIS

17 Tooth decay was a perennial national problem that meant a mouthful of silver for patients, and for dentists a pocketful of gold.
On decreasing occurrence of tooth decay, "Today's Dentistry: A New Drill" *Time* 9 Sep 85

ELIZABETH WHELAN, Amer Council on Science and Health

18 We recommend that no one eat more than two tons of turkey—that's what it would take to poison someone.
On toxins and carcinogens in holiday meals, *US News & World Report* 8 Dec 86

DR PAUL DUDLEY WHITE

19 The country will be very pleased—the country is so bowel-minded anyway . . . and it is important.
Reporting President Dwight D Eisenhower's condition following a heart attack, news summaries 10 Oct 55

FRED WITCH, District Staff Officer, St John's Ambulance Brigade

20 This is the moment when we get the most casualties. The adrenaline runs quick when the queen enters.
On Buckingham Palace garden parties, NY *Times* 15 Jul 83

DR ERNST WUNDER, President, Amer Health Foundation

21 Clearly, if disease is manmade, it can also be manprevented. It should be the function of medicine to help people die young as late in life as possible.
NY *Times* 30 Sep 75

BARBARA YUNCKER

1 In the medical sense now, birth is not the beginning but just a developmental transition.
"The Riddle of Birth" NY *Post* 23 May 69

Psychiatry & Psychology

RICHARD ABELL

2 Anxiety is the space between the "now" and the "then."
Own Your Own Life McKay 76

DR FRANZ ALEXANDER

3 We now feel we can cure the patient without his fully understanding what made him sick. We are no longer so interested in peeling the onion as in changing it.
Address marking 50th anniversary of organized practice of psychoanalysis in the US. *Time* 10 May 61

DR VICTOR ALTZHUL, Professor of Psychiatry, Yale

4 The practicing psychotherapist is perhaps better qualified than other serious human beings to discuss boredom.
New York 7 Apr 80

AMERICAN PSYCHIATRIC ASSOCIATION

5 Hardly a section of the country, urban or rural, has escaped the ubiquitous presence of ragged, ill and hallucinating human beings, wandering through our city streets, huddled in alleyways or sleeping over vents.
Report on transfer of the mentally ill from institutional to outpatient care. NY *Times* 13 Sep 84

ANONYMOUS

6 I'm a *consumer* of psychiatry but I can't accept being shut away—that's like cutting your throat without a knife.
Comment of "Harry" on *Full of Sound and Fury: Living with Schizophrenia* PBS TV 14 May 86

DR RUTH TIFFANY BARNHOUSE

7 Maturity is coming to terms with that other part of yourself.
News summaries 1 Mar 82

DR FRANK BARRON, Professor of Psychology, University of California, Santa Cruz

8 The creative person is both more primitive and more cultivated, more destructive and more constructive, a lot madder and a lot saner, than the average person.
Think Nov 62

DR JOHN V BASMAJIAN, McMaster University, Hamilton, Ontario

9 Back pain is just a tension headache that has slipped down the back.
On psychological aspects of backaches. *Time* 14 Jul 80

DR REX JULIAN BEABER, clinical psychologist, UCLA

10 A reservoir of rage exists in each person, waiting to burst out. We fantasize about killing or humiliating our boss or the guy who took our parking space. It is only by growing up in a civilized society of law that we learn the idea of proportionate response.
Quoted by Ed Magnuson "Up in Arms over Crime" *Time* 8 Apr 85

NEIL G BENNETT, Associate Professor of Sociology, Yale

11 It appears . . . that much of this marriage deferral is translating into marriage forgone.
On current marriage patterns, NY *Times* 22 Feb 86

DR RUTH BERKELEY

12 Heterosexuality is an attribute of the mature personality.
NY State Journal of Medicine 15 Nov 51

13 I see adult sexuality more as an expression of an emotional attitude than as a function of anatomy.
ib

DR ERIC BERNE

14 Losers spend time explaining why they lost. Losers spend their lives thinking about what they're going to do. They rarely enjoy doing what they're doing.
Games People Play Random House 64

15 Games are a compromise between intimacy and keeping intimacy away.
ib

DR LUDWIG BINSWANGER, Swiss psychiatrist

16 Loneliness is an unhappy compound of having lost one's point of reference, of suffering the fate of individual and collective discontinuity and of living through or dying from a crisis of identity to the point of alienation of one's self.
On his "naked horror" theory of loneliness, *National Observer* 12 Aug 72

DR PHILIP BONNET, psychiatrist, Princeton Brain Biological Center

17 The patient is always the ultimate source of knowledge.
W 27 Aug 76

DR FRANCIS J BRACELAND, Chief Psychiatrist, Institute for Living, Hartford CT

18 The sorrow which has no vent in tears may make other organs weep.
On psychosomatic disorders, "Living With Executive Tensions" *National Observer* 28 Dec 64

19 We can be sure that the greatest hope for maintaining equilibrium in the face of any situation rests within ourselves. Persons who are secure with a transcendental system of values and a deep sense of moral duties are possessors of values which no man and no catastrophe can take from them.
ib

DR NORMAN M BRADBURN, psychologist, University of Chicago

20 It is the lack of joy in Mudville, rather than the presence of sorrow that makes the difference.
In Pursuit of Happiness: A Pilot Study of Behavior Related to Mental Health National Opinion Research Center 63

JIMMY BRESLIN

21 When you stop drinking, you have to deal with this marvelous personality that started you drinking in the first place.
Table Money Ticknor & Fields 86

STEPHEN BROOK

1 Unpinned even by rudimentary notions of time and space, dreams float or flash by, leaving in their wake trails of unease, hopes, fears and anxieties.
The Oxford Book of Dreams Oxford 84

DR JOYCE BROTHERS

2 I don't give advice. I can't tell anybody what to do. Instead I say this is what we know about this problem at this time. And here are the consequences of these actions.
American Way 79

DR DONALD BROWN, Director, Morrisania Neighborhood Family Care Center, NYC

3 It's getting hard to find a pure schizophrenic anymore.
On the difficulty of differentiating between drug abuse and mental illness in the inner city, NY *Times* 17 Mar 86

ANATOLE BROYARD

4 The tension between "yes" and "no," between "I can" and "I cannot," makes us feel that, in so many instances, human life is an interminable debate with one's self.
NY *Times* 13 Jan 76

PEARL BUCK

5 Because psychologists have been able to discover, exactly as in a slow-motion picture, the way the human creature acquires knowledge and habits, the normal child has been vastly helped by what the retarded have taught us.
On her mentally retarded daughter, *The Child Who Never Grew* John Day 50

DR MARY S CALDERONE

6 Before the child ever gets to school it will have received crucial, almost irrevocable sex education and this will have been taught by the parents, who are not aware of what they are doing.
People 21 Jan 80

ELAINE CUMMING

7 We reveal the fullness of our devotion to individualism by keeping it as a reward for full participation in society. For the prisoner, the chronically ill, the bedridden old and the destitute, we reserve the forced collective life.
"Allocation of Care to the Mentally Ill, American Style" in Mayer N Zald ed *Organizing for Community Welfare* Quadrangle 67

VIOLET DE LAZLO

8 The edifice of C G Jung's work is reminiscent of a cathedral . . . With its altar, its cross and its rose window, this edifice has been erected *ad majorem Dei gloriam*, as is true of all valid creative efforts, often those which appear to be agnostically motivated.
Comment in her edition of Carl Jung *Psyche and Symbol* Doubleday 58

DR WILLIAM C DEMENT

9 Dreaming permits each and every one of us to be quietly and safely insane every night of our lives.
Newsweek 30 Nov 59

BELLA DePAULO, psychologist, University of Virginia

10 People tell about two lies a day, or at least that is how many they will admit to.
On a study in which participants kept a daily diary of lies, NY *Times* 12 Feb 85

PHIL DONAHUE

11 Suicide is a permanent solution to a temporary problem.
NBC TV 23 May 84

DR ROBERT L DuPONT, Director, Center of Behavioral Medicine, Washington DC

12 The malignant disease of the "what-ifs."
On phobias, quoted by Jerry Adler "The Fight to Conquer Fear" *Newsweek* 23 Apr 84

PAUL EKMAN, psychologist, University of California, San Francisco

13 Most liars can fool most people most of the time.
On research showing people to be surprisingly inept at detecting lies, NY *Times* 12 Feb 85

DR ERIK ERIKSON

14 Children love and want to be loved and they very much prefer the joy of accomplishment to the triumph of hateful failure. Do not mistake a child for his symptom.
Childhood and Society Norton 50

15 Doubt is the brother of shame.
ib

DR JACK R EWALT

16 The result was like preparing a plan to build a new airplane and ending up [with only] a wing and a tail.
On US policy that released many mentally ill people from institutional care, quoted in NY *Times* 30 Oct 84

DR VIKTOR E FRANKL, Professor of Neurology and Psychiatry, University of Vienna

17 Ultimately, man should not ask what the meaning of his life is, but rather he must recognize that it [is] he who is asked.
Man's Search for Meaning Beacon 59

18 Each man is questioned by life; and he can only answer to life by answering for his own life; to life he can only respond by being responsible.
ib

DR ERICH FROMM

19 In the 19th century inhumanity meant cruelty; in the 20th century it means schizoid self-alienation.
The Sane Society Holt, Rinehart & Winston 55

20 One cannot be deeply responsive to the world without being saddened very often.
ABC TV 25 May 58

21 Both dreams and myths are important communications from ourselves to ourselves. If we do not understand the language in which they are written, we miss a great deal of what we know and tell ourselves in those hours when we are not busy manipulating the outside world.
NY *Times* 5 Jan 64

DR WILLARD GAYLIN, President, Institute of Society, Ethics and the Life Sciences, Hastings-on-Hudson NY

1 A man may not always be what he appears to be, but what he appears to be is always a significant part of what he is.
NY *Times* 7 Oct 77

2 To probe for unconscious determinants of behavior and then define a man in their terms exclusively, ignoring his overt behavior altogether, is a greater distortion than ignoring the unconscious completely.
ib

3 Many of the quests for status symbols—the hot automobile, the best table in a restaurant or a private chat with the boss—are shadowy reprises of infant anxieties. . . . The larger office, the corner space, the extra window are the teddy bears and tricycles of adult office life.
The Rage Within Simon & Schuster 84, quoted in *Time* 24 Dec 84

DR RALPH GERARD, neurophysiologist

4 Activity of the nervous system improves the capacity for activity, just as exercising a muscle makes it stronger.
Time 29 Nov 63

DR HAIM GINOTT

5 Each of us carries within himself a collection of instant insults.
Between Parent and Teenager Macmillan 69

DR ERNEST HARTMANN, Professor of Psychiatry, School of Medicine, Tufts University

6 One important aspect of what makes a person an artist is having a psychological make-up of thin boundaries, which includes the ability to experience and take in a great deal from inside and outside, to experience one's own inner life in a very direct fashion and (sometimes an unwanted ability) to experience the world more directly, more painfully than others.
The Nightmare Basic Books 85, previewed in NY *Times* 23 Oct 84

ERNEST HAVEMANN

7 All of us, even the myriads among us who have emotional problems ranging from the light to the serious, have far more hope for the future.
On the outlook of modern psychiatry, *Life* 4 Feb 57

LESLEY HAZELTON

8 When depression is stigmatized as illness and weakness, a double bind is created: If we admit to depression, we will be stigmatized by others; if we feel it but do not admit it, we stigmatize ourselves, internalizing the social judgment. . . . The only remaining choice may be truly sick behavior: to experience no emotion at all.
The Right to Feel Bad Dial 84

9 Suffering, once accepted, loses its edge, for the terror of it lessens, and what remains is generally far more manageable than we had imagined.
ib

10 There is no perfect solution to depression, nor should there be. And odd as this may sound . . . we should be glad of that. It keeps us human.
ib

DR STANLEY A HERRING

11 We don't consider a patient cured when his sprain has healed or he's been restored to a minimal level of functioning. The patient is cured when he can again do the things he loves to do.
On a survey showing that several hundred orthopedists and neurosurgeons had never referred a patient to a psychiatrist for postoperative rehabilitation, NY *Times* 16 Apr 85

DR KAREN HORNEY

12 Life itself still remains a very effective therapist.
Recalled on her death 4 Dec 52

HOWARD HUGHES

13 Wash four distinct and separate times, using lots of lather each time from individual bars of soap.
Instructions from his procedure manual for staff who handled anything that he was to touch, quoted by Michael Drosnin *Citizen Hughes* Holt, Rinehart & Winston 85

14 The door to the cabinet is to be opened using a minimum of 15 Kleenexes.
ib

KATHRYN HULME

15 The dark-veiled silhouette . . . that solitary form patrolling without visible strain or vainglory a demented dreamland of fearful potential.
On a nun working in a psychiatric ward, *The Nun's Story* Little, Brown 56

MORTON HUNT

16 Being a good psychoanalyst, in short, has the same disadvantage as being a good parent: The children desert one as they grow up.
"How the Analyst Stands the Pace" NY *Times* 24 Nov 57

JILL JOHNSTON

17 The inmates are ghosts whose dreams have been murdered.
On Bellevue Hospital's psychiatric wards, *Paper Daughter* Knopf 85, quoted in NY *Times* 28 Jul 85

CARL JUNG

18 The brain is viewed as an appendage of the genital glands.
On Freudian theory of sexuality, *Time* 14 Feb 55

19 Understanding does not cure evil, but it is a definite help, inasmuch as one can cope with a comprehensible darkness.
Psyche and Symbol, edited by Violet de Lazlo, Doubleday 58

20 How indeed? He copes, like everybody else, as well as he can, that's all. And it's usually deplorably enough.
On how a psychiatrist deals with his personal problems, quoted by Yousuf Karsh *Portraits of Greatness* Nelson 60

21 Shrinking away from death is something unhealthy and abnormal which robs the second half of life of its purpose.
Recalled on his death 6 Jun 61

1 The greatest and most important problems of life are all fundamentally insoluble. They can never be solved but only outgrown.
>   *ib*

2 Neurosis is always a substitute for legitimate suffering.
>   *ib*

3 Man's task is to become conscious of the contents that press upward from the unconscious.
>   *Memories, Dreams, Reflections* Atlantic Monthly Press 62

4 As far as we can discern, the sole purpose of human existence is to kindle a light in the darkness of mere being.
>   *ib*

5 Everything that irritates us about others can lead us to an understanding of ourselves.
>   *ib*

6 Your vision will become clear only when you can look into your own heart. . . . Who looks outside, dreams; who looks inside, awakes.
>   To patient in Cambridge MA, quoted in Gerhard Adler ed *Letters Vol I* Princeton 73

7 Nobody, as long as he moves about among the chaotic currents of life, is without trouble.
>   To patient whose only son had drowned at age 21 while sailing off the coast of Maine. *ib*

DR RALPH KAUFMAN, Director of Psychiatry, Mt Sinai Hospital, NYC

8 Anybody who is 25 or 30 years old has physical scars from all sorts of things, from tuberculosis to polio. It's the same with the mind.
>   *Newsweek* 29 May 61

EUGENE KENNEDY, Professor of Psychology, Loyola University, Chicago

9 The future is religion and commerce, aphrodisiac and Benzedrine, a mother of mysterious comfort and a mistress of familiar ravishments ever on the verge of embracing or destroying us.
>   NY *Times* 2 Dec 79

10 We not only romanticize the future; we have also made it into a growth industry, a parlor game and a disaster movie all at the same time.
>   *ib*

CAROLE KLEIN

11 The tie is stronger than that between father and son and father and daughter. . . . The bond is also more complex than the one between mother and daughter. For a woman, a son offers the best chance to know the mysterious male existence.
>   *Mothers and Sons* Houghton Mifflin 84, quoted in *Time* 1 Oct 84

DR NATHAN S KLINE

12 There is nothing more productive of problems than a really good solution.
>   On tranquilizers and related drugs, *Time* 24 Apr 64

DR ELISABETH KÜBLER-ROSS

13 Those who have the strength and the love to sit with a dying patient in *the silence that goes beyond words* will know that this moment is neither frightening nor painful, but a peaceful cessation of the functioning of the body.
>   *On Death and Dying* Macmillan 69

14 Watching a peaceful death of a human being reminds us of a falling star; one of a million lights in a vast sky that flares up for a brief moment only to disappear into the endless night forever.
>   *ib*

WESTON LA BARRE

15 [We] feed upon each other's mouths and minds like ants with social stomachs.
>   *The Human Animal* University of Chicago 64

JOHN LE CARRÉ

16 The monsters of our childhood do not fade away, neither are they ever wholly monstrous. But neither, in my experience, do we ever reach a plane of detachment regarding our parents, however wise and old we may become. To pretend otherwise is to cheat.
>   *Book-of-the-Month Club News* May 86

DR ROBERT LINDNER

17 *You must adjust.* . . . This is the legend imprinted in every schoolbook, the invisible message on every blackboard.
>   *Must You Conform?* Holt, Rinehart & Winston 56

JOSHUA LOGAN

18 I would be going . . . until I went over the bounds of reality and was then caught up in a profound wish to be dead without having to go through the shaming defeat of suicide.
>   On "manic elations" over a 20-year period, NY *Times* 25 Jun 73

19 The aggravated agony of depression is terrifying, and elation, its nonidentical twin sister, is even more terrifying—attractive as she may be for a moment. You are grandiose beyond the reality of your creativity.
>   *ib*

JANET MALCOLM

20 Analysts keep having to pick away at the scab that the patient tries to form between himself and the analyst to cover over his wounds. [The analyst] keeps the surface raw, so that the wound will heal properly.
>   *Psychoanalysis: The Impossible Profession* Knopf 81, quoted in *Time* 28 Sep 81

DR ARNOLD J MANDELL, Professor of Psychology, University of California, San Diego

21 We will learn to think of ourselves, our personalities, as an orchestra of chemical voices in our heads.
>   *Time* 2 Apr 79

MICHAEL R MANTELL, San Diego police psychologist

22 You know what happens to scar tissue. It's the strongest part of your skin.
>   On psychological recovery of disaster victims, NY *Daily News* 14 Dec 86

Dr Vernon H Mark, Chief of Neurosurgery, Harvard Medical School

1 The proclivity for extraordinary violence is not just an ailment of the mind, as psychologists like to think. Nor is it only a malaise of the society, as sociologists believe. It is both of these things, but it is also a sickness of the body as distinct and definite as cancer or leprosy.
Life Aug 84

Dr William H Masters, codirector, Masters & Johnson Institute

2 The best sex education for kids is when Daddy pats Mommy on the fanny when he comes home from work.
NBC TV 16 Aug 71

3 Sex is a natural function. You can't make it happen, but you can teach people to let it happen.
NY *Times* 29 Oct 84

4 When things don't work well in the bedroom, they don't work well in the living room either.
NBC TV 23 Jun 86

Dr Rollo May

5 If we admit our depression openly and freely, those around us get from it an experience of freedom rather than the depression itself.
Paulus Harper & Row 73

Dr Joost Meerloo

6 It's among the intelligentsia . . . that we often find the glib compulsion to explain everything and to understand nothing.
The Rape of the Mind World 56

Dr Karl A Menninger

7 The voice of the intelligence . . . is drowned out by the roar of fear. It is ignored by the voice of desire. It is contradicted by the voice of shame. It is biased by hate and extinguished by anger. Most of all it is silenced by ignorance.
The Progressive Oct 55

8 Psychoanalysis has changed American psychiatry from a diagnostic to a therapeutic science, not because so many patients are cured by the psychoanalytic technique, but because of the new understanding of psychiatric patients it has given us and the new and different concepts of illness and health.
News summaries 29 Apr 56

9 It was his optimism that Freud bequeathed to America and it was the optimism of our youthfulness, our freedom from the sterner, sadder tradition of Europe which enabled us to seize his gift.
ib

10 Unrest of spirit is a mark of life.
This Week 16 Oct 58

11 Hope is a necessity for normal life and the major weapon against the suicide impulse.
Newsweek 2 Nov 59

12 Money-giving is a very good criterion . . . of a person's mental health. Generous people are rarely mentally ill people.
ib

13 To "know thyself" must mean to know the malignancy of one's own instincts and to know, as well, one's power to deflect it.
Vogue Jun 61

Dr William Menninger

14 Mental health problems do not affect three or four out of every five persons but one out of one.
NY *Times* 22 Nov 57

Arthur Miller

15 What is the most innocent place in any country? Is it not the insane asylum? These people drift through life truly innocent, unable to see into themselves at all.
On his 1964 play *After the Fall*, quoted in *Life* 7 Feb 64

Dr John W Money, Professor of Medical Psychology, Johns Hopkins Medical School

16 It puts an eggbeater in people's brains.
On the "liberating" aspects of pornographic films, NY *Times* 21 Jan 73

Ted Morgan

17 The stammer was a way of telling the world that he was not like others, a way of expressing his singularity.
Maugham Simon & Schuster 80

18 The stammerer is ambivalent about communicating with others—he desperately wants to communicate, but is afraid of revealing himself.
ib

Dr Willibald Nagler, Psychiatrist in Chief, NY Hospital–Cornell Medical Center

19 A psychiatrist has to be a person who commits himself to making a person better. Nothing should be too menial for a psychiatrist to do.
NY *Times* 16 Apr 85

Ulric Neisser, cognitive psychologist, Emory University, Atlanta

20 Most of our oldest memories are the product of repeated rehearsal and reconstruction.
Quoted by Sharon Begley "Memory" *Newsweek* 29 Sep 86

Dr Barry M Panter, Associate Professor of Psychiatry, UCLA, and director of annual conference on creativity and madness

21 The material artists use for their art comes from the primitive levels of their inner lives—aggression, sexual fantasy, polymorphous sexuality. . . . As we mature and are "civilized," we suppress [these drives]. But the artist stays in touch with and struggles to understand them. And to remain so in touch with that primitive self is to be on the fine line between sanity and madness.
NY *Times* 17 Nov 85

Dr M Scott Peck

22 It is only because of problems that we grow mentally and spiritually.
The Road Less Traveled Touchstone 80

Dr Wilder G Penfield, Montreal Neurological Institute

23 Among the millions of nerve cells that clothe parts of the brain there runs a thread. It is the thread of

time, the thread that has run through each succeeding wakeful hour of the individual's past life.
Reader's Digest Jul 58

V S PRITCHETT

1 The whole influence of psychology has turned our interest to . . . the failures of the will, the fulfillment of the heart, the vacillations of the sensibility, the perception of self-interest.
The Living Novel and Later Associations Random House 64

2 We do not wish to be better than we are, but more fully what we are.
ib

3 We live by our genius for hope; we survive by our talent for dispensing with it.
ib

HARRY REASONER

4 We're all controlled neurotics.
TV Guide 20 Mar 71

THEODOR REIK

5 The repressed memory is like a noisy intruder being thrown out of the concert hall. You can throw him out, but he will bang on the door and continue to disturb the concert. The analyst opens the door and says, "If you promise to behave yourself, you can come back in."
Saturday Review 11 Jan 58

6 In our civilization, men are afraid that they will not be men enough and women are afraid that they might be considered only women.
Quoted by Arthur M Schlesinger Jr "The Crisis of American Masculinity" *Esquire* Nov 58

7 Work and love—these are the basics. Without them there is neurosis.
Of Love and Lust Grove 59

ANN ROIPHE

8 In the office there was an old, soft and worn blue velvet couch, above which a hundred thousand dissected dreams floated in the peaceful, still air.
Recalling an interview with psychoanalyst Helene Deutsch, NY *Times* 13 Feb 71

DR MILTON ROKEACH

9 To say that a particular psychiatric condition is incurable or irreversible is to say more about the state of our ignorance than about the state of the patient.
The Three Christs of Ypsilanti Knopf 64

DR THEODORE I RUBIN

10 I must learn to love the fool in me—the one who feels too much, talks too much, takes too many chances, wins sometimes and loses often, lacks self-control, loves and hates, hurts and gets hurt, promises and breaks promises, laughs and cries. It alone protects me against that utterly self-controlled, masterful tyrant whom I also harbor and who would rob me of human aliveness, humility and dignity but for my fool.
Love Me, Love My Fool McKay 76

DR JOSEPH SANDLER

11 Blushing fulfills a most important function in propagation of the human species and is all the more interesting because it is involuntary and shows a readiness to be courted.
News summaries 9 Sep 55

JOHN SANFORD, priest-therapist

12 We can never cure a neurosis; the neurosis cures us and is resolved as the need for it no longer exists.
Your Church Jan 80

DR IRWIN SARASON, psychologist, University of Washington

13 Good friends are good for your health.
NY *Times* 27 Aug 85

DR STANLEY J SARNOFF, physiologist, National Institute of Health

14 The process of living is the process of reacting to stress.
Time 29 Nov 63

DR R W SHEPHERD

15 You handle depression in much the same way you handle a tiger.
Vogue Jul 78

16 If depression is creeping up and must be faced, learn something about the nature of the beast: You may escape without a mauling.
ib

R Z SHEPPARD

17 People once said they were "in" psychoanalysis, meaning they were committed to a long immersion. In a sense, they were writing their autobiographies.
Time 28 Sep 81

DR JUNE SINGER

18 Is it sufficient that you have learned to drive the car, or shall we look and see what is under the hood? Most people go through life without ever knowing.
Boundaries of the Soul Doubleday 72

19 The first half of life is spent mainly in finding out who we are through seeing ourselves in our interaction with others.
ib

PATRICIA MEYER SPACKS

20 Gossip, even when it avoids the sexual, bears around it a faint flavor of the erotic.
Gossip Knopf 85, quoted in NY *Times* 1 Sep 85

21 Poring over fragments of other people's lives, peering into their bedrooms when they don't know we're there, we thrill to the glamour and the power of secret knowledge, partly detoxified but also heightened by being shared.
ib

KARL STERN

22 Psychoanalysis . . . shows the human infant as the passive recipient of love, unable to bear hostility. Development is the learning to love actively and to bear rejection.
The Pillar of Fire Harcourt, Brace & World 51

ANTHONY-STORR

1 With the exception of certain rodents, no other vertebrate [except *Homo sapiens*] habitually destroys members of his own species.
Human Destructiveness Morrow 75

DR JOHN TALBOTT, former President, Amer Psychiatric Assn

2 The families have become the doctors, the nurses and the social workers.
On policies that have deinstitutionalized nearly a million schizophrenics, NY *Times* 17 Mar 86

3 The old philosophy was that parents, especially mothers, caused their kids to become schizophrenic. Now we see that when a kid is this crazy, he'll make the family begin to seem crazy.
ib

CAROL TAVRIS

4 The second sweetest set of three words in English is "I don't know," and it is to R D Laing's credit that he uses it often.
On R D Laing's *Wisdom, Madness and Folly* McGraw-Hill 85, NY *Times* 8 Sep 85

TIME MAGAZINE

5 Anxiety seems to be the dominant fact—and is threatening to become the dominant cliché—of modern life.
31 Mar 61

6 It shouts in the headlines, laughs nervously at cocktail parties, nags from advertisements, speaks suavely in the board room, whines from the stage, clatters from the Wall Street ticker, jokes with fake youthfulness on the golf course and whispers in privacy each day before the shaving mirror and the dressing table.
ib

DR PAUL TOURNIER

7 Recounting of a life story, a mind thinking aloud . . . leads one inevitably to the consideration of problems which are no longer psychological but spiritual.
The Meaning of Persons Harper 57

DR DAVID VISCOTT

8 This is really America in therapy, people trying to get themselves together and be whole.
On popularity of "nonoccasion" greeting cards, *Time* 12 May 86

DR CARL WHITAKER

9 The problem is that you have a disease, but the disease is abnormal integrity, loyalty to a view of the world that the schizophrenic is willing to stake his life on.
On schizophrenia, *Time* 23 Dec 85

TENNESSEE WILLIAMS

10 If I am no longer disturbed myself, I will deal less with disturbed people, but I don't regret having concerned myself with them because I think most of us are disturbed.
On psychological condition of his characters, NY *Herald Tribune* 5 Jan 58

DR STANLEY F YOLLES, Director, National Institute of Mental Health

11 It is rebellion without a cause, rejection without a program and a refusal of what is, without a vision of what should be.
On alienation as a major cause of drug abuse, NY *Times* 10 Mar 68

DR NORMAN ZINBERG, Professor of Psychiatry, Harvard

12 Nobody in the United States is more than one handshake away from virtually any drug they want to get.
NY *Times* 21 Mar 83

SCIENCE

WILTON ROBERT ABBOTT, aerospace engineer

13 To understand the place of humans in the universe is to solve a complex problem. Therefore I find it impossible to believe that an understanding based entirely on science or one based entirely on religion can be correct.
Quoted in *Who's Who in America, 43rd Edition 1984–85* Marquis 84

EDWIN E ("BUZZ") ALDRIN JR, US astronaut

14 Beautiful! Beautiful! Magnificent desolation.
On joining Neil A Armstrong in first walk on the moon 20 Jul 69

AMERICAN LIBRARY ASSOCIATION

15 The computer is only a fast idiot, it has no imagination; it cannot originate action. It is, and will remain, only a tool to man.
On Univac computer exhibited at the 1964 NY World's Fair

AMERICAN MUSEUM OF NATURAL HISTORY, NYC

16 A zebra is a light-colored animal with dark stripes; not a dark one with light stripes.
After discovery in South Africa that dark parts of zebras fade while light parts remain unchanged, *Newsweek* 16 Dec 57

ANONYMOUS

17 Here men from the planet Earth first set foot upon the moon, July 1969 AD. We came in peace for all mankind.
Plaque planted on the lunar surface by astronauts Neil A Armstrong and Edwin E Aldrin Jr 20 Jul 69

GEORGE ARCHIBALD, Director, International Crane Foundation

18 [They] thought the whole thing was a riot. I thought it was a miracle.
On the artificial insemination of a crane with sperm flown in from Maryland's Patuxent Wildlife Research Center and carried in a picnic cooler by stewardesses, *Life* Jul 86

NEIL A ARMSTRONG, US astronaut

19 Houston, Tranquillity Base here. The Eagle has landed.
First message to the earth from the Apollo 11 lunar module Eagle after landing on the moon 20 Jul 69

1 That's one small step for man, one giant leap for mankind.

> Message to the earth from the first man to walk on the moon 20 Jul 69; also reported as "That's one small step for *a* man"

ASSOCIATION OF AMERICAN COLLEGES

2 We have become a people unable to comprehend the technology we invent.

> *Integrity in the College Curriculum*, report on weakness of undergraduate programs, quoted in NY *Times* 11 Feb 85

ROBERT D BALLARD, senior scientist, Woods Hole Oceanographic Institution

3 It is a quiet and peaceful place—and a fitting place for the remains of this greatest of sea tragedies to rest.

> On descending to the wreck of the RMS *Titanic* 73 years after it sank with more than 1,500 passengers on board, NY *Times* 10 Sep 85

4 Forever may it remain that way. And may God bless these now-found souls.

> Expressing his hope that the *Titanic* would not be disturbed, *ib*

5 The *Titanic* will protect itself.

> On discovering that the ship's bow is too damaged and too deeply buried in the ocean bottom to be plundered by treasure hunters, *ib* 31 Jul 86

SHARON BEGLEY

6 The mind can store an estimated 100 trillion bits of information—compared with which a computer's mere billions are virtually amnesiac.

> "Memory: Science Achieves Important New Insights into the Mother of the Muses" *Newsweek* 29 Sept 86

7 The mind's cross-indexing puts the best librarian to shame.

> *ib*

KURT BENIRSCHKE

8 Extinct is forever.

> On work with endangered species at San Diego Zoo, *Christian Science Monitor* 29 May 80

LUCIEN M BIBERMAN, Associate Director, University of Chicago Military Research Laboratory

9 I think the school's involvement in the development of atomic energy and the bomb left a deep scar on the moral fiber of this place.

> NY *Times* 7 Jun 63

JIM BISHOP

10 Archaeology . . . is the peeping Tom of the sciences. It is the sandbox of men who care not where they are going; they merely want to know where everyone else has been.

> "Sifting the Sea for Time's Treasures" NY *Journal-American* 14 Mar 61

FRANK BORMAN, US astronaut

11 We have company tonight.

> Message from Gemini 7 on sighting Gemini 6 before they became the first two craft to rendezvous in space, NY *Times* 16 Dec 65

12 It's a vast, lonely, forbidding expanse of nothing . . . rather like clouds and clouds of pumice stone. And it certainly does not appear to be a very inviting place to live or work.

> Message from Apollo 8 during the first manned orbit of the moon 25 Dec 68

13 Exploration is really the essence of the human spirit.

> Address to joint session of Congress, NY *Times* 10 Jan 69

RAY BRADBURY

14 Touch a scientist and you touch a child.

> LA *Times* 9 Aug 76

15 The best scientist is open to experience and begins with romance—the idea that anything is possible.

> *ib*

LEWIS M BRANSCOMB, Director, National Bureau of Standards

16 Science is some kind of cosmic apple juice from the Garden of Eden. Those who drink of it are doomed to carry the burden of original sin.

> News summaries 9 Apr 71

WERNHER VON BRAUN

17 It will free man from the remaining chains, the chains of gravity which still tie him to this planet.

> On the meaning of space travel, *Time* 10 Feb 58

18 Our sun is one of 100 billion stars in our galaxy. Our galaxy is one of billions of galaxies populating the universe. It would be the height of presumption to think that we are the only living things in that enormous immensity.

> NY *Times* 29 Apr 60

JACOB BRONOWSKI

19 You will die but the carbon will not; its career does not end with you. . . . it will return to the soil, and there a plant may take it up again in time, sending it once more on a cycle of plant and animal life.

> "Biography of an Atom—And the Universe" NY *Times* 13 Oct 68

20 Sooner or later every one of us breathes an atom that has been breathed before by anyone you can think of who has lived before us—Michelangelo or George Washington or Moses.

> *ib*

21 The most wonderful discovery made by scientists is science itself.

> *A Sense of the Future* New American Library 77

MICHAEL CAREY

22 The thing about farming is it's so easy, half of it is learning to kill.

> On plowing under overabundant corn and soybean crops on his Iowa farm, quoted by Hugh Sidey "Bitter Harvest" *Time* 8 Sep 86

RACHEL CARSON

23 Over increasingly large areas of the United States, spring now comes unheralded by the return of the birds, and the early mornings are strangely silent where once they were filled with the beauty of bird song.

> On the effect of chemical insecticides and fertilizers, *Silent Spring* Houghton Mifflin 62

1 As crude a weapon as a cave man's club, the chemical barrage has been hurled against the fabric of life.
ib

CBS TV

2 Archaeologists dig up dirt on each other.
Advertisement for program with scientists holding conflicting opinions, 23 Sep 86

ROGER B CHAFFEE, US astronaut

3 Problems . . . look mighty small from 150 miles up.
In his last public interview before he died with astronauts Virgil I Grissom and Edward H White II in a fire aboard Apollo 1 during a simulated launch, *This Week* 23 Apr 67

4 The world itself looks cleaner and so much more beautiful. Maybe we can make it that way—the way God intended it to be—by giving everyone, eventually, that new perspective from out in space.
ib

ERWIN CHARGAFF, Professor of Biological Chemistry, Columbia University

5 Science is wonderfully equipped to answer the question "How?" but it gets terribly confused when you ask the question "Why?"
Columbia Forum Summer 69

6 We manipulate nature as if we were stuffing an Alsatian goose. We create new forms of energy; we make new elements; we kill crops; we wash brains. I can hear them in the dark sharpening their lasers.
ib

STEVEN CHU, Director, Quantum Electronics Research, Bell Laboratories

7 The atoms become like a moth, seeking out the region of higher laser intensity.
On isolating atoms with a laser for close study, NY *Times* 13 Jul 86

RUSSELL L CIOCHON

8 [It] is not a monkey, not an ape and not a human, but it's a common ancestor of them all.
On the discovery in Burma of a jawbone of the earliest known higher primate, NY *Times* 16 Aug 85

MICHAEL COLLINS, US astronaut

9 I think a future flight should include a poet, a priest and a philosopher . . . we might get a much better idea of what we saw.
News summaries 9 Nov 69

10 I knew I was alone in a way that no earthling has ever been before.
On his solo flight in the Apollo 11 command module while astronauts Neil A Armstrong and Edwin E Aldrin Jr explored the lunar surface, *Time* 11 Dec 72

WILLIAM G CONWAY, Director, NY Zoological Society

11 How can you expect to excite or educate by exhibiting an animal . . . in a concrete bathroom that provides him so little space and variety that he can do no more than men do in bathrooms.
On improvements at the Bronx Zoo, *Wall Street Journal* 2 Oct 84

ANN COOK

12 I'm a 44-year-old granny emotionally involved with toads.
On opening of the first of a chain of toad tunnels under British highways to protect migrating toads during mating season, NY *Times* 14 Mar 87

13 Our evenings won't be the same without a bucket of toads to carry.
On abandoning toad patrol, *ib*

JACQUES COUSTEAU

14 The sea is the universal sewer.
On the sea as a place "where all kinds of pollution wind up," to House Committee on Science and Astronautics 28 Jan 71

15 We must plant the sea and herd its animals . . . using the sea as farmers instead of hunters. That is what civilization is all about—farming replacing hunting.
Interview 17 Jul 71

16 Farming as we do it is hunting, and in the sea we act like barbarians.
ib

17 If we go on the way we have, the fault is our greed [and] if we are not willing [to change], we will disappear from the face of the globe, to be replaced by the insect.
ib

18 What is a scientist after all? It is a curious man looking through a keyhole, the keyhole of nature, trying to know what's going on.
Christian Science Monitor 21 Jul 71

19 I am not a scientist. I am, rather, an impresario of scientists.
Describing his role as an explorer and filmmaker associated with scientists in underwater exploration, *ib* 24 Jul 86

LEILA M COYNE, researcher, San Jose State University

20 The more science learns what life is, the more reluctant scientists are to define it.
On study of clay as an energy storehouse and transfer agent, *Christian Science Monitor* 4 Apr 85

LUTHER CRESSMAN, anthropologist

21 [The wearer of these sandals] did not look out on swirling dust devils or miles of alkali and sand flats, as we did that hot August day, but on a great lake with wavelets lapping against a beach below the cave.
On his 1938 discovery of a pair of 9,000-year-old sandals, the oldest dated New World artifacts, quoted by Jane Howard *Margaret Mead* Simon & Schuster 84

LORRAINE LEE CUDMORE

22 We are a sad lot, the cell biologists. Like the furtive collectors of stolen art, we are forced to be lonely admirers of spectacular architecture, exquisite symmetry, dramas of violence and death, mobility, self-sacrifice and, yes, rococo sex.
The Center of Life Quadrangle 77

23 Cells let us walk, talk, think, make love and realize the bath water is cold.
ib

ROBERT GORHAM DAVIS

1 In Genesis, seeing the world filled with violence, God decided to drown all mankind except Noah's family. But because that family carried the same genes as those who had drowned, violence continued unabated.
    Letter to the editor NY *Times* 15 Mar 87

JEANNETTE DESOR, research scientist, General Foods

2 Humans can learn to like anything, that's why we are such a successful species.
    Smithsonian May 86

3 You can drop humans anywhere and they'll thrive— only the rat does as well.
    ib

VLADIMIR DZANIBEKOV, Soviet cosmonaut

4 Without women, we stood in space on one leg only.
    Commenting on the first space walk by a woman, London *Times* 11 Aug 84

GERALD M EDELMAN, biochemist and 1972 Nobel laureate

5 We're inquiring into the deepest nature of our constitutions: How we inherit from each other. How we can change. How our minds think. How our will is related to our thoughts. How our thoughts are related to our molecules.
    Newsweek 4 Jul 76

KRAFFT A EHRICKE, rocket developer

6 Man, the cutting edge of terrestrial life, has no rational alternative but to expand the environmental and resource base beyond earth.
    On the "extraterrestrial imperative," recalled on his death 11 Dec 84

7 Its central goal is the preservation of civilization.
    ib

PAUL EHRLICH, Professor of Biological Sciences, Stanford

8 [The National Academy of Sciences] would be unable to give a unanimous decision if asked whether the sun would rise tomorrow.
    Look 1 Apr 70

ALBERT EINSTEIN

9 The grand aim of all science is to cover the greatest number of empirical facts by logical deduction from the smallest number of hypotheses or axioms.
    Life 9 Jan 50

10 I assert that the cosmic religious experience is the strongest and the noblest driving force behind scientific research.
    Recalled on his death 18 Apr 55

11 I think and think for months and years. Ninety-nine times, the conclusion is false. The hundredth time I am right.
    ib

12 The most beautiful experience we can have is the mysterious. . . . the fundamental emotion which stands at the cradle of true art and true science.
    From his 1931 book *Living Philosophies*, *ib*

13 When I examine myself and my methods of thought, I come close to the conclusion that the gift of fantasy has meant more to me than my talent for absorbing positive knowledge.
    Recalled on 100th anniversary of his birth, 18 Feb 79

14 I made one great mistake in my life—when I signed the letter to President Roosevelt recommending that atom bombs be made . . . but there was some justification—the danger that the Germans would make them.
    Quoted by Ted Morgan *FDR* Simon & Schuster 85

15 Concern for man and his fate must always form the chief interest of all technical endeavors . . . Never forget this in the midst of your diagrams and equations.
    Quoted in "Science and Values" London *Times* 1 Jul 85

LOREN EISELEY

16 One could not pluck a flower without troubling a star.
    The Immense Journey Random House 57

RICHARD P FEYNMAN, 1965 Nobel laureate in physics

17 If I could explain it to the average person, I wouldn't have been worth the Nobel Prize.
    People 22 Jul 85

18 Reality must take precedence over public relations, for nature cannot be fooled.
    On pinpointing reason for explosion of the space shuttle Challenger by showing that O-rings grow brittle when immersed in water, *Life* Jan 87

YURI A GAGARIN, Soviet cosmonaut

19 I could have gone on flying through space forever.
    On the first manned space flight, NY *Times* 14 Apr 61

ROBERT PETER GALE, bone-marrow specialist

20 There is a silent enemy lurking there.
    On dangerous radiation levels in western Russia, after his visit to treat victims of Chernobyl nuclear accident, *Time* 23 Jun 86

PAUL H GEBHARD, Director, Kinsey Institute for Sex Research, Indiana University

21 A crossing of a Rubicon in life history.
    On one's initial experience of sexual intercourse, to Amer Assn for the Advancement of Science, NY *Times* 30 Dec 67

LOUIS VAN GESTEREN

22 This will end the mythology of the dumb little Dutch boy with his stupid finger in the dike to save his country.
    On completion of new, technologically advanced sea barrier in the Netherlands, NY *Times* 5 Oct 86

RICCARDO GIACCONI, Director, Space Telescope Science Institute, Johns Hopkins University

23 The universe is popping all over the place.
    NY *Times* 8 May 84

HAROLD M GIBSON, Chief Meteorologist, NYC Weather Bureau

24 The best weather instrument yet devised is a pair of human eyes.
    NY *Times* 30 Mar 84

25 Looking out the window is the most important thing if you want to know what's going on.
    ib

JOHN GLENN, former astronaut

1 This is a day we have managed to avoid for a quarter of a century.

> On loss of seven lives in the explosion of the space shuttle Challenger, news summaries 28 Jan 86

ALBERT GORE JR, US Senator

2 To use a Southern euphemism, our space program has been snake-bit.

> On unsuccessful launch of an unmanned rocket shortly after the explosion of the space shuttle Challenger, *Nightline* ABC TV 5 May 86

DANIEL S GREENBERG

3 The scientific community . . . having made a rapid ascent from deep poverty to great affluence, from academe's cloisters to Washington's high councils, still tends to be a bit excitable—not unlike a nouveau riche in a fluctuating market.

> *The Politics of Pure Science* New American Library 68

JESSE L GREENSTEIN, Chairman, Department of Astronomy, California Institute of Technology

4 Knowing how hard it is to collect a fact, you understand why most people want to have some fun analyzing it.

> *Fortune* May 60

ROBERT GROVE JR, satellite engineer

5 It's like a big parking lot up there. There are lots of empty places, and you can park in one as long as it doesn't belong to someone else.

> On monitoring and transmitting satellite communications, *Newsweek* 29 Sep 86

KERRY GRUSON

6 An uncommon zoo specimen that survives on a diet of hamburgers, French fries and Coke went on display this weekend at Miami's MetroZoo.

> On the exhibition of an actor in the role of urban man, NY *Times* 22 Oct 84

WILL HARRISON, glaciologist

7 Glaciers are delicate and individual things, like humans. Instability is built into them.

> *Time* 1 Sep 86

CARYL P HASKINS, President, Carnegie Institution of Washington

8 A society committed to the search for truth must give protection to, and set a high value upon, the independent and original mind, however angular, however rasping, however socially unpleasant it may be; for it is upon such minds, in large measure, that the effective search for truth depends.

> NY *Times* 9 Dec 63

9 It is the gifted, unorthodox individual, in the laboratory, or the study, or the walk by the river at twilight, who has always brought to us, and must continue to bring to us, all the basic resources by which we live.

> *ib*

JOHN S HERRINGTON, US Secretary of Energy

10 Once again, this nation has said there are no dreams too large, no innovation unimaginable and no frontiers beyond our reach.

> On asking Congress for funds for giant $6-billion atom smasher, a project he likened to the 1969 manned landing on the moon, NY *Times* 31 Jan 87

EDMUND HILLARY

11 I am hell-bent for the South Pole—God willing and crevasses permitting.

> Comment eight days before he reached the South Pole via an overland route, news summaries 5 Jan 58

12 We knocked the bastard off.

> On his successful ascent of Mt Everest, London *Sunday Times* 21 Jul 74

13 Better if he had said something natural like, "Jesus, here we are."

> Commenting on Neil A Armstrong's 1969 message from the moon, "That's one small step for man, one giant leap for mankind," *ib*

GRACE MURRAY HOPPER

14 From then on, when anything went wrong with a computer, we said it had bugs in it.

> On the removal of a 2-inch-long moth from an experimental computer at Harvard in 1945, quoted in *Time* 16 Apr 84

15 In total desperation, I called over to the engineering building, and I said, "Please cut off a nanosecond and send it over to me."

> On using a piece of wire to represent maximum distance that electricity could travel in a billionth of a second, *60 Minutes* CBS TV 24 Aug 86

16 At the end of about a week, I called back and said, "I need something to compare this to. Could I please have a microsecond?"

> *ib*

JANE HOWARD

17 Anthropology [was] the science that gave her the platform from which she surveyed, scolded and beamed at the world.

> *Margaret Mead* Simon & Schuster 84

18 She was a patron saint of the peripheral.

> *ib*

J ALLEN HYNEK, Professor of Astronomy and Director of Dearborn Observatory, Northwestern University

19 Close encounters of the third kind.

> On physical contact with an alien being or an extraterrestrial craft, *The UFO Experience* Regnery 72

20 This intellectual Pearl Harbor, a real gutsy sock to the stomach.

> On success of the Soviet orbiter Sputnik, the earth's first artificial satellite, recalled on his death 27 Apr 86

LYNDON B JOHNSON, 36th US President

21 It may be, it just may be, that life as we know it with its humanity is more unique than many have thought.

> On awarding medals to NASA officials whose close-up photographs of Mars revealed a total lack of water, greatly reducing the possibility of the existence of human life there, 29 Jul 65

JOHN F KENNEDY, 35th US President

1 Let both sides seek to invoke the wonders of science instead of its terrors.
> On US and Soviet joint scientific ventures, inaugural address 21 Jan 61

2 In a very real sense, it will not be one man going to the moon . . . it will be an entire nation. For all of us must work to put him there.
> State of the Union address 30 Jan 61

3 America has tossed its cap over the wall of space.
> Quoted by William Safire NY *Times* 19 Aug 84

CHARLES F KETTERING, Vice President and Manager of Research, General Motors

4 People think of the inventor as a screwball, but no one ever asks the inventor what he thinks of other people.
> Recalled on his death 25 Nov 58

5 The Wright brothers flew right through the smoke screen of impossibility.
> *ib*

NIKITA S KHRUSHCHEV

6 He was . . . a crystal of morality among our scientists.
> On Andrei D Sakharov's concern for dangerous potential of experimental nuclear explosions, recalled at end of Sakharov's detention in Gorky, NY *Times* 20 Dec 86

ALFRED C KINSEY, founder, Institute for Sex Research, Indiana University

7 There are some who have questioned the applicability of scientific methods to an investigation of human sexual behavior. . . . as though the dietitian and biochemist were denied the right to analyze foods and the process of nutrition, because the cooking and proper serving of food may be rated a fine art, and because the eating of certain foods has been considered a matter for religious regulation.
> On critics of his pioneering investigations into human sexual behavior, *The Right to Investigate* Saunders 53

8 We are recorders and reporters of the facts—not judges of the behavior we describe.
> Recalled on his death 25 Aug 56

DANIEL KLEPPNER, Professor of Physics, MIT

9 Big machines are the awe-inspiring cathedrals of the 20th century.
> On large-scale equipment for physics experiments, NY *Times* 11 Jun 85

BRUCE KNAPP, physicist, Nevis Laboratory, Columbia University

10 It means you can try to answer questions you thought the universe was going to have to do without.
> On supercomputers, NY *Times* 3 Jul 84

ARTHUR KOESTLER

11 [They are] peeping Toms at the keyhole of eternity.
> Description of scientists, *The Roots of Coincidence* Hutchinson 72

VLADIMIR M KOMAROV, Soviet cosmonaut

12 In orbit now we have a small but harmonious collection of Soviet people.
> Message from the first spaceship to carry three people, NY *Times* 13 Oct 64

ARTHUR KORNBERG, biochemist, Stanford, and 1959 Nobel laureate

13 A scientist . . . shouldn't be asked to judge the economic and moral value of his work. All we should ask the scientist to do is find the truth—and then not keep it from anyone.
> San Francisco *Examiner & Chronicle* 19 Dec 71

ADRIAAN KORTLANDT

14 Once I saw a chimpanzee gaze at a particularly beautiful sunset for a full 15 minutes, watching the changing colors [and then] retire to the forest without picking a pawpaw for supper.
> "Chimpanzees in the Wild" *Scientific American* May 62

15 Behind their lively, searching eyes one senses a doubting, a contemplative personality, always trying to make sense out of a puzzling world.
> *ib*

CHARLES KURALT

16 This is a place where you can hear fall coming for miles.
> On Horicon Marsh in Wisconsin, *Sunday Morning* CBS TV 12 Oct 86

17 The sparrows are preparing for winter, each one dressed in a plain brown coat and singing a cheerful song.
> *ib* 7 Dec 86

STEPHEN LaBERGE, research associate, Stanford

18 Not all lucid dreams are useful but they all have a sense of wonder about them. If you must sleep through a third of your life, why should you sleep through your dreams, too?
> Quoted by Anne Fadiman "The Doctor of Dreams" *Life* Nov 86

19 Dream research is a wonderful field. All you do is sleep for a living.
> *ib*

MARY LEAKEY, paleontologist

20 I've found him—found our man!
> On 1959 discovery in Tanzania of a 1.8-million-year-old hominid skull, one of the earliest traces of human origin, quoted in NY *Times* 30 Oct 84

JOHN F LEHMAN JR, US Secretary of the Navy

21 We are opening up an enormous new era in archaeology. . . . time capsules in the deep oceans.
> On the underwater exploration of the *Titanic* and other wrecked ships, *Time* 11 Aug 86

JEROME LEJEUNE, geneticist

22 [I look forward] to the day when a mongolian idiot, treated biochemically, becomes a successful! geneticist.
> Deploring practice of aborting fetuses afflicted with Down's syndrome, quoted by Daniel J Kevles *In the Name of Eugenics* Knopf 85

CHARLES A LINDBERGH

1 I have seen the science I worshiped, and the aircraft I loved, destroying the civilization I expected them to serve.
Time 26 May 67

2 In wilderness I sense the miracle of life, and behind it our scientific accomplishments fade to trivia.
Declaring that if he were a young man he would choose a career that kept him more in contact with nature than with science, *Life* 22 Dec 67

WILLIAM N LIPSCOMB JR, 1976 Nobel laureate in chemistry

3 For me, the creative process, first of all, requires a good nine hours of sleep a night. Second, it must not be pushed by the need to produce practical applications.
NY *Times* 7 Dec 77

THOMAS E LOVEJOY, Executive Vice President, World Wildlife Fund

4 Natural species are the library from which genetic engineers can work.
Time 13 Oct 86

5 Genetic engineers don't make new genes, they rearrange existing ones.
ib

JAMES A LOVELL, US astronaut

6 The moon is essentially gray, no color. It looks like plaster of Paris, like dirty beach sand with lots of footprints in it.
Washington *Post* 25 Dec 68

JOHN JOSEPH LYNCH SJ

7 The laws of nature are written deep in the folds and faults of the earth. By encouraging men to learn those laws one can lead them further to a knowledge of the author of all laws.
On becoming president of NY Academy of Sciences, NY *Times* 5 Dec 63

8 Which would you rather have, a bursting planet or an earthquake here and there?
In defense of earthquakes, *ib*

JOHN MADSON

9 The wealth of the tall grass prairie was its undoing.
On overabundance of grain in the Midwest, quoted by Hugh Sidey "Bitter Harvest" *Time* 8 Sep 86

MAGAZINE PUBLISHERS ASSOCIATION

10 Scientists work better when they're all mixed-up.
Quoted in *Fortune* 14 Apr 86

SPYRIDON MARINATOS, Professor of Archaeology, University of Athens

11 To excavate is to open a book written in the language that the centuries have spoken into the earth.
NY *Times* 11 Jan 72

WILLIAM H MASTERS

12 Science by itself has no moral dimension. But it does seek to establish truth. And upon this truth morality can be built.
Life 24 Jun 66

BARBARA McCLINTOCK, 1983 Nobel laureate

13 It might seem unfair to reward a person for having so much pleasure over the years, asking the maize plant to solve specific problems and then watching its responses.
On her lifelong research into the genetic characteristics of Indian corn plants, *Newsweek* 24 Oct 83

14 I never thought of stopping, and I just hated sleeping. I can't imagine having a better life.
Time 24 Oct 83

JAMES S McDONNELL, builder of Mercury and Gemini space capsules

15 America is now a space-faring nation. . . . a frontier good for millions of years. The only time remotely comparable was when Columbus discovered a whole new world.
Time 31 Mar 67

16 The creative conquest of space will serve as a wonderful substitute for war.
ib

MARGARET MEAD

17 [Anthropology demands] the open-mindedness with which one must look and listen, record in astonishment and wonder that which one would not have been able to guess.
Sex and Temperament in Three Primitive Societies Morrow 63

18 The way to do fieldwork is never to come up for air until it is all over.
Letter from New Guinea, quoted by Jane Howard *Margaret Mead* Simon & Schuster 84

MIKE MELVILLE

19 I've got tooth marks on my heart.
Comment after *Voyager* pilot Richard G Rutan's plane dropped 3,000 feet during the last leg of the first nonstop flight around the world on one load of fuel, NY *Times* 24 Dec 86

20 What you want to do, and what you can do, is limited only by what you can dream.
Quoted by Charles Kuralt *Sunday Morning* CBS TV 28 Dec 86

RICHARD MELVILLE, Secretary, International Commission on Zoological Nomenclature

21 This isn't like naming your dog Spot.
On scientific Latin names for plants and animals, *Wall Street Journal* 13 Jul 84

DESMOND MORRIS

22 There are 193 species of monkeys and apes, 192 of them are covered with hair. The exception is a naked ape self-named *Homo sapiens*.
The Naked Ape McGraw-Hill 68

23 This unusual and highly successful species spends a great deal of time examining his higher motives and an equal amount of time ignoring his fundamental ones.
ib

LEONARD MOSLEY

24 Killing is practically a Filipino national pastime but on Mindanao it's an industry.
On Charles A Lindbergh's interest in the decline of native tribes, *Lindbergh* Doubleday 76

NATIONAL GEOGRAPHIC SOCIETY

1 Comets are the nearest thing to nothing that anything can be and still be something.
> Announcing discovery of a comet visible only by telescope, 31 Mar 55

DAVID R NELSON, Professor of Physics, Harvard

2 The main satisfaction we're getting . . . is the intellectual excitement. For me, that's plenty. Isn't that really the driving force of science?
> On crystal research, NY *Times* 30 Jul 85

STEPHEN A NESBITT, NASA Public Affairs Officer

3 Obviously a major malfunction.
> Announcement moments after the space shuttle Challenger exploded, quoted in NY *Times* 29 Jan 86

4 The vehicle has exploded.
> *ib*

RICHARD M NIXON, 37th US President

5 For one priceless moment in the whole history of man, all of the people on this earth are truly one. One in their pride at what you have done, one in our prayers that you will return safely to earth.
> Radio transmission to the first men to walk on the moon 20 Jul 69

J ROBERT OPPENHEIMER

6 The open society, the unrestricted access to knowledge, the unplanned and uninhibited association of men for its furtherance—these are what may make a vast, complex, ever growing, ever changing, ever more specialized and expert technological world, nevertheless a world of human community.
> *Science and the Common Understanding* Simon & Schuster 53

7 Both the man of science and the man of action live always at the edge of mystery, surrounded by it.
> Address at Columbia University 26 Dec 54

8 The atomic bomb . . . made the prospect of future war unendurable. It has led us up those last few steps to the mountain pass; and beyond there is a different country.
> Quoted by Richard Rhodes *The Making of the Atomic Bomb* Simon & Schuster 87

DR LOUIS ORR, President, Amer Medical Assn

9 Science will never be able to reduce the value of a sunset to arithmetic. Nor can it reduce friendship or statesmanship to a formula.
> Commencement address at Emory University, Atlanta, 6 Jun 60

HEINZ R PAGELS, Executive Director, NY Academy of Sciences

10 The world changed from having the determinism of a clock to having the contingency of a pinball machine.
> On quantum theory's break with classical Newtonian physics, *The Cosmic Code* Simon & Schuster 82

11 Stars are like animals in the wild. We may see the young but never the actual birth, which is a veiled and secret event.
> *Perfect Symmetry* Simon & Schuster 85

12 There was emptiness more profound than the void between the stars, for which there was no here and there and before and after, and yet out of that void the entire plenum of existence sprang forth.
> Reflecting on origin of the universe, *Vogue* Jan 86

LINUS C PAULING, 1954 and 1962 Nobel laureate

13 I like people. I like animals, too—whales and quail, dinosaurs and dodos. But I like human beings especially, and I am unhappy that the pool of human germ plasm, which determines the nature of the human race, is deteriorating.
> From 1959 paper on the effect of radioactive fallout on heredity, recalled on winning 1962 Nobel Peace Prize, NY *Times* 13 Oct 62

JOHN PIKE, Federation of Amer Scientists

14 Some agencies have a public affairs office. NASA is a public affairs office that has an agency.
> Criticism of statements made by image-conscious NASA officials after explosion of the space shuttle Challenger, NY *Times* 25 Apr 86

WARDELL B POMEROY

15 Like Everest, it was there and we conquered it. For the first time, a large body of sex information was gathered, so monumental and so comprehensive that it has not even been approached.
> Assessing his work with Alfred C Kinsey, *Dr Kinsey and the Institute for Sex Research* Harper & Row 72

16 If this project had been undertaken in Europe or Asia, it might never have attracted any attention or even succeeded, but in America we like to count things.
> *ib*

MICHAEL POTTS, spokesman, Beech Aircraft

17 The Wright brothers' design . . . allowed them to survive long enough to learn how to fly.
> On the wing formation used in the first successful powered flight, NY *Times* 17 Apr 84

WILBUR L PRITCHARD, President, Satellite Systems Engineering

18 NASA put all its eggs in one basket, and the basket fell on the concrete.
> On NASA's decision in the mid 1970s to de-emphasize unmanned rockets in favor of the space shuttle, *Time* 24 Mar 86

DAVID M RAUP, Professor of Geophysical Sciences, University of Chicago

19 [Extinctions occurred] with clocklike periodicity, every 26 million years.
> On computerized study of recorded ages of fossils, *The Nemesis Affair: A Story of the Death of Dinosaurs and the Way of Science* Norton 86, quoted in *International Herald Tribune* 23 Jul 86

RONALD REAGAN, 40th US President

20 You on the cutting edge of technology have already made yesterday's impossibilities the commonplace realities of today.
> To Nobel laureates and other scientists assembled at the White House 12 Feb 85

1 They had that special grace, that special spirit that says, "Give me a challenge and I'll meet it with joy."

> In a speech made a few hours after the death of seven astronauts in the explosion of the space shuttle Challenger 28 Jan 86

T R REID

2 It was a seminal event of postwar science, one of those rare demonstrations that changes everything.

> On the development of the microchip, *The Chip* Simon & Schuster 85, quoted in NY *Times* 11 Feb 85

BERTRAND RUSSELL

3 Science is what you know, philosophy is what you don't know.

> Quoted by Alan Wood *Bertrand Russell* Simon & Schuster 58

RICHARD G RUTAN

4 This was the last major event of atmospheric flight. That we did it as private citizens says a lot about freedom in America.

> On completing the first nonstop flight around the world on one load of fuel in the experimental craft *Voyager*, NY *Times* 24 Dec 86

5 Time goes by real slow when you're flamed out and going down into the dark—as dark as the inside of a cow.

> On engine failure over the Pacific, *Newsweek* 5 Jan 87

6 I flew in combat in Vietnam. I got shot at, I shot back, I got shot down. Compared to this flight, I felt a lot safer in combat.

> *ib*

CARL SAGAN, astronomer, Cornell University

7 To make an apple pie from scratch, you must first invent the universe.

> *Cosmos* PBS TV 23 Nov 80

ROALD Z SAGDEYEV, Soviet astrophysicist

8 I was looking at them as extraterrestrials.

> Recalling his first meeting with US scientists, NY *Times* 10 Mar 86

DAVID SARNOFF, Chairman, RCA

9 Freedom is the oxygen without which science cannot breathe.

> "Electronics—Today and Tomorrow," in Emily Davie ed *Profile of America* Crowell 54

10 Atoms for peace. Man is still the greatest miracle and the greatest problem on this earth.

> First message sent with atomic-powered electricity 27 Jan 54

11 I have learned to have more faith in the scientist than he does in himself.

> Recalled on his death, *Newsweek* 27 Dec 71

STUART L SCHREIBER, Associate Professor of Organic Chemistry, Yale

12 It was a flash of eureka.

> On 1983 Christmas Eve discovery of periplanon-B, a synthetic aphrodisiac that effectively controls *Periplaneta americana*, the common cockroach, NY *Times* 26 Sep 84

R TUCKER SCULLY, Director, US State Department Office of Oceans and Polar Affairs

13 You don't have three guys holed up there all winter with an American flag for nothing.

> In support of ad hoc exploratory missions rather than the establishment of a permanent Arctic research station. *Smithsonian* Nov 84

STUART LUMAN SEATON

14 The presence of humans, in a system containing high-speed electronic computers and high-speed, accurate communications, is quite inhibiting.

> To Amer Institute of Engineering, *Time* 17 Feb 58

FREDERICK SEITZ, President, Rockefeller University

15 A good scientist is a person in whom the childhood quality of perennial curiosity lingers on. Once he gets an answer, he has other questions.

> *Fortune* Apr 76

ALAN B SHEPARD JR, US astronaut

16 A-OK full go.

> Comment at blastoff from the first American in space 5 May 61

HUGH SIDEY

17 The Corn Belt is like John Bunyan's idyllic Beulah— or a dark Gehenna.

> "Bitter Harvest" *Time* 8 Sep 86

LORD SKELMERSDALE (Roger Bootle-Wilbraham), British Undersecretary of the Environment

18 This is the first time I've actually held a toad. And my sympathy goes very much to the toad.

> On opening of tunnel under highway to protect migrating toads during mating season, NY *Times* 14 Mar 87

C P SNOW

19 Technology . . . is a queer thing. It brings you great gifts with one hand, and it stabs you in the back with the other.

> NY *Times* 15 Mar 71

JOHN SPENCER, Professor of Science and Mathematics, Highlands University, Las Vegas NM

20 [The research rat of the future] allows experimentation without manipulation of the real world. This is the cutting edge of modeling technology.

> On computer program that simulates a human body's reaction to surgery, NY *Times* 12 Nov 85

ELVIN STACKMAN, President, Amer Assn for the Advancement of Science

21 Science cannot stop while ethics catches up . . . and nobody should expect scientists to do all the thinking for the country.

> *Life* 9 Jan 50

THOMAS P STAFFORD, US astronaut

22 Houston, this is Apollo 10. You can tell the world we have arrived.

> On reaching a lunar orbit that brought the spacecraft within nine miles of the moon's surface, NY *Times* 22 May 69

WILL STEGER

1 An incredible experience and humbling all the way through.

> Comment from a member of the first team to reach the North Pole without mechanical means since Adm Robert E Peary's expedition in 1909, NY *Times* 6 May 86

WALTER SULLIVAN

2 A black hole . . . an extremely dense concentration of matter equal in mass to millions or billions of suns.

> Describing the supermassive black hole thought to be in the center of the Milky Way galaxy, NY *Times* 7 Jun 85

ALBERT SZENT-GYÖRGYI, 1937 Nobel laureate

3 Research is four things: brains with which to think, eyes with which to see, machines with which to measure and, fourth, money.

> Recalled on his death 22 Oct 86

LEO SZILARD

4 We turned the switch, saw the flashes, watched for ten minutes, then switched everything off and went home. That night I knew the world was headed for sorrow.

> On 1939 Columbia University experiment that confirmed atoms could be split, making possible the use of atomic power, recalled on his death 30 May 64

5 A scientist's aim in a discussion with his colleagues is not to persuade, but to clarify.

> *ib*

LEWIS THOMAS

6 The uniformity of earth's life, more astonishing than its diversity, is accountable by the high probability that we derived, originally, from some single cell, fertilized in a bolt of lightning as the earth cooled.

> *The Lives of a Cell* Viking 74

7 It is from the progeny of this parent cell that we all take our looks; we still share genes around, and the resemblance of the enzymes of grasses to those of whales is in fact a family resemblance.

> *ib*

LIONEL TIGER, Professor of Anthropology, Rutgers University

8 Eternal vigilance is the price of sexual confidence.

> Quoted in *Time* 25 Nov 85

GHERMAN S TITOV, Soviet cosmonaut

9 Spring One. Spring One. I am Eagle. I am Eagle. I can hear you very well. I feel excellent. My feeling is excellent.

> Message from Vostok II using the call signal *Oriel*, or "Eagle," while orbiting the earth every 88 minutes, NY *Times* 7 Aug 61

10 Dear Muscovites, there are no changes in the cabin. The pressure is normal, perfect pressure . . . I am perfectly comfortable. I wish you the same.

> Said as Vostok II passed over Moscow, *ib*

11 Everything is going well, everything is going marvelously. I beg to wish dear Muscovites good night. I am turning in now. You do as you please, but I am turning in.

> *ib*

STEWART L UDALL, US Secretary of the Interior

12 [We stand] today poised on a pinnacle of wealth and power, yet we live in a land of vanishing beauty, of increasing ugliness, of shrinking open space and of an overall environment that is diminished daily by pollution and noise and blight. This, in brief, is the quiet conservation crisis.

> *The Quiet Crisis* Holt, Rinehart & Winston 63

13 The most common trait of all primitive peoples is a reverence for the life-giving earth, and the Native American shared this elemental ethic: The land was alive to his loving touch, and he, its son, was brother to all creatures.

> *ib*

14 Mining is like a search-and-destroy mission.

> *1976—Agenda for Tomorrow* Harcourt, Brace & World 68

15 Over the long haul of life on this planet, it is the ecologists, and not the bookkeepers of business, who are the ultimate accountants.

> To Congress of Optimum Population and Environment 9 Jun 70

HAROLD C UREY, 1934 Nobel laureate

16 I thought it might have a practical use in something like neon signs.

> On developing heavy water, vital to the atomic bomb, *Quote* 4 Apr 65

LARRY VAN GOETHEM

17 They travel with a constant companion, autumn.

> "Southward Stream of Birds of Prey" NY *Times* 14 Oct 84

NIKOLAI VERESHCHAGIN, Zoological Institute, Leningrad

18 I put my hand on the dark skin and felt the chill of centuries long gone. It was as if I had touched the Stone Age.

> On touching a recently discovered carcass of an infant mammoth, preserved in the Soviet permafrost for an estimated 40,000 years, London *Observer* 20 May 79

LANCE A WALLACE, environmental scientist

19 We're all living in a chemical soup.

> *Newsweek* 7 Jan 85

CLAUDIA WALLIS

20 They are babies in waiting, life on ice.

> On sperm cells frozen for preservation, "Quickening Debate over Life on Ice" *Time* 2 Jul 84

JAMES D WATSON, 1962 Nobel laureate and Director of Research, Cold Spring Harbor Laboratory, NY

21 Biology has at least 50 more interesting years.

> News summaries 31 Dec 84

22 Take young researchers, put them together in virtual seclusion, give them an unprecedented degree of freedom and turn up the pressure by fostering competitiveness.

> On his formula for breakthroughs in research, *ib*

HARVEY WHEELER

23 The same system that produced a bewildering succession of new-model, style-obsolescent autos and refrigerators can also produce an endless outpouring of new-model, style-obsolescent science.

> NY *Times* 11 Aug 75

EDWARD H WHITE II, US astronaut

1 I felt red, white and blue all over.

> On his walk in space, *Life* 25 Jan 65

JOHN NOBLE WILFORD

2 Alone among all creatures, the species that styles itself wise, *Homo sapiens*, has an abiding interest in its distant origins, knows that its allotted time is short, worries about the future and wonders about the past.

> On paleontology, NY *Times* 30 Oct 84

EDWARD O WILSON, Professor of Science, Harvard

3 It's like having astronomy without knowing where the stars are.

> On disappearance of plants and animals more quickly than scientists can find and describe them, *Time* 13 Oct 86

4 When you have seen one ant, one bird, one tree, you have not seen them all.

> *ib*

TOM WOLFE

5 What is it that makes a man willing to sit up on top of an enormous Roman candle, such as a Redstone, Atlas, Titan or Saturn rocket, and wait for someone to light the fuse?

> *The Right Stuff* Farrar, Straus & Giroux 79

TRAVEL

Travelers on Traveling

PHILIP ANDREW ADAMS

6 To many people holidays are not voyages of discovery, but a ritual of reassurance.

> *Australian Age* 10 Sep 83

FRED ALLEN

7 The American arrives in Paris with a few French phrases he has culled from a conversational guide or picked up from a friend who owns a beret.

> Introduction to Art Buchwald *Paris after Dark* Little, Brown 54

AMERICAN EXPRESS

8 When your business trip is running late, your room will be waiting up for you.

> Guaranteeing the holding of advance reservations, advertisement in *New York* 16 Sep 85

NIGEL ANDREW

9 The addictive semiconscious vice of *biblioscopy*—having to see what the other person is reading, usually on a train . . . peering over shoulders, bending down to attend simultaneously to a shoelace and a dust jacket, furtively changing seats.

> London *Times* 11 Mar 85

10 Commuter trains are packed with voyeurs of a similar bent.

> *ib*

ANONYMOUS

11 Is forbidden to steal towels, please. If you are not person to do such is please not to read notice.

> Sign in Tokyo hotel, quoted in *Holiday* 5 May 69

JEAN PAUL ARON

12 The hallucinatory frenzy of departure has its result in a pitiable monotony. One changes his décor, not his existence.

> Quoted on 50th anniversary of French law granting a week's paid vacation to every worker, NY *Times* 4 Aug 86

W H AUDEN

13 The train, panting up past lonely farms,
Fed by the fireman's restless arms . . .
Past cotton grass and moorland boulder,
Shoveling white steam over her shoulder.

> Quoted by Melvin Maddocks "The Case for the Train—With Feeling" *Christian Science Monitor* 24 Mar 80

RUSSELL BAKER

14 When it comes to cars, only two varieties of people are possible—cowards and fools.

> On use of seat belts, "The Belted Coward" NY *Times* 2 Feb 85

15 I was converted from fool [when] my spine [was] somewhat reorganized . . . What amazed me was how fast a perfectly robust man looking forward to nothing more terminal than a night in Toledo can cease being alive once he pulls the dreamboat out of the driveway.

> *ib*

16 A railroad station? That was sort of a primitive airport, only you didn't have to take a cab 20 miles out of town to reach it.

> *ib* 5 Nov 86

SARAH BALLARD

17 After nine days . . . I'd gotten used to the horizon, to the orderly rhythm of the ship, and all of a sudden the world came flooding back. I found myself looking at Nova Scotia and thinking about my mortgage.

> On Bermuda–Nova Scotia sailing competition, *Sports Illustrated* 1 Oct 84

CECIL BEATON

18 On close inspection, this device turned out to be a funereal juke box—the result of mixing Lloyd's of London with the principle of the chewing gum dispenser.

> On automatic insurance machines in US airline terminals, *It Gives Me Great Pleasure* John Day 55

19 Americans have an abiding belief in their ability to control reality by purely material means. . . . airline insurance replaces the fear of death with the comforting prospect of cash.

> *ib*

ELEANOR R BELMONT

20 A private railroad car is not an acquired taste. One takes to it immediately.

> *The Fabric of Memory* Farrar, Straus 57

BENEDICT OSB, Abbot of St Gregory's Episcopal Abbey, Three Rivers MI

21 Cruising through the countryside in my monk-mobile, listening to Bach, munching on cellophane-packaged snacks, provided me a space and time machine of incredible capacity.

> On sabbatical spent driving a van across the US, *Abbey Letter* Easter 85

HARVEY BERGENHOLTZ, NYC taxi driver

1 Our back seats are like psychiatrists' couches.
NY *Times* 18 Jul 84

2 I yell at my wife when I get home. I work 12 hours a day. I have no family life. I toss and turn all night. My wife tells me I yell at other drivers in my sleep!
ib

SHELLEY BERMAN

3 The sooner you are there, the sooner you will find out how long you will be delayed.
On "getting to the airport in plenty of time," CNN TV 12 Dec 86

RALPH BLUMENTHAL

4 The battle promises to be fought with bags of bagels and bran muffins, free beer and wine, expanded leg-room, baggage closets and overhead bins.
On inauguration of Pan American World Airways shuttle in competition with Eastern Air Lines between New York, Washington and Boston, NY *Times* 30 Sep 86

GEOFFREY BOCCA

5 Travel by sea nearly approximates the bliss of ba-byhood. They feed you, rock you gently to sleep and when you wake up, they take care of you and feed you again.
Quoted by Else and Bennet Daniels *Vacation at Sea* Cornerstone Library 79

JAMES BRADY

6 One very clear impression I had of all the Beautiful People was their prudence. It may be that they paid for their own airline tickets, but they paid for little else.
Superchic Little, Brown 74

FRANK BRAYNARD

7 We are all sailors on the spaceship Earth.
On his idea for Operation Sail, which brought 225 vessels from throughout the world to NY Harbor for US Bicentennial, *Newsweek* 4 Jul 76

PAT BUCKLEY

8 I've never made the trip to or from Connecticut without its resembling the worst excesses of the French Revolution.
Quoted in NY *Times* 20 Nov 84

DEIRDRE CARMODY

9 The windjammers . . . tall ships from around the world whose very presence bespeaks man's centuries-old struggle against the inexorabilities of the sea.
On boats assembled for 100th anniversary of the Statue of Liberty, NY *Times* 27 Jun 86

CHARLES, Prince of Wales

10 I'd rather go by bus.
When asked at age six if he was excited about sailing to Tobruk on the royal yacht, news summaries 21 May 54

ELLEN CHURCH

11 We could never get our coffee hot when flying out of Cheyenne because of the altitude—and we were too dumb to know why.
Recollection of being among the first airline hostesses in 1930, NY *Times* 15 May 60

AMANDA CROSS

12 One did not "hop" a plane. One took a long slow ride to an airport, and argued for hours with ticket agents who seemed to have been hired five minutes ago for what they supposed to be another job; and if one survived that, one got to Chicago only to join a "stack" over the airfield there, and then either died of boredom or crashed into a plane that thought it was in the stack over Newark.
In the Last Analysis Avon 66

CHARLOTTE CURTIS

13 His venture sounds like a banana peel awaiting its victim.
On plans of Nigel Nicolson to tour half the US while his son toured the other half for a book entitled *Two Roads to Dodge City*, NY *Times* 12 Nov 85

14 It does sound odd if by America [he] means 3,000 miles of superhighways, greasy spoons, HoJos, Ramada Inns and the thrill of arriving at sunset only to see the citizens evacuate downtown America and lock their doors for the night.
ib

ELIZABETH DAVID

15 Provence is a country to which I am always returning, next week, next year, any day now, as soon as I can get on a train.
W 12 Sep 80

RAYMOND DAVIDSON

16 I'm fed up with it. I'm sick and tired of the delays, tired of the waiting. I'm hanging it up. You can have it. This flight will be my last flight.
Announcement of Eastern Airlines pilot who taxied back to the terminal and walked off his plane in protest against delays at Atlanta's Hartsfield Airport, NY *Times* 25 Jul 86

MONICA DICKENS

17 The limitless jet-lag purgatory of Immigration and Baggage at Heathrow.
"A Modern Dickens Writes about Returning to the Land of Her Great-Grandfather" *Christian Science Monitor* 13 Mar 86

LUIGI DONZELLI, restaurant manager, Claridge's Hotel, London

18 Kings are no trouble. It's the queens.
Newsweek 5 Jun 78

LAWRENCE DURRELL

19 Journeys, like artists, are born and not made. A thousand differing circumstances contribute to them, few of them willed or determined by the will—whatever we may think.
Bitter Lemons Dutton 57, quoted in Washington *Post* 29 May 86

1 They flower spontaneously out of the demands of our natures—and the best of them lead us not only outward in space, but inward as well.
ib

2 Travel can be one of the most rewarding forms of introspection.
ib

TEMPLE FIELDING

3 As a member of an escorted tour, you don't even have to know the Matterhorn isn't a tuba.
Fielding's Guide to Europe Sloane 63

BETTY FORD

4 Have a nice trip, Dick.
Bidding farewell to resigning President Richard M Nixon, quoted in *RN: Memoirs of Richard Nixon* Grosset & Dunlap 78

ALAN FRANKS

5 Perhaps there is a sadist in me which delights in swimming against the gray onrush of commuters; of boarding an empty train in a teeming station—one of those coaches with the special fusty smell of aging . . . upholstery.
"A Walk on the Weald Side" London *Times* 29 Sep 84

LUCINDA FRANKS

6 In the railroads, some people read clearly printed departure signs and then proceed to ask several times what they say. On airplanes, they demand things they know they cannot have. In their cars, they load up, drive away and then suddenly realize they don't know where they're going.
"Thousands Ineptly Get Away from It All" NY *Times* 30 Aug 75

7 They can be cranky, bewildered, giddy, frustrated and sometimes moved to violence. In short, they are afflicted with the New York City Getaway Fever.
ib

OTTO FRIEDRICH

8 Americans have always been eager for travel, that being how they got to the New World in the first place.
Time 22 Apr 85

WILLIAM E GEIST

9 The 10 Frenchmen journeyed to America despite warnings from their mothers that they would be mugged within 5 minutes of their arrival in New York and mowed down by gangsters in Chicago—provided, of course, that they were not scalped by Indians along the way [or captured by] crowds of American women waiting at the airport to get their hands on a Frenchman.
NY *Times* 20 Apr 85

PAUL GOLDBERGER

10 Riding on the IRT is usually a matter of serving time in one of the city's most squalid environments—noisy, smelly, crowded and overrun with a ceaseless supply of graffiti.
On NYC subways, NY *Times* 27 Jul 85

DAN GREENBERG

11 Storing your car in New York is safer than entering it in a demolition derby. But not much.
On parking garages, *New York* 25 Jan 71

12 It should be done with the same degree of alacrity and nonchalance that you would display in authorizing a highly intelligent trained bear to remove your appendix.
ib

JOHN GUNTHER

13 One travels like a golf ball, hopping from green to green.
Inside Africa Harper 53

BEN HARTE

14 I always seem to be running into cyclists, every time I cross the road. There ought to be a law against me.
"Failing to Take a Problem by the Handlebars" NY *Times* 8 Mar 86

JIM HERRON

15 All they have to do is look down at the traffic and suddenly they don't feel like [flying is] that expensive a way to travel after all.
On $70 seaplane flights from Manhattan to Fire Island, NY *Times* 1 Jul 86

ROBERT HUGHES

16 [It] was a secular cathedral, dedicated to the rites of travel.
On the Gare d'Orsay in Paris, *Time* 8 Dec 86

ADA LOUISE HUXTABLE

17 Nothing was more up-to-date when it was built, or is more obsolete today, than the railroad station.
On railroad terminals in the air age, NY *Times* 19 Nov 72

18 Once benchmarks of civilization and style, these "gateways" to the cities were palaces of splendor and objects of civic pride. Now they are caverns of gloom.
ib

19 Summer is the time when one sheds one's tensions with one's clothes, and the right kind of day is jeweled balm for the battered spirit. A few of those days and you can become drunk with the belief that all's right with the world.
On vacationing in New England, *ib* 29 Sep 77

DONALD DALE JACKSON

20 Caboose, cabin car, crummy, way car, van, ape cage, throne room, hack, buggy, the office, shanty, monkey house, bedbug haven—American railroaders have known the last car on a freight train by all these names and more, [and] often [as] an ever-so-humble home.
"Cabooses May Be Rolling toward the End of the Line" *Smithsonian* Feb 86

21 The engine got most of the attention, but the "little red caboose," which was also brown, green, blue or yellow, was where the action was.
ib

JEROME A JACKSON

1 There is no way to avoid the birds in the air, but the pilots can avoid being where the birds are.

> On studying migration patterns to avoid aviation accidents, NY *Times* 7 May 85

ALFRED KAHN, Professor of Political Economy, Cornell University

2 People Express is clearly the archetypical deregulation success story and the most spectacular of my babies. It is the case that makes me the proudest.

> On no-frills airline company, *Time* 13 Jan 86

HELEN KELLER

3 It's wonderful to climb the liquid mountains of the sky. Behind me and before me is God and I have no fears.

> On her flight around the world at age 74, news summaries 5 Feb 55

JACQUELINE KENNEDY

4 A camel makes an elephant feel like a jet plane.

> On 1962 visit to India, quoted by Ralph G Martin *A Hero for Our Time* Macmillan 83

JACK KEROUAC

5 Whither goest thou, America, in thy shiny car in the night?

> *On the Road* Viking 57, quoted by Samuel G Freedman "Singing the Romance of the Open Road" NY *Times* 21 Apr 85

FRANCES G KNIGHT, Director, Passport Division, US State Department

6 I was well acquainted with the gag that if you looked like your passport picture, you needed a trip. I was unprepared for the proponderance of thuglike pictures which I found in the course of processing passports.

> Ruling that it is all right to smile in passport photographs, NY *Herald Tribune* 21 Feb 57

NOREEN KOAN, flight attendant

7 When tray tables get broken the standard fix is tape from the cockpit. People don't care about that. All they care about is their $29 ticket.

> On airline maintenance, NY *Times* 23 Mar 86

HANS KONING

8 The *Queen Elizabeth II* provides vast amounts of entertainment for an age that has forgotten how to amuse itself unaided.

> *International Herald Tribune* 15 Nov 85

CHARLES KURALT

9 Thanks to the interstate highway system, it is now possible to travel across the country from coast to coast without seeing anything.

> *On the Road* Putnam 85

PHILIP LARKIN

10 I wouldn't mind seeing China if I could come back the same day.

> NY *Times* 3 Dec 85

BOB LAVNER, spokesman for Automobile Club of NY

11 If a man needs his appendix taken out, his gallbladder treated and some brain surgery as well, I don't think too many doctors would do the jobs simultaneously.

> On concurrent road repairs clogging traffic, NY *Times* 29 Jun 84

BEA LILLIE

12 When does this place get to England?

> Aboard the *Queen Mary*, quoted in NY *Times* 3 Sep 67

ANDY LOGAN

13 Most people know the feeling. You've been away someplace, had a great time. You get home and before you can even unpack your souvenirs, dreary old problems surface, dreary new problems crowd in and soon some . . . person—all right, some wacko—asks who's been minding the store.

> *New Yorker* 9 Apr 84

STEVE LOHR

14 Gum-chewing Americans, loaded with money and ignorant of history, might succeed in appropriating the country as the 51st state [or] the United Kingdom Theme Park Inc.

> On high number of tourists in Great Britain in 1985, NY *Times* 30 May 86

LONDON TIMES

15 There are good dukes and bad dukes and they cannot all be worthy of the ultimate in airport lounges.

> On British Airport Authority's list of 42 official positions that rate use of VIP facilities, "Heathrow's Many Mansions" 15 Aug 78

ANITA LOOS

16 On a plane . . . you can pick up more and better people than on any other public conveyance since the stagecoach.

> NY *Times* 26 Apr 73

HAROLD MACMILLAN

17 But, my dear boy, it always has been.

> On being told that Cliveden, the Astor estate, had been turned into a hotel, NY *Times* 4 May 86

NORMAN MAILER

18 One will feel the same subtle nausea coming into the city or waiting to depart from it that one feels now in such plastic catacombs as O'Hare's reception center in Chicago.

> On plans for a rebuilt Pennsylvania Station in Manhattan, quoted in Maureen Howard ed *Penguin Book of Contemporary American Essays* Viking 84

ANDREW H MALCOLM

19 [A driver] is a king on a vinyl bucket-seat throne, changing direction with the turn of a wheel, changing the climate with a flick of the button, changing the music with the switch of a dial.

> NY *Times* 21 Apr 85

20 Every day all day, every night all night, cars, planes, trucks, trains, motorcycles and even pedestrians flow through that sprawling intersection like blood coursing through the arteries of the heartland, of which Chicago still reigns as the square-shouldered capital.

> On intersection near O'Hare Airport, *ib* 5 May 85

1 Calling [O'Hare] an airport is like calling the *Queen Elizabeth II* a boat.

ib

THOMAS MALLON

2 I have a picture of the Pont Neuf on a wall in my apartment, but I know that Paris is really on the closet shelf, in the box next to the sleeping bag, with the rest of [my] diaries.

NY *Times* 21 Jun 85

RAZA MANJI

3 You don't watch for potholes around here, you watch for a little roadway between them.

Quoted by Willliam E Geist "The Pothole: A Source of Perverse Civic Pride" NY *Times* 14 Jul 84

PAMELA MARSH

4 Enough scraps and rocks and countries are conveniently distributed across the face of the earth so that the sun still always shines on something British.

In review of Simon Winchester's *The Sun Never Sets* Prentice-Hall 86, *Christian Science Monitor* 3 Jul 86

GROUCHO MARX

5 I'm leaving because the weather is too good. I hate London when it's not raining.

News summaries 28 Jun 54

NEIL H MCELROY, US Secretary of Defense

6 In the space age, man will be able to go around the world in two hours—one for flying and the other to get to the airport.

Look 18 Feb 58

JAMES A MICHENER

7 If you reject the food, ignore the customs, fear the religion and avoid the people, you might better stay home.

Quoted by William Safire and Leonard Safir *Good Advice* Times Books 82

WALTER F MONDALE

8 I've traveled more this year than any other living human being, and if I'd traveled any more I wouldn't be living.

On campaigning for Democratic presidential nomination, NY *Times* 11 Jun 84

JAN MORRIS

9 [Worldwide] travel is not compulsory. Great minds have been fostered entirely by staying close to home. Moses never got further than the Promised Land. Da Vinci and Beethoven never left Europe. Shakespeare hardly went anywhere at all—certainly not to Elsinore or the coast of Bohemia.

"It's OK to Stay at Home" NY *Times* 30 Aug 85

10 Travel, which was once either a necessity or an adventure, has become very largely a commodity, and from all sides we are persuaded into thinking that it is a social requirement, too.

ib

11 [Travel seems] not just a way of having a good time, but something that every self-respecting citizen ought to undertake, like a high-fiber diet, say, or a deodorant.

ib

JAN MYRDAL

12 There is a third dimension to traveling, the longing for what is beyond.

The Silk Road Random House 80, previewed in NY *Times* 25 Aug 79

13 Traveling is not just seeing the new; it is also leaving behind. Not just opening doors; also closing them behind you, never to return. But the place you have left forever is always there for you to see whenever you shut your eyes. And the cities you see most clearly at night are the cities you have left and will never see again.

ib

ENID NEMY

14 My husband was getting his sea legs—rereading Joseph Conrad with a side order of C S Forester.

"In Search of Glamour on the Sea" *International Herald Tribune* 15 Feb 85

SYLVAINE ROUY NEVES

15 Dress impressively like the French, speak with authority like the Germans, have blond hair like the Scandinavians and speak of no American presidents except Lincoln, Roosevelt and Kennedy.

On how to gain respect while traveling in Europe, NY *Times* 30 Sep 84

NEW YORK STATE DRIVERS ASSOCIATION

16 When in doubt, don't start out.

Warning motorists not to drink and drive, NBC TV 3 May 85

PATRICK B OLIPHANT

17 Correct me if I'm wrong—the gizmo is connected to the flingflang connected to the watzis, watzis connected to the doo-dad connected to the ding dong.

Cartoon caption on questionable airline maintenance, *Time* 7 Jul 80

CYNTHIA OZICK

18 Traveling is *seeing*; it is the implicit that we travel by.

"Enchanters at First Encounter" NY *Times* 17 Mar 85

19 Travelers are fantasists, conjurers, seers—and what they finally discover is that every round object everywhere is a crystal ball: stone, teapot, the marvelous globe of the human eye.

ib

GLADYS PARRISH

20 The hotel was a forcing house for situations . . . every shade of behavior in public had significance, so that the choice of a seat could constitute a victory or a reverse, and a few words aside change the complexion of half the day.

Madame Solario Penguin 84

POPE PAUL VI

21 We see in these swift and skillful travelers a symbol of our life, which seeks to be a pilgrimage and a passage on this earth for the way of heaven.

Blessing 20,000 cars, buses, trucks and motor scooters assembled in St Peter's Square, *Newsweek* 13 Apr 64

DAVID PAULY

1 If airport traffic continues to snarl, the only sure way to get there on Tuesday will be to leave on Monday.
"Airport '84: Stalled Out" *Newsweek* 30 Jul 84

NANCY POND-SMITH, flight attendant

2 They are the passengers of the future, and we want them to have a good experience the first time they fly.
On increasing number of children who are traveling alone between homes of divorced parents, NY *Times* 21 Jun 86

WILLIAM PROXMIRE, US Senator

3 The limousine is the ultimate ego trip, the supreme sign of success. It shouts: "Hey, this guy is really and truly Mr Big."
Testimony to House Committee on Government Operations, NY *Times* 20 Sep 85

ANNA QUINDLEN

4 Green and amber and red lights shine in his sad eyes, and the track stretches before him, two silver strips converging in the distance, an art-school lesson in perspective.
On a subway engineer, NY *Times* 1 Jul 81

ANTHONY RAMIREZ

5 Flying first class is déclassé.
"The Decline of First Class" *Fortune* 26 May 86

ROBERT REINHOLD

6 The main . . . divorce routes are along the heavily traveled corridor between Boston and Washington in the Northeast and between nearby cities, such as Houston and Dallas in Texas and San Francisco and Los Angeles in California.
On increasing number of children who are traveling alone between homes of divorced parents, "Have Toys, Will Travel" NY *Times* 21 Jun 86

CHARLES RITZ

7 The Ritz is not ritzy.
Denying ostentatious luxury in his family's Parisian hotel, recalled on his death, NY *Times* 14 Jul 76

8 The guest is always right—even if we have to throw him out.
ib

WILLIAM ROBBINS

9 It provides an excuse for morning tardiness and an alibi for late returns. It provides grist for party talk and harrowing tales of accidents narrowly missed, potholes hit, tires blown and hubcaps lost.
On Philadelphia's Schuylkill Expressway, sometimes called "Surekill Stressway," NY *Times* 13 Jul 84

ANDY ROONEY

10 Crossing the street in New York keeps old people young—if they make it.
60 Minutes CBS TV 6 Jan 85

VICTOR ROSS, spokesman for NY Bureau of Traffic Operations

11 This was not a day of *Titanic* proportions. Maybe just *Lusitania*.
On road congestion after Labor Day, NY *Times* 5 Sep 84

12 My expressway runneth over.
After tractor trailer filled with wine casks split open on the Brooklyn-Queens Expressway, *ib* 7 May 85

RUMANIAN NATIONAL AIRLINES

13 Exit according to rule, first leg and then head. Remove high heels and synthetic stockings before evacuation: Open the door, take out the recovery line and throw it away.
Emergency instructions quoted in letter to London *Times* 27 Sep 84

ROBERT RUNCIE, Archbishop of Canterbury

14 I sometimes think that Thomas Cook should be numbered among the secular saints. He took travel from the privileged and gave it to the people.
Canadian Churchman Mar 80

CARL SANDBURG

15 I been a wanderin'
Early and late,
New York City
To the Golden Gate
An' it looks like
I'm never gonna cease my
Wanderin'.
Folk-music lyrics recalled on his death 22 Jul 67

MARY LEE SETTLE

16 She dreamed, lulled by the train, of getting off at heaven or New York City, whichever she got to first.
The Scapegoat Random House 80

GEORGE BERNARD SHAW

17 The great advantage of a hotel is that it is a refuge from home life.
Quoted in NY *Times* 10 Jul 83

MARGARET MARY SHEERIN

18 I read it all beforehand—"How to ditch without a hitch."
On preparing for a European flight that took her out of her Georgetown Visitation Convent for the first time in nearly 40 years, Washington *Post* 7 Jun 64

IGOR SIKORSKY

19 The helicopter . . . approaches closer than any other [vehicle] to fulfillment of mankind's ancient dreams of the flying horse and the magic carpet.
On the 20th anniversary of the initial flight of his invention, NY *Times* 13 Sep 59

RONALD STEEL

20 Discount air fares, a car in every parking space and the interstate highway system have made every place accessible—and every place alike.
"Life in the Last 50 Years" *Esquire* Jun 83

JOHN STEINBECK

21 Four hoarse blasts of a ship's whistle still raise the hair on my neck and set my feet to tapping.
Travels with Charley Viking 62

22 The sound of a jet, an engine warming up, even the clopping of shod hooves on pavement brings on the

ancient shudder, the dry mouth and vacant eye, the hot palms and the churn of stomach high up under the rib cage.

ib

ESTHER TALLAMY

1 I'm as self-contained as a turtle. When I put my key in the ignition, I have my home right behind me.

On convenience of motor homes for long-distance travel, NY *Times* 26 Jun 86

HENRIETTA, LADY TAVISTOCK

2 Traveling with a tiara is such a performance. Your hair has to be woven into [it], and I wouldn't think you would be able to find a hairdresser here who knows how.

Comment when a case of her tiaras was included in "The Treasure Houses of Britain" exhibit at Washington DC's National Gallery of Art, NY *Times* 31 Oct 85

ELIZABETH TAYLOR, novelist

3 In a café in Rhodes three Englishwomen walked in wearing the most outlandish holiday clothes and Panama hats, with lots of raincoats and cameras and walking sticks and rucksacks. They stood about looking for a waiter and one said in a loud voice, "How do we attract attention?"

1956 letter to Robert Liddell, quoted in London *Daily Telegraph*, 21 Mar 86

PAUL THEROUX

4 You define a good flight by negatives: you didn't get hijacked, you didn't crash, you didn't throw up, you weren't late, you weren't nauseated by the food. So you are grateful.

The Old Patagonian Express Houghton Mifflin 79

JAMES THURBER

5 A peril of the night road is that flecks of dust and streaks of bug blood on the windshield look to me like old admirals in uniform, or crippled apple women, or the front edge of barges, and I whirl out of their way, thus going into ditches and fields and up on front lawns, endangering the life of authentic admirals and apple women who may be out on the roads for a breath of air before retiring.

On driving with poor eyesight, quoted in Helen Thurber and Edward Weeks eds *Selected Letters of James Thurber* Atlantic–Little, Brown 81

TIME MAGAZINE

6 Down the road, as the Howard Johnson's tick by, all breathe easier. By mid-Pennsylvania, past the Amish country and into the Allegheny foothills, the father is almost counting cows with his children.

20 Jul 70

7 Local radio stations dissolve in static every five miles; insects detonate against the windshield. He stops and has the oil checked. The American is in his seasonal migration.

ib

PAUL TOURNIER

8 The real meaning of travel, like that of a conversation by the fireside, is the discovery of oneself through contact with other people, and its condition is self-commitment in the dialogue.

The Meaning of Persons Harper 57

CHARLES TURNER

9 It was a perfect night for a train. . . . The occasional whistle told Louis of all the farewells he had ever known.

The Celebrant Servant 82

10 When the whistle blew and the call stretched thin across the night, one had to believe that any journey could be sweet to the soul.

ib

ANNE TYLER

11 While armchair travelers dream of going places, traveling armchairs dream of staying put.

The Accidental Tourist Knopf 85, quoted in *Christian Science Monitor* 4 Oct 85

DONALD WEEKS

12 The crossroads of yesterday and tomorrow, Gatwick Airport.

In biography of Frederick William Rolfe, Corvo, *"Saint or Madman?"* McGraw-Hill 71

EUDORA WELTY

13 Writers and travelers are mesmerized alike by knowing of their destinations.

One Writer's Beginnings Harvard 84

JESSAMYN WEST

14 A big iron needle stitching the country together.

On Baltimore & Ohio Railroad, *The Life I Really Lived* Harcourt Brace Jovanovich 79

ROY WILKINS

15 The players in this drama of frustration and indignity are not commas or semicolons in a legislative thesis; they are people, human beings, citizens of the United States of America.

Testimony to Senate Commerce Committee on difficulties blacks experience in transcontinental travel, NY *Herald Tribune* 26 Apr 64

ROBIN WILLIAMS

16 The only people flying to Europe will be terrorists, so it will be, "Will you be sitting in armed or unarmed?"

Quoted in *US* 3 Nov 86

DARYL WYCKOFF

17 The airlines were always ending up like my beagle, 15 blocks from home and panting.

On bankruptcy of airlines that expanded routes too quickly after deregulation in 1978, *Time* 8 Oct 84

MELISSA ZEGANS

18 You have to run ahead of people sometimes and try to kill them.

On catching cabs in Manhattan, NY *Times* 18 Dec 86

The Eye of the Traveler

BARBARA ACTON-BOND

19 [Rain] hangs about the place, like a friendly ghost. . . . if it's not coming down in delicate droplets, then it's in buckets; and if neither, it tends to lurk suspiciously in the atmosphere.

"The Anglicization of Me" *Christian Science Monitor* 21 Jul 82

ANSEL ADAMS

1 Yosemite Valley, to me, is always a sunrise, a glitter of green and golden wonder in a vast edifice of stone and space.
   The Portfolios of Ansel Adams NY Graphic Society/Little, Brown 81

JAMES AGEE

2 This continent, an open palm spread frank before the sky.
   "The Great American Roadside" *Fortune* Sep 54

SHANA ALEXANDER

3 The graceful Georgian streets and squares, a series of steel engravings under a wet sky.
   "Dublin Is My Sure Thing" *Life* 2 Sep 66

NELSON ALGREN

4 Chicago is an October sort of city even in spring.
   Quoted by George F Will *Newsweek* 13 Aug 84

ANONYMOUS

5 London is a bad habit one hates to lose.
   Quoted by William Sansom *Blue Skies, Brown Studies* Hogarth 61

6 If the United States is a melting pot, then New York makes it bubble.
   Sign in Times Square, quoted in *US News & World Report* 14 Apr 86

R W APPLE JR

7 Aspects of life here—civility, courtesy, coziness—have always bound Britons to their country . . . They are part of the British myth, along with lovely countryside, dogs and horses, rose gardens, the Armada, the Battle of Britain.
   NY *Times* 9 Oct 85

ALFRED ARONOWITZ

8 Christened with a name that has come to be the color of its reputation, clasped to the bosom of Long Island and yet, somehow, closer to the South Seas than the South Shore.
   On Fire Island, NY *Post* 27 Jul 59

9 [It is] surrounded completely by Friday and Monday.
   ib

10 Reached only by boat, seaplane and, with less surety, telephone—this is Fire Island, a pile of sand beneath a pile of people.
   ib

BARBARA LAZEAR ASCHER

11 [A] red brick Presbyterian church . . . captured by kudzu vines as surely as a butterfly in a net.
   On a Natchez Trace ghost town, "An Old World the Mississippi Left Behind" NY *Times* 25 Nov 84

ANTHONY AUSTIN

12 The city charms you out of any mood of protest or anger or hopelessness. It is a city of sky and water, of stone lions and sphinxes gazing out over the Neva River, of delicate iron grillwork hanging over the canals, of sunsets that paint the riverfront houses with tender violet and pink.
   On Leningrad, NY *Times* 2 Jun 80

13 It is a city of fantasy, as Dostoyevsky called it, and sometimes, adrift amid so much beauty, one almost shares the expectation he described: that any moment one can imagine the city rising and floating away, leaving nothing but the swamp on which it was built.
   ib

ANTHONY BAILEY

14 As one comes down the Henry Hudson Parkway along the river in the dusk, New York is never real; it is always fabulous.
   New Yorker 29 Jul 67

MONICA BALDWIN

15 The Sussex lanes were very lovely in the autumn. . . . spendthrift gold and glory of the year-end . . . earth scents and the sky winds and all the magic of the countryside which is ordained for the healing of the soul.
   On the English countryside, *I Leap over the Wall* Rinehart 50

DJUNA BARNES

16 What is a ruin but time easing itself of endurance?
   Selected Works of Djuna Barnes Farrar, Straus & Giroux 62

CHARLES EDWIN WOODROW BEAN

17 Australia is a big blank map, and the whole people is constantly sitting over it like a committee, trying to work out the best way to fill it in.
   Quoted in Stephen Murray-Smith ed *The Dictionary of Australian Quotations* Heinemann 84

CECIL BEATON

18 More varied than any landscape was the landscape in the sky, with islands of gold and silver, peninsulas of apricot and rose against a background of many shades of turquoise and azure.
   On Egyptian sunset, quoted by Hugo Vickers *Cecil Beaton* Little, Brown 85

JIM BISHOP

19 Scoops of mint ice cream with chips of chocolate cows.
   On the English countryside, NY *Journal-American* 28 Sep 57

ARBIT BLATAS

20 In the winter, Venice is like an abandoned theater. The play is finished, but the echoes remain.
   Quoted by Erica Jong "A City of Love and Death: Venice" NY *Times* 23 Mar 86

MARY BLUME

21 The Englishman's telephone box is his castle. Like the London taxi, it can be entered by a gentleman in a top hat. It protects the user's privacy, keeps him warm and is large enough for a small cocktail party.
   Protesting replacement of Britain's bright-red phone booths, *International Herald Tribune* 30 Aug 85

ALAN BRIEN

1 The blue-rinse warbler and her horn-rimmed mate are rare and overdue this year.
>On annual migration of Americans to Great Britain, London *Sunday Times* 21 Jul 74

BRITISH TRAVEL ASSOCIATION

2 Tread softly past the long, long sleep of kings.
>On Henry VII Chapel in Westminster Abbey, advertisement in *New Yorker* 17 Jan 59

3 Henry, Mary and Elizabeth. Such are their simple names in sleep. No titles. No trumpets. The banners hang battle-heavy and becalmed. But still the royal crown remains—*honi soit qui mal y pense.*
>ib

ANATOLE BROYARD

4 Rome was a poem pressed into service as a city.
>NY *Times* 25 Mar 74

HOLLY BRUBACH

5 Nothing makes you feel that you've overstayed your welcome like a flower arrangement that has withered and died.
>In survey of London hotels, *Harper's* 8 Sep 84

6 Claridge's [is] elegant but determinedly unglamorous. . . . The only fantasy it has to offer is the illusion that the world is in good working order.
>ib

7 It's the punctilious attention to detail, in a time when nobody even bothers to get the spelling of your name right.
>ib

LENNY BRUCE

8 Miami Beach is where neon goes to die.
>Quoted by Barbara Gordon *Saturday Review* 20 May 72

TOM BUCKLEY

9 The voluptuous curve of the riverbank at 79th Street . . . escapes from the city's rigid grid of streets and avenues like a fat woman slipping out of a corset.
>On New York City, NY *Times* 13 Apr 75

TRUMAN CAPOTE

10 Venice is like eating an entire box of chocolate liqueurs in one go.
>News summaries 26 Nov 61

11 Holcomb stands on the high wheat plains of western Kansas, a lonesome area that other Kansans call "out there."
>*In Cold Blood* Random House 66

CLAUDIA CASSIDY

12 A Whistler mist washes the Thames beneath our Savoy windows, turning time back a century, softening the roar of the city and the bong of Big Ben.
>On London, Chicago *Tribune* 15 Sep 65

CHARLES, Prince of Wales

13 I sometimes wonder if two thirds of the globe is covered in red carpet.
>After Australian and US tour, quoted in *US* 16 Dec 85

ILKA CHASE

14 Wart hogs should sue for libel. It is a terrible name and they are fine fellows [and] devoted family men and it is rare to see one by himself; the little woman and the kiddies are usually close at hand.
>In African travelogue *Elephants Arrive at Half-Past Five* Doubleday 63

AGATHA CHRISTIE

15 It is ridiculous to set a detective story in New York City. New York City is itself a detective story.
>*Life* 14 May 56

WINSTON CHURCHILL

16 I shall always be glad to have seen it—for the same reason Papa gave for being glad to have seen Lisbon—namely, "that it will be unnecessary ever to see it again."
>On Calcutta, in 1896 letter to his mother, quoted by John Colville *The Fringes of Power* Norton 85

RICHARD COBB

17 France is getting younger. I am not.
>*London Illustrated News* Mar 86

ROBERT TRISTRAM COFFIN

18 Vermont's a place where barns come painted
Red as a strong man's heart,
Where stout carts and stout boys in freckles
Are highest forms of art.
>"Vermont Looks Like a Man," last poem contributed to NY *Herald Tribune* editorial page before his death 20 Jan 55

DAVID COHN

19 The Peabody is the Paris Ritz, the Cairo Shepheard's, the London Savoy . . . If you stand near its fountain in the middle of the lobby, where ducks waddle and turtles drowse, ultimately you will see everybody who is anybody in the Delta.
>Quoted by William E Schmidt "Memphis's Grand Hotel" NY *Times* 5 Oct 86

PAT COLANDER

20 Chicago is a city of contradictions, of private visions haphazardly overlaid and linked together.
>"A Metropolis of No Little Plans" NY *Times* 5 May 85

JOHN COLVILLE

21 The monastic republic of Mount Athos.
>Memory of a visit to Greece, *The Fringes of Power* Norton 85

ALISTAIR COOKE

22 People, when they first come to America, whether as travelers or settlers, become aware of a new and agreeable feeling: that the whole country is their oyster.
>*America* Knopf 73

23 Between a quarter and a third of Los Angeles's land area is now monopolized by the automobile and its needs—by freeways, highways, garages, gas stations, car lots, parking lots. And all of it is blanketed with anonymity and foul air.
>ib

EDWARD CRANKSHAW

1 That is a steppe; you always wanted to see [a steppe]; now you've seen it, and you never want to see it again. But all the time I knew Russia was tying itself around me.
Book-of-the-Month Club News Oct 76

WALTER CRONKITE

2 When Moses was alive, these pyramids were a thousand years old . . . Here began the history of architecture. Here people learned to measure time by a calendar, to plot the stars by astronomy and chart the earth by geometry. And here they developed that most awesome of all ideas—the idea of eternity.
Eternal Egypt CBS TV 28 Jun 80

CHARLOTTE CURTIS

3 The new, young, chic and acquisitive rich, the restless young Europeans and the beautiful people . . . still flit from Palm Beach's polo fields to Newport's yachts with refueling stops at Gucci, Yves Saint Laurent and Tiffany.
NY *Times* 7 Aug 84

CLIFTON DANIEL

4 Christmas morning in Russia . . . a cruel snow-laden wind blowing straight out of the pages of Russian history and literature whipped across roofs and through the frozen streets of Moscow.
Quoted by Gay Talese *The Kingdom and the Power* World 69

JAMES DEELY

5 With all due respect for the finger of John the Baptist, the shin of St George . . . most of the holy relics in Christendom pale in importance before the relic of the Holy Blood of Jesus.
On crystal flask venerated at Bruges, Belgium, "Pageantry and Passion" *Connoisseur* Apr 86

CHARLES DE GAULLE

6 Hearing Mass is the ceremony I most favor during my travels. Church is the only place where someone speaks to me . . . and I do not have to answer back.
Newsweek 1 Oct 62

LANDT DENNIS

7 The parks of Paris—the Bois de Boulogne, Parc Monceau, Vert Galant, Luxembourg, Tuileries, Buttes-Chaumont and others of varying size and fame—symbolize man's humanity to man.
"Parks of Paris" *Christian Science Monitor* 18 Aug 70

8 Appreciation, gratitude, affection—these are the qualities Parisians bestow on their parks. Beauty, serenity, tranquillity, majesty—these are the rewards they reap in return.
ib

ISAK DINESEN

9 In the Ngong Forest I have also seen, on a narrow path through thick growth, in the middle of a very hot day, the Giant Forest Hog, a rare person to meet.
From her 1937 book *Out of Africa*, recalled on her death 7 Sep 62

BOB DODSON

10 The Mississippi meanders down the spine of America.
CBS TV 26 Aug 84

DESMOND DOIG

11 The first tramcars rattled noisily through the empty streets, dilapidated monsters that just hours later would be festooned with people on their way to work.
On Calcutta, *Mother Teresa* Harper & Row 76

MARIA DONOVAN

12 The road turns and the town suddenly springs into view, presenting itself like a crown roast of lamb served up on a bed of fresh spring greens.
"Spoleto, Italy: A Festival Town" *Gourmet* Jun 74

ROBIN DOUGLAS-HOME

13 Scotland, thank God, is not for everyone.
"Scotland: The Dour and the Beautiful" *Vogue* 15 Apr 64

MARGARET DRABBLE

14 The yearning of the provincial for the capital is a quite exceptional passion. It sets in early, and until it is satisfied it does not let go. It draws its subjects into a strange world where trains and hotels take on an exceptional significance. Many suffering from it become travelers, but perhaps they are aware that travel is simply an extension of that first uprooting, a desire to repeat that first incomparable shock.
Arnold Bennett Knopf 74

GEORGIA DULLEA

15 The entire population of Liberty Island is small enough to fit into one copper-skinned palm of the colossal statue that serves as its only industry.
"In Miss Liberty's Shadow, A Tiny Village of Families" NY *Times* 2 May 86

ARNOLD EDINBOROUGH

16 We have never been a melting pot. The fact is we are more like a tossed salad. We are green, some of us are oily and there's a little vinegar injected when you get up to Ottawa.
On Canadians, NY *Times* 4 Aug 73

VICKY ELLIOTT

17 Colors that blend with the brick and the dark waters of the city's canals—greens, browns and the strong shade of oxblood that is known as Bruges red.
"Bruges, A City Sealed in the Past" *International Herald Tribune* 30 May 86

PATRICK LEIGH FERMOR

18 Looking backward we could almost see, suspended with the most delicate equipoise above the flat little island, the ghostly shapes of those twin orbs of the Empire, the cricket ball and the blackball.
On Barbados, *The Traveler's Tree* John Murray 51

19 Squares as small and complete and as carefully furnished as rooms.
On Vienna, *A Time of Gifts* Penguin 84

20 The statues of archdukes or composers presided with pensive nonchalance.
ib

JOHN FLEISCHMAN

1 Living as you do in New York, the navel of the universe, it is easy to confuse the Midwest and the South.

> Letter to the editor NY *Times* 7 Jun 85

2 North Carolina is the place you fly over on the way to Florida. Ohio is the flat place between Hoboken and Malibu.

> *ib*

E M FORSTER

3 A façade of skyscrapers facing a lake, and behind the façade every type of dubiousness.

> On Chicago, quoted in Mary Lago and P N Furbank eds *Selected Letters of E M Forster 1921–70* Belknap Press/ Harvard 84

FRANK FUSARO, observatory staff, Empire State Building

4 The visitors, they question you—they like to know what's that building, where's Brooklyn, which way's Jersey. They observe the view. That's why it's called an observatory.

> *New Yorker* 14 May 79

5 You think you could get this view from a mountain somewhere? No way.

> *ib*

WILLIAM E GEIST

6 New York is a city of conversations overheard, of people at the next restaurant table (micrometers away) checking your watch, of people reading the stories in your newspaper on the subway train.

> "A Quiet Sendoff at the Barbershop" NY *Times* 25 Oct 86

PENELOPE GILLIATT

7 Prague is like a vertical Venice . . . steps everywhere.

> *Vanity Fair* Jan 85

WILLIAM GOLDING

8 He who rides the sea of the Nile must have sails woven of patience.

> *An Egyptian Journal* Faber & Faber 85

NIGEL GOSLIN

9 New York is a granite beehive, where people jostle and whir like molecules in an overheated jar. . . . Houston is six suburbs in search of a center.

> *Saturday Review* 7 Oct 67

ROBERT GRAVES

10 I was last in Rome in AD 540 when it was full of Goths and their heavy horses. It has changed a great deal since then.

> NY *Times* 6 Jan 58

CEDRIC HARDWICKE

11 England is my wife, America my mistress. It is very good sometimes to get away from one's wife.

> NY *Herald Tribune* 7 Aug 64

ERNEST HEMINGWAY

12 If you are lucky enough to have lived in Paris as a young man, then wherever you go for the rest of your life it stays with you, for Paris is a moveable feast.

> *A Moveable Feast* Scribner's 64

JOHN HILLABY

13 Few things are more pleasant than a village graced with a good church, a good priest and a good pub.

> On cross-country walking in England, *Journey Home* Holt, Rinehart & Winston 84

PAUL HOGARTH and STEPHEN SPENDER

14 Chicago is at the base of that congress of lakes— Superior, Huron and Michigan—which, on the map, makes it look like the sensitive area of some vital organ—lungs or heart or liver drawing in and giving out blood—a meeting of waterways, airways and railways—the pulse of the continent.

> *America Observed* Potter 79, quoted in NY *Times* 1 Jul 79

ROBERT HUGHES

15 The prototypes of strong sensation: blazing lights, red earth, blue sea, mauve twilight, the flake of gold buried in the black depths of the cypress; archaic tastes of wine and olive, ancients smells of dust, goat dung and thyme, immemorial sounds of cicada and rustic flute.

> On Provence, *Time* 22 Oct 84

KATHRYN HULME

16 Lourdes was a bonfire . . . thousands of candles and burning cries and a week of rising suns over an esplanade where stretcher cases lay side by side, end to end, waiting for a priest to come with a monstrance that gathered sun to its gold and blazed in the sign of the cross above the stretchers.

> *The Nun's Story* Atlantic–Little, Brown 56

ELSPETH HUXLEY

17 [Africa] is a cruel country; it takes your heart and grinds it into powdered stone—and no one minds.

> *The Flame Trees of Thika* Morrow 59

ISRAELI TOURIST BUREAU

18 If you liked the book, you'll love the country.

> Urging tourists to visit Israel after reading the Old Testament, quoted by Episcopal Diocese of Chicago *Advance* Jul 79

BRIAN JACKMAN

19 Everything in Africa bites, but the safari bug is worst of all.

> "Close Encounters of the Rare and Violent Kind" London *Times* 15 Oct 83

RANDALL JARRELL

20 The Southern past, the Southern present, the Southern future . . . became one of red clay pine barrens, of chain-gang camps, of housewives dressed in flour sacks who stare all day dully down into dirty sinks.

> From his 1954 novel *Pictures from an Institution*, quoted by William Pritchard "Writing Well Is the Best Revenge" NY *Times* 27 Jul 86

MIKE JENKINS

1 Wives and children were miniatures
of the hill, the coal engrained
in enclosures on their skin.

> On Wales, quoted in Raymond Garlick and Roland Mathias eds *Anglo-Welsh Poetry 1480–1980* Poetry Wales Press 85

DENIS JOHNSON

2 As soon as the first drop of dawn dilutes the blackness, the neighbors begin their unbelievable racket, first the roosters, then the radios, then the live accompaniment to the radios—and then it's time to wind up the little children and start their screams and tears.

> On Managua, Nicaragua, *The Stars at Noon* Knopf 86, quoted in NY *Times* 13 Sep 86

PAMELA HANSFORD JOHNSON

3 The sky broke like an egg into full sunset and the water caught fire.

> On Bruges, Belgium, *The Unspeakable Skipton* Scribner's 81

ERICA JONG

4 It is the city of mirrors, the city of mirages, at once solid and liquid, at once air and stone.

> "A City of Love and Death: Venice" NY *Times* 23 Mar 86

5 The stones themselves are thick with history, and those cats that dash through the alleyways must surely be the ghosts of the famous dead in feline disguise.

> *ib*

BERN KEATING

6 Poets who know no better rhapsodize about the peace of nature, but a well-populated marsh is a cacophony.

> "Birders' Heaven" *Connoisseur* Apr 86

GEORGE F KENNAN

7 Russia, Russia—unwashed, backward, appealing Russia, so ashamed of your own backwardness, so orientally determined to conceal it from us by clever deceit.

> Quoted by Walter Isaacson and Evan Thomas *The Wise Men* Simon & Schuster 86

8 I shall always remember you—slyly, touchingly, but with great shouting and confusion—pumping hot water into our sleeping car in the frosty darkness of a December morning in order that we might not know, in order that we might never realize, to how primitive a land we had come.

> *ib*

GEORGE KIMBLE

9 The darkest thing about Africa has always been our ignorance of it.

> "Africa Today: The Lifting Darkness" *Reporter* 15 May 51

WAYNE KING

10 It is a picture postcard lost for eight decades in the mail.

> On Bisbee AZ, NY *Times* 20 Feb 84

JOHN LE CARRÉ

11 Berlin. What a garrison of spies! . . . what a cabinet full of useless, liquid secrets, what a playground for every alchemist, miracle worker and rat piper that ever took up the cloak.

> *A Perfect Spy* Knopf 86

12 Agents of disruption, subversion, sabotage and disinformation . . . tunnelers and smugglers, listeners and forgers, trainers and recruiters and talent spotters and couriers and watchers and seducers, assassins and balloonists, lip readers and disguise artists.

> *ib*

ANNE MORROW LINDBERGH

13 I have been overcome by the beauty and richness of our life together, those early mornings setting out, those evenings gleaming with rivers and lakes below us, still holding the last light.

> *War Within and Without* Harcourt Brace Jovanovich 80

14 Those fields of daisies we landed on, and dusty fields and desert stretches. Memories of many skies and earths beneath us—many days, many nights of stars.

> *ib*

CHARLES A LINDBERGH

15 I owned the world that hour as I rode over it. . . . free of the earth, free of the mountains, free of the clouds, but how inseparably I was bound to them.

> On flying above the Rocky Mountains, quoted by Leonard Mosley *Lindbergh* Doubleday 78

RICHARD E LINGENFELTER

16 The valley we call Death, isn't really that different from much of the rest of the desert West. It's just a little deeper, a little hotter and a little drier. What sets it apart more than anything else is the mind's eye.

> *Death Valley and the Amargosa* University of California 86, quoted in NY *Times* 6 Jun 86

17 For it is a land of illusion, a place in the mind, a shimmering mirage of riches and mystery and death. These illusions have distorted its landscape and contorted its history.

> *ib*

WALTER LIPPMANN

18 There is nothing so good for the human soul as the discovery that there are ancient and flourishing civilized societies which have somehow managed to exist for many centuries and are still in being though they have had no help from the traveler in solving their problems.

> Quoted by Ronald Steel *Walter Lippmann and the American Century* Atlantic–Little, Brown 80

LONDON TIMES

19 After the annual festival, Edinburgh reverts to its staid character, a stern old lady counting the cash from her annual fling.

> 17 Aug 81

WALTER LORD

20 Brilliantly lit from stem to stern, she looked like a sagging birthday cake.

> On the sinking *Titanic* on the night of April 15, 1912, *A Night to Remember* Holt, Rinehart & Winston 55

RUSSELL LYNES

1 Any real New Yorker is a you-name-it-we-have-it-snob . . . whose heart brims with sympathy for the millions of unfortunates who through misfortune, misguidedness or pure stupidity live anywhere else in the world.
Town & Country Aug 65

ARCHIBALD MACLEISH

2 Spring has many American faces. There are cities where it will come and go in a day and counties where it hangs around and never quite gets there. . . . Summer is drawn blinds in Louisiana, long winds in Wyoming, shade of elms and maples in New England.
"Sweet Land of Liberty" *Collier's* 8 Jul 55

ANDREW H MALCOLM

3 [The] brawny mix of extraordinary sights—weather, politics, races, imagination, corruption and athletics. They clash and mingle here where the broad prairies that are the world's most fertile collection of farm fields meet the vast Great Lakes that are the world's largest collection of fresh water.
On Chicago, NY *Times* 5 May 85

4 Ruthton looked like any of a thousand Midwestern towns, an aging collection of small homes on straight streets, all arranged around a two-block downtown where the brightest light after 9 PM is the Coca-Cola machine down by the Standard Oil station.
On Ruthton MN, "Murder on the Family Farm" *ib* 23 Mar 86

WILLIAM MANCHESTER

5 Our Boeing 747 has been fleeing westward from darkened California, racing across the Pacific toward the sun, the incandescent eye of God, but slowly, three hours later than West Coast time, twilight gathers outside, veil upon lilac veil.
Good-bye, Darkness: A Memoir of the Pacific War Little, Brown 80

6 The colors of the underwater rock [are] as pale and delicate as those in the wardrobe of an 18th-century marchioness.
On New Guinea, *ib*

7 The coconut trees, lithe and graceful, crowd the beach . . . like a minuet of slender elderly virgins adopting flippant poses.
ib

BERYL MARKHAM

8 I have a trunk containing continents.
Quoted on *World without Walls: Beryl Markham's African Memoir* WNET TV 8 Oct 86

FELIX MARTI-IBÁÑEZ

9 In Amsterdam the water is the mistress and the land the vassal. . . . throughout the city there are as many canals and drawbridges as bracelets on a Gypsy's bronzed arms.
MD Mar 80

10 People, houses, streets, animals, flowers—everything in Holland looks as if it were washed and ironed each night in order to glisten immaculately and newly starched the next morning.
ib

JOHN MASEFIELD

11 It is too maddening. I've got to fly off, right now, to some devilish navy yard, three hours in a seasick steamer, and after being heartily sick, I'll have to speak three times, and then [I'll] be sick coming home. Still, who would not be sick for England?
On touring America, letter quoted in NY *Times* 9 Jan 70

MILTON MAYER

12 The American goes to Paris, always has, and comes back and tells his neighbor, always does, how exorbitant and inhospitable it is, how rapacious and selfish and unaccommodating and unresponsive it is, how dirty and noisy it is—and the next summer his neighbor goes to Paris.
"Paris as a State of Mind" NY *Times* 9 Jun 85

DAVE MAZUR, Canisius College freshman

13 Beaches, beer and bikinis . . . sand, surf and sex.
On Ft Lauderdale FL during spring break, *Time* 7 Apr 86

PHYLLIS MCGINLEY

14 The East is a montage. . . . It is old and it is young, very green in summer, very white in winter, gregarious, withdrawn and at once both sophisticated and provincial.
"The East Is Home" *Woman's Home Companion* Jul 56

JOHN MCKAY, Lord Provost of Edinburgh

15 We are Boston, Glasgow is Cleveland.
Wall Street Journal 25 Oct 85

COLIN MCPHEE

16 [We] ran up the hills where, as you looked down toward the sea, the flooded rice fields lay shining in the sunlight like a broken mirror.
On Bali, quoted by Jane Howard *Margaret Mead* Simon & Schuster 84

THOMAS MERTON

17 Men in bowlers and dark suits . . . with their rolled-up umbrellas. Men full of propriety, calm and proud, neat and noble.
On the City of London, quoted by Monica Furlong *Merton* Harper & Row 80

18 [It is] a stately and grown-up city, a true city, life-size . . . anything but soulless.
On visit to NYC some 23 years after entering a Trappist monastery, *ib*

JAMES A MICHENER

19 Millions upon millions of years ago, when the continents were already formed and the principal features of the earth had been decided, there existed, then as now, one aspect of the world that dwarfed all others. . . . a mighty ocean, resting uneasily to the east of the largest continent, a restless ever-changing, gigantic body of water that would later be described as Pacific.
Hawaii Random House 59

TED MILLS and STEVEN WHITE

1 In every building of Paris there is a concierge, to serve as a human watchdog. Whoever you are, she knows about you.
Maurice Chevalier's Paris NBC TV 6 Mar 57

2 She knows all your friends. She does not like them. She talks about you secretly, and only to other concierges. The tell each other all they know. There is a good deal to tell.
ib

3 Without her, Paris could no more be Paris than it could be Paris without its art . . . and artists.
ib

NICHOLAS MONSARRAT

4 The marvelous maturity of London! I would rather be dead in this town than preening my feathers in heaven.
Breaking In, Breaking Out Morrow 66

BRIAN MOORE

5 As always on this boulevard, the faces were young, coming annually in an endless migration from every country, every continent, to alight here once in the long journey of their lives.
On Boulevard Saint-Michel in Paris, *The Doctor's Wife* Farrar, Straus & Giroux 76

DALE MORGAN

6 Great Salt Lake is an ironical joke of nature—water that is itself more desert than a desert.
Quoted by Rick Gore "No Way to Run a Desert" *National Geographic* Jun 85

7 Moody and withdrawn, the lake unites a haunting loveliness to a raw desolateness.
ib

JAMES MORRIS

8 There is a lull to the very air of the place, the creaking of the tall teak forests, the lapping of the canals, the gentle swaying of the little kingfishers who sit like neat blue idols on almost every telegraph wire.
On Thailand, *The Road to Huddersfield* Pantheon 63

9 The gentle, empty, haunting faces of the young prostitutes, in virginal white and vicarage embroidery.
On Addis Ababa, *Cities* Harcourt, Brace & World 64

10 A scent of jasmine and a rasp of sand.
On Algiers, *ib*

11 The gray, immense and unmistakably Central European sky. . . . air slightly perfumed with petrol and boiled potatoes.
On Warsaw, *ib*

12 Seduction but in a slightly medicinal way.
On Stockholm, *ib*

13 [New Delhi] is trying to show that greatness can be voted into office, if applied for in triplicate, through the proper channels.
ib

JAN MORRIS (James Morris)

14 There it stands, with a toss of curls and a flounce of skirts, a Carmen among the cities. . . . the last of the Middle Eastern fleshpots. . . . a junction of intrigue and speculation.
On Beirut, *Among the Cities* Oxford 85

15 Its origins are ancient but it burgeons with brash modernity, and it lounges upon its delectable shore, halfway between the Israelis and the Syrians, in a posture that no such city, at such a latitude, in such a moment of history, has any reasonable excuse for assuming.
ib

16 To the stern student of affairs, Beirut is a phenomenon, beguiling perhaps, but quite, quite impossible.
ib

17 Brooded over by mist more often than swirled about by cloud, drizzled rather than storm-swept, on the western perimeter of Europe lies the damp, demanding and obsessively interesting country called by its own people Cymru . . . and known to the rest of the world, if it is known at all, as Wales.
The Matter of Wales Oxford 85

18 Its smallness is not petty; on the contrary, it is profound.
ib

VERN MORTENSON

19 Have you listened still on a desert hill
At the close of a bitter day,
When the orange sun in wispy clouds
Has sat in a greenish haze?
In a cold white world the deepening drifts
That would cover the land like a pall,
Then the plaintive bawl of a hungry cow,
Is the loneliest sound of all.
"Range Cow in Winter," quoted in Hal Cannon ed *Cowboy Poetry* Western Folklife Center 85

H V MORTON

20 [The rain] descends with the enthusiasm of someone breaking bad news.
On Wales, quoted in NY *Times* 28 Jul 84

21 The exquisite steps of Rome . . . steps of marble and travertine; shallow Renaissance steps; steps curving left, right and center from Piazza di Spagna, as if to show what steps can do if given the chance; noble steps up to Santa Maria d'Aracoeli; elegant steps of the Quirinal Palace; majestic steps to St Peter's Basilica.
ib 3 Aug 86

PATRICIA MOYES

22 Suffolk . . . has something more than the coziness of Kent and Surrey. There is a hint of wildness in its tamed beauty, and the tang of the North Sea is never far away.
Night Ferry to Death Holt 85

V S NAIPAUL

23 I came to London. It had become the center of my world and I had worked hard to come to it. And I was lost.
An Area of Darkness André Deutsch 64

24 It was a good place for getting lost in, a city no one ever knew, a city explored from the neutral heart outward, until after many years, it defined itself into a jumble of clearings separated by stretches of the unknown, through which the narrowest of paths had been cut.
ib

NEW YORKER

1 Gypsy musicians whose expressions had gone beyond boredom to a sort of beatific madness.
    On Budapest during the first postwar Grand Prix race in an Eastern European country, 15 Sep 86

NEW YORK TIMES

2 The statue's 100th birthday is a time for marches, not madrigals. New York knows that, and the mayor and his people have labored for months on logistics, from toilets to terrorism.
    Editorial on the Statue of Liberty's centennial, "The Corny, Carny Spirit of '86" 29 Jun 86

SEÁN O'FAOLÁIN

3 God made the grass, the air and the rain; and the grass, the air and the rain made the Irish; and the Irish turned the grass, the air and the rain back into God.
    Holiday Jun 58

CAROL AND NEIL OFFEN

4 It used to mean a suspicious-eyed old woman with knitting needles who hustled you upstairs to sleep in itchy sheets and had fried eggs ready for you in the morning—ready since the night before.
    On improvement of Britain's "bed and breakfast" hotels, Esquire Apr 86

GEORGE ORWELL

5 The crowds in the big towns, with their mild, knobby faces, their bad teeth and gentle manners . . . solid breakfasts and gloomy Sundays, smoky towns and winding roads, green fields and red pillar boxes.
    On England during the blitz in World War II, quoted in London Times 10 Jun 85

ROBERT PAYNE

6 Those who suffer from [islomania] can be recognized by the faraway look in their eyes, their horror of enclosed spaces and their lust for certain colors, such as royal blue with depths upon depths of gold in it, which can only be seen in the Aegean and along the coasts of Greece.
    The Isles of Greece Simon & Schuster 65

V S PRITCHETT

7 London landladies are Britannias armed with helmet, shield, trident, and have faces with the word "No" stamped like a coat of arms on them.
    London Perceived Harcourt, Brace & World 62

8 [London] is sentimental and tolerant. The attitude to foreigners is like the attitude to dogs: Dogs are neither human nor British, but so long as you keep them under control, give them their exercise, feed them, pat them, you will find their wild emotions are amusing, and their characters interesting.
    ib

9 The very name London has tonnage in it.
    ib

STEPHEN J PYNE

10 In Antarctica . . . foreground and background were difficult to establish . . . On shelf and plateau the vision was of an immutable nothingness.
    The Ice: A Journey to Antarctica University of Iowa 86, quoted in NY Times 25 Jan 87

DAVID QUAMMEN

11 Stonehenge nowadays is a zoo animal, an imposing but humbled beast, captive behind a wire fence and a turnstile, embarrassed by the near presence of a visitors' car park.
    Christian Science Monitor 12 May 80

JONATHAN RABAN

12 They'll like you because you're a foreigner. They love foreigners; it's just strangers they hate.
    Citing a subtle distinction given him on a Mississippi River cruise, Old Glory: An American Voyage Simon & Schuster 81

13 In this part of the country taxidermy seemed as much a part of everyday culture as psychoanalysis in Manhattan.
    Visiting hunters and fishermen in the upper Midwest, ib

IVAN ROWAN

14 It's very nearly a Cecil B De Mille set. . . . a fixed backdrop of unrelenting sky and distant cathedral, and against it, the figures in magenta cassocks flowing across the plains like extras turning up for camera call.
    On England's University of Kent as scene of 11th Lambeth Conference, London Sunday Telegraph 22 Jul 78

JOHN RUSSELL

15 The bedrooms are just large enough for a well-behaved dwarf and a greyhound on a diet.
    On modern European hotels, NY Times 4 Aug 77

ERNESTO SÁBATO

16 The first time I passed through the country I had the impression it was swept down with a broom from one end to the other every morning by housewives who dumped all the dirt on Italy.
    On Switzerland, On Heroes and Tombs Godine 81

MORLEY SAFER

17 Arrogance and snobbism live in adjoining rooms and use a common currency.
    On the Ritz Hotel in Paris, 60 Minutes CBS TV 27 Jul 80

18 Pilgrims who are looking for a cure are soon looking for a curio.
    On "objects of plastic piety" in Lourdes, ib 28 Dec 86

HARRISON E SALISBURY

19 Here when I walk the hutungs of a summer's evening as the moon rises over the city I can hear a lover's flute sending a tender message beyond the courtyard walls or the mournful monotony of a three-stringed lute.
    "Capturing Old Echoes in the New Peking" NY Times 10 Feb 85

20 On an early November evening, the wind brisk from the north toward the great Gobi, lights dim, only an occasional man or woman on a bicycle, hurrying through the narrow alley, eager to be home and out of the cold, what poet may be sitting beside a charcoal brazier within one of the courtyards, delicately placing his brush in the new mixed ink, stroking onto paper verses that will be read and remembered, say, in the year 3220?
    ib

JEAN PAUL SARTRE

1 It is disappointing to realize that, hidden beyond these magnificent and promising names, is the same checkerboard city, the same red and green traffic lights and the same provincial look.

> On Albuquerque NM, recalled when the city sought a plan for urban renewal, NY *Times* 5 Feb 85

DOROTHY L SAYERS

2 There . . . within a stone's throw, stood the twin towers of All Souls, fantastic, unreal as a house of cards, clear-cut in the sunshine, the drenched oval in the quad beneath brilliant as an emerald in the bezel of a ring.

> On Oxford University, from her 1935 book *Gaudy Night*, recalled on her death 17 Dec 57

SERGE SCHMEMANN

3 [Leningrad] sits astride the Neva, frozen in time, a haunting mélange of pale hues, glorious façades and teeming ghosts.

> "Majesty Fading from Russia's Window on the West" NY *Times* 7 Apr 84

STERLING SEAGRAVE

4 [A realm of] cliff-lined seascapes and misty peaks that unrolled each dawn from the scroll of night.

> On Taiwan, *The Soong Dynasty* Harper & Row 85, quoted in NY *Times* 29 Apr 85

ROBERT B SEMPLE JR

5 In Britain it will connect you to all sorts of people you had no intention of speaking to in the first place.

> On London's telephone system, NY *Times* 6 Aug 76

LUCKY SEVERSON

6 Nome is as far west as west goes before it becomes east.

> On Nome AK, *1986* NBC TV 30 Dec 86

7 If you don't believe hell freezes over, you haven't been to Nome.

> *ib*

PETER SHAFFER

8 If London is a watercolor, New York is an oil painting.

> NY *Times* 13 Apr 75

R Z SHEPPARD

9 The San Francisco Bay Area [is] the playpen of countercultures.

> *Time* 8 Sep 86

DAVID K SHIPLER

10 Jerusalem is a festival and a lamentation. Its song is a sigh across the ages, a delicate, robust, mournful psalm at the great junction of spiritual cultures.

> *Arab and Jew: Wounded Spirits in a Promised Land* Times Books 86

11 Here among the constant ruins and rebuilding of civilizations lies the coexistence of diversity and intolerance.

> *ib*

TERENCE SMITH

12 The whole peninsula . . . remains what it has always been: one of the last great wildernesses of the world, a place of stunning beauty and harsh reality where history, religion and modern politics come together as nowhere else.

> "The Harsh Splendor of the Sinai" NY *Times* 18 Nov 84

PETER STOREY

13 Once a place becomes special, it's no longer special.

> On transformation of Cannes from fishing village to stylish resort, quoted by C David Heymann *Poor Little Rich Girl* Lyle Stuart 84

HORACE SUTTON

14 Ireland's ruins are historic emotions surrendered to time.

> *Saturday Review* 25 Jun 66

15 A leopard sprawled in the crook of an acacia tree, rising now and then to bite on the remains of a gazelle he had tucked away in a nearby branch, as one would get up from a couch to find some inviting edible in the refrigerator.

> "Out of Africa, Out of This World" *Signature* Dec 85

JUDITH THURMAN

16 This is the river of the great 19th-century landscapists; of Cole, Cropsey and Church, and at the end of the summer it lies motionless under the haze as under a light coat of varnish.

> On the Hudson River, *House & Garden* Dec 84

TIME MAGAZINE

17 Spain is a land of mystery where the dust of isolation has often settled on men's work and obscured their lives.

> 6 Jul 53

ARNOLD TOYNBEE

18 The immense cities lie basking on the beaches of the continent like whales that have taken to the land.

> On Australia, *East to West* Oxford 58

19 Angkor is not orchestral; it is monumental. It is an epic poem which makes its effect, like the *Odyssey* and like *Paradise Lost*, by the grandeur of its structure as well as by the beauty of the details. . . . an epic in rectangular forms imposed upon the Cambodian jungle.

> *ib*

JOHN UPDIKE

20 The city overwhelmed our expectations. The Kiplingesque grandeur of Waterloo Station, the Eliotic despondency of the brick row in Chelsea . . . the Dickensian nightmare of fog and sweating pavement and besmirched cornices.

> On London, in "A Madman" *New Yorker* 22 Dec 62

ELIZABETH GRAY VINING

21 Heidelberg in May was foaming with fruit blossoms.

> *Take Heed of Loving Me* Lippincott 66

JOHN VINOCUR

22 Real life in Paris, the waiting-for-a-bus kind of existence that goes on without ever crossing the tracks

to the city's elegance and worldly ambitions, moves on its own, without manifestoes or injunctions to stop it.

NY *Times* 18 Mar 85

MARK WALLINGTON

1 If any one of them deserves to be a shrine, it's Paddington. . . . [Its] departure board reads like a romantic novel, as it flicks its way through Oxford, Bath, the Cotswolds and the very heart of England.

On London's 19th-century railroad stations, *In Britain* Jan 84

2 It's still an emotional sort of place, an unforgettable crossroads for any traveler, where shoppers from suburbia mix with international businessmen, where kids with buckets and spades mingle with passengers for the Orient Express and where city gents carrying brollies step over more colorful travelers carrying guitars. Spend the morning here and you'll see every stereotype on earth.

On Victoria Station, *ib*

GORDON WEBBER

3 Flat-out flatness, the hard line of the horizon. I like the little towns with their handfuls of buildings huddled close to the grain elevators, like medieval towns clustered around their cathedrals.

On small cities of the Dakota plains, *The Great Buffalo Hotel* Little, Brown 79

JOSEPH WECHSBERG

4 The duality of St Petersburg and Leningrad remains. . . . They are not even on speaking terms.

In Leningrad Doubleday 77

5 Old St Petersburg remains a beautiful stage set . . . but to the Russians it is not what Rome is to the Italians or Paris to the French. The decisions are made in the Kremlin. The city of Peter remains a museum, open from 8:00 AM to 5:00 PM.

ib

TERRY WEEKS

6 The city in winter is rich with the bittersweet nuance and somber beauty of the once-was.

"Winter in Venice" *Gourmet* Jan 86

7 Here, seated on red velvet banquettes at marble-topped tables, one can't help wonder what sights these smoky, gilded mirrors have reflected for more than 250 years.

On Florian, a legendary café, *ib*

JESSAMYN WEST

8 The West is color. . . . Its colors are animal rather than vegetable, the colors of earth and sunlight and ripeness.

"The West—A Place to Hang Your Dreams" *Woman's Home Companion* May 56

PAUL WEST

9 Men in flat caps and collarless shirts wander around with a sprig of hawthorn between their teeth, their hands clamped behind them. . . . All you have to do is say "Ah," mingling pity, rage and stoicism in one breath, and everyone within earshot will echo you.

On Eckington, England, NY *Times* 8 Jul 84

PETER WESTBROOK, manager of London's Waldorf Hotel

10 So much of our future lies in preserving our past.

Christian Science Monitor 30 Jun 81

THEODORE H WHITE

11 I saw Chungking [now Chongqing] for the first time more than 40 years ago—a city of hills and mists, of grays and lavenders, 2 rivers shaping it to a point and the cliff rising above me like a challenge.

"Chongqing Transformed" NY *Times* 10 Feb 85

CRAIG R WHITNEY

12 A city of private lives, led in quiet resignation.

On Dresden, East Germany, NY *Times* 6 Nov 76

Humankind

FAMILY LIFE

Family Members

WERNHER VON BRAUN

1 For my confirmation, I didn't get a watch and my first pair of long pants, like most Lutheran boys. I got a telescope. My mother thought it would make the best gift.
Time 17 Feb 58

CAROL BURNETT

2 [This is to explain] just how your mom turned out to be the kind of hairpin she is.
Note to her daughters in *One More Time* Random House 86, quoted in NY *Times* 19 Oct 86

LILLIAN CARTER

3 Sometimes when I look at all my children, I say to myself, "Lillian, you should have stayed a virgin."
Comment to 1980 Democratic Convention that nominated her son for a second term as president, quoted in *Newsweek* 29 Dec 80

WHITTAKER CHAMBERS

4 When you understand what you see, you will no longer be children. You will know that life is pain, that each of us hangs always upon the cross of himself. And when you know that this is true of every man, woman and child on earth, you will be wiser.
Letter to his children, *Witness* Random House 52

JOHN CHEEVER

5 When I remember my family, I always remember their backs. They were always indignantly leaving places.
Quoted by Susan Cheever *Home before Dark* Houghton Mifflin 84

6 That's the way I remember them, heading for an exit.
ib

WINSTON CHURCHILL

7 Death came very easily to her. She had lived such an innocent and loving life of service to others and held such a simple faith, that she had no fears at all and did not seem to mind very much.
On death of his nanny Elizabeth Everest, quoted by William Manchester *The Last Lion* Little, Brown 83

8 It is a gaping wound, whenever one touches it and removes the bandages and plasters of daily life.
April 4, 1922, letter to his wife Clementine after his daughter Marigold's death, *ib*

MAY ROPER COKER

9 I never thought that you should be rewarded for the greatest privilege of life.
On being chosen Mother of the Year, NY *Daily News* 7 May 58

CLAUDETTE COLBERT

10 Why do grandparents and grandchildren get along so well? They have the same enemy—the mother.
Time 14 Sep 81

PAT CONROY

11 My mother thought of my father as half barbarian and half blunt instrument, and she isolated him from his children.
Book-of-the-Month Club News Dec 86

12 The children of warriors in our country learn the grace and caution that come from a permanent sense of estrangement.
ib

MARIO CUOMO, Governor of NY

13 I watched a small man with thick calluses on both hands work 15 and 16 hours a day. I saw him once literally bleed from the bottoms of his feet, a man who came here uneducated, alone, unable to speak the language, who taught me all I needed to know about faith and hard work by the simple eloquence of his example.
Commenting on his father, address to Democratic National Convention 16 Jul 84

14 I talk and talk and talk, and I haven't taught people in 50 years what my father taught by example in one week.
Time 2 Jun 86

15 I am a trial lawyer. . . . Matilda says that at dinner on a good day I sound like an affidavit.
NY *Times* 10 Nov 86

LOUISE SEVIER GIDDINGS CURREY

16 Spoil your husband, but don't spoil your children—that's my philosophy.
On being chosen Mother of the Year, NY *Post* 14 May 61

BETTE DAVIS

17 If you've never been hated by your child, you've never been a parent.
On publication of her daughter B D Hyman's book, CBS TV 5 May 85

DOROTHY DEBOLT

18 Of course I don't always enjoy being a mother. At those times my husband and I hole up somewhere in the wine country, eat, drink, make mad love and pretend we were born sterile and raise poodles.
On receiving 1980 National Mother's Day Committee Award as the natural mother of 6 and adoptive mother of 14, San Francisco *Chronicle* 22 Apr 80

YVONNE DE GAULLE

19 The presidency is temporary—but the family is permanent.
On her priorities as wife of French President Charles de Gaulle, quoted by Richard M Nixon *RN: Memoirs of Richard Nixon* Grosset & Dunlap 78

FRANCO DILIGENTI

1 They were becoming like a little Mafia. If one committed a mischief, the others would not tell.

> On why he sent his quintuplets to separate schools when they reached the age of seven, *Saturday Evening Post* 25 Jan 64

2 A man who has raised quintuplets has had enough of babies.

> *ib*

OLIVA DIONNE

3 I ought to be shot.

> On becoming father of quintuplets in 1934, recalled on his death 15 Nov 79

JILL EIKENBERRY

4 You have a wonderful child. Then, when he's 13, gremlins carry him away and leave in his place a stranger who gives you not a moment's peace.

> On raising teenagers, *Parade* 12 Jul 87

5 You have to hang in there, because two or three years later, the gremlins will return your child, and he will be wonderful again.

> *ib*

DWIGHT D EISENHOWER, 34th US President

6 I have found out in later years [that] we were very poor, but the glory of America is that we didn't know it then.

> On his childhood, *Time* 16 Jun 52

7 Our pleasures were simple—they included survival.

> On his childhood, *At Ease: Stories I Tell to Friends* Doubleday 67

8 That was and still is the great disaster of my life— that lovely, lovely little boy.

> On the death of his first son, recalled on *Ike* PBS TV 15 Oct 86

9 There's no tragedy in life like the death of a child. Things never get back to the way they were.

> *ib*

EARL EISENHOWER

10 The story of my boyhood and that of my brothers is important only because it could happen in any American family. It did, and will again.

> On growing up with Dwight and his other brothers, *American Weekly* 4 Apr 54

ELIZABETH II, Queen of England

11 They are not royal. They just happen to have me as their aunt.

> On children of Princess Margaret and Lord Snowdon, London *Daily Mail* 4 Oct 77

CLIFTON FADIMAN

12 My son is 7 years old. I am 54. It has taken me a great many years to reach that age. I am more respected in the community, I am stronger, I am more intelligent and I think I am better than he is. I don't want to be a pal, I want to be a father.

> *Newsweek* 16 Jun 58

GERALD R FORD, 38th US President

13 All my children have spoken for themselves since they first learned to speak, and not always with my advance approval, and I expect that to continue in the future.

> NY *Post* 13 Aug 74

HENRY FORD II

14 My grandfather killed my father in my mind. I know he died of cancer—but it was because of what my grandfather did to him.

> On Henry and Edsel Ford, quoted by Robert Lacey *Ford: The Men and the Machine* Little, Brown 86

SAM FRUSTACI

15 We thought it might be fun to have twins.

> On his wife's use of fertility pills that led to septuplets, the largest multiple birth in US history, *Time* 3 Jun 85

MAVIS GALLANT

16 [My father] had spent his own short time like a priest in charge of a relic, forever expecting the blessed blood to liquefy.

> *Home Truths* Random House 85, quoted in NY *Times* 5 May 85

VARTAN GREGORIAN

17 There she was in her bed. Dead. But nobody explained it to me. They told me later that she had gone to America.

> On his mother's death when he was age seven, *New Yorker* 14 Apr 86

HELEN HAYES

18 There's a little vanity chair that Charlie gave me the first Christmas we knew each other. I'll not be parting with that, nor our bed—the four-poster—I'll be needing that to die in.

> On auctioning furnishings of the house she shared with her husband Charles MacArthur, NY *Times* 21 Oct 63

19 When Charles first saw our child Mary, he said all the proper things for a new father. He looked upon the poor little red thing and blurted, "She's more beautiful than the Brooklyn Bridge."

> Quoted by Nancy Caldwell Sorel *Ever Since Eve: Personal Reflections on Childbirth* Oxford 84

20 Life . . . would give her everything of consequence, life would shape her, not we. All we were good for was to make the introductions.

> *ib*

KATHARINE HOUGHTON HEPBURN

21 If you want to sacrifice the admiration of many men for the criticism of one, go ahead, get married.

> Advice to her daughter Katharine before the actress's 1928 marriage to Ludlow Ogden Smith, quoted by Anne Edwards *A Remarkable Woman* Morrow 85

MARY JARRELL

22 Jarrell was not so much a father . . . as an affectionate encyclopedia.

> On her husband, *Randall Jarrell's Letters* Houghton Mifflin 85

CLAUDIA ("LADY BIRD") JOHNSON

23 This is something that I cherish. Once in a friend's home I came across this blessing, and took it down

in shorthand . . . it says something I like to live with: "Oh Thou, who dwellest in so many homes, possess Thyself of this. Bless the life that is sheltered here. Grant that trust and peace and comfort abide within, and that love and life and usefulness may go out from this home forever."

On her family's home, CBS TV 12 Aug 64

LYNDON B JOHNSON, 36th US President

1 This is a moment that I deeply wish my parents could have lived to share. My father would have enjoyed what you have so generously said of me—and my mother would have believed it.

Commencement address at Baylor University 28 May 65

NATASHA JOSEFOWITZ

2 My father died
many years ago,
and yet when something special
happens to me,
I talk to him secretly
not really knowing
whether he hears,
but it makes me feel better
to half believe it.

Is This Where I Was Going? Warner 83

JULIANA, Queen of the Netherlands

3 Our child will not be raised in tissue paper! We don't even want her to hear the word princess.

On hiring a nurse for her first child, Ladies' Home Journal Mar 55

EDWARD M KENNEDY, US Senator

4 Dad, I'm in some trouble. There's been an accident and you're going to hear all sorts of things about me from now on. Terrible things.

Informing his father of Chappaquiddick incident in which Mary Jo Kopechne was drowned, quoted by Peter Collier and David Horowitz The Kennedys Summit 84

JACQUELINE KENNEDY

5 Dear God, please take care of your servant John Fitzgerald Kennedy.

Inscription for mass cards at her husband's funeral 25 Nov 63

JOHN F KENNEDY JR

6 The three of us have been alone for such a long time. We welcome a fourth person.

Toast to Edwin Schlossberg at rehearsal dinner for his wedding to Caroline Kennedy, quoted in People 4 Aug 86

JOSEPH P KENNEDY

7 Jack doesn't belong anymore to just a family. He belongs to the country.

Comment a few weeks before his son's inauguration, quoted by Hugh Sidey John F Kennedy, President Atheneum 63

8 If there's anything I'd hate as a son-in-law, it's an actor; and if there's anything I think I'd hate worse

than an actor as a son-in-law, it's an English actor.

Tongue-in-cheek comment on Patricia Kennedy's marriage to English actor Peter Lawford, ib

9 He may be president, but he still comes home and swipes my socks.

On his son John, ib

10 He's a great kid. He hates the same way I do.

On his son Bobby, quoted by Richard J Whalen The Founding Father New American Library 64

ROSE KENNEDY

11 I looked on child rearing not only as a work of love and duty but as a profession that was fully as interesting and challenging as any honorable profession in the world and one that demanded the best that I could bring to it.

Times to Remember Doubleday 74

12 Make sure you never, never argue at night. You just lose a good night's sleep, and you can't settle anything until morning anyway.

Advice to her first married granddaughter, People 6 Jun 83

LOUISE HEATH LEBER

13 There's always room for improvement, you know—it's the biggest room in the house.

On being chosen Mother of the Year, NY Post 14 May 61

MADELEINE L'ENGLE

14 I love my mother, not as a prisoner of atherosclerosis, but as a person; and I must love her enough to accept her as she is, now, for as long as this dwindling may take.

The Summer of the Great-Grandmother Farrar, Straus & Giroux 74

15 She seems to have had the ability to stand firmly on the rock of her past while living completely and unregretfully in the present.

ib

CHARLES A LINDBERGH

16 He makes fuzz come out of my bald patch!

On his son's driving ability, quoted by Leonard Mosley Lindbergh Doubleday 76

ALISON LURIE

17 There is a peculiar burning odor in the room, like explosives. . . . the kitchen fills with smoke and the hot, sweet, ashy smell of scorched cookies. The war has begun.

On a wife's discovery of her husband's infidelity, The War between the Tates Warner 74

DOUGLAS MACARTHUR

18 Build me a son, O Lord, who will be strong enough to know when he is weak, and brave enough to face himself when he is afraid, one who will be proud and unbending in honest defeat, and humble and gentle in victory.

"A Father's Prayer," quoted by Courtney Whitney MacArthur Knopf 55

PETER MALKIN

19 Even a secret agent can't lie to a Jewish mother.

On his mother's suspicion that he was going on an important mission, NY Times 28 Apr 86

QUEEN MARY

1 Her old Grannie and subject must be the first to kiss her hand.

> On Elizabeth II's return to London from Kenya after her accession to the throne, quoted by John Pearson *The Selling of the Royal Family* Simon & Schuster 86

2 You are a member of the British royal family. We are *never* tired, and we all *love* hospitals.

> Reply to a protest of weariness with public engagements, *ib*

PHYLLIS MCGINLEY

3 God knows that a mother needs fortitude and courage and tolerance and flexibility and patience and firmness and nearly every other brave aspect of the human soul. But because I happen to be a parent of almost fiercely maternal nature, I praise *casualness*. It seems to me the rarest of virtues. It is useful enough when children are small. It is important to the point of necessity when they are adolescents.

> *McCall's* May 59

4 To be a housewife is . . . a difficult, a wrenching, sometimes an ungrateful job if it is looked on only as a job. Regarded as a profession, it is the noblest as it is the most ancient of the catalogue. Let none persuade us differently or the world is lost indeed.

> *Sixpence in Her Shoe* Macmillan 64

MARGARET MEAD

5 The pains of childbirth were altogether different from the enveloping effects of other kinds of pain. These were pains one could follow with one's mind.

> Quoted by Nancy Caldwell Sorel *Ever Since Eve: Personal Reflections on Childbirth* Oxford 84

LIZA MINNELLI

6 Whenever we were on a plane, we had a family.

> On life with her mother Judy Garland and father Vincente Minnelli, NBC TV 15 Jan 74

CHARLOTTE MONTGOMERY

7 One of my children wrote in a third-grade piece on how her mother spent her time. . . . "one-half time on home, one-half time on outside things, one-half time writing."

> *Good Housekeeping* May 59

JERROLD MUNDIS

8 I am years gone from my family and miles away . . . but they raid by telephone with jarring suddenness; they have the cyclic constancy of a mortgage; and they are inevitable and relentless, like the erosion of my remaining youth. Like certain frightening dreams, my family returns.

> *Gerhardt's Children* Atheneum 76

FRANK NIXON

9 This boy is one of five that I raised and they are the finest, I think, in the United States. If you care to give him a lift I would say the *Ohio State Journal* is still doing some good.

> Letter commending his son's 1953 vice-presidential candidacy, quoted by Richard M Nixon *RN: Memoirs of Richard Nixon* Grosset & Dunlap 78

HANNAH NIXON

10 I am sure you will be guided right in your decision, to place implicit faith in his integrity and honesty. Best wishes from one who has known Richard longer than anyone else. His mother.

> Telegram to Republican presidential candidate Dwight D Eisenhower, her son's running mate, on investigation of an alleged secret fund, quoted by Richard M Nixon *RN: Memoirs of Richard Nixon* Grosset & Dunlap 78

11 You have gone far and we are proud of you always. I know that you will keep your relationship with your Maker as it should be, for after all, that, as you must know, is the most important thing in this life.

> Note to her son on his inauguration as vice president on January 20, 1953, *ib*

RICHARD M NIXON, 37th US President

12 President Johnson and I have a lot in common. We were both born in small towns . . . and we're both fortunate in the fact that we think we married above ourselves.

> 5 Sep 69

13 I had come so far from the little house in Yorba Linda to this great house in Washington.

> On August 9, 1974, his last morning in the White House, *RN: Memoirs of Richard Nixon* Grosset & Dunlap 78

14 [He had] the poorest lemon ranch in California, I can assure you. He sold it before they found oil on it.

> On his father, address to White House staff, *ib*

15 I think of her, two boys dying of tuberculosis, nursing four others . . . she was a saint.

> On his mother, *ib*

NOOR, Queen of Jordan

16 Our planning may leave something to be desired, but our designs, thank God, have been flawless.

> On birth of fourth child in six years, *Time* 10 Mar 86

RICHARD OLTON

17 When I held you in my arms at your baptism, I wanted it to be a fresh start, for you to be more complete than we had ever been ourselves, but I wonder if we expected too much.

> Eulogy for 18-year-old nephew who committed suicide, quoted by James S Newton "Three Suicide Victims Buried in Jersey" NY *Times* 15 Mar 87

ALEXANDER ONASSIS

18 My father loves names and Jackie loves money.

> On marriage of his father Aristotle Onassis to Jacqueline Kennedy, quoted by Peter Evans *Ari* Summit 86

KATHERINE D ORTEGA, Treasurer of the US

19 In the next year or so, my signature will appear on $60 billion of United States currency. More important to me, however, is the signature that appears on my life—the strong, proud, assertive handwriting of a loving father and mother.

> Quoted by William Safire NY *Times* 19 Aug 84

MARGUERITE OSWALD

20 Lee was such a fine, high-class boy. . . . If my son killed the president he would have said so. That's the way he was brought up.

> On Lee Harvey Oswald, alleged assassin of President John F Kennedy, *Time* 13 Dec 63

1 Mr Johnson should remember that I am not just anyone and that he is only president of the United States
by the grace of my son's action.

On Lyndon B Johnson, *ib* 14 Feb 64

PABLO PICASSO

2 You can touch them with your eyes.

Forbidding his daughter Paloma to use his art materials
as playthings, recalled by her on *Live at Five* WNBC
TV 10 Dec 86

RAINIER, Prince of Monaco

3 I can be a good father but I'm a terrible mother.

After his daughter Stephanie went swimming fully clad
alongside models wearing swimwear she had designed,
Life Oct 85

RONALD REAGAN, 40th US President

4 You get a little stir crazy during the week.

On living in the White House, NY *Times* 27 Sep 83

5 Seventy-five years ago I was born in Tampico, Illinois, in a little flat above the bank building. We
didn't have any other contact with the bank than
that.

On his birthplace, NY *Times* 7 Feb 86

6 Now, here I am, sort of living above the store again.

ib

7 We were poor when I was young, but the difference
then was the government didn't come around telling
you you were poor.

Time 7 Jul 86

ARTUR RUBINSTEIN

8 It took great courage to ask a beautiful young woman to marry me. Believe me, it is easier to play the
whole of Petrushka on the piano.

Quoted by Samuel Chotzinoff *A Little Nightmusic* Harper & Row 64

9 The result was magnificent . . . I became the father
of two girls and two boys, lovely children—by good
fortune they all look like my wife.

ib

ANTONIN SCALIA

10 [In a big family] the first child is kind of like the first
pancake. If it's not perfect, that's okay, there are a
lot more coming along.

Recalled on his appointment to US Supreme Court,
Newsweek 30 Jun 86

WALTER M SCHIRRA SR

11 You don't raise heroes, you raise sons. And if you
treat them like sons, they'll turn out to be heroes,
even if it's just in your own eyes.

This Week 3 Feb 63

MAUDE SHAW

12 Your daddy's upstairs. You can call him "Mr President" now.

To Caroline Kennedy on morning after 1960 presidential
election, quoted by Ralph G Martin *A Hero for Our
Time* Macmillan 83

EARL SIMPSON

13 They say the best product off a farm is the children.

After losing 90 percent of corn crop to drought, quoted
by Hugh Sidey "Bitter Harvest" *Time* 8 Sep 86

STEPHEN SPENDER

14 When a child, my dreams rode on your wishes,
I was your son, high on your horse,
My mind a top whipped by the lashes
Of your rhetoric, windy of course.

On his father, from "The Public Son of a Public Man,"
quoted in *Time* 20 Jan 86

MARGARET THATCHER, Prime Minister of Great Britain

15 I just owe almost everything to my father [and] it's
passionately interesting for me that the things that I
learned in a small town, in a very modest home, are
just the things that I believe have won the election.

Quoted in *New Yorker* 10 Feb 86

HARRY S TRUMAN, 33rd US President

16 It is terrible—and I mean terrible—nuisance to be
kin to the president of the United States.

Letter to his mother and sister two weeks after assuming the presidency in 1945, *Year of Decision* Doubleday
55

17 I have found the best way to give advice to your
children is to find out what they want and then advise them to do it.

CBS TV 27 May 55

18 My father was not a failure. After all, he was the
father of a president of the United States.

Mr Citizen Geis 60

19 It seems like there was always somebody for supper.

On life in the White House, quoted by Merriman Smith
The Good New Days Bobbs-Merrill 62

20 I was the only calm one in the house. You see I've
been shot at by experts.

Recalling service in World War I after assassination attempt on November 1, 1950, quoted by Margaret Truman *Bess W Truman* Macmillan 86

21 We're going to be buried out here. I like the idea
because I may just want to get up some day and
stroll into my office. And I can hear you saying,
"Harry—you oughtn't!"

To his wife, on plans to be buried together at Truman
Library, Independence MO, *ib*

MARGARET TRUMAN

22 It's only when you grow up, and step back from him,
or leave him for your own career and your own
home—it's only then that you can measure his greatness and fully appreciate it. Pride reinforces love.

Address to joint session of Congress on centennial of
birth of her father President Harry S Truman, 8 May
84

GLORIA VANDERBILT

23 And it came to me, and I knew what I had to have
before my soul would rest. I wanted to belong—to
belong to my mother. And in return—I wanted my
mother to belong to me.

Once Upon a Time Knopf 85

EVELYN WAUGH

1 Of children as of procreation—the pleasure momentary, the posture ridiculous, the expense damnable.
> May 5, 1954, letter to Nancy Mitford, news summaries 31 Dec 54

MARY BETH WHITEHEAD

2 I gave her life, I can take life away.
> On her role as surrogate mother to Baby M, quoted in Washington *Post* 14 Oct 86

MARY GILLIGAN WONG

3 My husband would be Catholic and, I hoped, Irish, and if he happened to have played for Notre Dame, so much the better.
> *Nun* Harcourt Brace Jovanovich 83

4 We would have a picture of the Sacred Heart in the living room and holy-water fonts by each doorway, we would say the family rosary together every night and every Thursday night we would watch Bishop Fulton J Sheen on television.
> *ib*

JAMES C WRIGHT JR, Speaker of the House

5 That was the year when our family ate the piano.
> On his childhood during the Great Depression, NY *Times* 10 Dec 86

Observers & Critics

LADY MABELL AIRLIE

6 As the cortege wound slowly along, the queen whispered in a broken voice, "Here *he* is," and I knew that her dry eyes were seeing beyond the coffin a little boy in a sailor suit.
> On Queen Mary as she watched the funeral procession of her son King George VI, *Thatched With Gold* Hutchinson 62

7 She was past weeping, wrapped in the ineffable solitude of grief.
> *ib*

ANONYMOUS

8 Slow, Grandparents at Play
> Traffic sign in Orange Harbor FL mobile-home park, quoted in NY *Times* 24 Sep 84

9 Listen to me, little fetus,
Precious *homo incompletus*,
As you dream your dreams placental
Don't grow nothing accidental!
> Poem by prospective father, quoted by Jerry Adler "Every Parent's Nightmare" *Newsweek* 16 Mar 87

AHARON APPELFELD

10 People who lose their parents when young are permanently in love with them.
> *To the Land of the Cattails* Weidenfeld & Nicolson 86, quoted by Herbert Mitgang "Writing Holocaust Memories" NY *Times* 15 Nov 86

BARBARA LAZEAR ASCHER

11 The hot, moist smell of babies fresh from naps.
> *Playing after Dark* Doubleday 86, quoted in *Christian Science Monitor* 20 Aug 86

VIOLET ASQUITH

12 In his solitary childhood and unhappy school days Mrs Everest was his comforter, his strength and stay, his one source of unfailing human understanding. She was the fireside at which he dried his tears and warmed his heart. She was the night-light by his bed. She was security.
> On Winston Churchill's nanny Elizabeth Everest, quoted by William Manchester *The Last Lion* Little, Brown 83

LOUIS AUCHINCLOSS

13 With her high pale brow under her faded brown hair, she was like a rock washed clean by years of [her husband's] absences at conventions, dinners, committee meetings or simply at the office.
> *The Book Class* Houghton Mifflin 84

JOSEPH BARTH

14 Marriage is our last, best chance to grow up.
> *Ladies' Home Journal* Apr 61

ALAN BECK

15 Boys are found everywhere—on top of, underneath, inside of, climbing on, swinging from, running around or jumping to. Mothers love them, little girls hate them, older sisters and brothers tolerate them, adults ignore them and Heaven protects them. A boy is Truth with dirt on its face, Beauty with a cut on its finger, Wisdom with bubble gum in its hair and the Hope of the future with a frog in its pocket.
> "What Is a Boy?" pamphlet distributed by New England Life Insurance Co Boston 56

16 A boy is a magical creature—you can lock him out of your workshop, but you can't lock him out of your heart. You can get him out of your study, but you can't get him out of your mind. Might as well give up—he is your captor, your jailer, your boss and your master—a freckled-faced, pint-sized, cat-chasing bundle of noise. But when you come home at night with only the shattered pieces of your hopes and dreams, he can mend them like new with two magic words—"Hi, Dad!"
> *ib*

17 Little girls are the nicest things that happen to people. They are born with a little bit of angelshine about them, and though it wears thin sometimes there is always enough left to lasso your heart—even when they are sitting in the mud, or crying temperamental tears, or parading up the street in mother's best clothes.
> "What Is a Girl?" *ib*

18 A little girl can be sweeter (and badder) oftener than anyone else in the world. She can jitter around, and stomp, and make funny noises that frazzle your nerves, yet just when you open your mouth she stands there demure with that special look in her eyes. A girl is Innocence playing in the mud, Beauty standing on its head, and Motherhood dragging a doll by the foot.
> *ib*

19 What is a husband? He is the one who, with a touch, can bring back the starlight and glow of years long ago. At least he hopes he can—don't disappoint him.
> "What Is a Husband?" *Good Housekeeping* Jul 57

1 A girl becomes a wife with her eyes wide open. She knows that those sweetest words, "I take thee to be my wedded husband," really mean, "I promise thee to cook three meals a day for 60 years; thee will I clean up after; thee will I talk to even when thou art not listening; thee will I worry about, cry over and take all manner of hurts from."

"What Is a Wife?" *ib*

JAY BELSKY

2 Something's got to give, as they acquire a new role and the joys and burdens of their role. What gives is the marriage.

On women who work outside the home, NY *Times* 6 Jan 85

JIM BISHOP

3 Nobody understands anyone 18, including those who are 18.

"Age of Consent to What?" Shrewsbury NJ *Daily Register* 26 Apr 79

4 When you read about a car crash in which two or three youngsters are killed, do you pause to dwell on the amount of love and treasure and patience parents poured into bodies no longer suitable for open caskets?

ib

MARY KAY BLAKELY

5 Divorce is the psychological equivalent of a triple coronary by-pass. After such a monumental assault on the heart, it takes years to amend all the habits and attitudes that led up to it.

Quoted in *Parade* 12 Jul 87

HEINRICH BÖLL

6 His memories had never hinged on words and pictures, only on movement. Father was Father's gait, the spritely curve described, each step, by his right trouser leg.

Billiards at Half-Past Nine McGraw-Hill 62, recalled on his death, NY *Times* 17 Jul 85

NADIA BOULANGER

7 Loving a child doesn't mean giving in to all his whims; to love him is to bring out the best in him, to teach him to love what is difficult.

Quoted by Bruno Monsaingeon *Mademoiselle* Carcanet 85

HAL BOYLE

8 Whatever happened to that old-fashioned Grandpa? If he still survives, he must be hiding in the small towns. You sure don't see him very often in the big city. The big-city Grandpa has gone big time. . . . He is the life of every party, and out to prove he is just as young as he ever was. A grandchild who makes the mistake of calling him "Gramps" is lucky if he isn't rewarded by a quick kick in the stomach.

"Those Modern Grandpas" NY *Journal-American* 31 Jul 59

9 Does Grandpa love to baby-sit his grandchildren? Are you kidding? By day he is too busy taking hormone shots at the doctor's or chip shots on the golf course. At night he and Grandma are too busy doing the cha-cha.

ib

10 I used to envy kids who had an old-fashioned Grandpa. Not any more. I've got a new ambition. Now I just want to become a modern-type Grandpa myself—and really start living.

ib

ANTHONY BRANDT

11 Other things may change us, but we start and end with the family.

"Bloodlines" *Esquire* Sep 84

12 The most powerful ties are the ones to the people who gave us birth . . . it hardly seems to matter how many years have passed, how many betrayals there may have been, how much misery in the family: We remain connected, even against our wills.

ib

BARNETT BRICKNER

13 Success in marriage does not come merely through finding the right mate, but through being the right mate.

Quoted in Samuel Silver comp *The Quoteable American Rabbis* Droke House 67

BRITISH FAMILY PLANNING ASSOCIATION

14 Would you be more careful if it was you that got pregnant?

Urging birth control by men, advertisement quoted in *Time* 28 Apr 86

JOHN MASON BROWN

15 The comic book [is] the marijuana of the nursery, the bane of the bassinet, the horror of the home, the curse of the kids and a threat to the future.

News summaries 30 Nov 52

ANATOLE BROYARD

16 The first divorce in the world may have been a tragedy, but the hundred-millionth is not necessarily one.

On overemphasis on divorce in contemporary fiction, NY *Times* 25 Jun 80

PATRICIA L BRUECKNER

17 Knowing children
Surfeited with everything
Money could buy,
I rejoiced
At the children of poverty
Seeing their genius
As they invented games
Out of everything
Confronting them
In their joyous world
Of bare toughness of life
Light, sweet voices
Singing skip rope,
Throw the pie plate,
Pitch a stone
At the crack in the street,
Collect the broken bits of glass
And always,
Like a Jungian racial memory,
The elegant precision of hopscotch.

Privately published 64

GAIL LUMET BUCKLEY

1 Whites they pretended to ignore, as they busily lived mirror-image white lives.
The Hornes: An American Family Knopf 86

2 Family faces are magic mirrors. Looking at people who belong to us, we see the past, present and future.
ib

ROBERT C BYRD, US Senator

3 One's family is the most important thing in life. I look at it this way: One of these days I'll be over in a hospital somewhere with four walls around me. And the only people who'll be with me will be my family.
NY *Times* 27 Mar 77

MARY S CALDERONE

4 Our children are not going to be just "our children"—they are going to be other people's husbands and wives and the parents of our grandchildren.
NBC TV 18 Jan 74

RACHEL CARSON

5 If a child is to keep alive his inborn sense of wonder, he needs the companionship of at least one adult who can share it, rediscovering with him the joy, excitement and mystery of the world we live in.
The Sense of Wonder Harper & Row 65

STANLEY H CATH

6 Middle age is Janus-faced. As we look back on our accomplishments and our failures to achieve the things we wanted, we look ahead to the time we have left to us. . . . Our children are gaining life, and our parents are losing it.
NY *Times* 18 Apr 83

CHILDREN'S DEFENSE FUND

7 Will your child learn to multiply before she learns to subtract?
Poster on teen pregnancies, quoted in *Christian Science Monitor* 13 Mar 86

JEROME CHODOROV and JOSEPH FIELDS

8 I'll tell you the real secret of how to stay married. Keep the cave clean. They want the cave clean and spotless. Air-conditioned, if possible. Sharpen his spear, and stick it in his hand when he goes out in the morning to spear that bear; and when the bear chases him, console him when he comes home at night, and tell him what a big man he is, and then hide the spear so he doesn't fall over it and stab himself.
Anniversary Waltz Random House 54

FRANCIS X CLINES

9 He sits at the kitchen table, which is the only authentic way to touch down at home in Queens.
On a man's return home from prolonged hospitalization, NY *Times* 16 Jun 79

COLETTE

10 The faults of husbands are often caused by the excess virtues of their wives.
Recalled on her death 3 Aug 54

LAURIE COLWIN

11 That family glaze of common references, jokes, events, calamities—that sense of a family being like a kitchen midden: layer upon layer of the things daily life is made of. The edifice that lovers build is by comparison delicate and one-dimensional.
The Lone Pilgrim Knopf 81

HENRY STEELE COMMAGER

12 It's awfully hard to be the son of a great man and also of a half-crazy woman.
On Robert Todd Lincoln, NY *Times* 12 Feb 85

JOHN CORRY

13 Loneliness seems to have become the great American disease.
On NBC TV documentary *Second Thoughts on Being Single*, NY *Times* 25 Apr 84

JO COUDERT

14 The divorced person is like a man with a black patch over one eye: He looks rather dashing but the fact is that he has been through a maiming experience.
Advice from a Failure Stein & Day 65

QUENTIN CREWE

15 The children despise their parents until the age of 40, when they suddenly become just like them—thus preserving the system.
On British upper class, *Saturday Evening Post* 1 Dec 62

PATRICK DENNIS

16 The Upsons lived the way every family in America wants to live—not rich, but well-to-do. They had two of everything: two addresses, the flat on Park and a house in Connecticut; two cars, a Buick sedan and a Ford station wagon; two children, a boy and a girl; two servants, man and maid; two clubs, town and country; and two interests, money and position.
Auntie Mame Vanguard 55

17 Mrs Upson had two fur coats and two chins. Mr Upson had two chins, two passions—gold and business—and two aversions, Roosevelt and Jews.
ib

ANN DIEHL

18 I think we're seeing in working mothers a change from "Thank God it's Friday" to "Thank God it's Monday." If any working mother has not experienced that feeling, her children are not adolescent.
Vogue Jan 85

MARLENE DIETRICH

19 A king, realizing his incompetence, can either delegate or abdicate his duties. A father can do neither. If only sons could see the paradox, they would understand the dilemma.
NY *Journal-American* 21 Jun 64

MARGARET DRABBLE

20 Family life itself, that safest, most traditional, most approved of female choices, is not a sanctuary: It is, perpetually, a dangerous place.
Christian Science Monitor 10 Apr 85

DAVID ELKIND, Professor of Child Study, Tufts University

1 We see these adolescents mourning for a lost childhood.

> On children "pushed into sports or music or academics," quoted in NY *Times* 24 Sep 84

RALPH ELLISON

2 Some people are your relatives but others are your ancestors, and you choose the ones you want to have as ancestors. You create yourself out of those values.

> *Time* 27 Mar 64

DELIA EPHRON

3 As complicated as joint custody is, it allows the delicious contradiction of having children and maintaining the intimacy of life-before-kids.

> *Funny Sauce* Viking 86, quoted in NY *Times* 14 Sep 86

4 Your basic extended family today includes your ex-husband or -wife, your ex's new mate, your new mate, possibly your new mate's ex and any new mate that your new mate's ex has acquired.

> *ib* 12 Oct 86

5 [It] consists entirely of people who are not related by blood, many of whom can't stand each other.

> *ib*

NORA EPHRON

6 Summer bachelors, like summer breezes, are never as cool as they pretend to be.

> "The Truth about Summer Bachelors" NY *Post* 22 Aug 65

7 There are plenty of men who philander during the summer, to be sure, but they are usually the same lot who philander during the winter—albeit with less convenience.

> *ib*

TONI FALBO, Associate Professor, University of Texas

8 The only child is a world issue now.

> On importance of population control, NY *Times* 13 Aug 84

ELIZABETH FISHEL

9 A sister is both your mirror—and your opposite.

> *People* 2 Jun 80

10 Comparison is a death knell to sibling harmony.

> *ib*

TREVOR FISHLOCK

11 Babies here seem to be almost as rare as panda cubs.

> On New York City, London *Times* 9 May 85

F SCOTT FITZGERALD

12 Family quarrels are bitter things. They don't go according to any rules. They're not like aches or wounds, they're more like splits in the skin that won't heal because there's not enough material.

> Quoted by Nancy Milford *Zelda* Harper & Row 70

BETTY FRIEDAN

13 Each suburban wife struggled with it alone. As she made the beds, shopped for groceries, matched slip-cover material, ate peanut butter sandwiches with her children, chauffered Cub Scouts and Brownies, lay beside her husband at night—she was afraid to ask even of herself the silent question—"Is this all?"

> *The Feminine Mystique* Norton 63

14 American housewives have not had their brains shot away, nor are they schizophrenic in the clinical sense. But if . . . the fundamental human drive is not the urge for pleasure or the satisfaction of biological needs, but the need to grow and to realize one's full potential, their comfortable, empty, purposeless days are indeed cause for a nameless terror.

> *ib*

ROBERT FROST

15 You don't have to deserve your mother's love. You have to deserve your father's.

> Quoted in George Plimpton ed *Writers at Work* Viking 63

16 The father is always a Republican toward his son, and his mother's always a Democrat.

> *ib*

17 Home is the place where, when you have to go there,
They have to take you in.

> From 1914 poem "Death of the Hired Man," recalled on his death 29 Jan 63

18 The greatest thing in family life is to take a hint when a hint is intended—and not to take a hint when a hint isn't intended.

> Quoted in *Vogue* 15 Mar 63

LAVINA CHRISTENSEN FUGAL

19 Love your children with all your hearts, love them enough to discipline them before it is too late. . . . Praise them for important things, even if you have to stretch them a bit. Praise them a lot. They live on it like bread and butter and they need it more than bread and butter.

> On being chosen Mother of the Year, news summaries 3 May 55

GALLUP POLL

20 Only one woman in ten recognizes her husband as the same man he was before she married him. Nine out of ten say he's changed. One in three says he's changed for the worse.

> "The Woman's Mind" *Ladies' Home Journal* Feb 62

WILLIAM H GASS

21 We have scarcely gotten home . . . when our children's sneezes greet us, skinned knees bleed after waiting all day to do so. There is the bellyache and the burned-out basement bulb, the stalled car and the incontinent cat. The windows frost, the toilets sweat, the body of our spouse is one cold shoulder and the darkness of our bedroom is soon full of the fallen shadows of our failures.

> *Habitations of the Word* Simon & Schuster 85, quoted in NY *Times* 14 Feb 85

ANDRÉ GIDE

1 Families, I hate you! Shut-in homes, closed doors, jealous possessors of happiness.
Recalled on his death 19 Feb 51

RICHARD PERCEVAL GRAVES

2 People long dead were talked about as familiarly as though they had only just left the room.
On ancestral ties in family of Robert Graves, Robert Graves: The Assault Heroic 1895–1926 Viking 87, quoted in NY *Times* 6 Mar 87

VARTAN GREGORIAN

3 Dignity is not negotiable. Dignity is the honor of the family.
New Yorker 14 Apr 86

HENRY ANATOLE GRUNWALD

4 Home is the wallpaper above the bed, the family dinner table, the church bells in the morning, the bruised shins of the playground, the small fears that come with dusk, the streets and squares and monuments and shops that constitute one's first universe.
"Home Is Where You Are Happy" *Time* 8 Jul 85

5 Home is one's birthplace, ratified by memory.
ib

RICHARD C HALVERSON, Chaplain, US Senate

6 I like to remind them to be spouses and parents when they go home.
Wall Street Journal 31 Jan 85

ELIZABETH HARDWICK

7 I am alone here in New York, no longer a we.
On being divorced, Sleepless Nights Random House 79

SYDNEY J HARRIS

8 The beauty of "spacing" children many years apart lies in the fact that parents have time to learn the mistakes that were made with the older ones—which permits them to make exactly the opposite mistakes with the younger ones.
Leaving the Surface Houghton Mifflin 68

BROOKS HAYS

9 Back of every achievement is a proud wife and a surprised mother-in-law.
NY *Herald Tribune* 2 Dec 61

SUZANNE HELLER

10 Misery is when you make your bed and then your mother tells you it's the day she's changing the sheets.
Misery Eriksson 64

11 Misery is when grown-ups don't realize how miserable kids can feel.
ib

HELOISE (Heloise Cruse)

12 I think housework is the reason most women go to the office.
Editor & Publisher 27 Apr 63

LEWIS B HERSHEY

13 A boy becomes an adult three years before his parents think he does, and about two years after he thinks he does.
News summaries 31 Dec 51

THEODORE M HESBURGH

14 The most important thing a father can do for his children is to love their mother.
Reader's Digest Jan 63

MARJORIE HOLMES

15 What feeling is so nice as a child's hand in yours? So small, so soft and warm, like a kitten huddling in the shelter of your clasp.
Calendar of Love and Inspiration Doubleday 81

16 A child's hand in yours—what tenderness it arouses, what power it conjures. You are instantly the very touchstone of wisdom and strength.
ib

THOMAS HOLMES

17 A person often catches a cold when a mother-in-law comes to visit. Patients mentioned mothers-in-law so often that we came to consider them a common cause of disease in the United States.
Time 6 Jun 83

J EDGAR HOOVER

18 Above all, I would teach him to tell the truth . . . Truth-telling, I have found, is the key to responsible citizenship. The thousands of criminals I have seen in 40 years of law enforcement have had one thing in common: Every single one was a liar.
"What I Would Tell a Son" *Family Weekly* 14 Jul 63

McCREADY HUSTON

19 She invoked the understood silence of the long married.
The Platinum Yoke Lippincott 63

KENNETH HUTCHIN

20 The wife who always insists on the last word often has it.
On keeping husbands alive, NY Times 26 Feb 60

JOHN IRVING

21 To each other, we were as normal and nice as the smell of bread. We were just a family. In a family even exaggerations make perfect sense.
The Hotel New Hampshire Dutton 81

POPE JOHN XXIII

22 The family [is] the first essential cell of human society.
Pacem in Terris 10 Apr 63

POPE JOHN PAUL II

23 The great danger for family life, in the midst of any society whose idols are pleasure, comfort and independence, lies in the fact that people close their hearts and become selfish.
Sermon, Washington DC, 7 Oct 79

1 The fear of making permanent commitments can change the mutual love of husband and wife into two loves of self—two loves existing side by side, until they end in separation.
ib

2 To maintain a joyful family requires much from both the parents and the children. Each member of the family has to become, in a special way, the servant of the others.
ib

NORA JOHNSON

3 I doubt if there is one married person on earth who can be objective about divorce. It is always a threat, admittedly or not, and such a dire threat that it is almost a dirty word.
"A Marriage on the Rocks" *Atlantic* Jul 62

ELLEN KARSH

4 He is a teenager, after all—a strange agent with holes in his jeans, studs in his ear, a tail down his neck, a cap on his head (backward).
"A Teenager Is a Ton of Worry" NY *Times* 3 Jan 87

THOMAS H KEAN, Governor of New Jersey

5 The most painful death in all the world is the death of a child. When a child dies, when one child dies—not the 11 per 1,000 we talk about statistically, but the one that a mother held briefly in her arms—he leaves an empty place in a parent's heart that will never heal.
NY *Times* 20 Mar 85

ANN KENT

6 Grief and greed are as inextricably entwined as love and marriage should be.
"The Bitter Inheritance of Bereavement" London *Times* 12 Aug 85

7 Those terrible rows over who inherits what are not restricted to novels, soap operas or the families of the rich.
ib

CORETTA SCOTT KING

8 Mama and Daddy King represent the best in manhood and womanhood, the best in a marriage, the kind of people we are trying to become.
On the parents of her husband Martin Luther King Jr, recalled when her mother-in-law was slain, *Christian Science Monitor* 2 Jul 74

JEANE J KIRKPATRICK

9 Truth, which is important to a scholar, has got to be concrete. And there is nothing more concrete than dealing with babies, burps and bottles, frogs and mud.
On how the rearing of three sons prepared her for post as UN ambassador, *Newsweek* 3 Jan 83

LAWRENCE KUBIE

10 Today's family is built like a pyramid; with all the intrafamilial rivalries, tensions, jealousies, angers, hatreds, loves and needs focused on the untrained, vulnerable, insecure, young, inexperienced and incompetent parental apex . . . about whose incompetence our vaunted educational system does nothing.
Newsweek 7 Mar 60

NORMAN LEAR

11 Edith, stifle yourself!
Line for Archie Bunker to his wife, *All in the Family* ABC TV series 73

DAVID LEAVITT

12 Childhood smells of perfume and brownies.
On a son embracing his mother, *Family Dancing* Knopf 84, quoted in NY *Times* 30 Oct 84

MICHAEL LESY

13 In [family snapshots] the flow of profane time has been stopped and a sacred interval of self-conscious revelation has been cut from it by the edge of the picture frame and the light of the sun or the flash.
NY *Times* 16 Jan 78

GEORGE LEVINGER

14 What counts in making a happy marriage is not so much how compatible you are, but how you deal with incompatibility.
Quoted by Daniel Goleman "Marriage: Research Reveals Ingredients of Happiness" NY *Times* 16 Apr 85

GUY LOMBARDO

15 Many a man wishes he were strong enough to tear a telephone book in half—especially if he has a teenage daughter.
News summaries 19 Apr 54

NORMAN MAILER

16 There are four stages in a marriage. First there's the affair, then the marriage, then children and finally the fourth stage, without which you cannot know a woman, the divorce.
News summaries 31 Dec 69

ANDREW H MALCOLM

17 The car trip can draw the family together, as it was in the days before television when parents and children actually talked to each other.
"The Annual Automobile Migration" NY *Times* 21 Apr 85

FRANÇOIS MAURIAC

18 Where does discipline end? Where does cruelty begin? Somewhere between these, thousands of children inhabit a voiceless hell.
Second Thoughts World 61

ANDRÉ MAUROIS

19 A successful marriage is an edifice that must be rebuilt every day.
Quoted by Jacob Brande comp *Speaker's Encyclopedia* Prentice-Hall 55

20 Without a family, man, alone in the world, trembles with the cold.
Quoted by John D MacDonald *The Lonely Silver Rain* Knopf 85

MILLICENT CAREY MCINTOSH

21 The most important phase of living with a person [is] respect for that person as an individual.
"The Art of Living with Your Children" *Vogue* 1 Feb 53

1 There is no greater excitement than to support an intellectual wife and have her support you. Marriage is a partnership in which each inspires the other, and brings fruition to both of you.
NY *Herald Tribune* 4 Jun 58

MARGARET MEAD

2 Of all the peoples whom I have studied, from city dwellers to cliff dwellers, I always find that at least 50 percent would prefer to have at least one jungle between themselves and their mothers-in-law.
Recalled on her death 15 Nov 78

MAURICE MERLEAU-PONTY

3 Divorces as well as marriages can fail.
Signs Northwestern University 64

ARTHUR MILLER

4 He wants to live on through something—and in his case, his masterpiece is his son. . . . all of us want that, and it gets more poignant as we get more anonymous in this world.
On Willy Loman in *Death of a Salesman*, NY *Times* 9 May 84

LANCE MORROW

5 He vanished to the public in order to materialize for his family.
On Senator Paul Tsongas, who was diagnosed with cancer, *Time* 13 May 85

DAVID NASAW

6 The street bred a gritty self-reliance in its children. It was their frontier.
Children of the City Anchor 85, quoted in *People* 20 May 85

OGDEN NASH

7 An occasional lucky guess as to what makes a wife tick is the best a man can hope for,
Even then, no sooner has he learned how to cope with the tick than she tocks.
Marriage Lines Little, Brown 64

8 To keep your marriage brimming,
With love in the loving cup,
Whenever you're wrong, admit it;
Whenever you're right, shut up.
ib

9 Parents were invented to make children happy by giving them something to ignore.
Recalled on his death 19 May 71

NEW YORK TIMES

10 To be an American is to aspire to a room of one's own.
"Dream House" 19 Apr 87

CARROLL O'CONNOR

11 People see Archie Bunker everywhere. Particularly girls—poor girls, rich girls, all kinds of girls are always coming up to me and telling me that Archie is just like their dad.
On his role in *All in the Family*, quoted in NY *Times* 20 Mar 85

12 I think he's in every man my age, no matter what he does, whether he's a vice president at Chase or a cab driver.
ib

TIM PAGE

13 Born after sunset, dead by daybreak, his 11-hour scrap of existence was little more than a shuttle down fluorescent hallways, a tour of wards and laboratories.
On his son, "Life Miscarried" NY *Times* 27 Jan 85

POPE PAUL VI

14 Every mother is like Moses. She does not enter the promised land. She prepares a world she will not see.
Quoted by Jean Guitton *Conversations with Pope Paul* Meredith Press 67

JOHN PEARSON

15 Like the old motto of a famous Sunday paper, "All human life was there" in the stately circle of the Mountbatten-Windsors, as the family coped in semipublic with those everlasting elements of human interest—sickness, scandal, family tension and divorce.
The Selling of the Royal Family Simon & Schuster 86

16 The Queen Mother, with a lifetime's popularity, seemed incapable of a bad performance as national grandmother—warm, smiling, human, understanding, she embodied everything the public could want of its grandmother.
ib

DAVE POWERS

17 I had the strangest feeling that perhaps he was thinking, "This is the last time I'll ever read to her."
On President John F Kennedy and his daughter Caroline during the Cuban missile crisis, quoted by Ralph G Martin *A Hero for Our Time* Macmillan 83

IVY BAKER PRIEST, Treasurer of the US

18 Any woman who has a career and a family automatically develops something in the way of two personalities, like two sides of a dollar bill, each different in design. . . . Her problem is to keep one from draining the life from the other.
Green Grows Ivy McGraw-Hill 58

J B PRIESTLEY

19 As we read the school reports on our children, we realize a sense of relief that can rise to delight that— thank Heaven—nobody is reporting in this fashion on us.
Reader's Digest Jun 64

V S PRITCHETT

20 All writers—all people—have their stores of private and family legends which lie like a collection of half-forgotten, often violent toys on the floor of memory.
New Yorker 19 Feb 79

21 There is nothing like a *coup de foudre* and absorption in family responsibility for maturing the male and pulling his scattered wits together.
"Looking Back at 80" NY *Times* 14 Dec 80

RANDOLPH RAY

1 Kindness is the life's blood, the elixir of marriage. Kindness makes the difference between passion and caring. Kindness is tenderness. Kindness is love, but perhaps greater than love . . . Kindness is good will. Kindness says, "I want you to be happy." Kindness comes very close to the benevolence of God.

My Little Church around the Corner Simon & Schuster 57

SALLY AND JAMES RESTON

2 Age 17 is the point in the journey when the parents retire to the observation car; it is the time when you stop being critical of your eldest son and he starts being critical of you.

"So We Sent Our Son to College" *Saturday Evening Post* 5 May 56

3 Helping your eldest son pick a college is one of the great educational experiences of life—for the parents. Next to trying to pick his bride, it's the best way to learn that your authority, if not entirely gone, is slipping fast.

ib

ROGER ROSENBLATT

4 [They] do not leave home without American Express. . . . Blame the moral carelessness that parents pass off as the gift of freedom as they cut their children loose like colorful kites and wish them an exciting flight.

On wealthy teenagers and murder of 18-year-old girl in NYC's Central Park, "The Freedom of the Damned" *Time* 6 Oct 86

PHILIP ROTH

5 A Jewish man with parents alive is a 15-year-old boy.

Portnoy's Complaint Random House 69

BERTRAND RUSSELL

6 The fundamental defect of fathers is that they want their children to be a credit to them.

NY *Times* 9 Jun 63

JOHN RUSSELL

7 We coast along for years with an idea of what people are like and then—vroom! Our favorite uncle turns out to be the most terrible crook, the brother-in-law to whom we went for advice and support does not return our calls and our dull cousin in Australia, the one whose letters we always forgot to answer, gets the Nobel Prize for her pioneer work on the coccyx of the cassowary. What we get to know, in short, is not always what we hope to know.

NY *Times* 27 Jan 85

ELOISE SALHOLZ

8 To Tennessee Williams, children were "no-neck monsters," while William Wordsworth apotheosized the newborn infant as a "Mighty Prophet! Seer Blest!" Most adults know the truth is somewhere in between.

"Morals Minefield" *Newsweek* 13 Oct 86

CARL SANDBURG

9 A baby is God's opinion that the world should go on.

Remembrance Rock Harcourt, Brace 48, recalled on his death 22 Jul 67

RICHARD SCHICKEL

10 There is a limbo of the lost through which American males of a certain age and status almost inevitably must pass these days.

Time 2 Jul 84

11 Divorced, not loving their abandoned children as much as they loathe their former wives, directing a combination of need and hostility toward the women who drift in and out of their new lives, they are, as [one character] puts it, "involved in a variety of pharmaceutical experiments."

ib

GEORGE BERNARD SHAW

12 Never fret for an only son, the idea of failure will never occur to him.

Quoted by Alistair Cooke *America* Knopf 73

DAVID SHIRE

13 You can sort of be married, you can sort of be divorced, you can sort of be living together, but you can't sort of have a baby.

Quoted in *Time* 2 Jan 84

ALAN SIMPSON

14 A society like ours, which professes no one religion and has allowed all religions to decay, which indulges freedom to the point of license and individualism to the point of anarchy, needs all the support that responsible, cultivated homes can furnish. I hope your generation will provide a firmer shelter for civilized standards.

Commencement address at Vassar 31 May 65

C W SMITH

15 Divorced fathers are forced to recognize that there's no substitute for being there; or rather, there are only substitutes for it.

"Uncle Dad" *Esquire* Mar 84

ELINOR GOULDING SMITH

16 It sometimes happens, even in the best of families, that a baby is born. This is not necessarily cause for alarm. The important thing is to keep your wits about you and borrow some money.

The Complete Book of Absolutely Perfect Baby and Child Care Harcourt, Brace 57

MARGARET SMITH

17 The best contraceptive is the word *no*—repeated frequently.

To Women's Liberation Federation, Blackpool, England, *Quote* 27 Jun 71

CHARLES SPALDING

18 You watched these people go through their lives and just had a feeling that they existed outside the usual laws of nature; that there was no other group so handsome, so engaged.

On visiting the Kennedy's summer home at Hyannis MA in the early 1940s, quoted by Peter Collier and David Horowitz *The Kennedys* Summit 84

1 There was endless action—not just football, but sailboats, tennis and other things: movement. There was endless talk—the ambassador at the head of the table laying out the prevailing wisdom, but everyone else weighing in with their opinions and taking part.
ib

2 It was as simple as this: The Kennedys had a feeling of being heightened and it rubbed off on the people who came in contact with them. They were a unit.
ib

BENJAMIN SPOCK

3 What good mothers and fathers instinctively feel like doing for their babies is usually best after all.
Quoted in *Life* 26 Jun 50

4 All the time a person is a child he is both a child and learning to be a parent. After he becomes a parent he becomes predominantly a parent reliving childhood.
Quote 29 Aug 65

SPORTS ILLUSTRATED

5 Any parent who has ever found a rusted toy automobile buried in the grass or a bent sand bucket on the beach knows that objects like these can be among the powerful things in the world. They can summon up in an instant, in colors stronger than life, the whole of childhood at its happiest—the disproportionate affection lavished on some strange possession, the concentrated self-forgetfulness of play, the elusive expressions of surprise or elation that pass so transparently over youthful features.
"The Timeless House of Children's Games" 26 Dec 60

RONALD STEEL

6 Children, for whom suburban life was supposed to make wholesome little Johns and Wendys, became the acid-dropping, classroom-burning hippies of the 1960s.
"Life in the Last 50 Years" *Esquire* Jun 83

JOHN STEINBECK

7 The impulse of the American woman to geld her husband and castrate her sons is very strong.
Quoted in Elaine Steinbeck and Robert Wallsten comps *Steinbeck: A Life in Letters* Penguin 76

PRESTON STURGES

8 Daughters are a mess no matter how you look at 'em, a headache till they get married—if they get married—and, after that, they get worse. . . . Either they leave their husbands and come back with four children and move into your guest room or their husband loses his job and the whole *caboodle* comes back. Or else they're so homely you can't get rid of them at all and they hang around the house like Spanish moss.
From screenplay for his 1944 film *The Miracle of Morgan's Creek*, recalled on his death 6 Aug 59

PATRICIA SULLIVAN

9 We had our own baby boom.
On sailing to America on the *Queen Mary* during World War II, NY *Times* 15 Apr 85

ST CLAIR ADAMS SULLIVAN

10 Our children are here to stay, but our babies and toddlers and preschoolers are gone as fast as they can grow up—and we have only a short moment with each. When you see a grandfather take a baby in his arms, you see that the moment hasn't always been long enough.
The Father's Almanac Doubleday 80

JOHN TARKOV

11 This Melting Pot of ours absorbs the second generation over a flame so high that the first is left encrusted on the rim.
"Fitting In" NY *Times* 7 Jul 85

TIME MAGAZINE

12 To their deeply worried parents throughout the country, hippies seem more like dangerously deluded dropouts, candidates for a very sound spanking and a cram course in civics—if only they would return home to receive either.
7 Jul 67

ALVIN TOFFLER

13 Parenthood remains the greatest single preserve of the amateur.
Future Shock Random House 70

DESMOND TUTU

14 You don't choose your family. They are God's gift to you, as you are to them.
Address at enthronement as Anglican archbishop of Cape Town 7 Sep 86

ALAN VALENTINE

15 For thousands of years, father and son have stretched wistful hands across the canyon of time, each eager to help the other to his side, but neither quite able to desert the loyalties of his contemporaries. The relationship is always changing and hence always fragile; nothing endures except the sense of difference.
Fathers to Sons: Advice without Consent University of Oklahoma 63

ABIGAIL VAN BUREN

16 First, there is the rocket-boosted mother-in-law. . . . queen of the melodrama when her acts of self-sacrifice and martyrdom go unnoticed and unrewarded. Her banner is the tear-stained hanky. She is as phony as a colic cure, transparent as a soap bubble. And as harmless as a barracuda. But she is really more wretched than wicked and needs more help than she can give.
"After the Honeymoon" *McCall's* Sep 62

17 Then, there's the modern mother-in-law. In her mid 40s, she is the compact car of her breed: efficient, trim, attractive and in harmony with her times. . . . She's pretty stiff competition for the plain young matron who's overweight and underfinanced. If there is going to be friction in this relationship, it could start from envy and resentment in the younger woman. But Father Time is on her side, even if Mother Nature played her a dirty trick.
ib

JOHN VAN DE KAMP

1 If we can . . . get them to understand that saying "no" to drugs is rebelling against their parents and the generations of the past, we'd make it an enormous success.
On campaigning against drugs in rock videos, LA *Times* 16 Jul 86

AMY VANDERBILT

2 [Parents] must get across the idea that "I love you always, but sometimes I do not love your behavior."
On raising teenagers, *New Complete Book of Etiquette* Doubleday 63

GORE VIDAL

3 All children alarm their parents, if only because you are forever expecting to encounter yourself.
From his 1968 play *Weekend*

EVELYN WAUGH

4 Perhaps host and guest is really the happiest relation for father and son.
"Father and Son" *Atlantic* Mar 63

REBECCA WEST

5 She was like the embodiment of all women who have felt an astonished protest because their children have died before them.
On Queen Mary at funeral of her son King George VI, *Life* 25 Feb 52

GEORGE F WILL

6 Some parents . . . say it is toy guns that make boys warlike. . . . But give a boy a rubber duck and he will seize its neck like the butt of a pistol and shout "Bang!"
Newsweek 11 Dec 78

7 Childhood is frequently a solemn business for those inside it.
ib

EARL WILSON

8 For the parents of a Little Leaguer, a baseball game is simply a nervous breakdown into innings.
News summaries 31 Dec 79

CHARLES EDDIE WISEMAN

9 We're going to raise a lost generation of children unless they are properly disciplined and properly spanked.
On why members of the Northeast Kingdom Community Church, Island Pond VT, physically punish their children, NY *Times* 11 Jul 84

WORLD BANK

10 Parents may feel the need to have many babies to be sure that a few survive.
On high infant mortality rate in developing countries, *World Development Report*, quoted in NY *Times* 11 Jul 84

GEOFFREY WRANGHAM

11 Distrust all mothers-in-law. They are completely unscrupulous in what they say in court.
Boston *Herald* 10 Oct 60

12 The wife's mother is always more prejudiced against the husband than even the most ill-treated wife. If I had my way, I am afraid I would abolish mothers-in-law entirely.
ib

JONATHAN YARDLEY

13 An entire generation grew up unacquainted with the thwack of paddle against bottom.
On parental permissiveness promoted by Benjamin Spock's books, *American Heritage* Apr 85

LOVE

MORTIMER ADLER

14 There is only one situation I can think of in which men and women make an effort to read better than they usually do. [It is] when they are in love and reading a love letter.
Quote 26 Dec 61

AKIHITO, Crown Prince of Japan

15 I am marrying her because I love her.
On becoming first member of Japanese royal family to wed a commoner, news summaries 12 Apr 59

PRINCE ANDREW, Duke of York

16 [I am] over the moon! . . . We are both over the moon and will be even more so when this is over.
On his engagement to Sarah Ferguson, London *Daily Telegraph* 20 Mar 86

NOEL ANNAN

17 He was comforted by one of the simpler emotions which some human beings are lucky enough to experience. He knew when he died he would be watched by someone he loved.
On E M Forster, London *Observer* 11 Mar 79

ANTONY, Russian Orthodox Archbishop of England

18 So often when we say "I love you" we say it with a huge "I" and a small "you."
Beginning to Pray Paulist Press 70

BROOKS ATKINSON

19 We cheerfully assume that in some mystic way love conquers all, that good outweighs evil in the just balances of the universe and at the 11th hour something gloriously triumphant will prevent the worst before it happens.
Once around the Sun Harcourt, Brace 51

W H AUDEN

20 Among those whom I like, I can find no common denominator, but among those whom I love, I can; all of them make me laugh.
The Dyer's Hand Random House 62

21 He was my North, my South, my East and West,
My working week and my Sunday rest,
My noon, my midnight, my talk, my song;
I thought that love would last forever: I was wrong.
"Song: Stop All the Clocks," recalled on his death 28 Sep 73

JAMES BALDWIN

22 The face of a lover is an unknown, precisely because

it is invested with so much of oneself. It is a mystery, containing, like all mysteries, the possibility of torment.

Another Country Dial 62

PHYLLIS BATTELLE

1 If you haven't had at least a slight poetic crack in the heart, you have been cheated by nature.

NY *Journal-American* 1 Jun 62

2 A broken heart is what makes life so wonderful five years later, when you see the guy in an elevator and he is fat and smoking a cigar and saying long-time-no-see.

ib

ELIZABETH BLACK

3 He spoke of love and the Supreme Court.

On marriage proposal from Hugo L Black, quoted in *Christian Science Monitor* 27 Feb 86

ERMA BOMBECK

4 For years [my wedding ring] has done its job. It has led me not into temptation. It has reminded my husband numerous times at parties that it's time to go home. It has been a source of relief to a dinner companion. It has been a status symbol in the maternity ward.

Moneysworth Mar 80

CHARLES BOYER

5 A Frenchwoman, when double-crossed, will kill her rival; the Italian woman would rather kill her deceitful lover; the Englishwoman simply breaks off relations—but they all will console themselves with another man.

News summaries 20 Jul 54

PATRICIA L BRUECKNER

6 When
Then
I encountered the man,
I liked him
As I had known
I must.
But, with care,
Knowing danger,
I looked at him
And saw
Marriage
On his hand.
Carefully then
I turned away
As
Implicitly
The two of us
Sensed ourselves.
It was difficult
But it could be done.

Privately published 64

RICHARD BURTON

7 I might run from her for a thousand years and she is still my baby child. . . . Our love is so furious that we burn each other out.

After his second divorce from Elizabeth Taylor, recalled on his death 5 Aug 84

ROBERT FARRAR CAPON

8 I talk marriage; they talk weddings!

On counseling engaged couples, *Bed and Board: Plain Talk about Marriage* Simon & Schuster 65

MARC CHAGALL

9 Only love interests me, and I am only in contact with things that revolve around love.

Quoted by Diana Loercher "Marc Chagall—Capturing the Exuberant Spirit" *Christian Science Monitor* 1 Jul 77

10 In our life there is a single color, as on an artist's palette, which provides the meaning of life and art. It is the color of love.

Newsweek 8 Apr 85

GABRIELLE ("COCO") CHANEL

11 I never wanted to weigh more heavily on a man than a bird.

On why she never married her lovers, NY *Herald Tribune* 18 Oct 64

12 Jump out the window if you are the object of passion. Flee it if you feel it. . . . Passion goes, boredom remains.

McCall's Nov 65

ILKA CHASE

13 On the whole, I haven't found men unduly loath to say, "I love you." The real trick is to get them to say, "Will you marry me?"

This Week 5 Feb 56

NIKOLAI CHEPIK

14 Believing that a girl will wait is just like jumping with a parachute packed by someone else.

From diary of Soviet farm boy who died in action in Afghanistan, quoted by Seth Mydans NY *Times* 16 Jan 85

MAURICE CHEVALIER

15 Many a man has fallen in love with a girl in a light so dim he would not have chosen a suit by it.

News summaries 17 Jul 55

16 The crime of loving is forgetting.

Look 28 May 68

AGATHA CHRISTIE

17 An archaeologist is the best husband any woman can have: The older she gets, the more interested he is in her.

News summaries 9 Mar 54

WINSTON CHURCHILL

18 My most brilliant achievement was my ability to be able to persuade my wife to marry me.

Quoted by Jack Fishman *My Darling Clementine* McKay 63

FRANCIS X CLINES

19 In a party tent poised somewhere between romance and avarice, an auctioneer hammered out the sale of the first of the costly baubles that were scattered as love tokens across the lives of the Duke and Duchess of Windsor.

On jewels that brought $33.5 million at auction in Geneva, NY *Times* 3 Apr 87

JOSEPH COTTEN

1 [My wife] told me one of the sweetest things one could hear—"I am not jealous. But I am truly sad for all the actresses who embrace you and kiss you while acting, for with them, you are only pretending."

NY *Herald Tribune* 8 Jan 60

NOEL COWARD

2 I've sometimes thought of marrying—and then I've thought again.

Theatre Arts Nov 56

HARRY CREWS

3 He did not know what love was. And he did not know what good it was. But he knew he carried it around with him, a scabrous spot of rot, of contagion, for which there was no cure.

A Feast of Snakes Atheneum 76

MARNIE REED CROWELL

4 To keep the fire burning brightly there's one easy rule: Keep the two logs together, near enough to keep each other warm and far enough apart—about a finger's breadth—for breathing room. Good fire, good marriage, same rule.

Greener Pastures Funk & Wagnalls 73

E E CUMMINGS

5 Be of love (a little) more careful than of anything.

Line adapted for serigraph by artist Corita Kent, quoted in *Newsweek* 17 Dec 84

DAVID DEMPSEY

6 Most of them lead lives of unquiet desperation, continually seeking, in sex they wish was love and in the love they suspect is only sex, a center for their worlds to turn on.

On characters in Warren Miller's *The Way We Live Now* Little, Brown 58, NY *Times* 27 Apr 58

JACK DEMPSEY

7 Number 4 should have been number 1. Thanks, Honey.

Dedicating his autobiography to his fourth wife, quoted by John J Sirica "Unforgettable Jack Dempsey" *Reader's Digest* Nov 85

MARLENE DIETRICH

8 How do you know love is gone? If you said that you would be there at seven and you get there by nine, and he or she has not called the police—it's gone.

ABC Doubleday 62

9 Grumbling is the death of love.

ib

ISAK DINESEN

10 Man reaches the highest point of lovableness at 12 to 17—to get it back, in a second flowering, at the age of 70 to 90.

Shadows on the Grass Random House 60

DAVID HERBERT DONALD

11 Their correspondence was something like a duet between a tuba and a piccolo.

On love letters of Thomas Wolfe and Aline Bernstein, *Look Homeward* Little, Brown 87

MARTHA DUFFY

12 A fastidious person in the throes of love is a rich source of mirth.

In review of A N Wilson's *Wise Virgin* Viking 83, *Time* 5 Dec 83

WILL DURANT

13 The love we have in our youth is superficial compared to the love that an old man has for his old wife.

On his 90th birthday, NY *Times* 6 Nov 75

EDWARD, DUKE OF WINDSOR

14 I was shocked and angry . . . with the startling suggestion that I should send from my land, my realm, the woman I intended to marry.

Recalling political advice to send Wallis Warfield Simpson abroad "without further delay," *A King's Story* Putnam 51

15 I have found it impossible to carry the heavy burden of responsibility and to discharge my duties as king as I would wish to do without the help and support of the woman I love.

December 11, 1936, abdication broadcast, recalled on his death 28 May 72

16 A boy is holding a girl so very tight in his arms tonight.

July 23, 1935, letter to Wallis Warfield Simpson, quoted in Michael Bloch ed *Wallis and Edward: Letters 1931–37* Summit 86

M F K FISHER

17 When I write of hunger, I am really writing about love and the hunger for it, and warmth and the love of it . . . and it is all one.

Reply when asked why she wrote about eating and drinking, from her 1943 book *The Gastronomical Me*, quoted in *Time* 16 May 83

LYNN FONTANNE

18 One reason we lasted so long is that we usually played two people who were very much in love. As we were realistic actors, we became those two people. So we had a divertissement: I had an affair with him, and he with me.

On being married for 55 years to costar Alfred Lunt, NY *Times* 24 Apr 78

HARRY EMERSON FOSDICK

19 Bitterness imprisons life; love releases it. Bitterness paralyzes life; love empowers it. Bitterness sours life; love sweetens it. Bitterness sickens life; love heals it. Bitterness blinds life; love anoints its eyes.

Riverside Sermons Harper 58

JOHN FOWLES

20 Most marriages recognize this paradox: Passion destroys passion; we want what puts an end to wanting what we want.

The Aristos Little, Brown 64

ERICH FROMM

21 Love is the only sane and satisfactory answer to the problem of human existence.

The Art of Loving Harper 56, recalled on his death 18 Mar 80

1 If a person loves only one other person and is indifferent to all others, his love is not love but a symbiotic attachment, or an enlarged egotism.
ib

ROBERT FROST

2 Two such as you with such a master speed
Cannot be parted nor be swept away
From one another once you are agreed
That life is only life forevermore
Together wing to wing and oar to oar.
From "The Master Speed," inscribed on gravestone of Frost and his wife Elinor, *National Observer* 6 Jul 64

GEORGE GILDER

3 This is what sexual liberation chiefly accomplishes—it liberates young women to pursue married men.
Quoted in *Newsweek* 8 Dec 86

JEAN HARRIS

4 Loving an old bachelor is always a no-win situation, and you come to terms with that early on, or you go away.
On Dr Herman Tarnower, *Stranger in Two Worlds* Macmillan 86

ERNEST HAVEMANN

5 You can see them alongside the shuffleboard courts in Florida or on the porches of the old folks' homes up north . . . They are in love, they have always been in love, although sometimes they would have denied it. And because they have been in love they have survived everything that life could throw at them, even their own failures.
On a long-married couple, "Love and Marriage" *Life* 29 Sep 61

HELEN HAYES

6 The truth [is] that there is only one terminal dignity—love. And the story of a love is not important—what is important is that one is capable of love. It is perhaps the only glimpse we are permitted of eternity.
Guideposts Jan 60

SHIRLEY HAZZARD

7 The tragedy is not that love doesn't last. The tragedy is the love that lasts.
The Transit of Venus Viking 80

BEN HECHT

8 Love is a hole in the heart.
From his 1958 play *Winkelberg*

9 A man nearly always loves for other reasons than he thinks. A lover is apt to be as full of secrets from himself as is the object of his love from him.
Think Feb 63

LILLIAN HELLMAN

10 It was an unspoken pleasure, that having come together so many years, ruined so much and repaired a little, we had endured.
On her relationship with Dashiell Hammett, recalled on her death 30 Jun 84

ERNEST HEMINGWAY

11 You're beautiful, like a May fly.
To his future wife Mary Welsh, recalled on her death 26 Nov 86

KATHARINE HEPBURN

12 Only the really plain people know about love—the very fascinating ones try so hard to create an impression that they soon exhaust their talents.
Look 18 Feb 58

13 Marriage [is] a series of desperate arguments people feel passionately about.
Quoted by Charles Higham *Kate* Norton 75

MORTON HUNT

14 *Love* . . . is a quicksilver word; though you see plainly where it is, you have only to put your finger on it to find that it is not there but someplace else.
The Natural History of Love Knopf 59

15 Americans, who make more of marrying for love than any other people, also break up more of their marriages, but the figure reflects not so much the failure of love as the determination of people not to live without it.
ib

ALDOUS HUXLEY

16 No man ever dared to manifest his boredom so insolently as does a Siamese tomcat when he yawns in the face of his amorously importunate wife.
NY *Times* 2 Nov 63

POPE JOHN PAUL II

17 You will reciprocally promise love, loyalty and matrimonial honesty. We only want for you this day that these words constitute the principle of your entire life and that with the help of divine grace you will observe these solemn vows that today, before God, you formulate.
Solemnizing a marriage, news summaries 25 Feb 79

CLAUDIA ("LADY BIRD") JOHNSON

18 [Lyndon] was the most outspoken, straightforward, determined person I'd ever encountered. I knew I'd met something remarkable—but I didn't know quite what.
On meeting her future husband, *Saturday Evening Post* 8 Feb 64

LYNDON B JOHNSON, 36th US President

19 For Bird, still a girl of principles, ideals and refinement—from her admirer, Lyndon.
Inscription on a photograph presented to his wife on her 51st birthday, NY *Herald Tribune* 23 Dec 63

CARL JUNG

20 Where love rules, there is no will to power; and where power predominates, there love is lacking. The one is the shadow of the other.
Recalled on his death 6 Jun 61

JACQUELINE KENNEDY

21 We know you understand that even though people may be well known they still hold in their hearts the

emotions of a simple person for the moments that are the most important of those we know on earth—birth, marriage, death. We wish our wedding to be a private moment in the little chapel among the cypresses of Skorpios.

> Statement to press issued the day before her marriage to Aristotle Onassis, NY *Times* 20 Oct 68

1 It was a very spasmodic courtship, conducted mainly at long distance with a great clanking of coins in dozens of phone booths.

> On her romance with John F Kennedy, quoted by Doris Kearns Goodwin *The Fitzgeralds and the Kennedys* Simon & Schuster 87

PHILIP LARKIN

2 In everyone there sleeps
A sense of life lived according to love.
To some it means the difference they could make
By loving others, but across most it sweeps
As all they might have done had they been loved.
That nothing cures.

> "Faith Healing," recalled on his death 2 Dec 86

ESTÉE LAUDER

3 Look for a sweet person. Forget rich.

> Advice on choosing a spouse, *New Yorker* 15 Sep 86

JOHN LE CARRÉ

4 Love is whatever you can still betray . . . Betrayal can only happen if you love.

> *A Perfect Spy* Knopf 86

URSULA K LE GUIN

5 Love doesn't just sit there, like a stone; it has to be made, like bread, remade all the time, made new.

> *The Lathe of Heaven* Scribner's 71

C S LEWIS

6 This is one of the miracles of love: It gives . . . a power of seeing through its own enchantments and yet not being disenchanted.

> *A Grief Observed* Seabury 61

ANNE MORROW LINDBERGH

7 When the wedding march sounds the resolute approach, the clock no longer ticks, it tolls the hour. . . . The figures in the aisle are no longer individuals, they symbolize the human race.

> *Dearly Beloved* Harcourt, Brace & World 62

8 Don't wish me happiness—I don't expect to be happy . . . it's gotten beyond that, somehow. Wish me courage and strength and a sense of humor—I will need them all.

> 1928 letter to Corliss Lamont on her engagement to Charles A Lindbergh, *Bring Me a Unicorn* Harcourt Brace Jovanovich 72

9 Charles is life itself—pure life, force, like sunlight—and it is for this that I married him and this that holds me to him—caring always, caring desperately what happens to him and whatever he happens to be involved in.

> *War Within and Without* Harcourt Brace Jovanovich 80

10 Marriage is tough, because it is woven of all these various elements, the weak and the strong. "In love-ness" is fragile for it is woven only with the gossamer threads of beauty. It seems to me absurd to talk about "happy" and "unhappy" marriages.

> *ib*

LONDON TIMES

11 Eros goes in for repair tomorrow, with some abatement presumably of the transports and pains of love in central London.

> On restoration of Piccadilly Circus statue erected in 1893, 9 Aug 84

ISABEL G MacCAFFREY

12 Love is the source of language, and also its destroyer.

> In Frank Doggett and Robert Buttel eds *Wallace Stevens: A Celebration* Princeton 80

NORMAN MAILER

13 The highest prize in a world of men is the most beautiful woman available on your arm and living there in her heart loyal to you.

> On Joe DiMaggio's marriage to Marilyn Monroe, *Marilyn* Grosset & Dunlap 73, quoted by Ralph Novak *People* 10 Nov 86

SOMERSET MAUGHAM

14 The love that lasts longest is the love that is never returned.

> Recalled on his death 16 Dec 65

MIGNON McLAUGHLIN

15 A successful marriage requires falling in love many times, always with the same person.

> *Atlantic* Jul 65

H L MENCKEN

16 No normal man ever fell in love after 30 when the kidneys begin to disintegrate.

> Recalled on his death 29 Jan 56

17 Love is the delusion that one woman differs from another.

> *ib*

KARL A MENNINGER

18 Love cures people, the ones who receive love and the ones who give it, too.

> *Sparks* Crowell 73

ANDRÉ DE MISSAN

19 You study one another for 3 weeks, you love each other 3 months, you fight for 3 years, you tolerate the situation for 30.

> *Pink and Black* privately published 53

MISTINGUETT

20 A kiss can be a comma, a question mark or an exclamation point. That's basic spelling that every woman ought to know.

> *Theatre Arts* Dec 55

W Stanley Mooneyham

1 Love talked about can be easily turned aside, but love demonstrated is irresistible.

> *Come Walk the World* Word Books 78, quoted in *Reader's Digest* Oct 84

Charles Morgan

2 There is no surprise more magical than the surprise of being loved: It is God's finger on man's shoulder.

> Recalled on his death 6 Feb 58

Charles J V Murphy

3 The duke's kingdom had now shrunk to the duchess herself; for him and for her, there was nothing beyond; each had ended by defeating the other. The position she craved, he had forfeited irretrievably in order to have her. The love he craved, she could not give; perhaps she did not know the emotion at its deepest and purest.

> Preface to *The Windsor Story*, with J Bryan III, Morrow 79

Richard J Needham

4 Every woman needs one man in her life who is strong and responsible. Given this security, she can proceed to do what she really wants to do—fall in love with men who are weak and irresponsible.

> *The Garden of Needham* Macmillan 68

Paul Newman

5 So you wound up with Apollo
If he's sometimes hard to swallow
Use this.

> Inscription on silver sherry cup given to his wife Joanne Woodward, NY *Times* 28 Sep 86

Richard M Nixon, 37th US President

6 When the winds blow and the rains fall and the sun shines through the clouds . . . he still resolves as he did then, that nothing so fine ever happened to him or anyone else as falling in love with Thee—my dearest heart.

> Letter to his future wife Pat, quoted by Julie Nixon Eisenhower *Pat Nixon* Simon & Schuster 86

Joyce Carol Oates

7 Love commingled with hate is more powerful than love. Or hate.

> *On Boxing* Doubleday 87, quoted in NY *Times* 15 Mar 87

Seán O'Faoláin

8 Love lives in sealed bottles of regret.

> "The Jungle of Love" *Saturday Evening Post* 13 Aug 66

José Ortega y Gasset

9 Love is that splendid triggering of human vitality . . . the supreme activity which nature affords anyone for going out of himself toward someone else.

> *McCall's* Feb 82

Mary Parrish

10 Love vanquishes time. To lovers, a moment can be eternity, eternity can be the tick of a clock.

> "All the Love in the World" *McCall's* Jun 61

Boris Pasternak

11 Love is not weakness. It is strong. Only the sacrament of marriage can contain it.

> *Dr Zhivago*, translated by Max Hayward and Manya Harari, Pantheon 58

12 You fall into my arms.
You are the good gift of destruction's path,
When life sickens more than disease
And boldness is the root of beauty—
Which draws us together.

> "Autumn," quoted by Olga Ivinskaya *A Captive of Time: My Years with Pasternak*, translated by Max Hayward, Doubleday 78

M Scott Peck

13 Falling in love is not an extension of one's limits or boundaries; it is a partial and temporary collapse of them.

> *The Road Less Traveled* Simon & Schuster 78

14 Real love is a permanently self-enlarging experience. Falling in love is not.

> *ib*

Randolph Ray

15 I would like to have engraved inside every wedding band *Be kind to one another*. This is the Golden Rule of marriage and the secret of making love last through the years.

> *My Little Church around the Corner* Simon & Schuster 57

Ronald Reagan, 40th US President

16 Everywhere we go, Nancy makes the world a little better.

> On his wife, in film shown at Republican National Convention 22 Aug 84

17 Thank you, partner. . . . By the way, are you doing anything this evening?

> To Nancy, while convalescing from cancer surgery, radio address 20 Jul 85

Theodor Reik

18 Love is an attempt to change a piece of a dream world into reality.

> Recalled on his death 31 Dec 69

Ginger Rogers

19 When two people love each other, they don't look at each other, they look in the same direction.

> Quoted by Dotson Rader "'I Don't Want to Live without Love'" *Parade* 8 Mar 87

Ned Rorem

20 Quarrels in France strengthen a love affair, in America they end it.

> *The Paris Diary of Ned Rorem* Braziller 66

Howard Sackler

21 Affairs, like revolutions, should only have beginnings.

> From his 1980 play *Good-bye Fidel*

J D SALINGER

1 Sex is something I really don't understand too hot. . . . I keep making up these sex rules for myself, and then I break them right away.

The Catcher in the Rye Little, Brown 51

RICHARD SCHICKEL

2 That common cold of the male psyche, fear of commitment.

Time 28 Nov 83

JAROSLAV SEIFERT

3 But what you minded most
at our final parting
was that in my poor rags
—but was it not the costume of a beggar?—
you couldn't see our tears as in a suit of armor.

"Parting" in George Gibian ed *The Selected Poetry of Jaroslav Seifert* Macmillan 87, quoted in NY *Times* 15 Feb 87

MERLE SHAIN

4 It's terrifying to care, of course, and the young man whom I once heard say to the girl whose hand he was holding, "Shit, I think I love you," in the ominous tones of someone declaring that he was coming down with the plague, probably put the fear that accompanies loving as graphically as it can be put.

Some Men Are More Perfect Than Others Bantam 73

5 Loving can cost a lot but not loving always costs more, and those who fear to love often find that want of love is an emptiness that robs the joy from life.

ib

SIMONE SIGNORET

6 If Marilyn is in love with my husband it proves she has good taste, for I am in love with him too.

On rumors linking Yves Montand with Marilyn Monroe, NY *Journal-American* 14 Nov 60

ERNEST SIMPSON

7 I want you to believe—I do believe—that you did everything in your power to prevent the final catastrophe.

1936 letter to his estranged wife Wallis Warfield Simpson after Edward VIII's abdication, quoted in Michael Bloch ed *Wallis and Edward: Letters 1931–37* Summit 86

8 Could you possibly have settled down to the old life and forgotten the fairyland through which you had passed? My child, I do not think so.

ib

LIZ SMITH

9 The marriage didn't work out but the separation is great.

On a Hollywood relationship, NBC TV 13 Nov 85

10 All weddings, except those with shotguns in evidence, are wonderful.

NY *Daily News* 13 Apr 86

RALPH W SOCKMAN, Senior Minister Emeritus, Christ Church, Methodist, NYC

11 Love is the outreach of self toward completion.

Privately published 60

12 A true lover always feels in debt to the one he loves.

ib

13 The roads of life are strewn with the wreckage of run-down and half-finished loves.

ib

ROBERT C SOLOMON

14 Love can be understood only "from the inside," as a language can be understood only by someone who speaks it, as a world can be understood only by someone who lives in it.

Love: Emotion, Myth and Metaphor Anchor/Doubleday 81

MURIEL SPARK

15 It is impossible to repent of love. The sin of love does not exist.

New Yorker 10 Jul 65

WALLACE STEGNER

16 It is something—it can be everything—to have found a fellow bird with whom you can sit among the rafters while the drinking and boasting and reciting and fighting go on below.

On finding a loved one, *The Spectator Bird* Doubleday 76

ROBERT STERNBERG

17 Passion is the quickest to develop, and the quickest to fade. Intimacy develops more slowly, and commitment more gradually still.

NY *Times* 10 Sep 85

JESSICA TANDY

18 When he's late for dinner, I know he's either having an affair or is lying dead in the street. I always hope it's the street.

On her husband Hume Cronyn, *Kennedy Center Honors* CBS TV 26 Dec 86

DOROTHY THOMPSON

19 To have felt too much is to end in feeling nothing.

On waiting in Woodstock VT courthouse for divorce from Sinclair Lewis, quoted by Vincent Sheean *Dorothy and Red* Houghton Mifflin 63

JAMES THURBER

20 A lady of 47 who has been married 27 years and has 6 children knows what love really is and once described it for me like this: "Love is what you've been through with somebody."

Life 14 Mar 60

PAUL TILLICH

21 The first duty of love is to listen.

Recalled on his death 22 Oct 65

PAUL TOURNIER

22 It is a lovely thing to have a husband and wife developing together and having the feeling of falling in love again. That is what marriage really means: helping one another to reach the full status of being persons, responsible and autonomous beings who do not run away from life.

The Meaning of Persons Harper & Row 57

HARRY S TRUMAN, 33rd US President

1 In my Sunday School class there was a beautiful little girl with golden curls. I was smitten at once and still am.

    On his wife Bess, news summaries 31 Dec 52

PETER USTINOV

2 Love is an act of endless forgiveness, a tender look which becomes a habit.

    Christian Science Monitor 9 Dec 58

JUDITH VIORST

3 One advantage of marriage, it seems to me, is that when you fall out of love with him, or he falls out of love with you, it keeps you together until you maybe fall in again.

    "What *Is* This Thing Called Love?" *Redbook* Feb 75

DAVID VISCOTT

4 To love and be loved is to feel the sun from both sides.

    How to Live with Another Person Arbor House 74

SIMONE WEIL

5 The love of our neighbor in all its fullness simply means being able to say to him, "What are you going through?"

    Waiting for God Putnam 51

GLENWAY WESCOTT

6 It is not love, but lack of love, which is blind.

    NY *Herald Tribune* 19 Dec 65

MATTIE WHITE

7 I never married. Nobody ever asked me.

    On her 100th birthday, *Newsweek* 4 Jul 76

THORNTON WILDER

8 Love is an energy which exists of itself. It is its own value.

    Time 3 Feb 58

9 Love, though it expends itself in generosity and thoughtfulness, though it gives birth to visions and to great poetry, remains among the sharpest expressions of self-interest. Not until it has passed through a long servitude, through its own self-hatred, through mockery, through great doubts, can it take its place among the loyalties.

    Quoted by Edmund Fuller "The Notation of the Heart" in Hiram Hayden and Betsy Saunders eds *The American Scholar Reader* Atheneum 60

10 Many who have spent a lifetime in it can tell us less of love than the child that lost a dog yesterday.

    ib

EMLYN WILLIAMS

11 Cupid's dart had hit both targets and set the Nile on fire. And the Tiber. Even the Thames sizzled a bit.

    On 1963 romance of Richard Burton and Elizabeth Taylor while filming *Cleopatra* in Egypt, recalled on Burton's death, *People* 17 Sep 84

TENNESSEE WILLIAMS

12 The strongest influences in my life and my work are always whomever I love. Whomever I love and am with most of the time, or whomever I *remember* most vividly. I think that's true of everyone, don't you?

    NY *Times* 18 Mar 65

WALLIS, DUCHESS OF WINDSOR

13 Forgive me for not writing but this man is exhausting.

    On the Prince of Wales, February 12, 1934, letter to her Aunt Bessie, quoted in Michael Bloch ed *Wallis and Edward: Letters 1931–37* Summit 86

14 PS: It's all gossip about the prince. I'm not in the habit of taking my girlfriends' beaux.

    February 18, 1934, letter to her aunt, *ib*

15 I am so anxious for you not to *abdicate* and I think the fact that you do is going to put me in the wrong light to the entire world because they will say that I could have prevented it.

    December 6, 1936, letter to Edward VIII, written on her arrival at Cannes after fleeing England, *ib*

16 I look a hundred and weigh 110—you won't love me when you see the wreck England has made me.

    December 14, 1936, letter to Edward, after his abdication, *ib*

17 I hate this place. I shall hate it to my grave.

    On England in 1951, recalled on her death 24 Apr 86

SHELLEY WINTERS

18 Security is when I'm very much in love with somebody extraordinary who loves me back.

    News summaries 9 Jul 54

WOODROW WYATT

19 A man falls in love through his eyes, a woman through her ears.

    "To the Point" London *Sunday Times* 22 Mar 81

ISRAEL ZANGWILL

20 In how many lives does love really play a dominant part? The average taxpayer is no more capable of the grand passion than of a grand opera.

    Quoted on *Who Said That?* BBC TV 11 Feb 58

RELIGION

Spirituality

THOMAS J ALTIZER, Associate Professor of Religion, Emory University, Atlanta

21 We must recognize that the death of God is a historical event: God has died in our time, in our history, in our existence.

    Time 22 Oct 65

ANONYMOUS

22 God was more exciting then than he is now.

    Child's comment on the Old Testament, quoted by Gerald Kennedy *The Seven Worlds of the Minister* Harper & Row 68

23 May the Babe of Bethlehem be yours to tend;
May the Boy of Nazareth be yours for friend;
May the Man of Galilee his healing send;
May the Christ of Calvary his courage lend;
May the Risen Lord his presence send;
And his holy angels defend you to the end.

    "Pilgrim's Prayer," found in Oberammergau, West Germany, 80

1 From the cowardice that dare not face new truths,
From the laziness that is contented with half truth,
From the arrogance that thinks it knows all truth,
Good Lord, deliver me.

> Kenyan prayer, quoted in George Appleton comp *The Oxford Book of Prayer* Oxford 85

2 Oh priest of Jesus Christ, celebrate this Mass as if it were your first Mass, your only Mass, your last Mass.

> Sign in sacristy of Mother Teresa Hospice, NYC, 86

3 I sought my soul but my soul I could not see. I sought my God but my God eluded me. I sought my brother—and I found all three.

> Quoted by London Church News Service May 86

ANTONY, Russian Orthodox Archbishop of England

4 It was the spring of life . . . the beginning, when everything had total newness, when all things were possible, when duty entered into [the Disciples'] lives.

> Meditation on beginning of Christianity, Lambeth Conference 24 Jul 78

5 It was when faith exploded, when hope was fragrant and when they discovered the scope, the scale, the width and the depth of love they had never suspected.

> *ib*

W H AUDEN

6 Health is the state about which medicine has nothing to say: Sanctity is the state about which theology has nothing to say.

> *Atlantic* May 70

7 In a world of prayer, we are all equal in the sense that each of us is a unique person, with a unique perspective on the world, a member of a class of one.

> Recalled on his death 28 Sep 73

8 If time were the wicked sheriff in a horse opera, I'd pay for riding lessons and take his gun away.

> Lines used as part of offertory at his requiem in Cathedral Church of St John the Divine, NYC, 3 Oct 73

9 In the deserts of the heart
Let the healing fountains start,
In the prison of his days,
Teach the free man how to praise.

> "In Memory of W B Yeats," lines inscribed on Auden's stone in Poets' Corner of Westminster Abbey 2 Oct 74

KARL BARTH

10 Conscience is the perfect interpreter of life.

> *The Word of God and the Word of Man* Harper 57

11 Man can certainly keep on lying . . . but he cannot make truth falsehood. He can certainly rebel . . . but he can accomplish nothing which abolishes the choice of God.

> Recalled on his death 9 Dec 68

12 Man can certainly flee from God . . . but he cannot escape him. He can certainly hate God and be hateful to God, but he cannot change into its opposite the eternal love of God which triumphs even in his hate.

> *ib*

MARY CATHERINE BATESON

13 The Christian tradition was passed on to me as a great rich mixture, a bouillabaisse of human imagination and wonder brewed from the richness of individual lives.

> *With a Daughter's Eye* Morrow 84

STEPHEN BAYNE, Executive Officer, Anglican Communion

14 Obedience, judgment, witness . . . these are the signposts to our salvation, in all the perplexities and busyness of our life.

> Report to Archbishop of Canterbury Easter 63

HILAIRE BELLOC

15 The grace of God is courtesy.

> Quoted by Monica Baldwin *I Leap over the Wall* Rinehart 50

EDWARD M BERCKMAN, Episcopal priest

16 We are meant to be addicted to God, but we develop secondary addictions that temporarily appear to fix our problem.

> "Substitutes for God" *Living Church* 15 Feb 87

JOHN BETJEMAN

17 No love that in a family dwells, no caroling in frosty air,
Nor all the steeple-shaking bells
Can with this single Truth compare—
That God was Man in Palestine
And lives today in Bread and Wine.

> *Collected Poems* Houghton Mifflin 58

BOOK OF COMMON PRAYER

18 We thank you, Almighty God, for the gift of water.
Over it the Holy Spirit moved in the beginning of creation.
Through it you led the children of Israel out of their bondage in Egypt into the land of promise.
In it your Son Jesus received the baptism of John [and] we are buried with Christ in his death.
By it we share in his resurrection.
Through it we are reborn by the Holy Spirit.

> New baptismal rite for the Episcopal Church, Seabury 77

MALCOLM BOYD, Episcopal priest

19 I believe that God prays in us and through us, whether we are praying or not (and whether we believe in God or not). So, any prayer on my part is a conscious response to what God is already doing in my life.

> *Saturday Evening Post* 27 Aug 66

ROBERT McAFEE BROWN

20 Prayer for many is like a foreign land. When we go there, we go as tourists. Like most tourists, we feel uncomfortable and out of place. Like most tourists, we therefore move on before too long and go somewhere else.

> Introduction to John B Coburn *Prayer and Personal Religion* Westminster 67

Martin Buber

1 In Jewry, the way which leads to that promised time, the way of man's contribution to ultimate fulfillment, is whenever one generation encounters the next, whenever the generation which has reached its full development transmits the teachings to the generation which is still in the process of developing, so that the teachings spontaneously waken to new life in the new generation.
> *The Writings of Martin Buber* Meridian 56

2 God wants man to fulfill his commands as a human being and with the quality peculiar to human beings.
> *ib*

3 The law is not thrust upon man; it rests deep within him, to waken when the call comes.
> *ib*

4 God is the *mysterium tremendum* that appears and overthrows, but he is also the mystery of the self-evident, nearer to me than my I.
> Recalled on his death 13 Jun 65

Frederick Buechner

5 It is as impossible for man to demonstrate the existence of God as it would be for even Sherlock Holmes to demonstrate the existence of Arthur Conan Doyle.
> *Wishful Thinking: A Theological ABC* Harper & Row 73

6 If it seems a childish thing to do, do it in remembrance that you are a child.
> On the Eucharist, *ib*

7 In his holy flirtation with the world, God occasionally drops a handkerchief. These handkerchiefs are called saints.
> *ib*

8 Religion points to that area of human experience where in one way or another man comes upon mystery as a summons to pilgrimage.
> *Summons to Pilgrimage* privately published 84

Vannevar Bush

9 A belief may be larger than a fact. A faith that is overdefined is the very faith most likely to prove inadequate to the great moments of life.
> *Science Is Not Enough* Morrow 67

Jimmy Carter, 39th US President

10 You can't divorce religious belief and public service . . . I've never detected any conflict between God's will and my political duty. If you violate one, you violate the other.
> To National Conference of Baptist Men, 16 Jun 78

Fidel Castro

11 I never saw a contradiction between the ideas that sustain me and the ideas of that symbol, of that extraordinary figure [Jesus Christ].
> Quoted by Richard N Ostling "Castro Looks at Christianity" *Time* 30 Dec 85

Howard Hewlett Clark, Anglican Archbishop of Rupert's Land

12 Whatever task God is calling us to, if it is yours it is mine, and if it is mine it is yours. We must do it together—or be cast aside together.
> *Anglicans,* booklet published for Anglican Exhibition, 1964 NY World's Fair

William Sloane Coffin Jr, Senior Minister, Riverside Church, NYC

13 Hope arouses, as nothing else can arouse, a passion for the possible.
> *Once to Every Man* Atheneum 77, quoted in *Christian Science Monitor* 5 Jan 78

14 It's too bad that one has to conceive of sports as being the only arena where risks are, [for] all of life is risk exercise. That's the only way to live more freely, and more interestingly.
> *ib*

L Gordon Cooper Jr

15 Father, we thank you, especially for letting me fly this flight . . . for the privilege of being able to be in this position, to be in this wondrous place, seeing all these many startling, wonderful things that you have created.
> Prayer while orbiting the earth in a space capsule, quoted in NY *Times* 22 May 63

Harvey Cox, Professor of Divinity, Harvard

16 All human beings have an innate need to hear and tell stories and to have a story to live by. . . . religion, whatever else it has done, has provided one of the main ways of meeting this abiding need.
> *The Seduction of the Spirit* Simon & Schuster 73

17 There has never been a better raconteur than Jesus of Nazareth.
> *ib*

Wilford O Cross, Professor of Ethics and Moral Theology, Nashotah House Episcopal Seminary, Nashotah WI

18 Man does not bring to God's altar the stuff of nature in itself, in its initial structure, but something he has made and molded out of nature for the nourishment and the inspiration of men.
> *Prologue to Ethics* privately published 63

19 Within this thin wafer of bread is caught up symbolically the labor of plow and of sowing, of harvest and threshing, of milling, of packing, of transportation, of financing, of selling and packaging. Man's industrial life is all there.
> On the Eucharist, *ib*

Richard Cardinal Cushing, Archbishop of Boston

20 Mindful of the fact you live in an agricultural country, I presume you know what an ass is. We read in the New Testament that our blessed Lord rode on an ass in triumph into the city of Jerusalem. Today the Lord rides on another ass: myself.
> Preaching in the slums of Lima, Peru, *Time* 21 Aug 64

Dalai Lama

21 Sleep is the best meditation.
> *People* 10 Sep 79

Anthony Dalla Villa, Roman Catholic priest

22 What you are is God's gift to you; what you make of it is your gift to God.
> Eulogy at memorial Mass for Andy Warhol at NYC's St Patrick's Cathedral 1 Apr 87

23 Death gives life its fullest reality.
> *ib*

H B DEHQANI-TAFTI, exiled President Bishop, Episcopal Church in Jerusalem and the Middle East

1 The only remedy for a false view of the Cross is the Cross itself.

The Hard Awakening Seabury 81

LAKDASA J DE MEL, Anglican Metropolitan of India

2 Faith must not be slow to reason, nor reason to adore.

Sermon closing 10th Lambeth Conference, St Paul's Cathedral, London, 25 Aug 68

JEREMIAH A DENTON JR

3 A man does a lot of praying in an enemy prison. Prayer, even more than sheer thought, is the firmest anchor.

Quoted by George Esper and the Associated Press *The Eyewitness History of the Vietnam War 1961–75* Ballantine 83

ANGUS DUN, former Episcopal Bishop of Washington DC

4 I have learned that human existence is essentially tragic. It is only the love of God, disclosed and enacted in Christ, that redeems the human tragedy and makes it tolerable. No, more than tolerable. Wonderful.

Recalled on his death 12 Aug 71

WILL AND ARIEL DURANT

5 The soul of a civilization is its religion, and it dies with its faith.

The Age of Reason Begins Simon & Schuster 61

MARGARET WYVILL ECCLESINE

6 The life of a religious might be compared to the building of a cathedral . . . once a firm foundation has been laid, the building rises slowly.

A Touch of Radiance Bruce 66

7 Through it all there is order and symmetry and a vision of what the completed edifice will be; a vision of a perfect structure, dedicated wholly to the honor and glory of a great, good and loving God.

ib

OTIS EDWARDS, Dean, Seabury–Western Theological Seminary, Evanston IL

8 I go to the Eucharist day after day, every day I can, because that is what I am about.

Privately published 77

ALBERT EINSTEIN

9 I cannot imagine a God who rewards and punishes the objects of his creation [and] is but a reflection of human frailty.

Recalled on his death 18 Apr 55

10 My religion consists of a humble admiration of the illimitable superior spirit who reveals himself in the slight details we are able to perceive with our frail and feeble minds.

ib

11 That deep emotional conviction of the presence of a superior reasoning power, which is revealed in the incomprehensible universe, forms my idea of God.

ib

12 It was the experience of mystery—even if mixed with fear—that engendered religion.

From his 1931 book *Living Philosophies, ib*

13 God does not play dice [with the universe].

Quoted by Banesh Hoffman *Albert Einstein* New American Library 73

LESLIE FARBER

14 Out of disbelief [in God] we have impudently assumed that all of life is now subject to our own will. And the disasters that have come from willing what cannot be willed have not at all brought us to some modesty about our presumptions.

Quoted by Melvin Maddocks "Can Therapists Be Running out of Talk?" *Christian Science Monitor* 14 May 86

AUSTIN FARRER, Warden, Keble College, Oxford

15 Christ does not save us by acting a parable of divine love; he acts the parable of divine love by saving us. That is the Christian faith.

Faith and Logic Allen & Unwin 57

16 One of the silliest of all discussions is the question whether God is personal—it would be more useful to inquire whether ice is frozen.

Saving Belief Hodder & Stoughton 64

17 Religion is more like response to a friend than it is like obedience to an expert.

ib

RABBI LOUIS FINKELSTEIN

18 [A rabbi] should not despair if people do not do as much as they should. Every parent has that with children. God is merciful.

NY *Times* 1 Sep 85

GEOFFREY FISHER, Archbishop of Canterbury

19 There are only two kinds of people in the modern world who know what they are after. One, quite frankly, is the Communist. The other, equally frankly, is the convinced Christian. . . . The rest of the world are amiable nonentities.

Recalled on his death 14 Sep 72

20 Until you know that life is interesting—and find it so—you haven't found your soul.

ib

MARIE DE FLORIS OSB

21 Hunting God is a great adventure.

To novices making their vows, quoted by Peter Beach and William Dunphy *Benedictine and Moor* Holt, Rinehart & Winston 60

HARRY EMERSON FOSDICK

22 I would rather live in a world where my life is surrounded by mystery than live in a world so small that my mind could comprehend it.

"The Mystery of Life" in *Riverside Sermons* Harper 58

LUCINDA FRANKS

23 Christmas in Bethlehem. The ancient dream: a cold, clear night made brilliant by a glorious star, the smell of incense, shepherds and wise men falling to their knees in adoration of the sweet baby, the incarnation of perfect love.

"Pilgrimage" NY *Times* 23 Dec 84

1 The simple tableau is so rich with meaning that whether represented on the mantelpiece or in the mind, it seems suspended, complete unto itself, somewhere in eternity.

ib

R BUCKMINSTER FULLER

2 God, to me, it seems, is a verb not a noun, proper or improper.

No More Secondhand God Southern Illinois University 63

MONICA FURLONG

3 I have avoided the reverential approach, have tried to see him as the normal man he was, with his fair share, perhaps more than his fair share, of human frailties. It was this base metal which, in the marvelous alchemy of the spiritual journey, became transmuted into gold.

On Thomas Merton, *Merton* Harper & Row 80

4 The body . . . arrived at Gethsemani early on the afternoon of December 17, 1968. Monks and friends chanted the funeral liturgy in the church, and he was buried at dusk in the monastic cemetery under a light snowfall. He had, after all, returned home in time for Christmas.

On Merton's burial at the Monastery of Our Lady of Gethsemani in Kentucky, *ib*

GEORGE H GALLUP

5 I could prove God statistically. Take the human body alone—the chances that all the functions of an individual would just happen is a statistical monstrosity.

Recalled on his death 26 Jul 84

ERIC GILL

6 Without philosophy man cannot know what he makes; without religion he cannot know why.

Quoted in *Christian Science Monitor* 14 Aug 80

RUMER GODDEN

7 The motto was "Pax," but the word was set in a circle of thorns.

On a Benedictine motto, *In This House of Brede* Viking 69

8 Pax: peace, but what a strange peace, made of unremitting toil and effort, seldom with a seen result; subject to constant interruptions, unexpected demands, short sleep at night, little comfort, sometimes scant food; beset with disappointments and usually misunderstood; yet peace all the same, undeviating, filled with joy and gratitude and love.

ib

9 "It is My own peace I give unto you." Not, notice, the world's peace.

ib

LEON GOOD

10 Let us maintain our ability to wince as a people of faith.

On his Mennonite beliefs, NY *Times* 29 Nov 84

WILLIAM GORDON, Episcopal Bishop of Alaska

11 The really heroic people are not the ones who travel 10,000 miles by dog sled, but those who stay 10,000 days in one place.

Time 19 Nov 65

BILLY GRAHAM

12 The most eloquent prayer is the prayer through hands that heal and bless. The highest form of worship is the worship of unselfish Christian service. The greatest form of praise is the sound of consecrated feet seeking out the lost and helpless.

Chicago *American* 16 Apr 67

GREAT INVOCATION

13 From the point of light within the mind of God, let light stream forth into the minds of men. Let light descend on Earth. From the point of love within the heart of God, let love stream forth into the hearts of men.

WQXR Radio 15 Jul 83

14 May Christ return to Earth. From the center where the will of God is known, let purpose guide the little wills of men—the purpose which the masters know and serve.

ib

15 From the center which we call the race of men, let the plan of love and light work out and may it seal the door where evil dwells. Let light and love and power restore the plan on Earth.

ib

GRAHAM GREENE

16 You think it more difficult to turn air into wine than to turn wine into blood?

On a priest who pantomimes Mass, *Monsignor Quixote* PBS TV 13 Feb 87

DAG HAMMARSKJÖLD

17 God does not die on the day when we cease to believe in a personal deity, but we die on the day when our lives cease to be illumined by the steady radiance, renewed daily, of a wonder, the source of which is beyond all reason.

Markings Knopf 64

18 I am the vessel. The draft is God's. And God is the thirsty one.

ib

HENRY HANCOCK, Dean, St Mark's Cathedral, Minneapolis MN

19 Out of our beliefs are born deeds; out of our deeds we form habits; out of our habits grows our character; and on our character we build our destiny.

Alpha Xi Delta Magazine 57

ABRAHAM JOSHUA HESCHEL, Jewish Theological Seminary of America, NYC

20 A religious man is a person who holds God and man in one thought at one time, at all times, who suffers harm done to others, whose greatest passion is compassion, whose greatest strength is love and defiance of despair.

NY *Journal-American* 5 Apr 63

JOHN S HIGGINS, former Episcopal Bishop of Rhode Island

1 Read the Bible, first and foremost, always, every day, unremittingly and often with a concordance, until the history and prophecy and the wisdom literature of the Old Testament get into our very bones; and until the Gospels and Epistles of the New Testament become the foundation blocks of our thinking and way of life.

"Ten Commandments for Preachers" *Living Church* 13 Jan 85

STUART HINE

2 O Lord my God! When I in awesome wonder
Consider all the worlds thy hands have made,
I see the stars, I hear the rolling thunder,
Thy pow'r throughout the universe displayed,
Then sings my soul, my Savior God to thee;
How great thou art, How great thou art!

"How Great Thou Art," 1955 theme hymn for Billy Graham's revivals

JOHN E HINES, Presiding Bishop, Episcopal Church

3 It is only in the light of the inescapable fact of death that a person can adequately engage and enter upon the mysterious fact of life.

Easter message 65

4 Preaching is effective as long as the preacher expects something to happen—not because of the sermon, not even because of the preacher, but because of God.

On his retirement, *Witness* Jul 77

5 In the spectrum of God's mysteries, preaching is a sacrament: Because of its sacramental reality . . . some people have never again been the same.

ib

RICHARD HOLLOWAY, Anglican priest

6 God is waiting eagerly to respond with new strength to each little act of self-control, small disciplines of prayer, feeble searching after him. And his children shall be filled if they will only hunger and thirst after what he offers.

Beyond Belief Eerdmans 81

7 Simplicity, clarity, singleness: These are the attributes that give our lives power and vividness and joy as they are also the marks of great art. They seem to be the purpose of God for his whole creation.

ib

URBAN T HOLMES III, Dean, School of Theology, University of the South, Sewanee TN

8 The call to serve as priest or pastor is both internal and external—a matter of one's individual inner awareness and the ratification of that awareness by the church—and should manifest itself in the living out of that vocation through a lifetime.

Spirituality for Ministry Harper & Row 82

REUEL HOWE, Director, Institute of Advanced Pastoral Studies, Bloomfield Hills MI

9 I want them "dunked"—plunged deeply into life, brought up gasping and dripping, and returned to us humble and ready to learn.

On candidates for the priesthood, *Anglican World* Epiphany/Lent 64

10 Until all students are faced by the tragedies, the contradictions and the stark questions of life, they cannot understand the need for redemption or God's redemptive action.

ib

TREVOR HUDDLESTON CR, missionary in South Africa

11 My responsibility is always and everywhere the same: to see in my brother more even than the personality and manhood that are his. My task is always and everywhere the same: to see Christ himself.

Naught for Your Comfort Doubleday 56

12 God bless Africa,
Guard her people,
Guide her leaders,
And give her peace.

Composed for people who wanted to pray for Africa, quoted in address at Nashotah House Episcopal Seminary, Nashotah WI, 22 Apr 66

KATHRYN HULME

13 It is not easy to be a nun. It is a life of sacrifice and self-abnegation. It is a life against nature. Poverty, chastity and obedience are extremely difficult. But there are always the graces if you will pray for them. Pray that you may all become St Johns, lovers of Christ.

The Nun's Story Little, Brown 56

14 Never forget that [God] tests his real friends more severely than the lukewarm ones.

ib

ROZA JAKUBOWICZ, caretaker, Cracow Synagogue

15 In the city where the average age of Jews is 78, a Jewish boy has come to manhood and I have lived to see it.

On Eric Strom of Stamford CT who was invited to be bar mitzvahed in Poland, NY *Times* 8 Sep 85

JEWISH THEOLOGICAL SEMINARY OF AMERICA, NYC

16 A human life is like a single letter in the alphabet. It can be meaningless. Or it can be part of a great meaning.

From advertisement on Rosh Hashanah, "Who Takes Delight in Life" NY *Herald Tribune* 5 Sep 56

POPE JOHN XXIII

17 I am made to tremble and I fear!

On learning of his election to succeed Pius XII, 29 Oct 58

18 I have looked into your eyes with my eyes. I have put my heart near your heart.

To a prisoner on first papal visit to a prison since 1870, 26 Dec 58

19 I have been able to follow my death step by step and now my life goes gently to its end.

In his last hours, quoted in NY *Daily News* 2 Jun 63

20 The feelings of my smallness and my nothingness always kept me good company.

From his will, made public 6 Jun 63

21 Born poor, but of honored and humble people, I am particularly proud to die poor.

ib

POPE JOHN PAUL I

1 You know that I try to maintain a continuous conversation with you. I take comfort in the thought that the important thing is not for one person to write to Christ but for many people to love and emulate [you]. Fortunately, despite everything, this still occurs today.

> Letter to Jesus Christ, in volume of letters to historical figures published when he was patriarch of Venice, recalled on his death 28 Sep 78

POPE JOHN PAUL II

2 There are people and nations, Mother, that I would like to say to you by name. I entrust them to you in silence, I entrust them to you in the way that you know best.

> Prayer at Shrine of Mary, Jasna Gora Monastery, on return to Poland after election as pope, *Time* 18 Jun 79

3 This people draws its origin from Abraham, our father in faith . . . The very people that received from God the commandment "Thou shalt not kill" itself experienced in a special measure what is meant by killing. It is not permissible for anyone to pass by this inscription with indifference.

> On visiting Auschwitz concentration camp that he called "the Golgotha of the modern world," *ib*

4 Do not abandon yourselves to despair. . . . We are the Easter people and hallelujah is our song.

> Address in Harlem 2 Oct 79

5 When you wonder about the mystery of yourself, look to Christ, who gives you the meaning of life. When you wonder what it means to be a mature person, look to Christ, who is the fulfillness of humanity. And when you wonder about your role in the future of the world . . . look to Christ.

> To 19,000 students in NYC 3 Oct 79

6 Social justice cannot be attained by violence. Violence kills what it intends to create.

> To workers in São Paulo, Brazil, news summaries 4 Jul 80

7 Humanity should question itself, once more, about the absurd and always unfair phenomenon of war, on whose stage of death and pain only remain standing the negotiating table that could and should have prevented it.

> On arriving in Buenos Aires near end of conflict between Argentina and Great Britain over the Falkland Islands, 11 Jun 82

8 [I kiss the soil] as if I placed a kiss on the hands of a mother, for the homeland is our earthly mother. I consider it my duty to be with my compatriots in this sublime and difficult moment.

> On arriving in Poland during period of martial law, *Time* 27 Jun 83

9 What we talked about will have to remain a secret between him and me. I spoke to him as a brother whom I have pardoned and who has my complete trust.

> On visiting the imprisoned Mehmet Ali Agca, who wounded the pope in a 1981 assassination attempt, *Time* 9 Jan 84

10 In the context of Christmas and the Holy Year of Redemption, I was able to meet with the person that you all know by name, Ali Agca, who in the year 1981 on the 13th of May made an attempt on my life. But Providence took things in its own hands, in what I would call an extraordinary way, so that today . . . I was able to meet my assailant and repeat to him the pardon I gave him immediately.

> *ib*

LYNDON B JOHNSON, 36th US President

11 In our home there was always prayer—aloud, proud and unapologetic.

> To Washington prayer breakfast, quoted in *Time* 3 Apr 64

JIM JONES

12 To me death is not a fearful thing. It's living that's cursed.

> Final words tape-recorded before his death and mass suicide of his followers at Jonestown, Guyana, 18 Nov 78

CARL JUNG

13 I could not say I believe. I know! I have had the experience of being gripped by something that is stronger than myself, something that people call God.

> *Time* 14 Feb 55

14 Our heart glows, and secret unrest gnaws at the root of our being. . . . Dealing with the unconscious has become a question of life for us.

> *ib*

15 I have treated many hundreds of patients. . . . Among [those] in the second half of life—that is to say, over 35—there has not been one whose problem in the last resort was not that of finding a religious outlook on life.

> *ib*

16 In my case *Pilgrim's Progress* consisted in my having to climb down a thousand ladders until I could reach out my hand to the little clod of earth that I am.

> Letter to a former student on reassessing religious values outlined to Sigmund Freud a half century earlier, quoted in Gerhard Adler ed *Letters, Vol 1* Princeton 73

17 Knowing your own darkness is the best method for dealing with the darknesses of other people.

> *ib*

YASUNARI KAWABATA

18 Because you cannot see him, God is everywhere.

> Quoted by Susan Cheever *Home before Dark* Houghton Mifflin 84

HELEN KELLER

19 I can see, and that is why I can be happy, in what you call the dark, but which to me is golden. I can see a God-made world, not a manmade world.

> Reply to question,"Can you see a world?" in 1955 documentary *The Unconquered*

20 It gives me a deep comforting sense that "things seen are temporal and things unseen are eternal."

> On reading the Bible daily, news summaries 26 Jun 55

JOHN F KENNEDY, 35th US President

21 I know there is a God—I see the storm coming and I see his hand in it—if he has a place then I am ready—we see the hand.

> Paraphrasing Abraham Lincoln in notes on program for prayer breakfast, NY *Times* 15 May 64

MADELEINE L'ENGLE

1 We have much to be judged on when he comes, slums and battlefields and insane asylums, but these are the symptoms of our illness and the result of our failures in love.

The Irrational Season Seabury 77

2 In the evening of life we shall be judged on love, and not one of us is going to come off very well, and were it not for my absolute faith in the loving forgiveness of my Lord I could not call on him to come.

ib

3 Conversion for me was not a Damascus Road experience. I slowly moved into an intellectual acceptance of what my intuition had always known.

"Writer, Wife, Theologian" *Anglican Digest* Pentecost 83

C S LEWIS

4 I believe in Christianity as I believe that the sun has risen, not only because I see it but because I see everything by it.

Recalled on his death 22 Nov 63

5 Aim at heaven and you will get earth thrown in. Aim at earth and you get neither.

ib

6 The safest road to hell is the gradual one—the gentle slope, soft underfoot, without sudden turnings, without milestones, without signposts.

ib

7 What seem our worst prayers may really be, in God's eyes, our best. Those, I mean, which are least supported by devotional feeling. For these may come from a deeper level than feeling. God sometimes seems to speak to us most intimately when he catches us, as it were, off our guard.

Letters to Malcolm: Chiefly on Prayer Harcourt, Brace & World 64

8 Some people feel guilty about their anxieties and regard them as a defect of faith [but] they are afflictions, not sins. Like all afflictions, they are, if we can so take them, our share in the passion of Christ.

Episcopalian Apr 65

9 A man who is eating or lying with his wife or preparing to go to sleep in humility, thankfulness and temperance, is, by Christian standards, in an infinitely *higher* state than one who is listening to Bach or reading Plato in a state of pride.

To undergraduates at Oxford, quoted in W H Lewis ed *Letters of C S Lewis* Harcourt, Brace & World 66

10 I gave in, and admitted that God was God.

On relinquishing atheism at age 31 in 1929, quoted by William Griffin *Clive Staples Lewis* Harper & Row 86

STANLEY LINDQUIST, Professor of Psychology, California State University

11 God allows us to experience the low points of life in order to teach us lessons we could not learn in any other way. The way we learn those lessons is not to deny the feelings but to find the meanings underlying them.

Asbury Park NJ *Press* 25 Jul 75

SIDNEY LOVETT, Chaplain, Yale

12 The person who is truly religious is one who has come to be less at home in the world of sense, less moved by the things that appear, less confident in the weight and power of sheer material force and more assured of those verities that are hidden from the wise and prudent but revealed unto babes; more aware of those things which "eye hath not seen, nor ear heard," more at home in that greater and better part of life which is out of sight.

Recalled on his death 3 Apr 79

GEDDES MACGREGOR, Professor of Philosophy and Religion, Bryn Mawr

13 It is . . . in plunging into the stream of life itself and entering into the deepest involvement with the values that confront us, exercising our wills to the utmost—to the breaking point—that we find God in the very extremity of the battle.

Introduction to Religious Philosophy Houghton Mifflin 59

MOTHER MARY MADELEVA CSC

14 I like to go to Marshall Field's in Chicago just to see how many things there are in the world that I do not want.

My First Seventy Years Macmillan 59

MOTHER MARIBEL CSMV, Superior, Community of St Mary the Virgin, Wantage, England

15 So often we try to alter circumstances to suit ourselves, instead of letting them alter us, which is what they are meant to do.

Quoted by Sister Janet CSMV *Mother Maribel of Wantage* Society for Promoting Christian Knowledge 73

16 Our Lord did not try to alter circumstances. He submitted to them. They shaped his life and eventually brought him to Calvary. I believe we miss opportunities and lovely secrets our Lord is waiting to teach us by not taking what comes.

ib

17 Our real work is prayer. What good is the cold iron of our frantic little efforts unless first we heat it in the furnace of our prayer? Only heat will diffuse heat.

ib

18 Silence is not a thing we make; it is something into which we enter. It is always there. We talk about keeping silence. We keep only that which is precious. Silence is precious, for it is of God. In silence all God's acts are done; in silence alone can his voice be heard and his word spoken.

ib

CALVIN MARSHALL, evangelist

19 If we were nothing here, at least we were children of God. At some far-off point in time, all these things would be rectified and we would get our golden slippers.

On Christianity's traditional attraction for blacks, *Time* 6 Apr 70

20 Our religion *had* to mean more to us. We had to emote, we had to lose ourselves in it. We had to sing and shout, and after it was all over we had to have a big meal and have something going on Sunday

afternoon. Because when Monday came, it was back out into the fields, or back to the janitor's job, or back in Miss Ann's kitchen scrubbing the floor.
ib

MOTHER MARY AMBROSE MMS

1 The true vocation [is] settled on the day the girl looks around her and sees a young woman her own age in pretty clothes wheeling a baby carriage by the convent. Then her heart takes an awful flop and she knows what it is God really is asking of her. If she stays—then she has a true calling and the making of a good religious.
Life 15 Mar 63

ERIC MASCALL, Lecturer in Philosophy of Religion, Christ Church, Oxford

2 A very large amount of human suffering and frustration is caused by the fact that many men and women are not content to be the sort of beings that God has made them, but try to persuade themselves that they are really beings of some different kind.
The Importance of Being Human Columbia University 58

SUZANNE MASSIE

3 Evil is near. Sometimes late at night the air grows strongly clammy and cold around me. I feel it brushing me. All that the Devil asks is acquiescence . . . not struggle, not conflict. Acquiescence.
On the years of treating her son's hemophilia, *Journey*, written with her husband Robert, Knopf 75

4 Accept, accept that I have won, whispers the Devil. You can see for yourself that life is unjust, unfair, that suffering is ordinary. Who is stronger? I am, of course. Just despair, my dear, despair. Only tell me that I am strong, that Evil rules.
ib

W R MATTHEWS, Dean, St Paul's Cathedral, London

5 Naturally, we cannot say much about the spiritual body, because we cannot imagine what it would be like to have a spiritual body different from that which we now inhabit; but it seems to me reasonable to believe that we are weaving our spiritual bodies as we go along.
Recalled on his retirement, news summaries 31 Dec 67

JAN MAZUR, Roman Catholic Bishop of Siedlce, Poland

6 Dear youth, you have won through goodness. You were the ones who came to Christ and calmly stood by the cross. Stand by him all your lives.
After leading 450 Polish clerics on a bread and water fast in support of students who protested the removal of crucifixes from public buildings, NY *Times* 7 Apr 84

WILLIAM McGILL, Episcopal priest

7 The value of persistent prayer is not that he will hear us . . . but that we will finally hear him.
"Prayer Unceasing" *Living Church* 28 Sep 86

MARGARET MEAD

8 Prayer does not use up artificial energy, doesn't burn up any fossil fuel, doesn't pollute.
Quoted by Jane Howard *Margaret Mead* Simon & Schuster 84

THOMAS MERTON OCSO

9 By reading the scriptures I am so renewed that all nature seems renewed around me and with me. The sky seems to be a pure, a cooler blue, the trees a deeper green. . . . The whole world is charged with the glory of God and I feel fire and music . . . under my feet.
Thoughts in Solitude Farrar, Straus 58

10 The very contradictions in my life are in some ways signs of God's mercy to me.
Preface to *Thomas Merton Reader* Harcourt, Brace & World 62

11 So Brother Matthew locked the gate behind me, and I was enclosed in the four walls of my new freedom.
On entering the Trappist Monastery of Our Lady of Gethsemani, *The Seven Storey Mountain* Harcourt, Brace 48, recalled on his death 10 Dec 68

12 Solitude is not something you must hope for in the future. Rather, it is a deepening of the present, and unless you look for it in the present you will never find it.
Quoted by Monica Furlong *Merton* Harper & Row 80

13 Be good, keep your feet dry, your eyes open, your heart at peace and your soul in the joy of Christ.
ib

ERIC MILNER-WHITE, Dean of York Minster, England

14 Praised be St John, the glorified of God! Lord, grant me the prayers of St John, disciple and friend whom thou lovest, apostle of love. Thy love, forever, eternal, that my faith may become as complete, as flaming and tranquil, as his, and pierce as deep and speak as simply in the spirit.
My God, My Glory Society for Promoting Christian Knowledge 54

15 That I may apprehend thee as light lightening every creature and everything, every moment; that I may know thee as truth, hearing thy voice; that I may serve thee as love, loving thy people, asking for no reward, no place, but one only and for one instant—to lean on thy bosom.
ib

16 St John, on Christ's bosom, pray for me in the days of my discipleship, in the house of my faith, in the hour of my death.
ib

JOHN MONAGHAN, Roman Catholic priest

17 The religion of Christ is not aspirin to deaden the pain of living, it is not a discussion group, nor a miraculous medal nor a piety, nor bingo for God. Not anything less than a joyous adventure of being Christ in a world still skeptical of him.
"A Lenten Message" NY *Journal-American* 16 Feb 61

MOTHER HARRIET MONSELL CSJB

18 The one great aim of her life is the glory of God.
The one great example of her life is the incarnate God.
The one great devotion of her life is the will of God.
The one great longing of her life is union with God.
The one great reward of her life is the vision of God.
"My Ideal of a Religious," quoted by James B Simpson and Edward M Story *Stars in His Crown* Ploughshare Press 76

DEWI MORGAN, Rector, St Bride's, Fleet Street, London

1 Christianity is different from all other religions. They are the story of man's search for God. The Gospel is the story of God's search for man.
St Mary's Messenger Sep/Oct 66

ROBERT C MORTIMER, Anglican Bishop of Exeter, England

2 This was a splendid life. Splendid in its obscurity and humility, splendid in its strength and charity, splendid in its achievements.
At requiem for Anglican Franciscan Algy Robertson, quoted by Fr Denis SSF *Father Algy* Hodder & Stoughton 64

ROBERT MOSES, NYC Parks Commissioner

3 Here the skeptic finds chaos and the believer further evidence that the hand that made us is divine.
At reopening of Hayden Planetarium, NY *Herald Tribune* 3 Feb 60

J ROBERT MOSKIN

4 One of life's gifts is that each of us, no matter how tired and downtrodden, finds reasons for thankfulness: for the crops carried in from the fields and the grapes from the vineyard.
On ancient autumn holiday of Succoth, "The Heritage of Judaism" *Look* 5 Oct 65

5 Thanksgiving comes to us out of the prehistoric dimness, universal to all ages and all faiths. At whatever straws we must grasp, there is always a time for gratitude and new beginnings.
ib

ROBERT R MOTON, President, Tuskegee Institute

6 When you eat fish, you don't eat the bones. You eat the flesh. Take the Bible like that.
NY *Post* 17 May 64

MALCOLM MUGGERIDGE

7 Every happening, great and small, is a parable whereby God speaks to us, and the art of life is to get the message.
News summaries 31 Dec 78

JACK ("MURPH THE SURF") MURPHY

8 God had a sense of humor, a style of his own.
On his parole 10 Nov 86

JOHN COURTNEY MURRAY SJ

9 Today's barbarian may wear a Brooks Brothers suit and carry a ball-point pen. In fact, even beneath the academic gown there may lurk a child of the wilderness, untutored in the high tradition of civility, who goes busily and happily about his work, a domesticated and law-abiding man, engaged in the concoction of a philosophy to put an end to all philosophy.
Recalled on his death 16 Aug 67

MOHAMMED NAGUIB

10 Religion is a candle inside a multicolored lantern. Everyone looks through a particular color, but the candle is always there.
News summaries 31 Dec 53

REINHOLD NIEBUHR

11 Nothing that is worth doing can be achieved in a lifetime; therefore we must be saved by hope.
The Irony of American History Scribner's 52

12 Nothing which is true or beautiful or good makes complete sense in any immediate context of history; therefore we must be saved by faith.
ib

13 Nothing we do, however virtuous, can be accomplished alone; therefore we are saved by love.
ib

14 The final test of religious faith . . . is whether it will enable men to endure insecurity without complacency or despair, whether it can so interpret the ancient verities that they will not become mere escape hatches from responsibilities but instruments of insights into what civilization means.
Saturday Evening Post 23 Jul 60

15 God, give us grace to accept with serenity the things that cannot be changed, courage to change the things which should be changed and the wisdom to distinguish the one from the other.
Originally part of a sermon in 1943 and later used by Alcoholics Anonymous, quoted by June Bingham *Courage to Change* Scribner's 61

D T NILES

16 Christianity is one beggar telling another beggar where he found bread.
NY *Times* 11 May 86

WILLIAM BARR OGLESBY JR, Professor of Pastoral Counseling, Union Theological Seminary, Richmond VA

17 The presence of faith is no guarantee of deliverance from times of distress and vicissitude but there can be a certainty that nothing will be encountered that is overwhelming.
Virginia Seminary Journal May 83

C NORTHCOTE PARKINSON

18 Where life is colorful and varied, religion can be austere or unimportant. Where life is appallingly monotonous, religion must be emotional, dramatic and intense. Without the curry, boiled rice can be very dull.
East and West Houghton Mifflin 63

POPE PAUL VI

19 Of all human activities, man's listening to God is the supreme act of his reasoning and will.
Quoted by Curtis Pepper *The Pope's Backyard* Farrar, Straus & Giroux 66

NORMAN VINCENT PEALE

20 When you pray for anyone you tend to modify your personal attitude toward him. You lift the relationship thereby to a higher level. The best in the other person begins to flow out toward you as your best flows toward him. In the meeting of the best in each a higher unity of understanding is established.
The Power of Positive Thinking Prentice-Hall 52

PIO DA PIETREICINA, Capuchin monk

21 The wretchedness of men equals the mercy of God.
Time 24 Apr 64

POPE PIUS XII

1 Labor is not merely the fatigue of body without sense or value; nor is it merely a humiliating servitude. It is a service of God, a gift of God, the vigor and fullness of human life, the gauge of eternal rest.

Message for Labor Day, *Guideposts* Sep 55

2 I shall be able to rest one minute after I die.

To physicians who asked him to curtail his work, *Look* 22 Aug 55

3 Bodily pain affects man as a whole down to the deepest layers of his moral being. It forces him to face again the fundamental questions of his fate, of his attitude toward God and fellow man, of his individual and collective responsibility and of the sense of his pilgrimage on earth.

To a group of international heart specialists, news summaries 1 Sep 56

MICHAEL RAMSEY, Archbishop of Canterbury

4 Help one another, serve one another, for the times are urgent and the days are evil. Help one another, serve one another, as from this hundredth ceremony at St Augustine's throne there goes a band of those whose hearts God has touched.

Conclusion of enthronement sermon 27 Jun 61

5 Learning to laugh at ourselves, we did not lack other things to laugh about. How should we, if the Christian life is indeed the knowledge of him who is the author of laughter as well as tears?

On his days as a seminarian, quoted by James B Simpson *The Hundredth Archbishop of Canterbury* Harper & Row 62

6 Take heed to thyself, that self which can deceive itself unless it is revealed in naked simplicity before its God. It is in this taking heed that a true devoutness, simple, generous, Godward, has its root and its renewing.

To men about to be ordained, *ib*

7 The supreme question is not what we make of the Eucharist but what the Eucharist is making of us.

ib

8 There is a simplicity born of shallowness, and falsely so called; and there is a simplicity which is the costly outcome of the discipline of mind and heart and will. Simplicity in preaching is properly the simplicity of the knowledge of God and of human beings. To say of someone "he preaches simply" is to say "he walks with God."

ib

9 Reason is an action of the mind; knowledge is a possession of the mind; but faith is an attitude of the person. It means you are prepared to stake yourself on something being so.

ib

10 Christ comes to bind lives to God through reconciliation. He comes to bind human lives closely to one another in fellowship. He comes to bind up the individual human life that is lost and divided. Christian unity involves all these three aspects of peace.

Tennessee Churchman Dec 66

11 To be with God wondering, that is adoration. To be with God gratefully, that is thanksgiving. To be with God ashamed, that is contrition. To be with God

with people and things we care about in our hearts, that is intercession. But the center of it in desire and in design will be the being with God.

"The Heart of Prayer" *Christian World* 7 Dec 78

DAVID H C READ, Pastor, Madison Avenue Presbyterian Church, NYC

12 The Christian call . . . does not mean we are to become rigid and aggressive moralists with a strict and firm answer to every ethical problem. But it does mean we are committed to the conviction that there is an answer to be found.

Time 7 Feb 64

RONALD REAGAN, 40th US President

13 I miss going to church, but I think the Lord understands.

Explaining that security precautions prevented him from joining in public worship, reply in debate with Democratic candidate Walter F Mondale, Louisville KY, 7 Oct 84

BETTY ROBBINS

14 I sing what is in my heart. My only thought now is to sing as I have never sung before.

On being first woman cantor in Jewish history, news summaries 15 Aug 55

ROMAN CATHOLIC BISHOPS OF THE UNITED STATES

15 It is not the Christian vocation to canonize the human condition as such or to lament over it. It is our vocation to rise above it where it drags us down; to transform it where it might trap others; to ennoble it by the operation, through our agency, of that Spirit who continually refreshes the Church and renews the face of the earth.

Pastoral letter, NY *Times* 11 Jan 68

ROBERT RUNCIE, Archbishop of Canterbury

16 The New Testament never simply says "remember Jesus Christ." That is a half-finished sentence. It says "remember Jesus Christ is risen from the dead."

1980 Easter sermon, recalled in *Seasons of the Spirit* Eerdmans 83

17 The priest is concerned with other people for the sake of God and with God for the sake of other people.

Ordination sermon, "The Character of a Priest," *ib*

18 If our faith delivers us from worry, then worry is an insult flung in the face of God.

Address during April 1982 tour of Nigeria, *ib*

ANATOLY RYBAKOV

19 She returned home, to the empty and dark room, and there, lonely and suffering, uttered a prayer to the God whom she had long since abandoned, yet who remained the God of her ancestors, praying that the spirit of goodness and mercy, omnipresent and all-pervading, would soften the hearts of those who decided Sasha's fate.

On a mother seeking the whereabouts of her son during the Stalinist era in the USSR, quoted in NY *Times* 14 Mar 87

ST LEONARD'S HOUSE, Chicago

1 One can discard a warped chair, but one cannot discard a warped man. One can junk a car that doesn't function, but one cannot junk a man who doesn't. We can throw away anything we own. But we cannot throw away broken men. For we are made our brother's keeper . . . and in God's name we try to straighten and repair. And this is *our* redemption.

1966 brochure on rehabilitation of ex-convicts

FRANCIS B SAYRE, Dean, National Cathedral, Washington DC

2 Religion isn't yours firsthand until you doubt it right down to the ground.

Life 2 Apr 65

3 I don't think man comes to faith firsthand except through despair or to knowledge of God except through doubt. It has to be a kind of watershed experience.

ib

ALBERT SCHWEITZER

4 Day by day we should weigh what we have granted to the spirit of the world against what we have denied to the spirit of Jesus, in thought and especially in deed.

Guideposts Mar 56

5 Do not let Sunday be taken from you . . . If your soul has no Sunday, it becomes an orphan.

Quoted by Erica Anderson *The Schweitzer Album* Harper & Row 65

6 Example is not the main thing in influencing others. It is the only thing.

Recalled on his death 4 Sep 65

RICHARD SELZER

7 Each . . . is like a river that leaves behind its name and shape, the whole course of its path, to vanish into the vast sea of God.

On Benedictine monks in Venice, *Taking the World in for Repairs* Morrow 86, quoted in NY *Times* 19 Oct 86

FULTON J SHEEN, retired Roman Catholic Bishop of Rochester NY

8 The only way to win audiences is to tell people about the life and death of Christ. Every other approach is a waste.

To National Conference of Catholic Bishops, Chicago, NY *Times* 4 May 78

9 Show me your hands. Do they have scars from giving? Show me your feet. Are they wounded in service? Show me your heart. Have you left a place for divine love?

Good Friday sermon, quoted in *ib* 14 Apr 79

MASSEY SHEPHERD, Episcopal priest

10 The Magnificat is the loveliest flower of Hebrew Messianic poetry, blossoming on the eve of the Incarnation.

Oxford American Prayer Book Commentary Oxford 50

CARROLL SIMCOX, Editor, *Living Church*

11 When you want it, it's a handout; when I want it, it's seed money. When you're that way, you're naive; when I'm that way, I'm open. When you have it, it's a hang-up; when I have it, it's a priority. When you're that way, you're uptight; when I'm that way, I'm liberated. When you're that way, you're not hearing me; when I'm that way, I'm telling it like it is. When you're that way, you're being irrelevant; when I'm that way, I'm being prophetic.

On "semantic distinctions," at Episcopal convention 28 Sep 69

ISAAC BASHEVIS SINGER

12 Life is God's novel. Let him write it.

Quoted in Dom Moraes ed *Voices for Life* Praeger 75

13 Doubt is part of all religion. All the religious thinkers were doubters.

NY *Times* 3 Dec 78

SISTERS OF THE HOLY NATIVITY

14 We grow in Christ and Christ grows in us. In us, self must die, that we may rise from the grave of what we are, to the glory of what we should be.

Intercession paper quoted in Episcopal Diocese of Fond du Lac WI *Clarion* Aug 83

RALPH W SOCKMAN, Senior Minister, Christ Church, Methodist, NYC

15 A service of worship is primarily a service to God. When we realize this and act upon it, we make it a service to men.

Recalled on his death 29 Aug 70

16 The hope of free man in a frightened world is the values which man puts ahead of inventions when his back is to the wall. These values are beauty, truth, goodness and having a faith, all of which are bombproof.

ib

SOONG MEI-LING

17 No one who has had a unique experience with prayer has a right to withhold it from others.

"The Power of Prayer" *Reader's Digest* Aug 55

RABBI PINCHAS STOLPER, Executive Vice President, Union of Orthodox Jewish Congregations

18 [The yarmulke] is an indication that one recognizes that there is something above you. It says, "Above my intellect is a sign of godliness."

On Supreme Court ruling that allowed the military to prohibit an Orthodox Jewish officer from wearing a yarmulke indoors while in uniform, NY *Times* 26 Mar 86

IGOR STRAVINSKY

19 The Church knew what the psalmist knew: Music praises God. Music is well or better able to praise him than the building of the church and all its decoration; it is the Church's greatest ornament.

Quoted by Robert Craft *Conversations with Igor Stravinsky* Amer Biography Service 59

LÉON JOSEPH CARDINAL SUENENS, Archbishop of Mechlin-Brussels, Belgium

20 One is Christianized to the extent that he is a Christianizer. One is evangelized to the extent that he is an evangelist.

Catholic Digest Jun 64

1 I am a man of hope because I believe that God is born anew each morning, because I believe that he is creating the world at this very moment. He did not create it at a distant moment in time, then forget about it. It is happening now; we must therefore be ready to expect the unexpected from God.

> Quoted by Elizabeth Hamilton *Suenens* Doubleday 75

2 I believe in the surprises of the Holy Spirit.

> *ib*

WILLIAM SWING, Episcopal Bishop of California

3 I have a hunch that the last institution around at this moment which has a high doctrine of sex is the Church. We still believe sex is a good gift from God but it needs to be in context of a committed, loving, continuing relationship.

> *Episcopalian* Mar 86

4 Where there is an ongoing relationship of caring. Where there is a sense of humor. Where there is a sense of mutual mercy. Where there is a sense that God has given sex to you . . . there is nothing livelier. But when it is merchandised as a commodity for instant gratification, there is nothing deadlier than sex.

> *ib*

PIERRE TEILHARD DE CHARDIN SJ

5 Someday, after mastering the winds, the waves, the tides and gravity, we shall harness for God the energies of love, and then, for a second time in the history of the world, man will have discovered fire.

> Recalled on his death 10 Apr 55

6 Since once again, O Lord, in the steppes of Asia, I have no bread, no wine, no altar, I will raise myself above those symbols to the pure majesty of reality, and I will offer to you, I, your priest, upon the altar of the entire earth, the labor and the suffering of the world.

> Prayer composed on Easter Sunday in Inner Mongolia's Ordos Desert, quoted by John Kobler "The Priest Who Haunts the Catholic World" *Saturday Evening Post* 12 Oct 63

7 Receive, O Lord, in its totality the Host which creation, drawn by your magnetism, presents to you at the dawn of a new day. This bread, our effort, is in itself, I know, nothing but an immense disintegration. This wine, our anguish, as yet, alas! is only an evaporating beverage. But in the depths of this inchoate Mass you have placed—I am certain, for I feel it—an irresistible and holy desire that moves us all, the impious as well as the faithful to cry out: "O Lord, make us one!"

> *ib*

MOTHER TERESA MC

8 Our vow of chastity is nothing but our undivided love for Christ in chastity, then we proceed to the freedom of poverty—poverty is nothing but freedom. And that total surrender is obedience. If I belong to God, if I belong to Christ, then he must be able to use me. That is obedience. Then we give wholehearted service to the poor. That is service. They complete each other. That is our life.

> Quoted by Desmond Doig *Mother Teresa* Harper & Row 76

9 I do not pray for success, I ask for faithfulness.

> When asked if she was ever discouraged, NY *Times* 18 Jun 80

10 I am a little pencil in the hand of a writing God who is sending a love letter to the world.

> News summaries 1 Sep 82

11 Many people mistake our work for our vocation. Our vocation is the love of Jesus.

> From documentary film *Mother Teresa*, quoted by Vincent Canby NY *Times* 28 Nov 86

ROBERT TERWILLIGER, Director, Trinity Institute, NYC

12 Committing yourself is a way of finding out who you are. A man finds his identity by identifying. A man's identity is not best thought of as the way in which he is separated from his fellows but the way in which he is united with them.

> 1969 commencement address at General Theological Seminary, NYC

MOTHER CATHERINE THOMAS

13 A Carmelite nun should be, by the very nature of her vocation, a specialist in prayer. Or, to give it a more modern twist, she is a career woman in the field of prayer and contemplation.

> *My Beloved: The Story of a Carmelite Nun* McGraw-Hill 55

LIONEL TIGER

14 Cathedrals are an unassailable witness to human passion. Using what demented calculation could an animal build such places? I think we know. An animal with a gorgeous genius for hope.

> *Optimism: The Biology of Hope* Simon & Schuster 79

PAUL TILLICH

15 Being religious means asking passionately the question of the meaning of our existence and being willing to receive answers, even if the answers hurt.

> *Saturday Evening Post* 14 Jun 58

16 Faith consists in being vitally concerned with that ultimate reality to which I give the symbolical name of God. Whoever reflects earnestly on the meaning of life is on the verge of an act of faith.

> *Réalités* Aug 65

ELIO TOAFF, Chief Rabbi, Synagogue of Rome

17 The heart opens itself to the hope that the misfortunes of the past will be replaced by fruitful dialogue.

> Greeting John Paul II, first pope to visit a synagogue, 13 Apr 86

PAUL TOURNIER

18 Let us not seek to bring religion to others, but let us endeavor to live it ourselves.

> "Resources in Medical Training and Practice," lecture for Bishop Anderson Foundation, Chicago, 30 Mar 65

RABBI MATTHEW TROPP

19 We're looking into a mirror of godliness.

> On studying the Talmud, NY *Times* 7 Apr 86

CHARLES TURNER

1 Not until he stood at the altar did he achieve a sense of being hale and furnished. It was strange, he thought, that a man would find his surest current in the spot where he felt least worthy.
The Celebrant Servant 82

2 Open in his hand was a solid gift of the Church—or, as he thought of it at this moment, a gift from God to the Church, for a distilled grammar of faith and practice. The Book of Common Prayer . . . its treasure was great and always ready. . . . He loved the taste of the phrases in his mouth.
ib

ANN BELFORD ULANOV, Professor of Psychiatry and Mental Health, Union Theological Seminary, NYC

3 To be religious is to have a life that flows with the presence of the extraordinary.
Vogue Dec 85

ARTHUR VOGEL, Professor of Apologetics and Dogmatic Theology, Nashotah House Episcopal Seminary, Nashotah WI

4 The living God is related to the categories and formal arguments of our abstract thinking as fire is related to paper.
The Christian Person Seabury 63

5 There can be no true response without responsibility; there can be no responsibility without response.
ib

KURT VONNEGUT JR

6 It is a very mixed blessing to be brought back from the dead.
Palm Sunday sermon at St Clement's Episcopal Church, NYC, quoted by John Leonard NY *Times* 30 Apr 80

7 People don't come to church for preachments, of course, but to daydream about God.
ib

ALICE WALKER

8 I think it pisses God off if you walk by the color purple in a field somewhere and don't notice it.
The Color Purple Simon & Schuster 82

MAX WARREN, General Secretary, Church Missionary Society, London

9 If I think I meet him only in Bible and sacrament, and in the Christian fellowship, then I do not know who it is I meet.
Anglicans, booklet published for Anglican Exhibition, 1964 NY World's Fair

EVELYN WAUGH

10 Pray always for all the learned, the oblique, the delicate. Let them not be quite forgotten at the throne of God when the simple come into their kingdom.
Quoted by Richard Holloway *Beyond Belief* Eerdmans 81

SIMONE WEIL

11 The danger is not lest the soul should doubt whether there is any bread, but lest, by a lie, it should persuade itself that it is not hungry.
Waiting for God Putnam 51

EDGAR WELLS, Rector, Church of St Mary the Virgin, NYC

12 This morning this young man does what his time in seminary was preparing him to do, and what for the rest of his life will be the primary activity of his ministry.
Ordination sermon, quoted in *Ave* Jan 86

13 He takes bread, he raises his eyes to heaven, he breaks the bread, he blesses it, he eats the bread and he distributes it among us. And the bread that he will bless will be for us the true body of our Lord.
ib

EDWARD N WEST, former Subdean, Cathedral Church of St John the Divine, NYC

14 There is nothing in the world more dreary than a prayer that attempts to inform God of anything at all.
To NY School of Theology 2 Oct 83

MORRIS WEST

15 Once you accept the existence of God—however you define him, however you explain your relationship to him—then you are caught forever with his presence in the center of all things.
The Clowns of God Morrow 81

16 You are also caught with the fact that man is a creature who walks in two worlds and traces upon the walls of his cave the wonders and the nightmare experiences of his spiritual pilgrimage.
ib

THORNTON WILDER

17 Hope, like faith, is nothing if it is not courageous; it is nothing if it is not ridiculous.
The Eighth Day Harper & Row 67

18 Man is not an end but a beginning. We are at the beginning of the second week. We are children of the eighth day.
ib

19 When God loves a creature he wants the creature to know the highest happiness and the deepest misery . . . He wants him to know all that being alive can bring. That is his best gift. . . . There is no happiness save in understanding the whole.
ib

P J WINGATE

20 "Give us this day our daily bread" is probably the most perfectly constructed and useful sentence ever set down in the English language.
Wall Street Journal 8 Aug 77

JOHN J WRIGHT, Roman Catholic Bishop of Pittsburgh

21 Your lives, temporal and eternal, as well as those of your children, will be conditioned enormously by this council long after we who vote in it are silent in death. So we do well to weigh your place in all this and you do well to watch us.
Address to high-school newspaper editors on Vatican II, *Newsweek* 14 Oct 63

STEFAN CARDINAL WYSZYNSKI, Primate of Poland

22 I tell you, you will serve only your God, because man is too noble to serve anyone but God.
Sermon against Communist adversaries, NY *Times* 20 Mar 61

1 When the soil is covered with grass, the fiercest whirlwinds will not easily blow it away, even if it is sandy. But when the soil becomes a desert place, it is very easily conquered.

> On importance of "the bond of man to the land," April 2, 1981, statement supporting anti-Communist Rural Solidarity Movement, quoted by John Paul II during visit to Poland 20 Jun 83

2 A week before my arrest you asked me, in such a distinct voice, "Would you know how to be poor?" I answered then, "I think so, Christ." I now answer your question with my daily life.

> A Freedom Within: The Prison Notes of Cardinal Wyszynski Hodder & Stoughton 85, quoted by Timothy Garton Ash London Times 17 Jan 85

Polity & Religious Leaders

JOHN M ALLIN, Presiding Bishop, Episcopal Church

3 Being head of the Church is like putting together a jigsaw puzzle while riding on a roller coaster.

> To Trinity Institute, NYC, 22 Apr 75

4 I don't believe women can be priests any more than they can be fathers or husbands.

> Address to House of Bishops a year after constitutional amendment allowing ordination of women, NY Times 1 Oct 77

ANGLICAN MANIFESTO

5 Mission is not the kindness of the lucky to the unlucky, it is mutual, united obedience to the one God whose mission it is.

> Anglican Manifesto: Mutual Responsibility and Interdependence in the Body of Christ, approved at Anglican Congress, Toronto, 17 Aug 63

ANONYMOUS

6 Don't judge the quality of the gasoline by the filling station attendant.

> Heard at General Convention of the Episcopal Church, Houston TX, 13 Oct 70

7 It's good to have two priests on a parish staff; then everybody doesn't have to hate the same person.

> ib Louisville KY, 2 Oct 73

ATHENAGORAS I, Ecumenical Patriarch of Constantinople

8 There is only one theology, but there are many theologians.

> On first meeting since 1439 between the head of the Greek Orthodox Church and the pope, 5 Jan 64

KARL BARTH

9 Jews have God's promise and if we Christians have it, too, then it is only as those chosen with them, as guests in their house, that we are new wood grafted onto their tree.

> Time 25 Jun 65

STEPHEN BAYNE, Executive Officer, Anglican Communion

10 Some will have to cease thinking of the Church as a memorial association for a deceased clergyman called Christ.

> On Anglican Manifesto: Mutual Responsibility and Interdependence in the Body of Christ, approved at Anglican Congress, Toronto, 17 Aug 63, quoted in NY Herald Tribune 19 Aug 63

ANNE BIEZANEK

11 The Catholic wife is under great pressure. . . . If she uses contraceptives, she is called wicked by her parish priest. It she follows the advice of her priest and refrains from sexual intercourse, she is called cold by her husband. If she doesn't take steps, she is called mad by society at large.

> NY Times 21 May 64

THOMAS D BOWERS, Rector, St Bartholomew's Church, NYC

12 I don't go looking for trouble. It always finds me. I mean, it does. It comes right into the office.

> Quoted by Jonathan Larsen "Altar Egos" Manhattan Inc Jul 86

ROBERT MCAFEE BROWN, Professor of Theology, Stanford

13 Observermanship is the art of giving the impression that you are with it even though you don't know Latin very well.

> On being an official observer at Vatican II, Observer in Rome Doubleday 64

MARTIN BUBER

14 Justice and Christianity stand with each other in the mystery of our Father and Judge: So the Jew may speak of the Christian or the Christian of the Jew not otherwise than in fear and trembling before the mystery of God. On this foundation alone can genuine understanding exist between Jew and Christian.

> Quoted by Maurice Friedman Martin Buber's Life and Work: The Later Years 1945–65 Dutton 84

DORA CHAPLIN, Associate Professor of Pastoral Theology, General Theological Seminary, NYC

15 Our Lord said, "Feed my sheep"; he did not say, "Count them."

> On undue emphasis on church attendance, The Privilege of Teaching Morehouse-Barlow 62

SUSAN CHEEVER

16 His religious requirements—that the service come from Cranmer's rites in the old prayer book, that it take 33 minutes or less, that the church be within 10 minutes' driving distance and that the altar be sufficiently simple so that it wouldn't remind him of a gift shop—limited his choice of parishes.

> On her father John Cheever, Home before Dark Houghton Mifflin 84

KENNETH CLARK

17 The great achievement of the Catholic Church lay in harmonizing, civilizing the deepest impulses of ordinary, ignorant people.

> Civilization Harper & Row 70

RICHARD CARDINAL CUSHING, Archbishop of Boston

18 The bishops will govern the Church, the priests will do all the work and the deacons will have all the fun.

> On prospect of married diaconate, NY Times 2 Jul 67

JAN DARGATZ

19 He has no intention of living in the ghetto of heaven or even its suburbs.

> On Oral Roberts's religious aspirations, Boston Globe 20 Jan 87

JAY P DOLAN, Associate Professor of History, Notre Dame

1 In 1870 [during the first Vatican Council], Catholics were struggling with the question of what it meant to be an American; comfortably American in 1965, they now struggled with a more fundamental question: What it meant to be Catholic.

> On Vatican II, *The American Catholic Experience* Doubleday 85, quoted in NY *Times* 17 Nov 85

2 [The] council not only sanctioned reform, it accelerated it. What this meant was that Catholics tried to solve the riddle of religion and modernity overnight.

> *ib*

EPISCOPAL CHURCH

3 Good termination affirms what has been worthwhile and healthy, names what has been hurtful and diminishing, offers thanksgiving for what has been constructive, asks forgiveness for what has been destructive and enables everyone to move on.

> Guidelines for clergy employment, *Prayer in the Calling Process* Episcopal Church Center 85

GEOFFREY FISHER, Archbishop of Canterbury

4 This country and the Commonwealth last Tuesday were not far from the Kingdom of Heaven.

> On coronation of Elizabeth II, news summaries 30 Jun 53

5 I say to you Baptists, "Go on being good Baptists, thinking that you are more right than anybody else." Unless you think it, I have no use for you at all. The Church of England does precisely the same itself.

> To golden jubilee congress of Baptist World Alliance, news summaries 17 Jul 55

6 In one sense what may pass between the pope and myself may be trivialities. In another sense the fact of talking trivialities is itself a portent of great significance. But the pleasantries which we exchange may, as one church leader said, be pleasantries about profundities.

> To diocesan conference a month before first meeting of the heads of the Anglican and Roman Catholic churches in five centuries, 6 Nov 60

7 I hope that by going to visit the pope I have enabled everybody to see that the words *Catholic* and *Protestant*, as ordinarily used, are completely out of date. They are almost always used now purely for propaganda purposes. That is why so much trouble is caused by them.

> NY *Times* 11 Jan 61

8 My feelings are those of a schoolboy getting in sight of the holidays. Or more seriously, my feelings are perhaps those of a matador who has decided not to enter the bull ring.

> Announcing plans to retire, *ib* 18 Jan 61

JOHN P FOLEY, Director, Vatican Commission on Social Communications

9 It is essentially a matter of being clear on what your message is, and then preaching it, selling it, if you will, to the faithful and those you hope will become the faithful.

> On travel objectives of Pope John Paul II, NY *Times* 12 May 85

HARRY EMERSON FOSDICK, Senior Minister, Riverside Church, NYC

10 Preaching is personal counseling on a group basis.

> Recalled on his death 5 Oct 69

11 A good sermon is an engineering operation by which a chasm is bridged so that the spiritual goods on one side—the "unsearchable riches of Christ"—are actually transported into personal lives upon the other.

> *ib*

BILLY GRAHAM

12 I just want to lobby for God.

> On establishing national headquarters in Washington DC 12 Dec 55

13 If we had more hell in the pulpit, we would have less hell in the pew.

> NY *Herald Tribune* 25 May 64

ALISTER HARDY

14 My heart is in the Church of England but not my mind.

> *Time* 11 Mar 85

ULRICH HENN

15 All men, believing in God or not, are invited to enter. I wish to make them curious to see what God has to offer them within the cathedral.

> On designing bronze gates for Washington DC's National Cathedral, *Cathedral Age* Spring 80

ROBERT HOLTBY, Dean, Chichester Cathedral, England

16 Priests are ordained to apply the Gospel to the realities of history.

> Address at Episcopal Church of the Transfiguration, NYC, 4 Apr 85

EDWARD JEFFREY, British clergyman

17 People expect the clergy to have the grace of a swan, the friendliness of a sparrow, the strength of an eagle and the night hours of an owl—and some people expect such a bird to live on the food of a canary.

> NY *Times* 21 Jun 64

POPE JOHN XXIII

18 We ardently desire their return to the house of the common Father . . . they will not enter a strange house but their own.

> Calling for council to discuss unity of Christiandom, news summaries 9 Feb 59

19 The council now beginning rises in the Church like the daybreak, a forerunner of most splendid light.

> To Vatican II, *Newsweek* 22 Oct 62

20 It is now for the Catholic Church to bend herself to her work with calmness and generosity. It is for you to observe her with renewed and friendly attention.

> *Time* 28 Oct 62

POPE JOHN PAUL I

21 As books vary from one to the other, so too do bishops. Some bishops, in fact, resemble eagles, who sail loftily with solemn documents. Others are nightingales who marvelously sing the praise of the Lord. Others, instead, are poor wrens, who only twitter as

they seek to express a few thoughts on extremely profound subjects. I belong to the [last] category.

Letter to Mark Twain, in volume of letters to historical figures published when he was patriarch of Venice, recalled on his death 28 Sep 78

POPE JOHN PAUL II

1 [The vow of celibacy] is a matter of keeping one's word to Christ and the Church. . . . a duty and a proof of the priest's inner maturity; it is the expression of his personal dignity.

Letter to clergy 9 Apr 79

2 I hope to have communion with the people, that is the most important thing.

On his visit to six US cities, *Newsweek* 8 Oct 79

3 You are priests, not social or political leaders. Let us not be under the illusion that we are serving the Gospel . . . through an exaggerated interest in the wide field of temporal problems.

Admonishing clergy during visit to the Philippines, *ib* 2 Mar 81

4 Today, for the first time in history, a Bishop of Rome sets foot on English soil. . . . This fair land, once a distant outpost of the pagan world, has become, through the preaching of the Gospel, a beloved and gifted portion of Christ's vineyard.

Address at Westminster Cathedral, London, 28 May 82

5 Yours is a tradition embedded in the history of Christian civilization. The roll of your saints and of your great men and women, your treasures of literature and music, your cathedrals and colleges, your rich heritage of parish life speak of a tradition of faith. And it is to the faith of your fathers, living still, that I wish to pay tribute by my visit.

ib

6 When freedom does not have a purpose, when it does not wish to know anything about the rule of law engraved in the hearts of men and women, when it does not listen to the voice of conscience, it turns against humanity and society.

On visit to Holland, NY *Times* 12 May 85

7 Once again, through myself, the Church, in the words of the well-known declaration *Nostra Aetate*, "deplores the hatred, persecutions and displays of anti-Semitism directed against the Jews at any time and by anyone." I repeat, "By anyone."

On visit to the Synagogue of Rome, quoting document of Vatican II, 13 Apr 86

8 You are our dearly beloved brothers, and in a certain way, it could be said that you are our elder brothers.

ib

AIDAN KAVANAGH OSB

9 The liturgy, like the feast, exists not to educate but to seduce people into participating in common activity of the highest order, where one is freed to learn things which cannot be taught.

Elements of Rite Pueblo 66

GARRISON KEILLOR

10 A minister has to be able to read a clock. At noon, it's time to go home and turn up the pot roast and get the peas out of the freezer.

Lake Wobegon Days Viking 85

GEORGE A KELLY, Director, Institute for Advanced Studies in Catholic Doctrine, St John's University, Queens NY

11 Parishes will not revive without living priests, who will again go about their rounds of apostolic chores, working against powerful forces arrayed against them. . . . Their predecessors walked in the midst of cholera, fearless of dying because their people needed the Word, the Hand, the Presence, the Sacrament.

To National Conference of Catholic Charities, New Orleans, quoted in *Vital Speeches* 15 Nov 78

GEORGE FRENCH KEMPSELL, Rector, Episcopal Church of St James the Less, Scarsdale NY

12 If our Lord Jesus Christ had come back to earth in Scarsdale in time for the Holly Ball, he would not be allowed to escort a young lady of this parish to that dance.

On discrimination against Jews at Scarsdale Golf Club's annual ball, NY *Times* 13 Jan 61

CLIFFORD LONGLEY

13 [Its] language . . . is as bare as a monk's cell, and as uninviting.

On official English translation of the Mass, London *Times* 5 Nov 84

14 They cannot make it say what they want it to say. And this is the beginning and the end of the case for retaining the old language: If the churches give it up, who will remember how to say what is said?

ib

15 John Henry Newman was as English as roast beef, even if he lacked a passion for cricket.

ib 11 Mar 85

JOHN WESLEY LORD, Bishop, United Methodist Church, Washington DC

16 The Church recruited people who had been starched and ironed before they were washed.

On postwar religious revival that swelled church memberships with people drawn by fear of war, hope of social prestige or other nonreligious reasons, *Time* 1 Feb 63

JEAN MARIE CARDINAL LUSTIGER, Archbishop of Paris

17 I was born Jewish and so I remain, even if that's unacceptable for many. . . . For me, the vocation of Israel is bringing light to the goyim. That's my hope and I believe that Christianity is the means for achieving it.

Comment two years after becoming archbishop, quoted by John Vinocur "A Most Special Cardinal" NY *Times* 20 Mar 83

18 For me, this nomination was as if all of a sudden the crucifix began to wear a yellow star.

ib

PERCY LUTTON, Anglican Vicar, All Saints Church, Wribbenhall, England

19 On the outer fringe of the parish are the four-wheelers—those who come only by pram for their christening, taxi for their wedding and hearse for their funeral.

London *Illustrated News* Dec 78

RICHARD P McBRIEN, Roman Catholic priest and Professor of Theology, Notre Dame

1 It is clear that the Vatican does not know what a theologian is and what a university is.

> On efforts to impose orthodoxy in Roman Catholic colleges, quoted by Ari L Goldman "Catholic Colleges in US Debate Academic Freedom amid Disputes" NY *Times* 8 Oct 86

JAMES P McFADDEN, President, National Committee of Catholic Laymen

2 You don't need to be Catholic to be Catholic anymore. If you dissent, you don't get out. . . . Martin Luther looks like a prince compared to these people because he knew when it was time to go.

> On dissident Roman Catholics, NY *Times* 24 Dec 86

STERLING M McMURRIN, Professor of History, University of Utah

3 Mormonism is not simply a commitment to a theology or a church practice, but a social-cultural order.

> Quoted by Robert Lindsey "The Mormons: Growth, Prosperity and Controversy" NY *Times* 12 Jan 86

4 It becomes part of a person's second nature; he belongs to the church, like he belongs to his family, and he does not quit his family because someone in it turns out to be a rascal.

> On loyalty of Mormons despite suppression of 19th-century letters that question the credibility of Joseph Smith, founder of Mormonism, *ib*

CATHLEEN MEDWICK

5 That journeying metaphor that is Jewish history.

> On Primo Levi's *If Not Now, When?* Summit Books 85, *Vogue* May 85

GOLDA MEIR, Prime Minister of Israel

6 The man of the Cross, who heads the church whose symbol is the Cross, under which Jews were killed for generations. I could not escape the feeling. It stuck with me. And he felt it—that a Jewess was sitting opposite him.

> On audience with Pope Paul VI at the Vatican 20 Jan 73

S H MILLER, Dean, Harvard Divinity School

7 Religion which is interested only in itself, in its prestige and success, in its institutions and ecclesiastical niceties, is worse than vanity; it is essentially incestuous.

> Quoted by Paul Ferris *The Church of England* Hodder & Stoughton 62

8 Religion reveals itself in struggling to reveal the meaning of the world.

> *ib*

9 The task of organized religion is not to prove that God was in the 1st century, but that he is in the 20th.

> *Quote* 14 Nov 65

A A MILNE

10 The Old Testament is responsible for more atheism, agnosticism, disbelief—call it what you will—than any book ever written; it has emptied more churches than all the counterattractions of cinema, motor bicycle and golf course.

> Recalled on his death 31 Jan 56

GARTH MOORE, Corpus Christi College, Cambridge

11 It is not by Christ's *ordinance* that "the Sacrament is reserved, lifted up or worshiped." But because Our Lord did not command such practices, it does not mean that they are condemned.

> Reply to an Anglican priest's attack on Bishop of London's interpretation of adoration of the consecrated bread and wine of the Eucharist as covered in the 39 Articles of Religion, London *Times* 16 Apr 86

12 Indeed, were the Sacrament never carried about, it could never be received by the faithful.

> *ib*

LAURENCE MOORE

13 Mormons invented themselves just as other religious and ethnic groups invented themselves. But Mormons did so in such a singularly impressive way that we will probably always remain baffled as to how exactly it happened.

> NY *Times* 21 Jul 85

CLIFFORD P MOREHOUSE

14 The layman is not called to be an amateur or part-time priest. He is called to be an expert and full-time Christian.

> *A Layman Looks at the Church* Seabury 64

LANCE MORROW

15 Vatican II was a force that seized the mind of the Roman Catholic Church and carried it across centuries from the 13th to the 20th.

> "Triumphs of the Spirit" *Time* 60th anniversary issue Fall 83

16 The Church became both more accessible and less imposing. It threw itself open to risk.

> *ib*

C KILMER MYERS, Vicar, Chapel of the Intercession, NYC

17 We have relegated the saints to a pink and blue and gold world of plaster statuary that belongs to the past; it is a hangover, a relic, of the Dark Ages when men were the children of fantasy's magic.

> On lost role of saints in Christian tradition, NY *Times* 19 Mar 62

18 We are content to place a statue of Francis of Assisi in the middle of a birdbath and let the whole business of the saints go at that.

> *ib*

19 A real parish is a wondrously beautiful web of human relationship which is given meaning by the man who is Himself the meaning of life.

> As bishop of California, *Life* 13 Sep 68

AIDAN NICHOLS, Professor of Dogmatic Theology, Angelicum University, Rome

20 [Their thesis is that] everything in the Catholic Church's garden is or would be lovely, if only the pope and curial cardinals would refrain from meddling with healthy growth when they cannot in fact be trusted to distinguish weeds from plants and poison from fertilizer.

> On interpretation of Vatican affairs by the press, London *Times* 11 Mar 85

DANIEL NOONAN

1 Ambition is the ecclesiastical lust.
> *The Passion of Fulton Sheen* Dodd, Mead 72

JOHN CARDINAL O'CONNOR, Archbishop of NY

2 Are we to have a church in which everyone's judgment is equal to everyone else's? That's not a church, it's chaos. . . . Common sense dictates that you keep the fox out of the chicken coop.
> On barring parish speakers critical of Church teachings, NY *Times* 12 Sep 86

RICHARD N OSTLING

3 [It is] an ecclesiastical clone of the United Nations.
> On World Council of Churches, *Time* 22 Aug 83

POPE PAUL VI

4 We speak now to the representatives of the Christian denominations separated from the Catholic Church, who have nevertheless been invited to take part as observers in this solemn assembly. . . . If we are in any way to blame for that separation, we humbly beg God's forgiveness and ask pardon, too, of our brethren who feel themselves to have been injured by us.
> Opening second session of Vatican II 29 Sep 63

5 The pope is becoming a missionary, you will say. Yes, the pope is becoming a missionary, which means a witness, a shepherd, an apostle on the move.
> Announcing plans to visit India, NY *Times* 19 Oct 64

6 Liturgy is like a strong tree whose beauty is derived from the continuous renewal of its leaves, but whose strength comes from the old trunk, with solid roots in the ground.
> *Quote* 15 Nov 64

7 The Eucharistic mystery stands at the heart and center of the liturgy since it is the fount of life by which we are cleansed and strengthened to live not for ourselves but for God and to be united in love among ourselves.
> *Mysterium Fidei* 11 Sep 65

8 We consider Christmas as the encounter, the great encounter, the historical encounter, the decisive encounter, between God and mankind. He who has faith knows this truly; let him rejoice.
> Christmas address 23 Dec 65

9 The Church, then, has encountered in this act of reflection not herself alone but Christ whom she carries with her . . . She has felt the spirit of God flowing fresh within her, the Gospel message springing anew to her lips and the need to make new its preaching for her own sake and the world's. From this the Church has come back again. She has experienced her rebirth.
> On Vatican II, *ib*

10 You rebuild a bridge which for centuries has lain fallen between the Church of Rome and the Church of Canterbury; a bridge of respect, of esteem, and of charity. You cross over this yet unstable viaduct, still under construction, with spontaneous initiative and sage confidence—may God bless this courage and this piety of yours.
> Welcoming Michael Ramsey, first Archbishop of Canterbury in nearly five centuries to make official visit to the Vatican, 23 Mar 66

11 The pope—and we know this well—is without doubt the most serious obstacle on the ecumenical road.
> On papal infallibility, *Quote* 29 May 67

12 At times loneliness will weigh heavily on the priest, but not for that reason will he regret having generously chosen it. He who has chosen to belong completely to Christ will find, above all, in intimacy with him and in his grace, the power of spirit necessary to banish sadness and regret and to triumph over discouragement.
> *Sacerdotalis Caelibatus* 23 Jun 67

JAMES A PIKE, Episcopal Bishop of California

13 The 11 o'clock hour on Sunday is the most segregated hour in American life.
> *US News & World Report* 16 May 60

14 Fewer beliefs, more belief.
> On the Holy Trinity as "excess baggage," recalled in false report of his death, *Life* 19 Sep 69

15 Moslems have one God and three wives; Christians have three Gods and one wife.
> *ib*

16 My fee is $100, if hospitality is added it's $1,000.
> Quoted by Robert Runcie, Archbishop of Canterbury, interview 1 May 82

MICHAEL RAMSEY, Archbishop of Canterbury

17 When an Anglican is asked, "Where was your Church before the Reformation?" his best answer is to put the counterquestion, "Where was your face before you washed it?"
> Quoted by James B Simpson *The Hundredth Archbishop of Canterbury* Harper & Row 62

18 Perspectives change, and we must give the bag a good shake and see what happens.
> On foreseeing "the day when all Christians might accept the pope as presiding bishop," NY *Times* 7 Feb 72

19 To be an Anglican is to belong to a communion no longer limited by the English language or Anglo-Saxon culture.
> Quoted in Arthur Vogel ed *Theology in Anglicanism* Morehouse-Barlow 85

PAT ROBERTSON

20 I never thought God would hold someone accountable for not raising money.
> On Oral Roberts's warnings that God might "call him home" if supporters didn't send enough contributions, quoted in *Newsweek* 2 Feb 87

BARBARA ROSEWICZ

21 Christian religions mix about as well as holy water and holy oil.
> On disputes over sacred places in the Holy Land, *Wall Street Journal* 5 Apr 85

D DOUGLAS ROTH

22 Now Mellon Bank and US Steel have defrocked their first pastor.
> After discharge from Lutheran ministry because his efforts to help the unemployed defied his bishop and divided his Clairton PA congregation, NY *Times* 17 Mar 85

MOISH SACKS, Acting Rabbi, Intervale Avenue Jewish Center, Bronx NY

1 Let God come down and see we only have nine. He can count. And when he comes down, we'll count him in.

> On ways of achieving *minyan*, the minimum 10 men required by Jewish law for worship, NY *Times* 15 Dec 85

RABBI ALEXANDER M SHAPIRO, President, Rabbinical Assembly

2 The vote demonstrates that we accept the notion that all human beings are created in the image of God and have an equal right to preach and teach the word of God.

> On vote to amend its constitution to allow ordination of women, NY *Times* 14 Feb 85

WILFRID SHEED

3 For Catholics before Vatican II, the land of the free was pre-eminently the land of Sister Says—except, of course, for Sister, for whom it was the land of Father Says.

> *Frank and Maisie: A Memoir with Parents* Simon & Schuster 85

ISAAC BASHEVIS SINGER

4 The Jewish people have been in exile for 2,000 years; they have lived in hundreds of countries, spoken hundreds of languages and still they kept their old language, Hebrew. They kept their Aramaic, later their Yiddish; they kept their books; they kept their faith.

> NY *Times* 26 Nov 78

EDITH SITWELL

5 I have taken this step because I want the discipline, the fire and the authority of the Church. I am hopelessly unworthy of it, but I hope to become worthy.

> On becoming a Roman Catholic at age 67, news summaries 15 Aug 55

JOHN HALL SNOW, Professor of Pastoral Theology, Episcopal Divinity School, Cambridge MA

6 The wealthy don't go to church anymore; they go to a museum on Sunday afternoon. That's why we have magnificent museums being built instead of magnificent churches.

> Quoted by Paul Wilkes "The Episcopalians: A Church in Search of Itself" NY *Times* 1 Sep 85

RABBI CHAIM STAUBER, Satmar Chassidim, Brooklyn NY

7 If the retaliation for destroying lewd posters is to destroy a synagogue—if that is the equation—then there is something terribly wrong. You can't take pork and make it kosher.

> NY *Times* 7 Jul 86

SUPREME COURT OF ISRAEL

8 There are not two nations—one Jewish and one converted to Judaism.

> Ruling that non-Orthodox Jewish converts may also be citizens of Israel, *Time* 15 Dec 86

TIME MAGAZINE

9 Outward, for centuries, flowed the tide of British Empire; back, in hurried decades, it ebbed. . . . Empire is gone, the Church remains.

> On the Anglican Communion, 16 Aug 63

DAVID TRACY, Roman Catholic priest and Professor of Theology, University of Chicago

10 The problem *is* authority. But these Vatican officials seem unable to understand authority except as authoritarianism.

> On discipline of US clergy for liberal ideas, quoted by Eugene Kennedy "A Dissenting Voice" NY *Times* 9 Nov 86

11 Essentially, a church is a community that keeps alive the dangerous memories of its classics.

> *ib*

TRIAD, newsletter of Holy Trinity Episcopal Church, Oxford

12 Ladies who wear wide brimmed hats (they *are* in now) and gentlemen with hirsute adornments are asked to help guide the chalice to their lips, since the chalice bearer can't see what is going on.

> Quoted in *New Yorker* 2 Feb 87

VATICAN DOCTRINAL STATEMENT

13 What is technically possible is not for that very reason morally admissible.

> "Instruction on Respect for Human Life in Its Origin and on the Dignity of Procreation," quoted in NY *Times* 11 Mar 87

SPENCER WILSON, Anglican Chaplain, Haydock Hospital, St Helen's, England

14 The number of good preachers may have decreased. But so has the number of good listeners.

> Letter to the editor London *Times* 20 Aug 68

KENNETH L WOODWARD

15 The Anglican Church is like a boat with two oarsmen, one heading for Protestantism while the other rows toward Rome.

> On possibility of reconciliation with Roman Catholic Church, "A More Perfect Union" *Newsweek* 12 May 86

16 Thus the Church of England—and with it, the 64-million-member worldwide Anglican Communion—has remained intact chiefly by never drifting far in either direction.

> *ib*

HERMAN WOUK

17 I felt there's a wealth in Jewish tradition, a great inheritance. I'd be a jerk not to take advantage of it.

> On his return to Orthodox Judaism, *Time* 5 Sep 55

18 Deep in the heart of both critical Christian and alienated Jew, there is . . . a feeling, not even a feeling, a shadow of a notion, nothing more substantial than the pointless but compelling impulse to knock on wood when one talks of the health of children—*something* that says there is more to Jews than meets the eye.

> *This is My God* Doubleday 59

19 There is a mystery about the Jews . . . and within this mystery lies the reason for the folk pride of the house of Abraham. This pride exists despite the disabilities that come from many centuries of ostracism.

> *ib*

STEFAN CARDINAL WYSZYNSKI, Primate of Poland

1 You have to know the psychology of priests who spend a good part of their time praying and serving people and finally discover that they are not being rewarded properly by God on earth. They don't want to blame the Holy Ghost, so they turn to their peers and try to maneuver them into recognizing them as a little more than equal.

> On how his countryman Karol Wojtyla became Pope John Paul II, quoted by Antoni Gronowicz *God's Broker: The Life of John Paul II* Richardson & Snyder 84

MORT YOUNG

2 The aged nuns . . . struck out across the grounds, looking at the wonder of it all and seeming to passers-by like gentle, tired birds whose wings no longer had the strength to lift them beyond the clouds. It was an illusion. It was only their hurt bodies that were earthbound.

> On a group of 27 retired nuns who visited NY World's Fair, NY *Journal-American* 5 Jun 64

HUMOR & WIT

JONATHAN ADASHEK, age 12

3 To the best of my knowledge there has been no child in space. I would like to learn about being weightless, and I'd like to get away from my mother's cooking.

> Letter to President Ronald Reagan, *Life* Oct 84

FRED ALLEN

4 I have just returned from Boston. It is the only thing to do if you find yourself up there.

> Letter to Groucho Marx 12 Jun 53

5 A vice president in an advertising agency is a "molehill man" [who] has until 5 PM to make [a] molehill into a mountain. An accomplished molehill man will often have his mountain finished even before lunch.

> *Treadmill to Oblivion* Little, Brown 54

6 A celebrity is a person who works hard all his life to become well known, then wears dark glasses to avoid being recognized.

> *ib*

7 Batten, Barton, Durstine & Osborne—sounds like a trunk falling down a flight of stairs.

> On NYC advertising agency, recalled on his death 17 Mar 56

8 Life, in my estimation, is a biological misadventure that we terminate on the shoulders of six strange men whose only objective is to make a hole in one with you.

> *Forbes* 1 Aug 67

9 Everywhere outside New York City is Bridgeport, Connecticut.

> Quoted by Alistair Cooke *America* Knopf 73

STEVE ALLEN

10 Asthma doesn't seem to bother me any more unless I'm around cigars or dogs. The thing that would bother me most would be a dog smoking a cigar.

> News summaries 15 Jul 55

11 The hair is real—it's the head that's a fake.

> When asked if he wore a toupee, NBC TV 15 Dec 57

KINGSLEY AMIS

12 He resolved, having done it once, never to move his eyeballs again.

> On recovering from a hangover, *Lucky Jim* Jonathan Clowes 58

13 A dusty thudding in his head made the scene before him beat like a pulse. His mouth had been used as a latrine by some small creature of the night and then as its mausoleum.

> *ib*

CLEVELAND AMORY

14 A "good" family, it seems, is one that used to be better.

> *Who Killed Society?* Harper 60

15 The New England conscience . . . does not stop you from doing what you shouldn't—it just stops you from enjoying it.

> *New York* 5 May 80

RICHARD ARMOUR

16 I've suffered from all of the hang-ups known,
And none is as bad as the telephone.

> *Wall Street Journal* 11 Jul 85

ANONYMOUS

17 If you drink, don't dial.

> Reply to caller who dialed his social security number instead of the number he wished to reach, quoted in NY *Herald Tribune* 30 Apr 58

18 To hell with you. Offensive letter follows.

> Irate citizen's telegram, quoted by Alec Douglas-Home, British foreign secretary, *Wall Street Journal* 11 Jul 62

19 Wanted: Playpen, cot and highchair. Also two single beds.

> Advertisement in *Evening Standard*, quoted by David Frost and Antony Jay *The English* Stein & Day 68

20 Father, your sermons are like water to a drowning man.

> Churchgoer, quoted by James Montgomery, Episcopal bishop of Chicago, 30 Jul 72

21 Father, each of your sermons is better than the next.

> *ib*

22 There was a young lady from Kent
Who said she knew what men meant
When they asked her to dine
Private room, champagne, wine,
She knew what they meant and she went.

> Quoted by Brooke Astor NY *Times* 20 May 84

23 To our wives and sweethearts . . . and may they never meet.

> Favorite toast of the Royal Navy, quoted by Hugo Vickers *Cecil Beaton* Little, Brown 85

24 Don't cross this field unless you can do it in 9.9 seconds. The bull can do it in 10.

> Sign on bison range above underground quarters of Fermi National Accelerator Laboratory, Batavia IL, pictured in *People* 18 Nov 85

25 To be rich is no longer a sin; it's a miracle.

> Hand-stitched pillow pictured in *Vogue* Oct 86

26 Good girls go to heaven, bad girls go everywhere.

> T-shirt observed at Second World Whores Congress in Brussels, *Time* 13 Oct 86

1 Mr Holmes thanks you for your letter. At the moment he is in retirement in Sussex, keeping bees.

> Reply of a bank at 221B Baker Street, London, to 40 or so letters addressed daily to fictional sleuth Holmes, quoted in *US News & World Report* 19 Jan 87

ISAAC ASIMOV

2 If my doctor told me I had only six minutes to live, I wouldn't brood. I'd type a little faster.

> As author of 289 books, *Life* Jan 84

NANCY, LADY ASTOR

3 My vigor, vitality and cheek repel me. I am the kind of woman I would run from.

> To Washington reporters, news summaries 29 Mar 55

MURRAY BAIL

4 Vocal adjustments are needed to reduce the bloody velocity of words in the wide spaces of Orstraliah. By contrast . . . the British enunciate clearly in order to penetrate the humidity and hedges, the moist walls and alleyways.

> *Homesickness* Macmillan 80

TAMMY FAYE BAKKER

5 You don't have to be dowdy to be a Christian.

> On being the wife of a television evangelist, quoted in *Newsweek* 8 Jun 87

FRED BARTON

6 Monogamy is like good crystal—beautiful—but once you get it, all it takes is one chip and it's never the same again.

> Quoted in NY *Times* 14 Nov 85

BERNARD BARUCH

7 To me, old age is always 15 years older than I am.

> On his 85th birthday, news summaries 20 Aug 55

PHYLLIS BATTELLE

8 For her fifth wedding, the bride wore black and carried a scotch and soda.

> On Barbara Hutton's marriage to Porfirio Rubirosa, quoted by Cleveland Amory and Earl Blackwell eds *Celebrity Register* Harper & Row 63

STEPHEN BAYNE

9 I am rather like a mosquito in a nudist camp; I know what I ought to do, but I don't know where to begin.

> On becoming first executive officer of the Anglican Communion, *Time* 25 Jan 60

CECIL BEATON

10 A gardener not wholly herbivorous
From wilting was out to deliver us.
With blood, sweat and toil
She composted the soil
And made even the lilies carnivorous.

> Limerick on producer Irene Selznick, quoted by Hugo Vickers *Cecil Beaton* Little, Brown 85

LORD BEAVERBROOK (William Maxwell Aitken)

11 Buy old masters. They fetch a better price than old mistresses.

> Recalled on his death 9 Jun 64

MAX BEERBOHM

12 Most women are not so young as they are painted.

> "A Defense of Cosmetics," recalled on his death 20 May 56

BRENDAN BEHAN

13 New York is my Lourdes, where I go for spiritual refreshment. . . . a place where you're least likely to be bitten by a wild goat.

> Recalled on his death, NY *Post* 22 Mar 64

14 Ah, bless you, Sister, may all your sons be bishops.

> Last words to nun at his deathbed, quoted in *Time* 16 Jan 84

TERREL BELL, former US Secretary of Education

15 There's only one thing worse than an old fogy, and that's a young fogy.

> Commencement address at Longwood College, Farmville VA, *Time* 17 Jun 85

GUY BELLAMY

16 Life is a sexually transmitted disease.

> *The Sinner's Congregation* Secker & Warburg 84

HILAIRE BELLOC

17 I'm tired of love: I'm still more tired of rhyme.
But money gives me pleasure all the time.

> Quoted by James Reston NY *Times* 6 Jan 85

SAUL BELLOW

18 I've never turned over a fig leaf yet that didn't have a price tag on the other side.

> PBS TV 27 Jan 82

JACK BENNY

19 Age is strictly a case of mind over matter. If you don't mind, it doesn't matter.

> NY *Times* 15 Feb 74

MILTON BERLE

20 A committee is a group that keeps minutes and loses hours.

> News summaries 1 Jul 54

JOHN BETJEMAN

21 Lord, put beneath thy special care
One-eighty-nine Cadogan Square.

> Quoted in London *Church Times* 25 May 84

22 And now, dear Lord, I cannot wait
Because I have a luncheon date.

> *ib*

ALAN BLEASDALE

23 I've got a group who can't play music, one bad comedian plus boyfriend, a nervous breakdown calling himself a magician, two coachloads of 70-year-old religious maniacs looking for a fight and a fancy-dress contest that nobody knew about.

> Lines in his movie *No Surrender* for a troubled nightclub manager, *Time* 8 Sep 86

ROY BLOUNT JR

24 A good heavy book holds you down. It's an anchor that keeps you from getting up and having another gin and tonic.

> "Reading and Nothingness, Of Proust in the Summer Sun" NY *Times* 2 Jun 85

1 Many a person has been saved from summer alcoholism, not to mention hypertoxicity, by Dostoyevsky.
ib

ERMA BOMBECK

2 Guilt: the gift that keeps on giving.
Quoted by John Skow *Time* 2 Jul 84

3 You become about as exciting as your food blender. The kids come in, look you in the eye, and ask if anybody's home.
On housekeeping, *ib*

DANIEL J BOORSTIN, Librarian of Congress

4 [Reading is like] the sex act—done privately, and often in bed.
Smithsonian Apr 80

BOY GEORGE

5 I can do anything. In *GQ*, I appeared as a man.
Quoted in *US* 21 Apr 86

ROBERT BRADBURY, city official, Liverpool

6 After all, what is a pedestrian? He is a man who has two cars—one being driven by his wife, the other by one of his children.
NY *Times* 5 Sep 62

WERNHER VON BRAUN

7 We can lick gravity, but sometimes the paperwork is overwhelming.
On bureaucracy, Chicago *Sun Times* 10 Jul 58

HANK BRENNAN

8 His baroque is worse than his bite.
On Cecil Beaton, quoted by Hugo Vickers *Cecil Beaton* Little, Brown 85

MARIO BUATTA

9 Dust is a protective coating for fine furniture.
Quoted by John Taylor "Fringe Lunatic" *Manhattan Inc* Jul 86

ART BUCHWALD

10 A bad liver is to a Frenchman what a nervous breakdown is to an American. Everyone has had one and everyone wants to talk about it.
NY *Herald Tribune* 16 Jan 58

11 People are broad-minded. They'll accept the fact that a person can be an alcoholic, a dope fiend, a wife beater and even a newspaperman, but if a man doesn't drive, there's something wrong with him.
Have I Ever Lied to You? Putnam 68

LUIS BUÑUEL

12 Thank God, I am still an atheist.
Time 29 Nov 69

CAROL BURNETT

13 Adolescence is just one big walking pimple.
Phil Donahue show NBC TV 16 Oct 86

GEORGE BURNS

14 Happiness? A good cigar, a good meal, a good cigar and a good woman—or a bad woman; it depends on how much happiness you can handle.
NBC TV 16 Oct 84

15 I don't believe in dying. It's been done. I'm working on a new exit. Besides, I can't die now—I'm booked.
News summaries 20 Jan 87

HELEN CALDWELL

16 I don't say she was above reproach. She was above self-reproach.
On losing her husband Erskine Caldwell to Margaret Bourke-White, quoted by Timothy Foote NY *Times* 20 Jul 86

TRUMAN CAPOTE

17 Well, I'm about as tall as a shotgun, and just as noisy.
Self-description, *Time* 3 Mar 52

AL CAPP

18 The public is like a piano. You just have to know what keys to poke.
News summaries 1 Mar 54

19 Like all New York hotel lady cashiers she had red hair and had been disappointed in her first husband.
On cashing a check in Manhattan, NY *Herald Tribune* 29 Jan 61

JOHNNY CARSON

20 I know you've been married to the same woman for 69 years. That is marvelous. It must be very inexpensive.
Alluding to his exorbitant alimony payments in televised tribute to Jimmy Doolittle, quoted in NY *Times* 18 Aug 86

JEROME CAVANAGH, former Mayor of Detroit

21 He played football too long without a helmet.
On Congressman Gerald R Ford, quoted by Lyndon B Johnson and recalled when Richard M Nixon chose Ford as his vice president, *Newsweek* 22 Oct 73

HENRY ("CHIPS") CHANNON

22 Her appearance was formidable, her manner—well, it was like talking to St Paul's Cathedral.
On conversing with Queen Mary, quoted by Elizabeth Longford *The Queen: The Life of Elizabeth II* Knopf 83

HARRY CHAPMAN

23 Having served on various committees, I have drawn up a list of rules: Never arrive on time; this stamps you as a beginner. Don't say anything until the meeting is half over; this stamps you as being wise. Be as vague as possible; this avoids irritating the others. When in doubt, suggest that a subcommittee be appointed. Be the first to move for adjournment; this will make you popular; it's what everyone is waiting for.
Greater Kansas City Medical Bulletin 63

CHARLES, Prince of Wales

24 Father told me that if I ever met a lady in a dress like yours, I must look her straight in the eyes.
On Susan Hampshire's décolletage, *Reader's Digest* Oct 75

25 I learned the way a monkey learns—by watching its parents.
Quoted by Elizabeth Longford *The Queen: The Life of Elizabeth II* Knopf 83

ZEV CHAVETS

1 In Tel Aviv the weekends last 48 hours. In Jerusalem they last 6 months.
On moving from Jerusalem to Tel Aviv, Boston *Globe* 10 Apr 87

LYDIA CHAVEZ

2 An Argentine is an Italian who speaks Spanish and thinks he is British.
NY *Times* 9 Feb 86

JOHN CHEEVER

3 He had that spooky bass voice meant to announce that he had entered the kingdom of manhood, but Rosalie knew that he was still outside the gates.
The Wapshot Chronicle Harper 57

4 He was a tall man with an astonishing and somehow elegant curvature of the spine, formed by an enlarged lower abdomen, which he carried in a stately and contented way, as if it contained money and securities.
Description of a Yankee rector, *The Wapshot Scandal* Harper & Row 64

WINSTON CHURCHILL

5 A fanatic is one who can't change his mind and won't change the subject.
News summaries 5 Jul 54

6 An appeaser is one who feeds a crocodile—hoping it will eat him last.
Reader's Digest Dec 54

7 When you took your seat I felt as if a woman had come into my bathroom and I had only the sponge to defend myself.
To Nancy Astor, first women to sit in British Parliament, recalled on her death 2 May 64

8 Although present on the occasion, I have no clear recollection of the events leading up to it.
On his birth, recalled on his death 24 Jan 65

9 We have always found the Irish a bit odd. They refuse to be English.
ib

10 The monarchy is so extraordinarily *useful*. When Britain wins a battle she shouts, "God save the Queen"; when she loses, she votes down the prime minister.
Quoted by Anne Edwards *Matriarch* Morrow 84

JEAN COCTEAU

11 The trouble about the Académie is that by the time they get around to electing us to a seat, we really need a bed.
On election to Académie Française, recalled on his death 11 Oct 63

12 We must believe in luck. For how else can we explain the success of those we don't like?
ib

FREDERICK DONALD COGGAN, Archbishop of York

13 My ignorance of science is such that if anyone mentioned copper nitrate I should think he was talking about policemen's overtime.
NY *Journal-American* 20 Sep 61

CHRISTOPHER COLVEN, administrator, Anglican Shrine of Our Lady of Walsingham, England

14 Flew from London Heathrow to Boston and was met with a bunch of red roses. Culture shock sets in. . . . Evening Mass at St John's, Bowdoin Street. The deacon of the Mass had drop earrings and high-heeled shoes and turned out to be female—culture shock deepened.
Walsingham *Review* Christmas 84

BOB CONSIDINE

15 I believe in opening mail once a month, whether it needs it or not.
NY *Journal-American* 21 Jan 60

HENRY S F COOPER

16 A man who thinks too much about his ancestors is like a potato—the best part of him is underground.
Recalled on his death 10 Sep 84

ROBERT COOPER, Professor of Old Testament, Nashotah House Episcopal Seminary, Nashotah WI

17 There is no dilemma compared with that of the deep-sea diver who hears the message from the ship above, "Come up at once. We are sinking."
Episcopal Diocese of Chicago *Advance* Jul 79

BILL COSBY

18 When you become senile, you won't know it.
On growing older, quoted in NY *Times* 17 Mar 87

NORRIS COTTON, former US Senator

19 The boys are in such a mood that if someone introduced the Ten Commandments, they'd cut them down to seven.
Quoted in *A Guide to the 99th Congress* LTV Corp 85

NOEL COWARD

20 Success took me to her bosom like a maternal boa constrictor.
On having three hit plays running simultaneously in London, recalled on his death 26 Mar 73

21 It was not Café Society, it was Nescafé Society.
On entertaining at Desert Inn, Las Vegas, *ib*

22 I like long walks, especially when they are taken by people who annoy me.
ib

RUSSELL CROUSE and HOWARD LINDSAY

23 An optimist, in the atomic age, is a person who thinks the future is uncertain.
From their 1948 play *State of the Union*, recalled on Crouse's death 3 Apr 66

LAWRENCE CRUMB

24 If you want to see the sisters in their wimples with the pimples on their dimples, making laces for the faces of the acolytes in surplices, with purples for the trimmings of the cassocks of the canons of the bishop of the diocese of Fond du Lac—you're too late! They just passed by.
The Canons of the Bishop of the Diocese of Fond du Lac privately published 71

MARIO CUOMO, Governor of NY

1 I told them that my grandfather had died in the Great Crash of 1929—a stockbroker jumped out of a window and crushed him and his pushcart down below.
On meeting with a group assembled by David Rockefeller, NY *Times* 14 Sep 86

RICHARD J DALEY, Mayor of Chicago

2 We are proud to have with us the poet lariat of Chicago.
Introducing Carl Sandburg, NY *Times* 30 Jan 60

3 To higher and higher platitudes.
Citing goals for the future, *Life* 8 Feb 60

RODNEY DANGERFIELD

4 I'm at the age where food has taken the place of sex in my life. In fact, I've just had a mirror put over my kitchen table.
New York 5 May 80

GEORGE H DAVIES

5 What's all this fuss about fathers being present at the birth of their children? The way events are shaping, they'll be lucky to be present at the conception.
Letter to the editor Manchester *Guardian* 26 Aug 84

LAWRENCE DAVIES

6 He has shaken up a diocese founded by Episcopalians of innate conservatism. They accept as a truism that whereas Presbyterians, Methodists, Roman Catholics, Mormons and atheists came with the Gold Rush, they themselves waited for the Pullmans.
On James A Pike, Episcopal bishop of California, NY *Times* 3 Apr 60

BETTE DAVIS

7 She is the original good time that was had by all.
On another actress, *Parade* 15 Feb 81

CHARLES DE GAULLE, President of France

8 I always thought I was Jeanne d'Arc and Bonaparte. How little one knows oneself.
Reply to someone who compared him to Robespierre, *Time* 16 Jun 58

9 How can you be expected to govern a country that has 246 kinds of cheese?
Newsweek 1 Oct 62

ANNA DE NOAILLES

10 If God exists, I'd be the first to be told.
To Jean Cocteau, *Vogue* May 84

PETER DE VRIES

11 [Celibacy is] the worst form of self-abuse.
NY *Times* 12 Jun 83

MARLENE DIETRICH

12 Latins are tenderly enthusiastic. In Brazil they throw flowers at you. In Argentina they throw themselves.
On crowds in Buenos Aires, *Newsweek* 24 Aug 59

NORMAN DOUGLAS

13 Never take a solemn oath. People think you mean it.
Recalled on his death 9 Feb 52

WILLIAM O DOUGLAS, Associate Justice, US Supreme Court

14 Tell the FBI that the kidnappers should pick out a judge that Nixon wants back.
When told in 1970 of plot to hold for ransom a member of the Court in exchange for the release of federal prisoners, *The Court Years 1939–75* Random House 80

HUGH DOWNS

15 I've always thought that the stereotype of the dirty old man is really the creation of a dirty young man who wants the field to himself.
"The Seven Myths about Growing Old" *Family Weekly* 25 Mar 79

JAMES DUFFECY

16 A dead atheist is someone who's all dressed up with no place to go.
NY *Times* 21 Aug 64

RONALD DUNCAN

17 E M Forster was like a tea cozy, but I quite liked him. I was at a wedding party with him once, sitting opposite Queen Mary. I asked if he would like to be presented. "Good Lord," he said. "I thought it was the wedding cake."
London *Sunday Times* 14 Sep 80

EDWARD, Duke of Windsor

18 The thing that impresses me most about America is the way parents obey their children.
Look 5 Mar 57

ANNE EDWARDS

19 For the entire state of Georgia, having the première of *Gone With the Wind* on home ground was like winning the Battle of Atlanta 75 years late.
Road to Tara Ticknor & Fields 83

ALBERT EINSTEIN

20 When a man sits with a pretty girl for an hour, it seems like a minute. But let him sit on a hot stove for a minute—and it's longer than any hour. That's relativity.
Recalled on his death 18 Apr 55

21 I have just got a new theory of eternity.
On listening to a long after-dinner speech, quoted in Washington *Post* 12 Dec 78

DWIGHT D EISENHOWER, 34th US President

22 Oh yes, I studied dramatics under him for 12 years.
When asked if he knew Douglas MacArthur, quoted in *By Quentin Reynolds* McGraw-Hill 63

SUMNER LOCKE ELLIOTT

23 Imagine them adding insult to imagery.
On restaurant décor combining Yankee pewter with Muzak, *The Man Who Got Away* Harper & Row 72

EPISCOPAL THEOLOGICAL SEMINARY OF THE SOUTHWEST

1 You have in the course of a long career been the leader of a multitude of processions and have invariably brought your followers to higher places than they either desired or deserved.

> Citation honoring Edward Nason West, former subdean at Cathedral Church of St John the Divine, NYC, *Newsletter* Fall 84

WILLIAM FAULKNER

2 Why that's a hundred miles away. That's a long way to go just to eat.

> On declining invitation to White House dinner honoring Nobel laureates, *Life* 20 Jan 62

3 This is a free country. Folks have a right to send me letters, and I have a right not to read them.

> On discarding unopened mail, recalled on his death 6 Jul 62

4 Landlord of a bordello! The company's good and the mornings are quiet, which is the best time to write.
> On the ideal job, *ib*

DOUGLAS FEAVER, former Anglican Bishop of Peterborough, England

5 He'd believe anything provided it's not in Holy Scripture.

> On a liberal bishop, quoted in John Kelly comp *Purple Feaver* Northampton 85

6 His mouth is for export and his head has no entrance.

> On a member of the House of Lords, *ib*

7 I can't think why mothers love them. All babies do is leak at both ends.
> *ib*

ESTHER B FEIN

8 It may be a penny for your thoughts, but it is now a quarter for your voice.

> On increase in charge for pay-phone calls, NY *Times* 2 Jul 84

HARVEY FIERSTEIN

9 The great thing about suicide is that it's not one of those things you have to do now or you lose your chance. I mean, you can always do it *later*.

> *New York* 22 Aug 83

GEOFFREY FISHER, Archbishop of Canterbury

10 Dare I say that when he is at home I wish he was overseas, and still more profoundly when he is overseas I wish he was at home?

> On "Red Dean" of Canterbury Hewlett Johnson, *Time* 3 Jul 50

11 The long and distressing controversy over capital punishment is very unfair to anyone meditating murder.

> London *Sunday Times* 24 Feb 57

12 Once you start, there is no end to who is to go in and who is to be left out.

> On adding to the calendar of saints, *Look* 17 Mar 59

13 I have asked myself once or twice lately what was my natural bent. I have no doubt at all: It is to look at each day for the evil of that day and have a go at it, and that is why I have never failed to have an acute interest in each morning's letters.

> News summaries 18 Jan 61

JOE FLAHERTY

14 Farrell's Bar in Brooklyn had urinals so large they looked like shower stalls for Toulouse-Lautrec.

> *New York* 27 Dec 82

JANET FLANNER ("Genêt")

15 She was built for crowds. She has never come any closer to life than the dinner table.

> On Elsa Maxwell, recalled on Flanner's death 7 Nov 78

ERROL FLYNN

16 My problem lies in reconciling my gross habits with my net income.

> Recalled on his death 14 Oct 59

GERALD R FORD, 38th US President

17 The three-martini lunch is the epitome of American efficiency. Where else can you get an earful, a bellyful and a snootful at the same time?

> On tax-deductible entertaining, to National Restaurant Assn, Chicago, 28 May 78

18 Richard Nixon . . . was just offered $2 million by Schick to do a television commercial—for Gillette.

> At Humor and the Presidency Symposium, Ford Museum, Grand Rapids MI, quoted in *US* 3 Nov 86

GENE FOWLER

19 Never thank anybody for anything, except a drink of water in the desert—and then make it brief.

> NY *Mirror* 9 Apr 54

MARTIN FREUD

20 I didn't know the full facts of life until I was 17. My father never talked about his work.

> On being the son of Sigmund Freud, news summaries 15 Nov 57

B MICHAEL FROLIC

21 Foreigners in Moscow claim that, according to a Soviet statistic, there are only three brassieres for every five Russian women. In view of current Western women's fashion trends, they may be abreast of the times.

> NY *Times* 26 Oct 69

ROBERT FROST

22 I'm not confused. I'm just well mixed.

> *Wall Street Journal* 5 Aug 69

ZSA ZSA GABOR

23 A man in love is incomplete until he has married. Then he's finished.

> *Newsweek* 28 Mar 60

24 We were both in love with him. . . . I fell out of love with him, but he didn't.

> On ex-husband George Sanders, Chicago *American* 4 Sep 66

25 When I'm alone, I can sleep crossways in bed without an argument.

> On being between marriages, *Family Weekly* 7 May 76

ERLE STANLEY GARDNER

26 It's a damn good story. If you have any comments, write them on the back of a check.

> Note on manuscript submitted to hard-to-please editors, quoted by Dorothy B Hughes *Erle Stanley Gardner* Morrow 78

ANDRÉ GIDE

1 It is unthinkable for a Frenchman to arrive at middle age without having syphilis and the Cross of the Legion of Honor.
> Recalled on his death 19 Feb 51

FRANK L GILL, State Senator, Colorado

2 Last week we passed a birth-control bill. Now we are trying to pass a law to put the people to bed an hour earlier.
> On daylight-saving time legislation, *Quote* 18 Apr 65

SAMUEL GOLDWYN

3 Any man who goes to a psychiatrist ought to have his head examined.
> One of many Goldwynisms attributed to him, recalled on his death 31 Jan 74

MIKHAIL S GORBACHEV

4 If people don't like Marxism, they should blame the British Museum.
> On visit to British Museum Reading Room used by Karl Marx, NY *Times* 16 Dec 84

SONDRA GOTLIEB, wife of Canadian ambassador to US

5 For some reason, a glaze passes over people's faces when you say Canada.
> NY *Times* 8 Jul 82

BARRY GRAY

6 I get my exercise running to the funerals of my friends who exercise.
> *New York* 19 May 80

VARTAN GREGORIAN, President, NY Public Library

7 Everybody is somebody, so you don't have to introduce anybody.
> At dinner honoring authors, NY *Times* 13 Nov 84

EMMET GRIBBIN JR

8 The horse bit the pastor.
How came this to pass?
He heard the good pastor say,
"All flesh is grass."
> Letter to *Living Church* 12 Aug 84

ALAN HAMILTON

9 Some commoners are less common than others.
> On engagement of Prince Andrew to Sarah Ferguson, the niece of the Duchess of Gloucester, London *Times* 18 Mar 86

GRACE HANSEN

10 A wedding is just like a funeral except that you get to smell your own flowers.
> Recalled on her death, Eugene OR *Register-Guard* 14 Jan 85

AMANDA HILLIER, Administrator, Fauna and Flora Society of Britain

11 Driving round a bend and skidding on a mat of dead toads is very unpleasant for all concerned.
> On 20 tons of toads killed before opening of tunnels under roads to save them during mating season, quoted in NY *Times* 14 Mar 87

HERBERT HOOVER, 31st US President

12 The thing I enjoyed most were visits from children. They did not want public office.
> On his White House years, *On Growing Up* Morrow 62

13 About the time we can make the ends meet, somebody moves the ends.
> Recalled on his death 20 Oct 64

BOB HOPE

14 When she started to play, Steinway came down personally and rubbed his name off the piano.
> On comedian Phyllis Diller, WNEW TV 7 May 85

15 I have a wonderful make-up crew. They're the same people restoring the Statue of Liberty.
> At celebration of his 50 years in show business, NY *Times* 30 Apr 86

ROBERT HUGHES

16 One gets tired of the role critics are supposed to have in this culture: It's like being the piano player in a whorehouse; you don't have any control over the action going on upstairs.
> *Publishers Weekly* 12 Dec 86

CAROLINE HUNTER

17 Hostesses will usually divide their guest list between those who shoot the birds and those who shoot the breeze.
> "English Country Weekends" *M* Sep 84

BARBARA HUTTON

18 I've never seen a Brink's truck follow a hearse to the cemetery.
> On being told that she was being exploited, quoted by C David Heymann *Poor Little Rich Girl* Lyle Stuart 84

ANTONY JAY

19 From now on you can keep the lot.
Take every single thing you've got,
Your land, your wealth, your men, your dames,
Your dream of independent power,
And dear old Konrad Adenauer,
And stick them up your Eiffel Tower.
> On France's rejection of Great Britain as a member of the Common Market, *Time* 8 Feb 63

POPE JOHN XXIII

20 Here I am at the end of the road and at the top of the heap.
> On succeeding Pius XII, *Time* 24 Nov 58

21 It often happens that I wake at night and begin to think about a serious problem and decide I must tell the pope about it. Then I wake up completely and remember that I am the pope!
> *ib* 1 Feb 60

CARRIE JOHNSON

22 I for one appreciate a good form letter, having worked on Capitol Hill and learned several dozen cordial ways to say nothing.
> "Judging American Business by Its Writing Habits" NY *Times* 14 Jul 84

LYNDON B JOHNSON, 36th US President

1 When the burdens of the presidency seem unusually heavy, I always remind myself it could be worse. I could be a mayor.
   To US Mayors' Convention, *Newsweek* 3 Oct 66

2 Greater love hath no man than to attend the Episcopal Church with his wife.
   After a service at Bruton Parish Church, Williamsburg VA, in which the rector criticized the administration, 13 Nov 67

3 It's probably better to have him inside the tent pissing out, than outside the tent pissing in.
   On FBI director J Edgar Hoover, quoted in NY *Times* 31 Oct 71

ERICA JONG

4 Jealousy is all the fun you think they had.
   Fear of Flying Holt, Rinehart & Winston 73

YOUSUF KARSH

5 The trouble with photographing beautiful women is that you never get into the dark room until after they've gone.
   NY *Mirror* 2 May 63

GARRISON KEILLOR

6 It was luxuries like air conditioning that brought down the Roman Empire. With air conditioning their windows were shut, they couldn't hear the barbarians coming.
   Lake Wobegon Days Viking 85

7 Where all the women are strong, all the men are good-looking and all the children are above-average.
   On Lake Wobegon, fictional Minnesota town described on his radio show *Prairie Home Companion*, quoted in NY *Times* 18 Feb 87

WALT KELLY

8 We have met the enemy and he is us.
   From his comic strip *Pogo*, recalled on his death 18 Oct 73

JACQUELINE KENNEDY

9 The one thing I do not want to be called is First Lady. It sounds like a saddle horse.
   Quoted by Peter Collier and David Horowitz *The Kennedys* Summit 84

JOHN F KENNEDY, 35th US President

10 I am the man who accompanied Jacqueline Kennedy to Paris, and I have enjoyed it.
   Press conference 3 Jun 61

11 I think this is the most extraordinary collection of talent, of human knowledge, that has ever been gathered at the White House—with the possible exception of when Thomas Jefferson dined alone.
   At dinner for 49 Nobel laureates 29 Apr 62

12 It was absolutely involuntary. They sank my boat.
   On how he became a war hero, quoted in Bill Adler ed *The Kennedy Wit* Citadel 64

13 Let's not talk so much about vice. I'm against vice in all forms.
   Rejecting efforts to make him 1960 Democratic candidate for vice president, quoted by Ralph G Martin *A Hero for Our Time* Macmillan 83

14 The pay is good and I can walk to work.
   On becoming president, *ib*

CLARK KERR, President, University of California

15 I find that the three major administrative problems on a campus are sex for the students, athletics for the alumni and parking for the faculty.
   Time 17 Nov 58

JEAN KERR

16 I'm tired of all this nonsense about beauty being only skin-deep. . . . What do you want—an adorable pancreas?
   The Snake Has All the Lines Doubleday 60

17 A lawyer is never entirely comfortable with a friendly divorce, anymore than a good mortician wants to finish his job and then have the patient sit up on the table.
   Time 14 Apr 61

18 Life with Mary was like being in a telephone booth with an open umbrella—no matter which way you turned, you got it in the eye.
   Mary, Mary Doubleday 63

19 Being divorced is like being hit by a Mack truck—if you survive you start looking very carefully to the right and left.
   ib

LISA KIRK

20 A gossip is one who talks to you about others; a bore is one who talks to you about himself; and a brilliant conversationalist is one who talks to you about yourself.
   NY *Journal-American* 9 Mar 54

HENRY A KISSINGER

21 Next week there can't be any crisis. My schedule is already full.
   NY *Times* 28 Oct 73

22 The illegal we do immediately. The unconstitutional takes a little longer.
   On Watergate, *ib*

23 People are generally amazed that I would take an interest in any form that would require me to stop talking for three hours.
   On his fondness for opera, *Time* 15 Sep 80

24 Even a paranoid has some real enemies.
   Newsweek 13 Jun 83

25 The nice thing about being a celebrity is that when you bore people, they think it's their fault.
   Reader's Digest Apr 85

ANN LANDERS

26 You need that guy like a giraffe needs strep throat.
   Red Bank NJ *Register* 12 Oct 73

27 [I advise keeping] four feet on the floor and all hands on deck.
   From pamphlet "Teenage Sex and Ten Ways to Cool It," quoted in *Newsweek* 28 Jan 85

PAMELA LANSDEN

28 In show biz you are where you live. Real estate is the key to who has been signed, dumped, divorced, defrocked, deflowered, disbarred, arrested, disgraced, married and multiplied.
   People 13 Jul 87

JONATHAN LARSEN

1 Spectators came from far away. . . . The Queen of Camelot, the Duchess of Astor; the court architect, Philip of Glass (who has lately turned to stone); and the court's prose laureate, Brendan the Quill.
> On protest by Jacqueline Kennedy, Brooke Astor, Philip Johnson and Brendan Gill against proposed office tower on site of St Bartholomew's Church, "Altar Egos" *Manhattan Inc* Jul 86

GYPSY ROSE LEE

2 I have everything now I had 20 years ago—except now it's all lower.
> *Newsweek* 16 Sep 68

TOM LEHRER

3 First you get down on your knees
Fiddle with your rosaries
Bow your head with great respect
And genuflect, genuflect, genuflect.
> From his 1965 song "The Vatican Rag"

4 Get in line in that processional
Step into that small confessional
There the guy who's got religion'll
Tell you if your sin's original.
> *ib*

5 2–4–6–8
Time to transubstantiate!
> *ib*

STANISLAW LEM

6 Where do consequences lead? Depends on the escort.
> *Holiday* Sep 63

MADELEINE L'ENGLE

7 I didn't mean to give you the impression that life at the cathedral is like *Barchester Towers* as written by Dostoyevsky and heavily edited by John Updike.
> On Cathedral Church of St John the Divine, NYC, *A Severed Wasp* Farrar, Straus & Giroux 82

JOHN LEO

8 [By the mid 1920s the typical American town] was in full sexual bloom. The change came with erotic fashions, literature and movies, and an unsuspected sexual aid, the automobile.
> "Sex in the 80s" *Time* 9 Apr 84

OSCAR LEVANT

9 I don't drink. I don't like it. It makes me feel good.
> *Time* 5 May 58

10 I'm a study of a man in chaos in search of frenzy.
> *ib*

SAM LEVENSON

11 Insanity is hereditary—you get it from your children.
> *Diner's Club Magazine* Nov 63

C S LEWIS

12 There are two kinds of people: those who say to God, "Thy will be done," and those to whom God says, "All right, then, have it your way."
> From his 1943 book *The Screwtape Letters*, recalled on his death 22 Nov 63

LIBERACE

13 I cried all the way to the bank.
> On criticism of his flamboyant appearance and style as an entertainer, news summaries 30 Jun 54

14 You know that bank I used to cry all the way to? I bought it.
> Recalled on his death, *Newsweek* 16 Feb 87

ALICE ROOSEVELT LONGWORTH

15 My father always wanted to be the corpse at every funeral, the bride at every wedding and the baby at every christening.
> On President Theodore Roosevelt, quoted in Cleveland Amory and Earl Blackwell eds *Celebrity Register* Harper & Row 63

16 If you can't say something good about someone, sit right here by me.
> Motto embroidered on sofa pillow, quoted in *Time* 9 Dec 66

ANITA LOOS

17 The people I'm furious with are the women's liberationists. They keep getting up on soapboxes and proclaiming women are brighter than men. That's true, but it should be kept quiet or it ruins the whole racket.
> Quoted in NY *Times* 10 Feb 74

CLARE BOOTHE LUCE

18 I'm in my anecdotage.
> At age 77, *Town & Country* Jan 81

RUSSELL LYNES

19 The true snob never rests; there is always a higher goal to attain, and there are, by the same token, always more and more people to look down upon.
> *Snobs* Harper 50

HAROLD MACMILLAN, former Prime Minister of Great Britain

20 No man should ever lose sleep over *public* affairs.
> Interview with Dick Cavett ABC TV 16 Aug 82

MARCEL MARCEAU

21 Never get a mime talking. He won't stop.
> *US News & World Report* 23 Feb 87

FREDRIC MARCH

22 He has a terrific way with women. I don't think he has missed more than half a dozen.
> On Richard Burton, recalled on Burton's death, NY *Times* 6 Aug 84

GROUCHO MARX

23 A hospital bed is a parked taxi with the meter running.
> *Reader's Digest* Mar 73

24 I never forget a face, but in your case I'll make an exception.
> Quoted in news summaries 29 Jul 81

GALE W McGEE, US Senator

25 I'm going to introduce a resolution to have the postmaster general stop reading dirty books and deliver the mail.
> On efficiency over censorship, *Quote* 13 Sep 59

GERALD McKNIGHT

1 What the British must never believe about themselves is that they are good at games, strong in adversity, but lousy in bed. It is a myth invented by jealous foreigners.
Quote 11 Jun 67

MIGNON McLAUGHLIN

2 A woman telling her true age is like a buyer confiding his final price to an Armenian rug dealer.
Chicago *Tribune* 13 Sep 64

GEORGE MEANY, President, AFL

3 Anybody who has any doubt about the ingenuity or the resourcefulness of a plumber never got a bill from one.
CBS TV 8 Jan 54

BETTE MIDLER

4 When it's three o'clock in New York, it's still 1938 in London.
London *Times* 21 Sep 78

GEORGE MIKES

5 The world still consists of two clearly divided groups: the English and the foreigners. One group consists of less than 50 million people; the other of 3,950 million. The latter group does not really count.
How to Be Decadent Deutsch 77

EDNA ST VINCENT MILLAY

6 Please give me some good advice in your next letter. I promise not to follow it.
As an undergraduate at Vassar, quoted in Allen Ross Macdougall ed *Letters of Edna St Vincent Millay* Harper 52

ALICE-LEONE MOATS

7 The parties remind me of the Gay Nineties—the men are gay and the women are in their nineties.
On Philadelphia society, NY *Times* 5 Aug 86

MARILYN MONROE

8 I've been on a calendar, but never on time.
Look 5 Mar 57

9 It's not true that I had nothing on. I had the radio on.
On posing nude for a calendar, news summaries 31 Dec 57

ROBERT MORLEY

10 Names were not so much dropped as thrown in a perpetual game of catch.
On social life on the Riviera, London *Observer* 8 Aug 76

JOHN MORTIMER

11 All the flower children were as alike as a congress of accountants and about as interesting.
On conformist society in Great Britain in the 1970s, *TV Guide* 18 Oct 86

PETER MULLEN, Anglican priest

12 Even the end of the world is described as if it were only an exceptionally hot afternoon.
Criticizing the *New English Bible* translation, *Fair of Speech* Oxford 85, quoted in NY *Times* 22 Sep 85

OGDEN NASH

13 I would live all my life in nonchalance and insouciance
Were it not for making a living, which is rather a nouciance.
Reader's Digest Jun 67

GEORGE JEAN NATHAN

14 I drink to make other people interesting.
Recalled on his death 8 Apr 58

NEW YORKER

15 Gunther talks to his animals in English, French, German (when he's angry) and Baby Leopard. He also speaks fluent Elephant, several dialects of Tiger and Circus Horse.
On animal trainer Gunther Gebel-Williams, 21 Apr 75

NEW YORK TIMES

16 Uncle Frank and 12,999 former earthlings will be orbiting in a nose cone shiny to spot from the ground. True, he'll be dead, but what a way to go!
Editorial on plan to consign ashes of the dead to outer space, "Resting Places" 27 Jan 85

17 A New Yorker is a person with an almost inordinate interest in mental health, which is only natural considering how much of that it takes to live here.
"New Yorkers, By the Book" 4 Oct 86

ERIC NICOL

18 Was Lenin pro-Communist?
Russia, Anyone? A Completely Uncalled-for History of the USSR Harper & Row 63

DENNIS NINEHAM, Professor of Theology, University of Bristol, England

19 Generally speaking, bishops are generally speaking.
In consecration sermon, news summaries 6 Jul 84

CRAIG NOVA

20 She's got what I call bobsled looks: going downhill fast.
From his novel *Incandescence* Harper & Row 79

CAROL AND NEIL OFFEN

21 Kenya—along with Hollywood Boulevard—boasts one of the main animal crossings in the world.
Esquire Apr 86

ARISTOTLE ONASSIS

22 [Find a priest] who understands English and doesn't look like Rasputin.
To a business associate on planning Greek Orthodox marriage ceremony with Jacqueline Kennedy, quoted by Peter Evans *Ari* Summit 86

23 She's got to learn to reconcile herself to being Mrs Aristotle Onassis because the only place she'll find sympathy from now on is in the dictionary between shit and syphilis.
ib

THOMAS P ("TIP") O'NEILL, Speaker of the House

24 You better take advantage of the good cigars. You don't get much else in that job.
To Vice President Walter F Mondale, quoted in *Time* 4 Jun 84

ROBERT ORBEN

1 Life was a lot simpler when what we honored was father and mother rather than all major credit cards.
> *Wall Street Journal* 17 Mar 80

DOROTHY PARKER

2 He and I had an office so tiny that an inch smaller and it would have been adultery.
> On sharing space with Robert Benchley while working on *Vanity Fair* magazine, quoted in Malcolm Cowley ed *Writers at Work* Viking 58

3 How can they tell?
> On being told of the death of former President Calvin Coolidge, recalled on her death 7 Jun 67

4 [We look like] a road company of the Last Supper.
> On lunching with James Thurber and others at the Algonquin Round Table, quoted by Edmund Wilson *The Fifties*, edited by Leon Edel, Farrar, Straus & Giroux 86

HESKETH PEARSON

5 There is no stronger craving in the world than that of the rich for titles, except that of the titled for riches.
> *The Marrying Americans* Coward-McCann 61

S J PERELMAN

6 Under a forehead roughly comparable to that of Javanese and Piltdown man are visible a pair of tiny pig eyes, lit up alternately by greed and concupiscence.
> Self-description, *Quest* Nov 78

PRINCE PHILIP, Duke of Edinburgh

7 I have had very little experience of self-government. In fact, I am one of the most governed people in the world.
> NY *Times* 30 Dec 59

8 Dontopedology is the science of opening your mouth and putting your foot in it. I've been practicing it for years.
> To Britain's General Dental Council, *Time* 21 Nov 60

WILLIAM THOMAS PIPER, President, Piper Aircraft Corp

9 A speech is like an airplane engine. It may sound like hell but you've got to go on.
> *Time* 13 Jan 61

HENRY PORTER

10 The French and Italians seek solace by taking mistresses, but by and large the British retreat into a world of leather-bound misogyny.
> On men's clubs, "A User's Guide to London Clubs" *Illustrated London News* Sep 86

TOM POTTER, street person

11 I used to go to the movies on 42nd Street to sleep, but I can't stand those dirty movies they show there. They keep you awake.
> NY *Times* 17 May 76

IVY BAKER PRIEST, Treasurer of the US

12 We women don't care too much about getting our pictures on money as long as we can get our hands on it.
> *Look* 10 Aug 54

V S PRITCHETT

13 I shall never be as old as I was between 20 and 30.
> NY *Times* 16 Dec 85

BARBARA PYM

14 There was a reading from Ecclesiastes and a short eulogy, delivered by a younger colleague of the deceased, quietly triumphant in the prime of life.
> *Quartet in Autumn* Dutton 78

15 Miss Doggett again looked puzzled; it was as if she had heard that men only wanted one thing but had forgotten for the moment what it was.
> On an Oxford spinster, *Jane and Prudence* Dutton 81

16 There are no sick people in North Oxford. They are either dead or alive. It's sometimes difficult to tell the difference, that's all.
> *Crampton Hodnet* Dutton 85

JACQUES RABIO

17 People don't come here to learn to drive. They come here to get a driver's license.
> On his Paris driving school, *Newsweek* 20 Oct 69

GILDA RADNER

18 She's taken her good family name and put it on the asses of America!
> On Gloria Vanderbilt and her line of designer jeans, *Saturday Night Live* NBC TV 31 May 80

FREDERIC RAPHAEL

19 Miss Parker stood by her untalented husband through thick and thin, and thinner and thinner.
> On Dorothy Parker and Alan Campbell, "A Writer Stalks the Hollywood Myth" NY *Times* 6 Jan 85

RONALD REAGAN, 40th US President

20 Middle age is when you're faced with two temptations and you choose the one that will get you home by 9 o'clock.
> On his 66th birthday, quoted in Washington *Post* 7 Feb 77

21 Please tell me you're Republicans.
> To surgeons as he entered operating room after being wounded in an assassination attempt 30 Mar 81

22 A hippie is someone who looks like Tarzan, walks like Jane and smells like Cheetah.
> Quoted by Nat Shapiro ed *Whatever It Is, I'm Against It* Simon & Schuster 84

23 [Andrew Jackson] was actually 70 years old when he left the White House. . . . I know—he told me.
> To older volunteer workers at the White House whom he addressed as "my fellow septuagenarians," NY *Times* 27 Jun 84

24 I was recovering from young Mr Hinckley's unwelcome attentions.
> To Al Smith Memorial Dinner, recalling Terence Cardinal Cooke's visit to the White House after assassination attempt by John W Hinckley Jr, news summaries 18 Oct 84

25 I think we should keep the grain and export the farmers.
> On farm crisis, Washington Gridiron Club dinner 23 Mar 85

1 My doctors told me this morning my blood pressure is down so low that I can start reading the newspapers.

On recovering from prostate surgery, quoted in *US News & World Report* 23 Feb 87

2 Do you remember when I said bombing would begin in five minutes? Remember when I fell asleep during my audience with the pope? . . . Those were the good old days.

Washington Gridiron Club dinner 28 Mar 87

3 Since I came to the White House I got two hearing aids, a colon operation, skin cancer, a prostate operation and I was shot. The damn thing is, I've never felt better in my life.

ib

NAN ROBERTSON

4 Ever since Eve gave Adam the apple, there has been a misunderstanding between the sexes about gifts.

On Christmas shopping, NY *Times* 28 Nov 57

PATRICIA PEABODY ROOSEVELT

5 I felt like the Avon lady, breaking in on the reading of somebody's will.

On meeting her in-laws, *I Love a Roosevelt* Doubleday 67

BILLY ROSE

6 Never invest your money in anything that eats or needs repainting.

NY *Post* 26 Oct 57

JEAN ROSTAND

7 Concessions are essential at the outset of marital life, but after a certain lapse of time you can't afford to lose any more ground.

Maxims on Marriage Hachette 64

STANLEY RUDIN

8 Frustrate a Frenchman, he will drink himself to death; an Irishman, he will die of angry hypertension; a Dane, he will shoot himself; an American, he will get drunk, shoot you, then establish a million-dollar aid program for your relatives. Then he will die of an ulcer.

To International Congress of Psychology, NY *Times* 22 Aug 63

RITA RUDNER

9 If you never want to see a man again, say, "I love you, I want to marry you, I want to have children"— they leave skid marks.

NY *Times* 2 Aug 85

ROBERT O RUPP

10 We stopped counting his mistresses and started counting his accomplishments.

On commemorating Marion OH's best-known citizen, President Warren G Harding, NY *Times* 3 Nov 86

ANDREI D SAKHAROV, dissident Soviet scientist

11 [Bring] whatever else God prompts you to get. He won't suggest anything useless.

Final request on list of items for his wife to bring back from her trip to the US, *Time* 13 Oct 86

J D SALINGER

12 He probably passed on . . . of an overdose of garlic, the way all New York barbers eventually go.

Seymour: An Introduction Little, Brown 63

ANTHONY SAMPSON

13 Members rise from CMG (known sometimes in Whitehall as "Call Me God") to the KCMG ("Kindly Call Me God") to . . . the GCMG ("God Calls Me God").

On royal decorations ranging from Commander, Knight Commander and Grand Commander to the Order of St Michael and St George, *The Anatomy of Britain* Harper & Row 62

14 London clubs remain insistent on keeping people out, long after they have stopped wanting to come in.

ib

CHARLES M SCHULZ

15 You're a good man, Charlie Brown.

From *Peanuts* comic strip 75

16 No problem is too big to run away from.

Quoted by Al Ries and Jack Trout *Positioning: The Battle for Your Mind* McGraw-Hill 81

FRED ("THE FURRIER") SCHWARTZ

17 You have to remember. In the beginning we were *all* furriers.

Quoted in *Newsweek* 29 Dec 86

F R SCOTT

18 I am dying by honorary degrees.

On his many academic honors, news summaries 31 Dec 65

ARTIE SHAW

19 You have no idea of the people I *didn't* marry.

On his many marriages, NBC TV 8 Apr 85

FULTON J SHEEN, Auxiliary Bishop of NYC

20 Baloney is the unvarnished lie laid on so thick you hate it. Blarney is flattery laid on so thin you love it.

News summaries 22 Mar 54

21 I feel it is time that I also pay tribute to my four writers, Matthew, Mark, Luke and John.

On receiving award for television appearances, NY *World-Telegram & Sun* 24 Dec 54

22 An atheist is a man who has no invisible means of support.

Look 14 Dec 55

23 It's like being a Knight of the Garter. It's an honor, but it doesn't hold up anything.

On appointment as titular archbishop of Newport, Wales, NY *Times* 26 Jul 71

BARBARA BOGGS SIGMUND, Mayor of Princeton NJ

24 I think people have the impression that here in Princeton we won't go outside without alligators on our shirts to protect us.

NY *Times* 14 Feb 85

NEIL SIMON

1 People with honorary awards are looked upon with disfavor. Would you let an honorary mechanic fix your brand-new Mercedes?

> On receiving honorary degree from Williams College, NY *Times* 4 Jun 84

ANDREW SINCLAIR

2 He had a Puritan conscience and an Episcopalian sense of sin. The first pricked at him persistently, the second was excused through public piety.

> *Corsair: The Life of J Pierpont Morgan* Little, Brown 81

EDITH SITWELL

3 The aim of flattery is to soothe and encourage us by assuring us of the truth of an opinion we have already formed about ourselves.

> Quoted by Elizabeth Salter *The Last Years of a Rebel* Houghton Mifflin 76

JOHN SKOW

4 Housework, if it is done right, can kill you.

> "Erma in Bomburbia" *Time* 2 Jul 84

GERALD B H SOLOMON, US Congressman

5 [My dog] can bark like a congressman, fetch like an aide, beg like a press secretary and play dead like a receptionist when the phone rings.

> Entry in contest to identify Capitol Hill's Great American Dog, NY *Times* 9 Aug 86

SALLY STANFORD, madam and former Mayor of Sausalito CA

6 Madaming is the sort of thing that happens to you—like getting a battlefield commission or becoming the dean of women at Stanford University.

> *The Lady of the House* Putnam 66

WILL STANTON

7 Republicans sleep in twin beds—some even in separate rooms. That is why there are more Democrats.

> "How to Tell a Democrat from a Republican" *Ladies' Home Journal* Nov 62

BRENT STAPLES

8 Canceled checks . . . will be to future historians and cultural anthropologists what the Dead Sea Scrolls and hieroglyphics are to us.

> "Raw Meat for the Accountant" NY *Times* 15 Mar 87

JOHN STEINBECK

9 One man was so mad at me that he ended his letter: "Beware. You will never get out of this world alive."

> "The Mail I've Seen" *Saturday Review* 3 Aug 56

GLORIA STEINEM

10 She has become the Julia Child of sex.

> On "Dr Ruth" Westheimer, *Today* NBC TV 12 Feb 87

ADLAI E STEVENSON

11 Man does not live by words alone, despite the fact that sometimes he has to eat them.

> Recalled on his death 14 Jul 65

12 The relationship of the toastmaster to speaker should be the same as that of the fan to the fan dancer. It should call attention to the subject without making any particular effort to cover it.

> *ib*

13 Flattery is all right—if you don't inhale.

> *ib*

14 Do you know the difference between a beautiful woman and a charming one? A beauty is a woman you notice, a charmer is one who notices you.

> *ib*

15 I find Paul appealing and Peale appalling.

> On St Paul and Norman Vincent Peale, quoted in *Time* 20 Dec 68

16 A diplomat's life is made up of three ingredients: protocol, Geritol and alcohol.

> As US ambassador to UN, quoted by Elaine Sciolino "UN Parties: Quick Exits, Roasted Goats" NY *Times* 5 Nov 86

CASKIE STINNETT

17 Working for a federal agency was like trying to dislodge a prune skin from the roof of the mouth. More enterprise went into the job than could be justified by the results.

> *Out of the Red* Random House 60

18 A diplomat is a person who can tell you to go to hell in such a way that you actually look forward to the trip.

> *ib*

LEWIS THOMAS

19 Ants are so much like human beings as to be an embarrassment. They farm fungi, raise aphids as livestock, launch armies into war, use chemical sprays to alarm and confuse enemies, capture slaves, engage in child labor, exchange information ceaselessly. They do everything but watch television.

> *The Lives of a Cell* Viking 74

JAMES THURBER

20 Hundreds of hysterical persons must confuse these phenomena with messages from the beyond and take their glory to the bishop rather than the eye doctor.

> On retinal images caused by poor eyesight, quoted in Helen Thurber and Edward Weeks eds *Selected Letters of James Thurber* Atlantic–Little, Brown 81

ALICE B TOKLAS

21 This has been a most wonderful evening. Gertrude has said things tonight it will take her 10 years to understand.

> On leaving a dinner party with Robert M Hutchins, Gertrude Stein and Mortimer Adler, quoted by Adler WNET TV 15 Feb 76

ARNOLD TOYNBEE

22 America is a large, friendly dog in a very small room. Every time it wags its tail, it knocks over a chair.

> News summaries 14 Jul 54

PETER USTINOV

1 I'm convinced there's a small room in the attic of the Foreign Office where future diplomats are taught to stammer.
>Quoted by Israel Shenker *Words and Their Masters* Doubleday 74

ABIGAIL VAN BUREN

2 Kissing power is stronger than will power: Girls need to "prove their love" like a moose needs a hat rack.
>Quoted by Herbert R Mayes *The Magazine Maze* Doubleday 80

BILL VAUGHAN

3 Maybe the answer to Selective Service is to start everyone off in the army and draft them for civilian life as needed.
>*Half the Battle* Simon & Schuster 67

GEORGE VECSEY

4 One cannot help but be aware of the great scurrying to borrow, spend, invest, divest or just flat out hide things in the next three months before the wisdom of Congress falls upon us.
>On revision of US tax laws, NY *Times* 28 Sep 86

GORE VIDAL

5 A narcissist is someone better looking than you are.
>NY *Times* 12 Mar 81

ANDY WARHOL

6 It would be very glamorous to be reincarnated as a great big ring on Liz Taylor's finger.
>Quoted in eulogy at memorial mass, St Patrick's Cathedral, NY *Times* 2 Apr 87

ROBERT PENN WARREN

7 Storytelling and copulation are the two chief forms of amusement in the South. They're inexpensive and easy to procure.
>*Newsweek* 25 Aug 80

CHAIM WEIZMANN, President of Israel

8 Einstein explained his theory to me every day, and on my arrival I was fully convinced that he understood it.
>On transatlantic crossing with Albert Einstein, quoted by Nigel Calder *Einstein's Universe* Viking 79

ORSON WELLES

9 When you are down and out something always turns up—and it is usually the noses of your friends.
>NY *Times* 1 Apr 62

REBECCA WEST

10 Did St Francis preach to the birds? Whatever for? If he really liked birds he would have done better to preach to the cats.
>*This Real Night* Viking 85

RUTH WESTON

11 A fox is a wolf who sends flowers.
>NY *Post* 8 Nov 55

E B WHITE

12 I arise in the morning torn between a desire to improve (or save) the world and a desire to enjoy (or savor) the world. This makes it hard to plan the day.
>Recalled on his death, *Newsweek* 14 Oct 85

13 I can only assume that your editorial writer . . . tripped over the First Amendment and thought it was the office cat.
>Letter to NY *Herald Tribune* on its post–World War II insistence that its employees should "state their beliefs," *ib*

CHARLES A WHITTINGHAM, Publisher, *Life* magazine

14 The world should be in the kind of shape she's in!
>On his favorite *Life* cover, a photograph of actress Sophia Loren, *Live at Five* WNBC TV 3 Nov 86

CHARLOTTE WHITTON, Mayor of Ottawa

15 Whatever women do they must do twice as well as men to be thought half as good. Luckily, this is not difficult.
>*Canada Month* Jun 63

THYRA SAMTER WINSLOW

16 Platonic love is love from the neck up.
>News summaries 10 Aug 52

P G WODEHOUSE

17 There is only one cure for gray hair. It was invented by a Frenchman. It is called the guillotine.
>*The Old Reliable* Doubleday 51

18 He was white and shaken, like a dry martini.
>Describing a startled Englishman, *Cocktail Time* Simon & Schuster 58

LEONARD WOOLF

19 The London zoo is an animal microcosm of London, and even the lions, as a rule, behave as if they had been born in South Kensington.
>*Downhill All the Way* Harcourt, Brace & World 67

HENNY YOUNGMAN

20 I once wanted to become an atheist, but I gave up— they have no holidays.
>Quoted in Irving Wallace et al *Book of Lists #2* Morrow 80

21 When God sneezed, I didn't know what to say.
>NBC TV 28 Aug 86

MARGUERITE YOURCENAR

22 If I make it, I will carry a pencil instead of the ritual sword.
>On her chances of becoming the first woman elected to Académie Française, NY *Times* 3 Dec 79

JENNY ZINK

23 Santa is even-tempered. Santa does not hit children over the head who kick him. Santa uses the term *folks* rather than *Mommy and Daddy* because of all the broken homes. Santa does not have a three-martini lunch. Santa does not borrow money from store employees. Santa wears a good deodorant.
>To employees of Western Temporary Services, world's largest supplier of Santa Clauses, NY *Times* 21 Nov 84

WISDOM, PHILOSOPHY & OTHER MUSINGS

LIONEL ABEL

1 I have noted that persons with bad judgment are most insistent that we do what they think best.

> *Important Nonsense* Prometheus 86, quoted in NY *Times* 6 Feb 87

DEAN ACHESON

2 The great corrupter of public man is the ego. . . . Looking at the mirror distracts one's attention from the problem.

> To Society of Amer Historians, quoted in *Wall Street Journal* 22 Apr 66

3 The manner in which one endures what must be endured is more important than the thing that must be endured.

> Quoted by Merle Miller *Plain Speaking: An Oral Biography of Harry S Truman* Putnam 73

J DONALD ADAMS

4 There are times when I think that the ideal library is composed solely of reference books. They are like understanding friends—always ready to meet your mood, always ready to change the subject when you have had enough of this or that.

> NY *Times* 1 Apr 56

MORTIMER ADLER

5 Not to engage in the pursuit of ideas is to live like ants instead of like men.

> *Saturday Review* 22 Nov 58

RENATA ADLER

6 Bored people, unless they sleep a lot, are cruel.

> *Speedboat* Random House 76

AGA KHAN III

7 Every day has been so short, every hour so fleeting, every minute so filled with the life I love that time for me has fled on too swift a wing.

> Recalled on his death 11 Jul 57

BRIAN ALDISS

8 When childhood dies, its corpses are called adults.

> Manchester *Guardian* 31 Dec 77

SHANA ALEXANDER

9 Letters are expectation packaged in an envelope.

> "The Surprises of the Mail" *Life* 30 Jun 67

MUHAMMAD ALI

10 The man who views the world at 50 the same as he did at 20 has wasted 30 years of his life.

> *Playboy* Nov 75

STEWART ALSOP

11 A dying man needs to die as a sleepy man needs to sleep, and there comes a time when it is wrong, as well as useless, to resist.

> On his fight against cancer, *Stay of Execution* Bodley Head 74

MARIAN ANDERSON

12 I forgave the DAR many years ago. You lose a lot of time hating people.

> Announcing her retirement nearly 25 years after the DAR denied her concert space in Washington DC's Constitution Hall, NY *Times* 13 Dec 63

MAXWELL ANDERSON

13 If you practice an art, be proud of it and make it proud of you . . . It may break your heart, but it will fill your heart before it breaks it; it will make you a person in your own right.

> Quoted in NY *Herald Tribune* 7 Mar 59

MAYA ANGELOU

14 Self-pity in its early stages is as snug as a feather mattress. Only when it hardens does it become uncomfortable.

> *Gather Together in My Name* Random House 74

ANONYMOUS

15 Books are quiet. They do not dissolve into wavy lines or snowstorm effects. They do not pause to deliver commercials. They are three-dimensional, having length, breadth and depth. They are convenient to handle and completely portable.

> Notice posted at University of Wisconsin library, quoted in frontispiece to Hester Hoffman ed *The Reader's Adviser and Bookman's Manual* Bowker 60

16 Man himself is a visitor who does not remain.

> From proposed legislation to designate up to 10 million acres of government-owned land as wilderness preserves, quoted in NY *Times* 15 Jul 84

17 After ecstasy, the laundry.

> Zen statement, quoted in *Newsweek* 17 Dec 84

18 A person's right to smoke ends where the next person's nose begins.

> Public service announcement WNET TV 23 May 86

19 A neat house has an uninteresting person in it.

> Inscription on china plate, quoted by Enid Nemy NY *Times* 2 Nov 86

ROBERT ANTHONY

20 We neither get better or worse as we get older, but more like ourselves.

> *Think Again* Berkley 86

21 If you are not learning, no one will ever let you down.

> ib

22 If you let other people do it *for* you, they will do it *to* you.

> ib

DIANE ARBUS

23 Most people go through life dreading they'll have a traumatic experience. Freaks were born with their trauma. They've already passed their test in life. They're aristocrats.

> Quoted by Patricia Bosworth *Diane Arbus* Knopf 85

ELIZABETH ARDEN

24 Treat a horse like a woman and a woman like a horse. And they'll both win for you.

> Quoted by Alfred Allen Lewis *Miss Elizabeth Arden* Coward-McCann 72

HANNAH ARENDT

1 Nothing we use or hear or touch can be expressed in words that equal what is given by the senses.
New Yorker 12 Sep 70

2 Death not merely ends life, it also bestows upon it a silent completeness, snatched from the hazardous flux to which all things human are subject.
The Life of the Mind Harcourt Brace Jovanovich 78

BARBARA LAZEAR ASCHER

3 [There] is a need to find and sing our own song, to stretch our limbs and shake them in a dance so wild that nothing can roost there, that stirs the yearning for solitary voyage.
Playing after Dark Doubleday 86, quoted in *Christian Science Monitor* 20 Aug 86

4 [There is a need] to discover that we are capable of solitary joy and having experienced it, know that we have touched the core of self.
ib

BROOKE ASTOR

5 Mirrors in a room, water in a landscape, eyes in a face—those are what give character.
Architectural Digest Mar 82

NANCY, LADY ASTOR

6 The penalty of success is to be bored by people who used to snub you.
Recalled on her death 2 May 64

MARGARET ATWOOD

7 A divorce is like an amputation; you survive, but there's less of you.
Time 19 Mar 73

LOUIS AUCHINCLOSS

8 We were not as rich as the Rockefellers or Mellons, but we were rich enough to know how rich they were.
Lines for narrator in The Book Class *Houghton Mifflin 84, quoted in* People *13 Aug 84*

DOROTHY AUCHTERLONIE (Dorothy Green)

9 There is no moral virtue in being endowed with genius rather than talent: It is a gift of the gods or the luck of the genes.
Ulysses Bound Australian National University 73

10 Evil is the stone on which the good sharpens itself.
St Mark's Review Jun 76

W H AUDEN

11 Death is the sound of distant thunder at a picnic.
The Dyer's Hand Random House 68

12 We all have these places where shy humiliations gambol on sunny afternoons.
Quoted by Martha Graham NY Times *31 Mar 85*

DAVID AUGSBURGER

13 Since nothing we intend is ever faultless, and nothing we attempt ever without error, and nothing we achieve without some measure of finitude and fallibility we call humanness, we are saved by forgiveness.
Caring Enough to Forgive Regal 81

HAROLD AZINE

14 Happiness in the older years of life, like happiness in every year of life, is a matter of choice—*your* choice for yourself.
The House in Webster Groves NBC TV 16 Feb 58

15 Happiness in old age is, more than anything else, preserving the privileges of privacy.
ib

RICHARD BACH

16 Jonathan is that brilliant little fire that burns within us all, that lives only for those moments when we reach perfection.
On central metaphor in his best-seller Jonathan Livingston Seagull *Macmillan 70,* Time *13 Nov 72*

17 In the United States Christmas has become the rape of an idea.
ib

18 The more I want to get something done, the less I call it work.
Illusions Delacorte 77

FAITH BALDWIN

19 Time is a dressmaker specializing in alterations.
Face toward the Spring Rinehart 56

JAMES BALDWIN

20 I imagine one of the reasons people cling to their hates so stubbornly is because they sense, once hate is gone, they will be forced to deal with pain.
Notes of a Native Son Beacon 55

21 The price one pays for pursuing any profession or calling is an intimate knowledge of its ugly side.
Nobody Knows My Name Dial 61

22 It was books that taught me that the things that tormented me most were the very things that connected me with all the people who were alive, or who had ever been alive.
NY Times *1 Jun 64*

23 My father is dead. And he had a terrible life. Because, at the bottom of his heart, he believed what people said about him. He believed he was a "nigger."
ABC TV 10 Aug 64

24 To be a Negro in this country and to be relatively conscious is to be in a rage almost all the time.
Time 20 Aug 65

MONICA BALDWIN

25 I have always felt that the moment when first you wake up in the morning is the most wonderful of the 24 hours. No matter how weary or dreary you may feel, you possess the certainty that . . . absolutely anything may happen. And the fact that it practically always *doesn't*, matters not one jot. The possibility is always there.
I Leap over the Wall Holt, Rinehart & Winston 50

GEORGE BALL

26 Nostalgia is a seductive liar.
Newsweek 22 Mar 71

MARGARET CULKIN BANNING

1 Regrets are as personal as fingerprints.
"Living With Regrets" *Reader's Digest* Oct 58

CHRISTIAAN N BARNARD

2 Suffering isn't ennobling, recovery is.
Quoted in NY *Times* 28 Apr 85

SALO BARON

3 I oppose the lachrymose conception of Jewish history that treats Judaism as a sheer succession of miseries and persecutions.
Quoted by Israel Shenker *Coat of Many Colors* Doubleday 85

JOHN BARTH

4 Like an ox-cart driver in monsoon season or the skipper of a grounded ship, one must sometimes go forward by going back.
"Welcome to College—And My Books" NY *Times* 16 Sep 84

BRUCE BARTON

5 Conceit is God's gift to little men.
Coronet Sep 58

CECIL BEATON

6 Perhaps the world's second-worst crime is boredom; the first is being a bore.
Recalled on his death 18 Jan 80

SIMONE DE BEAUVOIR

7 One is not born, but rather becomes, a woman.
The Second Sex Knopf 53

8 That a whole part of the middle class detests me . . . is utterly normal. I would be troubled if the contrary were true.
Vogue May 79

ROY BEDICHECK

9 The so-called literature of escape, with its growing popularity, is in part a revolt against the tyranny of clocks.
Adventures with a Texas Naturalist University of Texas 61

10 It is not labor that kills, but the small attritions of daily routine that wear us down.
ib

11 A month of days, a year of months, 20 years of months in the treadmill, is the life that slays everything worthy of the name of life.
ib

LUCIUS BEEBE

12 All I want is the best of everything and there's very little of that left.
Quoted by Richard Kluger *The Paper: The Life and Death of the New York Herald Tribune* Knopf 86

MAX BEERBOHM

13 To say that a man is vain means merely that he is pleased with the effect he produces on other people.
Recalled on his death 20 May 56

BRENDAN BEHAN

14 I have a total irreverence for anything connected with society except that which makes the roads safer, the beer stronger, the food cheaper and the old men and old women warmer in the winter and happier in the summer.
Recalled on his death 20 Mar 64

GUY BELLAMY

15 Hindsight is an exact science.
The Sinner's Congregation Secker & Warburg 84

ELEANOR ROBSON BELMONT

16 I was trained by my husband. He said, "If you want a thing done—go. If not—send." I belong to that group of people who move the piano themselves.
NY *Times* 18 Dec 60

17 In retrospect, the past seems not one existence with a continuous flow of years and events that follow each other in logical sequence, but a life periodically dividing into entirely separate compartments. Change of surroundings, interests, pursuits, has made it seem actually more like different incarnations.
Recalled on her death 24 Oct 79

ERIC BENTLEY

18 Ours is the age of substitutes: Instead of language we have jargon; instead of principles, slogans; and instead of genuine ideas, bright suggestions.
The Dramatic Event: An American Chronicle Horizon 54

BERNARD BERENSON

19 A complete life may be one ending in so full an identification with the nonself that there is no self left to die.
Recalled on his death, *Time* 19 Oct 59

20 Life has taught me that it is not for our faults that we are disliked and even hated but for our qualities.
The Passionate Sightseer Abrams 60

21 From childhood on I have had the dream of life lived as a sacrament. . . . The dream implied taking life ritually as something holy.
ib

22 Boast is always a cry of despair except in the young, when it is a cry of hope.
Quoted by Umberto Morra *Conversations with Berenson* Houghton Mifflin 65

23 I would willingly stand at street corners, hat in hand, begging passers-by to drop their unused minutes into it.
Quoted on *A Renaissance Life* PBS TV 12 Apr 71

JOHN BERGER

24 We can become anything. That is why injustice is impossible here. There may be the accident of birth, there is no accident of death. Nothing forces us to remain what we were.
Pig Earth Pantheon 80, quoted by John Leonard NY *Times* 26 Aug 80

JOHN BERRY

25 The bird of paradise alights only upon the hand that does not grasp.
Flight of White Crows Macmillan 61

JOHN BETJEMAN

1 Now if the harvest is over
And the world cold
Give me the bonus of laughter
As I lose hold.
From *A Nip in the Air* Norton 76, recalled on his death, *Time* 28 May 84

STEPHEN BIRMINGHAM

2 What is known as success assumes nearly as many aliases as there are those who seek it.
"Young Men of Manhattan" *Holiday* Mar 61

JIM BISHOP

3 It is difficult to live in the present, ridiculous to live in the future and impossible to live in the past. Nothing is as far away as one minute ago.
NY *Journal-American* 7 May 61

4 Death is as casual—and often as unexpected—as birth. It is as difficult to define grief as joy. Each is finite. Each will fade.
Red Bank NJ *Register* 13 Aug 73

5 Books, I found, had the power to make time stand still, retreat or fly into the future.
A Bishop's Confession Little, Brown 81

LAWRENCE BIXBY

6 Each handicap is like a hurdle in a steeplechase, and when you ride up to it, if you throw your heart over, the horse will go along, too.
"Comeback from a Brain Operation" *Harper's* Nov 52

SHIRLEY TEMPLE BLACK

7 Make-believe colors the past with innocent distortion, and it swirls ahead of us in a thousand ways— in science, in politics, in every bold intention. It is part of our collective lives, entwining our past and our future. . . . a particularly rewarding aspect of life itself.
American Weekly 25 May 58

HARRY BLACKSTONE JR

8 Nothing I do can't be done by a 10-year-old . . . with 15 years of practice.
On being a magician, *Newsweek* 16 Oct 78

RONALD BLYTHE

9 He longed to be lost but he couldn't bear not to be found.
On T E Lawrence, *The Age of Illusion* Houghton Mifflin 64

10 Death used to announce itself in the thick of life but now people drag on so long it sometimes seems that we are reaching the stage when we may have to announce ourselves to death. . . . It is as though one needs a special strength to die, and not a final weakness.
The View in Winter Harcourt Brace Jovanovich 79

11 The ordinariness of living to be old is too novel a thing to appreciate.
ib

GEOFFREY BOCCA

12 Wit is a treacherous dart. It is perhaps the only weapon with which it is possible to stab oneself in one's own back.
The Woman Who Would Be Queen: A Biography of the Duchess of Windsor Rinehart 54

HUMPHREY BOGART

13 The whole world is about three drinks behind.
Recalled on his death 14 Jan 57

SISSELA BOK

14 Liars share with those they deceive the desire not to be deceived.
Lying Random House 78

15 We are all, in a sense, experts on secrecy. From earliest childhood we feel its mystery and attraction. We know both the power it confers and the burden it imposes. We learn how it can delight, give breathing space and protect.
Secrets Pantheon 83, quoted by Frank Trippett "The Public Life of Secrecy" *Time* 17 Jan 85

16 While all deception requires secrecy, all secrecy is not meant to deceive.
ib

EDWARD BOND

17 The English sent all their bores abroad, and acquired the Empire as a punishment.
Narrow Road to the Deep North Hill & Wang 68

DANIEL J BOORSTIN, Librarian of Congress

18 Technology is so much fun but we can drown in our technology. The fog of information can drive out knowledge.
On computerization of libraries, NY *Times* 8 Jul 83

19 The greatest obstacle to discovery is not ignorance—it is the illusion of knowledge.
Washington *Post* 29 Jan 84

VICTOR BORGE

20 Humor [is] something that thrives between man's aspirations and his limitations. There is more logic in humor than in anything else. Because, you see, humor is truth.
London *Times* 3 Jan 84

HAL BORLAND

21 Knowing trees, I understand the meaning of patience. Knowing grass, I can appreciate persistence.
Countryman: A Summary of Belief Lippincott 65

22 April is a promise that May is bound to keep.
A Promise—April 29, quoted in news summaries 31 Dec 82

RABBI EUGENE B BOROWITZ, Hebrew Union College, NYC

23 The peculiar malaise of our day is air-conditioned unhappiness, the staleness and stuffiness of machine-made routine.
Quoted on 1969 poster distributed by Argus Communications

NADIA BOULANGER

1 Life is denied by lack of attention, whether it be to cleaning windows or trying to write a masterpiece.

> Quoted by Bruno Monsaingeon *Mademoiselle* Carcanet 85

2 Everything we know by heart enriches us and helps us find ourselves. If it should get in the way of finding ourselves, it is because we have no personality.

> *ib*

3 The essential [conditions] of everything you do . . . must be choice, love, passion.

> *ib*

ELIZABETH BOWEN

4 Fate is not an eagle, it creeps like a rat.

> Recalled on her death 22 Feb 73

5 There is no end to the violations committed by children on children, quietly talking alone.

> *The House in Paris* Avon 79

HAL BOYLE

6 What makes a river so restful to people is that it doesn't have any doubt—it is sure to get where it is going, and it doesn't want to go anywhere else.

> *Help, Help! Another Day!* Lyle Stuart 70

TOM BRADLEY, Mayor of LA

7 People cut themselves off from their ties of the old life when they come to Los Angeles. They are looking for a place where they can be free, where they can do things they couldn't do anywhere else.

> Hilton Hotel Magazine *Guest Informant* Spring 80

FERNAND BRAUDEL

8 History may be divided into three movements: what moves rapidly, what moves slowly and what appears not to move at all.

> Surveying his work at age 73, NY *Times* 14 Jun 76

KINGMAN BREWSTER

9 There is no greater challenge than to have someone relying upon you; no greater satisfaction than to vindicate his expectation.

> Baccalaureate address as president of Yale 12 Jun 66

10 Judgment is more than skill. It sets forth on intellectual seas beyond the shores of hard indisputable factual information.

> Address at University of Exeter as US ambassador to Great Britain 26 Oct 78

JOSEPH BRODSKY

11 I do not believe in political movements. I believe in personal movement, that movement of the soul when a man who looks at himself is so ashamed that he tries to make some sort of change—within himself, not on the outside.

> NY *Times* 1 Oct 72

12 Life—the way it really is—is a battle not between Bad and Good but between Bad and Worse.

> *ib*

VAN WYCK BROOKS

13 Nothing is so soothing to our self-esteem as to find our bad traits in our forebears. It seems to absolve us.

> *From a Writer's Notebook* Dutton 58

CHARLES H BROWER

14 [This is] the great era of the goof-off, the age of the half-done job.

> May 20, 1958, address to National Sales Executive Convention, recalled on his death 23 Jul 84

JOHN MASON BROWN

15 So often we rob tomorrow's memories by today's economies.

> *The Arts of Living* Simon & Schuster 54

16 Charm is a glow within a woman that casts a most becoming light on others.

> *Vogue* 15 Nov 56

17 A good conversationalist is not one who remembers what was said, but says what someone wants to remember.

> *Esquire* Apr 60

ROSELLEN BROWN

18 When it comes time to do your own life, you either perpetuate your childhood or you stand on it and finally kick it out from under.

> *Civil Wars* Knopf 84

ANATOLE BROYARD

19 When friends stop being frank and useful to each other, the whole world loses some of its radiance.

> NY *Times* 1 Sep 85

MARTIN BUBER

20 An animal's eyes have the power to speak a great language.

> *I and Thou* Scribner's 70

21 I do, indeed, close my door at times and surrender myself to a book, but only because I can open the door again and see a human face looking at me.

> Quoted in Maurice Friedman ed *Martin Buber's Life and Work: The Later Years 1945–65* Dutton 84

PEARL BUCK

22 The secret of joy in work is contained in one word—excellence. To know how to do something well is to enjoy it.

> *The Joy of Children* John Day 66

GERALD BURRILL, retired Episcopal Bishop of Chicago

23 The difference between a rut and a grave is the depth.

> *Advance* Jul 79

RICHARD E BYRD

24 A static hero is a public liability. Progress grows out of motion.

> Recalled on his death 11 Mar 57

JAMES BRANCH CABELL

25 The optimist proclaims that we live in the best of all possible worlds, the pessimist fears this is true.

> Quoted on *Who Said That?* BBC TV 19 Sep 58

MARK CAINE

26 You cannot live on other people's promises, but if you promise others enough, you can live on your own.

> *The S-Man: A Grammar of Success* Houghton Mifflin 61

ALBERT CAMUS

1 There is no fate that cannot be surmounted by scorn.
The Myth of Sisyphus Knopf 55

2 Don't wait for the last judgment—it takes place every day.
The Fall Knopf 57

3 There is but one truly serious philosophical problem and that is suicide.
Recalled on his death 4 Jan 60

4 An intellectual is someone whose mind watches itself.
ib

5 At 30 a man should know himself like the palm of his hand, know the exact number of his defects and qualities, know how far he can go, foretell his failures—be what he is. And, above all, accept these things.
Notebooks Knopf 64

TRUMAN CAPOTE

6 Failure is the condiment that gives success its flavor.
The Dogs Bark Random House 73

AL CAPP

7 [The secret of] how to live without resentment or embarrassment in a world in which I was different from everyone else. . . . was to be indifferent to that difference.
"My Well-Balanced Life on a Wooden Leg" *Life* 23 May 60

AL CARMINE

8 She lived in capital letters.
Eulogy for Marion Tanner, model for Auntie Mame, NY *Times* 17 Nov 85

BENNETT CERF

9 For me, a hearty "belly laugh" is one of the beautiful sounds in the world.
Foreword to *An Encyclopedia of Modern American Humor* Doubleday 54

WHITTAKER CHAMBERS

10 On that road of the informer, it is always night. . . . I cannot ever inform against anyone without feeling something die within me. I inform without pleasure, because it is necessary.
Witness Random House 52

JOHN CHANCELLOR

11 The avenues in my neighborhood are Pride, Covetousness and Lust; the cross streets are Anger, Gluttony, Envy and Sloth. I live over on Sloth, and the style on our street is to avoid the other thoroughfares.
New York 24 Dec 84

LORD CHANDOS (Oliver Lyttelton)

12 Flattery is the infantry of negotiation.
Memoirs New American Library 63

GABRIELLE ("COCO") CHANEL

13 Nature gives you the face you have at 20; it is up to you to merit the face you have at 50.
Ladies' Home Journal Sep 56

14 How many cares one loses when one decides not to be something, but to be someone.
This Week 20 Aug 61

15 Those who create are rare; those who cannot are numerous. Therefore, the latter are stronger.
ib

16 Some people think luxury is the opposite of poverty. It is not. It is the opposite of vulgarity.
Recalled on her death 10 Jan 71

17 There is no time for cut-and-dried monotony. There is time for work. And time for love. That leaves no other time!
ib

JOHN CHEEVER

18 Homesickness is nothing . . . Fifty percent of the people in the world are homesick all the time.
From short story "The Bella Lingua" in *The Brigadier and the Golf Widow* Harper & Row 64, recalled on his death 18 Jun 82

SUSAN CHEEVER

19 Death is terrifying because it is so ordinary. It happens all the time.
On her father's last illness, *Home before Dark* Houghton Mifflin 84

MAURICE CHEVALIER

20 Old age isn't so bad when you consider the alternative.
At age 72, NY *Times* 9 Oct 60

SUSAN CHITTY

21 Never answer a question, other than an offer of marriage, by saying Yes or No.
The Intelligent Woman's Guide to Good Taste MacGibbon & Kee 58

WINSTON CHURCHILL

22 If you have an important point to make, don't try to be subtle or clever. Use a pile driver. Hit the point once. Then come back and hit it again. Then hit it a third time—a tremendous whack.
On public speaking, quoted by Edward, Duke of Windsor, *A King's Story* Putnam 51

23 Working hours are never long enough. Each day is a holiday, and ordinary holidays . . . are grudged as enforced interruptions in an absorbing vocation.
On work and pleasure, quoted by John Mason Brown "The Art of Keeping the Mind Refueled" *Vogue* 1 May 53

24 I am bored with it all.
Last words, recalled on his death 24 Jan 65

JOHN CIARDI

25 Nothing . . . goes further toward a man's liberation than the act of surviving his need for character.
Saturday Review 4 Aug 62

26 Intelligence recognizes what has happened. Genius recognizes what will happen.
Quote 30 Oct 66

27 The day will happen whether or not you get up.
Reader's Digest May 83

WISDOM, PHILOSOPHY & OTHER MUSINGS

EMILE M CIORAN

1 No one recovers from the disease of being born, a deadly wound if there ever was one.
The Fall into Time Quadrangle 70

LETA CLARK

2 Since women have been outside the system for so many centuries, it would be odd if they had not worked out an inner language that permitted them to puncture the pomposities.
NY *Times* 26 Nov 77

JAY COCKS

3 Yearning is not only a good way to go crazy but also a pretty good place to hide out from hard truth.
Time 15 Oct 84

JEAN COCTEAU

4 You've never seen death? Look in the mirror every day and you will see it like bees working in a glass hive.
Quoted by Ned Rorem, Dick Cavett show PBS TV 6 Oct 81

5 I have lost my seven best friends, which is to say God has had mercy on me seven times without realizing it. He lent a friendship, took it from me, sent me another.
Vogue May 84

6 Don't for a moment believe *He* was killing the young; He was costuming angels.
ib

WILLIAM SLOAN COFFIN

7 The world is too dangerous for anything but truth and too small for anything but love.
Address at Trinity Institute, San Francisco, 7 Feb 81

8 The woman most in need of liberation is the woman in every man and the man in every woman.
ib

COLETTE

9 January, month of empty pockets! . . . let us endure this evil month, anxious as a theatrical producer's forehead.
Recalled on her death 3 Aug 54

IVY COMPTON-BURNETT

10 Time . . . is not a great healer. It is an indifferent and perfunctory one. Sometimes it does not heal at all. And sometimes when it seems to, no healing has been necessary.
Darkness and Day Knopf 51

LESLEY CONGER

11 Every act of dishonesty has at least two victims: the one we think of as the victim, and the perpetrator as well. Each little dishonesty . . . makes another little rotten spot somewhere in the perpetrator's psyche.
Adventures of an Ordinary Mind Norton 63

CYRIL CONNOLLY

12 Our memories are card indexes—consulted, and then put back in disorder, by authorities whom we do not control.
The Unquiet Grave Harper & Row 72

JULIO CORTÁZAR

13 After the age of 50 we begin to die little by little in the deaths of others.
A Certain Lucas Knopf 84

NORMAN COUSINS

14 Life is an adventure in forgiveness.
Saturday Review 15 Apr 78

15 History is a vast early warning system.
ib

16 Wisdom consists of the anticipation of consequences.
ib

17 If something comes to life in others because of you, then you have made an approach to immortality.
Anatomy of an Illness Norton 79

18 What was most significant about the lunar voyage was not that men set foot on the moon but that they set eye on the earth.
Reader's Digest Sep 80

19 Optimism doesn't wait on facts. It deals with prospects. Pessimism is a waste of time.
Human Options Norton 81

20 Cynicism is intellectual treason.
ib

NOEL COWARD

21 I'll go through life either first class or third, but never in second.
NY *Post* 28 Mar 73

JAMES GOULD COZZENS

22 Real rebels are rarely anything but second rate outside their rebellion; the drain of time and temper is ruinous to any other accomplishment.
Children and Others Harcourt, Brace & World 64

DONALD CREIGHTON

23 History is the record of an encounter between character and circumstances.
Toward the Discovery of Canada Macmillan 72

WILFORD O CROSS

24 Our consciences are littered like an old attic with the junk of sheer conviction.
Prologue to Ethics Nashotah House 63

25 The rational mind of man is a shallow thing, a shore upon a continent of the irrational, wherein thin colonies of reason have settled amid a savage world.
ib

ELY CULBERTSON

26 The bizarre world of cards [is] a world of pure power politics where rewards and punishments [are] meted out immediately.
Recalled on his death 27 Dec 55

27 A deck of cards [is] built like the purest of hierarchies, with every card a master to those below it, a lackey to those above it.
ib

MARIO CUOMO, Governor of NY

1 When you've parked the second car in the garage, and installed the hot tub, and skied in Colorado, and wind-surfed in the Caribbean, when you've had your first love affair and your second and your third, the question will remain, where does the dream end for me?

Commencement address at Syracuse University, quoted in NY *Times* 12 May 86

SALVADOR DALI

2 Liking money like I like it, is nothing less than mysticism. Money is a glory.

NY *Times* 19 Mar 85

MARCIA DAVENPORT

3 A really interesting life has embraced everything from the most magnificent exultation to the depths of tragedy. I would say that's tremendous experience. But I wouldn't say enjoyment is an accurate summary of it.

NY *Post* 6 Apr 68

ROBERTSON DAVIES

4 Fanaticism is . . . overcompensation for doubt.

The Manticore Viking 72

CHARLES DE GAULLE

5 Old age is a shipwreck.

Quoted by Orson Welles NBC TV 14 Oct 85

MORARJI R DESAI, Prime Minister of India

6 Self-help must precede help from others. Even for making certain of help from heaven, one has to help oneself.

At conference of nonallied nations, NY *Times* 8 Apr 77

JOAN DIDION

7 To cure jealousy is to see it for what it is, a dissatisfaction with self, an impossible claim that one should be at once Rose Bowl princess, medieval scholar, Saint Joan, Milly Theale, Temple Drake, Eleanor of Aquitaine, one's sister and a stranger in a pink hat seen once and admired on the corner of 55th and Madison—as well as oneself, mysteriously improved.

"Jealousy: Is It a Curable Illness?" *Vogue* Jun 61

MARLENE DIETRICH

8 I love them because it is a joy to find thoughts one might have, beautifully expressed with much authority by someone recognizedly wiser than oneself.

On quotations, *ABC* Doubleday 62

NIELS DIFFRIENT

9 Today the ringing of the telephone takes precedence over everything. It reaches a point of terrorism, particularly at dinnertime.

NY *Times* 16 Oct 86

ISAK DINESEN

10 God made the world round so we would never be able to see too far down the road.

Recalled on her death 7 Sep 62

MACNEILE DIXON

11 Ideas, like individuals, live and die. They flourish, according to their nature, in one soil or climate and droop in another. They are the vegetation of the mental world.

Quoted by Norman Cousins *Human Options* Norton 81

12 The facts of the present won't sit still for a portrait. They are constantly vibrating, full of clutter and confusion.

ib

JIM DODGE

13 It just ain't possible to explain some things. It's interesting to wonder on them and do some speculation, but the main thing is you have to accept it—take it for what it is, and get on with your growing.

Fup Simon & Schuster 84

ANGELO DONGHIA

14 Assumption is the mother of screw-up.

NY *Times* 20 Jan 83

JOHN DOS PASSOS

15 People don't choose their careers; they are engulfed by them.

NY *Times* 25 Oct 59

W E B DU BOIS

16 One ever feels his twoness—an American, a Negro; two souls, two thoughts, two unreconciled strivings; two warring ideals in one dark body, whose dogged strength alone keeps it from being torn asunder.

Quoted in *Time* 3 Oct 69

JOHN FOSTER DULLES

17 A man's accomplishments in life are the cumulative effect of his attention to detail.

Quoted by Leonard Mosley *Dulles* Dial 78

WILL DURANT

18 To speak ill of others is a dishonest way of praising ourselves. . . . Nothing is often a good thing to say, and always a clever thing to say.

NY *World-Telegram & Sun* 6 Jun 58

19 In my youth I stressed freedom, and in my old age I stress order. I have made the great discovery that liberty is a product of order.

Time 13 Aug 65

20 When people ask me to compare the 20th century to older civilizations, I always say the same thing: "The situation is normal."

On winning Pulitzer Prize with his wife Ariel, NY *Times* 7 May 68

21 The ego is willing but the machine cannot go on. It's the last thing a man will admit, that his mind ages.

At age 90, NY *Times* 6 Nov 75

22 The most interesting thing in the world is another human being who wonders, suffers and raises the questions that have bothered him to the last day of his life, knowing he will never get the answers.

People 8 Dec 75

1 The trouble with most people is that they think with their hopes or fears or wishes rather than with their minds.
> Recalled on his death 7 Nov 81

ABBA EBAN

2 The Jews are the living embodiment of the minority, the constant reminder of what duties societies owe their minorities, whoever they might be.
> *Wall Street Journal* 2 Oct 84

UMBERTO ECO

3 The real hero is always a hero by mistake; he dreams of being an honest coward like everybody else.
> *Travels in Hyper Reality* Harcourt Brace Jovanovich 86

MARIAN WRIGHT EDELMAN

4 We must not, in trying to think about how we can make a big difference, ignore the small daily differences we can make which, over time, add up to big differences that we often cannot foresee.
> *Families in Peril* Harvard 87

ALBERT EINSTEIN

5 If A equals success, then the formula is A equals X plus Y plus Z. X is work. Y is play. Z is keep your mouth shut.
> Recalled on his death 18 Apr 55

6 Anger dwells only in the bosom of fools.
> *ib*

7 The tragedy of life is what dies inside a man while he lives.
> *ib*

8 A photograph never grows old. You and I change, people change all through the months and years but a photograph always remains the same. How nice to look at a photograph of mother or father taken many years ago. You see them as you remember them. But as people live on, they change completely. That is why I think a photograph can be kind.
> Recalled on centenary of his birth, *Christian Science Monitor* 6 Mar 79

9 The gift of fantasy has meant more to me than my talent for absorbing positive knowledge.
> Quoted in Washington *Post* 6 Mar 85

DWIGHT D EISENHOWER, 34th US President

10 Speeches are for the younger men who are going places. And I'm not going anyplace except six feet under the floor of that little chapel adjoining the museum and library at Abilene.
> On eve of his 75th birthday, NY *Times* 11 Oct 65

ALEXANDER ELIOT

11 Life is a fatal adventure. It can only have one end. So why not make it as far-ranging and free as possible?
> NY *Post* 28 Nov 62

T S ELIOT

12 The communication
Of the dead is tongued with fire beyond the language of the living.
> Inscription from *Little Gidding* on Eliot's memorial in Poets' Corner, Westminster Abbey, *Church Times* 13 Jan 67

WILLIAM EMERSON

13 Beware of the man who will not engage in idle conversation; he is planning to steal your walking stick or water your stock.
> *Newsweek* 29 Oct 73

PAUL ENGLE

14 Wisdom is knowing when you can't be wise.
> *Poems in Praise* Random House 59

LOUISE ERDRICH

15 In our own beginnings, we are formed out of the body's interior landscape. For a short while, our mothers' bodies are the boundaries and personal geography which are all that we know of the world. . . . Once we no longer live beneath our mother's heart, it is the earth with which we form the same dependent relationship, relying . . . on its cycles and elements, helpless without its protective embrace.
> "Where I Ought to Be" NY *Times* 28 Jul 85

CLIFTON FADIMAN

16 A sense of humor . . . is the ability to understand a joke—and that the joke is oneself.
> Santa Barbara *Center Magazine* Jul/Aug 77

WILLIAM FAULKNER

17 A gentleman can live through anything.
> *The Reivers* Random House 62

18 I love Virginians because Virginians are all snobs and I like snobs. A snob has to spend so much time being a snob that he has little time left to meddle with you.
> Recalled on his death, Memphis *Commercial Appeal* 7 Jul 62

19 I believe that man will not merely endure. He will prevail. He is immortal, not because he alone among creatures has an inexhaustible voice, but because he has a soul, a spirit capable of compassion and sacrifice and endurance.
> Accepting 1949 Nobel Prize, quoted in *Essays, Speeches and Public Lectures* Random House 65

HERMAN FEIFEL

20 It is a myth to think death is just for the old. Death is there from the very beginning.
> NY *Times* 21 Jul 74

CHARLES W FERGUSON

21 The essence of tragedy is to know the end.
> *Naked to Mine Enemies: The Life of Cardinal Wolsey* Little, Brown 58

GEOFFREY FISHER, Archbishop of Canterbury

22 Who knows whether in retirement I shall be tempted to the last infirmity of mundane minds, which is to write a book.
> On retiring, *Time* 12 May 61

MARGOT FONTEYN

23 Life forms illogical patterns. It is haphazard and full of beauties which I try to catch as they fly by, for who knows whether any of them will ever return?
> *Margot Fonteyn* Knopf 76

1 The one important thing I have learned over the years is the difference between taking one's work seriously and taking one's self seriously. The first is imperative and the second is disastrous.
ib

E M Forster

2 The only books that influence us are those for which we are ready and which have gone a little farther down our particular path than we have yet gone ourselves.
Recalled on his death 7 Jun 70

Harry Emerson Fosdick

3 He who cannot rest, cannot work; he who cannot let go, cannot hold on; he who cannot find footing, cannot go forward.
"Finding Unfailing Resources" in *Riverside Sermons* Harper 58

Gene Fowler

4 Men are not against you; they are merely for themselves.
Skyline Viking 61

5 Love and memory last and will so endure till the game is called because of darkness.
ib

John Fowles

6 Duty largely consists of pretending that the trivial is critical.
The Magus Little, Brown 66

Felix Frankfurter, Associate Justice, US Supreme Court

7 The mode by which the inevitable is reached is effort.
Quoted by Garson Kanin *Atlantic* Mar 64

8 I came into the world a Jew, and although I did not live my life entirely as a Jew, I think it is fitting that I should leave as a Jew. I don't want to . . . turn my back on a great and noble heritage.
ib

Betty Friedan

9 Men weren't really the enemy—they were fellow victims suffering from an outmoded masculine mystique that made them feel unnecessarily inadequate when there were no bears to kill.
Christian Science Monitor 1 Apr 74

Erich Fromm

10 The danger of the past was that men became slaves. The danger of the future is that men may become robots.
The Sane Society Holt, Rinehart & Winston 55

Robert Frost

11 You have freedom when you're easy in your harness.
News summaries 10 May 54

12 A civilized society is one which tolerates eccentricity to the point of doubtful sanity.
Quoted in *New Republic* 25 Oct 58

13 Forgive, O Lord, my little jokes on thee and I'll forgive thy great big one on me.
From *In the Clearing* Holt, Rinehart & Winston 62

14 Thinking isn't agreeing or disagreeing. That's voting.
Quoted in George Plimpton ed *Writers at Work* Viking 63

15 There is the fear that we shan't prove worthy in the eyes of someone who knows us at least as well as we know ourselves. That is the fear of God. And there is the fear of Man—fear that men won't understand us and we shall be cut off from them.
Quoted in *Newsweek* 11 Feb 63

16 What is this talked-of mystery of birth
But being mounted bareback on the earth?
"Riders" in *The Poetry of Robert Frost* Holt, Rinehart & Winston 66

Christopher Fry

17 Run on, keep your head down, cross at the double
The bursts of open day between the nights.
A Sleep of Prisoners Oxford 51

R Buckminster Fuller

18 Everyone is born a genius, but the process of living de-geniuses them.
Address at Ripon College, Ripon WI, NY *Post* 20 May 68

William Gaddis

19 Stupidity's the deliberate cultivation of ignorance.
Carpenter's Gothic Viking 85, quoted in *Newsweek* 15 Jul 85

John Kenneth Galbraith

20 [Economics] is a subject profoundly conducive to cliché, resonant with boredom. On few topics is an American audience so practiced in turning off its ears and minds. And . . . none can say that the response is ill advised.
Address at University of Arkansas 10 Jul 82

Paul Gallico

21 No one can be as calculatedly rude as the British, which amazes Americans, who do not understand studied insult and can only offer abuse as a substitute.
NY *Times* 14 Jan 62

John W Gardner, President, Carnegie Foundation

22 The society which scorns excellence in plumbing because plumbing is a humble activity, and tolerates shoddiness in philosophy because philosophy is an exalted activity, will have neither good plumbing nor good philosophy. Neither its pipes nor its theories will hold water.
Saturday Evening Post 1 Dec 62

23 Storybook happiness involves every form of pleasant thumb-twiddling; true happiness involves the full use of one's powers and talents.
Self-Renewal: The Individual and the Innovative Society Harper & Row 63

1 Self-pity is easily the most destructive of the non-pharmaceutical narcotics; it is addictive, gives momentary pleasure and separates the victim from reality.
   The Recovery of Confidence Norton 70

ANDRÉ GIDE

2 Sin is whatever obscures the soul.
   Recalled on his death 19 Feb 51

3 The most decisive actions of life . . . are most often unconsidered actions.
   ib

4 Believe those who are seeking the truth; doubt those who find it.
   ib

BERNARD GIMBEL

5 Two things are bad for the heart—running uphill and running down people.
   Reader's Digest Apr 67

LOUIS GINSBERG

6 Only in fetters is liberty.
   Without its banks,
   Can a river be?
   To Poetry Society of America, NY *Times* 2 Apr 66

WILLIAM GOLDING, 1983 Nobel laureate

7 An orotundity, which I define as *Nobelitis* . . . a pomposity [in which] one is treated as representative of more than oneself by someone conscious of representing more than himself.
   An Egyptian Journal Faber & Faber 85

EDWIN GOODGOLD

8 [The game of] Trivia, like camp, is a product of the heart, not of the mind. It's a social disease, it's little things for little minds. It's the last time you're able to act immature, to act like the college kid.
   NY *Post* 6 Dec 65

9 Trivia is a game played by those who realize that they have misspent their youth but do not want to let go of it.
   ib

GOOD LIFE ALMANAC

10 No man is the whole of himself. His friends are the rest of him.
   Solway Community Press 76

11 When in charge, ponder. When in trouble, delegate. When in doubt, mumble.
   ib

NADINE GORDIMER

12 Power is something of which I am convinced there is no innocence this side of the womb.
   News summaries 31 Dec 79

MARY GORDON

13 Waiting [is] the great vocation of the dispossessed.
   On immigrant-processing center at Ellis Island, NY *Times* 3 Nov 85

RUTH GORDON

14 Discussing how old you are is the temple of boredom.
   NY *Times* 23 Nov 79

15 Courage is very important. Like a muscle, it is strengthened by use.
   L'Officiel Summer 80

SUZANNE GORDON

16 To be alone is to be different, to be different is to be alone.
   Lonely in America Simon & Schuster 76

WILLIAM GORDON, Episcopal Bishop of Alaska

17 I believe that all of us have the capacity for one adventure inside us, but great adventure is facing responsibility day after day.
   Time 19 Nov 65

BILLY GRAHAM

18 Courage is contagious. When a brave man takes a stand, the spines of others are often stiffened.
   "A Time for Moral Courage" *Reader's Digest* Jul 64

MARTHA GRAHAM

19 You are unique, and if that is not fulfilled, then something has been lost.
   Newsweek 7 Apr 58

SHEILAH GRAHAM

20 You can have anything you want if you want it desperately enough. You must want it with an inner exuberance that erupts through the skin and joins the energy that created the world.
   The Rest of the Story Coward-McCann 64

CARY GRANT

21 My formula for living is quite simple. I get up in the morning and I go to bed at night. In between, I occupy myself as best I can.
   News summaries 28 Oct 79

ROBERT GRAVES

22 Marriage, like money, is still with us; and, like money, progressively devalued.
   "Real Women" *Ladies' Home Journal* Jan 64

DICK GREGORY

23 Just being a Negro doesn't qualify you to understand the race situation any more than being sick makes you an expert on medicine.
   Nigger Dutton 64

A WHITNEY GRISWOLD

24 Books won't stay banned. They won't burn. Ideas won't go to jail. In the long run of history, the censor and the inquisitor have always lost. The only sure weapon against bad ideas is better ideas.
   NY *Times* 24 Feb 59

ROBERT GRUDIN

25 Happiness may well consist primarily of an attitude toward time.
   Time and the Art of Living Harper & Row 82

1 Individuals we consider happy commonly seem complete in the present and we see them constantly in their wholeness: attentive, cheerful, open rather than closed to events, integral in the moment rather than distended across time by regret or anxiety.
ib

ALBERT GUERARD

2 Chivalry is the most delicate form of contempt.
Bottle in the Sea Harvard 54

CHARLES HAAR

3 Suburbs . . . have become the heirs to their cities' problems. They have pollution, high taxes, crime. People thought they would escape all those things in the suburbs. But like the people in Boccaccio's *Decameron*, they ran away from the plague and took it with them.
NY *Times* 16 Mar 80

DAG HAMMARSKJÖLD

4 Friendship needs no words—it is a loneliness relieved of the anguish of loneliness.
Markings Knopf 64

5 Destiny is something not be to desired and not to be avoided. . . . a mystery not contrary to reason, for it implies that the world, and the course of human history, have meaning.
ib

6 I believe that we should die with decency so that at least decency will survive.
ib

7 Do not seek death. Death will find you. But seek the road which makes death a fulfillment.
ib

OSCAR HAMMERSTEIN II

8 What is a sophisticate? He is a man who thinks he can swim better than he can and sometimes he drowns.
NY *Mirror* 15 Apr 60

KNUT HAMSUN

9 In old age . . . we are like a batch of letters that someone has sent. We are no longer in the past, we have arrived.
The Wanderer Farrar, Straus & Giroux 75

LORRAINE HANSBERRY

10 The thing that makes you exceptional, if you are at all, is inevitably that which must also make you lonely.
To Be Young, Gifted and Black Prentice-Hall 69

GRACE HANSEN

11 Don't be afraid your life will end; be afraid that it will never begin.
Recalled on her death, Eugene OR *Register-Guard* 14 Jan 85

HAN SUYIN

12 I really can't hate more than 5 or 10 years. Wouldn't it be terrible to be always burdened with those primary emotions you had at one time?
NY *Times* 25 Jan 85

SYDNEY J HARRIS

13 An idealist believes the short run doesn't count. A cynic believes the long run doesn't matter. A realist believes that what is done or left undone in the short run determines the long run.
Reader's Digest May 79

BARBARA GRIZZUTI HARRISON

14 To live exhilaratingly in and for the moment is deadly serious work, fun of the most exhausting sort.
Off Center Dial 80, quoted in NY *Times* 12 Jun 80

15 Beware of people carrying ideas. Beware of ideas carrying people.
Foreign Bodies Doubleday 84, quoted in *ib* 6 Jun 84

JOSEPH HELLER

16 When I grow up I want to be a little boy.
Something Happened Knopf 74

LILLIAN HELLMAN

17 People change and forget to tell each other.
Toys in the Attic Random House 60

ERNEST HEMINGWAY

18 The only thing that could spoil a day was people. . . . People were always the limiters of happiness except for the very few that were as good as spring itself.
A Moveable Feast Scribner's 64

19 All things truly wicked start from innocence.
Quoted by R Z Sheppard in review of Hemingway's posthumously published *The Garden of Eden* Scribner's 86, *Time* 26 May 86

KATHARINE HEPBURN

20 It's life isn't it? You plow ahead and make a hit. And you plow on and someone passes you. Then someone passes them. Time levels.
Quoted by Anne Edwards *A Remarkable Woman* Morrow 85

ABRAHAM J HESCHEL

21 Self-respect is the fruit of discipline; the sense of dignity grows with the ability to say no to oneself.
Quoted in Ruth M Goodhill ed *The Wisdom of Heschel* Farrar, Straus & Giroux 75

GEORGE HIGGINS, Minister, Congregational Church, Briarcliff NY

22 Egotism: The art of seeing in yourself what others cannot see.
Quoted in *Suburban People News* 2 Mar 86

LAURA Z HOBSON

23 I was thinking, 45—that's middle age. Well, I'm going to have the best damn middle age anybody ever had.
Laura Z Arbor House 83

ADAM HOCHSCHILD

24 Work is hard. Distractions are plentiful. And time is short.
"The Early Signs of Middle Age" NY *Times* 5 Feb 85

ERIC HOFFER

1 Craving, not having, is the mother of a reckless giving of oneself.
The True Believer Harper 51

2 I hang onto my prejudices, they are the testicles of my mind.
Before the Sabbath Harper & Row 79

3 Compassion alone stands apart from the continuous traffic between good and evil proceeding within us.
Christian Science Monitor 22 Apr 80

JOHN C HOLMES

4 To be beat is to be at the bottom of your personality, looking up.
"The Philosophy of the Beats" *Esquire* Feb 58

LARRY HOLMES

5 It's hard being black. You ever been black? I was black once—when I was poor.
Quoted by Joyce Carol Oates *On Boxing* Doubleday 87

MARJORIE HOLMES

6 The man who treasures his friends is usually solid gold himself.
Love and Laughter Doubleday 67

IRVING HOWE

7 The knowledge that makes us cherish innocence makes innocence unattainable.
Quoted by Louis Mumford *The City in History* Harcourt, Brace & World 61

ALDOUS HUXLEY

8 Most ignorance is vincible ignorance. We don't know because we don't want to know.
Recalled on his death 22 Nov 63

JOHN IRVING

9 You've got to get obsessed and stay obsessed.
The Hotel New Hampshire Dutton 81

INDRA JAHALANI

10 Camp is popularity plus vulgarity plus innocence.
NY *Times* 1 Jun 65

POPE JOHN XXIII

11 Every man has the right to life, to bodily integrity.
Pacem in Terris 10 Apr 63

POPE JOHN PAUL II

12 Work bears a particular mark of man and of humanity, the mark of a person operating within a community of persons.
1981 encyclical *On Human Work*, quoted in NY *Times* 9 Sep 84

CARL JUNG

13 The greatest and most important problems of life are all fundamentally insoluble. They can never be solved but only outgrown.
Recalled on his death 6 Jun 61

STEFAN KANFER

14 Sorrows cannot all be explained away . . . in a life truly lived, grief and loss accumulate like possessions.
Time 11 Jun 84

CONSTANTINE KARAMANLIS, Prime Minister of Greece

15 You do what you have to do in life, when you form a philosophy that you can't talk yourself out of.
News sumaries 14 Nov 56

16 People who decide they came to earth to work, who make work their personal philosophy, are kept very busy.
ib

YOUSUF KARSH

17 If there is a single quality that is shared by all great men, it is vanity.
Cosmopolitan Dec 55

NIKOS KAZANTZAKIS

18 Beauty . . . is merciless. You do not look at it, it looks at you and does not forgive.
Report to Greco Simon & Schuster 65

HELEN KELLER

19 Never bend your head. Always hold it high. Look the world straight in the eye.
To a five-year-old, recalled on her death 1 Jun 68

20 I long to accomplish a great and noble task, but it is my chief duty to accomplish small tasks as if they were great and noble.
ib

21 Death . . . is no more than passing from one room into another. But there's a difference for me, you know. Because in that other room I shall be able to see.
ib

JOHN F KENNEDY, 35th US President

22 The courage of life is often a less dramatic spectacle than the courage of a final moment; but it is no less than a magnificent mixture of triumph and tragedy.
As senator, *Profiles In Courage* Harper & Row 55

23 A man does what he must—in spite of personal consequences, in spite of obstacles and dangers and pressures—and that is the basis of all human morality.
ib

24 The credit belongs to the man who is actually in the arena, whose face is marred by dust and sweat and blood, who knows the great enthusiasms, the great devotions, and spends himself in a worthy cause; who at best, if he wins, knows the thrills of high achievement, and, if he fails, at least fails daring greatly, so that his place shall never be with those cold and timid souls who know neither victory nor defeat.
1961 comment quoted by William Manchester in frontispiece for *The Last Lion* Little, Brown 83

25 If I had to live my life over again, I would have a different father, a different wife and a different religion.
To John Sharon, former aide to Adlai Stevenson,

quoted by Ralph G Martin *A Hero for Our Time* Macmillan 83

ELIZABETH KENNY

1 It's better to be a lion for a day than a sheep all your life.
Quoted by Victor Cohn *Sister Kenny* University of Minnesota 76

CORITA KENT

2 Love the moment and the energy of that moment will spread beyond all boundaries.
Moments of 1984 Beacon 84

3 Flowers grow out of dark moments.
ib

4 Damn everything but the circus.
Quotation used on serigraph, *Newsweek* 17 Dec 84

5 Life is a succession of moments,
To live each one is to succeed.
ib

CHARLES F KETTERING

6 I object to people running down the future. I am going to live all the rest of my life there.
Quoted by T A Boyd *Professional Amateur* Dutton 57

7 Thinking is one thing no one has ever been able to tax.
Recalled on his death 25 Nov 58

NIKITA S KHRUSHCHEV, Soviet Premier

8 If you cannot catch a bird of paradise, better take a wet hen.
Quoted in *Time* 6 Jan 58

MARTIN LUTHER KING JR

9 There is nothing more tragic than to find an individual bogged down in the length of life, devoid of breadth.
The Measure of the Man Pilgrim 58

10 Everything that we see is a shadow cast by that which we do not see.
ib

11 I want to be the white man's brother, not his brother-in-law.
NY *Journal-American* 10 Sep 62

12 A nation or civilization that continues to produce soft-minded men purchases its own spiritual death on the installment plan.
Strength to Love Walker 63

13 We are not makers of history. We are made by history.
ib

14 Shallow understanding from people of good will is more frustrating than absolute misunderstanding from people of ill will.
Letter from a Birmingham jail 16 Jan 63

15 The sweltering summer of the Negro's legitimate discontent will not pass until there is an invigorating autumn of freedom and equality.
Address at Lincoln Memorial during March on Washington 28 Aug 63

16 I have a dream that one day on the red hills of Georgia, the sons of former slaves and the sons of former slave owners will be able to sit together at the table of brotherhood.
ib

17 I have a dream that my four little children will one day live in a nation where they will not be judged by the color of their skin, but by the content of their character.
ib

18 I have a dream that one day every valley shall be exalted, every hill and mountain shall be made low, the rough places will be made straight and the glory of the Lord shall be revealed and all flesh shall see it together.
ib

19 From the prodigious hilltops of New Hampshire, let freedom ring. From the mighty mountains of New York, let freedom ring. From the heightening Alleghenies of Pennsylvania, let freedom ring. But not only that: Let freedom ring from every hill and molehill of Mississippi.
ib

20 When this happens, when we let it ring, we will speed the day when all of God's children, black men and white men, Jews and Gentiles, Protestants and Catholics, will be able to join hands and sing in the words of the old Negro spiritual: "Free at last, free at last, thank God Almighty, we're free at last."
ib

21 Before the Pilgrims landed at Plymouth, we were here. Before the pen of Jefferson etched across the pages of history the majestic words of the Declaration of Independence, we were here. If the inexpressible cruelties of slavery could not stop us, the opposition we now face will surely fail.
On blacks in America, address at Birmingham AL, news summaries 31 Dec 63

22 A riot is the language of the unheard.
ib

23 Nonviolence is a powerful and just weapon. . . . which cuts without wounding and ennobles the man who wields it. It is a sword that heals.
Why We Can't Wait Harper & Row 64

24 If physical death is the price that I must pay to free my white brothers and sisters from a permanent death of the spirit, then nothing can be more redemptive.
On learning of threats on his life, St Augustine FL, 5 Jun 64

25 I believe that unarmed truth and unconditional love will have the final word in reality. This is why right, temporarily defeated, is stronger than evil triumphant.
Accepting Nobel Peace Prize 10 Dec 64

26 I just want to do God's will. And he's allowed me to go to the mountain. And I've looked over, and I've seen the promised land! I may not get there with you, but I want you to know tonight that we as a people will get to the promised land.
Address in Memphis the night before his assassination, 3 Apr 68

1 So I'm happy tonight. I'm not worried about anything. I'm not fearing any man. Mine eyes have seen the glory of the coming of the Lord!

ib

WALTER C KLEIN, Professor of Old Testament Literature and Languages, Seabury-Western Theological Seminary, Evanston IL

2 God bestows upon one man genius without patience and upon another man patience without genius. The relative achievements of the two are often surprising.

Clothed with Salvation Seabury-Western 53

LOUIS KRONENBERGER

3 The trouble with our age is all signposts and no destination.

Look 17 May 54

4 The closer and more confidential our relationship with someone, the less we are entitled to ask about what we are not voluntarily told.

Vogue 1 Mar 64

5 Nothing so soothes our vanity as a display of greater vanity in others; it make us vain, in fact, of our modesty.

ib

6 Highly educated bores are by far the worst; they know so much, in such fiendish detail, to be boring about.

Forbes 1 May 64

JOSEPH WOOD KRUTCH

7 [A] book . . . unlike a television program, moving picture or any other "modern means of communication" . . . can wait for years, yet be available at any moment when it happens to be needed.

More Lives Than One Sloane 62

WAUHILLAU LA HAY

8 Find a nice man, marry him, have babies and shut up.

Advice to career women, *Advertising Age* 26 Oct 59

JESSE LAIR

9 If you want something very, very badly, let it go free. If it comes back to you, it's yours forever. If it doesn't, it was never yours to begin with.

I Ain't Much, Baby—But I'm All I've Got Doubleday 74

HARPER LEE

10 Until I feared I would lose it, I never loved to read. One does not love breathing.

To Kill a Mockingbird Lippincott 60

STANISLAW LEM

11 To torture a man you have to know his pleasures.

Holiday Sep 63

12 Cannibals prefer those who have no spines.

ib

13 Do not trust people. They *are* capable of greatness.

ib

MADELEINE L'ENGLE

14 The great thing about getting older is that you don't lose all the other ages you've been.

Quoted in NY *Times* 25 Apr 85

JOHN LEONARD

15 In the cellars of the night, when the mind starts moving around old trunks of bad times, the pain of this and the shame of that, the memory of a small boldness is a hand to hold.

NY *Times* 2 Feb 77

OSCAR LEVANT

16 Happiness isn't something you experience; it's something you remember.

Recalled on his death, *Time* 28 Aug 72

HARRY LEVIN

17 The most protean aspect of comedy is its potentiality for transcending itself, for responding to the conditions of tragedy by laughing in the darkness.

Playboys and Killjoys Oxford 87, quoted in NY *Times* 18 Mar 87

C S LEWIS

18 Courage is not simply one of the virtues, but the form of every virtue at the testing point.

Recalled on his death 22 Nov 63

19 An explanation of cause is not a justification by reason.

ib

20 The long, dull, monotonous years of middle-aged prosperity or middle-aged adversity are excellent campaigning weather for the devil.

ib

21 The future is something which everyone reaches at the rate of 60 minutes an hour, whatever he does, whoever he be.

ib

22 It's so much easier to pray for a bore than to go and see one.

Letters to Malcolm Harcourt, Brace & World 64

VICTORIA LINCOLN

23 This is the art of courage: to see things as they are and still believe that the victory lies not with those who avoid the bad, but those who taste, in living awareness, every drop of the good.

"The Art of Courage" *Vogue* 1 Oct 52

ANNE MORROW LINDBERGH

24 The punctuation of anniversaries is terrible, like the closing of doors, one after another between you and what you want to hold on to.

Diary entry on the first anniversary of her son's kidnapping and death, *Locked Rooms and Open Doors* Harcourt Brace Jovanovich 74

CHARLES A LINDBERGH

25 It was a love of the air and sky and flying, the lure of adventure, the appreciation of beauty. It lay beyond the descriptive words of men—where immortality is touched through danger, where life meets death on equal plane; where man is more than man, and existence both supreme and valueless at the same time.

Contemplating his first parachute jump, *The Spirit of St Louis* Scribner's 53

1 Life [is] a culmination of the past, an awareness of the present, an indication of a future beyond knowledge, the quality that gives a touch of divinity to matter.
"Is Civilization Progress?" *Reader's Digest* Jul 64

2 If I had to choose, I would rather have birds than airplanes.
Recalled on his death 26 Aug 74

WALTER LIPPMANN

3 Industry is a better horse to ride than genius.
Quoted in Cleveland Amory and Earl Blackwell eds *Celebrity Register* Harper & Row 63

4 Men who are orthodox when they are young are in danger of being middle-aged all their lives.
ib

DONALD LLOYD

5 The American's conversation is much like his courtship. . . . He gives an inkling and watches for a reaction; if the weather looks fair, he inkles a little more.
"The Quietmouth American" *Harper's* Sep 63

LONDON TIMES

6 Our lives are like the course of the sun. At the darkest moment there is the promise of daylight.
Christmas editorial 24 Dec 84

CLARE BOOTHE LUCE

7 Courage is the ladder on which all the other virtues mount.
Reader's Digest May 79

RUSSELL LYNES

8 The only gracious way to accept an insult is to ignore it; if you can't ignore it, top it; if you can't top it, laugh at it; if you can't laugh at it, it's probably deserved.
Reader's Digest Dec 61

JOHN D MACDONALD

9 Friendships, like marriages, are dependent on avoiding the unforgivable.
The Last One Left Doubleday 67

ROBERT D MACDONALD

10 One German makes a philosopher, two a public meeting, three a war.
From his play *Summit Conference*, quoted in *International Herald Tribune* 13 May 82

JOAQUIM MARIA MACHADO DE ASSIS

11 In woman sex corrects banality, in men it aggravates it.
Esau and Jacob, translated by Helen Caldwell, University of California 65

SHIRLEY MACLAINE

12 When you look back on your life and try to figure out where you've been and where you are going, when you look at your work, your love affairs, your marriages, your children, your pain, your happiness—when you examine all that closely, what you really find out is that the only person you really go to bed with is yourself.
Washington *Post* 14 Nov 77

ARCHIBALD MACLEISH

13 The dissenter is every human being at those moments of his life when he resigns momentarily from the herd and thinks for himself.
"In Praise of Dissent" NY *Times* 16 Dec 56

HAROLD MACMILLAN

14 Tradition does not mean that the living are dead, it means that the dead are living.
Manchester *Guardian* 18 Dec 58

15 A man who trusts nobody is apt to be the kind of man nobody trusts.
NY *Herald Tribune* 17 Dec 63

16 When the curtain falls, the best thing an actor can do is to go away.
On withdrawing from Parliament in 1964, recalled on his death, *Time* 12 Jan 87

MOTHER MARY MADELEVA CSC

17 Thinking of things to be done, hopes to be realized, persons to be helped, I say laughingly that I go to a multitude of funerals daily, burying so many deceased projects, so much of what I have had to let die and must bury without regret.
My First Seventy Years Macmillan 59

BERNARD MALAMUD

18 Life is a tragedy full of joy.
NY *Times* 29 Jan 79

19 If you ever forget you're a Jew, a Gentile will remind you.
Quoted by Joseph Heller *Good as Gold* Pocket Books 80

MAXWELL MALTZ

20 Of all the traps and pitfalls in life, self-disesteem is the deadliest, and the hardest to overcome, for it is a pit designed and dug by our own hands, summed up in the phrase, "It's no use—I can't do it."
"You Can Do the Impossible" *This Week* 24 Jul 55

WILLIAM MANCHESTER

21 Abruptly the poker of memory stirs the ashes of recollection and uncovers a forgotten ember, still smoldering down there, still hot, still glowing, still red as red.
Good-bye, Darkness: A Memoir of the Pacific War Little, Brown 80

MARYA MANNES

22 For every five well-adjusted and smoothly functioning Americans, there are two who never had the chance to discover themselves. It may well be because they have never been alone with themselves.
"To Save the Life of 'I'" *Vogue* 1 Oct 64

PRINCESS MARGRETHE OF DENMARK

23 I have always had a dread of becoming a passenger in life.
On necessity of independent achievement, *Life* 12 Jan 68

FÉLIX MARTÍ-IBÁÑEZ

24 Even as a coin attains its full value when it is spent, so life attains its supreme value when one knows how to forfeit it with grace when the time comes.
"A Doctor Looks at Death" *MD* Sep 63

SUZANNE MASSIE

1 When one's own problems are unsolvable and all best efforts frustrated, it is lifesaving to listen to other people's problems.
Journey Knopf 75

MARCELLO MASTROIANNI

2 Woman is the sun, an extraordinary creature, one that makes the imagination gallop. Woman is also the element of conflict. With whom do you argue? With a woman, of course. Not with a friend, because he accepted all your defects the moment he found you. Besides, woman is mother—have we forgotten?
Atlas World Press Review Aug 78

SOMERSET MAUGHAM

3 I do not believe they are right who say that the defects of famous men should be ignored. I think it is better that we should know them. Then, though we are conscious of having faults as glaring as theirs, we can believe that that is no hindrance to our achieving also something of their virtues.
Quoted by Ted Morgan *Maugham* Simon & Schuster 80

4 Money . . . is the string with which a sardonic destiny directs the motions of its puppets.
ib

BILL MAULDIN

5 When we realize finally that we aren't God's given children, we'll understand satire. Humor is really laughing off a hurt, grinning at misery.
Time 21 Jul 61

ANDRÉ MAUROIS

6 People are what you make them. A scornful look turns into a complete fool a man of average intelligence. A contemptuous indifference turns into an enemy a woman who, well treated, might have been an angel.
News summaries 30 Jan 50

7 We owe to the Middle Ages the two worst inventions of humanity—romantic love and gunpowder.
Quoted on *Who Said That?* BBC TV 21 Jan 58

8 Growing old is no more than a bad habit which a busy man has no time to form.
Quoted by Milton Barron *The Aging American* Crowell 61

ELSA MAXWELL

9 Under pressure, people admit to murder, setting fire to the village church or robbing a bank, but never to being bores.
How to Do It Little, Brown 57

10 A bore is a vacuum cleaner of society, sucking up everything and giving nothing. Bores are always eager to be seen talking to you.
ib

11 Bores put you in a mental cemetery while you are still walking.
ib

12 I make enemies deliberately. They are the sauce piquante to my dish of life.
NY *Journal-American* 2 Nov 63

13 I don't hate anyone. I dislike. But my dislike is the equivalent of anyone else's hate.
Time 8 Nov 63

JOHN J MCCLOY

14 I found you could raise your voice and talk out loud in the world.
Discovery as prep student at Peddie School, quoted by Walter Isaacson and Evan Thomas *The Wise Men* Simon & Schuster 86

DAVID C MCCULLOUGH

15 A nation that forgets its past can function no better than an individual with amnesia.
LA *Times* 23 Apr 78

16 History is a guide to navigation in perilous times. History is who we are and why we are the way we are.
Address at Wesleyan University 3 Jun 84

PHYLLIS MCGINLEY

17 Gossip isn't scandal and it's not merely malicious. It's chatter about the human race by lovers of the same.
"A New Year and No Resolutions" *Woman's Home Companion* Jan 57

18 Gossip is the tool of the poet, the shoptalk of the scientist and the consolation of the housewife, wit, tycoon and intellectual. It begins in the nursery and ends when speech is past.
ib

19 Meanness inherits a set of silverware and keeps it in the bank. Economy uses it only on important occasions, for fear of loss. Thrift sets the table with it every night for pure pleasure, but counts the butter spreaders before they are put away.
Sixpence in Her Shoe Macmillan 64

MIGNON MCLAUGHLIN

20 What you have become is the price you paid to get what you used to want.
The Neurotic's Notebook Bobbs-Merrill 63

21 For the happiest life, days should be rigorously planned, nights left open to chance.
Atlantic Jul 65

MARSHALL MCLUHAN

22 The new electronic independence re-creates the world in the image of a global village.
The Gutenberg Galaxy: The Making of Typographical Man University of Toronto 62

23 Publication is a self-invasion of privacy.
Counterblast Harcourt, Brace & World 69

24 The more the data banks record about each one of us, the less we exist.
Playboy Mar 69

25 The winner is one who knows when to drop out in order to get in touch.
Quoted by Peter Newman "The Table Talk of Marshall McLuhan" *Maclean's* Jun 71

MARGARET MEAD

26 I was brought up to believe that the only thing worth doing was to add to the sum of accurate information in the world.
NY *Times* 9 Aug 64

1 All of us who grew up before the war are immigrants in time, immigrants from an earlier world, living in an age essentially different from anything we knew before. The young are at home here. Their eyes have always seen satellites in the sky. They have never known a world in which war did not mean annihilation.

> On generation gap of the late 1960s. *Culture and Commitment* Doubleday 70

2 As long as any adult thinks that he, like the parents and teachers of old, can become introspective, invoking his own youth to understand the youth before him, he is lost.

> *ib*

3 To cherish the life of the world.

> Recurring phrase in her manuscripts that was chosen for her gravestone, quoted by Mary Catherine Bateson *With a Daughter's Eye* Morrow 84

FRANK MEDLICOTT

4 Some people mistake weakness for tact. If they are silent when they ought to speak and so feign an agreement they do not feel, they call it being tactful. Cowardice would be a much better name.

> *Reader's Digest* Jul 58

ELISSA MELAMED

5 Men look *at* themselves in mirrors. Women look *for* themselves.

> *Mirror, Mirror: The Terror of Not Being Young* Linden Press 83

GIAN CARLO MENOTTI

6 A man only becomes wise when he begins to calculate the approximate depth of his ignorance.

> NY *Times* 14 Apr 74

THOMAS MERTON

7 A daydream is an evasion.

> *Conjectures of a Guilty Bystander* Doubleday 66

8 The biggest human temptation is . . . to settle for too little.

> *Forbes* 4 Aug 80

JAMES A MICHENER

9 Character consists of what you do on the third and fourth tries.

> *Chesapeake* Random House 78

ARTHUR MILLER

10 Where choice begins, Paradise ends, innocence ends, for what is Paradise but the absence of any need to choose this action?

> Foreword to 1964 play *After the Fall*, quoted in *Saturday Evening Post* 1 Feb 64

11 The apple cannot be stuck back on the Tree of Knowledge; once we begin to see, we are doomed and challenged to seek the strength to see more, not less.

> Commenting on *After the Fall, ib*

12 You specialize in something until one day you find it is specializing in you.

> From his 1967 play *The Price*

13 All we are is a lot of talking nitrogen.

> From his play *I Can't Remember Anything*, quoted in NY *Times* 9 Feb 87

HENRY MILLER

14 Life is 440 horsepower in a 2-cylinder engine.

> Recalled on his death 7 Jun 80

JAMES NATHAN MILLER

15 There is no such thing as a worthless conversation, provided you know what to listen for. And questions are the breath of life for a conversation.

> "The Art of Intelligent Listening" *Reader's Digest* Sep 65

LLEWELLYN MILLER

16 It's a sad truth that everyone is a bore to someone.

> *The Encyclopedia of Etiquette* Crown 68

PHILLIP MOFFITT

17 Always the rationalization is the same—"Once this situation is remedied, then I will be happy." But it never works that way in reality: The goal is achieved, but the person who reaches it is not the same person who dreamed it. The goal was static, but the person's identity was dynamic.

> "The Constancy of Change" *Esquire* Sep 84

18 A house is a home when it shelters the body and comforts the soul.

> "Everyman's Xanadu" *ib* Apr 86

ASHLEY MONTAGU

19 The cultured man is an artist, an artist in humanity.

> *The Cultured Man* World 58

20 He knows that human beings are still learning, by trial and error, how to be human and that many fall by the way. He knows that compassionate understanding and sympathy is the approach of the humane, while blame and censoriousness is the approach of the insufficiently humane.

> *ib*

21 The moments of happiness we enjoy take us by surprise. It is not that we seize them, but that they seize us.

> *The American Way of Life* Putnam 67

22 It is work, work that one delights in, that is the surest guarantor of happiness. But even here it is a work that has to be earned by labor in one's earlier years. One should labor so hard in youth that everything one does subsequently is easy by comparison.

> *ib*

23 Human beings are the only creatures who are able to behave irrationally in the name of reason.

> NY *Times* 30 Sep 75

MICHAEL MOONEY

24 When a civilization takes up the study of itself, it is always high noon.

> "The Ministry of Culture" *Harper's* Aug 80

BRIAN MOORE

25 If misery loves company, then triumph demands an audience.

> *An Answer from Limbo* Atlantic–Little, Brown 62

MARIANNE MOORE

1 The passion for setting people right is in itself an afflictive disease.

> Recalled on her death 5 Feb 72

LORD MORAN (Charles McMoran Wilson)

2 Courage is a moral quality; it is not a chance gift of nature like an aptitude for games. It is a cold choice between two alternatives, the fixed resolve not to quit; an act of renunciation which must be made not once but many times by the power of the will.

> *The Anatomy of Courage* Houghton Mifflin 67

ALBERTO MORAVIA

3 In life there are no problems, that is, objective and external choices; there is only the life which we do not resolve as a problem but which we live as an experience, whatever the final result may be.

> *The Time of Desecration* Farrar, Straus & Giroux 80

NEIL MORGAN

4 California is where you can't run any farther without getting wet.

> "California: The Nation within a Nation" *Saturday Review* 23 Sep 67

CHRISTOPHER MORLEY

5 There is only one success—to be able to spend your life in your own way.

> Recalled on his death 28 Mar 57

6 There are three ingredients in the good life: learning, earning and yearning.

> *ib*

7 When you sell a man a book you don't sell him just 12 ounces of paper and ink and glue—you sell him a whole new life.

> From his 1955 book *Parnassus on Wheels, ib*

TONI MORRISON

8 There is really nothing more to say—except why. But since why is difficult to handle, one must take refuge in how.

> *The Bluest Eye* Holt 69, quoted in NY *Times* 2 Jun 85

LANCE MORROW

9 Handwriting is civilization's casual encephalogram.

> "Scribble, Scribble, Eh, Mr Toad?" *Time* 24 Feb 86

ANNA MARY ROBERTSON MOSES ("Grandma Moses")

10 I look back on my life like a good day's work, it was done and I am satisfied with it.

> *Grandma Moses: My Life's History*, edited by Otto Kallir, Harper 52

MALCOLM MUGGERIDGE

11 Bad humor is an evasion of reality; good humor is an acceptance of it.

> BBC Publications 68

12 The truth is that a lost empire, lost power and lost wealth provide perfect circumstances for living happily and contentedly in our enchanted island.

> On British culture, London *Observer* 11 Aug 68

LEWIS MUMFORD

13 I would die happy if I knew that on my tombstone could be written these words, "This man was an absolute fool. None of the disastrous things that he reluctantly predicted ever came to pass!"

> To National Book Awards Committee, *My Works and Days* Harcourt Brace Jovanovich 79

EDWARD R MURROW

14 People say conversation is a lost art; how often I have wished it were.

> Quoted by George F Will *The Pursuit of Virtue and Other Tory Notions* Simon & Schuster 82

RALPH NADER

15 Every time I see something terrible, it's like I see it at age 19. I keep a freshness that way.

> *Esquire* Dec 83

TANCREDO NEVES, President of Brazil

16 I have never made a friend from whom I could not separate, and I have never made an enemy that I could not approach.

> Quoted in NY *Times* 16 Jan 85

NEW YORKER

17 People are like puzzles, and when somebody special dies there's a feeling that those particular pieces will never be assembled again—that particular picture is gone.

> "Talk of the Town" 27 Aug 79

NEW YORK TIMES

18 Who owns history? The public servants who make it, or the people who hire them and to whom they are accountable?

> Editorial on presidential memoirs, 19 Nov 83

19 Fear and ignorance about AIDS can so weaken people's senses as to make them susceptible to an equally virulent threat: bigotry.

> Editorial "AIDS and the New Apartheid" 7 Oct 85

MIKE NICHOLS

20 Being with an insanely jealous person is like being in the room with a dead mammoth.

> NY *Times* 27 May 84

MARTIN NIEMÖLLER

21 First they came for the Jews. I was silent. I was not a Jew. Then they came for the Communists. I was silent. I was not a Communist. Then they came for the trade unionists. I was silent. I was not a trade unionist. Then they came for me. There was no one left to speak for me.

> On resistance to Nazis, recalled on his death 6 Mar 84

RICHARD M NIXON, 37th US President

22 A man is not finished when he is defeated. He is finished when he quits.

> Dallas *Times-Herald* 10 Dec 78

23 You've got to learn to survive a defeat. That's when you develop character.

> *ib*

ALEX NOBLE

1 Success is a process, a quality of mind and way of being, an outgoing affirmation of life.

"In Touch with the Present" *Christian Science Monitor* 6 Mar 79

2 Success is not a place at which one arrives but rather . . . the spirit with which one undertakes and continues the journey.

ib

3 If I have been of service, if I have glimpsed more of the nature and essence of ultimate good, if I am inspired to reach wider horizons of thought and action, if I am at peace with myself, it has been a successful day.

ib

EDNA O'BRIEN

4 When anyone asks me about the Irish character, I say look at the trees. Maimed, stark and misshapen, but ferociously tenacious.

News summaries 31 Dec 65

SEAN O'CASEY

5 Laughter is wine for the soul—laughter soft, or loud and deep, tinged through with seriousness. . . . the hilarious declaration made by man that life is worth living.

"Saturday Night" in *Green Crows* Grosset & Dunlap 56

CLIFFORD ODETS

6 One night some short weeks ago, for the first time in her not always happy life, Marilyn Monroe's soul sat down alone to a quiet supper from which it did not rise.

"To Whom It May Concern: Marilyn Monroe" *Show* Oct 62, quoted by Dore Ashton *A Joseph Cornell Album* Viking 74

7 If they tell you that she died of sleeping pills you must know that she died of a wasting grief, of a slow bleeding at the soul.

ib

HERBERT O'DRISCOLL

8 I suspect that it is not without significance that the word *remembering* can be formed as *re-membering*. By its very nature the act of remembering is to offer a thing of patches, to try to put together again a once seamless garment of events totally and immediately experienced but now tattered by time.

A Doorway in Time Harper & Row 84

SEÁN O'FAOLÁIN

9 Pessimists are usually kind. The gay, bubbling over, have no time for the pitiful.

"In the Bosom of the Country" in *The Heat of the Sun* Atlantic–Little, Brown 66

LIAM O'FLAHERTY

10 I was born on a storm-swept rock and hate the soft growth of sun-baked lands where there is no frost in men's bones.

Recalled on his death 7 Sep 84

LAURENCE OLIVIER

11 Living is strife and torment, disappointment and love and sacrifice, golden sunsets and black storms. I said that some time ago, and today I do not think I would add one word.

LA *Times* 26 Feb 78

12 I take a simple view of living. It is keep your eyes open and get on with it.

ib

WILLIAM O'ROURKE

13 Regret is an odd emotion because it comes only upon reflection. Regret lacks immediacy, and so its power seldom influences events when it could do some good.

Idle Hands Delacorte 81

JOSÉ ORTEGA Y GASSET

14 I am I plus my circumstances.

Time 31 Oct 55

GEORGE ORWELL

15 The great enemy of clear language is insincerity. When there is a gap between one's real and one's declared aims, one turns, as it were, instinctively to long words and exhausted idioms, like a cuttlefish squirting out ink.

From his 1941 book *The Lion and the Unicorn*, recalled on his death 21 Jan 50

16 Sometimes the first duty of intelligent men is the restatement of the obvious.

Quoted by US Secretary of Education William J Bennett, address to National Press Club, Washington DC, 27 Mar 85

BOB PACKWOOD, US Senator

17 Judgment comes from experience and great judgment comes from bad experience.

NY *Times* 30 May 86

MARCEL PAGNOL

18 The most difficult secret for a man to keep is his own opinion of himself.

News summaries 15 Mar 54

DOROTHY PARKER

19 As only New Yorkers know, if you can get through the twilight, you'll live through the night.

Esquire Nov 64

BORIS PASTERNAK

20 Art has two constant, two unending concerns: It always meditates on death and thus always creates life. All great, genuine art resembles and continues the Revelation of St John.

Doctor Zhivago, translated by Max Hayward and Manya Harari, Pantheon 58

21 A corner draft fluttered the flame
And the white fever of temptation
Upswept its angel wings that cast
A cruciform shadow.

"Poems of Yurii Zhivago: Winter Night" *ib*

1 Our evenings are farewells
Our parties are testaments
So that the secret stream of suffering
May warm the cold of life.
  Quoted by his brother Alexander Pasternak *A Vanished Present* Harcourt Brace Jovanovich 85

KENNETH PATCHEN

2 Now is then's only tomorrow.
  Hallelujah Anyway New Directions 66

ALAN PATON

3 There is only one way in which one can endure man's inhumanity to man and that is to try, in one's own life, to exemplify man's humanity to man.
  "The Challenge of Fear" *Saturday Review* 9 Sep 67

CESARE PAVESE

4 We do not remember days, we remember moments.
  The Burning Brand Walker 61

NORMAN VINCENT PEALE

5 Getting people to like you is merely the other side of liking them.
  The Power of Positive Thinking Prentice-Hall 52

6 There is a real magic in enthusiasm. It spells the difference between mediocrity and accomplishment. . . . It gives warmth and good feeling to all your personal relationships.
  "Confident Living" NY *Herald Tribune* 5 Mar 61

7 Your enthusiasm will be infectious, stimulating and attractive to others. They will love you for it. They will go for you and with you.
  ib

WALTER PERSEGATI

8 Is life worth living? It is, so you take the risk of getting up in the morning and going through the day's work.
  NY *Times* 9 Jul 84

WILLIAM PHILLIPS

9 Boredom, after all, is a form of criticism.
  A Sense of the Present Chilmark 67

GEORGE PIERSON

10 The misfits and failures, the petty gangsters and confidence men, all follow a wandering star. Yet so, too, do many crusaders and missionaries in search of new sinners, new sufferings and new visions of perfection.
  The Moving American Knopf 73

BELVA PLAIN

11 All [life] is pattern . . . but we can't always see the pattern when we're part of it.
  Crescent City Delacorte 84

KATHERINE ANNE PORTER

12 I'm not afraid of life and I'm not afraid of death: Dying's the bore.
  At age 80, NY *Times* 3 Apr 70

13 You learn something the day you die. You learn how to die.
  Recalled on her death 18 Sep 80

PETER S PRESCOTT

14 Sociologists [are] academic accountants who think that truth can be shaken from an abacus.
  Newsweek 14 Apr 72

J B PRIESTLEY

15 One of the delights known to age, and beyond the grasp of youth, is that of Not Going.
  Delight Heinemann 66

16 Something in me resists the calendar expectation of happiness. *Merry Christmas yourself!* it mutters as it shapes a ghostly grin.
  Outcries and Asides Heinemann 74

V S PRITCHETT

17 The mark of genius is an incessant activity of mind. Genius is a spiritual greed.
  The Tale Bearers Random House 80

18 We live in a nervous, restless age, ourselves fragmented as we glance at one another. . . . We are forced to see our own and other people's lives in side glances; we ask for the essence, not the paragraph.
  Vogue Mar 81

19 The secret of happiness is to find a congenial monotony.
  Collected Stories Random House 82, quoted in NY *Times* 24 Apr 82

ROGER ALLAN RABY

20 A bad attitude is the worst thing that can happen to a group of people. It's infectious.
  Wall Street Journal 12 Apr 84

SARVEPALLI RADHAKRISHNAN

21 The worst sinner has a future, even as the greatest saint has had a past. No one is so good or so bad as he imagines.
  Recalled on his death 17 Apr 75

AYN RAND

22 I consider promiscuity immoral. Not because sex is evil, but because sex is too good and too important.
  Playboy Mar 64

23 Ever since Kant divorced reason from reality, his intellectual descendants have been diligently widening the breach.
  "The Cashing-In: The Student Rebellion" in *The New Left* New American Library 71

24 To achieve, you need thought. . . . You have to know what you are doing and that's real power.
  Christian Science Monitor 6 Jan 75

RONALD REAGAN, 40th US President

25 Heroes may not be braver than anyone else. They're just braver five minutes longer.
  Awarding Young American Medal for Bravery 22 Dec 82

VANESSA REDGRAVE

26 Integrity is so perishable in the summer months of success.
  Quoted by David Bailey *Good-bye Baby and Amen* Coward-McCann 69

JEAN RENOIR

1 When a friend speaks to me, whatever he says is interesting.
NY *Times* 28 Sep 69

FRANK H T RHODES

2 Without friendship and the openness and trust that go with it, skills are barren and knowledge may become an unguided missile.
Commencement address at Cornell 29 May 83

JOHN D ROCKEFELLER JR

3 I believe that the rendering of useful service is the common duty of mankind and that only in the purifying fire of sacrifice is the dross of selfishness consumed and the greatness of the human soul set free.
Credo engraved in plaza of Rockefeller Center, quoted in *New Yorker* 23 Mar 68

MARGARETTA ("HAPPY") ROCKEFELLER

4 Once you have been confronted with a life-and-death situation, trivia no longer matters. Your perspective grows and you live at a deeper level. There's no time for pettiness.
On recovery from cancer, *Family Weekly* 9 May 76

NELSON A ROCKEFELLER

5 There are three periods in life: youth, middle age and "how well you look."
NY *Times* 16 Dec 76

ANDY ROONEY

6 The closing of a door can bring blessed privacy and comfort—the opening, terror. Conversely, the closing of a door can be a sad and final thing—the opening a wonderfully joyous moment.
CBS TV 29 Feb 64

ELEANOR ROOSEVELT

7 Life was meant to be lived, and curiosity must be kept alive. One must never, for whatever reason, turn his back on life.
Autobiography of Eleanor Roosevelt Harper 61

FRANK ROWSOME JR

8 Getting in firewood is a many-faceted activity and not the least of its benefits is a sense of calm. . . . Woodcutting is a sovereign remedy for a churning mind, a specific for festering concern.
The Bright and Glowing Place Stephen Greene 75

LEONARD RUBINSTEIN

9 Curiosity is a willing, a proud, an eager confession of ignorance.
"Writing: A Habit of Mind" *Reader's Digest* Oct 84

BERTRAND RUSSELL

10 Three passions, simple but overwhelmingly strong, have governed my life: the longing for love, the search for knowledge and unbearable pity for the suffering of mankind.
The Autobiography of Bertrand Russell 1872–1914 Atlantic–Little, Brown 67

11 These passions, like great winds, have blown me hither and thither, in a wayward course, over a deep ocean of anguish, reaching to the very verge of despair.
ib

12 Work is of two kinds: first, altering the position of matter at or near the earth's surface relatively to other such matters; second, telling other people to do so.
Recalled on his death 2 Feb 70

13 Whenever one finds oneself inclined to bitterness, it is a sign of emotional failure.
ib

14 Boredom is a vital problem for the moralist, since at least half the sins of mankind are caused by the fear of it.
Life 13 Feb 70

WILLIAM SAFIRE

15 A sense of duty is moral glue, constantly subject to stress.
On the abdication of King Edward VIII. "'Lov'd I Not Honor More'" NY *Times* 23 May 86

16 When duty calls, that is when character counts.
ib

ADELA ROGERS ST JOHNS

17 Happiness is a sort of atmosphere you can live in sometimes when you're lucky. Joy is a light that fills you with hope and faith and love.
Some Are Born Great Doubleday 74

GEORGE SANTAYANA

18 Friendship is almost always the union of a part of one mind with a part of another: People are friends in spots.
Recalled on his death 26 Sep 52

19 There are books in which the footnotes or comments scrawled by some reader's hand in the margin are more interesting than the text. The world is one of these books.
ib

HELEN HOOVEN SANTMYER

20 [Time was] an accordion, all the air squeezed out of it as you grew older.
. . . *And Ladies of the Club* Putnam 84, quoted in *Time* 9 Jul 84

WILLIAM SAROYAN

21 The greatest happiness you can have is knowing that you do not necessarily require happiness.
News summaries 16 Dec 57

22 Good people are good because they've come to wisdom through failure. We get very little wisdom from success, you know.
NY *Journal-American* 23 Aug 61

23 Everybody has got to die, but I always believed an exception would be made in my case. Now what?
May 13, 1981, phone call to Associated Press reporter, quoted by Samuel G Freedman "Saroyan and His Plays Are Recalled at Tribute" NY *Times* 31 Oct 83

JEAN PAUL SARTRE

1 Hell is other people.
> From his 1947 play *No Exit*, recalled on his death 15 Apr 80

2 I think of death only with tranquillity, as an end. I refuse to let death hamper life. Death must enter life only to define it.
> *ib*

THOMAS SAVAGE

3 Cosmic upheaval is not so moving as a little child pondering the death of a sparrow in the corner of a barn.
> *Her Side of It* Little, Brown 81

DORE SCHARY

4 The true portrait of a man is a fusion of what he thinks he is, what others think he is, what he really is and what he tries to be.
> *Heyday* Little, Brown 80

RICHARD SCHICKEL

5 The law of unintended consequences pushes us ceaselessly through the years, permitting no pause for perspective.
> *Time* 28 Nov 83

JONATHAN SCHWARTZ

6 Most of us are only tuned in to distant stations where all kinds of things are happening to other people. We listen through the static to their heartbreaks as if we were in some well-protected receiving chamber.
> *Distant Stations* Doubleday 79

ALBERT SCHWEITZER

7 An optimist is a person who sees a green light everywhere, while the pessimist sees only the red stoplight. . . . The truly wise person is colorblind.
> News summaries 14 Jan 55

8 Reverence for life is the highest court of appeal.
> Recalled on his death 4 Sep 65

9 A man is ethical only when life, as such, is sacred to him, that of plants and animals as that of his fellow men, and when he devotes himself helpfully to all life that is in need of help.
> *ib*

10 The tragedy of life is what dies inside a man while he lives.
> *ib*

11 Hear our prayer O Lord . . . for animals that are overworked, underfed and cruelly treated; for all wistful creatures in captivity that beat their wings against bars; for any that are hunted or lost or deserted or frightened or hungry; for all that must be put to death. . . . and for those who deal with them we ask a heart of compassion and gentle hands and kindly words.
> Prayer for animals, *ib*

FLORIDA SCOTT-MAXWELL

12 The crucial task of old age is balance: keeping just well enough, just brave enough, just gay and interested and starkly honest enough to remain a sentient human being.
> *The Measure of My Days* Knopf 68

13 Life does not accommodate you, it shatters you. It is meant to, and it couldn't do it better. Every seed destroys its container or else there would be no fruition.
> *ib*

CHARLES SCRIBNER JR

14 Reading is a means of thinking with another person's mind; it forces you to stretch your own.
> *Publishers Weekly* 30 Mar 84

RICHARD SENNETT

15 Authority . . . is itself inherently an act of imagination.
> *Authority* Random House 80, quoted in *Newsweek* 5 May 80

ERIC SEVAREID

16 The chief cause of problems is solutions.
> *Reader's Digest* Mar 74

PETER SHAFFER

17 Everything we feel is made of Time. All the beauties of life are shaped by it.
> *The Royal Hunt of the Sun* Stein & Day 65

GEORGE BERNARD SHAW

18 The true joy of life [is] being used for a purpose recognized by yourself as a mighty one . . . being thoroughly worn out before you are thrown to the scrap heap . . . being a force of nature instead of a feverish, selfish clod of ailments and grievances.
> Recalled on his death 2 Nov 50

19 A perpetual holiday is a good working definition of hell.
> Quoted by Charles Krauthammer "Holiday: Living on a Return Ticket" *Time* 27 Aug 84

ANATOLY B SHCHARANSKY

20 All the resources of a superpower cannot isolate a man who hears the voice of freedom, a voice I heard from the very chamber of my soul.
> To NYC rally three months after his release from a Soviet prison, NY *Times* 12 May 86

FULTON J SHEEN, former Bishop of Rochester NY

21 Jealousy is the tribute mediocrity pays to genius.
> Quoted by Daniel P Noonan *The Passion of Fulton Sheen* Dodd, Mead 72

IGOR SIKORSKY

22 The work of the individual still remains the spark that moves mankind ahead even more than teamwork.
> Recalled on his death, NY *Times* 27 Oct 72

ALISTAIR SIM

23 It was revealed to me many years ago with conclusive certainty that I was a fool and that I had always been a fool. Since then I have been as happy as any man has a right to be.
> *Time* 30 Aug 76

GEORGES SIMENON

24 I adore life but I don't fear death. I just prefer to die as late as possible.
> *International Herald Tribune* 26 Nov 81

ISAAC BASHEVIS SINGER

1 The analysis of character is the highest human entertainment.
NY *Times* 26 Nov 78

2 When you betray somebody else, you also betray yourself.
ib

3 Our knowledge is a little island in a great ocean of nonknowledge.
ib 3 Dec 78

EDITH SITWELL

4 The aim of flattery is to soothe and encourage us by assuring us of the truth of an opinion we have already formed about ourselves.
Quoted by Elizabeth Salter *The Last Years of a Rebel* Houghton Mifflin 67

B F SKINNER

5 I did not direct my life. I didn't design it. I never made decisions. Things always came up and made them for me. That's what life is.
Particulars of My Life Knopf 76

C R SMITH

6 A problem is something you have hopes of changing. Anything else is a fact of life.
Publishers Weekly 8 Sep 69

C P SNOW

7 Civilization is hideously fragile [and] there's not much between us and the horrors underneath, just about a coat of varnish.
A Coat of Varnish Scribner's 79

RALPH W SOCKMAN, Senior Minister, Christ Church, Methodist, NYC

8 Whatever the right hand findeth to do, the left hand carries a watch on its wrist to show how long it takes to do it.
Triumph over Time NBC Radio sermon 12 Jan 58

9 Let us not bankrupt our todays by paying interest on the regrets of yesterday and by borrowing in advance the troubles of tomorrow.
ib

IRA SOLENBERGER

10 People who are getting up in years . . . die in the winter when the days are short, and in the hours after midnight. Life is at a low ebb after midnight and in the short days. Did you know that?
Quoted by Roy Redd "An Ozark Gardener, 86, Awaits Coming of the Greening Season" NY *Times* 12 Apr 76

SUSAN SONTAG

11 He who despises himself esteems himself as a self-despiser.
Death Kit Farrar, Straus & Giroux 67

ELLEASE SOUTHERLAND

12 God has plans which mortals don't understand. He rests in the womb when the new baby forms. Whispers the life dream to infinitesimal cells. It is God who lies under the thoughts of man. He is cartilage. Memory.
Let the Lion Eat Straw Scribner's 79

13 It is God in the house when the curtains lift gently at the windows, and a young child sucks his itching gums. We do not understand the mysteries of God. God the winter. Summer, Septembers. Moody dark tones of fathers dying. The splash and laughter. Children playing.
ib

MURIEL SPARK

14 It is impossible to persuade a man who does not disagree, but smiles.
The Prime of Miss Jean Brodie Lippincott 62

FRANCIS CARDINAL SPELLMAN

15 When you do say Yes, say it quickly. But always take a half hour to say No, so you can understand the other fellow's side.
Advice to Terence Cooke, recalled on Cooke's death 6 Oct 83

DANIELLE STEEL

16 If you see the magic in a fairy tale, you can face the future.
Family Album Delacorte 85, quoted in *Christian Science Monitor* 21 Mar 85

WALLACE STEGNER

17 Most things break, including hearts. The lessons of life amount not to wisdom, but to scar tissue and callus.
The Spectator Bird Doubleday 76

HARRY STEIN

18 Envy is as persistent as memory, as intractable as a head cold.
"Thy Neighbor's Life" *Esquire* Jul 80

JOHN STEINBECK

19 Men do change, and change comes like a little wind that ruffles the curtains at dawn, and it comes like the stealthy perfume of wildflowers hidden in the grass.
Sweet Thursday Viking 54

20 Where does discontent start? You are warm enough, but you shiver. You are fed, yet hunger gnaws you. You have been loved, but your yearning wanders in new fields. And to prod all these there's time, the Bastard Time.
ib

21 It is a common experience that a problem difficult at night is resolved in the morning after the committee of sleep has worked on it.
Recalled on his death 20 Dec 68

GEORGE STEINER

22 [The] most important tribute any human being can pay to a poem or a piece of prose he or she really loves . . . is to learn it by heart. Not by brain, by heart; the expression is vital.
Publishers Weekly 24 May 85

WALLACE STEVENS

23 The most beautiful thing in the world is, of course, the world itself.
Quoted in Frank Doggett and Robert Buttel eds *Wallace Stevens* Princeton 80

ADLAI E STEVENSON

1 You will find that the truth is often unpopular and the contest between agreeable fancy and disagreeable fact is unequal. For, in the vernacular, we Americans are suckers for good news.
   Commencement address at Michigan State, NY Times 9 Jun 58

2 Freedom is not an ideal, it is not even a protection, if it means nothing more than the freedom to stagnate.
   Putting First Things First Random House 60

3 We have confused the free with the free and easy.
   ib

HENRY L STIMSON

4 The only way to make a man trustworthy is to trust him.
   Recalled on his death 20 Oct 50

TOM STOPPARD

5 Life is a gamble, at terrible odds—if it was a bet you wouldn't take it.
   Rosencrantz and Guildenstern Are Dead Grove 67

6 Age is a very high price to pay for maturity.
   ib

7 The bad end unhappily, the good unluckily. That is what tragedy means.
   ib

MILDRED WITTE STRUVEN

8 A clay pot sitting in the sun will always be a clay pot. It has to go through the white heat of the furnace to become porcelain.
   Quoted by her daughter Jean Harris Stranger in Two Worlds Macmillan 86

THOMAS SZASZ

9 People often say that this or that person has not yet found himself. But the self is not something that one finds. It is something that one creates.
   The Second Sin Doubleday 73

BARRY TARGAN

10 Adventure is hardship aesthetically considered.
   Kingdoms State University of New York 81

EDWARD TELLER

11 Life improves slowly and goes wrong fast, and only catastrophe is clearly visible.
   The Pursuit of Simplicity Pepperdine University 80

12 No endeavor that is worthwhile is simple in prospect; if it is right, it will be simple in retrospect.
   ib

13 My experience has been in a short 77 years . . . that in the end when you fight for a desperate cause and have good reasons to fight, you usually win.
   To Israeli Institute for Advanced Political and Strategic Studies, quoted in Wall Street Journal 8 Aug 86

MARGARET THATCHER

14 Why do you climb philosophical hills? Because they are worth climbing . . . There are no hills to go down unless you start from the top.
   Recalling childhood maxims, New Yorker 10 Feb 86

ALEXANDER THEROUX

15 Silence [is] the unbearable repartee.
   "I Sing the Parrot!" Reader's Digest May 83

CAITLIN THOMAS

16 Fearful as reality is, it is less fearful than evasions of reality. . . . Look steadfastly into the slit, pinpointed malignant eyes of reality as an old-hand trainer dominates his wild beasts.
   Not Quite Posthumous Letter to My Daughter Atlantic–Little, Brown 63

DYLAN THOMAS

17 Do not go gentle into that good night.
   Title and first line of 1952 poem

18 Rage, rage against the dying of the light.
   ib

LEWIS THOMAS

19 Mistakes are at the very base of human thought . . . feeding the structure like root nodules. If we were not provided with the knack of being wrong, we could never get anything useful done.
   The Medusa and the Snail Viking 79

H W THOMPSON

20 There is a slippery step at every man's door.
   Quoted by William Safire "Countdown to Damage Control" NY Times 26 Sep 82

LORD THORNEYCROFT (Peter Thorneycroft)

21 Some men go through life absolutely miserable because, despite the most enormous achievement, they just didn't do one thing—like the architect who didn't build St Paul's. I didn't quite build St Paul's, but I stood on more mountaintops than possibly I deserved.
   London Sunday Telegraph 11 Feb 79

RODERICK THORP

22 We have to learn to be our own best friends because we fall too easily into the trap of being our worst enemies.
   Rainbow Drive Summit 86, quoted in NY Times 4 Nov 86

JAMES THURBER

23 Last night I dreamed of a small consolation enjoyed only by the blind: Nobody knows the trouble I've *not* seen!
   On his failing eyesight, Newsweek 16 Jun 58

24 Humor is emotional chaos remembered in tranquillity.
   NY Post 29 Feb 60

LIONEL TIGER

25 It is the formidable character of the species to routinely seek the improbable, the difficult, even the impossible, as a source of pleasure and self-justification. Who would try to write poems, or novels, or paint pictures unless he is an optimist?
   Optimism: The Biology of Hope Simon & Schuster 79

PAUL TILLICH

26 Decision is a risk rooted in the courage of being free.
   Systematic Theology Vol I University of Chicago 51

1 Astonishment is the root of philosophy.
Life 5 Nov 65

MIKE TODD

2 I've never been poor, only broke. Being poor is a frame of mind. Being broke is only a temporary situation.
Newsweek 31 Mar 58

ALVIN TOFFLER

3 Future shock [is] the shattering stress and disorientation that we induce in individuals by subjecting them to too much change in too short a time.
Future Shock Random House 70

J R R TOLKIEN

4 All that is gold does not glitter; not all those that wander are lost.
The Fellowship of the Ring Houghton Mifflin 54

PAUL TOURNIER

5 Acceptance of one's life has nothing to do with resignation; it does not mean running away from the struggle. On the contrary, it means accepting it as it comes, with all the handicaps of heredity, of suffering, of psychological complexes and injustices.
The Meaning of Persons Harper 57

6 The more refined and subtle our minds, the more vulnerable they are.
ib

ARNOLD TOYNBEE

7 Civilization is a movement and not a condition, a voyage and not a harbor.
Reader's Digest Oct 58

8 The right moment for starting on your next job is not tomorrow or next week; it is *instanter*, or in the American idiom, "right now."
Experiences Oxford 69

9 I do not believe that civilizations have to die because civilization is not an organism. It is a product of wills.
Recalled on his death, *Time* 3 Nov 75

10 History is a vision of God's creation on the move.
ib

11 There is a kind of intellectual provincialism in the dogma that "life is just one damned thing after another." . . . human affairs do not become intelligible until they are seen as a whole.
ib

CLAIRE TREVOR

12 What a holler would ensue if people had to pay the minister as much to marry them as they have to pay a lawyer to get them a divorce.
NY *Journal-American* 12 Oct 60

BARBARA TUCHMAN

13 The unrecorded past is none other than our old friend, the tree in the primeval forest which fell without being heard.
"Can History Be Served Up Hot?" NY *Times* 8 Mar 64

DESMOND TUTU

14 A person is a person because he recognizes others as persons.
Address at enthronement as Anglican archbishop of Cape Town 7 Sep 86

JOHN UPDIKE

15 A healthy male adult bore consumes each year one and a half times his own weight in other people's patience.
Assorted Prose Knopf 65

16 From infancy on, we are all spies; the shame is not this but that the secrets to be discovered are so paltry and few.
Bech: A Book Knopf 70

17 We take our bearings, daily, from others. To be sane is, to a great extent, to be sociable.
Christian Science Monitor 5 Mar 79

MAURICE VALENCY

18 We are all pretending . . . The important thing is to maintain a straight face.
Ashby Schocken 84, quoted in NY *Times* 30 Nov 84

MARK VAN DOREN

19 Nothing in man is more serious than his sense of humor; it is the sign that he wants all the truth.
Recalled on his death 10 Dec 72

GORE VIDAL

20 Every time a friend succeeds, I die a little.
Quoted in Nat Shapiro ed *Whatever It Is, I'm Against It* Simon & Schuster 84

21 One is sorry one could not have taken both branches of the road. But we were not allotted multiple selves.
On choosing writing over politics, *Newsweek* 11 Jun 84

DONALD WALKER, Associate Director, Branch Library Programs and Services, NY Public Library

22 These are the favored ones—year after year—read under dim spot lamps in taxis or air shuttles, balanced on subways, carried on boardwalks and into bathtubs. They develop broken spines, pages like prune skin or go to their reward in the land of lost umbrellas.
On library books that are most often worn out or stolen, NY *Times* 28 Sep 86

DEWITT WALLACE

23 The dead carry with them to the grave in their clutched hands only that which they have given away.
On philanthropic donations, recalled on his death, *Time* 13 Apr 81

JOHN WILLIAM WARD

24 Today the man who is the real risk-taker is anonymous and nonheroic. He is the one trying to make institutions work.
Time 17 Nov 65

ANDY WARHOL

25 In the future everyone will be famous for 15 minutes.
Prediction in the 1960s, quoted in Washington *Post* 15 Nov 79

1 I'm bored with that line. I never use it anymore. My new line is "In 15 minutes everybody will be famous."

> *ib*

2 I never think that people die. They just go to department stores.

> Manchester *Guardian* 3 Aug 86

3 I always wished I had died, and I still wish that, because I could have gotten the whole thing over with.

> On being gravely wounded in 1968, recalled on his death, *Newsweek* 9 Mar 87

4 During the 1960s, I think, people forgot what emotions were supposed to be. And I don't think they've ever remembered.

> *ib*

5 The most exciting thing is not doing it. If you fall in love with someone and never do it, it's much more exciting.

> *ib*

6 I always thought I'd like my own tombstone to be blank. No epitaph, and no name. Well, actually, I'd like it to say "figment."

> 1985 statement, *ib*

ROBERT PENN WARREN

7 A young man's ambition [is] to get along in the world and make a place for himself—half your life goes that way, till you're 45 or 50. Then, if you're lucky, you make terms with life, you get released.

> NY *Times* 2 Jun 81

ALAN WATTS

8 Trying to define yourself is like trying to bite your own teeth.

> *Life* 21 Apr 61

EVELYN WAUGH

9 Punctuality is the virtue of the bored.

> Quoted in Michael Davie ed *The Diaries of Evelyn Waugh* Little, Brown 76

10 We cherish our friends not for their ability to amuse us, but for ours to amuse them.

> *Forbes* 12 May 80

11 What is youth except a man or woman before it is ready or fit to be seen?

> Quoted in Donat Gallagher ed *A Little Order: A Selection from His Journalism* Little, Brown 81

12 Not everyone grows to be old, but everyone has been younger than he is now.

> *ib*

MAX WAYS

13 So many old landmarks have been set in motion that they have become misleading as guides. Newness has become an even more treacherous beacon.

> "New Strains on the System: The Era of Radical Change" *Fortune* May 64

LEE WEINER

14 We are all refugees of a future that never happened.

> On failure to achieve goals of the 1960s, *People* 12 Sep 77

EUDORA WELTY

15 The events in our lives happen in a sequence in time, but in their significance to ourselves they find their own order . . . the continuous thread of revelation.

> *One Writer's Beginnings* Harvard 84

REBECCA WEST

16 If the whole human race lay in one grave, the epitaph on its headstone might well be: "It seemed a good idea at the time."

> NY *Times* 2 Oct 77

17 A strong hatred is the best lamp to bear in our hands as we go over the dark places of life, cutting away the dead things men tell us to revere.

> Quoted in Jane Marcus ed *The Young Rebecca: Writings of Rebecca West 1911–17* Viking 81

18 Life ought to be a struggle of desire toward adventures whose nobility will fertilize the soul.

> Quoted by A L Rowse *Glimpses of the Great* University Press of America 86

19 It is the soul's duty to be loyal to its own desires. It must abandon itself to its master passion.

> *ib*

JOHN HALL WHEELOCK

20 It's almost two societies, the living and the dead, and you live with them both.

> To National Institute of Arts and Letters, NY *Times* 9 Apr 76

ELIE WIESEL

21 Not to transmit an experience is to betray it.

> *Christian Science Monitor* 18 Sep 79

22 Most people think that shadows follow, precede or surround beings or objects. The truth is that they also surround words, ideas, desires, deeds, impulses and memories.

> *The Fifth Son* Summit 84, quoted in NY *Times* 21 Mar 85

23 I do not recall a Jewish home without a book on the table.

> "Echoes of Yesterday" in advertisement marking centennial of Yeshiva University, *ib* 28 Sep 86

24 In Jewish history there are no coincidences.

> Quoted by Joseph Berger "Witness to Evil" *ib* 15 Oct 86

25 I decided to devote my life to telling the story because I felt that having survived I owe something to the dead. . . . and anyone who does not remember betrays them again.

> On writing about the Holocaust, *ib*

26 We have to go into the despair and go beyond it, by working and doing for somebody else, by using it for something else.

> *ib*

27 I have not lost faith in God. I have moments of anger and protest. Sometimes I've been closer to him for that reason.

> *ib*

28 Indifference, to me, is the epitome of evil.

> *US News & World Report* 27 Oct 86

1 The opposite of love is not hate, it's indifference. The opposite of art is not ugliness, it's indifference. The opposite of faith is not heresy, it's indifference. And the opposite of life is not death, it's indifference.
ib

2 Because of indifference, one dies before one actually dies.
ib

3 No one is as capable of gratitude as one who has emerged from the kingdom of night.
Accepting Nobel Peace Prize 10 Dec 86

4 Because I remember, I despair. Because I remember, I have the duty to reject despair.
Nobel lecture, Oslo, 11 Dec 86

5 A destruction, an annihilation that only man can provoke, only man can prevent.
ib

6 Just as despair can come to one only from other human beings, hope, too, can be given to one only by other human beings.
ib

7 Mankind must remember that peace is not God's gift to his creatures; peace is our gift to each other.
ib

THORNTON WILDER

8 Those who are silent, self-effacing and attentive become the recipients of confidences.
The Eighth Day Harper & Row 67

9 We do not choose the day of our birth nor may we choose the day of our death, yet choice is the sovereign faculty of the mind.
ib

10 It is only in appearance that time is a river. It is rather a vast landscape and it is the eye of the beholder that moves.
ib

11 The planting of trees is the least self-centered of all that we do. It is a purer act of faith than the procreation of children.
ib

12 A sense of humor judges one's actions and the actions of others from a wider reference and a longer view and finds them incongruous. It dampens enthusiasm; it mocks hope; it pardons shortcomings; it consoles failure. It recommends moderation.
ib

GEORGE F WILL

13 There may be more poetry than justice in poetic justice.
The Pursuit of Virtue and Other Tory Notions Simon & Schuster 82

14 Pessimism is as American as apple pie—frozen apple pie with a slice of processed cheese.
Statecraft as Soulcraft Simon & Schuster 83

TENNESSEE WILLIAMS

15 Time rushes toward us with its hospital tray of infi-

nitely varied narcotics, even while it is preparing us for its inevitably fatal operation.
The Rose Tattoo New Directions 51

16 All cruel people describe themselves as paragons of frankness.
The Milk Train Doesn't Stop Here Anymore New Directions 64

17 Hell is yourself [and the only redemption is] when a person puts himself aside to feel deeply for another person.
Recalled on his death 25 Feb 83

18 Once you fully apprehend the vacuity of a life without struggle, you are equipped with the basic means of salvation.
ib

VANESSA WILLIAMS

19 The past just came up and kicked me.
On losing Miss America title after *Penthouse* publication of nude pictures, *People* 6 Aug 84

BILL WILSON, cofounder, Alcoholics Anonymous

20 Years ago I used to commiserate with all people who suffered. Now I commiserate only with those who suffer in ignorance, who do not understand the purpose and ultimate utility of pain.
As Bill Sees It, AA World Services 67

21 In God's economy, nothing is wasted. Through failure, we learn a lesson in humility which is probably needed, painful though it is.
ib

22 AA is no success story in the ordinary sense of the word. It is a story of suffering transmuted, under grace, into spiritual progress.
ib

EDMUND WILSON

23 At 60 . . . the sexual preoccupation, when it hits you, seems sometimes sharper, as if it were an elderly malady, like gout.
The Fifties Farrar, Straus & Giroux 86

WALLIS, DUCHESS OF WINDSOR

24 I survived . . . by mastering my own emotions. . . . a kind of private arrangement within oneself—an understanding of the heart and mind—that one's life and purposes are essentially good, and that nothing from outside must be allowed to impair that understanding. . . . I learned that one can live alone.
On public criticism of her after Edward VIII's abdication, quoted in Michael Bloch ed *Wallis and Edward: Letters, 1931–37*, Summit 86

TOM WOLFE

25 The idea was to prove at every foot of the way up . . . that you were one of the elected and anointed ones who had *the right stuff* and could move higher and higher and even—ultimately, God willing, one day—that you might be able to join that special few at the very top, that elite who had the capacity to bring tears to men's eyes, the very Brotherhood of the Right Stuff itself.
The Right Stuff Farrar, Straus & Giroux 79

LOUIS B WRIGHT

1 More common sense can be induced by observation of the diversity of human beings in a small town than can be learned in academia.

Barefoot in Arcadia University of South Carolina 74

MAX WYLIE

2 Heartbreak is gratuitous wreckage. It is futility.

Response to murder of his daughter, *Ladies' Home Journal* Mar 64

YEVGENY YEVTUSHENKO

3 No monument stands over Babii Yar.
A drop sheer as a crude gravestone.
I am afraid.
     Today I am as old in years
as all the Jewish people.
Now I seem to be
     a Jew.

"Babii Yar" 19 Sep 61, quoted in George Reavey ed *The New Russian Poets, 1953–66* October House 66

4 I seem to be
     Anne Frank
transparent
     as a branch in April.
ib

5 I am
     each old man
          here shot dead.
I am
     every child
          here shot dead.
Nothing in me
     shall ever forget!
. . . .

For that reason
     I am a true Russian!
ib

B W M YOUNG, Headmaster, Charterhouse School, Godalming, England

6 Everyone should learn to do one thing supremely well because he likes it, and one thing supremely well because he detests it.

NY *Times* 12 Jan 64

MAURICE ZOLOTOW

7 In the lives of men and women who rise high in the world, there is a moment, while they are passing from obscurity to consequence, that is perhaps the most satisfying they will ever know. The difficulties of the old life are being abandoned; the difficulties of the new are still unknown.

Marilyn Monroe Harcourt, Brace 60

Communications & the Arts

ARCHITECTURE

Architects on Architecture

EMILIO AMBASZ

1 The large executive chair elevates the sitter. . . .
and it is covered with the skin of some animal, preferably your predecessor.
Smithsonian Apr 86

GAE AULENTI

2 Light *is* impressionism.
On positioning galleries for impressionist and post-impressionist paintings at the top of her design for Paris's Musée d'Orsay, *Time* 8 Dec 86

LUIS BARRAGÁN

3 Any work of architecture that does not express serenity is a mistake.
Time 12 May 80

4 Art is made by the alone for the alone.
ib

5 Solitude is good company and my architecture is not for those who fear or shun it.
On his austere Mexico City home, *Smithsonian* Nov 80

GOTTFRIED BOEHM, Cret Professor of Architecture, University of Pennsylvania

6 I think the future of architecture does not lie so much in continuing to fill up the landscape as in bringing back life and order to our cities and towns.
On winning Pritzker Architecture Prize, *International Herald Tribune* 18 Apr 86

ROBERTO BURLE MARX, landscape designer

7 I'm a plant eater.
On his use of plants for parks, offices and city streets, *Christian Science Monitor* 12 Aug 86

8 A garden is a complex of aesthetic and plastic intentions; and the plant is, to a landscape artist, not only a plant—rare, unusual, ordinary or doomed to disappearance—but it is also a color, a shape, a volume or an arabesque in itself.
ib

9 I did a salad, but I didn't do a garden.
Recalling the plethora of flora in the first garden he designed, *ib*

R BUCKMINSTER FULLER

10 My ideas have undergone a process of emergence by emergency. When they are needed badly enough, they are accepted.
On geodesic domes, *Time* 10 Jun 64

11 I just invent, then wait until man comes around to needing what I've invented.
ib

12 Let architects sing of aesthetics that bring
Rich clients in hordes to their knees;
Just give me a home, in a great circle dome
Where stresses and strains are at ease.
Lines for tune of "Home on the Range," *ib*

13 I look for what needs to be done. . . . After all, that's how the universe designs itself.
Christian Science Monitor 3 Nov 64

14 Tension is the great integrity.
On his belief that "tensegrity" gives coherence to the structure of the universe, *ib*

15 When I am working on a problem, I never think about beauty . . . but when I have finished, if the solution is not beautiful, I know it is wrong.
Reply to student at MIT about aesthetics in engineering and architecture, quoted by Clifton Fadiman comp *The Little, Brown Book of Anecdotes* Little, Brown 85

16 Man knows so much and does so little.
ib

WALTER GROPIUS

17 Architecture begins where engineering ends.
To Harvard Department of Architecture, quoted in Paul Heyer ed *Architects on Architecture* Walker 78

EDWARD HALL

18 Each organism, no matter how simple or complex, has around it a sacred bubble of space, a bit of mobile territoriality which only a few other organisms are allowed to penetrate and then only for short periods of time.
"The Anthropology of Space" *Architectural Review* Sep 66

GEORGE E HARTMAN

19 The architectural profession gave the public 50 years of modern architecture and the public's response has been 10 years of the greatest wave of historical preservation in the history of man.
Quoted by Barbara Gamarekian "New Game in Town: Façademanship" *NY Times* 31 Aug 83

HUGH NEWELL JACOBSEN

20 When you look at a city, it's like reading the hopes, aspirations and pride of everyone who built it.
NY Times 31 May 84

21 It is our art that has an opportunity to leave a footprint in the sand. They don't wrap fish in our work.
ib

PHILIP JOHNSON

22 The best thing to do with water is to use a lot of it.
On designing fountains, *New Yorker* 9 Jul 66

23 All architecture is shelter, all great architecture is the design of space that contains, cuddles, exalts, or stimulates the persons in that space.
1975 address at Columbia University, quoted in *Philip Johnson: Writings* Oxford 79

1 Architects are pretty much high-class whores. We can turn down projects the way they can turn down some clients, but we've both got to say yes to someone if we want to stay in business.
> *Esquire* Dec 80

2 I hate vacations. If you can build buildings, why sit on the beach?
> *ib*

3 I'm about four skyscrapers behind.
> On excusing himself from a dinner party, *Wall Street Journal* 20 Jun 84

LOUIS KAHN

4 Every time a student walks past a really urgent, expressive piece of architecture that belongs to his college, it can help reassure him that he does have that mind, does have that soul.
> On architecture for academia, *Fortune* May 63

5 A great building . . . must begin with the unmeasurable, must go through measurable means when it is being designed and in the end must be unmeasurable.
> *ib*

6 Consider . . . the momentous event in architecture when the wall parted and the column became.
> Quoted by John Lobell *Between Silence and Light* Shambhala 79

LE CORBUSIER

7 I prefer drawing to talking. Drawing is faster, and leaves less room for lies.
> *Time* 5 May 61

8 A hundred times have I thought New York is a catastrophe and 50 times: It is a beautiful catastrophe.
> NY *Herald Tribune* 6 Aug 61

9 Space and light and order. Those are the things that men need just as much as they need bread or a place to sleep.
> On need for spaciously separated skycrapers, recalled on his death 27 Aug 65

10 The home should be the treasure chest of living.
> *ib*

11 Architecture is the learned game, correct and magnificent, of forms assembled in the light.
> *ib*

12 The most beautiful bridge in the world. . . . so pure, so resolute, so regular that here, finally, steel architecture seems to laugh.
> Recalled on 50th anniversary of Manhattan's George Washington Bridge, NY *Times* 10 Oct 81

13 Vehement silhouettes of Manhattan—that vertical city with unimaginable diamonds.
> Quoted by Marilyn Hoffman "Window on Manhattan" *Christian Science Monitor* 23 Jun 86

S CHARLES LEE

14 For 50 cents we took the middle-class man out of his home and gave him an environment that only the Church had given before.
> On motion-picture palaces of the 1930s, *Newsweek* 10 Sep 79

LUDWIG MIES VAN DER ROHE

15 A chair is a very difficult object. A skyscraper is almost easier. That is why Chippendale is famous.
> *Time* 18 Feb 57

16 Less is more.
> On restraint in design, NY *Herald Tribune* 28 Jun 59

17 God is in the details.
> *ib*

18 Architecture starts when you carefully put two bricks together. There it begins.
> *ib*

19 Architecture is the will of an epoch translated into space.
> *ib*

RICHARD NEUTRA

20 I am an eyewitness to the ways in which people relate to themselves and to each other, and my work is a way of scooping and ladling that experience.
> *Christian Science Monitor* 1 Jul 77

21 [A building can] be designed to satisfy "by the month" with the regularity of a provider. . . . Or it can give satisfaction in a very different way, "by the moment," the fraction of a second, with the thrill of a lover.
> Quoted in NY *Times* 8 Sep 85

MIYOKO OHNO

22 Balance is beautiful.
> On designing bridges, *Christian Science Monitor* 22 May 86

RUSSELL PAGE, landscape designer

23 A discerning eye needs only a hint, and understatement leaves the imagination free to build its own elaborations.
> *The Education of a Gardener* Random House 62

24 I like the gardens with good bones and affirmed underlying structure. . . . well-marked paths, well-built walls, well-defined changes in level.
> *ib*

I M PEI

25 It is not an individual act, architecture. You have to consider your client. Only out of that can you produce great architecture. You can't work in the abstract.
> Washington *Post* 14 May 78

WILLIAM L PEREIRA

26 We have come to accept with enthusiasm the unprofessional, unappreciative, unskillful butchery of the land that goes under the name of planning.
> Recalled on his death, *Time* 25 Nov 85

JOHN PORTMAN

27 Thank God this isn't a play. Critics can kill a play. But not a hotel.
> On opening of Manhattan's Marriott Marquis Hotel, NY *Times* 12 Oct 85

28 It's like saying trousers with two legs is a design cliché.
> On criticism of his use of cavernous atriums, *ib*

1 People receive a spiritual release just watching the elevators fly up and down.
ib

T H ROBSJOHN-GIBBINGS

2 The surroundings householders crave are glorified autobiographies ghostwritten by willing architects and interior designers who, like their clients, want to show off.
"Robsjohn-Gibbings Names the Biggest Bore" *Town & Country* Jan 81

KEVIN ROCHE

3 The only real buildings are nonbuildings. The rest is theater.
On his design for a partially underground art gallery at Colonial Williamsburg, *Christian Science Monitor* 9 May 86

EERO SAARINEN

4 The purpose of architecture is to shelter and enhance man's life on earth and to fulfill his belief in the nobility of his existence.
Address at Dartmouth College, quoted in *Eero Saarinen on His Work* Yale 68

5 To me, the drawn language is a very revealing language; one can see in a few lines whether a man is really an architect.
NY *Times* 5 Jun 77

ELIEL SAARINEN

6 Always design a thing by considering it in its next larger context—a chair in a room, a room in a house, a house in an environment, an environment in a city plan.
Quoted by his son Eero, *Time* 2 Jun 77

ROBERT A M STERN

7 The dialogue between client and architect is about as intimate as any conversation you can have, because when you're talking about building a house, you're talking about dreams.
NY *Times* 13 Jan 85

8 Our greatest responsibility is not to be pencils of the past.
ib

9 Communities of tract houses, plopped on a grid, represent a way of throwing historical forms around like bouillabaisse.
ib

10 The American dream has always depended on the dialogue between the present and the past. In our architecture, as in all our other arts—indeed, as in our political and social culture as a whole—ours has been a struggle to formulate and sustain a usable past.
Pride of Place Houghton Mifflin 86

ROBERT VENTURI

11 Less is a bore.
1969 reaction to Mies van der Rohe's statement "Less is more," recalled on 100th anniversary of Mies's birth, *Time* 3 Mar 86

HAROLD E WAGONER

12 The great thing about being an architect is you can walk into your dreams.
Quoted by Episcopal priest Edward Chinn in tribute to Wagoner's restoration of All Saints' Church in Philadelphia, *Episcopalian* Oct 86

FRANK LLOYD WRIGHT

13 I doubt if there is anything in the world uglier than a Midwestern city.
Address at Evanston IL, news summaries 8 Aug 54

14 Clear out 800,000 people and preserve it as a museum piece.
On Boston, NY *Times* 27 Nov 55

15 New York: Prison towers and modern posters for soap and whiskey. Pittsburgh: Abandon it.
ib

16 If you're going to have centralization, why not have it!
Announcing plans for 510-story Chicago office building, news summaries 10 Sep 56

17 Early in life I had to choose between honest arrogance and hypocritical humility. I chose honest arrogance and have seen no occasion to change.
Recalled on his death 8 Apr 59

18 Architecture is life, or at least it is life itself taking form and therefore it is the truest record of life as it was lived in the world yesterday, as it is lived today or ever will be lived.
An Organic Architecture MIT 70

19 Here I am, Philip, am I indoors or am I out? Do I take my hat off or keep it on?
On Philip Johnson's glass house, *Architectural Digest* Nov 85

MINORU YAMASAKI

20 Man needs a serene architectural background to save his sanity in today's world.
Recalled on his death 6 Feb 86

21 We have built some real dogs!
ib

Observers & Critics

CHARLES ABRAMS, Chairman, Department of City Planning, Columbia University

22 A city . . . is the pulsating product of the human hand and mind, reflecting man's history, his struggle for freedom, creativity, genius—and his selfishness and errors.
The City Is the Frontier Harper & Row 65

23 A city has values as well as slums, excitement as well as conflict . . . a personality that has not yet been obliterated by its highways and gas stations.
ib

ANONYMOUS

24 An island of Indiana in the middle of Manhattan.
Roosevelt Island resident on newly built apartment towers, quoted in NY *Times* 23 May 86

25 The cost of less seemed more.
On attempts to cut costs while erecting the Statue of Liberty, *The Making of Liberty* PBS TV 28 Oct 86

R W APPLE JR

1 Maimed but still magnificent . . . Europe's mightiest medieval cathedral.

> On fire-ravaged York Minster in England, NY *Times* 15 Jul 84

2 The product of extraordinary wealth allied to a taste for the sumptuous.

> On Cliveden, the Astor estate in England turned into a hotel, *ib* 4 May 86

JOHN ASHBERY

3 A perfect example of the new republic's urge to drape itself with the togas of classical respectability.

> On 1824 bank façade selected as focal point of the Metropolitan Museum of Art's American Wing, *New York* 16 Jun 80

CLEMENT ATTLEE, Prime Minister of Great Britain

4 I think the British have the distinction above all other nations of being able to put new wine into old bottles without bursting them.

> On rebuilt House of Commons, *Time* 6 Nov 50

B DRUMMOND AYRES JR

5 A popcorn palace of gargantuan gaudiness.

> On the Fox Theater in Atlanta after it was saved from demolition, NY *Times* 6 Mar 78

ANTHONY BAILEY

6 Those massive between-the-wars brick apartment buildings that stand in dour solidity—their benefits, their endurance all turned inward, and not nervously flaunted in the manner of their flimsier postwar descendants.

> On apartment houses along the Henry Hudson Parkway approaching Manhattan, *New Yorker* 29 Jul 67

RUSSELL BAKER

7 The lobbies of the new hotels and the Pan American Building exhale a chill as from the unopened Pharaonic tombs. . . . And in their marble labyrinths there is an evil presence that hates warmth and sunlight.

> NY *Times* 19 May 64

8 What the New Yorker calls home would seem like a couple of closets to most Americans, yet he manages not only to live there but also to grow trees and cockroaches right on the premises.

> *ib* 18 Nov 78

CECIL BEATON

9 After 20 annual visits, I am still surprised each time I return to see this giant asparagus bed of alabaster and rose and green skyscrapers.

> On New York City, *It Gives Me Great Pleasure* John Day 55

LAURENCE BERGREEN

10 In its size and delicacy, [it] resembled a latter-day Chartres built in praise of a new god, the holy dollar. . . . In the lobby, the latest-model Chrysler revolved on a pedestal, as if the automobile were an object of reverence.

> On NYC's Chrysler Building, where *Fortune* magazine had its offices during James Agee's early employment, *James Agee* Dutton 84

LOUISE BERNIKOW

11 Objects that speak of the past, and look out at a skyline of concrete and steel, tokens of the present and hints of the future.

> On a high-rise apartment furnished with antiques, *Architectural Digest* Sep 86

MARILYN BETHANY

12 Suffering from terminal stodginess.

> On 1978 closing of the Chrysler Building's Cloud Club, *New York* 18 Jun 84

ALAN BIRD, English master builder

13 Most buildings now are glorified wallpaper.

> Comparing modern structures with his stonework for the Cathedral Church of St John the Divine, NY *Times* 19 Mar 86

PETER BLAKE

14 This book is not written in anger. It is written in fury.

> On his study of deteriorating towns and landscapes, *God's Own Junkyard* Holt, Rinehart & Winston 63

15 In our egalitarian democracy . . . we have just about empowered a branch of the government, the FHA, to specify the size and shape of the typical American suburban master bedroom in which all Americans are thus created equal.

> *ib*

16 There isn't much wrong with most of those summerhouses that a really good hurricane wouldn't cure [and] when it comes it may do for the Hamptons what Mrs O'Leary's cow did for Chicago.

> "Summerhouses: Eyefuls and Eyesores" *New York* 24 Aug 70

DANIEL J BOORSTIN, Librarian of Congress

17 When they built this building they were afraid to say that beauty is truth for fear that it wouldn't be by the time it was completed.

> On the library's 1980 Madison Building with its glass walls and unornamented linear spaces, NY *Times* 8 Jul 83

CHARLES D BREITEL, Judge, NY State Court of Appeals

18 The massive and indistinguishable public, governmental and private contributions to a landmark like the Grand Central Terminal are inseparably joined.

> Ruling that affirmed landmark status of Grand Central and denied real-estate developers permission to build a 55-story tower atop the beaux-arts structure, NY *Times* 24 Jun 77

JIMMY BRESLIN

19 Designed by architects with honorable intentions but hands of palsy.

> On a school in Queens NY, *Table Money* Ticknor & Fields 86

20 The auditorium, named after a dead Queens politician . . . is windowless in honor of the secrecy in which he lived and, probably, the bank vaults he frequented.

> *ib*

1 The other feature is a gymnasium named after an-other dead politician . . . who was gifted with fast and extremely sure hands.
> *ib*

DAVID BRINKLEY

2 The House Office Building is costing more than the combined cost of the Great Pyramids at Giza, the Colossus of Rhodes and the Hanging Gardens of Babylon. Three of the Seven Wonders of the World combined cost less money than an office building for 200 congressmen.
> NY *Herald Tribune* 16 Apr 64

BRITISH TRAVEL ASSOCIATION

3 A cathedral transcends the noblest single work of art. It is a pinnacle of faith and act of centuries. It is an offering of human hands as close to Abraham as it is to Bach.
> Advertisement in *New Yorker* 17 Jan 59

JOHN CANADAY

4 The Solomon R Guggenheim Museum . . . is a war between architecture and painting in which both come out badly maimed.
> On Manhattan museum designed by Frank Lloyd Wright, NY *Times* 21 Oct 59

ELLIOTT CARROLL, US Senate architect's office

5 It's strictly the schoolboy syndrome [and] seems to last well into adulthood.
> On senatorial tradition of carving initials on desks, NY *Times* 17 Mar 85

CHARLES, Prince of Wales

6 [It's] a kind of vast municipal fire station . . . a monstrous carbuncle on the face of a much-loved friend.
> On Peter Ahrends's design for an office building housing additional space for the National Gallery, address at 150th anniversary celebration of the Royal Institute of British Architects, NY *Times* 12 Oct 84

JOHN CHEEVER

7 I sometimes go back to walk through the ghostly remains of Sutton Place where the rude, new buildings stand squarely in one another's river views.
> "Moving Out" *Esquire* Jun 83

WINSTON CHURCHILL

8 We shape our buildings; thereafter they shape us.
> *Time* 12 Sep 60

FRANCIS X CLINES

9 [A] mass of Victorian wiles and granite . . . that resembles a battleship in the rain and a wedding cake in the sun.
> On Washington DC's Old Executive Office Building, NY *Times* 17 May 85

PAT COLANDER

10 Chicago is a city of contradictions, of private visions haphazardly overlaid and linked together. If the city was unhappy with itself yesterday—and invariably it was—it will reinvent itself today.
> "A Metropolis of No Little Plans" NY *Times* 5 May 85

11 Nor is it out of character that Chicago's grandest achievement—a largely manmade arc of lakefront parks and beaches—began as a mistake. . . . from waste thrown into Lake Michigan . . . a 75-year-old dump.
> *ib*

12 Big plans, elaborate schemes and grand designs sort of messily bleeding into one another [have] created Chicago's reputation for rawness. But that rawness is just ambition—sometimes ambition run amuck—that has acquired a life of its own.
> *ib*

CONGRESSIONAL MANAGEMENT FOUNDATION

13 Face it: Here you've got American government at its visual best: the marble, the columns, the rotundas, the sweeping staircases. You've got goals, you've got commitments, you've got aspirations and inspirations. . . . But have you got a place to sit?
> Report on overcrowding of legislative offices, quoted in NY *Times* 12 Nov 84

JOHN CORRY

14 The stars are . . . the great Gothic churches: spires, naves, delicate flying buttresses, massive conventional buttresses, stained glass and grandeur, grandeur, grandeur.
> On PBS TV's *Cathedral*, a "great plum pudding of a program," based on David Macaulay's *Cathedral* Houghton Mifflin 73, NY *Times* 30 Apr 86

E E CUMMINGS

15 The sensual mysticism of entire vertical being.
> On New York City, *Architectural Digest* Sep 86

GEORGE T DELACORTE, donor of fountain at City Hall Plaza, NYC

16 The fountain is my speech. The tulips are my speech. The grass and trees are my speech.
> *New Yorker* 14 May 79

ROBERT DiLEONARDO

17 My job is to create an environment that relaxes morality.
> On Atlantic City casinos, *Wall Street Journal* 10 Jan 83

DAVID W DUNLAP

18 An unusually tranquil skyscraping vantage—a kind of front porch 850 feet in the air.
> On closing of a midtown Manhattan observation deck to make room for the new entrance to a high-rise restaurant and nightclub, "A Quiet Place at RCA's Summit Drifts onto the Pages of the Past" NY *Times* 18 Jun 86

RICHARD T FELLER, Clerk of the Works and Chairman of the Building Committee, National Cathedral, Washington DC

19 The Gothic style historically, more perhaps than any other, released architecture from its earthbound confines.
> *An Act of Optimism*, 1980 cathedral booklet

JAMES FELT, Chairman, NYC Planning Commission

20 The smallest patch of green to arrest the monotony of asphalt and concrete is as important to the value of real estate as streets, sewers and convenient shopping.
> NY *Times* 28 Jun 60

HUGH FERRISS

1 A 60-story tower in New York evokes a 70-story tower in Chicago [and] a 60-story tower in New York evokes a 70-story tower directly across the street.

> From his 1929 book *The Metropolis of Tomorrow*, recalled on Whitney Museum's exhibition of his architectural drawings, NY *Times* 24 Jun 86

EDWARD FINLASON, British Army

2 Even the Germans did not succeed in doing the damage you propose to do.

> Protest against Mies van der Rohe's high-rise building in Mansion House Square, London *Times* 10 Jun 85

HENRY GELDZAHLER, Commissioner, NYC Department of Cultural Affairs

3 It is the theater God would have built if he had the money.

> On preservation of Radio City Music Hall, NY *Times* 2 Apr 78

PAUL GOLDBERGER

4 It fills one with a sense of architectural possibility.

> On Manhattan headquarters of AT&T, NY *Times* 28 Sep 83

5 [Buildings don't] exist to be pinned, like brooches, on the front of bigger structures to which they bear only the most distant of relationships.

> On "façadism" in NYC Landmarks Preservation Commission's tendency to allow high-rises behind the front of older structures, *ib* 15 Jul 85

6 A suburban mall turned vertical.

> On Marriott Marquis Hotel in Times Square, *ib* 31 Aug 85

7 A noble space, unlike any other of our time, for it is both strong and delicate. . . . It seems to call at once for a Boeing 747 and for a string quartet.

> On Jacob K Javits Convention Center, *ib* 31 Mar 86

8 Integrity has been enhanced.

> On restoration of NY Public Library, *ib* 19 May 86

9 It is something akin to boarding the Concorde and then discovering at the end of your trip that you had debarked at Grand Central Terminal.

> On using computers in the grandeur of the main card catalog room, *ib*

MARTHA GRAHAM

10 To me, a building—if it's beautiful—is the love of one man, he's made it out of his love for space, materials, things like that.

> NY *Times* 3 Mar 85

WILLIAM HAMILTON

11 Concrete is, essentially, the color of bad weather.

> *Gourmet* Dec 86

AUGUST HECKSCHER, NYC Parks Commissioner

12 The living generation is bound to support them, as it would an aged and slightly zany parent.

> On care of Grant's Tomb and Soldiers' and Sailors' Monument, NY *Times* 11 Aug 77

C DAVID HEYMANN

13 [It was] the last word in mortuary chintz.

> On dime-store magnate F W Woolworth's mausoleum, *Poor Little Rich Girl* Lyle Stuart 84

WARREN HOGE

14 The Moscow of these pageants is the old core city with its buildings of pastel hues and white trim that, with the season's continual dustings of snow, appear to be the work of confectioners.

> On funeral of Premier Konstantin U Chernenko, NY *Times* 14 Mar 85

SIDNEY HORENSTEIN

15 Saks is great for fossils.

> Commenting on his geologic tours of NYC with special attention to the marble used at Saks, the Fifth Avenue department store, and the pink breccia limestone in the lobby of the Trump Tower, NY *Times* 30 Apr 86

ROBERT HUGHES

16 [It was] an obsolete pachyderm of tawny limestone.

> On Paris's Gare d'Orsay, chosen as the new home of the Musée d'Orsay, *Time* 8 Dec 86

17 Nothing they design ever gets in the way of a work of art.

> On Kevin Roche, John Dinkeloo & Associates' design for new wing at the Metropolitan Museum of Art, *ib* 2 Feb 87

ADA LOUISE HUXTABLE

18 The New York Hilton is laid out with a competence that would make a computer blush.

> NY *Times* 30 Jun 63

19 Superfluous curtains that needlessly cover glass would give Salome a lifetime supply of veils.

> *ib*

20 A disaster where marble has been substituted for imagination.

> On $36-million expansion of Smithsonian Institution in Washington DC, *Saturday Evening Post* 9 May 64

21 A discreet study in expensive nonostentation.

> On Manhattan headquarters of the Ford Foundation, NY *Times* 26 Nov 67

22 An excellent job with a dubious undertaking, which is like saying it would be great if it wasn't awful.

> On Marcel Breuer's design for an office tower above Grand Central Terminal, *ib* 20 Jun 68

23 In the random way that democracy scatters art and monuments among its leaders, Lyndon Baines Johnson has a winner.

> On Johnson Presidential Library at the University of Texas in Austin, *ib* 23 May 71

24 The age of Lincoln and Jefferson memorials is over. It will be presidential libraries from now on.

> *ib*

25 The building is a national tragedy . . . a cross between a concrete candy box and a marble sarcophagus in which the art of architecture lies buried.

> On John F Kennedy Center for the Performing Arts in Washington DC, *ib* 6 Sep 71

ILLUSTRATED LONDON NEWS

1 The House of Lords [is] the finest specimen of Gothic civil architecture in Europe; its proportions, arrangements and decorations may be said to be perfect.

> On restoration of an ornate ceiling dating from 1847, Nov 84

WENDY INSINGER

2 Inside, the cathedral is a Gothic forest dappled in violet twilight and vast with quiet.

> "Hosanna for New York's St John the Divine" *Town & Country* Dec 81

JOHN F KENNEDY, 35th US President

3 I know that the White House was designed by [James] Hoban, a noted Irish-American architect, and I have no doubt that he believed by incorporating several features of the Dublin style he would make it more homelike for any president of Irish descent. It was a long wait, but I appreciate his efforts.

> Addressing the Irish Parliament in Dublin, assembled in a Georgian mansion that was the seat of Kennedy's maternal ancestors, NY *Times* 28 Jun 63

4 I look forward to an America which will not be afraid of grace and beauty, which will protect the beauty of our natural environment, which will preserve the great old American houses and squares and parks of our national past and which will build handsome and balanced cities for our future.

> Last major public address, at Amherst College 26 Oct 63

NEIL KINNOCK, Labor Party leader

5 The Parthenon without the marbles is like a smile with a tooth missing.

> Promising return of the Elgin marbles to Greece, London *Times* 5 Jan 84

E V KNOX ("Evoe")

6 The stately homes of England,
How beautiful they stood,
Before their recent owners
Relinquished them for good.

> Recalled on his death 2 Jan 71

SPIRO KOSTOF

7 [Architecture is] a social act [and] the material theater of human activity.

> *A History of Architecture* Oxford 85, quoted in NY *Times* 28 Apr 85

RUSSELL LYNES

8 The bungalow had more to do with how Americans live today than any other building that has gone remotely by the name of architecture in our history.

> *The Domesticated Americans* Harper & Row 63

NORMAN MAILER

9 Patterned after an Italian Renaissance palace, it is 88 times as large and one millionth as valuable to the continuation of man. . . . that Pentagon of traveling salesmen.

> On the Biltmore Hotel in Los Angeles, *Esquire* Nov 60

JOHN MAZZOLA, President, Lincoln Center, NYC

10 We patch and patch and patch and patch, but we work on the assumption that you can only keep a place beautiful by maintaining the hell out of it.

> On $6-million renovation during the center's 20th year, NY *Times* 11 Sep 81

DAVID McCORD

11 The high-ceilinged rooms, the little balconies, alcoves, nooks and angles all suggest sanctuary, escape, creature comfort. The reader, the scholar, the browser, the borrower is king.

> On the Boston Athenaeum, *Time* 15 Nov 82

CATHLEEN McGUIGAN

12 They may be America's last pioneers, urban nomads in search of wide open *interior* spaces.

> "The Soho Syndrome: Artists Are Revitalizing City Neighborhoods" *Newsweek* 22 Sep 86

ROBERT METZGER

13 It was the sort of house that glows with substance and savoir vivre in those advertisements for the best Scotch. . . . It had wonderful bones.

> On a Georgian-style Pennsylvania fieldstone house, *Architectural Digest* Mar 85

BRYAN MILLER

14 The Polo Lounge is like a fine old mink coat: opulent, dignified and warm.

> On the Westbury Hotel's bar, NY *Times* 9 Nov 84

MALCOLM MILLER

15 This building is like a book. Its architecture is the binding, its text is in the glass and sculpture.

> *Chartres Cathedral* Pitkin 80

16 If it were a person, it would be a woman, a very dignified old lady. She is beautiful. She is royal. She has kept her charms.

> *ib*

FREDERIC MORTON

17 A grand old odalisque should never deign to turn housewife.

> On trend to turn Manhattan's older hotels into cooperative apartment houses, *Holiday* Nov 64

18 Its oak paneling is rectory English; the marble in its bathrooms sometimes outdoes the tombstones of the Medici; and the salutes of the older bellhops seem imported from Windsor Castle.

> On Manhattan's St Regis Hotel, *ib*

19 The guests are often in key with the décor: beautifully preserved, highly pedigreed and finely burnished specimens of the *fin de siècle*.

> On patrons of the St Regis, *ib*

20 A glassy mountain range of exposed offices; on a clear day you can look through the windows and see as many as 6,000 coffee breaks at once.

> On Park Avenue skyscrapers, *ib*

ROBERT MOSES, NYC Parks Commissioner

21 Frank Lloyd Wright's inverted oatmeal dish and silo with their awkward cantilevering, their jaundiced skin and the ingenious spiral ramp leading down past the abstractions which mirror the tortured maladjustments of our time.

> On the Guggenheim Museum, NY *Times* 21 May 59

1 [It is] the most hideous waterfront structure ever inflicted on a city by a combination of architectural conceit and official bad taste. . . . the Cathedral of Asphalt.

> On arch-shaped municipal asphalt plant, recalled 40 years later when the structure had become a registered landmark and centerpiece for Manhattan's largest playing field, *ib* 24 Oct 84

LEWIS MUMFORD

2 New York is the perfect model of a city, not the model of a perfect city.

> *My Work and Days* Harcourt, Brace Jovanovich 79

3 Forget the damned motor car and build the cities for lovers and friends.

> *ib*

ENID NEMY

4 Windows . . . are as essential to office prestige as Christmas is to retailing.

> NY *Times* 13 Aug 80

5 Even at the United Nations, where legend has it that the building was designed so that there could be no corner offices, the expanse of glass in individual offices is said to be a dead giveaway as to rank. Five windows are excellent, one window not so great.

> *ib*

NEW YORKER

6 Given the proper cues, it can erupt in more ways than an angry parent.

> On City Hall Plaza's Delacorte Fountain, built atop a 24,000-gallon underground reservoir, 14 May 79

NEW YORK TIMES

7 Any city gets what it admires, will pay for and, ultimately, deserves.

> On demolition of Pennsylvania Station, 30 Oct 63

8 We want and deserve tin-can architecture in a tin-horn culture. And we will probably be judged not by the monuments we build but by those we have destroyed.

> *ib*

9 [It has] joined the Ritz Ballroom and the Astor Bar in that architectural graveyard whose monuments are the recollections of writers and lyricists.

> On closing of the Biltmore Hotel, 19 Aug 81

PATRICK O'DONOVAN

10 It is a gorgeous, great rose-pink cavern of highly unconventional Gothic, a marvelous enclosure of space, a dated and unforgettable masterpiece of breathtaking audacity and extravagance.

> On dedication of Liverpool Cathedral, begun in 1904, London *Observer* 22 Oct 78

RICHARD OULAHAN

11 The building has all the requisites of a great aunt. She is neither very pretty nor elegant, but she has enduring qualities of character.

> On Old Executive Office Building in Washington DC, *Smithsonian* Mar 86

JOSEPH R PAOLINO JR, Mayor of Providence RI

12 I'd like to see Providence become kind of like the baby brother of Boston.

> On renewal scheme that called for diverting two rivers and destroying the world's widest bridge, NY *Times* 1 Sep 85

PUNCH MAGAZINE

13 A stage set made in Hollywood for a musical about Oxford.

> On 50th anniversary of residential colleges at Yale, quoted in NY *Times* 27 Oct 83

ANNA QUINDLEN

14 It looms above the landscape like the cover drawing on a gothic novel, a true castle in the air.

> On Central Park's Belvedere Castle, NY *Times* 17 Jul 80

PAIGE RENSE, Editor, *Architectural Digest*

15 Everyone has, I think, in some quiet corner of his mind, an ideal home waiting to become a reality.

> Foreword to *Designers' Own Homes* Knapp 84

JOHN RICHARDSON

16 While American interiors are often designed to provide an idealized picture of their owner's circumstances, English interiors tend to tell the truth about the people who live in them.

> Quoted in NY *Times* 29 Jul 84

ANDY ROONEY

17 An arch is two curves trying to fall.

> *An Essay on Bridges* CBS TV 15 Feb 65

18 Man has made a sewer of the river—and spanned it with a poem.

> On completion of world's longest suspension span, the Verrazano-Narrows Bridge linking Brooklyn and Staten Island, *Time* 11 Jul 69

A L ROWSE, Emeritus Fellow, All Souls College, Oxford

19 It is the quintessence of England: gray, white and silvery stone, rose-red and rust-colored brick, embowered in greenery, ancient lawns running down to the water, and in spring starred with a million daffodils.

> "Cambridge through Oxford Eyes" NY *Times* 17 Mar 85

JOHN RUSSELL

20 Houses are like theater. . . . What is played out in them may be comedy or tragedy, historical drama or farce; but no matter what is on the program for the day, every house has its exits and its entrances, its upstage and its downstage, its good seats and its bad seats and, all too often, its prompter's box in full use.

> "Design Notebook" NY *Times* 5 Jul 79

CARL SANDBURG

21 We live in the time of the colossal upright oblong.

> To Chicago Dynamic Committee, *Life* 4 Nov 57

SAN DIEGO TRIBUNE

22 A Gothic cathedral is a hymn to God.

> On National Cathedral, Washington DC, 5 Jul 86

WOLFGANG SAXON

1 She presided over a community shuttling between Wisconsin and Arizona like the abbess of a medieval cloister.

On Olgivanna Lloyd Wright, widow of Frank Lloyd Wright and "keeper of his architectural legacy" at Taliesin East and Taliesin West, colonies for apprentice architects, NY Times 2 Mar 85

ALBERT SCARDINO

2 Not since the Battle of Britain has control over air space generated so much conflict.

On air rights for Manhattan skyscrapers, NY Times 21 Feb 86

ROGER SCRUTON

3 Architecture, like dress, is an exercise in good manners, and good manners involve the habit of skillful insincerity—the habit of saying "good morning" to those whose mornings you would rather blight, and of passing the butter to those you would rather starve.

London Times 14 Aug 84

MIMI SHERATON

4 Swirls of antique stained glass, blazes of brass, forests of carved wood and waterfalls of crystal combine to make up the city's most fabulously festive interior.

On Maxwell's Plum restaurant, NY Times 26 Oct 79

HUGH SIDEY

5 They can see the brave silhouette from almost anywhere in the District of Columbia and use it as a compass to locate other monuments and eventually to find their way out of the great, gray federal wilderness.

On 100th anniversary of the Washington Monument and its role as a landmark for pilots, Time 25 Feb 85

GAVIN STAMP

6 Sculpture married to architecture.

On frieze and statuary of the Chartered Accountants Building in London, Country Life 20 Sep 84

KEVIN STARR

7 Mission Revival . . . red-tiled roofs glowing carmine in the sunset.

Inventing the Dream: California through the Progressive Era Oxford 85, quoted in Newsweek 27 May 85

RALPH STEPHENSON, counterman at Savarin Restaurant

8 The city's got the right name—New York. Nothing ever gets old around here.

On demolition of Pennsylvania Station, NY Times 29 Oct 63

RICHARD L STROUT

9 Gingerbread in granite.

On Old Executive Office Building in Washington DC, Christian Science Monitor 1 Jul 77

GAY TALESE

10 The Park Avenue of poodles and polished brass; it is cab country, tip-town, glassville, a window-washer's paradise.

NY Times 23 Jun 65

JUDITH THURMAN

11 Here was a monument, in fieldstone, to the art of family life.

"Metamorphic Magic: Breathing New Life into a Pennsylvania Fieldstone House" Architectural Digest Mar 85

TIME MAGAZINE

12 In Hollywood's heyday the films were only celluloid, but the cinemas that showed them were marbled citadels of fantasy and opulence.

5 May 80

PATRICIA A TRETOUT

13 Our home, incredible as it may sound, was lovely: a true Victorian damsel absolved of her sins and her glory restored.

On remodeling an old house in Highlands NJ, NY Times 3 Mar 85

HARRY S TRUMAN, 33rd US President

14 I don't want it torn down. I think it's the greatest monstrosity in America.

1958 statement on the Old Executive Office Building, 19th-century structure adjoining the White House, quoted by Carleton Knight III "Dusting off History" Christian Science Monitor 1 Aug 86

KENNETH TYNAN

15 An office block made of prestressed celery.

"A Memoir of Manhattan" Holiday Dec 60

DAVID UTZ

16 There were no floors, no walls, no ceilings, no windows and the plumbing was nonexistent. Of course, I fell in love.

On renovating a loft apartment, NY Times 8 Jul 82

JOHN VINOCUR

17 No one has the right to change Paris, the protesters say, and argue that the city is the patrimony of all mankind.

On protests against building a glass pyramid in the courtyard of the Louvre, NY Times 18 Mar 85

MARK WALLINGTON

18 A strange collection of Victorian landmarks, now stranded around the Monopoly board of the modern city like brick dinosaurs.

On London railway stations, In Britain Jan 84

MICHAEL WALSH

19 Just build a classic horseshoe of wood and plaster, and fill it with statuary and curtains, then sit back and savor the beautifully blended results.

On the "vivid and unforced, warm and full-bodied" acoustics of the rebuilt Semper Opera House, Dresden, Germany, Time 25 Feb 85

EARL WARREN, Chief Justice, US Supreme Court

20 Before this distinguished assembly and the world, the bells today proclaim the joyous tidings of the completion of this quietly soaring tower.

At dedication of the bells in the new 301-foot-high Gloria in Excelsis Tower at Washington DC's National Cathedral, NY Times 8 May 64

P G Wodehouse

1 Few of them were to be trusted within reach of a trowel and a pile of bricks.
> On remodeled Victorian structures, *Country Life* 23 Oct 84

Trevor Wood

2 The pillars of this great cathedral church of God, roughhewn to perfection, spring from blessed roots at which the bones of St Cuthbert lay.
> On Durham Cathedral, *Illustrated London News* Oct 84

Lady Marjory Wright, wife of British ambassador to the US

3 When you come walking up that grand staircase you know you are in a bit of the Empire.
> On British Embassy in Washington DC, *NY Times* 26 Jun 84

Mina Wright

4 It does all the don'ts of architecture, mixing bits of everything from Moorish to Gothic. It's a rebel of a room that's characteristic of the whole building. I love it.
> On War Department Library in Washington DC's Old Executive Office Building, *NY Times* 17 May 85

ART

Painters & Sculptors

Leonard Baskin

5 Pop art is the inedible raised to the unspeakable.
> *Publishers Weekly* 5 Apr 65

Thomas Hart Benton

6 I lapsed into my favorite role as the old curmudgeon with the cotton-candy heart.
> On advising people in his "home country" of Joplin MO to "get some satisfaction out of this mural now—for it is now that you're stuck with it and now that you're going to pay for it, all $60,000," quoted in *NY Times* 26 Mar 73

Arbit Blatas

7 The surface of Venice is constantly metamorphosing [and] painting Venice is almost like being a restorer, peeling off the layers to find the picture after picture underneath.
> Quoted by Erica Jong "A City of Love and Death: Venice" *NY Times* 23 Mar 86

Georges Braque

8 Painting is a nail to which I fasten my ideas.
> Recalled on his death 31 Aug 63

Alexander Calder

9 I paint with shapes.
> On suspended sculptures that move with air—"mobiles," as Marcel Duchamp called them in 1932, *Saturday Evening Post* 27 Feb 65

Marc Chagall

10 I work in whatever medium likes me at the moment.
> Recalled on his death 28 Mar 85

11 One fine day (but all days are fine!) as my mother was putting the bread in the oven, I went up to her and taking her by her flour-smeared elbow I said to her, "Mama . . . I want to be a painter."
> *Newsweek* 8 Apr 85

12 Great art picks up where nature ends.
> *Time* 30 Dec 85

Winston Churchill

13 The first quality that is needed is audacity.
> *Painting as a Pleasure* Whittesay House 50

14 My hand seemed arrested by a silent veto.
> On trying to paint a pale-blue sky, quoted by William Manchester *The Last Lion* Little, Brown 83

15 I cannot pretend to be impartial about the colors. I rejoice with the brilliant ones, and am genuinely sorry for the poor browns.
> *ib*

Jean Cocteau

16 An artist cannot speak about his art any more than a plant can discuss horticulture.
> *Newsweek* 16 May 55

Gianluigi Colalucci

17 Around the dimmed and smoky view of Michelangelo a whole culture has formed itself. . . . and many will not accept the change.
> On his restoration of the Sistine Chapel ceiling to its original appearance, London *Times* 14 Apr 86

Joseph Cornell

18 Shadow boxes become poetic theaters or settings wherein are metamorphosed the element of a childhood pastime.
> Quoted by Dore Ashton *A Joseph Cornell Album* Viking 74

Gardner Cox

19 I do a bale of sketches, one eye, a piece of hair. A pound of observation, then an ounce of painting.
> On his portraits, Washington *Post* 31 May 75

Salvador Dali

20 Drawing is the honesty of the art. There is no possibility of cheating. It is either good or bad.
> *People* 27 Sep 76

21 Each morning when I awake, I experence again a supreme pleasure—that of being Salvador Dali.
> *NY Times* 1 Jan 80

22 Let my enemies devour each other.
> Replying at age 80 to reports that his assistants did much of his painting, *ib* 19 Mar 85

23 Painting is an infinitely minute part of my personality.
> *ib*

Jo Davidson

24 My approach to my subjects was very simple. I never had them pose, we just talked about everything in the world.
> On his sculpture, *Between Sittings* Dial 51

STUART DAVIS

1 The value of impermanence is to call attention to the permanent.

> Recalled on his death 24 Jun 64

BARBARA DONACHY

2 I didn't want to be so shortsighted as to be worrying about diaper rash, and not taking care of bigger things, like nuclear war.

> On *Amber Waves of Grain*, created—while she was pregnant—as a traveling exhibition of miniature representations of US weapons, *Christian Science Monitor* 28 Jan 86

JEAN DUBUFFET

3 For me, insanity is super sanity. The normal is psychotic. Normal means lack of imagination, lack of creativity.

> *New Yorker* 16 Jun 73

JACOB EPSTEIN

4 A wife, a lover, can perhaps never see what the artist sees . . . They rarely ever do. Perhaps a really mediocre artist has more chance of success.

> *Epstein: An Autobiography* Dutton 55

LUIS FRANGELLA

5 When something needs to be painted it lets me know.

> *Esquire* Apr 86

ALBERTO GIACOMETTI

6 Whores are the most honest girls. They present the bill right away.

> On his choice of models, quoted by James Lord *Giacometti* Farrar, Straus & Giroux 85

CHESTER GOULD

7 I usually start with a repulsive character and go on from there.

> On his *Dick Tracy* cartoons, NY *Daily News* 18 Dec 55

MORRIS GRAVES

8 I paint to rest from the phenomena of the external world—to pronounce and to make notations of its essences with which to verify the inner eye.

> On his unconventional paintings of conventional subjects, *Christian Science Monitor* 19 Feb 64

FREDERICK HART

9 One senses the figures as passing by the tree line and, caught in the presence of the wall, turning to gaze upon it almost as a vision.

> On his sculpture of a trio of soldiers near Vietnam Veterans Memorial in Washington DC, *National Geographic* May 85

EDWARD HOPPER

10 My aim in painting has always been the most exact transcription possible of my most intimate impression of nature.

> *Life* 17 Apr 50

11 What I wanted to do was to paint sunlight on the side of a house.

> Recalled on his death to mean "I want to paint the human soul," *Newsweek* 29 May 67

J STEWARD JOHNSON JR

12 The common strain in my work is that in each case I celebrate a moment when the individual responded to his or her own humanity.

> On his sculptures, "Capturing Moments" *Leaders* Oct 84

13 I see a man taking a break in his highly structured life, reading a newspaper in the park, or a young man sitting on a curb eating a sandwich and reading a book, taking the moment for himself. I celebrate these moments in bronze.

> *ib*

CORITA KENT

14 A painting [is] a symbol for the universe. Inside it, each piece relates to the other. Each piece is only answerable to the rest of that little world. So, probably in the total universe, there is that kind of total harmony, but we get only little tastes of it.

> *Newsweek* 17 Dec 84

15 That's why people listen to music or look at paintings. To get in touch with that wholeness.

> *ib*

ROCKWELL KENT

16 If to the viewer's eyes, *my* world appears less beautiful than his, I'm to be pitied and the viewer praised.

> Recalled on his death 13 Mar 71

DONG KINGMAN

17 Most artists are surrealists. . . . always dreaming something and then they paint it.

> Quoted in Mary Ann Guitar ed *Twenty-two Famous Painters and Illustrators Tell How They Work* McKay 64

18 Three men riding on a bicycle which has only one wheel, I guess that's surrealist.

> *ib*

ALEXANDER LIBERMAN

19 All art is solitary and the studio is a torture area.

> NY *Times* 13 May 79

ROY LICHTENSTEIN

20 I don't have big anxieties. I wish I did. I'd be much more interesting.

> Quoted by Deborah Solomon "The Art behind the Dots" NY *Times* 8 Mar 87

21 I like to pretend that my art has nothing to do with me.

> *ib*

MAYA LIN

22 It terrified me to have an idea that was solely mine to be no longer a part of my mind, but totally public.

> On her design for Vietnam Veterans Memorial in Washington DC, *National Geographic* May 85

JACQUES LIPCHITZ

23 Copy nature and you infringe on the work of our Lord. Interpret nature and you are an artist.

> NY *Times* 28 Apr 64

1 Imagination is a very precise thing, you know—it is not fantasy; the man who invented the wheel while he was observing another man walking—that is imagination!

Chicago *Tribune* 4 Jun 67

2 Cubism is like standing at a certain point on a mountain and looking around. If you go higher, things will look different; if you go lower, again they will look different. It is a point of view.

ib

3 All my life as an artist I have asked myself: What pushes me continually to make sculpture? I have found the answer. . . . art is an action against death. It is a denial of death.

ib

HENRI MATISSE

4 You study, you learn, but you guard the original naiveté. It has to be within you, as desire for drink is within the drunkard or love is within the lover.

Time 26 Jun 50

5 A picture must possess a real power to generate light [and] for a long time now I've been conscious of expressing myself through light or rather *in* light.

Quoted by Pierre Schneider *Matisse* Rizzoli 84

6 Impressionism is the newspaper of the soul.

ib

7 [I wouldn't mind turning into] a vermilion goldfish.

At age 80, *ib*

8 I have always tried to hide my efforts and wished my works to have the light joyousness of springtime which never lets anyone suspect the labors it has cost me.

Quoted by Theodore F Wolff in review of "The Drawings of Henri Matisse" exhibit at Manhattan's Museum of Modern Art, *Christian Science Monitor* 25 Mar 85

9 Drawing is like making an expressive gesture with the advantage of permanence.

ib

10 It is only after years of preparation that the young [artist] should touch color—not color used descriptively, that is, but as a means of personal expression.

ib

11 I have been no more than a medium, as it were.

Quoted in *Smithsonian* Nov 86

JOAN MIRÓ

12 My way is to seize an image that moment it has formed in my mind, to trap it as a bird and to pin it at once to canvas. Afterward I start to tame it, to master it. I bring it under control and I develop it.

London *Observer* 10 Jun 79

13 Art class was like a religious ceremony to me. I would wash my hands carefully before touching paper or pencils. The instruments of work were sacred objects to me.

ib

HENRY MOORE

14 It is a mistake for a sculptor or a painter to speak or write very often about his job. It releases tension needed for his work.

Henry Moore on Sculpture Viking 67

15 A sculptor is a person who is interested in the shape of things, a poet in words, a musician by sounds.

ib

16 A sculptor is a person obsessed with the form and shape of things, and it's not just the shape of one thing, but the shape of anything and everything: the growth in a flower; the hard, tense strength, although delicate form of a bone; the strong, solid fleshiness of a beech tree trunk.

ib

17 [Discipline in art is] a fundamental struggle to understand oneself, as much as to understand what one is drawing.

Recalled on his death 31 Aug 86

18 Seeing that picture, for me, was like Chartres Cathedral.

On a visit in student days to see Cézanne's *Large Bathers*, now in the Philadelphia Museum of Art, *ib*

ANNA MARY ROBERTSON MOSES ("Grandma Moses")

19 Paintin's not important. The important thing is keepin' busy.

News summaries 2 Jan 54

20 If you know somethin' well, you can always paint it [but] people would be better off buyin' chickens.

ib

ROBERT MOTHERWELL

21 If you can't find your inspiration by walking around the block one time, go around two blocks—but never three.

Nightline ABC TV 9 Aug 85

22 It may be that the deep necessity of art is the examination of self-deception.

On relationship between torment and creativity, NY *Times* 17 Nov 85

23 It's not that the creative act and the critical act are simultaneous. It's more like you blurt something out and then analyze it.

ib

24 Most painting in the European tradition was painting the mask. Modern art rejected all that. Our subject matter was the person behind the mask.

ib

MAUREEN MULLARKEY

25 A large-boned unexceptional young woman. . . . Yet as soon as she disrobed and took her place on the platform, she became not only a bare body but a splendid living design. She became a nude.

NY *Times* 29 Aug 85

26 Here was the drama of the flesh. . . . an architectonic system of skeleton and muscle, a musical arrangement of ellipsoids and undulating arcs.

ib

LOUISE NEVELSON

27 I see no reason why I should tickle stones or waste time on polishing bronze.

On her use of "found objects" showing traces of their original use, quoted in *Christian Science Monitor* 16 Jun 76

1 When you are doing a piece you are with it. You don't want to wait until next week, when experience will have given you something else.

> *ib*

2 A woman may not hit a ball stronger than a man, but it is different. I prize that difference.

> *ib*

GEORGIA O'KEEFFE

3 It was in the 1920s, when nobody had time to reflect, that I saw a still-life painting with a flower that was perfectly exquisite, but so small you really could not appreciate it.

> On the discovery that led to an approach synonymous with her name—the magnifying of flowers, bones and other aspects of nature, *Reader's Digest* May 79

4 I decided that if I could paint that flower in a huge scale, you could not ignore its beauty.

> *ib*

5 [Sun-bleached bones] were most wonderful against the blue—that blue that will always be there as it is now after all man's destruction is finished.

> On desert skies of New Mexico, *Newsweek* 17 Mar 86

PABLO PICASSO

6 When one starts from a portrait and seeks by successive eliminations to find pure form . . . one inevitably ends up with an egg.

> *Look* 6 Jun 56

7 If only we could pull out our brain and use only our eyes.

> On painting objectively, *Saturday Review* 1 Sep 56

8 Ah, good taste! What a dreadful thing! Taste is the enemy of creativeness.

> *Quote* 24 Mar 57

9 Art is a lie that makes us realize the truth.

> *ib* 21 Sep 58

10 The people no longer seek consolation in art. But the refined people, the rich, the idlers seek the new, the extraordinary, the extravagant, the scandalous.

> *Parade* 3 Jan 65

11 I have contented these people with all the many bizarre things that have come into my head. And the less they understand, the more they admire it.

> *ib*

12 By amusing myself with all these games, all this nonsense, all these picture puzzles, I became famous . . . I am only a public entertainer who has understood his time.

> *ib*

13 There are painters who transform the sun into a yellow spot, but there are others who, thanks to their art and intelligence, transform a yellow spot into the sun.

> *Quote* 21 Mar 65

14 Those trying to explain pictures are as a rule completely mistaken.

> Quoted in Dore Ashton ed *Picasso on Art* Viking 72

15 Every child is an artist. The problem is how to remain an artist once he grows up.

> Recalled on his death 8 Apr 73

16 For a long time I limited myself to one color—as a form of discipline.

> On his blue and rose periods, *ib*

17 For those who know how to read, I have painted my autobiography.

> *ib*

18 [He] must have an angel in his head.

> On Marc Chagall, recalled on Chagall's 97th birthday, NY *Times* 12 Jul 84

19 Everything I need to know about Africa is in these objects.

> On symbolism of primitive sculpture, quoted in *Time* 15 Oct 84

20 When I paint a woman in an armchair, the armchair is there to show illness and death—or as a protection.

> Recalled during televised tour of Paris museum housing much of his work, CBS TV 15 Mar 85

JACKSON POLLOCK

21 Abstract painting is abstract. It confronts you.

> Quoted by Francis V O'Connor *Jackson Pollock* Museum of Modern Art 67

22 He drove his kind of realism at me so hard I bounced right into nonobjective painting.

> On studying under Thomas Hart Benton at Manhattan's Art Students League, *Esquire* Dec 83

FAIRFIELD PORTER

23 To ask the meaning of art is like asking the meaning of life: Experience comes before a measurement against a value system.

> Quoted by Kay Larson *New York* 18 Jun 84

NORMAN ROCKWELL

24 I unconsciously decided that, even if it wasn't an ideal world, it should be and so painted only the ideal aspects of it—pictures in which there are no drunken slatterns or self-centered mothers . . . only foxy grandpas who played baseball with the kids and boys who fished from logs and got up circuses in the backyard.

> Washington *Post* 27 May 72

25 I cannot convince myself that a painting is good unless it is popular. If the public dislikes one of my *Post* covers, I can't help disliking it myself.

> Quoted by Arthur C Danto "Freckles for the Ages" NY *Times* 28 Sep 86

GEORGES ROUAULT

26 My only objective is to paint a Christ so moving that those who see him will be converted.

> *Look* 15 Apr 58

SAUL STEINBERG

27 I am among the few who continue to draw after childhood is ended, continuing and perfecting childhood drawing—without the traditional interruption of academic training.

> *Christian Science Monitor* 25 Nov 85

MACEDONLO DE LA TORRE

28 You cannot hear the waterfall if you stand next to it. I paint my jungles in the desert.

> NY *Times* 3 Feb 60

1 The imagination must not be given too much material. It must be denied food so that it can work for itself.
ib

MAURICE UTRILLO

2 The people here are idiots—idiots! . . . There's not an hour I don't think of it. . . . I'm shut out here and they won't let me go. I would rather be there than anywhere.
On his longing for Montmartre while living in an asylum outside Paris, *Life* 16 Jan 50

MARTINE VERMEULEN

3 Clay. It's rain, dead leaves, dust, all my dead ancestors. Stones that have been ground into sand. Mud. The whole cycle of life and death.
On her pottery, NY *Times* 3 Dec 75

ANDY WARHOL

4 I'd asked around 10 or 15 people for suggestions. . . . Finally one lady friend asked the right question, "Well, what do you love most?" That's how I started painting money.
Quoted in "Andy Warhol Inc, Portrait of the Artist as a Middle-Aged Businessman" *Manhattan Inc* Oct 84

5 If you want to know all about Andy Warhol, just look at the surface of my paintings and films and me, and there I am. There's nothing behind it.
Recalled on his death, *Newsweek* 9 Mar 87

JON WITCOMB

6 Portraits are supposed to "look within," but in my opinion very few people have an interior significantly different from the outside portrait.
Quoted in Mary Ann Guitar ed *Twenty-two Famous Painters and Illustrators Tell How They Work* McKay 64

GRANT WOOD

7 All the really good ideas I ever had came to me while I was milking a cow.
News summaries 1 Mar 54

ANDREW WYETH

8 I prefer winter and fall, when you feel the bone structure in the landscape—the loneliness of it—the dead feeling of winter. Something waits beneath it—the whole story doesn't show.
Quoted by Richard Meryman *The Art of Andrew Wyeth* NY Graphic Society 73

9 I think anything like that—which is contemplative, silent, shows a person alone—people always feel is sad. Is it because we've lost the art of being alone?
ib

10 There's an emotion in them that I feel very strongly about, and I don't want to stop that train of thought.
On why he hid a series of paintings of his model Helga Testorf for 15 years, NY *Times* 6 Aug 86

11 When you show it to someone, if they like it, you're stopped, and if they dislike it you're stopped—either way.
ib

12 I'm like a prostitute. . . . never off duty.
Time 18 Aug 86

13 I don't really have studios. I wander around—around people's attics, out in fields, in cellars, any-place I find that invites me.
ib

14 I dream a lot. I do more painting when I'm not painting. It's in the subconscious.
ib

JAMIE WYETH

15 Had I been born in New York, I'd probably be painting taxis . . . but because I live on this farm, I paint objects and landscapes I know and love.
Interviewed in his studio at Chadds Ford PA, *M* Aug 84

16 Trees or rooms I don't know don't interest me. A representational painter *has* to feel that way, otherwise the results would just be postcard junk.
ib

DEAN YOUNG

17 I don't deal in controversy. I deal in fun. It's separate from reality.
On continuing the comic strip *Blondie* begun by his father Chic Young, *Newsweek* 1 Oct 84

Photographers

ANSEL ADAMS

18 It is my intention to present—through the medium of photography—intuitive observations of the natural world which may have meaning to the spectators.
The Portfolios of Ansel Adams NY Graphic Society/Little, Brown 81

19 The negative is comparable to the composer's score and the print to its performance. Each performance differs in subtle ways.
ib

20 There is nothing worse than a brilliant image of a fuzzy concept.
Recalled on his death 22 Apr 84

21 Not everybody trusts paintings but people believe photographs.
ib

RICHARD AVEDON

22 It's in trying to direct the traffic between Artiface [*sic*] and Candor, without being run over, that I'm confronted with the questions about photography that matter most to me.
On maintaining authenticity, NY *Times* 27 Dec 85

DAVID BAILEY

23 My fashion pictures are documents just as much as my boat people or my pictures for Band-Aid of Sudan.
International Herald Tribune 15 Nov 85

24 When I die I want to go to *Vogue*.
ib

25 All pictures are unnatural. All pictures are sad because they're about dead people. Paintings you don't think of in a special time or with a specific event. With photos I always think I'm looking at something dead.
ib

CECIL BEATON

1 Mrs Woolf's complaint should be addressed to her creator, who made her, rather than me.

Answering Virginia Woolf's protest about his drawing of her, quoted by Hugo Vickers *Cecil Beaton* Little, Brown 85

2 An old Polish frog . . . with a huge casket of jewels. . . . and she clicks her teeth and shrugs, "Only Rubbish. Much more in Paris."

On Helena Rubinstein, *ib*

3 [He stared into the camera] like some sort of an animal gazing from across the back of its sty.

On Winston Churchill, *ib*

MARGARET BOURKE-WHITE

4 The beauty of the past belongs to the past.

On modern photojournalism, quoted by Mary Warner Marien *Christian Science Monitor* 5 Dec 86

HENRI CARTIER-BRESSON

5 He made me suddenly realize that photographs could reach eternity through the moment.

On Hungarian photographer Martin Munkacsi, *International Herald Tribune* 15 Nov 85

ALFRED EISENSTAEDT

6 I don't like to work with assistants. I'm already one too many; the camera alone would be enough.

On his 50-year career as a *Life* magazine photographer, *New York* 15 Sep 86

PHILIPPE HALSMAN

7 Of the thousands of people, celebrated and unknown, who have sat before my camera, I am often asked who was the most difficult subject, or the easiest, or which picture is my favorite. This last question is like asking a mother which child she likes the most.

Recalled on his death 25 Jun 79

YOUSUF KARSH

8 I have found that great people do have in common . . . an immense belief in themselves and in their mission. They also have great determination as well as an ability to work hard. At the crucial moment of decision, they draw on their accumulated wisdom. Above all, they have integrity.

Parade 3 Dec 78

9 I've also seen that great men are often lonely. This is understandable, because they have built such high standards for themselves that they often feel alone. But that same loneliness is part of their ability to create.

ib

10 Character, like a photograph, develops in darkness.

ib

ANDRÉ KERTESZ

11 Everything is a subject. Every subject has a rhythm. To feel it is the raison d'être. The photograph is a fixed moment of such a raison d'être, which lives on in itself.

The Concerned Photographer Grossman 67

12 I am still hungry.

When asked at age 90 why he continued to take pictures, recalled on his death, NY *Times* 30 Sep 85

ARNOLD NEWMAN

13 The subject must be thought of in terms of the 20th century, of houses he lives in and places he works, in terms of the kind of light the windows in these places let through and by which we see him every day.

One Mind's Eye Godine 74

NORMAN PARKINSON

14 A photographer without a magazine behind him is like a farmer without fields.

New Yorker 10 Dec 84

15 The camera can be the most deadly weapon since the assassin's bullet. Or it can be the lotion of the heart.

ib

EDWARD STEICHEN

16 Photography records the gamut of feelings written on the human face, the beauty of the earth and skies that man has inherited and the wealth and confusion man has created.

Time 7 Apr 61

17 Photography is a major force in explaining man to man.

ib

18 Every other artist begins [with] a blank canvas, a piece of paper . . . the photographer begins with the finished product.

Recalled on his death 25 Mar 73

19 When that shutter clicks, anything else that can be done afterward is not worth consideration.

ib

Collectors & Curators

ALFRED BARR, Director of Collections, Museum of Modern Art

20 This museum is a torpedo moving through time, its head the ever-advancing present, its tail the ever-receding past of 50 to 100 years ago.

Newsweek 1 Jun 64

FRANÇOISE CACHIN, Director, Musée d'Orsay, Paris

21 Certainly we have bad paintings. We have only the "greatest" bad paintings.

Time 8 Dec 86

HUGH CASSON, former President, Royal Academy of Art

22 Mine [was] the role of the oilcan in making the machinery clunk around.

Architectural Digest Dec 85

CLEMENT G CONGER, White House curator

23 If you do a president you're going to do it for the thrill of it.

On securing portraitists without cost, *International Herald Tribune* 18 Apr 86

Peggy Guggenheim

1 If Venice sinks, the collection should be preserved somewhere in the vicinity of Venice.
  Handwritten postscript to the final agreement on the disposal of her art collection, *Smithsonian* Jul 86

Gisberto Martelli, Superintendent of Monuments, Milan

2 Imagine 500 friars eating 500 plates of steaming minestrone every night—that's pollution.
  On the restoration of *The Last Supper*, Leonardo da Vinci's 1498 refectory fresco, NY *Times* 20 Aug 80

Paul Mellon

3 The horse is an archetypal symbol which will always find ways to stir up deep and moving ancestral memories in every human being.
  Foreword to John Baskett *The Horse in Art* Little, Brown 80

Walter Persegati, Secretary-Treasurer, Vatican Museum

4 You can't lock up art in a vault and keep it frozen for posterity. Then the artist is betrayed, history is betrayed.
  NY *Times* 9 Jul 84

Gaillard F Ravenel, National Gallery of Art, Washington DC

5 You begin with a group of objects and then you build a room like a glove to hold them.
  On the gallery's exhibit "The Treasure Houses of Britain," NY *Times* 10 Sep 85

S Dillon Ripley

6 I shall enjoy my freedom from the tyranny of the In and Out boxes.
  On his retirement after 20 years as secretary of the Smithsonian Institution, *Smithsonian* Sep 85

John Rothenstein, former Director, Tate Gallery, London

7 Art derives from the intention of the artist. But time is the only impeccable judge.
  Time 27 Jan 67

Robert C Scull, taxicab tycoon

8 It holds up in one object or one surface, in one bright, luminous and concentrated thing—whether a beer can or a flag—all the dispersed elements that go to make up our lives.
  On his collection of pop and minimal art, *Time* 21 Feb 64

9 I'd rather use art to climb than anything else.
  When asked if his purchases were for investment or social climbing, recalled on his death 1 Jan 86

Elizabeth Shaw, Public Relations Director, Museum of Modern Art

10 Dead artists always bring out an older, richer crowd.
  On a fauvism exhibition that drew 2,000 people, NY *Times* 26 Mar 76

Lowery Sims, Associate Curator, Metropolitan Museum of Art

11 [It was] like the wild child who belongs in a delinquent home.
  On status of modern art collection before $26-million, 110,000-square-foot addition to the museum, *Manhattan Inc* Aug 86

Baron Hans Heinrich Thyssen-Bornemisza

12 I chase works of art the way others chase *les jolies maîtresses*.
  M Jul 85

Peter C Wilson, Chairman, Sotheby's

13 Works of art are all that survive of incredibly gifted people.
  London Illustrated News Dec 78

Observers & Critics

Bernard Berenson

14 I am only a picture-taster, the way others are wine- or tea-tasters.
  Sunset and Twilight Harcourt, Brace & World 63

Jonathan Brown, Professor of Fine Arts, NY University

15 Whenever the occasion arose, he rose to the occasion.
  On Diego de Velázquez, quoted by Susan Heller Anderson NY *Times* 10 Aug 86

Linda Charlton

16 [It is] a statue that draws children as hot toast does butter.
  On José de Creeft's Central Park figure of Alice in Wonderland, NY *Times* 17 May 79

Winston Churchill

17 Without tradition, art is a flock of sheep without a shepherd. Without innovation, it is a corpse.
  To Royal Academy of Arts, *Time* 11 May 53

H E Clark

18 The photographer's palette [is] a thousand shades of gray.
  On a friend's black-and-white photographs, *Christian Science Monitor* 14 Apr 86

19 He carefully picked his cast of clouds, watched them intently as they swirled in before the lens and hoped the sun would break in concert.
  ib

Kenneth Clark

20 Ruthless, greedy, tyrannical, disreputable . . . they have had one principle worth all the rest, the principle of delight!
  Introduction to Douglas Cooper ed *Great Private Collections* Macmillan 63

Pat Colander

21 In Chicago, we may not think the Picasso presiding over the Richard J Daley Center plaza is art, but we know it's a big Picasso and it's the city's Picasso, and when the Cubs made the play-offs, the sculpture wore a baseball cap just like everything else.
  "A Metropolis of No Little Plans" NY *Times* 5 May 85

Richard Corliss

22 Every artist undresses his subject, whether human or still life. It is his business to find essences in surfaces, and what more attractive and challenging surface than the skin around a soul?
  On Andrew Wyeth's studies of Helga Testorf, *Time* 18 Aug 86

ARTHUR C DANTO, Johnsonian Professor of Philosophy, Columbia University

1 The Rockwell [magazine] cover was more a part of the American reality than a record of it.

In review of Laurie Norton Moffat's *Norman Rockwell: A Definitive Catalogue* Norman Rockwell Museum/University Press of New England 86, NY *Times* 28 Sep 86

2 His was a landscape of amiable codgers, nurturing moms, adorable dogs, callow soldiers with hearts of gold—grown-up Boy Scouts all.

ib

3 It really is impossible not to like him. His success was his failure.

ib

PETER DE VRIES

4 Murals in restaurants are on a par with the food in museums.

Madder Music Little, Brown 77

ALEXANDER ELIOT

5 So-called art restoration is at least as tricky as brain surgery. Most pictures expire under scalpel and sponge.

NY *Times* 20 Dec 86

HANS MAGNUS ENZENSBERGER

6 Culture is a little like dropping an Alka-Seltzer into a glass—you don't see it, but somehow it does something.

Quoted by painter Hans Haacke NY *Times* 25 Jan 87

EMILY GENAUER

7 Since nudes in all countries and centuries possess standard equipment, it's difficult to say precisely why the pictures at the Brooklyn Museum right now are so thoroughly American.

Reviewing a historical survey of the nude in American painting, NY *Herald Tribune* 10 Oct 61

BIL GILBERT

8 Audubon biographers and scholars [have noted], by various euphemisms, that all great men have their flaws, and their man's principal flaw was that he, well, he lied a lot.

On John James Audubon, *Sports Illustrated* 23 Dec 85

GRACE GLUECK

9 The studio, a room to which the artist consigns himself for life, is naturally important, not only as workplace, but as a source of inspiration. And it usually manages, one way or another, to turn up in his product.

NY *Times* 29 Jun 84

DAG HAMMARSKJÖLD

10 The breaking wave
and the muscle as it contracts
obey the same law.
Delicate line
gathers the body's total strength
in a bold balance.
Shall my soul meet
so severe a curve, journeying
on its way to form?

Poem inspired by sculptor Barbara Hepworth, recalled on the dedication of a Hepworth sculpture at the UN, *Christian Science Monitor* 18 Jun 64

HARVARD UNIVERSITY

11 Her creative spirit has transformed the fragments of a familiar world into sculptured wholes surprising, beguiling, demanding our visual appreciation.

Citation given with an honorary degree to Louise Nevelson, NY *Times* 7 Jun 85

ROBERT HUGHES

12 The protein of our cultural imagination.

On exhibits in newly acquired space at Manhattan's Museum of Modern Art, *Time* 14 May 84

13 Distanced from the work by crowds and railings, they may listen on their Acoustiguides to the plummy vowels of the Met's director, Philippe de Montebello, discoursing like an undertaker on the merits of the deceased.

On "Van Gogh in Arles" exhibit at the Metropolitan Museum of Art, *ib* 22 Oct 84

14 Hair like black ice cream.

On Caravaggio exhibit at the Metropolitan Museum of Art, *ib* 11 Mar 85

15 Popular in our time, unpopular in his. So runs the stereotype of rejected genius.

ib

16 An ideal museum show would . . . be a mating of *Brideshead Revisited* . . . with *House & Garden*. . . . provoking intense and pleasurable nostalgia for a past that none of its audience has had.

On "The Treasure Houses of Britain" exhibit at Washington DC's National Gallery of Art, *ib* 11 Nov 85

17 Landscape . . . is to American painting what sex and psychoanalysis are to the American novel.

On midcareer retrospective by Jennifer Bartlett, *ib* 30 Dec 85

18 "Less is more, and Moore is a bore" was what one heard from English art students.

On criticism of Henry Moore in the 1960s, *ib* 15 Sep 86

19 Matisses and Mirós hung transfixed like rabbits in the glare of spotlights.

On unsatisfactory exhibits in Paris's Centre National d'Art Contemporain, *ib* 8 Dec 86

20 [A Gustave Courbet] portrait of a trout . . . has more death in it than Rubens could get in a whole Crucifixion.

ib

21 Woven through these galleries are some of the most deliriously awful canvases of the 19th century . . . high-finance porn of the ripest sort.

On Musée d'Orsay's otherwise brilliant collection, *ib*

ALDOUS HUXLEY

22 A competent portraitist knows how to imply the profile in the full face.

Quoted in John Gassner and Sidney Thomas eds *The Nature of Art* Crown 64

ALEXANDRA JOHNSON

23 [It] is that rare impressionist painting where people don't judge the light, but rather are judged by it.

On *Terrace at Sainte-Adresse* by Claude Monet, *Christian Science Monitor* 1 Oct 80

1 It is a painting that exposes in oils what Chekhov so often did in print: sunlight mocking a dark isolation of the moment. A moment fixed in a brave, failing light.
ib

CLAUDIA ("LADY BIRD") JOHNSON

2 Art is the window to man's soul. Without it, he would never be able to see beyond his immediate world; nor could the world see the man within.
At opening of an addition to Manhattan's Museum of Modern Art, NY *Times* 25 May 64

LYNDON B JOHNSON, 36th US President

3 The ugliest thing I ever saw.
On portrait of him by Peter Hurd, recalled on Hurd's death 9 Jul 84

CARL JUNG

4 A "scream" is always just that—a noise and not music.
On Pablo Picasso, *Letters Vol 1* Princeton 73

JOHN F KENNEDY, 35th US President

5 The life of the artist is, in relation to his work, stern and lonely. He has labored hard, often amid deprivation, to perfect his skill. He has turned aside from quick success in order to strip his vision of everything secondary or cheapening. His working life is marked by intensive application and intense discipline.
From 1963 introduction to book about the National Cultural Center in Washington DC, quoted in NY *Post* 7 Jan 64

JESSE KORNBLUTH

6 Although one of his long-standing fantasies was to open a house of prostitution, the fantasy role he chose for himself was that of cashier.
On Andy Warhol, *New York* 9 Mar 87

RICHARD LACAYO

7 A museum show is the acid test for photojournalism.
On retrospective of Carl Mydans's work, *Time* 19 Aug 85

8 He found the egg-shaped perimeter of Nikita Khrushchev's head sweeping to a comic climax in the dark hole of his open mouth.
ib

MADELEINE L'ENGLE

9 Artistic temperament . . . sometimes seems a battleground, a dark angel of destruction and a bright angel of creativity wrestling.
A Severed Wasp Farrar, Straus & Giroux 82

10 When the bright angel dominates, out comes a great work of art, a Michelangelo *David* or a Beethoven symphony.
ib

MICHAEL LESY

11 Photographers represented occasions once. You dressed for them as you might for church, they cost money, they recorded important moments.
Wisconsin Death Trip Pantheon 73

12 You faced front, you seldom smiled, since levity was not the mark you wanted put across your face forever.
ib

RUSSELL LYNES

13 The Art Snob will stand back from a picture at some distance, his head cocked slightly to one side. . . . After a long period of gazing (during which he may occasionally squint his eyes), he will approach to within a few inches of the picture and examine the brushwork; he will then return to his former distant position, give the picture another glance and walk away.
Snobs Harper 50

14 The Art Snob can be recognized in the home by the quick look he gives the pictures on your walls, quick but penetrating, as though he were undressing them. This is followed either by complete and pained silence or a comment such as "That's really a very pleasant little water color you have there."
ib

HEATHER SMITH MACISAAC

15 Every American with a penny in his pocket carries a minute example of Daniel Chester French's work.
"Figures in a Landscape" *House & Garden* Jul 84

ANDRÉ MALRAUX, French Minister of Culture

16 Some pictures are in the gallery because they belong to humanity and others because they belong to the United States.
On visiting the National Gallery of Art, Washington DC, NY *Herald Tribune* 12 May 62

17 There has been talk of the risks this painting took by leaving the Louvre. . . . But the risks taken by the boys who landed one day in Normandy—to say nothing of those who had preceded them 25 years before—were much more certain.
At dinner honoring the exhibition of the *Mona Lisa* at the National Gallery, *ib* 8 Jan 63

18 To the humblest among them, who may be listening to me now, I want to say . . . that the masterpiece to which you are paying historic homage this evening . . . is a painting which he has saved.
ib

19 An art book is a museum without walls.
Quoted by Jonathan Cott *Conversations with Glenn Gould* Little, Brown 84

NIGEL MCGILCHRIST

20 It has always been difficult to get very close to the spirit of the Sistine Chapel; now that it is cleaned, it is like trying to get close to a trumpet.
London *Times* 14 Apr 86

HUGH MCKEAN

21 It was as though he had cut up the sky, melted down a flower garden, tossed in some jewels and made it into glass.
The Lost Treasures of Louis Comfort Tiffany Doubleday 80, quoted in *Christian Science Monitor* 26 Nov 80

MARSHALL MCLUHAN

1 I think of art, at its most significant, as a DEW line, a Distant Early Warning system that can always be relied on to tell the old culture what is beginning to happen to it.
Understanding Media McGraw-Hill 64

GEORGE MENDOZA

2 You never saw any husband writing an alimony check in Norman Rockwell's America.
Quoted in NY *Times* 20 Aug 85

THOMAS MERTON

3 Wheels of fire, cosmic, rich, full-bodied honest victories over desperation.
On Vincent van Gogh, quoted by Monica Furlong *Merton* Harper & Row 80

WRIGHT MORRIS

4 [His] special triumph is in the conviction his countrymen share that the mythical world he evokes actually exists.
On Norman Rockwell, *Time* 7 Jul 86

NEWSWEEK

5 Her face is like a wise Pekingese that has seen everything from a box by the bed, her bare arms are filled with spent cartridges of old age and she is packaged in fateful red, as if she has just received the final invitation.
On René Bouché's painting of "social mixmaster" Elsa Maxwell, 22 Jul 63

6 He paints the astonishingly complicated loneliness of the limbo hours in a coffee shop, like a glass-hulled boat trapped in the black ice of the city, lit by a slice of yellow light like stale lemon pie, and full of the sadness of a gray fedora, a red dress and a clean coffee urn.
On *Nighthawks* by Edward Hopper, 29 May 67

NEW YORKER

7 Like a *grande dame* caught in the middle of dressing for her birthday ball.
On preparations for centennial of the Metropolitan Museum of Art, 11 Oct 69

8 A unique, private world of imperious dowagers, decaying tycoons, lovesick spinsters and vaguely epicene young men.
Tribute to Mary Petty for her cover paintings spanning nearly 50 years, 12 Apr 76

BRIAN O'DOHERTY

9 He searched disorder for its unifying principle.
On Stuart Davis, abstractionist whose work prefigured pop art, NY *Times* 26 Jun 64

RONALD REAGAN, 40th US President

10 In an atmosphere of liberty, artists and patrons are free to think the unthinkable and create the audacious; they are free to make both horrendous mistakes and glorious celebrations.
To recipients of the National Medal of Arts, *Newsweek* 13 May 85

11 Where there's liberty, art succeeds.
ib

PAUL RICHARD

12 A mood of gloom or longing that people mistake for profundity.
On Andrew Wyeth's paintings, *Newsweek* 18 Aug 86

FRIDA KAHLO RIVERA

13 I cannot speak of Diego as my husband because that term, when applied to him, is an absurdity. He never has been, nor will he ever be, anybody's husband.
Acknowledging that art overruled everything in her husband's life, quoted by William Weber Johnson "The Tumultuous Life and Times of the Painter Diego Rivera" *Smithsonian* Feb 86

14 His capacity for work breaks clocks and calendars.
ib

JOHN RUSSELL

15 What makes people the world over stand in line for Van Gogh is not that they will see beautiful pictures [but] that in an indefinable way they will come away feeling better human beings. And that is exactly what Van Gogh hoped for.
NY *Times* 19 Oct 84

16 Though produced by a very old man who was mortally ill, they seem to come from the springtime of the world.
On Henri Matisse's paper cutouts, *ib* 25 Nov 84

17 Objects rarely if ever bore their natural hues: cows were likely to be blue, horses green, people red, [in] a world without gravity.
On Marc Chagall's paintings, *ib* 29 Mar 85

18 Henry Moore was . . . the Number 1 choice whenever a public sculpture was needed. . . . It was thought that a large Henry Moore work out front would add a final distinction.
ib 1 Sep 86

19 [He] was no less successful with his smaller sculptures, which worked their way up from toothbrush size to a scale that could dominate . . . a six-acre lawn.
ib

20 In a world at odds with itself, his sculptures got through to an enormous constituency as something that stood for breadth and generosity of feeling.
ib

21 They also suggested that the human body could be the measure of all things, for it was in terms of head, shoulder, breast, pelvis, thigh, elbow and knee that Mr Moore set the imagination free to roam across a vast repertory of connotations in myth and symbol.
ib

GEORGE SANTAYANA

22 Art is delayed echo.
Quoted in John Gassner and Sidney Thomas eds *The Nature of Art* Crown 64

23 Nothing is so poor and melancholy as an art that is interested in itself and not in its subject.
ib

JEAN PAUL SARTRE

24 What I see is teeming cohesion, contained dispersal. . . . For him, to sculpt is to take the fat off space.
On Alberto Giacometti's work, *Situations* Braziller 65

SUSAN SONTAG

1 Life is not significant details, illuminated by a flash, fixed forever. Photographs are.
On Photography Farrar, Straus & Giroux 77

MARK STEVENS

2 Shouldn't a great museum foster serious seeing before all else?
On poor presentation of a Van Gogh exhibit at the Metropolitan Museum of Art, *Newsweek* 15 Oct 84

3 One of the best things about paintings is their silence—which prompts reflection and random reverie.
Decrying guided tours by headphone, *ib*

GENE THORNTON

4 Magazine photography is the mural painting of modern times.
NY *Times* 15 Jul 79

TIME MAGAZINE

5 The doodle is the brooding of the hand.
16 Oct 78

WILLIAM TOBY JR, Regional Administrator, Health Care Financing Administration

6 During my 17 years of employment in this building, nothing has offended me and my staff more than the erection of this huge, rusted metal barrier.
On *Tilted Arc*, a 12-foot-high, 112-foot-long steel sculpture bisecting plaza of the Jacob K Javits Federal Building in Manhattan, NY *Times* 7 Mar 85

CALVIN TOMKINS

7 Each year, it seems, larger and more daunting mountains of text rise from the lush lowlands of visual reproduction. . . . You are likely to find yourself scaling craggy massifs of prose. . . . hacking a path through thickets of Nietzsche, Kierkegaard, Baudelaire and Marx.
On the "changing topography of coffee-table art books," *New Yorker* 11 Feb 85

LUCIE UTRILLO

8 I picked him up in a gutter, and saved him for France.
On her husband Maurice, recalled on his death 5 Nov 55

LILA ACHESON WALLACE

9 A painting is like a man. If you can live without it, then there isn't much point in having it.
Recalled on her death 8 May 84

THEODORE F WOLFF

10 It creates an enchanted world which draws the Hansel or Gretel in each of us into mysterious forms and structures.
On the Whitney Museum's exhibit "Louise Nevelson: Atmospheres and Environments," *Christian Science Monitor* 5 Jun 80

11 It may be big, bold and brilliantly effective, but it was painted with about the same degree of feeling with which new cars are painted in Detroit.
On *Persistence of Electrical Nymphs in Space* by James Rosenquist, *ib* 24 Jun 85

12 Piet Mondrian, with his precisely defined, irreducible images of right angles and primary colors, is modernism's champion painter of "nouns."
"Painters of Nouns and Verbs" *ib* 22 May 86

13 Jackson Pollock, with his passionate hurlings and dribblings of paint, is its outstanding producer of "verbs."
ib

FASHION

Designers

BILLY BALDWIN, interior designer

14 [Rich Palm Beach clients] all wanted the same kind of different thing.
NY *Times* 20 Oct 85

CRISTÓBAL BALENCIAGA

15 You don't have to have any taste at all. You are fitted by my fitter and that is it.
To Diana Vreeland, who had asked, "Does one need great taste to wear your clothes?" quoted by Colin McDowell *Country Life* 15 May 86

MANOLO BLAHNIK

16 About half my designs are controlled fantasy, 15 percent are total madness and the rest are bread-and-butter designs.
W 25 Aug 86

17 These are very dainty and superrefined, but really vile.
On shoes for winter 1986, *ib*

18 Women are wearing tight and sexy clothes again. It is the body-conscious mentality, and women are revealing every bulge.
ib

19 My shoes are special . . . shoes for discerning feet.
ib

BILL BLASS

20 When in doubt wear red.
News summaries 31 Dec 82

21 Sometimes the eye gets so accustomed that if you don't have a change, you're bored. It's the same with fashion, you know. And that, I suppose, is what style is about.
W 25 Feb 83

MARIO BUATTA, interior designer

22 I like all the chairs to talk to one another and to the sofas and not those parlor-car arrangements that create two Siberias.
New York 28 Jan 85

PIERRE CARDIN

23 The jean! The jean is the destructor! It is a dictator! It is destroying creativity. The jean must be stopped!
People 28 Jun 76

GABRIELLE ("COCO") CHANEL

24 I love luxury. And luxury lies not in richness and ornateness but in the absence of vulgarity. Vulgarity is the ugliest word in our language. I stay in the game to fight it.
Life 19 Aug 57

1 Luxury must be comfortable, otherwise it is not luxury.

NY *Times* 23 Aug 64

2 Fashion is made to become unfashionable.

ib

3 Look for the woman in the dress. If there is no woman, there is no dress.

ib

4 It is the unseen, unforgettable, ultimate accessory of fashion. . . . that heralds your arrival and prolongs your departure.

On perfume, NY *Herald Tribune* 18 Oct 64

5 Elegance is not the prerogative of those who have just escaped from adolescence, but of those who have already taken possession of their future.

McCall's Nov 65

LINDKA CIERACH

6 I wanted the Duchess of York's sense of fun and joy to come out in the dress. One day I woke up in the middle of the night and had dreamed it, and that was it.

On Sarah Ferguson's wedding gown, which included embroidered bees and thistles from the bride's coat of arms and anchors and waves for her husband Prince Andrew, news summaries 24 Jul 86

ANGELA CUMMINGS, jewelry designer

7 I think of Bergdorf's as being something like pastel sapphires.

On a fashionable clothing store, NY *Times* 20 Aug 84

LILLY DACHÉ

8 Glamour is what makes a man ask for your telephone number. But it also is what makes a woman ask for the name of your dressmaker.

News summaries 3 Dec 54

ELSIE DE WOLFE (Lady Mendl), interior designer

9 It's my color—beige!

On the Parthenon, recalled on her death 12 Jul 50

NIELS DIFFRIENT, industrial designer

10 The less there is of a phone, the more I like it.

At a Manhattan Phone City display, NY *Times* 16 Oct 86

11 It looks like a galosh with electronics in it.

On a rubber Italian telephone, *ib*

CHRISTIAN DIOR

12 My dream is to save them from nature.

On his desire to make all women look beautiful, *Collier's* 10 Jun 55

13 Women are most fascinating between the ages of 35 and 40 after they have won a few races and know how to pace themselves. Since few women ever pass 40, maximum fascination can continue indefinitely.

ib

ANNE FOGARTY

14 If you adore her, you must adorn her. There lies the secret of a happy marriage.

Wife Dressing Messner 59

FREDDIE FOX, milliner to Queen Elizabeth II

15 She is not a fashion plate, she is a monarch; you can't have both.

Replying to criticism of the queen's "awful hats," London *Times* 6 Oct 84

JEAN PAUL GAULTIER

16 I am 1952. . . . I masticate. I am like a big stomach.

On 1950s influence on his 1980s designs, NY *Times* 31 Oct 86

17 She was the first punk woman.

Referring to boyhood experience in which he caused his grandmother's hair to turn pink when he tried to dye it blue without first reading the directions, *ib*

RUDI GERNREICH

18 It was just a whimsical idea that escalated when so many crazy ladies took it up.

On his design for a topless bathing suit, Chicago *American* 26 Nov 66

HUBERT DE GIVENCHY

19 I absolutely believe my talent is God-given. I ask God for a lot, but I also thank him. I'm a very demanding believer.

W 12 Oct 79

20 Hair style is the final tip-off whether or not a woman really knows herself.

Vogue Jul 85

HALSTON

21 You are only as good as the people you dress.

Quoted by Lisa Belkin "The Prisoner of Seventh Avenue" NY *Times* 15 Mar 87

MARK HAMPTON

22 A nice, undercooked look—nothing too fake, nothing too rich.

Quoted by John Duka "One Decorator's World" NY *Times* 22 Nov 84

NORMAN HARTNELL

23 I despise simplicity. It is the negation of all that is beautiful.

London *Times* 30 Apr 85

EDITH HEAD, eight-time Oscar winner for costume design

24 A designer is only as good as the star who wears her clothes.

Saturday Evening Post 30 Nov 63

25 I have yet to see one completely unspoiled star, except for the animals—like Lassie.

ib

CALVIN KLEIN

26 I think there's something incredibly sexy about a woman wearing her boyfriend's T-shirt and underwear.

People 24 Dec 84

EILEEN ("BUTCH") KRUTCHIK

27 I don't do glitz, I do reverse chic.

On customized invitations and announcements, NY *Times* 21 Dec 85

RALPH LAUREN

1 I don't design clothes, I design dreams.
   NY *Times* 19 Apr 86

RAYMOND LOEWY

2 They looked like chrome-plated barges.
   On automobiles of the 1950s, recalled on his death 14 Jul 86

MAINBOCHER

3 To be well turned out, a woman should turn her thoughts in.
   Vogue 1 Apr 64

4 I have never known a really chic woman whose appearance was not, in large part, an outward reflection of her inner self.
   ib

BRUCE OLDFIELD

5 The bump I was trying to hide could be the future king of England.
   On designing maternity clothing for Diana, Princess of Wales, *Life* May 82

WILLIAM PAHLMANN, interior designer

6 Ambiance is an unstudied grace . . . the grace of human dignity.
   Insider's Newsletter 18 Jan 65

MRS HENRY PARISH ("Sister" Parish)

7 All decorating is about memories.
   Architectural Digest May 81

8 I *am* taste.
   W 14 Jun 85

9 I behaved quite well and I never kicked Caroline [Kennedy] as the story goes, but if I'd thought of it, I would.
   ib

10 It's me—shabby English.
   On furnishing her new apartment, NY *Times* 21 Mar 86

MARY QUANT

11 Legs stay throughout a woman's life.
   On ageless appeal of miniskirts, quoted by Marylin Bender *The Beautiful People* Coward-McCann 67

NETTIE ROSENSTEIN

12 It's what you leave off a dress that makes it smart.
   Recalled on her death 13 Mar 80

YVES SAINT LAURENT

13 I wish I had invented blue jeans. They have expression, modesty, sex appeal, simplicity—all I hope for in my clothes.
   New York 28 Nov 83

14 Dressing is a way of life.
   ib

15 Isn't elegance forgetting what one is wearing?
   ib

VIDAL SASSOON

16 We have come a long way from the youths who wore so much long hair it became a uniform—its own form of uniformity.
   Quote 13 Apr 75

VALENTINA

17 Mink is for football games . . . Please. Out in the fresh air, sit in it, eat hot dogs in it, anything. But not evening, not elegance, I beg of you.
   Ladies' Home Journal Mar 58

Manufacturers & Merchandisers

BROOKS BROTHERS

18 The well-dressed man still doffs his hat.
   On hats as "the classic finishing touch . . . a confident statement of your personal good taste," advertisement in NY *Times* 16 Sep 85

FLORENCE EISEMAN, manufacturer of children's clothing

19 Please do not have a fit in the fitting room. Your fashion life begins there.
   Advertisement in *New Yorker* 19 Mar 66

MAX FACTOR, cosmetics executive

20 A woman who doesn't wear lipstick feels undressed in public. Unless she works on a farm.
   Time 16 Jun 58

IRWIN GROSSMAN, Vice President, Groshire-Austin Leeds

21 If we knew how to get the label on the outside, we'd all be in clover.
   On men's suits, *Time* 28 Feb 64

HARRY LINDLEY, Kinloch Anderson kiltmakers

22 We don't just make a kilt. We build it.
   NY *Times* 13 Aug 80

JACK LIPMAN, Drizzle Inc

23 The trench coat is the only thing that has kept its head above water.
   Wall Street Journal 11 Oct 84

JOHN NEWTON, Chief, Tailors & Garment Workers Union, London

24 A bowler can make or break a chap.
   Time & Tide 4 Jun 64

25 To carry an umbrella without any headgear places a fellow in a social no man's land—in the category of one hurrying round to the corner shop for a bottle of stout on a rainy day at the behest of a nagging landlady.
   ib

ARTHUR ORTENBERG

26 Men's wear is an eight-lane highway with nobody on it.
   On opportunities in the manufacturing of men's fashions, NY *Times* 4 May 86

FRED PRESSMAN, President, Barney's New York

27 In the beginning, it looked quite elegant, but like a lot of trends, it soon became a fashion made by the wrong people, including guys with big bellies wearing gold chains.
   On Nehru jackets, quoted in *Wall Street Journal* 27 Jun 84

HELENA RUBINSTEIN, cosmetics executive

1 All the American women had purple noses and gray lips and their faces were chalk white from terrible powder. I recognized that the United States could be my life's work.
> Recalling her arrival in America on a cold day in 1914, *Time* 9 Apr 65

2 Some women won't buy anything unless they can pay a lot.
> *ib*

Observers & Critics

NORA ASTORGA, UN delegate, Nicaragua

3 You can't expect me to wear blue jeans to the Security Council.
> Defending her clothing expenditures, NY *Times* 28 Sep 86

RUSSELL BAKER

4 Skins tanned to the consistency of well-traveled alligator suitcases.
> On fashionable tans, NY *Times* 9 Aug 86

LETITIA BALDRIGE

5 She changed the White House from a plastic to a crystal bowl.
> On Jacqueline Kennedy, quoted by Ralph G Martin *A Hero for Our Time* Macmillan 83

6 The flower generation tore tradition to shreds, but in the 1980s some magic sewing machine has stitched it all up again.
> *Time* 5 Nov 84

MONICA BALDWIN

7 A wisp of gossamer, about the size and substance of a spider's web.
> On encountering modern lingerie after 27 years as a cloistered nun, *I Leap over the Wall* Rinehart 50

MAHARANI OF BARODA

8 After all, those emeralds used to be one of my anklets.
> Admiring a necklace of cabochon emeralds and diamonds worn by the Duchess of Windsor, quoted by Carol Vogel "Jewels of Windsor" NY *Times* 8 Feb 87

DAVE BARRY

9 [There is] a breed of fashion models . . . who weigh no more than an abridged dictionary.
> NY *News* 9 Nov 86

10 The leading cause of death among fashion models is falling through street grates.
> *ib*

ANNE BAXTER

11 My grandfather Frank Lloyd Wright wore a red sash on his wedding night. *That* is glamour!
> *Time* 5 May 52

CECIL BEATON

12 What is elegance? Soap and water!
> NY *Times* 30 Jan 59

13 Never in the history of fashion has so little material been raised so high to reveal so much that needs to be covered so badly.
> On miniskirts, news summaries 17 Jan 69

STELLA BLUM, Costume Institute, Metropolitan Museum of Art

14 Fashion is a social agreement. . . . the result of a consensus of a large group of people.
> Recalled on her death 31 Jul 85

15 After World War II society had to settle back for a moment before it picked up the 20th century.
> On Christian Dior's 1947 "New Look," characterized by full skirts and corseted waistlines suggestive of Victorian styles, *ib*

16 Fashion is so close in revealing a person's inner feelings and everybody seems to hate to lay claim to vanity so people tend to push it away. It's really too close to the quick of the soul.
> *ib*

DAVIS BUSHNELL

17 They are certainly fit to be tied.
> On designer shoelaces, *People* 10 May 82

TRUMAN CAPOTE

18 She is pure *Alice in Wonderland*, and her appearance and demeanor are a nicely judged mix of the Red Queen and a flamingo.
> On Diana Vreeland, quoted by Colin McDowell *Country Life* 15 May 86

PATRICK DENNIS

19 Chinchilla is said to be more chic than mink, though personally it reminds me of unborn burlap.
> *Life* 7 Dec 62

KAREN DEYOUNG

20 Britain's attention has to a large extent focused on Fergie's derrière—or bum, as they say here.
> On Sarah Ferguson, fiancée of Prince Andrew, "Fergie: Bedlam over the Bride" Washington *Post* 22 Jul 86

STEPHEN DRUCKER

21 The Lawson chair is the little black dress of the upholsterer: comfortable and safe.
> "A Revival of the Shapely Drawing-room Chair" NY *Times* 10 Jan 85

GEORGIA DULLEA

22 The Prince of Chintz . . . wears well and resists stains.
> On interior designer Mario Buatta, NY *Times* 24 Jan 86

DWIGHT D EISENHOWER, 34th US President

23 Ankles are nearly always neat and good-looking, but knees are nearly always not.
> Address to graduating class of one of his granddaughters, *National Observer* 19 Jun 67

JOHN FAIRCHILD, Publisher, *Women's Wear Daily*

24 "Style" is an expression of individualism mixed with charisma. Fashion is something that comes after style.
> Quoted in Dallas *Times Herald* 15 Jul 75

ALAN FUSSER

1 A plain white handkerchief is the sure sign of a confident and elegant dresser.

> On return of breast-pocket handkerchiefs in men's suit coats, *International Herald Tribune* 31 Dec 78

CATHERINE GALBRAITH, wife of former US ambassador to India

2 I used to put in a safety pin to make sure.

> On the art of wearing a sari, NY *Times* 11 Sep 85

WILLIAM HAMILTON

3 The salesgirl handed her a bright little wad of cloth that could be roomily stowed in a cigarette pack.

> On his 12-year-old daughter's purchase of a bikini, NY *Times* 1 Sep 85

GEORGE V HIGGINS

4 She had rouged her cheeks to a color otherwise seen only on specially ordered Pontiac Firebirds, and in her ears she wore two feathered appliances resembling surfcasting jigs especially appetizing to striped bass.

> On Diana Vreeland, *Wall Street Journal* 9 Jul 84

5 Rental formal wear of the sky-blue, brocade and shiny varieties [is] favored by upwardly mobile young gangsters drafted as groomsmen for weddings.

> *ib* 5 Feb 85

CHAUNCEY HOWE

6 Eclectic means you can put anything together as long as it's expensive.

> On decorators' show houses, NBC TV 6 May 85

JACQUELINE KENNEDY

7 A newspaper reported I spend $30,000 a year buying Paris clothes and that women hate me for it. I couldn't spend that much unless I wore sable underwear.

> Replying to charges that she was too chic to become First Lady, NY *Times* 15 Sep 60

8 It looks like it's been furnished by discount stores.

> Contemplating her move to the White House, quoted by Ralph G Martin *A Hero for Our Time* Macmillan 83

RENÉ KONIG

9 Fashion is as profound and critical a part of the social life of man as sex, and is made up of the same ambivalent mixture of irresistible urges and inevitable taboos.

> *The Restless Image: A Sociology of Fashion* Allen & Unwin 73

JOAN KRON

10 Sheets are fraught with meaning. . . . We cover the baby with them; hide nudity under them. Sheets are the beginning and the end: our first clothing (swaddling), and our last (the shroud). They are bandages in war, and rags when they're worn out. . . . We spend more time in contact with sheets than with any other item we own; they are almost a second skin.

> "Sheets: The New Security Blanket" *New York* 24 March 75

JAMES LAVER, Victoria and Albert Museum, London

11 Poor Englishwomen! . . . When it comes to their clothes—well, the French reaction is a shrug, the Italian reaction a spreading of the hands and a lifting of the eyes and the American reaction simply one of amused contempt.

> "Chic-ness Crosses the Channel" NY *Times* 24 Nov 63

DORIS LILLY

12 Men who wear turtlenecks look like turtles.

> NY *Post* 18 Dec 67

JOHN V LINDSAY, Mayor of NYC

13 The miniskirt enables young ladies to run faster, and because of it, they may have to.

> NY *Times* 8 Jun 67

LIN YUTANG

14 All women's dresses are merely variations on the eternal struggle between the admitted desire to dress and the unadmitted desire to undress.

> *This Week* 17 Feb 67

LONDON STAR

15 "Wow!" That's what Andy said when he saw Fergie at the Abbey . . . and so said all of us.

> On marriage of Sarah Ferguson and Prince Andrew, news summaries 24 Jul 86

ANITA LOOS

16 I've had my best times when trailing a Mainbocher evening gown across a sawdust floor. I've always loved high style in low company.

> NY *Times* 28 Mar 61

SOPHIA LOREN

17 A woman's dress should be like a barbed-wire fence: serving its purpose without obstructing the view.

> Quoted on *Good Morning, America* ABC TV 10 Aug 79

RUSSELL LYNES

18 The Good Quality Snob, or wearer of muted tweeds, cut almost exactly the same from year to year, often with a hat of the same material, [is] native to the Boston North Shore, the Chicago North Shore, the North Shore of Long Island, to Westchester County, the Philadelphia Main Line and the Peninsula area of San Francisco.

> *Snobs* Harper 50

19 It rides horses and is rare in Southern California, except in Pasadena. In Texas it trades at Neiman-Marcus.

> *ib*

20 What we are headed for is a sort of social structure in which the highbrows are the elite, the middlebrows are the bourgeoisie and the lowbrows are hoi polloi.

> *The Tastemakers* Harper 54

21 In my estimation, the only thing that is more to be guarded against than bad taste is good taste.

> *Confessions of a Dilettante* Harper & Row 66

MICHEIL MACDONALD, Scottish Tartans Museum, Comrie, Scotland

1 I called it the McVomit.

> On a computer-designed tartan for the state of Ohio, combining red for its steel and automotive industries, green and gold for its agriculture, blue for its lakes and white for its winter snows, London *Times* 21 Dec 84

2 Certainly in days past no one ever sat down to design a plaid for the MacLumphas and wove into the texture blue for the varicose veins, red for the bloodshot eyes and purple for the claret nose of the clan chief.

> *ib*

SAMORA M MACHEL, President of Mozambique

3 And you say Marxists don't have style!

> Showing off his double-breasted, double-vented, gray pinstripe suit to fellow delegates at the United Nations, NY *Times* 13 Oct 85

AXEL MADSEN

4 A 17-year-old from North London who called herself Twiggy made looking 17 and starved the fashion image of 1967.

> *Living for Design* Delacorte 79

WILLIAM MANCHESTER

5 An Edwardian lady in full dress was a wonder to behold, and her preparations for viewing were awesome.

> *The Last Lion* Little, Brown 83

6 As she sallied forth from her boudoir, you would never have guessed how quickly she could strip for action.

> *ib*

JUDITH MARTIN ("Miss Manners")

7 DEAR MISS MANNERS: Some time ago, a lady was dancing with her male friend at the White House and her underslip dropped off on the dance floor, and the lady just kept dancing as if nothing had happened. Was this the proper thing for the lady to do?

GENTLE READER: Yes, the thing to do is to ignore it. A general rule of etiquette is that one apologizes for the unfortunate occurrence, but the unthinkable is unmentionable.

> Quoted in *Time* 5 Nov 84

COLIN MCDOWELL

8 [Her] fingers are brandished as a crazed and half-starved Chinese would use chopsticks. . . . They prod and pinch the air, leaving it bruised and beaten.

> On Diana Vreeland, "The Vreeland Version" *Country Life* 15 May 86

9 When she speaks it is as if very thick olive oil is pouring vigorously over gravel chippings.

> *ib*

DAVID MCFADDEN, Curator of Decorative Arts, Cooper-Hewitt Museum, NYC

10 Outside of the chair, the teapot is the most ubiquitous and important design element in the domestic environment and almost everyone who has tackled the world of design has ended up designing one.

> *New York* 2 Aug 84

ANGUS MCGILL

11 Men's fashions . . . all start as sports clothes and progress to the great occasions of state . . . The tail coat, which started out as a hunting coat, is just finishing such a journey. The track suit is just beginning one.

> *Illustrated London News* Oct 86

12 [Edward VIII] replaced his fly buttons with a zip, a revolutionary move; and his Fair Isle pullovers, shorts and Windsor knots were considered by some to foreshadow the end of Empire.

> *ib*

SUZY MENKES

13 The Romanovs are overtaken by the Indian Maharajahs . . . as American heiresses pick over the carcasses of fallen Empire.

> In review of Hans Nadelhoffer's *Cartier: Jewelers Extraordinary* Abrams 84, London *Times* 11 Dec 84

LADY DIANA MOSLEY

14 The Duchess of Windsor never tried to hide her American upbringing or her love of fashion, even though the English prefer a royal family dressed in gum boots and head scarves.

> *W* brochure Summer 84

LOUIS MOUNTBATTEN, 1st Earl Mountbatten of Burma

15 If you've got it, wear it.

> Advice to Prince Charles on use of royal insignia and other medals, quoted by Stephen Barry *Royal Secrets* Villard 85

CARL M MUELLER, President of the Board of River House, exclusive NYC co-op

16 She is better known for her jeans than for her genes.

> On rejecting applications made by Gloria Vanderbilt. *People* 9 Jun 80

NEW YORK MAGAZINE

17 Most [of the rooms] looked like the duke had just gone out to bag a few birds . . . trademark tea-rinsed botanical chintzes and walls glazed strawberry-pink, pale shrimp, watermelon, corn-yellow or apple-green, the paintings of the alert King Charles spaniel school hanging from stretched taffeta ending in bows, their flower plates and cups, cabbage tureens, painted trellises and gazebos.

> On rooms designed by Mario Buatta, 28 Jan 85

NEW YORK JOURNAL-AMERICAN

18 They held on tight going around the curves.

> On gowns worn by actress Elizabeth Taylor, 22 Jun 64

NAVEEN PATNAIK

19 That left shoulder really has an aura of its own; it holds everything together.

> On wearing a sari, quoted by Marina Warner "Woven Winds" *Connoisseur* Apr 86

20 The sari's radiance, vigor and variety, produced by a single straight length of cloth, should give us in the West pause and make us think twice about the zipper, the dart and the shoulder pad.

> *ib*

ANNA QUINDLEN

1 I would even go to Washington, which is saying something for me, just to glimpse Jane Q Public being sworn in as the first female president of the United States, while her husband holds the Bible and wears a silly pillbox hat and matching coat.
NY *Times* 30 Jul 86

ELEANOR ROOSEVELT

2 You will feel that you are no longer clothing yourself, you are dressing a public monument.
Warning to wives of future presidents, NY *Herald Tribune* 27 Oct 60

JOHN RUSSELL

3 It is possible in England to dress up by dressing down, but it's a good idea to be a duke before you try it.
NY *Times* 9 Mar 86

DIANE SALZBERG

4 You take off a ski hat and you should immediately put a paper bag over your head. I hate those people out West who take off their hats, shake their blonde manes and look great. They aren't New Yorkers.
On attire for fashionable resorts, NY *Times* 5 Feb 86

5 "Oh, these? I got these in Zermatt. Everyone wears them there." That one remark is worth the cost of the vacation.
ib

6 You want them to know you are letting them know that you know what they know, am I right?
ib

CAROLINE SEEBOHM

7 World War I, that tiresome European engagement that threatened to close down French couture.
The Man Who Was Vogue Viking 82

GEORGE BERNARD SHAW

8 A fashion is nothing but an induced epidemic.
Recalled on his death 2 Nov 50

EUGENIA SHEPPARD

9 To call a fashion wearable is the kiss of death. No new fashion worth its salt is ever wearable.
NY *Herald Tribune* 13 Jan 60

JOHN R SILBER, President, Boston University

10 The younger generation finds a special value in the costumes of poverty and disarray simply because these aspects of life have become far scarcer for children of the middle class than good clothes and comeliness.
Wall Street Journal 23 Jul 75

UPTON SINCLAIR

11 I just put on what the lady says. I've been married three times, so I've had lots of supervision.
Interviewed at age 85, NY *Times* 7 Sep 62

EDITH SITWELL

12 The trouble with most Englishwomen is that they *will* dress as if they had been a mouse in a previous incarnation . . . they do not want to attract attention.
Recalled on her death 9 Dec 64

13 Why not be oneself? That is the whole secret of a successful appearance. If one is a greyhound, why try to look like a Pekingese?
ib

SUZANNE SLESIN

14 Chintz, it could rightly be said, is the basic black dress of the English-style interior.
"Floral Attributes" NY *Times* 14 Apr 85

CARMEL SNOW

15 Elegance is good taste *plus* a dash of daring.
The World of Carmel Snow McGraw-Hill 62

STEPHEN J SOLARZ, US Congressman

16 Compared to Imelda [Marcos], Marie Antoinette was a bag lady.
On viewing the elaborate wardrobe left behind by the wife of the overthrown Philippines president, NY *Times* 9 Mar 86

SUSAN SONTAG

17 "Camp" is a vision of the world in terms of style— but a particular style. It is the love of the exaggerated.
Against Interpretation and Other Essays Farrar, Straus & Giroux 66

TIME MAGAZINE

18 The first thing the first couple did after committing the first sin was to get dressed. Thus Adam and Eve started the world of fashion, and styles have been changing ever since.
"Gilding the Lily" 8 Nov 63

19 Pierre Cardin is a designer whose name can be worn, walked on, slept in, set upon, munched on, drunk, flown, pedaled or driven.
Quoted in introducing Cardin on *Good Morning America* ABC TV 22 Oct 86

DIANA VREELAND

20 I adore that pink! It's the navy blue of India!
On importation of bright pink silk from India, NY *Times* 28 Mar 62

21 The only real elegance is in the mind; if you've got that, the rest really comes from it.
Newsweek 10 Dec 62

22 What do I think about the way most people dress? Most people are not something one thinks about.
ib 2 Jan 78

23 [Blue jeans are] the most beautiful things since the gondola.
NY *Times* 14 Sep 80

24 Elegance is innate. It has nothing to do with being well dressed. Elegance is refusal.
ib

25 The two greatest mannequins of the century were Gertrude Stein and Edith Sitwell—unquestionably. You just couldn't take a bad picture of those two old girls.
Newsweek 22 Sep 80

26 I always wear my sweater back-to-front; it is so much more flattering.
Country Life 15 May 86

1 In a Balenciaga you were the only woman in the room—no other woman *existed*.
ib

2 No one cuts backs like he did. No one knows what a back *is* anymore.
On Cristóbal Balenciaga, *ib*

3 [Balenciaga] did the most delicious evening clothes. Clothes aren't *delicious* any more.
ib

WALL STREET JOURNAL

4 If anything is worse than your own tuxedo that doesn't fit, it's a borrowed one that doesn't fit.
1 Dec 58

IRV WILLIAMS, head gardener, White House

5 One administration will be more pink, another more yellow.
On the changes in the Rose Garden from Betty Ford yellow to Rosalynn Carter peach to Nancy Reagan red, NY *Times* 4 Apr 85

DAVID WINDER

6 It's toppers and tails for Ascot. Boaters and bow ties for Henley. And anything goes for Wimbledon.
On the proper attire for English races, regattas and tennis matches, *Christian Science Monitor* 25 Jun 85

TOM WOLFE

7 Radical chic.
On trendy NYC hostesses of the early 1970s, news summaries 31 Dec 75

8 By October of 1969 Funky Chic was flying through London like an infected bat, which is to say, silently, blindly, insanely and at night, fangs afoam . . . but with an infallible aim for the main vein.
Mauve Gloves and Madmen, Clutter and Vine Farrar, Straus & Giroux 76

9 [It was] much like the Sideburns Fairy, who had been cruising about the city since 1966, visiting young groovies in their sleep and causing them to awake with sideburns running down their jawbones.
ib

FILMS

Actors & Actresses

FRED ALLEN

10 You can take all the sincerity in Hollywood, place it in the navel of a fruit fly and still have room enough for three caraway seeds and a producer's heart.
Quoted by John Robert Colombo *Popcorn in Paradise* Holt, Rinehart & Winston 80

LAUREN BACALL

11 How many women do we know who were continually kissed by Clark Gable, William Powell, Cary Grant, Spencer Tracy and Fredric March? Only one: Myrna Loy.
Hosting Carnegie Hall tribute to Myrna Loy, NY *Times* 16 Jan 85

12 And to meet whom did Franklin D Roosevelt find himself tempted to call off the Yalta Conference? Myrna Loy. And to see what picture did John Dillinger risk coming out of hiding to meet his bullet-ridden death in an alley in Chicago? Myrna Loy, in *Manhattan Melodrama*.
ib

TALLULAH BANKHEAD

13 They made me sound as if I'd been castrated.
On early talking pictures, *People* 9 Feb 87

THEDA BARA

14 The reason good women like me and flock to my pictures is that there is a little bit of vampire instinct in every woman.
On her roles as the Vamp, recalled on her death 7 Apr 55

BRIGITTE BARDOT

15 I have been very happy, very rich, very beautiful, much adulated, very famous and very unhappy.
Interviewed on her 50th birthday, London *Times* 28 Sep 84

ETHEL BARRYMORE

16 Fundamentally I feel that there is as much difference between the stage and the films as between a piano and a violin. Normally you can't become a virtuoso in both.
NY *Post* 7 Jun 56

WARREN BEATTY

17 When you mutilate movies for mass media, you tamper with the hearts and minds of America.
On refusal to grant television rights for his movies because of cuts made for commercials, NY *Times* 21 Apr 85

INGRID BERGMAN

18 Hitch is a gentleman farmer who raises goose flesh.
On Alfred Hitchcock, recalled on his death 29 Apr 80

HUMPHREY BOGART

19 I came out here with one suit and everybody said I looked like a bum. Twenty years later Marlon Brando came out with only a sweatshirt and the town drooled over him. That shows how much Hollywood has progressed.
Recalled on his death 14 Jan 57

20 They'll nail anyone who ever scratched his ass during the National Anthem.
On House Un-American Activities Committee, *ib*

RAY BOLGER

21 How lonely it is going to be now on the Yellow Brick Road.
At 1979 funeral of Jack Haley, who played the Tin Man in *The Wizard of Oz*, recalled on Bolger's death 15 Jan 87

MARLON BRANDO

22 An actor's a guy who, if you ain't talking about him, ain't listening.
British *Vogue* Aug 74

LOUISE BROOKS

1 Every actor has a natural animosity toward every other actor, present or absent, living or dead.
Lulu in Hollywood Knopf 82

GEORGE BURNS

2 The most important thing in acting is honesty. If you can fake that, you've got it made.
News summaries 31 Dec 84

RICHARD BURTON

3 You may be as vicious about me as you please. You will only do me justice.
On being interviewed for cover story, *Time* 26 Apr 63

4 At 34 she is an extremely beautiful woman, lavishly endowed by nature with a few flaws in the masterpiece: She has an insipid double chin, her legs are too short and she has a slight potbelly. She has a wonderful bosom, though.
On Elizabeth Taylor, quoted in "His Liz: 'A Scheming Charmer'" *Life* 24 Feb 67

5 I rather like my reputation, actually, that of a spoiled genius from the Welsh gutter, a drunk, a womanizer; it's rather an attractive image.
On his own life as the best role he ever played, recalled on his death 5 Aug 84

6 Well, I don't want to kill myself.
When asked why he refused to see his performance in *Cleopatra*, quoted in NY *Times* 6 Aug 84

7 If you're going to make rubbish, be the best rubbish in it.
On his films, quoted in *Newsweek* 20 Aug 84

MICHAEL CAINE

8 The best research [for playing a drunk] is being a British actor for 20 years.
Quoted in *US* 2 Jun 86

CHARLIE CHAPLIN

9 I thought I would dress in baggy pants, big shoes, a cane and a derby hat. . . . everything a contradiction: the pants baggy, the coat tight, the hat small and the shoes large.
On his portrayal of the Tramp, *My Autobiography* Simon & Schuster 64

10 I had no idea of the character. But the moment I was dressed, the clothes and the make-up made me feel the person he was. I began to know him, and by the time I walked onto the stage he was fully born.
ib

11 A tramp, a gentleman, a poet, a dreamer, a lonely fellow, always hopeful of romance and adventure.
ib

12 All my pictures are built around the idea of getting in trouble and so giving me the chance to be desperately serious in my attempt to appear as a normal little gentleman.
Quoted by David Robinson *Chaplin* McGraw-Hill 85

13 That is why, no matter how desperate the predicament is, I am always very much in earnest about clutching my cane, straightening my derby hat and fixing my tie, even though I have just landed on my head.
ib

JOAN CRAWFORD

14 I think that the most important thing a woman can have—next to talent, of course—is her hairdresser.
Quoted by Helen Lawrenson "Star Gazing" *Esquire* Apr 57

BING CROSBY

15 Honestly, I think I've stretched a talent—which is so thick that it's almost opaque—over a quite unbelievable term of years.
Time 15 Oct 56

BETTE DAVIS

16 Evil people . . . you never forget them. And that's the aim of any actress—never to be forgotten.
Quoted in NY State Theater program Jun 66

17 The best time I ever had with Joan Crawford was when I pushed her down the stairs in *Whatever Happened to Baby Jane?*
Quoted by John Robert Colombo *Popcorn in Paradise* Holt, Rinehart & Winston 80

18 I'd luv to kiss ya, but I just washed my hair.
Citing "my favorite line in any movie I ever did," the 1932 film *The Cabin in the Cotton*, interview on *60 Minutes* CBS TV 20 Jan 80

19 You know what I'm going to have on my gravestone? "She did it the hard way."
CBS TV 5 May 85

20 People often become actresses because of something they dislike about themselves: They pretend they are someone else.
NBC TV 15 Nov 85

21 I am just too much.
When asked by Barbara Walters to describe herself in five words, ABC TV 30 Mar 87

SALLY FIELD

22 I can't deny the fact that you like me! You like me!
On winning an Oscar as best actress of 1984 for her role in *Places in the Heart*, quoted in *Newsweek* 8 Apr 85

ERROL FLYNN

23 I had now made about 45 pictures, but what had I become? I knew all too well: a phallic symbol. All over the world I was, as a name and personality, equated with sex.
My Wicked, Wicked Ways Putnam 59

AVA GARDNER

24 After my screen test, the director clapped his hands gleefully and yelled: "She can't talk! She can't act! She's sensational!"
On "crashing" Hollywood, news summaries 11 Dec 54

25 What's the point? My face, shall we say, looks lived in.
On not lying about her upcoming 65th birthday, *People* 10 Jun 85

JUDY GARLAND

26 I've never looked through a keyhole without finding someone was looking back.
On her lack of privacy, NBC TV 16 Mar 67

VITTORIO GASSMAN

1 A totally healthy actor is a paradox.
> Quoted in *Wall Street Journal* 2 Oct 84

2 In every real actor, there is a need to feel for a few hours like the center of the world. *Egocentrismo*, we say in Italian.
> *ib*

3 Acting is not that far from mental disease: An actor works on splitting his character into others. It is like a kind of schizophrenia.
> *ib*

LILLIAN GISH

4 Young man, if God had wanted you to see me that way, he would have put your eyes in your bellybutton.
> On a low camera angle, quoted by Richard Thomas on Amer Film Institute's *Salute to Lillian Gish* CBS TV 17 Apr 84

WHOOPI GOLDBERG

5 I told her her I would play a Venetian blind, dirt on the floor, anything.
> Letter to Alice Walker, author of *The Color Purple*, in which Goldberg eventually played a leading role, *Today* NBC TV 13 Jan 86

6 An actress can only play a woman. I'm an actor, I can play anything.
> *ib*

RUTH GORDON

7 Pan me, don't give me the part, publish everybody's book but this one and I will still make it!
> From her 1976 autobiography *My Side*, recalled on her death 28 Aug 85

8 Why? Because I believe I will. If you believe, then you hang on. If you believe, it means you've got imagination, you don't need stuff thrown out for you in a blueprint, you don't face facts—what can stop you?
> *ib*

9 If I don't make it today. I'll come in tomorrow.
> *ib*

CARY GRANT

10 We have our factory, which is called a stage. We make a product, we color it, we title it and we ship it out in cans.
> On the film industry as a form of merchandising, *Newsweek* 3 Jun 69

11 I pretended to be somebody I wanted to be until finally I became that person. Or he became me.
> On shaping his personality early in his career, *Parade* 22 Sep 85

CEDRIC HARDWICKE

12 I believe that God felt sorry for actors so he created Hollywood to give them a place in the sun and a swimming pool. The price they had to pay was to surrender their talent.
> *A Victorian in Orbit*, with James Brough, Doubleday 61

BARBARA HARRIS

13 The man with the navy-blue voice.
> On Alfred Hitchcock, London *Observer* 6 Aug 76

HELEN HAYES

14 I'm leaving the screen because I don't think I am very good in the pictures and I have this beautiful dream that I'm elegant on the stage.
> Statement on departing Hollywood in 1934, recalled on her 84th birthday, London *Times* 19 Dec 84

15 An actress always knows when she's hit it and mostly you haven't; but once or twice I think I hit it right, so maybe that's good enough for one life.
> *ib*

KATHARINE HEPBURN

16 It's a rather rude gesture, but at least it's clear what you mean.
> On spitting in the eye of director Joseph L Mankiewicz, quoted by Anne Edwards *A Remarkable Woman* Morrow 85

17 Living wasn't easy for you, was it? You couldn't enter your own life, but you could be someone else. You weren't you then; you were safe.
> To her late costar and friend Spencer Tracy on a televised tribute, quoted in *Newsweek* 17 Mar 86

BORIS KARLOFF

18 It grossed something like 12 million dollars and started a cycle of so-called boy-meets-ghoul horror films.
> On his role as Frankenstein, recalled on his death 2 Feb 69

DANNY KAYE

19 You bet I arrived overnight. Over a few hundred nights in the Catskills, in vaudeville, in clubs and on Broadway.
> On being an overnight film success in the 1940s, recalled on his death, Boston *Globe* 4 Mar 87

BERT LAHR

20 That was my one big Hollywood hit, but, in a way, it hurt my picture career. After that, I was typecast as a lion, and there just weren't many *parts* for lions.
> On his role in *The Wizard of Oz*, quoted in *New Yorker* 26 Jan 63

ELSA LANCHESTER

21 She looked as if butter wouldn't melt in her mouth—or anywhere else.
> On Maureen O'Hara, news summaries 30 Jan 50

SHIRLEY MacLAINE

22 I'd like to introduce someone who has just come into my life. I've admired him for 35 years. He's someone who represents integrity, honesty, art, and on top of that stuff I'm actually sleeping with him.
> Introducing a Broadway audience to Oscar, her award as best actress of 1983, *People* 7 May 84

RODDY McDOWALL

23 I really liked Lassie, but that horse, Flicka, was a nasty animal with a terrible disposition. All the Flickas—all six of them—were awful.
> On his roles as a child actor, Boston *Globe* 12 Feb 87

24 Intellectually I'd love to play Stanley Kowalski in *A Streetcar Named Desire* . . . Can't you just imagine me down in the streets yelling "Stella! Stella!" God, the critics would have a lot of fun with that one.
> *ib*

ROBERT MITCHUM

1 I never take any notice of reviews—unless a critic has thought up some new way of describing me. That old one about my lizard eyes and anteater nose and the way I sleep my way through pictures is so hackneyed now.

> NY *World-Telegram & Sun* 15 Aug 59

2 Every two or three years I knock off for a while. That way I'm constantly the new girl in the whorehouse.

> On maintaining his success in Hollywood, London *Observer* 18 Aug 68

MARILYN MONROE

3 The body is meant to be seen, not all covered up.

> Handwritten response to query about posing nude, which sold for $2,600 at auction in Boston, quoted in *International Herald Tribune* 5 Oct 84

4 Say good-bye to Pat, say good-bye to Jack and say good-bye to yourself, because you're a nice guy.

> Last words in 1962 to actor Peter Lawford, his wife Patricia and Patricia's brother President John F Kennedy, disclosed in the official report of Monroe's suicide released on September 23, 1985, quoted in *US News & World Report* 7 Oct 85

CLARENCE ("DUCKY") NASH

5 Words were written out for me phonetically. I learned to quack in French, Spanish, Portuguese, Japanese, Chinese and German.

> On his performance as the voice of Donald Duck in more than 150 cartoons and movies over 5 decades, recalled on his death 20 Feb 85

PAUL NEWMAN

6 I picture my epitaph: "Here lies Paul Newman, who died a failure because his eyes turned brown."

> Quoted by Maureen Dowd "Testing Himself" NY *Times* 28 Sep 86

7 I was always a character actor. I just looked like Little Red Riding Hood.

> *ib*

MARY PICKFORD

8 You would have thought I murdered someone, and perhaps I had, but only to give her successor a chance.

> On national furor when she bobbed her hair, recalled on her death 29 May 79

ROBERT PRESTON

9 There are lots of people in this country who can't shake off the idea that Pat O'Brien is a priest who has a parish in Pasadena and who coaches the Notre Dame football team on the side.

> On typecasting, NY *World-Telegram & Sun* 6 Feb 58

10 I'd get the best role in every B picture and the second best in the A pictures.

> On his career, recalled on his death, NY *Times* 23 Mar 87

11 I've done my best to avoid B pictures. Why should I go into them now and call it television?

> 1983 comment, *ib*

RONALD REAGAN

12 Sometimes those last few days seem like something I read in a book, but with your wire to cling to I get back to realization [*sic*] with a very satisfactory bump.

> Replying from Des Moines in 1937 to a telegram asking him to return to Hollywood to sign a contract with Warner Brothers, quoted in *Time* 17 June 85

13 I remain California-bound . . . I've got the telegram worn to a frazzle.

> *ib*

14 Kissing . . . in the old days was very beautiful. Actually the two people doing it were barely touching sometimes, in order to not push her face out of shape. You were doing it for the audience to see what in their minds they always think a kiss is. Now you see a couple of people start chewing on each other.

> Comparing films during his career with films of the 1980s, NBC TV 24 Mar 86

15 Today they show everything and do everything.

> *ib*

16 Someplace along the line the audience discovered you. In my case it was playing the Gipper.

> On his role as Notre Dame football hero George Gipp in the 1940 film *Knute Rockne—All American*, *ib*

17 No one goes Hollywood—they were that way before they came here. Hollywood just exposed it.

> *People* 9 Feb 87

ROBERT REDFORD

18 He has the attention span of a bolt of lightning.

> On Paul Newman, NY *Times* 28 Sep 86

19 I would go into life for a year. Go on the bum, so to speak.

> Advising Dartmouth film students to skip graduate school, Boston *Globe* 8 Feb 87

BURT REYNOLDS

20 You can only hold your stomach in for so many years.

> On retiring briefly from films, *Time* 9 Jan 78

MICKEY ROONEY

21 I was a 14-year-old boy for 30 years.

> On his film roles, quoted in NY *Journal-American* 15 Apr 58

22 It's confusing. I've had so many wives and so many children I don't know which house to go to first on Christmas.

> On his frequent marriages, quoted in NY *Post* 13 Nov 60

GEORGE SANDERS

23 I am leaving because I am bored.

> Suicide note 25 Apr 72

ROBERT STACK

24 These are icons to be treasured.

> Opposing colorization of black-and-white film classics such as *Casablanca*, NY *Times* 4 Nov 86

James Stewart

1 [It's well done] if you can do a part and not have the acting show.
On acting, WNET TV 13 Mar 87

Barbra Streisand

2 I was a personality before I became a person—I am simple, complex, generous, selfish, unattractive, beautiful, lazy and driven.
Interview with Barbara Walters ABC TV 13 Sep 85

Elizabeth Taylor

3 I have a woman's body and a child's emotions.
On her short-lived marriage at age 19 to Nicky Hilton, *Time* 4 Jan 51

4 Success is a great deodorant. It takes away all your past smells.
ABC TV 6 Apr 77

5 The Frank Sinatra of Shakespeare.
On Richard Burton, NY *Times* 6 Aug 84

Shirley Temple

6 When I was 14, I was the oldest I ever was. . . . I've been getting younger ever since.
Parade 7 Dec 86

Spencer Tracy

7 Know your lines and don't bump into the furniture.
Favorite advice to young actors, recalled on his death 10 Jun 67

8 Not much meat on her, but what's there is cherce.
Description of Katharine Hepburn, quoted by *People* 17 Mar 86

Lana Turner

9 I'm so gullible. I'm so damn gullible. And I am so *sick* of me being gullible.
On her seven marriages, *Life* 26 Sep 69

Johnny Weissmuller

10 How can a guy climb trees, say "Me, Tarzan, you, Jane," and make a million? The public forgives my acting because they know I was an athlete. They know I wasn't make-believe.
On his role as Tarzan in some 20 films between 1932 and 1949, recalled on his death 20 Jan 84

Orson Welles

11 Now I'm an old Christmas tree, the roots of which have died. *They* just come along and while the little needles fall off me replace them with medallions.
On receiving a special Academy Award in 1970, quoted by Barbara Leaming *Orson Welles* Viking 85

12 The word *genius* was whispered into my ear, the first thing I ever heard, while I was still mewling in my crib. So it never occurred to me that I wasn't until middle age.
Talking to biographer Barbara Leaming, quoted in *Wall Street Journal* 20 Sep 85

Oskar Werner

13 I'm married to the theater but my mistress is the films.
Vogue 1 Sep 65

Shelley Winters

14 He had a quality of sexual lightning.
On Montgomery Clift, NBC TV 19 Jun 80

Fay Wray

15 When I'm in New York I look at the Empire State Building and feel as though it belongs to me . . . or is it vice versa?
On her role in the 1933 film *King Kong*, NY *Times* 21 Sep 69

Writers, Producers & Directors

Michelangelo Antonioni

16 Hollywood is like being nowhere and talking to nobody about nothing.
London *Sunday Times* 20 Jun 71

Ingmar Bergman

17 I write scripts to serve as skeletons awaiting the flesh and sinew of images.
NY *Times* 22 Jan 78

Martin Brest

18 That the film turned out to be coherent is a miracle. That it is successful proves there is a God.
On directing *Beverly Hills Cop*, quoted in *Time* 7 Jan 85

James L Brooks

19 I spent two years telling studio heads that it wasn't a cancer picture. I hate cancer pictures. I don't want to see a cancer picture. There is only one thing worth saying about cancer, and that is that there are human beings in cancer wards.
On his production of *Terms of Endearment*, quoted in *Time* 23 Apr 84

Rita Mae Brown

20 You sell a screenplay like you sell a car. If someone drives it off a cliff, that's it.
Newsweek 19 Aug 85

Frank Capra

21 Do not help the quick moneymakers who have delusions about taking possession of classics by smearing them with paint.
1984 letter to Library of Congress on computer colorization of black-and-white films for television, quoted in NY *Times* 5 Aug 86

Leon Clore

22 If Americans didn't speak English, we'd have no problem.
On marketing British films in the US, NY *Times* 13 Jul 80

Jean Cocteau

23 A film is a petrified fountain of thought.
Quoted in *Esquire* Feb 61

Paul Del Rossi, President, Theater Division, General Cinema

24 People don't want to be umbilically connected to an electronic box.
On appeal of films shown in theaters rather than on television, NY *Times* 5 May 85

FILMS

CECIL B DE MILLE

1 Most of us serve our ideals by fits and starts. The person who makes a success of living is the one who sees his goal steadily and aims for it unswervingly. That is dedication.

> Introduction to Mary Pickford *Sunshine and Shadow* Doubleday 55

2 Creation is a drug I can't do without.

> NY *Times* 12 Aug 56

BARRY DILLER, Chairman, 20th Century-Fox

3 This is a world in which reasons are made up because reality is too painful.

> On the film industry, *Time* 3 Feb 86

WALT DISNEY

4 There is a natural hootchy-kootchy motion to a goldfish.

> On the fish ballet in *Fantasia*, quoted in *Profiles in America* Crowell 54

5 There's nothing funnier than the human animal.

> On changing from films with animals to films with people, news summaries 5 Dec 54

LESLIE DIXON

6 I noticed I had developed a fantasy about myself as a writer as opposed to actually doing it [so] I finally summoned up the bad taste to move to Los Angeles.

> On writing film scripts, NY *Times* 25 Jan 87

7 I attribute [success] to having the background of just loving the great stories of the world—and that's what makes the most successful films—combined with my trashy, vulgar appreciation of all that is modern Hollywood.

> *ib*

FEDERICO FELLINI

8 Even if I set out to make a film about a fillet of sole, it would be about me.

> On autobiographical nature of his films, *Atlantic* Dec 65

9 All art is autobiographical; the pearl is the oyster's autobiography.

> *ib*

10 Cinema is an old whore, like circus and variety, who knows how to give many kinds of pleasure. Besides, you can't teach old fleas new dogs.

> *ib*

TERRY GILLIAM

11 People in Hollywood are not showmen, they're maintenance men, pandering to what they think their audiences want.

> *Time* 3 Feb 86

EARL GLICK, Chairman, Hal Roach Studios

12 I could take 200 A-1 pictures, colorize them and turn them into solid gold.

> On computer colorization of black-and-white films for television, *Time* 8 Oct 84

SAMUEL GOLDWYN

13 A wide screen just makes a bad film twice as bad.

> *Quote* 9 Sep 56

14 The reason so many people turned up at his funeral is that they wanted to make sure he was dead.

> On producer Louis B Mayer, recalled on Goldwyn's death 31 Jan 74

15 Why only 12? Go out and get thousands.

> On restaging the Last Supper for one of his films, *ib*

16 Every director bites the hand that lays the golden egg.

> *ib*

17 Where they got lesbians, we'll use Albanians.

> When an associate questioned the taste of filming Radclyffe Hall's 1928 book *The Well of Loneliness, ib*

18 If people don't want to go to the picture, nobody can stop them.

> *ib*

19 Too caustic? To hell with the costs, we'll make the picture anyway.

> *ib*

JACK HANNAH

20 Mickey Mouse was the star in the early days, but he was too much of a Mr Nice Guy.

> On the creation of Donald Duck, *Wall Street Journal* 10 May 84

BEN HECHT

21 The honors Hollywood has for the writer are as dubious as tissue-paper cuff links.

> *Charlie* Harper 57

22 People's sex habits are as well known in Hollywood as their political opinions, and much less criticized.

> NY *Mirror* 24 Apr 59

ALFRED HITCHCOCK

23 I am a typed director. If I made *Cinderella*, the audience would immediately be looking for a body in the coach.

> *Newsweek* 11 Jun 56

24 Give them pleasure—the same pleasure they have when they wake up from a nightmare.

> On audiences, Asbury Park NJ *Press* 13 Aug 74

25 Self-plagiarism is style.

> Defending repetition of his filming techniques, London *Observer* 8 Aug 76

26 Blondes make the best victims. They're like virgin snow that shows up the bloody footprints.

> CBS TV 20 Feb 77

27 [This award is] meaningful because it comes from my fellow dealers in celluloid.

> On receiving Amer Film Institute's 1979 Lifetime Achievement Award, recalled on his death 29 Apr 80

JOHN HUSTON

28 The directing of a picture involves coming out of your individual loneliness and taking a controlling part in putting together a small world. A picture is made. You put a frame around it and move on. And one day you die. That is all there is to it.

> NY *Journal-American* 31 Mar 60

29 It's not color, it's like pouring 40 tablespoons of sugar water over a roast.

> On computer colorization of black-and-white films for television, to Directors Guild of America 13 Nov 86

NUNNALLY JOHNSON

1 She has no charm, delicacy or taste. She's just an arrogant little tail-twitcher who's learned to throw sex in your face.
>On Marilyn Monroe, quoted by John Robert Colombo *Popcorn in Paradise* Holt, Rinehart & Winston 80

RICHARD KAHN, Senior Vice President, Metro-Goldwyn-Mayer

2 Tarzan is direct; he doesn't ask Jane if they might have a meaningful relationship or if they can get together for lunch sometime.
>Arguing that audiences prefer simple solutions, *Wall Street Journal* 12 May 80

HERBERT T KALMUS

3 The only secret knowledge we have is know-how and you can't break up know-how by court order.
>Reply to a 1949 decree that Technicolor should not constitute a monopoly, recalled on his death, NY *Herald Tribune* 12 Jul 63

JOSEPH P KENNEDY

4 We must get into the picture business. This is a new industry and a gold mine. . . . it looks like another telephone industry.
>On his initial investment in motion pictures, quoted by Peter Collier and David Horowitz *The Kennedys* Summit 84

HERMAN J MANKIEWICZ

5 There, but for the grace of God, goes God.
>On Orson Welles, NY *Times* 11 Oct 85

JOSEPH L MANKIEWICZ

6 I've been in on the beginning, the rise, peak, collapse and end of the talking picture.
>*Washington Post* 1 Jun 86

7 And Kate Hepburn—God, she's beautiful, God, she plays golf well, God, she can get anyone in the world on the phone, God, she knows what to do all the time, God, she wears clothes well.
>*ib*

VINCENTE MINNELLI

8 I work to please myself. I'm still not sure if movies are an art form. And if they're not, then let them inscribe on my tombstone what they could about any craftsman who loves his job: "Here lies Vincente Minnelli. He died of hard work."
>Recalled on his death 25 Jul 86

DOROTHY PARKER

9 Hollywood money isn't money. It's congealed snow.
>On writing film scripts, *Paris Review* Summer 56

SAM PECKINPAH

10 I'm a student of violence because I'm a student of the human heart.
>Defending the violence in his films, *Newsweek* 7 Jan 85

S J PERELMAN

11 A dreary industrial town controlled by hoodlums of enormous wealth, the ethical sense of a pack of jackals and taste so degraded that it befouled everything it touched.
>On Hollywood, *Paris Review* Spring 64

12 There were times, when I drove along the Sunset Strip and looked at those buildings or when I watched the fashionable film colony arriving at some première . . . that I fully expected God in his wrath to obliterate the whole shebang.
>*ib*

ROMAN POLANSKI

13 It's easy to direct while acting—there's one less person to argue with.
>NY *Times* 22 Feb 76

JEAN RENOIR

14 I am interested in what happens to people when they must adapt to a new world.
>On his approach to filming, recalled on his death, *Time* 26 Feb 79

LENI RIEFENSTAHL

15 They killed me then. I am a ghost.
>Recalling at age 83 her 1936 film *The Olympic Games*, which identified her with Hitler and the Nazi Party, quoted by Frank Deford "The Ghost of Berlin" *Sports Illustrated* 4 Aug 86

ELDAR RYAZANOV

16 Even if you don't like your mother, she's still your mother.
>On popularity of Soviet films in new immigrant communities in the US, NY *Times* 20 Sep 85

MACK SENNETT

17 We never make sport of religion, politics, race or mothers. A mother never gets hit with a custard pie. Mothers-in-law—yes. But mothers—never.
>On slapstick comedy, NY *Times* 6 Nov 60

STEVEN SPIELBERG

18 I dream for a living.
>*Time* 15 Jul 85

ANDREI TARKOVSKY, Soviet director

19 Juxtaposing a person with an environment that is boundless, collating him with a countless number of people passing by close to him and far away, relating a person to the whole world, that is the meaning of cinema.
>*Sculpting in Time* Bodley Head 86

FRANÇOIS TRUFFAUT

20 An actor is never so great as when he reminds you of an animal—falling like a cat, lying like a dog, moving like a fox.
>*New Yorker* 20 Feb 60

JACK VALENTI, President, Motion Picture Association of America

21 I don't know any other business that tells you not to go in and buy their product.
>On the rating of films, NY *Times* 5 May 85

22 I don't care if you call it AO for Adults Only, or Chopped Liver or Father Goose. Your movie will still have the stigma of being in a category that's going to be inhabited by the very worst of pictures.
>On changing the X rating to an A for Adults, *ib* 5 Mar 87

JACK WARNER

1 I have a theory of relatives, too. Don't hire 'em.

> During a 1930s studio visit by Albert Einstein, quoted by Stephen Farber and Marc Green *Hollywood Dynasties* Delilah Books 84

2 You were very good playing a bitch-heroine, but you shouldn't win an award for playing yourself.

> To Bette Davis after she failed to win an Oscar as best actress for her 1935 portrayal of the Cockney waitress Mildred in *Of Human Bondage*, recalled in four-page advertisement "Reflections by Miss Bette Davis" *Time* 9 Apr 84

BILLY WILDER

3 Hollywood didn't kill Marilyn Monroe, it's the Marilyn Monroes who are killing Hollywood.

> Quoted in Nat Shapiro ed *Whatever It Is, I'm Against It* Simon & Schuster 84

4 Marilyn was mean. Terribly mean. The meanest woman I have ever met around this town. I have never met anybody as mean as Marilyn Monroe or as utterly fabulous on the screen.

> *ib*

FRANCO ZEFFIRELLI

5 I am a sultan in a harem of three women: Opera, Theater and Film!

> *Zeffirelli: An Autobiography* Weidenfeld & Nicolson 86

Observers & Critics

JAMES AGEE

6 He used this great, sad, motionless face to suggest various related things: a one-track mind near the track's end of pure insanity; mulish imperturbability under the wildest of circumstances; how dead a human being can get and still be alive; an awe-inspiring sort of patience and power to endure, proper to granite but uncanny in flesh and blood.

> On deadpan comedian Buster Keaton, "Comedy's Greatest Era" reprinted in *Life* Fall 86

7 When he ran from a cop his transitions from accelerating walk to easy jog trot to brisk canter to headlong gallop to flogged-piston sprint . . . were as distinct and as soberly in order as an automatic gearshift.

> *ib*

CECELIA AGER

8 Miss Hepburn's voice was lilting along as before: She is oblivious of her impact. Or inured to it. Or stuck with it.

> On Katharine Hepburn, NY *Times* 18 Jun 67

ANONYMOUS

9 What is Cannes? It is 10,000 people looking for the 10 people who really count . . . The 10,000 storm around trying to see the 10. They boast if they have seen them, keep it a secret if they haven't and try to give the impression that they know where they are, even if they don't.

> French publicity expert on Cannes Film Festival, quoted by Richard Bernstein "Cannes Starwatch" NY *Times* 17 May 86

DAVID ANSEN

10 Newman, with his clipped mustache and his whiskey-coated growl and his steely self-assurance, is an aristocrat of sleaze.

> On Paul Newman in *The Color of Money, Newsweek* 13 Oct 86

11 He has the body-fat content of a 20-year-old sprinter, the bone structure of a public monument and the eyes . . . well, we know about the blue eyes (which happen to be colorblind).

> *ib*

12 The world has lost its quintessential romantic icon.

> On death of Cary Grant, *ib* 8 Dec 86

SCOTT ARMSTRONG

13 The home of furs and Ferraris, glitter and glamour, the place where movie stars can be spotted in palm-fringed cafés and where limousines are as frequent as *Rocky* sequels.

> On idealized concept of Hollywood, *Christian Science Monitor* 19 May 86

CECIL BEATON

14 I can't afford a whole new set of enemies.

> When asked why he didn't go into films, quoted by Hugo Vickers *Cecil Beaton* Little, Brown 85

PAUL V BECKLEY

15 *The Entertainer* . . . has set itself to scratching the dandruff out of the mane of life.

> NY *Herald Tribune* 4 Oct 60

ROBERT BRUSTEIN

16 Olivier's idea of introspection was to hood his eyes, dentalize his consonants and let the camera circle his blondined head like a sparrow looking for a place to deposit its droppings.

> On Laurence Olivier as Hamlet in a 1948 film, *New Republic* 3 Nov 86

17 The invention of film has given our generation the dubious advantage of watching our acting heroes deteriorate before our eyes.

> *ib*

VINCENT CANBY

18 She was . . . a woman attempting to make some sense of, and get some satisfaction from, a life that seemed to have no more logic than a roulette wheel.

> On Jean Seberg, who committed suicide in Paris at the age of 40, NY *Times* 23 Sep 79

19 Through the magic of motion pictures, someone who's never left Peoria knows the softness of a Paris spring, the color of a Nile sunset, the sorts of vegetation one will find along the upper Amazon and that Big Ben has not yet gone digital.

> "A Reminder of Innocence Lost" *ib* 18 May 80

20 All of us knew the brownstone stoops in a Warner Brothers movie as well as we knew our own front porches.

> *ib*

21 [His acting] remains forever fixed in a time that never dates.

> On Cary Grant, *ib* 1 Dec 86

1 [It is] guaranteed to put all teeth on edge, including George Washington's, wherever they might be.
> On film production of Helene Hanff's *84 Charing Cross Road*, *ib* 13 Feb 87

2 [She] may be the only leading lady in America today with the ability to cross one eye without moving the other.
> On Anne Bancroft, *ib*

3 [It is] a movie of such unrelieved genteelness that it makes one long to head for Schrafft's for a double-gin martini, straight up, and a stack of cinnamon toast from which the crusts have been removed.
> *ib*

4 We attend to his later performances as a dramatic actor with respect, but watching the nondancing, nonsinging Astaire is like watching a grounded skylark.
> On Fred Astaire, *ib* 23 Jun 87

CHARLES CHAMPLIN

5 The wrong man at the studio saw the test and hired him. The right man had rejected him, but was fired before it made any difference.
> On Robert Preston's debut in films, Boston *Globe* 23 Mar 87

JEAN COCTEAU

6 He has the manner of a giant with the look of a child, a lazy activeness, a mad wisdom, a solitude encompassing the world.
> On Orson Welles, quoted in NY *Times* 11 Oct 85

ALISTAIR COOKE

7 Hollywood grew to be the most flourishing factory of popular mythology since the Greeks.
> *America* Knopf 73

RICHARD CORLISS

8 Hollywood was born schizophrenic. For 75 years it has been both a town and a state of mind, an industry and an art form.
> "Backing into the Future" *Time* 3 Feb 86

9 Today . . . is a time of turbulence and stagnation, of threat and promise from a competitor: the magic, omnivorous videocassette recorder (VCR). In other words, it is business as usual.
> *ib*

BOSLEY CROWTHER

10 Believe it or not, it is a picture about two young people romantically in love—in love with each other, that is, not with a tractor or the Soviet state . . . the Russians have finally found romance.
> On *The Cranes Are Flying*, NY *Times* 27 Mar 60

FRANK DEFORD

11 She glances at the photo, and the pilot light of memory flickers in her eyes.
> On Leni Riefenstahl, whose films of the 1930s tragically identified her with Hitler's Nazi Germany, "The Ghost of Berlin" *Sports Illustrated* 4 Aug 86

ALICE DEMORÉE

12 Mediocrity shuffles after banality in an unending process.
> On the French cinema, BBC Radio 20 Aug 68

DAVID DENBY

13 The action comes at us through a buzz of nattering remarks.
> On the film *Heartburn*, New York 4 Aug 86

14 Trivial details have been summoned, in part, to make a satirical point about upper-middle-class marriage—that the whole thing can slip away between the white wine and the arugula salad.
> *ib*

MAUREEN DOWD

15 He exists in the public mind as bits and pieces of his characters—Butch Cassidy's charm, Ben Quick's machismo, Cool Hand Luke's defiance, Harper's irony, Hud's disdain.
> On Paul Newman, "Testing Himself" NY *Times* 28 Sep 86

ANNE EDWARDS

16 She . . . claimed she loved the camera, its warmth, its familiarity. She responded to its naked glare, its slavish attention to every expression of her face and body, with the kind of immediacy a trusted lover could expect.
> On Katharine Hepburn's early years in Hollywood, *A Remarkable Woman* Morrow 85

DAVID ELLIOTT

17 It's time to put out an All Points Bulletin on Sylvester Stallone. Not for artistic crimes . . . but for so grossly abusing his license to pander.
> On *Over the Top*, San Diego *Union* 17 Feb 87

PETER B FLINT

18 [He] intuitively choreographed his motions with a body language that projected the image of an eager, bouncy terrier. His walk was jaunty and his manner defiant.
> On James Cagney, NY *Times* 31 Mar 86

PAUL GARDNER

19 Her eyebrows are clipped parentheses, and she paints her face for the last days of the Weimar Republic. Frizzy orange curls grow in her wild hair like snapdragons pleading for water.
> On Hollywood debut of Bette Midler, "The Divine Miss M" NY *Times* 29 Dec 72

DIANA GEDDES

20 With her unmistakable pout and jutting breasts . . . Brigitte Bardot was more than just a goddess. For a war-weary generation she came to personify a new, liberated, sun-soaked, carefree France.
> "Bardot at 50" London *Times* 28 Sep 84

WOLCOTT GIBBS

21 It is my indignant opinion that 90 percent of the moving pictures exhibited in America are so vulgar, witless and dull that it is preposterous to write about them in any publication not intended to be read while chewing gum.
> Quoted by John Robert Colombo *Popcorn in Paradise* Holt, Rinehart & Winston 80

SHEILAH GRAHAM

22 No one has a closest friend in Hollywood.
> *The Rest of the Story* Coward-McCann 64

LEWIS GROSSBERGER

1 That great menacing Easter Island face.

On Lee Marvin, "The Ultimate Drinking Buddy" *New York* 25 Aug 80

CHARLIE HAAS

2 From the German verb *tinzelle*—literally, "to book a turkey into 1,200 theaters and make one's money before word of mouth hits."

On Hollywood's nickname Tinseltown, *People* 9 Feb 87

LEARNED HAND

3 A self-made man may prefer a self-made name.

Granting court permission for Samuel Goldfish to change his name to Samuel Goldwyn, quoted by Bosley Crowther *The Lion's Share* Dutton 57

MOLLY HASKELL

4 *La Cage aux Folles* [is] a square love story in titillating drag that has become the *Charley's Aunt* of the 1980s.

On the original French film, "In Each Other's Clothing" NY *Times* 31 Mar 85

C DAVID HEYMANN

5 In the 1930s . . . people went [to see films] not just to be entertained or to escape the dreariness of their workaday lives but to gain an education, to see the world, to learn table manners and interior decoration, how to dress, kiss, to laugh and cry, how to react to tragedy and happiness, how to be brave, evil and good.

Poor Little Rich Girl Lyle Stuart 84

6 Hollywood was a silver-nitrate finishing school for a whole generation . . . with a faculty that included Lillian Gish, Douglas Fairbanks, Mary Pickford, John Gilbert, Pola Negri, Gloria Swanson, Clara Bow, Lon Chaney, Charlie Chaplin and Rudolf Valentino.

ib

JOY HOROWITZ

7 One is a young, pockmarked wiseacre with a smirk that won't quit, the other an aging but still gorgeous leading man with a sense of humor that won't start.

On Bill Murray and Robert Redford, "From Slapstick to Yuppie Fantasy" NY *Times* 15 Jun 86

CLIVE JAMES

8 As far as talent goes, Marilyn Monroe was so minimally gifted as to be almost unemployable, and anyone who holds to the opinion that she was a great natural comic identifies himself immediately as a dunce.

Commentary Oct 73

9 She was good at playing abstract confusion in the same way that a midget is good at being short.

On Marilyn Monroe, PBS TV 18 Jan 79

ERICA JONG

10 My reaction to porno films is as follows: After the first 10 minutes I want to go home and screw. After the first 20 minutes, I never want to screw again as long as I live.

Quoted by Norman Corwin *Trivializing America* Lyle Stuart 83

PAULINE KAEL

11 *Citizen Kane* is perhaps the one American talking picture that seems as fresh now as the day it opened. It may seem even fresher.

"Raising Kane" in *The Citizen Kane Book* Bantam 71

12 This movie is a toupee made up to look like honest baldness.

On *Nothing in Common, New Yorker* 8 Sep 86

ANNA KISSELGOFF

13 *Top Hat* and *Swing Time*, the quintessential [Fred] Astaire films, define his special contribution: Mr Astaire never lost sight of the fact that he was dancing on film.

NY *Times* 28 Jun 87

FLETCHER KNEBEL

14 Hollywood, to hear some writers tell it, is the place where they take an author's steak tartare and make cheeseburger out of it. . . . Upon seeing the film, they say, the author promptly cuts his throat, bleeding to death in a pool of money.

On how *Seven Days in May*, a novel he coauthored, was made into a motion picture, *Look* 19 Nov 63

JACK KROLL

15 Wrap up the 20th century; Fred Astaire is gone.

On death of Fred Astaire, *Newsweek* 6 Jul 87

16 He was one of those inexplicable gifts of nature, an artist who leaps over boundaries, changes our nervous systems, creates a new language, transmits new kinds of joy to our startled senses and spirits.

ib

17 Did any artist ever bring more pure joy to more people than Fred Astaire?

ib

RICHARD LACAYO

18 He was the embodiment of big-city scrappiness, a mean-streets survivor who got ahead on a good grin, good moves and better hustle.

On James Cagney, *Time* 14 Apr 86

HELEN LAWRENSON

19 These are the beautiful people, who, befitting their rank as gods and goddesses of a powerful modern mythology, lead beautiful lives in beautiful houses, attired in beautiful clothes and, ostensibly, thinking only beautiful thoughts.

"Star Gazing" *Esquire* Apr 57

OSCAR LEVANT

20 Strip away the phony tinsel of Hollywood and you'll find the real tinsel underneath.

Quoted in Nat Shapiro ed *Whatever It Is, I'm Against It* Simon & Schuster 84

DWIGHT MACDONALD

21 Charlton Heston throws all his punches in the first 10 minutes (3 grimaces and 2 intonations) so that he has nothing left long before he stumbles to the end, 4 hours later, and has to react to the Crucifixion. (He does make it clear, I must admit, that he quite disapproves of it.)

On *Ben Hur*, quoted in *Esquire's World of Humor* 64

MELVIN MADDOCKS

1 Cary Grant, born Archie Leach, was a poor boy who could barely spell *posh*. That's acting for you—or maybe Hollywood.
> *Christian Science Monitor* 3 Dec 86

JOSÉ MALDONADO

2 I've been beating up people for two years.
> On his job as an usher in a kung-fu movie theater in Manhattan's Times Square, NY *Times* 12 May 84

WILLIAM MANCHESTER

3 Actors who have tried to play Churchill and MacArthur have failed abysmally because each of those men was a great actor playing himself.
> *Book-of-the-Month Club News* Jun 83

MARGRETHE II, Queen of Denmark

4 [He is] the Pied Piper to the children of the world.
> On knighting Danny Kaye in 1983, recalled on his death, *US News & World Report* 16 Mar 87

EDWARD MARSH

5 How I dislike "Technicolor," which suffuses everything with stale mustard.
> *Ambrosia and Small Beer* Harcourt, Brace & Winston 65

SOMERSET MAUGHAM

6 In Hollywood, the women are all peaches. It makes one long for an apple occasionally.
> *Diners Club Magazine* Aug 64

MARGARET MITCHELL

7 [The house Rhett Butler built for Scarlett] could have been in Omaha so little does it resemble any dwelling in the Atlanta of the Reconstruction period.
> On film set for *Gone With the Wind*, quoted by Anne Edwards *The Road to Tara* Ticknor & Fields 83

NEW YORKER

8 Newman delivered his lines with the emotional fervor of a [railroad] conductor announcing local stops.
> 1954 review of Paul Newman's first film role as a Roman slave in *The Silver Chalice*, recalled by Newman in NY *Times* 28 Sep 86

NEW YORK TIMES

9 Cary Grant was not supposed to die. [He] was supposed to stick around, our perpetual touchstone of charm and elegance and romance and youth.
> Editorial 2 Dec 86

FREDERIC RAPHAEL

10 Hollywood was not a geographic location; it was a Fate Worse Than The *Reader's Digest*.
> On how young writers felt about writing screenplays, "A Writer Stalks the Hollywood Myth" NY *Times* 6 Jan 85

11 We all knew that unspeakable things happened to talent once it had crossed the Rockies. . . . The Warner Brothers' commissary, and similar places where they eat writers along with the caesar salad.
> *ib*

12 Strangely enough, the one universal myth of America—Show Business—flowered in a desert where a bunch of barely educated immigrants hoped to find the right conditions for shooting cheap movies and respite from the owners of the patents for film equipment whom they were ripping off.
> *ib*

13 During the years when the barely educated immigrants were being replaced by barely educated native sons, Hollywood . . . proved a more reliable, cost-effective means of securing world domination than any nuclear arsenal or diplomatic démarche.
> *ib*

14 It is, as they say, no accident that America's most popular president . . . emerged not from the legislators but from the star system.
> *ib*

15 Cheekbones scorched with this year's style in war paint, tears in their eyes and dears on their lips . . . they are often glowing with the effusive sentimentality to be found only among those who have stolen each other's ideas, deals and live-in companions.
> On Hollywood natives, *ib*

HARRY REASONER

16 Bond smoked like Peter Lorre, drank like Humphrey Bogart, ate like Sydney Greenstreet, used up girls like Errol Flynn . . . then went to a steam bath and came out looking like Clark Gable.
> On Ian Fleming's character James Bond in numerous films, NY *Journal-American* 13 Aug 64

17 The Legionnaire is Gary Cooper and Ray Milland, with just a touch of Brian Donlevy.
> On Hollywood's image of the French Foreign Legion, *60 Minutes* CBS TV 24 Aug 86

REX REED

18 It's hate at first sight.
> On Goldie Hawn's role as a football coach in *Wildcats*, Palm Beach *Daily News* 6 Apr 86

19 I don't think she ever remembered giving me the interview, but she sure remembered reading it.
> On May 1967 *Esquire* profile of Ava Gardner, quoted in *US* 19 May 86

MORT SAHL

20 I made the mistake early in my career, when I moved to Hollywood, of being attracted to actresses. I used to go out exclusively with actresses and all other female impersonators.
> *Heartland* Harcourt Brace Jovanovich 76

RICHARD SCHICKEL

21 He was the first to conceive of movies as . . . an art form. . . . His belief was that if the traditional art form would not find room for him, then he would make an art form of his own.
> *D W Griffith: An American Life* Simon & Schuster 84

22 A great novel is concerned primarily with the interior lives of its characters as they respond to the inconvenient narratives that fate imposes on them. Movie adaptations of these monumental fictions often fail because they become mere exercises in interior decoration.
> "The Adaptation as Antique Show" *Time* 15 Oct 84

1 This is a soul under perpetual migraine attack.
>On Vanessa Redgrave as Olive in *The Bostonians, ib*

GENE SHALIT

2 Some films could only have been cast in one way: Screen tests were given and the losers got the parts.
>NBC TV 18 May 71

IRWIN SHAW

3 On the terrace for two in springtime France, all the world was printed on sprocketed strips of acetate that passed through a projector at the rate of 90 feet per minute, and hope and despair and beauty and death were carried around the city in flat, round, shining cans.
>On Cannes Film Festival, *Evening in Byzantium* Delacorte 73

CLANCY SIGAL

4 Too many freeways, too much sun, too much abnormality taken normally, too many pink stucco houses and pink stucco consciences.
>On Hollywood, *Going Away* Houghton Mifflin 62

JOHN SIMON

5 The only real talent Miss Day possesses is that of being absolutely sanitary: her personality untouched by human emotions, her brow unclouded by human thought, her form unsmudged by the slightest form of femininity.
>On Doris Day, *Private Screenings* Macmillan 67

6 Miss Garland's figure resembles the giant-economy-size tube of toothpaste in girls' bathrooms: Squeezed intemperately at all points, it acquires a shape that defies definition by the most resourceful solid geometrician.
>On Judy Garland, *ib*

7 Sandy Dennis has balanced her postnasal condition with something like prefrontal lobotomy, so that when she is not a walking catarrh she is a blithering imbecile.
>On *The Fox*, news summaries 31 Mar 68

SIDNEY SKOLSKY

8 She was "discovered" for movies in the drugstore, sitting at the soda fountain. Thousands of girls have since sat at drugstore fountains drinking sodas and waiting to be discovered. They only got fat from the sodas.
>On Lana Turner, NY *Post* 12 Jan 58

KEVIN STARR

9 A city where everyone seemed to live in a bungalow on a broad avenue lined with palm, pepper or eucalyptus trees, where there was never any snow.
>On Mack Sennett's shaping of the public image of the West Coast by using Los Angeles backgrounds for early Keystone comedies, *Inventing the Dream: California through the Progressive Era* Oxford 85

WALLACE STEGNER

10 In an incredibly short time, Hollywood and the Sunset Strip were a fixed part of the world's consciousness, and the life of the stars, glamorous, public, exotic, full of romantic excess and as riddled with delightful scandal as it was crowded with role models, had invaded the consciousness of dreaming shop girls all around the globe.
>NY *Times* 24 Feb 85

GLORIA STEINEM

11 I'd like to be played as a child by Natalie Wood. I'd have some romantic scenes as Audrey Hepburn and have gritty black-and-white scenes as Patricia Neal.
>On casting a film about her life, *US* 3 Nov 86

IGOR STRAVINSKY

12 Film music should have the same relationship to the film drama that somebody's piano playing in my living room has on the book I am reading.
>Recalled on his death 6 Apr 71

TIME MAGAZINE

13 A British comedienne whose appearance suggests an overstuffed electric chair.
>On Margaret Rutherford in *Murder, She Says*, 2 Feb 62

14 Her writhing stare could reduce a rabid dog to foaming jelly.
>On Margaret Rutherford in *Mrs John Bull, Ltd*, 24 May 63

KENNETH TYNAN

15 What, when drunk, one sees in other women, one sees in Garbo sober.
>Recalled on his death 26 Jul 80

16 The vengeful hag is played by Ingrid Bergman, which is like casting Eleanor Roosevelt as Lizzie Borden.
>On *The Visit, ib*

17 Pearl is a disease of oysters. Levant is a disease of Hollywood.
>On Oscar Levant, quoted in news summaries 31 Dec 84

JOHN UPDIKE

18 The artistic triumph of American Jewry lay, he thought, not in the novels of the 1950s but in the movies of the 1930s, those gargantuan, crass contraptions whereby Jewish brains projected Gentile stars upon a Gentile nation and out of their own immigrant joy gave a formless land dreams and even a kind of conscience.
>*Bech: A Book* Knopf 70

19 It was one of history's great love stories, the mutually profitable romance which Hollywood and bohunk America conducted almost in the dark, a tapping of fervent messages through the wall of the San Gabriel Range.
>*ib*

HARRIET VAN HORNE

20 Closing these two books, a reader senses that Joan Crawford, idol of an age, would have made an exemplary prison matron, possibly at Buchenwald. She had the requisite sadism, paranoia and taste for violence.
>On books about Joan Crawford by the actress's adopted daughter Christina Crawford and Hollywood columnist Bob Thomas, NY *Post* 29 Oct 78

GORE VIDAL

1 Miss Georgia and Mr Shaker Heights.
> On Joanne Woodward and Paul Newman, quoted in NY
> *Times* 28 Sep 86

DWIGHT WHITNEY

2 [She was] dressed in a peignoir of beige lace . . .
with a blonde wig above false eyelashes—a kind of
Mt Rushmore of the cosmetician's art.
> On interviewing Mae West, *TV Guide* 28 Feb 65

FOOD & DRINK

Chefs & Restaurateurs

JEAN MARIE AMAT, chef, St James restaurant, Bordeaux,
France

3 Try to cook so that it will surprise a little, agree-
ably . . . and astonish slightly, without shocking.
> *Time* 19 Dec 77

JAMES BEARD

4 I believe that if ever I had to practice cannibalism,
I might manage if there were enough tarragon
around.
> Recalled on his death 23 Jan 85

5 I don't like gourmet cooking or "this" cooking or
"that" cooking. I like *good* cooking.
> Quoted in *Newsweek* 4 Feb 85

VICTOR J ("TRADER VIC") BERGERON

6 The real, native South Seas food is lousy. You can't
eat it.
> *Newsweek* 21 Apr 58

LYNNE BIEN, co-owner, Pie in the Sky restaurant, NYC

7 People are getting tired of going out to expensive
restaurants and spending lots of money for seven
pea pods and a two-inch steak.
> NY *Times* 3 Oct 84

8 Oh, that curdles my soul.
> On adding mace and nutmeg to a recipe for apple pie,
> *ib* 24 Sep 86

ALICE MAY BROCK

9 Tomatoes and oregano make it Italian; wine and tarragon make it French. Sour cream makes it Russian;
lemon and cinnamon make it Greek. Soy sauce
makes it Chinese; garlic makes it good.
> *Alice's Restaurant Cookbook* Random House 69

GIULIANO BUGIALLI

10 There are only two questions to ask about food. Is
it good? And is it authentic? We are open [to] new
ideas, but not if it means destroying our history. And
food is history.
> NY *Times* 9 May 84

ROBERT FARRAR CAPON, priest-chef

11 Give us this day our daily taste. Restore to us soups
that spoons will not sink in and sauces which are
never the same twice. Raise up among us stews with
more gravy than we have bread to blot it with . . .
Give us pasta with a hundred fillings.
> *People* 13 Oct 75

12 Older women are like aging strudels—the crust may
not be so lovely, but the filling has come at last into
its own.
> *ib*

13 At the root of many a woman's failure to become a
great cook lies her failure to develop a workmanlike
regard for knives.
> News summaries 31 Dec 76

JULIA CHILD

14 Nobody thinks it's silly to invest two hours' work in
two minutes' enjoyment; but if cooking is evanes-
cent, well, so is the ballet.
> NBC TV 1 Dec 66

15 In department stores, so much kitchen equipment is
bought indiscriminately by people who just come in
for men's underwear.
> *ib* 12 Dec 73

16 Life itself is the proper binge.
> *Time* 7 Jan 80

17 I was 32 when I started cooking; up until then, I just
ate.
> Quoted by Lynn Gilbert and Gaylen Moore *Particular*
> *Passions* Crown 81

18 I wouldn't keep him around long if I didn't feed him
well.
> When asked if her husband liked her cooking, NBC TV
> 18 Nov 85

19 In France, cooking is a serious art form and a national sport.
> NY *Times* 26 Nov 86

ALEXANDRE DUMAINE

20 The French peasant cuisine is at the basis of the
culinary art. By this I mean it is composed of honest
elements that *la grande cuisine* only embellishes.
> Recalled on his death 23 Apr 74

PHILIPPE GAERTNER, chef, Aux Armes de France
restaurant, Ammerschwihr, France

21 I'm taking only my toque blanche and my savoir-
faire.
> Comment on his departure for NYC as one of the 22
> French chefs chosen to cook during Statue of Liberty's
> centennial celebration, NY *Times* 14 May 86

OSCAR GIZELT, food and beverage manager, Delmonico's
restaurant, NYC

22 Fish should smell like the tide. Once they smell like
fish, it's too late.
> *Vogue* 15 Apr 64

OTTO GOEBEL, chef to Saudi Arabian royal family

23 We had too much camel in the fridge, so I tried some
ways to preserve it.
> To Le Club des Chefs des Chefs, NY *Times* 29 Aug 86

STANLEY KRAMER, chef, Grand Central Terminal's Oyster
Bar restaurant, NYC

24 George knows everything about every fish that
comes in here—where they came from, what they
were doing before they were caught, who their
mothers and fathers were.
> On assistant manager George Morfogen, in charge of
> purchasing $24,000 worth of fresh seafood a week, *Man-*
> *hattan Inc* Sep 84

WARNER LEROY, founder, Maxwell's Plum restaurant, NYC

1 A restaurant is a fantasy—a kind of living fantasy in which diners are the most important members of the cast.
NY *Times* 9 Jul 76

ERNEST MATTHEW MICKLER

2 Simmer til you can't stand it any more, then take it off the fire and dive in.
White Trash Cooking Jargon Society 86, quoted by Edwin McDowell NY *Times* 22 Sep 86

JEFF SMITH, minister-chef

3 Please understand the reason why Chinese vegetables taste so good. It is simple. The Chinese do not cook them, they just threaten them!
The Frugal Gourmet Cooks with Wine Morrow 86

4 I prefer the Chinese method of eating. . . . You can do anything at the table except arm wrestle.
Boston *Globe* 11 Jan 87

5 I don't go for the nouvelle approach—serving a rabbit rump with coffee extract sauce and a slice of kiwi fruit.
ib

6 The way I feel about it is: Beat me or feed me, but don't tease me. It's toy food; who needs it? Serve it to toy people.
ib

ANDRÉ SOLTNER, chef and proprietor, Lutèce restaurant, NYC

7 When you find a waiter who is a waiter and not an actor, writer, musician or poet, you've found a jewel.
Food & Wine Nov 84

RENÉ VEAUX, chef, Lasserre restaurant, Paris

8 One person cooking at home cannot pay attention to too many things. If a woman makes three dishes, she will get nervous on the first, the second will suffer and the third will be a disaster.
Quoted by Michael Demarest "Tips from the Toques" *Time* 19 Dec 77

9 A few years ago it was considered chic to serve Beef Wellington; fortunately, like Napoleon, it met its Waterloo.
On fads in cooking, *ib*

10 The feminist movement has helped open minds and kitchens to the notion that men can be at home on the range.
ib

ROGER VIARD

11 I started at 18 as a "young *commis*." I wore the traditional white apron then. I graduated to *chef de rang* (tails and white tie), *maître d'hôtel* (tails and black tie), then *assistant-directeur* (dinner jacket) and finally *directeur* (plain business suit—gray at midday, blue at night).
On his sartorial and gastronomical career during 47 years at Maxim's restaurant in Paris, *International Herald Tribune* 8 Jan 85

DONALD BRUCE WHITE

12 Catering is the cottage industry of New York. All a caterer needs is a Cuisinart, some pots and pans and a couple of food magazines to start out. They get jobs, though they don't necessarily get repeats.
NY *Times* 28 Nov 84

ANTONY WORRALL-THOMPSON, co-owner, Ménage à Trois restaurant, NYC

13 There are always minor hiccups along the line.
Acknowledging desirability of reduced prices during the first few weeks a new restaurant is in business, quoted by Marian Burros "Practical Prices for Practice Food" NY *Times* 27 Sep 86

Manufacturers, Merchants & Promoters

SAM AARON, owner, Sherry-Lehmann Wines and Spirits

14 What Freud was to psychoanalysis, I was to wine.
Quoted in "Wine Wars" *Manhattan Inc* Jul 85

GEORGES AUER

15 Suppose we had tried selective breeding of frogs and found we were developing the head instead of the legs? But a snail is just a walking intestine.
On why he and his partners chose to go into the snail-farming business, *Fortune* 7 Apr 80

BARRY BENEPE, Director, Greenmarkets

16 Bread and wine and thou—it's all there.
On selling wine at farmers' markets, NY *Times* 27 Sep 84

BRUCE R BYE, Director of Brand Management, Durkee Famous Foods

17 You can tell how long a couple has been married by whether they are on their first, second or third bottle of Tabasco.
On average shelf life of a hot sauce measured out in dashes and drops, NY *Times* 29 Jun 86

TERRENCE CONWAY, President, John T Handy Co

18 The best thing is not to do anything interesting.
Suggesting sautéing soft-shell crabs in clarified butter, *Christian Science Monitor* 8 May 85

JOSEPH DARGENT, French vintner

19 No government could survive without champagne. . . . In the throat of our diplomatic people [it] is like oil in the wheels of an engine.
NY *Herald Tribune* 21 Jul 55

BILL DEMMOND, Vice President, Inland Seafood Corp

20 If it swims, it's edible.
Time 18 Feb 85

FORTNUM & MASON, LONDON

21 It might have been Fortanon. It could have been Fortyahan. It hovered for years between Fortnam and Fortnane. It wasn't until 1707 that it settled down into Fortnum, collected its Mason and became the sweetest sound in the English language for those countless perceptive thousands who know that life can be sustained by bread and water, but it is given a sharp, upward boost by the more imaginative combination of caviar and champagne.
From booklet distributed to patrons, *The Delectable History of Fortnum & Mason* 72

DAVID GLICKMAN, President, Amer Kefir Co

1 More people think it's a new Israeli jet fighter than something to eat.
   On kefir, a low-calorie product originally fermented from mare's milk by Tartars wandering in Asia and now marketed under various trade names, quoted by Jonathan Probber "Yogurt's 'Cousin'" NY *Times* 25 Sep 86

ROBERTO C GOIZUETA, Chairman, Coca-Cola

2 Smoother, rounder, yet bolder.
   On the new formula that replaced the 99-year-old still-secret concoction originally called "Brain Tonic and Intellectual Beverage," *People* 13 May 85

SYLVAN N GOLDMAN

3 [The customers] had a tendency to stop shopping when the baskets became too full or too heavy.
   On why he designed the first grocery carts in the 1930s, recalled on his death, NY *Times* 27 Nov 84

JOHN JAY HOOKER

4 A Federal Express of fast food.
   Objective for Hooker's Hamburgers, NY *Times* 14 Apr 85

E THOMAS HUGHES, founder, Potato Museum, Washington DC

5 We're serious but not solemn about potatoes here. The potato has lots of eyes, but no mouth. That's where I come in.
   Christian Science Monitor 7 Jul 86

MACY'S DEPARTMENT STORE

6 Values like these only reach shallow waters twice a year.
   On salmon sales timed to coincide with Jewish holy days, advertisement in NY *Times* 1 Oct 86

JEAN MONNET, cognac distiller and statesman

7 The great thing about making cognac is that it teaches you above everything else to wait—man proposes, but time and God and the seasons have got to be on your side.
   Recalled on his death, *Time* 26 Mar 79

PETER MORRELL, vintner

8 I edit out the bad stuff and deliver the good stuff. Seventy-five percent of all wine is awful.
   Quoted in "Wine Wars" *Manhattan Inc* Jul 85

PAUL NEWMAN

9 For those of you who like to scarf your popcorn in the sack, the good news is that Newman's Own contains an aphrodisiac.
   On adding popcorn to his special line of products developed for a multimillion-dollar corporation run as a philanthropy, *Newsweek* 13 Aug 84

10 The star of oil and vinegar and the oil and vinegar of the stars.
   Label for his salad dressing, NY *Times* 25 Jan 85

NORTH CAROLINA TRAVEL DEPARTMENT

11 If you are what you eat, a visit to North Carolina could make you a very interesting person.
   Advertisement picturing grits soufflé, squab pie, wild persimmon pudding, green tomato pie and "pig-pickin' cake" to show that "a visit to North Carolina is more than food for the appetite. It's also food for the soul," *Sports Illustrated* 31 Mar 86

PHILIPPE DE ROTHSCHILD

12 Excellent wine generates enthusiasm. And whatever you do with enthusiasm is generally successful.
   W 9 May 80

HERSHEL SHAPIRO, co-owner, Brooklyn Bagel Co, Tulsa OK

13 We have cowboys coming in who have heard about bagels through word of mouth. They'll ask for a "bangle" or a "bockle," but after their first bite they love it. They come back.
   On spreading popularity of the bagel, NY *Times* 17 May 86

WILLIAM SOKOLIN, vintner

14 What is the definition of a good wine? It should start and end with a smile.
   Advertisement in NY *Times* 15 Dec 84

LEO STEINER

15 They didn't even have enough brains to take a couple of good pastrami sandwiches.
   On being robbed at the delicatessen he operated next to Carnegie Hall for 50 years, NY *Times* 7 Feb 86

ROY STOUT, Director of Market Research, Coca-Cola

16 They fell in love with the memory of old Coke.
   On the public's rejection of a new formula for the company's 99-year-old soft drink, NY *Times* 12 Jul 85

M TAITTINGER, French champagne vintner

17 You put your left index finger on your eye and your right index finger on the cheese . . . if they sort of feel the same, the cheese is ready.
   On how to test the ripeness of a Camembert cheese, *This Week* 10 Jul 66

ALAIN DE VOGUE, French vintner

18 Can you imagine opening a bottle of champagne with a bottle opener. I can't. It would eliminate half the fun.
   On movement to substitute bottle caps for corks, *National Observer* 1 Jul 63

JOSHUA WESSON, wine consultant

19 I didn't know which way I was going to die—run through, conked or poisoned.
   On approach of a man with a sword, a gnarled stick and a silver goblet during ceremony in which he became a knight in the prestigious wine society La Commanderies des Côtes du Rhône, NY *Times* 1 Feb 87

Observers & Critics

JONATHAN AITKEN

20 If you find an Australian indoors, it's a fair bet that he will have a glass in his hand.
   Land of Fortune Secker & Warburg 71

21 Breaking a glass in the northwest is rather like belching in Arabia, for it appears to be done as a mark of appreciation or elation.
   ib

22 In Port Headland, happiness comes smithereen-shaped.
   ib

GRACIE ALLEN

1 When my mother had to get dinner for 8 she'd just make enough for 16 and only serve half.
  News summaries 1 Dec 50

KINGSLEY AMIS

2 It scored right away with me by being the smooth, fine-grained sort, not the coarse, flaky, dry-on-the-outside rubbish full of chunks of gut and gristle to testify to its authenticity.
  On the pâté at London's Simpson's-on-the-Strand restaurant, *London Illustrated News* May 86

3 I sometimes feel that more lousy dishes are presented under the banner of pâté than any other.
  ib

4 I want a dish to taste good, rather than to have been seethed in pig's milk and served wrapped in a rhubarb leaf with grated thistle root.
  ib

MARTIN AMIS

5 I hire tea by the tea bag.
  On renting the essentials of life after breaking up with a lover, *Money: A Suicide Note* Viking 85, quoted in *Time* 11 Mar 85

SUSAN HELLER ANDERSON and DAVID W DUNLAP

6 There is nothing as American as a French chef from the Bronx.
  NY *Times* 14 Jan 85

BONNIE ANGELO

7 You balance the plate between the forefinger and three other fingers, which make a little platform, and with the forefinger and the thumb you grasp the glass and if you think that isn't hazardous, you haven't done it lately.
  On cocktail parties, quoted by Marian Burros "Buffets: Eat, Drink and Be Nervous" NY *Times* 26 Jul 86

JULIET ANNAN

8 No purist talk here of letting the flavors speak for themselves, the English let them sing in concert.
  "An English Summer Pudding" NY *Times* 25 Jul 84

ANONYMOUS

9 The new Condiment King of Camp Dudley is Adam Chamberlain. Adam ate a bowl of relish, a bowl of ketchup and a bowl of mustard.
  YMCA camp counselor, quoted by Michael Winerip NY *Times* 13 Jul 84

10 Bread is the warmest, kindest of words. Write it always with a capital letter, like your own name.
  Russian café sign, quoted by Seth Mydans *ib* 17 Aug 85

11 Protect your bagels, put lox on them.
  Sign at Bagel Connection, New Haven CT, quoted by Ron Alexander *ib* 5 Feb 86

12 Waitresses who are tipped don't spill.
  Sign in diner, quoted by Melvin Maddocks "Early Risers Get Their Reward" *Christian Science Monitor* 15 Aug 86

13 I've got only one other speed, and it's slower.
  ib

14 This has got to be the most expensive food ever laminated.
  On lunch or dinner for two from $80 to $100 at Manhattan's Casual Quilted Giraffe restaurant, quoted by Bryan Miller NY *Times* 15 Aug 86

R W APPLE JR

15 American Danish can be doughy, heavy, sticky, tasting of prunes and is usually wrapped in cellophane. Danish Danish is light, crisp, buttery and often tastes of marzipan or raisins; it is seldom wrapped in anything but loving care.
  "The Danish Worth an Ocean Voyage" NY *Times* 22 Nov 78

BROOKS ATKINSON

16 The cocktail party . . . is a device either for getting rid of social obligations hurriedly en masse or for making overtures toward more serious social relationships, as in the etiquette of whoring.
  Once around the Sun Harcourt, Brace 51

W H AUDEN

17 Murder is commoner among cooks than among members of any other profession.
  Forewords and Afterwords Random House 73

JACQUES BAEYENS, French consul general in NYC

18 Soufflé is more important than you think. If men ate soufflé before meetings, life could be much different.
  NY *Journal-American* 7 May 58

ROSS K BAKER

19 The $100-plus dinner in New York is a major speculative undertaking akin to going after sunken treasure. . . . the cost of the expedition is going to be steep [and] you'll come out of it enriched or just soaked.
  NY *Times* 29 Oct 86

RUSSELL BAKER

20 Goat cheese . . . produced a bizarre eating era when sensible people insisted that this miserable cheese produced by these miserable creatures reared on miserable hardscrabble earth was actually superior to the magnificent creamy cheeses of the noblest dairy animals bred in the richest green valleys of the earth.
  NY *Times* 27 Nov 85

21 It was dramatic to watch [my grandmother] decapitate [a turkey] with an ax the day before Thanksgiving. Nowadays the expense of hiring grandmothers for the ax work would probably qualify all turkeys so honored with "gourmet" status.
  ib

MONICA BALDWIN

22 The refectory is a cenacle in which the taking of food is transfigured almost into a sacrament.
  I Leap over the Wall Rinehart 50

OTILIA BARBOSA DE MEDINA, wife of Portugal's ambassador to the UN

23 Today we had a lunch for Jaime de Piniés, the president of the General Assembly, then we had cock-

tails with the foreign minister of Austria. We passed through a Chinese dinner, and now we are here. It's our life.

On diplomatic entertaining, at dinner given by Assn of Southeast Asian Nations, NY *Times* 4 Oct 85

MARY CATHERINE BATESON

1 Human beings do not eat nutrients, they eat food.
With a Daughter's Eye Morrow 84

JULIE BAUMGOLD

2 New York's own islands of watercress and Postum in seas of gastronomical exotica.
On "little old lady restaurants," *New York* 27 Oct 69

BRENDAN BEHAN

3 To get enough to eat was regarded as an achievement. To get drunk was a victory.
On Dublin in the 1930s, recalled on his death 20 Mar 64

LUDWIG BEMELMANS

4 The true gourmet, like the true artist, is one of the unhappiest creatures existent. His trouble comes from so seldom finding what he constantly seeks: perfection.
Recalled on his death 1 Oct 62

5 To be a gourmet you must start early, as you must begin riding early to be a good horseman. You must live in France, your father must have been a gourmet. Nothing in life must interest you but your stomach.
ib

6 Caviar is to dining what a sable coat is to a girl in evening dress.
ib

AMANDA BENNETT

7 Cantonese will eat anything in the sky but airplanes, anything in the sea but submarines and anything with four legs but the table.
Wall Street Journal 4 Oct 83

WILLIAM SAMUEL BENWELL

8 The soft extractive note of an aged cork being withdrawn has the true sound of a man opening his heart.
Journey to Wine in Victoria Melbourne 76

SUE BERKMAN

9 There has always been a food processor in the kitchen. But once upon a time she was usually called the missus, or Mom.
"Everything but the Kitchen Sink" *Esquire* Sep 84

JOHN BETJEMAN

10 Silver and ermine and red faces full of port wine.
On gatherings in London's financial district, *Church Times* 25 May 84

DANIEL J BOORSTIN, Librarian of Congress

11 Standing, standing, standing—why do I have to stand all the time? That is the main characteristic of social Washington.
NY *Times* 31 Jan 87

BENJAMIN C BRADLEE

12 The champagne was flowing like the Potomac in flood.
On a dinner party at the Kennedy White House, quoted by Ralph G Martin *A Hero for Our Time* Macmillan 83

LEONID I BREZHNEV, Soviet Premier

13 One sits the whole day at the desk and appetite is standing next to me. "Away with you," I say. But Comrade Appetite does not budge from the spot.
News summaries 13 May 73

ALAN BRIEN

14 New York waiters, probably the surliest in the Western world . . . are better images of their city than that journalistic favorite—the taxi driver.
Quoted in *Saturday Review* 5 Feb 66

15 The majority of them give the impression of being men who have been drafted into the job during a period of martial law and are only waiting for the end of the emergency to get back to a really congenial occupation such as slum demolition or debt collecting.
ib

D W BROGAN

16 Man does not live by bread alone, even presliced bread.
On decline of US baking industry, *Forbes* 1 Mar 64

LOUIS BROMFIELD

17 Bread is the king of the table and all else is merely the court that surrounds the king. The countries are the soup, the meat, the vegetables, the salad . . . but bread is king.
McCall's Cook Book Random House 63

J BRYAN III

18 The drink is slipping its little hand into yours.
On the start of a perfect weekend, *Travel & Leisure* Jul 74

ART BUCHWALD

19 The powder is mixed with water and tastes exactly like powder mixed with water.
On liquid diets, NY *Herald Tribune* 29 Dec 60

WILLIAM F BUCKLEY JR

20 To buy very good wine nowadays requires only money. To serve it to your guests is a sign of fatigue.
Quoted by Ellen Peck *Harper's Bazaar* Sep 79

MARIAN BURROS

21 It may not be possible to get rare roast beef . . . but if you're willing to settle for well done, ask them to hold the sweetened library paste that passes for gravy.
On the Bar Carvery restaurant at Rockefeller Center, NY *Times* 27 Jul 84

22 Fish sticks and beef stew that millions of children love to hate.
On food served in schools, *ib* 17 Oct 84

23 Today's restaurant is theater on a grand scale.
"Celebrities Take on New Roles as Restaurateurs" *ib* 28 May 86

1 If Broadway shows charge preview prices while the cast is in dress rehearsal, why should restaurants charge full price when their dining room and kitchen staffs are still practicing?

"Practical Prices for Practice Food" *ib* 27 Sep 86

2 Someone is putting brandy in your bonbons, Grand Marnier in your breakfast jam, Kahlua in your ice cream, Scotch in your mustard and Wild Turkey in your cake.

"Alcohol, the Ultimate Additive" *ib* 20 Dec 86

3 Americans may be drinking fewer alcoholic beverages, but they are certainly eating more of them than ever before. Wittingly or un.

ib

RICHARD BURTON

4 If you drink it straight down, you can feel it going into each individual intestine.

On raicilla, 180-proof distillate of the maguey plant, *Time* 8 Nov 63

GWEN CAFRITZ

5 With my little dinners I like to feel I am helping to save Western civilization.

On her Washington dinner parties, *Quote* 8 Jan 67

TRUMAN CAPOTE

6 I can see every monster as they come in.

On lunching at Manhattan's La Côte Basque restaurant, *New York* 29 Oct 84

LILLIAN CARTER

7 I know folks all have a tizzy about it, but I like a little bourbon of an evening. It helps me sleep. I don't much care what they say about it.

On attitudes toward drinking in Plains GA, where, according to another citizen, "most everybody who does, pretends they don't," NY *Times* 20 Dec 76

HUGH CASSON

8 All that changing of plates and flapping of napkins while you wait 40 minutes for your food.

On London restaurants, *Architectural Digest* 12 Dec 85

DAVID CECIL

9 You must be careful about giving any drink whatsoever to a bore. A lit-up bore is the worst in the world.

Quote 17 Jan 65

CENTURY CLUB OF NEW YORK

10 Members who never sit idly at the Long Table or loiter fecklessly at the Bar are missing the best features the Club has to offer. . . . savoring the pleasures of the commercially worthless discourse that is there in such plentiful supply.

Announcement from the House Committee, *Century Customs: The Spirit and the Letter* 85

11 Finally, a rule that isn't. A member may introduce himself to his bar or table neighbors at lunch but ancient and perhaps inexorable custom seems to render such politesse extraneous. You can, but you need not.

ib

B N CHAKRAVARTY

12 The Americans are a funny lot; they drink whiskey to keep them warm; then they put some ice in it to make it cool; they put some sugar in it to make it sweet, and then they put a slice of lemon in it to make it sour. Then they say "here's to you" and drink it themselves.

India Speaks to America John Day 66

LORD CHAMPION OF PONTYPRIDD (Arthur Joseph Champion)

13 I am such a great connoisseur that I can tell the difference between the tang of the Beaverbrook *Daily Express* and the mellow flavor of the *Times*.

On fish and chips wrapped in newspapers, NY *Times* 14 Jul 63

JEAN MICHEL CHAPEREAU

14 We were taken to a fast-food café where our order was fed into a computer. Our hamburger, made from the flesh of chemically impregnated cattle, had been broiled over counterfeit charcoal, placed between slices of artificially flavored cardboard and served to us by recycled juvenile delinquents.

Un Hiver Américain, quoted in news summaries 31 Dec 75

MME CHIANG KAI-SHEK

15 My good health is due to a soup made of white doves. It is simply wonderful as a tonic.

Time 27 Feb 56

WINSTON CHURCHILL

16 My wife and I tried two or three times in the last 40 years to have breakfast together, but it was so disagreeable we had to stop.

Letter to an American friend, news summaries 4 Dec 50

17 My rule of life prescribed as an absolutely sacred rite smoking cigars and also the drinking of alcohol before, after and if need be during all meals and in the intervals between them.

On dining with the abstinent King Ibn Saud of Saudi Arabia, *Triumph and Tragedy* Houghton Mifflin 53

18 I have taken more out of alcohol than alcohol has taken out of me.

Quoted in *By Quentin Reynolds* McGraw-Hill 63

19 There is no finer investment for any community than putting milk into babies.

Recalled on his death 24 Jan 65

CRAIG CLAIBORNE

20 Give me a platter of choice finnan haddie, freshly cooked in its bath of water and milk, add melted butter, a slice or two of hot toast, a pot of steaming Darjeeling tea, and you may tell the butler to dispense with the caviar, truffles and nightingales' tongues.

NY *Times* 31 Dec 77

21 He was an innovator, an experimenter, a missionary in bringing the gospel of good cooking to the home table.

On James Beard, *ib* 24 Jan 85

1 Physically he was the connoisseur's connoisseur. He was a giant panda, Santa Claus and the Jolly Green Giant rolled into one. On him, a lean and slender physique would have looked like very bad casting.
ib

2 When she goes about her kitchen duties, chopping, carving, mixing, whisking, she moves with the grace and precision of a ballet dancer, her fingers plying the food with the dexterity of a croupier.
On Seattle chef Kathy Pavletich Casey, *ib* 20 Aug 86

ELEANOR CLARK

3 If you don't love life you can't enjoy an oyster; there is a shock of freshness to it and intimations of the ages of man, some piercing intuition of the sea and all its weeds and breezes. [They] shiver you for a split second.
The Oysters of Locmariaquer Pantheon 64

4 You are eating the sea, that's it, only the sensation of a gulp of seawater has been wafted out of it by some sorcery, and are on the verge of remembering you don't know what, mermaids or the sudden smell of kelp on the ebb tide or a poem you read once, something connected with the flavor of life itself.
ib

FRANCIS X CLINES

5 At 5:30 the morning shift of commissary workers arrive to stock the coffee urns, bring in fresh food and prepare for the daylong job of feeding the humans.
On dining at the Bronx Zoo, NY *Times* 4 Oct 76

6 Rosie's is as simple as a hubcap and as unpretentious as its own rice pudding.
On Rosie's Diner, Little Ferry NJ, *ib* 15 Mar 79

ROBERT TRISTRAM COFFIN

7 My family dumplings are sleek and seductive, yet stout and masculine. They taste of meat, yet of flour. They are wet, yet they are dry. They have weight, but they are light. Airy, yet substantial. Earth, air, fire, water; velvet and elastic! Meat, wheat and magic! They are our family glory!
News summaries 31 Dec 55

WILLIAM COLE

8 A hundred standing people smiling and talking to one another, nodding like gooney birds.
On cocktail parties, NY *Times* 3 Dec 72

COLETTE

9 Truffles must come to the table in their own stock [and] as you break open this jewel sprung from a poverty-stricken soil, imagine—if you have never visited it—the desolate kingdom where it rules.
Quoted in Maria P Robbins comp *The Cook's Quotation Book* Pushcart Press 83

10 If I can't have too many truffles, I'll do without truffles.
ib

JAMES CONAWAY

11 He chopped up peppers, mixed them with vinegar and Avery Island salt, put the mixture in wooden barrels to age and funneled the resulting sauce into secondhand cologne bottles.
On Edmund McIlhenny's development of Tabasco sauce in post-Civil War days in Louisiana, *Smithsonian* May 84

ALISON COOK

12 People are getting really baroque with their perversions.
On new popularity of fajitas, including some with meat marinated in Coca-Cola and Dr Pepper instead of lime juice, NY *Times* 4 Aug 84

ALISTAIR COOKE

13 Las Vegas is Everyman's cut-rate Babylon. Not far away there is, or was, a roadside lunch counter and over it a sign proclaiming in three words that a Roman emperor's orgy is now a democratic institution. . . . "Topless Pizza Lunch."
America Knopf 73

14 Texas does not, like any other region, simply have indigenous dishes. It proclaims them. It congratulates you, on your arrival, at having escaped from the slop pails of the other 49 states.
The Americans Knopf 79

15 To the goggling unbeliever [Texans] say—as people always say about their mangier dishes—"but it's just like chicken, only tenderer." Rattlesnake is, in fact, just like chicken, only tougher.
ib

JOHN CORRY

16 One of the glories of New York is its ethnic food, and only McDonald's and Burger King equalize us all.
NY *Times* 10 Mar 75

BARBARA COSTIKYAN

17 In the childhood memories of every good cook, there's a large kitchen, a warm stove, a simmering pot and a mom.
"Holiday Entertaining" *New York* 22 Oct 84

CAROL CUTLER

18 A pâté is nothing more than a French meat loaf that's had a couple of cocktails.
Pâté, The New Main Course for the 80s Rawson 83, quoted in *Time* 21 Nov 83

PATRICK DEAN, British ambassador to the US

19 A plenitude of peanut butter and a dearth of hot mustard.
On US food, *Newsweek* 10 Feb 69

ROY ANDRIES DE GROOT

20 Lyon is full of temperamental gourmets, eternally engaged in a never-ending search for that imaginary, perfect, unknown little back-street bistro, where one can dine in the style of Louis XIV for the price of a pack of peanuts.
"A Weekend of Incredible Gluttony" *Esquire* May 70

WILLIAM DENTON

1 Food is to eat, not to frame and hang on the wall.
> On nouvelle cuisine, quoted by William E Geist NY *Times* 28 Mar 87

BERNARD DE VOTO

2 When evening quickens in the street, comes a pause in the day's occupation that is known as the cocktail hour. It marks the lifeward turn. The heart wakens from coma and its dyspnea ends. Its strengthening pulse is to cross over into campground, to believe that the world has not been altogether lost or, if lost, then not altogether in vain.
> In praise of the martini, *The Hour* Houghton Mifflin 51

3 The rat stops gnawing in the wood, the dungeon walls withdraw, the weight is lifted . . . your pulse steadies and the sun has found your heart, the day was not bad, the season has not been bad, there is sense and even promise in going on.
> *ib*

ELSIE DE WOLFE (Lady Mendl)

4 No, I don't take soup. You can't build a meal on a lake.
> Quoted by Jane S Smith and Diana Vreeland *Elsie de Wolfe: A Life in the High Style* Atheneum 82

PHIL DONAHUE

5 Miss Child is never bashful with butter.
> On Julia Child, NBC TV 18 Nov 85

JACK DOUGLAS

6 I personally prefer a nice frozen TV Dinner at home, mainly because it's so little trouble. All you have to do is have another drink while you're throwing it in the garbage.
> *Never Trust a Naked Bus Driver* Dutton 60

ELAINE DUNDY

7 I hate champagne more than anything in the world next to Seven-Up.
> *The Dud Avocado* Dutton 58

ELEANOR EARLY

8 Alcohol removes inhibitions—like that scared little mouse who got drunk and shook his whiskers and shouted: "Now bring on that damn cat!"
> News summaries 30 Jan 50

RENNIE ELLIS

9 Beer has long been the prime lubricant in our social intercourse and the sacred throat-anointing fluid that accompanies the ritual of mateship. To sink a few cold ones with the blokes is both an escape and a confirmation of belonging.
> On beer drinking in Australia, quoted in NY *Times* 13 Mar 85

WILLIAM EMERSON JR

10 New York is the greatest city in the world for lunch . . . That's the gregarious time. And when that first martini hits the liver like a silver bullet, there is a sigh of contentment that can be heard in Dubuque.
> *Newsweek* 29 Dec 75

NORA EPHRON

11 Whenever I get married, I start buying *Gourmet* magazine.
> News summaries 31 Dec 83

12 My mother was a good recreational cook, but what she basically believed about cooking was that if you worked hard and prospered, someone else would do it for you.
> *ib*

FLORENCE FABRICANT

13 Peanut butter [is] the pâté of childhood.
> "An Enduring American Passion" NY *Times* 21 May 86

CLIFTON FADIMAN

14 Cheese—milk's leap toward immortality.
> *Any Number Can Play* World 57

15 To take wine into our mouths is to savor a droplet of the river of human history.
> Comment included in a collection of food and wine memorabilia displayed at Hallmark Gallery, NY *Times* 8 Mar 67

16 A bottle of wine begs to be shared; I have never met a miserly wine lover.
> *ib*

17 Poetry in a bottle.
> Quoted in "Wine Wars" *Manhattan Inc* Jul 85

PETER FARB and GEORGE ARMELAGOS

18 Food to a large extent is what holds a society together and eating is closely linked to deep spiritual experiences.
> *Consuming Passions: The Anthropology of Eating* Washington Square 83

WILLIAM FAULKNER

19 Well, between Scotch and nothin', I suppose I'd take Scotch. It's the nearest thing to good moonshine I can find.
> *National Observer* 3 Feb 64

WILLIAM FERRIS, Director, University of Mississippi Center for the Study of Southern Culture

20 The Moon Pie is a bedrock of the country store and rural tradition. It is more than a snack. It is a cultural artifact.
> NY *Times* 30 Apr 86

M F K FISHER

21 When a man is small, he loves and hates food with a ferocity which soon dims. But at six years old his very bowels will heave when such a dish as creamed carrots or cold tapioca appears before him. His throat will close, and spots of nausea and rage swim in his vision.
> Interview 3 Nov 78

LYNN FONTANNE

22 Warm the pot first, please, then put two heaping teaspoonfuls in the pot—no bags—in boiling water, and when it's in, stir it. And when it comes here, I will stir it again.
> Telling a butler how to make good tea, NY *Times* 24 Apr 78

MALCOLM S FORBES

1 Their steaks are often good, but the lobsters—with claws the size of Arnold Schwarzenegger's forearms—are as glazed and tough as most of the customers.
> On Manhattan's Palm restaurant, *Forbes* 28 Apr 80

2 The Palm is a joint for sadists to entertain masochists.
> On crowded conditions at the restaurant, *ib*

GENE FOWLER

3 He has a profound respect for old age. Especially when it's bottled.
> On W C Field's fondness for aged bourbon, quoted in *Parade* 7 Apr 68

KENNEDY FRASER

4 He made a swirling motion with a chain-braceleted wrist. The wine mounted the inside of the glass in a sheet of gold, fell undulating back.
> On lunching at Manhattan's Le Cirque restaurant with photographer Norman Parkinson, *New Yorker* 10 Dec 84

5 Women's hands, heavy with diamonds, stirred coffee in tiny cups or alighted playfully on a neighboring sleeve. Young men's hands, with costly cuff links and the slimmest of watches, waved languorously at wine buckets and waiters.
> *ib*

BEATRICE AND IRA HENRY FREEMAN

6 The bagel [is] an unsweetened doughnut with rigor mortis.
> "About Bagels" NY *Times* 22 May 60

BRUCE FROEMMING, umpire

7 Dieting is murder on the road. Show me a man who travels and I'll show you one who eats.
> *Wall Street Journal* 8 Apr 85

ALICE FURLAND

8 If rich food can kill, people live dangerously here.
> On Alsatian restaurants, NY *Times* 14 May 86

MONIQUE GADAUD, wife of French consul general in NYC

9 You can forget about placing another tile on the roof of your country house.
> On the cost of entertaining in the US, NY *Times* 7 May 86

FRANKLIN GARRETT, official historian of Atlanta

10 My first reaction was that it seems to me they are fixin' something that ain't broke. I never saw anything wrong with it to start with.
> On Coca-Cola's announcement that it was changing its secret formula after 99 years, NY *Times* 26 Apr 85

WILLIAM E GEIST

11 Grown men have been seen fleeing after reading the menu posted outside.
> On the opening of Petrossian, a new "caviar restaurant," NY *Times* 17 Nov 84

12 Pressed caviar . . . has the consistency of chilled tar.
> *ib*

13 Drawn by warm nostalgic feelings for the place and by two sweet little words: "Open Bar."
> On the 20th anniversary of Lion's Head, a Greenwich Village bar, *ib* 15 Feb 86

14 They used to have a fish on the menu . . . that was smoked, grilled *and* peppered . . . They did everything to this fish but pistol-whip it and dress it in Bermuda shorts.
> On Manhattan's One Fifth restaurant, *ib* 28 Mar 87

MARK GIROUARD

15 [The pub] was a revolutionary invention [and] immediately began to erode the whole traditional image of the hotel as a house.
> *Victorian Pubs* Yale 84, quoted in NY *Times* 29 Jul 84

HOWARD G GOLDBERG

16 Wine books flow from printing presses like water from broken spigots.
> NY *Times* 28 Jan 87

BARBARA GOLDSMITH

17 Alcohol was the background color in the fabric of Reggie's life.
> On Gloria Vanderbilt's father, *Little Gloria . . . Happy at Last* Knopf 80

GAEL GREENE

18 We signal the captain, taking time out against the wall. He frowns. He groans. His feet hurt. His ulcer rages. He hates his wife. The risotto will take 25 minutes. Lasagna will take even longer.
> On Manhattan's Italian Pavilion restaurant, "That's Italian" *New York* 28 Jan 85

19 To be tempted and indulged by the city's most brilliant chefs. It's the dream of every one of us in love with food.
> From a *New York* column on Paris, quoted in American Express advertisement in *International Herald Tribune* 24 Aug 85

GRAHAM GREENE

20 Champagne, if you are seeking the truth, is better than a lie detector. It encourages a man to be expansive, even reckless, while lie detectors are only a challenge to tell lies successfully.
> *Travels with My Aunt* Viking 69

LEWIS GRIZZARD

21 The only way that I could figure they could improve upon Coca-Cola, one of life's most delightful elixirs, which studies prove will heal the sick and occasionally raise the dead, is to put rum or bourbon in it.
> On Coca-Cola's announcement that it was changing its secret formula after 99 years, quoted in NY *Times* 26 Apr 85

ARTHUR E GROSSER, Professor of Chemistry, McGill University

22 When we decode a cookbook, every one of us is a practicing chemist. Cooking is really the oldest, most basic application of physical and chemical forces to natural materials.
> NY *Times* 29 May 84

JOHN GUNTHER

1 All happiness depends on a leisurely breakfast.
Newsweek 14 Apr 59

JOAN GUSSOW, Assistant Professor of Nutrition and Education, Teachers College, Columbia University

2 As for butter versus margarine, I trust cows more than chemists.
NY *Times* 16 Apr 86

RICHARD GUTMAN

3 The diner is everybody's kitchen.
On renewed popularity of roadside diners, *Smithsonian* Nov 86

PHILLIP W HABERMAN JR

4 A gourmet is just a glutton with brains.
"How to Be a Calorie Chiseler" *Vogue* 15 Jan 61

DANIEL HALPERN

5 Light the candles and pour the red wine into your glass. Before you begin to eat, raise your glass in honor of yourself. The company is the best you'll ever have.
"How to Eat Alone" *Esquire* May 80

SYDNEY J HARRIS

6 In shape, it is perfectly elliptical. In texture, it is smooth and lustrous. In color, it ranges from pale alabaster to warm terra cotta. And in taste, it outstrips all the lush pomegranates that Swinburne was so fond of sinking his lyrical teeth into.
"Tribute to an Egg" in *Majority of One* Houghton Mifflin 57

S I HAYAKAWA, US Senator

7 So I will say it with relish. Give me a hamburger but hold the lawsuit.
Address to the Senate on legal debate over which fast-food chain makes the biggest hamburger, NY *Times* 6 Oct 82

STAN HEY

8 The pleasures of afternoon tea run like a trickle of honey through English literature from Rupert Brooke's wistful lines on the Old Vicarage at Grantchester to Miss Marple, calmly dissecting a case over tea cakes at a seaside hotel.
"Join the Tea-Set Ceremony" London *Times* 4 May 85

DUNCAN HINES

9 I've run more risk eating my way across the country than in all my driving.
Adventures in Good Eating 56

10 More people will die from hit-or-miss eating than from hit-and-run driving.
ib

11 We have to get away from the "bolt it and beat it" idea of eating.
ib

ALFRED HITCHCOCK

12 I'm frightened of eggs, worse than frightened, they revolt me. That white round thing without any holes . . . have you ever seen anything more revolting than an egg yolk breaking and spilling its yellow liquid? Blood is jolly, red. But egg yolk is yellow, revolting. I've never tasted it.
News summaries 31 Dec 63

HERBERT HOOVER, 31st US President

13 The pause between the errors and trials of the day and the hopes of the night.
Defining the cocktail hour, quoted by Richard Norton Smith *An Uncommon Man: The Triumph of Herbert Hoover* Simon & Schuster 84

PHILIP HOWARD

14 Jane Grigson is the nearest thing that we have on this side of the great green bouillabaisse to M F K· Fisher. . . . with learning and wit that are rarely devoted to such a banausic subject as stuffing food down one's cake hole.
London *Observer* 29 Nov 81

15 M F K Fisher is the dowager queen of writers on browsing and slicing.
ib

16 What is special about Fisher is not the tedious stuff about six teaspoons of dry mustard, but the literary dressing around the sides of the recipes.
ib

KATHRYN HULME

17 She could still taste the plump fine oysters from Zeeland that he had ordered for her last meal in the world, the dry sparkle of the vintage Budesheimer which had cost him the fees of at least five visits to patients and the ice cream richly sauced with crushed glazed chestnuts which she loved.
On the future Sister Luke's lunch with her physician father, *The Nun's Story* Atlantic–Little, Brown 56

18 Because he opposed her entering the convent, he had called for all the tempting things of life to speak to her where he had failed, unaware that what he was really putting into her like a probing pain was her last view of him tucking his napkin into the wing collar under his beard, smelling the wine cork before allowing the waiter to pour a drop and drinking the juice from the big rough oyster shells with gusty gourmet pleasure.
ib

STANLEY HUNT, nutritionist, Greater London Council

19 You're going out on a dangerous limb, making healthy sausages.
On introduction of leaner sausages, *Wall Street Journal* 12 Feb 85

SHIRLEY JACKSON

20 Cocoa? Cocoa! Damn miserable puny stuff, fit for kittens and unwashed boys. Did *Shakespeare* drink cocoa?
The Bird's Nest Farrar, Straus & Giroux 54

NANCY HARMON JENKINS

21 Italian wine was something rough and red that came in a straw-covered flask . . . with a candle stuck in its neck, [the empty bottle] was an unmistakable badge of sophomore sophistication.
On Italian wine in the 1960s, NY *Times* 6 Aug 86

POPE JOHN XXIII

22 When I eat alone I feel like a seminarian being punished. . . . I tried it for one week and I was not com-

fortable. Then I searched through Sacred Scripture for something saying I had to eat alone. I found nothing, so I gave it up and it's much better now.

On breaking the papal precedent of dining alone, recalled on his death 3 Jun 63

HUGH JOHNSON

1 [They] face each other across the road . . . like mad old duchesses in party clothes.

On vineyards of southwestern France, NY *Times* 2 Mar 86

STAN JOHNSON

2 You can't be a true bleacher creature drinking this kind of beer.

On low-calorie beer sold at Detroit's Tiger Stadium, NY *Times* 9 Apr 85

MARILYN KAYTOR

3 Condiments are like old friends—highly thought of, but often taken for granted.

"Condiments: The Tastemakers" *Look* 29 Jan 63

HANK KETCHAM

4 No more turkey, but I'd like some more of the bread it ate.

Lines for his cartoon *Dennis the Menace*, quoted by Marian Burros "At Thanksgiving, Trimmings Steal the Limelight" NY *Times* 20 Nov 85

NIKITA S KHRUSHCHEV, Soviet Premier

5 He who cannot eat horsemeat need not do so. Let him eat pork. But he who cannot eat pork, let him eat horsemeat. It's simply a question of taste.

NY *World-Telegram & Sun* 25 Aug 64

ALAN KING

6 As life's pleasures go, food is second only to sex. Except for salami and eggs. Now that's better than sex, but only if the salami is thickly sliced.

Quoted by Mimi Sheraton NY *Times* 28 Oct 81

WAYNE KING

7 Down she came, 1,500 pounds of longhorn beef with a speckled red hide, 4 feet of horns and a majestically glowering look in her red-rimmed eyes.

Reporting on the appearance of a prize-winning longhorn at a formal Houston auction and dinner attended by wealthy Texans, NY *Times* 26 Feb 85

EDWARD KOCH, Mayor of NYC

8 If they don't want to pay for it, they can stop drinking it.

On charging diplomatic missions for using city water, NY *Times* 21 Jan 80

9 The best way to lose weight is to close your mouth—something very difficult for a politician. Or watch your food—just watch it, don't eat it.

People 10 May 82

10 Water, water, everywhere
Atlantic and Pacific
But New York City's got them beat
Our aqua is terrific!

To Amer Water Works Assn convention in Dallas, NY *Times* 11 Jun 84

JEANINE LARMOTH

11 Marmalade in the morning has the same effect on taste buds that a cold shower has on the body.

Town & Country Feb 86

LAURIE LEE

12 In America, even your menus have the gift of language. . . . "The Chef's own Vienna Roast. A hearty, rich meat loaf, gently seasoned to perfection and served in a creamy nest of mashed farm potatoes and strictly fresh garden vegetables." Of course, what you get is cole slaw and a slab of meat, but that doesn't matter because the menu has already started your juices going. Oh, those menus. In America, they are poetry.

Newsweek 24 Oct 60

JOSEPH LELYVELD

13 More than any other in Western Europe, Britain remains a country where a traveler . . . has to think twice before indulging in the ordinary food of ordinary people.

"Fish and Chips: Britain's Bargain Fare" NY *Times* 16 Mar 86

HANK LESLIE

14 The men were so busy looking at the women, they didn't drink.

On the day that the Biltmore Hotel's Men's Bar first admitted women, NY *Times* 1 Jul 77

JOE E LEWIS

15 Whenever someone asks me if I want water with my Scotch, I say I'm thirsty, not dirty.

Quoted by Alan King and Mimi Sheraton *Is Salami and Eggs Better than Sex?* Little, Brown 85

A J LIEBLING

16 An Englishman teaching an American about food is like the blind leading the one-eyed.

Quoted by Alistair Cooke *Masterpiece Theater* PBS TV 20 Oct 74

PATRICIA LINDEN

17 Popcorn [is] the sentimental good-time Charlie of American foods.

"Popcorn!" *Town & Country* May 84

18 It's the national addiction: warmth on chilly winter nights, innocence on Saturday afternoons, the essence of hearth, home and blissful abandon.

ib

JOHN V LINDSAY, Mayor of NYC

19 Not only is New York City the nation's melting pot, it is also the casserole, the chafing dish and the charcoal grill.

To State Restaurant Assn, NY *Times* 10 Nov 66

LONDON TIMES

20 Anybody who minds his belly at all is nervously aware that the land is rich with regional delicacies: the jellied eels and mushy peas of the East End; the tripe and onions of the Northwest; the . . . haggis and bashed neeps of Scotland; the traditional English breakfast of fatty bacon and well-greased eggs.

"Gourmets of England Unite" 15 May 82

EDMUND G LOVE

1 When I was a small boy, my father told me never to recommend a church or a woman to anyone. And I have found it wise never to recommend a restaurant either. Something always goes wrong with the cheese soufflé.

> On eating his way through 5,000 NYC restaurants in alphabetical order, *Saturday Evening Post* 23 May 64

RONNI LUNDY

2 Onion soup sustains. The process of making it is somewhat like the process of learning to love. It requires commitment, extraordinary effort, time, and will make you cry.

> "The Seasoned Cook" *Esquire* Mar 84

DOUGLAS MACARTHUR

3 Found a little patched-up inn in the village of Bulson. . . . Proprietor had nothing but potatoes; but what a feast he laid before me. Served them in five different courses—potato soup, potato fricassee, potatoes creamed, potato salad and finished with potato pie. It may be because I had not eaten for 36 hours, but that meal seems about the best I ever had.

> Diary notes from World War I, *Life* 24 Jan 64

MELVIN MADDOCKS

4 It is beyond the imagination of the menu-maker that there are people in the world who breakfast on a single egg.

> On menus at diners, *Christian Science Monitor* 15 Aug 86

NORMAN MAILER

5 Short-term amnesia is not the worst affliction if you have an Irish flair for the sauce.

> *Vanity Fair* May 84

SOMERSET MAUGHAM

6 To eat well in England, you should have a breakfast three times a day.

> Recalled on his death 16 Dec 65

ELSA MAXWELL

7 Serve the dinner backward, do anything—but for goodness sake, do something weird.

> On entertaining, quoted in NY *Herald Tribune* 2 Nov 63

ANN L MAYTAG, appliance heiress

8 More than a pint, less than a quart.

> In suit against her former attorney, testimony when asked about her daily drinking habits, NY *Times* 9 Jul 86

PERLE MESTA

9 Oh, my dear, it's a buffet. I have chicken à la king. I have cold turkey. I have hot rolls. I have cold ham. I have a big watermelon, all filled with fresh fruit.

> Announcing menu for a series of parties for 1,700 persons attending the Democratic National Convention in Atlantic City, NY *Herald Tribune* 24 Aug 64

DAVID MICHAELIS

10 Under barrel-vaulted ceilings and among the vibrations of trains, in a spot 12.6 miles from the Atlantic Ocean, 28 feet above sea level and 22 feet below 42nd Street, at the epicenter of a metropolis that annually devours $1.5 billion worth of seafood, the most in the nation—stands Grand Central Terminal's celebrated seafood restaurant, the Oyster Bar.

> "Ode to the Oyster Bar" *Manhattan Inc* Sep 84

11 New York's Fulton Street is the Vatican City of fish markets.

> *ib*

12 The warehouse with all those crates, thousands of them, stretching out as far as the eye can see. . . . 227 metric tons of fish from around the world—fish with muscular tails wide as a weight lifter's chest, fish with big, open mouths and shining eyes, fish from deep places and deep dreams.

> *ib*

BRYAN MILLER

13 The qualities of an exceptional cook are akin to those of a successful tightrope walker: an abiding passion for the task, courage to go out on a limb and an impeccable sense of balance.

> "What Makes a Great Cook Great?" NY *Times* 23 Feb 83

14 The highway is replete with culinary land mines disguised as quaint local restaurants that carry such reassuring names as Millie's, Pop's and Capt'n Dick's.

> "Never Eat at Mom's" *ib* 16 Jul 83

15 Around every corner lurk greasy Fisherman's Platters that give children nightmares, Naugahyde minute steaks that put tofuburgers in a favorable light and all those ubiquitous fast-food indigestion huts.

> *ib*

16 The disparity between a restaurant's price and food quality rises in direct proportion to the size of the pepper mill.

> *ib*

17 The quality of food is in inverse proportion to a dining room's altitude, especially atop bank and hotel buildings (airplanes are an extreme example).

> *ib*

18 Never eat Chinese food in Oklahoma.

> *ib*

19 Contrary to popular notion, truck drivers know nothing about good restaurants. If you want a reliable tip, drive into a town, go to the nearest appliance store and seek out the dishwasher repair man. He spends a lot of time in restaurant kitchens and usually has strong opinions about them.

> *ib*

20 The moist, flavorful meat is concealed under a thick slab of crisp fat that would make a cardiologist blanch.

> On Pig Heaven, a Manhattan restaurant specializing in pork dishes, *ib* 28 Sep 84

21 I know a viscous butter sauce when I eat one, and that was one indeed!

> Responding to protests by Charles Masson, owner of Manhattan's La Grenouille, after an unfavorable review of the restaurant, *ib* 25 Mar 85

1 Lutèce [is] a culinary cathedral [but Mr Soltner] acts as if his four-star rating hinges on your satisfaction. . . . That is why the cathedral is packed to the choir loft twice daily.
> On André Soltner as his Manhattan restaurant celebrated its 25th anniversary, *ib* 17 May 85

2 The Model T of American cuisine.
> On the Coach House, a long-established restaurant in Greenwich Village, *ib* 20 Sep 85

3 Cheese steaks . . . are the gastronomic icons of this ethnic city.
> On a Philadelphia favorite since 1932, when a neighborhood chef offered an oversized hot dog bun with quickly cooked strips of lean steak smothered with chopped fried onions and melted cheese, *ib* 21 May 86

4 At lunchtime the place is jumping, while at night . . . the dining rooms could have been rented out for chess tournaments.
> On Manhattan's René Pujol restaurant, *ib* 26 Sep 86

5 Square meals, not adventurous ones, are what you should seek.
> *ib*

FRANÇOIS MINOT, Editor, *Guide Michelin*

6 Anybody can make you enjoy the first bite of a dish, but only a real chef can make you enjoy the last.
> Quoted in NY *Times* 19 Jul 64

ROBERT MORLEY

7 If people take the trouble to cook, you should take the trouble to eat.
> On why he opposes dieting, WNYW TV 3 Nov 78

SETH MYDANS

8 In the phrases of songs and poems . . . bread is gold, it is the motherland, it is the hard work of the masses, it is life itself.
> Reporting from Moscow on trial of a collective farm manager charged with feeding bread to pigs, NY *Times* 17 Aug 85

NATIONAL ASSOCIATION OF BROADCASTERS

9 Friends don't let friends drive drunk.
> Commercial announcement pictured in NY *Times* 31 Dec 86

NEW YORKER

10 In its prime, the drugstore was our closest approach to the European café—a warm, clean place where one could idle respectably, at no great expense, and feel the world flow in and out.
> "Talk of the Town" 4 Jun 84

11 It offered bright lights and healing essences—medicine, cosmetics, coffee, gossip and contemplation of chrome and marble, fizz and split bananas.
> *ib*

12 A drugstore now . . . is a place where you grab your vitamin supplements or pantyhose and get out. It smacks of controlled substances.
> *ib*

NEW YORK HERALD TRIBUNE

13 The unflappable hostess threw five soirees in what may be the longest running party in recreational history.
> On Perle Mesta, "Mostess Hostess's Marathon Bashes" 29 Aug 64

NEW YORK TIMES

14 The wild turkey is to the Thanksgiving offering what the tiger is to the tabby: a creature that knows better than to trust a human.
> Editorial 7 May 85

15 The wild turkey is no sitting duck. . . . It is not a bird to go gently into the roasting pan.
> *ib*

16 So fine a fowl deserves more than a place on a bourbon bottle.
> *ib*

17 The forests are taking over again and so, it seems, are the [turkeys]—eating well, laying eggs and thumbing their beaks at hunters. May they fly forever.
> *ib*

18 The day when the air in America's suburbs smells the same from sea to shining sea, flavored by a billion backyard barbecues.
> Editorial on Labor Day, "The Day When" 2 Sep 85

JOYCE CAROL OATES

19 When poets . . . write about food it is usually celebratory. Food as the thing-in-itself, but also the thoughtful preparation of meals, the serving of meals, meals communally shared: a sense of the sacred in the profane.
> "Writers' Hunger: Food as Metaphor" NY *Times* 19 Aug 86

20 If food is poetry, is not poetry also food?
> *ib*

JACQUELINE KENNEDY ONASSIS

21 You are about to have your first experience with a Greek lunch. I will kill you if you pretend to like it.
> On welcoming decorator Billy Baldwin to the island of Skorpios, quoted by Peter Evans *Ari* Summit 86

RICHARD OWEN

22 The relationship between a Russian and a bottle of vodka is almost mystical.
> On Soviet efforts to decrease drinking, London *Times* 17 May 85

CLEMENTINE PADDLEFORD

23 Beer is the Danish national drink, and the Danish national weakness is another beer.
> NY *Herald Tribune* 20 Jun 64

24 A tiny radish of passionate scarlet, tipped modestly in white.
> Recalled on her death 13 Nov 67

25 We all have hometown appetites. Every other person is a bundle of longing for the simplicities of good taste once enjoyed on the farm or in the hometown [he or she] left behind.
> *ib*

DEBORAH PAPIER

26 For months they have lain in wait, dim shapes lurking in the forgotten corners of houses and factories all over the country and now they are upon us, sodden with alcohol, their massive bodies bulging with strange green protuberances, attacking us in our homes, at our friends' homes, at our offices—there is no escape, it is the hour of the fruitcake.
> "Yecch! The Dreaded Fruitcake" *Insight* 23 Dec 85

DOROTHY PARKER

1 I misremember who first was cruel enough to nurture the cocktail party into life. But perhaps it would be not too much to say, in fact it would be not enough to say, that it was not worth the trouble.
Esquire Nov 64

LOUIS PARRISH

2 If you can organize your kitchen, you can organize your life.
Cooking as Therapy Arbor House 75

ELEANOR PERENYI

3 It is dazzling to discover smorgasbord at a South Carolina inn or a caesar salad in Arkansas. Surely, we think, such internationalism is a good sign, rather like the Daughters of the American Revolution voting for an increase in foreign aid.
"Whatever Happened to American Cooking?" *Saturday Evening Post* 15 Jun 63

PRINCE PHILIP, Duke of Edinburgh

4 I never see any home cooking. All I get is fancy stuff.
News summaries 5 Feb 55

ANTHONY POOLE

5 Dinner . . . possessed only two dramatic features—the wine was a farce and the food a tragedy.
Interview 3 Mar 53

SHONA C POOLE

6 Bread that doesn't loaf around.
On high-fiber bread, London *Times* 22 Aug 84

COLE PORTER

7 See that bivalve social climber
Feeding the rich Mrs Hoggenheimer,
Think of his joy as he gaily glides
Down to the middle of her gilded insides.
Proud little oyster.
From "The Tale of an Oyster," quoted in *Time* 11 Sep 64

FRANK J PRIAL

8 Bordeaux calls to mind a distinguished figure in a frock coat. . . . He enters his moderate enthusiasms in a leather pocketbook, observing the progress of beauty across his palate like moves in a game of chess.
"Days of Wine and Prose" NY *Times* 8 Jul 79

9 The haughty sommelier, with his talismanic tasting cup and sometimes irritating self-assurance, is perceived more as the high priest of some arcane rite than as a dining room functionary paid to help you enjoy the evening.
"Practitioners of the Sommelier's Art" *ib* 28 Mar 84

10 Like footmen and upstairs maids, wine stewards are portrayed as acolytes of the privileged, ever eager to intimidate the neophyte and spurn the unwary.
ib

11 A peculiar subgenre of the English language . . . has flowered wildly in recent years, like some pulpy jungle plant. It's called winespeak.
"Words, Words, Words" *ib* 1 Mar 87

J B PRIESTLEY

12 We plan, we toil, we suffer—in the hope of what? A camel-load of idol's eyes? The title deeds of Radio City? The empire of Asia? A trip to the moon? No, no, no, no. Simply to wake just in time to smell coffee and bacon and eggs.
Recalled on his death 14 Aug 84

JONATHAN PROBBER

13 The legume family is so talented, that if its members were humans, they would be the Leakeys, the Buckleys or perhaps the Osmonds.
"Nature's Bountiful Bean" NY *Times* 8 Oct 86

FREDERIC RAPHAEL

14 The food alone is adequate deterrent, unless you're very heavily into two-scoop tuna or best leather pastrami.
On Warner Brothers Studio commissary, "A Writer Stalks the Hollywood Myth" NY *Times* 5 Jan 85

15 [It is] the land where the Perrier never runs out.
ib

J D REED

16 The martini, once a symbol of American imbibing, memorialized in thousands of neon outlines of cocktail glasses, is becoming an amusing antique, like a downtown art deco apartment building.
Time 20 May 85

WILLIAM RICE, Editor in Chief, *Food & Wine*

17 I haven't had the rice pudding of my life today. But I guess I lost that opportunity with the end of my childhood.
On the First Ever Great Rice Pudding Tasting sponsored by the Rice Council of America, *New Yorker* 2 Jul 84

TOM ROBBINS

18 McDonald's is a reductive kitchen for a classless culture that hasn't time to dally on its way to the next rainbow's end.
Esquire Dec 83

19 When there are dreams to be chased, greener pastures to be grazed, deadlines to be met, tests to be taken, malls to be shopped, Little Leaguers to be feted, sitcoms to be watched or lonely apartments to be avoided, we refuel in flight. Places like McDonald's make it easy, if banal.
ib

DONALD ROGERS

20 Few things are more revolting than the spectacle of a normally reasonable father and husband gowned in one of those hot, massive aprons inscribed with disgustingly corny legends, presiding over a noisome brazier as he destroys huge hunks of good meat and fills the neighborhood with greasy, acrid smoke: a Boy Scout with five o'clock shadow.
"Cookout's Got to Go" NY *Herald Tribune* 21 Jul 61

ANDY ROONEY

21 The biggest seller is cookbooks and the second is diet books—how not to eat what you've just learned how to cook.
CBS TV 9 Aug 82

WAVERLEY ROOT

1 [Avocado growers] denied publicly and indignantly, the insidious, slanderous rumors that avocados were aphrodisiac. Sales immediately mounted.
> On publicity campaign to sell avocados, *Food* Simon & Schuster 80

2 The best peas are the smallest peas and . . . the sleaziest peas are the best peas.
> *ib*

WILLIAM SAFIRE

3 In the lexicon of lip-smacking, an *epicure* is fastidious in his choice and enjoyment of food, just a soupçon more expert than a *gastronome;* a *gourmet* is a connoisseur of the exotic, taste buds attuned to the calibrations of deliciousness, who savors the masterly techniques of great chefs; a *gourmand* is a hearty bon vivant who enjoys food without truffles and flourishes; a *glutton* overindulges greedily, the word rooted in the Latin for "one who devours."
> "The Post-Holiday Strip" NY *Times* 6 Jan 85

4 After eating, an *epicure* gives a thin smile of satisfaction; a *gastronome,* burping into his napkin, praises the food in a magazine; a *gourmet,* repressing his burp, criticizes the food in the same magazine; a *gourmand* belches happily and tells everybody where he ate; a *glutton* embraces the white porcelain altar, or, more plainly, he barfs.
> *ib*

ELIZABETH SAHATJIAN

5 A good custard pie is eggs and milk and sugar falling naturally into place and cooking up all tawny and soft on top of a tender butter crust that cracks clean like Georgia peanut brittle when you cut it. Dinner time, anytime.
> "The Seasoned Cook: A Slice of America" *Esquire* Apr 86

WILLIAM SANSOM

6 Coffee, whipped cream, hockish white wine, paprika and the curiously boiled beef—*Beinfleisch*—are the taste.
> On Viennese food, *Blue Skies, Brown Studies* Hogarth 61

DOROTHY L SAYERS

7 What? Sunday morning in an English family and no sausages? God bless my soul, what's the world coming to?
> Recalled on her death 17 Dec 57

ELSA SCHIAPARELLI

8 A good cook is like a sorceress who dispenses happiness.
> *Shocking Life* Dutton 54

RICK SCHMIDT

9 Charlie Kreuz started it that way and we are going to dance with the one who brung us.
> On unchanging recipe for barbecue (naturally-rendered tallow, salt and pepper, no sauce), quoted by Robert Reinhold "The Art of Small-Town Texas Barbecue" NY *Times* 17 Jul 85

SALLY SCHNEIDER

10 *Confit* is the ultimate comfort food, and trendy or not, it is dazzling stuff.
> *Food & Wine* Nov 86

DAVID SCHOENBRUN

11 People, like wines, have their moods and no restaurant is suited to every mood and every occasion . . . There are days when one does not feel like making love. There are days when I don't like to shave, and I have a favorite restaurant for these nonshaving days, which are not necessarily nonlove-making days.
> "The Foreign Correspondent's Guide to Europe" *Esquire* Feb 61

FRANK SCHOONMAKER

12 The more specific the name, the better the wine.
> *Frank Schoonmaker's Encyclopedia of Wine* Hastings House 65

FRAN R SCHUMER

13 What really distinguishes ice-cream parlors is their atmosphere and therein lies the difference between a sundae that satisfies the palate and one that satisfies the soul.
> "Flavors of Ice-Cream Parlors: Nostalgic to New" NY *Times* 20 Aug 86

DAVID SCHWARTZ

14 For two decades, the name of the author, Duncan Hines, was etched on the biting edge of the American appetite. . . . the best known and most purposeful vagabond.
> "He Made Gastronomes out of Motorists" *Smithsonian* Nov 84

15 In the large cities that received new Americans, there flowered a golden age of restaurants, manned by the available talent from abroad and fueled by the restless wealth of the newly rich.
> On 19th-century dining, *ib*

LAWRENCE CARDINAL SHEHAN, Archbishop of Baltimore

16 I am ready to defend the right of the tasty crab, the luscious oyster, the noble rockfish and the incomparable terrapin to continue their part in the penitential practice of Friday.
> Expressing his hope that Friday abstinence would remain a tradition even though it was rarely a hardship for Marylanders, NY *Times* 16 Jan 66

ISRAEL SHENKER

17 Savor sufficient to lure the wispiest ghost into corpulence.
> On food at Scotland's Culzean Castle, NY *Times* 4 Jul 82

18 Another assault by massed calories.
> *ib*

MIMI SHERATON

19 If it is true, as used to be said, that oversalting means the cook is in love, at least one cook at Le Cirque must be head over heels.
> On a Manhattan restaurant, NY *Times* 26 Aug 77

1 Before long it will be the animals who do the dieting so that the ultimate consumer does not have to.
> On leaner beef with less fat and fewer calories, *Time* 19 May 86

STRATFORD P SHERMAN

2 Brie with the rind sliced off is among the most essential tokens of yuppiedom.
> *Fortune* 18 Mar 85

ISAAC BASHEVIS SINGER

3 Take three quarts of duck's milk.
> First words of a recipe for high-priced cookies, *Stories for Children* Farrar, Straus & Giroux 84

HEDRICK SMITH

4 Russians will consume marinated mushrooms and vodka, salted herring and vodka, smoked salmon and vodka, salami and vodka, caviar on brown bread and vodka, pickled cucumbers and vodka, cold tongue and vodka, red beet salad and vodka, scallions and vodka—anything and everything and vodka.
> *The Russians* Random House 76

HERMANN SMITH-JOHANNSON, 103-year-old cross-country skier

5 The secret to a long life is to stay busy, get plenty of exercise and don't drink too much. Then again, don't drink too little.
> NY *Times* 20 Mar 79

RAYMOND SOKOLOV

6 Manhattan is a narrow island off the coast of New Jersey devoted to the pursuit of lunch.
> "Design for Lunching" *Wall Street Journal* 20 Jun 84

7 Reservations and cloth napkins are really minor pinnacles in the high sierra of the New York lunch. The zenith, the Mount Whitney of lunches, the noon meal at which all local lines of force converge [is] the Bar Room of the Four Seasons.
> *ib*

8 The Bar Room has a corner table placed strategically at a point diagonally across from the entrance. . . . the table of tables in the setting of settings in the building of buildings. In the religion of lunch, this is the holy of holies.
> *ib*

BASIL SPENCE

9 I could have done with some strong whiskey but . . . all I got was dry sherry. It was but the first of many such drinks, as I found that Anglican clergy favor it above all others.
> On winning architectural competition for Coventry Cathedral, *Phoenix at Coventry* Harper & Row 62

CONSTANTINE STACKELBERG

10 What do [I] eat an hors d'oeuvre for? Because I have a drink, and then I have to have blotting paper in my tummy.
> Washington *Post* 3 Aug 86

JOSEPH STALIN, Soviet premier

11 Well, all right, but it is cold on the stomach.
> Accepting a martini mixed by Franklin D Roosevelt at a Soviet–US meeting, quoted by Ted Morgan *FDR* Simon & Schuster 85

KEVIN STARR

12 In the luxuriance of a bowl of grapes set out in ritual display, in a bottle of wine, the soil and sunshine of California reached millions for whom that distant place would henceforth be envisioned as a sun-graced land resplendent with the goodness of the fruitful earth.
> *Inventing the Dream: California through the Progressive Era* Oxford 85

13 [The colors on citrus-crate labels] went beyond nature and spoke directly to fantasy: apricot, purple, cobalt blue, sea green, cinnamon, cinnabar, mauve, yellow, orange.
> *ib*

JOHN STEINBECK

14 So in our pride we ordered for breakfast an omelet, toast and coffee and what has just arrived is a tomato salad with onions, a dish of pickles, a big slice of watermelon and two bottles of cream soda.
> On traveling in the USSR, recalled on his death 20 Dec 68

JANE AND MICHAEL STERN

15 The slices are piled high on rye and each is beet red, lean except for a sultry halo of fat, edged with black pepper—profound pastrami, firm and muscular.
> On the main dish at a Queens delicatessen, NY *Daily News* 10 Nov 85

16 If it swims and it's Jewish, the Town Sturgeon Shop has it.
> *ib*

MARK STEVENS

17 They serve you your importance.
> On dining at a celebrity restaurant, *Summer in the City* Random House 84, quoted in *Time* 21 May 84

HORACE SUTTON

18 Whatever the regional differences, one thing is constant all over the nation—the cranberry. The red berry is jellied and cut in quivering slices, stewed and served with whole berries, squeezed and poured into glasses as a cocktail; nationwide it is spiked with spirits, baked in bread, chopped into a relish, embalmed in gelatin or cubed in a salad.
> "The Cranberry Connection" *Saturday Review* 26 Nov 77

ALEXANDER THEROUX

19 The parrot holds its food for prim consumption as daintily as any debutante, [with] a predilection for pot roast, hashed-brown potatoes, duck skin, butter, hoisin sauce, sesame seed oil, bananas and human thumb.
> "I Sing the Parrot!" *Reader's Digest* May 83

20 It's true, you can never eat a pet you name. And anyway, it would be like a ventriloquist eating his dummy.
> *ib*

VIRGIL THOMSON

21 I said to my friends that if I was going to starve, I might as well starve where the food is good.
> On life in Paris as a young man, PBS TV 23 Nov 86

JAMES THURBER

1 It's a naive domestic Burgundy without any breeding, but I think you'll be amused by its presumption.
> Cartoon caption from his 1943 collection *Men, Women
> and Dogs*, recalled on his death 2 Nov 61

TIME MAGAZINE

2 The kind of crunchy novelty snack that children and
their dentists dream about.
> On introduction of the Choco Taco in Philadelphia, 29
> Apr 85

ALICE B TOKLAS

3 What is sauce for the goose may be sauce for the
gander but is not necessarily sauce for the chicken,
the duck, the turkey or the guinea hen.
> *The Alice B Toklas Cookbook* Harper & Row 54

4 The carp was dead, killed, assassinated, murdered
in the first, second and third degree. Limp, I fell into
a chair, with my hands still unwashed reached for a
cigarette, lighted it and waited for the police to come
and take me into custody.
> Recalled on her death 7 Mar 67

ABIGAIL TRILLIN, age four

5 My tongue is smiling.
> On finishing a dish of chocolate ice cream, quoted by
> her father Calvin Trillin *Alice, Let's Eat* Random House
> 78

CALVIN TRILLIN

6 I never eat in a restaurant that's over a hundred feet
off the ground and won't stand still.
> Interview 29 Dec 79

7 There is no question that Rumanian-Jewish food is
heavy. . . . One meal is equal in heaviness, I would
guess, to eight or nine years of steady mung-bean
eating.
> *ib*

8 Following the Rumanian tradition, garlic is used in
excess to keep the vampires away.
> *ib*

9 Following the Jewish tradition, a dispenser of
schmaltz (liquid chicken fat) is kept on the table to
give the vampires heartburn if they get through the
garlic defense.
> *ib*

10 Even today, well-brought-up English girls are taught
by their mothers to boil all veggies for at least a
month and a half, just in case one of the dinner
guests turns up without his teeth.
> *Third Helpings* Houghton Mifflin 83

11 It happens to be a matter of record that I was first
in print with the discovery that the tastelessness of
the food offered in American clubs varies in direct
proportion to the exclusiveness of the club.
> *ib*

12 The food in such places is so tasteless because the
members associate spices and garlic with just the
sort of people they're trying to keep out.
> *ib*

13 Given the clientele, the restaurants on Capri might
resemble those fancy Northern Italian places on the
East Side of Manhattan where the captain has taken
bilingual sneering lessons from the maitre d' at the
French joint down the street and the waiter, whose
father was born in Palermo, would deny under torture that tomato sauce has ever touched his lips.
> *ib*

14 When it comes to Chinese food I have always operated under the policy that the less known about
the preparation the better. . . . A wise diner who is
invited to visit the kitchen replies by saying, as politely as possible, that he has a pressing engagement
elsewhere.
> *ib*

KENNETH TURAN

15 A book does not make bad jokes, drink too much or
eat more than you can afford to pay for.
> On reading a book while dining out, NY *Times* 13 Apr
> 83

LAWRENCE VAN GELDER

16 The mere fact of an undiscovered restaurant, in a
city where gourmands travel in ravening packs, creates an excitement unrelated to the quality of the
cuisine.
> NY *Times* 25 Apr 79

HARRIET VAN HORNE

17 Cooking is like love. It should be entered into with
abandon or not at all.
> *Vogue* 15 Oct 56

DIANA VREELAND

18 Poor, darling fellow—he *died* of food. He was killed
by the dinner table.
> On Christian Dior, *Country Life* 15 May 86

W MAGAZINE

19 Dining at Chatfield's is like kissing your kid sister—
it's just not worth the effort.
> On a Manhattan bistro, 10 Apr 81

JOHN WAIN

20 This book—amber-clear, cool and with a good
head—deserves a thoughtful swig even from people
who never drink.
> On Richard Boston's *Beer and Skittles*, a study of Eng-
> lish ales and pubs, London *Observer* 1 Aug 76

21 How much of our literature, our political life, our
friendships and love affairs, depend on being able to
talk peacefully in a bar!
> *ib*

ALICE WALKER

22 Tea to the English is really a picnic indoors.
> *The Color Purple* Simon & Schuster 82

LILA ACHESON WALLACE

23 If I displayed this cup, I might look at it once or
twice a week. By using it, I get pleasure from it
continually.
> On sipping a martini from a 4,000-year-old Egyptian
> cup, recalled on her death 8 May 84

NINA E WARREN

1 I let Earl go with me to a delicatessen just once. We never could afford it again.

> On shopping with her husband Chief Justice Earl Warren, recalled on his death 9 Jul 74

ALEC WAUGH

2 I am prepared to believe that a dry martini slightly impairs the palate, but think what it does for the soul.

> *In Praise of Wine and Certain Noble Spirits* Sloane 59

BRUCE WEBER

3 The condition of inebriation is very nearly a universal experience and the words come from all our societal venues—the fraternity house, debutante ball, literary luncheon, longshoreman's bar, the Wild West.

> "How to Talk to a Bartender" *Esquire* Sep 84

4 Wonderful, varied words. Blitzed, blasted, blotto, bombed, cockeyed, crocked, ripped, looped, loaded, leveled, wasted, wiped, soused, sozzled, smashed and schnockered. Stewed, stinko, stupid, tanked, totaled, tight and tipsy. Not to mention feeling no pain, three sheets to the wind, in one's cups, intoxicated, addle-pated and pixilated.

> *ib*

ELLIS WEINER

5 A perfectly reasonable slab of chicken . . . arrived coutured in garlands of watercress and crinolines of cilantro, but like Snow White was inevitably accompanied by a coterie of dwarfs—baby zucchini, baby carrots, tiny peas, small new potatoes "in their jackets."

> On abandonment of "adult vegetables" in trendy California cooking, "The Night They Ate Out" NY *Times* 8 Jun 86

EUDORA WELTY

6 When I was a child and the snow fell, my mother always rushed to the kitchen and made snow ice cream and divinity fudge—egg whites, sugar and pecans, mostly. It was a lark then and I always associate divinity fudge with snowstorms.

> Interviewed at Jackson MS during an unusually heavy snowfall, *New Yorker* 18 Feb 85

RICHARD WEST

7 It's a place people would go to even if the cook had just died of smallpox in the kitchen.

> On Manhattan's "21" Club, "The Power of 21" *New York* 5 Oct 82

DIANE WHITE

8 Printed menus are out, human menus are in.

> On "menu recitation roughly the length of *Hiawatha* and twice as dramatic," Boston *Globe* 5 Nov 86

KIM WILLIAMS

9 Page one is a diet, page two is a chocolate cake. It's a no-win situation.

> On so-called women's magazines, recalled on her death 6 Aug 86

WALLIS, DUCHESS OF WINDSOR

10 I never make a trip to the United States without visiting a supermarket. To me they are more fascinating than any fashion salon.

> NY *Journal-American* 8 Apr 64

TOM WOLFE

11 On their way into the Edwardian Room of the Plaza Hotel they all had that sort of dutiful, forward-tilted gait that East Side dowagers get after 20 years of walking small dogs up and down Park Avenue.

> On women meeting for lunch, NY *Herald Tribune* 8 Dec 63

HILMA WOLITZER

12 The waitress intoned the specialties of the day, "Chicken Cordon Bleu, Sole Amandine, Veal Marsala." She might have been a train conductor in a foreign country, calling out the strange names of the stations.

> *Hearts* Farrar, Straus & Giroux 80

HERMAN WOUK

13 This is an excellent martini—sort of tastes like it isn't there at all, just a cold cloud.

> *The Winds of War* ABC TV 10 Sep 86

Y YAKIGAWA, President, Kyoto University

14 My final warning to you is always pay for your own drinks. . . . All the scandals in the world of politics today have their cause in the despicable habit of swallowing free drinks.

> Advice to students, news summaries 13 Jun 54

DOUGLAS YORKE

15 The character of a diner built up the way grime does.

> On roadside diners, *Smithsonian* Nov 86

HENNY YOUNGMAN

16 My wife is a light eater . . . as soon as it's light, she starts to eat.

> Quoted in Irving Wallace et al *Book of Lists #2* Morrow 80

WILLIAM ZINSSER

17 Although the frankfurter originated in Frankfurt, Germany, we have long since made it our own, a twin pillar of democracy along with Mom's apple pie. In fact, now that Mom's apple pie comes frozen and baked by somebody who isn't Mom, the hot dog stands alone. What it symbolizes remains pure, even if what it contains does not.

> *Life* 9 Oct 69

18 The frank comes wrapped in its own napkin and is soon gone without a trace. It is the ultimate food of the disposable society.

> *ib*

ELSIE ZUSSMAN

19 I start with a chicken. A good chicken. A cheap chicken wouldn't make a rich soup. And it has to have gray feathers.

> On making chicken soup, NY *Times* 1 Apr 74

20 If they like it, it serves four; otherwise, six.

> *ib*

LITERATURE

Writers & Editors

PETER ACKROYD

1 I had to paraphrase the paraphrase.
> On how he avoided the ban imposed by T S Eliot's estate on directly quoting Eliot's works in his biography of the poet, *Illustrated London News* Apr 86

JAMES AGEE

2 We are talking now of summer evenings in Knoxville, Tennessee, in the time that I lived there so successfully disguised to myself as a child.
> Quoted by Laurence Bergreen *James Agee* Dutton 84

CLEVELAND AMORY

3 You can't make the Duchess of Windsor into Rebecca of Sunnybrook Farm.
> On resigning as collaborator on the memoirs of the former Wallis Warfield Simpson, new summaries 6 Oct 55

AHARON APPELFELD

4 The Holocaust is a central event in many people's lives, but it also has become a metaphor for our century. There cannot be an end to speaking and writing about it. Besides, in Israel, everyone carries a biography deep inside him.
> NY *Times* 15 Nov 86

RICHARD BACH

5 A professional writer is an amateur who didn't quit.
> *A Gift of Wings* Delacorte 74

SAMUEL BECKETT

6 I write about myself with the same pencil and in the same exercise book as about him. It is no longer I, but another whose life is just beginning.
> On being taken over by a fictional character, quoted by Hugh Kenner NY *Times* 13 Apr 86

7 It is right that he too should have his little chronicle, his memories, his reason, and be able to recognize the good in the bad, the bad in the worst, and so grow gently old down all the unchanging days, and die one day like any other day, only shorter.
> Cited by Kenner as "one of Beckett's great sentences," *ib*

HILAIRE BELLOC

8 When I am dead
I hope it may be said
"His sins were scarlet,
But his books were read."
> Quoted by A N Wilson *Hilaire Belloc* Atheneum 84

SAUL BELLOW

9 [There is] an immense, painful longing for a broader, more flexible, fuller, more coherent, more comprehensive account of what we human beings are, who we are and what this life is for.
> Accepting Nobel Prize 12 Dec 76

10 A novel is balanced between a few true impressions and the multitude of false ones that make up most of what we call life.
> *ib*

11 I discovered that rejections are not altogether a bad thing. They teach a writer to rely on his own judgment and to say in his heart of hearts, "To hell with you."
> NY *Times* 21 Jul 85

LUDWIG BEMELMANS

12 I don't keep any copy of my books around. . . . they would embarass me. When I finish writing my books, I kick them in the belly, and have done with them.
> NY *Herald Tribune* 15 Dec 57

NICHOLAS BENTLEY

13 To me it seems the sign of a second-rate imagination to assume that the impact of an obscene word can only be conveyed by showing it in cold print.
> *A Choice of Ornaments* Taplinger: André Deutsch 62

JIM BISHOP

14 It is impossible to read for pleasure from something to which you are both father and mother, born in such travail that the writer despises the thing that enslaved him.
> NY *Journal-American* 26 Jan 60

15 I can look at [my books] with pleasure from a distance. Four feet is close enough.
> *ib*

DANIEL J BOORSTIN, Librarian of Congress

16 I write to discover what I think. After all, the bars aren't open that early.
> On why he writes at home from 6:30 to 8:30 AM, *Wall Street Journal* 31 Dec 85

JORGE LUIS BORGES

17 Through the years, a man peoples a space with images of provinces, kingdoms, mountains, bays, ships, islands, fishes, rooms, tools, stars, horses and people. Shortly before his death, he discovers that the patient labyrinth of lines traces the image of his own face.
> Recalled on his death 14 Jun 86

CATHERINE DRINKER BOWEN

18 Writing, I think, is not apart from living. Writing is a kind of double living The writer experiences everything twice. Once in reality and once in that mirror which waits always before or behind.
> *Atlantic* Dec 57

19 Writers seldom choose as friends those self-contained characters who are never in trouble, never unhappy or ill, never make mistakes and always count their change when it is handed to them.
> *ib*

20 For your born writer, nothing is so healing as the realization that he has come upon the right word.
> *ib*

21 Will the reader turn the page?
> Note posted in her study, quoted in *MD* Jul 81

RAY BRADBURY

22 [My stories] run up and bite me on the leg—I respond by writing down everything that goes on during the bite. When I finish, the idea lets go and runs off.
> "Drunk and in Charge of a Bicycle," introduction to *The Stories of Ray Bradbury* Knopf 80

JOHN BRAINE

1 Being a writer in a library is rather like being a eunuch in a harem.
    NY *Times* 7 Oct 62

MAX BRAND

2 There has to be a woman, but not much of a one. A good horse is much more important.
    On writing Westerns, NY *Times* 16 Sep 85

MAEVE BRENNAN, alter ego of the Long-Winded Lady in *New Yorker* "Talk of the Town" column

3 The fewer writers you know the better, and if you're working on anything, don't tell them.
    Time 1 Jul 74

PETER BROOKS

4 We live immersed in narrative, recounting and reassessing the meaning of our past actions, anticipating the outcome of our future projects, situating ourselves at the intersection of several stories not yet completed.
    Reading for the Plot Knopf 84, quoted in NY *Times* 29 Sep 85

PEARL BUCK

5 In a mood of faith and hope my work goes on. A ream of fresh paper lies on my desk waiting for the next book. I am a writer and I take up my pen to write.
    My Several Worlds John Day 54

6 [I am] mentally bifocal.
    On being born to American parents living in China, recalled on issue of a commemorative postage stamp, NY *Times* 19 Jun 83

JAMES M CAIN

7 I write of the wish that comes true—for some reason, a terrifying concept.
    Recalled on his death 27 Oct 77

HORTENSE CALISHER

8 The words! I collected them in all shapes and sizes and hung them like bangles in my mind.
    Extreme Magic Little, Brown 64

ALBERT CAMUS

9 A guilty conscience needs to confess. A work of art is a confession.
    Notebooks 1935–42 Knopf 63

TRUMAN CAPOTE

10 I got this idea of doing a really serious big work—it would be precisely like a novel, with a single difference: Every word of it would be true from beginning to end.
    On *In Cold Blood* Random House 66, which he called "in my mind, a nonfiction novel," *Saturday Review* 22 Jan 66

11 To me, the greatest pleasure of writing is not what it's about, but the inner music that words make.
    McCall's Nov 67

12 When God hands you a gift, he also hands you a whip; and the whip is intended for self-flagellation solely.
    Vogue Dec 79

13 Writing stopped being fun when I discovered the difference between good writing and bad and, even more terrifying, the difference between it and true art. And after that, the whip came down.
    ib

BARBARA CARTLAND

14 A historical romance is the only kind of book where chastity really counts.
    To Romantic Novelists Assn of England, *Queen* 30 Jan 62

15 As long as the plots keep arriving from outer space, I'll go on with my virgins.
    On the publication of her 217th book, *New Yorker* 9 Aug 76

JOHN CHEEVER

16 The novel remains for me one of the few forms where we can record man's complexity and the strength and decency of his longings. Where we can describe, step by step, minute by minute, our not altogether unpleasant struggle to put ourselves into a viable and devout relationship to our beloved and mistaken world.
    Accepting National Book Award, *The Writer* Sep 58

17 Art is the triumph over chaos.
    The Stories of John Cheever Knopf 78

18 The need to write comes from the need to make sense of one's life and discover one's usefulness.
    Accepting Edward MacDowell Medal 8 Sep 79

19 I can't write without a reader. It's precisely like a kiss—you can't do it alone.
    Christian Science Monitor 24 Oct 79

20 For me, a page of good prose is where one hears the rain [and] the noise of battle. [It] has the power to give grief or universality that lends it a youthful beauty.
    Accepting National Medal for Literature, recalled on his death 18 Jun 82

21 What I am going to write is the last of what I have to say. I will say that literature is the only consciousness we possess and that its role as consciousness must inform us of our ability to comprehend the hideous danger of nuclear power.
    Entry in his journal before his last public appearance, the ceremony at which he received the National Medal for Literature, quoted by Susan Cheever *Home before Dark* Houghton Mifflin 84

22 Literature has been the salvation of the damned, literature has inspired and guided lovers, routed despair and can perhaps in this case save the world.
    ib

AGATHA CHRISTIE

23 I specialize in murders of quiet, domestic interest.
    Life 14 May 56

WINSTON CHURCHILL

24 I do hope you are right.
    Accepting Nobel Prize for Literature, news summaries 31 Dec 53

25 The short words are best, and the old words are the best of all.
    Quoted by Alistair Cooke *America* Knopf 73

MARCHETTE CHUTE

1 I've never signed a contract, so never have a deadline. A deadline's an unnerving thing. I just finish a book, and if the publisher doesn't like it, that's his privilege.
NY *Times* 18 Oct 53

TOM CLANCY

2 I've made up stuff that's turned out to be real, that's the spooky part.
On his books of international intrigue, NY *Times* 27 Jul 86

COLETTE

3 Sit down and put down everything that comes into your head and then you're a writer. But an author is one who can judge his own stuff's worth, without pity, and destroy most of it.
Casual Change Morrow 64

IVY COMPTON-BURNETT

4 At a certain point my novels set. They set just as hard as that jam jar. And then I know they are finished.
Quoted by Joyce Cary *Art and Reality* Harper & Row 58

5 There isn't much to say. I haven't been at all deedy.
When asked about her life, London *Times* 30 Aug 69

CYRIL CONNOLLY

6 Literature is the art of writing something that will be read twice.
Quote 12 Sep 65

7 The artist . . . one day . . . falls through a hole in the brambles, and from that moment he is following the dark rapids of an underground river which may sometimes flow so near to the surface that the laughing picnic parties are heard above.
Quoted by Christopher Lehmann-Haupt NY *Times* 15 Mar 84

8 The true function of a writer is to produce a masterpiece and . . . no other task is of any consequence.
Quoted in review of books reissued after his death, *Newsweek* 19 Mar 84

9 Whom the gods wish to destroy they first call promising.
ib

PAT CONROY

10 My mother, Southern to the bone, once told me, "All Southern literature can be summed up in these words: 'On the night the hogs ate Willie, Mama died when she heard what Daddy did to Sister.'" She raised me up to be a Southern writer, but it wasn't easy.
Book-of-the-Month Club News Dec 86

RAY COSSEBOOM

11 In your hands you feel a stir . . .
Someone comes in and asks you a question; someone
else is singing in the next room. But this does not disturb
you. You are writing a masterpiece.
"Flowing Secrets" *Christian Science Monitor* 13 Feb 80

12 A river's secret [is to] flow . . .
when an idea falls
out of a sentence
let it come back to the surface
  of its own
accord, finding any paragraph it wants later.
ib

JAMES GOULD COZZENS

13 I meditate and put on a rubber tire with three bottles of beer. Most of the time I just sit picking my nose and thinking.
On what he does in his study, *Time* 2 Sep 57

PATRICK DENNIS

14 I always start writing with a clean piece of paper and a dirty mind.
Vogue 15 Feb 56

JOAN DIDION

15 Call me the author.
Democracy Simon & Schuster 84

16 A young woman with long hair and a short white halter dress walks through the casino at the Riviera in Las Vegas at one in the morning. . . . It was precisely this moment . . . that made *Play It As It Lays* begin to tell itself to me.
NY *Times* 11 Aug 85

E L DOCTOROW

17 Writing is an exploration. You start from nothing and learn as you go.
NY *Times* 20 Oct 85

18 Planning to write is not writing. Outlining . . . researching . . . talking to people about what you're doing, none of that is writing. Writing is writing.
ib

JOHN DOS PASSOS

19 If there is a special Hell for writers it would be in the forced contemplation of their own works.
NY *Times* 25 Oct 59

20 A satirist is a man whose flesh creeps so at the ugly and the savage and the incongruous aspects of society that he has to express them as brutally and nakedly as possible in order to get relief.
Occasions and Protests Regnery 64

DAPHNE DU MAURIER

21 All autobiography is self-indulgent.
Myself When Young Doubleday 77

JOHN GREGORY DUNNE

22 Writing is manual labor of the mind: a job, like laying pipe.
Esquire Oct 86

23 I started all over again on page 1, circling the 262 pages like a vulture looking for live flesh to scavenge.
On resuming work on *The Red, White and Blue, ib*

24 The narrative was too constricted; it was like a fetus strangling on its own umbilical cord.
ib

WILL AND ARIEL DURANT

1 A book is like a quarrel: One word leads to another, and may erupt in blood or print, irrevocably.

A Dual Autobiography Simon & Schuster 77

LAWRENCE DURRELL

2 It takes a lot of energy and a lot of neurosis to write a novel. . . . If you were really sensible, you'd do something else.

Washington *Post* 29 May 86

UMBERTO ECO

3 A book is a fragile creature, it suffers the wear of time, it fears rodents, the elements and clumsy hands. . . . so the librarian protects the books not only against mankind but also against nature and devotes his life to this war with the forces of oblivion.

On librarians of the year 1327, *The Name of the Rose* Warner 84

LEON EDEL

4 Any biographer must of necessity become a pilgrim . . . a peripatetic, obsessed literary pilgrim, a traveler with four eyes.

NY *Times* 21 Jan 73

5 The biographer who writes the life of his subject's self-concept passes through a façade into the inner house of life.

"The Figure under the Rug" in Marc Patcher ed *Telling Lives: The Biographer's Art* New Republic Books 79

DEBORAH EISENBERG

6 I don't think things are ever exactly the way one expects, and I don't think things are ever the way one assumes they are at the moment. What I actually think is that one has no idea of what things are like, ever.

On her book of short stories *Transactions in a Foreign Currency* Knopf 86, NY *Times* 22 Apr 86

RALPH ELLISON

7 The act of writing requires a constant plunging back into the shadow of the past where time hovers ghostlike.

Quoted in George Plimpton ed *Writers at Work* Viking 63

LOUISE ERDRICH

8 Here I am, where I ought to be. A writer must have a place where he or she feels this, a place to love and be irritated with.

"Where I Ought to Be" NY *Times* 28 Jul 85

PETER EVANS

9 [He had] an accent that carried the longing cadence of the exile.

On interviewing Aristotle Onassis for his biography *Ari* Summit 86

10 The silence of the grave gagged the living; people who had talked with his incarnate approval became sepulchrally mute.

On continuing biography after Onassis's death in 1975, *ib*

WILLIAM FAULKNER

11 Everything goes by the board: honor, pride, decency . . . to get the book written.

Quoted in Malcolm Cowley ed *Writers at Work* Viking 58

12 If a writer has to rob his mother, he will not hesitate: The "Ode on a Grecian Urn" is worth any number of old ladies.

ib

13 The aim of every artist is to arrest motion, which is life, by artificial means.

ib

14 A writer is congenitally unable to tell the truth and that is why we call what he writes fiction.

Recalled on his death 6 Jul 62

15 A writer must teach himself that the basest of all things is to be afraid.

ib

16 It wasn't until the Nobel Prize that they really thawed out. They couldn't understand my books, but they could understand $30,000.

On reviewers, quoted in *National Observer* 3 Feb 64

17 It is my aim, and every effort bent, that the sum and history of my life, which in the same sentence is my obit and epitaph too, shall be them both: He made the books and he died.

Quoted by Joseph Blotner *Faulkner* Random House 74

EDNA FERBER

18 I sat staring up at a shelf in my workroom from which 31 books identically dressed in neat dark green leather stared back at me with a sort of cold hostility, like children who resent their parents. Don't stare at us like that! they said. Don't blame us if we didn't turn out to be the perfection you expected. We didn't ask to be brought into the world.

A Kind of Magic Doubleday 63

19 Life can't ever really defeat a writer who is in love with writing, for life itself is a writer's lover until death—fascinating, cruel, lavish, warm, cold, treacherous, constant.

Recalled on her death 16 Apr 68

20 Your idea of bliss is to wake up on a Monday morning knowing you haven't a single engagement for the entire week. You are cradled in a white paper cocoon tied up with typewriter ribbon.

On uninterrupted writing, *ib*

IAN FLEMING

21 My mental hands were empty, and I felt I must do something as a counterirritant or antibody to my hysterical alarm at getting married at the age of 43.

On writing 2,000 words each morning, without rereading or making corrections, on his 1953 novel *Casino Royale*, recalled on his death 12 Aug 64

THOMAS FLEMING

22 Actors yearn for the perfect director, athletes for the perfect coach, priests for the perfect pope, presidents for the perfect historian. Writers hunger for the perfect reviewer.

"The War between Writers and Reviewers" NY *Times* 6 Jan 85

1 But this is an imperfect world, as actors, athletes, priests and presidents soon discover. Writers have known this from the day they read their first review.
ib

C S FORESTER

2 My distaste for my own work lingers on surprisingly. A father looking down at his first-born for the first time may experience a sense of shock, but he generally recovers from it rapidly enough; after a day or two he thinks it is a very wonderful baby indeed. My life would be happier if I reacted in the same way toward my books. ·
The Hornblower Companion Little, Brown 64

3 I must be like the princess who felt the pea through seven mattresses; each book is a pea.
ib

E M FORSTER

4 Yes, oh dear, yes, the novel tells a story.
Aspects of the Novel Harcourt, Brace 54

5 It is the one orderly product our middling race has produced. It is the cry of a thousand sentinels, the echo from a thousand labyrinths; it is the lighthouse which cannot be hidden . . . the best evidence we can give of our dignity.
To PEN Congress, quoted by Huw Wheldon *Monitor* Macdonald 62

6 It is my fate and perhaps my temperament to sign agreements with fools.
Asserting that "booksellers are dishonest and publishers largely morons," quoted in Mary Lago and P N Furbank eds *Selected Letters of E M Forster 1921–70* Belknap Press/Harvard 84

7 I have been racking my brains and can find no reply [to] this very reasonable question. I can only suggest that the fictional part of me dried up.
Answer in 1966 to student who asked why *A Passage to India*, published in 1924, had not been followed by other novels, *ib*

GENE FOWLER

8 Sometimes I think [my writing] sounds like I walked out of the room and left the typewriter running.
Newsweek 1 Nov 54

PAULA FOX

9 A lie hides the truth. A story tries to find it.
A Servant's Tale North Point 84, quoted in NY *Times* 18 Nov 84

MAX FRISCH

10 The difference between an author and a horse is that the horse doesn't understand the horse dealer's language.
Quoted by Siegfried Unseld *The Author and His Publisher* University of Chicago 80

EDUARDO GALEANO

11 This work is a torture on the rump but a joy to the heart.
On doing research for a comprehensive history of the Western Hemisphere, *New Yorker* 28 Jul 86

MAVIS GALLANT

12 I began to ration my writing, for fear I would dream through life as my father had done. I was afraid I had inherited a poisoned gene from him, a vocation without a gift.
Home Truths: Sixteen Stories Random House 85, quoted by Maureen Howard NY *Times* 5 May 85

GABRIEL GARCÍA MÁRQUEZ

13 One of the things which makes me happier today is that I will never be a Nobel Prize candidate again.
On winning Nobel Prize, London *Times* 22 Oct 82

CAMPBELL GEESLIN

14 I then go miserably enough to the typewriter and I edit with tiny little pen scribbles until you can't read it anymore. And *then*, I put it into a word processor.
On editing his longhand drafts written on yellow legal pads, quoted by Eleanor Blau "The Long and Short of It: Yellow Pads Are Thriving" NY *Times* 4 Nov 86

THEODOR GEISEL ("Dr Seuss")

15 You can get help from teachers, but you are going to have to learn a lot by yourself, sitting alone in a room.
On becoming a writer, NY *Times* 21 May 86

ANDRÉ GIDE

16 What another would have done as well as you, do not do it. What another would have said as well as you, do not say it; what another would have written as well, do not write it. Be faithful to that which exists nowhere but in yourself—and thus make yourself indispensable.
Recalled on his death 19 Feb 51

17 Art begins with resistance—at the point where resistance is overcome. No human masterpiece has ever been created without great labor.
ib

BRENDAN GILL

18 I will try to cram these paragraphs full of facts and give them a weight and shape no greater than that of a cloud of blue butterflies.
Here at the New Yorker Random House 75

ELLEN GLASGOW

19 As far back as I remember, long before I could write, I had played at making stories. . . . But not until I was seven or more, did I begin to pray every night, "O God, let me write books! Please, God, let me write books!"
The Woman Within Harcourt, Brace 54

RUMER GODDEN

20 For a dyed-in-the-wool author, nothing is as dead as a book once it is written. . . . She is rather like a cat whose kittens have grown up.
NY *Times* 1 Dec 63

21 If books were Persian carpets, one would not look only at the outer side. . . . because it is the stitch that makes a carpet wear, gives it its life and bloom.
Book-of-the-Month Club News Sep 69

22 The stitch of a book is its words.
ib

HERBERT GOLD

1 Literature boils with the madcap careers of writers brought to the edge by the demands of living on their nerves, wringing out their memories and their nightmares to extract meaning, truth, beauty.

"There Are Normal Outpatients, and Then There Are Writers" NY *Times* 30 Dec 84

2 Diverting the internal traffic between the Writer as Angel of Light and the Writer as Hustler is that scribbling child in a grown-up body . . . wondering if anybody is listening.

ib

3 Sometimes he advertises himself assiduously, writing a few words and then rushing to the talk show to wave his flag.

ib

WILLIAM GOLDING

4 My yesterdays walk with me. They keep step, they are gray faces that peer over my shoulder.

On the influence of his naval service during World War II, after winning Nobel Prize 6 Oct 83

DORIS KEARNS GOODWIN

5 The past is not simply the past, but a prism through which the subject filters his own changing self-image.

On the shifting quality of Lyndon B Johnson's memories as he neared the end of his life, quoted in Marc Patcher ed *Telling Lives: The Biographer's Art* New Republic Books 79

NADINE GORDIMER

6 The creative act is not pure. History evidences it. Sociology extracts it. The writer loses Eden, writes to be read and comes to realize that he is answerable.

Paper quoted in Sterling McMurrin ed *The Tanner Lectures on Human Values* University of Utah 85

MARY GORDON

7 It's like walking into a cathedral. . . . It reminds me that what I do in the world is a valuable and important thing.

On the NY Public Library, quoted in NY *Times* 19 May 86

GRAHAM GREENE

8 My two fingers on a typewriter have never connected with my brain. My hand on a pen does. A fountain pen, of course. Ball-point pens are only good for filling out forms on a plane.

International Herald Tribune 7 Oct 77

9 The economy of a novelist is a little like that of a careful housewife who is unwilling to throw away anything that might perhaps serve its turn.

From 1959 journal kept while writing *A Burnt-Out Case*, quoted by Thomas Mallon *A Book of One's Own: People and Their Diaries* Ticknor & Fields 84

10 Perhaps the comparison is closer to the Chinese cook who leaves hardly any part of a duck unserved.

ib

11 A major character has to come somehow out of the unconscious.

NY *Times* 9 Oct 85

12 The moment comes when a character does or says something you hadn't thought about. At that moment he's alive and you leave it to him.

ib

A B GUTHRIE JR

13 If you are inclined to leave your character solitary for any considerable length of time, better question yourself. Fiction is association, not withdrawal.

The Blue Hen's Chick McGraw-Hill 65

14 Fiction is love and hate and agreement and conflict and common adventure, not lonely musings on have-beens and might-have-beens.

ib

SHIRLEY HAZZARD

15 It's a nervous work. The state that you need to write is the state that others are paying large sums to get rid of.

NY *Times* 25 Mar 80

ROBERT HEINLEIN

16 They didn't want it good, they wanted it Wednesday.

On writing science fiction for pulp magazines, NY *Times* 24 Aug 80

17 There is *no* way that writers can be tamed and rendered civilized or even cured. . . . the only solution known to science is to provide the patient with an isolation room, where he can endure the acute stages in private and where food can be poked in to him with a stick.

The Cat Who Walks through Walls Putnam 85, quoted in NY *Times* 22 Dec 85

18 If you disturb the patient at such times, he may break into tears or become violent. . . . and, if you shake him, he bites.

ib

LILLIAN HELLMAN

19 What a word is truth. Slippery, tricky, unreliable. I tried in these books to tell the truth.

"On Reading Again" in *Three: An Unfinished Woman, Pentimento, Scoundrel Time* Little, Brown 79

ERNEST HEMINGWAY

20 The most essential gift for a good writer is a built-in, shockproof shit detector. This is the writer's radar and all great writers have had it.

Paris Review Spring 58

21 I learned never to empty the well of my writing, but always to stop when there was still something there in the deep part of the well, and let it refill at night from the springs that fed it.

Quoted by Lillian Ross *Reporting* Simon & Schuster 64

22 All good books have one thing in common—they are truer than if they had really happened.

Quoted by A E Hotchner *Papa Hemingway* Random House 66

23 If a writer . . . knows enough about what he is writing about, he may omit things that he knows. . . . The dignity of movement of an iceberg is due to only one ninth of it being above water.

Quoted by Malcolm Cowley *A Second Flowering* Viking 73

1 When I have an idea, I turn down the flame, as if it were a little alcohol stove, as low as it will go. Then it explodes and that is my idea.

> Quoted by James Mellow *Charmed Circle: Gertrude Stein & Co* Praeger 74

2 If you have a success you have it for the wrong reasons. If you become popular it is always because of the worst aspects of your work.

> Quoted by Morley Callaghan *That Summer in Paris* Penguin 79

3 Forget your personal tragedy. We are all bitched from the start and you especially have to be hurt like hell before you can write seriously. But when you get the damned hurt, use it—don't cheat with it.

> Letter to F Scott Fitzgerald, quoted by William Safire and Leonard Safir *Good Advice* Times Books 82

4 It's none of their business that you have to learn how to write. Let them think you were born that way.

> On loss of a suitcase containing work that would have enabled critics to trace his first two years as a writer, quoted by Arnold Samuelson *With Hemingway* Random House 84

JOHN HERSEY

5 Journalism allows its readers to witness history; fiction gives its readers an opportunity to live it.

> *Time* 13 Mar 50

ROBERT HUGHES

6 Most of the untranscribed and unpublished manuscripts in the book popped out of boxes at me when I wasn't looking for them; I picked them up out of the corner of my eye.

> On use of convict records for his book about Australia, *The Fatal Shore* Knopf 86, quoted in *Publishers Weekly* 12 Dec 86

FANNIE HURST

7 Any writer worth the name is always getting into one thing or getting out of another thing.

> NY *Mirror* 28 Aug 56

ALDOUS HUXLEY

8 A bad book is as much of a labor to write as a good one, it comes as sincerely from the author's soul.

> *Newsweek* 2 Jan 56

CHRISTOPHER ISHERWOOD

9 I am a camera with its shutter open, quite passive, recording, not thinking.

> Opening lines from his 1939 book *Good-bye to Berlin*, recalled on his death 4 Jan 86

CHARLES JACKSON

10 [The writer] must essentially draw from life as he sees it, lives it, overhears it or steals it, and the truer the writer, perhaps the bigger the blackguard. He lives by biting the hand that feeds him.

> Recalled on his death 21 Sep 68

P D JAMES

11 [She was a] buxom grandmother noted for her detective stories, who gazed mournfully at the camera as if deploring either the bloodiness of her craft or the size of her advance.

> *A Taste for Death* Knopf 87, quoted in *Time* 27 Oct 86

12 In 1930s mysteries, all sorts of motives were credible which aren't credible today, especially motives of preventing guilty sexual secrets from coming out. Nowadays, people *sell* their guilty sexual secrets.

> LA *Times* 21 Jan 87

TOM JENKS

13 Editing Hemingway was like wrestling with a god.

> On turning 1,500 pages of manuscript into the 247-page posthumous novel *The Garden of Eden* Scribner's 86, quoted in *Time* 26 May 86

PAMELA HANSFORD JOHNSON

14 I have always wanted to write in such a way that will make people think, "Why, I've always thought that but never found the words for it."

> Recalled on her death, NY *Times* 20 Jun 81

GARSON KANIN

15 There are thousands of causes for stress, and one antidote to stress is self-expression. That's what happens to me every day. My thoughts get off my chest, down my sleeves and onto my pad.

> *Publishers Weekly* 23 Jan 78

ELIA KAZAN

16 The writer, when he is also an artist, is someone who admits what others don't dare reveal.

> NY *Times* 3 Dec 79

NIKOS KAZANTZAKIS

17 My entire soul is a cry, and all my work is a commentary on that cry.

> *Report to Greco* Simon & Schuster 65

ALFRED KAZIN

18 When a writer talks about his work, he's talking about a love affair.

> San Francisco *Examiner & Chronicle* 16 Jul 78

19 One writes to make a home for oneself, on paper, in time and in others' minds.

> Quoted in Marc Patcher ed *Telling Lives: The Biographer's Art* New Republic Books 79

CLARENCE B KELLAND

20 I get up in the morning, torture a typewriter until it screams, then stop.

> On how he wrote an estimated 10 million words in 61 years, recalled on his death, NY *Herald Tribune* 20 Feb 64

ELMER KELTON

21 [His characters] are always 7 feet tall and invincible, mine are 5 feet 8 and nervous.

> On fellow Western author Louis L'Amour, NY *Times* 16 Sep 85

PAUL MURRAY KENDALL

22 [The biographer] must be as ruthless as a board meeting smelling out embezzlement, as suspicious as a secret agent riding the Simplon-Orient Express, as cold-eyed as a pawnbroker viewing a leaky concertina.

> *The Art of Biography* Norton 65

WILLIAM KENNEDY

1 Without [a sense of place] the work is often reduced to a cry of voices in empty rooms, a literature of the self, at its best poetic music; at its worst a thin gruel of the ego.
   On winning Pulitzer Prize. *Time* 1 Oct 84

2 There's only a short walk from the hallelujah to the hoot.
   On the similarity between good writing and poor writing, CBS TV 28 Jul 85

JACK KEROUAC

3 It is not my fault that certain so-called bohemian elements have found in my writings something to hang their peculiar beatnik theories on.
   NY *Journal-American* 8 Dec 60

STEPHEN KING

4 [I work until] beer o'clock.
   On his 9 to 5 writing day, *Time* 6 Oct 86

5 [French is] the language that turns dirt into romance.
   ib

EDWARD KOCH, Mayor of NYC

6 I know many writers who first dictate passages, then polish what they have dictated. I speak, then I polish—occasionally I do windows.
   On his best-selling book *Politics*, NY *Times* 26 Feb 86

7 They have given me the imprimatur of a serious writer, which I knew I was but could not claim publicly until they gave it to me.
   On his election to membership in PEN society of writers, *ib* 27 Feb 86

MARGARET LAURENCE

8 When I say "work" I only mean writing. Everything else is just odd jobs.
   Quoted in Donald Cameron ed *Conversations with Canadian Novelists* Macmillan 73

JOHN LE CARRÉ

9 Writing is like walking in a deserted street. Out of the dust in the street you make a mud pie.
   Time 1 May 64

HARPER LEE

10 Well, they're Southern people, and if they know you are working at home they think nothing of walking right in for coffee. But they wouldn't dream of interrupting you at golf.
   On why she has done her best creative thinking while playing golf, *Time* 12 May 80

MADELEINE L'ENGLE

11 With each book I write, I become more and more convinced that [the books] have a life of their own, quite apart from me.
   "Collaborating with Inspiration" *Anglican Digest* Pentecost 83

12 A book comes and says, "Write me." My job is to try to serve it to the best of my ability, which is never good enough, but all I can do is listen to it, do what it tells me and collaborate.
   ib

MARIA LENHART

13 The fact that writers will go through so much to remain writers says something, perhaps everything. It would be far easier (and nearly always more profitable) to become a real estate agent.
   Christian Science Monitor 22 Aug 79

14 But for any writer worthy of the name . . . there are moments during the writing process when the rest of the planet might as well have gone to Venus. And those moments are not for sale.
   ib

ELMORE LEONARD

15 If it sounds like writing, I rewrite it.
   Newsweek 22 Apr 85

16 I leave out the parts that people skip.
   When asked about popularity of his detective novels, quoted by William Zinsser *A Family of Readers* Book-of-the-Month Club 86

DORIS LESSING

17 In the writing process, the more a story cooks, the better.
   NY *Times* 22 Apr 84

SINCLAIR LEWIS

18 There are dozens of young poets and fictioneers . . . most of them a little insane in the tradition of James Joyce, who, however insane they may be, have refused to be genteel and traditional and dull.
   "The American Fear of Literature," address as the first American to receive the Nobel Prize for Literature, recalled on his death 10 Jan 51

19 The middle class, that prisoner of the barbarian 20th century.
   Theme of his last novel, unfinished at his death, *ib*

ANNE MORROW LINDBERGH

20 I must write it all out, at any cost. Writing is thinking. It is more than living, for it is being conscious of living.
   Locked Rooms and Open Doors Harcourt Brace Jovanovich 74

NORMAN MAILER

21 When I read it, I don't wince, which is all I ever ask for a book I write.
   On publication of his first mystery, *Tough Guys Don't Dance* Random House 84, NY *Times* 8 Jun 84

22 I felt something shift to murder in me. I felt . . . that I was an outlaw, a psychic outlaw, and I liked it.
   On reaction to his publisher's rejection of *The Deer Park* because of "six salacious lines Mr Mailer would not remove," *ib* 21 Jul 85

BERNARD MALAMUD

23 Those who write about life, reflect about life. . . . you see in others who you are.
   Dublin's Lives Farrar, Straus & Giroux 79

24 It was all those biographies in me yelling, "We want out. We want to tell you what we've done to you."
   On how *Dublin's Lives* resulted from a lifetime of reading biographies, *W* 16 Feb 79

1 I for one believe that not enough has been made of the tragedy of the destruction of 6 million Jews. Somebody has to cry—even if it's a writer, 20 years later.
>Recalled on his death 18 Mar 86

2 With me, it's story, story, story.
>On the most important element of his writing, *ib*

3 The idea is to get the pencil moving quickly.
>On the task of beginning, *ib*

4 Once you've got some words looking back at you, you can take two or three—or throw them away and look for others.
>*ib*

WILLIAM MANCHESTER

5 Portly, balding, Brooks-Brothered.
>Self-description, *Good-bye, Darkness: A Memoir of the Pacific War* Little, Brown 80

THOMAS MANN

6 A writer is somebody for whom writing is more difficult than it is for other people.
>Recalled on his death 12 Aug 55

SOMERSET MAUGHAM

7 Have common sense and . . . stick to the point.
>On writing, quoted by Ted Morgan *Maugham* Simon & Schuster 80

8 Writing is the supreme solace.
>*ib*

ANDRÉ MAUROIS

9 Style is the hallmark of a temperament stamped upon the material at hand.
>*The Art of Writing* Dutton 60

10 Writing is a difficult trade which must be learned slowly by reading great authors; by trying at the outset to imitate them; by daring then to be original; by destroying one's first productions.
>NY *Journal-American* 31 Jul 63

11 There are deserts in every life, and the desert must be depicted if we are to give a fair and complete idea of the country.
>On the biographer's task, recalled on his death 9 Oct 67

MARY McCARTHY

12 I am putting real plums into an imaginary cake.
>On *The Group*, her 1963 novel about eight 1933 Vassar alumnae, NY *Herald Tribune* 5 Jan 64

13 I'm afraid I'm not sufficiently inhibited about the things that other women are inhibited about for me. They feel that you've given away trade secrets.
>*Look* 26 Feb 64

14 To be disesteemed by people you don't have much respect for is not the worst fate.
>On reviewers, quoted by Samuel G Freedman NY *Times* 27 Aug 84

CARSON McCULLERS

15 I live with the people I create and it has always made my essential loneliness less keen.
>Preface to *The Square Root of Wonderful* Houghton Mifflin 58

PHYLLIS McGINLEY

16 Let's make it clear from Maine to Kansas;
No sonnets, ballads, or rondeaux;
Is, Gentlemen, completely Prose.
Now once again, Sirs, please rehearse:
"All that's McGinley is not verse."
>Letter to the editor about *Sixpence in Her Shoe*, which had been reviewed as poetry rather than fiction, NY *Times* 27 Dec 64

THOMAS MERTON

17 There was this shadow, this double, this writer who had followed me into the cloister. . . . He rides my shoulders . . . I cannot lose him.
>*Elected Silence* Hollis & Carter 69

18 An author in a Trappist monastery is like a duck in a chicken coop. And he would give anything in the world to be a chicken instead of a duck.
>Quoted by Monica Furlong *Merton* Harper & Row 80

GRACE METALIOUS

19 Even Tom Sawyer had a girlfriend and to talk about adults without talking about their sex drives is like talking about a window without glass.
>Defending *Peyton Place*, NY *Mirror* 6 Feb 58

JAMES A MICHENER

20 Russia, France, Germany and China. They revere their writers. America is still a frontier country that almost shudders at the idea of creative expression.
>"A Spelunker in the Caves of History" *Modern Maturity* Aug 85

21 The arrogance of the artist is a very profound thing, and it fortifies you.
>Quoted by Caryn James "The Michener Phenomenon" NY *Times* 8 Sep 85

22 The really great writers are people like Emily Brontë who sit in a room and write out of their limited experience and unlimited imagination.
>*ib*

HENRY MILLER

23 My books are the books that I am, the confused man, the negligent man, the reckless man, the lusty, obscene, boisterous, scrupulous, lying, diabolically truthful man that I am.
>London *Observer* 26 Feb 79

24 Plots and character don't make life. . . . Life is here and now, anytime you say the word, anytime you let her rip.
>Recalled on his death 7 Jun 80

25 Whatever I do is done out of sheer joy; I drop my fruits like a ripe tree. What the general reader or the critic makes of them is not my concern.
>*ib*

BRIAN MOORE

26 When you're a writer you no longer see things with the freshness of the normal person. There are always two figures that work inside you.
>*Saturday Review* 13 Oct 62

TED MORGAN

1 When I slept, armies of footnotes marched across my dreams in close-order drill.

Preface to *Maugham* Simon & Schuster 80

2 A writer is always going to betray somebody. If you're going to be honest with your subject, you can't be genteel.

On writing biographies, quoted in *Publishers Weekly* 11 Oct 85

WILLIE MORRIS

3 When a writer knows home in his heart, his heart must remain subtly apart from it. He must always be a stranger to the place he loves, and its people.

"Coming on Back" *Life* Jun 81

4 His claim to his home is deep, but there are too many ghosts. He must absorb without being absorbed.

ib

5 When he understands, as few others do, something of his home . . . that is funny, or sad, or tragic, or cruel, or beautiful, or true, he knows he must do so as a stranger.

ib

VLADIMIR NABOKOV

6 Here lies the sense of literary creation: to portray ordinary objects as they will be reflected in kindly mirrors of future times. . . . To find in objects around us the fragrant tenderness that only posterity will discern when every trifle of our everyday life will become exquisite and festive in its own right.

Details of a Sunset McGraw-Hill 76

KATHLEEN NORRIS

7 Get a girl in trouble, then get her out again.

Describing her formula for 81 "relentlessly wholesome" novels, *Time* 28 Jan 66

JOYCE CAROL OATES

8 If you are a writer you locate yourself behind a wall of silence and no matter what you are doing, driving a car or walking or doing housework . . . you can still be writing, because you have that space.

NY Times 27 Jul 80

EDNA O'BRIEN

9 I am obsessive, also I am industrious. Besides, the time when you are most alive and most aware is in childhood and one is trying to recapture that heightened awareness.

NY Times 18 Nov 84

10 Recollection . . . is not something that I can summon up, it simply comes and I am the servant of it.

ib

11 My hand does the work and I don't have to think; in fact, were I to think, it would stop the flow. It's like a dam in the brain that bursts.

ib

12 Writing is like carrying a fetus.

Quoted in George Plimpton ed *Writers at Work* Viking 86

FLANNERY O'CONNOR

13 When a book leaves your hands, it belongs to God. He may use it to save a few souls or to try a few others, but I think that for the writer to worry is to take over God's business.

The Habit of Being Farrar, Straus & Giroux 79

14 I don't deserve any credit for turning the other cheek as my tongue is always in it.

ib

15 All my stories are about the action of grace on a character who is not very willing to support it, but most people think of these stories as hard, hopeless and brutal.

Quoted by Robert Cole *Flannery O'Connor's South* Louisiana State University 80

JOHN O'HARA

16 They say great themes make great novels. . . . but what these young writers don't understand is that there is no greater theme than men and women.

On publication of his 35th book, NY *Times* 13 Nov 67

17 An artist is his own fault.

Introduction to stories by F Scott Fitzgerald, recalled on O'Hara's death 11 Apr 70

18 Much as I like owning a Rolls-Royce, I could do without it. What I could not do without is a typewriter, a supply of yellow second sheets and the time to put them to good use.

Introduction to *And Other Stories* Random House 68, quoted in *National Observer* 20 Apr 70

GEORGE ORWELL

19 Writing a book is a horrible, exhausting struggle, like a long bout of some painful illness. One would never undertake such a thing if one were not driven on by some demon whom one can neither resist nor understand. For all one knows, that demon is simply the same instinct that makes a baby squall for attention.

Recalled on his death 21 Jan 50

20 It is also true that one can write nothing readable unless one constantly struggles to efface one's own personality. Good prose is like a windowpane.

ib

JOHN OSBORNE

21 Asking a working writer what he thinks about critics is like asking a lamppost what it feels about dogs.

Time 31 Oct 77

BORIS PASTERNAK

22 Immensely grateful, touched, proud, astonished, abashed.

Telegram accepting Nobel Prize, NY *Mirror* 26 Oct 58

23 In view of the meaning given to this honor in the community to which I belong, I should abstain from the undeserved prize that has been awarded to me. Do not meet my voluntary refusal with ill will.

Telegram reversing his acceptance of Nobel Prize after criticism by Soviets, NY *Times* 30 Oct 58

24 The writer is the Faust of modern society, the only surviving individualist in a mass age. To his orthodox contemporaries he seems a semi-madman.

London *Observer* 20 Dec 59

1 As in an explosion, I would erupt with all the wonderful things I saw and understood in this world.

> On planning the novel that became *Doctor Zhivago*, recalled on his death 30 May 60

2 I think that if the beast who sleeps in man could be held down by threats of any kind, whether of jail or retribution, then the highest emblem of humanity would be the lion tamer, not the prophet who sacrificed himself.

> On the central theme of *Doctor Zhivago, ib*

3 What for centuries raised man above the beast is not the cudgel but the irresistible power of unarmed truth.

> *ib*

4 They don't ask much of you. They only want you to hate the things you love and to love the things you despise.

> On Soviet bureaucrats, *Life* 13 Jun 60

5 I have been writing in spurts, bit by bit. It is incredibly difficult. Everything is corroded, broken, dismantled; everything is covered with hardened layers of accumulated insensitivity, deafness, entrenched routine. It is disgusting.

> Unpublished letter, quoted in NY *Times* 1 Jan 78

6 Work is the order of the day, just as it was at one time, with our first starts and our best efforts. Do you remember? Therein lies its delight. It brings back the forgotten; one's stores of energy, seemingly exhausted, come back to life.

> *ib*

ALAN PATON

7 Then you take it all—the chronology, the letters, the interviews, your own knowledge, the newspaper cuttings, the history books, the diary, the thousand hours of contemplation, and you try to make a whole of it, not a chronicle but a drama, with a beginning and an end, the whole being given form and integrity because a man moves through it from birth to death, through all the beauty and terror of human life.

> On completing his biography of South African statesman Jan Hofmeyr, quoted in *National Observer* 8 Nov 65

8 If you wrote a novel in South Africa which didn't concern the central issues, it wouldn't be worth publishing.

> Quoted in *Anglican Digest* Lent 82

WALKER PERCY

9 [Tuberculosis was] the best disease I ever had. If I hadn't had it, I might be a second-rate shrink practicing in Birmingham, at best.

> On convalescence that permitted him to read voraciously and turned his interest from psychiatry to writing, quoted by Malcolm Jones "Moralist of the South" NY *Times* 22 Mar 87

S J PERELMAN

10 The fact is that all of us have only one personality, and we wring it out like a dishtowel. . . . You are what you are.

> Quoted by William Zinsser "Learning to Be Funny Is No Joke" NY *Times* 2 Dec 79

JOAN PEYSER

11 Never . . . use the word *gossip* in a pejorative sense. It's the very stuff of biography and has to be woven in. To suggest that the personal life is not an essential element in the creative life is absurd.

> To her seminar students at NY University, *Publishers Weekly* 5 Jun 87

JAYNE ANNE PHILLIPS

12 If the first novel has been successful, the writer buys a serious, writerly object that bespeaks investment and confidence—a word processor, a new bookshelf, reams of white paper. . . . In any case, a new and bigger wastebasket.

> On writing a second novel, NY *Times* 17 Mar 85

13 As before, there is a great silence, with no end in sight. The writer surrenders, listening.

> *ib*

KATHERINE ANNE PORTER

14 I finished the thing; but I think I sprained my soul.

> On completing *Ship of Fools*, her 1962 novel, *McCalls's* Aug 65

15 I specialize in what the French call *la petite histoire*. I am interested in the individual thumbprint.

> Recalled on her death 18 Sep 80

16 I spent 15 years wandering about, weighed horribly with masses of paper and little else. Yet for this vocation of writing I was and am willing to die, and I consider very few other things of the slightest importance.

> *ib*

PADGETT POWELL

17 My craft was gathered by doing things other than actually spoiling paper. I knew I was supposed to be a writer; I had made that declaration in the closet of my soul.

> Quoted by Helen Dudar *Wall Street Journal* 26 Nov 86

J B PRIESTLEY

18 Most writers enjoy two periods of happiness—when a glorious idea comes to mind and, secondly, when a last page has been written and you haven't had time to know how much better it ought to be.

> *International Herald Tribune* 3 Jan 78

19 Much of writing might be described as mental pregnancy with successive difficult deliveries.

> *ib*

20 If there is one thing left that I would like to do, it's to write something really beautiful. And I could do it, you know. I could still do it.

> Interviewed on his 87th birthday, London *Times* 7 Sep 81

21 A synopsis is a cold thing. You do it with the front of your mind. If you're going to stay with it, you never get quite the same magic as when you're going all out.

> On the technique of planning a novel, *Illustrated London News* Sep 84

V S PRITCHETT

22 I am under the spell of language, which has ruled me since I was 10.

> "Looking Back at 80" NY *Times* 14 Dec 80

JONATHAN RABAN

1 The plot would be written by the current of the river . . . where the river meandered so would the book.
On writing a novel aboard a Mississippi River boat, *Old Glory: An American Voyage* Simon & Schuster 81

SANTHA RAMA RAU

2 Virtually nobody can help you deliberately—many people will help you intentionally.
On writing, *Harper's Bazaar* Aug 56

MICHAEL RAMSEY, Archbishop of Canterbury

3 Monday, a quarter of an hour; Tuesday, 10 minutes; Wednesday, rather better, half an hour; Thursday, not very good, but 10 minutes; Friday, a lull, an hour; Saturday, half an hour.
On how he found time to write books, NY *Herald Tribune* 28 Dec 65

MORDECAI RICHLER

4 Coming from Canada, being a writer and Jewish as well, I have impeccable paranoia credentials.
"It's a Plot" *Playboy* May 75

PHILIP ROTH

5 A kind of fever that flares up from time to time. . . . flared up again . . . to about 107 . . . Now there's just a low-grade fever running, nothing to worry about.
On criticism of his writing, NY *Times* 1 Aug 85

6 The best readers come to fiction to be free of . . . all that *isn't* fiction.
Quoted by John Updike *ib* 17 Aug 86

ANATOLY RYBAKOV

7 A society that wants to build the future must know its past, its real past, as it was.
On unprecedented publication in the USSR of his novel *The Children of Arbat*, set in 1934 and featuring Stalin as a major character, NY *Times* 31 Oct 86

8 If I, a living witness, one who experienced those times, don't speak about them, then others who did not experience or witness those times will invent their own version of them.
ib

FRANÇOISE SAGAN

9 Life has confirmed for me the thoughts and impressions I had when I was 18, as if it was all intuition.
W 17 May 74

10 There are moments when you feel trapped, ill at ease. A year later the same feeling can turn out to be the theme of a book.
ib

J D SALINGER

11 A confessional passage has probably never been written that didn't stink a little bit of the writer's pride in having given up his pride.
The Catcher in the Rye Little, Brown 51

12 [It's] like saying she's a beautiful girl, except for her face.
On an editor who praised a story while rejecting it, quoted in NY *Times* 30 Jan 87

CARL SANDBURG

13 I was up day and night with Lincoln for years. I couldn't have picked a better companion.
On his biography of Abraham Lincoln, NY *Times* 6 Jan 64

WILLIAM SANSOM

14 A writer lives, at best, in a state of astonishment.
Blue Skies, Brown Studies Hogarth 61

15 Beneath any feeling [he] has of the good or evil of the world lies a deeper one of wonder at it all. To transmit that feeling, he writes.
ib

JEAN PAUL SARTRE

16 A writer who takes political, social or literary positions must act only with the means that are his. These means are the written words.
Refusing Nobel Prize, NY *Times* 22 Oct 64

ERICH SEGAL

17 This isn't a watercolor, it's a mural.
On *The Class*, the longest of his popular novels, *People* 13 May 85

RICHARD SELZER

18 I don't dawdle. I'm a surgeon. I make an incision, do what needs to be done and sew up the wound. There is a beginning, a middle and an end.
On rewriting, NY *Times* 28 Sep 79

MAURICE SENDAK

19 You cannot write for children . . . They're much too complicated. You can only write books that are of interest to them.
Boston *Globe* 4 Jan 87

ROD SERLING

20 Every writer is a frustrated actor who recites his lines in the hidden auditorium of his skull.
Vogue 1 Apr 57

GEORGE BERNARD SHAW

21 Imagination is the beginning of creation. You imagine what you desire, you will what you imagine and at last you create what you will.
Recalled on his death 2 Nov 50

22 It was from Handel that I learned that style consists in force of assertion.
Quoted in *International Herald Tribune* 5 Dec 81

23 If you can say a thing with one stroke, unanswerably you have style; if not, you are at best a *marchande de plaisir*; a decorative littérateur, or a musical confectioner, or a painter of fans with cupids and cocottes. Handel had power.
ib

WILFRID SHEED

24 Every writer is a writer of the generation before.
On his parents, NY *Times* 10 Nov 85

25 I picked up the writing on the very day he died. It was the only consolation I could find.
On his father, *ib*

CLAUDE SIMON

1 To begin with, our perception of the world is deformed, incomplete. Then our memory is selective. Finally, writing transforms.

On winning Nobel Prize, NY *Times* 4 Nov 85

2 For me, the big chore is always the same: how to begin a sentence, how to continue it, how to complete it.

On writing his Nobel acceptance speech, *ib*

ISAAC BASHEVIS SINGER

3 I am thankful, of course, for the prize and thankful to God for each story, each idea, each word, each day.

On winning Nobel Prize, *Time* 16 Oct 78

4 A story to me means a plot where there is some surprise. . . . Because that is how life is—full of surprises.

NY *Times* 26 Nov 78

5 I don't invent characters because the Almightly has already invented millions. . . . Just like experts at fingerprints do not create fingerprints but learn how to read them.

ib

6 When I was a little boy, they called me a liar, but now that I am grown up, they call me a writer.

Time 18 Jul 83

OSBERT SITWELL

7 It is music to my ears. I have always said that if I were a rich man, I would employ a professional praiser.

On hearing his books read aloud, NBC TV 2 Jan 55

BETTY SMITH

8 I wrote about people who *liked* fake fireplaces in their parlor, who thought a brass horse with a clock embedded in its flank was *wonderful*.

On *A Tree Grows in Brooklyn* and other novels, *Parade* 29 Jun 58

ALEXANDER SOLZHENITSYN

9 For a country to have a great writer is like having a second government. That is why no regime has ever loved great writers, only minor ones.

The First Circle Bantam 76

10 This book is an agglomeration of lean-tos and annexes and there is no knowing how big the next addition will be, or where it will be put. At any point, I can call the book finished or unfinished.

On a manuscript written in sections in 1967, 1971, 1973 and 1974, *The Oak and the Calf* Harper & Row 80

SUSAN SONTAG

11 Volume depends precisely on the writer's having been able to sit in a room every day, year after year, alone.

"When Writers Talk among Themselves" NY *Times* 5 Jan 86

12 The writer is either a practicing recluse or a delinquent, guilt-ridden one; or both. Usually both.

ib

RONALD STEEL

13 Increasingly, I realized that I could not merely tell *his* story. Rather, I would have to tell my story about him.

"The Biographer as Detective: What Walter Lippmann Preferred to Forget" NY *Times* 21 Jul 85

JOHN STEINBECK

14 Writers are a little below clowns and a little above trained seals.

Quote 18 Jun 61

15 I am impelled, not to squeak like a grateful and apologetic mouse, but to roar like a lion out of pride in my profession.

Accepting Nobel Prize, quoted in *Newsweek* 24 Dec 62

16 I hold that a writer who does not passionately believe in the perfectibility of man has no dedication nor any membership in literature.

ib

17 The profession of book writing makes horse racing seem like a solid, stable business.

ib

18 In utter loneliness a writer tries to explain the inexplicable.

In diary used to warm up for his daily stint of writing, NY *Times* 2 Jun 69

19 The writer must believe that what he is doing is the most important thing in the world. And he must hold to this illusion even when he knows it is not true.

ib

20 I have owed you this letter for a very long time— but my fingers have avoided the pencil as though it were an old and poisoned tool.

Letter to his literary agent, found on his desk after his death in 1968, quoted in George Plimpton ed *Writers at Work* Viking 76

GLORIA STEINEM

21 Writing is the only thing that, when I do it, I don't feel I should be doing something else.

Publishers Weekly 12 Aug 83

WILLIAM STRUNK JR

22 Vigorous writing is concise. A sentence should contain no unnecessary words, a paragraph no unnecessary sentences, for the same reason that a drawing should have no unnecessary lines and a machine no unnecessary parts.

In *Elements of Style* 3rd ed, revised by E B White, Macmillan 79

WILLIAM STYRON

23 The good writing of any age has always been the product of *someone's* neurosis.

NY *Times* 27 Oct 63

24 Every writer since the beginning of time, just like other people, has been afflicted by what [a] friend of mine calls "the fleas of life"—you know, colds, hangovers, bills, sprained ankles and little nuisances of one sort or another.

Quoted in James L W West III ed *Conversations with William Styron* University Press of Mississippi 85

1 They are the constants of life, at the core of life, along with nice little delights that come along every now and then. . . . we all have them and they're a hell of a lot more invariable than nuclear fission or the revocation of the Edict of Nantes.
ib

GLORIA SWANSON

2 I've given my memoirs far more thought than any of my marriages. You can't divorce a book.
NY *Times* 10 Mar 79

PAUL THEROUX

3 Fiction gives us a second chance that life denies us.
NY *Times* 28 Jul 76

VIRGIL THOMSON

4 Let your mind alone, and see what happens.
On writing, *Christian Science Monitor* 12 Feb 85

JAMES THURBER

5 With 60 staring me in the face, I have developed inflammation of the sentence structure and a definite hardening of the paragraphs.
NY *Post* 30 Jun 55

J R R TOLKIEN

6 I am told that I talk in shorthand and then smudge it.
Acknowledging critics who said his writing was difficult to understand, NY *Times* 3 Mar 57

ARNOLD TOYNBEE

7 I don't believe a committee can write a book. . . . It can, oh, govern a country, perhaps, but I don't believe it can write a book.
NBC TV 17 Apr 55

P L TRAVERS

8 A writer is, after all, only half his book. The other half is the reader and from the reader the writer learns.
NY *Times* 2 Jul 78

LIONEL TRILLING

9 Immature artists imitate. Mature artists steal.
Esquire Sep 62

BARBARA TUCHMAN

10 Books are the carriers of civilization. Without books, history is silent, literature dumb, science crippled, thought and speculation at a standstill.
Authors' League Bulletin Nov 79

11 Books are humanity in print.
ib

12 Nothing sickens me more than the closed door of a library.
On raising funds for NY Public Library, *New Yorker* 21 Apr 86

13 For me, the card catalog has been a companion all my working life. To leave it is like leaving the house one was brought up in.
Informal talk to library staff when 8,000 oak drawers were replaced with 800 black-bound dictionary catalogs, *ib*

LOUIS UNTERMEYER

14 Write out of love, write out of instinct, write out of reason. But always for money.
NY *Times* 30 Sep 75

JOHN UPDIKE

15 I would especially like to recourt the Muse of poetry, who ran off with the mailman four years ago, and drops me only a scribbled postcard from time to time.
On completing a long novel, NY *Times* 7 Apr 68

16 When I write, I aim in my mind not toward New York but toward a vague spot a little to the east of Kansas.
Quoted in George Plimpton ed *Writers at Work* Viking 76

17 Each morning my characters
greet me with misty faces
willing, though chilled, to muster
for another day's progress
through the dazzling quicksand
the marsh of blank paper.
"Marching through a Novel" in *Tossing and Turning* Knopf 77

18 I moved to New England partly because it has a real literary past. The ghosts of Hawthorne and Melville still sit on those green hills. The worship of Mammon is also somewhat lessened there by the spirit of irony. I don't get hay fever in New England either.
London *Observer* 25 Mar 79

19 [Writers may be] disreputable, incorrigible, early to decay or late to bloom [but they] dare to go it alone.
Accepting Edward MacDowell Medal, NY *Times* 26 Aug 81

20 [Inspiration arrives as a] packet of material to be delivered.
Quoted by Joyce Carol Oates *ib* 11 Aug 85

21 Until the 20th century it was generally assumed that a writer had said what he had to say in his works.
"Writers on Themselves" *ib* 17 Aug 86

22 Writers take words seriously—perhaps the last professional class that does—and they struggle to steer their own through the crosswinds of meddling editors and careless typesetters and obtuse and malevolent reviewers into the lap of the ideal reader.
ib

23 One of the satisfactions of fiction, or drama, or poetry from the perpetrator's point of view is the selective order it imposes upon the confusion of a lived life; out of the daily welter of sensation and impression these few verbal artifacts, these narratives or poems, are salvaged and carefully presented.
ib

24 The creative writer uses his life as well as being its victim; he can control, in his work, the self-presentation that in actuality is at the mercy of a thousand accidents.
ib

MARIO VARGAS LLOSA

25 If you are killed because you are a writer, that's the maximum expression of respect, you know.
Time 5 Nov 84

1 Writing a book is a very lonely business. You are totally cut off from the rest of the world, submerged in your obsessions and memories.
Accepting Ritz Paris Hemingway Award, NY *Times* 30 Mar 85

GORE VIDAL

2 The greatest pleasure when I started making money was not buying cars or yachts but finding myself able to have as many freshly typed drafts as possible.
Interviewed on 30th anniversary of his 1st book, NY *Times* 24 Feb 76

3 I am an obsessive rewriter, doing one draft and then another and another, usually five. In a way, I have nothing to say, but a great deal to add.
ib

4 I don't want anything. I don't want a job. I don't want to be respectable. I don't want prizes. I turned down the National Institute of Arts and Letters when I was elected to it in 1976 on the grounds that I already belonged to the Diners Club.
Quoted in *Wall Street Journal* 3 Jul 84

ROBERT PENN WARREN

5 Most writers are trying to find what they think or feel. . . . not simply working from the given, but toward the given, saying the unsayable and steadily asking, "What do I really feel about this?"
National Observer 6 Feb 67

6 I've been to a lot of places and done a lot of things, but writing was always first. It's a kind of pain I can't do without.
ib 12 Mar 77

EUDORA WELTY

7 Writing a story or a novel is one way of discovering *sequence* in experience, of stumbling upon cause and effect in the happenings of a writer's own life.
One Writer's Beginnings Harper & Row 84

REBECCA WEST

8 Just how difficult it is to write biography can be reckoned by anybody who sits down and considers just how many people know the real truth about his or her love affairs.
"The Art of Skepticism" *Vogue* Nov 52

9 [Writing] has nothing to do with communication between person and person, only with communication between different parts of a person's mind.
ib

E B WHITE

10 Oh, I never look under the hood.
When asked for the sources of his short stories, NY *Times* 30 Aug 79

T H WHITE

11 I class myself as a manual laborer.
Letter to his publisher, recalled on his death, NY *Herald Tribune* 18 Jan 64

THEODORE H WHITE

12 I, alas, must present myself somewhat ignominiously as a chef in a busy kitchen. Somewhere a novel is bubbling on a back burner, an old attempt at history may come out of the freezer.
NY *Times* 19 Jul 79

THORNTON WILDER

13 I would love to be the poet laureate of Coney Island.
On his ultimate ambition, NY *Journal-American* 11 Nov 55

TENNESSEE WILLIAMS

14 When I stop [working] the rest of the day is post-humous. I'm only really alive when I'm writing.
Pittsburgh *Press* 30 May 60

WILLIAM CARLOS WILLIAMS

15 I think all writing is a disease. You can't stop it.
Newsweek 7 Jan 57

EDMUND WILSON

16 I am not quite a poet but I am something of the kind.
Note in his boyhood journal, quoted by David Castronovo *Edmund Wilson* Ungar 84

P G WODEHOUSE

17 I just sit at a typewriter and curse a bit.
On his writing technique, *Collier's* 31 Aug 56

18 Psmith . . . is the only thing in my literary career which was handed to me on a plate with watercress round it, thus enabling me to avoid the blood, sweat and tears inseparable from an author's life.
Quoted in Richard Usborne ed *A Wodehouse Companion* Elm Tree Books 81

HERMAN WOUK

19 I regard the writing of humor as a supreme artistic challenge.
Book-of-the-Month Club News May 85

RICHARD WRIGHT

20 I would hurl words into the darkness and wait for an echo. If an echo sounded, no matter how faintly, I would send other words to tell, to march, to fight.
American Hunger Harper & Row 77

MARGUERITE YOURCENAR

21 Leaving behind books is even more beautiful—there are far too many children.
On having no children, NY *Times* 5 May 80

22 I have never seasoned a truth with the sauce of a lie in order to digest it more easily.
ib

WILLIAM ZINSSER

23 I almost always urge people to write in the first person. . . . Writing is an act of ego and you might as well admit it.
On Writing Well Harper & Row 76

Poets

DIANE ACKERMAN

24 I don't want to get to the end of my life and find that I lived just the length of it. I want to have lived the width of it as well.
At age 37, looking back on two volumes of published poetry plus experiences as a teacher, cowhand and pilot, *Newsweek* 22 Sep 86

JOHN ASHBERY

1 I don't look on poetry as closed works. I feel they're going on all the time in my head and I occasionally snip off a length.
   London *Times* 23 Aug 84

2 I don't want to read what is going to slide down easily; there has to be some crunch, a certain amount of resilience.
   ib

3 I like poems you can tack all over with a hammer and there are no hollow places.
   ib

4 I write with experiences in mind, but I don't write about them, I write out of them.
   Quoted by John Updike NY *Times* 17 Aug 86

W H AUDEN

5 Before people complain of the obscurity of modern poetry, they should first examine their consciences and ask themselves with how many people and on how many occasions they have genuinely and profoundly shared some experience with another.
   Newsweek 17 Mar 58

6 A poet is, before anything else, a person who is passionately in love with language.
   NY *Times* 9 Oct 60

7 It's a sad fact about our culture that a poet can earn much more money writing or talking about his art than he can by practicing it.
   The Dyer's Hand Random House 68

8 A poet is a professional maker of verbal objects.
   Newsweek 29 Jan 68

9 Art is our chief means of breaking bread with the dead.
   NY *Times* 7 Aug 71

BRUCE BEAVER

10 I set the seal on a book of letters
   never to be posted, ever
   to the live poets of my knowing,
   not all writers, yet all conscious
   of the gift of the living word.
   Letters to Live Poets South Head Press 69

JOHN BETJEMAN

11 I don't think I am any good. If I thought I was any good, I wouldn't be.
   People 2 Jul 84

MAXWELL BODENHEIM

12 Poetry is the impish attempt to paint the color of the wind.
   Quoted in Ben Hecht's 1958 play *Winkelberg*

LOUISE BOGAN

13 Innocence of heart and violence of feeling are necessary in any kind of superior achievement: The arts cannot exist without them.
   Quoted in *Achievement in American Poetry: 1900–50* Regnery 51

14 [Your work] is carved out of agony as a statue is carved out of marble.
   In letter to Theodore Roethke, *ib*

JOSEPH BRODSKY

15 A language . . . is a more ancient and inevitable thing than any state.
   NY *Times* 1 Oct 72

16 For a writer only one form of patriotism exists: his attitude toward language.
   ib

17 Bad literature . . . is a form of treason.
   ib

18 Poetry is rather an approach to things, to life, than it is typographical production.
   ib

19 Who included me among the ranks of the human race?
   Response when asked at a 1964 trial, "Who included you among the ranks of the poets?" quoted in *ib*

20 Man is what he reads.
   Quoted by Thomas D'Evelyn *Christian Science Monitor* 21 May 86

JOHN CIARDI

21 Poetry lies its way to the truth.
   Saturday Review 28 Apr 62

22 You don't have to suffer to be a poet. Adolescence is enough suffering for anyone.
   Simmons Review Fall 62

23 What has any poet to trust more than the feel of the thing? Theory concerns him only until he picks up his pen, and it begins to concern him again as soon as he lays it down.
   Recalled on his death, NY *Times* 2 Apr 86

24 But when the pen is in his hand he has to write by itch and twitch, though certainly his itch and twitch are intimately conditioned by all his past itching and twitching, and by all his past theorizing about them.
   ib

JEAN COCTEAU

25 The poet never asks for admiration; he wants to be believed.
   Newsweek 7 Apr 58

E E CUMMINGS

26 A draftsman of words.
   Self-description, NY *Times* 30 Oct 63

J V CUNNINGHAM

27 I like the trivial, vulgar and exalted.
   On light verse, quoted by Thomas D'Evelyn *Christian Science Monitor* 26 Nov 86

T S ELIOT

28 [I am] an Anglo-Catholic in religion, a classicist in literature and a royalist in politics.
   Quoted in William Rose Benét ed *Reader's Encyclopedia* Crowell 65

29 Poetry is not a turning loose of emotion, but an escape from emotion; it is not the expression of personality, but an escape from personality.
   Recalled on his death 4 Jan 65

30 The Nobel is a ticket to one's own funeral. No one has ever done anything after he got it.
   On winning Nobel Prize in 1948, *ib*

1 [Poetry] may make us from time to time a little more aware of the deeper, unnamed feelings which form the substratum of our being, to which we rarely penetrate; for our lives are mostly a constant evasion of ourselves.

   Accepting Nobel Prize, ib

PAUL ENGLE

2 All poetry is an ordered voice, one which tries to tell you about a vision in the unvisionary language of farm, city and love.

   Life 28 May 56

3 Writing is like this—you dredge for the poem's meaning the way police dredge for a body. They think it is down there under the black water, they work the grappling hooks back and forth.

   ib

4 But maybe it's up in the hills under the leaves or in a ditch somewhere. Maybe it's never found. But what you find, whatever you find, is always only part of the missing, and writing is the way the poet finds out what it is he found.

   ib

5 Poetry is ordinary language raised to the Nth power. Poetry is boned with ideas, nerved and blooded with emotions, all held together by the delicate, tough skin of words.

   NY *Times* 17 Feb 57

6 Verse is not written, it is bled;
   Out of the poet's abstract head.
   Words drip the poem on the page;
   Out of his grief, delight and rage.

   A Woman Unashamed and Other Poems Random House 65

ROBERT FROST

7 I have never started a poem yet whose end I knew. Writing a poem is discovering.

   NY *Times* 7 Nov 55

8 I'd just as soon play tennis with the net down.

   On writing free verse, *Newsweek* 30 Jan 56

9 Modern poets talk against business, poor things, but all of us write for money. Beginners are subjected to trial by market.

   NY *Post* 18 May 58

10 Poets are like baseball pitchers. Both have their moments. The intervals are the tough things.

   ib

11 If you can bear at your age the honor of being made president of the United States, I ought to be able at my age to bear the honor of taking some part in your inauguration. I may not be equal to it but I can accept it for my cause—the arts, poetry—now for the first time taken into the affairs of statesmen.

   Reply to invitation from President-elect John F Kennedy, NY *Times* 15 Jan 61

12 I am glad the invitation pleases your family. It will please my family to the fourth generation and my family of friends and, were they living, it would have pleased inordinately the kind of Grover Cleveland Democrats I had for parents.

   ib

13 Life is tons of discipline. Your first discipline is your vocabulary; then your grammar and your punctuation . . . Then, in your exuberance and bounding energy you say you're going to add to that. Then you add rhyme and meter. And your delight is in *that* power.

   Life 1 Dec 61

14 You can be a little ungrammatical if you come from the right part of the country.

   Atlantic Jan 62

15 I alone of English writers have consciously set myself to make music out of what I may call the sound of sense.

   Quoted by Margaret Bartlett Anderson *Robert Frost and John Bartlett* Holt, Rinehart & Winston 63

16 The ear is the only true writer and the only true reader.

   ib

17 A poem . . . begins as a lump in the throat, a sense of wrong, a homesickness, a lovesickness.

   Quoted in *The Letters of Robert Frost to Louis Untermeyer* Holt, Rinehart & Winston 63

18 [Style is] that which indicates how the writer takes himself and what he is saying. . . . It is the mind skating circles around itself as it moves forward.

   ib

19 I would have written of me on my stone: I had a lover's quarrel with the world.

   Recalled on his death 29 Jan 63

20 Talking is a hydrant in the yard and writing is a faucet upstairs in the house. Opening the first takes the pressure off the second.

   Vogue 15 Mar 63

21 Poetry is a way of taking life by the throat.

   ib

22 I am a writer of books in retrospect. I talk in order to understand; I teach in order to learn.

   Quoted in Daniel Smythe ed *Robert Frost Speaks* Twayne 64

23 Humor is the most engaging cowardice.

   On wit as a form of evasiveness, quoted in L R Thompson ed *Selected Letters of Robert Frost* Holt, Rinehart & Winston 64

24 A poet never takes notes. You never take notes in a love affair.

   Quoted in Edward Connery Lathem ed *Interviews with Robert Frost* Holt, Rinehart & Winston 66

CHRISTOPHER FRY

25 [Poetry] has the virtue of being able to say twice as much as prose in half the time, and the drawback, if you do not give it your full attention, of seeming to say half as much in twice the time.

   Time 3 Apr 50

PHYLLIS GOTLIEB

26 You don't go after poetry, you take what comes. Maybe the gods do it through me but I certainly do a hell of a lot of the work.

   Quoted by Merle Shain *Chatelaine* Oct 72

ROBERT GRAVES

1 Prose books are the show dogs I breed and sell to support my cat.

> On writing novels to support his love of writing poetry, NY *Times* 13 Jul 58

2 Poetry is no more a narcotic than a stimulant; it is a universal bittersweet mixture for all possible household emergencies and its action varies accordingly as it is taken in a wineglass or a tablespoon, inhaled, gargled or rubbed on the chest by hard fingers covered with rings.

> *ib* 9 Oct 60

3 I believe that every English poet should read the English classics, master the rules of grammar before he attempts to bend or break them, travel abroad, experience the horror of sordid passion and—if he is lucky enough—know the love of an honest woman.

> Lecture at Oxford, *Time* 15 Dec 61

4 There's no money in poetry, but then there's no poetry in money either.

> Quoted by Huw Wheldon *Monitor* Macdonald 62

STANLEY KUNITZ

5 Old myths, old gods, old heroes have never died. They are only sleeping at the bottom of our mind, waiting for our call. We have need for them. They represent the wisdom of our race.

> To seminar at Manhattan's New School, NY *Times* 13 Oct 84

PHILIP LARKIN

6 I dream about that sometimes—and wake up screaming. With any luck they'll pass me over.

> When asked if he thought about becoming poet laureate, recalled on his death 2 Dec 85

7 I think writing about unhappiness is probably the source of my popularity, if I have any—after all, most people are unhappy, don't you think?

> *ib*

8 Deprivation is for me what daffodils were for Wordsworth.

> *ib*

9 You have to distinguish between things that seemed odd when they were new but are now quite familiar, such as Ibsen and Wagner, and things that seemed crazy when they were new and seem crazy now, like *Finnegans Wake* and Picasso.

> Quoted in George Plimpton ed *Writers at Work* Viking 86

10 I can't understand these chaps who go round American universities explaining how they write poems: It's like going round explaining how you sleep with your wife.

> Quoted by John Updike "Writers on Themselves" NY *Times* 17 Aug 86

C DAY LEWIS

11 No good poem, however confessional it may be, is just a self-expression. Who on earth would claim that the pearl *expresses* the oyster?

> "The Poet on His Work" *Christian Science Monitor* 24 May 66

ARCHIBALD MACLEISH

12 Journalism is concerned with events, poetry with feelings. Journalism is concerned with the look of the world, poetry with the feel of the world.

> "The Poet and the Press" *Atlantic* Mar 59

13 Journalism wishes to tell what it is that has happened everywhere as though the same things had happened for every man. Poetry wishes to say what it is like for any man to be himself in the presence of a particular occurrence as though only he were alone there.

> *ib*

14 To separate journalism and poetry, therefore—history and poetry—to set them up at opposite ends of the world of discourse, is to separate seeing from the feel of seeing, emotion from the acting of emotion, knowledge from the realization of knowledge.

> *ib*

15 A real writer learns from earlier writers the way a boy learns from an apple orchard—by stealing what he has a taste for and can carry off.

> *A Continuing Journey, Essays and Addresses* Houghton Mifflin 68

16 I think you have to deal with the confused situation that we're faced with by seizing on the glimpses and particles of life, seizing on them and holding them and trying to make a pattern of them. In other words, trying to put a world back together again out of its fragmentary moments.

> NY *Times* 5 Sep 68

JACQUES MARITAIN

17 Poetry proceeds from the totality of man, sense, imagination, intellect, love, desire, instinct, blood and spirit together.

> Quoted in Robert Fitzgerald ed *Enlarging the Change: The Princeton Seminars in Literary Criticism 1949–51* Northeastern University 85

18 The poet knows himself only on the condition that things resound in him, and that in him, at a single awakening, they and he come forth together out of sleep.

> *ib*

JOHN MASEFIELD

19 In the power and splendor of the universe, inspiration waits for the millions to come. Man has only to strive for it. Poems greater than the *Iliad*, plays greater than *Macbeth*, stories more engaging than *Don Quixote* await their seeker and finder.

> NY *Times* 1 Jun 58

JAMES MERRILL

20 He puts his right hand lightly on the cup, I put my left, leaving the right free to transcribe, and away we go. We get, oh, 500 to 600 words an hour. Better than gasoline.

> On deriving material for three volumes of poetry from Ouija-board sessions with a friend, quoted in George Plimpton ed *Writers at Work* Viking 84

MARIANNE MOORE

21 Any writer overwhelmingly honest about pleasing himself is almost sure to please others.

> *Vogue* 15 Aug 63

1 In a poem the excitement has to maintain itself. I am governed by the pull of the sentence as the pull of a fabric is governed by gravity.

> Quoted by Louis Untermeyer "Five Famous Poetesses" *Ladies' Home Journal* May 64

PABLO NERUDA

2 I grew up in this town, my poetry was born between the hill and the river, it took its voice from the rain, and like the timber, it steeped itself in the forests.

> On view of his childhood home of Temuco, Argentina, as he fled a new political regime in Chile, *Wall Street Journal* 14 Nov 85

3 Now, on the road to freedom, I was pausing for a moment near Temuco and could hear the voice of the water that had taught me to sing.

> *ib*

GEORGE OPPEN

4 Clarity, clarity, surely clarity is the
Most beautiful thing in the world,
A limited, limiting clarity
I have not and never did have any
Motive of poetry
But to achieve clarity.

> Recalled on his death 7 Jul 84

DOROTHY PARKER

5 My verses, I cannot say poems. . . . I was following in the exquisite footsteps of Miss Millay, unhappily in my own horrible sneakers.

> Quoted in Malcolm Cowley ed *Writers at Work* Viking 58

6 I can't write five words but that I change seven.

> *ib*

BORIS PASTERNAK

7 I come here to speak poetry. It will always be in the grass. It will also be necessary to bend down to hear it. It will always be too simple to be discussed in assemblies.

> Speech to International Congress of Writers in 1935, recalled on his death 30 May 60

8 Poetry is a rich, full-bodied whistle, cracked ice crunching in pails, the night that numbs the leaf, the duel of two nightingales, the sweet pea that has run wild, Creation's tears in shoulder blades.

> Quoted in *Life* 13 Jun 60

9 Even so, one step from my grave,
I believe that cruelty, spite,
The powers of darkness will in time
Be crushed by the spirit of light.

> From "Nobel Prize" in *Selected Poems* Norton 83

SAINT-JOHN PERSE

10 In these days of nuclear energy, can the earthenware lamp of the poet still suffice? Yes, if its clay reminds us of our own. And it is sufficient mission for the poet to be the guilt conscience of his time.

> Accepting Nobel Prize, NY *Times* 11 Dec 60

EZRA POUND

11 Use no word that under stress of emotion you could not actually say.

> Quoted in Patricia Willis ed *The Complete Prose of Marianne Moore* Viking 86

SALVATORE QUASIMODO

12 Poetry is the revelation of a feeling that the poet believes to be interior and personal [but] which the reader recognizes as his own.

> NY *Times* 14 May 60

CARL SANDBURG

13 I'll die propped up in bed trying to do a poem about America.

> On plans for his 79th birthday, news summaries 6 Jan 57

14 A sliver of the moon lost in the belly of a golden frog.

> Describing poetry, NY *Times* 13 Feb 59

15 Slang is a language that rolls up its sleeves, spits on its hands and goes to work.

> *ib*

16 I remember in my early 20s when I felt I couldn't live past 30. I was learning how to write. I had a lot of hard work ahead of me.

> Interviewed on his 86th birthday, *ib* 6 Jan 64

GIORGOS SEFERIS

17 I think the Swedish Academy . . . wished to manifest its solidarity with the living spirit of Greece today.

> On becoming the first Greek author to win Nobel Prize, NY *Herald Tribune* 25 Oct 63

18 For poetry there exists neither large countries nor small. Its domain is in the heart of all men.

> At dinner for Nobel laureates, NY *Times* 11 Dec 63

19 Don't ask who's influenced me. A lion is made up of the lambs he's digested, and I've been reading all my life.

> *Life* 17 Jan 64

JAROSLAV SEIFERT

20 If an ordinary person is silent, it may be a tactical maneuver. If a writer is silent, he is lying.

> On winning Nobel Prize 14 years after organizing resistance to Communist takeover of Prague, *Time* 22 Oct 84

EDITH SITWELL

21 Poetry is the deification of reality.

> *Life* 4 Jan 63

22 I am an unpopular electric eel in a pool of catfish.

> *ib*

23 The poet is a brother speaking to a brother of "a moment of their other lives"—a moment that had been buried beneath the dust of the busy world.

> Recalled on her death 9 Dec 64

STEPHEN SPENDER

24 Great poetry is always written by somebody straining to go beyond what he can do.

> NY *Times* 26 Mar 61

25 I'm struggling at the end to get out of the valley of hectoring youth, journalistic middle age, imposture, moneymaking, public relations, bad writing, mental confusion.

> On turning 70, *Journals 1939–83* Random House 86, quoted by R Z Sheppard *Time* 20 Jan 86

WALLACE STEVENS

1 Accuracy of observation is the equivalent of accuracy of thinking.
Opus Posthumous Knopf 57

2 Money is a kind of poetry.
Harper's Oct 85

3 Most people read [poetry] listening for echoes because the echoes are familiar to them. They wade through it the way a boy wades through water, feeling with his toes for the bottom: The echoes are the bottom.
Quoted in Beverly Coyle and Alan Filreis eds *Secretaries of the Moon: The Letters of Wallace Stevens and José Rodríguez Feo* Duke University 86

JOHN SYNGE

4 It is the timber of poetry that wears most surely, and there is no timber that has not strong roots among the clay and worms.
Quoted in *Christian Science Monitor* 26 Feb 85

DYLAN THOMAS

5 I hold a beast, an angel and a madman in me, and my enquiry is as to their working, and my problem is their subjugation and victory, downthrow and upheaval, and my effort is their self-expression.
Quoted by Constantine FitzGibbon *The Life of Dylan Thomas* Little, Brown 65

6 A born writer is born scrofulous; his career is an accident dictated by physical or circumstantial disabilities.
Quoted in Paul Ferris ed *The Collected Letters of Dylan Thomas* Macmillan 86

7 I went on all over the States, ranting poems to enthusiastic audiences that, the week before, had been equally enthusiastic about lectures on Railway Development or the Modern Turkish Essay.
ib

LOUIS UNTERMEYER

8 Every poet knows the pun is Pierian, that it springs from the same soil as the Muse. . . . a matching and shifting of vowels and consonants, an adroit assonance sometimes derided as jackassonance.
Bygones Harcourt, Brace & World 65

JOHN UPDIKE

9 There's a crystallization that goes on in a poem which the young man can bring off, but which the middle-aged man can't.
Quoted by Michiko Kakutani "When Writers Turn to Brave New Forms" NY *Times* 24 Mar 86

MARK VAN DOREN

10 When it aims to express a love of the world it refuses to conceal the many reasons why the world is hard to love, though we must love it because we have no other, and to fail to love it is not to exist at all.
On poetry and the world, *The Autobiography of Mark Van Doren* Harcourt Brace 58

ROBERT PENN WARREN

11 The poem . . . is a little myth of man's capacity of making life meaningful. And in the end, the poem is not a thing we see—it is, rather, a light by which we may see—and what we see is life.
Saturday Review 22 Mar 58

12 The urge to write poetry is like having an itch. When the itch becomes annoying enough, you scratch it.
NY *Times* 16 Dec 69

13 How do poems grow? They grow out of your life.
"Poetry Is a Kind of Unconscious Autobiography" *ib* 12 May 85

14 What is a poem but a hazardous attempt at self-understanding? It is the deepest part of autobiography.
ib

15 I don't expect you'll hear me writing any poems to the greater glory of Ronald and Nancy Reagan.
On being appointed first US poet laureate, Washington *Post* 27 Feb 86

RICHARD WILBUR

16 It is true that the poet does not directly address his neighbors; but he does address a great congress of persons who dwell at the back of his mind, a congress of all those who have taught him and whom he has admired; they constitute his ideal audience and his better self.
Accepting National Book Award, NY *Herald Tribune* 24 Mar 57

17 To this congress the poet speaks not of peculiar and personal things, but of what in himself is most common, most anonymous, most fundamental, most true of all men.
ib

WILLIAM CARLOS WILLIAMS

18 Nothing whips my blood like verse.
Quoted in John Thirlwall ed *The Selected Letters of William Carlos Williams* Astor-Honor 57

19 When they ask me, as of late they frequently do, how I have for so many years continued an equal interest in medicine and the poem, I reply that they amount for me to nearly the same thing.
Quoted in report on courses to train more sensitive physicians, NY *Times* 8 Apr 86

HELEN WORLEY

20 Dance, little words, on the end of your string.
I can make you do most anything I want to.
I can hide, anywhere
and watch you say the things
I would never dare.
"Puppetry and Poetry" in *The Soul Survivor* privately published 82

YEVGENY YEVTUSHENKO

21 A poet's autobiography is his poetry. Anything else can be only a footnote.
NY *Times* 3 Nov 63

22 Poetry is like a bird, it ignores all frontiers.
Quote 2 Jul 67

23 In Russia all tyrants believe poets to be their worst enemies.
A Precocious Autobiography Dutton 63, quoted by Robert Conquest "The Politics of Poetry" NY *Times* 30 Sep 73

24 In general, in poetry and literature, I am among those people who believe that too much is indispensable.
ib 2 Feb 86

1 [I] do not like poems that resemble hay compressed into a geometrically perfect cube. I like it when the hay, unkempt, uncombed, with dry berries mixed in it, thrown together gaily and freely, bounces along atop some truck—and more, if there are some lovely and healthy lasses atop the hay—and better yet if the branches catch at the hay, and some of it tumbles to the road. That's why I like Thomas Wolfe.
ib

2 Everything I do, I do on the principle of Russian borscht. You can throw everything into it—beets, carrots, cabbage, onions, everything you want. What's important is the result, the taste of the borscht.
ib

Observers & Critics

PETER ACKROYD

3 A triptych in which the presiding deities are Mother, England and Me.
On Noel Coward's memoirs, London *Times* 1 May 86

ALISON ADBURGHAM

4 The intimation of incest emerges from the imperceptible to the barely perceptible to the blindingly perceived.
On Gladys Parrish's *Madame Solario* Penguin 84, London *Times* 31 Dec 84

LORD ALTRINCHAM (John Edward Poynder Grigg)

5 Autobiography is now as common as adultery, and hardly less reprehensible.
London *Sunday Times* 28 Feb 62

A ALVAREZ

6 They read now like a single continuing work with the same heroine . . . and the same single, persistent, disconnected disaster of a life in which only four things can be relied on: loneliness, fear, booze and lack of money.
On novels by Jean Rhys, London *Observer* 20 May 79

KATRINE AMES

7 The best murder stories are often soufflés: light, delicately flavored and sometimes threatening to fall.
Newsweek 23 Aug 76

ANONYMOUS

8 Here lived, here died Colette, whose work is a window wide open on life.
Plaque placed by the city of Paris at the home of Colette, quoted by Maurice Goudeket *Close to Colette* Farrar, Straus & Cudahy 57

EDWARD ASWELL

9 Studying the mass of his manuscript was something like excavating the site of ancient Troy. One came upon evidences of entire civilizations buried and forgotten at different levels.
On editing Thomas Wolfe's writings into the posthumous novels *The Web and the Rock* and *You Can't Go Home Again*, quoted in NY *Times* 10 Sep 84

JAMES ATLAS

10 A penumbra of somber dignity has descended over his reputation.
On Edmund Wilson, in review of David Castronovo's *Edmund Wilson* Ungar 84, NY *Times* 28 Jul 85

11 To read Wilson . . . is to be instructed and amused in the highest sense—that is, to be educated.
ib

12 An account of some of these acts [makes] Henry Miller's crudest imaginations seem as chaste as a nun's diary.
On unexpurgated letters of James Joyce, "Putting One Letter after Another" *ib* 15 Mar 87

13 I doubt the garrulous archive bequeathed us by the tape recorder will prove as memorable as Henry James's thank-you notes.
On contemporary letter writers, *ib*

LOUIS AUCHINCLOSS

14 Perfection irritates as well as it attracts, in fiction as in life.
Pioners and Caretakers: A Study of Nine American Women Novelists University of Minnesota 65

15 A neurotic can perfectly well be a literary genius, but his greatest danger is always that he will not recognize when he is dull.
ib

16 The glittering structure of her cultivation sits on her novels like a rather showy icing that detracts from the cake beneath.
On Edith Wharton, *ib*

W H AUDEN

17 A real book is not one that's read, but one that reads us.
Recalled on his death 28 Sep 73

MARTHA BACON

18 She soothed and solaced and celebrated, destroying her gift by maiming it to suit her hearers.
On Phillis Wheatley, quoted in *Christian Science Monitor* 24 Jun 65

HERBERT SMITH BAILEY JR, Director, Princeton University Press

19 Books are the collective memory of mankind.
Bowker Memorial Lecture, news summaries 25 Jan 78

PAUL BAILEY

20 It is one of the ironies of biographical art that some details are more relevant than others, and many details have no relevance at all.
On Donald Spoto's *The Kindness of Strangers: The Life of Tennessee Williams* Little, Brown 85, *Country Life* 18 Jul 85

RUSSELL BAKER

21 Disguises thinner than a Chicago stripteaser's work clothes.
On characterizations in novels set in Washington DC, NY *Times* 28 Apr 62

22 Americans like fat books and thin women.
Quoted in James Charlton comp *The Writer's Quotation Book* Pushcart Press 80

1 Poetry is so vital to us until school spoils it.
> Introduction to *The Norton Book of Light Verse* Norton 86

2 Caution: These verses may be hazardous to your solemnity.
> *ib*

3 Anticipating that most poetry will be worse than carrying heavy luggage through O'Hare Airport, the public, to its loss, reads very little of it.
> *ib*

4 I gave up on new poetry myself 30 years ago when most of it began to read like coded messages passing between lonely aliens in a hostile world.
> *ib*

5 You can't enjoy light verse with a heavy heart.
> *ib*

RUSSELL BANKS

6 Lists of books we reread and books we can't finish tell more about us than about the relative worth of the books themselves.
> Quoted in "'Great Books' We Never Finished Reading" NY *Times* 3 Jun 84

JULIAN BARNES

7 The writer's life [is] full of frailty and defeat like any other life. What counts is the work. Yet the work can quite easily be buried, or half-buried, by the life.
> On biographies of writers, "The Follies of Writer Worship" NY *Times* 17 Feb 85

MARTHA BAYLES

8 If we are told of some four-volume epic. . . . we're apt to say "How interesting," but we never will read it unless we have both legs in traction.
> In review of *The Jewel in the Crown*, PBS television serial based on *The Raj Quartet* by Paul Scott, *Wall Street Journal* 17 Dec 84

LAURENCE BERGGREEN

9 He was not fit for marriage, only for work. A major writer, he conceded, required major torment.
> *James Agee* Dutton 84

ROGER BERTHOUD

10 Biographers, like actors, have to think their way into other people's minds and allow their own to be partially invaded by their subject's.
> Interview with Peter Ackroyd after Ackroyd had completed lives of Oscar Wilde and T S Eliot and had named his cat Dickens to mark the start of work on a biography of Charles Dickens, "A Writer Who Achieves His Goals" *Illustrated London News* Apr 86

JIM BISHOP

11 A good writer is not, per se, a good book critic. No more so than a good drunk is automatically a good bartender.
> NY *Journal-American* 26 Nov 57

HAROLD BLOOM

12 What matters in literature in the end is surely the idiosyncratic, the individual, the flavor or the color of a particular human suffering.
> *Newsweek* 18 Aug 86

13 [In the finest critics] one hears the full cry of the human. They tell one why it matters to read.
> *ib*

14 I have never believed that the critic is the rival of the poet, but I do believe that criticism is a genre of literature or it does not exist.
> *ib*

BOOKS ON TAPE NEWSLETTER

15 A lawyer in South Carolina cleans his garage every weekend so he can be alone with Churchill.
> On increasing popularity of recorded books, Feb 87

CATHERINE DRINKER BOWEN

16 In writing biography, fact and fiction shouldn't be mixed. And if they are, the fiction parts should be printed in red ink, the fact parts in black ink.
> *Publishers Weekly* 24 Mar 58

PIERS BRENDON

17 To make a criticism is a bit like complaining about the shape of the Pyramids.
> On Martin Gilbert's *Winston S Churchill* Houghton Mifflin 83, London *Times* 30 Jun 83

JIMMY BRESLIN

18 Speaks cheerful English and in the past has written this language with a paintbrush that talks.
> On Richard Condon, in review—worded as a police report—of *Prizzi's Family* Putnam 86, NY *Times* 28 Sep 86

19 Complainant . . . received immediate lacerations of the credibility.
> On his reaction to the book's chief character, *ib*

JOSEPH BRODSKY

20 Twentieth-century Russian literature has produced nothing special except perhaps one novel and two stories by Andrei Platonov, who ended his days sweeping streets.
> NY *Times* 1 Oct 72

21 [Robert] Frost's triumph was not being at John Kennedy's inauguration ceremony, but the day when he put the last period on "West-Running Brook."
> *ib*

22 This is the generation whose first cry of life was the Hungarian uprising.
> On "the large group of writers of the postwar generation, or more precisely, the so-called generation of 1956," *ib*

ANITA BROOKNER

23 It is my contention that Aesop was writing for the tortoise market. . . . hares have no time to read.
> Quoted by Rushworth M Kidder *Christian Science Monitor* 1 Mar 85

CLEANTH BROOKS

24 The cunning old codger knows that no emphasis often constitutes the most powerful emphasis of all.
> On Robert Frost, *Christian Science Monitor* 13 May 85

Van Wyck Brooks

1 No one is fit to judge a book until he has rounded Cape Horn in a sailing vessel, until he has bumped into two or three icebergs, until he has been lost in the sands of the desert, until he has spent a few years in the House of the Dead.
> *From a Writer's Notebook* Dutton 58

2 It is not that the French are not profound, but they all express themselves so well that we are led to take their geese for swans.
> *ib*

Anatole Broyard

3 It is one of the paradoxes of American literature that our writers are forever looking back with love and nostalgia at lives they couldn't wait to leave.
> On Curtis Harnack's *We Have All Gone Away* Doubleday 73, NY *Times* 16 Mar 73

4 The midnight snack of a life in its 70s.
> On Colette's 1946 book *The Evening Star*, *ib* 18 Sep 74

5 The epic implications of being human end in more than this: We start our lives as if they were momentous stories, with a beginning, a middle and an appropriate end, only to find that they are mostly middles.
> On Charles Simmons's *Wrinkles* Farrar, Straus & Giroux 78, *ib* 16 Nov 78

6 His father, Vincent, took him to La Coupole in Paris and, after sitting on the terrace for a while, walked off and forgot him. It was the perfect start in life for a writer.
> On Michael Korda, in review of *Charmed Lives* Random House 79, *ib* 3 Nov 79

7 She was a spendthrift of the spirit, an American in Paris when, as Evelyn Waugh said, the going was good.
> On Djuna Barnes, *ib* 28 Jun 80

8 We are all tourists in history, and irony is what we win in wars.
> On William Manchester's *Good-bye, Darkness: A Memoir of the Pacific War* Little, Brown 80, *ib* 17 Sep 80

9 Ruefulness is one of the classical tones of American fiction. . . . It fosters a native, deglamorized form of anxiety.
> On authors and characters who "reflect ruefully," *ib* 17 Jan 81

10 Lapped in poetry, wrapped in the picturesque, armed with logical sentences and inalienable words.
> On Evelyn Waugh, *ib* 7 Apr 84

11 A whole generation of writers dined out on the dialectic between original cultures and their culture by "progress." They became traveling salesmen of metaphors.
> On early travel writers, *ib* 31 May 84

12 Aphorisms are bad for novels. They stick in the reader's teeth.
> On Barbara Grizzuti Harrison's *Foreign Bodies* Doubleday 84, *ib* 6 Jun 84

13 To be misunderstood can be the writer's punishment for having disturbed the reader's peace. The greater the disturbance, the greater the possibility of misunderstanding.
> On Terry Garrity's *The Story of "J"* Morrow 84, *ib* 18 Jul 84

14 If a book is really good, it deserves to be read again, and if it's great, it should be read at least three times.
> "Rereading and Other Excesses" *ib* 3 Mar 85

15 The more I like a book, the more slowly I read. . . . this spontaneous talking back to a book [is] one of the things that makes reading so valuable.
> *ib*

16 The more I like a book, the more reluctant I am to turn the page. Lovers, even book lovers, tend to cling. No one-night stands or "reads" for them.
> "Confessions of a Page-Stayer, Staller, Stopper" *ib* 1 Sep 85

17 People . . . have no idea what a hard job it is for two writers to be friends. Sooner or later you have to talk about each other's work.
> *ib*

William F Buckley Jr

18 [Norman Mailer] decocts matters of the first philosophical magnitude from an examination of his own ordure, and I am not talking about his books.
> *National Review* 2 Jul 68

Claire Burch

19 The clear icy poet in her hated the spaghetti of contemporary prose.
> On her former teacher Eda Lou Walton of NY University, *Saturday Review* 29 Jun 63

James Branch Cabell

20 Poetry is man's rebellion against being what he is.
> Recalled on his death 5 May 58

Mary Cable

21 The best biographies leave their readers with a sense of having all but entered into a second life and of having come to know another human being in some ways better than he knew himself.
> On Louise Hall Tharp's *Saint-Gaudens and the Gilded Era* Little, Brown 69, NY *Times* 9 Nov 69

Vincent Canby

22 Good fiction reveals feeling, refines events, locates importance and, though its methods are as mysterious as they are varied, intensifies the experience of living our own lives.
> NY *Times* 3 Feb 80

23 Hack fiction exploits curiosity without really satisfying it or making connections between it and anything else in the world.
> *ib*

Cass Canfield

24 I am a publisher—a hybrid creature: one part stargazer, one part gambler, one part businessman, one part midwife and three parts optimist.
> Recalled on his death 27 Mar 86

25 [A publisher] should always be on the receiving end. He should take an interest in almost any subject and remain anonymous, letting the author take center stage.
> *ib*

TRUMAN CAPOTE

1 Adorned with cape, with tricorn, saintly soul singing in librarian tones an enameled song that coolly celebrates her chewing-gum enthusiasms.

On Marianne Moore, *Observations* Simon & Schuster 59

2 That's not writing, that's typing.

On the work of Jack Kerouac, quoted by Myrick Land *The Fine Art of Literary Mayhem* Holt, Rinehart & Winston 63

3 Most contemporary novelists, especially the American and the French, are too subjective, mesmerized by private demons; they're enraptured by their navels and confined by a view that ends with their own toes.

NY *Times* 16 Jan 66

JOHN CAREY

4 If you are unhealthily addicted to reading about murder trials, this book may cure you.

On Diana Trilling's *Mrs Harris: The Death of the Scarsdale Diet Doctor* Harcourt Brace Jovanovich 81, London *Sunday Times* 9 May 82

EDWARD CARPENTER, Dean, Westminster Abbey

5 Making a choice is like backing a horse—in a hundred years, they may decide you picked wrongly.

On choice of people to be memorialized in Poets' Corner, *New Yorker* 6 Jan 86

HUMPHREY CARPENTER

6 Autobiography is probably the most respectable form of lying.

NY *Times* 7 Feb 82

RAYMOND CARVER

7 Isak Dinesen said that she wrote a little every day, without hope and without despair. I like that.

Quoted in George Plimpton ed *Writers at Work* Viking 86

DAVID CASTRONOVO

8 A professor without a university, a critic without a "field," a historian without a "period," he became the exemplary intellectual of his generation.

Edmund Wilson Ungar 84

BENNETT CERF

9 There have been too many [books] in which some young man is looking forward, backward or sideways in anger. Or in which some Southern youth is being chased through the magnolia bushes by his aunt. She catches him on page 28 with horrid results.

News summaries 9 Jun 58

ANDREA CHAMBERS

10 A four-handkerchief novella.

On *Love Story*, by Erich Segal, *People* 13 May 85

ILKA CHASE

11 Neither an assembly line nor a stock market nor an oil well did it, simply what came from one small skull and that one right hand.

On Somerset Maugham's writing, quoted by Ted Morgan *Maugham* Simon & Schuster 80

JOHN CHEEVER

12 A collection of short stories is generally thought to be a horrendous clinker; an enforced courtesy for the elderly writer who wants to display the trophies of his youth, along with his trout flies.

Quoted in James Charlton comp *The Writer's Quotation Book* Pushcart Press 80

CHICAGO SUN-TIMES

13 Enough to give trash a bad name.

On Andrew Greeley's *The Cardinal Sins* Warner 81, with a character reportedly based on John Cardinal Cody, recalled on Cody's death 25 Apr 82

CAROLYN CHUTE

14 He uses a lot of big words, and his sentences run from here back to the airport.

On William Faulkner, NY *Times* 30 Jun 85

JOHN CIARDI

15 It's not a how-to-do-it school [but] more nearly a confessional in which people who have spent their lives at the writing process itemize their failures while clinging to their hopes.

On Bread Loaf Writers Conference, *Reporter* 26 Oct 63

16 Written by a sponge dipped in warm milk and sprinkled with sugar.

On traditional poetry for children, recalled on his death, NY *Times* 2 Apr 86

KENNETH CLARK

17 A visual experience is vitalizing. Whereas to write great poetry, to draw continuously on one's inner life, is not merely exhausting, it is to keep alight a consuming fire.

Moments of Vision Harper & Row 82

18 To hurry through the rise and fall of a fine, full sentence is like defying the role of time in human life.

Quoted by Anatole Broyard "Confessions of a Page-Stayer, Staller, Stopper" NY *Times* 1 Sep 85

GREGORY CLARK

19 You'll never get anywhere with all those damned little short sentences.

To fellow Toronto *Star* newspapermen Ernest Hemingway in the 1920s, quoted in Robert Thomas Allen ed *A Treasury of Canadian Humor* McClelland & Stewart 67

GERALD CLARKE

20 In the writing of memoirs, as in the production of shows, too much caution causes the audience to nod and think of other channels.

On CBS founder William S Paley's *As It Happened* Doubleday 79, *Time* 26 Mar 79

WALTER CLEMONS

21 Rebecca was a busy liar in her distinguished old age, reinventing her past for gullible biographers.

On Rebecca West, *Newsweek* 28 May 84

DUDLEY CLENDINEN

22 She realized as a girl of eight that if she sat down and wrote her stories, she could escape the parts of life she didn't like, embroider the parts she did and thus control the life she had.

On Carolyn Chute, author of *The Beans of Egypt, Maine* Ticknor & Fields 85, NY *Times* 30 Jan 85

A O J COCKSHUT

1 It is a privilege of a great autobiography to give us data for disagreeing with its conclusions.
The Art of Biography in 19th- and 20th-Century England Yale 84, quoted by Anatole Broyard NY *Times* 27 Jan 85

JEAN COCTEAU

2 That pile of paper on his left side went on living like the watch on a dead soldier's wrist.
On visiting the deathbed of Marcel Proust, quoted by Edmund White "Cocteau: The Great Enchanter" *Vogue* May 84

RICHARD L COE

3 He is the poet of solitude.
The Vision of Jean Genet Grove 68

ARTHUR A COHEN

4 Russia is a conspicious murderer of her poets and ennobler of their poems.
On Joseph Brodsky's *Selected Poems* Harper & Row 73, NY *Times* 30 Dec 73

JOHN COLVILLE

5 He fertilizes a phrase or a line of poetry for weeks and then gives birth to it in a speech.
On Winston Churchill, *The Fringes of Power* Norton 85

CYRIL CONNOLLY

6 Vulgarity is the garlic in the salad of life.
Quoted by Joseph Epstein *The Middle of My Tether* Norton 83

PETER CONRAD

7 Facts . . . have long since upstaged fiction, and the novelistic imagination now contents itself with documenting incidents it wouldn't have the temerity to invent.
On Diana Trilling's *Mrs Harris: The Death of the Scarsdale Diet Doctor* Harcourt Brace Jovanovich 81, London *Observer* 9 May 82

GEOFFREY COTTRELL

8 In America only the successful writer is important, in France all writers are important, in England no writer is important and in Australia you have to explain what a writer is.
NY *Journal-American* 22 Sep 61

NORMAN COUSINS

9 A book is like a piece of rope; it takes on meaning only in connection with the things it holds together.
Saturday Review 15 Apr 78

MALCOLM COWLEY

10 Authors are sometimes like tomcats: They distrust all the other toms but they are kind to kittens.
Introduction to *Writers at Work* Viking 58

11 It would have been the equivalent of Jackson Pollock's attempts to copy the Sistine Chapel.
On a manuscript John Cheever had submitted that seemed obviously based on a Hemingway story, quoted by Susan Cheever *Home before Dark* Houghton Mifflin 84

FREDERICK CREWS

12 "Little magazines" are, for the most part, the mayflies of the literary world.
Skeptical Engagements Oxford 87, quoted in NY *Times* 15 Mar 87

13 Ephemerality is the little magazine's generic fate; by promptly dying it gives proof that it remained loyal to its first program.
ib

MARIO CUOMO, Governor of NY

14 Lincoln isn't a man with ingrown toenails, he's an idea.
On reading a biography of Lincoln that "showed me the warts," NY *Times* 14 Sep 86

CHARLOTTE CURTIS

15 The nearest we have to a Henry James or an Edith Wharton of the East Coast's Wasp upper classes.
On Louis Auchincloss, NY *Times* 22 Apr 86

THOMAS D'EVELYN

16 He doesn't watch, he notices.
On Edward Hoagland, in review of *The Courage of Turtles* North Point 85, *Christian Science Monitor* 7 Jun 85

17 [It] reminds me of a piece of jade. The emerald light coming from within is refracted and dispersed according to the consistency of the impurities that gave it its quality.
On Nicolas Saudray's *The House of Prophets* Doubleday 85, *ib* 4 Oct 85

JAMES DICKEY

18 [She was] the Judy Garland of American poetry.
On Sylvia Plath, quoted in George Plimpton ed *Writers at Work* Viking 81

RONALD DUNCAN

19 I was lecturing to a group of English teachers about Dante. Suddenly one of them got up—English teachers, mind you—and said, "What is Dante?" "Well, Madam," I replied, "It is a kind of detergent."
London *Sunday Times* 14 Sep 80

CYRIL DUNN

20 A prose style as sharp and clean as a bleached bone on a beach.
On John Gale, London *Observer* 6 May 79

FERN MARJA ECKMAN

21 [He] is salt rubbed in the wounds of the nation's conscience. He is a scream of pain. He is an accusing finger thrust in the face of white America. He is a fierce, brilliant light illuminating the unspeakable and the shameful.
On James Baldwin, NY *Post* 13 Jan 64

RICHARD EDER

22 Artists and musicians have their impedimenta: easels and paint pots, blocks of marble, grand pianos. Writers' impedimenta are at least as large and awkward as a grand piano; and more cumbersome for being invisible . . . the silence they carry with them. Friends must squeeze past it, being careful not to leave scratches. Maids must be careful not to disturb it.
"For Writers, Separate Silences" NY *Times* 26 Mar 80

1 In the middle of the silence in a writer's house lies an invalid: the book being worked on.
ib

2 [He] is a tall, grandly built man; [she] tall and delicate. Both are narrow-faced with long, imperial noses; as they pose for pictures, it is a turkey buzzard sharing companionably with an egret.
On Jack Manning's photographs of husband and wife writers Francis Steegmuller and Shirley Hazzard, *ib*

3 A kind of duet—she as oboe, he as contrabassoon, and full of obbligato digressions.
ib

T S ELIOT

4 As things are, and as fundamentally they must always be, poetry is not a career, but a mug's game. No honest poet can ever feel quite sure of the permanent value of what he has written: He may have wasted his time and messed up his life for nothing.
Recalled on his death 4 Jun 65

STANLEY ELKIN

5 Life's tallest order is to keep the feelings up, to make two dollars' worth of euphoria go the distance. And life can't do that. So fiction does.
Introduction to *The Best American Short Stories 1980* Houghton Mifflin 80

6 It's fine, precise, detailed work, the infinitely small motor management of diamond cutters and safecrackers that we do in our heads.
Early Elkin Bamberger 85, quoted in NY *Times* 25 May 86

7 Once I opened books slowly, stately, plump imaginary orchestras going off in my head like overtures . . . humming the title page, whistling the copyright.
ib

GEORGE P ELLIOTT

8 A novel is not just a work of art: It is somehow a work of life as well.
A Piece of Lettuce Random House 64

NORA EPHRON

9 It shines like a rhinestone in a trash can.
On Jacqueline Susann's *The Love Machine* Simon & Schuster 69, NY *Times* 11 Mar 69

CLIFTON FADIMAN

10 The adjective is the banana peel of the parts of speech.
Reader's Digest Sep 56

MARK FEENEY

11 Once the implicit aim of biography was to *uplift* . . . now it is to *unveil*.
"Profitable Lives" Boston *Globe* 25 Jan 87

JAMES FENTON

12 When Mr Ackroyd says that in the 18th century, stranglers bit off the noses of their victims, I feel that he probably knows what he is talking about. I just wish he hadn't told me.
On Peter Ackroyd's *Hawksmoor* Hamish Hamilton 85, London *Times* 26 Sep 85

SAMUEL G FREEDMAN

13 Briefly leaving behind the molars and malocclusions to enter Yoknapatawpha County, the mythical realm of madmen and malingerers, drifters and grifters, funeral parties and lynch mobs.
On Karl Leone, "Under Faulkner's Spell, A Dentist from Staten Island" NY *Times* 26 Jul 86

OTTO FRIEDRICH

14 During the last months of the German Occupation in 1944, the young man who was to become France's most controversial contemporary philosopher and the woman who was to become its most controversial feminist met the professional criminal who was to become its most controversial playwright.
On Jean Paul Sartre, Simone de Beauvoir and Jean Genet, "The Mandarin and the Thief" *Time* 28 Apr 86

EDMUND FULLER

15 There's one irony . . . it has no pictures.
On biography of Henry R Luce, founder of photojournalism, *Wall Street Journal* 12 Mar 68

JOHN KENNETH GALBRAITH

16 Several times I concluded that there was too much detail; always I returned to continue and enjoy the book.
On W A Swanberg's *Whitney Father, Whitney Heiress* Scribner's 80, NY *Times* 27 Jul 80

17 We have escapist fiction, so why not escapist biography?
ib

MARILYN GARDNER

18 The gift of the family novelist is to turn the cleaning of a closet into an inventory of love and loss—to scan a poem from a shopping list.
On Anne Tyler's *The Accidental Tourist* Knopf 85, *Christian Science Monitor* 4 Oct 85

STEVE GARMAN

19 The lovely woman-child Kaa was mercilessly chained to the cruel post of the warrior-chief Beast, with his barbarian tribe now stacking wood at her nubile feet, when the strong clear voice of the poetic and heroic Handsomas roared, "Flick your Bic, crisp that chick and you'll feel my steel through your last meal."
Winning entry in Bulwer-Lytton Fiction Contest for the worst opening sentence for a novel, NY *Times* 13 May 84

WILLIAM H GASS

20 [For the speedy reader] paragraphs become a country the eye flies over looking for landmarks, reference points, airports, restrooms, passages of sex.
Habitations of the Word Simon & Schuster 85, quoted by Frank Kermode "Adornment and Fantastication" NY *Times* 10 Mar 85

21 The speeding reader guts a book the way the skillful clean fish. The gills are gone, the tail, the scales, the fins; then the fillet slides away swifly as though fed to a seal.
ib

1 Only the slow reader . . . will notice the odd crowd of images—flier, butcher, seal—which have gathered to comment on the aims and activities of the speeding reader, perhaps like gossips at a wedding.
ib

2 If you believed yourself to be a writer of . . . eminence, you are now assured of being over the hill—not a sturdy mountain flower but a little wilted lily of the valley.
Contending that "the Pulitzer Prize in fiction takes dead aim at mediocrity and almost never misses," *ib* 5 May 85

BRENDAN GILL

3 Parody is homage gone sour.
Here at the New Yorker Random House 75

REN GLASSER

4 He shows her through a magnifying glass which he holds in a velvet glove.
On Patrick O'Higgins's biography of Helena Rubinstein, *Madame* Viking 71, NY *Times* 22 Aug 71

HERBERT GOLD

5 He carried his childhood like a hurt warm bird held to his middle-aged breast.
On Sherwood Anderson, *The Age of Happy Problems* Dial 62

HARRY GOLDEN

6 Sex in a woman's world has the same currency a penny has in a man's. Every penny saved is a penny earned in one world and in the next every sexual adventure is a literary experience.
NY *Post* 13 Jan 64

WALTER GOODMAN

7 He uses anecdotes for the same reason other people climb mountains—they are there.
On Robert Sam Anson, in review of *Exile: The Unquiet Oblivion of Richard M Nixon* Simon & Schuster 84, NY *Times* 28 Jun 84

8 This is a book in which camels' backs are broken by straws, things stick in craws, people skate on thin ice, step into the breach and open cans of worms, cards are played close to the vest, cold shivers go down spines and time doesn't stand still. And that, to use another of Ms Sperber's inventions, is just the tip of the iceberg.
On A M Sperber's *Murrow* Freundlich 86, *ib* 2 Jul 86

ROBERT GRAVES

9 A remarkable thing about Shakespeare is that he is really very good in spite of all the people who say he is very good.
Recalled on his death 7 Dec 85

PAUL GRAY

10 Paperbacks blink in and out of print like fireflies. They also, as older collectors have ruefully discovered, fade and fall apart even more rapidly than their owners.
Time 3 May 82

11 He offers the never-never land of convenient clichés. . . . a world where statesmen say, "We've not heard the end of this," where people turn "scarlet with anger," where the price of gold goes "sky-high" and where the unsuspecting outsider "little knew what fate had in store for him."
On Gore Vidal's *Lincoln* Random House 84, *ib* 21 May 84

12 [It] even looks exactly like a real book, with pages and print and dust jacket and everything. This disguise is extremely clever, considering the contents: the longest lounge act never performed in the history of the Catskills.
On Joseph Heller's *God Knows* Knopf 84, *ib* 24 Sep 84

13 People joked that Forster became more renowned with every book he did not write.
On E M Forster, *ib* 31 Dec 84

14 Those who have spent time familiarizing themselves with the topography of Greeneland will have some idea of what must happen next.
On Graham Greene's *The Tenth Man* Simon & Schuster 85, *ib* 11 Mar 85

15 Muffled lives explode in . . . understatements.
On Ruth Prawer Jhabvala's *Out of India* Morrow 86, *ib* 12 May 86

JEFF GREENFIELD

16 Something about her eyes or voice has always suggested the hint of a free spirit, trapped in a Peck & Peck cage, dreaming of making rude noises at public gatherings of Republicans.
On Julie Nixon Eisenhower, in review of *Special People* Simon & Schuster 77, NY *Times* 31 Jul 77

JOHN GROSS

17 He has managed to capture the particular aura that made even the poet's more mundane activities—of which there were many—fascinatingly boring, so to speak, rather than merely boringly boring.
On Peter Ackroyd's *T S Eliot* Simon & Schuster 84, NY *Times* 7 Nov 84

18 The cliché is a hackneyed idiom that hopes that it can still palm itself off as a fresh response.
On Eric Partridge's *A Dictionary of Catch Phrases*, revised by Paul Beale, Stein & Day 85, *ib* 2 Jan 87

19 The catch phrase positively rejoices in being a formula, an accepted gambit, a ready-made reaction.
ib

PHILIP GUEDALLA

20 Biography, like big game hunting, is one of the recognized forms of sport, and it is [as] unfair as only sport can be.
Quoted by Robin Maugham "The Art of Biography" *MD* Mar 80

21 Autobiography is an unrivaled vehicle for telling the truth about other people.
Quoted by Hugh Leonard NY *Times* 23 Nov 80

MEL GUSSOW

22 On her pages sacred cows become blustering pachyderms.
On Anita Loos's *Kiss Hollywood Good-bye* Viking 74, NY *Times* 31 Aug 74

THEODOR HAECKER

1 One of the most arrogant undertakings, to my mind, is to write the biography of a man which pretends to go beyond external facts and gives the inmost motives. One of the most mendacious is autobiography.
Journal in the Night Pantheon 50

SYDNEY J HARRIS

2 The public examination of homosexuality in our contemporary life is still so coated with distasteful moral connotations that even a reviewer is bound to wonder uneasily why *he* was selected to evaluate a book on the subject, and to assert defensively at the outset that he is happily married, the father of four children and the one-time adornment of his college boxing, track and tennis teams.
On Jess Stearn's *The Sixth Man* Doubleday 61, *Saturday Review* 22 Apr 61

JOHN HEILPERN

3 He left the self-conscious literary demimonde of New York for the quiet infidelities of New England.
On John Updike, London *Observer* 25 Mar 79

ERNEST HEMINGWAY

4 His talent was as natural as the pattern that was made by the dust on a butterfly's wings. At one time he understood it no more than the butterfly did and he did not know when it was brushed or marred.
On F Scott Fitzgerald, *A Moveable Feast* Scribner's 64

5 All modern American literature comes from one book by Mark Twain called *Huckleberry Finn*.
Quoted in NY *Times* 9 Dec 84

DONAL HENAHAN

6 Next to the writer of real estate advertisements, the autobiographer is the most suspect of prose artists.
NY *Times* 11 Feb 77

GEORGE V HIGGINS

7 Writing is the only trade I know of in which sniveling confessions of extreme incompetence are taken as credentials probative of powers to astound the multitude.
Harper's Sep 84

8 The received image of a writer is that of an unproductive sensitive who suffers from the vapors, is enslaved by his gonads, falls victim to romantic swoons and passes out at deadlines.
ib

DAVID HOLAHAN

9 Your piece stinks. We fed it to the turtle.
Envisioning the ultimate, honest rejection by an editor, "Dining on Cardboard Au Gratin: A Free-lancer's Lament" *Christian Science Monitor* 13 Feb 85

HERBERT HOOVER, 31st US President

10 What this country needs is a great poem. *John Brown's Body* was a step in the right direction. I've read it once, and I'm reading it again. But it's too long to do what I mean. You can't thrill people in 300 pages.
Quoted in *Saturday Review Treasury* Simon & Schuster 57

11 The limit is about 300 words. Kipling's "Recessional" really did something to England when it was published. It helped them through a bad time. Let me know if you find any great poems lying around.
To Christopher Morley, an overnight White House guest, *ib*

A E HOUSMAN

12 Great literature should do some good to the reader: must quicken his perception though dull, and sharpen his discrimination though blunt, and mellow the rawness of his personal opinions.
Quoted in report on Great Books discussion groups, NY *Times* 28 Feb 85

PHILIP HOWARD

13 Ted Hughes has been appointed poet laureate to succeed Sir John Betjeman, which is a bit like appointing a grim young crow to replace a cuddly old teddy bear.
London *Times* 20 Dec 84

14 He brings a gust of acrid provincial air to the ancient office. He is an angry young prophet rather than a smooth courtier. His verse is angular, savage, robust and very good.
ib

IRVING HOWE

15 The cruelest thing anyone can do to *Portnoy's Complaint* is to read it twice.
On Philip Roth's novel, quoted by Thomas Fleming "The War between Writers and Reviewers" NY *Times* 6 Jan 85

RANDALL JARRELL

16 He thinks that Schiller and St Paul were just two *Partisan Review* editors.
On Delmore Schwartz, quoted in Mary Jarrell ed *Randall Jarrell's Letters* Houghton Mifflin 85

HORACE JUDSON

17 At his best he penerated the magnolia curtain of Southern illusions to the secret springs of motive and action. He said, in effect, "This is the way it feels to be Southern"—something the North needs to know and the South may even need to be reminded of.
On William Faulkner, *Time* 17 Jul 64

MICHIKO KAKUTANI

18 Glossy, efficient prose, garnished with a pinch of irony and a dab of melodrama.
On Louis Auchincloss's *The Book Class* Houghton Mifflin 84, NY *Times* 26 Jul 84

T E KALEM

19 The English language brings out the best in the Irish. They court it like a beautiful woman. They make it bray with donkey laughter. They hurl it at the sky like a paint pot full of rainbows, and then make it chant a dirge for man's fate and man's follies that is as mournful as misty spring rain crying over the fallow earth.
On Brendan Behan's 1958 play *Borstal Boy*, quoted in a *Time* advertisement, NY *Times* 17 Mar 79

1 Rarely has a people paid the lavish compliment and taken the subtle revenge of turning its oppressor's speech into sorcery.
ib

STEFAN KANFER

2 The catalogue of miseries seems to cry out for commercial spots and a station break: the stuff of noonday soap opera.
On Susan Kenney's *In Another Country* Viking 84, *Time* 11 Jun 84

3 Kenney . . . knows two essential truths about melodrama: First that it is most powerful when combined with irony and understatement; and second that it is a salient feature of modern life.
ib

4 They are the literary equivalent of sequins on an evening dress.
On prominent people in Gloria Vanderbilt's *Once Upon a Time* Knopf 85, *ib* 6 May 85

JOHN F KENNEDY, 35th US President

5 When power leads man toward arrogance, poetry reminds him of his limitations. When power narrows the area of man's concern, poetry reminds him of the richness and diversity of existence. When power corrupts, poetry cleanses.
Last major public address, at dedication of Robert Frost Library, Amherst College, 26 Oct 63

RUSHWORTH M KIDDER

6 He dropped into the Potomac, ever so casually, a few great thoughts. One can only hope their ripples will reach out to all the limousined and tuxedoed policymakers.
On Cleanth Brooks, speaking in Washington DC on illiteracy, *Christian Science Monitor* 13 May 85

ROSS KNOX

7 If you got to talking to most cowboys, they'd admit they write 'em. I think some of the meanest, toughest sons of bitches around write poetry.
Quoted by Michael Riley "In Arizona: Cowboy Poets" *Time* 25 Nov 85

RHODA KOENIG

8 Characters drop into whorehouses, have a little sex between paragraphs and leave without advancing the plot.
On Gore Vidal's *Lincoln* Random House 84, *New York* 18 Jun 84

9 [Readers] who like facts will be better off with a straight history that spares them all the forelock tugging and teacup tinkling.
ib

JOHN LAHR

10 His life was one long extravaganza, like living inside a Fabergé egg.
On Noel Coward, "Politics of Charm" *Harper's* Oct 82

F R LEAVIS

11 He doesn't know what he means, and doesn't know he doesn't know.
Two Cultures? The Significance of C P Snow Pantheon 63

DAVID LEAVITT

12 [She was] a copy editor, possessed of the rare capacity to sit all day in a small cubicle, like a monk in a cell, and read with an almost penitential rigor.
The Lost Language of Cranes Knopf 86, quoted in NY *Times* 3 Nov 86

13 It was an instinct to put the world in order that powered her . . . mending split infinitives and snipping off dangling participles, smoothing away the knots and bumps until the prose before her took on a sheen, like perfect caramel.
ib

CHRISTOPHER LEHMANN-HAUPT

14 Rice Krispies happens to be one of my favorite junk foods, just as I regard Michener as superior among junk writers.
On James A Michener, in review of *Chesapeake* Random House 78, *International Herald Tribune* 8 Aug 78

15 One misses the hiss of acid.
On Gore Vidal's *Lincoln* Random House 84, NY *Times* 30 May 84

16 We breathe, we think, we conceive of our lives as narratives.
On Peter Brooks's *Reading for the Plot* Knopf 84, *ib* 11 Jul 84

17 The beginning of a plot . . . is the prompting of desire.
ib

18 What they have in common is that if the reviewer did not already possess them, he would long for them most greedily.
On coffee-table books, *ib* 28 Nov 84

19 One is happy to report that Israel Shenker is still at the aerosol stage. His energy is still compressed. The result distinguishes him both as a Jew and as an observer of Jews.
In review of *Coat of Many Colors* Doubleday 85, *ib* 11 Mar 85

JOSEPH LELYVELD

20 His laughter, which was never far below the surface of his conversation, now sparkled like a splash of water in sunlight.
From interview with V S Pritchett at age 85, NY *Times* 16 Dec 85

JOHN LEONARD

21 He seems to have . . . gone to his icebox, pulled out all the cold obsessions, mixed them in a bowl, beat too lightly and baked too long.
On Gore Vidal's *Two Sisters* Little, Brown 70, NY *Times* 7 Jul 70

22 Aspiring to a soufflé, he achieves a pancake at which the reader saws without much appetite.
ib

23 There are too many ironies in the fire.
ib

24 His memoir is a splendid artichoke of anecdotes, in which not merely the heart and leaves but the thistles as well are edible.
On Brendan Gill's *Here at the New Yorker* Random House 75, *ib* 16 Feb 75

1 Books fall from Garry Wills like leaves from a maple tree in a sort of permanent October.
ib 15 Jul 79

2 [As] the Silks . . . walk around the Establishment and poke it with a stick . . . flocks of multicolored anecdotes rise into the air on flapping wings, and, occasionally, a bee stings.
On Leonard and Mark Silk's *The American Establishment* Basic 80, *ib* 15 Sep 80

3 A lollipop speaking baby talk.
On Suzanne Massie's *Land of the Firebird: The Beauty of Old Russia* Simon & Schuster 80, *ib* 8 Oct 80

C S LEWIS

4 Literature adds to reality, it does not simply describe it. It enriches the necessary competencies that daily life requires and provides; and in this respect, it irrigates the deserts that our lives have already become.
Quoted by Paul Holmer *C S Lewis* Harper & Row 76

A J LIEBLING

5 Henry Miller may write about revelers self-woven into a human hooked rug, because his ecstasy is solemn.
Between Meals: An Appetite for Paris North Point 86, quoted in NY *Times* 25 May 86

LIFE MAGAZINE

6 More delightfully than any other passage in the Bible, this episode drives home the rapport between the Hebrews and their deity, a rapport which allows God to drop in for dinner and a skeptical old lady to laugh at him.
On Genesis account of God's visitation to Abraham and his wife Sarah, declaring they shall have a son in their old age, 25 Dec 64

RON LOEWINSOHN

7 It's just this epidemic unimportance, this pervasive feeling that just about everything is "no big deal," that drives these ordinary people to those fast-food joints, there to try to fill with carbohydrates the spiritual and emotional emptiness gnawing inside them.
On Frederick Barthelme's *Second Marriage* Simon & Schuster 84, NY *Times* 30 Sep 84

8 Most of the people . . . are no thicker than Formica, yet they hunger obscurely for some continuity with the place and with each other.
ib

DWIGHT MACDONALD

9 The dominant rhetoric is academese relieved by flashes of cliché.
On NY *Times Book Review*, a criticism to which Sunday Editor Lester Markel replied, "Good people think I'm great, bad people think I'm a bastard," *Newsweek* 14 Sep 64

MARIAN MACDOWELL

10 It's what I've dedicated my life to prevent—the non-writing of the great poem.
On funding MacDowell Colony in Peterborough NH, quoted by Herbert Kubly "The Care and Feeding of Artists" *Horizon* Mar 63

MELVIN MADDOCKS

11 It is one test of a fully developed writer that he reminds us of no one but himself.
On Anthony Powell's *What's Become of Waring* Little, Brown 63, *Christian Science Monitor* 2 May 63

12 Discreet as an old teacup.
On Sylvia Townsend Warner's *Scenes of Childhood* Viking 82, *Time* 1 Feb 82

13 Writing is the most demanding of callings, more harrowing than a warrior's, more lonely than a whaling captain's—that, in essence, is the modern writer's message.
Christian Science Monitor 10 Apr 85

14 To choose art means to turn one's back on the world, or at least on certain of its distractions.
ib

GROUCHO MARX

15 From the moment I picked your book up until I laid it down I was convulsed with laughter. Someday I intend reading it.
On S J Perelman's 1929 book *Dawn Ginsbergh's Revenge*, quoted in *Life* 9 Feb 62

SOMERSET MAUGHAM

16 The crown of literature is poetry.
Saturday Review 20 July 57

17 The writer of prose can only step aside when the poet passes.
ib

18 It is unsafe to take your reader for more of a fool than he is.
Selected Prefaces and Introductions Doubleday 63

ANDRÉ MAUROIS

19 *Lost Illusion* is the undisclosed title of every novel.
The Art of Writing Dutton 60

20 In literature as in love, we are astonished at what is chosen by others.
NY *Times* 14 Apr 63

MARY McCARTHY

21 Every word she writes is a lie, including *and* and *the*.
On Lillian Hellman, a 1979 televised comment that resulted in a libel suit unresolved at the time of Hellman's death, recalled on opening of the play *Lillian*, NY *Times* 12 Jan 86

DAVID McCORD

22 Metaphorically these essays move as a quiet but observant coast-guard cutter among the rocks and islands up and down the littoral of our life.
On J B Priestley's *Essays of Five Decades* Little, Brown 68, NY *Times* 27 Oct 68

PHYLLIS McGINLEY

23 You'd better compile a collection
Of words that another has wrote.
It's the shears and the glue
Which will compensate you
And fashion a person of note.
For poets have common companions,
Their fame is a wraith in the mist,
But the critics all quarrel

To garland with laurel
The brow of the anthologist, my son,
The brow of the anthologist!
> "A Ballad of Anthologists," quoted in *The Saturday Evening Post Treasury* Simon & Schuster 54

CATHLEEN McGUIGAN

1 Don't think of . . . Diana Vreeland's memoir as a book; it's more like a lunch. A bit of soufflé, a glass of champagne, some green grapes—light, bubbly and slightly tart—all served up by an egocentric but inventive hostess.
> On *DV* Knopf 84, *Newsweek* 25 Jun 84

H L MENCKEN

2 There are some people who read too much: the bibliobibuli.
> *Minority Report: H L Mencken's Notebooks* Knopf 56

SUZY MENKES

3 This is a book lined with hard facts and stitched up with strong opinions.
> On *McDowell's Directory of 20th-Century Fashion*, London *Times* 11 Dec 84

EDNA ST VINCENT MILLAY

4 A person who publishes a book willfully appears before the populace with his pants down. . . . If it is a good book nothing can hurt him. If it is a bad book nothing can help him.
> Quoted in Alan Ross Macdougall ed *Letters of Edna St Vincent Millay* Harper & Row 52

BRIAN MOORE

5 As the flow of subliterary "news items" and anecdotes increases, the writer's work withers and stales until, in grim transference, his life becomes his oeuvre and he his only character.
> On effect of publicity, NY *Herald Tribune* 21 June 64

TED MORGAN

6 He saw them bearing not frankincense and myrrh but wormwood and hemlock.
> On Somerset Maugham's regard for biographers, *Maugham* Simon & Schuster 80

7 The Sitwells were less a family than a literary cartel with a gift for self-propagation.
> *ib*

8 He seemed embalmed in hatred.
> On Maugham's last years, *ib*

MALCOLM MUGGERIDGE

9 [Evelyn Waugh] was an antique in search of a period, a snob in search of a class.
> Quoted in Ian Hunter ed *Things Past: A Malcolm Muggeridge Anthology* Morrow 79

GLORIA NAYLOR

10 One should be able to return to the first sentence of a novel and find the resonances of the entire work.
> NY *Times* 2 June 85

JACK NEWFIELD

11 Koch has committed egocide with this book.
> On Edward Koch's *Mayor* Simon & Schuster 84, quoted in *People* 9 Apr 84

NEWSWEEK

12 The hotelkeeper's daughter is a nymphomaniac, the cab driver's wife is a prostitute, the druggist and the newspaper editor are rivals in lechery and the corresponding secretary of the WCTU is a dope addict. Just folks, one and all.
> On Day Keene and Dwight Vincent's *Chautauqua* Putnam 59, 29 Feb 60

13 Dipping into Marianne Moore is like trying potluck at Cartier's.
> 27 Nov 61

NEW YORK TIMES

14 Armed with a notebook, ingratiating grin and fine intelligence, he grew to be a most discerning witness of America's most distinctive rite, not just the election but the making of our presidents.
> Editorial on death of Theodore H White, 17 May 86

15 He had an acute eye for important bit players, and if his heroes tended to be a bit larger than life, they inhabited epics.
> *ib*

16 A New Yorker looks to Neil Simon for cheering-up, Sigmund Freud for shocks of recognition and Sir Thomas More for Utopia.
> Editorial on books most frequently stolen from NY Public Library, "New Yorkers, by the Book" 4 Oct 86

17 What he, or she, is looking for in the life of Miró we can't imagine, but he sure does like to read about it. Ditto the life of Michelangelo, and the days and nights of Holly Golightly and Holden Caulfield.
> *ib*

18 The best way to read [a poem] is off the top of your head, and out of the corner of your eye.
> "Noted with Pleasure" 15 Mar 87

JOYCE CAROL OATES

19 When people say there is too much violence in [my books], what they are saying is there is too much reality in life.
> NY *Times* 27 Jul 80

JOHN O'HARA

20 So who's perfect? . . . Washington had false teeth. Franklin was nearsighted. Mussolini had syphilis. Unpleasant things have been said about Walt Whitman and Oscar Wilde. Tchaikovsky had his problems, too. And Lincoln was constipated.
> Replying to criticism, *Carte Blanche* Fall 65

21 Little old ladies of both sexes. Why do I let them bother me?
> On reviewers, quoted by Thomas Fleming "The War Between Writers and Reviewers" NY *Times* 6 Jan 85

JACK PAAR

22 One gets the impression that this is how Ernest Hemingway would have written had he gone to Vassar.
> On Mary McCarthy's novel about Vassar's Class of '33, *The Group* Harcourt, Brace & World 63, quoted in *Look* 25 Feb 64

PRINCE PHILIP, Duke of Edinburgh

1 I don't enjoy writing, and I certainly would not do it for a living. Some people do, but some people enjoy flagellation.

> On completing a book about competition carriage driving, *Time* 10 May 82

CHARLES POORE

2 An essayist is a lucky person who has found a way to discourse without being interrupted.

> NY *Times* 31 May 62

3 Satire is the most aggressive form of flattery.

> On Gilbert Highet's *The Anatomy of Satire* Princeton 62, *ib* 29 Sep 62

4 Names are dropped throughout this glowing, witty, grave pageant of yesterdays so extravagantly that I imagine Harper's printers frequently borrowed cupfuls of capital letters from neighborly presses.

> On John Mason Brown's *The Worlds of Robert E Sherwood* Harper & Row 65, *ib* 12 Sep 65

CHRISTOPHER PORTERFIELD

5 The case against interviews with writers is historic: They exploit personalities, expose their subjects in verbal undress, without their styles hitched up, and they traffic in anecdotes and gossip.

> On George Plimpton ed's *Writers at Work* Viking 84, *Time* 10 Sep 84

EZRA POUND

6 A dirty book worth reading.

> On Henry Miller's 1934 book *Tropic of Cancer*, recalled on Miller's death 7 Jun 80

ANTHONY POWELL

7 The whole idea of interviews is in itself absurd—one cannot answer deep questions about what one's life was like—one writes novels about it.

> On failure of Edward Whitley's book *The Graduates*, which included interviews with famous people who had attended Oxford University, London *Times* 15 May 86

ORVILLE PRESCOTT

8 Scores of books a day, thousands in a year, many of them good and all of them dressed up in brightly colored jackets. And all of them free. Could a booklover imagine a better version of the earthly paradise?

> On being a book reviewer, NY *Times* 2 Dec 56

PETER S PRESCOTT

9 Let's hope the institution of marriage survives its detractors, for without it there would be no more adultery and without adultery two thirds of our novelists would stand in line for unemployment checks.

> *Newsweek* 8 Nov 76

10 Two things a novelist can do with a hat: Talk through it or pull a rabbit from it.

> On Muriel Spark's *The Only Problem* Putnam 84, *ib* 2 Jul 84

V S PRITCHETT

11 Detective stories are the art-for-art's sake of yawning Philistinism.

> *Books in General* Harcourt, Brace 53

12 I swallow Dickens whole and put up with the indigestion.

> Quoted by Richard Locke "In Praise of V S Pritchett" NY *Times* 29 Jun 80

13 A company of actors inside one suit, each twitting the others.

> On T S Eliot, quoted by Peter Ackroyd *T S Eliot* Simon & Schuster 84

14 The wrongs of childhood and upbringing have made a large and obsessional contribution to autobiography and the novel. [But] such wrongs are a static capital unless invested in matters far beyond the sense of personal injury.

> On Anthony West's *H G Wells* Random House 84, *New Yorker* 30 Jul 84

15 It is less the business of the novelist to tell us what happened than to show how it happened.

> *A Man of Letters* Random House 86

16 [He was] the autodidact of the jails.

> On Jean Genet, recalled on Genet's death, NY *Times* 16 Apr 86

PETER QUENNELL

17 [He had] the general look of an elderly fallen angel traveling incognito.

> On André Gide, *The Sign of the Fish* Viking 60

JONATHAN RABAN

18 Good travel books are novels at heart.

> Quoted by Christopher Lehmann-Haupt NY *Times* 26 Jan 87

J D REED

19 After 18 chapters of crudités and quiche, one longs for some meat and potatoes.

> On Mark Stevens's *Summer in the City* Random House 84, *Time* 21 May 84

CHRISTOPHER RICK

20 A cliché begins as heartfelt and then its heart sinks.

> Quoted by Anatole Broyard NY *Times* 20 Oct 83

PHILIP ROTH

21 Everybody else is working to change, persuade, tempt and control them. The best readers come to fiction to be free of all that noise.

> Quoted in George Plimpton ed *Writers at Work* Viking 86

HUGHES RUDD

22 *Texas* is . . . "trotting" journalism, history in a hurry.

> On James A Michener's 1,096-page novel, Random House 85, NY *Times* 13 Oct 85

EDWARD SACHS

23 Never underestimate an editor's intelligence and never overestimate a publisher's morality.

> *Publishers Weekly* 6 Jul 84

DOROTHY L SAYERS

24 As I grow older and older,
And totter toward the tomb,
I find that I care less and less
Who goes to bed with whom.

> On why she did not read modern novels, recalled on her death 17 Dec 57

WEBSTER SCHOTT

1 For all the "I's," he is a man of many masks.
   On W H Auden, *Christian Science Monitor* 26 Aug 65

DELMORE SCHWARTZ

2 I should like you to consider this letter as a resignation; I want to resign as one of your most studious and faithful admirers.
   Condemning Ezra Pound's anti-Semitism, quoted by James Atlas *Delmore Schwartz* Farrar, Straus & Giroux 77

GENE SHALIT

3 Her books were put down by most critics but readers would not put down her books.
   Eulogy for Jacqueline Susann, whose sales were greater at the time of her death than those of any other novelist, *Today* NBC TV 24 Sept 74

VINCENT SHEEAN

4 I have always thought that the surest proof of talent is its condescension to genius.
   On George Jean Nathan's tolerance of Sinclair Lewis, *Dorothy and Red* Houghton Mifflin 63

WILFRID SHEED

5 Mr Michener, as timeless as a stack of *National Geographic*s, is the ultimate Summer Writer. Just as one goes back to the cottage in Maine, so one goes back to one's Michener.
   On James A Michener, NY *Times* 6 Jul 80

ISRAEL SHENKER

6 From bar mitzvah on, [S J Perelman] had dreamed of being a Jewish Robert Louis Stevenson.
   Coat of Many Colors Doubleday 85, quoted by Hugh Nissenson NY *Times* 17 Mar 85

RICHARD F SHEPARD

7 Queens, as yet unheard from in the world of New York letters, has found its bard.
   On Jimmy Breslin, in review of *Table Money* Ticknor & Fields 86, NY *Times* 8 May 86

R F SHEPPARD

8 If one merely could name-drop most of the titles listed, he could be a social success; if one really read them all, he might be unbearable.
   "Good Reading: A Helpful Guide for Serious Readers" NY *Times* 20 Feb 63

R Z SHEPPARD

9 As a born actress, she instinctively understands that the world is more than a stage—it is an audience.
   On heroine of Louis Auchincloss's *The Dark Lady* Houghton Mifflin 77, *Time* 11 Jul 77

10 The short story is like an old friend who calls whenever he is in town. We are happy to hear from it; we casually fan the embers of past intimacies, and buy it lunch.
   On Ted Solotaroff ed's *The Best American Short Stories 1978* Houghton Mifflin 78, *ib* 9 Apr 79

11 His reserve of disdain appears endless. He could no sooner shut it off than a vampire could forgo his nightcap.
   On Gore Vidal, *ib* 13 Jun 83

12 An able practitioner of glitz lit.
   On Erich Segal, *ib* 13 May 85

FRANK SINATRA

13 Hell hath no fury like a hustler with a literary agent.
   On Judith Exner's *My Story* Grove 77, quoted in *US* 16 Dec 85

ISAAC BASHEVIS SINGER

14 We write not only for children but also for their parents. They, too, are serious children.
   Stories for Children Farrar, Straus & Giroux 85

EDITH SITWELL

15 A great many people now reading and writing would be better employed keeping rabbits.
   Recalled on her death 9 Dec 64

ROBERT SKIDELSKY

16 [It is] voyeurism embellished with footnotes.
   On modern biography writing, quoted by Mark Feeney "Profitable Lives" Boston *Globe* 25 Jan 87

JOHN SKOW

17 Nothing is more pleasurable than to sit in the shade, sip gin and contemplate other people's adulteries, and while the wormy apple of marriage still lives, the novel will not die.
   On Alison Lurie's *The War between the Tates* Random House 74, *Time* 29 Jul 74

JOSEF SKVORECKY

18 There is something that falls short of perfection in every book, without exception, something influenced by the age, even something ridiculous; just like everyone, without exception, has weaknesses.
   The Engineer of Human Souls Knopf 84, quoted by Robert Towers NY *Times* 19 Aug 84

19 Lovers of literature will . . . look for the remains of the golden treasure in that shipwreck on the bottom of the sea of criticism.
   ib

STEPHEN SPENDER

20 There is a certain justice in criticism. The critic is like a midwife—a tyrannical midwife
   Lecturing at Brooklyn College, NY *Times* 20 Nov 84

FRANCIS STEEGMULLER

21 I'm told that when Auden died, they found his Oxford [English Dictionary] all but clawed to pieces. That is the way a poet and his dictionary should come out.
   NY *Times* 26 Mar 80

JOHN STEINBECK

22 Syntax, my lad. It has been restored to the highest place in the republic.
   When asked his reaction to John F Kennedy's inaugural address, quoted by *Atlantic* Nov 69

GLORIA STEINEM

23 For the reader who has put away comic books, but isn't yet ready for editorials in the *Daily News*.
   On Jacqueline Susann's first novel, *Valley of the Dolls*, quoted in review of Susann's last book, NY *Times* 11 Jul 76

JEAN STROUSE

1 Book critics are a weird journalistic subspecies: We may pull all-nighters, but they tend to take place at home, where page 648 leads inexorably to page 649.
> In review of Osborn Elliott's *The World of Oz* Viking 80, *Newsweek* 12 May 80

ALLEN TATE

2 [Yevgeny Yevtushenko is] a ham actor, not a poet.
> Quoted by Robert Conquest "The Politics of Poetry" NY *Times* 30 Sep 73

DOROTHY THOMPSON

3 What was once Sinclair Lewis is buried in no ground. Even in life he was fully alive only in his writing. He lives in public libraries from Maine to California, in worn copies in the bookshelves of women from small towns who, in their girlhood, imagined themselves as Carol Kennicotts, and of medical men who, as youths, were inspired by Martin Arrowsmith.
> "The Boy From Sauk Center" *Atlantic* Nov 60

4 He is an ineradicable part of American cultural history in the 1920s and 1930s, and no one seeking to recapture and record the habits, frames of mind, social movements, speech, aspirations, admirations, radicalism, reactions, crusades and Gargantuan absurdities of the American demos during those 20 years will be able to do without him.
> *ib*

JAMES THURBER

5 Unless [artists] can remember what it was to be a little boy, they are only half complete as artist and as man.
> On John O'Hara, quoted in Helen Thurber and Edward Weeks eds *Selected Letters of James Thurber* Atlantic–Little, Brown 81

6 Laughter need not be cut out of anything, since it improves everything.
> *ib*

7 There is something about a poet which leads us to believe that he died, in many cases, as long as 20 years before his birth.
> *ib*

TIME MAGAZINE

8 When disaster causes the familiar ground to shudder beneath the feet of a child, a neurotic is sometimes born, or a writer, and often both.
> 20 May 57

9 Two of the most difficult tasks a writer can undertake, to write the truth about himself and about his mother.
> On Frank O'Connor's *An Only Child* Knopf 61, 31 Mar 61

10 Sex is too often not only Topic A, but also Topic B and C as well.
> On John O'Hara's novels, 7 Jun 63

11 The love that dare not speak its name has become the neurosis that does not know when to shut up.
> On reviewing "still another fictional treatment of homosexuality," 3 Apr 64

12 In full regalia, she looked like Lyndon B Johnson dressed up as Elizabeth I.
> On Edith Sitwell, 21 May 65

13 Her nerves were a shirt of nettles.
> On poems in Sylvia Plath's *Ariel*, published three years after her suicide, 10 Jun 66

14 She writes in ink as green as Irish grass—or vitriol.
> On Edna O'Brien, 16 May 67

15 As lovely and spare as a falcon swooping.
> On Thomas Keneally's *Bring Larks and Heroes* Viking 68, 16 Aug 68

16 One of the best-known, little-known writers now at work.
> 1977 evaluation of English novelist James Hanley, recalled on his death 11 Nov 85

17 This monumental survey deserves to be published to the strains of the triumphal march from *Aida*.
> On Kazimierz Michalowski's *The Art of Ancient Egypt* Abrams 85, 16 Dec 85

18 In any Krantz work, the good get loved, and that is what makes it romantic. The bad get punished, and that is what makes it fiction.
> On Judith Krantz's *I'll Take Manhattan* Crown 86, 28 Apr 86

19 Some men kiss and do not tell; they are called gentlemen. Some men tell but do not kiss; they are called liars. Some men kiss and tell; they are called best-seller writers.
> On Roger Vadim's *Bardot, Deneuve, Fonda* Simon & Schuster 85, *ib*

LIONEL TRILLING

20 Youth is a time when we find the books we give up but do not get over.
> NY *Times* 6 Mar 66

SIEGFRIED UNSELD

21 One of the signs of Napoleon's greatness is the fact that he once had a publisher shot.
> *The Author and His Publisher* University of Chicago 80, quoted by Herbert Mitgang NY *Times* 27 Jul 80

LOUIS UNTERMEYER

22 She has something to say about what life is like—which is all we ask of poetry.
> On Phyllis McGinley, *Time* 18 Jun 65

JOHN UPDIKE

23 The refusal to rest content, the willingness to risk excess on behalf of one's obsessions, is what distinguishes artists from entertainers, and what makes some artists adventurers on behalf of us all.
> On J D Salinger, *Christian Science Monitor* 26 Aug 65

24 The inner spaces that a good story lets us enter are the old apartments of religion.
> Introduction to *The Best American Short Stories 1984* Houghton Mifflin 84, quoted by Anatole Broyard NY *Times* 11 Nov 84

25 A narrative is like a room on whose walls a number of false doors have been painted; while within the narrative, we have many apparent choices of exit, but when the author leads us to one particular door, we know it is the right one because it opens.
> *ib*

1 Her sentences march under a harsh sun that bleaches color from them but bestows a peculiar, invigorating, Pascalian clarity.

> On Muriel Spark's *The Only Problem* Putnam 84, *New Yorker* 23 Jul 84

2 [He had a] sensation of anxiety and shame, a sensitivity acute beyond usefulness, as if the nervous system, flayed of its old hide of social usage, must record every touch of pain.

> On Franz Kafka, quoted in report on Great Books discussion groups, NY *Times* 28 Feb 85

3 But for a few phrases from his letters and an odd line or two of his verse, the poet walks gagged through his own biography.

> On Peter Ackroyd's *T S Eliot* Simon & Schuster 84, in which the Eliot estate forbade quotation from Eliot's books and letters, *New Yorker* 25 Mar 85

4 He skates saucily over great tracts of confessed ignorance.

> On T S Matthews's biography of Eliot, *Great Tom* Harper & Row 74, *ib*

RICHARD USBORNE

5 There are only two kinds of Wodehouse readers, those who adore him and those who have never read him.

> Quoted on centenary of P G Wodehouse's birth, *International Herald Tribune* 10 Oct 81

VANITY FAIR

6 Her acidic bons mots were the olives of the martini age.

> On Dorothy Parker, Jun 86

GORE VIDAL

7 What is in question is a kind of book reviewing which seems to be more and more popular: the loose putting down of opinions as though they were facts, and the treating of facts as though they were opinions.

> Taking issue with Dudley Fitt's review of his novel *Julian* Little, Brown 64, NY *Times* 5 Ju! 64

8 Many writers who choose to be active in the world lose not virtue but time, and that stillness without which literature cannot be made.

> *Réalités* Aug 66

9 That is sad until one recalls how many bad books the world may yet be spared because of the busyness of writers.

> *ib*

10 This is not at all bad, except as prose.

> On Herman Wouk's *The Winds of War* Little, Brown 71, quoted in *Time* 21 May 84

ELIZABETH GRAY VINING

11 Fragments came floating into his mind like bits of wood drifting down a stream, and he fished them out and fitted them together.

> On John Donne, *Take Heed of Loving Me* Lippincott 64

JOHN VINOCUR

12 Graham looks up . . . It is a still look, and it shuts the door gently on the subject.

> "The Soul-Searching Continues for Graham Greene" NY *Times* 3 Mar 85

DAVID WADE

13 Experience needs distance and what you write of at a distance tells not so much what you were like as what you have discovered since.

> On the BBC production *I, William Shakespeare*, London *Times* 8 May 82

JAMES WALCOTT

14 Irving can be devilishly readable—just as your attention begins to flag, he sends in a troupe of midgets, pulls back incestuous sheets, tosses off a daring piece of slapstick.

> On John Irving's *Hotel New Hampshire* Dutton 81, *Esquire* Sep 81

BARBARA WARD

15 The modern world is not given to uncritical admiration. It expects its idols to have feet of clay and can be reasonably sure that press and camera will report their exact dimensions.

> On *Autobiography of Eleanor Roosevelt* Harper 61, *Saturday Review* 30 Sep 61

EVELYN WAUGH

16 I think to be oversensitive about clichés is like being oversensitive about table manners.

> Quoted in Donat Gallagher ed *A Little Order: A Selection from His Journalism* Little, Brown 81

17 Professional reviewers read so many bad books in the course of duty that they get an unhealthy craving for arresting phrases.

> *ib*

H G WELLS

18 She writes like a loom, producing her broad rich fabric with hardly a thought of how it will make up into a shape, while I write to cover a frame of ideas.

> On work of his long-time companion Rebecca West, quoted in G P Wells ed *H G Wells in Love* Little, Brown 84

GLENWAY WESCOTT

19 Time is the nervous system of narration, whether factual or fictive. If it gets confused . . . some of the minutiae of human nature are certain not to work, not to glow, not to strike home.

> On memoirs of Somerset Maugham, NY *Times* 9 Oct 66

PAUL WEST

20 Purple is not only highly colored prose, it is the world written *up*, intensified and made pleasurably palpable, not only to suggest the impetuous abundance of Creation, but also to add to it by showing—showing off—the expansive power of the mind itself, its unique knack for making itself at home among trees, dawns, viruses, and then turning them into something else: a word, a daub, a sonata.

> "In Defense of Purple Prose" NY *Times* 15 Dec 85

E B WHITE

21 Thurber did not write the way a surgeon operates, he wrote the way a child skips rope, the way a mouse waltzes.

> Tribute to James Thurber, *New Yorker* 11 Nov 61

1 She would write 8 or 10 words, then draw her gun and shoot them down.
> On his wife Katharine S White, *Onward and Upward in the Garden* Farrar, Straus & Giroux 79

THORNTON WILDER

2 Literature is the orchestration of platitudes.
> *Time* 12 Jan 53

TENNESSEE WILLIAMS

3 [He is] a sweetly vicious old lady.
> On Truman Capote, *People* 11 Mar 85

EDMUND WILSON

4 The cruelest thing that has happened to Lincoln since he was shot by Booth was to fall into the hands of Carl Sandburg.
> *Time* 26 Jun 72

HERMAN WOUK

5 We are in the black theater of nonexistence. In an eye blink the curtain is up, the stage ablaze, for the vast drama of ourselves.
> On Genesis I as his favorite opening passage, NY *Times* 2 Jun 85

MARGUERITE YOURCENAR

6 A young musician plays scales in his room and only bores his family. A beginning writer, on the other hand, sometimes has the misfortune of getting into print.
> *Time* 16 Feb 81

MUSIC & DANCE

Artists & Entertainers

FRED ASTAIRE

7 Dancing is a sweat job.
> Recalled on his death 22 Jun 87

8 I don't want to be the oldest performer in captivity. . . . I don't want to look like a little old man dancing out there.
> On why he stopped dancing professionally at age 71, *ib*

JOAN BAEZ

9 Good morning, children of the 80s. This is your Woodstock, and it's long overdue.
> Opening Philadelphia Live Aid concert for African famine relief, NY *Times* 16 Jul 85

ROBERT BAKER

10 After you've designed and placed an organ as well as you possibly can, some well-meaning lady is able to ruin the whole thing by donating memorial carpeting.
> On modern organ building, *New Yorker* 23 Dec 61

GEORGE BALANCHINE

11 First comes the sweat. Then comes the beauty—if you're very lucky and have said your prayers.
> Quoted by Bernard Taper *Balanchine* Harper & Row 63

12 God creates, I do not create. I assemble and I steal everywhere to do it—from what I see, from what the dancers can do, from what others do.
> NY *Times* 16 Dec 63

13 Most ballet teachers in the United States are terrible. If they were in medicine, everyone would be poisoned.
> *Newsweek* 4 May 64

14 The ballet is a purely female thing; it is a woman, a garden of beautiful flowers, and man is the gardener.
> *Life* 11 Jun 65

15 In ballet a complicated story is impossible to tell. . . . we can't dance synonyms.
> *ib*

16 In my ballets, woman is first. Men are consorts. God made men to sing the praises of women. They are not equal to men: They are better.
> *Time* 15 Sep 80

MIKHAIL BARYSHNIKOV

17 The essence of all art is to have pleasure in giving pleasure.
> *Time* 19 May 75

18 There comes a moment in a young artist's life when he knows he has to bring something to the stage from within himself. He has to put in something in order to be able to take something out.
> *ib*

19 No dancer can watch Fred Astaire and not know that we all should have been in another business.
> Recalled on Astaire's death, *Newsweek* 6 Jul 87

THOMAS BEECHAM

20 [They] are quite hopeless—drooling, driveling, doleful, depressing, dropsical drips.
> On music critics, news summaries 13 Feb 54

21 Most of them sound like they live on seaweed.
> On sopranos, *Newsweek* 30 Apr 56

22 Movie music is noise. . . . even more painful than my sciatica.
> *Time* 24 Feb 58

23 No operatic star has yet died soon enough for me.
> Quoted on *Who Said That?* BBC TV 22 Aug 58

24 The English may not like music, but they absolutely love the noise it makes.
> NY *Herald Tribune* 9 Mar 61

TONI BENTLEY

25 A toe shoe is as eccentric as the ballerina who wears it; their marriage is a commitment.
> "The Heart and Sole of a Ballerina's Art: Her Toe Shoes" *Smithsonian* Jun 84

26 A brand-new pair of toe shoes presents itself to us as an enemy with a will of its own that must be tamed.
> *ib*

LEONARD BERNSTEIN

27 Any great work of art . . . revives and readapts time and space, and the measure of its success is the extent to which it makes you an inhabitant of that world—the extent to which it invites you in and lets you breathe its strange, special air.
> "What Makes Opera Grand?" *Vogue* Dec 58

1 Music, of all the arts, stands in a special region, unlit by any star but its own, and utterly without meaning . . . except its own.
The Joy of Music Simon & Schuster 59

2 Music . . . can name the unnamable and communicate the unknowable.
The Unanswered Question Harvard 76

3 I'm not interested in having an orchestra sound like *itself*. I want it to sound like the composer.
Quoted by Will Crutchfield "Orchestras in the Age of Jet-Set Sound" NY *Times* 6 Jan 85

E POWER BIGGS

4 The wonderful old paaah and chaah became just plain aaah.
On introduction of electric organs, *Newsweek* 21 Mar 77

LOIS BOOTSIN

5 One day I'm a prostitute and the next day I'm a nun. Where else could you get instant conversion like that?
On work as supernumerary at Metropolitan Opera, NY *Times* 19 Nov 84

NADIA BOULANGER

6 I've been a woman for a little over 50 years and have gotten over my initial astonishment. As for conducting an orchestra, that's a job where I don't think sex plays much part.
On becoming first woman to conduct Boston Symphony Orchestra, recalled on her death, *International Herald Tribune* 23 Oct 79

7 A great work is made out of a combination of obedience and liberty.
Quoted by Bruno Monsaingeon *Mademoiselle* Carcanet 85

PIERRE BOULEZ

8 The aim of music is not to express feelings but to express music. It is not a vessel into which the composer distills his soul drop by drop, but a labyrinth with no beginning and no end, full of new paths to discover, where mystery remains eternal.
Réalités Aug 65

BENJAMIN BRITTEN

9 Composing is like driving down a foggy road toward a house. Slowly you see more details of the house— the color of the slates and bricks, the shape of the windows. The notes are the bricks and the mortar of the house.
Life 7 Aug 64

10 The old idea . . . of a composer suddenly having a terrific idea and sitting up all night to write it is nonsense. Nighttime is for sleeping.
ib

LESLIE BROWNE

11 I don't want to feel a shoe; I want the shoe to become part of me.
Quoted by Daniel S and Stephanie R Sorine *Dancershoes* Knopf 79

JACK BRYMER

12 The ability to play the clarinet is the ability to overcome the imperfections of the instrument. There's no such thing as a perfect clarinet, never was and never will be.
London *Times* 24 Feb 85

13 It happens very rarely, but when it happens it's worth waiting for, that the instrument becomes part of your body.
ib

GRACE BUMBRY

14 I've gone from reluctance to acceptance to gung ho.
On singing title role in Metropolitan Opera's 1985 production of *Porgy and Bess*, NY *Times* 5 Feb 85

SAMMY CAHN

15 The popular song is America's greatest ambassador.
NY *Times* 17 Apr 84

MARIA CALLAS

16 It is like comparing champagne with cognac. No— with Coca-Cola.
On comparing her with Renata Tebaldi, quoted by Arianna Stassinopoulos *Maria Callas* Ballantine 81

17 An opera begins long before the curtain goes up and ends long after it has come down. It starts in my imagination, it becomes my life, and it stays part of my life long after I've left the opera house.
ib

18 I will not be sued! I have the voice of an angel!
On being presented with a court summons, *ib*

19 I cannot switch my voice. My voice is not like an elevator going up and down.
After being fired by Rudolf Bing for refusing to sing 3 performances of *Traviata* during a 26-performance contract, *ib*

20 When my enemies stop hissing, I shall know I'm slipping.
ib

21 I would like to be Maria, but there is La Callas who demands that I carry myself with her dignity.
ib

ELLIOT T CARTER

22 My compositions deserve the medal, not me.
On receiving MacDowell Medal, NY *Times* 22 Aug 83

PABLO CASALS

23 The cello is like a beautiful woman who has not grown older, but younger with time, more slender, more supple, more graceful.
Time 29 Apr 57

24 I am perhaps the oldest musician in the world. I am an old man but in many senses a very young man. And this is what I want you to be, young, young all your life, and to say things to the world that are true.
At a concert the summer before his death at age 96, NY *Times* 23 Oct 73

GOWER CHAMPION

25 I use dancing to embellish, extend or enlarge upon an existing emotion.
Recalled on his death 25 Aug 80

VAN CLIBURN

1 I'm not a success, I'm a sensation.

> After winning International Tchaikovsky Piano Competition in Moscow, news summaries 31 Dec 58

2 An artist can be truly evaluated only after he is dead. At the very 11th hour, he might do something that will eclipse everything else.

> NY *Times* 9 Jun 85

EDDIE CONDON

3 Someday we may have as many followers as the harpsichord.

> After financial failures of his early jazz guitar concerts, quoted in NY *Times* 17 May 64

4 As it enters the ear, does it come in like broken glass or does it come in like honey?

> On listening to jazz, recalled on his death 4 Aug 73

AARON COPLAND

5 When I speak of the gifted listener, I am thinking of the nonmusician primarily, of the listener who intends to retain his amateur status. It is the thought of just such a listener that excites the composer in me.

> *Music and Imagination* Harvard 52

6 There is something about music that keeps its distance even at the moment that it engulfs us. It is at the same time outside and away from us and inside and part of us. In one sense it dwarfs us, and in another we master it. We are led on and on, and yet in some strange way we never lose control.

> *ib*

7 You compose because you want to somehow summarize in some permanent form your most basic feelings about being alive, to set down . . . some sort of permanent statement about the way it feels to live now, today. So that when it's all gone, people will be able to go to the artwork of the time and get some sense of what it felt like to be alive in this year.

> *Bill Moyers Journal* WNET TV 14 Mar 76

8 So long as the human spirit thrives on this planet, music in some living form will accompany and sustain it and give it expressive meaning.

> London *Times* 27 Nov 80

9 Don't ever let him near a microphone.

> On Leonard Bernstein's tactlessness, quoted by Joan Peyser *Publishers Weekly* 5 Jun 87

MEYER DAVIS

10 What we provide is an atmosphere. . . . of orchestrated pulse which works on people in a subliminal way. Under its influence I've seen shy debs and severe dowagers kick off their shoes and raise some wholesome hell.

> On his orchestra, *Saturday Evening Post* 20 Apr 63

AGNES DE MILLE

11 A good education is usually harmful to a dancer. A good calf is better than a good head.

> News summaries 1 Feb 54

12 The practice mirror is to be used for the correction of faults, not for a love affair, and the figure you watch should not become your dearest friend.

> "To a Young Dancer" *Atlantic* Dec 60

13 The universe lies before you on the floor, in the air, in the mysterious bodies of your dancers, in your mind. From this voyage no one returns poor or weary.

> *ib*

14 Modern dancers give a sinister portent about our times.

> On teenage dance fads, NY *Times* 10 Jun 63

15 When you perform . . . you are out of yourself—larger and more potent, more beautiful. You are for minutes heroic. This is power. This is glory on earth. And it is yours nightly.

> *ib*

JAMES DEPREIST

16 I think [park] concerts tend to be, let's say, excessively accessible.

> On conducting NY Philharmonic in Central Park, NY *Times* 24 Jul 84

17 I thought it would be better to starve slowly over there than instantly over here.

> On living in Europe, *ib*

HARRY ELLIS DICKSON

18 I am looked upon with suspicion. I am on the "other side."

> On conducting orchestra of which he is also a member, *Gentlemen, More Dolce Please!* Beacon 69, quoted in *Christian Science Monitor* 18 Dec 85

19 My dearest colleagues seem to become metamorphosed into snarling beasts if I as much as glance at them, even if my glance is a complimentary one.

> *ib*

HOWARD DIETZ

20 Composers shouldn't think too much—it interferes with their plagiarism.

> News summaries 31 Dec 74

TODD DUNCAN

21 I knew the French were not ashamed of Carmen and she was a whore. I knew the Italians were not ashamed of Tosca and she was a high-class one. The Wagnerian operas had incest. So there was nothing in *Porgy and Bess* to be ashamed of. The thing to do was to bring out all the integrity, all the dignity.

> On singing title role in the original 1935 production, NY *Times* 3 Feb 85

BOB DYLAN

22 Chaos is a friend of mine.

> Defining his musical style in the mid 1960s, quoted in *Newsweek* 9 Dec 85

DUKE ELLINGTON

23 Playing "bop" is like playing Scrabble with all the vowels missing.

> *Look* 10 Aug 54

24 It's like an act of murder; you play with intent to commit something.

> On jazz, NY *Herald Tribune* 9 Jul 61

25 Roaming through the jungle of "oohs" and "ahs," searching for a more agreeable noise, I live a life of primitivity with the mind of a child and an unquenchable thirst for sharps and flats.

> *Music Is My Mistress* Doubleday 73

1 Now I can say loudly and openly what I have been saying to myself on my knees.
> When asked to compose sacred music, recalled on his death 24 May 74

2 Fate is being kind to me. Fate doesn't want me to be too famous too young.
> On being passed over for Pulitzer Prize in 1965, quoted in *Christian Science Monitor* 24 Dec 86

SIMON ESTES

3 Many people never treated this as an opera, but as a musical, a kind of musical ghetto.
> On singing title role in Metropolitan Opera's 1985 production of *Porgy and Bess*, NY *Times* 5 Feb 85

ARTHUR FIEDLER

4 It's nice to eat a good hunk of beef but you want a light dessert, too.
> On Boston Pops Orchestra, recalled on his death 10 Jul 79

MARGOT FONTEYN

5 Life offstage has sometimes been a wilderness of unpredictables in an unchoreographed world.
> *Margot Fonteyn: Autobiography* Knopf 76

6 Great artists are people who find the way to be themselves in their art. Any sort of pretension induces mediocrity in art and life alike.
> *ib*

IRA GERSHWIN

7 A song without music is a lot like H_2 without the O.
> *Connoisseur* Feb 86

BENNY GOODMAN

8 If a guy's got it, let him give it. I'm selling music, not prejudice.
> On including blacks in his orchestra, *Saturday Evening Post* 18 Dec 54

GLENN GOULD

9 The G-minor Symphony consists of eight remarkable measures . . . surrounded by a half-hour of banality.
> On Mozart, quoted in Tim Page ed *The Glenn Gould Reader* Knopf 84

10 A record is a concert without halls and a museum whose curator is the owner.
> Paraphrasing André Malraux, quoted in *Christian Science Monitor* 2 Aug 85

MARTHA GRAHAM

11 Think of the magic of that foot, comparatively small, upon which your whole weight rests. It's a miracle, and the dance . . . is a celebration of that miracle.
> Accepting Aspen Award in the Humanities, Aspen Institute for Humanistic Studies *Annual Report* 65

12 Dance is the hidden language of the soul of the body.
> NY *Times* 31 Mar 85

13 I did not want to be a tree, a flower or a wave. In a dancer's body, we as audience must see ourselves, not the imitated behavior of everyday actions, not the phenomenon of nature, not exotic creatures from another planet, but something of the miracle that is a human being.
> Quoted by Iris M Fanger "An American Modern" *Christian Science Monitor* 9 Jun 86

14 We learn by practice. Whether it means to learn to dance by practicing dancing or to learn to live by practicing living, the principles are the same. . . . One becomes in some area an athlete of God.
> Quoted in *ib* 5 Aug 86

15 Practice means to perform, over and over again in the face of all obstacles, some act of vision, of faith, of desire. Practice is a means of inviting the perfection desired.
> *ib*

BERNARD GREENHOUSE

16 [Trio life has] the wonderful advantage of not being alone, the pleasure of having success with two other people and the solace when you don't have success.
> On playing the cello in Beaux Arts Trio, NY *Times* 18 Nov 84

OSCAR HAMMERSTEIN II

17 I hand him a lyric and get out of his way.
> On partnership with Richard Rodgers, news summaries 12 May 55

JASCHA HEIFETZ

18 I occasionally play works by contemporary composers and for two reasons. First to discourage the composer from writing any more and secondly to remind myself how much I appreciate Beethoven.
> *Life* 28 Jul 61

19 If I don't practice one day, I know it; two days, the critics know it; three days, the public knows it.
> San Francisco *Examiner & Chronicle* 18 Apr 71

MARGARET HILLIS, choral director, Chicago Symphony Orchestra

20 There's only one woman I know of who could never be a symphony conductor, and that's the Venus de Milo.
> NY *Times* 13 Jun 79

VLADIMIR HOROWITZ

21 My future is in my past and my past is my present. I must now make the present my future.
> On resuming concert career after 12-year retirement, NY *Times* 17 Mar 65

22 Perfection itself is imperfection.
> Defending false notes, *Newsweek* 17 May 65

23 I am a general. My soldiers are the keys and I have to command them.
> NY *Times* 8 Jan 78

24 My face is my passport.
> To Soviet official on visit to USSR, *Time* 28 Apr 86

POOH KAYE

25 I think every dance is kind of an accumulation of information that goes one step farther along.
> On natural movement dance performed at Museum of Modern Art, NY *Times* 9 Aug 85

GELSEY KIRKLAND

26 I danced with passion to spite the music.
> On dancing title role in *The Firebird*, from her autobiography *Dancing on My Grave* Doubleday 86, quoted in *Vogue* Oct 86

ANDRÉ KOSTELANETZ

1 Everybody should have his personal sounds to listen for—sounds that will make him exhilarated and alive or quiet and calm.
> NY *Journal-American* 8 Feb 55

2 One of the greatest sounds of them all—and to me it is a sound—is utter, complete silence.
> *ib*

3 The conductor has the advantage of not seeing the audience.
> Recalled on his death 13 Jan 80

FRITZ KREISLER

4 Genius is an overused word. The world has known only about a half dozen geniuses. . . . I got only fairly near.
> News summaries 2 Feb 55

WANDA LANDOWSKA

5 I never practice; I always play.
> *Time* 1 Dec 52

LOTTE LEHMANN

6 You have always given me more than I gave to you. . . . You were the wings on which I soared.
> To farewell concert audience, *Life* 5 Mar 51

7 I had hoped you would protest, but please don't argue.
> Announcing her retirement, recalled on her death 26 Aug 76

JOHN LENNON

8 We're more popular than Jesus Christ now.
> Quoted in *Time* 12 Aug 66

9 I don't know which will go first—rock 'n' roll or Christianity.
> *ib*

10 The postman wants an autograph. The cab driver wants a picture. The waitress wants a handshake. Everyone wants a piece of you.
> Recalled on his death, *People* 22 Dec 80

ALAN JAY LERNER

11 You're an egghead with two yolks.
> On youthful self-confidence, recalled on his death 14 Jun 86

12 A schedule so tight that it would only work if I didn't sleep on Monday nights.
> On his early career, *ib*

JAMES LEVINE

13 We do not seem to be finding . . . tomorrow's Toscas.
> On shortage of great operatic voices, NY *Times* 23 Sep 79

LIBERACE

14 You can have either the Resurrection or you can have Liberace. But you can't have both.
> On billing with Easter show at Radio City Music Hall, *New York* 15 Sep 86

15 I had to dare a little bit. Who am I kidding—I had to dare a lot. Don't wear one ring, wear five or six. People ask how I can play with all those rings, and I reply, "Very well, thank you."
> Recalled on his death 4 Feb 87

JOSÉ LIMÓN

16 Dancers aren't pompous; they're too tired.
> NY *Times* 31 Jul 66

17 I saw the dance as a vision of ineffable power. A man could, with dignity and a towering majesty, dance. Not mince, cavort, do "fancy dancing" or "showoff" steps. No: Dance as Michelangelo's visions dance and as the music of Bach dances.
> Recalled on his death, *ib* 4 Dec 72

18 I try to be an atheist, but it's very hard. God is what makes you aspire beyond yourself, aspire incredibly. . . . God to me is what stops you from slicing the jugular because you choose not to. God is the Sistine Chapel, the Ninth Symphony, God is Bach and the Prado Museum! And this is what I've tried to show in my work.
> *ib*

FREDERICK LOEWE

19 It won't be long before we'll be writing together again. I just hope they have a decent piano up there.
> Letter read at Alan Jay Lerner's memorial service, *Time* 21 Jul 86

GUY LOMBARDO

20 The sweetest music this side of heaven.
> Slogan for Guy Lombardo and his Royal Canadians, recalled on his death 5 Nov 77

GEORGE LONDON

21 It was like a Japanese ball player being invited to play first base for the Yankees.
> On being first American to sing *Boris Godunov* in the USSR, *Time* 26 Sep 60

MARCEL MARCEAU

22 Music conveys moods and images. Even in opera, where plots deal with the structure of destiny, it's music, not words, that provides power.
> *US News & World Report* 23 Feb 87

23 Music and silence . . . combine strongly because music is done with silence, and silence is full of music.
> *ib*

24 In silence and movement you can show the reflection of people.
> *ib*

25 To communicate through silence is a link between the thoughts of man.
> *ib*

IGOR MARKEVITCH

26 Baton technique is to a conductor what fingers are to a pianist.
> Recalled on his death, *Time* 21 Mar 83

EVA MARTON

1 The public seems to like me here . . . Even my husband—I asked him, "What did you shout? Did you say brava, or viva, or what?" And he said, no, it was "wo-owww."
NY *Times* 27 Sep 84

2 What is important for me is finding what the composer wants in the character—what is deep in the character. I see it like an empty house.
Christian Science Monitor 13 Feb 85

ZUBIN MEHTA

3 Although I am flexible and ready to take advice, I can't carry an umbrella of thoughts over my head that would distract me and affect my music making.
On why he doesn't read reviews, *New York* 14 Jan 85

4 Essentially, the [New York] Philharmonic is just like any other orchestra—they all have the spirit of kids, and if you scratch away a little of the fatigue and cynicism, out comes a 17-year-old music student again, full of wonder, exuberance and a tremendous love of music.
ib

LAURITZ MELCHIOR

5 Regard your voice as capital in the bank. . . . Sing on your interest and your voice will last.
News summaries 1 Apr 56

GIAN CARLO MENOTTI

6 Not an audience but a habit.
On patrons of the Metropolitan Opera, *Time* 1 May 50

7 Melody is a form of remembrance. . . . It must have a quality of inevitability in our ears.
ib

8 Any subject is good for opera if the composer feels it so intently he must sing it out.
ib

YEHUDI MENUHIN

9 The violinist is that peculiarly human phenomenon distilled to a rare potency—half tiger, half poet.
The Compleat Violinist Summit 86

10 The violinist must possess the poet's gift of piercing the protective hide which grows on propagandists, stockbrokers and slave traders, to penetrate the deeper truth which lies within.
ib

ROBERT MERRILL

11 If you think you've hit a false note, sing loud. When in doubt, sing loud.
Saturday Evening Post 26 Oct 57

12 I felt I was painting with a Popsicle.
On singing *La Bohème* in English, NY *Times* 30 Dec 75

MIKE D

13 It's not as if we just insult women. Our insults go across the board.
On his rap group Beastie Boys, *Newsweek* 9 Feb 87

MITCH MILLER

14 Keep it simple, keep it sexy, keep it sad.
On popular music, *Time* 23 Feb 50

DIMITRI MITROPOULOS

15 I never use a score when conducting my orchestra. . . . Does a lion tamer enter a cage with a book on how to tame a lion?
News summaries 22 Jan 51

RUDOLF NUREYEV

16 A pas de deux is a dialogue of love. How can there be conversation if one partner is dumb?
On expanding role of danseur, *Newsweek* 19 Apr 65

17 My leg, make it more beautiful.
While being painted by Jamie Wyeth, *M* Aug 84

EUGENE ORMANDY

18 I'm one of the boys, no better than the last second violinist. . . . I'm just the lucky one to be standing in the center, telling them how to play.
NY *Times* 4 May 80

ITZHAK PERLMAN

19 You see, our fingers are circumcised . . . which gives them very good dexterity, particularly in the pinky.
On observation that many world-class violinists are Jewish, *60 Minutes* CBS TV 21 Dec 80

BERNADETTE PETERS

20 Singing lessons are like body building for your larynx.
NY *Times* 20 Sep 85

COLE PORTER

21 My sole inspiration is a telephone call from a producer.
News summaries 28 Feb 55

MENAHEM PRESSLER

22 There is a greater sense of brilliance when a trio plays, just because of the sheer volume that they can create and still be equals.
On playing the piano in Beaux Arts Trio, NY *Times* 18 Nov 84

DORY PREVIN

23 If I can say something honest about my feelings and thoughts and problems as a minority of one, then won't it be meaningful to all the other individual minorities of one?
On writing ballads, NY *Times* 16 Jan 72

LEONTYNE PRICE

24 The ghosts from the old house—Caruso, Flagstad—all those folks—have moved uptown, too. When I'd look up at the gold ceiling, there they'd be, swingin' around, saying to me, "Lee, you mess it up and we'll take care of you!"
On first performance in new Metropolitan Opera House, *Life* 30 Sep 66

25 It was the first operatic mountain I climbed, and the view from it was astounding, exhilarating, stupefying.
On her 1961 Metropolitan Opera debut, NY *Times* 31 Dec 84

26 I prefer to leave standing up, like a well-mannered guest at a party.
On her retirement from opera, *Newsweek* 14 Jan 85

1 I am here and you will know that I am the best and will hear me. The color of my skin or the kink of my hair or the spread of my mouth has nothing to do with what you are listening to.
Time 14 Jan 85

2 It makes me feel just wonderful to have this black god standing behind me.
On singing with Simon Estes in *Aida, ib*

RICHARD RODGERS

3 In America the musical theater is generally considered a whore. My ambition is to help make a good woman of her.
Quoted by Samuel Chotzinoff *A Little Nightmusic* Harper & Row 64

4 Listen to them when they are reacting as a mass—never listen to an individual reaction.
On audiences, quoted in tribute by Joshua Logan, NY *Times* 17 Mar 85

GAMBLE ROGERS

5 It was like the first time I ever made love. Terrifying to contemplate, wonderful when it happened and all too brief. And something I'll never forget.
On debut at Carnegie Hall, *New Yorker* 10 Jun 85

NED ROREM

6 Composition is notation of distortion of what composers think they've heard before. Masterpieces are marvelous misquotations.
The Paris Diary of Ned Rorem Braziller 66

7 If music could be translated into human speech, it would no longer need to exist.
Music from Inside Out Braziller 67

8 [Musical] themes are people, the notes are people's actions.
The Final Diary Holt, Rinehart & Winston 74

9 It isn't evil that's running the earth, but mediocrity. The crime is not that Nero played while Rome burned, but that he played badly.
ib

10 To see itself through, music must have idea or magic. . . . Music with neither dies young though rich.
Pure Contraption Holt, Rinehart & Winston 74

11 Music is the sole art which evokes nostalgia for the future.
Edition Peters Contemporary Music Catalogue 75

12 No artist wants to be "understood." If he's "understood," he feels superficial. What an artist wants is not to be misunderstood.
W 10 Oct 80

13 To have a large audience is not obscene. To want one is.
ib

14 Art means to dare—and to have been right.
ib

15 [He] is loved . . . as a fact of sonic geology, like a throbbing song-filled Rock of Gibraltar.
On Aaron Copland, NY *Times* 10 Nov 85

DIANA ROSS

16 We is terrific.
Motto of The Supremes, quoted by Mary Wilson *Dreamgirl* St Martin's 86

MSTISLAV ROSTROPOVICH

17 [It is my] wooden wife.
On his Stradivarius, *Wall Street Journal* 23 Feb 87

ARTUR RUBINSTEIN

18 Sometimes when I sit down to practice and there is no one else in the room, I have to stifle an impulse to ring for the elevator man and offer him money to come in and hear me.
Holiday May 63

19 Composing a concert is like composing a menu. . . . If you start with light pieces and play a 45-minute sonata after the interlude, it's like starting dinner with hors d'oeuvres and dessert and finishing with a Châteaubriand and vegetables.
Time 9 Apr 79

20 The first movement represented the struggles of my youth, the following andante the beginning of a more serious aspect of my talent, a scherzo represented well the unexpected success and the finale turned out to be a wonderfully moving end.
On final concert in London's Wigmore Hall, where he had given his first recital, *My Many Years* Knopf 80

ARTUR SCHNABEL

21 The notes I handle no better than many pianists. But the pauses between the notes—ah, that is where the art resides!
Chicago *Daily News* 11 Jun 58

ARNOLD SCHÖNBERG

22 There is still a lot of good music waiting to be written in C major.
News summaries 31 Dec 51

ANDRÉS SEGOVIA

23 Sometimes one is without the pleasure of playing. But when the silence of the audience is perfect, we recover that.
Christian Science Monitor 18 Mar 60

24 Among God's creatures two, the dog and the guitar, have taken all the sizes and all the shapes, in order not to be separated from the man.
NY *Times* 16 Feb 64

25 The advice I am giving always to all my students is above all to study the music profoundly. Because the music is like the ocean, and the instruments are little or bigger islands, very beautiful for the flowers and trees, or the contrary.
ib

26 Lean your body forward slightly to support the guitar against your chest, for the poetry of the music should resound in your heart.
ib

27 The guitar is a small orchestra. It is polyphonic. Every string is a different color, a different voice.
Christian Science Monitor 5 Aug 86

28 The piano is a monster that screams when you touch its teeth.
Quoted by Eugenia Zukerman *Sunday Morning* CBS TV 7 Jun 87

TED SHAWN

29 Dance is the only art of which we ourselves are the stuff of which it is made.
Time 25 Jul 55

1 I wanted to see if the American man in plain brown pants and a bare torso could speak profound things.

> On teaching men previously untrained in dance, *ib* 21 Aug 64

DIMITRI SHOSTAKOVICH

2 A creative artist works on his next composition because he was not satisfied with his previous one.

> NY *Times* 25 Oct 59

JEAN SIBELIUS

3 Pay no attention to what the critics say; no statue has ever been put up to a critic.

> Recalled on his death 20 Sep 57

BEVERLY SILLS

4 My voice had a long, nonstop career. It deserves to be put to bed with quiet and dignity, not yanked out every once in a while to see if it can still do what it used to do. It can't.

> On refusal to sing after her retirement from opera, *Time* 18 Jul 83

5 So long as it doesn't get to the point where you don't remember whose opera you're listening to, I'm willing to experiment.

> On set design at NYC Opera, quoted in *Newsweek* 8 Oct 84

6 I lived through the garbage. I might as well dine on the caviar.

> Answering speculation that NYC Opera's success would lead to her resignation as director, NY *Times* 15 Oct 84

7 Art is the signature of civilizations.

> NBC TV 4 May 85

FRANK SINATRA

8 The martial music of every sideburned delinquent on the face of the earth.

> On rock 'n' roll, *Look* 12 Jul 66

9 A rancid-smelling aphrodisiac.

> On rock 'n' roll, quoted by John Rockwell *Sinatra* Random House 84

10 The thing that influenced me most was the way Tommy played his trombone. . . . It was my idea to make my voice work in the same way as a trombone or violin—not sounding like them, but "playing" the voice like those instrumentalists.

> Quoted by Nancy Sinatra *Frank Sinatra* Doubleday 85

GIUSEPPE SINOPOLI

11 The conductor must make it possible to eliminate himself in the music. If the orchestra feels him doing that, then everything will go well.

> *Vogue* Apr 85

LEONARD SLATKIN

12 I use my hands like a sculptor, to mold and shape the sound I want, to clarify.

> Quoted by Tim Page "An American Conductor Succeeds at Home" NY *Times* 20 May 84

13 How could a New Yorker possibly take something called the Hollywood String Quartet seriously?

> *ib*

14 My first strong musical memory is of the Villa-Lobos Sixth Quartet which my parents were rehearsing. I remember that it reminded me of big teddy bears dancing around.

> *ib*

STEPHEN SONDHEIM

15 I prefer neurotic people. I like to hear rumblings beneath the surface.

> *Newsweek* 23 Apr 73

16 One difference between poetry and lyrics is that lyrics sort of fade into the background. They fade on the page and live on the stage when set to music.

> On Broadway musicals, quoted in NY *Times* 28 Mar 87

BRUCE SPRINGSTEEN

17 This music is forever for me. It's the stage thing, that rush moment that you live for. It never lasts, but that's what you live for.

> *Time* 27 Oct 75

18 Music was my way of keeping people from looking through and around me. I wanted the heavies to know I was around.

> On writing his own music, *ib*

19 Born in the USA.

> Title of 1984 song and concert tour

ISAAC STERN

20 Playing a concerto with Zubin is like being surrounded by a well-loved, cashmere-lined silk glove.

> On Zubin Mehta, *New York* 14 Jan 85

21 Everywhere in the world, music enhances a hall, with one exception: Carnegie Hall enhances the music.

> As president of Carnegie Hall, quoted in NY *Times* 17 May 85

22 Listen, I will now tell you the truth and there is no other.

> On what every conductor says to his artists, *60 Minutes* CBS TV 14 Dec 86

LEOPOLD STOKOWSKI

23 As a boy I remember how terribly real the statues of the saints would seem at 7 o'clock Mass—before I'd had breakfast. From that I learned always to conduct hungry.

> NY *Times* 18 Apr 67

24 A painter paints his pictures on canvas. But musicians paint their pictures on silence. We provide the music, and you provide the silence.

> Reprimanding talkative audience, *ib* 11 May 67

25 On matters of intonation and technicalities I am more than a martinet—I am a martinetissimo.

> Recalled on his death 13 Sep 77

IGOR STRAVINSKY

26 To listen is an effort, and just to hear is no merit. A duck hears also.

> News summaries 24 Jun 57

27 The real composer thinks about his work the whole time; he is not always conscious of this, but he is aware of it later when he suddenly knows what he will do.

> *Saturday Review* 9 Nov 57

1 My music is best understood by children and animals.
> London *Sunday Observer* 8 Oct 61

2 A plague on eminence! I hardly dare cross the street anymore without a convoy, and I am stared at wherever I go like an idiot member of a royal family or an animal in a zoo; and zoo animals have been known to die from stares.
> NY *Times* 12 May 66

3 Harpists spend 90 percent of their lives tuning their harps and 10 percent playing out of tune.
> Recalled on his death 6 Apr 71

4 I am an inventor of music.
> Declaring profession at French border during World War I, quoted in NY *Times* 7 Apr 71

5 My childhood was a period of waiting for the moment when I could send everyone and everything connected with it to hell.
> *ib*

6 The more constraints one imposes, the more one frees one's self. And the arbitrariness of the constraint serves only to obtain precision of execution.
> On obtaining dimensions of theater for which he was writing a ballet, *ib*

7 When I discovered that I had been made custodian of this gift, in my earliest childhood, I pledged myself to God to be worthy of it, but I have received uncovenanted mercies all my life. The custodian has too often kept faith on his all-too-worldly terms.
> Quoted by Paul Horgan *Encounters with Stravinsky* Farrar, Straus & Giroux 72

8 One has a nose. The nose scents and it chooses. An artist is simply a kind of pig snouting truffles.
> London *Observer* 16 Jul 72

GEORGE SZELL

9 Conductors must give unmistakable and suggestive signals to the orchestra—not choreography to the audience.
> *Newsweek* 28 Jan 63

LOUISE TALMA

10 Too many composers become involved in intellectual speculation which seems to matter more to them than the sound that comes out of all this speculation.
> NY *Times* 19 Oct 86

VIRGIL THOMSON

11 I thought of myself as a species of knight errant attacking dragons single-handedly and rescuing musical virtue in distress.
> On role as critic, quoted in NY *Times* 22 Nov 81

12 Falsely conceived and rather clumsily executed . . . crooked folklore and halfway opera.
> Review of *Porgy and Bess* première, recalled on the work's 50th anniversary, *ib* 3 Feb 85

13 I never learned to verbalize an abstract musical concept. No thank you. The whole point of being a serious musician is to avoid verbalization whenever you can.
> *Christian Science Monitor* 12 Feb 85

14 You explain how it went, and as far as you can figure out how it got that way.
> On role as critic, *ib*

15 The description and explanation is the best part of music reviewing. There is such a thing, and you know it too, as a gift for judgment. If you have it, you can say anything you like. If you haven't got it, you don't know you haven't got it. And everything you say will be held against you.
> *ib*

16 I don't have to worry . . . No matter what they do to it, it works.
> On his 1947 opera *The Mother of Us All*, *ib*

17 I don't care what [other critics] say, I only hope to be played.
> On being asked which of his compositions would endure, *ib*

18 Musicians . . . own music because music owns them.
> Commencement address at New England Conservatory of Music 18 May 86

19 I've never known a musician who regretted being one. Whatever deceptions life may have in store for you, music itself is not going to let you down.
> *ib*

20 I let her alone and when she got that finished she left me alone. We trusted each other.
> On collaborating with Gertrude Stein on *Four Saints in Three Acts*, NY *Times* 9 Nov 86

21 I don't go around regretting things that don't happen.
> On infrequency with which the Thomson-Stein opera has been produced, *ib*

22 They look better than we do; they can wear all colors on stage. We're sort of oyster-colored.
> On an all-black cast that was a sensation in the 1934 original production of *Four Saints in Three Acts*, *ib*

23 I seem to write an opera about every 20 years; if you live long enough you can write four operas. I finished my third in 1970.
> Interview at age 90, PBS TV 23 Nov 86

24 I look at you and I write down what I hear.
> To Picasso, when asked how he composed a musical portrait, *ib*

ARTURO TOSCANINI

25 God tells me how the music should sound, but *you* stand in the way.
> To a trumpet player, NY *Times* 11 Apr 54

26 After I die I shall return to earth as the doorkeeper of a bordello and I won't let a one of you in.
> To an orchestra that displeased him, recalled on his death 16 Jan 57

27 Assassins!
> After rehearsing an orchestra, *ib*

28 To some it is Napoleon, to some it is a philosophical struggle, to me it is allegro con brio.
> On Beethoven's Eroica, recalled on the opening of Toscanini archive at NY Public Library, NY *Times* 5 Apr 87

RICHARD TUCKER

29 To sing it right, Franco, you have to be Jewish.
> To Franco Corelli when asked to explain his success with Puccini, quoted by Ethan Mordden *Opera Anecdotes* Oxford 85

ALAIN VAËS

1 You translate paint to fabric, somebody gets into it and the ballet begins.
> On designing costumes, *Christian Science Monitor* 21 Jul 86

BENITA VALENTE

2 Why not say it? I'm bursting out of my cocoon. It was all too nice in the past—it never knocked anyone out. But last year, with *Rinaldo*—my first opening night at the Met—I looked out and heard all that cheering. And it was for me. And I loved it.
> After 25 years in opera, quoted in NY *Times* 3 Feb 85

3 Young singers ask me, "Do I have to live in New York?" I say, "You can live wherever you want—as long as people *think* you live in New York."
> *ib*

4 Inside I have been a stabber, a screamer, a die-er from way back.
> On portraying emotion in opera, *ib*

EDGARD VARÉSE

5 An artist is never ahead of his time but most people are far behind theirs.
> On composing, quoted in NY *Herald Tribune* 17 May 64

RALPH VAUGHAN WILLIAMS

6 I don't know whether I like it, but it is what I meant.
> On his *London* Symphony, quoted by Adrian Boult BBC Radio 1 Aug 65

FRED WARING

7 Be on your toes tonight—or I'll be on yours tomorrow.
> To his chorus, recalled on his death 29 Jul 84

LEONARD WARREN

8 Tenors are noble, pure and heroic and get the soprano, if she has not tragically expired before the final curtain. But baritones are born villains in opera. Always the heavy and never the hero—that's me.
> NY *World-Telegram & Sun* 13 Mar 57

ETHEL WATERS

9 We are all gifted. That is our inheritance.
> On black singers, CBS TV 8 Jan 54

LAWRENCE WELK

10 If they can't hum it after we play it, it's not for us.
> On music performed on his long-running television program, *Saturday Evening Post* Mar 80

11 It's the first time I ever got a standing ovation in the sky.
> After giving autographs on a flight from Florida to California, *ib*

MEREDITH WILLSON

12 Barbershop quartet singing is four guys tasting the holy essence of four individual mechanisms coming into complete agreement.
> NY *Herald Tribune* 6 Mar 60

Producers, Directors & Managers

RUDOLF BING

13 The opera always loses money. That's as it should be. Opera has no business making money.
> NY *Times* 15 Nov 59

14 I prefer to remember the happy things over 10 years, the things that went well. Let me see, what did go well?
> After a decade as manager of Metropolitan Opera, NY *Herald Tribune* 9 Oct 60

15 I will not enter into a public feud with Madame Callas, since I am well aware that she has considerably greater competence and experience at that kind of thing than I have.
> Quoted in Cleveland Amory and Earl Blackwell eds *Celebrity Register* Harper & Row 63

16 I don't want them to come in with a white tie, and I don't want them to come in a black tie. But I do want them to come in a tie.
> On standees, NY *Times* 16 Feb 64

17 Expressions of disapproval are on a level of vulgarity that cannot be tolerated. The way to express disapproval is to do without applause.
> NY *Herald Tribune* 9 Apr 64

18 It is becoming increasingly difficult to obtain the services of first-class conductors. . . . They are sick and tired of dealing with singers, as I am.
> *ib*

19 I never for a moment believed they would perform at 10 o'clock in the morning. It's hard enough getting them to perform at 8 at night.
> Apologizing to World's Fair audience for singers who overslept, NY *Times* 5 May 64

20 I am perfectly happy to believe that nobody likes us but the public.
> Replying to newspaper criticism of Metropolitan Opera, *Texaco Theater of the Air* 17 Apr 65

21 We are similar to a museum. My function is to present old masterpieces in modern frames.
> *Time* 8 Oct 65

22 There are two sighs of relief every night in the life of an opera manager. The first comes when the curtain goes up . . . The second sigh of relief comes when the final curtain goes down without any disaster, and one realizes, gratefully, that the miracle has happened again.
> *New Yorker* 17 Sep 66

23 She will sing only if her husband conducts, so I accept the old Viennese saying that if you want the meat, you have to take the bones.
> On Joan Sutherland, *5,000 Nights at the Opera* Doubleday 72

24 Miss Renata Tebaldi was always sweet and very firm. . . . she had dimples of iron.
> *ib*

25 We want an ensemble of stars, not comets.
> On continuity among performers, *National Observer* 29 Apr 72

26 How nice the human voice is when it isn't singing.
> *Newsweek* 1 May 72

1 They have a disease of the throat.
   On singers, *ib*

2 If that is not enough, will you please politely indicate that she can go to hell.
   November 21, 1957, letter to Metropolitan Opera's Italian representative on prolonged financial negotiations with Maria Callas, quoted in "A Century of Offstage Life at the Metropolitan Opera" NY *Times* 25 Sep 83

3 I never socialized with singers. It's very dangerous if you work with opera. . . . I don't think that in 30 years a singer has entered my apartment.
   News summaries 31 Dec 84

BOB GELDOF

4 It went beyond idealism and that ridiculous term *activism*, which basically means talking about something but doing nothing. . . . We made giving exciting.
   On organizing fund-raising concerts for African famine relief, *Time* 6 Jan 86

GOERAN GENTELE

5 Opera is an 18th- and 19th-century art that must find a 20th-century audience.
   On becoming general manager of Metropolitan Opera, NY *Times* 12 Sep 71

6 There are so many tensions involved in any creative activity . . . so when there is a catastrophe you never indicate that you think the end of the world has come. You examine it and say, "Well, this is a fine new catastrophe. Now, what else is important today?"
   ib

LORD HAREWOOD (George Henry Hubert Lascelles)

7 There is an old proverb much in evidence now at the [National Opera]: If you want the flowers in your garden to be glorious and to smell good, you must risk an occasional stink.
   On retiring, "A Lifetime of Undaunted Passion" London *Times* 20 Jun 85

8 My passion for opera—the eternal truth of drama through music—has grown, while my interest in performance . . . has diminished. Which is perhaps as good a reason as any other to go quietly.
   ib

JOAN INGPEN

9 I really love them but, of course, they tend to be more highly strung than actors because everything depends on those two little vocal cords and their life is a perpetual worry.
   On booking opera singers, NY *Times* 23 Sep 79

LINCOLN KIRSTEIN

10 In liberal democracy and anxious anarchy, the traditional classic dance, compact of aristocratic authority and absolute freedom in a necessity of order, has never been so promising as an independent expression as it is today.
   Classic Ballet, with Muriel Stuart, Knopf 52

11 A repertory, a patrimony of ballets, tended as carefully as the collection of 600-year-old bonsai in Tokyo's Imperial Palace conservatory, is not replaced; it is preserved, maintained, refreshed to give rebirth by grafting and seedlings.
   On NYC Ballet, NY *Times* 17 Mar 83

12 I've always had the idea . . . that we were conducting a military operation. It always seemed to me to be in a state of emergency.
   New Yorker 15 Dec 86

13 She was chronologically in luck. She corresponded to necessity.
   On Martha Graham, *ib*

14 He was trained as a dancer, and he had both a dancer's body and a dancer's capacity. He incarnated for me the most appealing and tragic aspects of American lower-class life.
   On Jimmy Cagney, *ib*

JOSHUA LOGAN

15 His music was direct from his heart and brain in the purest form possible.
   On Richard Rodgers, NY *Times* 17 Mar 85

16 Music has a poetry of its own, and that poetry is called melody.
   ib

ROUBEN MAMOULIAN

17 Critics complained it wasn't opera, it wasn't a musical. You give someone something delicious to eat and they complain because they have no name for it.
   Recalling his direction of the 1935 production of *Porgy and Bess*, NY *Times* 3 Feb 85

ROBERT MAYER

18 I look upon myself as a musical bricklayer with architectural aspirations.
   On his role as director of British Youth and Music Movement, *New Yorker* 21 Apr 80

ANDRÉ MERTENS

19 Singers' husbands! Find me stones heavy enough to place around their necks and drown them all!
   Time 1 Aug 60

20 Somewhere in the brain of every prima donna there is a deep craving for security and comfort, linked with a fear of old age. This causes her to pick a man who is prepared to act as a permanent wet nurse.
   ib

JAMES C PETRILLO, President, Amer Federation of Musicians

21 If I was a good trumpet player I wouldn't be here. I got desperate. I hadda look for a job. I went in the union business.
   NY *Times* 14 Jun 56

SEYMOUR ROSEN

22 One of the biggest problems today is the era of the guest conductor, and the music director who isn't.
   Quoted by Will Crutchfield "Orchestras in the Age of Jet-Set Sound" NY *Times* 6 Jan 85

Observers & Critics

SHANA ALEXANDER

23 Until quite recently dance in America was the ragged Cinderella of the arts. . . . Terpsichore was condemned to the chimney corner, and there she lan-

guished until the early 1930s, when Lincoln Kirstein, founding father of the New York City Ballet, stole Balanchine from Europe in the manner of Prometheus stealing fire.

Nutcracker Doubleday 85

1 An artificial style of dance confected for 18th-century kings evolved into a popular American art form. . . . an astonishing development for what until recently had been considered manna for aesthetes only, the quiche of the performing arts.

ib

2 The Sugarplum Fairy herself could have made no grander gesture.

On Ford Foundation grants to the NYC Ballet, *ib*

3 Every member of the inner ballet world, the entire peerage-pantheon of high culture-bearers, ladies bountiful, fiscal bigwigs, serious artists, jet-set sprinters, fading Tsarists, prima donnas, prime aesthetes, bursting stuffed-shirts, and the whole train of strenuous social mountaineers puffing uphill behind them all knew that Frances Schreuder was the great work's sole, albeit anonymous underwriter.

On Frances Schreuder's support of NYC Ballet, *ib*

4 Ballet's image of perfection is fashioned amid a milieu of wracked bodies, fevered imaginations, Balkan intrigue and sulfurous hatreds where anything is likely, and dancers know it.

ib

5 When the prima ballerina found ground glass in her toe slipper . . . every other dancer in the company was equally suspect.

ib

CHRISTOPHER ANDREAE

6 To the sound itself . . . the conductor adds the italics and punctuation of gesture, of strained arms, of startling tautness of the shoulders, of brisk nod, of hands flung apart in some wild appeal to the universe.

"Maestro" *Christian Science Monitor* 18 Dec 85

7 He is not all musician; he is also part bus conductor . . . in charge of a moving vehicle [who] dutifully hurries people off and onto it at designated intervals.

ib

W H AUDEN

8 No good opera plot can be sensible, for people do not sing when they are feeling sensible.

Time 29 Dec 61

9 [Music] can be made anywhere, is invisible and does not smell.

From 1951 poem "In Praise of Limestone," quoted in Kent Hieatt and William Clark eds *College Anthology of British and American Poetry* Allyn & Bacon 72

CLIVE BARNES

10 One of the few things in dance to match the Royal Ballet's curtain calls is the Royal Ballet's dancing.

"The Art of Acknowledgment" NY *Times* 10 Jun 66

JAMES BARRON

11 It was hard to make fun of him because he seemed to have so much fun making fun of himself.

On Liberace, NY *Times* 5 Feb 87

12 With his megawatt smile, his furry, feathery costumes, rhinestones as big as the Ritz and a unique blend of Beethoven and the "Beer Barrel Polka," Liberace charmed millions with a flashiness that was almost too much to be believed.

ib

KARL BARTH

13 Whether the angels play only Bach praising God, I am not quite sure. I am sure, however, that *en famille* they play Mozart.

Recalled on his death 9 Dec 68

JACQUES BARZUN

14 The piano is the social instrument par excellence. . . . drawing-room furniture, a sign of bourgeois prosperity, the most massive of the devices by which the young are tortured in the name of education and the grown-up in the name of entertainment.

Preface to Arthur Loesser *Men, Women and Pianos* Simon & Schuster 54

15 Music is intended and designed for sentient beings that have hopes and purposes and emotions.

Introduction to Joan Peyser *The New Music* Delacorte 71

SUZANNE BLUM

16 In every sense of the term, my client has been let down.

Defending ballerina whose partner failed to catch her, London *Sunday Times* 30 Nov 80

WILLIAM F BUCKLEY JR

17 The Beatles are not merely awful. . . . They are so unbelievably horrible, so appallingly unmusical, so dogmatically insensitive to the magic of the art, that they qualify as crowned heads of antimusic.

New summaries 8 Sep 64

ANGELA CARTER

18 This dance was the dance of death. [The clowns] danced it for the wretched of the earth, that they might witness their own wretchedness.

On an adaptation of the Mass for the Dead for one of their colleagues, *Nights at the Circus* Viking 85, quoted in NY *Times* 30 Jan 85

19 They danced the dance of the outcasts for the outcasts who watched them, amid the louring trees, with a blizzard coming on.

ib

PERCY CATER

20 It is no part of the functions of orchestral hall managers to tell me when I should cough. Anybody who wants to collect British seat money in the British winter must put up with the British cough.

On "coughing instructions" inserted in programs at London's Royal Festival Hall, *Newsweek* 18 Feb 63

JAY COCKS

21 He is a glorified gutter rat from a dying New Jersey town who walks with an easy swagger that is part residual stage presence, part boardwalk braggadocio.

On Bruce Springsteen, *Time* 27 Oct 75

JEAN COCTEAU

1 The ear disapproves but tolerates certain musical pieces; transfer them into the domain of our nose, and we will be forced to flee.
Recalled on his death 11 Oct 63

ALISTAIR COOKE

2 Cocktail music is accepted as audible wallpaper.
"The Innocent American" *Holiday* Jul 62

JOHN CORRY

3 His words and music weren't just joined; they were inseparably married.
On Cole Porter, NY *Times* 29 Jul 87

PETER DE VRIES

4 The tuba is certainly the most intestinal of instruments, the very lower bowel of music.
The Glory of the Hummingbird Little, Brown 74

RABBI CHAIM DRIZIN

5 Song is the pen of the soul.
At funeral for tenor Jan Peerce, NY *Times* 18 Dec 84

THOR ECKERT JR

6 The voice soared majestically, hugely, in the role, flooding the house with opulent, gleaming tones.
On Eva Marton in *Die Frau Ohne Schatten* at Metropolitan Opera House, *Christian Science Monitor* 13 Feb 85

RALPH ELLISON

7 Commercial rock 'n' roll music is a brutalization of the stream of contemporary Negro church music . . . an obscene looting of a cultural expression.
Shadow and Act Random House 64

THOMAS H FAY

8 It is a way of defining turf—a sonic turf.
On teenagers carrying oversize radios and tape players, NY *Times* 30 Jun 80

MARSHALL FISHWICK

9 As a student of American culture, I am willing to argue . . . that the Twist is a valid manifestation of the Age of Anxiety.
Saturday Review 3 Mar 62

CHET FLIPPO

10 [The star] had to be from humble beginnings, just like the audience.
On country music singers, NY *Times* 6 Sep 85

11 The star had to sing about those beginnings and the other things he shared with people from those beginnings: simple, everyday problems of life and frustration and mainly miseries of the heart and the troubles that caused.
ib

E M FORSTER

12 This opera is my *Nunc Dimittis*, in that it dismisses me peacefully and convinces me I have achieved.
On *Billy Budd*, in letter to collaborator Benjamin Britten, quoted in Mary Lago and P N Furbank eds *Selected Letters of E M Forster 1921–70* Belknap Press/Harvard 84

GEROLD FRANK

13 You heard a leaf fall, she heard a house crash.
On Judy Garland, NBC TV 9 Jul 75

ALFRED FRANKENSTEIN

14 Miss Farrell has a voice like some unparalleled phenomenon of nature. She is to singers what Niagara is to waterfalls.
On soprano Eileen Farrell, *Newsweek* 22 Sep 58

SAMUEL G FREEDMAN

15 His song "King of the Road" remains one of the anthems of the asphalt.
On Roger Miller, NY *Times* 21 Apr 85

FORD FRICK, baseball commissioner

16 I'd hate this to get out but I really like opera.
News summaries 8 Feb 54

WILLIAM E GEIST

17 Kristin Brown looks as though she could have been mailed first-class to New York for about a dollar and a half.
On 13-year-old ballerina from Dunwoody GA, NY *Times* 17 Jul 85

ARTHUR GELB

18 The girls are trotted out twice during each floor show, do nothing more strenuous than shake an ankle, wriggle a hip or twitch a shoulder—and it has taken choreographer Douglas Coudy weeks to teach them to do that.
On new program at Copacabana night club, NY *Times* 24 Jan 61

DONAL HENAHAN

19 Real folk music long ago went to Nashville and left no known survivors.
NY *Times* 8 May 77

20 It might be argued that genuine spontaneity is not really possible or desirable so long as printed scores of great works exist. . . . All modern musicians are, for better or worse, prisoners of Gutenberg.
"Whatever Happened to Spontaneity in Performance?" *ib* 13 May 84

21 [Rubinstein was] a fountain from which music spouted, not a recitalist.
On Artur Rubinstein, *ib*

22 The irrepressible spirit that made his playing seem like good conversation . . . is the Rubinstein legacy for pianists, if they can pick up their heads from the keyboard long enough to claim it.
ib

23 In her most taxing aria, "O patria mia," there were powerful reminders of the Price that we remember best and want to remember, a Price beyond pearls.
Reviewing Leontyne Price's farewell performance in *Aida*, *ib* 4 Jan 85

24 When her name is mentioned in the opera history books we will recall that vibrant, soaring tone—that and the blinding, high-beam-headlight smile that she flashed on her fans at each curtain call.
ib

1 The human brain can soften as a result of incessant listening to music with an intent to commit prose.

> On reviewing, "When Inspired Awfulness Becomes Interesting" *ib* 31 Aug 86

2 The more disastrous the mishaps the simpler the reviewing task.

> *ib*

3 Perhaps no hall of comparable size anywhere has served so nobly as a spawning ground for young talent and, it must be said, as a graveyard for the hopes of the mediocre.

> On renovated Weill Recital Hall in Carnegie Hall, *ib* 6 Jan 87

4 [It] will never be mistaken for a high school gymnasium or a meeting room in a Midwestern motel.

> *ib*

STEPHEN HOLDEN

5 You can get caught up in the visceral charge of its engines, sing along with its chunky tunes and dream its romantic dreams and still feel the cold wind of the history blowing through its pages.

> On *Bruce Springsteen & The E Street Band Live/1975–85*, NY *Times* 9 Nov 86

BERNARD HOLLAND

6 [The work] resembles a breech delivery—one which is expressed in rhythmic lurches, stabs of phrase and vocal ornamentation designed to express agitation rather than decorative grace.

> On Michael Tippett's composition "The Mask of Time," NY *Times* 9 Apr 84

KATHRYN HULME

7 The awesome antiphon swelled in the dark and expanded.

> On music at early morning mass in her convent, *The Nun's Story* Atlantic–Little, Brown 56

PAUL HUME

8 Miss Truman is a unique American phenomenon with a pleasant voice of little size and fair quality. . . . There are few moments during her recital when one can relax and feel confident that she will make her goal, which is the end of the song.

> On concert by Margaret Truman, *Time* 18 Dec 50

CLIVE JAMES

9 Disco dancing is . . . just the steady thump of a giant moron knocking in an endless nail.

> London *Sunday Observer* 17 Dec 78

POPE JOHN PAUL II

10 I have a sweet tooth for song and music. This is my Polish sin.

> Listening to folk-rock hymns on visit to Poland, NY *Daily News* 7 Oct 79

DENA KLEIMAN

11 A sea of red coats and white trousers, in perfect step, the airs of the Republic blasted with particular gusto, the kind of sing-along oom pah pah of which patriotism is made.

> On US Marine Band, NY *Times* 14 May 85

JON LANDAU

12 I saw rock 'n' roll future and its name is Bruce Springsteen.

> Quoted by Dave Marsh *Glory Days* Pantheon 87

PHILIP LARKIN

13 The chromatic scale is what you use to give the effect of drinking a quinine martini and having an enema simultaneously.

> *Required Writing* Farrar, Straus & Giroux 84, quoted in *Newsweek* 25 Jun 84

MADELEINE L'ENGLE

14 Her hands were broad and strong; the true pianist's sledgehammer hands, they had been called. They still moved to her bidding. . . . No matter to what she likened them—turnips, carrots—they were still as nimble as ever. The notes came clear and true.

> On heroine of *A Severed Wasp* Farrar, Straus & Giroux 83

CLAUDE LÉVI-STRAUSS

15 [Contemporary serial music] is like a sailless ship, driven out to sea by its captain, who is privately convinced that by subjecting life aboard to the rules of an elaborate protocol, he will prevent the crew from thinking nostalgically either of their home port or of their ultimate destination.

> Quoted by Howard Gardner *Art, Mind and Brain* Basic Books 82

GODDARD LIEBERSON

16 Show me an orchestra that likes its conductor and I'll show you a lousy conductor.

> Quoted by Herbet Kupferberg *Those Fabulous Philadelphians* Scribner's 69

LIFE MAGAZINE

17 Debonair, exultant, amused, he has imparted to the tap dance an elegance and mobility. He is the number 1 exponent of America's only native dance form.

> 1941 comment on Fred Astaire, recalled in special issue Fall 86

RUSSELL LYNES

18 [Ragtime] was a fanfare for the 20th century.

> *The Lively Audience* Harper & Row 85, quoted in *Christian Science Monitor* 18 Nov 85

MELVIN MADDOCKS

19 Giving jazz the Congressional seal of approval is a little like making Huck Finn an honorary Boy Scout.

> On resolution to designate jazz as a US national treasure, *Christian Science Monitor* 24 Dec 86

EDNA ST VINCENT MILLAY

20 The Englishman foxtrots as he fox-hunts, with all his being, through thickets, through ditches, through hedges, through chiffons, through waiters, over saxophones, to the victorious finish; and who goes home depends on how many the ambulance will accommodate.

> Recalled on her death 19 Oct 50

KENNETH MILLER

1 The piano's world encompasses glass-nerved virtuosi and stomping barrel-housers in fedoras; it is a world of pasture and storm, of perfumed smoke, of liquid mathematics.

"How to Buy a Piano "*Esquire* Apr 86

2 No other acoustic instrument can match the piano's expressive range, and no electric instrument can match its mystery.

ib

3 [The piano is] able to communicate the subtlest universal truths by means of wood, metal and vibrating air.

ib

HENRY MITCHELL

4 The choirs left the main tune and soared two octaves past heaven in a descant to rattle the bones and surge the heart.

On dedication of nave of Washington DC's National Cathedral, Washington *Post* 9 Jul 76

NBC TV NEWS

5 *The Pirates of Penzance* may have to walk the plank.

On closing of London's Old Vic, 15 May 81

NEWSWEEK

6 *La Sonnambula* is dull enough to send the most athletic sleepwalker back to bed.

On Bellini's opera, 4 Mar 63

7 The audience came out of its trance, transformed instantly from silence to cheers, from stillness to such vigorous applause that left and right hands might have been enemies.

On Rudolf Nureyev in *La Bayadère*, 19 Apr 65

8 And so it was good-bye at last. Good-bye to that broad and angular face and to that tall, forceful figure, like a Rodin sculpture, carved out of a giant block of ebony; and good-bye to those eyes which closed when she sang as if looking inward but which, when open, beamed warmth and quick response.

On Marian Anderson's farewell concert, 26 Apr 65

RALPH NOVAK

9 Her voice sounded like an eagle being goosed.

On Yoko Ono in television documentary *John and Yoko, People* 2 Dec 85

WALTER NURENA

10 The ballet people are champagne drinkers. They are a younger, more exciting crowd than the opera people.

On tending bar at Lincoln Center, NY *Times* 23 Nov 84

11 With each ballet we know what to expect. A pas de deux brings out a lot of excitement. And a lot of champagne.

ib

VANCE PACKARD

12 Rock 'n' roll might best be summed up as monotony tinged with hysteria.

Testimony to Senate Subcommittee on Interstate Commerce, news summaries 31 Dec 58

TONY PALMER

13 Wagner *was* a monster. He was anti-Semitic on Mondays and vegetarian on Tuesdays. On Wednesday he was in favor of annexing Newfoundland, Thursday he wanted to sink Venice and Friday he wanted to blow up the pope.

On directing a nine-hour biographical film about Richard Wagner, *TV Guide* 18 Oct 86

JOAN PEYSER

14 Musicians, even more than writers or artists, tend to be deified, and the institutions that surround them like to preserve that.

On why there are few unauthorized biographies of living musical figures, *Publishers Weekly* 5 Jun 87

HENRY PLEASANTS

15 [She] could hold a note as long as the Chase National Bank.

On Ethel Merman, *The Great American Popular Singers* Simon & Schuster 85, quoted in NY *Times* 16 Feb 85

16 One small town boy, born at the right time, in the right place, in the right environment and under the right circumstances [represented the convergence] of all the musical currents of America's subculture: black and white gospel, country and western and rhythm and blues.

On Elvis Presley, *ib*

ADAM CLAYTON POWELL JR

17 His personal blues are now finished. No more the problems of Beale Street. No more the irritations of Memphis. No more the vexation of the St Louis woman. No more the cynical "Love, Oh Love, Oh Careless Love."

Funeral tribute to W C Handy, NY *Times* 3 Apr 58

TOM PRIDEAUX

18 It wasn't a man singing a song. It was a man singing his autobiography.

On Irving Berlin singing "There's No Business Like Show Business," *Life* 3 May 63

DUNCAN PURNEY

19 I can see fiddling around with a banjo, but how do you banjo around with a fiddle?

Musical Notes WQXR Radio 16 May 84

ALAN RICH

20 No composer in history . . . has been so widely jazzed up, watered down, electrified and otherwise transmogrified, debated and admired as this German provincial.

On Johann Sebastian Bach, *Newsweek* 24 Dec 84

21 From the first, critics had no difficulty recognizing his talents: 10 omnipotent fingers at the command of a musical intelligence that made light of the most fearful musical challenges.

On Glenn Gould, *ib* 28 Jan 85

HAROLD C SCHONBERG

22 When Callas carried a grudge, she planted it, nursed it, fostered it, watered it and watched it grow to sequoia size.

On Maria Callas, *The Glorious Ones* Times Books 85, quoted in NY *Times* 21 Aug 85

GEORGE BERNARD SHAW

1 Let a short Act of Parliament be passed, placing all street musicians outside the protection of the law, so that any citizen may assail them with stones, sticks, knives, pistols or bombs without incurring any penalties.
> Recalled on his death 2 Nov 50

2 The real Brahms is nothing more than a sentimental voluptuary. . . . rather tiresomely addicted to dressing himself up as Handel or Beethoven and making a prolonged and intolerable noise.
> ib

3 I *hate* performers who debase great works of art; I long for their annihilation.
> ib

4 Orchestras only need to be sworn at, and a German is consequently at an advantage with them, as English profanity, except in America, has not gone beyond a limited technology of perdition.
> Quoted by Harold C Schonberg *The Great Conductors* Simon & Schuster 67

DAVID STEVENS

5 This vast piece of lyric theater, with its attempted fusion of music and ancient drama, has remained between the pages of musical encyclopedias. Often enough, that is where such enterprises ought to stay.
> "Fauré Opera—A Noble Bore" *International Herald Tribune* 18 Jun 70

ANITA T SULLIVAN

6 A piano is full of suppressed desires, recalcitrance, inhibition, conflict.
> *The Seventh Dragon* Metamorphous Press 85, quoted in NY *Times* 24 Aug 86

BERNARD TAPER

7 Balanchine has trained his cat to perform brilliant *jetés* and *tours en l'air*; he says that at last he has a body worth choreographing for.
> *Balanchine* Harper & Row 63

TIME MAGAZINE

8 Salome was 16 and slinky-slim. Birgit Nilsson is 46 and boatswain-burly. As for casting the Swede in the title role of Richard Strauss's *Salome*, the idea seemed roughly comparable to starring Judith Anderson as Lolita.
> On Metropolitan Opera's production of *Salome*, 12 Feb 65

9 Nilsson . . . sang as though her lungs were made of the finest Swedish steel . . . her tone as silver pure as a Nordic winterscape. Even John the Baptist would have lost his head.
> ib

HARRY S TRUMAN, 33rd US President

10 I have read your lousy review of Margaret's concert. I've come to the conclusion that you are an eight ulcer man on a four ulcer job . . . Some day I hope to meet you. When that happens you'll need a new nose, a lot of beefsteak for black eyes and perhaps a supporter below.
> Reply to critic Paul Hume, *Time* 18 Dec 50

11 I don't give a damn about "The Missouri Waltz" but I can't say it out loud because it's the song of Missouri. It's as bad as "The Star-Spangled Banner" so far as music is concerned.
> ib 10 Feb 58

KENNETH TYNAN

12 Not content to have the audience in the palm of his hand, he goes one further and clinches his fist.
> On Frankie Laine at London Palladium, recalled on Tynan's death 26 Jul 80

VARIETY

13 It will be gone by June.
> 1955 statement on rock 'n' roll, quoted by Christopher Cerf and Victor Navasky *The Experts Speak* Pantheon 84

MICHAEL WALSH

14 Opera stars know that biology is destiny. Sometime in their 50s or early 60s, the powerful, flexible and ultimately mysterious instrument that has been the source of their artistry frays, cracks and disappears.
> *Time* 14 Jan 85

15 Rich, supple and shining, it was in its prime capable of effortlessly soaring from a smoky mezzo to the pure soprano gold of a perfectly spun high C.
> On voice of Leontyne Price, ib

REBECCA WEST

16 Great music is in a sense serene; it is certain of the values it asserts.
> *This Real Night* Viking 85, quoted in *Time* 25 Mar 85

PRESS

Reporters & Editors

JOSEPH W ALSOP JR

17 The plain truth is that the reporter's trade is for young men. Your feet, which do the legwork, are nine times more important than your head, which fits the facts into a coherent pattern.
> On retiring at age 64, *Newsweek* 7 Oct 74

JACK ANDERSON

18 I don't like to hurt people, I really don't like it at all. But in order to get a red light at the intersection, you sometimes have to have an accident.
> *Newsweek* 3 Mar 72

ANONYMOUS

19 Mr Markel, I think you're a son of a bitch and I respect you.
> Reporter submitting resignation to Lester Markel, longtime editor of NY *Times Magazine*, quoted in NY *Times* 11 Jun 72

BEN BAGDIKIAN

20 Trying to be a first-rate reporter on the average American newspaper is like trying to play Bach's St Matthew Passion on a ukulele: The instrument is too crude for the work, for the audience and for the performer.
> Quoted by Melvin Maddocks *Christian Science Monitor* 23 Jan 85

CARL BERNSTEIN and BOB WOODWARD

1 From then on, any Watergate story would carry both names. [Our] colleagues melded the two into one and gleefully named [our] byline Woodstein.

On joint byline for Washington *Post* coverage of Watergate, *All the President's Men* Simon & Schuster 74

THEODORE M BERNSTEIN

2 If writing must be a precise form of communication, it should be treated like a precision instrument. It should be sharpened, and it should not be used carelessly.

On ideal writing and editing at the NY *Times*, recalled on his death 27 Jun 79

3 I favor *whom*'s doom except after a preposition.

Ending some years of ambivalence on the use of *who* and *whom*, *ib*

JIM BISHOP

4 A newspaper is lumber made malleable. It is ink made into words and pictures. It is conceived, born, grows up and dies of old age in a day.

Quill Oct 63

5 A reporter meets interesting people. If he endures, he will get to know princes and presidents, popes and paupers, prostitutes and panderers. And always, in the back of his head, there will be a dozen men and women he will never meet. And always, he will feel the poorer for it.

Shrewsbury NJ *Daily Register* 6 Sep 79

6 The reporter is the daily prisoner of clocked facts. . . . On all working days, he is expected to do his best in one swift swipe at each story.

A Bishop's Confession Little, Brown 81

ERMA BOMBECK

7 I was terrible at straight items. When I wrote obituaries, my mother said the only thing I ever got them to do was die in alphabetical order.

On her first newspaper job, *Time* 2 Jul 84

8 I was too old for a paper route, too young for Social Security and too tired for an affair.

On beginning her humor column, *ib*

JOHN BORRELL

9 Covering Africa is 80 percent logistics and 20 percent reporting.

Time 29 Aug 83

JIMMY BRESLIN

10 A job on a newspaper is a special thing. Every day you take something that you found out about, and you put it down and in a matter of hours it becomes a product. Not just a product like a can or something. It is a personal product that people, a lot of people, take the time to sit down and read.

On closing of NY *Mirror*, NY *Herald Tribune* 17 Oct 63

11 I busted out of the place in a hurry and went to a saloon and drank beer and said that for the rest of my life I'd never take a job in a place where you couldn't throw cigarette butts on the floor. I was hooked on this writing for newspapers and magazines.

On the day he almost went into advertising, *ib*

HELEN GURLEY BROWN, Editor in Chief, *Cosmopolitan*

12 I care. I care a lot. I think of *Cosmopolitan* all day, and I run scared. So it's a combination of fright, caring and anxiety.

To Amer Magazine Conference, NY *Times* 25 Oct 84

WILLIAM BUCHANAN

13 The general outlook is not that the person has died but that the person has lived.

On writing obituaries for the Boston *Globe*, quoted in Northwestern University *Byline* Winter 82

ERWIN CANHAM, Editor, *Christian Science Monitor*

14 The day of the printed word is far from ended. Swift as is the delivery of the radio bulletin, graphic as is television's eyewitness picture, the task of adding meaning and clarity remains urgent. People cannot and need not absorb meanings at the speed of light.

NY *Times* 5 Jan 58

HODDING CARTER III

15 I put a premium on responsibility. Too much of the television thing consists of the unseen hand with the up-front mouth, and the news magazine's separating the reporter and writer scares me. When you are clearly accountable, it breeds more rigorous reporting.

Quoted in report of libel suits against *Time* and CBS, NY *Times* 31 Jan 85

TURNER CATLEDGE

16 The composing room has an unlimited supply of periods available to terminate short, simple sentences.

Memo to staff of NY *Times*, quoted in *Time* 20 Dec 54

17 Hell, that's what the news is—an emergency. Why, we look at this as pretty much routine.

On sinking of *Andrea Doria*, covered in NY *Times*'s final edition seven hours after first reports of the accident, *ib* 6 Aug 56

RAY CAVE

18 If you don't have faith in your people in the field, you are lost. If that faith is blind faith, then it is not faith at all, just maladministration.

Interview during libel suit against *Time* brought by Ariel Sharon, former defense minister of Israel, NY *Times* 8 Jan 85

19 A quote is a personal possession and you have no right to change it.

To journalism alumni of Northwestern University 29 May 85

ARTHUR CHRISTIANSEN, Editor, London *Daily Express*

20 I saw their flat sallow faces, their Sunday-best clothes, their curious capacity for enjoying themselves without displaying any sign of emotion. I saw them all as a challenge.

On his paper's readership, *Headlines All My Life* Harper & Row 62

21 It was my job to interest them in everything that was happening, to make the arrival of the *Daily Express* each morning an event, to show them the world outside Bolton and Bacup, to give them courage and confidence to overcome the drabness of their lives.

ib

1 News, news, news—that is what we want. You cannot beat news in a newspaper.

> Recalled on his death, NY *Herald Tribune* 28 Sep 63

2 We never waste space saying, "On the one hand." We just state an opinion in a Godlike voice.

> *ib*

3 Good stories flow like honey. Bad stories stick in the craw. A bad story? One that cannot be absorbed on the first time of reading.

> *ib*

JOHN CIARDI

4 The reader deserves an honest opinion. If he doesn't deserve it, give it to him anyhow.

> "The Reviewer's Duty to Damn" *Saturday Review* 16 Feb 57

BOB CONSIDINE

5 Call it vanity, call it arrogant presumption, call it what you wish, but I would grope for the nearest open grave if I had no newspaper to work for, no need to search for and sometimes find the winged word that just fits, no keen wonder over what each unfolding day may bring.

> *It's All News to Me* Meredith Press 67

CLIFTON DANIEL

6 Write about society as news and . . . treat it like sociology.

> 1963 assignment for Charlotte Curtis, recalled on her death, NY *Times* 17 Apr 87

HEDLEY DONOVAN, Editor in Chief, Time Inc

7 The music, the news, is provided out there by Carter and Sadat and Begin and Reggie Jackson and others, who perhaps are the equivalent of Brahms and Bach and Beethoven. The editor doesn't make the news . . . but he does interpret it and shape it, as the conductor does. . . . Above all, he selects what's going to be on the program, which is one hell of a power.

> Quoted by his successor Henry Anatole Grunwald, address to Amer Society of Magazine Editors, *SMW Newsletter* 9 Dec 84

OSBORN ELLIOTT

8 Journalistic hours are odd and long and often tense, and newsmen seek each other out as natural allies in a world that is so much part of them, but which they visit so randomly.

> *The World of Oz* Viking 80

9 There is another reason journalists like to drink and eat together: they simply cannot think of better company.

> *ib*

JANET FLANNER ("Genêt")

10 I act as a sponge. I soak it up and squeeze it out in ink every two weeks.

> On her "Letter from Paris" published in the *New Yorker* over a 50-year period, recalled on her death 7 Nov 78

11 I keep going over a sentence. I nag it, gnaw it, pat and flatter it.

> *ib*

GENE FOWLER

12 News is history shot on the wing. The huntsmen from the Fourth Estate seek to bag only the peacock or the eagle of the swifting day.

> *Skyline* Viking 61

JAMES P GANNON, Editor, Des Moines *Register*

13 Every good newspaper is muckraking to some degree. It's part of our job. Where there's muck, we ought to rake it.

> NY *Times* 10 Apr 85

JOHN GATES

14 The first thing I am going to do is to rejoin the American people and find out what Americans are thinking about.

> On resigning after a decade as editor of the *Daily Worker* and 27 years as a Communist Party member, *Editor & Publisher* 18 Jan 58

WOLCOTT GIBBS

15 Our writers are full of clichés just as old barns are full of bats. There is obviously no rule about this, except that anything that you suspect of being a cliché undoubtedly is one and had better be removed.

> "Theory and Practice of Editing New Yorker Articles," quoted by James Thurber *The Years with Ross* Atlantic–Little, Brown 59

WILLIAM E GILES

16 Surprise, the stuff that news is made of.

> *National Observer* 19 Oct 64

BRENDAN GILL

17 It is in the nature of the *New Yorker* to be as topical as possible, on a level that is often small in scale and playful in intention.

> *Here at the New Yorker* Random House 75

18 The guns of the big events rumble through our pages, but the tiny firecrackers are constantly hissing and popping there as well; it appears that much of my life as a journalist has been devoted to sedulously setting off firecrackers.

> *ib*

ROBERT A GOTTLIEB

19 I don't have lunches, dinners, go to plays or movies. I don't meditate, escalate, deviate or have affairs. So I have plenty of time.

> On succeeding William Shawn as editor of the *New Yorker*, NY *Times* 13 Jan 87

REBECCA GREER

20 My chief responsibilities have been described as soliciting and procuring. The illegal variety would be easier. And it certainly would be more profitable.

> On her job as articles editor of *Woman's Day*, address to Society of Magazine Writers 12 Nov 70

WILLIAM H GRIMES, Editor, Wall Street Journal

21 We are not much interested in labels but if we were to choose one, we would say we are radical. Just as radical as the Christian doctrine.

> "A Newspaper's Philosophy," recalled by his successor Vermont Royster on the paper's 75th anniversary, *Wall Street Journal* 8 Jul 64

1 We have friends but they have not been made by silence or pussyfooting. If we have enemies, we do not placate them.

ib

HENRY ANATOLE GRUNWALD, Editor in Chief, Time Inc

2 Journalism can never be silent: that is its greatest virtue and its greatest fault. It must speak, and speak immediately, while the echoes of wonder, the claims of triumph and the signs of horror are still in the air.

Introduction to *Time* magazine's 60th anniversary issue, Fall 83

3 Libel actions, when we look at them in perspective, are an ornament of a civilized society. They have replaced, after all, at least in most cases, a resort to weapons in defense of a reputation.

Chet Huntley Memorial Lecture at NY University, NY *Times* 16 Nov 84

JOHN GUNTHER

4 It's the equivalent of putting on the brakes suddenly while driving uphill.

On writing magazine articles to pay the travel expenses engendered by writing books, *Saturday Review* 13 Dec 62

5 What interested me was not news, but appraisal. What I sought was to grasp the flavor of a man, his texture, his impact, what he stood for, what he believed in, what made him what he was and what color he gave to the fabric of his time.

On figures profiled in *Procession* Harper & Row 65

PETE HAMILL

6 The best newspapermen I know are those most thrilled by the daily pump of city room excitements; they long fondly for a "good murder"; they pray that assassinations, wars, catastrophes break on their editions.

NY *Times* 11 Nov 84

SYDNEY J HARRIS

7 Every morning I take out my bankbook, stare at it, shudder—and turn quickly to my typewriter.

On incentive as a journalist, quoted by Rosamund Essex *Church Times* 30 Dec 83

FRED M HECHINGER

8 I narrow-mindedly outlawed the word *unique*. Practically every press release contains it. Practically nothing ever is.

On resigning as education editor, NY *Herald Tribune* 5 Aug 56

BEN HECHT

9 We looked on the hopheads, crooks and gunsels and on their bawdy ladies as members of a family among whom we were privileged to move. . . . There was no caste system, moral or social, in our manners.

On crime reporting in Chicago, *Charlie* Harper 57

10 We trotted, coach-dog fashion, at the heels of the human race, our tails awag.

ib

11 Chicago is a sort of journalistic Yellowstone Park, offering haven to a last herd of fantastic bravos.

On hard-drinking, cynical, exuberantly emotional breed of newspapermen described in his play *The Front Page*,

written with Charles MacArthur, recalled on Hecht's death 18 Apr 64

HUGH HEFNER, Editor, *Playboy*

12 The interesting thing is how one guy, through living out his own fantasies, is living out the fantasies of so many other people.

On 25th anniversary of the magazine, *Newsweek* 1 Jan 79

ANTHONY HOLDEN

13 If you have an anecdote from one source, you file it away. If you hear it again, it may be true. Then the more times you hear it the less likely it is to be true.

International Herald Tribune 9 Jun 79

JENKIN LLOYD JONES, Editor, Tulsa *Tribune*

14 Let there be a fresh breeze of new honesty, new idealism, new integrity. . . . You have typewriters, presses and a huge audience. How about raising hell?

To Inland Daily Press Assn, *US News & World Report* 28 May 62

WILLIAM F KERBY, Executive Editor, *Wall Street Journal*

15 News work is highly addictive. It is the cocaine of crafts.

A Proud Profession: Memoirs of a Reporter, Editor and Publisher Dow Jones–Irwin 81

16 If the smell of printer's ink raises the hair on the back of your neck; if the mounting decibels of a rotary press moving up to top production speed cause your pulse rate to quicken and your heart to beat a faster rhythm; if you have a compulsion to share with the world anything interesting or unusual you have come upon; if you know no peace until you have the real answers—then you are hooked. You never will be truly happy doing anything else.

ib

JACK C LANDAU

17 If [newsmen] violate their promises of confidentiality, they may never again be able to operate effectively, except to cover news which is offered by government handout or is a matter of public record.

Testifying before House subcommittee as a member of the Reporters Committee for Freedom of the Press, LA *Herald-Examiner* 19 Feb 73

18 Consider what kind of nation we would be . . . if hundreds of scandals involving state and local government still lay locked in the mouths of citizens.

ib

ANN LANDERS

19 I was naive, but I certainly was not duplicitous.

On recycling her advice columns, *Time* 17 May 82

JOSEPH LELYVELD

20 If I have lived by any maxim as a reporter, it was that every person is an expert on the circumstances of his life.

On returning to South Africa, which he had first covered in the 1960s, *Move Your Shadow: South Africa, Black and White* Times Books 85

WALTER LIPPMANN

1 A long life in journalism convinced me many presidents ago that there should be a large air space between a journalist and the head of a state.
    Farewell to colleagues, quoted in NY *Times* 26 May 67

2 I would have carved on the portals of the National Press Club, "Put not your trust in princes." Only the very rarest of princes can endure even a little criticism, and few of them can put up with even a pause in the adulation.
    ib

DAVID LOW, British editorial cartoonist

3 Here lies a nuisance dedicated to sanity.
    Self-epitaph recalled on his death 19 Sep 63

4 I have learned from experience that, in the bluff and counterbluff of world politics, to draw a hostile war lord as a horrible monster is to play his game. What he doesn't like is being shown as a silly ass.
    ib

ROBERT MANNING, former Editor, *Atlantic*

5 Newspapermen, as journalists used to be called, have long been charged with the sin of cynicism. . . . a characterization that many of us encourage to deflect attention from our far more widespread flaw, incorrigible sentimentalism.
    NY *Times* 12 Jun 82

T S MATTHEWS

6 This is Choctaw, now try it in English.
    Marginal note asking for a rewrite, quoted by Henry Anatole Grunwald, address to Amer Society of Magazine Editors, *SMW Newsletter* 9 Dec 84

AILEEN MEHLE ("Suzy Knickerbocker")

7 Socialites kid each other, their way of life, their friends; and I kid the whole setup.
    On her role as society columnist for the Hearst newspapers, *Time* 24 Sep 65

8 What I do is kick them in the pants with a diamond-buckled shoe.
    NY *Times* 14 May 67

MALCOLM MUGGERIDGE

9 Good taste and humor are a contradiction in terms, like a chaste whore.
    Defending his editorship of *Punch*, quoted in *Time* 14 Sep 53

10 It was a somber place, haunted by old jokes and lost laughter. Life, as I discovered, holds no more wretched occupation than trying to make the English laugh.
    On *Punch* offices, *The Most of Malcolm Muggeridge* Simon & Schuster 66

NEW YORKER

11 The business ownership of the *New Yorker* may change hands, but the idea of the *New Yorker*—the tradition of the *New Yorker*, the spirit of the *New Yorker*—has never been owned by anyone and never will be owned by anyone.
    "Talk of the Town" statement after sale of magazine to Newhouse family, 22 Apr 85

12 Amid a chaos of images, we value coherence. We believe in the printed word. And we believe in clarity. And in immaculate syntax. And in the beauty of the English language.
    ib

13 We believe that the truth can turn up in a cartoon, in one of the magazine's covers, in a poem, in a short story, in an essay, in an editorial comment, in a humor piece, in a critical piece, in a reporting piece. And if any single principle transcends all the others and informs all the others, it is to try to tell the truth.
    ib

GERT NIERS, Executive Editor, *Aufbau*

14 Every obituary we put in, we know that's a reader we're losing.
    On readership of Manhattan German-language newspaper, NY *Times* 16 Nov 84

DOROTHY PARKER

15 Somebody was using the pencil.
    On why she missed a *New Yorker* deadline, quoted by James Thurber *The Years with Ross* Atlantic–Little, Brown 59

WESTBROOK PEGLER

16 My hates have always occupied my mind much more actively and have given greater spiritual satisfactions than my friendships.
    Quoted by Oliver Pilat *Pegler* Beacon 63

17 I am a member of the rabble in good standing.
    ib

WILLIAM REES-MOGG, Editor, London *Times*

18 Information, free from interest or prejudice, free from the vanity of the writer or the influence of a government, is as necessary to the human mind as pure air and water to the human body.
    Christian Science Monitor 22 Sep 70

ALASTAIR REID

19 In reporting with some accuracy, at times we have to go much further than the strictly factual. Facts are part of the perceived whole.
    On why he made up characters, rearranged events and invented dialogue in search of "a larger reality" for a nonfiction *New Yorker* article, *Wall Street Journal* 18 Jun 84

ROGER ROSENBLATT

20 The news on an ordinary day [is] a strange assembly that swoops down on one's life like cousins from Oslo one has never seen before, will never see again, and who, between planes, thought they would call to say hello.
    "The News: Living in the Present Tense" *Time* 12 Dec 83

21 People simply want to know that other people are around. . . . The day opens and closes with the reassuring noises of the species, and we seem taken with the news that we are here.
    ib

1 The principal reason journalists exist in society is that people have a need to be informed of and comprehend the details of experience.
"Journalism and the Larger Truth" *ib* 2 Jul 84

2 You slave to sound as if you knew it all along. You have to shape your column too—mostly Doric, a Corinthian fluting when they least expect it. It's work. Whatever the others say, it's work.
On writing a column, *ib* 27 Jan 86

3 It's not a career deep down; it is a protest against being overwhelmed by the speed of things, against letting the world get away from us.
ib

A M ROSENTHAL, Executive Editor, NY *Times*

4 It has been our policy not to use obscenities in the paper. It's a harmless little eccentricity of ours.
On not quoting presidential candidate Jimmy Carter's "vulgarism for sexual relations," *Time* 4 Oct 76

5 Other papers have added water to the soup, but we've added vegetables.
On new feature coverage that substantially increased the *Times*'s income and circulation, *ib* 15 Aug 77

6 If you don't have a sensation of apprehension when you set out to find a story and a swagger when you sit down to write it, you are in the wrong business.
On stepping down as executive editor, "Learning on the Job" NY *Times* 14 Dec 86

7 It was an interesting experience being metropolitan editor of the *Times*, in precisely the same way as being simmered in a saucepan for a few years is terribly interesting.
ib

8 The *Times* is a tough paper to work for, because if we fail to present the news fully and intelligently and with sophistication there are no rationalizations to fall back on—there is enough space and enough money, there are no taboos on subject, no pressures from wicked publishers and boards of directors and a world of land, sea and mind in which to roam.
ib

HAROLD ROSS, Editor, *New Yorker*

9 Editing is the same as quarreling with writers—same thing exactly.
On the magazine's 25th anniversary, *Time* 6 Mar 50

10 The *New Yorker* . . . hopes to reflect metropolitan life and affairs of the day, to be gay, humorous, satirical, but to be more than a jester . . . It is not edited for the old lady in Dubuque.
Recalled on his death 5 Dec 51

11 There will be a personal-mention column —a jotting down in the small-town newspaper style of the comings, goings and doings in the village of New York.
1924 prospectus for *New Yorker*, recalled by James Thurber, *The Years with Ross* Atlantic–Little, Brown 59

12 This will contain some josh and some news value.
ib

WILLIAM SAFIRE

13 A reader should be able to identify a column without its byline or funny little picture on top—purely by look or feel, or its turgidity ratio.
Quoted by Robert H Yoakum *Vanity Fair* Sep 84

14 Create your own constituency of the infuriated.
Formula for writing a column, *ib*

15 The most successful column is one that causes the reader to throw down the paper in a peak of fit.
ib

ROBERT SHAND, Managing Editor, NY *Daily News*

16 The real appeal of the *News*, I think, is that it lights up the narrow routine of millions of lives with gleams from the great outside. Its readers thrill with secondhand emotions they will never know, they shudder from crimes they will never commit, they quiver with courage that shall never be theirs.
Recalled on his death 25 Nov 66

17 We believe that motive is more interesting than murder. We think that consequences are more important than commission. We consider that what people think and feel is often more significant than what they do.
ib

WILLIAM SHAWN, Editor, *New Yorker*

18 We do not permit composites. . . . We do not create conversations.
Memo following a reporter's admission of having made up characters and conversations in a nonfiction article, NY *Times* 3 Jul 84

19 The *New Yorker* has devoted itself for 59 years not only to facts and literal accuracy but to truth. And truth begins, journalistically, with the facts.
ib

LIZ SMITH

20 Gossip is just news running ahead of itself in a red satin dress.
Dallas *Times-Herald* 3 Aug 78

MERRIMAN SMITH

21 The relationship between a reporter and a president is exactly the same as that between a pitcher and a batter. . . . They both are trying to keep each other away.
NBC TV 2 Aug 61

RED SMITH

22 I like to get where the cabbage is cooking and catch the scents.
On departure to cover California baseball games played by the Giants and Dodgers, *Newsweek* 21 Apr 58

23 The natural habitat of the tongue is the left cheek.
On covering sports, quoted by Richard Kluger *The Paper: The Life and Death of the New York Herald Tribune* Knopf 86

JAMES B STEWART

24 A newspaper reporter is related to a telephone as a musician is related to a piano.
On difficulty of reporting from India, lay sermon, St Michael's Church, NYC, 14 Apr 85

HERBERT BAYARD SWOPE, Editor, NY *World*

25 The first duty of a newspaper is to be accurate. If it be accurate, it follows that it is fair.
Letter to NY *Herald Tribune* 16 Mar 58

1 The secret of a successful newspaper is to take one story each day and bang the hell out of it. Give the public what it wants to have and part of what it ought to have whether it wants it or not.
> Recalled on his death 20 Jun 58

2 Don't forget that the only two things people read in a story are the first and last sentences. Give them blood in the eye on the first one.
> ib

FREDERICK TAYLOR, Executive Editor, *Wall Street Journal*

3 It's easier to make a reporter into an economist than an economist into a reporter.
> On the policy of his newspaper, quoted by Stephen Hess *Christian Science Monitor* 7 May 85

PETER UTLEY

4 An obituary should be an exercise in contemporary history, not a funeral oration.
> On writing candid obituaries for the London *Times*, NY *Times* 15 Mar 87

5 We never search for scandal, but we use it if it cries out to excess.
> ib

6 You never ring up the potential corpse because, you know, they'll be greatly upset.
> ib

AMY VANDERBILT

7 [I am] a journalist in the field of etiquette. I try to find out what the most genteel people regularly do, what traditions they have discarded, what compromises they have made.
> *Newsweek* 11 Aug 58

JOHN WALCOTT

8 You never stop, except occasionally to put a fork in your mouth.
> On breakfast and lunch with government sources as "information meals" vital for covering Washington DC, NY *Times* 30 Apr 85

THEODORE H WHITE

9 It was like walking through a field playing a brass tuba the day it rained gold. Everything was sitting around waiting to be reported.
> On writing *The Making of the President 1960* Atheneum 1961, quoted by Timothy Crouse *The Boys on the Bus* Random House 72

10 When that book came out, it was like Columbus telling about America at the court of Ferdinand and Isabella.
> ib

11 When a reporter sits down at the typewriter, he's nobody's friend.
> *Newsweek* 23 Oct 72

12 For those men who, sooner or later, are lucky enough to break away from the pack, the most intoxicating moment comes when they cease being bodies in other men's command and find that they control their own time, when they learn their own voice and authority.
> On becoming a foreign correspondent, *In Search of History: A Personal Adventure* Harper & Row 78

13 I'd get into a room and disappear into the woodwork. Now the rooms are so crowded with reporters getting behind-the-scenes stories that nobody can get behind-the-scenes stories.
> On his method of reporting, recalled on his death 15 May 86

ALDEN WHITMAN

14 Death, the cliché assures us, is the great leveler; but it obviously levels some a great deal more than others.
> Introduction to *The Obituary Book* Stein & Day 71

15 That's what an obit is supposed to be—a picture, a snapshot. It's not a full-length biography, it's not a portrait. It's a quick picture.
> *W* 18 Jul 80

WILLIAM WHITWORTH, Editor, *Atlantic*

16 All "little" magazines have the luxury of thinking the reader is the same person as their editors.
> *Christian Science Monitor* 31 Jul 85

WALTER WINCHELL

17 Today's gossip is tomorrow's headline.
> Quoted by Liz Smith Dallas *Times-Herald* 3 Aug 78

Publishers & Management

ANONYMOUS

18 Our professionals miscalculated on every major point. . . . Always their approach was "Give 'em nothing—and do it retroactively."
> Spokesperson for NY Publishers' Assn commenting on four-month newspaper strike, quoted in NY *Times* 1 Apr 63

FRANK H BARTHOLOMEW, President, United Press

19 The handout and the spokesman threaten our diligence, our ingenuity, our skepticism, our zeal. For zealots we must be. Not for a cause. For facts and for truth—and all of the truth.
> Address at University of Washington 21 Feb 58

20 Like the newspapers dependent upon us for news, ours will be a business organization, collecting and distributing one of the world's most perishable products, *news*.
> Announcing merger of United Press and International News Service, NY *Times* 25 May 58

LORD BEAVERBROOK (William Maxwell Aitken)

21 I suppose I will go on selling newspapers until at last will come the late night final.
> On 75th birthday, news summaries 7 Jun 54

OTTO BETTMANN, Director, Bettmann Archive

22 He outsells Jesus!
> On requests for pictures of Sigmund Freud, *Time* 23 Mar 81

LOREN GHIGLIONE, Publisher, Southbridge MA *News*

23 Ignorance, inertia and indifference are alive and well in America's newspapers. Minority still equals inferiority in the minds of many American editors and publishers.
> On need for more nonwhites in high-level management positions, NY *Times* 11 Mar 87

KATHARINE GRAHAM, Publisher, Washington *Post*

1 If we had failed to pursue the facts as far as they led, we would have denied the public any knowledge of an unprecedented scheme of political surveillance and sabotage.

> On Watergate coverage, Washington *Post* 3 Mar 73

PHILIP L GRAHAM, Publisher, Washington *Post*

2 I am insatiably curious about the state of our world. I revel in the recitation of the daily and weekly grist of journalism. . . . So let us drudge on about our inescapably impossible task of providing every week a first rough draft of a history that will never be completed about a world we can never understand.

> Addressing his editors and correspondents, recalled on his death 3 Aug 63

HARRY J GRANT, Publisher, Milwaukee *Journal*

3 It takes a long time to educate a community and it can't be done by spellbinders, moneybags, hypnotizers or magicians . . . or Aladdin's lamp. Character is what matters on a paper.

> *Time* 1 Feb 54

4 We're not a loved paper. But we're a respected one.

> *ib*

WILLIAM RANDOLPH HEARST JR

5 I don't have the umbilical cord Pop had with each paper.

> On closing of NY *Mirror*, founded by his father, NY *Times* 16 Oct 63

CHRISTIE HEFNER, President, Playboy Enterprises

6 She no longer has a staple in her navel.

> On the traditional nude centerfold after new binding techniques were developed for the magazine, NBC TV 28 Aug 85

ANDREW HEISKELL, former Chairman, Time Inc

7 A publication depends on a great idea, not there being a market out there. . . . You start with an idea rather than trying to get an idea which goes with that market.

> *New York* 3 Mar 86

ROY W HOWARD, Chairman, Scripps-Howard Newspapers

8 No date on the calendar is as important as tomorrow.

> Creed for newspaper personnel, recalled on his death, *Time* 27 Nov 64

INTERNATIONAL HERALD TRIBUNE

9 For more than half of its nearly 91 years, this newspaper has been published at 21 Rue de Berri, between the Étoile and the Elysée Palace, between the Paris that the tourists see and the Paris that governs France.

> Front-page announcement of move to new quarters in suburban Neuilly, 25 Mar 78

10 In moving to the Avenue Charles de Gaulle, the *International Herald Tribune* is not departing from the Paris or the France in which its roots are so deep; it is taking a step that will present more efficiently the mirror which it seeks to hold up to the swiftly moving events of our swiftly changing world.

> *ib*

JAMES A LINEN, Publisher, *Time* magazine

11 Moving a magazine is like ordering 100,000 gallons of alphabet soup, to go. Last week, in Manhattan, it went.

> On move to new headquarters, *Time* 21 Mar 60

HENRY R LUCE

12 To see, and to show, is the mission now undertaken by *Life*.

> Prospectus for *Life* magazine, quoted in *Saturday Evening Post* 16 Jan 65

13 Publishing is a business, but journalism never was and is not essentially a business. Nor is it a profession.

> Recalled on his death 28 Feb 67

14 Journalism is the art of collecting varying kinds of information (commonly called "news") which a few people possess and of transmitting it to a much larger number of people who are supposed to desire to share it.

> *ib*

15 There are men who can write poetry, and there are men who can read balance sheets. The men who can read balance sheets cannot write.

> On recruiting a staff for *Fortune* magazine, *ib*

16 Of necessity, we made the discovery that it is easier to turn poets into business journalists than to turn bookkeepers into writers.

> *ib*

17 I suggest that what we want to do is not to leave to posterity a great institution, but to leave behind a great tradition of journalism ably practiced in our time.

> *ib*

18 Show me a man who claims he is objective and I'll show you a man with illusions.

> Quoted in NY *Times* 1 Mar 67

19 I became a journalist to come as close as possible to the heart of the world.

> Quoted in *Esquire* Dec 83

20 I am all for titillating trivialities. I am all for the epic touch. I could almost say that everything in *Time* should be either titillating or epic or starkly, supercurtly factual.

> *ib*

21 *Time* should make enemies and *Life* should make friends.

> Quoted by Charles Whittingham, publisher of *Life*, on the magazine's 50th anniversary, *Live at Five* WNBC TV 3 Nov 86

RUPERT MURDOCK, newspaper magnate

22 I think a newspaper should be provocative, stir 'em up, but you can't do that on television. It's just not on.

> Declaring that he did not plan any television tabloids, *Business Week* 20 May 85

ALLEN NEUHARTH, founder, *USA Today*

23 We look like television in print.

> NBC TV 19 Nov 85

ELEANOR MEDILL ("CISSY") PATTERSON, Publisher, Washington *Times-Herald*

1 The trouble with me is that I am a vindictive old shanty-Irish bitch.
Time 13 Sep 54

LORD ROTHERMERE (Harold Sydney Harmsworth), Chairman, London *Daily Mail*

2 I buy wood pulp, process it and sell it at a profit.
Quoted by David Frost and Antony Jay *The English* Stein & Day 68

ARTHUR HAYS SULZBERGER, Publisher, NY *Times*

3 We tell the public which way the cat is jumping. The public will take care of the cat.
On impartial news reporting, *Time* 8 May 50

ARTHUR OCHS SULZBERGER, Publisher, NY *Times*

4 More than print and ink, a newspaper is a collection of fierce individualists who somehow manage to perform the astounding daily miracle of merging their own personalities under the discipline of the deadline and retain the flavor of their own minds in print.
Introduction to A M Rosenthal *Thirty-eight Witnesses* McGraw-Hill 64

5 In dread fear of sentimentality, another thing true is not said—that for its staff the paper is a source of pride and, I do believe, an object of affection and—yes, love.
ib

6 Anybody who claims to read the entire paper every day is either the world's fastest reader or the world's biggest liar.
Quoted in *Time* 15 Aug 77

7 Journalism's ultimate purpose [is] to inform the reader, to bring him each day a letter from home and never to permit the serving of special interests.
NY *Times* 28 Apr 83

8 The Defense Department's plan to ban newspaper reporters from [pool coverage of] military operations is incredible. It reveals the administration to be out of touch with journalism, reality and the First Amendment.
ib 11 Oct 84

LORD THOMSON OF FLEET (Roy Herbert Thomson)

9 I have a magpie mind. I like anything that glitters.
On profitability of newspapers, quoted in John Robert Colombo ed *Colombo's Canadian Quotations* Hurtig 74

10 I buy newspapers to make money to buy more newspapers to make more money.
Quoted in *Time* 15 Aug 77

11 As for editorial content, that's the stuff you separate the ads with.
ib

DEWITT WALLACE, founder, *Reader's Digest*

12 The final condensation.
Self-epitaph, recalled on his death, *Time* 13 Apr 81

LILA ACHESON WALLACE

13 I knew right away that it was a gorgeous idea.
On her husband's proposal for *Reader's Digest*, quoted in *Time* 13 Apr 81

JOHN HAY WHITNEY, Publisher, NY *Herald Tribune*

14 To be fair is not enough any more. We must be ferociously fair.
Address at Colby College, Waterville ME, *Time* 20 Nov 64

15 The role we can play every day, if we try, is to take the whole experience of every day and shape it to involve American man. It is our job to interest him in his community and to give his ideas the excitement they should have.
ib

CHARLES A WHITTINGHAM, Publisher, *Life* magazine

16 [It was] America's scrapbook.
On 50th anniversary of *Life* magazine, *Live at Five* WNBC TV 3 Nov 86

WILL WOODWARD, General Manager, Dubuque *Telegraph-Herald*

17 When I listen to people here who say that of course something was put in the paper because I ordered it in, it scares the hell out of me. That tells me what those people would do if they were in my place.
Quoted in "The Little Old Daily of Dubuque" NY *Times* 3 Feb 74

Observers & Critics

SPIRO T AGNEW, US Vice President

18 In the United States today, we have more than our share of the nattering nabobs of negativism.
Address at San Diego 11 Sep 70

19 [They have formed their own 4-H club—the] hopeless, hysterical hypochondriacs of history.
ib

SHANA ALEXANDER

20 At Gatling-gun tempo . . . word-perfect the first time out. . . . the journalistic equivalent of a high-wire front somersault without a net.
On fellow *Life* reporter Tommy Thompson meeting a deadline, *Nutcracker* Doubleday 85

PRINCESS ANNE

21 *You* are a pest, by the very nature of that camera in your hand.
To a photographer, quoted by John Pearson *The Selling of the Royal Family* Simon & Schuster 86

ANONYMOUS

22 Reporters are like alligators. You don't have to love them, you don't necessarily have to like them. But you do have to feed them.
White House source, on plans for frequent press briefings during Tokyo economic summit meeting, quoted in *US News & World Report* 5 May 86

CORAZON C AQUINO, President of the Philippines

23 You, the foreign media, have been the companion of my people in its long and painful journey to freedom.
To 400 guests at *Time*'s Distinguished Speakers Program, *Time* 29 Sep 86

1 The media's power is frail. Without the people's support, it can be shut off with the ease of turning a light switch.
ib

RUSSELL BAKER

2 Live by publicity, you'll probably die by publicity.
On President Ronald Reagan's changing image after news of Iranian arms sales, NY *Times* 3 Dec 86

THOMAS BARR

3 The press's job [is] to dig . . . to pick at things that may not be pleasant or comfortable for the people involved, to try to get as much of the story as possible into the hands of the public so that the public can make decisions about how we want to run our lives.
Summation for Time Inc in libel suit brought by Ariel Sharon, former Israeli defense minister, *Time* 21 Jan 85

BRUCE BARTON JR

4 Rumor, that most efficient of press agents.
On behind-the-scenes talk in Manhattan art galleries, *Time* 24 Nov 61

CELÂL BAYAR, President of Turkey

5 Photographers are the only dictators in America.
On US visit, news summaries 1 Feb 54

JIM BISHOP

6 The morning after a death, we learned an avalanche of goodies about the renowned, some of which persuaded the reader that he should have cultivated the deceased in life.
On NY *Times* obituary writer Alden Whitman, Shrewsbury NJ *Daily Register* 11 Jun 80

7 He dropped pejoratives like subliminal seasoning.
ib

HUGO L BLACK, Associate Justice, US Supreme Court

8 The Founding Fathers gave the free press the protection it must have [to] bare the secrets of government and inform the people.
On publication of the Pentagon Papers, NY *Times* 30 Jun 71

GWENDA BLAIR

9 *Newsweek*'s editors are known as the Wallendas, because like the famous family of trapeze artists, they have jobs requiring a strong measure of interdependence. They also have a very long way to fall.
"The Heart of the Matter" *Manhattan Inc* Oct 84

DANIEL J BOORSTIN

10 The celebrity is a person who is known for his well-knownness.
The Image Atheneum 61

ARNAUD DE BORCHGRAVE

11 *Newsweek* is a perpetual French Revolution. They keep eliminating their best people.
Quoted in *Manhattan Inc* Oct 84

JIMMY BRESLIN

12 Anything to the *Daily News* should be kept to two paragraphs, the first of which was to contain a personal insult to the paper or to the subject of an antilabor story. A letter to the *Times* newspaper should begin with a mention of the offending article, a factual presentation and not a personal insult [since] the editors were so ego-ridden that they needed to be told that even their obvious misdeeds were intellectually sound.
On letters to the editor, *Table Money* Ticknor & Fields 86

KINGMAN BREWSTER, President, Yale

13 It won't make for a quiet life but it will make for an interesting paper . . . vastly more significant because it is doing something only a daily paper can do.
Urging newspaper editors to indulge creativity of young reporters, NY *Times* 30 Oct 64

14 While the spoken word can travel faster, you can't take it home in your hand. Only the written word can be absorbed wholly at the convenience of the reader.
ib

15 The newspaper fits the reader's program while the listener must fit the broadcaster's program.
ib

PATRICK J BUCHANAN, White House director of communications

16 Saying the Washington *Post* is just a newspaper is like saying Rasputin was just a country priest.
On *Post* coverage of Watergate and arms sales to Iran, CNN TV 9 Dec 86

17 Dear Ted: Thanks for the invitation to question four distinguished liberal journalists. But 11:30 PM is long past my bedtime.
Declining invitation to appear with four White House correspondents on Ted Koppel's ABC TV special on coverage of Iran arms sales, quoted in *Newsweek* 29 Dec 86

WILLIAM F BUCKLEY JR

18 He invented the news magazine. He invested [it] with an interpretation . . . Tell what happened, tell it well, tell it concisely, but with attention to the belletristic imperative.
"The *Life* and *Time* of Henry Luce" *Esquire* Dec 83

19 Relate it to what *should* happen; fuse it into the long morality play that began, really, in the Garden of Eden.
ib

WARREN BUFFETT, Chairman, Berkshire, Hathaway Inc

20 The smarter the journalists are, the better off society is. [For] to a degree, people read the press to inform themselves—and the better the teacher, the better the student body.
Quoted by Walter Guzzardi *Fortune* 4 Mar 85

GEORGE BUSH, US Vice President

21 A bullpen seething with mischief.
On reporters covering his vice-presidential campaign, NY *Times* 7 Oct 84

JAY CARR

1 One of the things that will keep *The Front Page* burning bright as long as newspapers are alive is the myth that newspapermen are breezy and raffish. What other play has for so long fed the self-image of journalists?

> Reviewing Broadway revival of Ben Hecht and Charles MacArthur's 58-year-old play, Boston *Globe* 4 Dec 86

2 They were fast-moving opportunists encased in cynicism and proud of it.

> On Chicago reporters, *ib*

3 [Walter Burns is] the archetypal managing editor—ruthless, self-righteous, manipulative, downright maniacal if it means an exclusive, especially one that it can congratulate itself for on its own front page.

> *ib*

JIMMY CARTER, 39th US President

4 I look forward to these confrontations with the press to kind of balance up the nice and pleasant things that come to me as president.

> At first press conference after taking office, 9 Feb 77

FERN SCHUMER CHAPMAN

5 A big-city newsroom can be a snake pit. The politics put Mayor Daley's machine to shame, the competition proves beyond a doubt Darwin's theory of survival of the fittest and the hierarchy of editors is more complicated than the Vatican's.

> *Wall Street Journal* 26 Feb 85

FRANCIS X CLINES

6 Death's sting has a new meaning now that the *Times* of London is including candid descriptions of human peccadilloes in its obituaries.

> NY *Times* 15 Mar 87

7 The resultant tales from life are stirring reader interest, survivor passions and unease among Britons.

> *ib*

8 It is "lifestyle" journalism the way Chaucer first invented it, and the *Times*, onto a good thing, is uninhibitedly publishing articles on the passing of a cuckolded poet, a rock promoter strangely addicted to collecting orangutans and an Italian writer striving "to avoid becoming a bore."

> *ib*

9 Peter Utley, the newspaper's obituary editor . . . cheerfully checked with Primrose Palmer, his assistant, on the day's soul traffic. The late archbishop from New Zealand sounded promising, it was agreed, but then again it was lunch time, and who knew what had been happening in some now-ending life.

> *ib*

ALEXANDER COCKBURN

10 The pack slumbered and only a few watchdogs rattled their chains.

> On reluctance of press to criticize the first six years of the Reagan administration, *Wall Street Journal* 13 Nov 86

CHARLES W COLSON, White House aide

11 The first 20 stories written about a public figure set the tone for the next 2,000 and it is almost impossible to reverse it.

> NY *Times* 7 Jul 74

TIMOTHY CROUSE

12 A lightweight, by definition, is a man who cannot assert his authority over the national press, cannot manipulate reporters, cannot finesse questions, prevent leaks or command a professional public relations operation.

> On covering presidential candidates, *The Boys on the Bus* Random House 72

13 The press likes to demonstrate its power by destroying lightweights, and pack journalism is never more doughty and complacent than when the pack has tacitly agreed that the candidate is a joke.

> *ib*

JERRY DELLA FEMINA

14 A lot of its readers are of an age where they forget to cancel.

> On wide circulation of *Reader's Digest*, quoted by *Newsweek* 12 Jan 87

EVERETTE E DENNIS, Executive Director, Gannet Center for Media Studies, Columbia University

15 Broadcasters are storytellers, newspapers are fact-gatherers and organizers of information and news magazines are kind of a hybrid of both.

> NY *Times* 31 Jan 85

THOMAS D'EVELYN

16 [Russell] Baker writes columns as a poet writes light verse—with tongue in cheek and a steady hand.

> *Christian Science Monitor* 26 Nov 86

MARLENE DIETRICH

17 They want you to bring out your intestines.

> On interviewers, *People* 3 Sep 84

ERVIN S DUGGAN

18 The bad boy tweaking the nose of the Establishment [with] the countenance of a Jewish leprechaun.

> On Art Buchwald, *Washingtonian* Jan 85

DWIGHT D EISENHOWER, 34th US President

19 I don't attempt to be a poker player before this crowd.

> To press conference 30 Apr 58

20 Well, when you come down to it, I don't see that a reporter could do much to a president, do you?

> At his last and most candid press conference, quoted in NY *Times* 9 Aug 64

GEOFFREY FISHER, Archbishop of Canterbury

21 Some of the press who speak loudly about the freedom of the press are themselves the enemies of freedom. Countless people dare not say a thing because they know it will be picked up and made a song of by the press. That limits freedom.

> *Look* 17 Mar 59

FELIX FRANKFURTER, Associate Justice, US Supreme Court

1 Freedom of the press is not an end in itself but a means to the end of [achieving] a free society.
NY *Times* 28 Nov 54

FRED W FRIENDLY, Columbia School of Journalism

2 A composite is a euphemism for a lie. It's disorderly. It's dishonest and it's not journalism.
On *New Yorker* writer who admitted he made up characters, rearranged events and invented dialogue for nonfiction article, news summaries 19 Jun 84

PHIL GAILEY

3 If Washington were a circus, as some like to think it is, the Washington *Post* would be the ringmaster.
NY *Times* 26 Jun 84

WOLCOTT GIBBS

4 Backward ran sentences until reeled the mind.
In *New Yorker* parody on sentence structure of *Time*, recalled on his death 16 Aug 58

5 Where it all will end, knows God.
ib

6 He wrote about nothing that didn't carry either his name or his initials—sometimes his pieces were signed at both ends.
On Ralph Ingersoll, editor of *PM*, quoted by Roy Hoopes *Ralph Ingersoll* Atheneum 85

BRENDAN GILL

7 Questioning a comma, he will shake his head and say in his soft voice that he realizes perfectly well what a lot of time and thought have gone into the comma and that in the ordinary course of events he would be the first to say that the comma was precisely the form of punctuation that he would have been most happy to encounter at that very place in the sentence, but isn't there the possibility—oh, only the remotest one, to be sure, and yet perhaps worth considering for a moment in the light of the care already bestowed on the construction—that the sentence could be made to read infinitesimally more clearly if, say, instead of a comma a semicolon were to be inserted at just that point?
On editor William Shawn, *Here at the New Yorker* Random House 75

NEIL E GOLDSCHMIDT, US Secretary of Transportation

8 Editorial writers . . . enter after battle and shoot the wounded.
Wall Street Journal 5 May 80

BARRY M GOLDWATER, US Senator

9 I won't say that the papers misquote me, but I sometimes wonder where Christianity would be today if some of those reporters had been Matthew, Mark, Luke and John.
In first speech after accepting Republican presidential nomination, NY *Times* 11 Aug 64

PAUL GRAY

10 The image of the reporter as a nicotine-stained Quixote, slugging back Scotch while skewering city hall with an exposé ripped out of a typewriter on the crack of deadline, persists despite munificent evidence to the contrary.
In review of Richard Kluger's *The Paper: The Life and Death of the New York Herald Tribune* Knopf 86, *Time* 27 Oct 86

11 In the end, the *Tribune* lost touch with the world it was supposed to reach; it mattered passionately, but almost exclusively, to those who worked for it.
ib

BOB GREENE

12 The meat-and-potatoes work of world journalism is performed by the wire service reporters.
NY *Daily News* 5 May 85

13 The professionalism of wire service reporters is constantly being tested because reporters know that if they're late or sloppy on a story, it will show up because the competition is likely to be not late and not sloppy.
ib

THOMAS GRIFFITH

14 Editors may think of themselves as dignified headwaiters in a well-run restaurant but more often [they] operate a snack bar . . . and expect you to be grateful that at least they got the food to the table warm.
How True: A Skeptic's Guide to Believing the News Atlantic–Little, Brown 74

15 Journalism constructs momentarily arrested equilibriums and gives disorder an implied order. That is already two steps from reality.
ib

16 Anderson's muckraking is one of debatable ends constantly used to justify questionable works.
On Jack Anderson, "Muckraking Is Sometimes Sordid Work" *Time* 23 Jul 79

17 To the public, the press is not David among Goliaths; it has become one of the Goliaths, Big Media, a combination of powerful television networks, large magazine groups and newspaper chains that are near-monopolies.
"Credibility at Stake" *ib* 11 Mar 84

18 Its attitude, which it has preached and practiced, is skepticism. Now, it finds, the public is applying that skepticism to the press.
ib

19 The news is staged, anticipated, reported, analyzed until all interest is wrung from it and abandoned for some new novelty.
"Selling an Agreed Version" *ib* 30 Dec 85

20 As the final step, pollsters tell us how the public reacted to it, which becomes the agreed version—whether the event itself was a flop or a success.
ib

MURRAY I GURFEIN, Judge, US Court of Appeals, 2nd Circuit

21 A cantankerous press, an obstinate press, a ubiquitous press, must be suffered by those in authority in order to preserve . . . the right of the people to know.
1971 ruling affirming the NY *Times*'s right to publish the Pentagon Papers, recalled on his death 16 Dec 79

JAMES C HAGERTY, former White House press secretary

1 If you lose your temper at a newspaper columnist, he'll get rich or famous or both.
NY *Times* 17 Mar 68

WILLIAM A HENRY III

2 Any departure from fact is the first step on a slippery slope toward unbelievability.
On *New Yorker* reporter who admitted creating dialogue and composite characters for a nonfiction article, *Time* 2 Jul 84

HENRY HILLMAN, President, Hillman Co

3 A whale is harpooned only when it spouts.
On why he avoids interviews, *Fortune* 31 May 82

HAROLD L ICKES, Secretary of the Interior

4 That great, overgrown lummox of a Colonel Mc-Cormick, mediocre in ability, less than average in brains and a damn physical coward in spite of his size, sitting in the tower of the *Tribune* building with his guards protecting him while he squirts sewage . . . at men whom he happens to dislike.
1938 comment on Chicago publisher Robert Mc-Cormick, *The Secret Diary of Harold L Ickes Vol II The Inside Struggle* Simon & Schuster 54

LEE ISRAEL

5 Hatchet murders were the house speciality of the *Journal*, whose front page was a virtual abattoir of murder most foul.
On crime reporting in NY newspaper, *Kilgallen* Delacorte 79

HUGH NEWELL JACOBSEN

6 The permanent power brokers of this city are the columnists.
On Washington DC, NY *Times* 31 May 84

LYNDON B JOHNSON, 36th US President

7 I hear the headlines on the radio, see them on TV and read them in the paper. When I hear from the men out there, I sometimes don't believe they are talking about the same situation.
On coverage of Vietnam War, quoted by Hugh Sidey "Lyndon Johnson's Personal Alamo" *Time* 15 Apr 85

8 The fact that a man is a newspaper reporter is evidence of some flaw of character.
Quoted in *People* 2 Feb 87

JULIANA, Queen of the Netherlands

9 It must be wonderful sport to contradict each other.
To Washington correspondents during US visit, *Time* 14 Apr 52

10 You are interested in the kitchen of the world—you want to find out what is cooking . . . who has a finger in the pie and who will burn his finger.
ib

JACQUELINE KENNEDY

11 Whenever I was upset by something in the papers, [Jack] always told me to be more tolerant, like a horse flicking away flies in the summer.
Quoted by Ralph G Martin *A Hero for Our Time* Macmillan 83

12 [I want] minimum information given with maximum politeness.
Instructions to press secretary Pamela Turnure, *ib*

JOHN F KENNEDY, 35th US President

13 I am reading it more and enjoying it less.
On his treatment by the press, quoted by Pierre Salinger *With Kennedy* Doubleday 66

WALTER KERR

14 Seymour Peck's editorial hand ranged far, wide and deep, touching lightly but expertly . . . He seemed less an editor of any sort than the very best sort of guardian angel.
Tribute to *Times* drama editor, NY *Times* 5 Jan 85

15 He wove a great web of knowledge, linking everything together, and sat modestly at a switchboard at the center, eager to help.
ib

NIKITA S KHRUSHCHEV, Soviet Premier

16 They pay little attention to what we say and prefer to read tea leaves.
On interpretation of Soviet attitudes by members of the press, 5 Jul 55

17 The press is our chief ideological weapon.
NY *Times* 29 Sep 57

LANE KIRKLAND, President, AFL–CIO

18 My pappy told me never to bet my bladder against a brewery or get into an argument with people who buy ink by the barrel.
On labor reporting, *Fortune* 23 Dec 85

RICHARD KLUGER

19 Every time a newspaper dies, even a bad one, the country moves a little closer to authoritarianism; when a great one goes, like the New York *Herald Tribune*, history itself is denied a devoted witness.
The Paper: The Life and Death of the New York Herald Tribune Knopf 86

EDWARD KOCH, Mayor of NYC

20 The most guileful amongst the reporters . . . are those who appear friendly and smile and seem to be supportive. They are the ones who will seek to gut you on every occasion.
NY *Times* 18 Jan 84

ARTHUR KROCK

21 Every president after Jefferson has professed agreement with Jefferson's concept that the freedom of the American press to print its versions of the facts, background and likely consequences of human events was a constitutional principle permanently reserved from any form of interference by government. Consequently Jefferson denounced . . . either direct or indirect attempts by government to do what in current parlance has become known as "management of the news."
"Mr. Kennedy's Management of the News" *Fortune* Mar 63

LEWIS H LAPHAM

22 [He was] as uncommunicative as a vending machine.
On White House press secretary George E Reedy, *Saturday Evening Post* 11 Sep 65

G GORDON LIDDY

1 The press is like the peculiar uncle you keep in the attic—just one of those unfortunate things.
> Quoted in *Newsweek* 12 Jan 87

A J LIEBLING

2 People everywhere confuse what they read in newspapers with news.
> "A Talkative Something or Other" *New Yorker* 7 Apr 56

3 I take a grave view of the press. It is the weak slat under the bed of democracy.
> Quoted by Melvin Maddocks *Christian Science Monitor* 23 Jan 85

4 Freedom of the press is guaranteed only to those who own one.
> Quoted by Richard Kluger *The Paper: The Life and Death of the New York Herald Tribune* Knopf 86

WALTER LIPPMANN

5 The senator might remember that the Evangelists had a more inspiring subject.
> On Barry M Goldwater's speculation about how he might have fared at the hands of Matthew, Mark, Luke and John rather than the press, news summaries 13 Aug 64

PETER LISAGOR

6 We became spear carriers in a great televised opera. We were props in a show. I always felt we should have joined Actors Equity.
> On President John F Kennedy's press conferences, quoted by Ralph G Martin *A Hero for Our Time* Macmillan 83

7 Those of us who had a chance to ask questions should have charged that much for speaking lines. It was like making love in Carnegie Hall.
> *ib*

ALICE ROOSEVELT LONGWORTH

8 Dorothy is the only woman in history who has had her menopause in public and made it pay.
> On writing style of columnist Dorothy Thompson, quoted by Vincent Sheean *Dorothy and Red* Houghton Mifflin 63

CURTIS D MACDOUGALL, Professor Emeritus of Journalism, Northwestern University

9 A good reporter cannot afford to be cynical; a good reporter cannot afford to be skeptical.
> Recalled on his death 10 Nov 85

HAROLD MACMILLAN, Prime Minister of Great Britain

10 I read a great number of press reports and find comfort in the fact that they are nearly always conflicting.
> London *Observer* 20 Dec 59

MELVIN MADDOCKS

11 Nothing is more idealistic than a journalist on the defensive.
> "How Journalists Regard Their Field" *Christian Science Monitor* 23 Jan 85

12 Once we thought, journalists and readers alike, that if we put together enough "facts" . . . and gave them a fast stir, we would come up with something that, at least by the standards of short-order cooks, could be called the truth.
> *ib*

13 Journalists do not like to report on uncertainties. They would almost rather be wrong than ambiguous.
> *ib*

YAKOV MALIK, Soviet diplomat

14 It's like vodka without breakfast.
> On being photographed but not interviewed, NY *Times* 13 Feb 69

DAVID MARGOLICK

15 The *Review*'s labyrinthine editing process . . . does to the written word what the Cuisinart does to broccoli.
> On *Harvard Law Review*, NY *Times* 24 Sep 84

EDWIN MCDOWELL

16 There are serpents in that journalistic Eden.
> On the *New Yorker*'s policy of holding articles for several years before either publishing them or rejecting them, NY *Times* 26 Jan 87

ROBERT G MENZIES, Prime Minister of Australia

17 You don't have a democracy. It's a photocracy.
> On Washington news photographers, news summaries 6 Nov 54

ARTHUR MILLER

18 A good newspaper, I suppose, is a nation talking to itself.
> London *Observer* 26 Nov 61

FERDINAND MOUNT

19 One of the unsung freedoms that go with a free press is the freedom not to read it.
> London *Daily Telegraph* 22 May 86

BETTY SOUTHARD MURPHY, National Labor Relations Board

20 The broad spectrum of knowledge, the ability to probe into the meaning of an event and the ability to write clearly and concisely in newspaper style are the essence of professionalism.
> Dissenting opinion to board's ruling that journalists cannot be defined as professionals under federal law because their bargaining units also represent such employees as messengers and restaurant workers, NY *Times* 6 Apr 76

EDWARD R MURROW

21 Most of us probably feel we couldn't be free without newspapers, and that is the real reason we want the newspapers to be free.
> NY *Herald Tribune* 12 Mar 58

EDMUND S MUSKIE, US Secretary of State

22 Looking at yourself through the media is like looking at one of those rippled mirrors in an amusement park.
> *Newsweek* 26 May 80

NEW YORKER

1 It's a strange phenomenon of journalistic life today that the greatest potential "story" of our time—the self-extermination of mankind in a nuclear holocaust—is one that, by its very nature, can never be written.

21 Nov 83

NEW YORKER STAFF COMMITTEE

2 It is our strange and powerfully held conviction that only an editor who has been a long-standing member of the staff will have a reasonable chance of assuring our continuity, cohesion and independence.

Protest by 154 writers, cartoonists and editors against publisher's appointment of Robert A Gottlieb, Editor in Chief of Knopf, to succeed William Shawn as editor, NY *Times* 15 Jan 87

NEW YORK TIMES

3 Its history is the history of the newspaper and we owe it much, even—since it invented both the editorial and the editorial "we"—our voice.

On 200th anniversary of the London *Times*, 11 Jul 85

4 England would have been worse if governed without its tyranny.

ib

5 Those who live by secrecy can also perish by it.

Editorial on Soviet suppression of news about nuclear accident at Chernobyl, "Mayday! and May Day" 1 May 86

6 Secrecy is a disease and Chernobyl is its symptom, a threat both to the Soviet Union and its neighbors.

ib

7 The chance to work with William Shawn was like being asked to dance with Fred Astaire.

On retirement of veteran *New Yorker* editor, 18 Jan 87

RICHARD M NIXON, 37th US President

8 You won't have Nixon to kick around anymore, because, gentlemen, this is my last press conference.

After his defeat in California gubernatorial election, 7 Nov 62

9 The American people are entitled to see the president and to hear his views directly, and not to see him only through the press.

Press conference 10 Dec 70

10 Don't get the impression that you arouse my anger. You see, one can only be angry with those he respects.

To the press during Watergate investigation 26 Oct 73

11 It I talked about Watergate, I was described as struggling to free myself from the morass. If I did not talk about Watergate, I was accused of being out of touch with reality.

On press coverage, *RN: Memoirs of Richard Nixon* Grosset & Dunlap 78

12 Watergate had become the center of the media's universe, and during the remaining year of my presidency the media tried to force everything else to revolve around it.

ib

13 One thing, Ron, old boy. We won't have to have any more press conferences, and we won't even have to tell them that either!

To White House press secretary Ronald L Ziegler two days before resigning the presidency, *ib*

14 People in the media say they must look . . . at the president with a microscope. Now, I don't mind a microscope, but boy, when they use a proctoscope, that's going too far.

NBC TV 8 Apr 84

15 I've never canceled a subscription to a newspaper because of bad cartoons or editorials. If that were the case, I wouldn't have any newspapers or magazines to read.

ib

16 As far as I am concerned now, I have no enemies in the press whatsoever.

To Amer Society of Newspaper Editors, *Time* 21 May 84

DUNCAN NORTON-TAYLOR, former Managing Editor, *Fortune*

17 A gallery through which one can walk, passing from one decade to the next, viewing the pictures, or fragments of pictures, brought up from the basement—portraits of geniuses, heroes, rogues; landscapes of commercial and financial achievement and failure; artifacts of industry and science.

On compiling magazine's 50th anniversary issue, *Fortune* 11 Feb 80

PAUL O'NEIL

18 She was, for all her lifelong love affair with motion pictures, a reporter first. . . . She would skewer her best friend on the greasy spit of scandal if circumstances warranted it.

On Hollywood columnist Louella Parsons, *Life* 4 Jun 65

19 Lolly was possessed by a fiendish, auntielike excitement when on the trail of a hot "exclusive," and would sit at her telephone all night long if necessary, interpreting the denials of those she was interrogating as the great horned owl interprets the squeaking of distant mice.

ib

JOHN PEARSON

20 Given the chance, most people easily become voyeurs of royalty.

The Selling of the Royal Family Simon & Schuster 86

21 Hers was a face to sell a million million magazines, a story to inspire the lovelorn from Tennessee to Tokyo, and the worldwide media which had in a sense created her regarded her for what she was—their hottest property in years.

On Lady Diana Spencer, *ib*

PRINCE PHILIP, Duke of Edinburgh

22 You must sometimes stretch out your neck but not actually give them the ax.

On what he called "dontopedology" in dealing with the press, quoted by Elizabeth Longford *The Queen: The Life of Elizabeth II* Knopf 83

JODY POWELL, White House press secretary

1 If I had my way, I'd ask the f---ing Ayatollah to keep 50 reporters . . . Then you people who have all the answers could figure how to get them out.
> On the media during Iranian hostage crisis, quoted in *Newsweek* 2 Apr 84

ABE RASKIN

2 Of all the institutions in our inordinately complacent society, none is so addicted as the press to self-right-eousness, self-satisfaction and self-congratulation.
> Quoted by Melvin Maddocks *Christian Science Monitor* 23 Jan 85

WILLIAM RAUCH, NYC press secretary

3 Never trust a reporter who has a nice smile.
> NY *Times* 18 Jan 84

RONALD REAGAN, 40th US President

4 Now we shall get on with our first attempt at Reagan roulette.
> At his only press conference where questions were chosen by lottery 6 Mar 81

5 The District of Columbia is one gigantic ear.
> *Time* 23 Nov 81

6 I was going to have an opening statement, but I decided I wanted a lot of attention so I decided to wait and "leak" it.
> On first anniversary of his presidency 19 Jan 82

7 Just remember my best side is my right side—my *far* right side.
> To White House News Photographers Assn 18 May 83

8 I like photographers—you don't ask questions.
> *ib*

9 I like your motto: One picture is worth 1,000 denials.
> *ib*

HARRY REASONER, CBS News

10 Week after week their lead stories on [Watergate] have been more in the style of pejorative pamphlet-eering than objective journalism, and since they are highly visible and normally highly respected organs of our craft, they embarrass and discredit us all.
> On *Time* and *Newsweek*, quoted by Richard M Nixon *RN: Memoirs of Richard Nixon* Grosset & Dunlap 78

J D REED

11 From Puget Sound to Pennsylvania Avenue, type-writers clack at kitchen tables and computer screens glow in closets.
> On writers who seek to duplicate columnist Erma Bombeck's success, "And on Other Home Fronts" *Time* 2 Jul 84

12 Who cares if the roast burns or the dog sheds on the couch? . . . Such trifles must wait their turn behind dreams of hitting it big.
> *ib*

RICHARD REEVES

13 The White House Press Room [is] an adult day-care center built over what used to be the swimming pool where Lyndon Johnson skinny-dipped.
> In review of John Herbers's *No Thank You, Mr President* Norton 76, NY *Times* 21 Mar 76

JAMES RESTON

14 Somehow—I don't know why—peace seems to have a better chance in the [New York] *Times*.
> *New Leader* 7 Jan 63

15 People are always dying in the *Times* who don't seem to die in other papers, and they die at greater length and maybe even with a little more grace.
> *ib*

16 How do I know what to think if I can't read what I write?
> On NYC newspaper strike, *ib*

17 Like officials in Washington, we suffer from Afghan-istanism. If it's far away, it's news, but if it's close at home, it's sociology.
> To Columbia University convocation, *Wall Street Journal* 27 May 63

DOROTHY RIDINGS, President, League of Women Voters

18 We do not expect journalists to be political eunuchs.
> On respect for personal opinions of questioners selected for presidential campaign debates, *Time* 22 Oct 84

CHALMERS M ROBERTS

19 The trouble with daily journalism is that you get so involved with "Who hit John?" that you never really know why John had his chin out in the first place.
> *Newsweek* 6 Jan 58

ROGER ROSENBLATT

20 A flock of mad ducks flown north for the winter, descending noisily on this modest, good-mannered nation.
> On coverage of US–Soviet summit meeting at Reykja-vík, Iceland, *Time* 20 Oct 86

21 Merely the thought of the two big bosses sitting knee to knee, tossing the world's well-being back and forth, is enough to thump the journalistic heart.
> *ib*

CARL T ROWAN JR, US Ambassador to Finland

22 There aren't any embarrassing questions—just embarrassing answers.
> On press conferences, *New Yorker* 7 Dec 63

23 My advice to any diplomat who wants to have a good press is to have two or three kids and a dog.
> *ib*

DEAN RUSK, US Secretary of State

24 Communications today put a special emphasis on what happens next, for an able and sophisticated and competitive press today knows that what happens today is no longer news—it is what is going to happen tomorrow that is the object of interest and concern.
> To *Time*'s 40th anniversary dinner, *Time* 17 May 63

25 Unless we can find some way to keep our sights on tomorrow, we cannot expect to be in touch with to-day.
> *ib*

RENE SAGUISAG

26 [The word] *media* is the plural for *mediocre*.
> On press coverage of Philippines President Corazon C Aquino's administration, NY *Times* 22 Jan 87

1 Every day when I read the papers, I find out that I did or said or thought things that I did not do, say or think.
ib

J D SALINGER

2 Genius domus of the *New Yorker*, lover of the long shot, protector of the unprolific, defender of the hopelessly flamboyant, most unreasonably modest of born great artist-editors.
Dedication to William Shawn in *Franny and Zooey* Little, Brown 61, quoted in *New York* 28 Nov 83

ANTHONY SAMPSON

3 In America, journalism is apt to be regarded as an extension of history: in Britain, as an extension of conversation.
The Anatomy of Britain Harper & Row 62

4 I find it depressing, like a stately old home that has been thrown open to the public.
On changes in the 200-year-old London *Times* after its 1980 purchase by Rupert Murdoch, *Time* 11 Mar 85

DAVID SANFORD

5 Certain people seem to die in the *Times* more than others do. Doctors, for instance; obits give the impression that physicians die in droves.
On NY *Times* obituaries, *Wall Street Journal* 29 Aug 85

SERGE SCHMEMANN

6 The art of reading between the lines is as old as manipulated information.
On distortion of news, NY *Times* 10 Nov 85

DANIEL SCHORR, CBS News

7 There was a vacuum in investigation, and the press began to try men in the most effective court in the country.
On Watergate investigations, quoted by Richard M Nixon *RN: Memoirs of Richard Nixon* Grosset & Dunlap 78

R Z SHEPPARD

8 [Ken] Kesey practices what has come to be known as gonzo journalism. The reporter, often intoxicated, fails to get the story but delivers instead a stylishly bizarre account that mocks conventional journalism.
Time 8 Sep 86

GEORGE P SHULTZ, US Secretary of State

9 If there are ways in which we can make Qaddafi nervous, why shouldn't we? . . . That is not deceiving you, but just using your predictable tendencies to report things that we try to keep secret.
On Libya, NY *Times* 3 Oct 86

10 The higher the classification [of secrecy], the quicker you will report it.
ib

HUGH SIDEY

11 The legions of reporters who cover politics don't want to quit the clash and thunder of electoral combat for the dry duty of analyzing the federal budget. As a consequence, we have created the perpetual presidential campaign.
Time 5 Nov 84

FRANK SINATRA

12 All day long, they lie in the sun, and when the sun goes down, they lie some more.
On Hollywood reporters, *US* 16 Dec 85

ISAAC BASHEVIS SINGER

13 If Moses had been paid newspaper rates for the Ten Commandments, he might have written the Two Thousand Commandments.
NY *Times* 30 Jun 85

JOHN SKOW

14 In journalistic terms, syndication is equivalent to ascending to heaven on a pillar of cloud.
On Erma Bombeck, "Erma in Bomburbia" *Time* 2 Jul 84

RED SMITH

15 My best girl is dead.
On August 15, 1966, closing of NY *Herald Tribune*, quoted by Richard Kluger *The Paper: The Life and Death of the New York Herald Tribune* Knopf 86

FRANKLIN BLISS SNYDER, President, Northwestern University

16 The greatest privilege in our society is to be a purveyor of news.
1949 commencement address at Medill School of Journalism, recalled on his death 11 May 58

ALEXANDER SOLZHENITSYN

17 Woe to that nation whose literature is cut short by the intrusion of force. This is not merely interference with freedom of the press but the sealing up of a nation's heart, the excision of its memory.
Time 25 Feb 74

18 Hastiness and superficiality are the psychic diseases of the 20th century, and more than anywhere else this disease is reflected in the press.
Commencement address at Harvard 7 Jun 78

LARRY SPEAKES, White House press spokesman

19 You don't tell us how to stage the news and we don't tell you how to cover it.
Sign on his desk, quoted by Steven Weisman "The President and the Press" NY *Times* 14 Oct 84

20 Those who talk don't know what is going on and those who know what is going on won't talk.
On news blackout at Geneva summit meeting, *ib* 20 Nov 85

21 Being a press secretary [is like] learning to type: You're hunting and pecking for a while and then you find yourself doing the touch system and don't realize it. You're speaking for the president without ever having to go to him.
ib 10 Oct 86

22 I would dodge, not lie, in the national interest.
ib

23 This job has probably got the most screwing-up potential in the world.
On retiring, ABC TV 31 Jan 87

LADY DIANA SPENCER

24 I know it's just a job they have to do, but sometimes I do wish they wouldn't.
On photographers who followed her during her engagement to Prince Charles, NY *Times* 25 Feb 81

RONALD STEEL

1 [There is a] curious relationship between a candidate and the reporters who cover him. It can be affected by small things like a competent press staff, enough seats, sandwiches and briefings and the ability to understand deadlines.
> NY *Times* 5 Aug 84

ADLAI E STEVENSON

2 An editor is one who separates the wheat from the chaff and prints the chaff.
> Quoted in Bill Adler comp *The Stevenson Wit* Doubleday 66

GAY TALESE

3 Most journalists are restless voyeurs who see the warts on the world, the imperfections in people and places. . . . gloom is their game, the spectacle their passion, normality their nemesis.
> *The Kingdom and the Power* World 69

4 News, if unreported, has no impact. It might as well have not happened at all.
> *ib*

5 The reporter . . . wrote with the hope that he would get a by-line in the *Times*, a testimony to his being alive on that day . . . and all the tomorrows of microfilm.
> *ib*

6 Even after they had stopped modeling for *Playboy* and had settled down with other men to raise families of their own, [Hugh] Hefner still considered them his women, and in the bound volumes of his magazine he would always possess them.
> *Thy Neighbor's Wife* Doubleday 80

7 He was a sex junkie with an insatiable habit.
> On Hugh Hefner. *ib*

FRANCISCO S TATAD

8 If you want unverified gossip passed on as truth, it is there. If you want a person's private fault reported as public fact, it is there, too. If you want the most inconsequential nonsense blown up into an earth-shaking event, you will find no shortage of it.
> On press coverage of Philippines President Corazon C Aquino's administration, quoted in NY *Times* 22 Jan 87

MARGARET THATCHER, Prime Minister of Great Britain

9 [Democratic nations] must try to find ways to starve the terrorist and the hijacker of the oxygen of publicity on which they depend.
> Calling for ban on headlines that offer publicity for political causes, to London meeting of Amer Bar Assn 15 Jul 85

10 Ought we not to ask the media to agree among themselves a voluntary code of conduct, under which they would not say or show anything which could assist the terrorists' morale or their cause while the hijack lasted.
> *ib*

ROGER THÉROND, Editor in Chief, *Paris-Match*

11 Look, it is our *Dallas*, our serial, and they are our Kennedys, and we didn't invent any of it. The scenario is beyond belief.
> On covering Monaco's royal family, NY *Times* 28 Aug 84

12 The public has invested in this story. It participates, it judges, it condemns, it pities. It's a second life for a lot of people.
> *ib*

VIRGIL THOMSON

13 Reviewing music or reviewing anything is a writing job. It's nice if you are experienced in the field you are writing about, but writing is what you are doing.
> On role of the critic, *Christian Science Monitor* 12 Feb 85

JAMES THURBER

14 No other editor has ever been lost and saved so often in the course of a working week. When his heart leaped up, it leaped a long way, because it started from so far down, and its commutings over the years from the depths to the heights made Ross a specialist in appreciation.
> On *New Yorker* editor Harold Ross, *The Years with Ross* Atlantic–Little, Brown 59

15 The story of Harold Ross, the *New Yorker* and me is a mere footnote to the story of our time, and we might as well face the truth that to researchers of the future, poking about among the ruins of time, we shall all be tiny glitters. But then, so are diamonds.
> Quoted in Helen Thurber and Edward Weeks eds *Selected Letters of James Thurber* Atlantic–Little, Brown 81

TIME MAGAZINE

16 Her friends stand by her: When she prematurely published the claim that a certain actress was pregnant, the actress's husband hastened to prove her correct.
> On Hollywood columnist Louella Parsons, 24 Nov 61

MARTIN TOLCHIN

17 The stakeout [is] the lowest form of journalism and a boring penance for . . . journalistic sins.
> On reporters' vigil outside closed Senate Intelligence Committee hearings about Iran arms sales, NY *Times* 20 Dec 86

CALVIN TRILLIN

18 Ross begat Shawn. He handed down the crown of St Peter to Shawn.
> On "apostolic succession" of *New Yorker* editors Harold Ross and William Shawn, *Wall Street Journal* 20 Jan 87

HARRY S TRUMAN, 33rd US President

19 To hell with them. When history is written they will be the sons of bitches—not I.
> On criticism by what he called the "sabotage press," quoted by Margaret Truman *Bess W Truman* Macmillan 86

MARGARET TRUMAN

20 Mother . . . considered a press conference on a par with a visit to a cage of cobras.
> *Bess W Truman* Macmillan 86

JOHN UPDIKE

21 [We] hope . . . the "real" person behind the words will be revealed as ignominiously as a shapeless snail without its shapely shell.
> On "consumeristic appetite for interviews," NY *Times* 17 Aug 86

UPPER & LOWER CASE MAGAZINE

1 Regardless of the devices that are conjured up by the technicians, designers have the last word with the words.
Jun 80

2 The job to entice, surprise, engage, entertain, inform, persuade—in short, communicate with readers—has been the burden of the artist from Day 1.
ib

3 Every age has had its specialists. When smoke signals were the medium, there were surely some Indians a little more nimble with their blankets . . . in the jungles, some drummers had a better beat . . . in the medieval cloisters, almost any brother could grind the pigment, but only a few penned the manuscripts.
ib

PETER USTINOV

4 Her virtue was that she said what she thought, her vice that what she thought didn't amount to much.
On Hollywood columnist Hedda Hopper, quoted by Herbert R Mayes *The Magazine Maze* Doubleday 80

JOHN VINOCUR

5 The public relations warriors fought and lost Monte Carlo's Battle of the Magazine Covers.
On Monaco's attempt to curb unfavorable publicity about its royal family, NY *Times* 28 Aug 84

JAMES G WATT, US Secretary of Interior

6 They kill good trees to put out bad newspapers.
Newsweek 8 Mar 82

THEODORE H WHITE

7 Those 40 or 50 national correspondents who had followed Kennedy since the beginning of his electoral exertions into the November days had become more than a press corps—they had become his friends and, some of them, his most devoted admirers.
The Making of the President 1960 Atheneum 61

8 When the bus or the plane rolled or flew through the night, they sang songs of their own composition about Mr Nixon and the Republicans in chorus with the Kennedy staff and felt that they, too, were marching like soldiers of the Lord to the New Frontier.
ib

RADIO & TELEVISION

Personalities

FRED ALLEN

9 When a radio comedian's program is finally finished it slinks down Memory Lane into the limbo of yesteryear's happy hours. All that the comedian has to show for his years of work and aggravation is the echo of forgotten laughter.
Treadmill to Oblivion Little, Brown 54

10 Ed Sullivan will be around as long as someone else has talent.
On 10th anniversary of Sullivan's Sunday night variety show, *TV Guide* 21 Jun 58

STEVE ALLEN

11 Is it larger than a bread box?
Favorite question for guests on the panel show *What's My Line* CBS TV 2 Feb 50 to 3 Sep 67

LUCILLE BALL

12 Use a make-up table with everything close at hand and don't rush; otherwise you'll look like a patchwork quilt.
Family Weekly 6 Jul 75

MILTON BERLE

13 With comedy, niceness counted. People turned on television and said, "Hey, he looks like Cousin Charlie and acts like Uncle Joe."
NY *Times* 16 Apr 85

JIMMY BRESLIN

14 ABC Television Network: Your services, such as they are, will no longer be required as of 12/20/86.
Page 1 advertisement that he intended to quit as host of his short-lived late-night program, NY *Times* 24 Nov 86

DAVID BRINKLEY and CHET HUNTLEY

15 Good night, Chet.
Good night, David.
Sign-off lines on *Huntley-Brinkley Report* NBC TV 29 Oct 56 to 30 Jul 70

TOM BROKAW, NBC News

16 It's all storytelling, you know. That's what journalism is all about.
Northwestern University *Byline* Spring 82

CAROL BURNETT

17 I liked myself better when I wasn't me.
On her high-school drama classes, *One More Time* Random House 86, quoted by Andrea Carla Michaels *Wall Street Journal* 28 Sep 86

JOHNNY CARSON

18 We're more effective than birth control pills.
On late-night television programs, *Time* 19 May 67

JOHN CHANCELLOR, NBC News

19 Other administrations have had a love-hate relationship with the press. The Nixon administration has a hate-hate relationship.
Quoted by Osborn Elliott *The World of Oz* Viking 80

20 The American government is doing whatever it wants to, without any representative of the American public watching what it is doing.
On Reagan administration's exclusion of reporters during the invasion of Grenada, *Time* 12 Dec 83

21 [There's] the Ronald Reagan cupped-ear gambit. The press is deliberately and systematically kept away from him. All you hear is a bunch of monkeys screaming at him when they could easily have been brought right up and the president could have stood and talked in a conversational tone.
On White House manipulation of television coverage, *ib* 11 Mar 84

ALISTAIR COOKE

1 People in America, when listening to radio, like to lean forward. People in Britain like to lean back.
Quoted in Cleveland Amory and Earl Blackwell eds *Celebrity Register* Harper & Row 63

2 It's an acting job—acting natural.
On his television commentaries, *New York* 17 Dec 79

3 [I] talk to my typewriter . . . and that is what I've been working on for 40 years—how to write for talking.
Christian Science Monitor 5 Sep 86

WALTER CRONKITE, CBS News

4 And that's the way it is, March 6, 1981.
Sign-off line on his last night as anchor

5 Everything is being compressed into tiny tablets. You take a little pill of news every day—23 minutes—and that's supposed to be enough.
On superficiality of television news, *Newsweek* 5 Dec 83

6 Television [is] a high-impact medium. It does some things no other force can do—transmitting electronic pictures through the air. Still, as an explored, comprehensive medium, it is not a substitute for print.
NY *Times* 18 Jul 84

7 The great sadness of my life is that I never achieved the hour newscast, which would not have been twice as good as the half-hour newscast, but many times as good.
ib

PHIL DONAHUE

8 In order to keep this feather in the air—and that's what it is—my people have to *stay on fire* creatively.
On moving his long-running interview show from Chicago to New York, *60 Minutes* CBS TV 24 Feb 85

9 I see all those Solomons out there, I can't wait to hear your wisdom.
Hosting program on adoption, NBC TV 9 Jan 86

SAM DONALDSON, ABC News

10 News conferences are the only chance the American public has to see Ronald Reagan use his mind.
NY *Times* 27 Sep 86

11 The questions don't do the damage. Only the answers do.
On presidential press conferences, *Hold On, Mr President!* Random House 87

12 Call me a braggart, call me arrogant. People at ABC (and elsewhere) have called me worse. But when you need the job done on deadline, you'll call me.
ib

JIMMY DURANTE

13 Good night, Mrs Calabash, wherever you are!
Sign-off line referring to nickname of his late wife, recalled on his death, *Time* 11 Feb 80

LINDA ELLERBEE

14 We call them Twinkies. You've seen them on television acting the news, modeling and fracturing the news while you wonder whether they've read the news—or if they've blow-dried their brains, too.
"And So It Goes" Putnam 86

15 Some of my colleagues want to be The Anchorman on the Mount. Others see themselves as the Ace Reporter. Because of *60 Minutes*, there's a whole herd of them determined to be The Grand Inquisitor and . . . a heady number want only to be The Friendliest Anchor on the Block. At least one wants to be Jesus.
ib

16 When the anchorman is wearing a colonel's uniform, it tells you something.
On countries where "good" news is presented regularly on television, *ib*

17 The new national campfire—radio.
Our World: The Year 1938 ABC TV 30 Oct 86

AVA GARDNER

18 For the loot, honey, for the loot.
On why she came out of retirement to appear on a prime time soap opera, *People* 10 Jun 85

JACKIE GLEASON

19 I only made $200 a week and I had to buy my own bullets.
On his early film career, recalled on his death, NY *Times* 26 Jun 87

20 How sweet it is!
Stock phrase used in his television programs, *ib*

21 One of these days, Alice. Pow! Right in the kisser!
Line from his 1950s series *The Honeymooners*, quoted in *People* 13 Jul 87

MAX HEADROOM (Matt Frewer)

22 I think it was Shakespeare who once said:
"Blipverts may come
And blipverts may go
But the laziness upon which they breed is with us always."
Actually, that's quite good; perhaps it was me who said it.
As computer-generated television character, quoted in *Newsweek* 20 Apr 87

GARRISON KEILLOR

23 I want to resume the life of a shy person.
On retiring after 13 years as the host of his radio show *Prairie Home Companion*, quoted in *US News & World Report* 2 Mar 87

TED KOPPEL, ABC News

24 I have the necessary lack of tact.
On interviewing guests on *Nightline*, quoted by Nancy Collins "The Smartest Man on TV" *New York* 13 Aug 84

25 Emotions get in the way [but] they don't pay me to start crying at the loss of 269 lives. They pay me to put some perspective on the situation.
ib

26 In the days of Caesar, kings had fools and jesters. Now network presidents have anchormen.
People 17 Dec 84

27 I think we're glazing eyes all across America.
Interrupting a long-winded guest, *Nightline* ABC TV 13 Feb 87

JACK LESCOULIE

1 The closer you come to being yourself on the screen, the longer you last [because] on television there's always the risk of a quick shot in an off-guard moment, a chance insight; and if you're playing a part, you'll be exposed.

On hosting NBC TV's *Today*, *TV Guide* 30 Jan 65

ROBERT MACNEIL, PBS TV

2 [Television] has created a nation of news junkies who tune in every night to get their fix on the world.

Time 25 Feb 80

GROUCHO MARX

3 I read in the newspapers they are going to have 30 minutes of intellectual stuff on television every Monday from 7:30 to 8. . . . to educate America. They couldn't educate America if they started at 6:30.

Boston *Globe* 22 Jan 60

DON MCNEIL

4 It's a beautiful day in Chicago!

Traditional opening for *The Breakfast Club*, Chicago-based variety show 1933–68

CLAYTON MOORE

5 I will continue wearing the white hat and black mask until I ride up into the big ranch in the sky.

On his costume as the Lone Ranger, *Time* 4 Feb 85

BILL MOYERS

6 A journalist is basically a chronicler, not an interpreter of events. Where else in society do you have the license to eavesdrop on so many different conversations as you have in journalism? Where else can you delve into the life of our times? I consider myself a fortunate man to have a forum for my curiosity.

Channel Maker 29 Feb 79

7 The printed page conveys information and commitment, and requires active involvement. Television conveys emotion and experience, and it's very limited in what it can do logically. It's an existential experience—there and then gone.

NY *Times* 3 Jan 82

8 A producer is a saboteur who tries to infiltrate the passivity of viewers and to create impressions that are lasting.

ib

9 I own and operate a ferocious ego.

ib

EDWARD R MURROW, CBS News

10 Don't be deluded into believing that the titular heads of the networks control what appears on their networks. They all have better taste.

To convention of radio and television news directors, Chicago, news summaries 15 Oct 58

11 We cannot make good news out of bad practice.

Reply as director of US Information Agency to Senate critics who wanted him to ignore racial strife in order to project a better image abroad, recalled on his death, *Life* 7 May 65

12 The speed of communications is wondrous to behold. It is also true that speed can multiply the distribution of information that we know to be untrue.

On receiving 1964 Family of Man Award, quoted by Alexander Kendrick *Prime Time* Little, Brown 69

13 [A] satellite has no conscience.

ib

14 The newest computer can merely compound, at speed, the oldest problem in the relations between human beings, and in the end the communicator will be confronted with the old problem, of what to say and how to say it.

ib

15 If we were to do the Second Coming of Christ in color for a full hour, there would be a considerable number of stations which would decline to carry it on the grounds that a Western or a quiz show would be more profitable.

ib

16 Good night, and good luck.

Sign-off line, quoted by A M Sperber *Murrow* Freundlich 86

17 We are in the same tent as the clowns and the freaks—that's show business.

Quoted by Bill Moyers CBS TV 10 Sep 86

JACK PAAR

18 Statistics show that many people watch our show from the bedroom. . . . and people you ask into your bedroom have to be more interesting than those you ask into your living room. I kid you not!

As host of NBC TV's *Tonight Show*, NY *Herald Tribune* 22 Apr 58

ROBERT PIERPOINT, CBS News

19 Most people are not worth interviewing if they are not known to the public, and . . . once known, they often don't want to be interviewed.

Time 27 Dec 82

DAN RATHER, CBS News

20 They know where the levers of power are.

On White House officials who criticized CBS News coverage, NY *Times* 14 Nov 83

21 The mine field doesn't have any end. You think, "If I could just get through it to the other side . . . But there's no getting through it.

On job of CBS president Howard Stringer, quoted by Peter J Boyer "CBS News in Search of Itself," *ib* 28 Dec 86

22 Every time Howard puts his foot down he runs the risk of stepping on something that will maim him, if not destroy him.

ib

23 You'd better do what you feel good about doing. If we [try] to figure out what it is the audience wants and then try to deliver it to them, we're lost souls on the ghost ship forever.

ib

24 News is a business, but it is also a public trust.

ib 10 Mar 87

1 Anyone who says network news cannot be profitable doesn't know what he is talking about. But anyone who says it must *always* make money is misguided and irresponsible.

ib

ANDY ROONEY

2 It's not so much that I write well—I just don't write badly very often, and that passes for good on television.

On his essays for CBS TV's *60 Minutes, Time* 11 Jul 69

3 I've had 30 bosses at CBS. I've outlived them all.

On his disagreements with network management, Boston *Globe* 8 Apr 87

JOHN RUBINSTEIN

4 I always say I would be content—maybe not fulfilled, but content—playing the piano in the bar of a hotel lobby in Wichita.

NY *Times* 30 Jul 85

MORLEY SAFER, CBS News

5 BBC Radio is not so much an art or industry as it is a way of life . . . a mirror that reflects . . . the eccentricities, the looniness that make Britons slightly different from other humans.

60 Minutes CBS TV 15 Sep 85

6 The BBC is a perfect example of uncontrolled growth, [occupying] old churches and manor houses, the old Langham Hotel where Sherlock Holmes once met Moriarty and where this correspondent once shared an office with an 8-foot bathtub.

ib

7 [The] BBC was known as Auntie—suggesting someone prudish and Victorian—and that she still is on some days. On others she's a champagne-soaked floozie, her skirts in disarray, her mind in the gutter, and the mixture can be quite wonderful.

ib

8 BBC Radio is a never-never land of broadcasting, a safe haven from commercial considerations, a honey pot for every scholar and every hare-brained nut to stick a finger into.

ib

9 It's back to the future.

On new management at CBS, quoted in *US* 3 Nov 86

DANIEL SCHORR, CBS News

10 All news is an exaggeration of life.

Newsweek 11 Jul 83

RED SKELTON

11 His death was the first time that Ed Wynn ever made anyone sad.

Time 1 Jul 66

MIKE WALLACE, CBS News

12 I determined that if I was to carve out a piece of reportorial territory for myself . . . it would be [doing] the hard interview, irreverent if necessary, the façade-piercing interview.

NY *Daily News* 14 Oct 84

BARBARA WALTERS

13 Wait for those unguarded moments. Relax the mood and, like the child dropping off to sleep, the subject often reveals his truest self.

On interviewing, *Christian Science Monitor* 10 Dec 79

WALTER WINCHELL

14 Good evening Mr and Mrs America, from border to border and coast to coast and all the ships at sea. Let's go to press.

Opening for Sunday evening newscasts, recalled on his death 20 Feb 72

Writers, Producers & Directors

ROONE ARLEDGE, President, ABC News

15 They're indispensable. They're the glue that holds a newscast together.

On anchors, *US News & World Report* 20 Nov 78

JAMES T AUBREY, President, CBS

16 If I had my way we'd have some guy come on at 11 AM and say, "The following six men made horses' asses of themselves at the Republican Convention," and then he'd give the six names and that would be it.

Quoted by David Halberstam *The Powers That Be* Knopf 79

DON BRESNAHAN

17 I am always apologizing for it, criticizing it, defending it, praising it, damning it, loving it and hating it . . . that glamorous enfant terrible of journalism, television news.

On producing documentaries, *Newsweek* 19 Apr 82

18 We are guilty of giving you too little because we are desperately afraid that you don't really want any more.

ib

HERBERT BRODKIN

19 The curse of television [is] the programming department—all trained to look for the same kind of show.

On producing television dramas, NY *Times* 19 Mar 85

20 They have reduced the audience's level of receptivity to a bunch of monkeys asking for the same peanuts. And they are the same organ grinders giving it to them. If that sounds extreme, it's not. It's true.

ib

HENRI DIEUZEIDE

21 The bright gray blackboard.

On educational television, *Réalités* Jul 63

BARRY DILLER, Chief of Programming, ABC

22 The American public tunes in every night hoping to see two people screwing. Obviously, we can't give them that . . . but let's always keep it in mind.

Quoted in *Newsweek* 20 May 85

REUVEN FRANK, President, NBC News

23 The printed press does not show the reporter asking the question. What is peculiar to television is that the intrusiveness is part of the story.

Time 12 Dec 83

ROBERT FRASER, Chief, British Independent Television Authority

1 Television should be kept in its proper place—beside us, before us, but never between us and the larger life.
  Look 18 Feb 58

STEVE FRIEDMAN, Producer, NBC *Today* Show

2 It's *The Mourning Show*. Is it true that the theme song is going to be "Taps"?
  On new format for rival CBS *Morning Program*, NY *Times* 4 Jan 87

LARRY GELBART

3 If vaudeville had died, television was the box they put it in.
  To Museum of Broadcasting, NY *Times* 3 Oct 84

4 It was like electronic euthanasia.
  On short life span of *United States*, his situation comedy about marriage, *ib*

5 Today's audience knows more about what's on television than what's in life.
  ib

LAWRENCE GROSSMAN, President, NBC News

6 You wait for a gem in an endless sea of blah.
  On television coverage of political conventions, NY *Times* 20 Jul 84

DON HEWITT, CBS TV producer

7 Let's give the conventions back to the politicians. . . . If we think there's any news, we can tack it on afterward as commentary. But the conventions should be their show, not ours.
  Quoted by Theodore H White *Time* 19 Nov 84

8 Confrontation is not a dirty word. . . . Sometimes it's the best kind of journalism as long you don't confront people just for the sake of a confrontation.
  Minute by Minute Random House 85

9 He can thread a needle with a well-turned phrase.
  On Morley Safer, *ib*

ALFRED HITCHCOCK

10 [Television is] like the invention of indoor plumbing. It didn't change people's habits. It just kept them inside the house.
  NY *Journal-American* 25 Aug 65

11 One of television's great contributions is that it brought murder back into the home, where it belongs.
  National Observer 15 Aug 66

12 Seeing a murder on television can . . . help work off one's antagonisms. And if you haven't any antagonisms, the commercials will give you some.
  ib

ARTHUR MILLER

13 In the theater, while you recognized that you were looking at a house, it was a house in quotation marks. On screen, the quotation marks tend to be blotted out by the camera.
  On television production of *Death of a Salesman*, NY *Times* 15 Sep 85

14 The problem was to sustain at any cost the feeling you had in the theater that you were watching a real person, yes, but an intense condensation of his experience, not simply a realistic series of episodes.
  ib

15 It isn't easy to do in the theater, but it's twice as hard in film.
  ib

GLORIA MONTY

16 Some people call it a rape. *We* call it a seduction.
  On controversial 1981 story line for the soap opera *General Hospital*, quoted in *US* 13 Jul 87

TONY PALMER

17 I think my greatest single achievement . . . took place on a Tuesday in March, when, with much bribery and corruption, I got them to clear the Grand Canal. . . . *That* was truly Wagnerian.
  On re-creating Richard Wagner's funeral cortège in Venice for *Wagner*, multipart PBS TV presentation, TV *Guide* 18 Oct 86

C WREDE PETERSMEYER, Chairman, Corinthian Broadcasting Corp

18 The size of television's footprint is as long and as wide as the country itself. . . . measured by the allegiance of audiences and advertisers.
  "Born of the Vitality of Advertising" *Printers' Ink* 20 Mar 64

19 This sight, sound and motion medium has made mass salesmanship an indispensable facet of mass production and mass employment.
  ib

FRANK PIERSON

20 After all, what was *Medea*? Just another child custody case.
  On lack of originality in television plots, NY *Times* 23 Mar 62

JOHN B SIAS, President, ABC

21 We're going to run that program come rain, blood or horse manure.
  On controversial miniseries *Amerika*, about a peaceful Soviet takeover of the US, NY *Times* 28 Jan 87

HENRY SIEGEL, Chairman, LBS Communications

22 I don't think anybody in our business is creative. What we do is copy something better than the next person.
  NY *Times* 5 Sep 85

FRANK STANTON, President, CBS

23 [It is] ominous [because] it is made upon the journalism of a medium licensed by the government of which he is a high-ranking officer.
  On Vice President Spiro T Agnew's attack on the power of network news divisions, quoted in NY *Times* 14 Nov 83

ALAN WAGNER, Vice President, CBS

24 I'm afraid we felt the wrong end of the elephant first.
  On failure of pioneering nighttime drama series *Beacon Hill*, NY *Times* 28 Oct 75

CHRISTY WELKER, Vice President, ABC

1 There has to be a strong love story. That gives the audience an easily identifiable, emotional umbilical cord.

On her "biovid" *Napoleon and Josephine*, quoted in *Newsweek* 20 May 85

PAUL W WHITE, Director of Special Events, CBS

2 A gent I know whose life is superfluidity
Took a job in CBS Continuity.
One night after too much Scotch paregoric,
He turned in a script just too prehistoric.
He was fired and said, as he read his doxology . . .
"I thought they would like my Paley-ontology."

On CBS chairman William S Paley, quoted by A M Sperber *Murrow* Freundlich 86

Observers & Critics

DEAN ACHESON

3 Between 9 and 10 AM the American radio is concerned almost exclusively with love. . . . It seems a little like ending breakfast with a stiff bourbon.

On soap operas, *Reporter* 19 Sep 57

ROBERT MCC ADAMS, Secretary, Smithsonian Institution

4 Television probably has become the most evocative, widely observed signpost we have.

On adding television memorabilia to the museum's collection, *Smithsonian* Jul 85

RICHARD P ADLER, Institute of the Future, Palo Alto CA

5 *All* television is children's television.

Quoted by Jonathan Rowe "Modern Advertising: The Hidden Persuasion" *Christian Science Monitor* 29 Jan 87

SPIRO T AGNEW, US Vice President

6 A tiny and closed fraternity of privileged men, elected by no one, and enjoying a monopoly sanctioned and licensed by government.

On network news divisions, nationally televised address 13 Nov 69

PETER ALFANO

7 The first thing a television viewer realizes when watching a golf tournament is how the sport tends to make one inclined to whisper and avoid sudden movements, such as walking to the refrigerator [during] a possible birdie putt.

"A Weekend of Whispering at Augusta" NY *Times* 17 Apr 84

8 One almost expects [one of the players] to peer into the monitor and politely request viewers to refrain from munching so loudly on cheese and crackers while the golfers are trying to read the greens.

ib

WOODY ALLEN

9 The whole country was tied together by radio. We all experienced the same heroes and comedians and singers. They were giants.

On *Radio Days*, his film about the 1940s, NY *Times* 25 Jan 87

BURNETT ANDERSON

10 Sports broadcasters are the only reporters . . . who describe past events in the future tense.

Quoted by William Safire NY *Times* 6 Nov 83

ANONYMOUS

11 You'll never have a nervous breakdown, but you sure are a carrier.

To CBS's Fred W Friendly, quoted in *Newsweek* 27 Mar 72

12 [He is] the gynecologist of the airways.

On Phil Donahue, known for provoking frank discussions on his program, quoted by Mike Wallace *60 Minutes* CBS TV 24 Feb 85

13 Daddy, Daddy, there's the man who lives in our TV.

Child who spotted Florida Governor Bob Graham at a rally during Graham's US Senate campaign, quoted in Boston *Globe* 21 Nov 86

R W APPLE JR

14 The sense of national catastrophe is inevitably heightened in a television age, when the whole country participates in it.

On explosion of Challenger space shuttle, NY *Times* 29 Jan 86

15 A first hint of the power of the electronic media to bring disaster directly into living rooms came with the radio broadcast of the explosion of the zeppelin *Hindenburg* in 1937; but that was as nothing compared with the pictures . . . of the space shuttle exploding, disintegrating and etching chaotic, sickening contrails against the blue sky.

ib

W H AUDEN

16 What the mass media offer is not popular art, but entertainment which is intended to be consumed like food, forgotten and replaced by a new dish.

The Dyer's Hand Random House 68

RUSSELL BAKER

17 [I] know it's public television if: 1) Bert and Ernie are performing, 2) Julia Child is cooking, 3) Mr Rogers is talking to small children, 4) Beverly Sills is introducing Luciano Pavarotti, 5) Leo Buscaglia is lecturing on the value of love, 6) the Monty Python company is satirizing the BBC, 7) mulch is being discussed on the Victory Garden or, what is more likely, 8) I am watching the 10th rerun of any of the above.

"TV's Identity Crisis" NY *Times* 2 Mar 86

CLIVE BARNES

18 Television is the first truly democratic culture—the first culture available to everyone and entirely governed by what the people want. The most terrifying thing is what people do want.

NY *Times* 30 Dec 69

MARTHA BAYLES

19 If we think of [television] programming as an all-American menu, then the detective show is definitely the hamburger.

"What Makes a Formula Work?" *Wall Street Journal* 22 Oct 84

KENNETH BILBY

1 [He] had come to view [television] as a force of nearly preternatural dimensions, life-transforming in its impact.
> The General: David Sarnoff and the Rise of the Communications Industry Harper & Row 86, quoted by Charles Fountain Christian Science Monitor 10 Dec 86

MICHAEL BOBICK

2 You get these small-town feuds because people don't have cablevision. You don't have anything else to do.
> On warring factions in Pine Hill NY, NY Times 20 Nov 84

DANIEL J BOORSTIN, Librarian of Congress

3 Nothing is really real unless it happens on television.
> NY Times 19 Feb 78

JIMMY BRESLIN

4 Why something in the public interest such as television news can be fought over, like a chain of hamburger stands, eludes me.
> NY Daily News 8 Mar 87

5 The only reason this country is different from any place else is that once in a great while, this huge, snobbish, generally untalented news reporting business stops covering stories of interest only to itself and actually serves the public.
> ib

6 If a man, for private profit, tears at the public news, does so with the impatience of one who thinks he actually owns the news you get, it is against the national interest.
> ib

JOHN MASON BROWN

7 Some television programs are so much chewing gum for the eyes.
> Recalled on his death 16 Mar 69

LES BROWN

8 Unlike productions in the other arts, all television shows are born to destroy two other shows.
> Harper's Mar 85

9 When a show fails to destroy the competition—and it can fail while attracting 20 million viewers—it is itself destroyed.
> ib

ART BUCHWALD

10 Every time you think television has hit its lowest ebb, a new . . . program comes along to make you wonder where you thought the ebb was.
> Have I Ever Lied to You? Putnam 68

WARREN E BURGER, Chief Justice, US Supreme Court

11 It is not possible to arrange for any broadcast of any Supreme Court proceeding, but when you get the Cabinet meetings on the air, call me.
> Reply to Mutual Broadcasting System's request for live radio coverage, quoted in International Herald Tribune 24 Mar 86

VINCENT CANBY

12 When Uncle Bob (or Ted or Ray) promised to send a shooting star over the house to mark a young listener's birthday, the young listener, who had hung out the window for an hour without seeing the star, questioned not Uncle Bob (or Ted or Ray), but his own eyesight.
> On the Golden Age of radio, NY Times 30 Jan 87

13 Radio wasn't outside our lives. It coincided with—and helped to shape—our childhood and adolescence. As we slogged toward maturity, it also grew up and turned into television, leaving behind, like dead skin, transistorized talk-radio and nonstop music shows.
> ib

LILLIAN CARTER

14 I'm not a homosexual and I don't smoke pot, so what would I say?
> On being asked to appear on Phil Donahue's talk show, 60 Minutes CBS TV 24 Feb 85

HUGH CASSON, President, Royal Academy of Art

15 Strangers often come up to me and say, "I saw you on television." To them it's a sort of confirmation that I exist.
> Architectural Digest Dec 85

CHARLES, Prince of Wales

16 That's called a microphone. It's a big sausage that picks up everything you say—and you're starting early.
> To his two-year-old son Prince William at his first press conference, Newsweek 25 Jun 84

FRANCIS X CLINES

17 Delegates crane their gaze at overhead screens. The producers, using fast-cutting close-up shots, have added the narcissistic touch of allowing delegates to watch themselves watch themselves at a convention of people watching them.
> On televised proceedings of Democratic National Convention in San Francisco, NY Times 18 Jul 84

18 Britain's gnawing hunger for retrospection is of Proustian proportions; historical confections of past glory are always being sugared up and nibbled at somewhere in the land.
> On 50th anniversary of BBC's first telecast, ib 9 Nov 86

19 The grand institution, at once hoary and ethereal, that some call Auntie and others call the Beeb, and that most, it seems, must call controversial.
> ib

20 The wine and special video samplings of five decades of funny, nostalgic programs—Benny Hill so young and foolish, Elizabeth so young and regal, Joan Collins so young and vampy—had a number of the mass pack of TV writers chuckling or at least struck glassy-eyed by mortal identity with the grainy ghosts of TV past.
> ib

21 The earnest weatherman is even more hilarious than in America because his forecasts of change are even more unchanging, and his wondrous maps are always pocked with countless rain cloud symbols that seem permanently rooted across the beloved isle.
> ib

1 Thus does the Beeb ease the English into another gray familiar day, another half-century of magic mystic rays.

ib

THAD COCHRANE, US Senator

2 The camera is a natural attraction for a politician. And if a camera is here, we're going to be here. And we're going to say something, even if we have nothing to say.

On allowing televised coverage of Senate floor debates, NY *Times* 16 Sep 85

JOHN CONDRY, Department of Human Development, Cornell University

3 Advertising causes conflicts at exactly the most vulnerable age for children to be in conflict with parents.

Quoted by Jonathan Rowe "Modern Advertising: The Subtle Persuasion" *Christian Science Monitor* 29 Jan 87

JOHN CORRY

4 His voice is his great weapon. It is not an orator's voice. It is husky, and sometimes it fades to a whisper. Meanwhile, it is extraordinarily intimate. Mr Reagan does not speak to audiences; he speaks to individuals.

On televised debate between Ronald Reagan and Walter F Mondale, NY *Times* 9 Oct 84

5 He bullied, soothed and cajoled. In fact, he's awfully good at what he does, but how one wishes he didn't work quite so hard doing it.

On Phil Donahue, *ib* 8 Jan 85

6 He's still not interviewing other people; he's still interviewing himself.

ib

JOHN CROSBY

7 He is forced to be literate about the illiterate, witty about the witless and coherent about the incoherent.

On role of a television critic, news summaries 20 Mar 55

BRAD DARRACH

8 Gross in physique, gargantuan in gourmandise, oceanic in liquid capacity, prodigal of purse, a fire hose of libido and a Niagara of comic invention, the man was excess personified and one of the great entertainers of the age.

On Jackie Gleason, *People* 13 Jul 87

LEE DE FOREST, inventor of triode electron tube

9 You have debased [my] child . . . You have made him a laughingstock of intelligence . . . a stench in the nostrils of the gods of the ionosphere.

To National Assn of Broadcasters, recalled on his death, *Time* 7 Jul 61

CHARLES DE GAULLE, President of France

10 I might have had trouble saving France in 1946—I didn't have television then.

Newsweek 19 Aug 63

ROBERT DUVALL

11 They have a tourniquet on the brain.

On producers of some soap operas, *Live at Five* WNBC TV 24 Sep 86

T S ELIOT

12 It is a medium of entertainment which permits millions of people to listen to the same joke at the same time, and yet remain lonesome.

On television, NY *Post* 22 Sep 63

ELIZABETH II, Queen of England

13 It's inevitable that I should seem a rather remote figure to many of you—a successor to the kings and queens of history; someone whose face may be familiar in newspapers and films but who never touches your personal lives. But now, at least for a few minutes, I welcome you to the peace of my own home.

First televised Christmas address 25 Dec 57

EDWARD ROBB ELLIS

14 The world is going mad at an accelerating rate and television is the Typhoid Mary of this madness.

NY *Times* 25 Feb 81

HENRY FAIRLIE

15 There is a middlebrow snobbery in America that praises everything on public television and disdains everything on the commercial networks as a blight.

On US reaction to television presentation of Evelyn Waugh's *Brideshead Revisited*, London *Times* 1 Feb 82

FRED W FRIENDLY

16 Television makes so much at its worst that it can't afford to do its best.

After becoming professor of broadcast journalism at Columbia University, *US News & World Report* 12 Jun 67

17 Television was supposed to be a national park. [Instead] it has become a money machine. . . . It's a commodity now, just like pork bellies.

Quoted by Rushworth M Kidder "Videoculture" *Christian Science Monitor* 10 Jun 85

GEORGE GERBNER, Dean, Annenberg School of Communications, University of Pennsylvania

18 The product is the delivery of the largest number of people at the least cost.

On television programmers, *Christian Science Monitor* 10 Jun 85

DAVID GERGEN, White House director of communications

19 Ronald Reagan is clearly to television what Franklin Roosevelt was to radio.

Newsweek 18 Apr 83

PETER GOLDMAN

20 A debate before 70 million people is in fact a distorting glass, a fun-house mirror in which wrinkles look like canyons and hesitation like an attack of amnesia.

On debate between presidential candidates Ronald Reagan and Walter F Mondale, *Newsweek* special election issue Nov/Dec 84

SAMUEL GOLDWYN

21 Why should people go out and pay money to see bad films when they can stay at home and see bad television for nothing?

Recalled on his death 31 Jan 74

JACK GOULD

1 It's like being called up in the draft. The peculiar joy of hemorrhaging without bleeding starts when the evil little red light glows on the monstrous camera.

> On telecasting his columns during a prolonged newspaper strike, *Time* 15 Feb 63

2 There is something supremely reassuring about television; the worst is always yet to come.

> NY *Times* 3 Nov 66

THOMAS GRIFFITH

3 Journalism as theater [is what] TV news is.

> On coverage of return of Iranian-held hostages, *Time* 9 Feb 81

4 Just to be seen strolling to or from a helicopter on the White House lawn, shouting an evasive answer to Sam Donaldson, must seem to the Reagans not quite satisfactory enough of a 7 PM presence, and this inane scene certainly galls the press.

> On White House move to supply "appropriate soapboxes and visual backdrops" for the president, "Making News and Non-News" *ib* 1 Sep 86

SUE HALPERN

5 The resident kvetch of *60 Minutes*. . . . an unabashed fogy.

> On Andy Rooney, NY *Times* 7 Oct 84

ALAN HAMILTON

6 In the opulence of its set, its cast was remarkably adept . . . and it was richly endowed with character actors able, indeed anxious, to play cameo roles.

> On initial telecasts from House of Lords, "Cast of the Lords' TV Show in Sparkling Form" London *Times* 24 Jan 85

7 Its plot is loose and tortuous and will take some time for its stars to emerge.

> *ib*

8 There is, as yet, no Beast and definitely no Bitch.

> *ib*

GARY HART, US Senator

9 You can get awful famous in this country in seven days.

> On television coverage of his presidential campaign, NY *Times* 7 Oct 84

BEN HECHT

10 Television excites me because it seems to be the last stamping ground of poetry, the last place where I hear women's hair rhapsodically described, women's faces acclaimed in odelike language.

> NY *Herald Tribune* 26 May 58

CARRIE HEETER, Director, Communications Technology Laboratory, Michigan State University

11 They don't watch programs anymore; they watch pieces of programs.

> On viewers' tendency to change channels, NY *Times* 9 Oct 85

HOWELL HEFLIN, US Senator

12 I see a little better grooming. Some might even be trying a little powder.

> On first day of televised Senate proceedings, NY *Times* 2 May 86

ROBERT M HUTCHINS

13 We can put television in its proper light by supposing that Gutenberg's great invention had been directed at printing only comic books.

> News summaries 31 Dec 77

PICO IYER

14 For citizens who think themselves puppets in the hands of their rulers, nothing is more satisfying than having rulers as puppets in their hands.

> On *Spitting Image*, British television comedy "in which some 400 latex and foam-rubber puppets reduce the antics of the powerful to a mess of funny faces, pratfalls and spasmodic jerks," *Time* 28 Apr 86

HUGH NEWELL JACOBSEN

15 [Washington] is the only city in the world where you can go to a black-tie dinner and there at the foot of the table is a television set up to catch a press conference.

> NY *Times* 31 May 84

JEFF JARVIS

16 Now that's a case of the pot calling the kettle metal.

> On criticism by Robin Leach, host of television's *Lifestyles of the Rich and Famous*, of a similar program, *On Top All Over the World*, quoted in *People* 22 Apr 85

NICHOLAS JOHNSON, Federal Communications Commission

17 All television is educational television. The only question is what is it teaching?

> *Life* 10 Sep 71

18 A viewer who skips the advertising is the moral equivalent of a shoplifter.

> To Amer Magazine Conference, NY *Times* 25 Oct 84

WARD JUST

19 Watching a baseball game on television is like chasing the great white whale in a goldfish bowl. It trivializes everything: men two inches high, a ball the size of a bee. It is like looking at the heavens through a dime-store telescope.

> "Your Ear on the Ball" NY *Times* 17 Apr 84

E J KAHN

20 Looking at *60 Minutes*, in full or in part, has roughly the impact on Hewitt that standing at the edge of an unruffled pool had on Narcissus.

> On CBS TV producer Don Hewitt, *New Yorker* 19 Jul 82

ALEXANDER KENDRICK

21 He believed that . . . there had to be a message to start with, that in the beginning was the Word. Otherwise, he said, "all you have is a lot of wires and lights in a box."

> *Prime Time: The Life of Edward R Murrow* Little, Brown 69

CHARLES KRAUTHAMMER

22 In the old days one merely gawked at these unfortunates. Donahue's genius is to get them to talk.

> On guests of Phil Donahue's talk show, *Cutting Edges: Making Sense of the 80s* Random House 85, quoted in NY *Times* 12 Nov 85

LOUIS KRONENBERGER

1 For tens of millions of people [television] has become habit-forming, brain-softening, taste-degrading.
> *The Cart and the Horse* Knopf 64

2 Privacy was in sufficient danger before TV appeared, and TV has given it its death blow.
> *ib*

CHRISTOPHER LEHMANN-HAUPT

3 There is no medical proof that television causes brain damage—at least from over five feet away. In fact, TV is probably the least physically harmful of all the narcotics known to man.
> NY *Times* 24 Sep 69

JOHN LEONARD

4 The British Broadcasting Corporation, like the British tabloids, adores aristocrats. Their houses are big and their servants are cute and, when they aren't eating immense amounts of overcooked food, they stand around on their broad, rolled lawns like croquet hoops waiting for history to pop through the holes in their heads.
> "Television: Costumes without Drama" *New York* 30 Apr 84

LEE LOEVINGER, Federal Communications Commission

5 Television is the literature of the illiterate, the culture of the lowbrow, the wealth of the poor, the privilege of the underprivileged, the exclusive club of the excluded masses.
> To New Jersey Broadcasters Assn, *National Observer* 17 Oct 66

6 Television is a golden goose that lays scrambled eggs; and it is futile and probably fatal to beat it for not laying caviar. Anyway, more people like scrambled eggs than caviar.
> *ib*

7 Television is simply automated daydreaming.
> *Vogue* Jun 67

LONDON TIMES

8 The BBC will wear a brisk morning face.
> On plans for first venture into early morning television, 12 Apr 82

DMITRI LYUBOSVETOV, *Pravda* columnist

9 Journalistic clichés migrate from broadcast to broadcast.
> On Soviet television coverage of the West, NY *Times* 20 May 86

ARCHIBALD MACLEISH

10 You burned the city of London in our houses and we felt the flames.
> On wartime coverage by CBS Radio correspondent Edward R Murrow, quoted by A M Sperber *Murrow* Freundlich 86

ALBERT A MARKS JR, Chief Executive Officer, Miss America Pageant

11 He really did put Vaseline on his teeth, you know that?
> On long-time host Bert Parks, quoted in *US* 20 Oct 86

CLEO MAUER, cook in a Long Island rectory

12 I could have stayed home and watched it on [television], but if you see anyone on TV it's always different. Face to face, there's a special quality. And when it's over, you keep with you the idea that you were really there—not in a room a long way off, looking at a picture.
> On why she went to see Pope John Paul II at Battery Park, *New Yorker* 15 Oct 79

MARSHALL MCLUHAN

13 The medium is the message.
> Assessing the impact of television, *Understanding Media* McGraw-Hill 64

JOHN MCNULTY, Vice President of Public Relations, General Motors Corp

14 They'll leave anything incompatible with their view on the cutting-room floor. *60 Minutes* is to journalism what *Charley's Aunt* is to criminology.
> Quoted by Walter Guzzardi Jr "How Much Should Companies Talk?" *Fortune* 4 Mar 85

MARGARET MEAD

15 Thanks to television, for the first time the young are seeing history made before it is censored by their elders.
> Recalled on her death 15 Nov 78

NEWTON N MINOW, Federal Communications Commission

16 You will observe a vast wasteland.
> On television, to National Assn of Broadcasters, NY *Times* 10 May 61

17 Children will watch anything, and when a broadcaster uses crime and violence and other shoddy devices to monopolize a child's attention, it's worse than taking candy from a baby. It is taking precious time from the process of growing up.
> To Senate Subcommittee on Juvenile Delinquency, NY *Post* 19 Jun 61

18 When television is good, nothing is better. When it's bad, nothing is worse.
> Recalled on 25th anniversary of his "vast wasteland" speech, *Nightline* ABC TV 9 May 86

WALTER F MONDALE

19 Modern politics today requires a mastery of television. I've never really warmed up to television and, in fairness to television, it's never warmed up to me.
> After losing presidential election, NY *Times* 8 Nov 84

20 I hope we don't lose in America this demand that those of us who want this office . . . must be prepared not to handle the 10-second gimmick that deals, say, with little things like war and peace.
> *ib*

21 By instinct and tradition, I don't like the thing. I like to look someone in the eye.
> On television, *Newsweek* 19 Nov 84

SAM MOORE

22 It came from nowhere, blazed up like a brush fire, pulled us together at the bottom of the Depression, held us together through a war, galloped up to the brink of television and fell over dead.
> On radio, *Life* 13 Nov 64

1 Radio invented a new kind of drama called soap opera, a form of serial in which the main rule was, "Don't let anything happen!"—because if something happened on a Wednesday and you were at the dentist, on Thursday you wouldn't know what the hell was going on and you'd get mad and switch soap operas, and soap, too.
ib

2 Radio tried everything, and it all worked. It invented a new kind of singer whose voice wasn't even loud enough to carry across a hotel bedroom, and Americans, as it turned out, would rather hear these "crooners" than any big-bellied tenor who ever shook an opera house chandelier.
ib

NATIONAL COMMISSION ON CAUSES AND PREVENTION OF VIOLENCE

3 Children are inclined to learn from television [because] it is never too busy to talk to them, and it never has to brush them aside while it does household chores.
On influence of violent television programs, quoted in NY *Times* 25 Sep 69

4 Unlike their preoccupied parents, television seems to want their attention at any time, and goes to considerable lengths to attract it.
ib

NEWSWEEK

5 Almost from the moment the horror occurred, television changed. It was no longer a small box containing entertainment, news and sports; suddenly, it was a window opening onto violently unpredictable life in Washington and in Dallas.
On coverage of President John F Kennedy's assassination, 9 Dec 63

6 More than a hundred million Americans watched the late president's funeral, but the funeral did not take place in Arlington Cemetery alone. It took place in a living room in Los Angeles, in Grand Central Terminal in New York, in kitchens and offices across the United States. John F Kennedy's casket did not ride down Pennsylvania Avenue only. It rode down Main Street.
ib

NEW YORK TIMES

7 His fans eat it up, along with their toast and morning coffee.
On 25th anniversary of John Gambling's radio show, 20 Oct 84

8 Radio let people see things with their own ears.
Editorial, 30 Jan 86

9 Once upon a time—from 1974 to 1977, to be precise—Sunday night went like this: After you washed the dishes and put the kids to bed and made sure you had enough cigarettes (lots of us were smoking then, remember?) and maybe poured yourself a little something, you sat down in front of the television set and thought of England.
On return of PBS series *Upstairs, Downstairs*, 15 Mar 87

10 There is now a good reason to live through March.
ib

RICHARD M NIXON, 37th US President

11 I knew if I continued to look around . . . it would be difficult for me to contain my own emotions. So I turned away from the red eyes of the crowd and looked only at the red eye of the camera, talking to all the nation.
On his departure from the White House, *RN: Memoirs of Richard Nixon* Grosset & Dunlap 78

12 In the television age, the key distinction is between the candidate who can speak poetry and the one who can only speak prose.
After 1984 presidential campaign between Ronald Reagan and Walter F Mondale, *New York* 19 Nov 84

MARTIN F NOLAN

13 [Television executives] are afraid to advertise condoms that could save lives, but do not blush about telecasting a National Geographic special on President Reagan's pelvic plumbing.
Boston *Globe* 9 Feb 87

14 If the Barons of Bad Taste known as network executives believe in chastity as an anti-AIDS measure, it doesn't show on the soaps, night or day.
ib

JOHN J O'CONNOR

15 [They are] the video equivalent of junk food.
On miniseries, NY *Times* 16 Nov 78

16 Silly sitcoms are designed to attract juveniles of all ages.
News summaries 31 Dec 79

17 Benito Mussolini is being put through the grinder of a television biography and . . . the result resembles Italian sausage—of the spicy variety.
On NBC TV's three-part presentation *Mussolini*, NY *Times* 22 Nov 85

TERRENCE O'FLAHERTY

18 No wonder the audiences for the late-night talk shows are growing. Who can get to sleep after hearing the 11 PM news?
Reader's Digest Nov 72

MIKE PETERS

19 What do you want to watch tonight? The president's enlarged prostate on 2, his benign polyp on 4 or a colonoscopy on 5?
Cartoon caption on obsessive coverage of President Ronald Reagan's health, *Newsweek* 12 Jan 87

IVER PETERSON

20 Eighty channels in the sky, offering a glimpse of anything from sunrise prayers to soft-core pornography.
On satellite dishes used to pick up programs without charge, NY *Times* 15 Jan 86

RONALD REAGAN, 40th US President

21 I usually never walk by a microphone.
On abiding love of broadcasting, NY *Times* 31 Mar 85

NELSON A ROCKEFELLER, Governor of NY

22 Others looked at radio and saw a gadget; his genius lay in his capacity to look at the same thing . . . but to see far more.
On David Sarnoff, *Newsweek* 27 Dec 71

1 [To] David Sarnoff, the word *visionary* meant a capacity to see into tomorrow and make it work.
ib

CLAUDIA ROSETT

2 Diamonds, high finance and convulsive sex are crammed into thick books like so much mint cream into imported chocolates. . . . As with soft-centered candy, there seem to be standard ingredients.
On books used for miniseries, *Wall Street Journal* 9 Apr 85

CARL SANDBURG

3 The impact of television on our culture is . . . indescribable. There's a certain sense in which it is nearly as important as the invention of printing.
News summaries 30 Dec 55

ARTHUR M SCHLESINGER JR

4 [Television] has spread the habit of instant reaction and stimulated the hope of instant results.
Newsweek 6 Jul 70

MARTIN SCHRAM

5 Television . . . often cannot cover the passing of the torch without fanning the flames in the process.
New York 26 Mar 84

MURRAY SCHUMACH

6 Television is the bland leading the bland.
The Face on the Cutting Room Floor Morrow 64

FULTON J SHEEN, Auxiliary Bishop of NY

7 You should realize that the community with which you deal is not the one of 42nd Street and Broadway, or Hollywood and Vine. These are the crusts on the great American sandwich. The meat is in between.
To broadcasting executives, news summaries 9 Nov 55

HUGH SIDEY

8 [Kennedy] did not have to run the risk of having his ideas and his words shortened and adulterated by a correspondent. This was the television era, not only in campaigning, but in holding the presidency.
John F Kennedy, President Atheneum 63

9 [He is] television's sultan of splutter.
On ABC News correspondent Sam Donaldson, *Time* 30 Sep 85

G ROYCE SMITH, Executive Director, Amer Booksellers Assn

10 Book sales have always been largely by word of mouth . . . and television is the biggest word of mouth there is. It's substituted for a lot of conversation, for that matter.
NY *Times* 21 Dec 73

LARRY SPEAKES, White House press spokesman

11 "Ol' Shoot from the Lip," we call him.
On ABC TV news correspondent Sam Donaldson, quoted in *Wall Street Journal* 18 Mar 87

12 When, at the age of seven, he blew up the family truck by dropping a match down the gas tank, we should have known he'd grow up to make his living hurling verbal firebombs at presidents.
ib

A M SPERBER

13 Little figures on a little screen showed newsreel footage, talked about the war with maps and pointers, unable to compete as yet with radio.
On television coverage of the Korean War in the 1950s, *Murrow* Freundlich 86

14 [He had] a cheekiness bordering at times on nail-file abrasive.
On producer Fred W Friendly, *ib*

RONALD STEEL

15 Television has made places look alike, and it has transformed the way we see. A whole generation of Americans, maybe two, has grown up looking at the world through a lens.
"Life in the Last 50 Years" *Esquire* Jun 83

16 Television has changed how we choose our leaders. It elected Ronald Reagan and a host of Kennedy-look-alike congressmen with blow-dried hair and gleaming teeth. It destroyed Senator Joe McCarthy by showing him in action and it created Jerry Falwell.
ib

JAMES THURBER

17 The chill Miss Trent has her men frustrated to a point at which a mortal male would smack her little mouth, so smooth, so firm, so free of nicotine, alcohol and emotion.
On soap opera heroine Helen Trent, recalled on his death 2 Nov 61

TIME MAGAZINE

18 Political conventions are the intramural Olympics of television.
On Republican National Convention in San Francisco, to which the networks sent 1,825 employees to cover the activities of 1,308 delegates, 24 Jul 64

19 Most of its investigative pieces are playlets in which a Lone Ranger journalist corners a villain, not with a gun but with an interview.
On CBS TV's *60 Minutes*, 12 Dec 83

JOHN UPDIKE

20 I secretly understood: the primitive appeal of the hearth. Television is—its irresistible charm—a fire.
On child doing homework near the family's television set, *Roger's Version* Knopf 86, quoted in NY *Times* 31 Aug 86

HARRIET VAN HORNE

21 There are days when any electrical appliance in the house, including the vacuum cleaner, seems to offer more entertainment possibilities than the [television] set.
NY *World-Telegram & Sun* 7 Jun 57

22 One who roams the channels after dark, searching for buried treasure.
On her role as television critic, *ib* 27 Feb 58

23 The time of the rack and the screws is come. Summer television has set in with its usual severity. And the small screen, where late the sweet birds sang, is now awash with repeats, reruns, rejects, replacements and reversions to the primitive.
"Time to Buy a Polo Mallet" *ib* 2 Jun 58

1 Rarely in broadcasting history has so much been riding on the whimsical flick of a few thousand wrists.
"The Battle for TV's Midnight Millions" *Look* 11 Jul 67

GORE VIDAL

2 Television is now so desperately hungry for material that they're scraping the top of the barrel.
News summaries 20 Jul 55

TOM WALTERS

3 You own anything which comes down in your yard, and you have a right to use it.
On selling satellite dishes, *Time* 16 Sep 85

ANDY WARHOL

4 When I got my first television set, I stopped caring so much about having close relationships.
Recalled on his death, *Newsweek* 9 Mar 87

JOHN W WARNER, US Senator

5 I remain unchanged, defiantly unchanged. Let the raw material stay rough and raw.
On first day of televised Senate proceedings, NY *Times* 2 May 86

HARRY F WATERS

6 [They favor] flashy packages of bite-size stories that . . . are to serious journalism what McNuggets are to a full-course dinner.
On network news magazine programs, *Newsweek* 2 Jul 82

7 Titanic clashes in this video courtroom are likely to swirl around botched paint jobs, unshoveled sidewalks, defective toasters, aggressive guard dogs and every conceivable, and sometimes inconceivable, mishap involving a dry cleaner.
On *The People's Court*, television program featuring "real litigants arguing real small-claims cases before a real judge," *ib* 16 Jun 86

8 No soap opera has so engrossingly captured the wondrous banality of the human condition.
ib

9 He was both [television's] first celebrity and its most persistent conscience.
On Edward R Murrow, *ib* 23 Jun 86

10 Max Headroom, if overly exposed, could end up as just another Muppet . . . Nothing would be more distressing than to witness a brilliant parody of TV turn into a TV cliché.
On computer-generated character Max Headroom, *ib* 20 Apr 87

HENRY A WAXMAN, US Congressman

11 The routine promotion of condoms through advertising has been stopped by networks who are so hypocritically priggish that they refuse to describe disease control as they promote disease transmission.
US News & World Report 23 Feb 87

ORSON WELLES

12 I hate television. I hate it as much as peanuts. But I can't stop eating peanuts.
NY *Herald Tribune* 12 Oct 56

WILLIAM C WESTMORELAND

13 Television is an instrument which can paralyze this country.
On Vietnam as the first war ever reported without censorship, *Time* 5 Apr 82

14 I was participating in my own lynching, but the problem was I didn't know what I was being lynched for.
On being interviewed by Mike Wallace for *CBS Reports: The Uncounted Enemy: A Vietnam Deception*, which prompted Westmoreland to sue CBS for $120 million, NY *Times* 20 Nov 84

E B WHITE

15 [Television] should be our Lyceum, our Chautauqua, our Minsky's and our Camelot.
Quoted by Alexander Kendrick *Prime Time* Little, Brown 69

16 It should restate and clarify the social dilemma and the political pickle. Once in a while it does, and you get a quick glimpse of its potential.
ib

THEODORE H WHITE

17 With electricity we were wired into a new world, for electricity brought the radio, a "crystal set" [and] with enough ingenuity, one could tickle the crystal with a cat's whisker and pick up anything.
In Search of History: A Personal Adventure Harper & Row 78

18 He who is created by television can be destroyed by television.
Television and the Presidency WOR TV 24 Jun 84

GEORGE F WILL

19 They seem to have a license to lie.
On docudramas, programs that blend reality and entertainment, quoted by Victor Lasky *Reader's Digest* Apr 86

WALTER WINCHELL

20 The only ones who like Milton Berle are his mother—and the public.
Recalled by Berle in address at Museum of Broadcasting dinner honoring him as Mr Television, NY *Times* 16 Apr 85

LOIS WYSE

21 You don't laugh with me;
I don't laugh with you.
All the wit comes pouring out of the tube.
And we laugh at it together.
The more we avoid talking
the more passive the relationship becomes.
Television permits us to walk through life
with minor speaking parts.
And the more we fail to speak,
the more difficult speaking becomes.
Lovetalk Doubleday 73

LINDA YGLESTAS

22 Nostrils flaring, every muscle in his face working overtime while his right index finger beat his point into the table. . . . That smirking half-smile of righteousness that lands its blow with the coolness of Carrara marble.
On Mike Wallace, NY *Sunday News* 14 Oct 84

VLADIMIR ZWORYKIN

1 The technique is wonderful. I didn't even dream it would be so good. But I would never let my children come close to the thing.
> Comments of developer of television, interviewed on his 92nd birthday, news summaries 31 Dec 81

SPORTS

Athletes & Players

HENRY ("HANK") AARON, NY Yankees

2 Didn't come up here to read. Came up here to hit.
> To Casey Stengel, who had told him to hold the bat in such a way that he could see its trademark, quoted by Bob Uecker and Mickey Herskowitz *Catcher in the Wry* Putnam 82

MUHAMMAD ALI, prizefighter

3 I'm not the greatest; I'm the double greatest. Not only do I knock 'em out, I pick the round.
> As US 1960 Olympic gold medalist in boxing, NY *Times* 9 Dec 62

4 I'll be floating like a butterfly and stinging like a bee.
> Before defeating Sonny Liston for world heavyweight championship, NY *Herald Tribune* 26 Feb 64

5 I'll beat him so bad he'll need a shoehorn to put his hat on.
> On fight with Floyd Patterson, quoted in NY *Times* 21 Nov 65

6 I know I got it made while the masses of black people are catchin' hell, but as long as they ain't free, I ain't free.
> *Playboy* Nov 75

7 There are no pleasures in a fight but some of my fights have been a pleasure to win.
> *ib*

8 It's just a job. Grass grows, birds fly, waves pound the sand. I beat people up.
> NY *Times* 6 Apr 77

9 When you can whip any man in the world, you never know peace.
> On beginning treatment for Parkinson's syndrome, *Newsweek* 1 Oct 84

10 Superman don't need no seat belt.
> Comment to flight attendant, who replied, "Superman don't need no airplane, either," quoted by Clifton Fadiman comp *The Little, Brown Book of Anecdotes* Little, Brown 85

11 I'm the best. I just haven't played yet.
> On his golf game, *ib*

12 Only the nose knows
Where the nose goes
When the door close.
> Response when asked about sex in relationship to athletic prowess, *ib*

ANONYMOUS

13 When he says "Sit down!" I don't even look for a chair.
> Green Bay Packers player on coach Vince Lombardi, recalled on Lombardi's death 3 Sept 70

JOHN BACHAR, rock climber

14 Soloing is serious business, because you can be seriously dead.
> On climbing sheer rock faces alone without mechanical aid, *Newsweek* 1 Oct 84

ED BARRY, rock climber

15 Sooner or later . . . you are going to be looking at God saying, "We're going to be lucky if we get out of here." Your life is going to be in front of you and then you are going to realize that you'd rather be grocery shopping.
> *Newsweek* 1 Oct 84

YOGI BERRA, NY Yankees catcher

16 So I'm ugly. So what? I never saw anyone hit with his face.
> Quoted in Bert Sugar comp *The Book of Sports Quotes* Quick Fox 79

JIM BURT, NY Giants nose tackle

17 I was a dirt-bag. Now I'm an All-Pro.
> On winning first NFC championship since 1956, quoted by Eric Pooley "True Blue: From Giants to Supermen" *New York* 26 Jan 87

ROGER CLEMENS, Boston Red Sox pitcher

18 I was pitching on all adrenaline . . . and challenging them. I was throwing the ball right down the heart of the plate.
> On breaking record by striking out 20 batters in a 9-inning game, NY *Times* 1 May 86

DENNIS CONNER, yachtsman

19 Design has taken the place of what sailing used to be.
> After 1983 loss of America's Cup to Australia, recalled before he regained the cup, *Time* 9 Feb 87

20 Sailing is just the bottom line, like adding up the score in bridge. My real interest is in the tremendous game of life.
> *ib*

21 It basically was an art before. We're just starting to scratch it into a science.
> On yacht racing, after regaining America's Cup, *ib* 16 Feb 87

JIMMY CONNORS, tennis player

22 People don't seem to understand that it's a damn war out there.
> Quoted by Thomas Tutko and William Bruns *Winning Is Everything and Other American Myths* Macmillan 76

ANGEL CORDERO JR, jockey

23 He's good enough for me. I won't say he's a super-horse because you're never a superhorse until you're retired. Any horse can be beaten on any given day.
> On Spend a Buck, winner of Kentucky Derby, NY *Times* 5 May 85

TOM COURTNEY, US 1956 Olympic gold medalist, track

24 My head was exploding, my stomach ripping, and even the tips of my fingers ached. The only thing I could think was, "If I live, I will never run again!"
> *Life* Summer 1984

ROB DE CASTELLA, Australian marathon runner

1 Not unless they have Dutch elm disease.
> When asked if there was a disadvantage to having legs that look as heavy as tree trunks, NY *Times* 3 Nov 86

JACK DEMPSEY, prizefighter

2 Honey, I forgot to duck.
> Comment to his wife after losing 1926 fight to Gene Tunney, recalled on his death 31 May 83.

3 Tell him he can have my title, but I want it back in the morning.
> On a drunk who challenged him, *ib*

JOE DiMAGGIO, NY Yankees outfielder

4 A ball player's got to be kept hungry to become a big leaguer. That's why no boy from a rich family ever made the big leagues.
> NY *Times* 30 Apr 61

ROBERTO DURAN, prizefighter

5 I am not an animal in my personal life. But in the ring there is an animal inside me. Sometimes it roars when the first bell rings. Sometimes it springs out later in a fight. But I can always feel it there, driving me and pushing me forward. It is what makes me win. It makes me enjoy fighting.
> Comments before defeating Sugar Ray Leonard for world welterweight championship, *Newsweek* 23 Jun 80

6 Getting hit motivates me. It makes me punish the guy more. A fighter takes a punch, hits back with three punches.
> *ib*

EL CORDOBÉS (Manuel Benítez Pérez), Spanish matador

7 Where is the university for courage? . . . The university for courage is to do what you believe in!
> Quoted by Larry Collins and Dominique Lapierre *Or I'll Dress You in Mourning* New American Library 70

8 Bravery is believing in yourself, and that thing nobody can teach you.
> *Newsweek* 22 Mar 71

ROGER ERICKSON, NY Yankees pitcher

9 I don't want to be in your future. It's frustrating enough being in your present.
> On retiring after being demoted to the Yankees' farm team, *Sports Illustrated* 2 May 83

CHRIS EVERT LLOYD, tennis player

10 If you can react the same way to winning and losing, that's a big accomplishment. That quality is important because it stays with you the rest of your life, and there's going to be a life after tennis that's a lot longer than your tennis life.
> Quoted by William Safire and Leonard Safir *Good Advice* Times Books 82

BOBBY FISCHER, chess player

11 I like the moment when I break a man's ego.
> *Newsweek* 31 Jul 72

GEORGE FOREMAN, US 1968 Olympic gold medalist, boxing

12 My mother was watching on television and she doesn't want me to hurt anyone.
> On not knocking out his Soviet opponent in final bout, news summaries 31 Dec 68

JOE FRAZIER, prizefighter

13 I want to hit him, step away and watch him hurt. I want his heart.
> Before losing 1975 fight to Muhammad Ali, *Newsweek* 29 Sep 75

MITCH GAYLORD, US 1984 Olympic gold medalist, gymnastics

14 A team championship doesn't happen because three people score 10s, it happens because all the guys score well. In my opinion, everyone deserved 10s, we're all 10s on this team.
> NY *Times* 2 Aug 84

FRANK GIFFORD, NY Giants halfback

15 Pro football is like nuclear warfare. There are no winners, only survivors.
> *Sports Illustrated* 4 Jul 60

HAROLD ("RED") GRANGE, Chicago Bears halfback

16 If you can't explain it, how can you take credit for it?
> On his extraordinary ability to elude tacklers, news summaries 31 Dec 51

FRANCO HARRIS, Seattle Seahawks fullback

17 After 12 years, the old butterflies came back. Well, I guess at my age you call them moths.
> On playing for a new team, *Sports Illustrated* 1 Oct 84

BOBBY JONES, golfer

18 You might as well praise a man for not robbing a bank.
> On penalizing himself one stroke that cost him a national championship, quoted by Alistair Cooke *America* Knopf 73

19 I will tell you privately it's not going to get better, it's going to get worse all the time, but don't fret. Remember, we "play the ball where it lies," and now let's not talk about this, ever again.
> On being stricken by a rare disease in his mid 40s, *ib*

HENRY JORDAN, Green Bay Packers right tackle

20 He's fair. He treats us all the same—like dogs.
> On Vince Lombardi, recalled on Lombardi's death 3 Sep 70

MICHAEL JORDAN, Chicago Bulls basketball player

21 The game is my wife. It demands loyalty and responsibility, and it gives me back fulfillment and peace.
> Quoted by Pete Axthelm *Newsweek* 5 Jan 87

22 My body could stand the crutches but my mind couldn't stand the sideline.
> On broken foot bone that caused him to miss 64 games in 1985–86 season, *ib*

JOE KAPP, former Minnesota Vikings quarterback

23 Is it normal to wake up in the morning in a sweat because you can't wait to beat another human's guts out?
> News summaries 31 Dec 79

BILLIE JEAN KING, tennis player

24 Tennis is a perfect combination of violent action taking place in an atmosphere of total tranquillity.
> *Billie Jean* Harper & Row 74

SANDY KOUFAX, Los Angeles Dodgers pitcher

1 Pitching is . . . the art of instilling fear.
> Quoted by Robert Hood *The Gashouse Gang* Morrow 76

VERNON LAW, Pittsburgh Pirates pitcher

2 Experience is a hard teacher because she gives the test first, the lesson afterward.
> "How to Be a Winner" *This Week* 14 Aug 60

3 Some people are so busy learning the tricks of the trade that they never learn the trade.
> *ib*

SUGAR RAY LEONARD, prizefighter

4 I figure it's like something that has to be, before Marvin and me can be content with ourselves. There is a burning desire in me now.
> On challenge to fight middleweight champion Marvin Hagler, *Sports Illustrated* 8 Sep 86

BEN LEXCEN, Australian yachtsman

5 We don't have any sailors in Australia, we have rowers.
> On US victory at America's Cup races, NY *Times* 3 Feb 87

6 Even when we did win, we were using a rifle against a club . . . It's our sunburned minds. We need more Crocodile Dundees down here.
> On winning the cup in 1983, *ib*

GENE LITTLER, golfer

7 Golf is not a game of great shots. It's a game of the most misses. The people who win make the smallest mistakes.
> News summaries 22 Mar 69

BOBBY LOCKE, golfer

8 You drive for show but putt for dough.
> Recalled on his death 9 Mar 87

ROGER MARSHALL, mountain climber

9 Having seen all the Sherpas who are mutilated, the Sherpanis who are without husbands, I would never employ a Sherpa.
> On not using Sherpa porters for his ascent of Mt Everest, NY *Times* 10 Aug 86

10 I believe in an extraconsciousness that looks after you. It only comes into play in extreme circumstances, which for me is in the mountains. That's where I fit in best.
> *ib*

VINCE MATTHEWS, US 1972 Olympic gold medalist, track

11 Twenty years from now, I can look at this medal and say, "I was the best quarter-miler in the world on that day." If you don't think that's important, you don't know what's inside an athlete's soul.
> News summaries 31 Dec 72

JOHN MCENROE, tennis player

12 You are the pits of the world! Vultures! Trash!
> To the umpire, spectators and reporters at Wimbledon, quoted in *Time* 28 Dec 81

13 I'll let the racket do the talking.
> On defending his title as Wimbledon champion, London *Times* 26 Jun 84

14 This taught me a lesson, but I'm not sure what it is.
> On losing to Tim Mayotte in the Ebel US Pro Indoor Championships, NY *Times* 9 Feb 87

15 If, in a few months, I'm only number 8 or number 10 in the world, I'll have to look at what off-the-court work I can do. I will need to do something if I want to be number 1.
> *ib*

MICHAEL MCGUIRE, adventurer

16 I like to collect experiences the way other people like to collect coins and stamps.
> On hiking across the polar ice cap, *Christian Science Monitor* 26 Feb 85

RON MCLEAN, California State–Fullerton defensive tackle

17 They need rest, too.
> On sleeping with his shoulder pads and helmet the night before a game, *Sports Illustrated* 17 Nov 86

REINHOLD MESSNER, mountain climber

18 I do this for myself because I am my own fatherland, and my handkerchief is my flag.
> On climbing the world's 14 tallest mountains, *Time* 27 Oct 86

FRANK MUNDUS

19 This is it. There are no world records after this.
> On fellow fisherman Donnie Braddick's landing of a 17-foot, 3,450-pound great white shark, believed to be the largest ever caught with rod and reel, *Sports Illustrated* 18 Aug 86

JOE NAMATH, NY Jets quarterback

20 Till I was 13, I thought my name was "Shut Up."
> *I Can't Wait until Tomorrow* Random House 69

21 When we won the league championship, all the married guys on the club had to thank their wives for putting up with all the stress and strain all season. I had to thank all the single broads in New York.
> News summaries 31 Dec 79

MARTINA NAVRATILOVA, tennis player

22 I hope, when I stop, people will think that somehow I mattered.
> *International Herald Tribune* 22 Jul 86

23 I just try to concentrate on concentrating.
> On strategy for winning the US Open, quoted in *US* 20 Oct 86

JACK NICKLAUS, golfer

24 It's hard not to play golf that's up to Jack Nicklaus standards when you *are* Jack Nicklaus.
> On winning his 70th PGA tournament, WINS Radio 28 May 84

TENZING NORGAY, Sherpa guide

25 If I know I make this much trouble, I never climb Everest.
> On trying to secure a passport, news summaries 29 Mar 54

BRIAN ORSER, ice skater

26 It's not who does the most tricks, but the total package.
> On refusal to perform a quadruple jump in his free-skating program at the world figure skating championships, NY *Times* 12 Mar 87

DON OTT, Athletes in Action basketball player

1 You might say they did unto us as we did unto others.
    On loss to UCLA, *Sports Illustrated* 24 Jan 83

JESSE OWENS, US 1936 Olympic gold medalist, track and field

2 Another old friend gone!
    On learning that his last remaining world record had been broken, news summaries 31 Dec 60

WILLIAM ("REFRIGERATOR") PERRY, Chicago Bears defensive tackle

3 Even when I was little, I was big.
    On his weight, quoted in *Life* Jan 86

4 Some people call me the Kitchen, some call me the Dining Room—and some call me the Cafeteria!
    NBC TV 23 Sep 86

GARY PLAYER, golfer

5 Golf asks something of a man. It makes one loathe mediocrity. It seems to say, "If you are going to keep company with me, don't embarrass me."
    Christian Science Monitor 24 Jun 65

SUGAR RAY ROBINSON, prizefighter

6 My business is hurting people.
    Comment to NY State Boxing Commission, news summaries 23 May 62

JOHN ROSKELLEY, mountain climber

7 You've got to know when to turn around.
    On those who have failed to duplicate the feat of two men who climbed Mt Everest without bottled oxygen in 1975, NY *Times* 10 Aug 86

TOM SANDERS, former Boston Celtics center

8 Learn to compartmentalize yourself. You're an athlete for only a few more years. You have to live 80 or 90 years, so you better find more things to do.
    To student athletes, NY *Times* 20 May 86

ARNOLD SCHWARZENEGGER, body builder

9 I just use my muscles as a conversation piece, like someone walking a cheetah down 42nd Street.
    News summaries 31 Dec 79

WILLIE SHOEMAKER, jockey

10 If Jack Nicklaus can win the Masters at 46, I can win the Kentucky Derby at 54.
    Quoted by *Life* Jan 87

LEON SPINKS, prizefighter

11 I know a lot of people think I'm dumb. Well, at least I ain't no educated fool.
    LA *Times* 28 Jun 78

MARK SPITZ, US 1972 Olympic gold medalist, swimming

12 I swam my brains out.
    On winning seven gold medals, a record number for a single Olympiad, news summaries 31 Dec 72

LAWRENCE TAYLOR, NY Giants linebacker

13 He's a cocky sumbitch. That's what makes him such a great player.
    On quarterback Phil Simms, quoted by Eric Pooley "True Blue: From Giants to Supermen" *New York* 26 Jan 87

BILL TILDEN, tennis player

14 Hit at the girl whenever possible.
    On how to play mixed doubles, quoted by Phil Pepe and Zander Hollander *The Book of Sports Lists* Pinnacle 79

WILLYE WHITE, US 1956 Olympic silver medalist, woman's long jump

15 I was nervous, so I read the New Testament. I read the verse about have no fear, and I felt relaxed. Then I jumped farther than I ever jumped before in my life.
    Quoted in *Life* Summer 84

CHRISTOPHER WILLIAMS, yachtsman

16 It evokes another age of shipbuilding when the clippers reigned. It's like the Parthenon, showing off lovely, immutable laws of aesthetics.
    On the restored 1930 yacht *Jezebel*, NY *Times* 4 May 85

YUN LOU, Chinese 1984 Olympic gymnast

17 Suit too big. Grabbed pants instead of pommel.
    On scoring low in pommel horse competition, news summaries 30 Jul 84

Coaches, Officials & Owners

ALEX AGASE, University of Michigan, assistant football coach

18 If you really want to advise me, do it on Saturday afternoon between 1 and 4 o'clock. And you've got 25 seconds to do it, between plays. Not on Monday. I know the right thing to do on Monday.
    Quoted by Thomas J Peters and Nancy K Austin "A Passion for Excellence" *Fortune* 13 May 85

YOGI BERRA, professional baseball manager

19 What difference does the uniform make? You don't hit with it.
    On becoming coach of the Houston Astros, NY *Times* 8 May 86

20 It ain't over till it's over.
    As 1973 manager of NY Mets in National League pennant race, quoted by William Safire *ib* 15 Feb 87

TERRY BRENNAN, University of Notre Dame football coach

21 If you're old and you lose, they say you're outmoded. If you're young and you lose, they say you're green. So don't lose.
    Life 25 Mar 57

DAVE BRISTOL, Cincinnati Reds manager

22 Boys, baseball is a game where you gotta have fun. You do that by winning.
    On becoming manager, *Time* 26 May 67

AVERY BRUNDAGE, President, International Olympic Committee

23 Sport must be amateur or it is not sport. Sports played professionally are entertainment.
    This Week 14 Jan 68

BOBBY CLARKE, Philadelphia Flyers manager

24 I've discovered that the less I say, the more rumors I start.
    Sports Illustrated 15 Jul 84

DAVE CURREY, University of Cincinnati football coach

1 We don't have any refrigerators. We have a few pot-belly stoves, but they're on the coaching staff.
> Referring to Chicago Bears player William "Refrigerator" Perry, *Sports Illustrated* 2 Dec 85

MARVIN DAVIS, Oakland Athletics owner

2 As men get older, the toys get more expensive.
> On purchase of team for a rumored $12 million, news summaries 31 Dec 79

LEO DUROCHER, NY Giants manager

3 You don't save a pitcher for tomorrow. Tomorrow it may rain.
> NY *Times* 16 May 65

4 There are only five things you can do in baseball—run, throw, catch, hit and hit with power.
> *Time* 16 Jul 73

5 Nice guys finish last.
> 1946 remark as manager of Brooklyn Dodgers, quoted in Eric Partridge *A Dictionary of Catch Phrases*, edited by Paul Beale, Stein & Day 86

JAMES ("SUNNY JIM") FITZSIMMONS, horse trainer

6 It can be set down in four words: the best of everything. The best hay, oats and water.
> On how to train winning horses, *Life* 18 Jun 63

AL FORMAN, National League umpire

7 I occasionally get birthday cards from fans. But it's often the same message: They hope it's my last.
> *Time* 25 Aug 61

JIM FREY, Chicago Cubs manager

8 I'm only interested in winning ball games and I can't be worrying about whether the sun's out or the moon's out.
> On controversy over night baseball, NY *Times* 17 Jun 85

TOM GORMAN, National League umpire

9 It's a strange business, all jeers and no cheers.
> Recalled on his death, NY *Times* 17 Aug 86

GEORGE HALAS, professional football coach

10 When they boo you, you know they mean *you*.
> On San Francisco, his "favorite booing city," recalled on his death 31 Oct 83

LOU HOLTZ, University of Arkansas football coach

11 The man who complains about the way the ball bounces is likely the one who dropped it.
> LA *Times* 13 Dec 78

12 A lifetime contract for a coach means if you're ahead in the third quarter and moving the ball, they can't fire you.
> NY *Times* 17 Dec 78

FRANK LEAHY, former University of Notre Dame football coach

13 Egotism is the anesthetic that dulls the pain of stupidity.
> *Look* 10 Jan 55

VINCE LOMBARDI, professional football coach

14 A game that requires the constant conjuring of animosity.
> On football, NY *Times* 10 Dec 67

15 Winning isn't everything, it's the only thing.
> Recalled on his death 3 Sep 70

16 Some people try to find things in this game that don't exist but football is only two things—blocking and tackling.
> *ib*

17 A school without football is in danger of deteriorating into a medieval study hall.
> *ib*

BOB MALOIT, Supervisor, Montana State Department of Fish, Wildlife & Parks

18 That way, someone will always come along and tell you to play the black 9 on the red 10.
> On why to play solitaire when you are lost in the woods, NY *Times* 17 Nov 84

BILL PARCELLS, NY Giants coach

19 I *like* linebackers. I *collect* 'em. You can't have too many good ones.
> Quoted by Eric Pooley "True Blue: From Giants to Supermen" *New York* 26 Jan 87

20 Something goes wrong, I yell at them—"Fix it"—whether it's their fault or not. You can only really yell at the players you trust.
> *ib*

21 Don't *worry* about it. It's just a bunch of guys with an odd-shaped ball.
> On football, *ib*

RUSS PERRY, ski resort owner

22 It's a gold mine. We can see the green falling.
> On a heavy snowfall, NY *Times* 7 Dec 81

RICHARD W POUND, International Olympic Committee

23 Watching Carl Lewis run against his countrymen is little short of boring. But put him, as an American, in a race against the rest of the world, and suddenly everything changes.
> "Sport Is a Point of Contact for a Shrinking World" NY *Times* 29 Jun 86

24 Even baseball instinctively recognized that the "World Series" is better than simply a national championship.
> *ib*

LOU SCHULTZ, trainer of Alaskan Huskies

25 First you learn a new language, profanity; and second you learn not to discipline your dogs when you're mad, and that's most of the time when you're training dogs.
> NY *Times* 15 Mar 80

26 "No" is something you use a lot, and when you start using it you have a whip in your hands.
> *ib*

27 A good snow machine will cost $2,000 and last four to five years. With dogs, you've got regenerative powers. Snow machines don't have pups.
> *ib*

WILLIAM E SIMON, President, US Olympic Committee

1 Explaining something sensible to Lord Killanin is akin to explaining something to a cauliflower. The advantage of the cauliflower is that if all else fails, you can always cover it with melted cheese and eat it.
> On former president of International Olympic Committee, NY *Times* 29 Jul 84

CASEY STENGEL, professional baseball manager

2 The team has come along slow but fast.
> On NY Mets, NY *Times* 6 Oct 69

3 There comes a time in every man's life and I've had many of them.
> Recalled on his death 29 Sep 75

4 Managing is getting paid for home runs someone else runs.
> *ib*

5 Sure I played, did you think I was born at the age of 70 sitting in a dugout trying to manage guys like you?
> At age 72 when asked by Mickey Mantle if he had ever played ball, *ib*

6 I was not successful as a ball player, as it was a game of skill.
> *ib*

BARRY SWITZER, University of Oklahoma football coach

7 It was like a heart transplant. We tried to implant college in him but his head rejected it.
> On player who dropped out of school, *Sports Illustrated* 12 Nov 73

GEORGE THOMA, grounds keeper

8 Grass grows by inches but it's killed by feet.
> On care of Kansas City football field, NBC TV 21 Jan 87

MIKE TRAINER, boxing manager

9 [Sugar] Ray Leonard is the kind of guy who's always looking at the edge of the cliff, fascinated as to how close he can get to it. He hasn't gotten to the edge yet.
> *Sports Illustrated* 8 Sep 86

PETER UEBERROTH, baseball commissioner

10 The integrity of the game is everything.
> Urging players to submit to drug tests, NY *Times* 12 May 85

11 Other sports play once a week . . . but this sport is with us every day.
> *ib* 9 Aug 85

12 Baseball is a public trust. Players turn over, owners turn over and certain commissioners turn over. But baseball goes on.
> *ib*

13 A cloud hangs over baseball. It's a cloud called drugs and it's permeated our game.
> *ib* 25 Sep 85

ED VARGO, Supervisor of Umpires, National League

14 You're expected to be perfect the day you start, and then improve.
> *Wall Street Journal* 8 Apr 85

BILL VEECK, Chicago White Sox owner

15 The most beautiful thing in the world is a ballpark filled with people.
> Recalled on his death, NY *Times* 4 Jan 86

DOUG WEAVER, former Kansas State University football coach

16 I'm glad it happened in front of the library. I've always emphasized scholarship.
> On being hanged in effigy, *Sports Illustrated* 9 Jun 86

Observers & Critics

JOEY ADAMS

17 If you break 100, watch your golf. If you break 80, watch your business.
> News summaries 31 Dec 82

PETER ALFANO

18 Coverage of golf's most prestigious tournament . . . was filled with odes to Augusta, plus numerous shots of the picture-postcard setting, bees pollinating and what the host . . . called "azaleas screaming at you and dogwoods whispering to you."
> "A Weekend of Whispering at Augusta" NY *Times* 17 Apr 84

DAVE ANDERSON

19 The perfect going-away gift for a college student-athlete. A dictionary.
> NY *Times* 20 May 86

20 In the America's Cup, you can't go to your backup quarterback. You can't juggle your batting order. . . . You can't fire the manager either, although Iain Murray might not be safe if George Steinbrenner were the principal owner of the *Kookaburra III*.
> On *Kookaburra III*'s loss to the US yacht *Stars & Stripes*, *ib* 3 Feb 87

21 Dennis Conner is Pete Rose in deck shoes.
> On skipper of *Stars & Stripes*, *ib* 5 Feb 87

22 Instead of sailing off into the sunset, he hopes to sail into the next century.
> On Conner's plan to defend the cup in future races, *ib*

ANONYMOUS

23 If God had meant Wimbledon to be played in great weather, he would have put it in Acapulco.
> British tennis official, quoted in *Newsweek* 4 Jul 77

24 I resent the charges that we intentionally blacked out the city to help save the Yankees. The blackout was an act of God, and even God couldn't save the Yankees.
> Spokesman for Consolidated Edison, quoted in news summaries 14 Jul 77

25 In Chicago, the bums are all gentlemen.
> After damage by fans at NYC's Shea Stadium, quoted on NBC TV 18 Sep 86

26 Cricket . . . You have two sides: one out in the field and one in. Each man that's in the side that's in goes out and when he's out he comes in and the next man goes in until he's out.
> Printed on tea towel sold to overseas visitors, quoted by David Winder *Christian Science Monitor* 27 Jan 87

1 When they are all out the side that's out comes in and the side that's been in goes out and tries to get those coming in out.
ib

2 When both sides have been in and out including the not outs, that's the end of the game.
ib

SUSAN BARRANTES

3 They met on the polo fields. But then, doesn't everybody?
Comment by mother of Prince Andrew's fiancée Sarah Ferguson, *Time* 31 Mar 86

JACQUES BARZUN

4 Whoever wants to know the heart and mind of America had better learn baseball, the rules and realities of the game—and do it by watching first some high-school or small-town teams.
Quoted in NY *Times* 31 May 81

DICK BEDDOES

5 The sportswriting confraternity is burdened with hacks who make tin-can gods out of cast-iron jerks.
Quoted in John Robert Colombo ed *Colombo's Concise Canadian Quotations* Hurtig 76

IRA BERKOW

6 If millionaires and corporations want to spend their money trying to drown one another in the Indian Ocean—the movers and shakers are still millionaires and corporations at that level, and the rest of them are glorified galley slaves—then who am I to try to stop them.
On America's Cup races, NY *Times* 10 Feb 87

HUGO L BLACK, Associate Justice, US Supreme Court

7 When I was 40, my doctor advised me that a man in his 40s shouldn't play tennis. I heeded his advice carefully and could hardly wait until I reached 50 to start again.
Think Feb 63

ERMA BOMBECK

8 If a man watches three football games in a row, he should be declared legally dead.
Quoted by Phil Donahue, NBC TV 22 May 86

JOSEPH R BOYLE, President, Amer Medical Assn

9 It seems to us an extraordinarily incongruous thing that we have a sport in which two people are literally paid to get into a ring and try to beat one another to death, or at least beat them into a state of senselessness which will then leave them permanently brain-damaged.
On resolution calling for abolition of boxing, NY *Times* 6 Dec 84

RICHARD BRAUTIGAN

10 The sun was like a huge 50-cent piece that someone had poured kerosene on and then had lit with a match, and said, "Here, hold this while I go get a newspaper," and put the coin in my hand, but never came back.
Trout Fishing in America Delta 69

TOM BROKAW

11 I'm honored that you invited me, especially when for $10,000 and a new convertible you could have had the top running-back prospect at SMU.
As master of ceremonies for NCAA's honors luncheon. *Sports Illustrated* 27 Jan 86

HEYWOOD HALE BROUN

12 Sweat is the cologne of accomplishment.
On rodeos, CBS TV 21 Jul 73

NELSON BRYANT

13 A stream is music and motion: smooth glides, fast, turbulent riffles and deep pools, each posing a special challenge.
"Plumbing the Subtle Joys of Trout Ponds" NY *Times* 28 May 84

14 At some moment in September when there is an intimation of fall—perhaps a certain slant of light across the browning meadow in the hush of a late afternoon when the wind from the sea has suddenly died—I think of the fiercely independent ruffed grouse, a game bird without peer.
"Grouse Hunting Has Its Ritual" *ib* 27 Sep 84

TOM CALLAHAN

15 [He] was blessed to have forgotten his binoculars.
On veteran horse trainer Charlie Whittingham when his horse Ferdinand won the Kentucky Derby, *Time* 12 May 86

16 The America's Cup, yachting's great and garish grail, is a tumorous tureen no handsomer than a camel.
"Going for the Cup" *ib* 9 Feb 87

17 Only a few millionaires with wet bottoms were very disappointed.
On US loss to Australia in 1983, *ib*

JIMMY CANNON

18 A sportswriter is entombed in a prolonged boyhood.
Quoted in Jerome Holtzman ed *No Cheering in the Press Box* Holt 74

JOHN CHEEVER

19 All literary men are Red Sox fans—to be a Yankee fan in a literate society is to endanger your life.
Quoted in *Newsweek* 20 Oct 86

WINSTON CHURCHILL

20 [Playing golf is] like chasing a quinine pill around a cow pasture.
Despairing of his numerous efforts to enjoy golf, quoted by William Manchester *The Last Lion* Little, Brown 83

MARSHALL S COGAN

21 I couldn't buy the Red Sox. They're both in the entertainment business.
On why he bought the "21" Club in NYC, NY *Times* 15 Feb 87

BUD COLLINS

22 Is the quick and stoic stepper . . . going to spawn a secondary event—a maternithon for expectant mothers?
On Joan Benoit's decision to run in the Boston Marathon while pregnant, Boston *Globe* 27 Mar 87

1 Benoit should get one adult first prize ($41,000 and a Mercedes sedan) if she wins, plus one child's portion ($20,500 and a stroller).
> *ib*

ALISTAIR COOKE

2 Golf is an open exhibition of overweening ambition, courage deflated by stupidity, skill soured by a whiff of arrogance.
> Quoted in Bob Chieger and Pat Sullivan eds *Inside Golf* Atheneum 85

3 These humiliations are the essence of the game.
> *ib*

HOWARD COSELL

4 Sports is the toy department of human life.
> News summaries 31 Dec 77

JACQUES COUSTEAU

5 From birth, man carries the weight of gravity on his shoulders. He is bolted to earth. But man has only to sink beneath the surface and he is free.
> *Time* 28 Mar 60

6 Buoyed by water, he can fly in any direction—up, down, sideways—by merely flipping his hand. Under water, man becomes an archangel.
> *ib*

JOHN CROSBY

7 If they hit the ball out, they'd say "Sorry." If they hit it in but too hot for me to handle, they'd say "Sorry." If it was too well hit, they were sorry; too badly hit, they were sorry.
> On playing tennis in England, NY *Herald Tribune* 4 Nov 63

MARIO CUOMO, Governor of NY

8 It was anticipating self-defense.
> On why he once hit a catcher in the face mask while playing minor league baseball, CBS TV 30 Dec 84

RICHARD L CURRY, Judge, Cook County Circuit Court, Chicago

9 Do those who schedule play time
For the games of our national pastime
Have the right to interfere with bedtime
By starting the game at nighttime
Instead of the customary daytime?
> Upholding ban against lighting Chicago's Wrigley Field, *Christian Science Monitor* 3 Apr 85

FRANK DEFORD

10 It almost seemed as if the Statue of Liberty had gone on tour, turning in her torch for a Yonex racket.
> On Martina Navratilova's return to her native Czechoslovakia to lead the US team to victory in the Federation Cup tournament, "Yes, You Can Go Home Again" *Sports Illustrated* 4 Aug 86

DENNIS DIAZ

11 I fished a lot, dove a lot, boated a lot—and made Johnny Walker Red about a quarter of a million dollars richer.
> On why he started breeding horses, including 1985 Kentucky Derby winner Spend a Buck, two years after his retirement at age 38, *People* 20 May 85

PHIL DONAHUE

12 It's like threading a needle while walking on a water bed.
> On detecting drug use by athletes, NBC TV 23 Mar 87

EDWARD, Duke of Windsor

13 I like going there for golf. America's one vast golf course these days.
> Recalled on his death 28 May 72

DWIGHT D EISENHOWER, 34th US President

14 A lot more people beat me now.
> On how his golf game had fared since he left the White House, recalled on his death 28 Mar 69

BILL EMERSON

15 A bicycle does get you there and more . . . And there is always the thin edge of danger to keep you alert and comfortably apprehensive. Dogs become dogs again and snap at your raincoat; potholes become personal. And getting there is all the fun.
> On bicycling, *Saturday Evening Post* 29 Jul 67

WILLIAM FAULKNER

16 There is something about jumping a horse over a fence, something that makes you feel good. Perhaps it's the risk, the gamble. In any event it's a thing I need.
> *National Observer* 3 Feb 64

JAMES FIXX

17 The qualities and capacities that are important in running—such factors as will power, the ability to apply effort during extreme fatigue and the acceptance of pain—have a radiating power that subtly influences one's life.
> *The Complete Book of Running* Random House 77, recalled on his death, *Newsweek* 30 Jul 84

18 [Eventually the] hoopla will die down [and people will] run the same way we brush our teeth—every day, without a fuss.
> *ib*

JOE FLAHERTY

19 When the Dodgers left, it was not only a loss of a team, it was the disruption of a social pattern. . . . a total destruction of a culture.
> Quoted by Peter Golenbock *Bums: An Oral History of the Brooklyn Dodgers* Putnam 84

PHYLLIS ORLIKOFF FLUG, Judge, Queens Criminal Court

20 'Twas Game Six of the Series when out of the sky,
Flew Sergio's parachute, a Met banner held high.
His goal was to spur our home team to success,
Burst Beantown's balloon claiming Sox were the best.
> "Ode to a Criminal Trespasser," written with law secretary Peter Kelly, included with $500 fine and sentencing of actor Michael Sergio, who had parachuted into Shea Stadium during the World Series, NY *Times* 20 Dec 86

21 The fans and the players cheered all they did see,
But not everyone present reacted with glee.
"Reckless endangerment!" the DA spoke stern.
"I recommend jail—there, a lesson he'd learn!"
> *ib*

1 But jail's not the answer in a case of this sort,
To balance the equities is the job of this court.
So a week before Christmas, here in the court,
I sentence defendant for interrupting a sport.
Community service, and a fine you will pay.
Happy holiday to all, and to all a good day.
ib

GERALD R FORD, 38th US President

2 The pat on the back, the arm around the shoulder,
the praise for what was done right and the sympa-
thetic nod for what wasn't are as much a part of golf
as life itself.
At dedication of World Golf Hall of Fame, Pinehurst
NC, NY *Times* 12 Sep 74

3 I would hope that understanding and reconciliation
are not limited to the 19th hole alone.
ib

ASHRITA FURMAN

4 Everything is in slow motion down there and silent.
It could replace psychotherapy.
On aqua pogo, NY *Times* 22 Mar 86

PAUL GALLICO

5 If there is any larceny in a man, golf will bring it out.
NY *Times* 6 Mar 77

WILLIAM E GEIST

6 The crack of a bat sounded amplified in cavernous
Yankee Stadium, sprinkled lightly with fans on a
cool September evening.
"At Yankee Stadium, a Wistful September Song" NY
Times 22 Sep 84

CLARA GERMANI

7 Their tails are high and tongues awag—the twin banners of sled dog contentment.
On Alaskan Huskies in thousand-mile sled dog race following the Klondike gold rush trail, *Christian Science
Monitor* 29 Jan 85

RICHARD GILMAN

8 Being a sports fan is a complex matter, in part irrational . . . but not unworthy . . . a relief from the
seriousness of the real world, with its unending pressures and often grave obligations.
"The Wounded Giant Regains His Dignity" NY *Times*
25 Jan 87

9 There's an appreciation, not unlike that for dancers
or tightrope walkers, of the body undergoing tests
and coming through them by courage and technique;
a desire for "clean" results.
ib

10 The Giants will always represent New York [in] the
sort of in-your-face move that being in the Super
Bowl presents to the way the rest of the country
mostly thinks of us: huge, cold, rich, conceited, *unnatural*, deserving therefore of all our misfortunes.
ib

LUIS GONZÁLEZ SEARA

11 Some violent spectacle is normal in most countries.
On bullfighting as compared to boxing in the US and fox
hunting in Great Britain, NY *Times* 17 Sep 85

HANK GREENBERG

12 The Pied Piper . . . enjoyed people enjoying themselves. He was colorblind and race-blind and relig-
ion-blind.
On Bill Veeck, owner of Chicago White Sox, NY *Times*
4 Jan 86

MAURICE GRIMAUD, Prefect of Paris Police

13 Not to open the hunting season on the pretext that
there is no game would be as if one gave up cele-
brating Christmas because there was not enough
snow to go by sleigh to midnight Mass.
NY *Times* 3 Oct 68

DAG HAMMARSKJÖLD, UN Secretary-General

14 Never measure the height of a mountain until you
have reached the top. Then you will see how low it
was.
On his love of mountain climbing, *Markings* Knopf 64

SANFORD HANSELL, bowling center manager

15 The bowling alley is the poor man's country club.
NY *Times* 11 May 75

THEODORE M HESBURGH, President, Notre Dame

16 The fundamental difference between intercollegiate
and professional athletics is that in college the players are supposed to be students first and foremost.
This does not mean that they should all be Phi Beta
Kappas or physics majors, but neither should they
be subnormal students majoring in Ping-Pong.
Sports Illustrated 27 Sep 54

HERBERT HOOVER, 31st US President

17 Fishing is much more than fish. . . . It is the great
occasion when we may return to the fine simplicity
of our forefathers.
Recalled on his 90th birthday, NY *Times* 9 Aug 64

18 All men are equal before fish.
ib

BOB HOPE

19 If you watch a game, it's fun. If you play it, it's
recreation. If you work at it, it's golf.
Reader's Digest Oct 58

ROGER KAHN

20 A major league baseball team is a collection of 25
youngish men who have made the major leagues and
discovered that in spite of it, life remains distress-
ingly short of ideal. A bad knee still throbs before a
rainstorm. Too much beer still makes for an unpleasant fullness. Girls still insist on tiresome pre-
liminaries. And now there is a wife who gets headaches or a baby who has colic.
"Intellectuals and Ball Players" *American Scholar* 3
Nov 57

21 Football is violence and cold weather and sex and
college rye. Horse racing is animated roulette. Boxing is smoky halls and kidneys battered until they
bleed. Tennis and golf are best played, not watched.
ib

1 Basketball, hockey and track meets are action heaped upon action, climax upon climax, until the onlooker's responses become deadened. Baseball is for the leisurely afternoons of summer and for the unchanging dreams.
> *ib*

2 I was showing early symptoms of becoming a professional baseball man. I was lying to the press.
> On becoming part owner of minor league baseball team, *Good Enough to Dream* Doubleday 85, quoted in NY *Times* 8 Sep 85

STANLEY KUBRICK

3 You sit at the board and suddenly your heart leaps. Your hand trembles to pick up the piece and move it. But what chess teaches you is that you must sit there calmly and think about whether it's really a good idea and whether there are other, better ideas.
> *Newsweek* 26 May 80

CHARLES KURALT

4 If there are bleachers in heaven and a warm sun, that's where you'll find Bill Veeck.
> On owner of Chicago White Sox, *Sunday Morning* CBS TV 27 Dec 86

JACK LEMMON

5 If you think it's hard to meet new people, try picking up the wrong golf ball.
> *Sports Illustrated* 9 Dec 85

JOHN LEONARD

6 Baseball happens to be a game of cumulative tension but football, basketball and hockey are played with hand grenades and machine guns.
> NY *Times* 2 Nov 75

LONDON TIMES

7 [The Bears victory] was almost incidental to the three-and-a-half hours of novelty, noise and relentless sideshows . . . in which two teams of padded and helmeted carnivores, looking like extras from a low-budget space epic, run headlong into each other like rival stags at the rut.
> On exhibition game between the Chicago Bears and the Dallas Cowboys at Wembley Stadium, quoted in *Sports Illustrated* 18 Aug 86

8 American football is an occasion at which dancing girls, bands, tactical huddles and television commercial breaks are interrupted by short bursts of play.
> *ib*

OREN LYONS JR, adviser to chiefs of the Onondaga Nation

9 When you talk about lacrosse, you talk about the lifeblood of the Six Nations. The game is ingrained into our culture and our system and our lives.
> NY *Times* 15 Jun 86

10 There are two times of the year that stir the blood. In the fall, for the hunt, and now for lacrosse.
> *ib*

11 When you look at where team sports are going, the National Football League is turning into organized warfare.
> *ib*

CHARLES BLAIR MACDONALD, golf course architect

12 The object of a bunker or trap is not only to punish a physical mistake, to punish lack of control, but also to punish pride and egotism.
> Quoted in Bob Chieger and Pat Sullivan eds *Inside Golf* Atheneum 85

MELVIN MADDOCKS

13 Watching baseball under the lights is like observing dogs indoors, at a pedigree show. In both instances, the environment is too controlled to suit the species.
> "Baseball—The Difference between Night and Day" *Christian Science Monitor* 3 Apr 85

DEAN MARTIN

14 If you drink, don't drive. Don't even putt.
> News summaries 31 Dec 79

JOHN ALLAN MAY

15 The king and queen of games [hold] court.
> On tennis, "100th Wimbledon: Masterpiece Tennis Theater" *Christian Science Monitor* 23 Jun 86

GORDON McLENDON, sportscaster

16 What harm is there in making 100,000 people happy on a hot summer afternoon?
> On "fictionalizing" baseball games, recalled on his death, *Sports Illustrated* 29 Sep 86

H L MENCKEN

17 I hate all sports as rabidly as a person who likes sports hates common sense.
> Recalled on his death 29 Jan 56

PAUL MOORE, Episcopal Bishop of NY

18 This summer I tried to take up golf, after many years of avoiding that particular temptation to blasphemy.
> To diocesan convention 21 Oct 86

JAMIE MURPHY

19 Chess, like mathematics and music, is a nursery for child prodigies.
> On Budapest's chess-playing Polgar sisters, *Time* 21 Apr 86

OGDEN NASH

20 Basketball, a game which won't be fit for people until they set the basket umbilicus-high and return the giraffes to the zoo.
> *The Old Dog Barks Backward* Little, Brown 72

NEW JERSEY STATE COMMISSION OF INVESTIGATION

21 No truly viable social or economic benefits can be derived from such legal savagery.
> On boxing, NY *Times* 12 Dec 85

JOYCE CAROL OATES

22 To be knocked out doesn't mean what it seems. A boxer does not have to get up.
> Quoted by George Vecsey NY *Times* 4 Mar 87

23 [Boxing is] a celebration of the lost religion of masculinity all the more trenchant for its being lost.
> *On Boxing* Doubleday 87, quoted in *Newsweek* 9 Mar 87

24 [The] third man in the ring makes boxing possible.
> On introduction of referees in late 19th century, *ib*

GEORGE ORWELL

1 Serious sport has nothing to do with fair play. It is bound up with hatred, jealousy, boastfulness, disregard of all rules and sadistic pleasure in witnessing violence. In other words, it is war minus the shooting.
Shooting an Elephant Harcourt, Brace 50

DAN PARKER

2 The reason the Yankees never lay an egg is because they don't operate on chicken feed.
Sports Illustrated 7 Apr 58

LESTER B PEARSON, Prime Minister of Canada

3 This fastest of all games has become almost as much of a national symbol as the maple leaf or the beaver.
On hockey, quoted in John Robert Colombo ed *Colombo's Canadian Quotations* Hurtig 74

4 Most young Canadians . . . are born with skates on their feet rather than with silver spoons in their mouths.
ib

GEORGE PLIMPTON

5 The smaller the ball used in the sport, the better the book.
Theory on why books about football don't sell as well as those about baseball, tennis or golf, NY *Times* 25 Sep 86

MARTIN QUIGLEY

6 The story of the curve ball is the story of the game itself. Some would say of life itself.
The Curve Ball in American Baseball History Algonquin 84

STEVE RATINETZ

7 I only save decent fights. . . . I can't be bothered with every two-minute penalty.
On his videotape collection of 120 hours of televised hockey fights, NY *Times* 2 Feb 86

RONALD REAGAN, 40th US President

8 There's nothing better for the inside of a man than the outside of a horse.
On horseback riding, NY *Times* 2 Oct 81

9 It ought to be remembered by all [that the Olympic] Games more than 2,000 years ago started as a means of bringing peace between the Greek city-states. And . . . if a war was going on, they called [it] off . . . I wish we were that civilized.
On Soviet withdrawal from 1984 Olympics, *Time* 21 May 84

10 You will be competing against athletes from many nations. But, most important, you are competing against yourself. All we expect is for you to do your very best, to push yourself just one second faster, one notch higher, one inch further.
To US Olympic team 28 Jul 84

HARRY REASONER

11 Statistics are to baseball what a flaky crust is to Mom's apple pie.
60 Minutes CBS TV 20 Oct 85

CHRIS REDMAN

12 When icicles hang by the wall and blood is nipped and ways be foul, when the Great Lakes freeze into ice packs the size of Rhode Island and shipping is stilled, then folks in the Midwest are moved to fish through the ice, a curious, seasonal madness for which there is no known cure except spring.
Time 16 Feb 81

GRANTLAND RICE

13 For when the One Great Scorer comes
To write against your name,
He marks—not that you won or lost—
But how you played the game.
Recalled on his death 13 Jul 54

JIM ROBBINS

14 Throughout the city, the talk now is of the kill or of the near kill. Some of it may even be true.
On Helena MT during hunting season, NY *Times* 17 Nov 84

SYBIL ROBINSON

15 Many manufacturers are competing for your foot.
On production of running shoes, news summaries 30 Jun 86

JOHN D ROCKEFELLER

16 Golf courses are the best place to observe ministers, but none of them are above cheating a bit.
Quoted by William Manchester *A Rockefeller Family Portrait* Little, Brown 59

WILLIAM SAFIRE

17 The perfect Christmas gift for a sportscaster, as all fans of sports clichés know, is a scoreless tie.
NY *Times* 6 Nov 83

HAROLD SEGALL

18 Golf is not just exercise; it is an adventure, a romance. . . . a Shakespeare play in which disaster and comedy are intertwined [and] you have to live with the consequences of each action.
"Golf Is a Funny Game; Tennis Not So" NY *Times* 15 Jun 86

SUE SIMMONS

19 The cup that went down under has now come up again.
On regaining America's Cup after 1983 loss to Australia, NBC TV 9 Feb 87

RED SMITH

20 He had splendid conformation—broad shoulders, white hair and erect carriage—and was beautifully turned out in an ensemble of rich brown. One was inclined to hope he would, in the end, award first prize to himself.
On a judge at a dog show, *Newsweek* 21 Apr 58

TED SOLOTAROFF

21 A professional football team warms up grimly and disparately, like an army on maneuvers: the ground troops here, the tanks there, the artillery and air force over there.
NY *Times* 11 Jun 72

1 Basketball teams, after the perfunctory lay-up drill, fall into the crowded isolation and personal style of 10 city kids shooting at the same basket or playing one-on-one.
> *ib*

RAY SONS

2 The best use of fat since the invention of bacon.
> On Chicago Bears rookie William "Refrigerator" Perry, *Time* 30 Dec 85

JOHN STEINBECK

3 Sectional football games have the glory and the despair of war, and when a Texas team takes the field against a foreign state, it is an army with banners.
> *Travels with Charlie* Viking 62, quoted in NY *Times* 5 Mar 87

GEORGE STEINER

4 Chess may be the deepest, least exhaustible of pastimes, but it is nothing more. As for a chess genius, he is a human being who focuses vast, little-understood mental gifts and labors on an ultimately trivial human enterprise.
> *Fields of Force* Viking 74

PHIL STONE

5 He looks like he's just been told there's no cannelloni in the world.
> On LA Dodgers manager Tommy Lasorda's dejection after a loss to the San Francisco Giants, *Sports Illustrated* 12 May 86

E M SWIFT

6 A traveling traffic jam of one-night stands.
> On the 23-day Tour de France bicycle race, "An American Takes Paris" *Sports Illustrated* 4 Aug 86

DALE TALLON

7 I wouldn't say it's cold, but every year Winnipeg's athlete of the year is an ice fisherman.
> On covering hockey game between Chicago Blackhawks and Winnipeg Jets, *Sports Illustrated* 22 Dec 86

PATRICK THOMPSON

8 He rides in the game like heavy cavalry getting into position for the assault. . . . trots about, keenly watchful, biding his time, a master of tactics and strategy.
> On polo style of Winston Churchill, quoted by William Manchester *The Last Lion* Little, Brown 83

TIME MAGAZINE

9 Ideally, the umpire should combine the integrity of a Supreme Court justice, the physical agility of an acrobat, the endurance of Job and the imperturbability of Buddha.
> "The Villains in Blue" 25 Aug 61

TED TURNER

10 Sports is like a war without the killing.
> *60 Minutes* CBS TV 24 Jul 77

UNITED STATES DEPARTMENT OF COMMERCE

11 Baseball, like cricket, is an elegant and leisurely summer game during which tension builds up slowly.
> Travel information booklet prepared for British tourists, quoted in NY *Times* 9 Aug 79

UNITED STATES INFORMATION AGENCY

12 Americans are achievers. They are obsessed with records of achievement in sports and they keep business achievement charts on their office walls and sports awards displayed in their homes.
> Booklet for foreign students, quoted in NY *Times* 15 Apr 85

GEORGE VECSEY

13 For about 15 minutes, Doug Flutie was the toast of New York—not just the toast but the challah and the pita and the croissants, too.
> On the day financier Donald J Trump signed Flutie to play for the New Jersey Generals, NY *Times* 28 Sep 86

JOHNNY WALKER

14 The players on the Maryland football team all made straight As. Their Bs were a little crooked.
> *Sports Illustrated* 23 Dec 85

EARL WARREN, former Chief Justice, US Supreme Court

15 I always turn to the sports page first. . . . They record people's accomplishments; the front page, nothing but man's failure.
> Quoted by Marabel Morgan *Total Joy* Revell 76

GEORGE F WILL

16 It is committee meetings, called huddles, separated by outbursts of violence.
> On football, *Newsweek* 6 Sep 76

17 Scholars concede but cannot explain the amazing chemistry of Cub fans' loyalty. But their unique steadfastness through thin and thin has something to do with the team's Franciscan simplicity.
> On the Chicago Cubs, *ib* 27 Jun 77

THEATER

Actors & Actresses

TALLULAH BANKHEAD

18 Nobody can be exactly like me. Sometimes even I have trouble doing it.
> News summaries 1 Jan 51

19 If you really want to help the American theater, don't be an actress, dahling. Be an audience.
> *ib* 31 Dec 52

20 Dahling Congressman Boykin: 10 AM is an unprecedented time for a child of the grease paint to cope with the sandman.
> Response to invitation to speak at a fund-raising rally for a new civic auditorium in Washington DC, *ib* 15 Jan 55

ETHEL BARRYMORE

21 I never let them cough. They wouldn't dare.
> On control of audiences during dramatic moments, NY *Post* 7 Jun 56

INGRID BERGMAN

22 I have had my different husbands, my families. I am fond of them all and I visit them all. But deep inside me there is the feeling that I belong to show business.
> Interview after opening in a Broadway play, NY *Times* 20 Apr 75

SHIRLEY BOOTH

1 Actors should be overheard, not listened to, and the audience is 50 percent of the performance.
News summaries 13 Dec 54

YUL BRYNNER

2 I am just a nice, clean-cut Mongolian boy.
Self-description, NY *Post* 24 Sep 56

3 When I am dead and buried, on my tombstone I would like to have it written, "I have arrived." Because when you feel that you have arrived, you are dead.
ib 30 Sep 56

LYNNE CARTER

4 I much prefer being a man. Women have to spend so much time pulling themselves together, and their shoes kill your feet.
On his appearance as a female impersonator at Carnegie Hall, recalled on his death 11 Jan 85

BETTE DAVIS

5 Wave after wave of love flooded the stage and washed over me, the beginning of the one great durable romance of my life.
On her first solo curtain call, *People* 21 Mar 77

6 You can't say I didn't fall for you.
To the audience after fainting on stage during Broadway opening of *Two's Company*, quoted by B D Hyman *My Mother's Keeper* Morrow 85

RUTH DRAPER, monologist

7 Try to look at everything through the eyes of a child.
To Alec McCowen, recalled on the actor's recitation of St Mark's Gospel before 400 Anglican bishops, quoted by James B Simpson and Edward M Story *Discerning God's Will* Nelson 79

ALBERT FINNEY

8 To be a character who feels a deep emotion, one must go into the memory's vault and mix in a sad memory from one's own life.
International Herald Tribune 29 Mar 85

LYNN FONTANNE

9 I lied to everybody. I lie very well, being an actress, naturally.
On refusal to reveal her true age, even to her husband Alfred Lunt, NY *Times* 24 Apr 78

10 We can be bought, but we can't be bored.
On offers from Hollywood, interview on Milwaukee's WMVS TV, aired in NYC 22 Jun 80

JUDY GARLAND

11 You are never so *alone* as when you are ill on stage. The most nightmarish feeling in the world is suddenly to feel like throwing up in front of four thousand people.
Life 2 Jun 61

JOHN GIELGUD

12 Acting is half shame, half glory. Shame at exhibiting yourself, glory when you can forget yourself.
Quoted in Ronald Harwood ed *The Ages of Gielgud* Limelight 84

13 Your English style will no doubt put all the other gentlemen to bed. I speak figuratively, of course.
On Cecil Beaton's decision to act in a production of *Lady Windermere's Fan*, quoted by Hugo Vickers *Cecil Beaton* Little, Brown 85

ALEC GUINNESS

14 An actor is totally vulnerable. . . . his total personality is exposed to critical judgment—his intellect, his bearing, his diction, his whole appearance. In short, his ego.
NY *Times* 17 May 64

15 A superb tenor voice, like a silver trumpet muffled in silk.
On John Gielgud, quoted in Ronald Harwood ed *The Ages of Gielgud* Limelight 84

16 An actor is . . . at his best a kind of unfrocked priest who, for an hour or two, can call on heaven and hell to mesmerize a group of innocents.
Blessings in Disguise Knopf 86

17 She flung herself full-length on the stage, drummed with her feet and, taking the corner of a small Persian rug in her teeth, worried it [while] I sat rigid and appalled on the sofa, pressed back against the chintz cushions.
Reaction at an Edith Evans tantrum, *ib*

KENNETH HAIGH

18 You need three things in the theater—the play, the actors and the audience, and each must give something.
Theatre Arts Jul 58

CEDRIC HARDWICKE

19 When [actors] are talking, they are servants of the dramatist. It is what they can show the audience when they are not talking that reveals the fine actor.
Theatre Arts Feb 58

20 Actors must practice restraint, else think what might happen in a love scene.
NY *Herald Tribune* 7 Aug 64

JULIE HARRIS

21 God comes to us in theater [in] the way we communicate with each other, whether it be a symphony orchestra, or a wonderful ballet, or a beautiful painting, or a play. It's a way of expressing our humanity.
Christian Science Monitor 15 May 79

REX HARRISON

22 Whatever it is that makes a person charming, it needs to remain a mystery . . . once the charmer is aware of a mannerism or characteristic that others find charming, it ceases to be a mannerism and becomes an affectation. And good Lord, there is nothing less charming than affectations!
LA *Herald-Examiner* 24 Jun 78

HELEN HAYES

23 An actress's life is so transitory—suddenly you're a building.
On Broadway theater named in her honor, news summaries 9 Nov 55

KATHARINE HEPBURN

1 Drive on. We'll sweep up the blood later!

> To her chauffeur, on fans at a London theater, quoted by Anne Edwards *A Remarkable Woman* Morrow 85

EDWARD EVERETT HORTON

2 A low trick I hate to stoop to is tying and untying my shoelaces. It seems to fascinate audiences . . . probably because so many women in the audience have their shoes off, or wish they did.

> On scene-stealing, news summaries 14 Dec 54

JOSEPHINE HULL

3 Playing Shakespeare is so tiring. You never get a chance to sit down unless you're a king.

> *Time* 16 Nov 53

MARGARET LEIGHTON

4 It's like being in a dark tunnel, walking over treacle.

> On stage fright, NY *Times* 18 May 64

THIERRY LE LURON

5 My rifle always remains the same. It's the pigeons who change.

> Denying that political motives prompt his celebrated imitations of French politicians, recalled on his death, NY *Times* 14 Nov 86

JACK LEMMON

6 I won't quit until I get run over by a truck, a producer or a critic.

> On returning to the stage, *Newsweek* 5 May 86

MARCEL MARCEAU

7 I have designed my style pantomimes as white ink drawings on black backgrounds, so that man's destiny appears as a thread lost in an endless labyrinth. . . . I have tried to shed some gleams of light on the shadow of man startled by his anguish.

> *Wall Street Journal* 19 Nov 65

MARY MARTIN

8 They hadn't even started writing it, but it didn't matter; I knew that anything that had that song in it would be beautiful.

> On impact of Rodgers and Hammerstein's "Some Enchanted Evening" for the musical *South Pacific*, NY *Times* 26 Feb 87

LAURENCE OLIVIER

9 When you're a young man, Macbeth is a character part. When you're older, it's a straight part.

> On playing Macbeth at age 30 and age 48, *Theatre Arts* May 58

10 Autograph-hunting is the most unattractive manifestation of sex-starved curiosity.

> NY *Journal-American* 9 Apr 65

11 I don't know what is better than the work that is given to the actor—to teach the human heart the knowledge of itself.

> *Look* 27 Jan 70

12 I'm rather bored by the subject—meaning me. It's a sort of a yoke, but at times you know, a yoke is a kind of comfort. And it's always there.

> Interviewed at age 72, NY *Times* 27 Feb 80

13 I'd like [people] to remember me for a diligent . . . expert workman. . . . I think a poet is a workman. I think Shakespeare was a workman. And God's a workman. I don't think there's anything better than a workman.

> *Christian Science Monitor* 16 Jun 80

14 The office of drama is to exercise, possibly to exhaust, human emotions. The purpose of comedy is to tickle those emotions into an expression of light relief; of tragedy, to wound them and bring the relief of tears. Disgust and terror are the other points of the compass.

> *Confessions of an Actor* Simon & Schuster 82

15 There is a spirit in us . . . that makes our brass to blare and our cymbals crash—all, of course, supported by the practicalities of trained lung power, throat, heart, guts.

> *ib*

16 I believe in the theater; I believe in it as the first glamorizer of thought. It restores dramatic dynamics and their relations to life size.

> First address in House of Lords, 1971, *ib*

17 I believe that in a great city, or even in a small city or a village, a great theater is the outward and visible sign of an inward and probable culture.

> *ib*

18 It's just like a nursery game of make-believe.

> On the theater, *60 Minutes* CBS TV 2 Jan 83

19 Surely we have always acted; it is an instinct inherent in all of us. Some of us are better at it than others, but we all do it.

> "Olivier on Acting" NY *Times* 26 Oct 86

20 We have all, at one time or another, been performers, and many of us still are—politicians, playboys, cardinals and kings.

> *ib*

21 We ape, we mimic, we mock. We act.

> *ib*

22 The actor should be able to create the universe in the palm of his hand.

> *ib*

23 I often think that could we creep behind the actor's eyes, we would find an attic of forgotten toys and a copy of the Domesday Book.

> *ib*

24 Lead the audience by the nose to the thought.

> *ib*

25 I should be soaring away with my head tilted slightly toward the gods, feeding on the caviar of Shakespeare. . . . An actor must act.

> On resentment at his forced retirement from the stage after he was fired by Britain's National Theater, *On Acting* Simon & Schuster 86, quoted by Robert Brustein *New Republic* 3 Nov 86

26 My stage successes have provided me with the greatest moments outside myself, my film successes the best moments, professionally, within myself.

> *ib*

27 If he was lost for a moment, he would dive straight back into its honey.

> On belief that John Gielgud was infatuated with his own voice, *ib*

RALPH RICHARDSON

1 You've got to perform in a role hundreds of times. In keeping it fresh one can become a large, madly humming, demented refrigerator.
Time 21 Aug 78

2 I know he's a boring old scoutmaster on the face of it, but being that it's Shakespeare, he's the exaltation of all scoutmasters. He's the cold-bath king, and you have to glory in it.
To Laurence Olivier on title role in *Henry V*, quoted by Olivier *Confessions of an Actor* Simon & Schuster 82

3 Actors are the jockeys of literature. Others supply the horses, the plays, and we simply make them run.
Recalled on his death 10 Oct 83

4 Acting is merely the art of keeping a large group of people from coughing.
Quoted in *Time* 24 Oct 83

CYRIL RITCHARD

5 Two thousand dear ladies. All very careful and diplomatic with one another. Ever so sweet and catty, you know. I can hear that sweet-and-catty sound through the curtain while the house lights are still on. They all applaud with their gloves on, never too hard or too much. They're busier watching each other than the show.
On matinee audiences, *Holiday* Sep 60

JASON ROBARDS

6 All the abstract nouns that are involved become more real—forgiveness, pity, peace, love, hate, all become much deeper in the outcome.
On reviving role he played nearly 30 years earlier in Eugene O'Neill's *The Iceman Cometh*, NY Times 23 Jul 85

7 Acting is make-believe. . . . If you make believe well enough, [audiences] make believe, too.
On being honored at Library of Congress dinner, *ib*

BARBRA STREISAND

8 What does it mean when people applaud? . . . Should I give 'em money? Say thank you? Lift my dress? The *lack* of applause—that I can respond to.
Life 22 May 64

9 They're called "angels" because they're in heaven until the reviews come out.
On financial backers, *Playbill* Oct 69

LAURETTE TAYLOR

10 I sometimes forget a face, but I *never* forget a back.
On meeting a man who had walked out during a performance, quoted in Clifton Fadiman comp *The Little, Brown Book of Anecdotes* Little, Brown 85

SYBIL THORNDIKE

11 It's only people who are hysterical who can play hysterical parts.
On Noel Coward's stage roles, quoted by John Lahr "The Politics of Charm" *Harper's* Oct 82

PETER USTINOV

12 Critics search for ages for the wrong word, which, to give them credit, they eventually find.
BBC Radio Feb 52

13 By increasing the size of the keyhole, today's playwrights are in danger of doing away with the door.
Christian Science Monitor 14 Nov 62

14 Playwrights are like men who have been dining for a month in an Indian restaurant. After eating curry night after night, they deny the existence of asparagus.
ib

SHELLEY WINTERS

15 I think on-stage nudity is disgusting, shameful and damaging to all things American. But if I were 22 with a great body, it would be artistic, tasteful, patriotic and a progressive religious experience.
News summaries 13 Sep 65

ESTELLE WINWOOD

16 My advice to actresses is don't worry about your looks. The very thing that makes you unhappy in your appearance may be the one thing to make you a star.
Prompted by the recollection that as a child her classmates called her "Cow Eyes," recalled on her death 20 Jun 84

ED WYNN

17 A comedian is not a man who says funny things. A comedian is one who says things funny.
Recalled on his death, *Time* 1 Jul 66

Playwrights, Producers & Directors

MARCEL ACHARD

18 The career of a writer is comparable to that of a woman of easy virtue. You write first for pleasure, later for the pleasure of others and finally for money.
Quote 3 Jul 66

EDWARD ALBEE

19 One must let the play happen to one; one must let the mind loose to respond as it will, to receive impressions, to sense rather than know, to gather rather than immediately understand.
On his play *Tiny Alice*, quoted in *National Observer* 5 Apr 65

20 I'm not suggesting that the play is without fault; all of my plays are imperfect, I'm rather happy to say— it leaves me something to do.
ib

21 Good writers define reality; bad ones merely restate it. A good writer turns fact into truth; a bad writer will, more often than not, accomplish the opposite.
Saturday Review 4 May 66

22 A play is fiction—and fiction is fact distilled into truth.
NY *Times* 18 Sep 66

23 Your source material is the people you know, not those you don't know, [but] every character is an extension of the author's own personality.
ib

24 What people really want in the theater is fantasy involvement and not reality involvement.
Quote 4 Jun 67

1 Oh, Mother, you go home too early!

> When asked by his mother if people really talk to each other as they do in *Who's Afraid of Virginia Woolf?* interview 24 Dec 67

ROBERT ANDERSON

2 The mission of the playwright . . . is to look in his heart and write, to write whatever concerns him at the moment; to write with passion and conviction. Of course the measure of the man will be the measure of the play.

> *Theatre Arts* Mar 58

JEAN ANOUILH

3 Talent is like a faucet, while it is open, one must write.

> NY *Times* 2 Oct 60

4 Inspiration is a farce that poets have invented to give themselves importance.

> *ib*

EMANUEL AZENBERG

5 This is an industry that doesn't have the common cold. . . . It has cholera.

> Quoted by Samuel G Freedman "The Last of the Red-Hot Producers" NY *Times* 2 Jun 85

6 The short-term problems are economic—royalties, unions, irresponsible management. The long-term problems are artistic, and they started 40 years ago with the advent of television and the upgrading of films.

> *ib*

7 Will the theater disappear? No. Is it healthy? Also no.

> *ib*

CECIL BEATON

8 Be daring, be different, be impractical; be anything that will assert integrity of purpose and imaginative vision against the play-it-safers, the creatures of the commonplace, the slaves of the ordinary. Routines have their purposes, but the merely routine is the hidden enemy of high art.

> Advice to theatrical designers, "The Secret of How to Startle" *Theatre Arts* May 57

9 I have the *worst* ear for criticism; even when I have created a stage set I like, I *always* hear the woman in the back of the dress circle who says she doesn't like blue.

> BBC TV 18 Feb 62

SAMUEL BECKETT

10 [James] Joyce was a synthesizer, trying to bring in as much as he could. I am an analyzer, trying to leave out as much as I can.

> Quoted by Mel Gussow "Beckett at 75—An Appraisal" NY *Times* 19 Apr 81

11 My characters have nothing. I'm working with impotence, ignorance. . . . that whole zone of being that has always been set aside by artists as something unusable—something by definition incompatible with art.

> London *Times* 10 Apr 86

12 Nothing matters but the writing. There has been nothing else worthwhile. . . . a stain upon the silence.

> *ib*

BRENDAN BEHAN

13 Ninety-seven saint days a year wouldn't affect the theater, but two Yom Kippurs would ruin it.

> Recalled on his death, NY *Post* 22 Mar 64

14 Critics are like eunuchs in a harem. They're there every night, they see it done every night, they see how it should be done every night, but they can't do it themselves.

> Quoted by Gyles Brandreth *Great Theatrical Disasters* St Martin's 83

ALINE BERNSTEIN

15 When I say I like raw scenery, it is much the same as a cook feels about the assembled ingredients of her dishes—a bowl of eggs, a quart of cream, the beauty of an uncooked cabbage or a basket of tomatoes.

> On her set designs, quoted by Carole Klein *Aline* Harper & Row 79

ALLAN CARR

16 It's *Charley's Aunt* and *The Odd Couple* rolled into one.

> On his production of *La Cage aux Folles*, interview with Merv Griffin WNYW TV 15 Nov 84

JEAN COCTEAU

17 Commissions suit me. They set limits. Jean Marais dared me to write play in which he would not speak in the first act, would weep for joy in the second and in the last would fall backward down a flight of stairs.

> On *The Eagle Has Two Heads*, quoted in *Vogue* May 83

NOEL COWARD

18 *Private Lives* was described variously as "tenuous, thin, brittle, gossamer, iridescent and delightfully daring," all of which connoted to the public mind cocktails, evening dress, repartee and irreverent allusions to copulation, thereby causing a gratifying number of respectable people to queue up at the box office.

> Recalled on his death 26 Mar 73

19 If you must have motivation, think of your paycheck on Friday.

> Advice to actors, *ib*

20 Consider the public. . . . Never fear it nor despise it. Coax it, charm it, interest it, stimulate it, shock it now and then if you must, make it laugh, make it cry, but above all . . . never, never, never bore the living hell out of it.

> Advice to playwrights, *ib*

21 Work is much more fun than fun.

> *ib*

22 Someday I suspect, when Jesus has definitely got me for a sunbeam, my works may be adequately assessed.

> Quoted by Cole Lesley *Remembered Laughter* Knopf 76

EDWARD GORDON CRAIG

1 That is what the title of artist means: one who perceives more than his fellows, and who records more than he has seen.
On the Art of the Theater Theatre Arts Books 57

BILL C DAVIS

2 Audiences cry in the theater when people make a hard choice—for life.
On his plays *Mass Appeal* and *End Zone*, NY *Times* 30 Dec 84

PATRICK DENNIS

3 No, Virginia, there is no Auntie Mame, she is a distillation and a moonbeam and nothing more.
On the eve of Broadway première of *Auntie Mame*, NY *Times* 28 Oct 56

4 Auntie Mame [is] a froth of whipped cream and champagne and daydreams and Nuit de Noël perfume. She's not mortal at all.
ib

HOWARD DIETZ

5 A day away from Tallulah is like a month in the country.
On Tallulah Bankhead, news summaries 31 Dec 68

JOSEPH J DIOGUARDI

6 You can't kiss an oil well.
On his investment in a play, NY *Times* 17 Aug 83

JAMES DUFF

7 I realized there was something I didn't quite like in myself that I didn't want to hear about.
On expressing his feelings about the Vietnam War in *Home Front*, NY *Times* 30 Dec 84

T S ELIOT

8 My greatest trouble is getting the curtain up and down.
On writing plays, *Time* 6 Mar 50

9 Playwriting gets into your blood and you can't stop it. At least not until the producers or the public tell you to.
Quote 17 Dec 59

10 A play should give you something to think about. When I see a play and understand it the first time, then I know it can't be much good.
NY *Post* 22 Sep 63

ZELDA FICHANDLER, Director, Arena Stage, Washington DC

11 There is a hunger to see the human presence acted out. As long as that need remains, people will find a way to do theater.
Christian Science Monitor 5 Jun 86

CHRISTOPHER FRY

12 In my plays I want to look at life—at the commonplace of existence—as if we had just turned a corner and run into it for the first time.
Time 20 Nov 50

13 In tragedy every moment is eternity; in comedy, eternity is a moment.
ib

JOHN GOODWIN, Producer, National Theater, London

14 Theater people work by instinct. . . . I've never known a really calculated artistic decision.
Christian Science Monitor 11 Feb 85

PETER HALL

15 Whoever becomes the head of the National Theater finds himself in a position like that of Nelson's Column—pigeons dump on you because you're there.
On directing Britain's National Theater, *W* 6 Apr 84

TERRY HANDS, Director, Royal Shakespeare Company

16 Our contention has always been that Shakespeare is our greatest living author. If he can survive a season on Broadway, he must be.
On production of *Much Ado about Nothing*, NY *Times* 6 Jan 85

17 My real pleasure is that 4 times a week 1,800 people are standing up and shouting on Broadway for an author who died hundreds of years ago.
ib

MOSS HART

18 Charity in the theater begins and ends with those who have a play opening within a week of one's own.
Act One Random House 59

MICHAEL HASTINGS

19 She has been Stalinized out of literary history on the theory that she messed up Eliot's life.
On why he wrote *Tom and Viv* about T S Eliot and his wife Vivien, NY *Times* 3 Feb 85

BEN HECHT

20 I have written a raucous valentine to a poet's dream and agony.
On *Winkelberg*, 1958 play based on life of his friend Maxwell Bodenheim, recalled on Hecht's death 18 Apr 64

LILLIAN HELLMAN

21 If you believe, as the Greeks did, that man is at the mercy of the gods, then you write tragedy. The end is inevitable from the beginning. But if you believe that man can solve his own problems and is at nobody's mercy, then you will probably write melodrama.
Answering critics' complaints that her plots were melodramatic, recalled on her death 30 Jun 84

22 Tallulah was sitting in a group of people, giving the monologue she always thought was conversation.
On Tallulah Bankhead, quoted in portrayal of Hellman by Zoe Caldwell, *Time* 27 Jan 86

SOL HUROK

23 When people don't want to come, nothing will stop them.
On his philosophy as a producer, NY *Times* 25 Feb 69

24 The sky's the limit if you have a roof over your head.
ib

25 If I would be in this business for business, I wouldn't be in this business.
ib 28 Aug 70

1 If they're not temperamental, I don't want them. It's in the nature of a great artist to be that way.

ib 6 Mar 74

WILLIAM INGE

2 Theater is, of course, a reflection of life. Maybe we have to improve life before we can hope to improve theater.

Saturday Review 22 Feb 64

ROBERT KASS, agent

3 Years of training mean absolutely nothing. . . . it's a disgusting, despicable business, and you should all know what you're up against.

Addressing Actor's Survival Seminar, NY *Times* 25 Sep 84

GEORGE S KAUFMAN

4 They're not understudies, they're overstudies.

On substitute actors who overplay their roles, recalled on his death 2 Jun 61

5 Satire is what closes on Saturday night.

Quoted by Howard Teichmann *George S Kaufman* Atheneum 72

6 I understand your new play is full of single entendres.

Remark to Howard Dietz about his play *Between the Devil, ib*

ALAN JAY LERNER

7 We used to say that inside Cecil Beaton there was another Cecil Beaton sending out lots of little Cecils into the world. One did the sets, another did the costumes. A third took the photographs. Another put the sketches in an exhibition, then into magazines, then in a book.

Quoted by Hugo Vickers *Cecil Beaton* Little, Brown 85

CLARE BOOTHE LUCE

8 The women who inspired this play deserved to be smacked across the head with a meat ax and that, I flatter myself, is exactly what I smacked them with.

On her 1936 play *The Women*, quoted by Stephen Shadegg *Clare Boothe Luce* Simon & Schuster 70

9 They are vulgar and dirty-minded and alien to grace, and I would not, if I could, which I hasten to say I cannot, cross their obscenities with a wit which is foreign to them and gild their futilities with the glamour which by birth and breeding and performance they do not possess.

ib

CARSON MCCULLERS

10 The theme is the theme of humiliation, which is the square root of sin, as opposed to the freedom from humiliation, and love, which is the square root of wonderful.

On her play *The Square Root of Wonderful*, NY *Herald Tribune* 27 Oct 57

ARTHUR MILLER

11 I know that my works are a credit to this nation and I dare say they will endure longer than the McCarran Act.

On being refused a passport for supposed disloyalty, NY *Herald Tribune* 31 Mar 54

12 I have made more friends for American culture than the State Department. Certainly I have made fewer enemies, but that isn't very difficult.

ib

13 The structure of a play is always the story of how the birds came home to roost.

Harper's Aug 58

14 A play is made by sensing how the forces in life simulate ignorance—you set free the concealed irony, the deadly joke.

ib Nov 60

15 The best of our theater is standing on tiptoe, striving to see over the shoulders of father and mother. The worst is exploiting and wallowing in the self-pity of adolescence and obsessive keyhole sexuality. The way out, as the poet says, is always *through*.

On *After the Fall*, quoted in *National Observer* 20 Jan 64

16 I think now that the great thing is not so much the formulation of an answer for myself, for the theater, or the play—but rather the most accurate possible statement of the problem.

ib

17 The job is to ask questions—it always was—and to ask them as inexorably as I can. And to face the absence of precise answers with a certain humility.

ib

18 Certainly the most diverse, if minor, pastime of literary life is the game of Find the Author.

Reply to charges that his former wife Marilyn Monroe was portrayed in *After the Fall*, quoted in *Life* 7 Feb 64

19 The number of elements that have to go into a hit would break a computer down. . . . the right season for that play, the right historical moment, the right tonality.

On Broadway revival of *Death of a Salesman*, NY *Times* 9 May 84

20 The theater is so endlessly fascinating because it's so accidental. It's so much like life.

ib

21 I understand [Willy Loman's] longing for immortality . . . Willy's writing his name in a cake of ice on a hot day, but he wishes he were writing in stone.

ib

22 If I see an ending, I can work backward.

ib 9 Feb 86

23 A playwright lives in an occupied country. . . . And if you can't live that way you don't stay.

ib

24 Well, all the plays that I was trying to write . . . were plays that would grab an audience by the throat and not release them, rather than presenting an emotion which you could observe and walk away from.

ib

JONATHAN MILLER

25 Being a doctor has taught me a lot about directing. . . . You're doing the same thing: You're reconstructing the manifold of behavior to the point where an audience says, yes, that's exactly like people I know.

Christian Science Monitor 1 May 86

MIKE NICHOLS

1 Opening night . . . you will find a sizable number of people with severe respiratory infections who have, it appears, defied their doctors, torn aside oxygen tents, evaded the floor nurses at various hospitals and courageously made their way to the theater to enjoy the play—the Discreet Choker and the Straight Cougher.

> "Let's Hear It for (Cough) Opening Nights" NY *Times* 2 Oct 77

EDNA O'BRIEN

2 Writers really live in the mind and in hotels of the soul.

> Interviewed when she brought her play *Virginia* to the US, *Vogue* Apr 85

SEAN O'CASEY

3 The hallway of every man's life is paced with pictures; pictures gay and pictures gloomy, all useful, for if we be wise, we can learn from them a richer and braver way to live.

> On *Pictures in the Hallway*, NY *Times* 16 Sep 56

4 Between the writing of plays, in the vast middle of the night, when our children and their mother slept, I sat alone, and my thoughts drifted back in time, murmuring the remembrance of things past into the listening ear of silence; fashioning thoughts to unspoken words, and setting them down upon the sensitive tablets of the mind.

> *ib*

SEÁN O'FAOLÁIN

5 I have learned in my 30-odd years of serious writing only one sure lesson: Stories, like whiskey, must be allowed to mature in the cask.

> *Atlantic* Dec 56

EUGENE O'NEILL

6 I love every bone in their heads.

> On critics, quoted by Brooks Atkinson on accepting a medal from the Theater Committee for Eugene O'Neill, NY *Times* 1 Dec 80

7 [Her] love and tenderness . . . gave me the faith in love that enabled me to face my dead at last and write this play—write it with deep pity and understanding and forgiveness for all the four haunted Tyrones.

> Dedication to his wife Carlotta in *Long Day's Journey into Night*, recalled on play's Broadway revival, *Christian Science Monitor* 1 May 86

JOHN OSBORNE

8 The British public has always had an unerring taste for ungifted amateurs.

> Speaking as one of the Angry Young Men of the London theater, BBC TV 18 Feb 58

HOWARD OTWAY, theater owner

9 If you have a hit, the best thing that can happen to you is having a bigger hit open next door.

> Explaining that pleased playgoers tend to seek yet another evening of entertainment, NY *Times* 14 Mar 86

JOSEPH PAPP

10 It will be like some sort of painting with huge chunks missing.

> On future perception of a generation of theater talent depleted by AIDS, NY *Times* 16 Mar 87

J B PRIESTLEY

11 I'm in the business of providing people with secondary satisfactions. It wouldn't have done me much good if they had all written their own plays, would it?

> Interviewed at age 89, *Illustrated London News* Sep 84

JOSÉ QUINTERO

12 A great man for the arts should be celebrated not because of the past, but for the future.

> At Broadway memorial service for William Saroyan, NY *Times* 31 Oct 83

TERENCE RATTIGAN

13 A playwright must be his own audience. A novelist may lose his readers for a few pages; a playwright never dares lose his audience for a minute.

> NY *Journal-American* 29 Oct 56

WILLIAM SAROYAN

14 One of us is obviously mistaken.

> To British critic who had panned his latest play, NY *Mirror* 10 Jun 60

15 The role of art is to make a world which can be inhabited.

> Recalled at his Broadway memorial service, NY *Times* 31 Oct 83

GEORGE BERNARD SHAW

16 Why, except as a means of livelihood, a man should desire to act on the stage when he has the whole world to act in, is not clear to me.

> Recalled on his death 2 Nov 50

17 General consultant to mankind.

> Self-description, *ib*

18 The utmost I can bear for myself in my best days is that I was one of the hundred best playwrights in the world, which is hardly a supreme distinction.

> Letter to W D Chase, president of US Shaw Society, *ib*

19 A drama critic is a man who leaves no turn unstoned.

> Quoted in NY *Times* 5 Nov 50

20 Go on writing plays, my boy, One of these days one of these London producers will go into his office and say to his secretary, "Is there a play from Shaw this morning?" and when she says, "No," he will say, "Well, then we'll have to start on the rubbish." And that's your chance, my boy.

> Advice to a young playwright, quoted by William Douglas Home *ib* 7 Oct 56

21 Am reserving two tickets for you for my première. Come and bring a friend—if you have one.

> Wire inviting Winston Churchill to opening night of *Pygmalion*; Churchill wired back, "Impossible to be present for the first performance. Will attend the second—if there is one," quoted by William Manchester *The Last Lion* Little, Brown 83

1 I absolutely forbid any such outrage.

> Postcard dismissing proposal to make a musical version of *Pygmalion*; after Shaw's death his estate granted rights to the play, which became the successful musical *My Fair Lady*, recalled on death of lyricist Alan Jay Lerner, *Time* 21 Jul 86

2 If *Pygmalion* is not good enough for your friends with its own verbal music, their talent must be altogether extraordinary.

> *ib*

ROBERT E SHERWOOD

3 To be able to write a play . . . a man must be sensitive, imaginative, naive, gullible, passionate; he must be something of an imbecile, something of a poet, something of a liar, something of a damn fool.

> Quoted by John Mason Brown *The Worlds of Robert E Sherwood* Harper & Row 65

4 He must be a chaser of wild geese, as well as of wild ducks. He must be prepared to make a public spectacle of himself.

> *ib*

5 He must be independent and brave, and sure of himself and of the importance of his work, because if he isn't he will never survive the scorching blasts of derision that will probably greet his first efforts.

> *ib*

NEIL SIMON

6 You must realize that honorary degrees are given generally to people whose SAT scores were too low to get them into schools the regular way. As a matter of fact, it was my SAT scores that led me into my present vocation in life, comedy.

> On receiving an honorary degree, NY *Times* 4 Jun 84

7 Everyone thinks they can write a play; you just write down what happened to you. But the art of it is drawing from all the moments of your life.

> *ib* 24 Mar 85

8 I felt like writing about a time when I was probably, and I think all of us are, the happiest in our lives—before the obligations start in.

> On his play *Brighton Beach Memoirs*, *ib* 25 Jan 87

WOLE SOYINKA

9 [It] takes a jaundiced view of the much-vaunted glorious past of Africa. And I suppose since then I've been doing nothing but the danse macabre in this political jungle of ours.

> On his play *A Dance of the Forests*, recalled on winning Nobel Prize, NY *Times* 17 Oct 86

ROGER L STEVENS, Chairman, Kennedy Center for the Performing Arts, Washington DC

10 A quarter of the time I have big hits, a quarter of the time artistic successes, a quarter of the time the critics were crazy and a quarter of the time I was crazy.

> Quoted in NY *Times* 7 Oct 85

TOM STOPPARD

11 Skill without imagination is craftsmanship and gives us many useful objects such as wickerwork picnic baskets. Imagination without skill gives us modern art.

> News summaries 31 Dec 72

JAMES THURBER

12 We are a nation that has always gone in for the loud laugh, the wow, the belly laugh and the dozen other labels for the roll-'em-in-the-aisles gagerissimo. This is the kind of laugh that delights actors, directors and producers, but dismays writers of comedy because it is the laugh that often dies in the lobby.

> "The Quality of Mirth" NY *Times* 21 Feb 60

13 The appreciative smile, the chuckle, the soundless mirth, so important to the success of comedy, cannot be understood unless one sits among the audience and feels the warmth created by the quality of laughter that the audience takes home with it.

> *ib*

GORE VIDAL

14 A talent for drama is not a talent for writing, but is an ability to articulate human relationships.

> NY *Times* 17 Jun 56

15 The theater needs continual reminders that there is nothing more debasing than the work of those who do well what is not worth doing at all.

> *Newsweek* 25 Mar 68

16 Each writer is born with a repertory company in his head. Shakespeare has perhaps 20 players, and Tennessee Williams has about 5, and Samuel Beckett one—and maybe a clone of that one. I have 10 or so, and that's a lot. As you get older, you become more skillful at casting them.

> Dallas *Times-Herald* 18 Jun 78

17 Some writers take to drink, others take to audiences.

> NY *Times* 12 Mar 81

DAVID WATSON, director, Sharon CT summer playhouse

18 It's for that little bit of Judy Garland and Mickey Rooney in all of us.

> On summer stock, NY *Times* 18 Jun 84

THORNTON WILDER

19 Many plays—certainly mine—are like blank checks. The actors and directors put their own signatures on them.

> NY *Mirror* 13 Jul 56

20 A dramatist is one who believes that the pure event, an action involving human beings, is more arresting than any comment that can be made upon it.

> Quoted in Malcolm Cowley ed *Writers at Work* Viking 58

21 On the stage it is always *now*; the personages are standing on that razor edge, between the past and the future, which is the essential character of conscious being; the words are rising to their lips in immediate spontaneity . . . The theater is supremely fitted to say: "Behold! These things are."

> *ib*

22 I am not interested in the ephemeral—such subjects as the adulteries of dentists. I am interested in those things that repeat and repeat and repeat in the lives of the millions.

> NY *Times* 6 Nov 61

TENNESSEE WILLIAMS

1 My own creed as a playwright is fairly close to that expressed by the painter in Shaw's play *The Doctor's Dilemma*, "I believe in Michelangelo, Velásquez and Rembrandt; in the might of design, the mystery of color, the redemption of all things by beauty everlasting and the message of art that has made these hands blessed. Amen."
> Afterword to his 1953 play *Camino Real*

2 Some mystery should be left in the revelation of character in a play, just as a great deal of mystery is always left in the revelation of character in life, even in one's own character to himself.
> Stage directions for *Cat on a Hot Tin Roof* New Directions 55

3 If the writing is honest it cannot be separated from the man who wrote it.
> Preface to William Inge *The Dark at the Top of the Stairs* Random House 58

4 I have found it easier to identify with the characters who verge upon hysteria, who were frightened of life, who were desperate to reach out to another person. But these seemingly fragile people are the strong people really.
> NY *Times* 18 Mar 65

5 Most of the confidence which I appear to feel, especially when influenced by noon wine, is only a pretense.
> "I Am Widely Regarded as the Ghost of a Writer" *ib* 8 May 77

6 Maybe they weren't punks at all, but New York drama critics.
> On being mugged in Key West FL, *People* 7 May 79

7 This country of endured but unendurable pain.
> On the emotional environment of his characters, whether they live in New Orleans, St Louis or abroad, NY *Times* 18 May 86

P G WODEHOUSE

8 Has anybody ever seen a dramatic critic in the daytime? Of course not. They come out after dark, up to no good.
> NY *Mirror* 27 May 55

Observers & Critics

BROOKS ATKINSON

9 It seems not to have been written. It is the quintessence of life. It is the basic truth.
> On Tennessee Williams's *Cat on a Hot Tin Roof*, NY *Times* 25 Mar 55

10 Good plays drive bad playgoers crazy.
> *Theatre Arts* Aug 56

11 In the 1920s dramatists attacked their subjects as if the inequities could be resolved. Some of the traditional optimism of America lurked behind most of the early plays. But not now. There is no conviction now that the problem will be solved.
> *The Lively Years* Association Press 73

12 Ethel Waters, the flaming tower of dusky regality, who knows how to make a song stand on tiptoe.
> Recalled on her death 1 Sep 77

13 There is no joy so great as that of reporting that a good play has come to town.
> Recalled on his death 13 Jan 84

PAUL BAILEY

14 Blanche is written with a terrible authority, the authority that comes from artistic necessity when the writer is compelled to write by his demon, rather than by his agent or promoter.
> On the central character of *A Streetcar Named Desire*, quoted by Donald Spoto *The Kindness of Strangers: A Life of Tennessee Williams* Little, Brown 85

CLIVE BARNES

15 Dialogue more tame than Wilde.
> On revival of Somerset Maugham's *The Constant Wife*, NY *Times* 15 Apr 75

16 As hard as the nails on a crucifix.
> On Mildred Dunnock's portrayal of the mother in *Days in the Trees*, *ib* 28 Sept 76

17 The mother is not dying exactly, but has reached a point in life where death is a familiar on the staircase.
> *ib*

18 I am convinced that anyone can be a great writer . . . if he can only . . . tell the naked truth about himself and other people. That, a little technique with words and the willingness to bare heart, soul and body are really all it takes. But few people know the truth, and fewer have the artistic intent and perhaps ruthlessness to tell it.
> *ib* 17 Jan 77

PHYLLIS BATTELLE

19 A reporter discovers, in the course of many years of interviewing celebrities, that most actors are more attractive behind a spotlight than over a spot of tea.
> NY *Journal-American* 30 Apr 61

ERIC BENTLEY

20 A play has two authors, the playwright and the actor.
> NY State Theater Program Jun 66

JOHN MASON BROWN

21 Among the Round Tablers [at the Algonquin Hotel], Sherwood stood out like a grandfather's clock. The tick of his talk was measured, his words seeming to be spaced by minutes, but when he chimed he struck gaily.
> *The Worlds of Robert E Sherwood* Harper & Row 65

22 The more one has seen of the good, the more one asks for the better.
> "More Than 1,001 First Nights" *Saturday Review* 29 Aug 65

23 A critic is a man who prefers the indolence of opinion to the trials of action.
> *Town & Country* May 66

ANATOLE BROYARD

24 There is something about seeing *real people* on a stage that makes a bad play more intimately, more personally offensive than any other art form.
> NY *Times* 6 Feb 76

ROBERT BRUSTEIN

1 The people who spoke [those lines] were inhabitants of the earth, not brocaded humanoids from some far-flung planet.

On Laurence Olivier's "immediate, coherent, engrossing" rendering of Shakespearean characters, *New Republic* 3 Nov 86

2 Forty years later, people swear they can still hear his offstage scream.

On Olivier in *Oedipus Rex, ib*

JOHN BRYSON

3 The intimate, even incestuous Circle in the Square where the audience was close enough to be patrons of the saloon.

On theater housing scaled-down production of *The Iceman Cometh* by Eugene O'Neill, *New York* 16 Sep 85

ANTHONY BURGESS

4 Life is a wretched gray Saturday, but it has to be lived through.

On Samuel Beckett's *Waiting for Godot*, London *Times* 10 Apr 86

VINCENT CANBY

5 Miss Dietrich is not so much a performer as a one-woman environment.

On Marlene Dietrich's first Broadway appearance, NY *Times* 10 Oct 67

DEIRDRE CARMODY

6 Like an immense flock of chattering birds observing precise migratory habits, every Wednesday, just a few minutes before noon, they swoop down upon the midtown area.

"Ladies' Day at the Theater" NY *Times* 13 Mar 75

JAY CARR

7 [*The Front Page*] is still full of peppy banter as it sends its seedy knights after cheap scoops.

On Broadway revival of Ben Hecht and Charles MacArthur's 58-year-old play, Boston *Globe* 4 Dec 86

MARC CHAGALL

8 I adore the theater and I am a painter. I think the two are made for a marriage of love. I will give all my soul to prove this once more.

On painting new ceiling for the Paris Opéra, *Newsweek* 14 Oct 63

JOHN CHAPMAN

9 It is three and a half hours long, four characters wide and a cesspool deep.

On Edward Albee's *Who's Afraid of Virginia Woolf?* NY *Daily News* 15 Oct 62

HAROLD CLURMAN

10 From the holocausts of the day he lights his own flaming torch. It illuminates what we are, what we have wrought, what we must renounce.

On Jean Genet, recalled on Genet's death, NY *Times* 16 Apr 86

JEAN COCTEAU

11 There are too many souls of wood not to love those wooden characters who do indeed have a soul.

On marionettes, NY *Times* 15 Feb 87

RICHARD CORLISS

12 By dint of dogged charisma, Brynner has identified himself with a role more than any other actor since Bela Lugosi hung up his fangs.

On Yul Brynner's performance as the king of Siam in a revival of a role he first played in 1951, *Time* 21 Jan 85

13 Mausoleum air and anguished pauses: If this production were a poem, it would be mostly white space.

On Max Stafford-Clark's direction of Michael Hastings's *Tom and Viv, ib* 25 Feb 85

14 [Michael Hastings] has composed a dirge to incompatibility, which, because it raises expectations only to defeat them, leaves a taste of exhumed ashes.

ib

ROBERTSON DAVIES

15 The drama may be called that part of theatrical art which lends itself most readily to intellectual discussion: what is left is theater.

A Voice in the Attic Knopf 60

MAUREEN DOWD

16 They have been painting the barn red and white. . . . chasing skunks from the stage, clearing bird nests from the spotlights, scraping mildew from costumes and very gingerly, in the manner of city slickers, shooing snakes out of the yard.

On managers of summer theaters, NY *Times* 18 Jun 84

17 It is empty and dark now, with green paint covering the windows, and a jagged hole where the orchestra once played, and cats roaming after rats, and plaster everywhere. But the imagination dances back 70 years to scenes of Fanny Brice introducing "Secondhand Rose" and Eddie Cantor mugging his way through "Makin' Whoopee" and Will Rogers cracking wise.

On Manhattan's New Amsterdam Theater, *ib* 2 Aug 84

HELEN DUDAR

18 She saw *Death of a Salesman* from the balcony. From the evidence of her essay, it was close enough.

On Mimi Kramer, who lost her theater press pass because of her acerbic criticism, *Wall Street Journal* 9 Jul 84

RICHARD EDER

19 A prettiness mummified by years of chalk dust.

On Estelle Parson's portrayal of a schoolteacher in *Miss Margarida's Way*, NY *Times* 1 Aug 77

20 This sentimental comedy by the Soviet playwright Aleksei Arbuzov is said to have had a great success in its own country. So do fringed lamp shades.

On *Do You Turn Somersaults? ib* 10 Jan 78

ANNE EDWARDS

21 She represented the distilled essence of the battle between the sexes.

On Katharine Hepburn in her early Broadway performances, *A Remarkable Woman* Morrow 85

T S ELIOT

22 I must say Bernard Shaw is greatly improved by music.

On being asked by Rex Harrison for his opinion of the opening night performance of *My Fair Lady*, recalled by Robert Giroux NY *Times* 21 Dec 84

ESTHER B FEIN

1 The first thing they were told was how to hone their talent. Then they were told how to market their talent, discipline their talent and type their talent. And then they were told they might as well forget about talent.

> On theatrical agent Robert Kass's address to Actor's Survival Seminar, NY *Times* 25 Sep 84

E M FORSTER

2 I am so used to seeing the sort of play which deals with one man and two women. They do not leave me with the feeling I have made a full theatrical meal . . . they do not give me the experience of the multiplicity of life.

> On seeing Santha Rama Rau's 1960 dramatization of *A Passage to India*, recalled by Vincent Canby in review of the motion-picture version of the novel, NY *Times* 14 Dec 84

SAMUEL G FREEDMAN

3 When St Genesius, the patron saint of actors, refused to act in a Roman play that ridiculed Christianity, the legend goes, the producers executed him. It reminds some people of Broadway today.

> NY *Times* 29 Dec 83

JEAN JACQUES GAUTIER

4 Men who love humanity have all dreamed at least once during their lives of bringing all their fellow men together in a state of carefree happiness. And only the world of the theater ever really succeeds in doing this.

> "A Thousand and One First Nights" *Réalités* Jan 58

5 For a minute or perhaps two—and this is a long time—the theater makes man better and happier on this earth.

> *ib*

WILLIAM E GEIST

6 George, a camel, stepped on the foot of a Rockette; six sheep came off the elevator as three kings bearing gifts got on; human Christmas trees bumped into eight maids-a-milking at the water cooler and an elf came down with the flu.

> On the day "pandemonium paid a visit backstage" at opening of Radio City Music Hall's Christmas spectacular, NY *Times* 29 Nov 86

7 Scrooge pushed past Mary number 1 and Joseph number 2 in the wings without so much as an "excuse me." Typical.

> *ib*

BRENDAN GILL

8 If it were better, it wouldn't be as good.

> On *Butterflies Are Free* by Leonard Gershe, *New Yorker* 1 Nov 69

9 Of . . . plays by authors of high reputation and of the most serious dramaturgic intentions, [*The Iceman Cometh*] is *the* most boring play ever written. [But] immediately after *The Iceman Cometh*, O'Neill sat down and wrote *Long Day's Journey into Night*. It is easily the greatest play written in English in my lifetime.

> On Eugene O'Neill's plays, *ib* 7 Oct 85

STANLEY GREEN

10 They were not merely quipsters and storytellers, nor were they only song and dance entertainers. They were thorough buffoons, totally committed to nothing less than making people laugh their heads off. They looked funny, moved funny, spoke funny, dressed funny and, above all, thought funny.

> *The Great Clowns of Broadway* Oxford 84, quoted in *Christian Science Monitor* 20 Dec 84

11 They didn't portray comic characters, they *were* comic characters.

> *ib*

MEL GUSSOW

12 Though the clown is often deadpan, he is a connoisseur of laughter.

> On Avner Eisenberg in his one-man show *Avner the Eccentric*, NY *Times* 21 Sep 84

13 Bring a child and ignore your inhibitions.

> *ib*

14 Genet was . . . an actor in the play of his life, putting on masks, rearranging facts to suit his purpose and clouding himself in mystique.

> On Jean Genet, *ib* 16 Apr 86

DASHIELL HAMMETT

15 The truth is you don't like the theater except the times when you're in a room by yourself putting the play on paper.

> To Lillian Hellman, recalled on her death 30 Jun 84

JOHN HARVEY

16 Inevitably, a dramatist writes one play, his director interprets another, the actors perform a third and the public sees a fourth and altogether different one.

> Preface to *Anouilh, A Study in Theatrics* Yale 64

WILLIAM A HENRY III

17 A poet laureate of adolescent sexuality and middle-age longing.

> On William Inge, *Time* 23 Jul 83

18 The title refers to the wife's calling for a lost puppy, yet it is clear that hers is in truth a *cri de cœur* for the unassuageable pain of growing old before she has even grown up.

> On Inge's *Come Back, Little Sheba*, *ib*

19 Inge did not transform his characters: They end where they began. But he understood them. In their interplay was genuine life, often blunted but ever resilient.

> *ib*

20 What you get is first-draft Neil Simon.

> On interviewing the playwright, noted for producing many drafts of his plays, *ib* 15 Dec 86

DAVID RICHARD JONES

21 Starting with its title, everything about this play is designed to crack the spectator on the jaw, then douse him with ice-cold water, then force him to assess intelligently what has happened to him, then give him a kick . . . then bring him to his senses again.

> On Peter Brook's production of Peter Weiss's *Marat/ Sade*, quoted by Robert Brustein NY *Times* 27 Jul 86

T E Kalem

1 He sometimes ran a purple ribbon through his type-writer and gushed where he should have dammed.
On Tennessee Williams, *Time* 7 Mar 83

Walter Kerr

2 Me no Leica.
On John Van Druten's *I Am a Camera*, news summaries 31 Dec 51

3 Wherever it came from, the musical came with its hair mussed and with an innocent, indolent, irreverent look on its bright, bland face.
On musical comedy, NY *Herald Tribune* 1 Sep 63

4 It has an air about it of having strolled in from the street with a few tricks up its sleeve, and if everybody would relax, please, it would do its best to pass the time whimsically.
ib

5 Harpo Marx looks like a musical comedy.
ib

6 A serious and composed young actress who won't let a line pass without making certain she's had it in for a private talk and perhaps tea.
On Catherine Burns, *International Herald Tribune* 26 May 68

7 Reviewers . . . must normally function as huff-and-puff artists blowing laggard theatergoers stageward.
1975 statement quoted in NY *Times* 30 Sep 83

Dena Kleiman

8 A virtually uninterrupted duet of seduction, an exquisitely choreographed collage of tickling, kneeling, lounging, smoking, reading, sliding, leaping, posing, massaging, pushing, shaking, pulling, bouncing, tugging, stretching, crawling, limping, yanking, waving—not to mention singing as well.
On *Me and My Girl*, "A Pas de Deux of Flirting and Fun" NY *Times* 18 Aug 86

John David Klein

9 I saw this show under adverse circumstances—my seat was facing the stage.
On *Three Guys Naked from the Waist Down*, WNET TV 5 Feb 85

Stewart Klein

10 I have seen stronger plots than this in a cemetery.
On *Break a Leg*, WNYW TV 29 Apr 79

Jan Kott

11 When I met Genet I could not conceive of him as the author of his plays. He looks like a terrified baby.
On Jean Genet, NY *Times* 2 Feb 85

Pia Lindstrom

12 *Tom and Viv* is a literary whodunit and a medical what-did-it.
On Michael Hastings's *Tom and Viv*, about T S Eliot and the illness of his first wife, NBC TV 6 Feb 85

Anita Loos

13 Tallulah never bored anyone, and I consider that humanitarianism of a very high order indeed.
Eulogy for Tallulah Bankhead, NY *Times* 17 Dec 68

Donald Malcolm

14 [It is] a genuine delight to those amiable qualities that thrive best when the critical sense is out to lunch.
On *Little Mary Sunshine* in an off-Broadway production, *New Yorker* 28 Nov 59

James McCourt

15 A kind of cross between Helen Traubel and Martha Raye . . . an uncanny amalgam of Joan Sutherland and Phyllis Diller.
On Anna Russell, NY *Times* 15 Dec 85

Robert D McFadden

16 Tall, bald and pouch-eyed, with a velvet voice, a droll wit and the face of a cunning bloodhound . . . a performer who made audiences twitter and roar with subtle ease.
On Alastair Sim, NY *Times* 21 Aug 76

John McPhee

17 A tympanic resonance, so rich and overpowering that it could give an air of verse to a recipe for stewed hare.
On Richard Burton, recalled on Burton's death 5 Aug 84

Ted Morgan

18 A round ball of a man with protruding lower lip and seal-colored eyes, [he] spun like a top from continent to continent, jabbing a pudgy forefinger at everything that stood in his way.
On Charles Frohman, developer of the "star system," *Maugham* Simon & Schuster 80

19 It is less artificial than his other comedies. The epigrams do not seem to have been added on like candied cherries on a cake.
On Somerset Maugham's 1921 play *The Circle*, *ib*

Sheridan Morley

20 There is something remarkably and peculiarly English about the passion for sitting on damp seats watching open-air drama . . . only the English have mastered the art of being truly uncomfortable while facing up to culture.
London *Times* 18 Jun 83

21 Her education was erratic, though she learned to add by counting the nightly box-office takings.
On Helen Hayes, *ib* 19 Dec 84

George Jean Nathan

22 [It is] bosh sprinkled with mystic cologne.
On T S Eliot's *The Cocktail Party*, quoted in Charles Angoff ed *The World of George Jean Nathan* Knopf 52

23 So long as there is one pretty girl left on the stage, the professional undertakers may hold up their burial of the theater.
Theatre Arts Jul 58

New Yorker

24 [It is] a comedy that verges on autohagiography, the hero being the author.
Review of Neil Simon's *Biloxi Blues*, 28 Oct 85

BENEDICT NIGHTINGALE

1 [William Inge] handles symbolism rather like an Olympic weight lifter, raising it with agonizing care, brandishing it with a tiny grunt of triumph, then dropping it with a terrible clang.
> On Broadway revival of *Come Back, Little Sheba*, NY *Times* 29 Jul 84

GEORGES POMPIDOU, President of France

2 He imitated me so well that I couldn't stand myself any longer.
> On impersonation by satirist Thierry Le Luron, recalled on Le Luron's death, NY *Times* 14 Nov 86

FRANK RICH

3 As synthetic and padded as the transvestites' cleavage.
> On *La Cage aux Folles*, NY *Times* 22 Aug 83

4 The actor doesn't merely command the stage, he seems to own it by divine right.
> On Richard Burton's revival of *Camelot* role he created in 1960, recalled on Burton's death, *ib* 6 Aug 84

5 Yul Brynner's performance in *The King and I* . . . can no longer be regarded as a feat of acting or even endurance. After 30-odd years . . . Mr Brynner is, quite simply, The King.
> On opening night of Brynner's farewell engagement in the title role he created in 1951, *ib* 8 Jan 85

6 There's something endearingly crackpot about this play—it speaks to us from the century's boom time, when our culture, like the author, was at once naive and inordinately ambitious.
> On revival of Eugene O'Neill's *Strange Interlude*, *ib* 22 Feb 85

7 The playwright starts off angry, soon becomes furious and then skyrockets into sheer rage.
> On Larry Kramer's *The Normal Heart*, about AIDS, *ib* 22 Apr 85

8 Lillian Hellman brought out the knee-jerk in almost everyone.
> *ib* 23 Nov 86

9 A confusing jamboree of piercing noise, routine roller-skating, misogyny and Orwellian special effects, *Starlight Express* is the perfect gift for the kid who has everything except parents.
> *ib* 16 Mar 87

ELEANOR ROOSEVELT

10 An excellent play . . . but I have no feeling of reality about it. It had no more to do with me than the man in the moon.
> On *Sunrise at Campobello*, about her family in the 1920s, *Theatre Arts* Apr 58

RICHARD SCHICKEL

11 Memory is the personal journalism of the soul.
> On Harold Pinter's plays, *Time* 23 Jan 84

RICHARD SEVERO

12 [Monty] Woolley reduced the nurse in *The Man Who Came to Dinner* to the potency of a pound of wet Kleenex. It was probably the best thing that had happened to the art of the insult since the Medicis stopped talking in the 16th century.
> NY *Herald Tribune* 7 May 63

JOEL SIEGEL

13 His Texas accent doesn't come closer than Perth Amboy.
> On Carroll O'Connor in *Home Front*, WNYW TV 2 Jan 85

JOHN SIMON

14 Diana Rigg is built like a brick mausoleum with insufficient flying buttresses.
> On nude scene in *Abelard and Heloise*, *New York* 15 May 70

15 Like springs, adaptations can only go downhill.
> On Broadway production of *Singin' in the Rain*, *ib* 15 Jul 85

MERVYN STOCKWOOD, Bishop of Southwark, England

16 As boring as a boarding school on bath night.
> On nudity in *Oh! Calcutta*, London *Sunday Times* 2 Nov 80

DAN SULLIVAN

17 She presents no beauty but the memory of beauty, sustained by cosmetics, clever lighting, good health and will power . . . At times she seems to join the audience in watching the image she is creating, and she winks a little as if to say: not bad.
> On Broadway appearance by Marlene Dietrich, NY *Times* 4 Oct 68

TIME MAGAZINE

18 While tragedy moves from sanity toward madness, comedy moves from madness toward sanity. In his pride, the tragic hero overreaches human limits and dies. In his folly, the comic hero ludicrously pounds his head against those limits, is brought to his senses and lives.
> 22 Jan 65

19 The measuring out of life in tepid teacups.
> On contemporary English drama, 26 Mar 65

20 Man, as they see him, is a creature trapped between two voids, prenatal and posthumous, on a shrinking spit of sand he calls time.
> On European dramatists such as Beckett, Ionesco, Genet, Pinter and Osborne, "The Modern Theater, or the World as a Metaphor of Dread" 8 Jul 66

KENNETH TYNAN

21 A good many inconveniences attend playgoing in any large city, but the greatest of them is usually the play itself.
> NY *Herald Tribune* 17 Feb 57

22 The sheer complexity of writing a play always had dazzled me. In an effort to understand it, I became a critic.
> NY *Mirror* 6 Jun 63

23 No theater could sanely flourish until there was an umbilical connection between what was happening on the stage and what was happening in the world.
> Recalled on his death 26 Jul 80

E B WHITE

24 The critic leaves at curtain fall
To find, in starting to review it,
He scarcely saw the play at all
For starting to review it.
> NY *Times* 19 Sep 65

Index by Sources

Index by Subjects and Key Lines

Fulbright scholarships, 114:5, 118:3–6
"full of single entendres," 401:6
fund-raising
    for charities, 73:18–19, 76:16
    political, 31:6
funerals, 94:12, 104:10, 200:19, 211:17
    See also graves
furniture, fine, 206:9
furs, 215:17, 268:17, 269:19, 289:6
    sable, 270:7
future, the, 133:9–10, 231:6, 232:21, 241:16, 344:11
    See also tomorrow
future shock, 243:3

Gable, Clark, 283:16
galaxy, Milky Way, 145:2
Gale, John, 327:20
gambling, 32:13
Gambling, John, 381:7
games, card, 224:26–27, 388:18
Gandhi, Indira, assassination of, 5:10–11
Garbo, Greta, 284:15
Garden of Eden, 81:16
gardens and gardening, 205:10, 247:8, 248:24
Gardner, Ava, 283:19
Garland, Judy, 166:6, 284:6, 350:13
garlic, 285:9, 301:8, 301:12
gastronomes, 299:3–4
Gebel-Williams, Gunther, 213:15
Gemini space mission, 137:11
"general consultant to mankind," 402:17
General Motors, 94:17, 99:14, 100:16, 107:23
generals, 57:15, 59:9
    See also military
generation gap, 16:11, 235:1
"generous people are rarely mentally ill people," 134:12
genes, 139:1, 145:7, 219:9
Genesis, 338:5
    See also Bible
Genesius, Saint, 406:3
Genet, Jean, 327:3, 328:14, 334:16, 405:10, 406:14, 407:11
genetic engineering, 126:25, 142:4–5
genetic research, 127:1, 142:13–14
Geneva summit conference, 369:20
genius, 219:9, 223:26, 227:18, 232:2, 233:3, 238:17, 240:21, 263:15, 277:12
    chess, 395:4
genocide, 67:3
    See also Holocaust
genteel people, 359:7
"gentleman farmer who raises goose flesh," 273:18
gentlemen, 226:17
gentlemen's agreement, 70:2
"genuflect, genuflect, genuflect," 212:3
geodesic dome, 247:10–12
George VI, King of England, 168:6, 177:5
Georgia, 208:19

Germany
    Berlin, 157:11–12
    Berlin Wall, 8:16, 14:14
    concentration camps. *See* concentration camps;
        Holocaust
    Dresden, 162:12, 255:19
    East Berlin, 8:19
    Heidelberg, 161:21
    language of, 116:18
    Nuremberg trials, 59:10
    people of, 233:10
    terrorists in, 14:10
    West Berlin, 1:1, 7:15–16, 7:20–21
    West Germany. *See* West Germany
    and World War II, 18:3
"get the pencil moving quickly," 311:3
Giacometti, Alberto, 265:24
"giant panda, Santa Claus and the Jolly Green Giant
    rolled into one," 291:1
Gide, André, 334:17
Gielgud, John, 396:15, 397:27
Gill, Brendan, 212:1, 331:24
girls, 168:17–18
GIs, 60:16
"give me back my reputation," 17:10
glamour, 267:8
Glasgow, Scotland, 158:15
glasnost, 5:16
Gleason, Jackie, 378:8
Glendon, Michael, 59:13
glitz lit, 335:12
"global town meeting," 51:9
"gloom is their game," 370:3
"glorified gutter rat," 349:21
gluttons, 299:3–4
"go ahead—make my day," 13:19
God, 193:7–8, 197:4, 241:12–13, 342:18
    addiction to, 185:16
    adoration of, 194:11
    belief in, 187:9–11, 190:13
    disbelief in, 187:14
    energies of, 196:5
    escaping from, 185:12
    existence of, 197:15–16
    faith in, 244:27
    finding, 191:13
    grace of, 185:15
    listening to, 193:19
    mercy of, 193:21
    mystery of, 186:4
    proof of, 186:5, 188:5
"God and President Truman did not see eye to eye,"
    56:18
"God does not play dice," 187:13
"God does not take sides in . . . politics," 35:7
"God give us grace to accept," 193:15
"God . . . is a verb," 188:2
"God is in the details," 248:17
"God's a workman," 397:13
"God's gift to little men," 220:5
"God will not forgive us if we fail," 1:21